WORLD DRAMA

WORLD DRAMA

FROM ÆSCHYLUS TO ANOUILH

by

ALLARDYCE NICOLL

With contributions by Arthur
Wilmurt, Gareth Lloyd Evans,
Pierre Paul Auger,
Hilde Haider-Pregler, Jens
Kistrup, Małgorzata Semil-Jakubowicz,
Rodolfo Cardona,
Katharine Brisbane and
Lewis Nkosi

With Fifty-six Plates in Half-tone

*REVISED, ENLARGED
AND COMPLETELY RESET*

BARNES & NOBLE
BOOKS
10 East 53d St., New York 10022
(a division of Harper & Row Publishers, Inc.)

This edition first published in Great Britain 1976
by GEORGE G. HARRAP & CO. LTD
182–184 High Holborn, London WC1V 7AX

Copyright Allardyce Nicoll 1949, © 1976

Published in the U.S.A. 1976 by
HARPER & ROW PUBLISHERS, INC.,
BARNES & NOBLE IMPORT DIVISION

ISBN 0–06–495157–X

Made in Great Britain

PREFACE TO THE FIRST EDITION

THIS book attempts to provide a general conspectus of the drama's development from its earliest days in ancient Greece down to latest times. Confessedly it is prejudiced, since without prejudice no essay of this kind can be other than a mere record of facts, and the endeavour here is to present something beyond a collection of statistical information.

Judgments on individual plays and on the work of various playwrights are, therefore, coloured by the light in which the entire progress of the theatre is viewed. Still further, it must be emphasized that these judgments are based on standards or values independent of particular times and places. In a volume devoted to a period of dramatic activity restricted both in time and in place certain plays may justifiably be selected for praise because they rise above the general tone of their companions: in a book dealing with the whole development of the drama such plays may, with equal justification, be omitted or dealt with cursorily. If we take Sophocles and Shakespeare, Aristophanes and Shaw, as our standards, many lesser authors, although perhaps important for their own time and country, must of necessity be ignored.

An attempt, of course, has been made to refer to many plays which, because of their historical significance, are worthy of notice even though they may no longer make appeal to us, but always my object has been to make a distinction between such historical significance and intrinsic value. Should any reader in another country feel that I have not done justice to authors whose local fame is greater than their general esteem, I refer to my treatment of certain periods of English dramatic history, wherein numerous plays of decided interest have been weighed against others of greater importance and found wanting.

Particular difficulty has arisen, naturally, in dealing with contemporary contributions to the stage. In this region there is no perspective supplied by time to aid us; yet modern efforts are those which most attract our attention. Because of these considerations I have devoted to the dramatic work of the twentieth century perhaps greater space than would have been accorded to it had this book been written, not in 1949, but in 2049—and certainly greater space than a strict balancing of worth with that of earlier times might warrant.

In this connexion another thing must be emphasized. A purely factual account of theatrical development would presumably treat of plays in all countries, East and West, according to their position in time; and it would, moreover, seek to deal with all manifestations of the art dramatic no matter where they were exhibited. Thus, for example, in a work of such a kind an account of the Sanskrit theatre would appear alongside an account of the medieval stage in Europe, and presumably space would be devoted to the extraordinarily interesting religious 'mysteries' of India, Persia, and Tibet. In the present volume a definite orientation has been adopted. It begins with Æschylus and ends with Anouilh. This means that it is concerned chiefly with the Western drama and that other kinds of drama are dealt with largely in so far as they have aided in the evolution of Western forms. An account of the Oriental theatre is thus placed, not in medieval times, but in the modern period—when first these Oriental conventions came to be appreciated and were deemed worthy of imitation.

Naturally a book of this sort presents many and serious language problems. So far as possible, I have read (or seen, when opportunity offered itself) plays in their original tongues, but obviously only some half a dozen countries could so be dealt with. This meant application to translations, and fortunately there is a fairly extensive library, prepared by authors British and American, of theatrical works originally composed in other tongues. Even these large resources, however, sometimes proved inadequate, and consequently, as a third choice, I have turned to versions in French, Italian, or German. Thus, for instance, a rather important Hungarian drama has been read in Italian, a Czech drama in German, and a Bulgarian in French, since apparently none of these had been put into English dress. I fully realize that in the perusal of works at second, or even at third hand, much of the flavour of the original must inevitably be lost, particularly if the author was a poet; but I have sought, so far as possible, to make allowances for this inevitable loss.

After due deliberation, I have decided not to add a bibliography to the text of this volume. Partly this decision has been determined by the fact that divers such reading-lists have been published during recent years and are readily available; partly I have been influenced by the thought that any reading-list based merely on material in English must necessarily be inadequate because of the many dramatic literatures dealt with, and that a really appropriate bibliography would become inconveniently lengthy and would perforce include scores of titles in other tongues. If any reader wishes to devote particular attention to a selected period of dramatic development or to the contributions of an individual country, there should be no difficulty in his obtaining references to such books as will aid him in his course of study.

At the same time, it should be emphasized that in the following pages great care has been taken to make the factual information, and, in especial, the dating of plays, as accurate as might be. This has not proved by any means an easy task. Frequently even those critical works which might have been thought to provide authority were found to differ among themselves, while in certain instances the obtaining of absolutely definitive information proved impossible. All that may be said is that every endeavour has been exercised to make this volume as correct as possible in the presentation of statistical information, although it is too much to hope that, with so wide a scope, errors have been entirely avoided.

For aid in locating elusive documentary evidence I have to thank many of my colleagues and friends, at the University of Birmingham, at other British universities, in the United States of America, and in continental Europe. The Cultural Attachés at the Embassies of the U.S.S.R. and Norway have also been most kind in helping me in this task. For all such assistance I am deeply grateful.

Some of the translated quotations from plays have been specially prepared for the present book, but many have been taken from already published versions. For permission to include both extracts from these versions and quotations from original works by British and American authors I have to thank the following:

Messrs ACTAC (Theatrical and Cinematic), Ltd, for extracts from Christopher Fry's *Venus Observed* (Oxford University Press).

Messrs George Allen and Unwin, Ltd, and Messrs Alfred A. Knopf, Inc., for an extract from Arthur Waley's *The No Plays of Japan* (copyright 1922).

Messrs George Allen and Unwin, Ltd, and the Oxford University Press, Inc., New York, for extracts from Dr Gilbert Murray's translations of Euripides' *The Trojan Women* and *Bacchæ* (from *Euripides: Five Plays;* copyright 1906, 1910, 1915, by the Oxford University Press, Inc., N.Y.)

Messrs Allen and Unwin, Ltd, and Random House, Inc., for extracts from J. M. Synge's *Riders to the Sea* and *The Playboy of the Western World.*

Messrs G. Bell and Sons, Ltd, for extracts from E. P. Coleridge's translations of Euripides' *Orestes, Hecuba,* and *Helen*; from Sir George Young's translation of Sophocles' *Œdipus at Colonus*; from F. M. Stawell's translation of Euripides' *Iphigenia in Aulis*; from B. B. Rogers' translations of Aristophanes' *The Acharnians* and *The Birds*; and from Sir Theodore Martin's translation of Schiller's *William Tell.*

The Executors of the late Ugo Betti for an extract from his *Frana allo Scalo nord.*

The Bodley Head, Ltd, for an extract from Roy Campbell's translation of Krog's *Triad.*

The Bodley Head, Ltd, and W. Sloan Associates, Inc., New York, for an extract from Maxwell Anderson's *Winterset.*

The Executors of the late Dr Gordon Bottomley and Messrs Constable and Co., Ltd, for an extract from Dr Bottomley's *Fire at Callart*.

Constable and Co., Ltd, for extracts from *Tobias and the Angel* and *The Sleeping Clergyman*, by James Bridie, and extracts from *St Joan*, *Caesar and Cleopatra*, and *Too True to be Good*, by G. B. Shaw.

The Syndics of the Cambridge University Press for an extract from F. L. Lucas's translations of Seneca's *Thyestes* and *Hercules Furens* appearing in that author's *Seneca and Elizabethan Tragedy* (1922).

Messrs Chatto and Windus, Ltd, for an extract from C. St John's translation of the *Plays of Roswitha*.

Mr Barrett H. Clark for extracts from his translations of Beaumarchais and Dumas appearing in his *European Theories of the Drama*, and for an extract from Ethel van der Veer's translation of *The Chalk Circle*.

Messrs Jonathan Cape, Ltd, and Messrs Random House, Inc., for extracts from Eugene O'Neill's *The Hairy Ape*, *All God's Chillun got Wings*, and *Mourning becomes Electra*.

The Columbia University Press, Inc., for an extract from A. E. Zucker's translation of *The Redentin Easter Play*.

Messrs Curtis Brown, Ltd, for an extract from Barrett H. Clark's translation of Sardou's *La Patrie*.

Messrs J. M. Dent and Sons, Ltd, and Messrs E. P. Dutton and Co., for an extract from Barker Fairlie's translation of Hebbel's *Maria Magdalena* ("Everyman's Library"), for extracts from Pirandello's *Six Characters in Search of an Author*, *Clothing the Naked*, and *Each in his Own Way* (translated by the present author).

Dobson Books, Ltd, and Messrs Alfred A. Knopf, Inc., for an extract from Harold Clurman's *The Fervent Years*.

Messrs Doubleday and Co., Inc., for an extract from C. H. Meltzer's translation of Gerhart Hauptmann's *The Sunken Bell*.

Messrs Gerald Duckworth and Co., Ltd, and Messrs Charles Scribner's Sons for extracts from E. Björkmann's translations of Strindberg's *The Dance of Death* and Introduction to *The Dream Play* in *Eight Famous Plays*, by A. Strindberg (*Plays by August Strindberg*, copyright 1912).

Mr S. A. Eliot, Junior, for an extract from his translation of Hans Sachs' *Wandering Scholar*.

Messrs Faber and Faber, Ltd, and Messrs Harcourt, Brace Jovanovich, Inc., for an extract from T. S. Eliot's *Murder in the Cathedral*.

The Librairie Gallimard for an extract from Albert Camus' *Caligula*.

The Executors of John Galsworthy, Messrs Gerald Duckworth and Co., Ltd, and Messrs Charles Scribner's Sons for an extract from John Galsworthy's *Justice* (copyright 1910).

Mme Jean Giraudoux for an extract from Jean Giraudoux' *Electre*.

Messrs Gollancz, Ltd, for an extract from *Counsellor-at-Law*, by Elmer Rice.

Messrs Harcourt, Brace Jovanovich, Inc., for an extract from D. Fitts' and R. Fitzgerald's translation of Sophocles' *Antigone*.

Messrs A. M. Heath and Co., Ltd, Victor Gollancz, Ltd, and Random House, Inc., for an extract from Clifford Odets' *Golden Boy*.

Messrs William Heinemann, Ltd, for extracts from William Archer's translations of Ibsen's *Emperor or Galilean, Pillars of Society, The Wild Duck*, and *When We Dead Awaken*.

Messrs William Heinemann, Ltd, and Messrs Doubleday and Co., Inc., for an extract from Noel Coward's *Private Lives*.

Messrs Holt, Rinehart and Winston, Inc., N.Y., and Victor Gollancz, Ltd, for an extract from Marc Connelly's *Green Pastures* (copyright 1929 by Marc Connelly).

The Editors of the Loeb Classical Library for extracts from F. Storr's translation of Sophocles' *Electra* and from Arthur S. Way's translation of Euripides' *Electra*.

Messrs Longman Group, Ltd, for an extract from *Man and Superman*, by G. B. Shaw.

Messrs Longmans, Green and Co., Inc., New York, for an extract from M. P. Baker's translation of Molnar's *The Swan*.

Mr James Graham Lujan and Mr Richard O'Connell for an extract from their authorized translation of Lorca's *The Shoemaker's Prodigious Wife*.

The Princeton University Press for an extract from Lacy Lockert's translation of Racine's *Andromaque*.

Messrs Random House, Inc., for extracts from the translations of Aristophanes' *Acharnians, The Clouds*, and *The Wasps* appearing in *Complete Greek Drama* (ed. Whitney J. Oates and Eugene O'Neill, Junior), and from Paul Landis's translation of Corneille's *Cinna* and Robert Henderson's translation of Racine's *Phèdre* appearing in "The Modern Library."

Messrs Routledge and Kegan Paul, Ltd, for an extract from L. A. Post's translation of Menander's *Arbitration*.

Messrs Charles Scribner's Sons for extracts from J. G. Underhill's translations of Lope de Vega's *El mejor alcalde el Rey, Fuente Ovejuna*, and *El perro del hortelano*, and of Benavente's *Bonds of Interest*.

Messrs Simon and Schuster, Inc., for an extract from H. Thayer Kingsbury's translation of Rostand's *Cyrano*.

Mrs Bella and Samuel Spewack and Messrs Victor Gollancz Ltd, for an extract from *Boy Meets Girl*.

The Executors of August Strindberg and Messrs Jonathan Cape, Ltd, for extracts from E. Classens's translation of *Lucky Peter's Travels*, and from C. D. Locock's translations of *The Saga of the Folkungs* (*Master Olof and Other Plays*), and the Introduction to *Lady Julia*.

Mr Louis Untermeyer for an extract from his translation of Toller's *Man and Masses* (produced by the Theatre Guild at the Garrick Theatre, April 14, 1924).

The Viking Press, Inc., New York, for extracts from translations of Gerhart Hauptmann's *Before Sunrise* and *Schluck und Jau*, in *Dramatic Works of Gerhart Hauptmann*, translated by Ludwig Lewisohn (copyright 1913, 1915, by B. W. Huebsch; 1941, 1943, by Ludwig Lewisohn).

The University of Washington Press, for an extract from Edward N. Stone's translation of *Adam*.

The Yale University Press and the Oxford University Press for an extract from C. W. Mendell's *Our Seneca*.

Mrs W. B. Yeats, Messrs Macmillan and Co., Ltd, and the Macmillan Co, New York, for extracts from W. B. Yeats' *At the Hawk's Well* and *The King's Threshold*, from *Collected Plays of W. B. Yeats (Four Plays for Dancers)*.

A. N.

PREFACE TO THE SECOND EDITION

The present edition of *World Drama* carries the general story of the stage onwards through the quarter-century which has passed by between the years 1946 and the early seventies—a period of numerous vast changes in social life and of many experimental efforts in dozens of theatres. These changes and experiments, indeed, have been so marked a feature of this age that it seemed an impossible task for any single person satisfactorily to survey and to evaluate all the diverse post-war contributions to the drama—and I wish here to express my indebtedness to those who have contributed to this volume interpretative essays on recent theatrical developments within their own countries. Without their assistance and co-operation no truly effective account of what has been happening in the playhouses during those twenty-five years would have been possible.

The chief objective in preparing this new edition has been, of course, to bring the survey up to date, but, in addition, in its preparation the opportunity has been taken to revise the text throughout, with the making of such corrections and modifications as have appeared desirable both because of historical information recently published and because of the fresh light which certain current theatrical trends have cast on at least a few playwrights of the past.

In the preparation of this material I have been greatly aided by the care and expertise with which the publisher's editorial department has dealt with the text, and to all those concerned I wish to express my gratitude and thanks.

A. N.

CONTENTS

PART I

FROM ATHENS TO ROME

PART II

RELIGIOUS DRAMA AND PROFANE DURING THE MIDDLE AGES

PART III

THE DRAMA OF THE RENAISSANCE

PART IV

THE DRAMA OF THE RENAISSANCE: ENGLAND

PART V

THE TRIUMPH OF CLASSICISM

PART VI

THE AGE OF GENTILITY, PHILOSOPHY, AND SENTIMENTALISM

PART VII

THE ROMANTIC THEATRE

PART VIII

FROM THE MEDIEVAL TO THE MATERIALISTIC

PART IX

REALISM'S TRIUMPH

PART X
THE DRAMA OF THE ORIENT

PART XI

ENTERING THE TWENTIETH CENTURY

PART XII

DRAMA BETWEEN TWO WARS

PART XIII
CHANGES AND CHANCES

PART XIV
THE TRANSFORMATION SCENE: 1945–73

ILLUSTRATIONS

PART I

FROM ATHENS TO ROME

1

THE FIRST DRAMATIST: ÆSCHYLUS

FOR US the story of the drama may properly be said to start towards the beginning of the fifth century B.C. when the earliest extant tragedies composed by Æschylus were performed in Athens.

It is possible that dramatic entertainment existed hundreds, perhaps thousands, of years before this date; it is possible that Æschylus and the other early playwrights of Greece owed a considerable debt, for both the content and the form of their plays, to priestly performers of sacred dramas in ancient Egypt; it is certain that Æschylus was no inventor of tragedy, but merely elaborated upon a growing Greek tradition which gradually brought the theatre as we know it to full fruition. But in all of these realms we move darkling, unable to do more than guess at what may be around us.

What forms were assumed by mimetic dances in prehistoric communities we can only vaguely conjecture; we do not know whether the tellers of tales, the acrobats, and the singers of songs amid these tribes mingled dramatic material with their own wares. However strongly we may suspect that the dances took on something approaching a theatrical appearance, and that the popular entertainers made their contributions to later dramatic artistry, there is no evidence available by which we can formulate any assured statements.

Egypt offers us a trifle more, yet, despite all our wealth of knowledge concerning this ancient empire, we are barely better off, in so far as our knowledge of the theatre is concerned, than when we contemplate prehistoric times. There was, we are aware, an *Abydos Passion Play* existent in the second, perhaps even in the third, millennium before Christ. This drama celebrated the death of Osiris, and apparently told how his limbs were torn apart, to be brought together again by Isis, his sister and his wife; but no text survives, and its action can be only tentatively reconstructed from a record by one Ikhernofret, who refashioned older material for a presentation before Sesostris III (1887–1849 B.C.). Even after such a tentative reconstruction, however, we remain unsure whether this presentation was truly dramatic—whether it may not have been, after all, merely a piece of expanded ritual. And if we are in doubt concerning the *Abydos Passion Play*, still greater doubt attends any consideration of the "Pyramid Texts" and the so-called "Memphite Drama." We are in the presence of a kind of dramatic exercise here, undoubtedly; yet there is so little evidence of a concrete nature that regretfully we must leave these ritual plays aside. For the specialist their exploration is fascinating, but to the specialist they must be left.

Safer and firmer ground is reached when we move to Greece. The tragic dramas of Æschylus and his successors sprang from the ancient dithyramb, a choral song chanted in honour of Dionysus. Again, however, even although the way be clearer, certainties are lacking, and we can but guess at the probable line of development. At first the dithyramb was, in all probability, an improvised affair, words and music alike issuing from the excitement of the festival occasion. At first, too, the dithyramb must have been largely or wholly narrative in form, telling some legend relating to the god. Gradually changes came. At least by the days of Arion of Methymna (between the seventh and sixth centuries B.C.) individual poets were composing lines for the celebrants; and at the same time the separation of a choral leader (the *exarchos*, ἔξαρχος) from the crowd led to the possibility of genuine dramatic action—or, rather, for the transformation of narrative into direct representation.

Then came the truly decisive step, traditionally attributed to Thespis (sixth century B.C.), when an actor (as distinct from a choral leader) was introduced. With the use of masks—whereby the single actor might impersonate several characters during the course of the action—the way was opened for the exploitation in dramatic form of many and complex themes.

With Thespis we move close to Æschylus, for this actor-dramatist seems, after having exhibited his plays in his native Icaria, to have transferred his activities to Athens about the year 560 B.C. Precise records are wanting, but such evidence as remains tends to suggest that from this date Thespis gave public performances of his works in the city, and it is certain that when Pisistratus established the first dramatic festival in 534 B.C. he won the prize for one of his tragedies.

His activities, aided by the incentive of the festival-contests, immediately had their effect. Other dramatists followed his lead: the fecund Choirilos, who is credited with some hundred and sixty plays, and who is said to have improved on the masks introduced by Thespis; Pratinas, who specialized in the 'satyric' drama; Phrynichos, the inventor of women's masks, a writer famous in his own days, yet, unlike the happier Æschylus, without a single one of his works extant.

The earliest play-texts which have come down to us out of the past are seven tragedies by this last-named author, and among these it may be profitable to start with *The Suppliants*: even although a fragmentary entry in a recently discovered papyrus suggests (although it does not prove) that this was not the earliest of his extant plays, its structure most certainly best illustrates the characteristic form assumed by the Greek drama in its days of infancy—with the chorus playing a central role in the action.

The First Theatre: "The Suppliants"

It is sunrise, and a great crowd of Athenian citizens is gathered on the bare hillside below the Acropolis, some standing, some squatting among the rocks, some seated on rudely constructed tiers of wooden benches. Below them the slope of the hill levels out, and on the small plateau thus formed a great circle has been marked out, in its midst an altar. Near by the dim light reveals the outline of a temple.

The crowd is expectant and eager, though physically tired. Already there have been days and nights of ecstatic festivity, beginning with a solemn procession, during which the statue of Dionysus has been carried from its temple down towards the Academy on the road to Eleutherae, and including a tumultuous torchlit return, when the god's statue has been placed, where it is now visible, beside the great orchestral circle. There has been sacrifice and ritual, flute music and the chanting of hymns, solemnity and ribald laughter, in the atmosphere of release and reverence.

Now once more the crowd has gathered, in this dawn, anxious to see the presentations which are to be placed before them in further honour of Dionysus.

A sudden silence descends as the nightingale-clear tones of a flute issue from the half-darkness below, and vaguely can be seen a group of fifty figures robed in white garments with strange embroideries moving into the circle's precincts and arranging themselves about the altar. Among them is one man, clad in rich robes, high-soled boots on his feet, with a venerable mask so fashioned as to indicate that he is a monarch.

For a moment there is silence, and then a choral chant begins:

> Zeus! Lord and guard of suppliant hands!
> Look down benign on us who crave
> Thine aid—whom winds and waters drave
> From where, through drifting, shifting sands,
> Pours Nilus to the wave.
> From where the green land, god-possest,
> Closes and fronts the Syrian waste,
> We flee as exiles, yet unbanned
> By murder's sentence from our land;
> But—since Ægyptus had decreed
> His sons should wed his brother's seed—
> Ourselves we tore from bonds abhorred,
> From wedlock not of heart but hand,
> Nor brooked to call a kinsman lord!

Only one section of the chorus has been singing; now another takes up the tune:

> And Danaus, our sire and guide,
> The king of counsel, pond'ring well
> The dice of fortune as they fell,
> Out of two griefs the kindlier chose,
> And bade us fly, with him beside,
> Heedless what winds or waves arose,
> And o'er the wide sea waters haste,
> Until to Argos' shore at last
>   Our wandering pinnace came.

Already sufficient has been told to permit the attendant audience of Athenian citizens, their minds fed with the legends of their land, to know that the stalwart man in the orchestral circle is Danaus, and that the fifty women in the chorus are his daughters. All the spectators know the bare outline of their fate. Danaus was the brother of Ægyptus, two princes descended from a union of the god Zeus and the poor tormented Io. The fifty sons of Ægyptus had proffered marriage with, and had later threatened violence upon, Danaus' daughters, who in terror had taken ship with their father to seek Io's native land, Argos, and beg the protection of its king, Pelasgus.

The audience, then, know the antecedents of the action about to be unfolded before them, and are even aware of the course to be taken by the coming scenes. They ask no thrill of novelty in the plot: unhindered by ignorance of the events, they give their whole minds to listening to the poet's words and to appreciating his skill in handling this age-old theme.

Through complex strophe and antistrophe, in subtle melody the chorus has continued its chant, accompanying the stanzas with intricate dance movement. Now, their voices and their bodies stilled, the maidens gather close to the altar, while Danaus, left alone at the edge of the circle, addresses them, warning them to be wary, and telling them that they must expect the arrival of the King of Argos and his soldiers:

> Adore this altar consecrate
> To many lesser gods in one; then crouch
> On holy ground, a flock of doves that flee,
> Scared by no alien hawks, a kin not kind,
> Hateful, and fain of love more hateful still. . . .
>   Take heed, draw hitherward,
> That from this hap your safety ye may win.

At this the actor playing Danaus remains silent, while his active rôle is taken by another, clad in a royal mask. Addressing the chorus, this second actor announces himself as Pelasgus, comments on the strange Eastern robes of the chorus, and asks why they are come to Argive land.

Eagerly the audience listen, for now is come a scene of crisis. How will these maidens defend themselves? What will the King of Argos say? The answer to the first question is soon given. "Short is my word and clear," declares the leader of the chorus. "Of Argive race we come." Pelasgus stands amazed, unable to credit that women so strange in attire should be of his country, but gradually, as the choral leader retells the story of Io and the fortunes of her descendants, he becomes convinced; and thereupon the chorus breaks out into a wild chant pleading for protection and justice. Through the clear air, in the brilliant light of morn, the words come singing to the crowd above:

> Justice, the daughter of right-dealing Zeus,
> Justice, the queen of suppliants, look down,
>> That this our plight no ill may loose
>>> Upon your town!
> This word, even from the young, let age and wisdom learn:
> If thou to suppliants show grace,
> Thou shalt not lack Heaven's grace in turn,
> So long as virtue's gifts on heavenly shrines have place.

This is the maidens' plea: what now of Pelasgus' reply? It comes equally short and direct:

> Not at my private hearth ye sit and sue;
> And if the city bear a common stain,
> Be it the common toil to cleanse the same:
> Therefore no pledge, no promise will I give,
> Ere counsel with the commonwealth be held.

And, hearing these words, the crowd stirs eagerly, for this audience belongs to a democracy, proud that common opinion, not the will of tyrants, rules its fate; and this ancient Argos over which Pelasgus is chieftain is the land of Athens. Thus is the antique tale brought close to them in spirit.

With the threat in his ears that these maidens will hang themselves should succour be refused, the Argive king retires, while the chorus chants melodiously a hymn to Zeus. To the audience gathered there the five strophes and antistrophes take but a brief space of time, yet, as the song is being sung, winged imagination accompanies Pelasgus on his mission, pictures him summoning his free council of citizens, creates in fancy the scene wherein the case is set and argued. With no shock of surprise or resentment, the spectators see Danaus return and hear him announce the verdict: time is foreshortened here in this highly conventional presentation of bygone action:

> With one assent the Argives spake their will,
> And, hearing, my old heart took youthful cheer.
> The very sky was thrilled when high in air
> The concourse raised right hands and swore their oath:
> *Free shall the maidens sojourn in this land.*
> *Unharried, undespoiled by mortal wight:*
> *No native hand, no hand of foreigner,*
> *Shall drag them hence.*

Immediately the chorus break into a passionate song of thankfulness to the gods; but no sooner is this ended than Danaus, gazing down the hill-side towards the sea far beneath him, cries out that he discerns there the ship of their pursuers. Danaus leaves the stage, while the maidens cluster miserably round the altar, uttering cries of fear:

> O land of hill and dale, O holy land,
> What shall befall us? whither shall we flee,
> From Apian land to some dark lair of earth? . . .

> For the race of Ægyptus is fierce, with greed and with malice afire;
> They cry as the questing hounds, they sweep with the speed of desire.

In a moment a new figure enters, the Herald of Ægyptus. Rudely he attempts to force the women from the altar; the air is rent with their cries, all is tumult and dismay. Then suddenly Pelasgus appears, and with him hope:

> Know that if words unstained by violence
> Can change these maidens' choice, then mayest thou,
> With full consent of theirs, conduct them hence
> But thus the city with one voice ordained—
> *No force shall bear away the maiden band.*
> Firmly this word upon the temple wall
> Is by a rivet clenched, and shall abide:
> Not upon wax inscribed and delible,
> Nor upon parchment sealed and stored away.—
> Lo, thou hast heard our free mouths speak their will:
> Out from our presence—tarry not, but go!

At this, but threatening war, the Herald withdraws, and the chorus, overjoyed, release their emotions in a passionate song in praise of Argos, in praise of the land of Athens:

> Pass and adore ye the Blessed, the gods of the city who dwell
> Around Erasinus, the gush of the swift immemorial tide.

So rings out one pæan, to be caught up excitedly by another:

> Chant ye, O maidens; aloud let the praise of Pelasgia swell;
> Hymn we no longer the shores where Nilus to ocean doth glide.

Thus ends the play on an apparent note of hope.

The audience, however, does not move. There is a restless moment of intermission, but soon expectancy and silence once more fall upon the crowd: once more the sound of a flute, playing a fresh melody, comes from below; once more the maidens of the chorus flock into the orchestra. A new play begins.

We do not possess this second drama, but its content is easily to be reconstructed. Here is shown the rape of the daughters of Danaus by Ægyptus' sons. Nor is this even the end, for the second play in turn is

THE THEATRE AT EPIDAURUS
This theatre is among the best preserved and the most beautiful
of the earlier type.
Photo E. P. Co.

ANDROMEDA
Attic vase, Berlin Museum.
From Margarete Bieber,
*The History of the Greek
and Roman Theater*

MASK OF A TRAGIC HERO
From Margarete Bieber, *Die
Denkmäler zum Theaterwesen
im Altertum.*

followed by a third, which tells their final fate—tells how all the maidens but one (Hypermnestra, moved by new-won love for her Lynceus) slay their hated husbands. Only then does the dramatic movement reach its conclusion.

For those gathered on the bare hillside by the little Athenian city, the single play of *The Suppliants* becomes by a strange paradox at once complete and incomplete, a dramatic whole in itself, and yet only part of a trilogy, a single act·in a larger unity.

The Dramatic Conventions of the Greek Drama

The space thus given to *The Suppliants*, even although that play cannot be regarded as the greatest of Æschylus' writings, seems fully justified by the fact that it manifests so excellently the dramatic form which the young Æschylus inherited from Thespis and his immediate followers.

As yet there is hardly any theatre as such: as yet only rude provision is made for the audience, and the actors all move within the levelled area of the orchestra, with no background save what is provided by the open sky and the long, noble landscape stretching far below. The drama is close to the form of its origin, the dithyramb; action is kept to a minimum, and the chorus, these daughters of Danaus, become, as it were, a collective protagonist; of individual portraiture there is virtually nothing. This is drama, certainly, and not ritual, but it is drama of the most rudimentary kind.

Already, however, the main conventions of the Greek stage have been set. Very soon a stage-building, designed at once to give the actors opportunity for the changing of mask and dress and to provide for them an architectural background, is to come into being, but even in its absence the conditions of performance for *The Suppliants* are characteristic of the entire course of the Greek theatre. This theatre was never at any time more than a collection of parts—the auditorium remained separate from the orchestra and the orchestra from the stage—and always the central part was the extensive acting space assigned to the chorus. Out of the chorus the drama had originally sprung, and with the chorus (albeit at the end a trifle unwillingly) it remained until the tragic spirit vanished completely.

This hillside theatre of *The Suppliants* was already a festival theatre, in which plays were presented, in competition, by actor-dramatists who trained their own performers and found the cost of the production defrayed by some rich citizen who gladly accepted the onus of payment as a kind of religious offering, or at least as a public duty. Already the system of appointing judges by lot had been established; already the dates had been set for the two great Athenian dramatic festivals, the City Dionysia, in the spring (March), and the Lenæa, in the winter (January). The actors were costumed as they were to be costumed for the entire space of the production of Greek tragedy, and their dress was virtually the creation of Æschylus himself. Basing his model upon antique traditional forms, he was responsible for the theatrical adoption of the long-sleeved robe, generally embroidered more richly than was the attire of the contemporary Athenian and, when occasion offered, assuredly taking advantage of barbaric ornament. In *The Suppliants*, for example, Pelasgus at once recognizes that the fifty women of the chorus come from some strange, far-off land, and we may presume that Egyptian motifs appeared on their flowing draperies. Æschylus, too, was credited with having introduced the *cothurnus* as the characteristic footwear for the principal characters in tragedy, and there is also the suggestion that he was responsible for the employment of the *onkos*, the relic of an ancient method of dressing the hair, which produced a crown-like addition to the tragic masks. The examination of early archaeological remains, however, tends to indicate that the high-soled boot and the lofty *onkos* were later theatrical developments; yet, even if we find ourselves forced to believe that these were not worn by the earliest actors, it seems probable, indeed certain, that even from the very start there must have been an effective contrast between the majestic-seeming chief characters in tragic performances, solemn and statuesque in their proportions and movements, and the fleet-footed persons who collectively made up the chorus. The early Greek commentators who ascribed the invention of the tragic costume to Æschylus may have been wrong in fact without necessarily having erred in spirit.

The Suppliants was originally part of a trilogy, and we must remember that, from the time of Æschylus at least, the poets who entered into the festival competition were compelled to present, not one play, but four plays—a tetralogy, consisting of three tragedies (a trilogy) and a satyr play. Æschylus' habitual method was to use the trilogy for the purpose of revealing a dramatic story—as that of the daughters of Danaus —extending in action over a considerable period of time. Theoretically each individual drama had a fictional action corresponding to the time of representation: the presence of the chorus in the orchestra from the beginning to the end seemed to make this obligatory. In practice, however, two devices could be used to obviate the severe limitations thus imposed. The use of the trilogy enabled Æschylus to show the daughters of Danaus in Argos, later—after the passage of many months—in Egypt, and still later—again after the passage of months—at their final death-scene. Between the parts of a trilogy, as between the acts of a modern play, time might lapse. In addition to this device was another, once more exemplified in *The Suppliants*. These dramas of Æschylus were poetic dramas, not bound by the petty restrictions of the realistic stage: the actual might therefore easily be forgotten in the contemplation of the imaginative. For the audience there was no shock, or wrenching of the mind, when, during the chanting of a few verses by the chorus, it was presumed that Pelasgus, the king, had journeyed back to his palace, had summoned his council, had explained the problem set before him, had received their answer, and had travelled back again to the sea-shore. Ideal time, not real time, rules in the Greek tragic theatre.

The fourth part of the tetralogy was a satyr play. This is a peculiar form of drama, the characteristic property of the Greek stage, about which we know but little. Only one complete work of the kind has come down to us—the *Cyclops* of Euripides, presumably performed about the year 410 B.C.—but another, the *Ichneutæ*, or *Trackers*, of Sophocles (about 460 B.C.), has fairly recently come to light in incomplete form. From these, and from some representations on vases, it would seem that the typical play of this kind was a drama in which the chorus were satyrs, dressed in pieces of skin, with attached tails, round their middles, led by old Silenus himself. The themes must have been tales of adventure, involving a fair amount of merriment and ending happily. The *Cyclops* tells how Odysseus (Ulysses) out-tricks the one-eyed giant who seeks to destroy him; the *Trackers* is the earliest detective-drama on record, in which the chorus take in hand the search for Apollo's stolen cattle and discover the culprit in Hermes. In view, however, of the facts that so little is extant of this kind of play and that it is so dependent upon the ancient and forgotten cult of Dionysus, lord of the satyrs, we may pass it rapidly by; although, in any endeavour to reconstruct in our minds the conditions of an Athenian festival performance, the inclusion of these satyr shows should always be remembered. They formed part of the offerings of the tragic poets.

The chorus, as *The Suppliants* amply reveals, was the original core of the tragic drama. Here in this play the number of performers was fifty, and that number, the established size of the dithyrambic chorus also, appears to have been the traditional chorus strength when tragedy first took shape. Very soon, however, modifications were introduced. Perhaps because it was difficult for the performers to train themselves in the intricate melodies and in the complex dance movements demanded in the four parts of the tetralogy, Æschylus was responsible for splitting the fifty performers into four groups of twelve each; and twelve remained the stable size of the chorus until, some years later, Sophocles increased the number to fifteen. If the reduction of the chorus to twelve persons was due to practical considerations it has been presumed that the subsequent increase to fifteen was due to æsthetic reasons. Since the chorus was always split into parts, with a general chorus-leader and subsidiary leaders for the separate portions, the presence of fifteen performers permitted the entry of three lines of five persons each, and at the same time allowed the main chorus-leader to detach himself on occasion from his fellows, leaving still a balanced array of two half-choruses each consisting of seven persons.

On the rôle of the chorus it is wise to concentrate when reading the Greek drama, for the modifications introduced in its theatrical function provide a kind of record of the development of the tragic concept from the beginnings in Æschylus to the end in Euripides. In *The Suppliants*, as we have observed, the chorus is virtually the protagonist. This is the earliest, most primitive form, when the drama is dragging itself with difficulty out of the dithyramb. Sporadically, similarly composed plays are to be found much later in date, but in general the history of the Greek stage shows a gradual reduction of the chorus's participation in the dramatic action. It never disappears completely—that with which Æschylus started remains to the very conclusion—but less and less, as the years go by, does it play the major part assigned to it in earliest times.

At the very beginning Thespis drew drama out of the dithyramb by placing a single actor in opposition to the choral group and to its *exarchos*, or leader. When we speak of a single actor, however, two things must be understood. First, by the use of different masks and dress, one performer might, within the course of a single drama, assume various parts. And, second, the reference to a single actor does not imply that the Greek drama, from beginning to end, did not make free theatrical use of other, but mute, persons. In imaginatively reconstructing the productions of these dramas we must think of a king, Pelasgus or Menelaus or Agamemnon, entering the stage powerfully and richly attended; we must think of the Herald in *The Suppliants* as accompanied by many warriors ready to lay hands on the petitioning women; we must, too, be prepared to accept the appearance of named characters often of some considerable importance, who, in excess of the stipulated number of 'actors,' come on the stage in silent rôles.

The allusion to 'stipulated number of actors' reminds us that Thespis' single player was soon given companions. Very hesitantly, as *The Suppliants* shows, Æschylus brought in a second actor—so hesitantly, in fact, that, with the slightest of changes, the entire action of this drama might have been carried through with the utilization of one performer only. There are only two scenes—when Danaus speaks to Pelasgus and when Pelasgus confronts the Herald—that positively demand the presence of two speaking actors on the stage at one time.

With this second actor Æschylus remained content until Sophocles, his younger contemporary, introduced a third speaking part. This, however, was the limit to which the Greek stage moved. Even the rebellious Euripides dared not go further, but was prepared to make use of diverse dramatic devices to cover up the consequences of the restriction in speaking rôles. A good example appears in his *Orestes*. During the earlier scenes Pylades appears as the traditional friend of the hero. At the close of the drama, however, the author needs to have on the stage Menelaus, Orestes, and the god Apollo, three actors all with speeches to deliver; in addition he needs the presence of a girl, Hermione, and of Pylades. There is no difficulty in leaving Hermione mute, but a slight problem arises in connexion with Pylades. Silent he stands throughout the scene, and then Menelaus turns to him with a question.

Art thou too, Pylades, a partner in this bloody work?

he asks, and Orestes quickly intervenes with the words

> His silence says he is; so my saying it will suffice.

Later, to get him off the stage, Orestes gives his friend a cue for exit:

> Ho there! fire the palace from beneath, Electra; and, Pylades, my trusty friend, kindle the parapet of yonder walls.

Thus bidden, the mute hastily retires.

Conventions such as these must obviously be fully understood if we are to appreciate the Greek drama aright—although at the same time, despite these conventions born of a stage so unlike our own, we must ever stand amazed at the likeness between the dramatic concepts and methods of this age and those operative more than two thousand years later. The dramatist's task was essentially the same then as now: the presence of particular theatrical conventions creates no chasm between Æschylus and O'Neill, between Sophocles and Shaw.

The Stalwart Warrior: "The Persians"

Æschylus, author of *The Suppliants*, was born at Eleusis in the year 525 B.C., at the very time when Cambyses, monarch of Persia, led his victorious forces down into Egypt. Great things were happening as he grew to boyhood: the shuttle of destiny was weaving a glorious future for the city of his adoption, the little sea-town of Athens, although for a time the oracles seemed dark. Closer and closer came the looming power of Persia. When the dramatist-to-be was aged thirteen Darius, the successor of Cambyses, swept down over the Balkan peninsula; when he was thirty-five years old, even while *The Suppliants* was being performed at Athens, he stood alongside his brother and a band of his countrymen at Marathon, a plain on the eastern coast of Attica, and there helped to shatter the Persian hosts sent to destroy his city. The event was long remembered, and the poet's prowess on the occasion became almost legendary. When, an old man of sixty-nine, as he lay dying, afar off from his own land, in Sicily, he wrote his epitaph he recalled the event in bold Miltonic words. "Here Æschylus lies," he wrote:

> Here Æschylus lies, 'neath Gela's fertile soil, a guest
> From the Athenian land he loved the best:
> How stalwart in the fight was this Euphorion's son
> May the long-tressed Persian tell that fled from Marathon.

These were the words they carved in honour on his tomb.

Marathon, however, did not end the struggle. Ten years later, at Thermopylæ, a pass leading from Thessaly to the south, an heroic company of Spartans fought a long and weary battle with the invaders and were eventually overwhelmed by the force of numbers. Athens soon was in flames, and its memory would have perished had not the city's tiny ships, anticipating the great fight of the Armada, battled with the mightier Persian fleet at Salamis and so shattered the encroaching power of the East. Rebuilt, the Athenian state was freed to produce its inspiration for the world.

Remembering these things, we need feel no surprise that in the works of Æschylus there appears a grandeur, an elemental strength, that gives to his plays a quality of monumental majesty. He was, we feel, close to Olympus in his heroic stature and conceptions. Legend said that he was inspired by the god Dionysus, and it is known that he had been initiated into the mysteries of his native Eleusis, the mysteries that brought men near to the power of Demeter, the goddess of the Earth. In his plays the human seems very close to the godlike, the gods walk like men, and we breathe the air of ecstasy.

Nor need we feel surprise that in his second extant play, *The Persians*, produced in 472 B.C., eight years after the battle of Salamis, he has presented us with a drama at once unique in the annals of the Greek stage because of its adoption of contemporary subject-matter, and almost unique in the entire history of the theatre because it succeeds in viewing a stirring contemporary struggle from an almost Olympian height. This was no catchpenny theatrical exploitation of recent war; by his extraordinary strength Æschylus has attained to what might have appeared the impossible—the contemplation of living events, in which he himself had been directly and physically involved, *sub specie æternitatis.*

It is a magnificent achievement, this. Set in distant Susa and thus removed from the contemporary spectators in space if not in time, rich in sonorous Persian names, which give to it an element of strangeness, it introduces a chorus of Persian Elders at a period shortly after the battle of Salamis. Xerxes, the son of Darius, is in Greece with his army, and the chorus expresses anxiety concerning the king's return and his "arm'd host blazing with gold." Atossa, the queen-mother, joins them in their talk, and this gives the author dramatic opportunity for the introduction of a reference to Athens and what that city stands for. Atossa inquires, "Where, in what clime, the tow'rs of Athens rise?" and the choral leader answers her:

LEADER: Far in the west, where sets th' imperial sun.
ATOSSA: Yet my son will'd the conquest of this town.
LEADER: May Greece through all her states bend to his power!
ATOSSA: Send they embattled numbers to the field?
LEADER: A force, that to the Medes hath wrought much woe. . . .
ATOSSA: From the strong bow wing they the barbed shaft?
LEADER: They grasp the stout spear, and the massy shield.
ATOSSA: What monarch reigns, whose power commands their ranks?
LEADER: Slaves to no lord, they own no kingly power.

A messenger now enters and relates, in memorable words, the progress of that battle of Salamis in which Æschylus himself had participated. A long catalogue of fallen Persian nobles is recited, but to the intensely dramatic query of the queen,

> Who is not fallen?
> What leader must we wail? What sceptred chief
> Dying hath left his troops without a lord?

the Messenger is able to reply,

> Xerxes himself lives, and beholds the light—

small comfort when the flower of Persian youth is gone.

After a long dirge by the chorus Atossa now calls upon the spirit of Darius, and that king's ghost rises from the tomb. This gives Æschylus the opportunity of introducing his basic tragic concept: the disaster fallen upon Persia has been wrought by *hubris*, overweening pride and ambition:

> With what a winged course the oracles
> Haste their completion! With the lightning's speed
> Jove on my son hath hurl'd his threaten'd vengeance:
> Yet I implor'd the gods that it might fall
> In time's late process: but when rashness drives
> Impetuous on, the scourge of Heav'n uprais'd
> Lashes the fury forward; hence these ills
> Pour headlong on my friends.

At the end of the drama, tattered, weary, worn, Xerxes enters. In the lament chanted by him and the chorus there is no idle indulgence in triumph, on Æschylus' part, over a defeated enemy. Rather is there a profound sympathy with the despair that has come upon this land through pride and a deep, tragic appreciation of the meaning of these contemporary events.

The Persians is a 'static' drama in that but little or no action occurs in it and that there is no real conflict involved in the presentation of the characters, yet its majesty of conception gives it an intensity that makes up for any absence of movement. The greatness of Æschylus is revealed nowhere more clearly than in this play wherein he invests the immediate and the topical with almost mythological grandeur.

Among the Gods: "Prometheus Bound"

In Æschylus' thought the relation of God to man was ever paramount. It was, indeed, through this preoccupation that he succeeded with such power in establishing the tragic form of drama, for tragedy is in essence the theatrical representation of themes wherein man is set in relation to the universe. It is an essay, not in social relationships, but in the eternal problem of good and evil. Its quality is metaphysical. In tragedy the supernatural becomes, as it were, part of the natural: man and fate become one.

How deeply Æschylus was obsessed with such considerations is revealed in *Prometheus Bound* (*c.* 470 B.C.), a baffling drama in view of the fact that we have in it only a fragment of a trilogy and can but guess at the solution. We do not even know whether this play was a first part or a second. Presumably it was preceded by an action showing Prometheus —who, although a mortal, had been admitted to the secrets of Olympus —defying the anger of Zeus and bearing the precious treasure of fire to man, but of this we may not be sure. All that is certain is that the end of the trilogy must have introduced some kind of a reconciliation between the god and his enemy: beyond this we may only vaguely conjecture. Our feet are on sure ground nowhere save on the basis of the one extant portion of the greater whole.

This drama, since it showed Prometheus bound by Zeus' orders to a crag in the Caucasus, presented to the poet a serious problem in dramaturgy, and a measure of Æschylus' skill is to be found in a consideration of the manner in which he keeps our interest alive in the necessarily static action. At the beginning two symbolic characters, Force and Power, enter with the blacksmith god Hephaistos, commissioned to nail Prometheus to the rocks. Their attitude towards the task assigned to them immediately captures our attention: although compelled to do Zeus' bidding, Hephaistos shrinks from its necessity: "It must needs be done," he says to Power, "yet urge me not overmuch." In the contrast between these two figures the essential problem of the tragedy is set. Prometheus has betrayed his trust and therefore must be punished, yet even a god may feel pity at his fate, for his crime was motivated by pity for mankind.

Left alone, Prometheus cries out to the elements, and as he cries the chorus, consisting of the daughters of Oceanus, enter the orchestra. "What murmur hovereth near?" asks Prometheus:

> Once more the murmur
> I hear as of hovering birds;
> And the air is whirring with quick
> Beating of wings. For me
> There is fear, whatever approaches.

The chorus, however, is come in sympathy with the hero, and the skill of the dramatist is shown in the manner by which he thus draws a sharp contrast first between the dark, mighty figure of the man nailed to the rock and these women, light and free as the ocean's waves, and, second, between the gloom of the Caucasian rocks, elements of earth, and the bright elemental sprites of water. In a moment their father, Oceanus, appears, and once more contrast is afforded, since this monarch of the seas is presented as a goodwilled but craven-hearted time-server, who is eager to give advice, unwilling to take any risks. In a choral chant Prometheus tells of his hopes for mankind, and again his words are broken by the appearance of the wretched Io, another victim of divine wrath, half demented as she flees from land to land pursued by a gadfly. Akin to her in misery, Prometheus reveals that Zeus' power cannot last for ever, and dares the gods' anger a second time by counselling her to a certain yet perilous way of escape. Still further contrast is provided by the entry of Hermes, the impertinent herald of Zeus: Prometheus remains obdurate, and at the end of the drama, amid lightning from heaven, the entire crag to which Prometheus has been bound sinks downward out of sight.

How to explain this tragedy it is difficult to say. One thing alone seems certain—that Æschylus viewed Zeus in what may be styled a progressive light. In his thought Zeus becomes a character, domineering and tyrannical at first, and later wrought, through experience and its accumulated wisdom, to assume the benign and just features of the monarch to whom pray the daughters of Danaus. Prometheus because of pride has done wrong in breaking his trust, yet his opposition to the tyrannical power is worthy of admiration. His pride and the cruel implacability of the god will alike be modified and tempered in the final reconciliation.

Perhaps, with its wealth of mythological reference, this drama set at the very beginning of time may not make as great appeal to modern readers as others among the plays of the Greeks, yet its majestic proportions allied to the skill by which the contrasting characters are endowed with vitality reveal, more than any other of his plays, the essential secret of Æschylus.

The Tale of the House of Atreus: the "Oresteia"

Out of all the poet's ninety plays only seven remain, but among these seven there is fortunately one complete trilogy, the *Oresteia* (458 B.C.), comprising *Agamemnon, The Choephori,* and *The Eumenides.* Of another trilogy we possess the final part, *The Seven against Thebes* (467 B.C.), but, being nothing save an act in a larger drama, this deserves less attention than the later complete work.

Before commencing to read *Agamemnon* one must have in clear view those antecedent events which would have been known to practically every Greek spectator, and the knowledge of which placed the tragic dramatist in a peculiar position with respect to his subject-matter. In a fragment of one of Antiphanes' comedies, *Poetry,* we listen to a comic playwright complaining:

> The writer of tragedy is a lucky fellow! The audience always knows the plot as soon as his play begins. All the poet has to do is to give a jog to their memories. He just says "Œdipus": they know all the rest—father, Laius; mother, Jocasta; daughters, sons, what's to come and what is past. If he but utter the one word "Alcmeon," the very children at once repeat: "He went mad and killed his mother; in a minute Adrastus will come in a rage and go out again. . . ." We can't do that, we have to invent everything—new names, the action before the play begins, the present situation, the climax, the opening. If a comic character forgets any of this, he's hissed off the stage, but a tragic character can forget as much as he likes.

This complaint, exaggeratedly as it may be expressed, is basically justified, and in our reading of the tragic dramas we must make full imaginative allowance for this body of common knowledge on the part of the
spectators. Thus, in witnessing a play on Agamemnon, the memories of
the audience would have carried them far back in time to the story of two
brothers, Atreus and Thyestes, sons of Pelops. Thyestes sins by seducing
his sister-in-law, and Atreus takes a grisly vengeance. Pretending to be
reconciled, he bids Thyestes to his house and sets before him a rich banquet—a banquet, however, which he reveals to be composed of the
bodies of his brother's own children, thus served up before their father.
As a result a curse has descended on the house of Atreus. Agamemnon,
son of Atreus, has married Clytemnestra, and, when the former is absent
in Troy, his wife is seduced by Ægisthus, son of Thyestes. Living in
Agamemnon's palace, the pair of lovers await the return of its lord. It is
at this moment in time, ten years after the departure of Agamemnon for
Troy, that the trilogy begins.

When we turn to the *Oresteia* we immediately recognize that the drama
has moved far from the early days of *The Suppliants* and *Prometheus Bound*,
and, in particular, that three changes have occurred to influence its composition. The first is a change in physical representation. *The Suppliants*
was set on a lonely sea-coast, *Prometheus Bound* amid the Caucasian wilds;
Agamemnon opens before a palace front. By this time the scene-building,
or the *skene* (σκηνή)—which gave us our word 'scene'—has been added
to the early auditorium and orchestra. No doubt simpler in appearance
than was the *skene* of later theatres, it still must have had some slightly
raised platform in front and a background consisting of a wall, ornamented with columns and broken by one large centre door or entrance,
together with two smaller doors placed at the sides. From now on there
was a tendency on the part of the dramatists to choose for their fictional
localities the courtyard of a palace or of a temple: rudimentary scene-
painting already had been introduced—it is said at the inspiration of
Æschylus—but the playwrights found their easiest path was to accept
the wall and the columns as they stood and to utilize these directly.

The second change concerns the actors. About the year 470 B.C.
Sophocles appeared as a successor to Æschylus, and very soon after his
début he added a third to the two speaking parts allowed by his predecessor. This immediately made for a rapid development of dramatic dialogue as opposed to choral chant; it offered greater opportunities for
interplay of character; it permitted variety of incident; above all, it
induced the playwrights to consider more closely the question of dramatic technique.

This development of dramatic technique is the third great change
that had come into being under the influence of Sophocles. The Greek
tragedy now assumed a definite form and was divided into a number of
recognized parts. First came the prologue introducing the theme, indi-

cating the locality, sometimes even the time of day; this was followed by the entrance-song of the chorus, known as the *parodos*; thereafter followed five 'episodes,' portions of dialogue, separated by five choral odes; finally, the drama was brought to a conclusion with the exodus, or exit-song, of the chorus. From this division of parts came, in later Hellenistic times, the traditional five acts of drama.

These altered circumstances must be taken fully into account as we turn to the *Oresteia.*

The *Agamemnon* opens in front of a palace, and in the dim light of dawn we can discern a lonely figure on the roof. His words at once proclaim the palace to be the home of Agamemnon, son of Atreus, and we learn that he himself is a Watchman, placed here by Clytemnestra to give news when a beacon-fire appears on a distant height. This will be the herald of Troy's fall. Suddenly a distant light is seen, and the Watchman retires to present his tidings, while the chorus enter singing of the house of Atreus, of the long, ten-year absence of their lord, and particularly of one episode of the Trojan expedition—when the Greek fleet was held back by contrary winds, and when Agamemnon, the leader of the host, sacrificed his own daughter Iphigenia that the gods might be propitious:

> And so he steeled his heart—ah, well-a-day—
>   Aiding a war for one false woman's sake,
>   His child to slay,
>   And with her spilt blood make
> An offering, to speed the ships upon their way!
>
>   Lusting for war, the bloody arbiters
> Closed heart and ears, and would not hear nor heed
>   The girl-voice plead,
> "Pity me, Father!" nor her prayers,
>   Nor tender, virgin years.
>
>   So when the chant of sacrifice was done,
>   Her father bade the youthful priestly train
> Raise her, like some poor kid, above the altar-stone,
>   From where amid her robes she lay
>   Sunk all in swoon away—
> Bade them, as with the bit that mutely tames the steed,
>   Her fair lips' speech refrain,
> Lest she should speak a curse on Atreus' home and seed.

"Lest she should speak a curse on Atreus' home and seed"—these words give us our first clue to Æschylus' treatment of the Agamemnon story. Outwardly there is a curse upon this house; in a certain sense all the characters are doomed by fate, have no choice but to pursue paths allotted to them. Yet a strange paradox exists here. Already it is evident that this absent king, Agamemnon, has committed a crime, and since, immediately after these words, the queen, Clytemnestra, appears, our

imagination connects the story of Iphigenia with her: she, queen and
mother, has been sadly wronged that thus her daughter has been sacrificed in order that a fleet might sail. In this paradoxical sense character is
destiny: whatever happens to Agamemnon in this ill-fated house will be
of his own creation.

In their chant the members of the chorus have revealed themselves to
be old men—"grey dishonoured eld, feeble of frame, unfit . . . to join the
warrior array that then went forth unto the fray." Once more, in providing a contrast between the woman Clytemnestra and these aged men
—a contrast similar to that between the man-god Prometheus and the
daughters of Oceanus—Æschylus has shown his innate dramatic sense.
She tells them of the meaning of the beacon-fire: Troy is fallen. Some
there are who doubt her word, think she may be deluding herself; there is
a confusion of thought and of talk, when, in this idealized time of Greek
tragedy, a Herald arrives to announce the truth of the tidings and to say
that Agamemnon, homeward bound, has been separated from the rest of
his fleet. With fine dramatic irony the chorus now sings of the woe fallen
upon Troy through a woman, and hints unknowingly of what is to come
to this palace and its occupants:

> Woe springs from wrong, the plant is like the seed—
> While Right, in honour's house, doth its own likeness breed.
>   Some past impiety, some grey old crime,
>   Breeds the young curse, that wantons in our ill,
>   Early or late, when haps th'appointed time—
>   And out of light brings power of darkness still,
> A master-fiend, a foe, unseen, invincible;
>   A pride accursed, that broods upon the race
>   And home in which dark Atè holds her sway—
> Sin's child and Woe's, that wears its parents' face.

Again in the world of idealized time, Agamemnon now appears,
royally attended, seated in a chariot, while another chariot bears the
person of Cassandra, daughter of Priam and dedicated vestal, to touch
whom is impiety, and yet whom Agamemnon has reft away from her
altar and her home. With a rather heavy, bombastic speech he addresses
the chorus and is greeted in honeyed words by Clytemnestra, who, to
honour him, spreads rich crimson tapestries from the chariot to the
palace. Agamemnon knows that such honour is fit only for the gods,
refuses to set foot on the "rich dyes," but, puffed up with self-esteem and
guiled by her flattery, at length consents and walks over the crimson
cloth into the palace. As he goes he adds another to the grievances of Clytemnestra by bidding her care for his mistress, Cassandra.

Left alone, the chorus gives expression to its dark foreboding:

> Wherefore for ever on the wings of fear
>   Hovers a vision drear
> Before my boding heart? a strain,

> Unbidden and unwelcome, thrills mine ear,
> Oracular of pain.

Immediately thereafter Clytemnestra comes from the palace and cruelly, rudely, addresses Cassandra, bidding her also go within. Although she maintains silence in the presence of the queen, as soon as Clytemnestra departs Cassandra, the priestess-prophetess, dismally foreshadows what is to follow. First, in dark words, she shows her awareness of the blood-stained story of the house of Atreus, and then her chanting ecstasy hints at what must be:

> God! a new sight! a net, a snare of hell,
> Set by her hand—herself a snare more fell!
> A wedded wife, she slays her lord,
> Helped by another hand!

The chorus chides her for her boding speech, but becomes disturbed as her words continue, and still more disturbed when, after she has entered the palace, a loud cry is heard from within. There follows a highly dramatic scene where the individual members of the chorus speculate confusedly on the meaning of the cry—confusion stilled when Clytemnestra appears, blood on her forehead, and when the palace doors open to display the slain bodies of Agamemnon and Cassandra. The queen exults in her crime, the while the chorus upbraids her: their words are full of love and honour for their dead lord, hers emphasize the foul wrongs done to her by his faithlessness and by his sacrifice of Iphigenia. A moment later Ægisthus comes upon the stage, proud of having avenged himself upon the son of the man who had set the ghastly banquet before Thyestes. So incensed is he by the reproaches of the old men of the chorus that he is about to fall upon them when Clytemnestra intervenes. She will have no more of killing and stays Ægisthus' angry hand: in her words as she addresses him one senses a hint of weariness:

> Nay, enough, enough, my champion! we will smite and slay no more.
> Already have we reaped enough the harvest-field of guilt:
> Enough of wrong and murder, let no other blood be spilt. . . .
> > Let the cur-pack growl and yell!
> I and thou will rule the palace and will order all things well.

Her speech is instinct with unconscious dramatic irony, for the next play, *The Choephori*, is to tell of the vengeance fallen on the murderers: murder is not, as Clytemnestra thinks, an end, but is merely a beginning. Before turning to the second drama, however, it is essential to survey Æschylus' dramatic purpose as revealed in *Agamemnon*. That this play is executed with consummate skill and majestic mastery is at once apparent. The tension is subtly built up and varied: the calm opening in the darkness before dawn, with the sleepy Watchman at his weary vigil; the sudden glow of the beacon; the nervous excitement of Clytemnestra; the doubts of the chorus; the triumphant entry of Agamemnon, and his wife's steel-lipped greeting; the insulting of Cassandra, followed by the priestess's ecstatic ravings; Clytemnestra's defence after the murder, and the approach towards a physical struggle between Ægisthus and the chorus —all these give to the play a dramatic movement intense and absorbing. In the midst of the movement characters shine forth brightly: Clytemnestra nursing her wrongs; Ægisthus, love-besotten and querulously intent on vengeance; Agamemnon, of true heroic stature, yet guilty of the sin of pride, willing to step like a god into his house, willing like a god to make the dedicated Cassandra his mistress. This stress upon character-delineation makes *Agamemnon* a much more human play than any we have so far considered; yet we must not lose sight of the fact that here we are confronted with no domestic drama: here we are in the presence of essential tragedy, metaphysical, baffling, infinite in its implications. The problem of evil is that on which Æschylus sets his gaze, and the gods are ever in his mind as he deals with the human action.

The story, of course, is not yet done. When Clytemnestra greets Agamemnon she makes excuse for the absence of his son, the boy Orestes. This Orestes is the hero of *The Choephori*, so called because the chorus is composed of a band of 'Libation-bearers,' who are the companions of Orestes' sister Electra. The action opens before the tomb of Agamemnon. Two men, seen from their dress to have travelled from afar, enter the stage and reveal themselves as Orestes, now grown to manhood, and his close friend, Pylades. On the altar the former reverently places two locks of his own hair. This prologue scene is followed by the entry of the chorus, together with Electra: at the altar she finds the locks, and immediately recognizes them as belonging to her brother. Orestes reveals himself to her, and, after a moment of doubting suspicion, tearfully she embraces him and learns that he has come at the god Apollo's command to seek vengeance. A great wave of ecstatic song from the chorus ensues, and Orestes hastily outlines his plan of action. He enters the palace; the cry of Ægisthus in his death-agony is heard; and at last the vengeful son confronts his mother. A moment's compassion comes to him:

CLYTEMNESTRA: Woe, woe! Ægisthus, spouse and champion, slain!
ORESTES: What, lov'st the man? then in his grave lie down,
    Be his in death, desert him nevermore!
CLYTEMNESTRA: Stay, child, and fear to strike. O son, this breast
    Pillowed thine head full oft, while, drowsed with sleep,
    Thy toothless mouth drew mother's milk from me.
ORESTES: Can I my mother spare? speak, Pylades.
PYLADES: Where then would fall the hest Apollo gave
    At Delphi, where the solemn compact sworn?
    Choose thou the hate of all men, not of gods.

Thus bidden, Orestes drives Clytemnestra within, but hardly has she been slain before the murderer sees what is visible to him alone—a grisly throng of "Gorgon shapes" with "dusky robes and hair unwound," the

Furies sent to torment him.

It is difficult to interpret *The Choephori* aright. Brilliant as is the conception and glorious the language, one has the impression that Æschylus is not as deeply interested in this part of the theme as he was in *Agamemnon*. He is inclined, as it were, to hurry on with the action, laying no stress, for example, on such potentially dramatic scenes as the recognition by Electra of the brother she has not seen for so long or the confronting of Clytemnestra by her son. The whole of the action might almost be regarded as merely the necessary preliminary for that which is to follow—the expiation and reconciliation of spirit revealed in *The Eumenides*.

The Furies form the final chorus in this third play. The scene now is the temple at Delphi, to which Orestes, worn with suffering, has at last come in his wanderings. A Pythian priestess goes to the shrine and shrinks back in terror: at the central altar she has seen a tattered, blood-stained figure, and

> Lo, in front of him,
> Crouched on the altar-steps, a grisly band
> Of women . . . not like women they,
> But Gorgons rather . . . black, and all their shape
> The eye's abomination to behold.

At this the main doors of the temple open, showing the scene as the priestess has described it, and revealing also the god-figure of Apollo. The ghost of Clytemnestra rises, awakening the Furies from their sleep; they demand their prey while Apollo tries to protect his suppliant. Sternly he admonishes them:

> Know, that above the marriage-bed ordained
> For man and woman standeth Right as guard,
> Enhancing sanctity of troth-plight sworn;
> Therefore, if thou art placable to those
> Who have their consort slain, nor will'st to turn
> On them the eye of wrath, unjust art thou
> In hounding to his doom the man who slew
> His mother.

Pallas, he declares, Pallas, the goddess of reason, shall decide.

After this the scene is supposed to change. In all probability Orestes and the Furies simply move over to one of the side-doors and imaginatively are presumed to have made the long journey from Apollo's temple at Delphi to the temple, in Athens, of Pallas Athene. Thus in this movement time and place are alike truncated: both exist in an imaginatively ideal world. Before the goddess Orestes and the Furies put their case. For the latter the old law of implacable vengeance alone has validity:

> When from womb of Night we sprang, on us this labour
> Was laid and shall abide.
> Gods immortal are ye, yet beware ye touch not
> That which is our pride!

> None may come beside us gathered round the blood-feast—
> > For us no garments white
> Gleam on a festal day; for us a darker fate is,
> > Another darker rite.
> That is mine hour when falls an ancient line—
> > When in the household's heart
> The God of blood doth slay by kindred hands,—
> > Then do we bear our part:
> On him who slays we sweep with chasing cry:
> > Though he be triply strong,
> We wear and waste him; blood atones for blood,
> > New pain for ancient wrong.

Athene decides that the case must be tried and argued before the twelve judges of the Areopagus, the highest court in Athens. On the one side, the Furies mutter and grumble:

> Now they are all undone, the ancient laws,
> > If here the slayer's cause
> Prevail—

while, on the other, Apollo comes as witness in Orestes' defence. The judges place their votes in an urn, and it is found that they are equally divided—whereupon Athene gives her voice for Orestes, and to the threatening chorus, who cry that they have been dishonoured by the younger gods, she offers a new rôle: if they agree to follow her they will win honour as spirits of mercy. After some hesitation they accept, and the play ends with a kind of mystical chant as the Furies, now become Eumenides, figures of goodwill, leave the stage:

> With loyalty we lead you; proudly go,
> Night's childless children, to your home below!
> > (*O citizens, awhile from words forbear!*)
> To darkness' deep primeval lair,
> Far in Earth's bosom, downward fare,
> > Adored with prayer and sacrifice.
> > (*O citizens, forbear your cries!*)
> Pass hitherward, ye powers of Dread,
> With all your former wrath allayed,
> > Into the heart of this loved land;
> With joy unto your temple wend,
> The while upon your steps attend
> > The flames that feed upon the brand—
> > (*Now, now ring out your chant, your joy's acclaim!*)
> > Behind them, as they downward fare,
> > Let holy hands libations bear,
> > > And torches' sacred flame.
> > All-seeing Zeus and Fate come down
> > To battle fair for Pallas' town!
> *Ring out your chant, ring out your joy's acclaim!*

This is the very apotheosis of patriotism. For Æschylus the problem of evil, which he sought to explore in the *Oresteia*, is to be explained only by taking it to the uttermost extremes—to primeval times before the birth of history when the universe was peopled by titans and by gods, and to the conditions of his own age, into the very halls of the Areopagus. That final chorus chant of *The Eumenides* is a fitting epilogue to his entire dramatic achievement, with its supernatural figures of the old law, led by Pallas Athene, trooping downward towards the elements that gave them being, and with its direct appeal to those citizens, the fellows of the poet, who sit watching the first performance of his tragic trilogy. Fitting, too, is the concept they embody. Evil has been set loose in the world; death and torment and darkness have come in its wake, and Clytemnestra's hope that by the mere exercise of the human will it can be, at any point, given an end has been proved naught save an idle dream; yet the end does come, and out of the suffering new vision arises: the Furies are transformed into the spirits of mercy.

The first dramatist whose work has come down to us was a mighty master.

2

THE GLORY OF THE GREEK THEATRE: SOPHOCLES

ÆSCHYLUS was obviously a pioneer: he was compelled to forge the very instruments from which his art was fashioned, and there must ever be amazement that, thus handicapped, he was able to accomplish so much. His position in relation to the theatre of his time bore many parallels to that of Marlowe in the Elizabethan Age. If he wrought deeper and finer things than Marlowe in the course of his brief existence was permitted to create, like him he served as a forerunner to one, if not greater, at least more fortunately circumstanced than himself. If Æschylus is Marlowe, Sophocles is Shakespeare.

When Sophocles was born in the lovely town of Colonus about 495 B.C. the struggle with Persia was at its fiercest, but by the time he was a boy of fifteen Athens had secured her independence. Events were moving rapidly in these distant days, and there was a world of difference between the man who, at forty-five, fought at Salamis and the youth, thirty years his junior, who was chosen for his beauty and his skill in music to lead the chorus of boys who sang a pæan of joy round the trophy erected to commemorate that victory. The one spent his early years in conflict, the other was destined to reap full advantage of the peace which brought Athens to its greatest glory. Under Pericles he saw the Parthenon rise majestically: he was privileged to gaze on the wonders of Pheidias' art when these were fresh and young.

Contemporary records tell of his wide accomplishments. Extraordinarily handsome, he was a noted athlete; the gifts of learning were his; for his dancing and his musical talents he was famous. Surrounded by friends, esteemed by his countrymen, he lived a life of even tenor, balanced, calm, and classically triumphant. He was καλὸς κ'ἀγαθός —beautiful and good—the ideal of perfection. Even in his death he was fortunate, for, passing away at eighty-nine years of age, he was spared seeing the might of the Athenian navy annihilated at Ægospotami in 405 B.C. This was the decisive battle in the Peloponnesian War and the ominous sign that Athens' brief flowering was near its end.

Amid these surroundings Sophocles might readily have become an easy sentimentalist, but the basis of his city's culture was not of so light a kind. There was strength here, and thought, and passion. Above all, there was deep interest in man and in man's relations to the universe. The dark and the terrible formed part of the woof of Greek philosophy. Of a consequence most of Sophocles' dramas, instead of dealing—as they might well have done—with the easy loveliness of life, take us through the world of suffering: Antigone dies immured in a rock and the eyes of Œdipus are cruelly torn out. The tragic sense was deeply implanted in him, and his calm was not won by a refusal to contemplate suffering. It was this fortunate man who wrote: "Never to have been born is much the best."

As a dramatist he necessarily benefited much from the pioneering efforts of his predecessor Æschylus. To the latter's two actors, as we have seen, he added a third, and the consummate skill with which he handled his dialogue showed that he had learned much from the earlier works. Æschylus had improved the stage: Sophocles improved it further and gave it flexibility. Contemporary record testifies to his inventions in the field of scene-painting, and there is reason to believe that he was the first to provide the persons of his tragedies with a defined background. A still more significant step was taken when he discarded the Æschylean trilogy and substituted therefor separate dramas, each with its own beginning, middle, and end, works self-inclusive and self-complete. By taking this step he moved the early theatre vastly nearer the dramatic form of the later Western stage.

Æschylus had been, like his immediate predecessors, the entire director of his own writings. It was expected then that the poet, besides penning his lines, should provide the accompanying music, train the chorus, and even take the leading histrionic rôles. With Sophocles, despite his varied accomplishments, we begin to see the breaking-up of these functions: the actor becomes an interpreter of the poet's words, the musician is a separate artist, and the chorus may be trained by one other than the author. Perhaps this breaking-up of theatrical functions came by chance. Although record tells of Sophocles' magnificent performance in the parts of the maiden Nausikaa, when he held an audience spellbound as he gave an exhibition of expert ball-playing, and of the youthful lyric Thamyras, it is known that his voice was too weak for weightier rôles. As a result, he was forced to depend on the services of another. At the same time, this separation of actor and poet was a natural development. In the early days of Æschylus there were no trained actors, and the poet was consequently forced to be his own interpreter, but when Sophocles came to write there must have been a number of men in Athens with stage experience, and clearly it was to the author's advantage to relieve himself of this part of the performance in order to concentrate on his writing and on general direction. Here is the true beginning of professional playing, and it is interesting to observe that in the Greek age the actor, instead of being the despised slave of Roman times or a person only half removed from an

Elizabethan vagrant, held a high position in public esteem.

The House of Atreus again: "Electra"

Of all Sophocles' one hundred and twenty dramas only seven have come down to us complete, together with a sorry yet precious fragment of one of his satyr plays. Although he first appeared in 471 B.C. and had already won a victory over Æschylus in 468 B.C., the first of these seven tragedies, the *Antigone*, was not written until about the year 441, when his position was fully established. About the same time came his *Ajax*; *Œdipus Tyrannus* dates from about ten years later; *Electra* and the *Trachiniæ* must have come between 420 and 414, *Philoctetes* in 409, when the playwright was eighty-six years old; while *Œdipus at Colonus*, his last work, was presented posthumously in 401.

Of these *Antigone* is perhaps the most appealing to the modern consciousness, but, before dealing with this drama, we may do well to examine the later *Electra*, since this treats of the same theme as Æschylus' *Oresteia*, and in its modifications well indicates the essential differences between the two playwrights.

In this *Electra*, as at the beginning of the *Agamemnon*, it is time of dawn. Three figures appear before us—an aged Tutor, Orestes, and Pylades. Orestes has returned to effect his revenge and is discussing his plans with the old man when a cry from within the palace reminds him of the sister whom he has not seen for so many years. Electra now enters with a chorus of women of Mycenæ, the latter sympathetic but counselling her to forget her woes and to give stay to her self-torment. Suddenly a new character enters—Chrysothemis, Electra's sister. Anxiously she advises caution and the acceptance of authority:

> Sister, why com'st thou once more to declaim
> In public at the outer gate? Has time
> Not schooled thee to desist from idle rage?
> I too, my sister, chafe no less than thou
> At our sad fortunes, and had I the power,
> Would make it plain how I regard our masters.
> But in the storm 'tis best to reef the sail,
> Nor utter threats we cannot execute.
> I would thou wert likeminded; yet I know
> Justice is on thy side, and I am wrong.
> Yet if I am to keep my liberty,
> I needs must bow before the powers that be.

At once, in a flash of anger, Electra displays her true temper. "O shame," she cries,

> that thou, the child of such a sire,
> Should'st him forget and take thy mother's part! . . .
> Shall we to all our ills add cowardice?

Her spirit is implacable; unshakeable the devotion she bears to the memory of her father.

After this scene follows a scene between Electra and her mother. It is apparent that there is deadly enmity between them; their words to each other are bitter, smouldering in hate. Now the Tutor appears, in accordance with the plan devised by Orestes. Pretending to have been sent by a Phocian known to Clytemnestra, he tells her that Orestes is dead, that his ashes are in the urn he bears. While Electra sinks in woe, Clytemnestra is troubled by mingled passions:

> *CHORUS-LEADER:* Alas, alas! our ancient masters' line,
>   So it appears, hath perished root and branch.
> *CLYTEMNESTRA:* Are these glad tidings? Rather would I say
>   Sad, but of profit. Ah, how hard my lot
>   When I must look for safety to my losses!
> *TUTOR:* Why, lady, why downhearted at my news?
> *CLYTEMNESTRA:* Strange is the force of motherhood; a mother,
>   Whate'er her wrongs, can ne'er forget her child.
> *TUTOR:* So it would seem our coming was in vain.
> *CLYTEMNESTRA:* Nay, not in vain. How canst thou say "in vain,"
>   If of his death thou bring'st convincing proof,
>   Who from my life drew life, and yet, estranged,
>   Forgat the breasts that suckled him, forgat
>   A mother's tender nurture, fled his home,
>   And since that day has never seen me more,
>   Slandered me as the murderer of his sire
>   And breathed forth vengeance?—Neither night nor day
>   Kind slumber closed these eyes, and imminent dread
>   Of death each minute stretched me on the rack.
>   But now on this glad day, of terror rid
>   From him and her, a deadlier plague than he,
>   That vampire who was housed with me to drain
>   My very life blood—now, despite her threats
>   Methinks that I shall pass my days in peace.

Left alone as Clytemnestra and the Tutor enter the palace, Electra gives vent to expression of her woe. The chorus in vain endeavours to comfort her, and bitter gall comes when Chrysothemis arrives, eager and excited, to say that Orestes must have returned, for she has found his locks on the altar. Miserably Electra tells her of the news of their brother's death, but warns her that, although he is gone, she is determined to act unaided: Chrysothemis, who a moment before had been saying she would assist Electra to the limit of her power, now shrinks back, looks timorously around to see if her words have been overheard, advises caution—while the chorus adds to her prudent arguments. Electra, however, is adamant:

> *CHORUS-LEADER:* Hearken! for mortal man there is no gift
>   Greater than forethought and sobriety.

> *ELECTRA:* 'Tis as I thought: before thy answer came
> I knew full well thou wouldst refuse thine aid.
> Unaided then and by myself I'll do it,
> For done it must be, though I work alone.

A choral chant follows, and immediately after it is completed Orestes
and Pylades enter: Electra takes the urn supposed to contain the ashes,
and there is a scene of gentle pathos as brother and sister, she not knowing who he is, converse together, until at last he reveals himself:

> *ELECTRA:*   Ah! woe for thee, Orestes, woe is me,
> If I am not to give thee burial.
> *ORESTES:* Guard well thy lips; thou hast no right to mourn.
> *ELECTRA:* No right to mourn a brother who is dead!
> *ORESTES:* To speak of him in this wise is not meet.
> *ELECTRA:* What, am I so dishonoured of the dead?
> *ORESTES:* Of none dishonoured; this is not thy part.
> *ELECTRA:* Not if Orestes' ashes here I hold?
> *ORESTES:* They are not his, though feigned to pass for his.
>   [*He gently takes the urn from her.*
> *ELECTRA:* Where then is my unhappy brother's grave?
> *ORESTES:* There is no grave; we bury not the quick.
> *ELECTRA:* What sayst thou, boy?
> *ORESTES:*   Nothing that is not true.
> *ELECTRA:* He lives?
> *ORESTES:*   As surely as I am alive.

In joy she embraces him, and eagerly they discuss what they shall do
—too eagerly, for now the Tutor comes to warn them:

> *TUTOR:* Fools! madmen! are ye weary of your lives?
> Or are your natural wits too dull to see
> That ye are standing, not upon the brink,
> But in the midst of mortal jeopardy?
> Nay, had I not kept watch this weary while,
> Here at the door, your plot had slipped inside
> Ere ye yourselves had entered.

Orestes, Pylades, and the Tutor enter the palace while Electra
remains to guard against the return of Ægisthus: Clytemnestra cries out
in death agony, and Orestes comes on the stage once more—a wisp of
doubt in his mind:

> *ELECTRA:* How have ye sped, Orestes?
> *ORESTES:*   All within
> Is well, if Phœbus' oracle spake well.

On the arrival of Ægisthus the doors are opened to display the shrouded
corpse of Clytemnestra, which he believes to be that of Orestes, and a
tensely dramatic scene ensues:

> *ÆGISTHUS:* Take from the face the face-cloth; I, as kin,
> I too would pay my tribute of lament.

ORESTES:　Lift it thyself, 'tis not for me but thee
　　To see and kindly greet what lieth here.
ÆGISTHUS:　Well said, so will I. [*To ELECTRA*] If she be within,
　　Go call me Clytemnestra, I would see her—
ORESTES:　She is beside thee; look not otherwhere.
　　　　　　　　　　　[*ÆGISTHUS removes the face-cloth from the corpse.*

ÆGISTHUS:　O horror!
ORESTES:　　　　　　Why dost start? is the face strange?
ÆGISTHUS:　Who spread the net wherein, O woe is me,
　　I lie enmeshed?
ORESTES:　　　　　Hast thou not learnt ere this
　　The dead of whom thou spakest are alive?
ÆGISTHUS:　Alas! I read thy riddle; 'tis none else
　　Than thou, Orestes, whom I now address.
ORESTES:　A seer so wise, and yet befooled so long!
ÆGISTHUS:　O I am spoiled, undone! yet suffer me,
　　One little word.
ELECTRA:　　　　　Brother, in heaven's name
　　Let him not speak a word or plead his cause.
　　When a poor wretch is in the toils of fate
　　What can a brief reprieve avail him? No,
　　Slay him outright and having slain him give
　　His corse to such grave-makers as is meet,
　　Far from our sight.

Ægisthus is driven within and dies. The end has come.

Even from such a brief summary as the above it must be immediately apparent that Sophocles' *Electra* moves in a world different from that of Æschylus' *Oresteia*. Quite apart from the subtler building of dramatic climaxes, we see that his purpose is entirely distinct from what his predecessor had aimed at. There is no doubt expressed concerning the justice of Orestes' action: a very slight ironic hint is in the words he speaks after the murder of his mother—"All within is well, if Phœbus' oracle spake well"—but that is all. The whole action of the play has been taken down from the elemental world, closer to the world of ordinary life. Condensed as the conversations are, they approach reality more closely than those of Æschylus, and the practical considerations of common life now play their part. In Æschylus' plays the characters stand and speak in idealized isolation; Sophocles causes the Tutor to warn the brother and sister that their words might have been overheard in the palace. We are in the world of men here, not in the world of eternity.

Sophocles' aim is to explain the legendary story in human terms, and to effect this aim he concentrates, not on the theme itself, but on one character. All else is subordinated to Electra. The chorus does not take any dominant position; Orestes and the Tutor are but broadly outlined. In Electra, however, there is a psychological study such as appears nowhere in any of Æschylus' works. Her position in this household is clearly indicated, and as scene follows scene her personality unfolds before us. If any persons stand beside her they are Chrysothemis and Clytemnestra—for this is a tragedy of women rather than of men—but even they are largely foils for the heroine. What Sophocles is interested in is the situation in which one main and two subsidiary characters appear: the mother, unable to hate her son yet living in deadly terror of his return; one daughter, devoted to her father's memory and passing her days in impotent hate; the other, sympathetic towards Electra, yet timorous, prudent, cautious. The drama is one composed of a single fully drawn portrait set against a background of interplay of character.

Electra is a much more assured piece of dramatic art than *The Choephori*, yet something essential has been lost. The metaphysical has ceded place to the natural, and, despite the high idealization in the treatment of the story, we feel that we have drawn somewhat away from the presence of majesty, that we are coming tremblingly near to the realm of the domestic drama.

The Human Law and the Law of the Spirit: "Antigone"

The scene between Electra and Chrysothemis has a close parallel in an earlier and a greater play by Sophocles. *Antigone* presents what *Electra* lacks.

In approaching this drama, once more the preceding events associated with a doomed house must be appreciated. The house is the house of Laius in Thebes. Laius has sinned, and upon his son Œdipus the curse has descended. After many torments Œdipus dies, leaving behind him two sons, Eteocles and Polyneices, who, quarrelling, die by each other's hands in battle. The lordship of Thebes is taken by Creon, who gives the body of Eteocles all due rites, but issues a proclamation to the effect that the body of his brother—because he led an alien host against his native city—shall remain unburied. Of the children of Œdipus only two are left, the girls Antigone and Ismene, the former betrothed to Creon's son, Hæmon.

In the prologue to Sophocles' drama the two sisters enter. Antigone has heard of the proclamation, and, although she knows that death is decreed for anyone who defies the proclamation, she is determined to give honour to her brother's corpse. In a few short lines the personality of the pair is searingly revealed to us—Antigone, devoted to her brother, obdurately intent on her self-appointed mission, herself perhaps half in love with easeful death, Ismene, more fragile, afraid of what her sister's obstinacy may bring. "Listen, Ismene," says Antigone,

> Creon buried our brother Eteocles
> With military honours, gave him a soldier's funeral,
> And it was right that he should; but Polyneices,
> Who fought as bravely and died as miserably—
> They say that Creon has sworn
> No one shall bury him, no one mourn for him,

> But his body must lie in the fields, a sweet treasure
> For carrion birds to find as they search for food.
> That is what they say, and our good king Creon is
> To announce it publicly; and the penalty—
> Stoning to death in the public square!
>   There it is,
>
> And now you can prove what you are:
> A true sister, or a traitor to your family.

In Ismene's reply her character is enshrined: "Poor Antigone! But what can I do about it?" How can Polyneices' body be buried, she inquires: "You have just said the new law forbids it. . . . Think of the danger! Think what Creon will do!" Equally characteristic are Antigone's words:

>   If that is what you think,
> I should not want you, even if you asked to come.
> You have made your choice, you can be what you want to be.
> But I will bury him; and if I must die,
> I say that this crime is holy: I shall lie down
> With him in death, and I shall be as dear
> To him as he to me.
>   It is the dead,
> Not the living, who make the longest demands:
> We die for ever.

Ismene's terror is partly for herself, but largely also for her sister:

> *ISMENE:*   Antigone,
>   I am so afraid for you!
> *ANTIGONE:*   You need not be:
>   You have yourself to consider, after all.
> *ISMENE:* But no one must hear of this, you must tell no one!
>   I will keep it a secret, I promise!
> *ANTIGONE:*   Oh, tell it! Tell every one!
>   Think how they'll hate you when it all comes out
>   If they learn that you knew about it all the time!

To this last cry Ismene's reply is once again revealing, but now rather of Antigone than of herself: "You are so on fire with a plan so ghastly cold!"

The entry-song of the chorus follows, and the isolation of the heroine is increased when we realize that this chorus is made up, not of women or even of youths, but of old men, grown chill and cautious with age. With fine irony they chant of the Theban success in battle; this will be a day of joy:

> Our temples shall be sweet with hymns of praise,
> And the long night shall echo with our chorus.

Creon now comes on stage and, in a kind of parody of a political oration, pompously announces his proclamation. No sooner is this done than, in a comic scene, a half-crazed soldier tells of his finding Polyneices' body with earth sprinkled upon it. In a burst of anger, Creon lashes out with fury: rejecting contemptuously the chorus's suggestion that this deed might have been done by the gods, he declares his belief that some one has been bribed to do it. That every man has his price and that 'money talks' is the mainspring of his thoughts:

> Money!
> There's nothing in the world so demoralizing as money.
> Down go your cities,
> Homes gone, men gone, honest hearts corrupted,
> Crookedness of all kinds, and all for money!

The choral song that follows anticipates a famous passage in *Hamlet.* "What a piece of work is a man" forms its theme:

> Numberless are the world's wonders, but none
> More wonderful than man; the storm grey sea
> Yields to his prows, the huge crests bear him high;
> Earth, holy and inexhaustible, is graven
> With shining furrows where his plows have gone
> Year after year, the timeless labour of stallions.

And its conclusion is a plea for reason:

> O clear intelligence, force beyond all measure!
> O fate of man, working both good and evil!
> When the laws are kept, how proudly his city stands!
> When the laws are broken, what of his city then?
> Never may the anarchic man find rest at my hearth,
> Never be it said that my thoughts are his thoughts.

From this moment the tragedy rushes swiftly on. The soldier returns triumphant with the culprit, Antigone. "You dared defy the law?" inquires Creon incredulously, and her reply is calm:

> I dared.
> It was not God's proclamation. That final Justice
> That rules the world below makes no such laws.
>
> Your edict, King, was strong,
> But all your strength is weakness itself against
> The immortal unrecorded laws of God.
> They are not merely now: they were, and shall be,
> Operative for ever, beyond man utterly.

In a passion, Creon orders Ismene also to be brought before him, and, with the skilled dramatist's sensitive use of the unexpected, she professes to have been a co-partner in her sister's guilt, even while Antigone in her pride wishes to suffer alone:

ISMENE: Yes, if she will let me say so. I am guilty.
ANTIGONE [*coldly*]: No, Ismene. You have no right to say so.
  You would not help me, and I will not have you help me. . . .
    Save yourself. I shall not envy you.
  There are those who will praise you; I shall have honour too.

The chorus now sings of impending doom; the gods are at work; "Man's little pleasure is the Spring of Sorrow." Hæmon, the betrothed of Antigone, comes to plead her cause. On Creon's side is the argument that law and order must be preserved; on Hæmon's the argument that no single man, however wise, can be absolutely sure of the rightness of his judgments. "The State is the King!" cries Creon, to which Hæmon's answer is: "Yea, if the State is a desert." The monarch remains resolute, although, again with a touch of the unexpected, he announces that he will spare Ismene, while the chorus sings of the power of love over intellect, the force that has made Hæmon dare to brave his father's wrath. Antigone goes to her doom, ordered to be walled up in a rock, but hardly has she been taken away before the old blind Tiresias, the seer, approaches Creon, warning him that he stands "once more on the edge of fate." The king rejects his counsel, claiming that he too has been bribed, but his mind becomes troubled as the prophet lashes out with a dark prediction of disaster. The words are so solemn that suddenly Creon reverses his decision and commands his attendants to rescue the girl he has condemned. By this time, however, it is too late. A messenger tells how Antigone has been found hanged and how Hæmon in misery has committed suicide, while Creon's wife, Eurydice, broken by the death of her son, perishes also. A shattered Creon is left standing lonely on a dark stage.

In *Antigone* there is obviously present a quality the presence of which in *Electra* we seek for in vain. Here, too, emphasis is upon human character, but, even although no supernatural beings appear among the other *dramatis personæ*, the gods have come mysteriously close to the action. The human persons, together with their actions, are illuminated by the light of a basic theme, a theme essentially metaphysical. Throughout the entire play runs a refrain, the refrain of the two laws. For Creon reason and civic order are of paramount import; for Antigone, led by faith and emotion, the spiritual commandment is all. Between these conflicting forces Sophocles holds an even course, for this is no propaganda play. True, our deepest sympathies are for Antigone and for Hæmon, yet, as she is drawn in clear terms before us, she is not ideally perfect. In her pride she is selfish, and about her clings a neurotic robe of world weariness: she is almost enamoured of death.

Unquestionably this is the finest and most delicately balanced of all the tragedies the Greek stage has to offer us.

The House of Laius: "Œdipus Tyrannus" and "Œdipus at Colonus"

The story of the Theban kingdom was one that had deep attractions for Sophocles. Shortly after writing *Antigone* he created his terrible *Œdipus Tyrannus*, and five years after his death his *Œdipus at Colonus* was performed.

The former is perhaps the play by which he is most widely known, and one must agree that its planning is magnificent, its dialogue supremely fashioned, its revelation of character profound. Before the action begins much of basic significance for an understanding of the plot has occurred, but with great skill the dramatist makes allusion to these events in the process of unfolding his story, so that past and present become interfused. Œdipus has now been monarch of Thebes for several years, having married the widow of Laius, Jocasta. In reality Jocasta is his mother, and Laius has died, although Œdipus knows it not, by his son's hand. A plague has descended on the city, and the king, desperately anxious for the fate of his kingdom, has sent Creon, his brother-in-law, to the oracle in an endeavour to find what sin has brought this ruin upon them.

The oracle declares that the plague is due to the presence in Thebes of the murderer of Laius, and Œdipus pledges himself to discover this criminal. He summons the blind seer Tiresias, who darkly accuses him, but whom Œdipus curtly and angrily dismisses as suborned by Creon. An angry scene between the king and his brother-in-law is interrupted only by the hurried entry of Jocasta from the palace. Left alone with Œdipus, she laughs aside Tiresias' accusation by describing the way in which Laius was killed, by robbers, "at a place where three highways meet." From this moment the tragedy develops rapidly. Œdipus is aghast, for the description of the spot tallies with his own memory of an event when, in anger, he once slew a wayfarer who obstructed his path. Jocasta comforts him by pointing to the oracle's declaration that Laius should die by the hand of his own son, arguing that clearly therefore the murder of this king cannot be true to prophecy. Further comfort arrives when a messenger announces the death of Polybus, whom Œdipus thinks to be his father and from whose presence he had departed in order that another oracle might not be fulfilled.

"Thou dreadest to be stained with guilt through thy parents?" inquires the Messenger:

> *ŒDIPUS:* Even so, old man—this it is that ever affrights me.
> *MESSENGER:* Dost thou know, then, that thy fears are wholly vain?
> *ŒDIPUS:* How so, if I was born of those parents?
> *MESSENGER:* Because Polybus was nothing to thee in blood.
> *ŒDIPUS:* What sayest thou? Was Polybus not my sire?
> *MESSENGER:* No more than he who speaks to thee, but just so much.

With inexorable logic the truth is gradually revealed. Œdipus was found as a child by a shepherd and reared by Polybus as his son. By this time Jocasta has divined the terrible secret, tries to stay him from obtaining the final proof from the old shepherd, but is powerless to stop the progress of events. She commits suicide, while Œdipus in torment tears out his own eyes and prepares to leave the city.

The entire play is executed with masterly precision, event following on event, the passion continually on the build. Because of its dramatic skill Aristotle, when he sought for support of his arguments in his *Poetics*, took it as the prime example of tragedy. There is hardly a line that is unnecessary in the dialogue, hardly an opportunity that has been missed for the creation of emotional tension. As in *Electra* and *Antigone*, the chief emphasis is on character—on Creon, the honest courtier; on Jocasta, half-wife, half-mother; on Œdipus, noble and magnanimous, yet cursed with too quick a temper, obstinate and rash. By his well-nigh perfect handling of the theme Sophocles has been able to let us see the story in a kind of double vision. Externally considered, this is a tragedy of fate; the oracles prove true in the end; whatever Œdipus and Jocasta do to escape, fate twists and turns their lives to their own undoing. On the other hand, as Œdipus is delineated here he was responsible for the events which prove the oracles true. The sudden anger directed against Tiresias and, more particularly, against the faithful Creon is symbolic of what formed a basic weakness in his character; the aged Laius would never have been slain had the young prince not been possessed then as now, of ungovernable fits of anger. Nor does he plead ignorance in defence at the close of the play. Very easily he might have indulged in self-pity, laying the entire blame on the curse that thwarted his every action: instead he accepts full responsibility, for once more character is being shown as destiny. Contemplation on the strangeness of life's passage is the mood with which we are left as the chorus departs from the stage:

> While our eyes wait to see the destined final day, we must call no one happy who is of mortal race, until he hath crossed life's border, free from pain.

The slightest error may have the most grievous consequence.

Once again, at the very close of his life, Sophocles turned to the Œdipus story, showing the aged king, as self-appointed exile for many years from his home in Thebes, blind and feeble, led from land to land by his faithful Antigone. The plot possesses at once a grand simplicity and a peculiarly complex structure. We are now at the moment in time when Eteocles is preparing to meet the great Argive army that Polyneices has gathered against his brother, and when an oracle has declared that Thebes will prove fortunate only if the exiled Œdipus dies there, that if his body is buried in Attica the city of Athens will flourish instead. It is at Colonus, in Attica, by the grove sacred to the Furies, or Eumenides, that Œdipus is found.

The action of the play shows Creon endeavouring to trick the old man into returning to Thebes, the while Theseus offers him protection. But it is not the action that is important: the prime quality of this drama consists in its depiction of peace of spirit won out of suffering. In the Œdipus presented here breathes a nobility such as could come to no man who has not plumbed the very depths of despair and risen triumphant above them. And at the end an almost mystical scene rivets our attention. Rising to his full height, the grey figure of the king stands facing his daughters and King Theseus; blind though he is, he knows he will find his final resting-place unaided, guided not by human hands but by the light of his own new-found inner strength:

> I will inform thee, son of Ægeus,
> Of what shall be in store for this thy city
> Beyond the harm of time. Of my own self,
> Without a hand to guide me, presently
> I will explore a spot where I must die. . . .
> Now—to the place! The message from on high
> Urges me forth; let us not linger now.
> Here, follow me, my daughters! in my turn.
> Look, I am acting as a guide to you,
> As you were mine, your father's. Come along!—
> Nay, do not touch me; let me for myself
> Search out the hallowed grave where, in this soil,
> It is my fate to lie. . . .
> O Light—my Dark—once thou wast mine to see;
> And now not ever shall my limbs again
> Feel thee! Already I creep upon my way
> To hide my last of life in Hades. Thou,
> Dearest of friends—thy land—thy followers—all,
> May you live happy; and in your happiness
> Fortunate ever, think of me, your dead!

The last words of the chorus form a fitting conclusion to this drama: "Come, cease lamentation, lift it up no more; for verily these things stand fast."

In these mystically conceived scenes once more appears an apotheosis of patriotism, but gentler, and perhaps for that reason even more profound, than in the work of Æschylus. No lines are more lovely in the play than the choral ode in honour of Attica:

> Stranger, thou art come to rest
> Where the pasturing folds are best
> Of this land of goodly steeds
> In Colonos' glistening meads,
> Where the clear-voiced nightingale
> Oftenest in green valley-glades
> Loves to hide her and bewail;
> Under wine-dark ivy shades,
> Of the leafy ways, untrod,
> Pierced by sun or tempest never,
> Myriad-fruited, of a God;

> Where in Bacchanalian trim
> Dionysus ranges ever
> With the Nymphs who fostered him.

In these last days of his life Sophocles turned in fond recollection to "white Colonos," city of his birth, and to praise of the Attica that had reared him. The golden words shimmer in the sunlight of memory, and the present scene becomes tinged with the radiance of eternity.

The Dream of Life: "Ajax" and "Philoctetes"

Among the dramatist's early works is his *Ajax*, among his latest the *Philoctetes*. Basically, these are far apart from each other, the one instinct with passion, tempestuous and fierce, the other tinged with an almost romantic strangeness of quiet mood. Yet these two plays, taken together, help to reveal an essential quality in Sophocles' outlook upon the world and help to explain the atmosphere of his *Œdipus at Colonus*.

The former drama is a terrible study of tragic error. Ajax, one of the most renowned warriors among the Greeks, deems that a prized honour, the arms of Achilles, should fall to his lot. These arms are, however, given to Odysseus, and Ajax, bitterly wounded in his pride, sets out by night to murder the leaders of the expedition, Agamemnon and Menelaus, whom he believes responsible for this insult.

Angered at this exhibition of overweening pride, the goddess Athene comes from Olympus, and darkens his mind with madness so that he falls upon the army's flock of sheep in the fond delusion that he is slaying his enemies. In the end, having recovered from his frenzy, and consumed by shame, he commits suicide.

As a study in character the tragedy possesses great force, but beyond the character-portrayal resides a peculiar quality of even greater import. The opening scene displays this clearly. Athene appears above and speaks to Odysseus, but, although he hears her voice, she remains to him invisible. After a short conversation between the man and the goddess she summons forth the crazed Ajax from his tent. Cruelly she mocks him, leading him on from pathetic boast to boast, while Odysseus the wise stands silent, wondering. At last, when Ajax has again retired, he gives expression to his thoughts. "I know none nobler," he declares.

> and I pity him
> In his misery, albeit he is my foe,
> Since he is yoked fast to an evil doom.
> My own lot I regard no less than his,
> For I see well, nought else are we but mere
> Phantoms, all we that live, mere fleeting shadows.

The thought that life is but a dream is one that has haunted the minds of several of the greatest playwrights in the theatre's history: that this thought was first expressed by Sophocles over two thousand years ago indicates the quality of his genius. In this scene of madness and of wonder is, as it were, the adumbration of Shakespeare's vision in *The Tempest* and of Calderón's in *Life's a Dream*.

The spirit of *The Tempest* is recalled even more potently in the drama of *Philoctetes*, written when Sophocles was nearing ninety years of age. Strange is the story of this drama and strange its atmosphere. The scene is the lonely isle of Lemnos, where for years Philoctetes, deserted by the Greeks when he had had the misfortune to be stung by a serpent and consequently to suffer from a loathsome disease, has been living in a cave; his life he has preserved only because he possesses the famous bow and arrows of the heroic Herakles. Although there are many complications in the plot, briefly the drama tells how Neoptolemus, the youthful son of the dead Achilles, and the wily Odysseus arrive at Lemnos, sent thither by the leaders of the Greek forces at Troy because an oracle had declared that success would come to them only if they could obtain possession of the Herakles arms.

For Odysseus all that matters is the acquiring of this bow; pity stirs him not, and he is entirely content to trick the helpless Philoctetes in the pursuit of this one object. For the young Neoptolemus, however, the matter is not so simple: the calm nobility of the dweller upon this island casts its spell on him, so that questions of honour and loyalty conflict with Odysseus' single-minded expediency.

Throughout the whole play an atmosphere of wonder enwraps the action. From the moment Odysseus and Neoptolemus set foot on the shore of this "sea-girt Lemnos, desart and forlorn, where never tread of human step is seen, or voice of mortal heard," we are caught in the spell. By skilled words Sophocles conjures up before us an image of the desolate spot, so that we seem to feel the very silence of the place, disturbed until now only by the breaking of waves upon the rocks and by the sighing of the pitiless winds. With consummate art the dramatist weaves his tapestry of human character set against this scene; contrasts the conscienceless intrigues of Odysseus both with the fresh bloom of Neoptolemus' enthusiasm and the nobility, rendered greater through suffering, of Philoctetes; sets the physical torment of the hero against the healing balm of sleep:

> Sleep, thou patron of mankind,
> Great physician of the mind,
> Who dost nor pain nor sorrow know,
> Sweetest balm of ev'ry woe,
> Mildest sov'reign, hear us now
> Hear thy wretched suppliant's vow;
> His eyes in gentle slumbers close,
> And continue his repose;
> Hear thy wretched suppliant's vow,
> Great physician, hear us now.

DRUNKEN MEN
n Museum.
Margarete Bieber, *The History*
e Greek and Roman Theater

A MAN AND A WOMAN
Kunstgeschichtliches Museum,
Würzburg University.
Photo Rudolph Hartzold

A COMIC
HERAKLES
Berlin Museum.
From Margarete
Bieber. *The History
of the Greek and
Roman Theater*

A WORRIED
SLAVE
*By courtesy of the
Metropolitan
Museum of Art,
New York*

TERRA-COTTA STATUETTES OF GREEK COMIC CHARACTERS

MENANDER
WITH HIS
MASKS
From the original
in the Museo
Laterano, Rome.
Photo Anderson

We are close to Shakespeare here, with his deep appreciation of nature, his wide observation of mankind, his sense of the intermingling of fate and of character, his profound realization of the suffering of life, and his concept of the nobility of spirit that comes when the human soul has been tested and tried by pain. Sophocles, more than the rugged Æschylus, approaches near to us. His dramas may be bound by the strict conventions of the Greek stage, but no conventions, however strange, can conceal the essential humanity which breathes out of his lines.

3

THE DAWN OF REALISM: EURIPIDES

WHEN WE turn to the plays of Euripides as presented, for example, in the translations of Gilbert Murray and read the lyrical chants of their choruses, it is somewhat difficult to think of them in relation to the term 'realism'; yet, placed in comparison with the work of Æschylus or Sophocles, they undoubtedly reveal, on careful examination, qualities which bring them close to the characteristic theatrical form of our time. If Sophocles shows himself akin to Shakespeare, Euripides, with his prevailing intellectualism and disillusionment, frequently reminds us of Shaw.

For this mood in him there were causes in the conditions of his life. True, he was born only ten years after Sophocles, but these ten years were fateful. In 480, as we have seen, Æschylus was a man of middle age fighting at Salamis, Sophocles was a youth of fifteen leading a chorus in honour of the victory. Euripides was a child of only five years. The relationship between Sophocles and Euripides in connexion with the Peloponnesian War is also instructive: they both died about the same time, but when the first part of this long struggle broke out in 431 B.C. the former was already an old man, while Euripides was still in full manhood —not so much older, indeed, than Æschylus at the time of the battle of Salamis. By then Sophocles was already moving towards the mysticism of his final years, while his younger contemporary was actively interested in the political affairs around him.

Euripides seems to have addressed himself primarily to the young intelligentsia of his time. Scepticism was in the air about the middle of the fifth century, and the Sophists came to exercise much influence on the young. The older idealism was fading; expedient calculations rapidly were taking its place. To this school of thought Euripides belonged. For him the gods were no longer the awful forces they had been in the imagination of Æschylus; the old legends of Athens were scanned now with doubting eyes; the heroic was reduced to terms of the common life of the day. There is an ugly modern word that saw much service in the twenties of the present century—'debunking': it might well be applied to much of Euripides' work.

His tendency to doubt the truth of the ancient legends, to question the wisdom of the past, presented him with a peculiar dramatic problem, and through his solution to that problem he drew the theatre still nearer to our age. For the most part the playwright was restricted to choice among a limited number of legendary histories, and, even although Euripides sought more widely than his predecessors, the restriction still kept him within fairly narrow bounds. Two things, however, Euripides was eager to do—to make the characters real and ordinary, and to use them for the purpose of 'philosophizing' on the events. From these two endeavours came his changes in dramatic structure. Obviously the chorus was a theatrical element out of keeping with his central idea, and, as a consequence, in most of his plays he tended to reduce its participation in the main action until it became nothing save a detached group of singers indulging in the presentation of chants only slightly related to the major theme. To compensate for what was thus lost Euripides provided brilliant and beautiful lyrics for this group to sing, and at the same time steadily enriched the musical accompaniments, but the fact remains that in the majority of his plays our attention is concentrated almost entirely on the 'episodes' involving the main characters: his plays are dramas in which appears a collection of choral interludes rather than dramas built from the interplay of chorus and characters.

A further modification in dramatic structure was necessitated by his individualistic attitude towards the legendary themes. Not seldom he found himself compelled to introduce, at the very beginning of his plays, explanatory matter designed to give the audience the information essential for an understanding of his point of view; hence evolved the typical Euripidean 'prologue,' in which a single person becomes almost the mouthpiece of the poet himself. Had Euripides lived at a later age he would have written prefaces.

If this was obligatory at the beginning of the piece, a similar device was needed at the end. So boldly did he deal with the ancient stories that often there remained no possible solution for the complicated action that would have been acceptable on the Greek stage. As a result Euripides fell back on the trick ever afterwards associated with his name—the use of the *deus ex machina*. The 'machine' in question was a theatrical device introduced towards the close of the fifth century by which a deity could be lowered from the roof of the scene-building. Since Euripides frequently used the device to huddle his drama to an illogical end—the god announcing his divine commands to the characters below—the phrase about the *deus ex machina* came to bear the transferred significance which it has to-day. Even when the gods are gone Euripides' practice remains.

In noting these innovations, however, we must not think that all of Euripides' eighteen or nineteen extant plays are of one kind or that he did not have within him both sincerity of purpose and depth of feeling. Although he frequently sinks to sentimentalism and is driven to the exploitation of the sensational—the two curses that ever dog the footsteps of the realistic playwright—he does have the power at times of rising to true tragic perceptions. However much he would wish to belittle the mystery of man, the impress of his age was sufficiently strong on his spirit to make him present, in at least some of his plays, profound expression of the problems of evil and of good.

"*Electra*"

It may be well to start an examination of his work by choosing a play which stands, as it were, in the middle of his dramatic career and which provides opportunities for comparison with kindred dramas by Æschylus and Sophocles. *Electra* was presented about the year 413 B.C., when he was seventy-two years of age, and, as its title indicates, it deals with the same theme as that of Sophocles' similarly named tragedy and that of *The Choephori*. A scrutiny of its structure is revealing.

Instead of a palace courtyard, we stand before a peasant's hut, from which the owner comes dressed in poor raiment, a figure worn by toil. In his prologue speech he rapidly reviews the events leading to Agamemnon's murder, and then turns to tell of subsequent events. Electra has grown of an age to marry, and all the princes of Greece seek her hand, but Ægisthus, afraid lest she bear a high-born son to wreak vengeance upon him, would not betroth her to any—would, indeed, have slain her had his hand not been held back by Clytemnestra. At last he conceived a wily scheme: he married off the girl to a poor peasant, believing that no low-born son could give him cause to fear. For himself, this peasant declares, he has ever respected her maidenhood.

As he finishes his talk Electra enters with a water-pitcher on her head. Asked why she toils in this manner, she replies that she does so because of the peasant's kindness:

> High fortune this, when men for sore mischance
> Find such physician as I find in thee,
> I ought, as strength shall serve, yea, though forbid,
> To ease thy toil, that lighter be thy load,
> And share thy burdens.

Immediate comment is demanded on this scene. The effect created is obvious. Electra, heroic in the hands of Æschylus and idealized in those of Sophocles, becomes an ordinary girl going to the well for water. The antique legend is dragged down to earth. Besides this, the characters are, as it were, related now to a real environment. While the peasant talks of taking his steers to the fields to sow his crop, Electra speaks of keeping the house in order so that the labourer at the day's end will find comfort. Not only is the legend dragged down to earth, it is being made domestic. At the same time an implicit comment is being made. Euripides is a kind of socialist before his time, and his presentation of noble qualities in this poor toiler seems designed to indicate that high thought and passion are not the exclusive property of those kings and princes who are the persons of early myth. That such was indeed his purpose is clearly indicated later when Orestes makes direct reference to the magnanimity of mind enclosed in an outward form so impoverished. Above all, the new situation invented by the dramatist provides an opportunity for the arousing of pity: pathos is one of Euripides' main devices; if he does not know how to express that hardness of temper so characteristic of Æschylus, he is adept at causing tears to flow.

The following scene introduces us to Orestes and his friend Pylades. Electra and a chorus of Argive maidens come on the stage, and when their chant is done Orestes detains her, tells her he has news of her brother, and indulges in a lengthy conversation with her, during which her love for her brother is fully displayed, and the information is given to the audience that, were Orestes to return, only one person, an aged servant who tended him as a child, would recognize his features. The pathetic note is increased. "Since thou dost wake the tale," says Electra:

> I pray thee, stranger,
> Report to Orestes all mine ills and his.
> Tell in what raiment I am hovel-housed,
> Under what squalor I am crushed, and dwell
> Under what roof, after a palace-home;—
> How mine own shuttle weaves with pain my robes,—
> Else must I want, all vestureless my frame;—
> How from the stream myself the water bear;—
> Banned from the festal rite, denied the dance.

If this contributed added pathos, added realism appears when the peasant returns and complains that it is unseemly for a woman to stand talking with young men, while she begs him not to be "suspicious." Being satisfied, he then chides her for not bidding the strangers welcome to his hut, and Orestes makes the comment on natural nobility:

> Lo, there is no sure test for manhood's worth;
> For moral natures are confusion-fraught,
> I have seen ere now a noble father's son
> Proved nothing-worth, seen good sons of ill sires,
> Starved leanness in a rich man's very soul,
> And in a poor man's body a great heart.
> How then shall one discern 'twixt these and judge?
> By wealth?—a sorry test were this to use.
> Or by the lack of all?—nay, poverty
> Is plague-struck, schooling men to sin through need.
> To prowess shall I turn me?—who, that looks
> On spears, can swear which spearman's heart is brave?
> Leave Fortune's gifts to fall out as they will!
> Lo, this man is not among Argive's great,
> Nor by a noble house's name exalted,
> But one of the many—proved a king of men!
> Learn wisdom, ye which wander aimless, swoln
> With vain imaginings: by converse judge
> Man, even the noble by their daily walk.
> For such be they which govern states aright

> And homes: but fleshly bulks devoid of wit
> Are statues in the market-place.

Obviously this is extra-dramatic material, the reflections of the author rather than of the character, material for preface rather than for play.

The scene continues in the same strain. Electra criticizes her husband for asking such noble strangers to so poor an abode, but, since he has made this social error, she bids him send for Orestes' old servant; he will aid in entertaining the guests and at the same time take joy in hearing of his young master.

A choral ode, beautiful but inconsequent, gives time for this old man to arrive. He says a few words to Electra, and then starts to examine Orestes' figure and features, declaring eventually that here in person is Electra's brother. She at first doubts (in terms that show Euripides ridiculing the recognition scene in Sophocles' *Electra*), but becomes convinced when the old man points out a scar on the young man's brow, the result of a fall in childhood's days. All now sit down to discuss plans. The palace is closely guarded, and only careful strategy may prevail. It is settled that Orestes will go to Ægisthus where he is sacrificing at an altar outside the palace, while Electra, who cries that she will make preparation for her mother's slaying, proposes to entice Clytemnestra to her hut by sending false news that she has been delivered of a son.

The chorus sings another lyrically lovely but obscure song, when a noise is heard in the distance. Electra is in despair, thinking Orestes has been detected and slain, but news soon comes that it is Ægisthus who is dead. Orestes returns with the body, and Electra, after a moment's hesitation, indulges in a brutal reviling of the corpse; her hate knows no bounds, and in her long tirade we guess at the long-pent-up emotions that have for so many years seared her spirit.

This done, Clytemnestra is seen approaching. Orestes trembles at thought of completing his vengeance:

ORESTES: What shall we do? Our mother—murder her?
ELECTRA: How? Hath ruth seized thee, seeing thy mother's form?
ORESTES: Woe!
  How can I slay her—her that nursed, that bare me?
ELECTRA: Even as she thy father slew and mine.
ORESTES: O Phœbus, folly exceeding was thine hest.
ELECTRA: Nay, where Apollo erreth, who is wise?
ORESTES: Who against nature bad'st me slay my mother!
ELECTRA: How art thou harmed, avenging thine own sire?
ORESTES: Arraigned for a mother's murder—pure ere this.
ELECTRA: Yet, impious if thou succour not thy sire.
ORESTES: Her blood-price to my mother must I pay.
ELECTRA: And *Him*!—if thou forbear to avenge a father.
ORESTES: Ha!—spake a fiend in likeness of the God?—
ELECTRA: Throned on the holy tripod!—I trow not.
ORESTES: I dare not trust this oracle's utter faith!

ELECTRA: Wilt thou turn craven—be no more a man?
ORESTES: How? must I lay the self-same snare for her?
ELECTRA: Ay! that which trapped and slew the adulterer!
ORESTES: I will go in. A horror I essay!—
 Yea, will achieve! If 'tis Heaven's will, so be it.
 Oh bitter strife, which I must needs hold sweet.

By this treatment Euripides is completely rewriting the age-old scene. Clytemnestra's murder is placed last, with ample time given for reflection. Instead of killing her in the heat of passion, Orestes is made to sacrifice her in the light of reason. The new situation permits the dramatist to emphasize his conception of Electra, a starved soul rendered neurotic by hate and thwarted love, dominating her brother through the intensity of her passion. It also permits him to cast characteristic doubt upon the ways of the gods: confronted by his terrible task, Orestes goes so far as to question whether the inviolate oracle may truly be trusted.

Equally characteristic is the debate between Clytemnestra and her daughter that immediately follows. The queen justifies herself, while Electra castigates her as the mere wanton. "Child," says Clytemnestra, not unwisely and rather pathetically,

> Child, still thy nature bids thee love thy sire.
> 'Tis ever thus: some cleave unto their father,
> Some more the mother than the father love.
> I pardon thee. In sooth, not all so glad
> Am I, my child, for deeds that I have done.

These are almost her last words, for, entering the hut to do sacrifice—"take care that my smoke-grimed walls soil not thy robes," remarks Electra in cruel sarcasm—she is slain by Orestes. No sooner is she dead, however, than a great revulsion of feeling descends upon Electra; in tears she and Orestes think of her pitiful words to them; they are abjectly conscience-stricken—and at last when it is hard to see how the playwright can reach a fitting conclusion a heavenly vision appears. Castor and Pollux descend in the machine. They declare the deed to be unrighteous, and Castor confirms Orestes' suspicions by himself condemning Apollo's command:

> Thou, thou hast sinned;
> And Phœbus—Phœbus—since he is my king,
> I am dumb. . . . He is wise:—not wise his hest for thee!
> **We must needs say " 'Tis well."**

Things being as they are, the twin gods bid Electra to marry Pylades (a nice sentimental tying-up of knots), while Orestes is to journey to Argos that Athene may release him from the torment of the Furies. In a final pathetic scene, when Electra throws her arms tearfully about her brother's neck, Orestes bids a last farewell to his native land.

The fate of Orestes is the same as that in *The Choephori*, yet in spirit we are here far indeed from Æschylus' high concept. Tears, not emotions too deep for tears, afflict us; and in place of an attempt to justify the ways of god to man is a sneering at religious belief: the divine Apollo is treated as a fool.

Some Studies of Women:
"Alcestis," "Medea," "Hippolytus,"
"Andromache," "Hecuba," "The Trojan Women"

Having gained some conception of Euripides' dramatic style, we may now turn to examine his other plays briefly in their chronological sequence. In the *Electra* all attention is concentrated upon the heroine, and it may be said that in general this dramatist was more interested in his women characters than in his men. He understood well the neurotic types; their presentation gave him opportunity for the exploitation of those pathetic scenes he so dearly loved. Not without considerable justification did Aristophanes satirically depict him as the playwright most detested by womenkind, because he had revealed to the world many of their innermost secrets.

With the exception of the *Cyclops*, his solitary extant satyric drama, the first play we have from his pen is *Alcestis*, produced in 438 B.C. Strangely, it was the fourth element in a tetralogy—a position usually taken by a satyr drama—and very probably its romantic, almost fairy-tale-like quality, together with its comic scenes, is explainable by reference to its original purpose. Nevertheless the characteristic elements of the Euripidean play are already amply apparent. The plot deals with an ancient legend which told how King Admetus of Thessaly was promised by the Fates, through the intervention of Apollo, that death would spare him for a time if only he could find some person willing to go to Hades in his place. With complete lack of heroic nobility, Admetus hurries from kinsman to kinsman, seeking help in his predicament and finding aid from none save his wife, the loyal Alcestis. As the play opens she is just on the point of going to her doom, calm, matter-of-fact, but with just a faint tremor that betrays her humanity.

What precise purpose Euripides had in writing this drama is hard to tell: perhaps he had no thought other than that the story gave him a pathetic situation, romantic in colouring; that it allowed him to reveal, not too blatantly, his utter scepticism concerning the gods; and that it offered opportunity for subtle revelations of human character. "The King will not know his loss until he suffers it," is an appropriate comment, made by a servant to the leader of the chorus, on his attitude towards Admetus. This monarch is depicted as a thoroughly respectable, convention-loving middle-class citizen. To Alcestis he makes all the proper promises: he will look after the children, he will not marry again, gone for ever are the merry drinking-parties that used to send their music through the house. He is desperately anxious lest she should decide not to carry the business through to the bitter end, yet he is as desperately afraid to be left alone. He is mightily affronted by his father, Pheres, who counsels him sarcastically to "woo many women, so that more may die for you," yet there is more than a trifle of shamefacedness in his talking about the whole matter to Herakles. As for Herakles, he is presented as a kind of softened version of the comic caricature that passed under his name on the farcical stages of the time—a self-assured braggart who goes out to wrestle with death for Alcestis, not unfortified with wine and somewhat uncertain in his gait. Beautiful as portions of *Alcestis* are, disbelief and cynicism appear to be the mainsprings of its action.

Far different in character is *Medea* (431 B.C.), a sensational tragedy of love turned to hatred, and the first drama extant written on the theme of miscegenation. Medea is a princess of distant Colchis and a sorceress, a strange barbaric figure from the mysterious East. She has aided Jason to obtain the Golden Fleece, and, later, wedded to him, she has contrived the death of his uncle, Pelias, in an endeavour to place her husband on the throne of his native land. The plot, however, miscarries; Jason, Medea, and their two sons have to flee into exile; and there Jason deserts her, marrying the daughter of Creon, monarch of Corinth.

This, then, is a study of ill-mated husband and wife. Jason is nothing but a self-seeking, self-deluding male, willing to accept the results of any crime committed on his behalf by his wife, but absolutely incapable of accepting any joint responsibility. His love for her is an intoxicated affair, the desire for physical possession of her body, in no wise a true marriage. She, on the other hand, is the barbarian who gives her whole being to the man she loves, and when that love fails finds herself consumed by a hate no less fierce and incandescent. Tremble though she may at the thought of killing her children, this sacrifice, in her mind, must be made to expiate the treachery to which she has been exposed. In the end, and not inappropriately, she flies from human sight in a magical chariot drawn by dragons.

The intensity of this play, its bold presentation of the two main characters, its theme of sex-strife accentuated by racial disparities, and also, be it said, its inherently sensational qualities have made it the happy hunting-ground for modern playwrights of the realistic school. It strikes an inherently 'modern' note, and, if that modern note possesses less power than the ancient strength of Æschylus, less calm than the assured mastery of Sophocles, our regret at the loss can avail us nothing.

Hippolytus (428 B.C.), which, in spite of its title, again focuses attention upon a heroine rather than on a hero, has something of the same elements. *Medea* is the first of its kind of drama; *Hippolytus* is the earliest-known full-length study of criminal passion—the love of Phædra, wife of King Theseus, for her husband's illegitimate son Hippolytus. As Euripides traces the course of the action we watch the young queen struggling against her infatuation and finally succumbing to it; we see Hippolytus, the cold, uprighteous youth, incapable of even faintly appreciating the power that wraps her in its folds. The contrast between these two is the more stressed in that Artemis and Aphrodite, the symbols of chastity and love, appear in person to provide a kind of symbolic commentary on the course of events and upon the personalities of the two opposed human figures. Between them stands Theseus, troubled of mind, credulous, an inefficient judge of character. When Phædra, scorned by the pure Hippolytus, accuses him of making love to her, and when he, for his father's sake, remains silent under the accusation, the king all too readily accepts his wife's word and puts such a curse upon him as to lead him to his death. While obviously Euripides was most interested in the heroine here, we might perhaps agree that the tragedy is one produced by three conflicting types, each with its own peculiar failing: Theseus, finding his youthful incontinence the ultimate cause of his present miseries, and obtusely unable to deal with any circumstances beyond the ordinary commonplace affairs of daily life; Phædra, consumed by her fatal passion; and Hippolytus, wrapped up in the dignified silence of his own self-esteem and frigidity of spirit. If ever Euripides came close to capturing the true tragic spirit it was in this play; although, even in the making of this statement, one must recognize that only in one or two of his scenes does he rise above the depiction of the psychological and reach a metaphysical plane.

About the same time came his *Hecuba* (about 425 B.C.) and *Andromache* (about 430 B.C.). The latter reveals clearly two of Euripides' chief failings—his tendency towards contriving complex incident and allowing plot to dominate over other dramatic elements, and his corresponding tendency towards exaggeration of pathos. In *Andromache* is a whole tangle of incident. Andromache, widow of the Trojan hero Hector, is shown as the slave and mistress of Neoptolemus, son of Achilles. Neoptolemus has married Hermione, daughter of Menelaus, and she, consumed with jealousy, plots to murder both Andromache and her son. There is intrigue in the device by which the unhappy widow is tricked by Menelaus and Hermione; there is pathos in the scene wherein she stands helpless and bound while her little son vainly clings to her robes. Almost as though this were a nineteenth-century melodrama, this situation is saved by the opportune arrival of Peleus, who unties her bonds and rescues the child. Virtually the dramatic action is now over, but suddenly a fresh movement begins. Hermione is tormented by the thought of what she had intended to do, when suddenly Orestes makes his appearance, claims that she had been betrothed to him, leads her off the stage, murders Neoptolemus. Finally comes the usual Euripidean *deus ex machina* —Thetis this time—who gives commands for the care of the corpse, and orders Andromache, without any previous warning, to be married to Helenus.

Little may be honestly said in praise of this tissue of sensational and pathetic episodes. Likewise sharply split into two parts, *Hecuba* deserves a somewhat different judgment. Here also a slave-queen appears

—Hecuba, formerly ruler of Troy along with Priam, now the captive property of Agamemnon. First, we are shown the sacrifice of her daughter Polyxena, whom the Greeks slay as a sacrifice to the spirit of Achilles; next we are introduced to the murder of her son Polydorus and to the cruel revenge she takes upon the treacherous perpetrator of this deed, Polymestor.

In order to understand this play, we need to remember that already Athens had become involved in the Peloponnesian War and that Euripides was becoming obsessed with the thought of war's follies in general. Hecuba's plight is the result of the long, disastrous struggle round Troy; and as the aftermath of war youth perishes, evil is let loose. With bitter irony the dramatist puts into Agamemnon's mouth the last words of the play. He, who was to have such a dismal homecoming, turns to the wretched Hecuba:

> Go thou, unhappy Hecuba, and bury thy two corpses; and you, Trojan women, to your masters' tents repair, for lo! I perceive a breeze just rising to waft us home. God grant we reach our country and find all well at home, released from troubles here!

During this period Euripides may have suffered deeply from divided loyalties. In the *Herakleidæ* (about 430 B.C.) and *The Suppliants* (about 421 B.C.) he indulges in some patriotic tub-thumping, vastly different from the calmly assured praises of Athens that came from the lips of Æschylus and of Sophocles (although in *The Madness of Herakles* (about 421 B.C.) he succeeds in striking a surer patriotic note), but in *The Trojan Women* (415 B.C.) he turns once more to the mood of *Hecuba*, and seems to have become so immersed in it that all sense of dramatic structure is lost. There is in reality no play here, simply one long lament over the consequences of war and an eloquent lyrical cry of despair. No special power of divination is required to see reflected in it the image of contemporary events. The year before it was produced the Athenians had attacked neutral Melos and with unparalleled savagery had put all its men to the sword: the same year saw the laying of plans for the ill-fated Sicilian expedition and demonstrated clearly the total lack of concerted purpose among the new rulers of Athens. From the very beginning of his career Euripides had been a doubter and a sceptic: now his doubts and scepticism overflowed. As the flames light up the ruined city of Troy the chorus is left on the stage uttering its miserable cries:

> Woe, woe, woe!
> Thou of the Ages, O wherefore fleest thou,
>   Lord of the Phrygian, Father that made us?
> 'Tis we, thy children; shall no man aid us?
> 'Tis we, thy children! Seest thou, seest thou?
>
> He seeth, only his heart is pitiless;
>   And the land dies: yea, she,
> She of the Mighty Cities perisheth citiless!
>   Troy shall no more be!

From disbelief in the gods Euripides is moving towards belief in a cruel and pitiless universe.

Probably induced by reflection on these contemporary events, Euripides produced in his latter years a series of plays of a peculiarly baffling kind. *Helen* (412 B.C.) may be selected as an extreme example. Every one knows the legend of Helen, how she, the wife of Menelaus, was taken to Troy by Paris and caused that proud city to fall. She is the supreme *femme fatale* of ancient myth. In the hands of Euripides her whole story becomes a jest, for he has seized upon, and elaborated, a story far different from that hallowed by the Homeric epic. According to this, Helen never went to Troy: the pother of the ten years' siege of that city was not over a real woman, but over her wraith, a mere phantom semblance of her person. All the time that Paris thinks he has possessed her, all the time that Menelaus has been afflicted with jealous pangs, the real Helen has lived a pleasant and blameless life in Egypt under the protection of King Proteus. As the play opens, however, she reveals in her prologue address to the audience that since Proteus' recent death conditions in Egypt are beginning to change; his son, Theoclymenus, wishes to marry her, and she is troubled by his unwanted attentions. Shortly thereafter Menelaus enters, tattered, worn, shipwrecked on this Egyptian shore while on his journey home from Troy. With him he has brought Helen from Troy —that is to say, the wraith of Helen—and has concealed her in a cave, but now he learns from a rude portress at the palace that some one is living here in Egypt under Helen's name. The poor man is at an utter loss, the more particularly since he is depicted here as a rather obtuse and dull-witted individual. Had he been a clown, we might have said he goggled at the news. Suddenly he spies the real Helen:

MENELAUS: Who art thou? whom do I behold in thee, lady?
HELEN: Nay, who art thou? the self-same reason prompts us both.
MENELAUS: I never saw a closer resemblance.
HELEN: Great God! Yea, for to recognize our friends is of God.
MENELAUS: Art thou from Hellas, or a native of this land?
HELEN: From Hellas; but I would learn thy story too.
MENELAUS: Lady, in thee I see a wondrous likeness to Helen.
HELEN: And I in thee to Menelaus; I know not what to say.
MENELAUS: Well, thou hast recognized aright a man of many sorrows.
HELEN: Hail! to thy wife's arms restored at last!
MENELAUS: Wife indeed! Lay not a finger on my robe. . . .
HELEN: In me thou beholdest no spectre of the night, attendant on the queen of phantoms.
MENELAUS: Nor yet am I in my single person the husband of two wives.
HELEN: What other woman calls thee lord?

MENELAUS: The inmate of yonder cave, whom I from Troy convey. . . .
        Herein is my dilemma; I have another wife.

Helen, thus spurned, is in despair. The situation seems to offer no remedy, when suddenly one of Menelaus' attendants rushes in excitedly to
announce that the lady in the cave has vanished into thin air, being so
thoughtful, before her departure, as to give an unsolicited testimonial to
Helen's purity. Husband and wife fall into each other's arms.

Grievous thoughts, however, soon assail the pair. If Theoclymenus
hears of Menelaus' arrival the Greek prince undoubtedly will be slain;
and that he will be informed of the arrival appears certain, since his sister
is Theonoe, a damsel gifted with the power of divination, one who knows
all. As a last resort Helen falls on her knees before this lady, begging her
not to tell her brother, and, somewhat to her own surprise, receives the
promise of silence. This hurdle surmounted, she devises a plan of escape:
she will tell Theoclymenus that Menelaus has perished at sea, beg from
him a funeral ship so that she may offer the dead man's spirit the appropriate rites, and so bid good-bye to Egypt. The plot succeeds; Helen and
Menelaus step on board the proffered vessel, the sails are set and the miserable Theoclymenus is left raging on the strand, impotent, until the
Dioscuri descend from heaven to pacify him.

There is an air of *The Private Life of Helen of Troy* about this play: there is
a flavour of melodrama, at times even a flavour of farce. It is unlikely, as
some have thought, that here Euripides was burlesquing his own tragic
style: what he was doing was to provide the audience with excitement
and adventure and stage thrill in a colourful setting, and at the same time
express his cynical view both of the gods and of the ancient myths. We
are far from the spirit of tragedy, yet we are not in the presence of burlesque; rather we inhabit the world of tragic comedy and come close
indeed to the atmosphere of *Cæsar and Cleopatra* or *The Man of Destiny*.

Closely akin to *Helen* stands *Iphigenia in Tauris* (about 414 B.C.), where
a similar situation is dealt with. This too is a romantic tale of adventure
with a happy ending, and, like *Helen*, it deliberately exploits a variant legend of a famous event in the history of the house of Atreus. It will be recalled that when the Greek fleet was stayed by contrary winds in its
expedition against Troy Agamemnon had sacrificed his young daughter
Iphigenia on the altar of the gods. Euripides supposes that, like Helen,
the girl was in reality saved, carried off by divine power to a distant land
—the land of the Taurians—while a mere phantom was placed upon the
altar-stones. In this land of Tauris she has lived for many years, a dedicated priestess in a temple, where all strangers who set foot in the barbarian country are cruelly sacrificed.

All goes reasonably well until Iphigenia's brother, Orestes, and his
friend Pylades arrive. In a tense scene of recognition, specifically praised
by Aristotle as a prime model of its kind, brother and sister are united

after their many years of separation, only to realize that they stand in mortal peril. Once the presence of these travellers is known it will be her duty to prepare them for sacrificial death. The greater part of the drama is taken up with an account of the trick, very close to that used by Helen, through which Iphigenia deceives Thoas, King of the Taurians, and saves them all. Delineation of character is here, but again Euripides' main object would seem to have been the creation of a kind of romantic escape play, half serious and half cynically amused.

Closely akin in spirit is the strange *Orestes* (408 B.C.), which, after a brilliant opening wherein Electra is seen tending her brother in his madness after Clytemnestra's murder, degenerates into a perplexing farrago of sensational incident and undramatic argumentation. There is truth in the depiction of his abnormal state of mind, falsity in the succeeding events. Orestes, Pylades, and Electra are condemned to death by an Argive court, but, in a series of exciting scenes, they seize Helen as a hostage and murder her, later lay hands on Menelaus' daughter, Hermione, and set fire to the palace. The tumult subsides only when the inevitable *deus ex machina* creaks down from the roof and reconciles all strife.

What Euripides was aiming at here is quite uncertain; perhaps his sensationalism was merely going to seed. This sensationalism, we should remember, must have been accompanied in those times by increasing sensationalism in the scenic production. Again and again in reading such plays as those just dealt with one feels that Euripides was relying upon stage effects, and this impression is confirmed by diverse contemporary evidence.

The stage was certainly becoming more spectacular: painted scenery was more freely employed, and machines of all kinds were being introduced. The device for lowering gods from above was one of these; another was the frequently used *ekkuklema* (ἐκκύκλημα) a sort of turntable set in the doorway of the scene-building, through which might be displayed the bodies of characters murdered behind the scenes. In all probability, too, the actors' costumes had been made richer, while at the same time realistic touches appeared in harmony with the familiar quality of many of his scenes. How these actors seemed to their original audiences we are, fortunately, able to tell with a certain amount of assurance, since a number of painted vases of the latter part of the fifth century B.C. were obviously made by artists who had been witnesses of the theatrical events they depicted.

One such vase shows us the characters in the *Iphigenia in Tauris*. In the background we get a glimpse of the noble temple front, its great doors slightly ajar. Iphigenia is there, clad in her finely embroidered theatrical robes, with an attendant priestess behind her. Before her sits forlorn the wretched Orestes, dressed in rags, and near by Pylades stands, leaning on a staff.

Even more revealing of the appearance these dramas assumed in his own times is a scene from his lost drama, *Andromeda*. The central figure here is the heroine herself, a barbarian princess, as is at once indicated by the Eastern crown upon her head: her dress is peculiarly ornamented, and her arms are spread wide in the gesture which the artist had seen in the theatre, for she has been chained to a rock and awaits a dismal fate at the mercy of a sea-monster. To her right sits her father, Kepheus, a royal staff in his hands and on his head a crown of the same pattern as that worn by his daughter. Towards her comes Perseus, with a skull-cap showing that he has voyaged far, bearing in his hand the curved sword with which he had slain Medusa: behind him the goddess Aphrodite, much bejewelled, is crowning him for his exploits in the name of love. Particularly interesting is the maiden seated at the extreme left: with great naturalness her mask shows her to be an Ethiopian, and we may presume that she was one of a dark-skinned chorus designed to give an atmosphere of strangeness to this drama of romantic adventure.

The whole impression here is of an ornate stage, far different from the simple orchestral circle that satisfied Æschylus not a hundred years before; in looking at these vases we realize that we are well on our way towards the decorated theatres of modern times. The fact reminds us that the history of the drama presents one unassailable truth: when the drama declines scenic adornment begins to flourish. Perhaps we might even say that when scenery and show become dominant poetry and passion are forced to retire. The theatre cannot nobly feast the ear if the eye is distracted.

The Final Dramas: "Phœnissæ," "Bacchæ," "Iphigenia in Aulis"

Fortunately we do not need to take our farewell of Euripides with *Helen* and *Orestes* in our minds. During his last years the aged playwright seems to have had a fresh vision and discovered a hitherto untapped fount of strength. From this time three plays come before us, each of great interest.

In the extraordinary lengthy *Phœnissæ* (about 409 B.C.) he struck a new note—new in many ways. The canvas is greater than that of any other Greek drama, and even approaches the scope of a modern play; the chorus occupies a peculiar position, being formed of a group of Phœnician girls sanctified to the cult of Apollo who happen to be in Thebes at the time of the action and who therefore act as observers of the events displayed before them; the characters are dealt with sincerely and with deepened vision.

For a Greek play the character list is enormous. Here we meet the blind Œdipus and his aged queen-mother, Jocasta; here are his sons, Eteocles and Polyneices; here is Jocasta's brother, Creon, and his son, Menœceus; here is the blind seer, Tiresias, and his guardian child; here is the ill-fated Antigone. The whole story of Thebes is caught up into one single play.

There is much to attract our attention in the *Phœnissœ*, but perhaps, despite its brilliance in portraiture and some of its incisive scenes, it must be regarded as a comparative failure. This failure, however, is of a kind different from that of *Orestes*, for it comes from the very largeness of the attempt made by the playwright. The weaknesses are the weaknesses of supreme genius, not those of mediocre talent.

Genius too breathes throughout that most puzzling of all Greek plays, the *Bacchœ*, written presumably after the poet had departed in exile from his native city, and produced posthumously. No one will ever be able to say what this strange drama intends; but no one can deny its power, its intensity, and its beauty. Fundamentally it is a study of religious frenzy. Set in Thebes during the time of King Pentheus, it shows the city caught up in hysterical orgies in honour of Dionysus, and the god himself not only speaks the prologue, but plays an important rôle in the action.

The scenes are complex, but briefly the story told is that of Pentheus' attempt, in the name of reason, to combat the frenzy that has gripped all the citizens. Between the god and the king stand the old Tiresias and Cadmus, rather contemptuous of the follies of the worshippers, yet prepared to pursue a cautious path. Resolutely Pentheus sets forth to rid his kingdom of the Dionysiac rites, but is confronted by the magic-working god, is himself seized by a group of intoxicated women, including his own mother, Agave, and killed. Peculiarly intense is the scene wherein this Agave, who holds her son's head in her hands under the delusion that it is a lion's head, comes slowly back to reason and realization of the truth:

Enter from the mountain AGAVE, mad; and to all seeming wondrously happy, bearing the head of PENTHEUS in her hand. The CHORUS MAIDENS stand horror-struck at the sight; the LEADER, also horror-struck, strives to accept it and rejoice in it as the God's deed.

AGAVE: Ye from the lands of Morn!
LEADER: Call me not; I give praise!
AGAVE: Lo, from the trunk new-shorn
   Hither a Mountain Thorn
   Bear we! O Asia-born
     Bacchanals, bless this chase.
LEADER: I see. Yea; I see.
   Have I not welcomed thee?
AGAVE [*very calmly and peacefully*]:
   He was young in the wildwood:
   Without nets I caught him!
   Nay, look without fear on
     The Lion; I have ta'en him!

Cadmus enters and argues her back to sanity:

AGAVE [*troubled*]: I know not what thou sayest; but my will
   Clears, and some change cometh, I know not how.
CADMUS: Canst hearken then, being changed, and answer, now?
AGAVE: I have forgotten something; else I could.

CADMUS: What husband led thee of old from mine abode?
AGAVE: Echion, whom men named the Child of Earth.
CADMUS: And what child in Echion's house had birth?
AGAVE: Pentheus, of my love and his father's bred.
CADMUS: Thou bearest in thine arms an head—what head?
AGAVE [*beginning to tremble, and not looking at what she carries*]:
   A lion's—so they all said in the chase.
CADMUS: Turn to it now—'tis no long toil—and gaze.
AGAVE: Ah! But what is it? What am I carrying here?
CADMUS: Look once upon it full, till all be clear.
AGAVE: I see . . . most deadly pain! Oh, woe is me!
CADMUS: Wears it the likeness of a lion to thee?
AGAVE: No; 'tis the head—O God!—of Pentheus, this!

As will be realized, it is indeed difficult to discern Euripides' purpose. The most likely explanation is that, as in the *Hippolytus*, he is suggesting imaginatively that the extreme of reason and frigidity is as false as the extreme of passion. There is no jeering at the gods now: their terrible power has been amply revealed, and the final words of the chorus testify to their omnipotence:

> There be many shapes of mystery.
> And many things God makes to be,
>   Past hopes or fear.
> And the end men looked for cometh not,
> And a path is there where no man thought.
>   So hath it fallen here.

Finally we reach *Iphigenia in Aulis*, perhaps the last dramatic effort of Euripides' career and one completed by his son. The scene of the maiden's sacrifice forms its subject-matter, but, although it provides a sort of prelude to the story of *Iphigenia in Tauris*, it displays a greater depth and a higher seriousness. Euripides' interest seems concentrated less on the story and more on the characters, and it is interesting to observe that, whereas in his earlier dramas, the playwright had tended to fix his attention on a limited group of main persons, sometimes merely on one outstanding hero or heroine, here he depicts interplay of human personalities.

The central character is Agamemnon, a good-willed but feckless individual, obsessed by thought of his position as general of the Greek forces, easily influenced by his restless brother, Menelaus, who, fretting at the delay in recapturing Helen and so at restoring his honour, eggs him on to follow the advice of the seer Calchas that he shall sacrifice his daughter, Iphigenia. After some hesitation Agamemnon sends a missive to Clytemnestra declaring that Achilles wishes to marry their daughter, and bidding her bring the girl to the camp. Hardly has this missive gone, however, before he suffers from afterthoughts and dispatches a second message countermanding the first. Unfortunately it miscarries; Clytemnestra and Iphigenia arrive, much to Agamemnon's dismay, and the scene wherein they greet him not only exhibits high dramatic skill in the handling of an ironic situation, but throws brilliant light on all their characters:

> *CLYTEMNESTRA:* There comes your father! Let us greet him, girl!
>   Most honoured lord, King Agamemnon, hail!
>   We came at your behest.
> *IPHIGENIA:* O mother, blame me not! Let me go first
>   And put my arms about my father's neck.
> *CLYTEMNESTRA:* Go, go, my girl. You have always loved your father
>   More than the other children.
> *IPHIGENIA:* Father, how glad it makes my heart to see you!
>   It is so long since you have been away!
> *AGAMEMNON:* Yes, and mine too; your words are for us both!
> *IPHIGENIA:* How good it was of you to send for me!
> *AGAMEMNON:* No, child, not good; and yet there's good in it.
> *IPHIGENIA:* Why, what is it? There's trouble in your face,
>   Your eyes are sad. You are not glad to see me.
> *AGAMEMNON:* A general and a king has many cares.
> *IPHIGENIA:* O, stay with me now; send your cares away!
> *AGAMEMNON:* Why, all my cares are only for your sake.
> *IPHIGENIA:* Then smooth your face, unknit your brows, and smile!
> *AGAMEMNON:* I am as glad as I can be, my child.
> *IPHIGENIA:* And all the while the tears are in your eyes!
> *AGAMEMNON:* The parting that must come will be for long.
> *IPHIGENIA:* O, father dear, I do not understand.
> *AGAMEMNON:* Had you the sense I should but suffer more.
> *IPHIGENIA:* Then I'll talk nonsense, if that pleases you.

Here breathes a spirit of pathos vastly different from what we have met with in others of Euripides' plays: the pity here arises not from the situation itself, but from contemplation of the characters involved.

Step by step Agamemnon treads deeper in the mire of his own deceit. With difficulty he satisfies the questioning of Clytemnestra, but a moment later the queen encounters Achilles, addresses him as the future husband of her daughter, and is met by his blank wonder at her words. Finally a faithful old servant reveals to her the dire secret, while she in turn tells it to Achilles. In the preceding scenes Euripides had already given sufficient hints to indicate that no true harmony existed between Agamemnon and his wife; now Clytemnestra throws off the veil completely in a magnificent tirade:

> Then hear me now. I'll speak the naked truth,
> No dark hints now! By force you wedded me,
> I never loved you! Tantalus you slew,
> My first dear husband; and my little son,
> You tore him from my breast. And when my brothers,
> The sons of God, flashed to me on their steeds,
> My father pitied you, his suppliant,
> Gave me to you for wife. And a true wife I was,

Yes, chaste and true, and cared well for your home.
Such wives are not so common!—
Three girls I bore you and a son, and now
You rob me of the first! Your reason, pray,
If men should ask it? Oh, I'll answer that,—
To win back Helen! Your own child for a wanton,
Your dearest for a foe! A proper bargain!
If you do this, if you are long at Troy,
What will my heart be like, think you, at home,
When I look on my daughter's empty chair,
And empty room, sitting there all alone,
Companied by my tears, still muttering,
"Your father killed you, child, killed you himself!"
What will your wages be when you come back?
We who are left, we shall not want much urging
To greet you with the welcome you deserve!
O, by the gods, drive me not thus to sin,
Nor sin yourself!
If once you killed your child, how could you pray?
What good thing ask for? Rather for defeat,
Disgrace, and exile! Nor could I pray for you:
We make fools of the gods if we suppose
They can love murderers. If you come home.
Will you dare kiss your girls? Or they dare come,
That you may choose another for the knife?
Have you once thought of this? Are you a man?
Or nothing but a sceptre and a sword?
You should have gone among the Greeks and said,
"You wish to sail for Troy? Good, then draw lots,
And see whose child must die." That had been fair;
Or Menelaus should have slain his own,—
Hermione for Helen. But I, the chaste,
I must be robbed, and she come home in triumph
To find her daughter! Answer, if I am wrong!

The human heart is crying here; the vision of the woman's heart thus bared is brilliant with incandescent tensity.

Iphigenia, terrified, flings herself at her father's feet, but the plans for the sacrifice go on. Achilles, who had tried to save her, is stoned for his pains, and at last the girl, wearied out with the confusion, breaks down and pitifully accepts the fact of her coming death.

It is good to end our survey of Euripides' work on this high note. A puzzling, and at times irritating, dramatist, he contributed much towards the decay of the tragic theatre at the end of the fourth century B.C., but in him too there were brave, translunary things. The only regret is that the world outside of Greece seized on his writings rather than on those of Sophocles or Æschylus for imitation, and, among these writings, often tended to select the most sensational.

4

ARISTOPHANES AND THE OLD COMEDY

CONSIDERATION of the further fate of tragedy in classical times must be put aside for the moment until we gain a general picture of the comedy that developed during the period from the appearance of Æschylus to the death of Euripides. Greek audiences were capable of appreciating deep, tragic sensations: they could listen spellbound to the sonorous words given to choruses and actors in the serious plays; but they also enjoyed their merriment, and enjoyed it to the full. They were alert for beauty and wit and bawdry alike.

Comedies were first admitted to the Dionysiac Festivals in the year 486 B.C., but for many decades before that the comic form had been slowly evolving out of a diverse series of popular entertainments and rituals. In its earliest shape it was, indeed, a strange admixture, and for long it betrayed, in its absence of a precise structure, the variety of the elements out of which it had been wrought.

Its foundation was the Attic *comus* ($\kappa\widehat{\omega}\mu o\varsigma$), a popular ritual wherein a group of revellers organized processions and sang songs of doubtful propriety in honour of Dionysus. From this *comus* comedy takes its name. Often the *comus* group wore masks, or dressed themselves up in a kind of animal masquerade, appearing as birds, horses, or frogs, and this element also was incorporated into the literary comedy when finally that assumed an independent existence. The near-by town of Megara, too, contributed something to the general joy by providing burlesque sketches of a rudely farcical kind, while hilarious dances, such as the licentious *kordax*, contributed to the total ensemble.

The general result was the creation of that type of play which came to be known as the Old Comedy—grotesque, wanton, vulgar, sharp with stinging wit, and richly lyrical; a fantastic exhibition in which the latest gossip of the city was intermixed with material of the most imaginative sort; in which serious political and philosophical purpose jostled with buffoonery of the lowest. This is the Gilbert and Sullivan opera in a land where no Victorian taboos were set upon playwrights or performances, where anything might be said and almost anything done. The shriek of the magpie and the chattering of apes mingle here with the exquisite melodies of the nightingale.

In performance everything was done to make this an hilarious occasion. Animal figures freely appeared in the chorus, and for the main actors there was a rude comic dress. Tights were worn on the legs; a kind of jerkin was exaggeratedly padded; over this a short cloak barely came down to the non-existent waist; and prominently displayed was the indecent *phallus*, the emblem of fertility. The masks were equally exaggerated, rollicking in their distortion and caricature, yet underneath all the slapstick costuming, underneath the unbridled hilarity, there was always the sense of significant purpose, often the unexpected appearance of beauty.

Comedies of War, Philosophy, and Peace

Of this Old Comedy we know much from extant vases and statuettes, but the only literary relics that have been spared for us are the eleven precious plays written by Aristophanes. He was not the earliest nor was he by any means the only exponent of the form, but contemporaries recognized him as the greatest, so that this treasure not only has the value of displaying to us the content of the Old Comedy, but also, and more importantly, of revealing it at its best.

Aristophanes was born about 448 B.C., and the first play of his that we possess was produced in 425, at the time when Euripides was oppressed by bitterness on account of the Peloponnesian War and the decline of the democratic principle in Athens. In his opposition to the conduct of the war itself Aristophanes was at one with his elder contemporary, but the two differed violently in their basic philosophies. Where Euripides belonged to the coterie of young, advanced thinkers and in disillusioned spirit sought to discredit the legends of the past, Aristophanes, for all his boisterous fun, was made of Æschylean marble, and endeavoured, with every power that in him lay, to recall the degenerating citizenry of his age to the virtues of their predecessors. His is the conservatism of faith; Euripides fed on a rather superficial disbelief and a facile liberalism.

Since the structure of Old Comedy presents features unique and peculiar, it may be of service to take the first of Aristophanes' plays, *The Acharnians*, and rapidly review its contents. The scene we must suppose to be the Pnyx at Athens, with three doors representing the entrances to the houses of an ordinary citizen Dicæopolis, of the poet Euripides, and of the military general Lamachus (the last two being, of course, prominent contemporaries of the comic dramatist). On to the stage wanders Dicæopolis alone; in his prologue speech he grumbles about the discomforts consequent upon the current war, and declares that when the assembly meets he will press for peace. His aim, however, is thwarted when the officers of the court rudely repress another citizen, Amphitheus, who rises to raise the same issue, and when a group of ambassadors, newly returned from Persia and all togged-up in Eastern fineries, enter to present their reports. With burlesqued dignity the envoys explain that they went on their mission on a miserable salary of two drachmas a day, that they "suffered horribly on the plains of the Cayster, sleeping under a tent, stretched deliciously on fine chariots, half dead with weariness," and were "forced to drink delicious wine out of golden or crystal flagons." In vain Dicæopolis tries to expose the lies with which they flatter the assembly, and disgustedly he sends off Amphitheus to conclude a private truce with Sparta on behalf of himself, his wife, and his children. Meanwhile another ambassador returns, dressed in Thracian costume, and Dicæopolis, to put an end to the business, announces an omen: he pretends he has just felt a drop of rain. Immediately the court is adjourned, while Amphitheus runs in, panting, with a group of angry Acharnians at his heels, irate because of the proposed truce.

All of this provides the first part of the action, and the way is now clear for the *parodos*, or entrance-song, of the chorus. They enter, a group of Acharnian charcoal-burners, and after their first chant proceed to assail Dicæopolis. By the burlesque trick of taking a basket of coal from the house and threatening to destroy it, he commands their attention, and then proposes that he should be permitted to present his defence. At the same time he knows that if he is to prevail he must arouse their pity, and a brilliant thought occurs to him: off he goes to seek Euripides, in order to borrow some of the realistic stage rags worn by characters in that poet's pathetic plays. Knocking at the door, he is answered by a slave:

SLAVE [*opening the door and poking his head out*]: Who's there?

DICÆOPOLIS: Is Euripides at home?

SLAVE: He is and he isn't: understand that, if you can.

DICÆOPOLIS: What's that? He is and he isn't?

SLAVE: Certainly, old man; busy gathering subtle fancies here and there, his mind is not in the house, but he himself is; perched aloft, he is composing a tragedy.

DICÆOPOLIS: Oh, Euripides, you are indeed happy to have a slave so quick at repartee! Now, fellow, call your master.

SLAVE: Impossible!   [*He slams the door.*

DICÆOPOLIS: Too bad. But I will not give up. Come, let us knock at the door again. Euripides, my little Euripides, my darling Euripides, listen; never had man greater right to your pity. It is Dicæopolis of the Chollidian Deme who calls you. Do you hear?

EURIPIDES [*from within*]: I have no time to waste.

DICÆOPOLIS: Very well, have yourself wheeled out here.

EURIPIDES: Impossible.

DICÆOPOLIS: Nevertheless . . .

EURIPIDES: Well, let them roll me out; as to coming down, I have not the time.

[*The ekkuklema turns and presents the interior of the house. EURIPIDES is lying on a bed, his slave beside him. On the back wall are hung up tragic costumes of every sort, and a multitude of accessories is piled up on the floor.*

Dicæopolis asks for the costume of one of the tragic poet's most wretched characters. After refusing some that are proffered to him he selects those of Telephus, which the slave finds on top of the rags of Thyestes and mixed with those of Ino. Holding this costume up for the audience to see, he soliloquizes:

> Oh! Zeus, whose eye pierces everywhere and embraces all, permit me to assume the most wretched dress on earth. Euripides, cap your kindness by giving me the little Mysian hat, that goes so well with these tatters. I must to-day have the look of a beggar; "be what I am, but not appear to be"; the audience will know well who I am, but the Chorus will be fools enough not to, and I shall dupe them with my subtle phrases.

He now bothers Euripides for a whole set of hand-properties—a beggar's staff, a little pot with a sponge for a stopper; these, to get rid of the nuisance, Euripides gives him, although he complains that Dicæopolis is stealing an entire tragedy.

Now comes Dicæopolis'.speech, in which he gives a grotesque yet not essentially false account of the origins of the war, with the result that the chorus splits into two parts, those for him and those against. The latter call to their aid the general Lamachus, who enters in full warlike panoply and acts the braggart, but, rather discomfited by Dicæopolis' words, soon retires.

This leaves the stage free for what was a cardinal element of the Old Comedy, the *parabasis*, wherein the chorus wheeled round and made direct address to the audience in a long melodic ode. There follows a series of detached episodes. Dicæopolis marks out a square in front of his house and declares that this will be a market-place where all but Lamachus may trade. A starved Megarian enters, followed by a well-fed Bœotian, and in their farcical scenes further comment is made both on the effects of the war and on the political dangers within the city. Dicæopolis, prospering in his own peaceful little market-square, prepares himself a fine feast, and while he does so the braggart Lamachus comes out of his house to get ready for a military expedition commanded by the General Staff. The scene in which the joyous Dicæopolis sits at one side of the stage and the gloomy Lamachus at the other is replete with ironic comedy:

LAMACHUS: Bring me the plumes for my helmet.
DICÆOPOLIS: Bring me wild pigeons and thrushes.
LAMACHUS: How white and beautiful are these ostrich feathers!
DICÆOPOLIS: How fat and well browned is the flesh of this wood-pigeon!
LAMACHUS [*to DICÆOPOLIS*]*:* My friend, stop scoffing at my armour.
DICÆOPOLIS [*to LAMACHUS*]*:* My friend, stop staring at my thrushes.
LAMACHUS [*to his slave*]*:* Bring me the case for my triple plume.
DICÆOPOLIS [*to his slave*]*:* Pass me over that dish of hare.
LAMACHUS: Alas! the moths have eaten the hair of my crest.
DICÆOPOLIS: Shall I eat my hare before dinner?

Both soon go off, but immediately re-enter—Lamachus wounded and woeful, Dicæopolis gloriously drunk, accompanied by two pretty girls.

The whole comedy is spattered with indecent references, and there is much vulgar by-play, yet its serious purpose is amply apparent. Aristophanes does not like the new school of thought represented by Euripides, and he detests the political developments in his city. There is no doubt about his mission, or about his consciousness of it. In the parabasis to this play of *The Acharnians* the chorus specifically points out to the audience what the poet is trying to do and what benefit will accrue to the city if attention is given to his words:

> He therefore affirms,
> In confident terms,
> That his active courage and earnest zeal
> Have usefully served the common weal.
> . . . He for his part
> Will practise his art
> With a patriot heart,
> With the honest views
> That he now pursues,
> And fair buffoonery and abuse;
> Not rashly bespattering, or basely beflattering,
> Not pimping, or puffing, or acting the ruffian;
> Not sneaking or fawning;
> But openly scorning
> All menace and warning,
> All bribes and suborning:
> He will do his endeavour on your behalf;
> He will teach you to think, he will teach you to laugh.
> So Cleon again and again may try;
> I value him not, nor fear him, I!
> His rage and rhetoric I defy.
> His impudence, his politics,
> His dirty designs, his rascally tricks
> No stain of abuse on me shall fix.
> Justice and right, in his despite,
> Shall aid and attend me, and do me right:
> With these to friend, I ne'er will bend,
> Nor descend
> To a humble tone
> (Like his own),
> As a sneaking loon,
> A knavish, slavish poor poltroon.

That he was permitted in the midst of a serious war to produce this stinging anti-war comedy, to refer to the "tricks and plotting" of the popular leader Cleon, and to bring a burlesque Lamachus on the stage testifies to the fact that the Athenian democracy was still, in spite of all he said, healthy and robust. To think of a modern parallel to *The Acharnians* one would have to imagine a bitingly anti-war play of, say, 1943, in which an Eisenhower and a Montgomery were ridiculed in person, and in which a

Roosevelt and a Churchill were openly attacked: it would have to be, too, the success of the season, for Aristophanes' comedy was awarded the first prize when it was produced at the Lenæan Festival in 425.

The attack was continued in *The Knights* (424 B.C.), which unfortunately no amount of admiration of Aristophanes' style can make us call a good play; in it indignation has banished laughter. Why it also gained the first prize we cannot tell; nor can we tell why *The Clouds* was rated lowest in the competition of the following year. In this latter work Aristophanes turns from politics to philosophy, and an assessment of its merits is rendered difficult in view of the fact that as his chief figure he has chosen the person of Socrates, presented in such a distorted caricature as to leave the original far behind. If our attention is fixed mainly on the subject of the caricature, then we are bound to deem this play unjust, absurd, and even crassly stupid; but if, as seems the more proper approach, we consider it as a comedy designed to ridicule the follies of the new sophistries then in fashion, with the person of Socrates conveniently taken in symbolic wise, the drama becomes one of prime importance, full of pleasant sallies and amusingly plotted. The story tells of an old man, Strepsiades, who is much worried because of the debts incurred by his son's addiction to horse-racing. Creditors are pressing for their money, and the idea occurs to him that if only the youth will study for a time under the guidance of Socrates he will learn how to argue his way out of paying what he owes. The son, Pheidippides, refuses, whereupon the aged Strepsiades himself determines to go to school. Approaching Socrates' Thought-shop, he finds the philosopher strung up in a basket contemplating the heavens (a burlesque of the tragic *deus ex machina*), and is treated to a discourse in which the Clouds, and not the gods, are made the authors of all things. The Chorus of Clouds now appears, and Socrates explains how everything has a cause that goes back to them:

STREPSIADES: But you have not told us what makes the roll of the thunder.

SOCRATES: Have you not understood me, then? I tell you, that the Clouds, when full of rain, bump against one another, and that, being inordinately swollen out, they burst with a great noise.

STREPSIADES: How can you make me credit that?

SOCRATES: Take yourself as an example. When you have heartily gorged on stew at the Panathenæa, you get throes of stomach-ache, and then suddenly your belly resounds with prolonged rumbling.

STREPSIADES: Yes, yes, by Apollo! I suffer, I get colic, and then the stew sets to rumbling like thunder and finally bursts with a terrific noise. At first it's but a little gurgling *Pappax, pappax!* then it increases, *Papapappax!* and when I take my crap, why, it's thunder indeed, *papapappax! pappax! papapappax!* just like the clouds!

After the chorus has sung its odes Socrates comes out again, exhausted with the attempt to teach anything to Strepsiades: the latter's mind is set on learning nothing but "the art of false reasoning," but he is incapable of study. The philosopher bids him lie down on a pallet and cogitate.

"Well, now!" he inquires. "What are you doing? Are you reflecting?"

> *STREPSIADES:* Yes, by Poseidon!
> *SOCRATES:* About what?
> *STREPSIADES:* Whether the bugs will entirely devour me.
> *SOCRATES:* May death seize you, accursed man!

At last Socrates can stand it no longer, and Pheidippides is persuaded to come in the old man's stead, and we are regaled with a long debate between "Just Reason" and "Unjust Reason"—which might be interpreted as Valid Argument and Specious Argument. So well does Pheidippides prosper that, returning home, he is able to give his father a thorough thrashing, and prove that in taking this course with his parent a son is completely justified.

Purposeful laughter becomes at once gayer and more deeply loaded with serious ore in *The Wasps*, which won the first prize in 422 B.C. The attack returns again to Cleon, and specifically to the large juries which, under his administration, consumed much precious time and proved a political danger. In the first portion of the play we find an elderly gentleman, Philocleon, shut up in his house by his son, Bdelycleon, because of his inordinate love of serving in the courts. Vainly the old man tries, by every trick he can think of, to get away: he pretends he is smoke coming out of the chimney, he attempts to escape by clinging to the belly of an ass, he gets on the roof and endeavours to persuade his gaolers that he is a bird. To his aid come a chorus of his fellow-jurymen, costumed as wasps, but eventually he is persuaded to stay at home, provided he can set up his own private law-court. Here the trial is begun of the house-dog Labes, flagrantly caught in the act of stealing a Sicilian cheese, who is accused by a fellow-dog. There is no doubt about the defendant's guilt, but Bdelycleon puts up a spirited argument on his behalf.

> *BDELYCLEON:* Gentlemen of the jury, it is a difficult thing to speak for a dog who has been calumniated, but nevertheless, I will try. He is a good dog, and he chases wolves finely.
> *PHILOCLEON:* He is a thief and a conspirator.
> *BDELYCLEON:* No, he is the best of all our dogs; he is capable of guarding a whole flock.
> *PHILOCLEON:* And what good is that, if he eats the cheese?
> *BDELYCLEON:* What? he fights for you, he guards your door; he is an excellent dog in every respect. Forgive him his larceny! he is wretchedly ignorant, he cannot play the lyre. . . . Take pity on the unfortunate. . . . Have pity, Father, pity, I adjure you; you would not have him dead. Where are his puppies? [*A group of children costumed as puppies comes out.*] Come, poor little beasties, yap, up on your haunches, beg and whine!

Partly by this moving address and partly by a trick, Philocleon is persuaded to do what he has never done before, acquit the accused —whereupon he faints from shame and is revived only on his son's promise of a lively banquet.

The parabasis of the chorus follows, a stirring ode in which the praise of the jurymen of old is sung, of the men who saved Athens at Marathon. In rich melodies the music takes the audience back in memory to the days of Æschylus, when the city repelled the barbarian might of Persia.

Not yet, however, is the comedy over. The old man Philocleon has to be tutored in social graces by his son, and this gives occasion for further digs at Cleon:

> *BDELYCLEON:* The flute-player has finished the prelude. The guests are Theorus, Æschines, Phanus, Cleon, Acestor. . . . You are with them. Shall you know exactly how to take up the songs that are started?
> *PHILOCLEON:* Quite well.
> *BDELYCLEON:* Really?
> *PHILOCLEON:* Better than any born mountaineer of Attica.
> *BDELYCLEON:* That we shall see. Suppose me to be Cleon. I am the first to begin the song of Harmodius, and you take it up: "There never yet was seen in Athens—"
> *PHILOCLEON:* "—such a rogue or such a thief."
> *BDELYCLEON:* Why, you wretched man, it will be the end of you if you sing that. He will vow your ruin, your destruction, to chase you out of the country.

Having gone to the banquet, Philocleon gets thoroughly drunk, and the comedy ends in an hilarious dance.

The next year, 421 B.C., Aristophanes' theme was once again the Peloponnesian War; his *Peace* is a lyrical cry for a cessation of the stupid internecine conflict which was destroying both Athens and Sparta. Emulating Dicæopolis, a certain worthy Athenian citizen, Trygæus by name, has determined on ending the fight, and at the beginning of the play there is a glorious scene in which he and his slaves are busily engaged in feeding dung to a large beetle which he hopes will become sufficiently large to carry him up to the heavens, where he intends to solicit the aid of Zeus.

· At last all is ready. Up he goes in his beetle-machine (another hit at Euripides), and discovers that most of the gods, tired and wearied at contemplation of the follies of men, have gone off, leaving War to do his worst. For his part, War has made a huge mortar in which he proposes "to pound up all the cities of Greece." When he has departed Trygæus realizes that the only hope lies in rescuing Peace from the deep cave into which War has thrust her, and he summons a chorus of Greek peasants and workmen to aid him in this task. After many difficulties they get her out and, again amid difficulties, prepare for a wedding feast. A prophet angrily declares that to war there can be made no end, while an Armourer, equally angry, protests that if peace comes he will be utterly ruined—all his helmets and spears will have to be scrapped or sold at a loss. There is, of course, a happy ending, as Trygæus sings:

> While eating and drinking deep draughts of wine,
> continue to repeat: Oh! Hymen! oh! Hymenæus!

> Oh! Hymen! oh! Hymenæus! Hail, hail, my
> friends. All who come with me shall have
> cakes galore!

The whole play, written just before the deceptive Peace of Nicias, is full of
joyousness, and the choral odes, with their lyric praise of the peaceful
countryside, are trembling with ecstasy.

From "The Birds" to "The Frogs"

The beetle-flight of *Peace* was followed by the aerial delights of *The
Birds*, but between these two plays six long years had elapsed. *The Birds*
appeared in 414 B.C., and the delusive hope of a truce in the Peloponnesian War had gone: indeed, the time was rapidly approaching when
Athens was to experience her heaviest blows and to see her democracy
overthrown. Small wonder is it, therefore, that Aristophanes sought
refuge in a dream-world of his own creation, and endeavoured to find expression for his disgust at the real in the building for himself of an imaginative, fantastic world of Utopian quality.

Again we are introduced to the ordinary sensible Athenian citizen,
this time presented by a couple of figures, Euelpides and Peisthetærus,
who, wearied out with the discomforts of war and the follies of human
politics, set off to consult Epops, the hoopoe. Arrived at his habitation,
they suddenly have a brilliant idea: why, they inquire, should the birds
not be made masters of all things, building a city in the air in such a stra-
tegic situation as might permit them to overawe the gods by controlling
the sacrificial smoke from the altars and to rule men by having power
over the earth's weather?

Epops is impressed by the grandeur of the plan and summons all the
birds to counsel. At first they are prepared to attack the humans who
have invaded their sanctuary, but gradually order prevails; they endorse
the proposal and indulge in an exquisitely beautiful chant, in which the
notes of the nightingale form a lovely refrain—so lovely and so gay it
must be quoted almost in full:

> O darling! O tawny-throat!
> Love, whom I love the best,
> Dearer than all the rest,
> Playmate and partner in
>   All my soft lays,
> Thou art come! Thou art come
> Thou hast dawned on my gaze,
> I have heard thy sweet note,
> Nightingale! Nightingale!
> Thou from thy flute   Softly sounding canst bring
> Music to suit   With our songs of the spring.
>   Begin then I pray
>   Our own anapæstic address to essay.

Ye men who are dimly existing below, who perish and fade as the leaf,

Pale, woebegone, shadowlike, spiritless folk, life feeble and wingless and brief,

Frail castings in clay, who are gone in a day, like a dream full of sorrow and sighing,

Come listen with care to the Birds of the air, the ageless, the deathless, who flying

In the joy and the freshness of Ether, are wont to muse upon wisdom undying. . . .

O woodland Muse,

tio, tio, tio, tiotinx,

Of varied plume, with whose dear aid

On the mountain top, and the sylvan glade,

tio, tio, tio, tiotinx,

I sitting up aloft on a leafy ash, full oft,

tio, tio, tio, tiontinx,

Pour forth a warbling note from my little tawny throat,

Pour festive choral dances to the mountain mother's praise,

And to Pan the holy music of his own immortal lays;

totototototototototinx,

Whence Phrynichus of old,

Sipping the fruit of our ambrosial lay,

Bore, like a bee, the honied store away,

His own sweet songs to mould.

tio, tio, tio, tio, tiotinx.

Is there any one amongst you, O spectators, who would lead

With the birds a life of pleasure, let him come to us with speed.

All that here is reckoned shameful, all that here the laws condemn,

With the birds is right and proper, you may do it all with them.

Is it here by law forbidden for a son to beat his sire?

That a chick should strike his father, strutting up with youthful ire,

Crowing, "Raise your spur and fight me," that is what the birds admire.

Come, you runaway deserter, spotted o'er with marks of shame,

Spotted Francolin we'll call you, that, with us, shall be your name.

You who style yourself a tribesman, Phrygian pure as Spintharus,

Come and be a Phrygian linnet, of Philemon's breed, with us.

Come along, you slave and Carian, Execestides to wit,

Breed with us your Cuckoo-rearers, they'll be guildsmen apt and fit.

Son of Peisias, who to outlaws would the city gates betray,

Come to us, and be a partridge ("cockerel like the cock," they say),

We esteem it no dishonour knavish partridge-tricks to play.

Even thus the swans,

tio, tio, tio, tiotinx,

Their clamorous cry were erst up-raising,

With clatter of wings Apollo praising,

tio, tio, tio, tiotinx,

As they sat in serried ranks on the river Hebrus' banks.

tio, tio, tio, tiotinx,

Right upward went the cry through the cloud and through the sky.

Quailed the wild-beast in his covert, and the bird within her nest,

And the still and windless Ether lulled the ocean-waves to rest,
>   *totototototototototototinx.*
> Loudly Olympus rang!
And every Muse within that heavenly place
Amazement seized the kings; and every Grace
>   Took up the strain, and sang.
>   *tio, tio, tio, tio, tiotinx.*
Truly to be clad in feathers is the very best of things.
Only fancy, dear spectators, had you each a brace of wings,
Never need you, tired and hungry, at a Tragic Chorus stay,
You would lightly, when it bored you, spread your wings and fly away,
Back returning, after luncheon, to enjoy our Comic Play. . . .
If a gallant should the husband on the Council-bench behold
Of a gay and charming lady, one whom he had loved of old,
Off at once he'd fly to greet her, have a little converse sweet,
Then be back, or e'er ye missed him, calm and smiling in his seat.
Is not then a suit of feathers quite the very best of things?

The city is now a-building and named Nephelococcygia—Cloud-cuckoo-town—but soon its founders are confronted by a set of self-seeking Athenians. A poet ready to pen civic odes, a seer who would provide it with oracles, a town-planning expert, an inspector, and a law-maker are dealt with summarily; but a herald announces that there is a positive bird-mania down below, that thousands are applying for wings, and once again a series of objectionable characters flocks in—a Parricide who wants to live in Nephelococcygia because there, he thinks, he can kill his father with impunity, Cinesias the poetaster, and an Informer, who thinks his professional pursuits would be the better carried out if he could fly from place to place. Finally creeps in a heavily cloaked figure who turns out to be Prometheus, traditional friend of man: he brings news that the gods are in a sorry state since the founding of the city, and that they may be forced to accept whatever terms may be imposed.

Thus ends a joyous and a lovely play in gladness and in mirth.

Three years later (411 B.C.) *Lysistrata* repeats the mirth, although the gladness is more than a trifle bitter. This magnificent comic conception, in which Lysistrata, a woman of Athens, plans to stop the war by swearing all the wives of the warring states to refrain from intercourse with their husbands until the latter abandon their stupidities and call a truce, has the brilliance of simplicity. The fortunes of the women's revolution are related with gusto—both the anxieties of the men to have their wives back, and the pathetic little tricks employed by the weaker among the sisterhood, who wish to escape from the austere fervour of Lysistrata, are handled with consummate ease and obvious enjoyment. Here Aristophanes' inventive powers are at their finest; scene follows scene in unflagging merriment. The oath that the revolutionaries rather dismally are forced to swear; the almost pitiful combat between the chorus of old men, who bear faggots to the Acropolis in the hope of smoking out Lysistrata's friends, and the chorus of old women, who bear buckets wherewith to douse the flames; the discomfiture of the Athenian magistrate; the comic misery of Cinesias as he attempts to recapture his wife, while she tortures him beyond endurance; followed by the equally comic misery of the Spartan herald—episode after episode is daringly vulgar and gloriously amusing.

The same season (411 B.C.) Aristophanes offered to the public another comedy of women, the *Thesmophoriazusæ*, in which the theme of war is laid aside and the poet returns to the attack, begun many years before, on Euripides. Again, the comic invention is boldly and brilliantly simple. The tragic dramatist has learned that the women of Athens are to try him in their meeting at the Thesmophoria, accusing him of betraying the secrets of their sex; and, terrified of what may happen, he determines he must have an advocate to speak in his defence. First, he approaches his effeminate tragic colleague, Agathon, begging him to dress up as a woman and go on his behalf to the Thesmophoria, but fails to find the assistance he needs. Now, however, unexpected aid comes from a kinsman, Mnesilochus, who, after a comic shaving scene, gets himself ready. At the meeting all would have been well had this advocate not chosen to deliver a hearty but exceedingly tactless oration, pleading that the assembly should remember how many feminine sins and failings Euripides had *not* revealed. Infuriated, the women set upon him; he is found to be a man and placed under strong guard pending the announcement of his doom.

There follows a series of delicious episodes in which the wretched Mnesilochus tries device after device from the plays of his kinsman in an attempt to escape. Remembering how Œax in the (now lost) *Palamedes* had carved messages on wooden oars, he tries to send word of his fate to Euripides by similarly carving on small wooden images. Next he starts reciting from the *Helen*, while Euripides enters in the part of Menelaus, and there is fine merriment when Mnesilochus, whose face is lacerated from his shaving, quotes Helen's line: "My cheeks show the marks of the insults I have been forced to suffer." A magistrate enters and causes him to be bound to a post, but Euripides, retiring, declares he will never abandon him "as long as I draw breath and one of my numberless artifices remains untried." Given a cue, the prisoner sings a doleful ditty from *Andromeda*, while Euripides, peering round the edge of the scene-building, pretends to be Echo, and later poses as Perseus. All these tricks, however, fail, and in the end the dramatist has to forget his dramas, is forced to dress up as an old bawd and come in leading two pretty girls. These he parades across the stage, thus distracts the guardian policeman, and is enabled to release Mnesilochus.

The comedy is replete with good-humour and incisive wit, and its episodes are instinct with the sense of the ludicrous.

To Euripides Aristophanes returned some years later in *The Frogs* (405 B.C.), a short time after the tragic dramatist had died. Dionysus, god of the theatre, is worried lest the stage be left without any good plays and determines to go to Hades to try to get the deceased Euripides back. Remembering that Herakles had once made the journey to the nether regions with impunity, he goes with his slave Xanthias to seek advice from that hero:

DIONYSUS: Just tell us what's the best and quickest road to Hades. And, please, give us the most comfortable route.
HERAKLES: Well, let's see. Now, which would be best? Oh, yes, I have it. Get a sturdy seaman to tug a hawser round your neck.
DIONYSUS: A chokey sort of journey, that.
HERAKLES: Well, then, there is one very quick way—smoothly pounded up in a mortar.
DIONYSUS: The road of hemlock?
HERAKLES: Precisely.
DIONYSUS: Too cold for me. I'm freezing already.
HERAKLES: What about a short steep road?
DIONYSUS: That would suit me fine. I'm not a great walker.
HERAKLES: Then just walk down to Ceramicus—
DIONYSUS: Yes?
HERAKLES: Ascend the tower there—
DIONYSUS: That's all right: and then?
HERAKLES: Wait till they start the races down below, lean over till they give the signal to go, and then go.
DIONYSUS: Where?
HERAKLES: Over.

At last, after this badinage, the pair set out, Dionysus dressed in Herakles' skin and bearing his club. He is ferried across Charon's lake of the dead while Xanthias pants round the edge, and a group of frogs raucously chants the "Brekekekex koax koax" chorus. Ludicrous scenes occur in Hades and gradually work up to the climax, when Æschylus and Euripides contest to see which of them is the weightier playwright by placing lines from their dramas on a great pair of scales. Although the latter displays wit, subtlety of argument, and an ability to anger his opponent by his sophistries, the scales weight down on Æschylus' side, and he is chosen to return to earth. Even as a contemporary, Aristophanes realized how far Euripides was injuring the spirit of tragedy: only a return to Æschylean passion could save it from complete ruin.

Thus is enclosed, between the bird chorus and the chorus of frogs, the gayest, the most serious, the wittiest, and the most lyrical period of Aristophanes' genius.

The Last Plays: "Ecclesiazusæ" and "Plutus"

In the year 405 B.C. the doom of Athens had been firmly engraved by the hand of destiny and the foolish hands of its citizenry. The great fleet was routed at Ægospotami, and the once proud city-state surrendered ignominiously to Sparta; the Piræus and the Long Walls were razed,

A SCENE FROM THE
NEW COMEDY
From the original in the
Museo Nazionale, Naples.
Photo Anderson

OLD MAN AND SLAVE
Bari Museum. From Margarete Bieber,
*Die Denkmäler zum Theaterwesen
im Altertum.*

THE BIRTH OF HELENA
Bari Museum. From Margarete Bieber,
*Die Denkmäler zum Theaterwesen
im Altertum.*

ZEUS VISITING ALCMENA
Vatican Museum.
Photo Alinari

ZEUS VISITING ALCMENA
British Museum.

COMIC SCENES FROM 'PHLYAX' VASES

only twelve ships were permitted to remain in her navy, her foreign possessions all were lost. Very soon the Thirty Tyrants took control, the
moderate Theramenes was murdered, and the brief-lived despotism was
overthrown by a violent revolution under Thrasybulus. Amid these
events the civic life of the state inevitably altered: excesses were rife and
the old freedom had gone. Socrates, instead of merely being laughed at
on the stage, was grimly forced to take the chilly hemlock road to Hades
jokingly recommended to Dionysus by Herakles.

Under such conditions the spirit of comedy gradually changed; the
Old Comedy was transformed into what was known as the Middle
Comedy. In this, it would seem, the licences of the earlier Aristophanic
style were curbed, political references were cautiously introduced, and
the general structure was changed through the influence of Euripides,
but largely, too, because rich men no longer were prepared to defray the
high costs of production of these pieces. In the *Ecclesiazusæ* (392 B.C.) the
familiar Aristophanic fantasy is still apparent, but subdued in tone. Like
the *Lysistrata*, it deals with a women's revolution, led by Praxagora,
designed to establish a genuine communist state, in which property
belongs to all and where free love is allowed—with modifications, the
chief of these being that the old women and the ugly are given priority
over the young and the lovely. This piece of legislation furnishes the principal merriment at the end, when a young man, attracted by a girl, finds
he must satisfy first an elderly woman; rescued from her, he is captured
by one yet older; and finally, a second time rescued, he finds himself in
the clutches of a hideous and aged harridan.

The spirit is the spirit of the Old Comedy, but the form is changing.
Gone is the central element in the more ancient type of play, the parabasis of the chorus, and although the basic action is fantastic, the language is more nearly akin to the speech of common life. That we are
entering a new world is revealed, too, in one character name, Chremes,
which in the New Comedy, soon to follow, was destined to become a
stock title for the comic old man.

Aristophanes' last play is the peculiar *Plutus*, presented in 388 B.C., a
kind of morality drama, in which the blind god of riches, Plutus, is protected (incognito) by the worthy citizen Chremylus, at length is cured,
and regains his sight. The spectre of Poverty rises and enters into a debate by trying to prove that she, not Plutus, has most aided mankind;
discomfited, she retires, and the god is left to dispense his blessings more
equably than in the past. The play has some quality, and a few flashes of
the Aristophanic humour irradiate the dialogue, but, compared with the
outpouring of invention in *The Birds* or the roistering joy of *Thesmophoriazusæ*, it is a tame, and rather dull, affair. The time of unbridled, uproarious, purposeful laughter had gone for Aristophanes, for Athens,
and, one might even say, for the world.

5

FROM MENANDER TO THE MIMES

THE STYLE known as the Middle Comedy endured from the first quarter of the fourth century to about 330 B.C., but concerning its qualities we can but make broad guesses. The literary evidence consists of no more than a number of fragments, and our chief guide is a set of statuettes which evidently reproduce the stage appearance of its characters. From these we may hazard the conjecture that the Middle Comedy was basically a transitional form of drama, inheriting some of the features of the Old Comedy, but definitely tending towards an entirely different concept of the comic.

The costumes worn by the characters still bear traces of the attire of the actors in the fifth century, with the padded stomachs, the tights, the short cloak, but when we examine the figures in greater detail we realize that the exaggeration of feature has been softened and that the characters represented must have been much closer to the living persons to be seen on Athens' streets than the grotesques beloved by Aristophanes. There are still some burlesque mythological persons, such as the braggart Herakles, but most of the statuettes represent a series of stock types of the day—an old woman holding a child, a modest-seeming courtesan, old men and young men, rascally slaves, some seated in impertinent attitude on altars where they have sought sanctuary. We receive the impression—fortified from other sources—that the actions in which these characters were involved must have been of a more domestic kind than the earlier fantasies and that their behaviour must have been much more realistic.

A Changing Theatre

Meanwhile both audience and theatre were in process of change. The old gusty days of the Athenian democracy were gone, and a bourgeois civilization had taken its place. Civic interests had ceded to domestic. Having argued the gods out of existence, men had no other deity than Plutus, god of wealth. The ancient culture was sufficiently strong to leave its deep impress on all the peoples of the Mediterranean basin, but its vitality had been dissipated; the culture had become polite.

Gradually Athens ceased to be the core of this civilization. Power passed from state to state, and it was not to be long before Alexander the Great, Greek in outlook but a monarch of Macedon, became lord of the ancient world. Nor was it to be long after that before this civilization was to find its chief home in Egypt, at Alexandria under the Ptolemies.

All over the Greek countries there was the building of new theatres and the remodelling of old during this time, for the impetus of the three great Athenian tragic dramatists and of Aristophanes was powerful enough to maintain prime interest in the stage; but the forms assumed by these new theatres were different from those of the fifth century. True, the Greek playhouse to the very end retained its chief characteristic feature—the combination of three essentially separate parts, auditorium, orchestra, and scene-building. At the same time the functions of these parts were being altered. The great sweep of stone seats tended to approach more nearly to the shape of a semicircle. Although the orchestra still kept its central position, the reduced importance of the chorus permitted an encroachment upon its area, with the *skene* pushing itself forward; in some theatres, even, such as those at Assos and Priene, the circular form was deliberately abandoned, and the new orchestra took the shape of a semicircle extended by lines drawn at right angles to the diameter.

It was, however, the scene-building that altered most, taking shape as a structure clearly modelled on the richer domestic architecture of the time. Because the chorus and the actors were now separate, with more emphasis placed upon the individual characters in the dramas presented, the way was open for the erection of a high stage. Normally, this high stage was placed upon a long line of low pillars and jutted out in front of the *skene* proper: it was, accordingly, styled the proscenium (*proskenion*), literally signifying that which was before the *skene*. Behind it was the second storey of the *skene*, with a row of columns supporting a roof and providing a kind of rear or inner stage in the space between the columns and the front wall of the scene-building.

In this new type of theatre scenery could be, and was, more freely used than in the past, and we must think of the actors appearing against backgrounds of panels (*pinakes*), painted either to give the suggestion of walls and doors or more elaborately to convey an impression of buildings in perspective. We must think, too, of these actors becoming more and more important, until Aristotle could observe that in theatrical productions they were generally of greater consequence than the dramas they interpreted. This is a playhouse intended not for those who have come to a religious exercise, intent upon listening to rich words, but for those who see in the theatre a place of entertainment merely, whose interests are more mundane and whose eyes need showy scenes.

The New Comedy: Menander

The characteristic dramatic genre in this theatre was the New Comedy, established, during the time of Alexander the Great, about 330

B.C. Even had we possessed nothing but the terracottas and other visible records of the actors in these plays, we could have made a fair guess at its tone and contents. Gone is the old grotesque comic dress; the mythological types have vanished. Instead on the stage now appear figures garbed in the costumes of the day. Here are the fathers and sons of Hellenistic society, the slaves and the cooks and the musicians, the old gossips and the parasites, the young wives, and, above all, the courtesans. Some of the masks still retain an element of grotesquerie, but in general the features are closely modelled on the real.

Happily some literary record also remains, and this enables us to corroborate the impression received from contemplation of the little histrionic statuettes and to round out our imaginative reconstruction of the productions. Apart from fragments from a number of authors of the New Comedy style, a happy discovery at Cairo has given us some four thousand lines of the writing of the most famous of these authors, Menander, amply sufficient to allow us to shape general conclusions concerning the entire development of this comic style.

One of a group of playwrights including Philemon, Diphilus, Poseidippus, and Apollodorus, Menander was born in 343 B.C. (he died in 292), the nephew of a Middle Comedy dramatist, Alexis. Well-born, he was interested in social manners and the graces of culture; the life of the city appealed to him, and its types he studied with sympathetic care. The contemporary and friend of Epicurus, he imbibed some of that philosopher's ideas, while from Theophrastus he probably acquired his interest in the delineation of character types.

Before turning to an examination of those works of his which are still, though fragmentarily, extant, we may do well to consider, in general terms, the style of play which he was largely responsible for establishing on the stage. This style of play is essentially realistic. Aristophanes' fantasies are forgotten, and the characters are familiar; nor need we be surprised, since the comedies were penned for a bourgeois civic audience, to find that, despite the changed conventions of life, a peculiarly 'modern' note is struck in the dialogue. When we hear the persons of New Comedy speaking about 'gold-digging' and 'shop-keeping minds' we recognize the world we are in.

With the fantastic has vanished, too, the old uproarious laughter. Menander seldom allows more than a smile to curve his lips. Indeed, we encounter here a quiet, contemplative mood which might almost have seemed more proper to the tragic stage.

> When you wish to know what you are, look at the tombs in the cemeteries. There are bones there, and the ashy dust of men who were monarchs, tyrants, sages, men proud of their birth and their riches, their estates and their handsome figures. Naught of these defended them against Time: Death comes to all things mortal. Look on these and learn what you are.

Passages such as this remind us that we are far off from boisterous comedy, that we are in the world of a realistic, reflective, sentimental comedy of human manners.

And here the influence of Euripides upon the New Comedy becomes clearly apparent. From Euripides two great streams of influence are to be traced. His inspiration was a dominant influence on all the tragic playwrights who followed him. This was a direct channel, but no less direct was the passage from his dramas to those of Menander. In Euripides' plays certain characteristic features attract attention: his suppression of the chorus, his emphasis upon character (particularly the characters of women), his carefully wrought plots with their complications, his reflective, rhetorical tone, his introduction of love-themes, his development of a kind of tragi-comedy. The chief trend of his art was from the heroic to the realistic, from the ideal to the ordinary, from the rigours of tragedy to the sentimentalities of the drama of ideas. Already, in *Helen* and other plays, these features have been amply revealed, but there still remains at least one of his works to be considered, and this may now be glanced at, since it demonstrates in an extreme form qualities later on to be taken up by the comic playwrights of the fourth century. The date of *Ion* is unknown, but almost certainly it came late in Euripides' career; with one or two changes its plot might easily have been the plot of one of Menander's plays. The familiar situation is here—a girl ravished in the dark and a child exposed with trinkets; only here the girl is a princess, Creusa, the ravisher is a god, Apollo. As the plot proceeds we find Creusa married to a king, Xuthus; the couple are childless and go to Delphi for aid. Apollo's oracle declares that the first person whom Xuthus meets as he leaves the temple will be his son; this person is, in reality, Ion, the child of Creusa. Not knowing who he is, Creusa, enraged, determines to destroy him, is prevented, and discovers the boy's real paternity by means of the jewels she herself had left with the exposed babe. Gods appear in this story, and princesses, but they behave like middle-class citizens; bourgeois romance surrounds them, sentimentalism colours their actions, the atmosphere in which they dwell is not that highly charged mountain air out of which tragedy is wrought, but the quiet, reflective comic air of the plains. Tragedy is rapidly becoming drama.

Fundamentally, then, we may say that the style of Menander and his fellows was wrought out of the Euripidean manner. In their structure, in their romantic theme, in their concentration on the domestic, and in their rhetorical quality a direct link exists between the tragedies of the one school and the sentimental comedies of the other.

The first play from which we have fragments of Menander's writing is *Samia (The Girl from Samos)*, which, although more carefree, perhaps one might almost say farcical, than his other extant works, nevertheless reveals the typical features of his art. Only a small portion of the text has come down to us, sufficient, however, for a reconstruction of the plot. Romantic love is the core, with misunderstandings complicating the action, providing opportunity for character portrayal and creating scenes of laughable disorder. Moscion, son of the kindly, good-willed Demeas, is deeply in love with Plangon, daughter of the poor, irascible, touchy Niceratus. She has a child, and, fearing her father's wrath, has it taken by Chrysis, Demeas' mistress and housekeeper, who gives out that it is her child by her guardian. The complications may be imagined: Demeas suddenly rendered jealous when he imagines that Chrysis has been unfaithful with his own son; Niceratus so hasty in his passions that he will not listen to reason; slaves trying to conceal secrets and making confusion worse confounded by their efforts. There is in some lines a sort of brittle wit, as when the slave Parmeno addresses the Cook:

> Cook, I'm damned if I know why you carry knives with you. Your chatter would reduce anything to mincemeat.

There is abundance of comic irony when characters blunder over issues quite plain to the audience. There is pathos, as in the scene where the unfortunate and falsely suspected Chrysis is driven out-of-doors by her protector.

Misunderstandings—symbolized by the abstract figure of Misapprehension—teem also in *Perikeiromene* (*The Girl with Shorn Hair*), a comedy of separated twins, Glycera and Moschion. Abandoned in infancy, the former has been brought up by a poor woman and later finds a protector in the soldier Polemon, while the latter has been adopted and lavishly cared for by a wealthy old lady, Myrrhine. From the scene in which Polemon, enraged by ill-founded jealousy, shears off Glycera's hair the play takes its title, but jealous rages of such sort do not long endure in Menander's comedies, and, of course, the pair are reconciled; of course Glycera and Moschion discover their relationship; of course the pair are united to their long-lost father. It is all very pretty, very romantic, and yet at the same time very close to real life.

How far Menander carried the comic drama along these lines is revealed even more patently in *Epitrepontes* (*The Arbitration*), still another play of love, in which pathos battles with laughter as to which shall win. Since more of this comedy has been preserved than of any other of Menander's works, and since in this New Comedy the true basis is to be found for the characteristic modern theatre, its plot may be more fully summarized.

In the first act we are introduced to a young wife, Pamphila, daughter of the tight-fisted Smicrines, and her strait-laced husband, Charisius, a very serious and proper youth. There has just been a crisis in the household. Barely five months after her marriage Pamphila has borne a son, and we learn that this was the result of an attack made upon her, before her wedding, by a drunken man at one of the city's festivals: since the assault was in the dark, she has no idea of the identity of her seducer. The child has been taken by a slave to be exposed, and all would have been well had not Onesimus, Charisius's slave, revealed the secret. Charisius is shocked but, being genuinely in love with his wife, he does not cast her off: instead, he leaves the house and indulges in extravagant orgies in which a girl harpist, Habrotonon, figures largely.

The second act opens with the appearance of Smicrines, who, not knowing about the child, is in a rage at his son-in-law, not so much for having deserted Pamphila as for squandering his fortune on riotous living. His reflections are interrupted when a slave, Davus, and Syriscus, a charcoal-burner, enter in lively and acrimonious argument. They agree to put their case to arbitration and beg Smicrines to be the judge. Davus explains that some time ago he found an exposed babe along with some trinkets:

> I picked it up and went back home with it and was going to raise it. That's what I intended then. In the night, though, like everybody else, I thought it over to myself and argued it out: "Why should I bring up a baby and have all that trouble? Where am I to get all that money to spend? What do I want with all that worry?" That's the state I was in. Early next morning I was tending my flock again, when along came this fellow, he's a charcoal-burner, to this same spot to get out stumps there. He had made friends with me before that. So we got talking together and he saw that I was gloomy and said: "Why so thoughtful, Davus?" "Why indeed," said I, "I meddle with what doesn't concern me." So I tell him what had happened, how I found the baby and how I picked it up. And he broke in at once, before I had finished my story, and began entreating me: "As you hope for luck, Davus," he kept saying, "do give me the baby, as you hope for fortune, as you hope for freedom. I've a wife, you see," says he, "and she had a baby, but it died." Meaning this woman who is here now with the child. Did you entreat me, Syriscus?

The charcoal-burner admits this, but, having heard about the trinkets, he claims he ought to have them. In a spirited speech he argues that these trinkets must go with the child:

> Perhaps this babe is better born than we. He may, though brought up among labourers, look down on our condition, seek his own native level, have pluck to ply some noble occupation, hunt lions, bear arms, take part in races at the games. You have seen actors, I am sure, and all these things are familiar to you. A certain Neleus and Pelias, the famous ones, were found by an aged goat-herd clad in a goat-skin just like mine. When he saw that they were nobler born than he, he told them all, how he found and picked them up, and he gave them a wallet full of tokens and from that they found out everything about themselves for certain and, goat-herds before, now became kings.

Convinced by such arguments, Smicrines immediately commands Davus to hand over the trinkets. As Syriscus examines his booty Onesimus enters, and at once recognizes a ring as belonging to his master, Charisius.

The third act reveals, through the words of Onesimus and Habrotonon, that Charisius, despite his semblance of rioting, is really pining for his wife and curses the day he was told her secret—so much so that Onesimus is afraid to reveal the secret of the ring to him. He knows Charisius lost it at a festival, and he is almost sure he must have assaulted some girl there; before taking further action he wishes to find that girl. Here Habrotonon comes to his aid: she was at the festival, she says, when a young girl was apparently attacked:

> *ONESIMUS:* You were there?
> *HABROTONON:* Yes, last year at the Tauropolia. I was playing the lute for some young ladies, was joining in the sport myself; at that time I hadn't—I mean I didn't know yet what a man is. [*ONESIMUS smiles knowingly.*] Indeed I didn't, by Aphrodite.
> *ONESIMUS:* Yes, but do you know who the girl was?
> *HABROTONON:* I could ask. She was a friend of the women that I was with.
> *ONESIMUS:* Did you hear who her father was?
> *HABROTONON:* I don't know anything about her except that I should recognize her if I saw her. A good-looking girl, goodness, yes, and rich too, they said.
> *ONESIMUS:* Perhaps it's the same one.
> *HABROTONON:* I don't know about that. Well, while she was with us there, she strayed off and then suddenly came running up alone, crying and tearing her hair. She had utterly ruined a very fine Tarantine shawl, and delicate, my goodness. Why, it was all in tatters.

It is arranged between them that Habrotonon will wear the ring and, if Charisius notices it, will profess to have been the wronged maiden. The plot works: Charisius acknowledges the child and is prepared to pay heavily in order to secure Habrotonon's liberty; while Smicrines, outraged, determines to take his daughter home with him.

In the fourth act Pamphila protests to her father (Charisius overhearing her words) that, despite all the ill-usage she has received, she will not desert her husband. A moment later she meets Habrotonon and receives the joyous news that Charisius is the father of her child, while as for Charisius himself, the words of Onesimus are sufficient testimony:

> He's not quite sane. By Apollo, he's mad. He's really gone mad. By the gods he *is* mad. My master, I mean, Charisius. He's had an atrabilious stroke or some such thing. How else can you explain it? He spent a long time by the door inside just now craning his neck and listening. His wife's father was having a talk with her about the business, I suppose. The way he kept changing colour, gentlemen, I don't even care to mention. Then he cried out: "O darling! what a wonderful thing to say!" and beat his head violently. Then again after a while: "What a wife I had and now have lost, alas!" And to cap it all, when he had heard them to the end and had gone in at last, inside there was groaning, tearing of hair, continual frenzy. Over and over again he'd repeat: "Criminal that I am, when I had myself done a thing like that, when I had myself got an illegitimate child, to be so unfeeling, so utterly unforgiving to her in the same unhappy situation. No humanity; no mercy." He calls himself names as hard as he can, his eyes are bloodshot with fury. I'm shaking in my shoes; I'm all wilted with terror. If he catches sight of me, who told on her, anywhere, while he's in this state, he'll maybe kill me. That's why I've quietly slipped out here. Where am I to turn though? What can I think of? It's all over. I'm done for. He's at the door coming out. O Zeus Saviour, help me if you can.

Poor Charisius now comes in, berating himself for his superiority and determining to make amends to Pamphila. Learning that she is really the mother of the child, his self-abasement knows no bounds, his new-found resolve no limits.

The last act shows the discomfiture of Smicrines, who, arriving in a passion to abduct his daughter by force, is suddenly deflated by the truth. "By all the gods and spirits," he cries, and Onesimus cynically questions him:

> *ONESIMUS:* Do you believe, Smicrines, that the gods can spare the time to mete out daily to every individual his share of good or evil?
> *SMICRINES:* What's that?
> *ONESIMUS:* I'll make it quite plain. The total number of cities in the world is approximately a thousand. Each has thirty thousand inhabitants. Are the gods busy damning or saving each of them one by one? Surely not, for so you make them lead a life of toil. Then are they not all concerned for us, you'll say. In each man they have placed his character as commander. This ever present guardian it is that ruins one man, if he fails to use it aright, and saves another. [*Indicating himself*] This is our god, this is the cause of each man's good or evil fortune. Propitiate this by doing nothing absurd or foolish, that good fortune may attend you.

Thus ends *The Arbitration*, on a strangely modern note. All the ingredients are here for the drama of to-day—the emphasis on manners, the mingled smiles and tears, the growth of character in the persons represented, the concept of the single moral law for men and for women alike, even, we may say, the building of the entire play about an idea, for Menander's comedy is, in essence, a problem drama.

The Mimes, Rough and Refined

The style of Menander was handed on and taught to Rome, but before we turn to the Latin playwrights we must consider, very briefly, the characteristics of a largely unliterary theatre which, taking many and diverse shapes, ran its course from earliest days to latest, independently of the Old, Middle, and New Comedy traditions.

It will be recalled that the Aristophanic kind of drama owed something to the burlesque, farcical episodes put upon the stage at Megara. Down through the years from Aristophanes to Menander, and beyond, dim relics of these popular farces may be traced, sometimes very faint and uncertain, sometimes firm and sure. An example of the latter is the stage of the so-called Phlyakes (Φλύακες) of Southern Italy and Sicily, as depicted on numerous vases and revealed in contemporary record. In the pieces played by these actors a wooden stage was used, sometimes at least with an upper gallery which could serve as an acting-area. Their costumes were based on the costumes of the Old Comedy (themselves probably derived from the Megarean farce), and the basis of their efforts was burlesque.

Some authors, whose names are preserved for us by commentators—such as Rhinthon, who flourished about 300 B.C.—lent their talents to the penning of plays for the Phlyakes, but one gets the impression, on studying the vase paintings in which the players appear, that most of this activity was unliterary, perhaps largely improvised. In most of the scenes depicted the gods and the heroes are unmercifully mocked. Zeus is a pathetic creature, Herakles a brutal savage, Apollo an effeminate æsthete; Zeus appears dragging a ladder with which to mount to Alkmena's window, Apollo takes refuge on the top of his own temple from the threats of Herakles. Scenes of ordinary life are here too, burlesqued in like manner; old men are stupid, slaves ridiculous; life's amusing panorama is broadly set before us.

This *mimus*, or mime, as it came to be styled, spread out in two directions, the one untheatrical and literary, the other becoming ever more and more popular. Far back in the fifth century the Sicilian Epicharmus won fame for his handling of this kind of play, and later came Herodas, a native of Kos, who apparently lived and wrote in the third century B.C. Of the former's works nothing save titles and a few fragments remain, but fortune has preserved eight sketches by Herodas—lively, frank little studies of life. About the same time were composed the mimes of Theocritus, in which a polished style and a delicate refinement in the handling of subject-matter cannot conceal the popular origin of the idyllic poetry.

In these, however, we are being steadily drawn away from the stage, and for our purposes it is much more important to trace the movement of the mimic drama in its more definitely theatrical forms. From Sicily the mime seems to have moved northward, through the Greek settlements on the Italian peninsula, to Tarentum and Pæstum, and thence it reached the Oscans, producing a kind of associated drama which the Romans called the *fabula Atellana*—a name derived from the Campanian town of Atella. Little is known of the *fabula Atellana*, but certain facts seem clear: it was inspired by Greek models, apparently of the Phlyakes type; it became popular in Rome as early as the third century B.C., and was the genre particularly favoured by Pomponius of Bononia and by Novius a couple of centuries later; it introduced a set of stock characters among whom the stupid Bucco, the Punch-like Dossennus, the greedy Maccus, the senile Pappus, are clearly indicated. In tone the spirit of these Atellan plays cannot have been far removed from that of the Sicilian popular drama.

The Comic World of Plautus

The Greek inspiration in the development of the Atellan farce is a symbol of a general truth regarding the entire development of Roman literature and Roman theatre alike. The Greek genius was inventive; the Romans knew best how to adapt; the Greeks felt an innate demand for spiritual expression; the Romans delighted more in practical things. The result is that the Roman theatre is built out of what the Greeks created, and the Latin plays were based confessedly on Athenian models. At the same time we must ever bear in mind the fact that, while Rome did not introduce anything fundamentally new, the manner in which it took over and firmly stamped the older forms made it, and not Athens, produce the models on which the whole of the subsequent Western stage is based.

So far as the theatre building is concerned, certain dominant features are worthy of special attention. To Rome the theatre came late, but when it did it took characteristic shape as a single architectural structure; the three separate parts of the Greek theatre (auditorium, orchestra, and stage) were crushed within continuous containing walls. The effect was achieved by making the first and second elements exact semicircles and by elaborating the *skene* so that it occupied the entire diameter. Thus the spectators, entering such a playhouse, no longer sat watching a performance in which the actors were at least partly revealed against a natural background of sea and mountainous landscape, but, instead, remained enclosed by the lofty theatre's retaining structure. Plays, as it were, became more indoor affairs, and the impression was no doubt intensified by the roofs, which in some buildings jutted out over the stage, and by the awnings, which could even be spread, as occasion demanded, above the audience. No longer was there any advantage in erecting theatres on lofty positions, and, therefore, in Roman times the followers of Thespis brought their baggage down from the hillsides and performed on the plains. In such playhouses scenery could be more effectively introduced than in any of the early Greek structures, and scenic display, we know, was freely presented on the lofty, ornate façades against which the actors were revealed. There even came into use the theatrical front curtain, raised on posts at the side of the stage and lowered into specially prepared trenches at the rear of the attenuated orchestra.

The development of these structures, with their characteristic Roman features, was, however, mainly the result of architectural activity during the period of the Empire; the plays of Plautus, the first Latin playwright known to us, and, indeed, virtually the first Roman author, were produced in no such grandiose structures. For him simple wooden erections, apparently based on the kind of stage used by the Phlyakes, had to suffice.

Titus Maccius Plautus was born about 254 B.C. and died, at the age of seventy, in 184. Reared in poor circumstances and forced to make a living by hard labour, he seems to have turned to the theatre in the hope of easing his lot, and consequently all his works have a strongly popular flavour: he wanted success and was fully prepared to give the audience precisely what it wanted. Rough and ready, he sought no literary esteem and was content if he could make his audience laugh.

His inspiration was twofold. First, he was well acquainted with the writers of the Greek New Comedy, Menander in particular, and from them he freely borrowed plots, character, and dialogue. For an ordinary

Roman audience, however, the refinements of Menander's style would have been too dull, and therefore this author, with an eye on the public, freely borrowed also from the Atellan farces, themselves based on the Sicilian Phlyakes which in turn have at least a nodding acquaintanceship with the work of Aristophanes. His middle name, Maccius or Maccus, he took from the stock character of the greedy fool of the *fabula Atellana*. The general result is a strange admixture of diverse elements. In the plays of Plautus there are scenes modelled on Menander's sentimental realism, farcical scenes in the style of the mime, burlesque like that introduced into the Sicilian comedy. He reflects the style of Menander's comedy of manners, of the mime's realistic scenes, and even (as in *Amphitryon*) of the ancient burlesque drama. The very form of his comedies is mixed—a jumbling together of spoken dialogue (*diverbium*) and lyrics (*cantica*)—reminding us of the forms assumed by the ballad opera in the eighteenth century.

Naturally his pieces exhibit wide diversity, for all was fish that came to his net; but throughout run certain dominant qualities. The characters are for the most part broadly delineated types. Chief of all is the comic slave, an intriguing, bustling, impertinent fellow, ever in danger of a whipping or worse, ever meddling, ever ingenious. In nearly every one of the extant twenty comedies he is the moving spirit of the piece. Old men also figure prominently; some are irascible, some are kindly, most are willing to have a gay time if they can. 'Mother,' as Edith Hamilton so aptly emphasizes, is a prominent influence in these plays, and her romanticized figure reminds us of the very strong sentimental concept which colours so many of the Plautan scenes. Indeed, his characteristic recipe for a successful piece seems to have been a sentimentally romantic plot, with a touch of heart-interest and an occasional stock reflection, intrigue in plenty, with many a dash of farcical episode. The formula for the modern drama is being set.

For the most part he avoids the use of surprise: little is kept concealed from his simple-minded spectators, who are thus flattered by being made little gods watching the blunderings of characters immersed in a slough of misapprehensions. By this means he has been able to make what, in the end, may perhaps be regarded as his principal contribution to drama —the development of comic irony. The device was, of course, more ancient than he. It appears markedly in Menander's work, and Aristophanes makes free use of it in individual scenes—as, for example, in that ludicrous if indecorous episode when the wretched Cinesias in *Lysistrata* thinks his wife, Myrrhine, is to give him satisfaction, while we know that by her delays she is intent merely on increasing his wretchedness. But it was in Plautus that the device was first used to its fullest extent. His characteristic method is to let the audience fully into the secrets of his plot at the very beginning and allow them to take delight, not from the unexpected in action, but from the mistakes and errors resultant from the fact that what the audience knows remains unknown to the characters.

Some of his pieces are little more than uproarious farce. Of these the *Miles Gloriosus* (*The Bragging Soldier*) may be taken as an example. The plot is complex, but is reducible to a simple plan: all depends upon the follies of Pyrgopolinices, the braggart, who, full of strange oaths, is discomfited in love and deflated in spirit. The very first words of the play introduce him as he addresses one of his men:

> See that my shield be polished so that its sheen is more resplendent than the noon-day sun. When the battle is joined, it must dazzle the eyes of the fierce ranks of the enemy before me. But ah! my sword: how doleful and sad is its spirit, lamenting its long disuse! How eagerly it pines to make havoc of my foes!

In the final scene we see him wretchedly cudgelled and abject in his protestations: "By Venus and Mars," he swears, "I bear no malice for this affront. You were quite right, entirely right. If you let me off now, I'll consider it just punishment and let it go." The merriment creaks a trifle nowadays, yet we must remember the influence of this and other Plautan plays on the later course of the theatre: the *miles gloriosus* was a popular figure on the Renaissance stage, and had Pyrgopolinices not been created we might not now be laughing at Falstaff's gay and scoundrelly bombast.

Of somewhat similar sort, and equally popular among later dramatists, is the *Menæchmi* (*The Menæchmuses*), from which Shakespeare wrought his *Comedy of Errors*—extracting fun from the misadventures caused by the presence in one city of long-separated twins. In the *Asinaria* (*The Comedy of the Asses*) a young man, Argyrippus, applies to his father, Demænetus, for some money wherewith to purchase a pretty young courtesan, Philenium. The father, also attracted by the girl, gladly gives his aid, but unfortunately has no ready cash, since his wife, Artemona, holds the purse-strings tight: hence comes the main intrigue of the farce, in which money due to the wife for the sale of some asses is transferred, by devious means, into his control. At the end of the play the elderly gentleman, greatly pleased with himself, is sitting pleasantly with Philenium and about to amuse himself with her caresses, while the wife, apprised of the affair, listens, fuming, in concealment, until, unable to control her temper, she bursts in and drags him off home.

Financial intrigues designed for the same purpose—this time to enable Calidorus procure his beloved Phœnicium—provide the theme for *Pseudolus*; although there is one well-drawn character here, Ballio the procurer, the trickery, ingenious as it is, wears a trifle thin. Money, it may be noted, plays a major rôle in these plays, and its constant presence serves as a reminder, if that were needed, of the materialistic and bourgeois character of the audience whom Plautus is addressing. *Trinummus* is entirely taken up with the subject of treasure buried under a house and of the transactions by which the house is sold; *Curculio* concerns itself with an impoverished young man who, desiring to purchase a slave-girl, Planesium, is induced to steal a ring from another *miles gloriosus*, Therapontigonus by name; in the *Bacchides*, a sort of female *Menæchmi*, money is extracted by the slave Chrysalus from the old Nicobulus on behalf of the latter's son, Mnesilochus (once more for an identical end); buried treasure reappears in the *Aulularia* (*The Comedy of the Little Pot*), in which the portrait of the aged miser Euclio imprinted itself on the imagination of many later dramatists, especially of Molière: Harpagon in *L'avare* is Euclio Parisianized.

In this last-mentioned Plautan comedy occurs a close parallel to one part of the plot of Menander's *Arbitration*. Euclio's daughter, Phædra, has been ravished, at the feast of Ceros, by a young man, Lyconides. This youth, repentant of his behaviour and now genuinely in love with the girl, desires to marry her, and such scenes as are not devoted to showing the old man's frantic devices for the concealment of his money are concerned with this affair. Like the audience whom Menander addressed, the Roman audience of Plautus' time was apt to welcome a romantic theme with strong sentimental colouring, provided always that this portion of the story did not take away too much from the farcical merriment. Certainly this romantic, sentimental element must not be forgotten amid the raucous merriment and the play of comic irony. It suffuses, for example, the entire drama called *Rudens* (*The Rope*), one of the most interesting among Plautus' productions, in which is told the pathetic story of Palæstra, an earlier Marina, who, having been stolen from her home in childhood, has fallen into the clutches of the procurer Labrax. How a storm has been raised by the star-god Arcturus, how Palæstra is cast up from a shipwrecked vessel on the very shore where her father has his house, how a fisherman drags from the deeps a box containing Labrax' gold and the trinkets proving the girl's identity, how she is restored to her father and to her lover, Plesidippus, is a tale told in scenes not unreminiscent of the style of Shakespeare's later comedy. Akin in its sentimentalism is the *Captivi* (*The Captives*), which relates the fortunes of the two sons of Hegio, seized in their boyhood, the one by pirates and the other by a runaway slave. Through a number of almost serious scenes, enlivened by misunderstandings, the plot is carried forward until the old man recovers the two youths, ironically finding that one of them is a slave of his own whom he has been punishing severely. The *Cistellaria* (*The Casket*) brings a foundling girl back to her parents (again by means of trinkets), and something of the same theme appears in *Casina*, while in *Pœnulus* (*The Little Carthaginian*) two girls are restored to their home. *Epidicus* combines the theme of the long-lost daughter with the tricks by which a cunning slave draws an old man's money into the hands of his son.

Comedy after comedy rings the changes on farce and sentiment, romantic love and carnal love, trickery and caricature. In *Mercator* (*The Merchant*), as typical as any, a young man brings back with him from abroad a lovely Rhodian girl; his father spies her and determines to have her for his own, persuades a friend to buy her on his behalf, and sets in train a series of ludicrous misunderstandings and errors. The scene in which old Demipho reveals his infatuation to his neighbour Lysimachus has true comic spirit:

DEMIPHO: How old do I look?

LYSIMACHUS: One foot in the grave: a broken-down, decrepit old fellow.

DEMIPHO: Oh, you're not looking at me right. I'm just a child, Lysimachus, seven years old.

LYSIMACHUS: What's all this nonsense? A child?

DEMIPHO: Really just a child.

LYSIMACHUS: Oh, I see. Lost your senses: second childhood, eh?

DEMIPHO: No, no, not that at all. I'm twice as lusty as I've ever been.

LYSIMACHUS [*getting bored*]: Is that a fact? Excellent.

DEMIPHO: And I can see much better now than before.

LYSIMACHUS: That's good.

DEMIPHO [*shyly*]: I'm almost ashamed to tell you——

LYSIMACHUS: What?

DEMIPHO: May I?

LYSIMACHUS: What?

DEMIPHO: Well, then.

LYSIMACHUS: Come on, man.

DEMIPHO: I've been going to school to-day, Lysimachus. I've learned four letters already.

LYSIMACHUS [*puzzled*]: What's that? Four letters?

DEMIPHO: L O V E.

Much as Lysimachus laughs at his friend, however, he goes to the dock and purchases Pasicompsa on his behalf, and we meet the pair coming back to town. The girl is in tears:

LYSIMACHUS [*aside*]: Well, I've done what he asked. He wanted me to buy her, and here she is. [*To PASICOMPSA*] You now belong to me. Come on. Stop blubbering. [*More kindly*] Really, it's quite stupid your spoiling these lovely eyes. There's more reason for laughter than tears.

PASICOMPSA: Please, sir, do tell me.

LYSIMACHUS: Ask me what you like.

PASICOMPSA: Why did you buy me?

LYSIMACHUS: Why? To do what you're bidden. [*After a pause, slyly*] But then what you bid, I'll do.

PASICOMPSA: I'm ready, I'm sure, to give every satisfaction.

LYSIMACHUS: Of course, I shan't ask you to do anything very hard.

PASICOMPSA: My goodness, I hope not. I haven't learned, sir, to do hard work.

LYSIMACHUS: If you promise to be a good girl, you'll be all right.

PASICOMPSA: My gracious, that's terrible.

LYSIMACHUS: What do you mean?

PASICOMPSA: Where I come from it was the bad girls that had a good time.

LYSIMACHUS [*aside*]: By Jove, her talk itself's worth all I paid for her.

This is followed immediately by a characteristic Plautan scene of equivoque. Pasicompsa is in love with and is loved by Demipho's son, and in the ensuing conversation she refers to the latter, while Lysimachus speaks of his elderly friend:

LYSIMACHUS: Can you spin?

PASICOMPSA: Yes, sir.

LYSIMACHUS: Fine, and coarse?

PASICOMPSA: There's not another who's my match at spinning.

LYSIMACHUS: You've been well brought up, my dear.

PASICOMPSA: Yes, I was well taught, sir.

LYSIMACHUS: Well, then, what do you say if I give you a sheep of your very own, sixty years old.

PASICOMPSA [*laughing*]: As old as that?

LYSIMACHUS: Pure Greek breed. If you take care of it, you can shear it very easily.

PASICOMPSA [*not understanding, a trifle puzzled*]: It's very good of you, sir. Thanks a lot.

LYSIMACHUS: To put it quite straight, you're not mine, so don't think you are.

PASICOMPSA [*astonished*]: Then whose am I?

LYSIMACHUS: I've bought you for your own master. He asked me to.

PASICOMPSA: That's fine.

LYSIMACHUS: You'll get freed, I'm quite sure. He's madly in love with you.

PASICOMPSA: Yes, it's two years we've been lovers.

LYSIMACHUS [*amazed*]: What? Two years?

PASICOMPSA: Sure it is. We pledged ourselves, him and me: he wasn't to look at any other girl, I wasn't to look at any other man.

LYSIMACHUS [*nonplussed*]: My goodness gracious! What about his wife?

PASICOMPSA: He's not got a wife.

LYSIMACHUS: I wish he hadn't. Goodness gracious me, he's been committing perjury.

PASICOMPSA: I don't love any young man as much as him.

LYSIMACHUS [*slowly*]: Young man? Well, yes, of course he really is a child, my dear.

In *Persa* (*The Persian*) sport is made of the outwitting of a procurer; in *Truculentus* (*The Churl*) a courtesan makes hay while the sun shines; in *Mostellaria* (*The Ghost*) an astute slave causes an old man to believe that his house is haunted; a hungry parasite is held up to ridicule in *Stichus*. All the familiar doings of Rome are here, treated in a spirit of wanton levity: of the grandeur of the Republic there is no sign—that was left to the historians to depict; Plautus was interested in the characters of his day, not when they donned their togas, when they fought or philosophized, but rather when they stepped out of their front doors in undress and indulged in domestic strife instead of battle, in bickering instead of noble oratory.

Terence and the Young Men About Town

If Plautus wrote to please the crowd, his successor Terence sought the esteem of the intelligentsia; if Plautus derived his comic style from many sources, Terence tried to follow only the one master, Menander. Between the two men, although frequently their names are linked together, there was a world of difference.

Publius Terentius Afer was born about 195 B.C. and died in 159. A native of Carthage, he was probably negroid in origin and had been brought, in his youth, to Rome as a slave. Educated by his master, he seems to have become the protégé of a little circle of literary wits, and for their delectation rather than for the plaudits of the crowd he confessedly penned his comedies. In all, six of his pieces are extant—*Andria* (166 B.C.), *Hecyra* (165 B.C.), *Heautontimorumenos* (163 B.C.), *Eunuchus* (161 B.C.), *Phormio* (161 B.C.), and *Adelphi* (160 B.C.).

This "half-Menander" (*dimidiate Menander*), as Cæsar styled him, based all his art upon the New Comedy, deliberately revealing the sources of his plots, and making no claims to anything beyond purity of style and skill in the weaving together of plots taken from the Greek plays: "Nullum est iam dictum quod non dictum sit prius," he cheerfully remarks. "There's nothing new under the sun; everything one says has been said before." Like Menander, he aims at arousing smiles, not laughter; and like his master, he is a sentimentalist. Perhaps the essential difference between him and Plautus is revealed most clearly by a consideration of the general orientation of their works. Whereas the latter brings his merchants, his young sons, his slaves, his pimps, and his courtesans in a tumultuous, seething mass on stage, Terence endeavours to secure an exact perspective, and this perspective has as its focal-point the elegant young Roman gentleman. Highly trained, eminently conscious of the value of good manners (or at least of the manners considered good by his society), eager for enjoyment, and more than a little annoyed by the fretting restraints put upon his freedom by men less youthful than himself, this Roman gallant is the centre of every Terentian play; here is his image, and the actions are those in which, at least, he would like to have been involved. "What partial judges of all sons are fathers!" soliloquizes Clitipho in *Heautontimorumenos* (*The Self-tormentor*),

> Who ask grey wisdom from our greener years,
> And think our minds should bear no touch of youth;
> Governing by their passions, now kill'd in them,
> And not by those that formerly rebell'd.
> If ever I've a son, I promise him
> He shall find me an easy father; fit
> To know, and apt to pardon his offences!

These young gallants, like the gallants of the Restoration period in England, savour fine phrases and delight in epigram, and Terence must have endeared himself to them not only by the fond picture he gives of their lives and aspirations, but also by his skill in forging the delicate phrase—"quot homines, tot sententiæ," "hinc illæ lacrimæ," "amantium iræ amoris integratiost"—these, and others, have become proverbial.

Andria (*The Girl of Andros*), his first drama, is as representative as any, and it may be of value to follow its plot act by act. First, we have conversations between Simo, father of Pamphilus, and his devoted slave Sosia. The old man explains that his son, a youth of infinite perfection and promise, has of late been devoting himself to a certain girl, Glycerium by name, sister of the courtesan Chrysis. So open has this scandal become that old Chremes, who had been willing to have his daughter marry Pamphilus, now refuses to go through with the match. In order to catch his son, Simo is, however, pretending to go on with the preparations for the wedding. Having retired, he leaves the stage free for Pamphilus, who enters in desperation, and whose words have the true romantically sentimental ring of Menander. To Glycerium's maid, Mysis, he protests his undying devotion:

MYSIS: I only know
    That she deserves you should remember her.
PAMPHILUS: I should remember her? O Mysis, Mysis!
    The words of Chrysis touching my Glycerium
    Are written in my heart. On her death-bed
    She call'd me. I approach'd her. You retir'd.
    We were alone; and Chrysis thus began:
    My Pamphilus, you see the youth and beauty
    Of this unhappy maid: and well you know
    These are but feeble guardians to preserve
    Her fortune or her fame. By this right hand
    I do beseech you, by your better angel,
    By your tried faith, by her forlorn condition,
    I do conjure you, put her not away,
    Nor leave her to distress. If I have ever,
    As my own brother, lov'd you; or if she
    Has ever held you dear 'bove all the world,
    And ever shown obedience to your will—
    I do bequeath you to her as a husband,
    Friend, guardian, father: all our little wealth
    To you I leave, and trust it to your care.
    She join'd our hands, and died. I did receive her,
    And once receiv'd will keep her.

This pathetic narrative out-Menanders Menander in its sentimental implications: it even introduces the golden-hearted courtesan.

The second act introduces another character, Charinus, a friend of Pamphilus, who, it appears, loves Chremes' daughter, Philumena, as much as Pamphilus detests her. He is cheered by his friend's frank declaration of disinterest in the girl, while Pamphilus receives the welcome news, from Davus, his slave, that the marriage preparations are all a pretence. As a result Pamphilus, for his part, pretends to agree to a wedding. Unfortunately Simo becomes apprised that Glycerium has had a child and that Pamphilus has acknowledged himself the father, but the day is saved when, in his self-conceit, he refuses to believe that this is anything more than a device designed to trick him. Davus takes his cue and anxiously helps to confirm the old man in his belief; but in this the slave overreaches himself, since Simo immediately communicates the news to Chremes and once more re-arranges the marriage.

In the course of the fourth act all is in confusion. Charinus is enraged at what he regards as Pamphilus' perfidy: Mysis is in despair because she thinks her mistress deserted. The ever-resourceful Davus, however, has a device: he takes Glycerium's child and convinces old Chremes that he is being deluded by Simo. Meanwhile a new character, Crito, arrives, and through him it is discovered (we almost guess it at the beginning) that, of course, Glycerium is a well-born Athenian girl—none other, in fact, than the daughter of Chremes himself. She is thus free to marry her beloved Pamphilus, while Charinus is allowed to wed her sister.

In general terms, the plot is similar to that of many a Plautan comedy, but the atmosphere is vastly different. Here all is refined, toned down, softened. No broad farcical scenes shatter the atmosphere of well-to-do politeness, of romantic sentiment, and of moral reflection. The young men are more worthy than their Plautan brothers, the old men far less ridiculous, the jests of the slave are more subdued, and the (supposed) courtesan's maid becomes a pretty little Columbine whose one thought is of her mistress's happiness.

The closeness of Terence to Menander—and yet at the same time the gulf that separates them—is well revealed in his second play, *Hecyra* (*The Step-mother*), the plot of which is a variant of that of *The Arbitration*. Pamphilus, the hero, has, very unwillingly, been persuaded to abandon his mistress Bacchis and marry Philumena. Trouble breaks out between the young wife and her stepmother, and the latter ferrets out a dark secret —that shortly after her wedding Philumena has given birth to a child. It turns out, of course, that, like Menander's heroine, the girl had been violated in the darkness of night, and, by means of a ring, the violator is proved to have been Pamphilus himself. Fundamentally the plot is the same, but the manners are Roman. The awful power of the Roman mother is patently revealed, and above all there is the excessive sentiment associated with the golden-hearted courtesan. Although Pamphilus, after swearing that he would never marry, has deserted Bacchis, the happy discovery at the end is made largely through that young lady's disinterested efforts. "What joy have I procur'd to Pamphilus by coming here to-day!" she reflects.

> What blessings brought him!
> And from how many sorrows rescu'd him!

> His son, by his and their means nearly lost,
> I've sav'd; a wife, he meant to put away
> I have restor'd. . . . That I've been
> The instrument of all these joys I'm glad,
> Tho' other courtesans would not be so;
> Nor is it for our profit and advantage
> That lovers should be happy in their marriage.
> But never will I, for my calling's sake
> Suffer ingratitude to taint my mind.
> I found him, while occasion gave him leave,
> Kind, pleasant and good-humour'd: and this marriage
> Happen'd unluckily I must confess.
> Yet I did nothing to estrange his love,
> And since I have receiv'd much kindness from him,
> 'Tis fit I should endure this one affliction.

Another Bacchis appears in *Heautontimorumenos* (*The Self-tormentor*), where again the sentimental is laid on thickly. The self-tormentor is Menedemus, who toils and sweats in voluntary penance for the harsh treatment he had meted out to his son Clinia. "Homo sum: humani nihil a me alienum puto," says his friend Chremes. "I am a man and feel for all mankind"—and the epigrammatic phrase has become a proverb—as he seeks out his secret sorrow and chides him gently:

> You I believe a tender parent, him
> A duteous son, if govern'd prudently.
> But you were unacquainted with his nature,
> And he with yours: sad life, where things are so!
> You ne'er betray'd your tenderness to him,
> Nor durst he place that confidence in you
> Which well becomes the bosom of a father.
> Had that been done, this had not happen'd to you.

Thus are the fathers romantically conceived by the world of youth that Terence represents: thus fathers ought to behave were life ordered properly. Clinia's sole fault was that he had fallen in love with Antiphila, the supposed daughter of a poor Corinthian woman. On this basis the plot develops. Clinia returns to his native town and stays with his friend Clitipho (Chremes' son), who is spending his money freely on the courtesan Bacchis. Says Bacchis to Antiphila:

> Well, I commend you, my Antiphila:
> Happy that you have made it still your care
> That virtue should seem fair as beauty in you!
> Nor gracious Heaven so help me, do I wonder
> If ev'ry man should wish you for his own;
> For your discourse bespeaks a worthy mind.
> And when I ponder with myself, and weigh
> Your course of life, and all the rest of those
> Who live not on the common, 'tis not strange
> Your morals should be different from ours.

Virtue's your int'rest; those with whom we deal
Forbid it to be ours—for our gallants,
Charm'd by our beauty, court us but for that,
Which fading, they transfer their love to others.
If then meanwhile we look not to ourselves,
We live forlorn, deserted and distressed.
You, when you've once agreed to pass your life
Bound to one man, whose temper suits with yours,
He too attaches his whole heart to you:
Thus mutual friendship draws you each to each;
Nothing can part you, nothing shake your love.

At the end of this sentimental drama the virtuous Antiphila is, of course, found to be Chremes' long-lost daughter.

A courtesan, Thais, who is anxious to return a free-born girl to her family, figures as a prominent character in *Eunuchus* (*The Eunuch*), where also is included a braggart soldier, Thraso, and a rather delightful parasite, Gnatho, in addition to the usual collection of young men. The main episode, which gives its title to the play, concerns the device by which the young Chærea, enamoured of the girl who is being befriended by Thais, poses as a eunuch in order to find an opportunity for ravishing her: when she turns out to be one of the collection of long-lost daughters a marriage is, of course, immediately arranged. Witty, reflective, epigrammatic, the style here is even more polished than in Terence's earlier plays, and for this reason it has ever maintained a high position in the list of this dramatist's work.

Nearer in plot to a Plautan comedy is *Phormio*, in which a young man, Antipho by name, marries a poor orphan (who turns out to be the daughter of Chremes), and another young man, Phædria, aided by the astute parasite who provides the title for the comedy, goes to extraordinary lengths to secure money wherewith to purchase a music-girl with whom he is in love. The plot is complicated by the fact that old Chremes, while away on a journey, has been consorting with a prostitute, and in his endeavours to recover some money inveigled from him by Phormio this is, to his dismay, brought to light.

Perhaps more thoroughly Terentian is the *Adelphi* (*The Brothers*), in which a sentimentally conceived plot is worked out almost in the style of a modern problem drama. Demea, a harsh old disciplinarian, has two sons: one, Ctesipho, he himself rears in the country, the other, Æschinus, is cared for, in town, by his kind-hearted, genial, indulgent uncle, Micio. As might have been expected from the pen of one who so persistently takes the side of youth, Æschinus, although for a time under a considerable cloud owing to his own kind-heartedness, is revealed as a man of the best intentions and the warmest feelings, while Ctesipho, who had been hypocritical enough to deceive his father into thinking him the very model of moral discretion, is shown to be a profligate. In essence the whole comedy is an essay in education, a propaganda piece designed on the part of the young gentlemen about town to persuade their fathers that liberality and lack of discipline will, in the end, produce the best results. We are well on our way here towards modern romantic concepts of how to bring up the young: "Apply the rod and spoil the child" is Terence's motto. Here the modern sentimental drama is becoming fully formed.

Seneca and the End of the Roman Stage

In the *Hecyra* Terence mournfully relates how at the first performance of his play the audience had given it no attention:

> When I first
> Began to play this piece, the sturdy boxers—
> The dancers on the rope expected too—
> The increasing crowds, the noise and women's clamour
> Obliged me to retire before my time.

The truth is that the Roman public had but little taste for the drama. Give them raucous horse-play of the Plautan sort, and they would suffer a comedy, but their interests lay rather in watching rope-dancers, boxers, and the still more brutal displays presented in their one original type of entertainment-building, the amphitheatre.

If for comedy they had but little use, they had practically none for tragedy. From the Hellenistic period, indeed, tragedy's fate seems to have been but a sorry one. Throughout the fourth century and onward writer after writer sought to assume the mantle of Euripides, but Aristophanes had been in the right when he made his Dionysus believe that the only hope of preserving the tragic stage was to make the dangerous journey to Hades and to bring back the ghost of one of the old giants.

Although virtually nothing remains either of the later Greek efforts in tragedy or of those made later in Rome, we know sufficient to realize that rhetoric was being substituted for vibrant poetry, artificialities for living texture, sensationalism for passion. As creative writing declined actors became famous and, again anticipating the ways of the present age, insisted on altering the works of the classical masters in order to make their own individual rôles the more effective. By the third century they had their own trades unions (the guilds of the Dionysiac artists, οἱ περὶ τὸν Διόνυσον τεχνῖται), through which they succeeded in escaping both from military service and the payment of taxes. From extant vase-paintings and terracottas we can imagine that their styles of performance were much more muscular, much more gesticulatory, than had been those of their predecessors, and that they contributed towards forcing the remnants of tragic drama along the channel of sensationalism. One particular vase-painting of the fourth century gives us a vivid picture of a production of a play on the theme of *Medea*, written probably some fifty years after Euripides' death. The stage is filled with action; the dresses are rich; there is a suggestion of scenic effect in Medea's dragon-borne car. A sense of restlessness is here in sharp contradiction to the impression of monumental calm in the preceding century.

In Rome the actors, too, took a prominent place, especially about the first century B.C. Although at first recruited from the ranks of slaves, they won social prominence, became 'stars' in their own time, and even —as with Roscius—had their names reverently handed down to afterages as masters of their art. In watching the actors' tricks the spectators were apt to forget the dramatist.

There being no indigenous Latin tragedy, the first steps towards establishing this form were made by the preparing of translations, and even the earliest of these were made, not by a native of Rome, but by a man who, born at Tarentum (a Greek settlement), was, like Terence, a slave. Between 240 and 207 B.C. Livius Andronicus thus introduced to a Latin-speaking public some of the plays of Sophocles and Euripides, and one of these, presented in the former year, was the earliest tragedy to be produced in the Eternal City. About the same time a certain Nævius, a native of Campania and a naturalized Roman citizen, took the next steps by preparing what seem to have been original dramas based on the Greek (called, because of the use in their production of the Hellenic cloak, or *pallium, fabulæ palliatæ*), and by writing tragedies on Roman historical or legendary themes (named *fabulæ prætextæ*, from the togas in which the actors were dressed). During the second century B.C. the impact of Athens became even more pronounced, and three tragic dramatists, all of whom were influenced by Euripides, have had their names, if not their works, preserved for posterity—Ennius, Pacuvius, and Accius.

As the years wore on, so interest declined in this newly discovered form. Still-existing mosaics and similar records prove that on special occasions tragedies continued to be performed both in Rome and the provinces until at least the end of the second century A.D., but all the evidence seems to indicate, firstly, that the performances were sporadic, secondly, that they were not widely popular, and, thirdly, that they were weakened by pathetic sensationalism and suffocated by show. When the *Clytemnestra* of Accius was produced at the opening of Pompey's theatre in 55 B.C. we are informed that five hundred mules and three thousand chariots, besides elephants and giraffes innumerable, took hours to pass over the stage: they formed a processional spectacle of the trophies borne from ruined Troy. Thinking of some modern efforts in this direction, Terence's dictum comes to mind again: there truly is nothing new under the sun, and it is not only the theatre of to-day that has been taught to ruin creative writing by a passion for spectacle.

In the midst of these sporadic theatrical activities the nine or ten tragedies of Seneca stand out as a puzzle and an enduring, if not wholly worthy, monument. Lucius Annæus Seneca, a native of Corduba, in

Spain, was born about 4 B.C. and took his own life, by Nero's command, in A.D. 65. A kind of earlier Bacon, he was a noted writer of philosophical and scientific works, and, like Bacon, did not always permit his moral sentiments to coincide with his practical political actions. The plays were probably composed late in his life, and include nine dramas on traditional Greek themes—*Hercules Furens, Medea, Troades, Phædra, Agamemnon, Œdipus, Hercules Œtæus, Phœnissæ, Thyestes*—with one *fabula prætexta, Octavia*, on a Roman topic. This tenth tragedy is often denied to his pen, and several scholars believe it to be a work of considerably later date.

The puzzle is to determine whether these plays were intended for stage representation or whether they were designed merely as literary exercises suitable for private 'readings.' That Seneca did take an interest in the theatre and had studied the art of acting is certain from one of his letters, and it has been observed that the spirit of his verses is not unlike that expressed in contemporary reproductions of tragic scenes. On the other hand, the custom of reading tragic compositions aloud before small literary coteries was then well established, and it is easier to explain many peculiarities in the Senecan structure by treating the plays as literary exercises than by regarding them as intended for the theatre. Most of the external evidence, corroborated by examination of the works themselves, appears to show that Seneca was the first-known closet playwright.

If the puzzle leaves much uncertain, there is no doubt about the solidity of the monument. It was at the fount of Seneca that the early dramatists of the Renaissance fed, and without the influence of his writings we might never have had, in their existing form, the tragedies of Shakespeare. For an entire century, at the most formative period in the development of the modern drama, his was the model towards which all young writers reverently gazed. His mantle may be a trifle tattered now and his bust more than a little tarnished, but for what he meant to the dramatic authors of the sixteenth century he can never be forgotten or completely despised.

To examine Seneca's plays in detail would be useless, for in his treatment of the old themes he introduced no intrinsically worthy elements. All we need do is consider the principal features of his dramatic work, and in particular those characteristics which exerted most influence upon the playwrights of the new world born in the Renaissance.

Although he based his conceptions on Euripides, little of the Greek tragedian's realism appears in Seneca's scenes. Rather does he seize upon, and exaggerate, the sensational, melodramatic qualities which existed along with that realism in such plays as *Medea* and *Orestes*. Blood, torment, and the sense of impending doom delight him: all he feels is a mood—dark, gloomy, fateful. He adores an out-and-out villain, whose mind is set on naught but the accomplishment of his crimes. In *Thyestes* Atreus thus soliloquizes:

> Fall now this mighty house of famous Pelops,
> And crush me, so it crush my brother too.
> Come dare, my heart, a crime no age shall pardon,
> But no age e'er forget. Venture some deed
> Bloody and fell, such as my brother would
> Wish to be *his*. Nothing avenges crimes
> But what surpasses them.

So, too, he adores a dramatic figure who, for no apparent reason, is conscious of a terrible future, of one who invokes the divinities of hell. Thus does Medea introduce her story:

> Ye gods of wedlock and thou guardian queen
> Lucina, watcher o'er the marriage couch,
> And thou that taughtest mankind to master ships
> To dominate the sea, thou ruler fierce
> Of all the vasty deep, thou Titan too
> Dividing with thine orb the coursing days,
> Thou Hecate of triple form whose beams
> Glance at all secret rites, ye gods by whom
> Jason once swore to me and whom methinks
> 'Tis seemlier far Medea should invoke:
> Chaos of night eternal, realms the gods
> See not, all impious shades and thou the lord
> Of blackest hell and thou its mistress too—
> I call ye all with my ill-omened cry.

Characteristic of the Senecan bombast is the way in which a single metaphor or simile is monotonously carried through a long speech; characteristic also is the vast amount of equally monotonous moralizing. A heavy cloud of pessimism weighs down upon these plays, but it is a pessimism which lacks vitality, which dully creeps and heavily drags its slow length along. Darkness can be inspiring; ebony's blackness may have almost the quality of light: Seneca's gloom is merely oppressive.

It cannot, however, be denied that, within his own chosen field of rhetorical expression, the Roman playwright had more than common skill. In his interminable tirades, in his rapid fire of dialogue, and in his contemplative choruses alike he was able to strike out sparks which, although they perhaps themselves had no warmth, had the power later of producing passionate flame. In *Hercules Furens* the hero thus declaims:

> What Tanais, what Nile or swirling flood
> Of Persian Tigris, what wild Rhine or Tagus,
> Rolling in spate the rich Iberian gold,
> Will wash this right hand clean? Though cold Mæotis
> Should deluge me with all her Arctic waves,
> Or all the Ocean flood across these hands,
> The stain of blood will stay.

The flint has struck the steel here; the spark is cold yet, but the flame comes from it:

> Will all great Neptune's ocean wash this blood
> Clean from my hand? No, this my hand will rather
> The multitudinous seas incarnadine,
> Making the green one red.

In the form of his plays Seneca, together with Terence, established a structure which was destined to endure up to the nineteenth century. His dramas are all cast in five formal acts, and the old Greek prologue is incorporated into the action; Terence's plan is fundamentally the same, although he takes the further step of separating the prologue from the body of the drama and of making it, like the Aristophanic parabasis, a mouthpiece for the poet. The five-act shape for tragedy and comedy alike was thus definitely set.

The chorus Seneca retains, but in retaining it he carries to further limits the trends already noted in the works of Sophocles and, more particularly, of Euripides. The choral odes in his tragedies, some of them gifted with a cold loveliness, are in general unrelated, or at best only slightly related, to the events narrated in the main action. Fundamentally the chorus has now become merely a purveyor of interludes.

In the dialogue long speeches tend to alternate with passages of a kind of battledore-and-shuttlecock quality, wherein two characters thrust and parry through some fifty or sixty staccato lines. Thus it is in *Hercules Furens*:

LYCUS: Art thou so proud of a husband lost in Hell?
MEGARA: He entered Hell, that he might scale the Heavens.
LYCUS: Well, now he's crushed beneath the massive earth.
MEGARA: The back that bore the sky *no* load can crush.
LYCUS: I'll force thee.
MEGARA: None is forced that dares to die.
LYCUS: Nay, tell me, what royal gift shall I prepare
       To grace our bridals?
MEGARA: Thy death or mine own.
LYCUS: Fool, thou shalt die.
MEGARA: So I shall meet my lord.
LYCUS: Dost prize a slave above our royal crown?
MEGARA: How many kings that 'slave' has sped to death!
LYCUS: Then why serves he a king, and bears a yoke?
MEGARA: Remove all harsh commands: and what is virtue?

Such dialogue, the so-called *stichomythia*, based on the Greek but made exaggerated, played its part, too, in the creation of the Elizabethan tragic style.

With Seneca the impulse that began with Æschylus and his immediate predecessors reached its lurid end—at least in so far as the direct line of development from Athens to Rome was concerned. It is true that a kind of side-stream carried the current of the Greek theatre to Byzantium, where apparently the Euripidean influence succeeded in producing a series of dramas based in structure and style on the Greek, but intent on Christian themes. Of these plays one, Χριστός πάσχων (*Christ's Suffering*), dating from the eleventh century A.D., has come down to us. This stream of dramatic activity, however, interesting though it is, has no direct bearing on the main growth of the Western stage. From Rome the early writers of the Renaissance received their first introduction, at second hand, to the theatre of Greece; Seneca, Terence, and Plautus were the masters whom they acknowledged and followed.

One further development of the Roman stage, on the other hand, may have combined with the dramas of these three men to make an impress on the later playhouse. Between the second and the fourth centuries of our era Rome produced little or nothing of dramatic literature, but the mimes energetically and successfully pursued their popular activities. Out of tragedy came the *pantomimus*, a kind of ballet, in which a chorus chanted words while an actor mimed the parts one after another. This *pantomimus* seems to have been mainly a toy of the degenerate imperial Courts, but the *mimus*, or comic mime, certainly appealed to a wider public. With mingled memories of the Atellan farces and of the indigenous mimes of Greece, these shows were diversified in character, sometimes taking shape as burlesque knock-and-tumble comedy, sometimes presenting dramas of a tragi-comic sort, sometimes capable of being performed by a small troupe of half a dozen itinerant entertainers, sometimes demanding the services of companies as large as those called for in a modern musical comedy.

When Rome fell before the invading might of the barbarians at the beginning of the fifth century these mimic actors were freely presenting their shows throughout the entire extent of the Empire. Under the new conditions of life no doubt they fell on evil days. The Goths, the Vandals, and the Huns were hardly equipped to appreciate even their crude dramatic efforts, and the Christian church, wrathful at the manner in which its rites had been burlesqued on the stage, ceased not to fulminate at the iniquities of the mimes. Nevertheless they seem to have carried on their profession into the ages of darkness: one of our last pictorial records of the classical theatre is a sixth-century ivory tablet with a scene in relief showing a mimic hero amid a group of comic, bald-headed gesticulating slaves. To this had the heritage of Æschylus come, and yet out of this was later to arise a new flowering of the popular stage. If there is any dramatic continuity between the world of the Greek and Roman temples and the world dominated by the fantastic imagination of the Gothic cathedral we must look for it in the pitiful and despised gesturings of the mimes.

PART II

RELIGIOUS DRAMA AND PROFANE
DURING THE MIDDLE AGES

RELIGIOUS DRAMA AND PROFANE
DURING THE MIDDLE AGES

THE MIMIC actors thus take their itinerant way into the darkness. Occasionally we catch half-glimpses of them, entertaining gaping village crowds and the rude denizens of medieval castles with their jests, their juggling, their acrobatic tricks, but the path they tread is a long, a dim, and a tortuous one before they come clearly before us again. Their grimacings and their gesticulations are lost in the night of the Dark Ages.

Here and there, in monastery cell or in nunnery, a black-robed figure will turn from the Scriptures and the theological commentaries and take down from the heavy oak presses a manuscript of Terence, appeasing his conscience by remembering that a good Latinity is next to godliness and that Terence is a master of style. Sometimes a worthy clerk, or even a pious nun, will dare a little more and attempt, afar off, to imitate Terence by a few pages of dramatic dialogue, and it is possible to imagine the occasional reciting of these lines of dialogue within the closed walls of a convent, the hearts of the little audience fluttering with a conflict of emotions—the joy of daring to participate in exercises so closely associated with the pagan, the fear that this might be but another bait of Satan's designed to trap the unwary.

Such reading and imitation of Terence is attested for us by the naïve playlets of a certain tenth-century nun of Gandersheim, in Saxony: Hrotswitha or Roswitha she called herself. Concerning the inception of her dramatic work she leaves us in no doubt; her desire is to give to her sisters, worthily, holy matter in the form used by the Roman comedians for their doubtful stories of love and intrigue:

> There are many Catholics, and we cannot entirely acquit ourselves of the charge, who, attracted by the polished elegance of the style of pagan writers, prefer their works to the holy scriptures. There are others who, although they are deeply attached to the sacred writings and have no liking for most pagan productions, make an exception in favour of the works of Terence, and, fascinated by the charm of the manner, risk being corrupted by the wickedness of the matter. Wherefore I, the strong voice of Gandersheim, have not hesitated to imitate in my writings, a poet whose works are so widely read, my object being to glorify, within the limits of my poor talent, the laudable chastity of

Christian virgins in that self-same form of composition which has been used to describe the shameless acts of licentious women.

The plays themselves are exceedingly short, and it is difficult to tell whether they were intended for performance. The fact, however, that there are scenes which require their action to be visualized before they can be understood seems to suggest that the nuns of Gandersheim may have enlivened their winter evenings with attempts to act them in person. Thoroughly typical of the series is *Dulcitius*, which narrates the martyrdom of the Christian maidens Agape, Chionia, and Irena. These girls are first shown rejecting the order of the Emperor Diocletian that they should marry; in anger he throws them into prison under the control of the governor Dulcitius. The latter is enflamed by their beauty and commands his soldiers to place them in a room more easy of access, "the one leading out of the passage where the pots and pans are kept." There he goes to ravish them, but by a miracle he is led to believe that the pots and pans are the girls; fervidly he kisses them, gets his face thoroughly blackened, and is thus made a laughing-stock. Other miracles of a like kind follow, but in the end the Christian maidens are executed by the Count Sisinnius, Agape and Chionia being burned, Irena shot to death by arrows.

The admixture of tragedy and comedy has a definitely theatrical flavour, and, if we believe that these plays were indeed intended for amateur performance, we recognize that—at least afar off—the spirit of Terence was being kept alive in surroundings which were vastly different from those he had enjoyed in pagan Rome. The tenth century has nothing to show us more interesting or more revealing.

Such dramatic activities, however, as are exemplified in the plays of Hrotswitha do not illustrate the main current of dramatic development. They may have contributed towards the growth of the medieval stage, but it was from another source, and in an even humbler manner, that the new Western drama arose.

The Liturgy and the Drama

The story of the evolution of drama out of the liturgy has often been told; although some portions of it remain dark, and although, after all the attention devoted to it, some puzzles remain, the main lines of progress are clearly to be traced. It is now recognized that, after all the wealth of Greek endeavour and of imitation of the Greek in Rome, the theatre in the tenth century made a fresh start in the form of a tiny, four-line playlet inserted into the Easter service. The cue is taken from the Bible. In the Gospel according to Mark we read:

> And entering into the sepulchre, they saw a young man sitting on the right side, clothed in a long white garment; and they were affrighted. And he saith unto them, Be not affrighted: ye seek Jesus of Nazareth, which was crucified: he is risen; he is not here; behold the place where they laid him. But go your

THE THEATRE
AT ORANGE
'Radio Times'
Hulton Library

A SLAVE
Terra-cotta statuette, Berlin.
From Margarete Bieber, *The
History of the Greek and
Roman Theater,* Fig. 416.

A MONEYLENDER (?)
Terra-cotta statuette in the
British Museum.

**A ROMAN
ACTOR**
Bronze statuette.
*By courtesy of the
Museum of Fine
Arts, Boston*

A POTTER (?)
Terra-cotta
statuette in the
British Museum.

way, tell his disciples and Peter that he goeth before you into Galilee: there shall ye see him, as he said unto you.

Here is the plot, as it were, and thus the play takes shape. One priest, clad in a white robe, sits near the altar, where a cloth has been laid over a cross: three other priests advance towards him, and he addresses them: "Quem quæritis in sepulchro, O Christicolæ?" ("Whom do ye seek in the sepulchre, O Christian women?") At this the others reply in unison: "Jesum Nazarenum crucifixum, O cælicola!" ("Jesus of Nazareth who was crucified, O Heavenly One!") Raising the cloth, the first replies: "Non est hic: surrexit sicut prædixerat. Ite, nuntiate quia surrexit de sepulchro." ("He is not here: He has risen even as He said. Go, announce that He has arisen from the sepulchre.")

This is the entirety of the drama, but, short as it is, there can be no doubt of its being a play. A locality is clearly indicated—the sepulchre; the short dialogue, moreover, in its additions to the Gospel texts adds just those words that are so necessary in drama, demonstrating to the spectators the rôles that are being interpreted by the actors and suggesting appropriate action. The three priests are no longer priests, but Christian women—the three Marys; the single priest has become, for the space of the brief action, an angel.

Thus was born the *liturgical drama*, that form of medieval play wherein the dialogue and the movement formed part of the regular liturgy or service of the day. Even from the very beginning it must have begun to expand in several ways; by the introduction of mimetic action, by the utilization of properties and appropriate dress; and by the expansion of the simple plot through the addition of related episodes. Being part of the liturgy, these plays were written in Latin, and we must presume that their representation always retained a hieratical character: at the same time, there is plentiful evidence to demonstrate that as the years went by elaboration in form drew them out of their simple four-line shape into something much more complex.

Already in the tenth century instructions are given for the behaviour of the clerical actors. The first priest must approach the sepulchre without attracting attention, and sit there quietly with a palm in his hand; the others must walk up the nave, "stepping delicately as those who seek something," and come to the sepulchre "like folk lost." Later the rubrics to various texts show how this mimetic action becomes enlarged, while at the same time additional Latin words are given to the actors. Here, for example, is a specimen of a text, still liturgical, that well illustrates both developments. The three Marys are lamenting:

MAGDALEN [*here she turns to the men with her arms extended*]: O my brothers! [*Here to the women*] O my sisters! Where is my hope? [*Here she beats her breast.*] Where is my consolation? [*Here she raises her hands.*] Where is my whole well-being? [*Here, head inclined, she throws herself at Christ's feet.*] O my Master!
MARY MAJOR [*here she points to MARY MAGDALEN*]: O Mary Magdalen,

> [*here she points to CHRIST*] sweet disciple of my Son, [*here she embraces MAGDALEN, putting both her arms round her neck*] weep with me, in grief, [*here she points to CHRIST*] over the death of my sweet Son, [*here she points to MAGDALEN*] and the death of your Master, [*here she points to CHRIST*] the death of Him [*here she points to MAGDALEN*] who so loved you, [*still pointing to MAGDALEN*] who all your sins [*here she lets her arms fall*] has taken from you. [*Here she embraces MAGDALEN, as before, while she says*] Most sweet Magdalen.
>
> *MAGDALEN* [*here she greets MARY with her hands*]: Mother of Jesus crucified, [*here she weeps*] with you do I weep over the death of Christ.
>
> *MARY, MOTHER OF JAMES* [*here she makes a wide gesture over the audience and then puts her hands before her eyes*]: Who is there here who would not weep, seeing the Mother of Christ [*here she beats her breast*] in such misery?

The stage directions indicate here a highly stylized approach towards the interpretation of the parts, and this is precisely what we should expect so long as the play remained within the walls of the church, was connected with the ecclesiastical services, and was performed by the clergy.

The reference above to the early tenth-century liturgical playlet comes from an English manuscript; the very first record we have of the "Quem quæritis" issues from France; the last quotation given here is taken from an Italian text several centuries later. These facts illustrate, firstly, the extensive geographical distribution of the liturgical drama, and, secondly, the lengthy period of time during which it remained a feature of the Church's celebrations. Everywhere the Catholic creed was established the liturgical drama developed, and in all probability expansions of the primitive dialogue, together with the addition of fresh episodes, were being introduced now here, now there, and carried from country to country by the last of the true internationalists—those clerks who acknowledged themselves the servants of no particular country, and whose universal Latin tongue made them as much at home in Paris or Winchester as in Rome itself.

The accretions that grew around the simple sepulchre scene can easily be imagined. At the close of the original four-line dialogue the Marys are told to announce the arising of Christ: it was natural that the carrying out of this command should be the first additional scene, wherein the choir becomes, as it were, the body of Christ's disciples or wherein two members of the choir take the rôles of Peter and John. But the Gospel narrative tells us how these two apostles hurry to the tomb, how John "did outrun Peter, and came first to the sepulchre." This at once adds materially to the dramatic action. Still a further episode is the appearance of the risen Christ to Magdalen, who mistakes him for a *hortolanus*, or gardener. Later comes a scene showing the Marys purchasing perfumes and spices from an *unguentarius*, or spice-seller.

Thus grew the liturgical play, and, growing, it gradually created its own characteristic method of staging. At first no locality is demanded save the altar, taken for the sepulchre, or the erection within the church of a special structure representing this sepulchre. Even then, however, the entirety of the nave has to be considered part of the 'theatre,' since the three Marys come from a supposedly distant point and move slowly up to the Angel. The episode of the Announcement calls for movement to a second locality, that of the garden for a third, and when the Marys stop to buy their spices something representing a stall has to be supplied for the *unguentarius*. Thus, without any conscious planning, the earliest medieval theatre is evolved with three main characteristic features: (*a*) the mingling of audience and actors; (*b*) the establishment of a series of platforms or small structures indicating special localities (sepulchre, garden, spice-seller's booth); and (*c*) the utilization of the space between these platforms or structures as an acting area. On these principles was the entire medieval stage to develop during the course of the centuries from the tenth to the fifteenth.

The Liturgical Plays break their Bonds

Obviously, the original intention of the clergy in thus introducing the liturgical drama was to make the chief episode in the Christian story more real and more vivid for the assembled congregation. The effect must, we imagine, have exceeded their expectations: for the people of the early medieval period, starved of entertainment of all kinds, the little shows were assuredly things not only of devotion but also of delight; and no doubt the clergy themselves found a secret joy in participation in the exercise of amateur theatricals. Pressure from within and without, therefore, guaranteed the rapid elaboration of the new-found stage.

After dealing with the Easter story it was natural that the story of Christmas should similarly be exploited, with the substitution of the opening line, "Quem quæritis in præsepe, pastores, dicite?" ("Whom seek ye in the manger, shepherds, say?") for the original "Quem quæritis in sepulchro, O Christicolæ?" Here progress was even more rapid. We hear of priests appearing "quasi obstetrices" ("like midwives"), we hear of the introduction of an ox and an ass, even of simple theatrical machinery, such as a movable star. Herod becomes a character; the three Magi are introduced. The play is expanded into a drama of many scenes.

The next step is also an obvious one. Scenes are written, still in Latin, for separate performance; they belong yet to the church, but they are no longer extensions of the church service, and, as they become more elaborate, they are brought out of the church itself and played in the open. Here for the first time in the medieval theatre do we encounter anything of genuine dramatic worth—the twelfth-century Anglo-Norman *Adam* —and fortunately the stage directions in the original manuscript of this drama give extraordinarily clear indications of the way in which it was intended to be performed.

We must imagine ourselves standing outside a great Norman cathedral. On the steps leading to the west door a platform has been built, "with curtains and cloths of silk hung round it at such a height that persons" there "may be visible from the shoulders upward." This place represents Paradise, and here appears God, rather peculiarly named the Figura, or Figure. He is clothed in a dalmatic, and before him come Adam, in a red tunic, and Eve, dressed in a woman's robe of white, with a white silk cloak. The author is exact in his demands.

> *ADAM must be well trained when to reply and to be neither too quick nor too slow in his replies. And not only he, but all the personages must be trained to speak composedly, and to fit convenient gesture to the matter of their speech. Nor must they foist in a syllable or clip one of the verses, but must enounce firmly and repeat what is set down for them in due order. Whoever names Paradise is to look and point toward it.*

The direction regarding 'pointing' reminds us of the stylized hieratic gesture demanded for the Marys: obviously the acting required here is akin to that of the priests before their altars.

The Figura gives his commands to Adam and Eve and departs into the church, while they "walk about Paradise in honest delight." At the same time a number of devils run out "per plateas"—that is to say, on the open ground, or *platea*, immediately in front of the Paradise platform. Adam is tempted, but remains loyal to the Figura's behest, whereupon the chief devil,

> *sadly and with downcast countenance, shall leave ADAM, and go to the doors of Hell, and hold council with the other demons. Thereafter he shall make a sally amongst the people, and then approach Paradise on EVE'S side, addressing her with joyful countenance and insinuating manner.*

It is clear that the liturgical principles of staging are being observed: there must be a distinct place representing Hell, the open ground between this and Paradise is an acting area, and the spectators are almost involved in the action: the devil makes "a sally amongst the people."

Now comes a scene of true dramatic insight:

DEVIL: Eve, hither am I come, to thee.
EVE: And prithee, Satan, why to me?
DEVIL: Seeking thy weal, thine honour, too.
EVE: God grant it!
DEVIL: Then thy fears eschew.
  Long since, I've mastered by my pains
  Each secret Paradise contains;
  A part of them to thee I'll tell.
EVE [*her curiosity aroused*]:
  Begin, then, and I'll listen well.
DEVIL: Thou'lt hearken to me?
EVE: Hearken?—yea,
  Nor vex thy soul in any way.
DEVIL: Thou'lt keep it hidden?

EVE: Yea, in truth.
DEVIL: Nor publish it?
EVE: Not I! forsooth.
DEVIL: Then, to this contract I'll agree,
    Nor further pledge require of thee.
EVE: Might'st safely trust my promise, though.
DEVIL: Thou'st been to a good school, I trow!
    Adam I've seen—a fool is he.
EVE [*considering*]: A little hard.
DEVIL: He'll softer be;
    But harder now than iron is.
EVE: A noble man!
DEVIL: A churl! I wis.
    Thought for himself he will not take;
    Let him have care, e'en for thy sake.
    Thou art a delicate, tender thing,
    Thou'rt fresher than the rose in spring;
    Thou'rt whiter than the crystal pale,
    Than snow that falls in the icy vale.
    An ill-matched pair did God create!
    Too tender thou, too hard thy mate.
    But thou'rt the wiser, I confess;
    Thy heart is full of cleverness.

At this, of course, Eve begins to consider the devil a very discerning
young man and is all ready to listen when he tells her of the wonders of
the forbidden fruit. "What savour hath't?" she asks, and is told, "'Tis
heavenly food!'":

                    To thy fair body, to thy face,
                    Most meet it were to add this grace:
                    That thou be queen of the world—of this,
                    Of the firmament, and of the abyss—
                    And know all things that shall befall,
                    And be the mistress of them all.

Carefully she reviews the situation, but, womanlike, delays. Only
when the serpent arrives does she taste of the fruit and bring it to
Adam. When he demurs she taunts him with cowardice and munches
the apple, declaiming at its delicious taste; and at last he consents to
eat of it. Immediately, however, he takes "knowledge of his sin," bows
down out of sight behind the curtains, and changes his fine dress for
"poor garments of fig-leaves sewn together." His lament is pitiful:

                    And whom shall I beseech for aid,
                    When mine own wife hath me betrayed,
                    Whom God gave me my fere to be?
                    An evil counsel gave she me!
                    Alas! O Eve!

The Figura returns, "wearing a stole, and looking about him, as if

seeking to know where Adam is. But Adam and Eve shall be hidden in
a corner of Paradise, as if conscious of their wretchedness." Adam confesses his sin as the terrible figure ironically denounces the miserable
pair:

> Didst reckon thus my peer to be?
> I do not think thou'lt jest with me! . . .
> Didst think through him to be my peer?
> Hast learned to make things hidden clear?
> Erstwhile thou heldest sovereignty
> Over all living things that be;
> How quickly hast thou lost thy crown! . . .
> I'll render thee thy just desert;
> Thy service I will thus repay.

They are driven out of Paradise and toil wearily. Adam turns upon his
wife with bitter sarcasm, crying:

> O wretched Eve! How seemeth it to thee?·
> This hast thou gained thee as thy dowery—

while she expresses her contrition pathetically:

> Forgive me!—no atonement can I see,
> Else would my sacrifice be offered free . . .
> I gave it thee, to serve thee was mine aim . . .
> The fruit was sweet, bitter will be the pain!

This tense treatment of the Fall is followed by a great scene of diablerie:

> *Then shall the devil come, and three or four other devils with him, bearing in their hands
> chains and iron shackles, which they shall place on the necks of ADAM and EVE. And cer-
> tain ones shall push them on, others shall drag them toward hell; other devils, however, shall
> be close beside Hell, waiting for them as they come, and these shall make a great dancing and
> jubilation over their destruction; and other devils shall, one after another, point to them as
> they come; and they shall take them up and thrust them into Hell; and thereupon they shall
> cause a great smoke to arise, and they shall shout one to another in Hell, greatly rejoicing;
> and they shall dash together their pots and kettles, so that they may be heard without.*

After this comes a scene of Cain and Abel, and when the latter has
been slain there follows a great procession of the Prophets, ending with a
dialogue between Isaias and an unnamed Jew:

> *JEW:* Now, Sir Isaias, answer me:
>   Is this a tale or prophecy?
>   This thing thou'st told—pray, what is it?
>   Didst it invent, or is it writ?
>   Thou'st been asleep—didst dream the rest?
>   Speak'st thou in earnest, or in jest?
> *ISAIAS:* This is no tale, 'tis very truth!
> *JEW:* Then, let's know all of it, forsooth!
> *ISAIAS:* What I have spoke is prophecy.

JEW: Writ in a book?
ISAIAS: Yea, verily,
  —In Life's! I've dreamed it not, but seen!
JEW: And how?
ISAIAS: Through grace of God, I ween.
JEW: Thou seem'st to me a dotard grey,
  Thy mind and sense all gone astray!
  A soothsayer thou seem'st, indeed,
  Skilled in the glass, perchance, to read;
  Come, read me now this hand, and tell
    [*then shall he show him his hand*]
  Whether my heart be sick or well.
ISAIAS: Thou hast sin's murrain in thy soul,
  Ne'er in thy life shalt thou be whole.

The last words of the drama are a vision of the Redeemer:

> His face shone, full of majesty,
> The Son of God he seemed to be!

We are in the presence here of something quite extraordinary. There is a simple passion and a sly, humorous observation in *Adam* that is hard to match in the entire course of the medieval drama until we reach, at the very end of its development, that other anonymous play of quiet faith, *Everyman.*

The Great Mystery Cycles

In *Adam* the setting is close to a church; Latin anthems are sung; and, although the first two episodes are written wholly in the Anglo-Norman vernacular, Latin appears, along with the vulgar tongue, in the speeches of the Prophets, as in the words of Isaias:

> Egredietur virga de radice Jesse, et flos de radice eius ascendet, et requiescat super cum spiritus Domini.
>> Or vus dirrai merveillus diz:
>> Jesse sera de sa raïz.
>> Verge eu istra, qui fera flor,
>> Qui ert digne de grant unor
>> Saint esprit l'avra si clos,
>> Sor cest flor iert sun repos.

The play, though attached still to the Church, is straining towards the people.

Gradually the final step is made; the ties are broken; the drama becomes entirely vernacular and belongs to the laity. When this finally occurred vast expansion became possible—indeed, imperative. Hundreds of worthy medieval citizens wanted, like Bottom and his crew, to amuse themselves with the delightful new toy, and consequently there grew into being those vast collections of separate playlets known as the

Mystery Cycles, the word 'mystery,' from *ministerium* (service or office), still denoting the religious origin of these pieces.

The actors now were, for the most part, the ordinary burghers and artisans of the towns and countryside. In England the trades guilds undertook the performance of the plays, especially after the establishment of the Corpus Christi festival in 1311, a feast set apart specifically for the performance of these pieces. The guilds defrayed the expenses for the costumes and scenery, and from their members came the acting personnel. In France arose special organizations, amateur groups, named *confréries*, of which the most famous was the Confrérie de la Passion at Paris, founded in 1402, although there the craft corporations also concerned themselves with theatrical performances. In certain parts of Italy the actors were youths who formed themselves into devotional associations named after their patron saints—la Compagnia di San Francesco or la Compagnia dell'Agnesa.

There is no festival competition here, as in the Greek theatre, and, although there may have been a sincerity in the presentation of the parts, we must assume that in many instances the interpretation was naïve and ludicrously inadequate. At least in one district of France in the sixteenth century record declares that the performers of mystery plays

> are an ignorant set of men, mechanics and artisans, who know not an A from a B, untrained and unskilled in playing such pieces before the public. Their voices are poor, their language unfitting, their pronunciation wretched. No sense do they have of the meaning of what they say.

Nevertheless they took their job seriously. They were willing to rehearse for long hours, to be up betimes at 4.30 in the morning, and, although their labours were freely interspersed with collations of ale and beef, the task they set themselves must have been a hard one.

For the presentation of their pieces they followed, and expanded, the stage principles established by the liturgical drama, setting up a series of decorated platforms, now named 'mansions,' before the audience in a straight line, in a semicircle, or, as in Cornwall, in a circle. Each mansion represented a distinct and separate locality, while the open space in front or in the middle, the *platea*, could be used much in the manner in which it had formerly served when the drama was in the hands of the clergy.

Already in the twelfth century a *Conversion de l'apôtre Saint Paul (Conversion of St Paul)*, of French composition, shows the principle in full development. Instructions are there given for the preparation "in a convenient place of a platform for the Prince of Priests: this will stand for Jerusalem. Another platform must be prepared also, where a young man dressed as Saul will be seated, with armed guards before him." At the other side are platforms representing Damascus, one for Judas and one for the Prince of the Synagogue, and in addition to these there is a bed for Ananias. This system of 'multiple staging' or 'simultaneous setting' was the characteristic medieval contribution to the art of the theatre, although in some places, notably in England and Flanders, another device was adopted whereby individual mansions were set upon wheels (and named pageants) and drawn from group to group of spectators.

As the years went by the productions became more and more elaborate. Guild vied with guild, confraternity with confraternity, in enriching the mansions, while at the same time machinery and 'effects' were freely introduced, especially in France. The great director's script of the mysteries played at Mons gives us a clear insight into the marvels shown to the public, and the impression made upon a contemporary is well revealed in an account of a production at Valenciennes in 1547:

> The effects associated with Heaven and Hell were veritably prodigious and might well have seemed to the audience the result of magic. One saw Truth, the Angels and diverse characters descend from a great height. . . . From Hell, Lucifer rose, how one could not tell, on a dragon's back. Moses' staff, dry and withered, suddenly burst forth with flowers and fruit; the souls of Herod and Judas were borne into the air by devils. . . . Water was seen to change into wine, so extraordinarily that one could hardly credit it, and more than a hundred persons tasted the wine; the five loaves and two fish were multiplied and distributed to more than a thousand people, yet notwithstanding there were a dozen baskets over. . . . The eclipse, the earthquake, the shattering of rocks and other miracles that accompanied the death of Our Lord were represented with still further miracles.

While we cannot assume that in all districts such wonders were reproduced—while in some areas the plays certainly must have been presented in a very humble manner—we must not lose sight of the fact that those who lived at least in the later medieval period were acquainted with theatrical effects of no mean kind.

The plays thus produced essayed to tell the entire Biblical story from the Creation of the World to the Last Judgment. In many countries they took shape in fundamentally similar forms. The Italian *sacre rappresentazioni* were akin to the French *mystères*, the *mystères* to the German *Passionsspiele*, and those to the English 'miracle plays' and to the Cornish *guary* plays. Taking days to perform, the cycles consisted of thirty, forty, fifty, and even more separate dramas, each telling some salient portion of the Bible's account of events human and supernatural. In England there are still extant the cycles of York, Wakefield, Coventry, Chester; in France there are riches innumerable, from the early thirteenth-century plays of a Chantilly manuscript to the later vast *Passions* of Eustache Marcadé, Arnoul Greban, and Jehan Michel, and to the *Mystère du Vieil Testament*; other lands similarly add their quota to the total treasury.

In the composition of the dramas clearly a variety of different impulses was at work. First was the basic object of presenting dramatically the Biblical story, with accretions from apocryphal gospels as well as from the writings of commentators. In this sense the mystery cycle was an historical drama. But truth to the original narrative frequently was permitted to give way to a desire for symbolic and allegorical treatment of persons and events. Mary Magdalen, for example, thus becomes, not so much a real woman as an abstract figure representing sin repentant. This trend towards symbolism is, of course, a general characteristic of medieval art, but it is intensified here because these plays, besides being drama of an historical and symbolic kind, are also propaganda theatre, designed to instruct men to avoid vice and cling to virtue. Even when the mysteries strayed farthest from the Church, their devotional, or, at least, instructional, quality remained dominant.

Beyond all of this, however, there was something else. All the marvels involved in the production of the plays were designed obviously to delight the audience, and we recognize that those concerned with their presentation were fully aware of what we should now call their 'entertainment value.' This awareness led to the invention of subject-matter for which no valid authority was forthcoming. In general it assumed certain clearly defined forms: the introduction of realistic elements, of comic scenes, and of sensational scenic devices such as those indicated in the staging of the later French *mystères*. While possibly all of these were natural developments such as might have been expected to arise unbidden within the mystery-play framework, there is more than a suspicion that as the amateurs pursued their path and sought for new ways of delighting their audiences they may have turned to professional entertainers—the minstrels and *jongleurs*, who were the descendants of the mimes—for aid and inspiration. The comic elements brought into the plays were of just that kind in which the early mimics had delighted, and there is undoubtedly a professional touch in the magical wonders described for us by contemporaries. The realistic element, too, provides further suggestions of a similar kind: it is, for example, noteworthy that in precisely those portions of the mystery cycles to which the entertainers might have been expected to contribute their skill—the scenes of the devils and the comic episodes—the characters, instead of being left anonymous (first, second, third devil or first, second, third soldier), are provided with names and to a certain extent at least are given individual rôles. In all countries do we find this feature. Mak, the good-humoured predecessor of Autolycus, appears in England; Italy brings its Nencio, Bobi, and Randello, its Filino, Schirnio, and Thesino; France its Aloris, Ysambert, and Pellion. Looking at these, we may well suspect that the secularization of certain scenes in these prevailingly devotional plays was materially aided by the activities of those obscure descendants of the *mimi* who strutted forth, on the fall of Rome, into the Dark Ages.

To reach a valid appreciation of the artistic quality of the mystery cycles is difficult. We are inclined to do no more nowadays—unless we are specialized students of literature—than read a few selected examples of individual plays in anthologies; yet we must always bear in mind that for contemporary audiences the entire cycle, and not merely separate portions of it, was the object of attention. The cycle, on the other hand, possessed no formal unity: playlets might be added to or extracted from the collection at will. If there is a unity, it is such as we find in a Gothic cathedral, wherein Norman elements are set side by side with the work of later builders, where there need be no symmetry, where elaboration in one transept may be in no wise paralleled in another, where the very pillars of the nave may be of the most diverse forms. The unity here is rather a unity of impression than one of formally associated parts.

Within the various countries of Europe different elements were stressed in these productions, even although the main features were the same in all lands. The Germans loved grotesque, nightmarish scenes of devils, were adept at Jew-baiting, and enjoyed a kind of rude realistic satire in which contemporary personalities were set cheek-by-jowl with figures from the Bible. An excellent example is provided in the fifteenth-century *Redentiner Osterspiel (Redentin Easter Play)*, a work which, despite the extraordinary diversity of its material, illustrates well the Gothic unity referred to above as well as the characteristic qualities of the German medieval mind. Divided into two parts, the play first tells, with some rude-handed humour and broad satire, how the Jews beg Pilate to see that Christ's body is not taken from the tomb: their efforts fail, and Jesus rises to effect the harrowing of Hell. The devils are in dismay; and consternation is among the soldiery appointed by Pilate to guard the tomb. In the second part of the drama Lucifer is shown lamenting; Hell must be repopulated, and Satan is sent to gather in as many souls as he can. "Bring the poor and the rich," he is ordered,

> And let none escape from you:
> The usurer and also the robber;
> The counterfeiter and the milk-thief;
> The magician and the pastry-cook;
> The liar and the dog-trainer;
> The brewer, the maltster,
> And also the dealer in tripe.

Then comes a long procession of miserable sinners—a baker who has cheated his customers, a shoemaker who has left his leather untanned, a tailor who has stolen cloth, a barmaid who has given short measure:

> Why should I try to cover it up?
> I don't think I could deceive you anyway.
> I was always able to make a lot of beer,
> Chiefly for this reason:
> I used an ample quantity of water—
> Otherwise my need for water was small.
> Also, when I sold beer or wine,
> Then this was my custom:
> I put my thumb into the glass
> And served beer with a lot of foam.
> Whenever I measured out beer for some one,
> I believe that I never once forgot

> To serve part from the second boiling;
> And thus I earned many a penny.

The procession continues, with a weaver, a butcher, a huckster, a robber, and, finally, a priest—all depicted in vivid contemporary terms. Obviously here, although the aim is highly moral, the story of Christ is being forgotten amid the clamour of the devils and their prey.

Farcical satirical scenes are frequent in many of the German plays of the time. In the *Wiener Osterspiel* (*Vienna Easter Play*), for example, the episode of the unguent-seller is much elaborated. He is represented as a quack doctor, just arrived from Paris with a stock of tinctures and drops. He is worried because his assistant has left him. Luckily, however, the rascally Rubin appears—a thief and a rogue—and accepts the vacant position. The whole scene is a vivid picture of contemporary life. From the realistic trend which gave it birth also derives a number of scenes of more serious import. Thus in the *Hessisches Weihnachtsspiel* (*The Hessian Christmas Play*) there appears a remarkable and touching picture of the homeless Joseph and Mary wearily seeking a humble lodging. The appeal made by their words springs from the same source as gives vitality to the quack doctor's bargaining with Rubin.

The vast mystery cycles of France are broader in their scope, and in general one is inclined to regard them as unnecessarily prolix. Rhetoric and intellectual argument only too often are substituted in them for dramatic passion. They too, however, possess their characteristic interest. Diablerie is much stressed here, as in the German plays, but what most attracts our attention is the occasional appearance of an intensely lyrical note and of scenes as realistic as the German, but more polished and refined. Even the usually tedious Greban can thus rise to his song of Hell, with its refrain,

> La dure mort éternelle
> C'est la chanson des damnés—

and to the haunting appeal of Christ's prayer to His Father:

> Heavenly Father, sovereign creator,
> Who first adorned these beautiful heavens,
> Who know all in Thy infinite wisdom,
> Look on me Thy lowly human son,
> Bowed down with an intolerable burden
> Such as heart of man cannot guess at.

As representative of the realistic note we may take the lively scene in Marcadé's *mystère* in which Magdaleine is shown, before her conversion, with her waiting-maids Pasiphée and Perusine:

PASIPHÉE: You are all the rage;
  They talk of nothing else but you. . . .
MAGDALEINE: I must get myself ready,
  Dressed, laced, made-up:
  I must look my best.

PASIPHÉE: There's not a lady your equal;
  You're so lovely
  You don't need make-up. . . .
    [*MAGDALEINE washes her face and looks in her mirror.*]
MAGDALEINE: Have I not a radiant face?
PERUSINE: Indeed, yes.
  You're quite a picture.
MAGDALEINE: And my bonnet?
PERUSINE: The latest fashion.

A trifle more polished, and this might have been an episode from a comedy of manners.

The English mystery plays, compared with the German and the French, seem more subdued, but perhaps because of that there may be justification for those who believe that their contents have more structural harmony and more directness of appeal than any of the others. Here the devils play just such a part as they ought and no more; here comedy appears rather as a relief and a contrast than as an entity by itself; here at times there is a simple passion and a naïve tenderness of a strangely appealing sort. There is a peculiarly restrained emotional impact in the scene where Abraham unwillingly prepares to sacrifice his son:

ABRAHAM: Oh, my son! I am sorry
  To do thee this great annoy,
  God's commandment do must I,
  His works are aye full mild.
ISAAC: Would God, my mother were here with me!
  She would kneel upon her knee,
  Praying you, father, if it might be,
  For to save my life.
ABRAHAM: Oh, comely creature, but I thee kill,
  I grieve my God, and that full ill:
  I may not work against his will
     But ever obedient be. . . .
ISAAC: Is it God's will I should be slain?
ABRAHAM: Yea, son, it is not for to layne;
  To his bidding I will be bane,
     Ever to his pleasing.
  But that I do this doleful deed,
  My Lord will not quit me my meed.
ISAAC: Marry, father, God forbid
     But you do your off'ring.
  Father, at home your sons you shall find
  That you must love by course of kind.
  Be I at once out of your mind,
     Your sorrow may soon cease.
  But you must do God's bidding.
  Father, tell my mother of nothing.

A homely quality is present in the gentle Coventry Nativity Play, with its lovely shepherds' song:

> As I outrode this enderes' night,
> Of three jolly shepherds I saw a sight,
> And all about their fold a star shone bright;
> They sang, Terli, terlow—
> So merrily the shepherds their pipes can blow.

In the Torturers of the Towneley Crucifixion appears a grim humour, and a gay atmosphere surrounds Noah's wife in the Chester Deluge. She is a true artisan's wife, and her words are racy as she flouts her husband:

> Yea, sir, set up your sail
> And row forth with evil heale,
> For, without any fail,
> I will not out of this town.
> But I have my gossips every one,
> One foot further I will not go.
> They shall not drown, by Saint John,
> If I may save their life.
> They loved me full well, by Christ!
> But thou wilt let them in thy chest,
> Else row forth, Noah, whither thou list,
> And get thee a new wife.

And, of course, above all others, there is the famous Wakefield *Second Shepherds' Play*, the first part of which presents an incisive picture of the three shepherds, cold and weary, watching their flocks as they grumble about the exactions of the "gentlery men" and their minions. The thievish Mak comes and steals one of their flock, carries it to his home, and, aided by his wife Gill, puts it in a cradle and swaddles it with clothes. Found out at last, Mak is "tossed for his sins," and immediately after this merriment an Angel's voice is heard sweetly intoning the announcement of Christ's birth. The contrast is severe, yet the quiet scene by the manger gains in simple dignity, not loses, from this sharp juxtaposition with the comic episodes preceding it. Although the author of this play may have been untutored, he possessed an innate sense of the dramatic.

For us to-day the medieval mystery plays may have historic rather than intrinsic interest. We still flock to Oberammergau, but the mood in which these pieces were written is gone; at best we can be but spectators at, not participators in, the performance. On the other hand, the historic interest is no ordinary one, for this vast endeavour of the Middle Ages is, as it were, the rock upon which Shakespeare's palaces and towers were firmly erected. It is possible, of course, to argue that, since Christ is a perfect character and a symbol rather than a man, the mystery play could offer no basis for the later secular tragic drama, but such arguments seem to lose sight of the most important contributions of this form to the theatre. The tragic drama depends fundamentally on what we may call

high seriousness; it is an exploration of the deepest, the most fundamental problems of the universe; the slightest breath of cynicism is fatal
to its being. So far as form is concerned, the mystery plays had nothing to
give to the later theatre, but their spirit is the illimitable landscape
against which the tragic figures of the Elizabethan stage stand gloriously
illumined. Their atmosphere of unquestioning faith, their breadth of
scope, and the variety of tone through which they contrasted the solemn
with the ludicrous all contributed materially towards building the
strength that reached its culmination in Shakespeare.

The Theatre of the Saints

In many respects the mystery cycles were inhibited from the possibility of organic growth. Once a cycle had been composed additions and
alterations might be, and, indeed, were, undertaken, but there was no incentive or opportunity for the building of things new. Partly this was due
to the fact that the Biblical material was the be-all and the end-all for the
dramatists; partly it was due to the fact that the actors were amateurs
who engaged in the presentation of the plays only once a year. For the
preparation of fresh dramatic compositions there was the impulse
neither of the Athenian competitions nor of professional needs. Apart
from this, the cycle itself weighed heavily upon the theatre: too vast to be
lightly rewritten, it prohibited the growth of a more readily perceivable
unity. A new playwright might on occasion substitute another "Abraham and Isaac" or "Deluge" for those which had been previously performed, but in general he was fettered by the thought that these separate
dramas could be no more than parts of a very much larger whole. The
process could be little beyond the exercise of a modern dramatist engaged in the rewriting of a single scene—the thirtieth or fortieth part—of
an already existent tragedy or comedy.

Besides the Biblical play, however, the medieval stage had plays of the
saints, and these offered some more promising possibilities. Although
owing their being to the development of the liturgical drama, these miracle plays early sprang into being alongside the mysteries, and exhibited
not so much a development from as a growth parallel to the others. As
early as the beginning of the twelfth century a chance accident provides
us with a record of a play of *St Catherine* (*ludus de Sancta Katarina*) performed at Dunstable. The accident occurred to a certain Norman clerk
named Geoffrey who had borrowed some vestments from the abbey for
the performance; fire broke out in his house, the ecclesiastical property
was destroyed, and the poor man, conscience-stricken, became a monk.
For Geoffrey the ill-wind had the advantage of bringing him in time to be
the abbot of St Albans; for us it has given us our first authentic record of a
saint's play, or miracle, in Europe.

This record will illustrate some of the problems confronting a student
of the medieval theatre. Although the twelfth century thus reveals the

existence of a play of St Catherine in England, and although later allusions testify to the flourishing of miracles alongside the mysteries, there is virtually no single text of an English play of the kind now extant. For our knowledge of what the saint's play provided we must turn to other lands, notably to France, where fortunately so much has been preserved, from the thirteenth to the sixteenth century, that a clear picture both of the growth of the genre and of its diverse manifestations is readily obtainable.

Le jeu de Saint Nicolas (*The Play of St Nicholas*) is known to have been written by a certain Jean Bodel, and, since he died in 1210, its date can be at least approximately determined. Its trailing plot well exemplifies some of the elements which were later to be so fully exploited in this kind of drama. The background is that of the Crusades, romantic, adventurous, with a King of the Pagans, surrounded by his "amiraus," or emirs; there is noise of battle and slaughter of the Christians; there are effective prayers to St Nicholas and an overthrowing of the great idol Terragan. But there also appear scenes of a different character—scenes in an inn, with rollicking, racy dialogue born of the Arras soil. *Le jeu de Saint Nicolas* is ostensibly a religious drama, and it ends with the singing of the *Te Deum*; but it is at least half-secular, a mixture of an adventure story and a comedy of ordinary life.

From the same period comes an even more interesting play, *Le miracle de Théophile* (*The Miracle of Theophilus*), the work of a thirteenth-century minstrel, Rutebeuf. The plot here deals with the tale of the man who gives his soul to the devil. Dissatisfied with his lot, Théophile, a clerk, effects the sale of his immortal being through the office of a magician named Salatin, "who talks to the devil as often as he wants." The hero is not untroubled by doubts, and the devil, for his part, is treated, amusingly, as a character much annoyed by the way in which he is continually being tormented by human conjurations, and very cautious in this transaction because he has so frequently been cheated in the past. After a career of sin, suddenly, without any warning, Théophile repents, prays to the Virgin, is first repulsed and then aided by her. She succeeds in recovering the paper that Théophile had signed; he takes it triumphantly to his bishop, who indulges in some suitable moralizations; and the play ends with the *Te Deum*.

Here we are approaching the great treasury of the French miracles —the wonders wrought by Our Lady—which was to produce the lengthy series of diverse dramas entitled *Les miracles de Nostre-Dame* (*The Miracles of Our Lady*). Already in *Théophile* the shape of these pieces has been determined. Each play is now a separate entity, and, even when miracle cycles develop, the component parts remain independent: the cycle now is not a lengthy story stretching from Creation to Resurrection, but merely a collection of individual dramas. These dramas consist of two parts, showing first the sins of the protagonists and secondly the wonder-working miracle, the repentance, the finding of the true way;

and since the miracle comes necessarily at the conclusion of the plot, it is to be understood that the greater part of the story is concerned with secular, and often comic, material.

The variety of such material is astounding. In general, one may divide the *Miracles de Nostre-Dame* into three groups: (*a*) those in which the miracle is the climax of the plot, in which the playwright has tried to build his tale towards the final wonder; (*b*) those in which the miracle, while necessary for the resolving of the plot, tends to be overshadowed by the secular material; and (*c*) those in which the miracle is a mere appendage to an entirely secular theme. A few examples will illustrate the types.

In *Jehan le Paulu* an anchorite is tempted by the devil, who poses as his servant, and when the king's daughter comes to his cell after losing her way during a hunt he ravishes and kills her at the demon's suggestion. The body is thrown into a pit. Repenting, he vows he will make penance by going on all-fours like a beast and feeding himself on roots. Seven years pass, when the king revisits the place where his daughter was lost. Word from heaven comes to Jehan saying he is pardoned; he rises, confesses his crime, prays that the princess be restored. The prayer is granted, and all the company thanks the Virgin for her intercession. Although the plot has an element of romantic wonder about it, clearly its design has been determined by the fact of the miracle; the end is anticipated in the beginning.

Somewhat different is the *Miracle de Nostre Dame, comment elle guarda une femme d'estre arse* (*The Miracle of Our Lady: how She protected a Woman from being burned*). The first part of the story is a domestic melodrama. Guillaume, the mayor of Chiefvi (Chivy), and his wife, Guibour, live happily with their daughter and their son-in-law, Aubin, until rumour starts to whisper that Guibour and Aubin are lovers. Informed of this, she comes to a terrible decision: Aubin must die. Two harvesters are commissioned to trap him as he goes to his wine-cellar and to strangle him. A brilliantly conceived scene follows when the mayor cheerily prepares for the family meal and sends his daughter to call Aubin, while Guibour astutely conceals her guilty knowledge. After the arrival of officers of justice it is discovered that the youth has been murdered; the whole family is arrested; Guibour confesses and is sentenced to be burned alive. The play might now be considered finished, but the marvel is still to come. So well does she pray to the Virgin that a miracle is wrought: the cords that bind her are consumed by the flames, but her body remains untouched.

With this drama we are well on the way to the secular theatre, and when we move to the miracles of the third type we are almost wholly within that sphere. Here we encounter a variety of themes of diverse moods. In *La femme du Roy de Portugal* (*The Wife of the King of Portugal*) a king proposes to a girl, but declares that, since the marriage day has to be delayed, he will die if he does not have her immediately. She pleads the cause of honour, then succumbs and gives him the key of her room, with the words: "You have in your hands now the key of my honour, and of your own." This is a plot of ordinary life, not a religious exercise. The story of *Amis et Amille* appears here, a tale of friendship in the realm of chivalry. *Robert le Diable* makes his entry. There are stories of romantic pathos and adventure, such as *La fille du Roy de Hongrie* (*The Daughter of the King of Hungary*), in which is told how a monarch, in order to keep his vow to his now dead wife that he will never remarry save it be to "a woman of her likeness," obtains the Pope's blessing for a wedding with his own daughter. The girl, to escape incest, dares her father's wrath, is condemned to death, escapes, marries the King of Scotland, is accused by her mother-in-law of faithlessness to her husband and set adrift on the sea in a small boat. From a dismal fate she is saved by intercession of Our Lady. The same story, it may be noted, although wrapped up in pseudo-classical robes, appears in the interesting fifteenth-century Latin *Comœdia sine nomine* (*The Comedy without a Title*).

So much has been lost of this kind of drama that it is difficult to assess rightly its true significance in the development of the romantic stage. A few years ago we should have been inclined to believe, for example, that England had nothing to offer in this kind, but towards the beginning of the present century there was discovered a manuscript, written about 1380, containing the part of an actor who took the chief rôle in a play which may be called *Duke Moraud*. Penned in stanza form which is similar to the style of the miracles, it tells a melodramatic story of a duke who conceives an incestuous passion for his own daughter; his wife threatens to expose them and is killed by the girl; a child is born of the liaison, and, at the duke's command, it too is slain. At the end he is shown joyous at the thought that now their secret is safe, but, going to church, he becomes conscious of his sin, falls into a decline, and dies begging Christ to have mercy upon him. Here in the fourteenth century is a wholly secular drama, with as sensational a theme as any of those exploited by the later Elizabethans.

One after another these plays ring the changes on episodes and characters akin to those familiar to us in the worlds of romance and balladry, and we realize that the genre of the miracle play was offering to the playwrights of the time innumerable opportunities for the exploitation of new material. There are no inhibitions in this realm, as there were in the realm of the mystery dramas; the tales of miracles were legion, and if necessary it was a simple feat to take any theme, no matter whether grave or gay, sordidly realistic or replete with romantic wonder, and tack on to its close a miracle of the Virgin. If the mysteries provided the element of high seriousness and vastness of conception, the miracles taught men how to give theatrical expression to domestic scenes and legends of adventure.

The Moralities

In the mystery plays we occasionally meet with personifications among the Biblical and invented characters, and it is probable that the growth of yet another type of medieval drama, the *morality play*, was inspired from this source. In the moralities all the persons introduced upon the stage are abstract figures, most of them representing vices and virtues. Already in the twelfth century Germany could show, in the *Ludus de Antichristo*, a morality-type drama introducing Paganism and Synagogue, Hypocrisy and Heresy, as speaking characters.

At first glance it would seem as though this were a retrograde movement in the theatre, a moving away from living characters to characters of a purely symbolic cast; but examination of the plays themselves must lead us to beware of too hasty judgments. The typical morality handles a plot in which a central figure, called Mankind or Humanum Genus or Infans, is tempted, falls, and comes again to grace. The pens of some of the playwrights may be heavy and dull and uninspiring; others may permit their moralizing aims to suppress dramatic tensity; but in general it will be found that this basic theme aids rather than hinders the medieval dramatist in the writing of vividly conceived scenes, many of them based on the life he has seen around him.

Of all the moralities the Anglo-Dutch *Everyman*, or *Elckerlijk*, is both the most typical and the best. Its story is well known. God summons Everyman by ordering Death to take him for his own:

> Go thou to Everyman,
> And show him in my name
> A pilgrimage he must on him take,
> Which he in no wise may escape;
> And that he bring with him a sure reckoning
> Without delay or any tarrying.

Everyman pleads delay, and then seeks around for anyone who may bear him company. First he turns to Fellowship:

EVERYMAN: Well met, good Fellowship, and good morrow!
FELLOWSHIP: Everyman, good morrow by this day.
   Sir, why lookest thou so piteously?
   If anything be amiss, I pray thee, me say.
   That I may help to remedy.
EVERYMAN: Yea, good Fellowship, yea,
   I am in great jeopardy.
FELLOWSHIP: My true friend, show to me your mind;
   I will not forsake thee, unto my life's end
   In the way of good company.
EVERYMAN: That was well spoken, and lovingly.
FELLOWSHIP: Sir, I must needs know your heaviness;
   I have pity to see you in any distress;
   If any have you wronged ye shall revenged be,
   Though I on the ground be slain for thee,—
   Though that I know before that I should die.

EVERYMAN: Verily, Fellowship, gramercy.
FELLOWSHIP: Tush! by thy thanks I set not a straw.
   Show me your grief, and say no more.

When, however, he hears what is wanted he quickly draws back. A similar answer is given by Kindred and Goods; Knowledge, Confession, Beauty, Strength, Discretion, Five-wits, all fail Everyman; in the end only Good Deeds, although faint and "lying cold" in the ground, is prepared to stand at his side.

The quality of this drama has deservedly rescued it from oblivion. In the original form and in the rather voluptuously expanded German *Jedermann* it has seen many performances during recent years and has always worked its magic on its audiences. This magic derives, of course, largely from the universal appeal of its theme, but it is contributed to by the manner in which the unknown playwright has made his figures, despite their abstract names, vital human characters—and this is true of all the moralities. Even in the dullest of these pieces there are flashes of this quality. Sensual Appetite is one of the deadly sins, but he becomes a man when he meets Studious Desire in *The Four Elements*:

SENSUAL APPETITE: Aha! now good even, fool, good even!
   It is even thee, knave, that I mean.
   Hast thou done thy babbling?
STUDIOUS DESIRE: Yea, peradventure, what then?
SENSUAL APPETITE: Then hold down thy head like a
   Pretty man, and take my blessing.
   Benedicite! I grant to thee this pardon
   And give thee absolution
   For thy sooth saws. Stand up, jackdaw! . . .
   Make room, sirs, and let me be merry,
   With huffa, gallant, sing tirl on the berry
     And let the wide world wind!
   Sing friska jolly, with hey trolly lolly,
   For I see well it is but a folly
     For to have a sad mind.

In France the 'morality' went even further, and, although it preserved its ethical colouring, actually sloughed off the personifications and substituted real or type names in their place. Thus, for example, we find a *Nouvelle moralité d'une pauvre fille villageoise, laquelle ayma mieux avoir la teste coupée par son père que d'estre violée par son seigneur, faicte à la louenge et honneur des chastes et honnestes filles* (*A New Morality of a Poor Village Girl who chose rather to have her Head cut off by her Father than be violated by her Lord, in honour of all Chaste and Honest Maids*). The plot reveals to us, first, a poor domestic interior, with a widower, Le Père, and his beloved daughter, Eglantine, without whom his life would be dark. Into this humble setting comes Le Seigneur, who has been informed of her beauty by his valet. The Seigneur demands to have her, but father and daughter prefer to brave his threats. In order to escape him and at the same time to avoid the punishment of eternal damnation on account of suicide, she begs her father to slay her, hands him the sword herself. But the Seigneur has overheard her pitiful plea and steps forward in time to prevent this action, crying:

> O venerable creature!
> I renounce my former folly.
> Pardon me, gentle maid.

Thus converted, he makes atonement by appointing the father the governor of his territory, and places a "crown of chastity" on Eglantine's head. All ends happily, and the valet presents the moral in terms that the sentimental Richardson would have approved:

> Good comes to her who favours good:
> Maidens, take good heed!

Before taking leave of these edifying dramas one aspect of their production requires attention. Although some, like the English *Castle of Perseverance*, called for a simultaneous setting akin to that which served the mysteries, the majority, both French and English, asked for no more than a single simple platform. This meant that they could step out of the world of the amateurs with their elaborate, cumbersome, and costly mansions or pageants and adapt themselves to the needs of those small professional companies which came into being towards the end of the fifteenth century. The morality, therefore, formed the true link between the medieval theatre and the modern. Shakespeare almost certainly witnessed performances of mystery plays in his youth, but there was a vast gulf between the stages they demanded and the London stages upon which he became an actor. On the other hand, whatever company he first joined almost certainly must have had some moralities in its repertoire. When Sir Thomas More is shown, in the drama to which he gives his name, greeting, like Hamlet, a group of comedians who come to his house, he finds on inquiry that their plays include *The Cradle of Security, Impatient Poverty, Lusty Juventus,* and *The Marriage of Wit and Wisdom.* In carrying such plays with them these comedians in *Sir Thomas More* were undoubtedly typical of all their fellows.

Farces and Interludes

Lusty Juventus is extant, and is called in the original text "An Interlude." The interlude is a term difficult to define: here, for example, it is applied to what unquestionably is a morality, and from the diversity of its use it might almost be taken to mean a short play of any kind, and particularly one suited for professional production. While the word does have this wider significance, however, it also bears a narrower and more specialized significance, indicating in the more particular sense a short play of purely secular nature, without any very obvious ethical moral, and usually farcical in tone. The existence of this form reminds us that just as the miracle play rapidly tended to transform itself into romantic drama of adventure, the morality gradually threw off its ethical attire and came to exist entirely for sheer entertainment.

These farces or interludes of the late medieval and early Renaissance periods are of prime importance in the history of the theatre. In many countries they arose. Germany had her Nuremberg Shrovetide Plays (*Fastnachtsspiele*), out of which sprang the farces of Hans Sachs, a prolific and not untalented author who set an individual seal on the anonymous forms of his predecessors. One cannot claim him as a genius, but undoubtedly he did succeed in writing scenes of a not unamusing if rough sort. There is, for instance, considerable good humour and a nice sense of dramatic contrasts in his *Der fahrende Schüler im Paradies* (*The Wandering Scholar from Paradise*, 1550). The story is a simple one. A Wife, whose first husband is dead, dreams fondly of the days when he was with her; her new husband is a surly brute; she did not appreciate her first as he deserved. To her comes a wandering student. He tells her he has just come from Paris, and she, a creature illiterate and credulous, thinks he said Paradise. Immediately she inquires whether the Student has seen her old man; all he had when he died, she says, was a blue hat and a winding-sheet. The Student soon catches on and declares that the poor man is a perfect sight in heaven:

> He goes about there without boots,
> Breeches, or smock—or substitutes!
> As queer as he was laid in earth!
> Cock his hat as he may, or girth
> His shroud around him,—when others feast
> He stays outside, penniless, fleeced,
> Lingering there with longing eyes,
> Living on alms the rest despise—
> Dirty and wretched beyond expression!

The tale is so moving that the Wife gets together a bundle of her husband's clothes and begs the Student to take these, together with a purse of gold, to the poor man when next he goes to Paradise. The Husband comes home, and there is a pleasant scene in which she, glad-eyed, twittering with excitement, tells him of this wonderful piece of good-fortune:

> *WIFE* [*beginning to realize the miraculous nature of her news*] :
> Oh, how shall I the marvel say?
> A strolling scholar, to still my sighs,
> Came by here out of Paradise!
> There he had seen my former man—
> And swears that he is poorer than
> The meanest, without shirt or shoes
> Or money—nothing he can use
> But hat and sheet! Think!—nothing save
> What we thrust with him in the grave!

HUSBAND [*with a grim smile*]:
  Wouldst thou not send him something fit?
WIFE [*surprised at the suggestion from him, accepting it eagerly*]:
  Oh, husband dear, I did!

With excitement he asks what road this man has taken, and sarcastically adds:

> Thou gav'st him far too little money
> For thy dead husband's alimony!
> He cannot well live long therewith!
> Go, have the fast horse saddled forthwith.

The Wife takes these words literally and blesses him for his thoughtfulness, while he dashes off in pursuit of the Student. Arriving at a muddy patch of ground, he encounters his quarry, but the astute Student, after dropping his pack, pretends to be a peasant, sends the Husband on foot over the mire, and gaily steals his horse. Returned home, the good man haltingly explains to his Wife that out of kindness he has given away the horse, but counsels her to keep the whole affair quiet:

WIFE [*jubilantly*]: Nay, the whole parish knows and agrees!
HUSBAND [*much startled*]: Eh? Who told them of it so quick?
WIFE: Why, before thou hadst reached yon rick
  I had told them all from beginning to end:
  What to my husband I would send,
  With all respect, to Paradise.
  And everybody was so nice—
  Laughed aloud and made sport with me.

This little playlet is but one among many others. In *Der Rossdieb zu Fünsing mit den tollen Bauern* (*The Horse Thief*, 1553) three farmers are deliberating about the hanging of a horse thief. They decide the execution shall be on Monday, and then recall that, if it takes place then, the corn in their fields will be spoiled: the crowds will trample it down. To save the crops and at the same time to avoid the cost of feeding the thief they eventually determine to free him on his promise that he will return to the gaol four weeks hence—after the harvest. The thief, hearing of their proposal, soon estimates with whom he has to deal. Shall it be said, he asks, that the village was so mean as to leave him to find his own food during the time of waiting? They are all impressed by this argument and quickly collect money for his keep, while he leaves a worthless cap in pledge. Gaily he proceeds to steal right and left, sells his booty to others in the village, and finally has them all soundly belabouring one another. *Das heisse Eisen* (*The Hot Iron*, 1551) has a similar mood. A Wife wonders, first, why she no longer loves her husband as passionately as she did at first, and, secondly, whether he is faithful to her. She determines to test his virtue by the trial of the hot iron. When she proposes this to him he at once feels suspicious and begins to wonder whether she perhaps may

not be leading a double life. For himself he prepares to pass the test by
concealing a piece of wood in the hand that is to hold the red-hot iron.
His trick succeeds beautifully, and at once he turns the table. Now that
he has submitted to the trial, he says, she must follow suit. In horror she
confesses that the chaplain had been her lover:

> HUSBAND: The Devil take the chaplain!—well;
> He was a priest, and threatened Hell.
> I give you up the priest. Now take
> The iron for thy honour's sake.

At this she blubbers out that there were two others, and then asks him to
forgive her "four more men—all, as I live!" The four soon grow to seven,
and at the end she is abject in submission. The play closes with the Husband, duly virtuous, exulting in a new-found authority in his household.

These farces of Hans Sachs are akin to many another similar playlet
produced about this time. From Holland comes a set of peasant comedies of kindred spirit. In one a foolish Lippijn is cheated by his slatternly
wife; in another an old farmer is tricked by a quack at the fair; in still
another a dull-witted Rubben whose wife bears a child three months
after marriage is persuaded by her relations that all is well. Italy gives us
the farces of Giorgio Alione da Asti; Spain produces its *Dialogo entrel
Amor y un Viejo* (*Dialogue between Love and an Old Man*).

Most prolific in this field, however, were France and England. In the
former, amid the many *sotties* presented by those associations of
'fools'—*sots* or *fous*—that flourished in the later Middle Ages, there are
several works which, because of their dramatic structure, characterization, and individual spirit may truly be brought among the
theatre's masterpieces. Such a play is the famous *Pierre Pathelin* (*c*. 1469),
an anonymous work, vivid and gay, in which the hero, Pathelin, succeeds
in cozening a draper out of a roll of cloth, and then, feeling proud of his
skill, instructs a shepherd how to get out of paying his debts, only to find
that his seemingly stupid pupil has learned so well that he is able to
escape from tendering a fee to his mentor. The trickster is himself
tricked. Here is something more than mere peasant buffoonery: the farce
is coming close to comedy.

Even more true is this of the peculiar plays written many years before,
in the thirteenth century, by Adam de la Halle (or Adan de la Hale),
extraordinary achievements for their time, at once reaching back
towards Aristophanes and stretching forward towards the modern
world. One of these dramas, which might almost be regarded as the earliest of comic operas, is named *Robin and Marion* after its two chief persons, a shepherd and his shepherdess. The pastoral opens with a song by
Marion, testifying to her love:

> Robin m'aime, Robin m'a;
> Robin m'a demandée, il m'aura.

A Chevalier arrives, makes love to her, even offers violence, and departs; Marion sings out to her Robin, who comes running, and there is a pleasant little rustic interlude. The Chevalier returns, but Marion says her lines so prettily that he is discomfited, and the play charmingly ends, as it had begun, on the note of pastoral song and dance. To find such delightful scenes in the thirteenth century is surprising, but even more surprising is the same author's *Jeu de la feuillée* (*The Play of the Greenwood*), in which the real and the fantastic are inextricably intermingled, and in which the spirit of Aristophanes is recalled by the sharp juxtaposition of satire directed at contemporaries and of soaring adventures in the world of the imagination. Adam himself comes on stage, and with him his father, Maistre Henris de la Halle, but the play also includes a kind of dream scene, a vision of the land of fairy. Whether there were other plays of this age akin in spirit to the *Jeu de la feuillée* we cannot tell; as it stands, it is unique; but even if nothing like it existed at that time it testifies to a potential dramatic power that awaited only the coming of the Renaissance to break free and enlarge itself. The oak that was Molière already existed in the acorn of *Pathelin* and the plays of Adam de la Halle.

In much the same manner the new 'profane' drama developed in England. From the early fourteenth century comes a fragment of a piece entitled *Interludium de clerico et puella* (*The Play of a Clerk and a Girl*) in which the former, failing to win the love of the latter, goes off for aid to an old bawd, Mome Helwis; and some two hundred years later appeared the first writer of English comedy, John Heywood, to whom are assigned six plays: *A Play of Love, A Dialogue of Witty and Witless, The Play of the Weather, The Pardoner and the Freer, The Four PP,* and *Johan Johan.* If these are indeed all by the same author it is easy to see how he advanced both in dramatic skill and in his sense of the comic. The first is nothing but a debate among four abstractly named characters: Loved-not-Loving, Loving-not-Loved, Neither-Loved-nor-Loving, and Both-Loved-and-Loving. In *The Four PP* a similar debate makes its appearance, but with more point, the Palmer, the Pardoner, the Pothecary, and the Pedlar vying with each other as to which is the most skilled in lying. The prize goes to the Palmer, who, after listening to the Pardoner's tale of a shrew in Hell, innocently remarks that he is much surprised to hear it—since in all his wanderings he has never yet known a single woman out of patience.

Something more of dramatic movement enters into *The Play of the Weather*, wherein Jupiter, worried because of human complaints regarding the weather he supplies to the world, commissions Merry-report to conduct an investigation. After hearing a Gentleman ask for days

Dry and not misty, the wind calm and still,

a Merchant request suitable gentle winds for his ships, a Ranger seek "blustering and blowing," a Water Miller demand rain and a Wind Miller no rain at all, a Gentlewoman pray for weather undamaging to

her complexion, and a Launderer bright sunshine, and finally a Boy
(described as "the least that can play") beg for frost,

> And plenty of snow to make my snowballs,

Jupiter decides to let matters stand as they have been in the past.
Although there is nothing but a succession of entries here, at least some
action appears; characters come and go on their cues instead of merely
standing still and debating. Action becomes more pronounced in *The
Pardoner and the Freer*, while in *Johan Johan* a fully outlined plot is developed.

This last play is easily the best of all that Heywood had to give to the
stage. Its complete title, *A Mery Play, betwene Johan Johan, the Husbande,
Tyb, his Wyfe, and Syr Jhan, the Priest*, introduces the three characters
whose interrelations provide the comic episodes. At the start appears
Johan Johan, the henpecked husband, but for the moment irate and
boastful:

> God speed you, masters, every one!
> Wot ye not whither my wife is gone?
> I pray God the devil take her,
> For all that I do I cannot make her—
> But she will go a-gadding very much
> Like an Antony pig with an old witch
> Which leadeth her about hither and thither—
> But, by Our Lady, I wot not whither.
> But, by Goggis' blood, were she come home
> Unto this my house, by our Lady of Crome,
> I would beat her ere that I drink.

In a lengthy tirade he permits his fancy to imagine all he would do, but
on her entry his tone changes:

> *TYB:* Why, whom wilt thou beat, I say, thou knave?
> *JOHAN:* Who? I, Tyb? None, so God me save.
> *TYB:* Yes, I heard thee say thou would'st one beat.
> *JOHAN:* Marry, wife, it was stockfish in Thames Street,
>   Which will be good meat against Lent.
>   Why, Tyb, what had'st thou thought that I had meant?

The wife pretends to be satisfied and, announcing that she has made a
fine pie, sends Johan off to bid the priest, Sir Jhan, to partake of the fare.
The scene now changes to the priest's house; Johan gives his message;
and once more we are back in his dwelling. Thinking to sit down and eat
of the pie, he is rudely disillusioned; first, he is sent out to get some water;
next, it is discovered that the pail has a hole in it; after that, he has to sit
by the fire chafing wax wherewith to mend it. And all the while the priest
and the wife make merry at the table:

> *SIR JHAN:* What dost, Johan Johan, I thee require?
> *JOHAN:* I chafe the wax here by the fire.

TYB: Here is good drink, and here is good pie.

SIR JHAN: We fare very well, thanked be Our Lady.

TYB [*aside to SIR JHAN*]: Look how the cuckold chafeth the wax that is hard,
 And for his life dareth not look hitherward.

SIR JHAN: What doth my gossip?

JOHAN: I chafe the wax—

[*aside*] And I chafe at it so hard that my fingers cracks,
 And eke the smoke putteth out my eyes two.
 I burn my face and ray my clothes also—
 And yet I dare not say one word,
 And they sit laughing yonder at the board.

So the scene proceeds until, unable to stand it any longer, Johan Johan kicks over the traces, smashes down the pail, and chases Priest and Wife out of the house.

It is a simple and perhaps crude playlet, but true comedy is peering round the side-wings of farce.

PART III

THE DRAMA OF THE RENAISSANCE

1

COMEDY, TRAGEDY, AND MELODRAMA IN ITALY

ALREADY, at the time when these farces of Heywood were being written and performed, a new movement was afoot in the world of the theatre. *Johan Johan* looks back to the medieval comic realm that Chaucer so well knew how to depict; perhaps indirectly and afar off it has connexions with the work of the wandering mimes, but certainly it exhibits no tie with the literary comedy of Rome or of Greece.

By the end of the fifteenth century, however, the whole of Europe was being changed by the impact of that revolution of spirit to which has been given the name of the Renaissance. Essentially it was a forward-looking development, in which new concepts—political, religious, and artistic—came to supplant those which had so long served men's needs. It is true that the more its diverse manifestations are studied the more we realize how much the men of the sixteenth century unconsciously incorporated into their new philosophies the core of medieval thought, how freely they made use of medieval forms in their ecstatic searching for fresh means of expression. Certainly strength came from the incorporation of the long tradition of the Middle Ages; but now the medieval elements were incorporated into something else, not pursued in their original forms: in the process of combination with elements different from themselves they suffered a complete transmogrification. Shakespeare, the brightest star in this firmament, owes his being to a subtle fusing of three forces: the classical influence contributes to his sense of structural form, the spirit of his age is strong upon him, and beyond these stretches the powerful tradition of the medieval theatre. Out of those three something entirely new has been created.

The Theatres of Italy

How necessary for absolute success was a fusing of the three forces is amply demonstrated by a comparison of the Italian theatre with the theatres of Spain and of England during the sixteenth and seventeenth centuries. The union that so gloriously was effected in England, and that gave strength to Spain, in Italy failed of realization, largely because diverse groups laid their hands on particular elements and attempted to develop these independently.

The story starts with the endeavour, at several Italian Courts, during the last years of the fifteenth century, to put plays by Plautus, Terence, and Seneca upon the stage. At this time we must not think of 'Italy,' but merely of a collection of Italian states, each under its own ruler and each, although maybe allied with its neighbours, existing in tremulous or passionate rivalry among the rest. Only one thing brought them together—love of art and admiration of the classics. Amid conditions of life dangerous and often depraved, amid the clashing of arms and the perilous intrigue of palace politics, this passion ruled in every city, and princes vied with one another in attracting to their service men of literary and pictorial genius, philosophers, scholars. In Rome the Popes and Cardinals were the patrons, in Florence the Medici, in Milan the Sforza; Ferrara owed its esteem to the efforts of the Este, Mantua to those of the Gonzaga, and Urbino to those of the Della Rovere.

At the start Rome and Ferrara took the lead. Under the inspiration of Julius Pomponius Laetus, Latin plays were given before specially invited audiences in the Eternal City, while Duke Ercole I eagerly encouraged similar efforts at Ferrara. This was an amusement that appealed to all. Princes gained esteem from the performances they sponsored; scholars were delighted to assist in presenting the texts they studied; painters and architects found in the stage new opportunities for the exercise of their skills.

From first to last these activities put firm stress on the visual effects to be secured, and in general two main lines of development are to be traced. The one was the endeavour to recreate the form of the classical stage in an indoor hall; the other was the attempt to achieve in three-dimensional terms the effects currently aimed at two-dimensionally by the artists of the time. For the early productions at Rome and Ferrara apparently no more was done than the building of what has come conveniently to be known as "the bathing-box" stage, illustrated in some fifteenth-century editions of Terence. Here a platform some four or five feet high was raised upon trestles, and at the rear was a façade formed by pillars supporting round ornamented arches and by curtains between the pillars. Each entry was supposed to be the 'house' of a particular character, and on occasion the curtains might be drawn to reveal small interiors within. The classical façade with its doors of entrance is thus interpreted in a manner not unreminiscent of the contemporary simultaneous setting used for the production of the mystery plays.

Soon, however, more was attempted. In 1484 the work of the Roman architect and author Vitruvius was discovered, and when men read of the scenery devised in ancient times for tragedy, comedy, and satyr play, and when they found plans for the arrangement of auditorium, orchestra, and stage, they set happily to work in diverse directions. One series of experiments culminated in the famous Teatro Olimpico (1584) of Vicenza, wherein a semicircular auditorium faces a long, narrow stage backed by a richly designed façade with one large central opening and with four

MIMIC FOOLS
Terra-cotta statuettes in the British
Museum.

A MIMIC FOOL
Bronze (probably Greek).
*By courtesy of the Metropolitan
Museum of Art, New York*

ERRA-COTTA MASKS
rom the originals in the British
Museum.

GREEK AND ROMAN MASKS AND MIMES

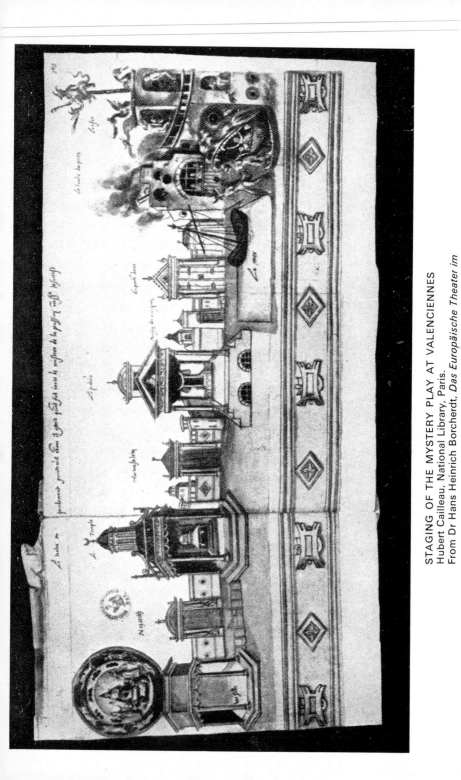

STAGING OF THE MYSTERY PLAY AT VALENCIENNES
Hubert Cailleau, National Library, Paris.
From Dr Hans Heinrich Borcherdt, *Das Europäische Theater im*

other doors of entrance. Here the attempt to reproduce the Roman theatrical form comes to its logical end.

Beyond the entrance-ways of the Teatro Olimpico, however, were set what no Roman theatre had known, perspective vistas of city streets; these, designed by the architect Vincenzo Scamozzi, belong to the other tradition—the tradition of the artists, not of the scholars. Easy to trace is the development of these pictorial scenes from the type of fixed settings illustrated in Serlio's *Architettura* (1551) on to the elaborate displays, so fashioned as to admit of sudden breathtaking changes, popular at the Courts in the early seventeenth century. Easy, too, is it to see how, with these settings, a proscenium frame—no doubt not uninfluenced by such large central openings as that which appears in the Teatro Olimpico —became necessary. At first these frames were merely flat and painted, each constructed especially for its own production, but by 1618 had come into being the great Teatro Farnese at Parma, with its elongated' auditorium and its richly sculptured proscenium arch. Thus the modern theatre was born.

In watching the progress of this theatrical architecture three things are worthy of special note. First, the playhouses thus described were essentially courtly. Most of them were built within the vast halls of the princely palaces of the Renaissance, and the rest, like the Teatro Olimpico, were the efforts of academies closely associated with and sponsored by noble patrons. Into them entered no ordinary spectators: when they were used for the performance of plays the audience was a splendid one of princes and their guests. Secondly, they were all closed structures, so that a theatrical element unknown in the past, lighting, made its first appearance and was destined to play, later at least, an important rôle. Thirdly, the forms assumed by these theatres did not provide a harmony between the needs of the time, its dramatic theory, and its creative effort.

This last aspect is the most important and deserves some further attention. With the rediscovery of ancient Greece and Rome came the finding of Aristotle, and the scholars of the sixteenth century had a pretty time poring over his *Poetics* and enunciating theatrical laws which they fondly thought were based on his injunctions. Thus came into being the famous or notorious Rule of the Three Unities, which demanded that a play should have unity of action (with a single plot), unity of place (permitting no change of scene), and unity of time (the fictional action being restricted to twelve or twenty-four hours). These were fettering laws, yet the age was one of adventuresome existence, vivid in colour, when men sought rich show and rapid movement. The validity of scholarly theory, firmly set on the unassailable rock of Aristotelian authority, could not be denied, while at the same time the whole desire of the time was for an expansive display fundamentally opposed to these circumscribing limitations.

No organic solution for the problem thus set was reached in Italy. Instead the theatre found itself hopelessly divided at heart. The dramatists were compelled to accept the unities and to fashion their scenes within one setting, while the desires of the century, craving for change and excitement, called for, and obtained, satisfaction in the presentation of richly spectacular shows between the acts of comedy or of tragedy. The result may readily be imagined: dramatists found that their efforts were bound by the restrictive laws, at the same time as licence revelled tumultuously about them; spectators, bored with the plays, gave all their attention to the *intermedii* (or *intermezzi*) between the acts. The words of the poet were lost in a riot of show.

Italian Comedy

Of the two dramatic forms, comedy and tragedy, the former obviously had more chance than the latter to preserve some vitality under these conditions, but even the laughing muse, although at first promising liveliness of spirit, soon languished and miserably died.

The first signs of life came from Ferrara, where Tito Livio dei Frulovisi wrote an interesting series of Latin plays of Plautan flavour and romantic sentiment (1432–34), and where, later, Lodovico Ariosto, the Court poet, applied himself energetically to the stage, producing plays which, although too heavily imitative of Latin models, suggested that from this beginning much might come. Despite the fact that his comedies were composed only a few years after the first experiments in the presentation of the Plautan and Terentian originals, he showed an eye keenly observant of contemporary manners and a hand apt to infuse into the classical material the qualities of his own time.

Ariosto's first extant play, *La cassaria* (*The Casket*, originally (1508) written in prose and later (1529) recast in verse), reveals the dramatist at his apprentice stage. The plot is a tissue of episodes culled from Latin sources, telling how Erofilo and Caridoro, loving two slave-girls owned by the bawd Lucrano, are involved in a series of escapades and misunderstandings in their attempt to obtain the wherewithal to purchase them. There is nothing original in this story, but the language is crisp and direct, while some of the characters bear features that give them individuality. In *I suppositi* (*The Counterfeits*, also originally written in prose (1509) and reworked (1529) in verse), translated by George Gascoigne as *The Supposes* (1572) and used by Shakespeare for *The Taming of the Shrew*, the *dramatis personæ*, although still heavily bound by their classical fetters, are making more determined efforts to break free. The episodes may be borrowed from Plautus' *Captivi* and the *Eunuchus* of Terence, but the scene is set in Ferrara, the spirit is that of Ariosto's own time, and the characters are drawn from the life of his day. The story tells how Erostrato, a Ferrarese student, has dressed as his own servant in order to gain entry to the house of Damone, father of Polinesta, a girl wooed also by the old Cleandro, who offers two thousand ducats as her dowry. Since Erostrato cannot cap this offer, his servant Dulippo (dressed as his master) induces a Sienese traveller to pose as the young man's father. The complications attendant upon the arrival of the real father, and upon the discovery of Polinesta's relations with the supposed servant (Erostrato in disguise), may be left to the imagination: it is not these that challenge our attention. What is noteworthy is the vividity and ease of the style. Ariosto commands an easy pen and is as happy when allowing Dulippo to recount his intrigue with the stranger from Siena as when devising the flow of talk among the masters and their attendants.

Ariosto's other three plays, *La lena* (*The Bawd*, 1529), *Il negromante* (*The Charlatan*, 1520), and *La scolastica* (*The Academic Comedy*, left uncompleted at the author's death and finished by his brother about 1543), show considerable developments along similar lines. For *Il negromante* both the plot and the principal character, the charlatan Jachelino, seem to have been the invention of the poet: the whole spirit of the play, with its adumbration of Jonson's *Volpone*, breathes of the sixteenth century, when astrologers and quacks abounded, feeding luxuriously on popular credulity. Satire of modern life appears in a different guise in *La lena*, with its prostitute and its complacent husband, while in *La scolastica* we find a gay dramatic record of contemporary academic life. Here the chief persons are a couple of students who have come from Paris to the University of Ferrara, and their adventures with their lady-loves provide many scenes of hilarious comedy.

When we consider that *La cassaria* is the first true modern comedy, and that consequently Ariosto had to create his own style, his achievement indeed must be deemed remarkable. The episodes are lively, the language is crisp, the characters have vitality, and the atmosphere of Plautus is subtly altered so that what was in his hands a comedy of crude sexual appetite tends to take shape as a comedy of romantic adventure. One might readily have thought that with this beginning the Italian stage was due to exhibit wonders.

Nor was Ariosto alone. Already in 1513 his friend, Cardinal Bernardo Dovizi da Bibbiena, had produced his *La Calandria* (*The Comedy of Calandro*) at Urbino. Based on Plautus' *Casina* and *Menæchmi*, it introduces a pair of twins, Lidio and Santilla, the former dressed as his sister, the latter dressed as her brother. Although lacking Ariosto's grace and, like *La cassaria*, heavily indebted to its classical models, this play too presents a vivid picture of sixteenth-century life. And about the same time came Niccolò Machiavelli's deliciously salacious exposure of contemporary stupidity and corruption, *La mandragola* (*The Mandrake*; Florence, *c.* 1520). The action here concerns the journey of Callimaco from Paris to Florence for the purpose of seeing the famed beauty of Lucrezia, wife of Messer Nicia Calfucci. Consumed with passion for this lady, he seeks the aid of the parasite Ligurio, who devises a subtle trick. Knowing that Messer Nicia is concerned because he has no heir, and, at the same time, knowing his abject credulity, he induces Callimaco to pose as a wonder-working doctor. The latter advises that the wife be given a potion of mandragola, but warns that the first man to lie with her must, because of the potion, inevitably die; whereupon he further proposes that they shall kidnap some young fellow after dark and bring him to Nicia's house for the purpose of taking off the effects of the medicament. On hearing that the King of France and his leading nobles have consented to adopt just such procedure, the silly little husband agrees, and the more he is drawn into the device the more eager he becomes. To persuade Lucrezia to accept the plan they call on the aid of her mother and her confessor. In tears she is won by their arguments: Callimaco is, of course, the supposed kidnapped stranger, and at night he wins Lucrezia's heart by declaring his passion and demonstrating the crass stupidity of her husband. The comedy ends in satiric laughter:

NICIA: Master, take my wife here by the hand.
CALLIMACO: Gladly.
NICIA: Lucrezia, here's the man who will be responsible for our having a staff to support our old age.
LUCREZIA [demurely]: I hold him very dear, and I hope he'll be our friend.
NICIA: Now bless you! And I want him and Ligurio to come and dine with us to-day.
LUCREZIA: Of course.
NICIA [with a sudden new thought, beaming fatuously]: I want to give them the key to the ground room by the loggia, so that they can come here just to suit their convenience. . . .
CALLIMACO: I accept it, and I'll use it when I can.

Although by far his finest work is *La mandragola*, Machiavelli proved in his companion plays, *La Clizia* (1525) and his unnamed *Commedia in prosa*, that he possessed a wide and varied power of comic invention. *La Clizia* in particular is memorable for its mordantly satirical portrait of the old Messer Nicomaco.

After this brilliant start in romantic comedy and in satire, although nearly all the prominent writers of the time turned their hands to the stage, and although the classical episodes came to be mingled with invented material and with material taken from the *novelle* of the time, comedy, unfortunately, shows little progress. Plays such as Trissino's *I simillimi* (*The Identical Twins*; Venice, 1548) and Lodovico Dolce's *Il capitano* (*The Captain*; Venice, 1545) we may neglect as being little more than reworkings of Plautan themes, but it is strange that more life was not infused into others in which contemporary events were exploited, and particularly into those written by authors intent on shaking off the undue influence of the classics. Even in such a play as Dolce's *Fabrizia* (1549), where an attempt is made to break away from overgreat reliance on the classical, the intrigue is apt to creak.

In many ways the devices for arousing the spirit of comedy were here being expanded, as, for instance, in Lorenzino de Medici's interesting portrait (*L'Aridosia, The Play of Aridosio*; Florence, 1536) of a timid, prevaricating miser, or in Agostino Ricchi's use of foreign speech (*I tre tiranni,*

The Three Tyrants; Bologna, 1530) for the arousing of laughter, yet as a
whole these plays remain lifeless and dull. Even Antonfrancesco Grazzini (called Il Lasca), despite his "proud Florentinity" and his aggressive
modernism, failed. His *La gelosia* (*Jealousy*; Florence, 1550) has interest
in that it introduces the trick which plays such a vital part in
Shakespeare's *Much Ado about Nothing*, but its scenes, although full of
invention, rarely have sparkle. Grazzini may justly lay claim (as he specifically does for this comedy) that he is introducing fresh matter to the
stage, but he may hardly be accounted one of those who, by their wit and
vigour, have advanced comedy's cause. Much the same verdict must,
regretfully, be passed on *La spiritata* (*The Possessed*; Florence, 1560),
although for us it has considerable historical value, both because of its
Elizabethan adaptation as *The Bugbears* and because of the frequent later
use of its plot—wherein a girl, to escape the unwanted attentions of an
undesirable suitor, pretends to be possessed or mad. Perhaps the most
amusing of his plays is *La pinzochera* (*The Devotee*; printed 1582), which
entertainingly tells how old Gerozzo, a henpecked husband, tries to win
the favour of Diamante, wife of Alberto Catelani. A rascally servant
makes him believe that the lady would agree were it not that she fears discovery, and gives Gerozzo a couple of supposedly magic cherrystones
which, it is claimed, will make him invisible. When they have been put in
the old man's mouth the servant and his associates pretend they cannot
see him; off he goes on his love-tryst, with the expected result that he is
soundly beaten for his pains.

Another author who sought to break new ground, but with hardly
greater success, was the self-styled Scourge of Princes, Pietro Aretino. Of
all his work perhaps *La cortigiana* (*The Play of the Court*; Venice, 1534) is
the best—a bitter attack on the Papal Court, containing an excellent picture of little Messer Maco, who comes to Rome full of piety and is gradually taught to do as Romans did in the sixteenth century. All his work,
however, has interest, from the vividity of the farcical scenes in *Il
marescalco* (*The Blacksmith*; printed 1533) to the satirical sallies of
L'ipocrito (*The Hypocrite*; Venice, 1541).

Angelo Beolco, nicknamed Il Ruzzante, essayed still another path in
trying to wed a native Paduan farcical style to the comic style of Plautus:
an interesting example of this mixed form of comic invention is to be
found in his *L'Anconitana* (*The Girl of Ancona, c.* 1530), in which romantic
and classical elements are intermingled. Still freer in subject-matter and
tone are *La moschetta* (*The Coquette, c.* 1520) and *La Fiorina* (*The Little
Flower, c.* 1520), both of which take their inspiration from the Paduan
countryside and deal realistically with rustic love affairs. How strongly
the impress of the age was striving to substitute a contemporary romantic for a classical seal is to be seen when we compare, for example, the
two plays of Gigio Artemio Giancarli: *La Capraria* (*The Comedy of the Goats
c.* 1540) is almost entirely Roman in concept, whereas *La zingana* (*The
Gipsy, c.* 1550) is rich in the life of the day. The movement too is easily

traceable in the various comedies written by a better-known author, Giambattista Della Porta. *La Cintia* (*c.* 1580), with its girl dressed as a boy and its man dressed as a girl, is thoroughly imitative; when we come to *L'astrologo* (*The Astrologer*, 1570), however, we find a classic plot enlivened by the introduction of a strongly drawn portrait of a fake astrologer whose actions and words are those of the sixteenth century; while in *I due fratelli rivali* (*The Two Rival Brothers, c.* 1580) we are in the midst of romantic subject-matter with only a few vague echoes of Plautus and Terence, and the atmosphere of romance is still further developed in *La furiosa* (*The Desperate Girl, c.* 1590) and *Il moro* (*The Moor*; printed 1607). The student life of the time, which had attracted Ariosto's attention in *La scolastica*, is treated in *La Cecca* (*c.* 1550) by Girolamo Razzi, author of an extraordinary drama of sentimental heroics named *La Gostanza* (printed 1564). A playwright such as Raffaello Borghini can deal in tragi-comic manner with a Romeo and Juliet theme in *La donna costante* (*The Constant Lady*; printed 1582); and a Francesco d'Ambra can make vivacious some scenes of *I Bernardi* (*The Bernardos*, 1547) by allowing popular elements to intrude into his imitative plot. The list of dramatic works is impressive in quantity if not in quality. Niccolò Secchi comes forward with his *Gli inganni* (*The Cheats*, 1549), introducing some reasonably lively scenes based on the ancient theme of long-lost children, and with his farcical *L'interesse* (*Self-interest*; printed 1584); an anonymous author gives us the rather delightful *Gli ingannati* (*The Cheated*, 1531), to which, perhaps, Shakespeare owed a debt in *Twelfth Night*; to Plautan intrigue Giovanni Maria Cecchi adds some witty dialogue in *Gli incantesimi* (*The Charms*; printed 1550); in *Flora* (1555) Luigi Alamanni attempts to regularize the contemporary stage by reference back to classic models; a fairly graceful style marks Giambattista Gelli's story of an elderly lover in *L'errore* (*The Error, c.* 1550) and the not dissimilar story told by Agnolo Firenzuola in *I Lucidi* (*The Lucidos*, 1549); in *Il Granchio* (1566) of Lionardo Salviati echoes of folk speech are substituted for polish of phrase. There is variety here; there is the desire to achieve things of value; there is obviously superabundant energy. Yet, despite this infusion of new material, not one of these plays possesses enduring quality.

What it was that prevented these plays from achieving richer proportions than they were in fact able to realize is difficult to determine. One restrictive element was, of course, the impress of the classics, and, in particular, the rule of the unities which forced the playwrights to fit their themes to a Procrustean bed of fixed time and place; but this in itself cannot be cited as the sole explanation. More important, perhaps, was the fact that all these comedies were being written for highly select audiences unleavened by what existed outside the courtly halls—indeed, by the fact that, even so, the audiences were not those of one centre but of several independent cities, each small and almost parochial in spirit. If Ariosto's Ferrara could have been united with Bibbiena's Urbino, Grazzini's Florence, and Aretino's Venice, more might have come from these endeavours. Chief of all, however, was the failure of the dramatists to create that world of romance which permitted Shakespeare and Lope de Vega such wide opportunities. There is a hint of it in Ariosto's scenes, but no more than a hint; it appears, but dully expressed, in Alessandro Piccolomini's *L'amor costante* (*Constant Love*; Siena, 1536) and in his *Alessandro* (1543); but for the most part all these plays are dull and antiquated. Love, ideal and romantic yet close to earth, was the major theme of the time, but whereas the Elizabethan drama incorporated that theme into the harmony of its comedy, Italy allowed it to be endlessly and tiresomely discussed in her philosophical *dialoghi d'amore* while her stage fed, not on the spirit of poetry, but on the physical intrigues of prose.

The Tragedies

The tale of tragedy during these years is much similar to that of comedy, although here the rules were more insistent in their demands, and the models—the plays of Seneca—less inspiring.

Early in the fourteenth century Albertino Mussato was responsible for a Latin tragedy *Ecerinis* (1315), in which the story is told of a fairly recent Paduan tyrant, Ezzelino III, in Senecan terms. The following century produced Antonio Cammelli's *Filostrato e Panfila* (Ferrara, 1499), the first tragedy written in Italian wherein elements of the mystery plays were combined with suggestions taken from the Roman playwright—a drama of illicit love and horror, the theme of which had been narrated by Boccaccio in his tale of Gismonda.

Soon came severer efforts at classical imitation, heralded by the first 'regular' tragedies, the *Rosmunda* (1515) of Giovanni Rucellai, in which Seneca is taken as a guide, and the *Sofonisba* (1515) of Gian Giorgio Trissino, who went beyond Seneca back to Greek models. *Sofonisba* is an important work historically, but, despite contemporary esteem which praised it even above the *Œdipus* of Sophocles, incredibly dull. The themes of *Ecerinis*, *Filostrato e Panfila*, and *Sofonisba* indicate that the same spirit was at work as operated in the realm of comedy: playwrights, although dominated by admiration of the classics, were prepared to exploit subject-matter distinct from that used by the authors of Rome and of Athens, but once more failed to produce any work of a truly noteworthy sort.

In vain, for example, did Giraldi Cinthio, at Ferrara, endeavour to establish a new form based on the Senecan by developing the theme of romantic love and sensational horrors. Of the latter element his *Orbecche* (1541) is full. The prologue promises the spectators "tears, sighs, anguish, terrors and frightsome deaths," and the five acts that follow, introduced by the ghost of Selina, former wife of Sulmone, clamouring for revenge, do not disappoint that promise. Apparently Selina had been executed because of her incestuous relations with Sulmone's son, discovered through the intermediary of that young man's sister, Orbecche. Orbecche is now secretly married to the humbly born Oronte—which gives the ghost her chance. Gradually the tension increases until in the fourth act we are informed that Sulmone has cut off Oronte's hands, murdered his children, cut off his head, put the head and the bodies into vases for some obscure purpose. The Chorus guesses that these vases will perhaps be sent to Orbecche. The guess is justified: Orbecche kills her father, Sulmone, cutting off his head in turn, and finally stabs herself—leaving the ghost of Selina presumably the only satisfied character in the play.

Obviously little promise could come from such efforts (although we must remember that the young Shakespeare started his career with the equally bloody *Titus Andronicus*), but Cinthio by no means confined his writing to this style. His most interesting dramas, indeed, are those in which he exploited the material of romance and contrived to bring tragic material to a happy close. Thus, for example, his *Arrenopia* (printed 1583) frankly deals with the world of the adventuresome, narrating how Arrenopia, a princess of Scotland, is secretly married to the King of Ireland, and how her husband, having become infatuated with another lady, plans to murder her. Confusion follows confusion until, in an atmosphere not unreminiscent of that of such a play as *Cymbeline*, the plot is brought to a fortunate conclusion.

The reference to *Cymbeline* reminds us that Cinthio, more than any of his companion dramatists, was making a contribution to the Elizabethan comedy of romance. This is even more marked in *Gli antivalomeni* (*The Interchanged*; printed 1583), where we learn of children of a king exchanged for the children of a usurper, of girls donning men's clothes, of threatened death and sudden recognitions. We might almost, but for the lack of poetic magic, be in a Forest of Arden, a mythical Thebes, or a fantastic Sicily.

Unhappily there were none to follow his lead. The *Canace* (1542) of Sperone Speroni, a famous work of its day, outdoes the gruesome follies of *Orbecche*, opening with a speech uttered by the ghost of a child not born until the third act. Lodovico Dolce brings in a new element by introducing, in his *Marianna* (1565), the theme of jealousy for the first time into Italian tragedy, while Luigi Groto crowds into *La Dalida* (1572) all the horrors of which his fevered imagination can dream. Other playwrights, with no more dramatic skill, essayed to explore the realms of chivalric romance, but mostly their scenes are dull, as in Torquato Tasso's *Il Re Torrismondo* (*King Torrismondo*, 1587), or replete with artificial absurdities, as in the ludicrous *Almerigo* (1590) of Gabriele Zinano. Even the interesting experiments made by Giovanni Maria Cecchi in his 'religious dramas' can hardly be said to offer anything of enduring import.

There is but little good to be said of this field of endeavour. Once more we feel the impress of the classical, the frantic endeavours to escape, and the resultant disharmony of effort.

Pastorals and Operas

The audience before whom such plays were presented had interests which found satisfaction in more artificial realms of dramatic expression than tragedy could, or should, offer. Far back, in 1480, Angelo Poliziano produced at Mantua his *Orfeo*, and in this play he achieved a finer unity of effect than anything attained by the tragic dramatists of the period. There is a fantastic charm here and a delicacy of utterance which rings truer than many a comic scene of the time or the mouthing rhetoric of the serious dramas. Although *Orfeo* is hardly a pastoral, in its scenes the pastoral is being born. The line of development from this play to the *Aminta* (Ferrara, 1573) of Torquato Tasso and the *Pastor fido* (*The Faithful Shepherd*, 1585) of Battista Guarini is a direct one. In these works the Italian Renaissance theatre comes as near as anywhere to perfection of expression: yet neither of the works can be styled a great play. Charm they have, and smiles, rippling verse and artificiality of sentiment, but to these they add none of those qualities which make for true strength in the theatre. Here is the world of escape. Shakespeare entered this world too in *As You Like It*, but his shepherds and shepherdesses are treated in a mood of ironic amusement, while Touchstone and Jacques arouse thoughts far other than those appropriate to idyllic joy and bucolic simplicity.

The pastoral virtually closed its career with *Il pastor fido*, although many other plays in the same style, such as the not uncharming *L'amoroso sdegno* (*Lovers' Trials*; printed 1597), by Francesco Bracciolini, were still to be written and performed, but a kindred form of drama, closely connected with it in origin, was destined to develop rapidly in this time and to have a long and distinguished career. During the latter years of the sixteenth century the age of madrigals discovered that the Greek plays were originally chanted, and this discovery led to the desire to present modern plays in the same way. In 1574, at Venice, a tragedy was "produced in the manner of the ancients"; it had music composed by Claudio Merulo, and "all the actors sang in most pleasant harmony, both in solos and in choruses." Already Poliziano's *Orfeo* had made a gesture towards the opera, while the *intermezzi* usually added a musical element to their preponderating element of scenic decoration. This last step, therefore, was not without its forerunners, and the manner in which the 'melodrama'—or musical drama—met the desires of the time is indicated by its immediate popularity.

For the full establishment of the form a group of Florentine enthusiasts was responsible. Under the presiding genius of Giovanni Bardi, Count of Vernio, a little academe gave its anxious thought to the development of the music-drama. Here was Vincenzo Galilei, father of the famous Galileo, Giulio Caccini, an able musician, Jacopo Peri, the composer, and

Ottavio Rinuccini, the poet. After much talk and many experiments the first true opera took final shape in 1594—a *Dafne*, with libretto by Rinuccini and music by Peri. A short time later came Peri's *Euridice* and Caccini's *Il ratto di Cefalo* (*The Rape of Cephalus*)—and the opera was well launched on its early lines of classical mythology.

The Bardi group had always intended to achieve a true marriage of poetry and music; but the charm of novelty lay in the singing, and it is easy to see how, as the 'melodrama' developed and became the '*opera*, or work, in music,' the libretto more and more faded in importance. Within a few years a composer of genius, Claudio Monteverde, had seized on the newly devised dramatic genre and stamped it as the property of the musician, not of the poet. In the year 1607 appeared at Mantua his *Orfeo*, followed the next year by *Arianna*, in both of which the restrained academic character of Peri's efforts was discarded in favour of a full-blooded theatricality. The bored intellectuals at the Courts eagerly cast aside dull tragedy and trivial comedy in order freely to embrace the new form. From Mantua the vogue of opera spread among the principalities and dukedoms of Italy, penetrated into bourgeois Venice (where the first public opera-house was opened in 1637), crossed the Alps into France and Austria, becoming ever more and more ornate. All that lavish theatre-building of the seventeenth century, all that labour expended in creating majestic settings, all that inventive power applied to the devising of stage machinery, was associated, not with drama, but with opera. Words were lost in the splendour of the scene and in the harmonies of the music. During the seventeenth century Italy has nothing to give us of worth in the realm of the literary play. The opera had triumphed.

2

THE POPULAR PLAY:
THE COMMEDIA DELL' ARTE

INSTEAD of sitting in a palace hall, let us imagine ourselves standing in the great square of Venice about the year 1600.

It is spring-time, and the lazy Italian sun is falling gently on the flag-stones, on the roofs of the surrounding buildings, on the gay façade of the Cathedral of San Marco.

At one corner of the square a platform stage has been erected; in front of it are benches for specially privileged spectators; around, in a widely expectant semicircle, stands a jostling, excited crowd. The comedians are about to present a play, announced as *Arcadia incantata* (*Enchanted Arcady*).

Of scenic decoration there is little. Two little box-like side-wings are set at the sides of the stage, and at the rear is a backcloth painted with trees to represent a wood.

Suddenly an actor steps forward, and the crowd is silent. His heavy robe is decorated with astrological signs; he bears a heavy, leather-bound volume and leans upon a peculiarly carved staff; obviously he is a magician. Alone on the stage he addresses the audience, declaring that by his art he has become lord of this island of Arcadia and of its silly in-habitants, the shepherds and the nymphs of the woods; but now he has learned by his magic skill that the privacy of his lonely retreat is about to be broken: strangers are approaching.

At this he departs, and the backcloth of the forest is changed to repre-sent a stormy sea with, in the distance, a ship foundering upon rocks. From one of the side-wings staggers in a strangely dressed creature, hump-backed, with a dark half-mask showing a sharply curved nose and a wrinkled receding brow on which a large wart is prominent. There is no doubt about his identity, for he has appeared in countless other plays; his name is Pulcinella. Gaspingly he tells us that he has just escaped from the wreck; alone of all his companions he has been saved.

As he is speaking, from the other side comes in a second character, also masked but even more grotesque, with a long, drooping nose and exag-geratedly large spectacles perched precariously on its bridge. His dress consists of a jacket, flapping trousers, a short cloak, and a beret with two long, curving feathers. He too is immediately recognizable as Coviello. In a kind of echo of Pulcinella's words, he also relates how he, alone of all his companions, has escaped a watery grave.

Gradually the pair move over towards the centre of the stage until, the one looking to the right and the other to the left, they bump into each other, start back in fear, take one another for ghosts, make as if to run away, then cautiously, timorously, draw near again, put out tremulous fingers, touch each other's arms, and finally, realizing the truth, embrace ecstatically. This done, they move aside in doleful converse over the loss of the others.

Meanwhile the same scene is repeated with another pair—the first, bespectacled like Coviello, and the other, older and ridiculously pompous, dressed like a savant of the University of Padua—Tartaglia and the Dottore. First, these two recognize each other as Coviello and Pulcinella had done, and then the two couples go through the scene of fear as a foursome. The more the crowd laughs at their ridiculous antics the more absurd their gestures become, until at last, the tumult over, they sit down and, talking all at once, gabble excitedly about their adventures. Then the thought of food comes into their minds; they are all hungry, and with one accord they decide to go off on a foraging expedition.

The scene now changes back to the wood, and four pastoral figures enter—the shepherd Silvio, who tells us he is in love with the shepherdess Clori, who tells us she is in love with Fileno, who tells us he is in love with Filli, who tells us she is in love with Silvio. Blundering into the midst of this idyllic tangle comes Pulcinella, and they all run off. Pulcinella has become separated from his companions, and, having failed to stay the shepherds, he is delighted when a company of richly costumed Priests enters. He begs them for food, and they ask him to come to their temple —where, they explain to the audience, they intend to sacrifice him.

Again the scene changes, this time to a temple. A great procession of Priests and Shepherds comes in, with Pulcinella, ludicrously unaware of the fate intended for him, borne on a chair. In a scene of equivoque he asks for food, while they exhort him to make a good end. At last he realizes what is intended; the knife is just descending when the Magician makes an impressive entry, bids them desist, and, when they prove obdurate, calls up two fiery Spirits who drive the whole crowd off the stage.

The first act is now over, and, after a pause, the scene is altered to the wood again, with a large property fruit-tree set in front of the backcloth. The Dottore, Tartaglia, and Coviello wander in, abjectly miserable, hungry, and lost. Wild beasts have terrified them in the forest, and they fear that Pulcinella has been eaten by one of these. At this moment Pulcinella dashes across the stage convulsed with fear. Forcibly they stay him, and in stammering words he relates his adventures in the temple, while they laugh at his words, thinking he has gone off his mind through lack of food. Suddenly the Dottore spies the fruit-tree and calls the attention of his companions, whereupon, with ridiculously cautious movements, they start to peer into every corner of the stage to see if anyone is

looking; satisfied at last, they approach to take the fruit—only to be terrified at the rising of flames, which consume the tree and drive them back.
As they are going a shepherdess, Silvana, enters complaining about a
shepherd, Dameta, who, having loved, has left her. All the four comic
characters at once fall in love with her, and there is a ridiculous struggle
among them, when the Magician enters with words of reproof. Thinking
him powerless in the face of their numbers, they are about to attack him,
but he charms them into immobility and releases them only if they promise to be good. Off they go with the kind-hearted Silvana to have some
supper.

Once more there is a pastoral interlude, Fileno lamenting the cruelty
of Filli, Clori suing Fileno, Silvio in despair, and Filli making vain love to
him. Now the Magician places a magic garland on a tree, explaining that
if anyone puts it on his temples he will seem to be the person beloved by
another.

First comes Pulcinella, satisfied after having had a good repast: he sees
the garland, puts it on, and is immediately taken for Clori by Silvio. Pulcinella jeers at him, and he goes off; but a moment later Filli enters and
takes Pulcinella to be Silvio; then Fileno thinks he is Filli, while Clori
deems him Fileno. As Pulcinella stands amazed at this madness his companions enter, assume that he is Silvana, and attempt to embrace him;
and matters become more complicated when, in the resultant confusion,
the Magician enters invisible and shifts the garland from head to head.

At last he desists and carries the garland away; Silvana comes on stage
and, hearing them all woo her, declares she cannot belong to all four, but
will marry the one who is the best sleeper—whereupon all settle themselves down to display their prowess in repose, only to be awakened by
four Spirits who chase them off the stage. Thus ends the second act amid
cries of fear and strange noises.

The third act opens with the pastoral characters, all of whom are bearing gifts to the temple and propose to pray for success in love. Coviello,
who has overheard their words, immediately outlines a plan to his companions: the Dottore shall dress as Jove, Tartaglia as Venus, Pulcinella
as Cupid, and Coviello as a Priest; seated in the temple, they will be able
to appropriate all the rustic sacrifices for themselves. In a richly ludicrous scene this project is realized, and the four conspirators set themselves down for a good feast. Again, however, Pulcinella becomes
separated from the other three and, when they depart, remains alone.

The Magician now enters and creates him King of Arcadia, handing
to him the magic book, the crown, and the sceptre. Pulcinella opens the
book, and at once a Spirit appears and declares he is at his lord's service.
Just at first Pulcinella is terrified, but he soon gains assurance, bids the
Spirit bring him a chair, and seats himself royally upon it. Silvio enters,
jeers at him, is beaten for his pains by the Spirit, begs for pardon, and is
admitted to Pulcinella's retinue: and a similar scene is enacted with
Fileno, Clori, Filli, and Silvana. Finally the Dottore, Tartaglia, and

Coviello come on stage and mock him unmercifully, until in a rage he opens his book and a Spirit appears. First he orders them to be beaten, and they are duly chastised; then he commands them to be hanged. Ropes are put round their necks, while they weep and implore, and the execution is about to take place when the Magician enters, stops the Spirit, chides Pulcinella, and marries off Silvio to Clori, Fileno to Filli, and Silvana to Dameta.

So the play ends.

The Professional Players

Clearly this is something entirely different from the tragedies and comedies, the *intermezzi* and the *opere*, acted at Court. The performers are professionals, not courtly amateurs; and, were we able to go backstage, we should find that their entire method of approach towards the play is different from that familiar in the palace theatres. There a poet composed his drama and the actors learned their lines. Here, search where we will, we shall find no written text. All that the manager of the company has is a brief scenario, specifying entries and exits, with a summary indication of what is to be done in each scene; all that the actors have is a short set of instructions pinned up behind the wings. When, for example, Pulcinella and Coviello are to make their first appearance on the stage they have as guidance only a general sketch of what they are expected to do and to say:

> *Enter PULCINELLA, from the sea; he speaks of the storm, the shipwreck and loss of his master and his companions. At this enter COVIELLO, from the other side; he speaks of the same things as PULCINELLA; they see one another and make the* lazzi *of fear. At last, after* lazzi *of touching one another, they realize that they have been saved and speak of the loss of their comrades and their master.*

The players, therefore, were expected to be their own authors, providing in their various scenes such dialogue as might appear necessary. Thus the type of performance illustrated by *Arcadia incantata* could be carried out only by men and women trained for long years in a special kind of acting technique; and consequently, in contradistinction to the *commedia erudita*—the 'erudite,' or 'amateur,' play of the Court—men were accustomed to speak of this other sort of drama as the *commedia dell' arte*, the play of 'the quality' (as the Elizabethans would have said), or, as we say now, of '*the* profession.'

Even for well-trained professionals, however, the creation of such scenes could not have been effectively realized without the acceptance of a number of conventions. The *commedia dell' arte* plays were improvised, certainly, so that no two performances of any given scenario could be quite the same in action and in dialogue, but the players were aided in diverse ways towards the successful securing of their ends. While it is true that over eight hundred scenarios have come down to us from the sixteenth, seventeenth, and eighteenth centuries, and that we must presume this number to have been but a small proportion of those originally in existence, we must observe, first, that many of these are almost duplicates, and, second, that any single company would have been content to use only a dozen or score out of the entire list.

Besides this fact, there is another still more important. In play after play of this kind the same characters put in an appearance and similar scenes occur. Each company was made up of a limited number of actors, each of whom, in every play, interpreted the same stock rôle. Normally there were four lovers, dressed either as gallants and ladies of the day or, as in *Arcadia incantata*, as shepherds and their nymphs. Alongside these were two old men, Pantalone, the Venetian merchant, and Dottore, the Paduan academic. Then came the Capitano, a boasting soldier, and an indeterminate number of so-called *zanni*, servants or clowns, each with his own particular name and characteristics—Pulcinella, Tartaglia, Coviello in *Arcadia incantata*, or elsewhere Arlecchino, Brighella, Bertolino, Fritellino, Pedrolino—together with a clownish maid or two, Colombina or Arlecchina. Occasionally other types appeared; occasionally the Capitano took the rôle of one of the *zanni* or Pantalone played the part of another old man (as probably he did in *Arcadia incantata*); but generally the dramatic characters were fixed and constant.

This meant that each actor from experience could build up for himself a long range of set speeches suitable for particular occasions: the lover might memorize Petrarchan sonnets for quoting to his lady; the Dottore might at leisure compose and learn long rigmaroles full of Latin tags; the Capitano might rehearse at length his mouth-filling oaths and rhodomontades. Business, too, could be established and used on different occasions. In the scenario of *Arcadia incantata* reference is made to the '*lazzi* of fear,' and whenever we come across the word *lazzi* (and no scenario is without it) we recognize that we are in the presence of stock business. If the manager bade two *zanni* to do a scene with the *lazzi* of fear they knew precisely what was required of them; they had enacted this scene together many times before, and their comic tricks were all ready to hand.

In this way a *commedia dell' arte* performance took shape as a repatterning of well-established, familiar stock-types and of well-known 'acts' or 'turns' similar to those we associate now with circus clown and music-hall comedian. A modern Christmas pantomime, although the words are here provided for the actors, is not dissimilarly composed: from the music-hall come the players with their diverse turns, and these are incorporated into the framework provided by the theme of a *Cinderella* or a *Puss-in-Boots*.

The performers in these companies set their eyes mainly upon broadly popular audiences. It is true that often, indeed, generally, the larger troupes were attached to particular Courts and that some of the actors were on such familiar terms with the dukes and princes that they might dare to address their lords with impertinent levity: regularly, *commedia dell' arte* productions were given in palace halls, while the time and energy of ambassadors were occupied in trying to persuade the sovereigns to whom they were accredited to grant leave for foreign tours of the toupes acting under their licence. At the same time the roots of even the most famous companies ran deep into the common soil; most of their performances were given before the people of the cities they visited. No doubt they purchased their trinkets out of moneys allotted to them by Court treasurers; but their bread and butter came from the takings at public performances. And beside these more famous troupes, with skilled actresses, like Isabella Andreini, who were the companions of queens and the stars of poets, with expert *zanni* like Drusiano Martinelli or Giuseppe Domenico Biancolelli, honoured guests at Court, were dozens of smaller companies, some engaged solely in producing plays, some merely appendages to the booth of some quack or charlatan, eager, through their antics, to gather gaping spectators apt to buy his nostrums.

The Fortunes of the Commedia dell' Arte

No one knows for certain whence the *commedia dell' arte* arose. It may have been born independently out of the social conditions of sixteenth-century Italy; on the other hand, there seems to be sufficient evidence to suggest that in this Renaissance form of entertainment we may trace the inspiration of medieval *jongleurs*, who themselves were the inheritors of the tradition of the Roman mimes.

All that is sure is that about the middle of the sixteenth century we begin to catch glimpses of dramatic shows which included some of the later stock characters—the Venetian Pantalone, the Bolognese Dottore, and the *zanni*—and that with extraordinary rapidity these small early groups of players expanded into the internationally renowned troupes of the Gelosi, the Confidenti, and the Fedeli.

At first their activities were confined to Italian cities, but before the sixteenth century had drawn to a close they were giving performances in France, while during the following century their fame spread widely over the entirety of Europe, where the various countries welcomed them and gradually modified their stock personages. In German lands Hanswurst is a native type born of Italian inspiration; France created the pathetic Pierrot out of Pedrolino, and refined the early rough Colombina into the dainty Columbine; in England Pulcinella became Punch, and the pantomime clown was born out of the Italian *zanni*. For nearly two hundred years the *commedia dell' arte* was the most popular form of dramatic entertainment in most countries of the Continent.

In itself, of course, it has vanished; these improvised plays have left no record of their original productions such as come from the production of written dramas. Yet the debt of the theatre to the *commedia dell' arte* cannot be exaggerated. Continually, in the pictorial records of the stage during the time of the Renaissance, an Arlecchino or a Dottore is peering impertinently from the wings, and in the writings of even the greatest authors of the time the spirit of the lost improvised comedies is to be traced. The theme of *Arcadia incantata* is so close to that of *The Tempest* that we are almost bound to assume a connexion between Shakespeare's last comedy and some similar piece played by the Italians; in *The Taming of the Shrew* Gremio is specifically named as the 'pantalowne,' while the *zanni*, or zany, well known to the English playwright, seems to have left his impress on more than one Elizabethan clown. Nearly a century later Molière was finding his genius stimulated by the *commedia dell' arte*, while a few decades after that Goldoni began his artistic career among these players.

There can be no doubt concerning the influence of the *commedia dell' arte* upon the drama, yet this very influence serves to indicate why the Renaissance in Italy failed to produce great plays. To create worthy tragedies and comedies an age requires to put all its strength into the theatre; part of its effort will not do. In Italy the stage was split. The literary qualities were reserved for the *commedia erudita*, and that remains lifeless or dull. There is a closet atmosphere, a preciousness, a smell of the wax candle, about every one of these Court productions, and their very weakness led to the expenditure of excessive effort upon costly scenic production. The atmosphere they breathe is so heavy with perfume, their surroundings are so stiff with brocade, that one sighs for at least a faint whiff of good honest garlic and the feel of homespun. In exchange for a few sincere kersey 'yeas' and 'noes' we would willingly sacrifice much of their artificial and turgid rhetoric.

Yet when we turn to the popular play we find something, instinct with life, no doubt, but like life mortal. Of the elements making for permanence in art there was none. Hence the strange double paradox: that, although the Italian stage has left us virtually no memorable play from this time, it established the form of theatre which still endures to-day, and that it created a dramatic form which, though evanescent, appealed throughout the whole of Europe not only to popular audiences, but also to the greatest dramatists of the seventeenth and eighteenth centuries. There was no lack of theatrical inspiration in Renaissance Italy, but the delicate balance of forces out of which alone a great dramatic expression can come was absent. Only rarely, and then without the power of a Goldoni, did any Italian author of this time succeed in fusing the literary and the popular. Although Giovan Battista Andreini, the son of the famous actress Isabella Andreini and himself an actor in the *commedia dell' arte* tradition, essayed the task in such plays as *Amor nello specchio* (*Love in the Looking-glass*; printed 1622) and *Le due commedie in commedia* (*The Two Plays within a Play*; printed 1623) with spirit and a certain grace, he failed, partly because his own talents were not equal to the occasion, partly because already it was too late to hope for the achieving of an end which, if it were to have proved fruitful, ought to have been secured nearly a century before.

3

FRENCH ROMANTICISM AND CLASSICISM

THE STORY of the stage in France during these years is at once similar and dissimilar. Here, as in Italy, imitation of the classics led to the writing of independent tragedies and comedies; here too there is virtually nothing of worth produced from the beginnings of the new movement in the theatre up to the middle of the seventeenth century. If there is this agreement, however, there are three marked differences: the French theatre presents no vital popular movement such as is marked in the *commedia dell' arte*, but, on the other hand, it does exhibit the development, albeit crude, of a kind of drama more appealing to ordinary tastes than the Senecan tragedies and the Plautan comedies, and it was destined, at a time when the Italian stage had sunk to its lowest ebb, to flourish forth gloriously towards the end of the seventeenth century. In a sense, the rather dull record of the French theatre from 1500 to 1650 is but the preliminary introduction to the glories of Molière and Racine.

The Classical Tradition

In the Courts and academies of France the same restless search for classical inspiration is to be traced as aroused the Courts of Italy—and, since the Italians had begun their questing at an earlier date, it was but natural that the French should often have approached their Seneca and their Terence through transalpine intermediaries.

Seneca appeared in Paris in 1485; Greek tragedy in Latin dress was represented by Erasmus' translations of two Euripidean dramas in 1506; by the middle of the sixteenth century these, or similar, plays were being issued in French versions. At the same time Italian tragedy was being introduced to Gallic readers through the renderings of Trissino's *Sofonisba* by Mellin de Saint-Gelais (1559) and Claude Merinet (1585), while the *commedia erudita* made its bow before French royalty as early as 1548, when Bibbiena's *La Calandria* was performed at Lyons, by Italian players, at the command of Henri II.

The real start of the French 'literary' drama was made in 1552 when Étienne Jodelle produced his historically significant, but intrinsically worthless, *Cléopâtre captive* (*Cleopatra Captive*), in which the old classical chorus is retained, the unities are preserved, and rhetoric rules.

The model thus established, other academically minded amateurs eagerly pursued the same path. The ghost of Seneca sits heavily on the *Médée* (1555) of La Péruse (Jean Bastier) and Jacques Grévin's *Jules César* (1558), on Gabriel Bounin's *La Soltane* (*The Sultana*, 1561) and André de Rivaudeau's *Aman* (1561). These are all hopelessly dull; in the kindred works of Robert Garnier a faint spark of light illuminates the darkness, although on them, too, the oppressive influence lays its sterile hand. Look where we will—at the early *Porcie* (printed 1568), *Hippolite* (printed 1573), and *Cornélie* (printed 1574), or at the later *Bradamante* (printed 1582) and *Les Juifves* (*The Jews*; printed 1583), we find but little to excite our admiration. Contemporaries—at least those who belonged to the intelligentsia—thought his work marvellous; he was lauded above Seneca, above the Greeks; his plays ran into an enormous number of editions. Yet the truth is that before the tribunal of time he stands shorn of his glory, exposed as a poor imitator of Seneca and as one who sacrificed dramatic effect for rhetorical commonplace. It is indeed difficult for us to realize what the men of his time, however besotted with passion for the 'rules,' saw in his dramas to admire so much. Almost the only element in his work which calls for special note is the manner in which he applied (as, for example, in *Bradamante*) the classical form to subject-matter derived from romantic sources, going so far, indeed, as to allow this subject-matter to break the rule of exact genres and to evolve a tragi-comic kind of drama.

A similar tale, only slightly more encouraging, is to be told of the efforts to establish regularized comedy during these years. The active and indomitable Pléiade, bent on reforming French literature, set out from the beginning to substitute for the medieval farces and moralities a more consciously artistic form of comic expression, based, of course, on the familiar Terence and Plautus. Already by 1500 the latter's *Amphitryon* had been translated by Jean Meschinot; the former's *Andria* appeared in French dialogue in 1537; two years later (1539) came *Le Grant Térence tant en rime qu'en prose*, a collection of renderings by diverse hands.

Then, as in Italy, arrived the time for the writing of plays, heavily influenced by the classic authors, but more or less independent—and almost wholly valueless. In 1552 was produced the *Eugène* of Étienne Jodelle, who thus takes rank as the creator, not only of the first regular tragedy in France, but also of her first Renaissance comedy, although in this satirical piece the traces of the long-established medieval farce are clearly to be seen beneath the framework ostensibly erected in an entirely different manner. Others soon followed: Jacques Grévin, whose *Jules César* was among the earliest of French tragedies, contributed to the comic stage his *Maubertine, ou la trésorière* (*Maubertine; or, The Paymistress*, 1558) and his *Esbahis* (1560), in both of which he attacked the older models and declared his determination to set up new. In his theatre, he asserts, the audience will not "see either farce or morality," but instead true comedy based on the Roman pattern. Jean de la Taille, author of an interesting critical tract entitled *De l'art de la tragédie* (printed as the preface to his *Saül le furieux*, 1573), brought forward *Les corrivaux* (*The Rivals*) in 1562, a comedy in prose; in 1567 appeared *Le brave* (*The Boaster*), by Antoine de Baïf, based mainly on Plautus' *Miles Gloriosus*.

   Already the classical inspiration was being confused and intermingled with that of Italy. Translations of the *commedia erudita*, such as de la Taille's version of Ariosto's *Il negromante* (1573), were creeping in among the renderings of the Roman plays. The double force of Roman comedy and of the Italian *commedia erudita* is well illustrated in the writings of that author who, before Corneille and Racine, was perhaps the most important playwright this Renaissance French theatre had to offer—Pierre de Larivey, an Italian by origin, but born in Troyes, who set himself the task of introducing the transalpine plays to the audiences of Paris and the provinces. Six plays were published in 1579 and another three in 1611—of which the best-known is *Les esprits* (*The Wits*), based on Lorenzino de Medici's *L'Aridosia*, and destined to be used later by Molière in *L'avare*, Regnard in *Le retour imprévu*, and Montfleury in *Le comédien poète*. The very fact that it was thus employed by later authors testifies to Larivey's skill in translating the Italian scenes into French vestments. His style is easy; he has a true sense of the theatre; and his feeling for gentle comedy is assured. In *Les esprits* and in its companions—*Le laquais* (*The Lacquey*; from Lodovico Dolce's *Il ragazzo*), *La veuve* (*The Widow*; from Niccolò Buonaparte's *La vedova*), *Le morfondu* (*The Abashed Lover*; from Antonfrancesco Grazzini's *La gelosia*), *Les jaloux* (*The Jealous Couple*; from Vicenzio Gabiani's *I gelosi*), *Les escolliers* (*The Students*; from Girolamo Razzi's *La Cecca*), *La constance* (*Constancy*; from the same author's *La Gostanza*), *Le fidelle* (*The Faithful Lover*; from Luigi Pasquaglio's *Il fedele*), and *Les tromperies* (*The Tricks*; from Niccolò Secchi's *Gli inganni*)—he provided the stage with livelier examples of comic material than had been produced by his predecessors. The Italian plays he used were perhaps not brilliant comedies, but at least they had more grace than the original French comedies composed before his time, and his influence is to be widely traced in the following years. In the sprightly *Les contens* (*The Merry Ones*, 1580?) of Odet de Turnèbe reminiscences of Italian comedy are present, but are becoming transformed more definitely into French shapes: its delightfully drawn Louise and her daughter Geneviève, its bombastic soldier, Rodomont, and its inimitable old Françoise are characters well worthy of remembrance. This play can be honestly praised, yet, when one considers how few companions it has, one realizes the essential poverty of this French classical stage of the sixteenth century. The foundations are being laid for something to come, but in itself this ambitious activity, this endeavour to establish a regular tragedy and comedy in Paris, failed as the kindred endeavours in Italy had failed.

The Public Theatres

To a large extent this was due to a similar cleavage between the 'intellectual' and the 'popular,' although we must also recognize that the political conditions in France, amid the heat of religious controversies and the ever imminent threat of civil war, were not propitious to the producing of a vital drama.

During the time when the young academicians were intently eager upon establishing a regularly composed literary drama plays of another sort were being performed before less precious audiences than normally attended the productions of classic tragedy and comedy. In 1402 the Confrérie de la Passion had been granted a royal privilege virtually establishing them as the sole acting group in Paris, their special mission being to present annually the great medieval mysteries, which they had been created to interpret. A hundred years later, however, conditions had changed: both Catholics and Protestants were looking askance at the Biblical plays, and as a consequence came a decree of 1548 sternly forbidding the setting upon the stage of religious dramas, but, instead, establishing the Confrérie as controllers of whatsoever secular forms of entertainment might be given in the city. From being an association of amateurs engaged in performing the mystery cycles, therefore, the Confrérie became a corporation of theatre managers, with the rare good fortune of having absolute monopoly in their own field. They hurriedly fitted up a theatre in the famous Hôtel de Bourgogne and prepared themselves to receive the high rent they were determined to exact from its occupants.

For years this theatre was leased by a variety of troupes—French players acting those farces and moralities so severely frowned upon by the intellectuals, English and Spanish actors appearing for brief spells with their characteristic repertoires, and, most importantly, Italian comedians—among them the outstanding Gelosi—introducing to Parisian audiences the style of improvisation already popular in their native cities. Only with the beginning of the seventeenth century did a relatively permanent troupe settle itself within its walls, when Valleran Le Conte, after performing at Court, established himself there with a company he named Les Comédiens du Roi (The King's Men), which included the then popular favourites among Parisian actors—"Gros-Guillaume" (Robert Guérin), the fat, farcical clown, "Gaultier-Garguille" (Hugues Guéru), the comic old man, and "Turlupin" (Henry Le Grand), the rascally servant. As the prominence of these performers indicates, the Comédiens du Roi were adapted for the interpretation, not of academic drama, but of essentially popular scenes rougher in fabric.

At the Hôtel de Bourgogne medieval traditions still lingered. Two methods of staging were used there, and both stemmed from the Middle Ages. The first, employed for the production of farces, was a simple adaptation of the open platform used by the popular actors of the late fifteenth century and carried on by those troupes (the most renowned of which was the company headed by Tabarin) permitted to give their out-of-doors performances at the fairs. The other, more complex, inter-estingly showed an adaptation of Italian scenic method to more ancient principles. In this the medieval device of the separate 'mansions,' with foreshortening of space, was translated into terms suitable for a small stage set at the end of an indoor hall and for the utilization of the perspec-tive wings evolved by the Italian architects. At first, no doubt, the rem-nants of the scenery used for the mystery plays were put to profaner use, and in all probability there was a time of transition when back-curtains, with openings for entrances and exits, served the players, but certainly by 1633, as the well-known *Mémoire* of the scene-directors Mahelot and Laurent amply testifies, the stage was being set for divers plays by means of side-wings representing the most widely separated localities, backed by a cloth indicating either a distant prospect or still another specific locality. Thus, for the earliest of the productions noted by Mahelot —that of Rotrou's *Les occasions perdues* (1633)—the setting shows, at the rear, a palace in a garden, with practicable windows, doors, and stairs, and, at the two sides, a fountain in a wood and a ruined building—places which in the play are supposed to lie far apart from one another.

Just how far this method of stage-setting was in use during the early years of the seventeenth century cannot now be determined with any surety, but the fact that, although it adopts the style of scene-painting habitual in Italy, its basis is unquestionably to be traced back to the medieval 'mansions' gives us assurance for believing that the forms so fully illustrated in the *Mémoire* are the final results of a continuous tra-dition from the time when, in 1548, the Hôtel de Bourgogne had turned from the religious to the secular drama.

The interest of this device rests in its attempt to find a compromise suited to the needs of the time. As we have seen, the Italian theatre failed in this respect, so that two sharply opposed principles clashed with one another and never found harmony. On the other hand, there was the set perspective scene, providing a background for plays which, theoretically at least, preserved the unity of place, and on the other was the open, gen-erally undecorated platform of the *commedia dell' arte*. The age, however, demanded more liberty than the severer classicists would allow, and hence the Court theatres lost themselves in the riotous display of the *inter-mezzi* while the *commedia dell' arte* troupes fumblingly experimented with crude scenic changes. In the type of decoration associated with the work of Mahelot we see an endeavour to find another solution for the prob-lem—the adoption of the architectural side-wings and backcloth fam-iliar in Italy, but the arrangement of these in such a manner as to put three, four, or even five different localities on the stage at one time.

Early Romanticism

The appearance of this staging method reminds us that the French public, fed with the restlessness of the Renaissance spirit, was by no means inclined to endure the dull classic immobility of the tragedies and comedies written by the academicians. They loved their free farces, and when they turned to more serious fare they demanded that the scene should be full of action and that the dramatic tales should be restrained by no artificial bonds.

As a result, the first French professional dramatist, Alexandre Hardy, found his *métier*, not in the realm of the unities, but in a land of romantic adventure where change of locality was frequent and no bars were set against the presentation, in full view of the audience, of scenes of violence. It has been said that "Hardy was irregular enough to have become a Shakespeare, had he had the genius," but irregularity in itself presents no highroad to mastery of the theatre, and, although perhaps we may find a trifle more of interest in his plays than in those of his predecessors, we recognize that the path he trod was not one likely to yield greatness. A man with no resources save what might come from the exercise of his pen, he early attached himself to a provincial troupe of comedians, and throughout several decades wrote feverishly in an attempt to keep body and soul together with the meagre sums then offered to a practising playwright. In all he penned over six hundred dramas (of which only forty-one are extant), some of them composed, rehearsed, and produced within a period of three days.

Obviously little could be expected from such conditions, and the expectation is not out of harmony with the reality. Most of his works are tragedies or tragi-comedies, and although they move their stories forward with commendable vigour, they lack all the qualities making for dramatic power. Their sole interest for us now is that they were the earliest professional plays written in France, and that they indicate a desire on the part of the public for a type of drama utterly at variance with that cultivated by Garnier and his companions. Love themes are frequently exploited here, and sensationalism is not absent; the classical elements are well concealed under romantic trappings.

From his work stems a long but not particularly inspiring line of similarly romantic plays—the Marquis de Racan's pastoral *Les bergeries* (*The Pastoral Comedy, c.* 1619), Théophile de Viau's tragic *Pyrame* (1621), the various dramas of Jean Mairet and of Jean de Rotrou, the last of whom was claimed by Voltaire to have been "le véritable fondateur du théâtre français."

Mention of Rotrou in this company reminds us, however, that the style which these men had cultivated—the drama of romance—was nearing the end of its not very glorious career, for he was one of the famous group of 'Five Poets' commissioned by Cardinal Richelieu to reform the French stage by leading it back to classicism. In taking this course Richelieu displayed true judgment. The age had passed the excitements of Renaissance passion, and the quality of romanticism was becoming tarnished. There might have been the hope of a virile, untrammelled French drama had Hardy come, not in the seventeenth century, but towards the middle of the century preceding: as it was, his example arrived too late; and although Mairet and Rotrou endeavoured to pursue the path he had trod, that path itself was becoming so entangled by the briers of undisciplined fancy that it could give no promise of reaching any worthy goal. A different way, as Richelieu (with surprisingly correct judgment) realized, had to be taken: instead of an irregular Shakespeare, France was to have a most regular Racine.

During all these years the French drama was handicapped, and the handicaps, not uninterestingly, throw light on what qualities are demanded if a theatre is to produce work of permanent worth. It took long before Paris became the prime centre of the world of the stage, and even when that time arrived the dramatic activities of the city were inhibited by cluttering restrictions. All through these years the theatre was looked upon with not a little disdain by those who esteemed themselves on account of their wealth or intellectual attainments; all through, the dramatists were wretchedly remunerated. Despite experimentation, the stage itself never succeeded in evolving a form truly suited to the needs of the age: the modification of the medieval simultaneous setting was, at best, a cumbersome device and unimaginative.

Looking at these facts, we may perhaps suggest that a vital theatre requires to have a geographical focus, relative freedom, the support of both the populace and the intellectuals, the provision of encouragement for the professional author, and, at the same time, a stage-form adapted to the time's demands. None of these prerequisites was satisfied in France until the reforms of Richelieu had established a fresh tradition.

4

THE SPANISH STAGE UNDER LOPE DE VEGA AND CALDERÓN

THE FAILURE of Italy and France is made the more pronounced when we contrast it with the success of Spain and the triumph of England.

Concerning the remoter developments of the stage in Spain not much need, or perhaps can, be said. Most of what must once have existed has now perished, and such fragments as remain have no more than an historical interest. Nothing is worthy of engaging our attention until we reach the rather crude 'Comedias' written by Bartolomé de Torres Naharro, confessedly under Italian inspiration, and the better-known works of Lope de Rueda, the latter of whom may be regarded, despite the more earthy quality of most of his writings, as the true founder of that style of play which was destined to become the characteristic expression of the Spanish genius—free from restraint, romantic in tone, lyrical in medium, and in texture weaving together the serious and the comic. At the same time attention should be called to the work of the Portuguese Gil Vicente, particularly to his trilogy of the *Barca do Inferno* (*The Boat of Hell*, 1517), the *Barca do Purgatorio* (*The Boat of Purgatory*, 1518), and the *Barca do Gloria* (*The Boat of Glory*, 1519)—devotional morality-type presentations that certainly had a considerable influence in the development of the Spanish religious plays.

When Lope de Rueda was composing his *comedias* professional playing was at its most primitive. "The whole apparatus of a manager," wrote Cervantes,

> was contained in a large sack, and consisted of four white shepherds' jackets, turned up with leather, gilt and stamped; four beards and four sets of hanging locks; and four shepherd's crooks more or less. . . . The theatre was composed of four benches, arranged in a square, with five or six boards laid across them, providing a platform a few feet from the ground. . . . The furniture of the theatre was an old blanket drawn aside by two cords, making what they call a tiring-room, behind which were the musicians, who sang old ballads without a guitar.

Before more could be expected of the drama this theatre had to reach nobler proportions.

The Theatres of Spain

Fortunately the audiences and the playwrights of Madrid and Seville had not long to wait, and when the theatre was set up on a firmer foundation it assumed a form at once more fitting and more flexible than that of the French or Italian stages.

The model was that of the *corrales*, or courtyards, where the earliest dramatic troupes had been accustomed to play. We must imagine for ourselves a square formed by the walls of houses, with windows and balconies providing box-accommodation for privileged spectators. In the yard there was standing-room for the less fortunate, while some tiers of benches at the side opposite the stage offered seats for the gentlemen, and above these a wooden gallery, nicknamed the *cazuela*, or stewpan, was apportioned to women of the poorer classes. Already in 1574 a troupe of Italian *commedia dell'arte* players at Madrid had fitted up such a theatre at the Corral de la Pacheca, while a few years later (1579 and 1582) the success attending the production of plays inspired the erection, in the manner of those improvised in the *corrales*, of two permanent houses, the Corral de la Cruz and the Corral del Príncipe.

For the actors there was a long, rather narrow platform, without any front curtain, but curtained at the back and at the sides in such a way that, when necessary, a kind of inner stage could be revealed. Above, a gallery extended over the acting-platform, and this was employed regularly for the representation of the upper window of a house or of a city wall. It is obvious that essentially this stage was built on the same principles as those operative in contemporary London, and the fact that the two were almost identical suggests that the dramatic strength developed in these two lands was at least partly dependent upon the harmony thus reached between the desires of the time and the opportunities offered to the actors. Here was a theatre where the players' rich clothes presented a continually moving panorama of kaleidoscopic colours before the spectators; here was a stage well adapted for the uttering of poetic lines; here the imagination of the audience was called actively into play. Only later, in the seventeenth century, did scenic effects and machinery begin to be put to frequent use, with the result that, as Lope de Vega observed, the true spirit of the drama started to evaporate: when "the managers avail themselves of machinery," he said, then "the poets avail themselves of the carpenters and the auditors of their eyes."

No doubt there were many shortcomings in these theatres and many abuses; no doubt managers, actors, and playwrights had justification for their occasional grumblings; but fundamentally the conditions were well adapted for the production of a vital drama. Spain was not dominated, as Italy was, by the supposedly classical rules of the academic theorists; artisans and aristocrats joined together in their love of the stage; the actors had free opportunity for movement; and the authors found that their flights of poetry could be spoken to good effect on the open stage for which they wrote. Once a fitting medium of expression was devised the way was open for a rich, flamboyant drama such as these men and women of the Renaissance were avid to receive.

Lope de Vega

After the first efforts of Lope de Rueda a number of other writers eagerly attempted to exploit the theatrical form, each—like the immediate predecessors of Shakespeare—contributing something to the creation of a national drama, so that when, in 1585, Lope Félix de Vega Carpio attached himself to the stage he found not only a well-established playhouse but a reasonably lively and inspiring literary tradition to give him aid.

Interestingly, the career of this author and the career of Shakespeare exhibit a strange parallel. Born in 1562, Lope was two years older than his English contemporary, but both came to attach themselves to the stage about the same time—towards the middle of the second-last decade of the sixteenth century. Separated by that vast gulf which is symbolized historically by the Spanish Armada, each ignorant of the other's very existence, their positions in their respective countries were virtually the same, and their writings, diverse though they are, display many features in common. Only in the length of their lives and in the extent of their contributions to the stage do they essentially differ; Shakespeare, dying at the age of fifty-two, left thirty-seven dramas behind him; Lope lived to be seventy-three and left behind him, apart from several hundred miscellaneous entertainments, an incalculable number of plays. Although the greater proportion of these has vanished, even so over 470 of his dramas are still extant. No poet has ever displayed greater ease and fertility.

Nor are these works merely imitative. Much in Lope's plays may be inspired by the efforts of his predecessors, but the greater part was his own, and to him the Spanish theatre owes many of its most characteristic features. His concept of tragic action set its impress on the work of his successors; his style of tragi-comedy was that accepted by others; it was he who developed the thoroughly representative genre of *comedias de capa y espada*—the cloak-and-sword drama—tending sometimes towards romantic incident, sometimes towards the style of the comedy of manners; recently we have become aware of his surprising invention of what has been acclaimed as a true proletarian theatre; even particular stage characters, such as the *gracicso*, or humorous clown, although adumbrated before, were virtually of his creation.

In writing his plays Lope set above all other things the desire to capture the attention of his auditors, and one imagines that if Shakespeare had found time to put down his critical precepts in essay form they would have been expressed very similarly to the way the Spanish dramatist expounds his aims in the *Arte nuevo de hacer comedias en este tiempo* (*The New*

Art of Writing Plays in this Age, 1609). The tone of this short discourse is clear and uncompromising—I know all the rules, says Lope, but

> when I have to write a comedy I lock in the precepts with six keys, I banish Terence and Plautus from my study . . . and I write in accordance with that art which they devised who aspired to the applause of the crowd.

He was intent on pleasing first, and the theatre was his testing-place. He might have wished to write more 'correct' dramas, but in practice he was prepared to give his audience what obviously it wanted.

His plays are lyrical in tone, for the Spanish audiences of the 'Golden Age,' like those in contemporary England, loved to listen to words instinct with passion and rich in melody. There is realism in Lope's work, but it is realism inspired and deepened by the imagination—not the dull, pale, miserable thing which creeps pitifully into many a modern scene. Here is true theatre—bold, emotional, built on terms appropriate to the theatre's conventionalism, and made powerful by strong contrasts.

For the most part Lope's dramas defy exact classification. Nearly all include elements high and low, tragic and comic, some veering more in the one direction, some more in the other. Many of the plots are based on history, but the historical events are rendered theatrical; many are derived from romances, but the romantic matter is made vital by effective portraiture. All we can say is that within the course of his work we find certain dramas which we may call tragedies, because in them the greatest stress is laid on dark actions conditioned by the social codes then universally maintained by the aristocracy; that we find others in which the dark and the light provide a tragi-comic impression; that still others emphasize the interests of the peasantry or the gallantries of youth or the clowneries of the ignorant. At moments we are in the presence of a *Twelfth Night*, at moments we are conversing with Bottom, at moments we approach the mood of a *Romeo and Juliet*. The ranges of Shakespeare and Lope are not far different from each other: what is lacking in the latter is the intensity of a *Hamlet* and the wonder of a *Tempest*. With Lope we move from the spirit of *Love's Labour's Lost* through *Much Ado about Nothing* to *All's Well that Ends Well*; we have much of the atmosphere of the histories, too; but of the tragic temper and the metaphysical tone there is but little in his plays.

The darker side of his work is well illustrated by *El castigo sin venganza* (*Punishment without Revenge*; printed 1635), which tells the story of a Duke of Ferrara, whose illegitimate and beloved son, Federico, falls in love with the young Duchess. On discovering this liaison the Duke's mind is cast into a torment of conflicting passions, but at last he devises a scheme whereby vengeance—and, more important, the clearing of his honour —will be secured without his own hands being dipped in blood. In a darkened room he binds up his wife, casts a cloth over her, and tells Federico that a trapped traitor is seated there. The son stabs his stepmother-mistress, and is himself slain by men outside the palace when the Duke informs them that the Duchess has been murdered. Basically the plot is that of a sensational melodrama, but Lope—although he wants the power to conjure forth the spirit of tragedy—contrives by his bold delineation of consuming emotion and by the sombre passion of his verse to give the theme enduring interest. With sympathetic understanding is revealed the course of the illicit intrigue; with flashing grandeur the twisted mentality of the Duke is bravely illuminated.

More commonly, however, the potentially tragic atmosphere in such plays is converted, generally by means of surprising intrigue, into a tragi-comic sentiment. Jealousy and love, for example, suggest that the plot of *Lo cierto por lo dudoso* (*A Certainty for a Doubt*; printed 1625) must end in disaster. The King, Don Pedro, is consumed with jealousy of his brother, Don Enrique, who is the accepted lover of Doña Juana; in turn, Juana's lady-in-waiting, Doña Inés, devoted to Don Enrique, strives to get him for her own. The action threatens royal displeasure, decrees of banishment, and death, yet in the end, by a rather conventional trick, Enrique and Juana are married, while the King casts off his earlier humour and accepts the event:

> What is done
> Admits no remedy. I pardon him,
> And I confirm the match.

So far as the movement of the dramatic story is concerned, there is little here of value, but once more the play takes life from the intimate and penetrating relations of human character presented in its various scenes. On the one hand, there are the little wisps of doubt in the faithful Juana's mind when she weighs the passion of Don Enrique against the joy of being a queen; on the other, there is the contorted jealousy of the King, who is led to lay suit to Juana only because he knows her the object of his brother's attentions. As a whole, the tragi-comedy has but small intrinsic interest, yet its action is carried on with vigour, and life pulsates beneath the inanimate mask. Much the same judgment may be passed on such plays as *Los embustes de Celauro* (*Celauro's Machinations, c.* 1600), where a villainous Iago is foiled in his plans to wreck connubial happiness, and *El halcón de Federico* (*The Falcon of Federico*; printed 1620), based on the same story of Boccaccio's on which is founded Tennyson's *The Falcon*.

Of particular interest, because of its theme, among these tragi-comedies is *Castelvines y Monteses* (*The Castelvines and the Monteses, c.* 1608), Lope's treatment of the story of Romeo and Juliet, a strange mixture of lyrical ecstasy and clownish merriment. The drama opens with the ball at which Roselo Montes first meets his Julia, but the action is complicated by the fact that Julia is also beloved by her cousin Otavio, and that, after giving Roselo some token of her affection, she is inclined cautiously to withdraw her words, only reluctantly being persuaded by his protestations:

> *ROSELO:* I'd have thee all mine own sweet star,
>   In secret, if thou wilt: a close friendship
>   With a holy friar I have, and he, I know,
>   Will aid us; but should his conscience scruples hold,
>   I'll find some subtle means of cure.
> *JULIA:* My very soul doth tremble at thy words.
> *ROSELO:* What fears my dearest Julia?
> *JULIA:* More than a thousand ills.
> *ROSELO:* They are but fancied ills; once wed,
>   All rivalry would cease, all hatred should be dead.
>   Love beckons by this safe and secret road
>   To hold our houses free from hate,
>   And through our love shall smile everlasting peace. . . .
> *JULIA:* Look that thou no promise dost forget.
> *ROSELO:* Nay, this I swear; forgetting such,
>   May heaven desert me at my need.
> *JULIA:* Swear not, for I have read
>   That ready swearers have
>   Scant credit with the world or God.
> *ROSELO:* What shall I say, sweet maid?
> *JULIA:* Say that I am thy heart's desire.

Immediately after their secret wedding a broil springs up between the two houses, in the midst of which Otavio is slain by Roselo, who is forthwith banished. During his journey to Ferrara the latter hears that Julia has promised to marry Count Paris, while she, forced by her father to give consent, finds her only remedy in a philtre concocted by the friar and supposed by Julia herself to be a deadly poison. In the vault she wakens and there meets Roselo; both proceed in disguise to her father's house, where they are engaged as servants. Shortly after Julia calls out to her father from an upper room, persuades him that the voice he hears is that of an angel, and acquaints him with the truth of the marriage: the result is that when Roselo, discovered, is about to be executed for his breaking the order of banishment the old father pleads for him, Julia reveals herself, and all ends happily.

Perhaps the basic theme of *Romeo and Juliet* is more suited for romantic tragi-comic than for tragic treatment, and in so far Lope's handling of the story is more harmonious with the events than is that of Shakespeare; yet, even granting this, we must recognize how much he has sacrificed for the sake of plot intrigue and stage thrill. There is nothing here that corresponds to the homely garrulousness of the Nurse or to the exquisitely youthful fancies of the debonair Mercutio; all is on a level—the level of intrigue and of sensational events.

Something worthier of esteem enters into *La estrella de Sevilla* (*The Star of Seville,* c. 1615)—although in dealing with this play one must draw attention to the fact that recent study tends to deny it to Lope. The basic theme concerns the action of a Spanish knight who, bidden by his monarch, slays a man who is not only his friend, but also the brother of the girl whom he is on the point of marrying. Although the King attempts to protect him after this deed has been committed, the judges refuse to allow the law to be tampered with by arbitrary practice, and at length the hero escapes death only when his royal master makes full confession. The important element is the presentation of the final scenes of the play. We are living here in a world wherein the courtiers are all but slaves of their king, wherein they will not, even to escape execution, betray the secrets of their lords, yet beyond the walls of the palace another world is suggestively revealed. Even the King himself must bow to a force greater than his own—the force of justice, incorruptible and supreme.

The existence of this world gives to certain of Lope's plays a peculiar intensity. Among these may be singled out *El mejor alcalde el Rey* (*The King the Best Alcalde*; printed 1635) and *Fuente Ovejuna* (*The Sheep Well*, *c.* 1614). The plots of both are worthy of careful scrutiny. At the opening of the first drama Sancho soliloquizes on his pastoral love of Elvira, daughter of the farmer Nuño. In a delightfully playful scene he obtains Nuño's blessing, provided that his lord, Don Tello, will promise to give him a gift or offer him constant employment. All is rustic joy and jollity. The next scene shows Don Tello just returned from hunting; he is pleased with the world and, on hearing Sancho's request, gladly gives him a marriage gift of twenty cows and a hundred sheep. When, however, he graces the betrothal with his presence he is consumed with passion for Elvira, and, with the aid of his minion Celio, raids Nuño's house and carries her off. In the second act Don Tello is shown trying to persuade the girl to become his mistress; Sancho and Nuño come and seek his aid, but are driven out by his servants. They have, however, one other course open to them; Sancho goes to the Court of the King and solicits his justice, eventually obtaining from him an order for Elvira's release—only to find that Don Tello treats it with contumely. On hearing his news the King decides to go in person to Galicia:

> *KING:* Though all the world should question who I am,
>   You are to say a noble of Castile,
>   And lay your hand upon your mouth like this—
>   Take heed and mark me well—and never be
>   Without these first two fingers on your lips. . . .
> *SANCHO:* Consider, Sire, a peasant's humble honour
>   Touches you not so near. Despatch some judge,
>   Some just Alcalde to Galicia
>   To do your will.
> *KING:*   The King the greatest Alcalde!

At the very time when Don Tello is preparing to force Elvira to his will the monarch arrives at Nuño's house: kindly he greets the farmers, the labourers, the shepherds, and then proceeds to Tello's palace, announces himself, condemns the seducer to death, but decrees that first he shall marry Elvira in order that she, as an honest woman, may wed Sancho with a dower of half his "lands and hoarded revenues."

Lope's sympathetic treatment of the peasantry is even more pronounced in *Fuente Ovejuna*, in which he unconsciously develops a dramatic form later to be associated with experiments in the 'proletarian' theatre. Essentially the hero of this play is, not one person, but a crowd of peasants in the village of Fuente Ovejuna. The Commander (Fernán Gómez de Guzmán) is a libertine, who, in seeking to seduce Laurencia, is threatened and foiled by the baseborn Frondoso. Enraged, he seizes the wretched youth, beats Laurencia's father, and carries off this maid. The villagers thereupon gather to take council:

> *ESTEBAN:* Is the Town Board assembled?
>
> *BARRILDO:* Not a person can be seen.
>
> *ESTEBAN:* Bravely we face danger!
>
> *BARRILDO:* All the farms had warning.
>
> *ESTEBAN:* Frondoso is a prisoner in the tower, and my daughter Laurencia in such plight that she is lost save for the direct interposition of heaven.   [*JUAN ROJO enters with the SECOND REGIDOR.*
>
> *JUAN ROJO:* Who complains aloud when silence is salvation? Peace, in God's name, peace!
>
> *ESTEBAN:* I will shout to the clouds till they re-echo my complaints while men marvel at my silence.   [*Enter MENGO and PEASANTS.*
>
> *MENGO:* We came to attend the meeting.
>
> *ESTEBAN:* Farmers of this village, an old man whose grey beard is bathed in tears inquires what rites, what obsequies, we poor peasants, assembled here, shall prepare for our ravished homes, bereft of honour? And if life be honour, how shall we fare since there breathes not one among us whom this savage has not offended? Speak! Who but has been wounded deeply, poisoned in respect? Lament now, yes, cry out! Well? If all be ill, how then say well? Well, there is work for men to do.

The peasants are inclined to caution, when Laurencia enters, her hair dishevelled, after having been ravished by the Commander, and in a stirring speech rouses them to action:

> My face is bruised and bloody in this court of honest men. Some of you are fathers, some have daughters. Do your hearts sink within you, supine and cowardly crew? You are sheep, sheep! Oh, well-named, Village of Fuente Ovejuna, the Sheep Well! Sheep, sheep, sheep! Give me iron, for senseless stones can wield none, nor images, nor pillars—jasper though they be—nor dumb living things that lack the tiger's heart that follows him who steals its young, rending the hunter limb from limb upon the very margin of the raging sea, seeking the pity of the angry waves.
>
> > But you are rabbits, farmers,
> > Infidels in Spain,
> > Your wives strut before you
> > With the cock upon their train!

MEDIEVAL DEVILS' MASKS
Collection in the Ferdinandeum, Innsbruck.
Photo Ferdinandeum

BICCI DI LORENZO: MIRACLES OF ST NICHOLAS AT
BARI. THE THREE PICKLED BOYS
By courtesy of the Metropolitan Museum of Art, New York

BICCI DI LORENZO: MIRACLES OF ST NICHOLAS AT
BARI. THE THREE GOLDEN BALLS
By courtesy of the Metropolitan Museum of Art, New York

Tuck your knitting in your belts,
Strip off your manly swords,
For, God living, I swear
That your women dare
Pluck these fearsome despots,
Beard the traitors there!
No spinning for our girls;
Heave stones and do not blench.
Can you smile, men?
Will you fight?

The crowd storms the palace, and the Commander is slain by Esteban. Knowing that this crime cannot remain unavenged, the villagers, in a highly interesting scene, rehearse what they will do when the officers of justice arrive, and all agree that, even under torture, they will assert that the Commander was killed by the entire populace, by Fuente Ovejuna itself. This is followed by another scene, in which Frondoso and Laurencia listen to the examination of their fellows; the royal judge, in another chamber, takes them one by one:

JUDGE [within]: Old man, I seek only the truth. Speak!
FRONDOSO: An old man tortured?
LAURENCIA: What barbarity!
ESTEBAN [within]: Ease me a little.
JUDGE [within]: Ease him. Who killed Fernando?
ESTEBAN [within]: Fuente Ovejuna.
LAURENCIA: Good, Father! Glory and praise!
FRONDOSO: Praise God he had the strength!
JUDGE [within]: Take that boy there. Speak, you pup, for you know! Who was it? He says nothing. Put on the pressure there.
BOY [within]: Judge, Fuente Ovejuna.
JUDGE [within]: Take that boy there. Speak, you pup, for you know! Who killed the Commander?
FRONDOSO: They torture the child, and he replies like this?
LAURENCIA: There is courage in the village.
FRONDOSO: Courage and heart.
JUDGE [within]: Put that woman in the chair. Give her a turn for her good.
LAURENCIA: I can't endure it.
JUDGE [within]: Peasants, be obstinate and this instrument brings death. So prepare! Who killed the Commander?
PASCUALA [within]: Judge, Fuente Ovejuna.
JUDGE [within]: Have no mercy.
FRONDOSO: I cannot think: my mind is blank!
LAURENCIA: Frondoso, Pascuala will not tell them.
FRONDOSO: The very children hold their peace!
JUDGE [within]: They thrive upon it. More! More!
PASCUALA [within]: Oh, God in heaven!
JUDGE [within]: Again, and answer me! Is she deaf?
PASCUALA [within]: I say Fuente Ovejuna.
JUDGE [within]: Seize that plump lad, half undressed already.

LAURENCIA: It must be Mengo! Poor Mengo!
FRONDOSO: He can never hold out.
MENGO [*within*]: Oh, oh, oh!
JUDGE [*within*]: Let him have it.
MENGO[*within*]: Oh!
JUDGE [*within*]: Prod his memory.
MENGO [*within*]: Oh, oh!
JUDGE [*within*]: Who slew the Commander, slave?
MENGO [*within*]: Oh, oh! I can't get it out! I'll tell you—
JUDGE [*within*]: Loosen that hand.
FRONDOSO: We are lost!
JUDGE [*within*]: Let him have it on the back!
MENGO [*within*]: No, for I'll give up everything!
JUDGE [*within*]: Who killed him?
MENGO [*within*]: Judge, Fuente Ovejuna.

Hardly another scene in Renaissance drama is more surprising than this, and the surprise is the greater when we remember that it comes, not from an England where already democratic sentiment was growing in power, but from proud, aristocratic Spain.

Although so far little attention seems to have been paid to another of Lope's plays, *La bella mal maridada* (*Marriages of Convenience*; printed 1609), it would seem worthy of being associated with the dramas just discussed, since in effect it is the very first theatrical work on record which deals, almost in the style of an eighteenth-century *drame*, with the theme of love and money. Strangely modern is its subject. Lucrecia, impelled partly by poverty and partly by her mother's ambitions, finds herself forced to abandon Don Juan, the man she loves, for a Milanese millionaire. He dies after a few years and leaves her his wealth provided that she marries his nephew, a weak, malformed youth, and only fortunate circumstances enable her to escape from an even more disastrous second marriage and to unite herself to the man whose image has been in her mind all these years. Hardly any play of this period more startlingly attests to Lope's originality: some of its scenes might have been written in 1900. Almost equally extraordinary is the strangely philosophic *El villano en su rincón* (*The Peasant in his Acres*; printed 1617), which, set in an idealized France, presents as hero a rich peasant Juan Labrador who, though loyal to his king, prides himself on being a king in his own acres. When he is called to Court it is evident that instead of depending on the monarch, it is the monarch who depends on him. Still another surprise comes in *Las famosas asturianas* (*The Famous Asturian Women*; printed 1623), where nearly all the dialogue is cast in an out-of-date form of speech—obviously in an effort at a kind of historical realism.

Among the many plays written by Lope de Vega, works of another kind abound—comedies of love and gallantry, charmingly light essays in the display of manners. Of these *El perro del hortelano* (*The Gardener's*

Dog, c. 1615) may be taken as an example. The plot of this play, artificial, delicate, and gracious, toys with the characters as a juggler with his balls. Teodoro, the handsome secretary to Diana, Countess of Belflor, makes love to Marcella, and the Countess, led, like numbers of Lope's men and women, to love through jealousy, finds him attractive. She first pretends to aid his suit of Marcella, then—on the ground that their embracements are too public—locks the maid in her room. Love combats in her breast with the sense of honour, and not the least sign of Lope's originality lies in the solution he finds. Teodoro claims to a rival that he is a Count's son: both he and Diana know this to be false, but she is willing to let the lie remain, since this will allow her to marry him. If others think he is noble all is well. We are far on the way here towards the world of Pirandello.

Lope's skill is nowhere more clearly displayed. Nothing could be better, theatrically, than the opening scene, a room in the Countess's palace, at night. Teodoro and Tristan cross the stage at a run:

TEODORO: Quick, Tristan! Run!
TRISTAN: Who's there?
TEODORO: Discovered!
TRISTAN: Down quickly!

As they vanish Diana enters:

DIANA: Stay, sir, stay! Such effrontery before my door? Turn, stop, stay! Up, my people! Not a man astir in the house? I have seen a solid shade, no wisp of dreams. Hello! Does the Palace sleep?

[*Enter FABIO*

FABIO: My lady calls—
DIANA: You are as cool by my troth as I hot by my call. Run, fool, thou quintessence of folly, and bring me the scoundrel's name who this moment passed my door.
FABIO: I see no scoundrel, lady.
DIANA: Reply by speed. Fly quickly!
FABIO: I vanish.
DIANA: His name on your life!
FABIO: In this wicked world? . . . Ah me!

[*Exit. Enter OTTAVIO, the majordomo.*

OTTAVIO: Though I heard your voice, I could not believe that at this hour your Excellency called so loudly.
DIANA: O thou Flicker of the Faltering Flare, at what hour crept you to sleep? You rouse from a soft bed right smartly. There are men in my house making the dark hours hideous even at the very portal of my chamber! Can such insolence be, Ottavio? And when I call, like a faithless squire you nod in my extremity.
OTTAVIO: Though I heard your voice, I could not believe that at this hour your Excellency called so loudly.
DIANA: No, I did not call. Back to bed! To dream! Repose!

Again and again in Lope's comedies the seeming is contrasted with the real, the belief with the actuality. His lovers in *El premio del bien hablar* (*The Prize for Good Speech*, 1625) are wrapped in a maze of doubts and suppositions; true love triumphs over conventional manners in the gay *Las Bizarrías de Belisa* (*Belisa's Tricks*, 1634), in which the heroine, Belisa, gifted with teeming fancy and independence of spirit, wins Don Juan de Cardona from her rival, Lucinda; there is even, as in Pirandello, the contrast between sanity and madness: in *La boba para los otros y discreta para sí* (*There's Method in't, c.* 1630) a witty Diana pretends to be a simpleton in order to gain her own ends, while in *Los locos de Valencia* (*The Lunatics of Valencia, c.* 1600) there are real madmen, pretended madmen, and some folk deemed mad.

Love themes are dominant in these plays, and it is interesting to observe that the social codes that form the basis of so many Spanish tragedies are habitually turned here into the cause of merriment. Jealousy becomes a thing of laughter, and ladies indulge in escapades which, in other dramas, would have been deemed ample cause for their public dishonouring, if not for their death. *Los melindres de Belisa* (*Belisa's Caprices*; printed 1617), also known as *La dama melindrosa* (*The Capricious Lady*), shows a pair of lovers taking menial positions in a rich household and occasioning much disturbance thereby. A jealous lover in *¡Si no vieran las mujeres!* (*If Women didn't see!, c.* 1631) is forced to confess that he really has less interest in the code of honour than in the love of his mistress, and in *El mayor imposible* (*The Greatest Impossibility*, 1615) the title of the play refers to what is seen to be the utmost in folly—the belief that any power on earth can constrain a woman if her heart is set upon a man.

With infinite ease Lope plays variations on such themes, continually startling us by the introduction of some unexpected reflection or some quick turn in the development of what seems to be a conventional situation. In other comedies, such as *El acero de Madrid* (*Madrid Steel*; written 1603), heroines restrained by dragon-like chaperones find means of meeting their lovers: in this particular play Belisa, infatuated with Lisandro, escapes the clutches of Teodora by getting Lisandro's servant Beltran to pose as a doctor and to prescribe for her residence in Madrid, where she must drink a medicine compounded of water strongly impregnated with iron ("agua de acero") and take long walks in the city, when, of course, she has ample opportunity for meeting her sweetheart. *Amar sin saber a quien* (*Loving without knowing Whom*; printed 1630), with its complex story of Don Juan and Leonarda, typically presents Lope's skill in handling stage intrigue; the character of Fenisa in *La discreta enamorada* (*The Clever Girl*; written *c.* 1606) adds to the same kind of intrigue something of character-portrayal; while the similarly named but vastly different heroine of *El anzuelo de Fenisa* (*Fenisa's Bait*; printed 1617) demonstrates that when he desired Lope could depict men and women with sure and subtle touches.

In the midst of these gay, artificial works we are suddenly encountered by that peculiar play *La Dorotea* (printed 1632), in which Lope, evidently incorporating into it much of his own life's story, almost anticipates Musset in his delicate analysis of the unpredictable movements of the human heart. This story of Dorotea, a married woman attached to the poet Fernando, yet faithless both to lover and husband—this story of the poet-devotee who tries to escape from his infatuation, now by fleeing to another city, now by joining the Armada in its expedition against England—shows a power of psychological observation and spiritual subtlety well-nigh unique in its time.

A final judgment on his work is difficult to arrive at. There can be no doubt but that he is a dramatist of amazing invention and extraordinary fecundity. This is a teeming world he sets before us, widely diversified and rich in colour. Yet he exhibits many defects. No man could write as much as he did and hope that his work might possess that final perfection which is the mark of highest genius. Only too often his plots betray the haste of their planning, and his scenes present rather an inspiring suggestion of what might have been had he had more time to develop lines and characters. Perhaps that is why his plays have had a rather peculiar fate outside of Spain. Productions of his work have been rare, yet his influence has been strong on many another dramatist. The Parisian stage did not wish to present his plays as they stood, although Rotrou and Molière owed much to his writings: on the English stage he is virtually unknown, but there too his scenes peer through numberless dramas from the time of Fletcher onward. In approaching Shakespeare men have felt the harmony between content, conception, and execution; with Lope they have rather experienced a wonder at the inventive powers displayed and an accompanying disappointment with the manner in which the dramatic material has been handled.

On the other hand, there is a chance that after so many years of neglect by the public abroad he may now be coming to his own. Recent study has revealed afresh the almost incredible diversity of his work, and dramas —such as *Fuente Ovejuna*—which had remained known only to a few specialists are now being translated and presented in their original forms. All too few are to be found in English dress, but the way is being opened, and it is possible that the coming years will make him more than he has been hitherto—a name attached to works unknown.

Calderón

Lope's immediate successor, Pedro Calderón de la Barca, has had more favourable fortunes, both because his Court position offered him financial security and because, not having to invent so much as the earlier dramatist and not attempting to emulate his fertility, he had more time to polish and refine his work. Even so, however, his output of plays was larger than that of most theatrical authors: in 1680 his own list included 111 dramas, together with 70 *autos* (plays on religious themes), and to these a fair number of other writings for the stage must be added.

In turning from Lope's theatre to his we are struck primarily by its greater elevation of tone and by what might almost be styled its stiffness. Lope reflects the severe code of behaviour which dominated Spanish life in these decades, but there is about him a breezy naturalness which constantly brings the air of nature into his palace interiors. With Calderón all is mannerism; his nature is nature methodized into courtly convention; he is orientating himself, we feel, towards the aristocrats rather than towards a general audience. The result is that, while unquestionably we feel ourselves more in the presence of a finished artist, the glow of vitality that comes from a perusal of Lope's plays is absent. Despite the often misplaced enthusiasm of the romantics for his writings, Calderón is seen as a lesser genius than Lope. It has been said that "Lope de Vega incarnated the genius of a nation; Calderón expresses the genius of an age"—but maybe the truth might be rephrased: Calderón expresses the genius of a nation at a particular epoch in its development, while in Lope's work common humanity, timeless and unchangeable, peers through the contemporary masks of his characters.

Symbolic of this difference between the two men is the fact that, while Lope's plays are based mainly on the theme of love, Calderón's frequently concentrate on a peculiar and restricted concept of honour. The first makes universal appeal; the second is based entirely upon the social conventions operative in Calderón's own time. When Lope's peasants in *Fuente Ovejuna* speak of honour their words are those of men; when Calderón's characters talk of honour their accents are narrowly Castilian.

At the same time, we cannot escape from the respective fortunes of these two playwrights: Calderón has achieved an international reputation, while Lope remains largely unknown outside of Spain. Perhaps there is a lesson for us here. Lope has ebullience, vigour, keenness of eye, but his writing is careless, and it is this carelessness that has formed a barrier to his fuller appreciation. The theatre needs the qualities he brought to it, but on these alone it cannot subsist. Its conventional nature cries out continually for form and precision. Had Shakespeare been the utterly careless artist so many have thought him we should not now be esteeming his plays so highly. Lope fails because his form is deficient; Calderón's reputation is founded on his skill as a craftsman. Although deficient in the eager understanding of theatrical values so patent in all Lope's plays, he has been able by his sense of balanced form and by his delicate lyricism to conceal weaknesses left manifest by his fellow-dramatist.

Beyond this there is a further distinction to be made between the two authors. Both Lope and Calderón lay great stress on the stories they have to tell, and this is entirely right: but, whereas the former is content, in the main, with plot and character, Calderón introduces what might be called a 'philosophical' note. Where the drama rests on plot and character it can never attain greatness: only when these elements are illuminated by an informing purpose can the true heights be reached.

The 'philosophical' quality in Calderón is well exemplified in the success of his *autos*, a peculiarly characteristic kind of play that flourished in Spain and found in him its greatest exponent. While the word *auto* (from the Latin *actus*) has a wide interpretation, in application to this dramatist it generally bears a particular significance and refers to the *autos sacramentales* presented on Corpus Christi Day in honour of the Mystery of the Blessed Eucharist. These plays were allegorical; their characters, like the characters of the moralities, were usually abstractions.

The occasion of their performance was a religious procession. In the year 1654 a Dutch visitor to Madrid left a detailed account of the manner of their production. The festival started with a great parade, in which the king, his nobles, the common people, and grotesque statues of giants, in strange array, accompanied the sacrament as it was carried through the streets. After an intermission the *autos* were played, the more privileged spectators seated in balconies, the others standing on the ground below.

To gain some idea of the way in which these shows were produced we cannot do better than turn to George Ticknor's account of *El divino Orfeo* (*The Divine Orpheus*, 1663):

> It opens with the entrance of a huge black car, in the shape of a boat, which is drawn along the street toward the stage where the auto is to be acted, and contains the Prince of Darkness, set forth as a pirate, and Envy, as his steersman; both supposed to be thus navigating through a portion of chaos. They hear at a distance sweet music, which proceeds from another car, advancing from the opposite quarter in the form of a celestial globe, covered with the signs of the planets and constellations, and containing Orpheus, who represents allegorically the Creator of all things. This is followed by a third car, setting forth the terrestrial globe, within which are the Seven Days of the Week, and Human Nature, all asleep. These cars open, so that the personages they contain can come upon the stage and retire back again, as if behind the scenes, at their pleasure—the machines themselves constituting, in this as in all such representations, an important part of the scenic arrangements of the exhibition. . . .
>
> On their arrival at the stage, the Divine Orpheus, with lyric poetry and music, begins the work of creation, using always language borrowed from Scripture; and at the suitable moment, as he advances, each Day presents itself, roused from its ancient sleep, and clothed with symbols indicating the nature of the work that has been accomplished; after which Human Nature is, in the same way, summoned forth, and appears in the form of a beautiful woman, who is the Eurydice of the fable. Pleasure dwells with her in Paradise; and, in her exuberant happiness, she sings a hymn in honour of her Creator, founded on the hundred and thirty-sixth Psalm. . . .
>
> The temptation and fall succeed; and then the graceful Days, who had before always accompanied Human Nature and scattered gladness in her path, disappear one by one, and leave her to her trials and her sins. She is overwhelmed with remorse, and endeavouring to escape from the consequences of her guilt, is conveyed by the bark of Lethe to the realms of the

Prince of Darkness, who, from his first appearance on the scene, has been labouring, with his coadjutor Envy, for this very triumph. But his triumph is short. The Divine Orpheus, who has for some time represented the character of our Saviour, comes upon the stage, weeping over the fall, and sings a song of love and grief to the accompaniment of a harp made partly in the form of a cross; after which, rousing himself in his omnipotence, he enters the realms of darkness, amidst thunders and earthquakes; overcomes all opposition; rescues Human Nature from perdition; places her, with the seven redeemed Days of the Week, on a fourth car, in the form of a ship, so ornamented as to represent the Christian Church and the mystery of the Eucharist; and then, as the gorgeous machine sweeps away, the exhibition ends with the shouts of the actors in the drama, accompanied by the answering shouts of the spectators on their knees wishing the good ship a good voyage and a happy arrival at her destined port.

With this may be compared *El gran teatro del mundo* (*The Great Theatre of the World, c.* 1635) in which the Author (God), in a gorgeous starry cloak, addresses the World He has created, and summons representatives of humanity—the rich and the poor, the king and the slave, the beautiful and the learned. Some of the characters object to their parts, but the Author stills their complaints; these actors must play their rôles without rehearsal, even without knowing the precise times of their entrances and exits. Appropriate garments and properties are furnished for all, and the World utters a kind of prologue:

> Since the stage is now supplied
> With its motley company,
> For I there a monarch see
> With his kingdoms broad and wide
> And a beauty that with pride
> Of her charms all senses awes,
> Great men having great applause,
> Clownish hinds and beggars bare,
> Or who in still cloisters fare,
> All brought forward for this cause
> That the persons they may play
> Of this present comedy,
> To whom I a stage supply,
> Fit adornments and array,
> Robes or rags, as suit it may,
> Oh look forth, the pageant see,
> Divine Author, which to Thee
> Mortals play; this earthly ball
> Let unfold, for there of all
> That is done, the scene must be.

Two great globes now open simultaneously, the one with a throne for the Author, the other with a stage, at each end of which are doors, painted respectively with representations of a cradle and a coffin. The Author seats Himself, the Law of Grace makes ready to act as prompter, and a morality play is presented. As the characters utter their lines the Law of Grace keeps up a kind of refrain. Beauty and Discretion part company; the Beggar complains of his lot, while the Rich Man boasts:

> *RICH MAN:* How shall I make ostentation
> Best of all my wealth?
> *BEGGAR:* My woe
> How shall I best endure?
> *LAW OF GRACE: Doing well; for God is God.*
> *RICH MAN:* Oh, how that voice wearies me!
> *BEGGAR:* Oh, how that voice me consoles!

"What do *I* need in the world?" inquires the King, and to him comes the voice of the Law of Grace: "*To do well; for God is God.*"

So they play their parts, while one after another is summoned towards the door of death. At last the stage is left empty save for the World, who now seeks to claim from each of the actors the properties lent for the purposes of the action. The King is miserably stripped of crown and rich array—"for naked they must go, who naked came"; Beauty loses her loveliness, the Labourer gives up his spade—and all the actors prepare to pass in to a great banquet beyond:

> *DISCRETION:* All of us are equal now,
> Having laid aside our garments;
> For in this poor winding-sheet
> No distinction more remaineth.
> *RICH MAN:* Do you go before me, villain?
> *LABOURER:* Leave this foolish dream of greatness;
> For, once dead, thou art the shadow
> Of the sun which thou wast lately.
> *RICH MAN:* Some strange fear in me the prospect
> Of the Author's presence wakens.
> *BEGGAR:* Author of the earth and heaven,
> All Thy company, the players,
> Who that briefest comedy
> Played of human life so lately,
> Are arrived, of that they promise
> Mindful, of that noble banquet.
> Let the curtains be drawn back,
> And Thy glorious seat unveiled.

Closely associated with the *autos* are Calderón's religious dramas, mostly concerned with miracles of the saints. These include *La devoción de la cruz* (*The Devotion of the Cross, c.* 1633)—a tale of the saving of a sinner because of his worshipping of whatever is cruciform; *El purgatorio de San Patricio* (*The Purgatory of St Patrick*, 1635)—in which also a sinner reaches salvation and is instrumental in converting a heathen court to Christianity; *Los dos amantes del cielo* (*The Two Lovers of Heaven*; printed 1636)—wherein a peculiarly lyrical tone enwraps a theme presenting the conflict between paganism and the Christian faith; and the better-known *El mágico prodi-*

gioso (*The Wonder-working Magician*, 1637)—a drama distinguished through the translation of several of its scenes by the poet Shelley. The plot of the last work deals with the life of St Cyprian, who in the first scene is shown as still a heathen, but one searching for the ultimate truth: he has retired for solitary contemplation while

> with glorious festival and song
> Antioch now celebrates the consecration
> Of a proud temple to great Jupiter,
> And bears his image in loud jubilee
> To its new shrine.

In the midst of his deliberations the Devil enters, dressed as a courtier, pretending to have lost his way in the forest. He offers to debate on any topic that Cyprian cares to choose, and an argument on the essential nature of God ensues. In this Cyprian outwits his opponent, but the Devil now tries another plan. Floro and Lelio prepare to fight a duel over the poor but beautiful Justina; staying their hands, Cyprian agrees to adjudicate their quarrel, visits Justina, and immediately falls in love with her. After returning in perturbation of spirit to a lonely sea-shore he is again confronted by the Devil in another guise, that of a shipwrecked mariner:

> *DÆMON:* And who art thou, before whose feet my fate
>   Has prostrated me?
> *CYPRIAN:*   One who, moved with pity,
>   Would soothe its stings.
> *DÆMON:*   Oh, that can never be!
>   No solace can my lasting sorrows find.
> *CYPRIAN:* Wherefore?
> *DÆMON:*   Because my happiness is lost.
>   Yet I lament what has long ceased to be
>   The object of desire or memory,
>   And my life is not life.
> *CYPRIAN:*   Now, since the fury
>   Of this earthquaking hurricane is still,
>   And the crystalline Heaven has reassumed
>   Its windless calm so quickly, that it seems
>   As if its heavy wrath had been awakened
>   Only to overwhelm that vessel—speak,
>   Who art thou, and whence comest thou?
> *DÆMON:*   Far more
>   My coming hither cost, than thou hast seen
>   Or I can tell. Among my misadventures
>   This shipwreck is the least. Wilt thou hear?
> *CYPRIAN:*   Speak.
> *DÆMON:* Since thou desirest, I will then unveil
>   Myself to thee;—for in myself I am
>   A world of happiness and misery;

This I have lost, and that I must lament
Forever. In my attributes I stood
So high and so heroically great,
In lineage so supreme, and with a genius
Which penetrated with a glance the world
Beneath my feet, that, won by my high merit,
A king—whom I may call the King of kings,
Because all others tremble in their pride
Before the terrors of His countenance,
In His high palace roofed with brightest gems
Of living light—call them the stars of Heaven—
Named me His counsellor. But the high praise
Stung me with pride and envy, and I rose
In mighty competition, to ascend
His seat and place my foot triumphantly
Upon His subject thrones. Chastised, I know
The depth to which ambition falls; too mad
Was the attempt, and yet more mad were now
Repentance of the irrevocable deed:—
Therefore I chose this ruin, with the glory
Of not to be subdued, before the shame
Of reconciling me with Him who reigns
By coward concession—Nor was I alone,
Nor am I now, nor shall I be alone;
And there was hope, and there may still be hope,
For many suffrages among His vassals
Hailed me their lord and king, and many still
Are mine, and many more perchance shall be.
Thus vanquished, though in fact victorious,
I left His seat of empire, from mine eye
Shooting forth poisonous lightning, while my words
With inauspicious thunderings shook Heaven,
Proclaiming vengeance, public as my wrong,
And imprecating on His prostrate slaves
Rapine, and death, and outrage. Then I sailed
Over the mighty fabric of the world,—
A pirate ambushed in its pathless sands,
A lynx crouched watchfully among its caves
And craggy shores; and I have wandered over
The expanse of these wide wildernesses
In this great ship, whose bulk is now dissolved
In the light breathings of the invisible wind,
And which the sea has made a dustless ruin,
Seeking ever a mountain, through whose forests
I seek a man, whom I must now compel
To keep his word with me. I came arrayed
In tempest, and although my power could well
Bridle the forest winds in their career,
For other causes I forbore to soothe
Their fury to Favonian gentleness.

His curiosity excited, Cyprian leagues himself with this magician, who in the meantime proceeds to torment the poor Justina's mind with thoughts of love. She, however, is a Christian devotee, and although the impress of passion is on her heart, she remains firm. In the end, after many trials, Cyprian and she reach peace of spirit and are martyred for their faith. The Dæmon is vanquished.

The concept of purity of spirit thus presented in *El mágico prodigioso* finds a strange metamorphosis in the concept of honour introduced into many of his secular dramas. Perhaps *El médico de su honra* (*The Physician of his own Honour*, 1635) may be taken as a prime example. This play tells of a lady, Doña Mencía de Acuña, who is the wife of Don Gutierre Alfonso de Solís. Before her marriage she had been the object of the affections of Don Enrique, the King's brother, and this prince, against her will, pays her a visit. The husband's suspicions are aroused: interrupted while writing a letter to Don Enrique bidding him trouble her no more, she faints, and on recovering finds that her husband has written on the paper the fatal words:

> Love adores thee, but honour abhors thee; and thus while one condemns thee to death, the other gives thee this admonition: thou hast but two hours to live—thou art a Christian—save thy soul, for as to thy life it is impossible to save it.

In terror she calls on her maid: no one answers. She rushes to the door: it has been locked. The windows are stoutly barred. Within two hours' space the husband returns with a blindfolded surgeon. "Come," he says,

> Look within this chamber:
> What do you see in it?
> *SURGEON:*   An image
> Of pale death—an outstretch'd body
> Which upon a bed is lying:—
> At each side a lighted candle
> And a crucifix before it,—
> Who it is I cannot say,
> As the face is covered over
> With a veil of taffeta.
> *GUTIERRE:* To this living corse—this body
> Which you see, you must give death.

On threat of his own demise if he disobeys, the surgeon is compelled to bleed the wife to death, and is led blindfold back to his house again. There follows an amazing series of scenes. The surgeon finds the place to which he had been conducted and hastens to inform the King. In order to protect his honour—that is to say, in order not to let anyone know the cause of his crime—Gutierre claims that his wife's death was an accident, whereupon the King immediately commands him to marry Doña Leonor, a lady to whom he had made promises in the past. Hinting at what has happened, he inquires what he should do after a second wedding if he were to find Don Enrique disguised at night within his house:

> KING: Do not give faith to mere suspicion.
> GUTIERRE: And if behind the very arras
> Of my bed, I find the dagger
> Of the Infante Don Enrique?
> KING: Remember there are thousand servants
> In the world by gold corrupted.
> And thy better self invoke.
> GUTIERRE: How many times then must I do so,
> If night and day I see him haunting
> The very precincts of my house?
> KING: Complain to me . . .
> GUTIERRE: And, if, unto my house returning,
> I find a certain letter, asking
> The Infante not to go?
> KING: There is a remedy for all things.
> GUTIERRE: What! Is it possible? For this one?
> KING: Yes, Gutierre.
> GUTIERRE: What, my lord?
> KING: It is your own.
> GUTIERRE: What is it?
> KING: Bleeding!

Gutierre gives his hand to Leonor, warning her it is bathed with blood, but she does not flinch:

> LEONOR: 'Tis no matter: that doth neither
> Wake my wonder nor my fear.
> GUTIERRE: Remember, too, I am Physician
> Of my own Honour, and my skill
> Is not forgotten.
> LEONOR: Cure with it
> My life, when deadly danger threatens.

This scene, so popular in the Spanish theatre, amply demonstrates how alien to almost all other sentiment is the social code on which Calderón built his scenes.

A kindred play is *El pintor de su deshonra* (*The Painter of his own Dishonour, c.* 1645), in which a queer romantic story is told of Serafina, who has married, at her father's command, Don Juan Roca, although her memory still holds fondly the love of Álvaro, whom she thinks dead. Álvaro unexpectedly returns and forcibly abducts her. The husband slays them both and is applauded for the deed by the fathers of the wife and the lover (Don Pedro and Don Luis). As the Prince and other characters enter upon the tragic scene Don Juan Roca stands boldly forward:

> *JUAN:*   A picture
> Done by the Painter of his own Dishonour
> In blood.
> I am Don Juan Roca. Such revenge
> As each would have of me, now let him take,
> As far as one life holds. Don Pedro, who
> Gave me that lovely creature for a bride,
> And I return to him a bloody corpse;
> Don Luis, who beholds his bosom's son
> Slain by his bosom friend; and you, my lord,
> Who, for your favours, might expect a piece
> In some far other style of art than this.
> Deal with me as you list; 'twill be a mercy
> To swell this complement of death with mine;
> For all I had to do is done, and life
> Is worse than nothing now.
> *PRINCE:*   Get you to horse,
> And leave the wind behind you.
> *LUIS:*   Nay, my lord,
> Whom should he fly from? not from me at least,
> Who lov'd his honour as my own, and would
> Myself have help'd him in a just revenge,
> Ev'n on an only son.
> *PEDRO:*   I cannot speak,
> But I bow down these miserable grey hairs
> To other arbitration than the sword;
> Ev'n to your Highness' justice.

Jealousy and an exaggerated belief in honour—these form staple themes in Calderón's work. In *El mayor monstruo del mundo los celos* (*No Monster like Jealousy, c.* 1634) he deals horribly with Herod's determination to have his beloved wife, Mariamne, slain lest she become another's after his death, while in *A secreto agravio, secreta venganza* (*For a Secret Wrong, Secret Revenge*, 1635) a tale hardly less terrifying is narrated.

In strange contrast to such pieces, revolting in their calm delineation of tortured emotions, are Calderón's romantic comedies, delightful in their gay humour. In *Nadie fíe su secreto* (*Keep your own Secrets, c.* 1624) Prince Alexander explains to Don Arias how he has suddenly become smitten with love for Doña Anna; he had seen her often, but not till now has he looked upon her with passion:

> Know you not
> That not an atom in the universe
> Moves without some particular impulse
> Of heaven? What yesterday I might abhor,
> To-day I take delight in: what to-day
> Delight in, may as much to-morrow hate.
> All changes; 'tis the element the world,
> And we who live there, move in.

This philosophy of love is soon further extended. He is informed that this lady and his secretary, Don César, are bethrothed. "Oh, wretched fate!" he cries,

> Desperate ere jealous—jealous ere in love!
> If César but loved her, I could, methinks,
> Have pardon'd, even have advanc'd, his suit
> By yielding up my own. But that *she* loves,
> Blows rivalry into full blaze again.

To torment César he draws him into his company at the very hour when he had trysted his Anna; he tells Anna's brother that a kinsman of his own desires the lady in marriage; he harries César by his commands, and at the end bids him bear a letter to the brother purporting to make arrangements for the wedding with the rival prince. When, however, this letter is read they discover that, with princely magnanimity, César's name is set as that of the bridegroom.

A similar atmosphere breathes through *El secreto a voces* (*The Secret in Words*, 1662), with its gay group of ladies—Florida, the Duchess of Parma, Laura, Flora, and Livia—and its sprightly lyric dialogue of passion, in which the characters vie with one another in describing and evaluating the various states of the heart—loving and loved, loving not loved —in a manner reminiscent of Heywood's interlude. So too in *Guárdate del agua mansa* (*Beware of Smooth Water*, 1649) the scenes are tremulous with happy though conflicting emotion; ludicrous intrigue, although not without the threat of dark consequence, dominates in *Antes que todo es mi Dama* (*My Lady First of All*, c. 1636), the charming *La banda y la flor* (*The Scarf and the Flower*, c.1632), and the hardly so charming *El astrólogo fingido* (*The Feigned Astrologer*; printed 1633).

As in Lope's works, so in Calderón's, the aristocratic code is frequently shattered when comedy is in view. The *Casa con dos puertas mala es de guardar* (*It's Difficult to guard a House with Two Doors*, 1629) shows a heroine evading the angry eye of her brother, and *No siempre lo peor es cierto* (*Don't always believe the Worst*, c. 1650) gleefully attacks just such excessive jealousy as was condoned in *The Physician of his own Honour*. No play shows this trend better than the delightful *La dama duende* (*The Fairy Lady*, c. 1629), with its charming portrait of the mischievous and unconventional Doña Angela. This lady, by means of a concealed secret door between her apartments and those of Don Manuel, succeeds in persuading the latter's servant, Cosme, that she is a goblin and is mightily perplexing the master. It is true that in this play honour is rampant, and two duels are introduced into its action, but the defiance of conventions by Angela infuses its scenes with a delicious gaiety.

Still a further class of play is illustrated in *El príncipe constante* (*The Constant Prince*, 1629). The opening scene has a haunting loveliness. We are in the gardens of the King of Fez, and some Christian captives enter with Zara, attendant upon the Princess:

> *ZARA:* Sing, from out this thicket here,
>   While the beauteous Phenix dresses;
>   Those sweet songs, whose air expresses
>   Fond regrets; which pleased her ear
>   Often in the baths,—those strains
>   Full of grief and sentiment.
> *FIRST CAPTIVE:* Can music, whose strange instrument
>   Was our clanking gyves and chains—
>   Can it be, our wail could bring
>   Joy unto her heart? Our woe
>   Be to her delight?
> *ZARA:*   'Tis so:
>   She from this will hear you; sing.
> *SECOND CAPTIVE:* Ah! this anguish doth exceed,
>   Beauteous Zara, all the rest—
>   Since from out a captive's breast
>   (Save a soulless bird's indeed)
>   Never has a willing strain
>   Of music burst.
> *ZARA:*   But have not you
>   Yourselves sung many a time?
> *THIRD CAPTIVE:*   'Tis true;
>   But then it was no stranger's pain
>   To which we hoped some ease to bring;
>   It was our own too bitter grief
>   For which in song we sought relief.

Thus set in an atmosphere of captivity, the action proceeds. The hero is Don Fernando, who, although taken prisoner and suffering the worst indignities, is stalwart in his determination not to win his ransom from the Moors by ceding the city of Ceuta—the price of his freedom. His fixed resolution remains firm even unto death, and, although much romantic nonsense has been written concerning the virtues of the play, it must be agreed that Calderón has here succeeded in painting an arresting picture of inflexibility of purpose and devoted gallantry.

Two other dramas deserve attention. In *El alcalde de Zalamea* (*The Mayor of Zalamea, c.* 1640), based on a similarly named play by Lope, he comes closer perhaps to that author than in any other of his plays, dealing with a theme that recalls the story of *Fuente Ovejuna*. There is, however, an essential difference. Lope had daringly made the entire population of the village a collective hero; the quality of his work ultimately depends on the memorable scene in which they all unite in accepting common responsibility for the crime that has been committed. In *The Mayor of Zalamea* all stress is laid on one man, Pedro Crespo, a farmer who has been elected *alcalde* and who, low-born though he is, dares to avenge his daughter's violated honour by executing Don Álvaro de Ataide. There can be no doubt but that Crespo is an interestingly delineated character and that here, as in Lope's play, we are made aware of the sense of justice which transcends the pride of the aristocrats, but the story is one treated on a plane by far less interesting than that on which *Fuente Ovejuna* is based.

Finally we reach *La vida es sueño* (*Life's a Dream, c.* 1636), the true triumph of Calderón's art. Outwardly this play is but another romantic tale, set this time in Poland, with a heroine, Rosaura, and a miserable captive, Segismundo; but what gives the whole action its distinction is the way in which the author has, as it were, imposed a theme upon his plot. Segismundo is being kept in durance because an oracle had declared that he, the true prince, would prove a fatal enemy to his father and his country. As the King, his parent, grows old, however, remorse comes to him, and he determines that his son shall be granted a trial. Given a potion, the young man is brought, drugged, to the palace, and when he opens his eyes he finds himself surrounded by the trappings of royalty. Almost at once, however, he betrays ungovernable brutality of spirit even while he wonders in his mind whether all of this may not merely be a dream. His actions are so savage and arbitrary that once more he is returned to his dungeon, and there he reflects, now with regret and horror, on what he is convinced must have been an hallucination:

> And let us then restrain
> This the fierceness of our pride,
> Lay this wilfulness aside,
> Lest perchance we dream again:
> And we shall so, who remain
> In a world of wonder thrown,
> Where to live and dream are one.
> For experience tells me this,
> Each is dreaming what he is,
> Till the time his dream is done.
> The king dreams himself a king,
> And in this conceit he lives,
> Lords it, high commandment gives,
> Till his lent applause takes wing,
> Death on light winds scattering,
> Or converting (Oh, sad fate!)
> Into ashes all his state:
> How can men so lust to reign,
> When to waken them again
> From their false dream death doth wait?
> And the rich man dreams no less
> 'Mid his wealth which brings more cares,
> And the poor man dreams he bears
> All his want and wretchedness;
> Dreams, whom anxious thoughts oppress,
> Dreams, who for high place contends,
> Dreams, who injures and offends;
> And though none are rightly ware,
> All are dreaming that they are

In this life, until death ends.
I am dreaming I lie here,
Laden with this fetter's weight,
And I dreamed that I of late
Did in fairer sort appear.
What is life? a frenzy mere;
What is life; e'en that we deem;
A conceit, a shadow all,
And the greatest good is small,
Nothing is, but all doth seem,
Dreams within dreams, still we dream.

With these words, in their intensity and spiritual exploration beyond anything Lope ever wrote, we may take leave of Calderón. Had he but been granted some of his predecessor's verve and his theatrical sense, had he not been bound and fettered by the narrow code of honour that dominated his age, he might have been another Shakespeare. As it is, despite his skill and the beauty of much of his work, he just fails to achieve ultimate dramatic greatness. The concept of *Life's a Dream* is universal, but all too much of Calderón's writing is tied to a particular place and time, thus preventing his scenes from making such appeal to all ages and races as is made by the dramatist of Elizabethan England.

Cervantes, Moreto, and Others

Lope de Vega and Calderón are sun and moon of the firmament of the Spanish theatre, but beside them glitter—gaily or ominously—many another star.

The names of the early playwrights are many, and the influence of their works is not inconsiderable. *La comedia de Calisto y Melibea* (known also as *Celestina*; printed 1499), probably written by Fernando de Rojas, although unsuited for theatrical representation, won international repute and inspired numerous other dramas. The author of *Don Quixote*, Miguel de Cervantes Saavedra, turned to dramatic composition, although without much distinction in style or concept. As yet the secular play had not thrown off the trammels of the morality; even his best drama, the *Numancia* (c. 1587), is a strange, rambling affair, with abstract characters jostling historical personages; his *entremeses* are little more than farces in the medieval mode; and, when he tries to handle romantic material, as in *La gran sultana* (*The Great Sultana*; printed 1615), his treatment of characters and events often becomes ludicrous.

The great period of the Spanish stage came much later, between 1620 and 1665; from this age derive numerous writers of worth. During these years flourished Augustín Moreto y Cavaña, a man who vied in popularity with Lope himself. Thoroughly conversant with the theatre, his scenes have life, vigour, and interest. Less successful in serious efforts, he has left several comedies which, because of their skilful planning and interesting character portraits, have been instrumental in inspiring later playwrights. His rôle was that of the elaborator and refiner rather than that of the inventor, and most of his pieces—such as *El desdén con el desdén* (*Scorn for Scorn*; printed 1654), *No puede ser* (*You Can't, c.* 1660), *De fuera vendrá quien de casa nos echará* (*The Cuckoo in the Nest*; printed 1654), and *El lindo Don Diego* (*Don Diego the Fop, c.* 1662)—are based on plays by Lope and others. As typical of Moreto's work the last-mentioned play may be briefly noted. Don Diego is a foolish provincial booby who gives himself absurd airs, and when Doña Inés finds herself betrothed to him against her will she and her sweetheart, Don Juan, play upon his pretensions, finally exposing him after he has laid suit to a supposed countess, who is really Inés' maid in disguise. Moreto delighted in such farcical situations and knew well how to handle them: he knew, too, how to enliven his scenes with a delicate, fresh, and vivacious wit.

Allied to Calderón rather than to Lope is Francisco de Rojas Zorrilla, who carries both romantic intrigue and the idea of honour—as diversely exemplified in the popular *Del rey abajo ninguno* (*All Equal below the King*), *Entre bobos anda el juego* (*The Boobies' Sport*), and *Lo que son mujeres* (*What Women are*) (all printed 1640–54)—to an extreme.

From Tirso de Molina (Gabriel Téllez) comes the dramatic story of Don Juan. This author, almost as prolific as Lope, has among his four hundred odd plays *El burlador de Sevilla y convidado de piedra* (*The Deceiver of Seville and the Stone Guest*; printed 1630), the first presentation of the legendary libertine on the stage. Although the play is episodic and chaotic in form, the author has the power to reveal to us a sinner whose very daring and flamboyancy charm our senses. No doubt we agree with the retribution that comes to him in the end, but until that time arrives we are held intent by his prodigious villainy and the spell of his personality. Like Lope and Calderón, Tirso de Molina also has a number of witty comedies of intrigue, best known among which are *Don Gil de las calzas verdes* (*Don Gil of the Green Trousers*; printed 1635), in which Don Gil is found to be a lady less fortunate than, but as mischievous as, the heroine of *La dama duende*, and *El vergonzoso en palacio* (*The Timid Fellow at Court*; printed 1621), which transports a clown into aristocratic circles. Perhaps one of the best is *Marta la piadosa* (*Martha the Devotee*; also known as *La beada enamorada, The Blessed Mistress*; printed 1634), in which a girl, in order to escape an unwished marriage, feigns to have received a heavenly call.

With these go other plays that demonstrate in the author a range of interests almost as wide as Lope's. *La villana de Vallecas* (*The Peasant Woman of Vallecas*; printed 1627) tells a pathetic story of intrigue in which a ravished maiden, Violante, after disguising herself as a peasant, succeeds in discovering her seducer. Not least powerful among them all is the religious drama *El condenado por desconfiado* (*Damned for Lack of Faith*; printed 1635), distinguished by the fact that, through the concrete story of a hermit, Paul, it introduces to the theatre discussion of theological problems deeper and more abstract than those essayed by other playwrights.

Somewhat more original in concept, but less virile, is Juan Ruiz de Alarcón y Mendoza, a native of Mexico, among whose twenty-seven dramas a few stand out either for their strong characterization or for their themes. *La verdad sospechosa* (*Truth Suspected*; printed 1628) interestingly deals with a hero, Don García, whose ready wit, keen fancy, and careless disposition cause him to tell so many lies that no one will believe him. He falls in love with a girl, Jacinta, but he labours under the impression that she is really Lucrecia, while he lays official suit to the true Lucrecia under the name of Jacinta. Normally in a comedy of this kind one would have expected to find this lover relieved of his tangles in the end, but Alarcón takes the unconventional course of causing his hero to marry Lucrecia, with whom he is not in love, because of his failure to distinguish between truth and reality. At the opposite pole this author produces such a study of loyalty, treachery, and passion as *La crudeldad por el honor* (*Cruelty for Honour*, *c*. 1625) or such an 'heroic' play as *Ganar amigos* (*Gaining Friends*, *c*. 1621), which glorifies generosity of spirit in its story of how a noble marquis, by conquering his own passions, gains a devoted friend in Don Fernando, and how the latter proves true to the loyal Doña Flor. While Alarcón clearly bases his style on that of Lope and Calderón, equally clearly demonstrated in his work is an individual sincerity of purpose.

In between these two comes such a play as *El examen de maridos* (*The Husband's Examination*; printed 1634), where the heroine, Inés, who has loudly proclaimed her intention of testing her suitors before making choice of a husband, falls in love and is, unwillingly, forced to impose the examination she would now fain dispense with. For its character delineation the comedy is noteworthy.

A somewhat similar originality of treatment appears in *Las paredes oyen* (*Walls have Ears*; printed 1628), in which the hero, Don Mendo, is severely punished both for his vacillation in affection and for the stories he tells about his two lady-loves. Juan Ruiz de Alarcón has severe moral standards, and the logic with which he applies these in comedy give him an undoubted, but a rather unsympathetic, distinction among his fellows.

All these authors became known, at least to playwrights if not to the general public, beyond the boundaries of Spain, and there were many others who, although noted among their fellow-citizens, have remained outside of the Iberian peninsula nothing but names—Álvaro Cubillo de Aragón, Antonio Coello, Antonio de Solís y Ribadeneira, Fernando de Zárate y Castronovo, Juan Bautista Diamante, Juan de la Hoz y Mota, and others. The galaxy of talent is as great, and as diversified, as that which graced the English theatre during the reigns of Elizabeth and her Stuart successors. Without question the Spanish drama is the closest rival to the Elizabethan, and was prevented from vying with it more closely only by the carelessness of texture that mars so much of Lope's work and by the provincially Castilian code on which Calderón based so many of his writings.

5

THE INTERNATIONAL THEATRE OF THE JESUITS

BEFORE leaving the Renaissance theatre of Europe we must cast at least a fleeting glance on what was, in effect, the last relic of the international stage of the medieval mysteries. In the year 1540 St Ignatius of Loyola, a Spanish soldier turned ecclesiastic, succeeded in obtaining Papal approval for his new religious order, the Society of Jesus. Designed to combat the heresies of the Reformation, the order of the Jesuits eagerly seized on all devices likely to be of use in testifying to the glory of the Church, and among such devices the theatre, because of its appeal to eye and ear, was particularly favoured. Especially in the Germanic territories and in the lands of Eastern Europe, this Jesuit drama flourished, serving at once as a continuation of the medieval and as a forerunner of secular drama to come.

The Jesuits were thoroughly eclectic. For their stage and plays they took suggestions from a diversity of sources. The mysteries, miracles, and moralities, of course, provided them with many ideas, but they were not prepared to rest on ancient traditions. Nothing if not modern, they looked around them on the contemporary stages and infused new material into old forms. In especial, they gazed with favour upon the 'school-drama,' and upon the tableau type of production which had grown up in the Netherlands.

The school-drama was a direct result of those early amateur productions of Roman comedies and tragedies which ushered in the theatre of the Renaissance. Performed for the most part simply on an open hall-stage backed by curtains or by a skeleton façade, the original Latin plays soon were succeeded by Latin dramas of later vintage. Dozens of learned authors, in places as diverse as Western Oxford and Eastern Vienna and Cracow, turned their pens towards the creation of scenes, usually but not always on sacred subjects, imitated from Plautus or from Terence. Although hardly any one of these early efforts is worthy of special attention (unless it be for historical reasons), their collective influence was by no means negligible, for they brought to their restricted publics examples of the new methods of dramaturgy. Their subject-matter may have been the same as that of the mysteries: their technique was entirely different.

From these school-dramas the early Jesuit authors took many ideas for their later Latin plays. In addition, they saw and took advantage of opportunities presented to them in the Netherlands. There two theatrical developments are of interest to us. The first is the long series of *tableaux vivants*, presented usually on platforms framed by archways and revealed by the drawing of curtains, which, while not restricted to Dutch cities, especially flourished there. The second, and more important, is the dramatic activities associated with the Rederyker Kamers, or "Chambers of Rhetoric," that played such a vigorous rôle in the sixteenth century. These companies of Rederykers were collections of amateur enthusiasts who banded themselves together into societies, each distinguished by a particular emblem, linked loosely together by means of annual competitions. Much of their energy was spent on the arranging of processions, the reciting of poems, and the singing of songs: nevertheless the dramatic art was the real core of their being, and to this style of literary composition they gave themselves eagerly.

These Rederyker Kamers developed their own kind of theatre—usually an outdoor platform backed by an arcaded façade provided with curtains which could be drawn to reveal such scenes as might be desired—and eventually in 1638 out of these relatively simple platforms there came into being the famous Schouwburg at Amsterdam. Most of the early plays were strongly influenced by the morality tradition, but some—notably *De Spaansche Brabander* (*The Spaniard of Brabant*, 1617), by Gerbrand Adriaensen Bredero)—were racily comic, while the Schouwburg itself was formally opened with the performance of a patriotically inspired historical drama, *Gysbreght van Aemstel*, which even now is still annually presented at Amsterdam every New Year's Day. The author of this work, Joost van den Vondel, clearly stood out predominant among his playwriting companions—a poet deeply influenced by the classical tradition yet firmly set on his native Dutch stage, and one who, despite his admiration for Euripides and Seneca and also despite his patriotic political interests, generally preferred to deal with Biblical themes. His very first play was *Pascha* (*Passover*, 1610) and his greatest achievement was a tragic *Lucifer* (1654).

From just such stages, too, the Jesuits drew inspiration, but in taking over the 'Rederyker' style they characteristically elaborated, so that what at the beginning was tied closely to the school performances and to the *tableaux vivants* in the end was almost indistinguishable from the opera. The first step was the extension of the curtained façade so that the spectators were presented with a series of arched frames, each with its own stage, and all capable of being used at once if occasion demanded. Thus the earlier Terence façade or that used in the Netherlands was adapted for the use of representational scenery, while at the same time the traditions of the medieval 'simultaneous setting' were pressed again into service. From this type of stage, established by the third quarter of the sixteenth century, to the adoption of the single proscenium opening favoured by seventeenth-century Italian architects was an easy progress.

In this later form of Jesuit stage relics of the old frequently remain in the shape of small (and by then useless) side-arches, but the visual appeal is concentrated on the central picture.

Naturally the plays presented by the Jesuits were didactic. An authoritarian order, its self-appointed mission was to display the glories of the true Church and to demonstrate to men the evils of free thought. Against the individualism expressed in the Reformation, it set forth to deny the right of man to think for himself, and, like some dictators, richly extolled the virtues of authority. Loyalty to the Church and loyalty to a king were its two main virtues. On the other hand, in order to exhibit these virtues most effectively and appealingly, the Jesuits were willing to employ all means of attracting attention, and hence their drama has interest not only for the potentially romantic material incorporated into its being, but also for the impetus it gave to the development of scenic decoration already richly sponsored by the opera.

Most of the playwrights have no more than a minute value, but two or three deserve to be remembered, and it must be confessed that under the bare Latin exteriors of their scenes there rests a quality of significance and distinction. Jakob Gretser merits mention, partly because he was among the first of his school with the composition of his *Comœdia de Timone* (*Timon*) in 1584, partly because he succeeds in many of his scenes in striking a note of genuine passion. His power, however, rests much inferior to that of his follower, Jakob Bidermann, a writer of unquestioned talent. Among his nine dramas one stands out pre-eminent, the *Cenodoxus* of 1602. This tragedy, which interestingly begins with a comic episode and is as free in construction as any secular romantic play, puts Heaven and Hell upon the stage, uses almost every stage device known to contemporary theatre-workers, and definitely opens the way towards the still more elaborate functioning of the Jesuit playhouses during the course of the seventeenth century. In its dramatic concretion of the struggle between free thought and divine faith, it obviously made tremendous appeal in its own day and was frequently reproduced in the later Jesuit repertory.

Cenodoxus is a kind of morality play of Faustian flavour. Others among Bidermann's plays seize on historical subject-matter, on material from the Bible, and on themes of romantic style (for example, *Philemon*, which deals with the ancient tale of the Roman comedian who suffers martyrdom, and *Cosmarchia* or *Mundi Respublica*, with its folk-tale, 'life-is-a-dream' structure). In all of these the religious author shows himself possessed of an innate dramatic sense, of a skill in character-portrayal, and of a true concept of the tragic.

Of his immediate companions Joseph Simeons (*alias* Emanuel Lobb), an English Jesuit, perhaps comes nearest to him in power of expression, with his five tragedies printed in 1656—*Zeno sive ambitio infelix* (*Zeno; or, Unfortunate Ambition*), *Mercia sive pietas coronata* (*Mercia; or, Piety Crowned*), *Theoctistus sive constans in aula virtus* (*Theoctistus; or, Virtue Constant at Court*),

Virtus sive Christiana fortitudo (*Virtue; or, Christian Fortitude*), and *Leo Armenius sive impietas punita* (*Leo Armenius; or, Impiety Punished*). Of his followers most important was Nikolaus of Avancini, author of over thirty plays —allegories, mysteries, miracles, and the like. His varied style is characteristically revealed in his *Susanna Hebræa, Cyrus, Dei bonitas de humana pertinacia victrix sive Alphonsus X* (*The Goodness of God Victorious over Human Obstinacy; or, Alfonso X*), and *Pietas Victrix sive Flavius Constantinus Magnus* (*Piety Victorious; or, Flavius Constantinus the Great*).

Nor was it only in the Germanic lands that the Jesuit theatre won some dramatic success. In Sicily Ortensio Scamacca produced a long series of such plays, and the impulse that brought these into being lasted well into the eighteenth century, when minor masterpieces appeared in *La santa infanzia di Gesù Cristo* (*The Holy Infancy of Jesus Christ*; printed 1708), by Presepio Presepi (Giuseppe Antonio Patrignani), and *Eustachio* (printed 1758), by Agostino Palazzi. Still further, it must be observed that the Jesuit theatre did not always remain within the walls of the colleges. In 1644 Sforza Pallavicino urged in the 'discourse' prefaced to his *Martire Ermengilda* (*Hermengild the Martyr*) the general adoption of religious themes such as the Jesuit authors dealt with, pleading that the fate of martyrs was more fitting material for tragedy than the subjects of classical myth. The way in which this influence worked may be traced too in the works of the German Andreas Gryphius. His *Catharina von Georgien, oder bewährte Beständigkeit* (*Catharine of Georgia; or, True Constancy*; written 1647) is a drama of martyrdom cast in the style that the author had learned from his early association with the Jesuit stage. No doubt the choice of theme in *Carolus Stuardus, oder die ermordete Majestät* (*Charles Stuart; or, Majesty Murdered*; printed 1657) was selected because Charles I could be regarded as a martyr; but *Cardenio und Celinde* (printed 1657) is a tragedy of love, while in *Die geliebte Dornrose* (*The Beloved Thorny Rose*, 1660) Gryphius was able to write not merely an imaginative comedy of intrigue, but a comedy composed almost entirely in dialect, thus pointing forward to dramatic developments that as yet lay far in the future.

The early influence of the humanist stage and of Italian theatrical activities, followed by the later influence of the Jesuit stage, is to be traced in diverse localities during the sixteenth and seventeenth centuries. Typical are the plays that came into being in the vicinity of Ragusa (or Dubrovnik) on the shores of the Adriatic. Here flourished a native Croat drama, inspired by Italian example yet instinct with individual vitality. Already in the sixteenth century playwrights were at work, and one of them, Marin Držić, succeeded in creating comic scenes which even yet retain their appeal on the stage; in the following century came the still more notable epic and tragic poet Ivan Gundulić, a man who symbolized his age and time by dealing both with classical themes and with themes culled from the legend and history of his own land. Slightly later the Jesuit Latin theatre induced other writers to turn to the composition of plays moral and religious. Although all this vigorous flourishing of the dramatic form was destined soon to wither and vanish, it deserves notice both for such intrinsic excellence as it attained and for its testimony to the strength and widespread appeal of Renaissance enthusiasm for the theatre.

There can be no doubt but that the activities of the Jesuits were of prime importance in developing dramatic interest among lettered audiences, particularly in the countries to the east of Europe, and that everywhere they had a widespread influence on theatrical form. Even although their dialogue was commonly in Latin, and even although their basic philosophy was destined to be confronted with philosophies alien and antagonistic to the Papal Court they aimed to extol, they too set their seal on the stage of the time. To neglect the school-drama and this its offshoot is to omit an essential chapter—albeit a short one—in the history of the modern playhouse.

PART IV

THE DRAMA OF THE RENAISSANCE: ENGLAND

1

THE POPULAR BEGINNINGS

IF ONLY because of Shakespeare, the English drama of this time demands treatment apart from that of Italy, France, and Spain. It has its close ties with all of these, yet it stands apart by its realization of a broader spirit and of a richer harmony than its companions succeeded in attaining.

The First Attempts

At the beginning it offered no more promise than any of the others; indeed, for many decades it seemed to be lagging grievously behind the drama of Italy. Before 1560—and even much later—England could show nothing to compare with Ariosto's clean-cut comedies of contemporary life or with Machiavelli's penetrating satire. In 1583, when Sir Philip Sidney, writing his *Apology for Poetry*, utterly condemned the contemporary popular stage, no one, whether academically classical in trend or romantically revolutionary, could have dared to dream that the English theatre would, within the course of a few decades, produce such riches as to make even the gold of Greece seem less glorious a treasure. After the event, of course, it is easy to discern in the early works the shadows cast by what was to come, but if the development of the English stage had suddenly ceased in 1580 one would have said that here, as in Italy and France, was interesting material utterly failing to find adequate realization in artistic form.

The fact remains, however, that the London theatres did succeed in reaching this realization and that their magnificent contribution to the drama was not due simply to the fortuitous appearance of one author or of a group of authors. Something in the conditions of the English stage permitted the growth stifled in Italy, stunted in France, and only partly developed in Spain. In our survey obviously one of our chief tasks must be to suggest what these conditions were.

To England the Renaissance came as it did to other lands. There was a great stirring of spirit and an eager-eyed enthusiasm; the wonders of the long-lost classical world were being suddenly revealed to men's wondering gaze. At the Court of Henry VIII Latin plays were presented, just as they had been elsewhere.

There was, however, an essential difference in the atmosphere in which these performances were set. They were being given, not at a variety of different Courts, as in Italy, not against a background of civil war, as in France, not in the midst of a narrowly repressive *milieu*, as in Spain. It is true that many years were to pass before the burning hatreds between Catholics and Protestants in England began to smoulder down —after Henry VIII was to arise the bloody Mary; but, fundamentally, Henry's reforms became the established tradition of the land, and most men, no matter what their private beliefs, gradually united in a common good. It was a Catholic who commanded the little English fleet confronting the might of the Catholic Armada. For England the Renaissance meant not merely the rediscovery of the classics and the opening up of fresh vistas for art, but also the finding of a new sense of national unity, expressed clearly in the establishment of a national Church, but embracing all—even those who would not bow to the reformed creed—within its folds. Italy and France lacked that unity, while in Spain the sense of common purpose was vitiated by obscurantism.

And by more than obscurantism. To a large extent Spain was living on its past. At a time when hardly anyone thought of England seriously as a power Spanish galleons were sailing home laden with untold wealth, the whole of the New World was in the grasp of her monarchs, and over much of the Old World they had set their imperial seal. In the sixteenth century the English were just becoming conscious of their strength; their eyes were on the future. It is characteristic that, while in England a new national Church was born, with the sweeping away of so many cluttered and outworn traditions, Spain endeavoured through the Inquisition to stamp out the new by force of rack and fire. No doubt the new Church was created as a political device by the astute Henry VIII, but, whatever its inception, it met the needs of the time and succeeded because it accorded with the will of the people; and it was a symbol of an England realizing her own promise.

In another way, too, these early performances of Latin plays were placed against a different setting. Much as men in England paid homage to the classic civilization, there was always in England a healthy spirit of scepticism. The other three countries could never forget that they were forged out of the Roman Empire and that their Romance tongues were but Latin vulgarized. Despite the long centuries of Roman occupation of Britain, this mould of form was never so deeply felt in the land where successive invasions had left a race, and a language, which owed its being to many diverse cultures. Even beyond that there were Englishmen who prided themselves in the fact, or in the belief, that their ultimate being derived not from proud Rome and haughty Greece, but from the ancient land of Troy. The belief was, perhaps, no more than a pleasant fiction even for those who expressed it most warmly, but its very existence as a fiction is also symbolic. Dreams are woven out of desires.

The result is that we search almost in vain during the early years for any faithful reproduction of classical dramatic forms in English dress. Sir

Philip Sidney, in 1583, deplored the fact that even *Gorboduc*, the only tragedy that might in any respect be regarded as regular, was manifestly impatient of the rules. Only later did a number of academically minded playwrights endeavour to provide stricter examples, but by that time the popular theatre had grown to full stature and its course was not to be stayed. The voices of the little group of English Senecans were drowned by the accents of Shakespeare and his fellows—whereas had they been uttering their Aristotelian notes fifty years before they might well have altered the entire development of the English drama. In Italy the model presented by *Sofonisba* came very early; England had no such model until the years had passed when it might have been an object of reverent admiration.

It is true, of course, that the same kind of amateurism as flourished a¹ road also played an important part in London, but the Court plays were at once less elaborate and more closely associated with professionalism than was common in Italian palaces. Elizabeth's parsimony held expenses down, so that, although scenery assuredly was used at Court, we may be sure it was kept simple. At the Inns of Court, at the Universities, and in the schools young men and boys amused themselves with acting, but rapidly the Queen and her Court came to depend rather upon the skilled services of professional players than upon the exhibitions of the amateurs. From the year 1493 we have record of a troupe of "Lusores Regis" (the King's Players), and these are known to have given regular performances before royalty during the early part of the sixteenth century, while the companies of boys (the Children of Paul's, the Children of the Chapel and the Queen's Revels, and the Children of Windsor) became, in Elizabeth's reign, virtually professionals. The account of Court performances during the middle of the century shows the performance of many masques by the amateurs, but of comparatively few plays; these were given by those of 'the quality,' and necessarily included, for the most part, popular dramas.

As a consequence the list of purely 'classical' plays in England during this era is a meagre one, while at the same time there is a goodly show of dramatic works, even those amateur in origin, in which elements taken from Seneca, Plautus, and Terence are subordinated to the needs of audiences unapt to welcome the severer forms beloved of the academics.

In comedy Plautus' *Amphitruo* is just faintly discernible beneath the careless vesture of *Jacke Juggler* (printed 1555), described as "A new Enterlude for Chyldren to playe," while the learned authors of the *Ryght Pithy, Pleasant and merie Comedie: Intytuled Gammer gurtons Nedle* (*c.* 1550–53; printed 1575) and *Ralph Roister Doister* (1553–54; printed 1566) were not prepared to allow their knowledge of classical methods to prevent them from producing work of a popular sort. *Gammer Gurton's Needle* is a gay and good-humoured farcical comedy, much of it written in rustic dialogue, with the characters firmly rooted in an English village; while

Roister Doister, by Nicholas Udall, although a trifle more imitative, not only shows the delineation of contemporary types, but also borrows largely from the native morality tradition.

The same is true of the gestures made in the direction of tragedy. *Gorboduc* (1562), by Thomas Norton and Thomas Sackville, is certainly 'classical' when compared with some other dramas of the time, but it displays a healthy independence and a native power of invention. The plot is taken, not from the writings of some Greek or Roman historian, but from the legendary material of Geoffrey of Monmouth; the unities are disobeyed; there is a flavour of the morality in the development of its theme; and the use made of the dumb-show at the beginning of the acts is apparently unique.

No doubt numerous plays written and acted in the earlier years of the sixteenth century are now irretrievably lost, but a sufficient number has been preserved to show how the drama was gaining in strength and variety. Thomas Hughes follows the authors of *Gorboduc* in going to Geoffrey of Monmouth for the plot of *The Misfortunes of Arthur* (1588), and Robert Wilmot discovers in Boccaccio the material for his *Tancred and Gismund* (1567–68). Henry Medwall's *Fulgens and Lucrece* (printed about 1515) deals with true love and nobility; George Whetstone's *Promos and Cassandra* (printed 1578) is akin in spirit; in the hands of John Pikeryng the tale of Orestes is transformed into a tragi-comedy with a Cockney accent as *A Newe Enterlude of Vice, Conteyninge the Historye of Horestes* (printed 1567); in *The Commody of the most vertuous and Godlye Susanna* (printed 1578) the Biblical story is used as an excuse for the composition of a typical morality play, with a character-list including the Devil, a Vice named Ill Report, and such persons as Voluptas and Sensuality. All these plays delight in action, and perhaps none is more typical than Thomas Preston's *Lamentable Tragedie, mixed full of plesant mirth, containing the life of Cambises King of Percia* (probably 1561). The plot is based on ancient history, but the numerous characters include such abstract figures as Councell, Murder, Commons Cry, and Cruelty, as well as such humorous characters as Huf, Ruf, and Snuf, companions of Ambidexter the Vice. Although the parts include no fewer than thirty-eight speaking rôles, the author has been careful to arrange them so that a company of but six men and two boys can perform the play, while this evidence of his keen attention to its theatrical possibilities is corroborated by the numerous racy stage directions running throughout its length. Ambidexter enters "with an old capcase on his head, an olde paile about his hips for harnes, a scummer and a potlid by his side, and a rake on his shoulder"; he "swinges" Huf, Ruf, and Snuf; a Meretrix comes in, and there is a ludicrous brawl in which Ruf "falleth downe; she falleth upon him, and beats him, and taketh away his weapon." There is a constant impression of movement here: Commons Cry comes "running in," and after speaking his verse goes "out againe hastily." We are told of drinking, kissing, shooting, executions; the hands of Cruelty and Murder are "bloody." No reticence is

THE TEATRO
OLIMPICO, VICENZA,
1594
Photo Alinari

THE TEATRO
FARNESE, PARMA,
1618
Photo Alinari

shown; no attempt is made to avoid displaying scenes of violence; rather are these freely exploited for the merriment or the thrilling of the audience. Lamentable tragedies mixed full of pleasant mirth may later have become somewhat ridiculous, retaining their hold only on the Bottoms of the last years of the sixteenth century, but they were healthily unrestrained, and, despite Shakespeare's good-humoured but satirical allusions to them, were to prove the model on which his comedy of romance and even his tragedy were fashioned.

The Growth of Professional Drama and Public Theatres

In the Christmas season of 1567–68 Queen Elizabeth had eight plays acted for her delight—*As Plain as can be, The Painful Pilgrimage, Jack and Jill, Six Fools, Wit and Will, Prodigality, Orestes, The King of Scots*. When the authors of *Sir Thomas More* pictured a group of actors, consisting of four men and a boy, presenting their repertoire to the hero of that drama, they listed *The Cradle of Security, Hit Nail o' th' Head, Impatient Poverty, The Four PP, Dives and Lazarus, Lusty Juventus*, and *The Marriage of Wit and Wisdom*.

These titles may be taken as fairly typical of what the professional actors were engaged in performing about the middle of the century. By far the majority of the plays are moralities—nine out of a total of fifteen; *As Plain as can be, Jack and Jill*, and *Hit Nail o' th' Head* sound as though they were comedy farces; *Orestes* is presumably the *Horestes* mentioned above among the early tragi-comedies; only one tragedy, and that an historical play, appears in either list. We receive the impression of a repertoire composed mainly of late medieval or early humanist moralities and interludes, with a faint infusion of popular romantic drama based on classical legend and of chronicle history. From what we know of the extant examples we can assert with assurance that all these dramas must have been crude affairs, but they possessed what the theatre of Italy lacked—a sound foundation and a tradition. The moralities brought into the sixteenth century the high seriousness of the medieval stage and the interludes its sense of fun.

As the years went by certainly new plays were added to the store. In the Court records of the seventies titles of a different kind begin to appear: *Lady Barbara, Iphigenia, Fortune, Alcmæon, Quintus Fabius, The Painter's Daughter, The Three Sisters of Mantua, The Cruelty of a Stepmother*, and *Murderous Michael*—titles suggestive of a dual development of classical themes and of realistic material. Along with these, however, plays of a thoroughly romantic sort seem to predominate: *Cloridon and Radiamanta, Theagenes and Chariclea, Perseus and Andromeda, Predor and Lucia, Mamillia, Herpetalus the Blue Knight and Perobia, The Solitary Knight, The Irish Knight*. None of these have come down to us, but one precious example of a kindred play almost certainly demonstrates their general characteristics.

This is *The Historie of the two valiant Knights, Syr Clyomon Knight of the Golden Sheeld, sonne to the King of Denmarke And Clamydes the white Knight, sonne to the King of Suavia*. Although not printed until 1599, there can be no doubt but that it belongs to a period about 1570 and that it represents the kind of chivalric adventurous drama which, from the evidence of the titles of plays given at Court, we may assume to have been popular then.

A stranger farrago of diverse elements has hardly ever been included in a single set of scenes. In the old 'fourteener' measure—"Well," says Quince to Bottom, "we will have such a prologue; and it shall be written in eight and six"—the author concentrates on the story of his two knights, but introduces along with them personages of the most diverse kinds. The opening lines might almost have been uttered by the artisans in the enchanted wood near Athens. Clamydes enters:

> As to the weary wandering wights, whom waltering waves environ,
> No greater joy of joys can be than when from out the ocean
> They may behold the altitude of billows to abate,
> For to observe the longitude of seas in former rate—
> And having then the latitude of sea-room for to pass,
> Their joy is greater through the grief than erst before it was.

Shortly afterwards Sir Clyomon comes on stage to enact a comic scene with Subtle Shift the Vice. Crude intrigue and excitement follow at the Court of the King of Suavia, and then suddenly we are confronted by "King Alexander the Great, as valiantly set forth as may be, and as many soldiers as can." Soon he is associated with a giant, Bryan Sans Foy, and with Patranius, "King of the Strange Marshes." There is fighting, there is love-making, there are horn-pipes and funerals.

The whole drama is almost as ludicrous as "Pyramus and Thisbe," yet within it is embedded the seed out of which grew the rich flourish of the Elizabethan stage. Alexander and Bryan and Subtle Shift meet on one platform: the classic age unites with chivalric romance and with the spirit of the moralities. *Clyomon and Clamydes* is absurd, but it is absurd in the right way. Its tissue of diverse elements is no more ridiculous than the mingling together of a mythical Theseus and Hippolita, a King and Queen of Fairy, and a group of Elizabethan artisans in a wood near Athens. Shakespeare knew this, realizing that the best in this kind are but shadows, and the worst are no worse if imagination amend them.

With plays such as these the players delighted their audiences. They began, too, to exploit the realm of the history play. Before 1548 John Bale had penned his *Kynge Johan*, in which the morality drama with its abstractions was beginning to assume a new form. King John is paired in this play with Cardinal Pandulph and the Pope, but their companions are England, Clergy, Private Wealth, Dissimulation, Usurped Power, and Treason. Not more than forty years later we hear of the comic actor Tarlton doubling the parts of a judge and a clown in a play of Henry V, and there is some reason to believe that in *The Famous Victories of Henry the Fifth* (printed 1598) we may have a mangled text of the very drama in which, as one of the Queen's Men, he appeared on that occasion.

The Famous Victories, well known for its connexions with Shakespeare's later tetralogy, is the earliest dramatic chronicle extant, and no doubt gives a fair picture of what its lost companions were like. As it has come down to us it possibly represents a rough running-together of a pair of plays, but, faulty as its text may be, its general tone, we may believe, reflects the spirit in which such works were written. Comic scenes preponderate, and in the serious portions nothing more is attempted than a bare presentation of sentiment. A barrenness in language and concept is everywhere evident. Yet the scenes have movement, and it is easy to understand how appealing this panorama of history must have proved to audiences as yet untutored in the possibilities of the poetic drama.

The episode recorded of Tarlton took place "at the Bull in Bishopsgate," and this fact reminds us that the rapidly growing professional companies were now giving regular performances in London and elsewhere. Just as the Spanish actors seized upon the convenient *corrales*, their English contemporaries found the Elizabethan inn-yard excellently suited to their purposes. The main archway provided an entrance where money could be taken by door-keepers; the galleries offered more comfortable accommodation for those who desired to be separated from the crowd in the yard below; a platform stage could readily be erected on trestles at the farther end, and to this access was easy from the inn-doors themselves. We may imagine *Clyomon and Clamydes* and *The Famous Victories* presented in such surroundings, without scenery, but with full appeal made to the imaginations of the audience.

In the year 1576 a long step forward was made. The Red Lion Inn, the Bull, the Bell, the Bel Savage, and the Cross Keys found the actors moving into a newly erected building just outside Bishopsgate: the work of James Burbage, it was called the Theatre. Immediately successful, this first permanent home of theatrical entertainment in London was soon followed by the near-by Curtain (1577), by Newington Butts (before 1580), by the Rose (1587), south of the river, by the Swan (*c.* 1595), and by the famous Globe (1599).

For the model of his theatre Burbage might have gone to the kind of staging utilized by the boy-players associated with the Court. The same year that the Theatre was opened (1576) a room in the ancient Blackfriars monastery was converted into a playhouse by Richard Farrant, Master of the Children of Windsor Castle and deputy to the Master of the Children of the Chapel Royal. Here, apparently, they established the type of production which was already familiar to them in their command performances—wherein various localities were, as in France, set upon the stage at the same time.

The device was liable and congruent, as Holofernes might have said, and we could very easily imagine its being adapted by Burbage for his first theatrical venture. Happily, it was not. Had it been, the development of the Elizabethan drama would almost certainly have been seriously retarded. What was needed by the age was freedom and an air of expansiveness: the restrictions imposed by the simultaneous setting might well have proved fatal to the genius of Shakespeare and his companions.

Instead a highly effective compromise was—by design or not we cannot tell—arrived at. A great open platform provided ample scope for movement; beyond was an inner stage, which could serve, when occasion demanded, as a particular locality; while above, a gallery divided by pillars and curtains gave opportunity for vertical action as opposed to the horizontal action on the stage below. Intimacy between audience and actors was effected; the actors were not tempted to ruin themselves by spending vast sums on scenery; the imagination of the spectators was freely called into play; and the authors were left free to develop their themes as they cared, with the knowledge that here was an excellent platform for the speaking of noble lines and that such noble lines were imperatively demanded from them if the imperfections of the stage were to be overcome. There was a challenge to the poet here, and an incentive.

Basically, as we have already suggested, this Elizabethan stage was similar in principle, and even in particular form, to the Spanish, but there was one essential difference. The *corrales* appear always to have been makeshift affairs, and even in the time of Calderón the arrangements made for both actors and audiences were crude. When foreign visitors came to London—even those who were acquainted with the theatres of Italy—they agreed that the English playhouses were sumptuous. They possessed a dignity and a distinction lacking in Spain. The players attained an appropriate home, and, although there were Puritans who grumbled, the acting profession secured a position of no mean rank. Servants of lords, even of royalty, Shakespeare's fellows were no vagabonds; the poet-actor could write himself gentleman and retire in his latter years to the best house in his native town; his contemporary, Edward Alleyn, could establish the College of God's Gift at Dulwich.

With the erection of the Theatre in 1576 the scene was set, with every augury propitious. As yet the English drama had produced nothing of any significance, but, if an Ariosto and a Machiavelli were wanting, the conditions were such as to provide fertile soil for the flourishing of genius. In a united kingdom looking eagerly towards the future men of all ranks were displaying interest in the stage—in the one stage, that of professional actors. Love of words was universal, and audiences were eager to listen to high-astounding terms. No single writer had appeared, as in Italy, to stamp his impress too soon on dramatic material; no critics of any consequence were giving laws to the liberty-loving age. In the theatre a new stage form had been evolved, with its potentialities still to explore, and orientated not towards the scenic decorator, but towards the actor interpreting the playwright's words.

Where the playhouse of Italy was ruined by its cleavage into amateur and professional, by the weight of classical theory, and by the dispersed interests of its Courts; where that of France was inhibited by the confining political conditions of the time, by the failure to develop a suitable stage, and by the late appearance of its first professional dramatist, Hardy; where that of Spain, despite the near approach it made to complete success, was prevented from reaching the highest levels because of its provincialism and because its greatest author came at a time when already the force of the Renaissance was being dissipated; the stage in England in 1580 found itself most fortunate. There was now a home for the drama, while a group of eager young university men were preparing themselves for the exercise of playwriting in popular terms. Robert Greene was then twenty-two years of age, Thomas Lodge twenty-three, John Lyly twenty-six, George Peele twenty-three; with them was associated Thomas Kyd, a learned if not an academic man, aged twenty-two; while there were another two youths, both then aged sixteen, the one a student at St John's College, Oxford, and the other possibly acting as assistant to his wool-dealing father, who were soon to join the ranks of London's dramatists. Again, fortunately, the former of the latter pair, Christopher Marlowe, hurried to the theatre a few years before his companion, so that the young William Shakespeare, coming to the stage at about twenty-eight years of age, arrived not only in time to catch the Renaissance spirit at its most glorious, but with models immediately behind him unstaled by custom and awaiting his refinement.

2

SHAKESPEARE AND HIS PREDECESSORS

WILLIAM SHAKESPEARE began and ended his work with comedies. At the beginning of his career stand *Love's Labour's Lost* (*c*. 1594), *The Taming of the Shrew* (1594), and *The Comedy of Errors* (*c*. 1593); at its conclusion stands *The Tempest* (1611). He it was who gave colour and composition to the comedy of romance, but many suggestions for its development he owed to his younger contemporaries.

The Comedy of Romance

The romantic comedy ultimately takes its tone from the tragi-comic efforts of the kind exemplified in *Clyomon and Clamydes*, but plays of this kind clearly had two outstanding weaknesses: they were dominated by no general mood and in style they were deplorably weak. They lacked both form and spirit.

About the year 1584 a young Oxford student named John Lyly became associated with the boy-players of the Chapel Royal and St Paul's, and for them he wrote a play, *Campaspe*, described on the title-page as "A most excellent Comedie" and in the title-headings to individual pages as "A tragical Comedie." The same year saw the appearance of a second drama, *Sapho and Phao*, and shortly after came *Galathea*. In these works appeared a tone at once old and new.

The author quite clearly is one who knows his classic authors; there is no jumbling of Alexander and Subtle Shift here. The scene of *Campaspe* is Athens, and the characters are all suitably named. He is, too, a man interested in style. The old fourteeners have vanished, and in their place appears a highly artificial form of elegant prose: "Parmenio," says Clitus, at the very beginning of the play,

> Parmenio, I cannot tell whether I should more commend in Alexander's victories courage or courtesy, in the one being a resolution without fear, in the other a liberality above custom. Thebes is razed, the people not racked; towers thrown down, bodies not thrust aside, a conquest without conflict, and a cruel war in a mild peace.

This may sound stilted, and the antithetical balancing of the phrases seem tedious; but at least there is no mere blundering and floundering here. The author of *Clyomon and Clamydes* stamps his way through the world of words ignorant of his goal; Lyly is sure-footed, and, certain of his purpose, he steps delicately.

The style accords with the contents. Tragic elements are here softened, comic scenes are made less clownish; over all is spread a strange illumination, so that high and low lose their contrasts, so that thrill is reduced to interest and laughter to delight. Listen to three servants talking—Manes, attendant upon the crusty Diogenes, Granichus, upon Plato, and Psyllus, upon Apelles, the painter:

> *MANES:* I serve instead of a master a mouse, whose house is a tub, whose dinner is a crust, and whose bed is a board.
>
> *PSYLLUS:* Then art thou in a state of life which philosophers commend: a crumb for thy supper, a hand for thy cup, and thy clothes for thy sheets—for "*Natura paucis contenta.*"
>
> *GRANICHUS:* Manes, it is pity so proper a man should be cast away upon a philosopher; but that Diogenes, that dog, should have Manes, that dog-bolt, it grieveth nature and spiteth art: the one having found thee so dissolute—absolute, I would say—in body, the other so single—singular—in mind.

Their accents are different, but their tone is the same as that of Apelles while he stands at his canvas painting the fair Campaspe:

> *APELLES:* I shall never draw your eyes well, because they blind mine.
>
> *CAMPASPE:* Why then, paint me without eyes, for I am blind.
>
> *APELLES:* Were you ever shadowed before of any?
>
> *CAMPASPE:* No: and would you could so now shadow me that I might not be perceived of any!

There can be no possibility of claiming that Lyly was a great genius, but in his application of form and style to the popular tragi-comedy he laid the foundation-stone for the later comedy of romance. He showed that this tragi-comedy could be made truly effective only by creating a particular mood in the minds of the audience, and he indicated how an appreciation of classical forms could be put into service for the creation of a kind of drama of which neither Rome nor Greece could even have dreamed.

His plays, however, were written for the boy-players, and although these boys were virtually professionals too, the strength of the new theatre lay in the hands of the adult companies. Lyly's delicately graceful comedies were suited for boyish treble; the other actors sought for deeper tones. For the Children of the Chapel George Peele penned his *Arraignment of Paris* about the same time as Lyly wrote his *Campaspe*, and in its verse, delicate and fantastic though it be, we hear these deeper tones being sounded. They become more pronounced in *The Old Wives' Tale* (*c.* 1591), while they sound clearly enough in the plays written for the adult actors by his friend Robert Greene—*Friar Bacon and Friar Bungay* (*c.* 1589) and *James the Fourth* (*c.* 1591). In these the tradition of *Clyomon and*

Clamydes is perhaps more apparent than in Lyly's writings, yet at the same time there is both a firmer handling of dramatic tools and a greater variety of material. The main scenes of *James the Fourth* concern love and intrigue at the Court of Scotland, but the whole action is preceded by an introduction in which figure Oberon, King of the Fairies, and a misanthropic Bohan: in *Friar Bacon and Friar Bungay* the supernatural joins with the natural; in both we move from high to low, from clownery to romantic seriousness. The staple instrument for dialogue here is the blank-verse medium, a form introduced many years before by the poet Surrey and put to dramatic use, but dully and awkwardly, in *Gorboduc*. In Greene's hand blank verse begins to give out some of its true melodies. Individual lines, such as

> Why, thinks King Henry's son that Margaret's love
> Hangs in the uncertain balance of proud time?

exhibit ease and strength, while throughout the measure is employed effectively for the give-and-take of dramatic speech. "My lord," asks Ida, "why are you thus impatient?" and Ateukin replies:

> Not angry, Ida, but I teach this knave
> How to behave himself among his betters.
> Behold, fair countess, to assure your stay
> I here present the signet of the king,
> Who now by me, fair Ida, doth salute you;
> And since in secret I have certain things
> In his behalf, good madam, to impart,
> I crave your daughter to discourse apart.

There is no distinction in these lines, but there is here something of great significance—an instrument for dramatic language capable of almost any note that a greater poet may care to play.

In his earliest essays in comedy the young Shakespeare shows himself a follower of these men, but as yet a trifle unsure. We do not know the precise order of his first plays, but the impression we have is of a young man experimenting. *Love's Labour's Lost* is satirical and impertinent, the work of a youth who looks with amused contempt at the follies around him; *The Taming of the Shrew* is a gay flight on the wings of Italianate farce; in *The Comedy of Errors* homage is paid to the spirit of Plautus. Yet, if we look with care, the quality which enriches the later dramas is to be discerned here in embryo. The satire in *Love's Labour's Lost* turns in upon itself; laughing at Berowne, Shakespeare smiles at his own follies, and even Holofernes is not merely an objectively conceived figure of fun, a butt for the intellectuals. There is a warmth here and an originality in concept unlike anything contributed by the preceding playwrights; the structure may be somewhat mechanically composed, the characters may want depth, and the merriment may be more than a little forced, but, imperfect as these comedies are, we recognize in them the presence of a distinctive atmosphere.

From these plays alone, however, we could not have told what course in the realm of comedy this dramatist would pursue. The satire of *Love's Labour's Lost*, the farcical laughter of the other two plays, might indeed have suggested that this young recruit to the stage was likely to depart from the line of romantic comedy and to aim rather at the creation of scenes instinct with wit and replete with ludicrous situation.

Soon, however, comes the full achievement, and all doubt is set at rest. In *A Midsummer Night's Dream* (*c*. 1595) there is complete technical mastery and a brilliant development of the romantic mood through which Lyly and Greene had been able to harmonize diverse elements. The heroic Theseus, the commonplace Ægeus, the lovers, the fairies, the artisans, are all swept into one pervasive melodic pattern. We are in a world of dreams where everything seems double: the fanciful and the real may barely be separated, and a charm is wrought upon our senses. Nothing quite like this has previously appeared in the history of the drama.

In *A Midsummer Night's Dream* the fancy-weaving imagination is given free play, but Shakespeare is not prepared to make this a model for his other romantic comedies. Oberon is not to find a companion until, at the close of the dramatist's career, Ariel is created to minister to Prospero's magic. The main line of development is marked much more clearly in a less distinguished play, *The Two Gentlemen of Verona* (*c*. 1593). With its Sir Eglamour, the squire of dames, with its fancifully conceived outlaws, and with its basic theme of friendship and love, its chivalric-romantic origins are manifest, and with its choice of an Italian setting it is linked with most of the comedies immediately to follow. For background Lyly had selected a vaguely classical world of history or legend, Greene had chosen an equally vague pseudo-historical realm. It would seem as though the young Shakespeare quite deliberately had decided, after experimenting with the legendary in *A Midsummer Night's Dream*, to make Italy the spiritual home of his comic characters. The device has certain obvious advantages. It provides distance, but not too great distance: the events are taking place in a far-off land of music, of colour, and of sunshine, and yet, by the exercise of the imagination, they may be conceived of as almost contemporaneous. There is the opportunity here for the creation of what, after all, is the basic paradox of the theatre—the arousing of a mood of strange wonder and at the same time the making of this wonder seem real and true.

The Merchant of Venice (*c*. 1596), *Much Ado about Nothing* (*c*. 1598), *Twelfth Night* (*c*. 1601)—all of these take Italy for their scene, and in all the quality of romantic realism is dominant. To keep this quality in perfect equilibrium, however, is a task hard even for one of Shakespeare's genius; sentimental romanticism is easy of attainment, but realistic romanticism demands for its preservation and development such delicate handling of characters and of actions as to make the path of any dramatist essaying its creation fraught with perils. *Much Ado about Nothing* and

Twelfth Night catch the mood perfectly, but *The Merchant of Venice* and *Measure for Measure* (*c.* 1604) show signs of its shattering. Even if we are prepared to see in the portrait of Shylock nothing more than a comic composition or to view the theme of *Measure for Measure* merely as a kind of fairy-tale, we must recognize that the presence of evil and the ever-looming threat of death tend to disrupt the quiet mood and the good-humoured laughter. There are accents here as threatening as those which rudely interrupt the pastoral grace of *Lycidas*.

The spirit of Shakespeare's comedy of romance is something entirely new, differing alike from the ecstatic abandonment of Aristophanes, from Plautan scenes of hilarious merriment, from Terence's sophisticated sentimentalism, and from the crudities of medieval farce. There is a kind of transcendentalism here, where the objective and the subjective meet; where the author is at one with his characters and yet, godlike, above them; where intellectual laughter becomes emotional; where clowns become wise and wise men fools. We scoff at ridiculous absurdities in these plays and discover that we are mocking ourselves; in superior manner we look down on the Dogberries and find that they alone hold the true secrets in their clumsy hands. Over all breathes an atmosphere of natural beauty wherein the common flowers of the fields have ideal implications and the hedgerows are invested with a strange unwonted grace.

This is not mere pastoralism, such as was being exploited by Guarini and Tasso. Its difference from that, indeed, is seen nowhere more clearly than in Shakespeare's one play of shepherds and their nymphs—*As You Like It* (*c.* 1600). Superficially considered, the comedy seems an ordinary pastoral, with its banished lords in the leafy greenwood, its Corins and its Sylviuses, yet throughout all its scenes runs a strain that is the very antithesis of pastoralism. With consummate art Shakespeare plays upon his rustic pipes, and then, in a single line, reveals smilingly that he realizes not only the rusticity, but also the artificiality, of his instrument. "Pray you, no more of this," cries Rosalind after she has taken part with Phebe and Sylvius in a highly artificial melodic dialogue; "'tis like the howling of Irish wolves against the moon." We listen to pleasant praise of the free life of the forest and are almost persuaded that the author would wish for himself nothing better than a bed of leaves and a drowsy peace far from the busy hum of men, when suddenly, on news that the banished exiles may return to their homes, the Duke turns from extolling "this life more sweet than that of painted pomp," and from protestations that he would change his condition on no account, to frank admission of the unhappiness of his existence and of the "shrewd days and nights" he and his companions have suffered in their enforced retirement. All through the course of the play a gentle ironic scepticism irradiates its sentiments: Shakespeare loves the greenwood, but no one is more conscious of its prickly discomforts.

Although the scene of these dramas be the Forest of Arden, or antique

Athens, or an Italian city, the characters are all recognizably Elizabethan, and little attempt is made to disguise their native habiliments. At the same time, Shakespeare reveals a power far beyond that of Lope de Vega or Calderón, who also peopled their strange localities with persons of their own age and clime. To a supreme measure, the English dramatist possessed knowledge of basic human nature, so that where the Spanish playwrights were unable or unwilling to distinguish the temporary from the eternal and that which depends on social convention from that which is essential, he is granted the skill to present, in his Elizabethan persons, figures of permanent interest. We need no knowledge of life in sixteenth-century London or Stratford to understand a Rosalind or a Viola; Touchstone wears a vanished motley, but his thoughts are not of one age; Claudios and Dogberries, Lysanders and Bottoms, are as common today, and everywhere, as they were in Shakespeare's time.

If an exquisite sense of balance, poising these plays between the two extremes of reality and the ideal, distinguishes the characters and the themes, no less is this sense of balance evident in the medium employed. Taking over the blank verse of his immediate predecessors, Shakespeare gives it flexibility in body and spirit. It hovers between rich lyricism and the common speech of men. At moments the dialogue sings melodiously, at others it has the simple directness of familiar utterance. The blank verse may be richly stocked with ore, or it may descend to such phrases as: "When are you married, madam?—Why, every day, to-morrow. Come, go in"; "If you go on thus, You will kill yourself"; "Away! I will not have to do with you." For further variety there is the medium of prose itself, with its diverse stops capable of making it the appropriate utterance of a Doll Tearsheet or of Hamlet's reflections upon man. Here too is a distinction between the English and the Spanish stages. The measures that Lope de Vega and Calderón knew were supple, but their artificiality could not permit of the scope that the Elizabethan blank verse and prose can give. The former are inclined to tinkle, where the latter yield subtle harmonies and deep diapasons. In the end drama is a creation in words, and for its development it depends more than perhaps we are accustomed to realize upon the provision of a suitable instrument—an instrument which may be exquisitely attuned to one age, but which may not serve for another. Shakespeare's genius must have been aided considerably by the fortunate circumstances that he found such an instrument—the potentialities of which had not yet been fully explored—apt in its accord with the ordinary language of his time.

The Later Tragi-Comedies

With *Measure for Measure* the series of Shakespearian comedies of romance comes to an end, although some of its tones were to be sounded again, with variations, in the tragi-comedies of his last years. *Cymbeline* (c. 1609), *The Winter's Tale* (c. 1610), and *The Tempest* (1611) are plays difficult to assess aright. Some readers find in them a groping towards a newer, and more 'philosophical,' form of theatre; others see them merely as essays made by the aging Shakespeare in the style of his younger contemporaries Beaumont and Fletcher; by some they are treated as deeply symbolic; others are equally certain that they are mere fairytales.

Three things are incontrovertible: that they differ markedly in spirit from the early comedies, even although we may trace likenesses in themes and in characters; that they do betray kinship of mood with the plays of Beaumont and Fletcher; and that in this mood they come closer than any of the other plays to the spirit of the Spanish stage. What is not sure is the precise relationship between Shakespeare's work and that of his companions, and to that is added the still greater doubt concerning the purpose which impelled him to adopt this style of drama.

In *Cymbeline* the atmosphere of *King Lear* has turned tragi-comic. We are back in Roman Britain, and villainy unadulterated reveals itself; a heroine self-reliant as Cordelia, and as tender, is the centre of the plot. Whereas, however, in the one drama the tempest of passion rises until it engulfs all the characters, in the other looming clouds suddenly part and sunshine descends on the world. If *Cymbeline* reminds us of *Lear, The Winter's Tale* recalls *Othello*. The passion of Leontes almost parallels that of the Moor, but again the sun shines forth and the tragic gloom is dissipated: the maligned wife is condemned to death, but lives, through seventeen long years, to bless with her forgiving smiles the repentant husband. It is as though a Desdemona of forty were greeting with mature love an Othello with silver in his hair. Both these plays agree in having extensive canvases, in time and in place, but in the third of the series, *The Tempest*, we encounter a drama almost as strict in its retention of the unities as even the severest of the classicists would have wished. This fact alone separates it from its companions, and that separation is increased by its basic theme. Where they recall the tragedies, this is reminiscent of the early comedies. Prospero has no kinsman in all Shakespeare's work save Oberon, Ariel none save Robin Goodfellow. The mood in which the three plays were written must have been fundamentally the same, yet perhaps we do wrong to treat them together as though they were all manifestations of an exactly similar spirit. A subtle difference divides them: *Cymbeline* and *The Winter's Tale* are the creation of a tragic dramatist prepared to ease the tensity of his passion; in *The Tempest* we have a drama written by a comic playwright whose vision of life has been deepened, enriched, and made more solemn. There is, indeed, justification for interpreting this play of Prospero as a deliberately conceived farewell to the stage.

The History Plays

From *The Tempest*, at the close of Shakespeare's career, return must now be made to the very start of his apprentice work. At the same time as he was experimenting in comedy he also found exercise for his pen in the composition of drama based on the history of England. Unfortunately, once more the relationship between his work in this kind and that of his contemporaries is unsure. *Henry VI* is now tending to be credited wholly or largely to his pen, rather than to those of his elder contemporaries. *Richard III* probably, but not certainly, came in 1592 or 1593, *King John* about 1595, and *Richard II* either the same or the following year. Peele's *Edward I* was printed in 1593, but it is impossible to say what time elapsed between its composition and its publishing; Marlowe's *Edward II* was printed the following year, and may be dated about 1592. All we can say with assurance is that the history play, probably in a crude form, was being exploited in the years before Shakespeare came to London, but that the development of the form seems to have been his own characteristic contribution to the theatre. He may have owed in inspiration to Marlowe, but just as easily can we argue for his impress on that author's single history drama.

Whether or not *Edward II*—not the most interesting but decidedly the best-fashioned of all the plays left by that rebellious and ill-starred genius of the Renaissance, Christopher Marlowe—was written before Shakespeare presented the stage with his first history dramas, it serves a useful purpose for comparison with these. In Marlowe's hands the story of Edward's reign becomes an isolated study of conflicting temperaments, with an analysis of kingly weakness. Opposite the astute, ambitious, and ruthless Mortimer is placed the figure of the dissolute, perverted monarch, gifted with a certain royalty of character, but fatally irresolute in his purposes. The scenes have undoubted strength, yet a reading of them leaves us unsatisfied. Edward's death does not arouse the tragic passions; rather do we experience a feeling of pitiful contempt as the gay king at the end lies in his unsavoury dungeon and goes miserably to his death. If it came first, Shakespeare could have gained from this work a conception of the manner in which the old chronicles might be vivified by the interpretation of their chief characters, but for the characteristic quality of his own histories he had to rely on his own genius.

That characteristic quality is suggested, if but crudely, in the three parts of *Henry VI* (*c.* 1592), where, on a vast canvas, the story of Henry's reign is discursively told, leaving Edward as the reigning king, but with threats of future disaster in the ominous person of Richard, Duke of Gloucester. There is not much of highest praise that can be given to this rambling trilogy, yet we recognize an element in it lacking in *Edward II*. Whereas that was an isolated drama, these plays, besides dealing with that cardinal fact in English medieval history—the cleavage between the red rose and the white, with the resultant Wars of the Roses—suggest, at least vaguely, an action preceding the opening scenes of the first part, and very definitely hint at what is to come after the close of the third part's final scene. The initial lines bewail the death of King Henry V; at the end there is sharp juxtaposition of Gloucester's self-confessed villainy and of King Edward's dream of happiness:

> And now what rests but that we spend the time
> With stately triumphs, mirthful comic shows,
> Such as befits the pleasures of the court?
> Sound drums and trumpets! farewell sour annoy!
> For here, I hope, begins our lasting joy.

When these lines were written, it would seem, *Richard III* (*c*. 1593) was already in the author's mind, and with this play we enter a new realm. Here the discursive arrangement of scenes has vanished, and in its stead all concentration is placed on the personality of one man. Richard is a demon incarnate, made sympathetic only by the very flamboyance of his evil, by his flashes of sardonic humour, and by that rift in his armour of baseness which eventually causes his assurance to crack and crumble. Already Shakespeare has achieved, at least in rough terms, his vision of tragic action, with the forces of hell let loose upon the world, only to dissipate themselves in their self-destroying hate, leaving us worn with travail yet conscious that a new era is to begin. When Henry of Richmond ascends to Richard's throne there is an anticipation of Malcolm's succession to Macbeth. In addition, Shakespeare has made his characteristic contribution to the history play—the creation of a drama with its own unity which is yet merely part of a larger concept.

Why, after thus creating *Richard III*, the dramatist turned to the isolated *King John* (*c*. 1595) we cannot tell: perhaps it was merely because his fellows in the theatre desired to have a reworking of an older drama on this monarch's reign; perhaps he had boyish memories of Worcester, where John lies buried, to urge him on. In handling his material he has striven to paint a picture of an irresolute monarch who, however, possesses sufficient royalty to summon forth the devoted service of the only truly living person in the play, the Bastard Faulconbridge.

The irresolution of John is paralleled, but with a notable variation, in the king who gives his name to *Richard II* (1595–96), a play in which is inaugurated another and a greater tetralogy. The three parts of *Henry VI* and *Richard III* had narrated events following the death of Henry V; *Richard II* is the initial section of a second dramatic sequence telling of the actions which led to the reign of the hero of Agincourt. Once more Shakespeare has created a tragedy, although of a sharply diverse kind. Where Richard of Gloucester was a villain and the moving spirit in the circle within which he moved, Richard II is depicted as a man of worth placed in circumstances false to his nature. He is a poet who loves to play with fancies, not a man of action such as a king should be. His irresolution, unlike that of King John, is at once motivated and made dramatically arresting.

In misery Richard goes to his death, overawed and overpowered by the masterful Henry Bolingbroke, Duke of Hereford, who ascends to the throne as King Henry IV. The play, like *Henry VI*, ends on a continuing note of ironic content. Mourning the Richard whom he has slain, Henry declares:

> I'll make a voyage to the Holy Land,
> To wash this blood off from my guilty hand:
> March sadly after; grace my mournings here;
> In weeping after this untimely bier.

The first part of *Henry IV* opens with the King's reference to the conflicts which have prevented him from fulfilling his vow; a moment of peace has come, and now he proposes at last to seek "the sepulchre of Christ." No sooner have these words been uttered, however, than news comes of the breaking out of fresh trouble in Wales, and there is the commencement of a fresh unfolding of evil strife.

Yet in the second scene we are suddenly carried into a world utterly alien to anything in the earlier histories. With the first line spoken by a greasy, corpulent, white-haired knight—"Now, Hal, what time of day is it, lad?"—we move unexpectedly out of the tragic into the comic world. For this Shakespeare had the cue in the earlier drama, *The Famous Victories of Henry V*, already mentioned, but its crude farce is here deepened into a humour pre-eminent among all the comedies of the age. With consummate mastery Shakespeare keeps these Falstaff scenes as a foil to the serious action, and at the same time makes use of them to reveal the humanity of the man who was to be the hero of this tetralogy—Prince Hal, the later Henry V. There is an almost epic sweep in this series of plays, from the lyrically poetic and tragic tone of *Richard II*, through the variegated spirit of *Henry IV*, on to the triumphant conclusion, when the son of Bolingbroke reveals the true kingly qualities so lacking in all the other monarchs whose failures Shakespeare had previously depicted.

This, except for the later *Henry VIII* (*c.* 1610), possibly written in collaboration with Fletcher, marks the close of Shakespeare's career as a writer of history plays, and it was virtually the close of the Elizabethan history play itself. The great reigns of the past had been exhausted, and the devastating Wars of the Roses had been given profound theatrical presentation. For others there was but little left to do. Here and there, sporadically, a history drama made its appearance during the years immediately following, but since Shakespeare had given such consummate expression to the form, the excitement of invention, the joy of exploration, had gone.

The Tragedies

If Shakespeare owed much to his predecessors for his comedy of romance and no less for his exploitation of the history play, and if, paradoxically, these two genres were his own creation in their final achievement, the same paradox is equally true of his tragedy. That came from his predecessors, yet was unmistakably his own.

In the complete realization of the tragic spirit exemplified in the four great dramas written between 1602 and 1606 several distinct elements are fused into unity. These elements may be described as the medieval-philosophical, the morality, the Marlovian, and the Kydian.

By the medieval-philosophical is intended that concept of tragedy which sees it as any story (not necessarily dramatic) showing great princes at the height of their estates about to fall calamitously to disaster. The moralists declared that the mission of these stories was to demonstrate the vanity of earthly happiness or to warn us of the instability of fortune. Basically such a definition of tragedy agrees with that of the early classical critics, who found the criteria of the tragic in its disastrous conclusion and in its concentration upon royal personages.

The morality tradition, while by no means directly concerned with the arousing of the tragic mood, laid stress upon the eternal conflict of good and evil, while in practice it set forth, crudely but not ineffectively, the inner struggle within man of these two forces. Here good was always triumphant in the end, but that end might come—and generally did come—only at the very conclusion of each drama, so that essentially the morality play was concerned with an exhibition of evil rampant against a field of eternity.

In the hands of the authors of *Gorboduc, Tancred and Gismund*, and their like attempts had been made to create a native English tragedy, but all evidence seems to show that until about 1587 the popular stage had failed to produce anything of worth in this kind. Rude tragi-comedies, not tragedies, satisfied the general audiences to whom the early dramatists made their appeal. That these general audiences, however, were ready to welcome something sterner is proved conclusively by the immediate success of Marlowe's plays.

Christopher Marlowe, born in the same year as Shakespeare, was a more fiery spirit than his greater contemporary. Where Shakespeare's genius manifested itself comparatively late in his career and continued to burn steadily through two decades, Marlowe's flared forth in rich splendour and vanished, with his own death, after a brief few years. No one, of course, can say what he might or might not have accomplished had he lived, but the very brilliance of the flame suggests—though it cannot prove—that its endurance might have been slight. It burned too fiercely to have lasting qualities.

Of the brilliance of the torch he held Marlowe was thoroughly conscious. Throughout the plays of Shakespeare there is little evidence of any flamboyant vainglory; there is no indication that he himself realized the extent to which he was recreating the material he found to hand. He may have known his own power, but of such knowledge no indication is given in his writings. The very first words of Marlowe uttered on the stage are a declaration of defiance and of self-assurance. From jigging veins of rhyming mother-wits he loudly promises to bring us to the high-astounding terms in which his *Tamburlaine* (*c.* 1587) is expressed.

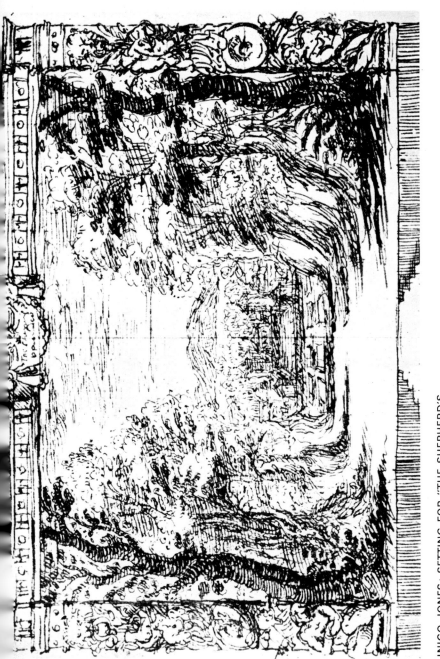

INIGO JONES: SETTING FOR "THE SHEPHERD'S PARADISE"

By courtesy of the Duke of Devonshire

INIGO JONES: FOUR COSTUME DESIGNS
By courtesy of the Duke of Devonshire

INIGO JONES: SETTING FOR
"OBERON"
By courtesy of the Duke of
Devonshire

THE SWAN THEATRE,
1595

DUTCH REDERIJKER
STAGE
Pieter Balten (after P.
Breughel the Elder).
*Photo Commissie
Rijksmuseum,
Amsterdam*

This was precisely what the age had been waiting for: the stage in 1587 needed a man sure of his aims and deliberately intent on dramatic reform. Before Shakespeare, with consummate ease, could consolidate and give culminating expression to the spirit of the Elizabethan audiences a forerunner had to blaze a bold trail for his feet to tread.

Tamburlaine is not a great play, but it was an inspiration. In terms apt to catch the attention of the spectators it set forth in glowing words an heroic theme with consistent seriousness. Marlowe proved that admiration and wonder alone could hold a crowded theatre silent, that no vulgar clownage was necessary as a sop to the public, and that lofty rhetoric, expressed in impassioned lines suited for an actor's delivery, held a charm of potent worth.

The success of *Tamburlaine* was followed by that of an entirely different kind of play, *Dr Faustus* (*c.* 1588), in which a closer approach was made to the familiar tragic form. Fundamentally the former drama had depended upon a record of achievement rather than a display of disaster. It called on men to gaze in wonderment at the power of a man who might from humblest origins rise to greatest heights; in *Dr Faustus* we are bidden to look upon a human being whose ambition leads him to uttermost ruin, and, furthermore, we are shown this hero encircled about with the insidious spirit of evil. So different was *Tamburlaine* from all preceding concepts of the tragic that men might have failed to relate it to earlier essays in this form; about *Dr Faustus* there could be no doubt: it is definitely, as the first quarto of the play states, a "tragical history."

Its innovations are many. First, it utterly defies authority and practice by abandoning completely the convention of royalty. The central figure makes not the slightest pretensions to princely lineage. He is naught but a poor scholar, distinguished from his companions solely through the extent and the intensity of his learning. Tamburlaine, if not born a king, at least becomes one, and the greater part of the drama in which he appears bears the trappings of a monarch's Court: from first to last Faust moves within the orbit of his study.

This revolutionary conception of the hero is of profound significance, since it led men to substitute a spiritual, or an inner, for an external, or a material, interpretation of the tragic essence. So long as the kingly rank was sufficient qualification the playwrights were offered no incentive to do other than clothe a dummy with ermine and gold; now Marlowe showed them that the true spirit of tragedy lay within and that the presentation of even the humblest character could arouse the deepest emotions.

The second innovation is the uniting of the tragic elements with the elements of the morality play. In every respect *Dr Faustus* is an example of the dramatic movement that produced *Everyman*. The one difference—and it is, of course, an essential difference—lies in the fact that, whereas the hero of *Everyman* is every man, the hero of *Dr Faustus* is a human being whose exceptional qualities call forth our admiration.

Otherwise the forms are the same, even to the introduction of abstract personifications and the display of the seven Deadly Sins.

By linking the morality to the tragic drama Marlowe revealed to his companions the essential business of tragedy: disaster and calamity are merely incidental consequences in the tragic play, the pith and core of which is the demonstration of evil.

This innovation is connected with a third. In classical tragedy there was comparatively little opportunity for revelation of what may be called character-growth within the scope of a single drama. Something of the quality appears when we compare, for example, the *Œdipus Tyrannus* with the *Œdipus at Colonus*, but these are two distinct plays. Where the effect is produced, as in the *Philoctetes*, its manifestation is slight and almost incidental. *Dr Faustus* depends wholly for its impression upon the moving of Faust from confident assurance and untroubled ambition to a realization of his error and to an abject dismay at the forces of hell surrounding him. The man who so proudly set forth the scope of human longing and whose words might have been those of Tamburlaine—

> Nature that framed us of four elements,
> Warring within our breasts for regiment,
> Doth teach us all to have aspiring minds.
> Our souls, whose faculties can comprehend
> The wondrous architecture of the world
> And measure every wandering planet's course,
> Still climbing after knowledge infinite,
> And always moving as the restless spheres,
> Will us to wear ourselves and never rest—

is a person entirely different from the wretched victim of Mephistopheles who hears in the striking of the clock the rapid approach of his doom:

> Ah, Faustus,
> Now hast thou but one bare hour to live
> And then thou must be damned perpetually.
> Stand still, you ever-moving spheres of heaven,
> That time may cease and midnight never come!
> Fair Nature's eye, rise, rise again, and make
> Perpetual day, or let this hour be but
> A year, a month, a week, a natural day.
> That Faustus may repent and save his soul—
> *O lente, lente currite noctis equi!*

These lines illustrate well the fourth quality distinctive of this play. In earlier tragedies there had been long speeches full of argumentative rhetoric, but no theatrical author in England had demonstrated the effect of poetic passion on the stage. Then, as now, the power of *Dr Faustus* must have lain essentially in those passages in which the grave harmonies of words charmed the ear. In action the play is absurd and petty; when we think of its worth it is on the opening speeches we concentrate, on the dialogue with Mephistopheles, on the invocation to Helen, above all on that last long soliloquy when Faust, alone on the stage, contemplates the speed of the flying hours.

This, above all other dramas, is the foundation of Shakespeare's tragedy. There is much of value in *The Jew of Malta* (*c.* 1589), and even in *Dido Queen of Carthage* (*c.* 1593); suggestions for the treatment of tragic scenes appear in *Edward II*; but, when all is said, Marlowe's reputation, and immediate influence, rests on his dramatic exposition of the story of Faust.

About the same time as *Dr Faustus* came one other tragedy of prime importance for a study of Shakespeare's art. *The Spanish Tragedy* (*c.* 1589), by Thomas Kyd, has not the poetic splendour of Marlowe, but it does possess what all Marlowe's plays lacked—skill in play construction. To a certain extent, accordingly, we may view these two plays as complementary, the one bringing to the theatre poetic distinction and depth of passion, the other contributing variety of appeal and the skilled management of episode.

It is interesting to observe that, like Marlowe, Kyd has chosen for his main characters persons not of royal birth. In his treatment of these figures, on the other hand, he has taken a variant course. The author of *Dr Faustus* had done well in insisting that tragedy must have a single hero dominant in its action; Kyd did equally well in showing how such a central person might be harmonized with his associates. Old Hieronimo is the man on whom our attentions are set, but hardly less significant for the development of the plot are Bellimperia, Balthazar, and Lorenzo. Where Marlowe succeeds by his flamboyancy, Kyd's strength depends on his skill in composition.

One particular feature of *The Spanish Tragedy* merits attention. This is a revenge drama, and in so far it has affiliations with many of the plays of Spain. It differs from them, however, in that its motivation is general rather than particular. No narrow concept of honour colours the handling of the theme. Hieronimo's son has been cruelly and treacherously murdered, and the father's search for the criminals is dictated, not by any desire to clear his injured name, but by a human passion —independent of time and place—to bring to justice those who have destroyed his happiness.

In introducing this type of revenge play to the stage, Kyd unwittingly did tremendous service. To win success in this genre a dramatist must pay close attention to the weaving of his scenes, and in a period as dominated by the inconsequences of the earlier style of tragi-comedy the new authors required, above all other things, experience in strict dramatic construction. Nothing could have been better adapted for the purpose of urging them towards such exercise than the play of revenge.

Thus was the stage set for Shakespeare. At first, as in comedy, the young writer failed to indicate the path he was later to take. In *Richard III* he had concentrated on a Marlovian superman, melodramatically evil as the Jew of Malta, ambitious as Tamburlaine; in *Titus Andronicus* (1594) he waded into a sea of horror and of blood. From that he moved, with startling suddenness, to *Romeo and Juliet* (*c.* 1595), which is to his tragedy what *Love's Labour's Lost* is to his comedy. Instinct with the spirit of youth, its lyric ecstasy attempts to wrest the tragic mood from a pitiful romantic tale, but the quality which animates a *Hamlet* or a *Lear* is absent from its scenes. Basically its story is akin to such plots as Shakespeare was currently using for his comedies, and although he has enwrapped the action in an atmosphere of fate or of adverse fortune, and although the very intensity of his poetic utterance carries us onward in a torrent of words, there can be no doubt but that the final impression leaves us without the soul-searing experience which comes from contemplation of the deepest forms of the tragic.

In *Richard II*, perhaps, a clearer advance towards this deeper tragic concept may be discerned. Richard's disaster springs not from the influence of external stars but from within, and this failing which leads to his downfall is closely and intimately related to the circumstances in which he finds himself. He is by no means a despicable character, but the very qualities that might otherwise have won our admiration are the cause of his ruin. Moreover, the failing in his nature, when related to the circumstances by which he is surrounded, releases an evil force engulfing both him and his country. In dim form and as yet not fully expressed the essential foundations of the later tragedies are outlined—as they were not outlined in *Romeo and Juliet*.

With *Hamlet* (*c.* 1601) the tragic idea is clear and the form exact: Shakespeare has found that for which he had been seeking and has succeeded in welding together harmoniously all the various elements passed on to him by his predecessors. The close connexion with Kyd's revenge tragedy is patent: it is even possible that an early *Hamlet* may have come from his pen. Marlowe contributes the feeling of admiration with which the Prince's person is invested. Hamlet in a sense is Everyman, and the general plot of the play would make it fit with ease into the early definitions of the tragic.

No play has attained to greater fame than this of Shakespeare's, and its universal appeal is seen to rise from the manner in which the poet-creator has infused into a story of apparently peculiar circumstance qualities of common and eternal import. Age after age has seen itself reflected in the hero of this play, because Shakespeare, in depicting this central figure, has seized upon human qualities of wide diffusion. The result is a strange paradox: we feel admiration for Hamlet; here is the courtier, the scholar, the soldier, the man who was eminently fitted for kinghood; and at the same time we feel that Hamlet is a representative of ordinary humanity; in Hamlet is something of ourselves.

This is the effect that Lope de Vega and Calderón so frequently missed: in their heroes the inessential and the temporary concealed the basic and the eternal.

In *Othello* (*c*. 1604) Shakespeare turned to attempt a somewhat different kind of theme. *Hamlet*, with its extensive canvas, is unquestionably romantic; the tightness of *Othello's* structure has a classic simplicity. In *Hamlet* a prince is the hero; *Othello* takes us more into the realm of the ordinary: its setting is republican Venice and its hero a man who, although general of the Doge's forces, is placed before us mainly in his domestic capacity. Powerful as this play is, its quality is less than that of *Hamlet*. Only Shakespeare could have conceived the latter, whereas *Othello*, while possessing a strength of poetic passion, might have been conceived by another. We are moving here on a less exalted plane, and the element of mystery is absent.

King Lear (1605–6) swings us tempestuously back into the realm of the metaphysical and the exalted. As a play calculated for the stage, its virtues are perhaps below those of *Othello*, but in majesty of concept and in tensity of emotion it attempts heights far beyond. The word 'elemental' has frequently been applied to this play, and the epithet is just. In *Othello* the force of evil was symbolized in a single human figure—that of Iago; in *King Lear* the whole of nature seems to become impregnated with the vapours of hell. The storm at sea in *Othello* is only reported; the actual scenes are ironically vaulted by calm Italian and Cyprian skies.

Better than any other drama the tragedy of Lear indicates those qualities which mark out Shakespeare's power. In this play the superficial sources are readily to be traced. The plot has affinities both with the typical themes of the early tragi-comedies and of the histories; bold, flamboyant portraiture appears as in Marlowe's plays, and the gloomy intrigue of Kyd is not lacking; in structure and concept, too, the spirit of the moralities is evident. Yet *King Lear* is like none of these; a new being has been wrought out of the many forces fused into one. No tragic drama had sought to achieve so much in the course of its action, and, if there is less that is strictly theatrical in its structure than there is in *Othello*, the reason lies in the fact that Shakespeare is here moving over to the very boundaries of the stage, is straining the walls of the Globe until they groan and crack.

Reference to the Globe reminds us that this, above all other plays by Shakespeare, must be visualized in terms of the stage for which he wrote. To see its illimitable conceptions degraded to the pettiness of canvas scenery is certain ruin to the idea it expresses. Here Shakespeare is calling for the fullest possible exercise of the imagination on the part of his audience, and any attempt to reproduce in artificial terms the forms surrounding the characters immediately conflicts with, and destroys, the spell of his poetic utterance. If the storm scene is enacted on a bare stage it can achieve its effect; if painted scenery is set behind the aged Lear his figure becomes tawdry and his words mere rant. If an actor succeeds in conquering such hindrances the victory is merely a personal *tour de force*.

With *Macbeth* (1605–6) we reach the end of this magnificent series of tragic dramas, and once more—although almost certainly in mangled form—there is placed before us a play of elemental scope. Already in *Julius Cæsar* (1599) Shakespeare had essayed the presentation, in theatrical form, of evil let loose upon the world, consuming and destroying in its terrible path. The earlier play, however, did not provide him with the fullest scope for the development of this conception, largely because of the presuppositions which any spectator inevitably must bring with him to a drama on such a well-known story, but partly also because the historical material could not permit of apt moulding to the dramatist's basic theme. The result was an effective theatrical piece, but not a play of deepest import.

For *Macbeth* Shakespeare could work as he willed. True, the plot was 'historical,' but only vaguely so: no member of the audience would be likely to know much of almost legendary Scottish chronicles, and the way was thus entirely open for the creation of characters and episodes best calculated to reveal the cardinal idea that called the tragedy into being. This cardinal idea was the release of evil through an individual crime, its sweeping course of destruction, and its final self-destruction, leaving a world shattered and broken, yet in some strange way the richer for its experience. Magnificently as the central characters are placed before us, it is the theme rather than the persons that seizes on our imagination and stirs our emotions. As de Quincey so clearly realized and so brilliantly put into words, this is a play of hell in which Macbeth's dark castle, with its great doors shutting out the world of humanity, is endowed with a symbolic significance:

> All action in any direction is best expounded, measured and made apprehensible, by reaction. Now apply this to the case of Macbeth. Here . . . the retiring of the human heart, and the entrance of the fiendish heart, was to be expressed and made sensible. Another world has stepped in, and the murderers are taken out of the region of human things, human purposes, human desires. They are transfigured: Lady Macbeth is "unsexed"; Macbeth has forgot that he was born of woman; both are conformed to the image of devils; and the world of devils is suddenly revealed. But how shall this be conveyed and made palpable? In order that a new world may step in, this world must for a time disappear. The murderers, and the murder, must be insulated—cut off by an immeasurable gulf from the ordinary tide and succession of human affairs—locked up and sequestered in some deep recess; we must be made sensible that the world of ordinary life is suddenly arrested—laid asleep—tranced —rocked into a dread armistice; time must be annihilated; relation to things without abolished; and all must pass self-withdrawn into a deep syncope and suspension of earthly passion. Hence it is that, when the deed is done, when the work of darkness is perfect, then the world of darkness passes away like a pageantry in the clouds: the knocking at the gate is heard; and it makes known audibly that the reaction has commenced; the human has made its reflux upon the fiendish; the pulses of life are beginning to beat again; and the reestablishment of the goings-on of the world in which we live, first makes us profoundly sensible of the awful parenthesis that had suspended them.

Such comment on *Macbeth* well illustrates the gulf that separates Shakespeare from Calderón and Lope de Vega. They were skilled dramatists with easily moving pens, but not a single one of their works, not even the philosophically conceived *autos*, bears a quality worthy of contemplation in this way. Their ideas are surface ideas, readily appreciated and capable of interpretation in intellectual terms; for the interpretation of Shakespeare an imaginative process is demanded, and intellectually conceived words must fail in the attempt to indicate his meaning.

The effect he produces is achieved by the utilization of every device offered to him by the theatre, from the physical movement of his actors upon the stage to the subtlest use of poetic imagery. In *Antony and Cleopatra* (*c.* 1606), for example, he takes a story of grand passion which had already been told and retold both by historians and by playwrights and invests it with a quality of his own. Even he, perhaps, cannot wrest out of its material a tragic atmosphere so intense as that of *Hamlet* or *Macbeth*, but, by the pervasive imagery through which he excites our minds into conceiving illimitable spaces and the very vastness of the universe, he takes a tale of consuming sexual passion, all too human, and gives it superhuman proportions. Here the temporary is wrought into the eternal.

3

EARLY SEVENTEENTH-CENTURY TRAGEDY AND COMEDY

A Changing Theatre

By THE time that Shakespeare retired from the stage the theatre was beginning to change its form. James VI of Scotland travelled southward in the year 1603 to assume the throne left vacant by Elizabeth's death, and very soon he showed that the royal parsimony which had prevented the fuller development of Court theatricals in the sixteenth century was to be replaced by lavish expenditure on scenic productions. Under the direction of the architect-designer Inigo Jones the masque rapidly assumed a position of importance.

Like the *intermezzi* and later operas of Italy, these masques existed more for show than for sense. Care no doubt went into their composition; at least one author, Ben Jonson, never ceased to press the claims of poetry, while another, John Milton, produced in *Comus* (1634) a work of delicate literary art. But, fundamentally, appeal to the eyes was inherent in the genre. When the courtiers gathered at Whitehall to witness one of these productions they forgot the words in the wonder of the scenery, the richness of the costumes, and the glittering lights with which Inigo Jones and his assistants bespangled the stage.

In the published texts of the masques we may find many lovelinesses. There are lyrics with words that sing, delicate fancies, and charmingly turned phrases, but, with the exception of *Comus*, there is not a single example in this kind, from Jonson's *Masque of Blackness* (1605) on to the elaborate productions of the reign of Charles I, culminating in Sir William D'Avenant's *Salmacida Spolia* (1639–40), which possesses any true dramatic worth. It may be amusing to revive one of these pieces for an occasional performance, yet the amusement can go little beyond historical interest and dilettante curiosity.

What is significant in the development of the Court masque is the change it wrought in the shape of the public theatre. To Whitehall Inigo Jones brought the perspective scenery of Italy, with its proscenium stage, its wings, its backcloths, its 'machines,' and its indoor lighting. The novelty was too great and too alluring not to be without its influence abroad. As the seventeenth century advanced we can easily trace a

change in the typical theatre audiences, with the gradual retirement of
the puritanically inclined middle classes and the taking over of the stage
by the Cavaliers. That which had been in 1590 a genuinely popular entertainment, attracting all classes of the community, became by 1640 an
almost exclusively courtly delight. Thus, increasingly, the same spectators as joyed in the production of the masque at Whitehall came to form
the greater part of the audiences in the public playhouses: and, this being
so, it would have been strange indeed had they not sought to introduce,
or had they not inspired the introduction of, theatrical effects similar to
those with which they were familiar at Court.

Thus is explained the general shifting from the open air to the roofed-
in theatre during the early years of the seventeenth century. By 1608
Shakespeare's company was using the closed Blackfriars theatre as their
winter headquarters; by 1617 the Phœnix in Drury Lane had been established, and by 1629 the Salisbury Court Playhouse. These were the typical theatres of the Caroline period, and in these scenery could be, and
was, introduced—perhaps tentatively at first, but nevertheless in such a
manner as to indicate that the bare, flexible stage that Shakespeare knew
would soon be superseded.

Domestic and Horror Tragedy

Amid these changing conditions new forms of drama necessarily
arose, but, since the process of change was slow, the qualities we may call
'Elizabethan' maintained their integrity well into the reign of James I,
and of these qualities two call for particular attention here.

Already about the year 1590 the public stage had witnessed the production of a tragedy called *Arden of Feversham*, in which is presented, not a
story of a kingdom's downfall, but a tale of the murder of a Mr Arden by
his wife, Alice. Nothing could be further removed from the principles of
the 'classic' drama, yet no theatrical development could have been more
natural in the circumstances of the romantic theatre. In Spain a similar
set of conditions produced *The Physician of his own Honour*; although this
has a courtly background and deals with aristocratic figures, the weaving
of tragic scenes out of ordinary domestic circumstances is fundamentally
the same as that which inspired the unknown Elizabethan author to pen
his tragedy of middle-class passions. Out of romantic fervour and liberty
the realistic drama was being born.

Although only one drama of this kind in England—Shakespeare's
Othello—reaches any great height (and even this tragedy veers from the
true 'domestic' scene to exploit a background of Venetian splendour and
of Eastern war), the vogue of plays dealing with common characters has
unquestioned interest for us as we survey the development of dramatic
art in the early seventeenth century. Various records show that many
dramas of domestic sort must have perished, while even those which have
been preserved form a goodly little company. A flash of lurid genius il-

luminates *A Yorkshire Tragedy* (*c.* 1606); the murder of a "Master George Sanders of London, Merchant," is narrated in *A Warning for Fair Women* (printed 1599); while *Two Lamentable Tragedies* (printed 1601) tells of several similar crimes. Here, definitely, is middle-class realism, with all the sensational and moral qualities associated with that style of composition.

The middle-class atmosphere enwraps many of the works of two authors of this time—Thomas Dekker and Thomas Heywood—both of whom added to the mere delineation of murders an element which pointed unmistakably towards the problem drama of later times. The latter started his career with a peculiar romantic play entitled *The Four Prentices of London* (*c.* 1592), and in the course of a long journeyman's service in the theatre turned out dozens of diverse pieces exploiting historical and legendary themes; among these stand out two domestic dramas —*A Woman killed with Kindness* (1603) and *The English Traveller* (*c.* 1627). The former presents a happily married, fairly well-to-do gentleman, Frankford by name, who generously offers hospitality to a friend, Wendoll, and is betrayed by him. At first he will not allow his suspicions to fall on his wife; then as he watches them doubts arise in his mind, until certainty eventually is forced upon him. It is at this stage in the development of his theme that Heywood shows his originality. Instead of stabbing the guilty lovers when he finds them in each other's arms, Frankford refrains from vengeance and, in broken accents, dreams passionately and fondly for ignorance of his wife's guilt:

> O God! O God! that it were possible
> To undo things done—to call back yesterday—
> That Time could turn up his swift sandy glass,
> To untell the days and to redeem these hours;
> Or that the sun
> Could, rising from the west, draw his coach backward—
> Take from the account of Time so many minutes
> Till he had all these seasons called again,
> Those minutes and those actions done in them,
> Even from her first offence, that I might take her
> As spotless as an angel in my arms.
> But Oh! I talk of things impossible
> And cast beyond the moon!

As punishment for her sin she is sent to a neighbouring house, there to be well cared for, but condemned never to see him or her children again. Her conscience will not, however, permit her to live; gradually she fades, and as she lies dying her husband comes to see her, and, calling her wife and mother, bids her a sad farewell:

> Both those lost names I do restore thee back,
> And with this kiss I wed thee once again.

That a prolific but not particularly outstanding playwright could conceive such scenes testifies to the inherent strength of the Elizabethan theatre.

The English Traveller, although marred by a comic sub-plot, has a somewhat similar atmosphere. The hero of the play, young Geraldine, returns from abroad and meets again a love of his boyhood, now the wife of the elderly Wincott. He realizes that he is still passionately in love with ·her, yet his fineness of temper will not allow him to wrong the husband. In a peculiarly emotional scene he pledges chastity, although the wife and he vow to marry when the old man has died. Here, as in *A Woman killed with Kindness*, Heywood introduces an original twist in the plot. By chance Geraldine discovers that this woman whom he adores is playing false with a young gallant, Delavile. His rage is that of an injured husband, but, like Frankford, he forbears from taking a bloody revenge, while she, broken by the nobleness of his spirit, dies of shame.

Thomas Dekker was a dramatist somewhat akin to Heywood, author of a large number of plays, tinged with a similar middle-class colouring, but possessed too of a romantically poetical quality. *Old Fortunatus* (1599), with its strange allegorical scenes, is a queer farrago of episodes illuminated by passages of melodious verse; *The Shoemakers' Holiday*, produced the same year, presents a racy, 'realistic' picture of master-journeymen and their apprentices in late-Elizabethan London. These first two plays of his indicate the wide range of Dekker's style, a style which led him to not ineffective satire in *Satiromastix* (1601), to exploitation of the morality play in *The Whore of Babylon* (*c*. 1605), and to the depiction of common scenes of contemporary life in such works as *Westward Ho!* (1604), *Northward Ho!* (1605), and *The Roaring Girl* (*c*. 1610). Many of these plays were composed in collaboration with others, as was *The Honest Whore* (*c*. 1604–5), a drama in two parts written with Thomas Middleton. Typical of several similar theatrical writings of the time, this last work infuses into a plot of palace intrigue a story of common life. Bellafront is the courtesan referred to in the title; falling in love with Hippolito, she declares she will "prove an honest whore in being true to one, and to no more," but is rejected angrily by the man on whom she has set her affections. The second section of the drama reverses the situation, for here Hippolito sues her to be his mistress, while she, having been converted by his earlier words, refuses his suit. Although not strictly like the other domestic plays already noted, the treatment of this part of the story shows Dekker influenced partly at least by the realistic tragedies and tragi-comedies of the time.

Under the new conditions operative in the theatre, however, this vogue of bourgeois scenes rapidly disappeared, and the tragic stage more and more was given over to sensationalism and the presentation of horror. Palace intrigue rather than domestic problems interested the courtly audiences: the theme of revenge, which already had attracted attention in the Elizabethan period, now became of greater interest, while the bold passions that had served the earlier theatres were supplanted by strange and tortured emotions.

Playwrights such as George Chapman, Philip Massinger, and Thomas Middleton form a link between the old and the new. The first of these won some virtue out of the writing of historical tragedies with philosophic content, failing to reach the highest levels only because of a lack of variety in his utterance and by a failure to develop unity out of his diverse material. Listening to Chapman's words, we have the impression of hearing Marlowe's boldly vigorous terms turned incoherent, of passion that has become forced, and of scenes framed rather for their intellectual than for their theatrical content. There is strength in the flamboyant *Bussy d'Ambois* (1604); there are flashes of true insight in the two parts of *Charles, Duke of Byron* (1608); there is an interesting attempt to present a wholly virtuous hero in *Chabot, Admiral of France* (*c.* 1613); but not a single one of these leaves us with a clear picture. The stage is cluttered with useless characters; never do we feel that Chapman is thorough master of his own conceptions.

The rhetorical note so strongly sounded in Chapman's plays becomes intensified in those of Massinger, while the glaring colours to which Dryden objected in *Bussy d'Ambois* are rendered still more blatant. With Dekker he collaborated in *The Virgin Martyr* (*c.* 1620), exploiting all the current love of spectacle and sensation. The main theme concerns the constancy of the Christian maid Dorothea, but about her circle a motley collection of wonders, from the 'fearful shape' of the devil Harpax to the heavenly Angelo, while full use is made of the dire torments meted out at the end to the heroine and her fellow-martyrs. Although six hundred years separate the two plays, *The Virgin Martyr* is strangely akin, in its mingled buffoonery and concentration upon pagan rage, to Hrotswitha's primitive little *Dulcitius*.

Rhetoric, horror, sensationalism, mar all of Massinger's other tragic dramas. Character is sacrificed to effect, and self-conscious argumentation takes the place of self-revealing lines. *The Duke of Milan* (printed 1623) is full of surprises and grisly episodes; we can take no interest in it as a whole, since sensational scenes crowd upon each other in such wise that any possibility of capturing a dominant central emotion is utterly lost. Incest and murder form the theme of *The Unnatural Combat* (*c.* 1620); torture and torment are freely exploited in *The Roman Actor* (1626).

Thomas Middleton has something of greater worth to offer. His atmosphere may be dark, with flashes of lurid light, but there is a passionate tensity in his writing that holds our attention. He too could sup on crude horror, as in *The Witch* (*c.* 1616), but a more serious purpose animated some of his other works, and, where Chapman and Massinger showed a failure to grasp their material firmly, he displays a concentration of power and an insistence in aim that reminds us of the Shakespearian model. In *Women beware Women* (*c.* 1620) the darkness of passion is almost unrelieved. One plot tells of an incestuous relation between Hippolito and his niece Isabella; another relates how Bianca, wife of Leantio, is seduced by an amorous Duke of Florence. In the end Leantio is slain in a duel, while Hippolito, Isabella, the Duke, and Bianca all perish in a masque presented in a manner reminiscent of that in *The Spanish Tragedy*. Sensationalism is beginning to run riot here, yet there is a strength, albeit tormented with loathing, inherent in the succession of dismal scenes. More impressive is *The Changeling* (1622), in which Middleton collaborated with William Rowley, a play akin to *Macbeth* in its delineation of evil breeding evil. Falling in love with Alsemero, a girl, Beatrice Joanna, commissions a needy gentleman, De Flores, to murder the man whom her father bids her marry. Although she does not know it, De Flores lusts after her and gladly accepts the task. The murder done, he returns to claim his reward; she offers him money, only to learn that it is herself he desires. In a magnificently planned scene Middleton reveals the capricious, proud, aristocratic woman, who has imagined that she can easily control this insignificant creature, gradually forced to a sense of the terrible reality. "Why," she cries, in incredulous accents,

> Why, 'tis impossible thou canst be so wicked,
> Or shelter such a cunning cruelty,
> To make his death the murderer of my honour!
> Thy language is so bold and vicious
> I cannot see which way I can forgive it
> With any modesty.

The imperious words, just faintly broken by a trembling fear, are stilled by his reply:

> Pish! You forget yourself!
> A woman dipped in blood, and talk of modesty!

When she speaks of "the distance that Creation set 'twixt thy blood and mine," she finds for answer only his contemptuous

> Look but into your conscience, read me there:
> 'Tis a true book; you'll find me there your equal.

She has truly become, as he says, "the deed's creature"—and the deed will not let her rest. Relentlessly she is driven on until she is slain by her minion.

Something of the same quality appears in *The Maid's Tragedy* (c. 1611) by Beaumont and Fletcher, two playwrights whose work in the field of tragi-comedy will call for further treatment. With a simple plot, the authors drive steadily towards their goal, and although there is here no dominant theme illuminating the actions, the characters stand out in bold and vital terms. Evadne, the King's mistress, is married by royal command to the loyal courtier Amintor, who is thus forced to abandon his first love, Aspatia. Coldly she informs him after the wedding of the truth, and he, although fired with anger, cannot lift his hand against his monarch. Evadne, however, finds herself oppressed by his reproaches and by those of his friend Melantius; secretly she prepares to destroy her royal lover, binds him to the bed in which he lies, and stabs him. Expecting Amintor's praise, she is dismayed at his horror of her deed and dies by her own hand. Unfortunately, with that tendency towards sentimentalism which becomes so patent in the plays of the seventeenth century, the authors have followed these truly impressive scenes with others in which the fragile Aspatia, dressed as a man, challenges Amintor to a duel and perishes by his hand.

Many plays of this time might merit consideration here, but obviously selection must be made if proportion is to be kept. That the dramatic urge which produced Shakespeare maintained some of its power during the reigns of James I and Charles I is certain, yet when the tragedies written during this time are put to the highest test we must admit that, brilliant though individual scenes may be, they fall far short of perfection. Sense of character-drawing becomes increasingly weaker; larger compositional values are lost; novelties in the exploitation of sensational incident grow more and more frequent; almost frenzied rhetoric and splenetic outbursts replace the rich sounds of balanced poetic utterance; for boldness of passion appears subtly degenerate emotion.

Out of the run of the earlier tragedies stand *The White Devil* (*c.* 1610) and *The Duchess of Malfi* (1613–14) of that dark genius John Webster. The 'White Devil' is Vittoria Corombona, wife of the spiritless Camillo, whose tempestuous desire for power causes her to encompass the murder both of her husband and of the innocent Isabella, wife of the Duke whose mistress she has become. Her character is brilliantly drawn, and her resolute will receives ample illumination in the scene wherein, brought to justice, she clearly renders herself intellectual master of the Court. As in so many other of these Jacobean dramas, the stage becomes cluttered here with inessentials and with a very plethora of horrors, but no one can deny that Webster has with singular skill created an atmosphere of courtly evil or that he has succeeded in presenting to us one of the most memorable, although at the same time one of the most unsympathetic, heroines in the entire course of the drama.

The mood of *The Duchess of Malfi* is similar, but the personality of the heroine is vastly different. She is here presented as a woman of highest lineage, offering her love to, and marrying, a low-born steward. Her action enrages her brothers—one a great Cardinal, the other a Duke. They engage a villainous agent for their purpose in the criminal Bosola; they torment her with grim pageants, culminating in a cruel dance of madmen; they proceed to strangle her and her children. Webster's genius is shown nowhere more clearly than in the famous line with which her brother the Duke turns from the cold corpses of his victims. He has displayed no feeling when Bosola reveals them to him, but finally breaks when he looks closer at his sister:

Cover her face: mine eyes dazzle: she died young.

In the final act complete eclipse descends on this palace interior. The Cardinal is slain by his own brother; Bosola and the Duke fall by each other's hands. This indeed is, in Webster's own words, a "gloomy world," a "deep pit of darkness."

An even deeper pit is dug by Cyril Tourneur, author of *The Atheist's Tragedy* (*c.* 1607) and probably of *The Revenger's Tragedy* (*c.* 1607). The latter is immeasurably the finer work, and, despite the fact that its conglomeration of sensational scenes becomes almost ludicrous for a modern reader, its ghastly impressiveness cannot be denied. There is a grim tragic irony in the development of the plot; a refulgent beauty appears in its unrelieved delineation of fathomless evil. From the moment when, at the very beginning of the drama, we listen to Vindice apostrophizing the skull of his murdered mistress to the very last scene a kind of evil spell is wrought upon us. Few authors of the time could rise to that sombrely bitter denunciation of sexual passion delivered in searing words by Vindice as he gazes on the skull:

> Does every proud and self-affecting dame
> Camphire her face for this? And grieve her maker
> In sinful baths of milk—when many an infant starves—
> For her superfluous outside, all for this?
> Who now bids twenty pounds a night, prepares
> Music, perfumes and sweet meats? All are hushed:
> Thou may'st lie chaste now! It were fine, methinks,
> To have thee seen at revels, forgetful feasts
> And unclean brothels. Sure, 'twould fright the sinner
> And make him a good coward, put a reveller
> Out of his antic amble
> And cloy an epicure with empty dishes.
> Here might a scornful and ambitious woman
> Look through and through herself. See, ladies, with
>   false forms
> You deceive men, but cannot deceive worms.

Such frenzy, as is obvious, could not long maintain its intensity, and when we trace the fortunes of the tragic drama in England up to the closing of the theatres in 1642 we clearly see how the dark sensationalism of the earlier years becomes a mere mannerism, and how the fiery bitterness of spirit is reduced to a staleness of utterance. One author of the later years, John Ford, retains elements of the pristine strength, but the worm is upon his pages, the rose is cankered; we are out of the honest breath of heaven breathing hot-house air. *'Tis Pity she's a Whore* (*c.* 1624) ventures daringly into the realm of incest: with hardly a backward thought Giovanni woos his sister, Annabella, gains her love, and calmly watches her being married off (for the purpose of preserving her 'honour') to a gentleman named Soranzo. Knowing that the husband plans revenge, Giovanni kills Annabella, and in a scene of sensational incident dashes in among Soranzo's assembled guests with her heart impaled on his dagger, stabs him, and is himself slain. Despite the fact that the author has inserted here and there some pious reflections of a suitable moral tendency, there seems to be no doubt but that he was flaunting his daring theme before a jaded public for whom ordinary passions had well-nigh lost their savour. Degenerate sensuality, wrapped in an intoxicating riot of words, casts its orchidian clamminess over every scene.

Sensationalism of a like kind flourishes in *The Broken Heart* (*c.* 1629), where two lovers, Orgilus and Penthea, are separated by Ithocles, who forces the latter to marry the noble blackguard Bassanes. Under the stress of her emotions she goes mad and finally dies, while Orgilus plans vengeance on Ithocles. Trapping him in a specially devised chair with movable arms, he stabs him to death. At this point in the drama we suddenly discover, to our astonishment and dismay, that Ford's main purpose is to concentrate attention, not upon any of these characters, but upon the princess Calantha who had been betrothed to Ithocles: it is she who dominates the latter part of the tragedy. Such disruption of interest reveals strikingly the inherent weakness in the later Jacobean and Caroline drama. The authors have lost the virtue of simplicity, because their audiences, affected and blasé courtiers, are not content with the consistent dramatic development of a single story. Each scene has to have its horror or excitement; each act has to have its catastrophe and climax.

After Ford little remains worthy of mention. The stages are closed by Puritan ordinance on the violence and strained passions of James Shirley and Sir William D'Avenant. The former's *The Traitor* (1631) and *The Cardinal* (1641) and the latter's *Albovine* (1626) and *The Cruel Brother* (1627), each presenting, in Shirley's words, a "heap of tragedies," show the Elizabethan fervour at its last panting gasp. Phrenetic emotions, allied to madness, infect these plays: were it not for their obvious mannerism and artificiality they would be unbearable; as it is, save for a few individual scenes, they are merely dull. Renaissance romanticism had here run its course.

The Growth of Realistic Comedy: Ben Jonson

One man had stood out stalwartly against romanticism during the first years of the seventeenth century. Ben Jonson, although largely self-educated, made himself one of the best classical scholars of his time, and tried with desperate seriousness to convert the stage to imitation of the models he so deeply admired. Had he been born twenty years earlier, he might have altered the entire course of the Elizabethan drama—and, incidentally, might have denied us the works of Shakespeare; as it was, his comparatively late appearance permitted the Elizabethan romanticism to develop unchecked while it served the salutary purpose of revivifying the spirit of comedy, which, after Shakespeare, otherwise would certainly have exhibited signs of progressive debility.

In his attempt to establish 'classical' tragedy among the courtly audi-

SBARCO DI VENERE E DELLA SVA CORTE CONDOTTA DA ZEFFIRO NELLE SPIAGGE TIRRENE

Alfonso Parigus del: et fecit 1628.

ALFONSO PARIGI: "THE DISEMBARKING OF VENUS,"
SETTING FOR AN INTERMEZZO

CLOUD MACHINES AT TURIN IN THE SEVENTEENTH
CENTURY

ences of his time he failed utterly. *Sejanus* (1603) and *Catiline* (1611) are ponderously dull, and their heavy solemnity pleased not at all the spectators before whom Shakespeare's own company presented them. Far diverse was the fate of his comedies. At a time when men were seeking for new styles in their scenes of merriment Jonson stepped forward with a self-conscious, deliberately planned programme which caught the attention of men who inclined to look on the Shakespearian comedy of humour as more than a trifle old-fashioned, and perhaps even lacking in gentility.

Fundamentally this programme of Jonson's was based on three precepts: he sought for precision of form, condemning the discursiveness of the romantic mood; he wanted 'realism,' believing that it was the mission of comedy to depict contemporary life with moral intent, not tell pleasing tales of fairies and Calibans; he believed in the presentation of boldly conceived types, each representative of some folly or vice, in order that through the resultant satire men might laugh and be cured of their errors. The age was ready for satire, and thus Jonson rolled forward gloriously on the crest of the wave.

Like Marlowe before him, but with greater explicitness, Jonson announced his purposes in prologue and 'induction.' He sought to give in his plays

> Deeds and language such as men do use,
> And persons such as Comedy would choose
> When she would show an image of the times
> And sport with human follies, not with crimes.

His plots were to be "near and familiarly allied to the time," and not concerned with romantic incident:

> As of a Duke to be in love with a Countess, and that Countess to be in love with the Duke's son, and the son to love the Lady's waiting-maid—some such cross-wooing, with a Clown to their serving-man.

Above all, the characters in these realistically conceived plots were to be based on the 'humours' of men, their eccentricities. The word 'humour,' connected etymologically with our modern 'humid,' is to be explained by the belief that in the human body coursed four separate fluids (or 'humours'); in proper balance and proportion these produced even perfection, but when one or more were in excess the character concerned was carried out of the level path and became obsessed or dominated by melancholy, choler, and the like. Jonson insisted strongly that he was concerned, not with mere mannerism, but with basic human traits. For him 'humour' arose

> When some one peculiar quality
> Doth so possess a man that it doth draw
> All his affects, his spirits and his powers
> In their confluctions all to run one way.

"This," he declares, "may be truly said to be a humour," but it is "more than most ridiculous" to imagine that a 'humour' is to be found when a gallant sports some strange fashions in clothes: this is merely an external affectation and does not indicate any inner quality.

The result is that Jonson's comedies are more closely tied to the London world in which he lives than are the typical comedies of Shakespeare (although the comic scenes of *Henry V* and *The Merry Wives of Windsor* approach towards the former's ideal), and at the same time are concerned not so much with the presentation of rounded characters as with the delineation, almost caricature-wise, of living eccentricities. Instead of drawing a man, Jonson takes a 'humour' and invests it with seemingly human form, so that, in one sense, Greed and Folly and Jealousy, not living persons, stalk his stage.

Were his programme all, we should not now be regarding him as Shakespeare's greatest rival in dramatic art; fortunately, to his deliberateness of purpose he added a full-blooded, lusty strength, a keen eye, and a style incisive and theatrical. His inventive power is rich, his vigour unsurpassed: in his plays there crowd before us a great gathering of grotesques whom he has invested with vitality, presenting a vast and motley panorama of caricature, boldly coloured, unforgettable.

Towards his final aim he seems to have moved slowly, although ponderously and surely. Before 1600 he had written several plays, now lost, which from their titles must certainly have been in the romantic manner; *The Case is Altered*, which may date from this period, shows his style by no means fully fashioned; and even *Every Man in his Humour* (1598), as first composed, had an Italianate, not an English, scene.

This is the play, however, in which he realized his peculiar strength, and, after listening to the author's pronouncement of aim, we find it something of a shock when we discover that its quality depends by no means entirely upon the 'classical' plan that Jonson designed for himself. It is true that in the relation between the testy Knowell and his poetic son there is a clear utilization of Plautan and Terentian comedy scenes, but the central figure in the play, the inventive Brainworm, is much more than adaptation to modern conditions of the intriguing slave of Rome. This character, who is singled out by the wise and kindly Justice Clement as the best fellow of them all, gains his vitality more from the tradition of the morality Vice than from that of the Latin *servus*. His gusto is medieval rather than classical.

The whole racy action, vaguely based though it may be on Jonson's knowledge of the ancients, is instinct with the life of his own time. The jealousy of Kitely, the pretence of Cob, the absurdities of the 'gulls' Matthew and Stephen, the melancholy grandeur of Bobadil—all these derive from native sources and Jonson's own imaginative power.

As his art developed, we become conscious both of the possibilities of this new form of comedy and of the dangers inherent in it. A man with a programme may incline both towards overweening self-esteem and towards exaggeration of purpose; and such inclinations unquestionably prevented Jonson from achieving more than he did. *Every Man out of his Humour* (1599) pushes his ideas too far; *Cynthia's Revels* (1600) and *The Poetaster* (1601), brilliant though some of their scenes may be, are marred by the incursion of personal bitterness; in the plays of his latter years determination to keep to his self-appointed plan makes the aging dramatist falter and stumble, become incoherent and dull.

But all of the complete or partial failures count as nothing against the brilliance of four plays of his maturity—*Volpone; or, The Fox* (1606), *Epicœne; or, The Silent Woman* (1609), *The Alchemist* (1610), and *Bartholomew Fair* (1614). The first of these is incomparably the greatest, rising from the merely laughable to levels worthy of comparison with tragedy itself. With magnificent conception Jonson here presents a play with which there is none to compare in that age save the contemporary dramas of Shakespeare. The author's grasp is sure; his delineation of character types is superb; his weaving of plot and theme indicates the presence of theatrical genius.

The scene is Venice and the central figure the luxurious, cynical, contemptuous Volpone. Aided by his rascally servant Mosca, he pretends to be on his death-bed in order to tempt a miserable crew of self-seekers —Corbaccio, Corvino, Voltore—to make him presents of gold and jewels in the expectation of being named his heir. Volpone's active mind, his sensuality, his overweening belief in his own cunning and his underrating of the intelligence of all mankind, will not, however, let him rest with such a simple piece of ironic villainy. He becomes enamoured of Corvino's beautiful young wife, Celia, and in his attempt to seduce her oversteps himself. Ordered before the Venetian courts, he has himself brought in on a litter, and Mosca claims he is so enfeebled he cannot even open his mouth to speak. This trick has its effect; his detractors are silenced; while he, intoxicated by success, is induced to attempt a more daring device still: he gives out that he is dead, and that Mosca is his heir. In his savage joy at the discomfiture of his dupes he does not see the danger into which he has blundered: Mosca, invested with his riches, calmly refuses to part with his booty; Volpone's only course left is to reveal the trick, and this leads to his punishment and disgrace.

There is an intensity and a directness in this play which give it uncommon distinction. Its vision of a world of rapacious birds and beasts of prey has the simplicity and the searing light of true genius.

The play that immediately followed, *Epicœne*, is more mirth-provoking. Taking as his central figure an elderly Morose, whose ears can brook no noise, Jonson devises an intrigue of the kind he knew so well how to manage. Tricked into marrying an apparently ideal, soft-spoken wife, poor Morose is dismayed to find he has brought a loud-tongued termagant into his household, and is released from the torment (by the discovery that the supposed wife is in reality a boy) only after he has agreed to make suitable provision for his nephew Dauphine. The whole piece is masterly in its handling of a complex and amazing intrigue, although it is to be questioned whether Jonson was wise in avoiding Plautan practice and in endeavouring to keep the audience as much in the dark as the main characters of the play.

From the merriment of *Epicœne* he next turned to a milder and less bitter essay in the *Volpone* style. In *The Alchemist* the scene is plague-stricken London, when many a rich householder fled the city, leaving their houses tenanted only by servants. One such house is being looked after by Face, who, in order to make some money on the side, leagues himself with a charlatan-alchemist, Subtle, and a prostitute, Dol Common. Into their spider's web come a variegated collection of stupid flies—the young tobacconist, Abel Drugger; Dapper, a clerk; Sir Epicure Mammon, a would-be millionaire; Ananias and Tribulation Wholesome, the needy Puritans.

With consummate skill Jonson handles his types and their characteristic speech. The play is full of racy idiom, slang, and spurious 'alchemical' jargon, but the author succeeds in making the entire action richly fraught with interest and meaning, even although much of the language must have been almost as obscure to a Jacobean audience as to modern readers. Indeed, the very obscurity points to a peculiar paradox in Jonson's work as a whole. With his learning and his 'classical' leanings, it might have been thought that his writings would have yielded more in the study than on the stage, whereas precisely the opposite is true. When we read the lines of Abel Drugger we may find it hard to understand why David Garrick chose this rôle for himself, or how, having chosen it, he succeeded in winning such acclaim for its interpretation. Any theatrical production will explain the conundrum: on the stage Jonson's lines achieve an individuality, a verve, and a significance which are hard to wrest from them when they are merely conned on the printed page.

The final drama in this great quartet is *Bartholomew Fair*, an uproarious, breezy delineation of low life in London, where character and plot alike become subordinate to the noisy clamour of the Fair itself. There is, indeed, in this play no 'plot' in the ordinarily accepted sense of that word; the persons, from Lantern, the maker of toys and verses, and Rabbi Zeal-of-the-Land Busy to the sweaty pig-woman Ursula and the thievish Edgeworth, move in and out of the scenes, passing from raucous booth to booth, as though they truly lived.

Here Jonson's realism is stretched to its farthest limits.

Romance and Wit: From Beaumont and Fletcher to Shirley

During the years that Jonson was thus fighting to establish a realistic, 'classical' form of English comedy Elizabethan romance continued to flourish in the hands of many playwrights, although gradually the romantic elements were taking such new shapes that eventually they coalesced with his style and, combined with that, produced a new comedy of manners.

A typical author of the early years of the century, John Day, illustrates well the way in which the Jonsonian plan was being tentatively fused with the romantic. *The Blind Beggar of Bethnal Green* (1600), with its plethora of disguises, need not detain us, but *The Isle of Gulls* (1606) and *Humour out of Breath* (1607–8), although not great works of art, deserve some brief attention. The story of the first, dealing with a Duke of Arcadia and chivalric adventure, is thoroughly in the 'Elizabethan' mood, but the fact that all the characters are 'gulled' at the close brings the comedy near to *Every Man in his Humour*; chivalric adventure, general challenges offered to the world, provide the chief stuff of the second play also, but when the witty Florimell engages in a duel of wits with the melancholic hero Aspero we come at last to the threshold of another world, a world of realistic vision and sharp repartee.

The comedies of Thomas Heywood and Thomas Dekker likewise display transitional features, middle-class realism here marrying with sentimental and romantic fancies; *The Fair Maid of the West* (printed 1631) and *The Roaring Girl* (*c.* 1610) reveal these amply. The latter comedy was written by Dekker in collaboration with Thomas Middleton, an author who, besides contributing largely to the sensational domestic tragedy, made characteristic contribution to the realistic comedy. His affiliations with the earlier comedy of romance may easily be traced in *The Old Law* (1599) and *Blurt Master Constable* (1601–2). In the former a Duke of Epire publishes a decree condemning to death all men over eighty, all women over sixty, and as a result several characters are led to ludicrous intrigue. Simonides rejoices because his aged father will go; Eugenia receives suitors since her husband will be eighty in a few months; Gnatho the clown suborns a clerk to alter his wife's date of birth. With considerable verve the scenes are vividly brought before us, and the dialogue is frequently amusing. "When dies thy husband?" says one wife to another. "Is't not July next?" The second play provides us with a strange admixture of elements reminiscent of *Romeo and Juliet* and *Much Ado about Nothing*, with humours of a Jonsonian sort.

Something different, however, appears in *A Trick to catch the Old One* (*c.* 1605), with its group of gallants who live on their wits. Here, as in others of Middleton's realistic comedies, the Jonsonian element is heavily emphasized, but to that element a new quality is being added. Jonson's humours depend almost entirely on their own natures; in Middleton the humours are beginning to be related to the classes to which the various persons belong. A social note is being introduced.

With *A Trick to catch the Old One* may be associated the much darker comedy of Philip Massinger, and in particular *A New Way to pay Old Debts* (*c.* 1620) and *The City Madam* (1632). Both of these have the downrightness which was an inheritance from Elizabethan days, but both breathe a new air. The former is distinguished by the magnificently drawn portrait of Sir Giles Overreach, a man of money who has risen from lowly rank; he is a Sir Epicure Mammon without that character's voluptuousness—hard, cruel, self-seeking. Here Massinger clearly shows his awareness of social conditions apart from, yet operative on, character. In *The City Madam* it is a woman, Lady Frugal, who seeks to rise in the social scale, and Massinger spares nothing in listing her absurdities.

All of these plays bear about them an unmistakably bourgeois flavour, but the new audiences in the theatre, now predominantly courtly, were waiting for something of a different kind. Before that something different could come, however, there was needed both a fresh instrument and a fresh concept. An easy, witty style was required and a self-conscious presentation of aristocratic manners. Both of these were furthered in the plays written by John Fletcher in collaboration with Francis Beaumont and others. In these the English stage begins to assume the colouring of the Spanish. Tragi-comic episode is frequent, often with patent absurdities, but the manner in which the aristocrats are depicted is realistic, and their codes are unhesitatingly adopted as the correct behaviour. Courtly love begins to triumph over natural love, and much is being said of honour. Witty gallants come to take centre stage, and laughter is meted out to those not born to the manner who strive to ape the ways of the palace.

In *Wit at Several Weapons* (printed 1647) Wittypate Oldcraft is a young gallant who lives on his wits; he is companioned by several others in *Wit without Money* (c. 1614; printed 1639), in which, characteristically, the hero, Valentine, esteems intelligence, quickness of fancy, and ease in conversation above wealth; in *The Nice Valour; or, The Passionate Madman* (printed 1647) Shamont is "a superstitious lover of reputation," reminiscent of Spanish types: we are stepping now out of the old Globe into the new Drury Lane.

The enormous variety of the 'Beaumont and Fletcher' plays makes any kind of classification difficult, and perhaps all we need to do is to note a few examples typical of their style. Some are frankly satirical in a farcical way—such as *The Little French Lawyer* (c. 1620), with its brilliantly incisive picture of La Writ, who comes to imagine himself a great duellist because in the first combat he attends he has the almost unbelievably good fortune to disarm two of his opponents. Others concentrate most on tragi-comic incident, as in *The Woman Hater* (c. 1606), which the printer "dare not call Comedy or Tragedy; 'tis perfectly neither; a Play it is." Since this work excellently illustrates the complexity of intrigue introduced in dramas of this kind, the two strands of its plot may summarily be indicated. In the first appears a mischievous girl, Oriana, not unlike the heroine of *La dama duende*. Although beloved by the Duke of Milan, she forces herself on Gondarino, the woman-hater, in order to plague him. In return he slanders her reputation, and she is in danger of utter disgrace when a fortunate turn saves her. The second element in the plot centres on Lazarillo, a poor courtier whose eccentricity it is to dote on strange viands. Hearing of a rare fish which has been given to the Duke, he struggles to get an invitation to the palace; successful in this, he finds the fish has been presented to Gondarino, who in turn has handed it over to his Mercer, who gives it to a Courtesan; in order to taste it, Lazarillo agrees to marry the last-named.

In these and similar plays the authors of the 'Beaumont and Fletcher' comedies have, quite unconsciously, achieved certain ends. They have stressed unconditionally the world of fashionable youth, making the witty gallant their main character. They have introduced a gay, high-spirited aristocratic maiden to be fit match for him. They have suggested, but only slightly, an opposition to the citizen class, and have transferred the quality of humours from character defects to social manners. Above all, they have forged a new instrument of dialogue—delicate, intellectual, acute: in their scenes we listen to the quick repartee of the superficially brilliant Cavaliers in tavern and salon.

The comedy of manners was thus nearly formed. A further step taken towards its perfection was made by one of Jonson's protégés, Richard Brome, a man of no great talent, but one who more clearly than Fletcher recognized both the inherent opposition of the citizens and the Cavaliers and the existence of a special code of manners on which the society of the latter was founded. Where Fletcher unconsciously reflected this code, Brome consciously exploited it. Here satire directed at citizens who dare to ape the courtly manners—as in *Sparagus Garden* (1635), *A Mad Couple well matched* (printed 1653), and *The New Academy* (printed 1658)—derives, not only from a sense of the ridiculous, but still more from an awareness of social values.

Then came James Shirley, and the search was ended. In some of his comedies, such as *The Constant Maid* (printed 1640) and *The Gamester* (1634), Elizabethan features are predominant, but even in these class-consciousness is strongly marked. In the latter play Hazard asks Old Barnacle why, since he is a citizen, he does not bring up his nephew in his own way of life; the answer is clear:

> We that had
> Our breeding from a trade—cits, as you call us,
> Though we hate gentlemen ourselves, yet are
> Ambitious to make our children gentlemen.

Three plays in particular reveal Shirley's true accomplishment—*The Witty Fair One* (1628), *Hyde Park* (1632), and *The Lady of Pleasure* (1635). Here the comedy of manners if fully shaped and awaits only perfection in style to reach culmination. The fundamental basis of these plays is ease of courtly behaviour. Equally fundamental is the equality of men and women, and the frank, realistic appraisal of an intellectual duel of the sexes. Everywhere there is emphasis on polished wit, and brilliant conversation carries each scene. It is noteworthy, for example, that such a play as *Hyde Park* presents not a single 'comic' character as such figures were conceived in earlier years: the interest is concentrated almost entirely on the erratic and fanciful Mistress Carol and her three lovers—not so much on the intrigue which brings her into Fairfield's arms at the end, but on the display of wit occasioned by their wooing.

Shirley lived on into the period of the Restoration, and thus was an elder contemporary of Dryden and of Etherege: it was his style that they adapted and wrought into the finely aristocratic form, graceful and graceless, which eventually found its culmination in Congreve's *The Way of the World*—the world of Society, the world of manners, the world of artificiality and polish and scintillating wit.

PART V

THE TRIUMPH OF CLASSICISM

1

RACINE AND THE TRAGEDY OF SENTIMENT

BEFORE pursuing farther the fortunes of the English stage and examining the heroic drama and the comedy of manners produced at the Court of Charles II we must once more return, and in happier circumstances, to the theatre of Paris. Only two countries in Europe during the latter half of the seventeenth century produced dramatic writing of any significance, and of these two France is without even a film of doubt vastly the superior. She had failed utterly to create anything of real value during the period of the Renaissance, but now, under conditions far more propitious for her than those of 1600, her stage rapidly assumed an assurance and a power which made it the immediate inspiration for other lands, and which nourished the genius of two authors, Molière and Racine, who have been universally recognized as prime masters of their art, the one supreme in comedy, the other in tragic drama.

The Revival of the French Stage

The change in conditions came slowly yet with determined sureness as the seventeenth century was approaching its middle years. Throughout the whole of the Western world a longing for order and settled social state was supplanting the hardy adventurings, the bold individualism, and the emotional excitements of the Renaissance. England was still to plunge herself into civil war and execute her king, but even there the impress of the age was sufficiently strong to make men welcome the firm rule of Oliver Cromwell and, later, to induce them to call back the son of the monarch whom they had tried and condemned to death. Romanticism ruled at the beginning of the century: fifty years later the world was ready for classical precision and control.

Whereas England won through to acceptance of this spirit only after years of bloody conflict, France steadily moved forward from social chaos to order. The fury of the wars of religion died away, and under the astute hands of Cardinal Richelieu, from 1624 to 1642 the chief Minister of Louis XIII, the troublesome power of the nobles was reduced and the foundation was laid for a strong monarchical rule. Had his efforts been less sure, serious strife might well have broken out afresh when Louis XIII, dying in 1643, left his throne to a child of but five years of age, but the basis he had built was laid upon rock, and, despite the Fronde, it proved not impossible for his successor, Cardinal Mazarin, trained by Richelieu himself, to tide over the dangerous years until Louis XIV was able to assume control and in his long and glorious reign to become famous as the 'Grand Monarque' and 'Le Roi Soleil.'

Thus the particular conditions in France harmonized perfectly with the temper of the world in which she played her part. That part too was to prove a major rôle. With the coming of national unity, national greatness followed, and in the affairs of Europe French politics exercised decisive sway. To the sense of new-found unity, therefore, there was added something of the aspiration that had animated England fifty or sixty years before.

This aspiration was political, but it was also cultural. From the thirties of the century, when Richelieu was beginning to reap the certain fruits of his efforts, on to the latter years of Louis XIV, there was evident in Paris a desire to create a national literature, to penetrate the secrets of taste, to devise sure standards of critical judgment; and the success that attended these endeavours is attested by the dominant position French culture assumed in the other countries of Europe. For the authors of England, of Germany, of Russia, French writers provided the models of literary excellence.

So far as the stage in particular was concerned, the path of achievement was made the smoother by the fact that, while the provinces still retained independent interests, Paris rapidly came to be the centre of cultural activities. Theatres might flourish in other cities; dramatic authors and actors might train themselves there; but Paris was their ultimate goal, and from Paris alone the artists could receive final, assured acclaim.

To this may be added another consideration. The French stage of the mid-seventeenth century was assisted materially by its very poverty in the years immediately preceding. The age needed, and sought for, adequate means of expression in classical form, and the absence of any great romantic models permitted freer scope to the Parisian authors than they would have had if the shadow of romantic genius had fallen on their pages. If the French theatre had possessed a Shakespeare, even a Marlowe or a Webster, the task would have been infinitely harder. As it was, the new generation of classically minded authors started their work largely unimpeded. The tragi-comedies and farces with which they were surrounded could call forth little or no critical esteem, and thus no temptations offered themselves for the infusion of romantic elements in their classical conceptions. This meant, too, that in seeking for a fresh kind of tragedy and comedy the authors were not simply acting negatively, opposing old forms with new; their efforts were positive, uninhibited, and free.

With the development of the classical drama the names of princes and their Ministers are closely associated. Louis XIV was the patron of

Molière and Racine, and during the earlier, formative years Richelieu, by his direct personal encouragement, was responsible for the creation of the new theatre. Interested generally in the development of French literature, Richelieu was particularly intent on the drama. Partly at least through his influence the stage came to abandon the old type of simultaneous setting and to adopt the Italian proscenium frame with its perspective scenery. The theatre known as the Palais Cardinal, and later as the Palais Royal, established under his direct orders by the architect Mercier, opened with the performance of *Mirame* in 1641, and was the model that finally and definitely ousted the old. In place of the multiple settings that had been used for the popular tragi-comedies at the Hôtel de Bourgogne, and that trailed with them memories of the Middle Ages, men now were provided with classically simple, unified stage-scenes created by means of side-wings and backcloths, framed by a deep proscenium arch as though in a picture-frame. Although the Palais Cardinal was originally a courtly playhouse, its influence was widely spread among the public theatres that followed. Another Court theatre that had considerable influence was the great Salle des Machines, built by Vigarani in the Tuileries (1661)—so large and with such vast space for scenic equipment that in 1763, when the Palais Royal was burned, the architect Soufflot created an entirely new and sufficiently commodious playhouse out of its stage alone.

At the same time the more settled conditions of life and the growth of Paris as the capital of France permitted the development of more permanent companies than had commonly prevailed in the past. The Hôtel de Bourgogne came under settled management, and its company gradually evolved into the Théâtre Français, playing in various houses, including the Théâtre Guénégaud (1670) and, later, a new Théâtre Français, converted out of a tennis-court in 1689; its rivals, the company of the Théâtre Marais, boasted the attraction of the great tragic actor Mondory; the Comédie Italienne won attention for its gay freedom and its vitality; above all, there was the famous Illustre Théâtre, formed by the young Molière in 1643, which after many vicissitudes in the provinces achieved glory on its return to Paris in 1659.

Although there were numerous abuses in the theatre during those days, the general conditions were right for the development of fruitful creative activity, and it is by no means surprising that France, producing Corneille, Racine, and Molière, became the leader of the world dramatic.

The Forerunner: Pierre Corneille

The drama that first gave distinction to the French tragic stage was *Le Cid* (1636), the work of Pierre Corneille. Its author, a lawyer of Rouen, had been impelled towards the theatre by the visit to his native city of the Marais troupe, and when, in 1629, Mondory returned to Paris he carried with him the manuscript of a comedy, *Mélite*, by the young author. During the succeeding years Corneille trained himself in the penning of comedy, and then set all literary Paris in an uproar with his heroic drama on a Spanish theme.

At the time that this drama appeared classic theory and practice had not as yet fully established itself. Tragi-comedies were still being produced by men such as Rotrou and Benserade, and for some years these dramatists were to remain moderately popular. Along with their vogue was a vogue for dramas on English history—a kind of gesture on the part of romantic playwrights to the claims of tragedy. Here came La Calprenède's *Jeanne, Royne d'Angleterre* (printed in 1638) and this play was accompanied by other similar works. Already, however, the classical style was making headway. In 1634 Jean Mairet came forward with his *Sophonisbe*, the first tragedy in France truly based on the rules, and it was followed by a series of dramas which treated ancient themes in accordance with the critical precepts supposed to be found in Aristotle's *Poetics*. Mairet himself followed his *Sophonisbe* with *Marc Antoine, ou la Cléopâtre* (*c.* 1635), Scudéry produced his *La mort de César* (*The Death of Caesar*, 1635) and Pierre Corneille his *Médée* (*Medea*, 1634–35).

At the same time the critics were eagerly discussing the precepts that should be followed. Some men of independent judgment agreed with François Ogier in objecting to the stricter application of the rules, but the majority welcomed Mairet as the leader of the classical legion. As yet, however, the debate was rather abstract, since no really important tragic drama, whether classically inclined or the reverse, had appeared to provide a concrete issue. It was precisely such a concrete issue that *Le Cid* gave to Parisian society. No one could deny its power; the question was whether that power was secured by legitimate means.

The plot of Corneille's drama was derived from a Spanish source. Chimène is the daughter of Don Gomès, and is the love of the gallant Rodrigue. Unfortunately Don Gomès insults and strikes Rodrigue's father, and the young man, at the very moment of his wedding, is forced to challenge the former; in the ensuing duel Don Gomès is slain. Chimène now is in turn forced to wish Rodrigue's death, and he, rather than commit suicide, takes command of a small troop of soldiers prepared to attempt the apparently forlorn hope of preventing the advance of a great Moorish army. Instead of perishing on the field, however, Rodrigue is triumphant, and returns home in glory. Still impelled by her sense of loyalty to her dead father, Chimène causes Don Sanche, who seeks her hand in marriage, to challenge Rodrigue, but, on hearing that he proposes to let himself be killed, she herself bids him to use his strength in order to obtain victory—even although (or because) she is aware that by the King's order she must marry the survivor. Rodrigue wins the duel, and the lovers are united.

The storm that broke around this drama may at first seem inexplicable; but consideration of *Le Cid* in its setting dissipates all difficulty. Its brilliant, forceful verse and its bold, arresting presentation of character marked it out as a tremendous achievement. Here was a literary effort that could not be ignored, and in this period when men were so eagerly searching for the true road the question as to whether Corneille, by his very genius, might not be leading the world astray became a theme of profound significance.

Externally the author keeps the rules. All the action is supposed to take place within a period of twenty-four hours, and the entire action is pursued near the royal palace. Yet the five acts of the drama are crowded with incident, straining dangerously our sense of probability, and the end, instead of being tragic, bears a happy conclusion. Several questions were paramount for the dramatic authors of that time: Was probability or retention of the rules the more important? Could these two be reconciled, and, if so, in what way? What was the true end of the tragic drama? *Le Cid* provided a practical test for the establishing of opinion.

Anyone who wades through the spate of controversy which flooded upon *Le Cid* at that time may well deem that the critical comments are frequently weak, absurd, and beside the point; yet a general understanding of the situation shows that, although the authors were frequently arguing about problems of lesser import, their passionate advocating of even trivial views sprang from a consciousness of the ultimate importance of the quarrel.

Almost immediately following its presentation on the stage, Mairet (perhaps stung by jealousy) and others started debating its merits, and so bitter did the debate prove that within a few months the Academy was formally asked to judge the issue, with the result that Jean Chapelain, assisted by the learned institution to which he belonged, soon published the famous *Sentimens de l'Académie Françoise sur la tragi-comédie du Cid*.

Much space is taken up in the *Sentimens* with criticism of minor points, and even more with what seems utterly futile—the moral questions involved. In particular, the authors of that essay fix their attention on the impropriety of causing Chimène to marry the man who has slain her father, of allowing her to permit love to sway her heart above the dictates of duty. Unquestionably this appears to be but foolish criticism, yet, perhaps unconsciously, the *Sentimens* here have, although rather crudely, concentrated their attention upon what is ultimately the core of the entire controversy. Corneille, while he bows formally to the unities, has in reality a romantic soul. There is a strength about him that rebels against restraint: into the age of classicism he carries a bold, truculent individualism. But individualism of this sort is exactly that which the age was seeking to restrain, and in the criticisms directed at Chimène's conduct the Academy was, in effect, testifying to its desire for order, restraint, and social unity. Marlowes and their like could find place in the Renaissance; in this later age no room might be allowed to them.

The emphasis laid upon the improbabilities of the action of *Le Cid* also has deeper implications. The old tragi-comedies had extended actions, but their structure was formless. Form was needed, hence the inculcation of the unities. At the same time form must harmonize with content, and the truth is that Corneille, despite the vigour and beauty of his work, failed to secure such harmony. In plays of romantic structure it may be proper to have variety of incident; in plays of classical restraint the subject-matter, and the passions, must be so conceived as to accord with the conventions employed. The Academy, rightly, recognized that what Corneille aimed at was a type of drama which could not provide the age with what it needed. Some of its members may have been animated by personal jealousies, some may have been too academic to recognize true genius when it appeared; but basically the general criticism of the *Sentimens*, in the light of what was then demanded of the theatre, must be deemed fully justified. The path indicated by Corneille could have led to nothing but chaos; the way of the *Sentimens* leads towards the work of Racine.

That Corneille himself took the lesson to heart is indicated in his later dramas. In *Horace* (1640) he selects a classical subject and attempts to deal with it more simply than he had treated the content of *Le Cid*. Basically this tragedy deals with conflicting loyalties. Rome is at war, and against the background of the conflict the dramatist sets Horace, the patriot of untroubled mind; Sabine, his wife, and a native of the enemy country; Camille, his sister, in love with a soldier, Curiace, also of that country. Each character, clearly etched, is presented without any inner conflict. Horace is so assured of the rightness of his views that he slays his sister when he finds her cursing her own country; for Camille nothing matters save love of Curiace. There is a noble grandeur about the entire conception; and with subtle sensitivity Corneille has been able to hammer out lines of almost Roman brevity, pith, and grandeur: "Qui veut mourir ou vaincre est vaincu rarement"; "Et qui veut bien mourir peut braver les malheurs"; "Mais Rome ignore encor comme on perd des batailles"—these and other epigrammatic lines linger in the memory.

Yet *Horace*, even although its author has taken the *Sentimens* to heart, still fails to point in the true direction. Its very boldness is too strong for the temper of the age, and its lack of inner conflict causes it to miss an opportunity such as Racine knew later how to embrace.

In *Cinna, ou la clémence d'Auguste* (*Cinna; or, The Clemency of Augustus, c.* 1641) Corneille turned once more to a tragedy with a happy ending, but, as in *Horace*, simplified the contents of the work. Auguste is the all-powerful Emperor, and among his closest protégés are Emilie, burning with a desire to avenge her father's death; Cinna, induced to join in a conspiracy against Auguste because of his love for Emilie; and Maxime, another member of the conspiracy and also secretly in love with the heroine. With admirable conciseness and economy of means Corneille reveals these characters in their relations with the Emperor, and rises to a magnificent conclusion in Auguste's decision to pardon the offenders.

Peculiarly effective is the monarch's soliloquy in the fourth act, which might be regarded as the classical equivalent of the romantic soliloquy put into the mouth of Henry V by Shakespeare:

> O Heaven, to whom is it your will that I
> Entrust my life, the secrets of my soul?
> Take back the power with which you have endowed me,
> If it but steals my friends to give me subjects,
> If regal splendours must be fated ever,
> Even by the greatest favours they can grant,
> To foster only hate, if your stern law
> Condemns a king to cherish only those
> Who burn to have his blood. Nothing is certain.
> Omnipotence is bought with ceaseless fear. . . .

Polyeucte (*c.* 1642) carries us into a different world, for here Corneille moved from pagan character to Christian. Polyeucte is a descendant of Armenian princes who has accepted the material power of Rome and is married to the daughter of the Governor, Pauline. A quality of mystical faith enters in here, for the author is intent upon showing how this man, becoming dedicate to a higher law, is forced to a way of life different from that of his companions. The contrast is well revealed in his relations with Pauline. This Roman lady has married him only at her father's command; in reality her heart has been given to a fellow-Roman, Sévère. Faithful to her husband, the other love cannot be stilled, but when, towards the close of the tragedy, she finds Polyeucte, recognizing her passion, offering her happiness with Sévère when he himself is dead, while Sévère tacitly accepts the proposal, a sudden new light floods in upon her. She becomes a Christian in order that, even in death, she may be with the heroic soul whose virtues have thus been revealed to her.

The qualities displayed in these dramas are reproduced in the succeeding tragedies of Corneille—*Pompée* (1642), *Rodogune, Princesse des Parthes* (printed 1646), *Héraclius* (1646), and *Nicomède* (1650–51), as well as the later works, *Œdipe* (1659), *Sertorius* (1662), and *Sophonisbe* (1663)—but the times were rapidly leaving him as a monument of the past. His stalwart figure, strayed out of the Renaissance, stood somewhat awkwardly among the polite and delicate gallantries of the age. His characters were rough-hewn, bold in their proportions, massive; what the ladies and gentlemen of the Paris Court desired was something subtler and more polished. These audiences had the power to be aroused by "greatness of soul," as Charles Saint-Évremond expressed it, but even more they sought "tender admiration." There is a rugged masculinity about Corneille; more appropriate to the age were Racine's sensitive heroines.

The New Tragedy: Racine

Jean Racine was born in 1639; by 1664 he had produced his first play, and before his death in 1699 he had established himself as the supreme master in that particular style of French classicism which distinguished the age of Louis XIV.

Unlike Corneille, he was content to mould his own desires absolutely to the form of his age—or perhaps it might be said that basically his desires were harmoniously attuned to the desires of the Parisian society in which he found himself. Behind him were many models, each of which offered something of inspiration, but in the dramas of his maturity he so wrought the elements he had taken from others to his own image that they became converted into shapes far other than those they had originally exhibited, and everywhere the mould was formed in the image of his times.

Chief of his predecessors was, of course, Pierre Corneille, but before *La Thébaïde, ou les frères ennemis* (*The Theban; or, The Enemy Brothers*) appeared in 1664 there were other writers who had essayed the tragic path, and even while he was engaged in producing his series of classical plays numerous companions vied with him for supremacy. Thomas Corneille, younger brother of Pierre, stalwartly contributed a series of tragedies to the stage, but even the best of these, *Timocrate* (1656), lacks brilliance. Philippe Quinault also pursued the Corneillian way, but soon, in collaboration with Lulli, was drawn into the sphere of opera, when among other works he produced his famous *Armide* (1686), one of the tragedies most influential in establishing 'Grand Opera' in France. None of the tragic plays produced during the years immediately before Racine's appearance had given any indication of true greatness: *Le Cid, Horace*, and *Cinna* still remained the finest serious dramas that the French stage had created.

To the theatre of his time Racine brought certain qualities which immediately distinguish him from his companions. The beauty of his verse is dependent not so much upon vigorous utterance as upon delicacy and precision. Corneille's dialogue is that of a romantic constrained to speak in classical tones; Racine's lines are perfectly adjusted to the general speech-character of his age. His epigrams are chiselled to perfection, where Corneille's are heavily and sometimes even impatiently hammered out. This verse he made both eminently theatrical—so that it has been acclaimed by generations of French actors—and dramatic, in that it is at once the expression of character and expresses character with almost epigrammatic poise. The single line in Racine may carry a weight that only a paragraph of Corneille could counterbalance. The very simplicity of Hermione's cry in *Andromaque*—

> Where am I? What have I done? What ought
> I to do now? What fury sways me? What
> Anguish devours my heart? All aimlessly
> Hither and thither through this palace I
> Have rushed. Alas! Is there no way I can
> Know if I love or hate?

—has a quality far beyond its ordinary meaning. Lacking flamboyant features, Racine's verse is virtually untranslatable. Its delicacy depends on the author's exquisite sensibility to the tones of his own tongue; and when other tongues attempt to reproduce his forms they falter with embarrassment.

To this simplicity of language Racine adds simplicity of action. He knew, as Corneille did not, how to adjust his plots to the requirements of current conventions. No improbabilities mar his scenes: it seems eminently proper—nay, inevitable—that what he shows us should take place in a few hours and in one place. There are no digressions here, and the directness which is appropriate to the classic style finds perfect realization.

His greatest achievement, however, was the evolving of a pattern suited to the classical tendencies of his particular time. Corneille had aimed at the arousing of heroic admiration for his characters, and although the theme of love played a considerable part in his dramas, he specifically stated his belief that in tragedy the love element should be made subordinate to other issues. "The dignity of tragedy," he stated in his discourse of 1660,

> needs some great state interest or passion nobler and more virile than love, such as ambition or vengeance, which leads us to expect greater misfortune than the loss of a mistress. It is fit to mix love in it because it always has much attraction and can serve as a basis to those other interests and other passions of which I speak. But it must content itself with second rank in the poem and leave the first to the other.

Unquestionably in setting forth this point of view Corneille was correctly estimating the general requirements of the tragic genre, but the age in which he lived was one of gallantry, where the theme of love was of paramount importance and where the sterner emotions of which he spoke could make little appeal. Racine realized that if tragic drama were to be truly successful in this time the passion of love must form the centre, or at least the determining element, in the composition.

This in turn implied the exercise of greater subtlety than Corneille commanded. His figures were simply and boldly fashioned: Racine set out to secure interest and develop interest by means more delicate. Inner conflict became obligatory, and this spectator of the human heart knew well how to weave a tissue of conflicting passions in such a manner as to arouse a feeling of almost unbearable tension. He began to search down into the domain below consciousness, and in effect laid the basis for the modern 'psychological' drama.

As his aim was not to encourage heroic admiration or to deal preeminently with other emotions than love, he wisely took another step. Corneille had concentrated most of his attention upon his heroes; Racine explored a fresh realm by emphasizing his heroines. Nor was it the heroines of hard, almost masculine quality that most attracted his attention—an Electra consumed by hate or a Medea tormented by the desertion of her husband: the heroines he displayed were women of more tender structure. Where Æschylus reveals the classical tragic style at its most masculine, where Corneille's genius is romantically masculine, subdued and restricted by the impress of classic form, Racine's spirit is essentially feminine.

To a realization of his mission he came but slowly. In the preface to *La Thébaïde* he drew attention to the fact that he had practically neglected the love element, deeming lovers' tenderness and jealousies to have no legitimate place amid the severities of the plot he had selected. Moreover, in *Alexandre le Grand* (1665) he followed Corneille, and to a certain extent Quinault, in dealing with a theme calculated to call forth admiration for the heroic qualities of his hero.

Two years later, however, he showed that these were but trial essays by producing his first feminine tragedy, the *Andromaque* (*Andromache*, 1667). Here the simple classical framework was definitely established: not only were the unities preserved and the story stripped of every vestige of extraneous matter, but the very movement of the actors on the stage was reduced to a minimum. There are but four persons of any interest in the play—Oreste, in love with Hermione, Hermione in love with Pyrrhus, Pyrrhus in love with Andromaque, and Andromaque herself, with her devotion set upon her dead Hector. Their names are Greek; but they step forth before us as idealized portraits of ordinary human types. Rising and falling in intensity, the five acts of the tragedy are given over to an analysis of the torments of these four love-intoxicated persons. The ancient Greek tale is retold in delicate terms; Andromaque's mind is in conflict because of the clash between self-dedication to the memory of her first husband and devotion to her living son; Hermione hardly knows whether to love or hate, can barely distinguish these passions in her soul. "Hate him, Cleone?" she asks:

> All my dignity,
> My honour, is at stake, such kindness I
> Have shown to him, whereof all memory
> He yet hath lost—yea, e'en he that was so
> Dear to me, and who could betray me. Oh,
> Too much I have loved him, not to hate him now!

Oreste stands lost in his melancholy abstraction, enfeebled both by his obsession for Hermione and by his sense of being doomed by the gods to disaster:

> I understand. My doom
> Is this: that Pyrrhus hath thy heart; thy head,
> Orestes.

We are far here from the world of the heroic: Andromaque calls for our sincere admiration, but the others are tortured souls, each disturbed within its own being, and each selfishly intent upon its own desires, its own miseries. The difference between Corneille's aims and Racine's is perhaps revealed most characteristically in the contrast between Chimène and Hermione: the former is prepared to seek, or at least to sanction, her lover's death because the claims of honour demand it; the latter is led only by her own inner rage to bid Oreste slay Pyrrhus.

For Racine, now sure of his own powers and of the path he wished to travel, tragedy had assumed clear proportions: it was to be "a simple action, charged with little matter, as becomes an action which occupies a single day, advancing gradually to its end, and sustained by the interests, the sentiments, and the passions of the characters." In *Britannicus* (1669) he essayed, brilliantly, a drama more in the manner of Corneille, but adapted to his own peculiar pattern—almost as though he were determined to demonstrate that the theme of love did not embrace the entire range of his conceptions. Corneillian influence of the same kind is traceable in *Bajazet* (1672) and *Mithridate* (1673), but in *Bérénice* (1670), *Iphigénie* (1674), and *Phèdre* (1677) he moved firmly on his own elected soil. In *Bajazet*, dealing with an almost contemporary event, he tried to secure tragic 'distance' by treating of life in a far-off Oriental world, painting excellent portraits of the politician Acomat and of the impassioned Roxane—indeed, it is Roxane who becomes the central figure in the play, and Racine assuredly was wise in concentrating, in his three classically derived dramas, upon the character of a woman.

These three tragedies boldly announce in their titles the predominating feminine interest. *Iphigénie* presents a delicate interplay of character and carries its action to a happy conclusion, although the atmosphere throughout is serious and threatening disaster. Central in the composition stands the frail, lovely Iphigénie, firm in her constancy both to her lover, Achille, and to her father, Agamemnon. On one side she is flanked by her weak, ambitious, vacillating parent, desperately anxious not to lose his post as commander-in-chief of the Greek forces, yet almost equally anxious not to stir up domestic trouble—a man whose absence of will makes him take what seems the easier of two disturbing alternatives, and whose mind changes and shifts with every breeze. On the other side is Clytemnestre, desperately intent on saving the life of her child, balanced against her husband by her fixity of purpose, stronger than he in character, yet rendered impotent by circumstance. And in sharp contrast to Iphigénie are the young Achille and Ériphile—the former a blunt, single-minded man of action, the latter a pathologically miserable girl, jealous of others and suicidal in tendency. It is, indeed, by her self-inflicted death that Racine succeeds in giving a fortunate conclusion to his action, for the seer Calchas declares that she may be accepted instead of Iphigénie as the victim-sacrifice demanded by the gods.

This play naturally challenges comparison with Euripides' *Iphigenia in Aulis*, and it must be confessed that it stands up well in the test. It does not possess the boldness with which even Euripides—so much less monumental in his work than Æschylus—knew how to invest his characters, but such boldness in execution is not its aim. Racine seeks to probe into secret recesses of the soul, while Euripides attempts to present a picture classically etched.

Bérénice had preceded *Iphigénie* by four years, but consideration of the latter first is justified in view of the fact that it more clearly shows Racine's full mastery of his peculiar tragic style. In a sense *Bérénice* may be regarded as transitional, since although the theme is love and the chief figure is a woman, the dictates of duty and the 'state' quality demanded by Corneille are clearly present. Rome imperiously calls upon Titus for abandonment of his passion for Bérénice, yet the claims of her beauty batter down his resolution, while Antiochus, sent by his master to give her the stern command to leave the city, falls dangerously under her spell. *Bérénice*, like *Andromaque*, is a drama of conflicting love; it differs from the latter in introducing the clash between love and honour; yet the fact that duty triumphs cannot conceal from us the dominant power of passion or take from the pervading atmosphere of tenderness. One line spoken by Antiochus might be taken as typical of its whole mood:

> Je cherchais en pleurant les traces de vos pas.

In rejecting the Corneillian pattern, and in penning such a drama of renunciation, Racine undoubtedly strikes a note that appears strangely modern.

In *Phèdre* Racine exhibits to the full both his strength and his weakness. The dialogue has an exquisite delicacy beyond almost anything he had previously accomplished, and the figures of the drama stand out in clearly limned perfection. For his plot the French author once more has turned to Euripides, and reveals the encroaching obsession of Phèdre, wife of Theseus, for her husband's son by a former marriage, Hippolyte. In order to help her mistress, the faithful Œnone, believing that Theseus has died on a foreign expedition, counsels Phèdre to disclose her passion to the stepson. Indignantly he rejects her offer of love, but when, on Theseus' unexpected return, he is accused by Œnone of having tried to seduce Phèdre he refuses to say a word: cursed by his father, he goes to his doom, while Phèdre herself, overwhelmed by mingled shame and grief at her loss, commits suicide.

With consummate artistry, the dramatist has presented an unforgettable portrait of a woman whose very being is consumed by a fire she cannot quench. Her first entry shows her pitifully weakened. "Yes, this is far enough," she says to Œnone:

> Stay here, Œnone.
> My strength is failing. I must rest a little.
> I am dazzled with the light; it has been long
> Since I have seen it.

Before she confronts Hippolyte he is displayed to us as having fallen in love with Aricie: he confesses that to him, the scorner of the tender passion, has come an unwonted emotion:

> I leave your presence:—leaving, I find you near,
> And in the forest's darkness see your form.
> Black night, no less than daylight brings the vision
> Of charms that I avoid. All things conspire
> To make Hippolytus your slave. The fruit
> Of all my sighs is only that I cannot
> Find my own self again.

The tension rises steadily up to Phèdre's great speech in the fourth act, in which she thinks with bitterness of that which she cannot have. When Œnone asks her, "What fruit can they desire from fruitless love?" her reply reveals the torment of her spirit:

> That love will stay,
> And it will stay for ever. While I speak—
> O dreadful thought—they laugh and scorn my madness
> And my distracted heart. In spite of exile,
> In spite of that which soon must come to part them,
> They make a thousand oaths to bind their union.
> Œnone, can I bear this happiness
> Which so insults me? I would have your pity.
> Yes, she must be destroyed. My husband's fury
> Against her hated race shall be renewed.
> The punishment must be a heavy one.
> Her guilt outruns the guilt of all her brothers.
> I'll plead with Theseus, in my jealousy—
> What do I say? Oh, have I lost my senses?
> Is Phædra jealous? Will she, then, go begging
> For Theseus' help? He lives—and yet I burn.
> For whom? Whose heart is this I claim as mine?
> My hair stands up with horror at my words,
> And from this time, my guilt has passed all bounds!
> Hypocrisy and incest breathe at once
> Through all I do.

The tempestuous passion, despite her will, cannot be controlled.

At this point in Racine's career a new mood came upon him. Not, as some have supposed, because of the disgraceful attacks of his ill-wishers, but because of a genuine religious conversion, he left the theatre. In the peace of faith he found refuge from the torments of the characters of his own creation, and he abandoned the public stage. One great play, however, he still had to give to the world. At the age of fifty-two, in 1691, he produced his Christian drama, *Athalie*. The theme of love is now far off, and a bare lyric grandeur takes the place of the earlier searchings of spirit. Its simple plot contrasts the ambitious queen Athalie, her hands stained with blood, and the youthful Joas, heir to the true vision. This story of faith and purpose he has exhibited with much the same subtlety as, but with calmer assurance of spirit than, he had revealed the tormented emotions of *Phèdre* and *Andromaque*, achieving, however, a deeper impression because of the way in which the individual characters are silhouetted against the background provided by a chorus of maidens. The first choral ode celebrates the power of God:

> His glory fills the universe sublime,
> Lift to this God for aye the voice of prayer!
> He reign'd supreme before the birth of Time;
> Sing of His loving care.

And the final words of this choral group are devoted to the same subject: in a sense the invisible God is the hero of the play. The hand that created such concise, memorable lines for the delineation of Andromaque and Phèdre has lost none of its skill: such a person as Joas, for example, is put before us with peerless simplicity in less than a dozen words; when, shortly after his first appearance, he utters the line

> Je crains Dieu, cher Abner, et n'ai point d'autre crainte,
> —I fear my God, and know no other fear,—

his entire rôle in the play is indicated in a single illuminating flash. In its own time *Athalie* won little esteem, but the nineteenth-century romantics, in spite of their general reaction against Racine's classicism, found qualities in this play lacking in the others, so that for many it has come to stand as his highest achievement.

To assess Racine's position aright is a hard task. That he cannot be compared with the very greatest dramatists is certain, since his range and his style are both limited. Shakespeare and Sophocles, despite the power and the subtlety of their poetic medium, still retain much of their quality even in translation: the very precision and simplicity of Racine make his plays somewhat dull and bare when the poise of their original language is rendered into other tongues. Allied to this is the fact that they imperiously demand a particular kind of theatrical interpretation, and certainly do not offer either to actor or to director the rich possibilities that have given the Shakespearian tragedies their triumphant career upon the stage. As a result, the performance of Racine's dramas outside of France—and even there very largely only by the company which inherited the traditions of the age of Louis Quatorze—is rare: French actresses for over two and a half centuries have won fame in the rendering of Racine's rôles, but it is seldom that these rôles receive stage realization abroad.

These are limiting factors, but against them may be placed other considerations—and among such considerations the most significant is the power that Racine exhibits to achieve dramatic interest and tension by the simplest possible means. He demonstrated that violent action and richness of incident were not necessary to engage an audience's attention, that excitement could be induced by concentrating upon the delicate delineation of inner movement, that subtle suggestion could play a part almost as forceful as bold enunciation. He showed how the dramatist could exhibit characters whose whole beings are consumed by desires beyond their reach, so that with the impossibility of satisfying these desires life becomes empty and death is a merciful deliverance. Through these qualities he taught much to the stage, and his influence, indirect if not direct, is far-flung. The entire development of the modern psychological drama owes much to his inspiration.

2

MOLIÈRE AND THE COMEDY OF MANNERS

THE GROWTH of classical tragedy in France moved steadily forward alongside a corresponding growth of comedy. Racine himself inserted among his serious dramas a witty *Plaideurs*, and Pierre Corneille started his theatrical career with a comic *Mélite*. The very fact that classical theory stressed the purity of genres, or kinds, induced men to seek expression now in the tragic style, now in the comic, and this stress on purity led towards the creation of comic scenes of peculiar excellence and individual quality.

The Precursors of Molière: Pierre Corneille

In the year 1638 there was published—with, rather extraordinarily, a dedication to Sir Kenelm Digby—a play manufactured under highest auspices. It had been especially commissioned by Richelieu himself, and for its composition he had selected five authors—Boisrobert, Colletet, Corneille, l'Estoile, and Rotrou. His object was to set up a model for a new comedy.

In harmony with his political desires, which sought order, precision, and unity, Richelieu definitely approved of those critics who endeavoured to apply the pseudo-classic rules. The formlessness of the popular tragi-comedy was to him anathema, and all his efforts to encourage the drama were orientated towards the creation of pure comedy and tragedy, towards simplicity, and towards the preservation of the unities. The play he had commissioned, and of which he was, indeed, part-author, *La comédie des Tuileries*, was designed to show what comedy of this kind should be.

Of the five authors of the piece the only man of true genius was Corneille. With his *Mélite* of 1629 he had shown himself possessed of genuine dramatic skill, apt in the delineation of manners, and interested in depicting social life in a realistic manner. Between the composition of this play and the *Comédie des Tuileries* came several other similar works from his pen—*La veuve* (*The Widow*, 1633), *La galerie du palais* (*The Palace Gallery*, 1634), *La Place Royale* (1634), and *L'illusion comique* (*The Comic Illusion*; printed 1639)—all of which marked him out as a writer of promise.

It cannot be claimed that the experiment in joint authorship was a signal success, yet there can be no doubt but that Richelieu's emphasis on classical precision, concretely exemplified in the simple plot and symmetrically balanced scenes of his comedy, was in accord with the needs of the time, was to prove of prime importance in the development of the French theatre, and was not alien to the genius of Corneille himself, who, although a trifle restive under the excessive strictness which some critics would have desired to impose upon the stage, was well equipped to experiment in the style of classic comedy.

In so far as these comic efforts of his are concerned, however, we must admit that Corneille was a precursor, not a thoroughly accomplished master. In *Mélite* he demonstrated to contemporaries how the pattern of real life, the life of society, could with propriety and delicacy be reproduced in dramatic form; in *L' illusion comique* he created a comic spirit richer than anything that had hitherto been shown on the Parisian stage; and in his later comedies—particularly *Le menteur* (*The Liar*, 1644), based on *La verdad sospechosa*, in which he opened up the way for a true comedy of character—he led the van of those among his companions who discovered fresh inspiration in the Spanish theatre.

This Spanish influence on the French comic writers of the time is a force which must be fully appreciated. Paul Scarron's *Jodelet, ou le maître valet* (*Jodelet; or, The Man the Master*; printed 1645), Thomas Corneille's *Les engagements du hazard* (*Fortune's Favours*; printed 1657), the same author's *Le feint astrologue* (*The Feigned Astrologer*; printed 1650), and the anonymous *L'amour à la mode* (*Love à la Mode*; printed 1653)—all of them full of wit and vitality, and all destined to inspire other plays abroad—are derived from this source. So too is what must be regarded as among the very best of these mid-seventeenth-century comedies, Scarron's *L' héritier ridicule* (*The Foolish Heir*; printed 1650), a gay dramatic picture of cross-purposes in love, with its amusing scenes in which Filipin poses grandiloquently as Dom Pedro de Buffalos.

The Advent of Molière: The Early Farces

During the decades immediately to follow the stage was well supplied by comic authors. The earlier group, headed by the two Corneilles and by Paul Scarron, soon were succeeded by others such as Philippe Quinault, whose very first play, *Les rivales* (*The Rivals*; printed 1655), was a comedy, and who produced in *La comédie sans comédie* (*The Comedy without Comedy*, printed 1657) a work of genuine interest; Samuel Chappuzeau, a restless spirit who contributed several lively pieces to the contemporary stage; Racine, whose *Les plaideurs* (*The Litigants*, 1668) is an amusing satire on lawyers; and Raymond Poisson, an actor who wrote a number of farcical comedies not without merit.

All the comic authors of the second half of the seventeenth century, however, fade into insignificance when we turn to Jean-Baptiste

Poquelin, who, under the name of Molière, stood forward in this time as one of the greatest masters in the art of comedy that the world has known. However, it was not until 1655, when he was thirty-three years of age, that his first important work, *L'étourdi, ou les contretemps* (*The Blunderer; or, The Mishaps*), was written and acted. Up to that time he had been gaining experience in the playhouses. His own company, L'Illustre Théâtre, had been formed in 1643, and since then had been touring the provinces with a repertory consisting mainly of farce; now the future author of *Tartuffe*, trained in his profession of actor, felt himself ready to add to that repertory by plays in which his sense of the stage and his wide observation of life could find free scope.

Before *L'étourdi* it is possible, even likely, that Molière had written one or two short farces; if so, we have a suggestion of their style in two pieces, *La jalousie du Barbouillé* (*The Jealousy of Le Barbouillé*) and *Le médecin volant* (*The Flying Doctor*), first published in 1819 from an early manuscript. Clearly based on the style of the *commedia dell' arte*, yet displaying affinities with medieval farce, they well illustrate the manner in which their author may have served his apprenticeship, drawing strength and assurance from the popular French tradition, and enlivening that with material taken from Italian sources. The former play introduces to us a jealous fool, Le Barbouillé, married to Angélique. At a loss to know what to do, he consults a doctor, who, refusing to listen to him, gives him a long discourse on his own merits. In the end, thinking to trap his wife as she returns home late from a party, he is himself locked out of his house and severely chided by Angélique's father. Equally slight is the plot of *Le médecin volant*. Here also a doctor appears, but in this case a pretended one. Gorgibus, father of Lucile, does not wish his daughter to marry Valère, whereupon the young man's servant, Sganarelle (played by Molière himself), takes upon him to dress as a doctor, and, despite his ridiculous patter, completely dupes Gorgibus and is thus enabled to effect the union of the lovers. Gorgibus greets him:

> *GORGIBUS:* Doctor, I am your very humble servant. I sent for you to come and see my daughter who is ill; I put all my hopes in you.
> *SGANARELLE:* Hippocrates says, and Galen, too, with strong reasoning, argues, that a person does not feel well when he is ill. You are right to put all your hopes in me, for I am the greatest, the cleverest, the wisest doctor in the vegetable, animal and mineral faculty.
> *GORGIBUS:* I am delighted to hear it.
> *SGANARELLE:* Do not imagine that I am an ordinary doctor, a common doctor. All other doctors compared to me are abortions. I possess wonderful talents; I am a master of many secrets. *Salamec, salamec.* "Hast thou courage, Rodrigo?" *Signor, si; signor, non. Per omnia sœcula sœculorum.* Still, let us see a little. [*Feels GORGIBUS' pulse.*
> *SABINE:* Eh! He is not the patient; it is his daughter who is ill.
> *SGANARELLE:* It does not matter: the blood of the father and that of the daughter are the same; and by the deterioration of the blood of the father, I

can know the illness of the daughter.
GORGIBUS: Ah! doctor, I am greatly afraid that my daughter will die.
SGANARELLE: S'death! she must not! She must not indeed have the pleasure of dying before she has the doctor's prescription.

The title of the farce comes from the fact that in the course of his intricate deception Sganarelle is forced to impersonate not only the doctor, but also his own supposed twin brother—all of which necessitates his flying on and off the stage in disguise and without.

For the longer and more pretentious comedy of *L'étourdi* Molière passed from the *commedia dell' arte* to the *commedia erudita*, choosing for inspiration *L'inavvertito (The Indiscreet Man)*, by Nicolò Barbieri, already used by Quinault for his *L'amant indiscret.* The plot is little more than a series of episodes. Lélie is in love with Célie, and in order to win her agrees that his servant, Mascarille, should indulge in a series of stratagems. To the disgust of this witty and ingenious rogue, however, Lélie destroys plot after plot by his blunderings. Sometimes he wrecks his servant's plans through ignorance of what is being arranged, sometimes through excessive honesty, sometimes through his own love obsession. There is an undoubted advance here upon the style of the short farces, but dramatic intricacy is lacking, the characters are as yet only surface-drawn, and there is no sign of that comedy of social criticism which later was to prove Molière's greatness.

After the series of episodes in this play we move to a mass of complication in *Le dépit amoureux (Lovers' Spite*; acted first at Béziers in 1656), another work based on an Italian comedy—*L'interesse (Self-interest)*, by Niccolò Secchi. Although it can hardly be considered to show an advance upon *L'étourdi*, individual scenes exhibit a widening of the author's dramatic skill. Such episodes, for example, are the lovers' quarrels, which are the core of the play, and the scene in which Albert tries in vain to get the attention of the pedant Métaphrase:

MÉTAPHRASE: Mandatum tuum curo diligenter.
ALBERT: Master, I wish to——
MÉTAPHRASE: Master is derived from *magister*; it is as if you said "three times greater."
ALBERT: May I die if I knew this. But let it be. Master, then——
MÉTAPHRASE: Proceed.
ALBERT: I will proceed, but do not you proceed to interrupt me thus. Well then, master (mark, this is the third time!), my son causes me some anxiety. You know that I love him dearly, and that I have always carefully brought him up.
MÉTAPHRASE: It is true: *filio non potest præferri nisi filius.* . . .
ALBERT: He seems to me to have set his heart against matrimony, and whatever match I propose to him he is cold and indifferent, and rejects my offer.
MÉTAPHRASE: Perhaps he is of the temper of the brother of Marcus Tullius, who discoursed about it to Atticus; and as the Greeks also say that: "*Athanaton*——"

ALBERT: For Heaven's sake, you irrepressible pedagogue, leave in peace the Greeks, the Albanians, the Sclavonians, and all the other nations you want to talk about. What can my son have to do with them?

MÉTAPHRASE: Very well, then, your son—?

ALBERT: I often wonder if some secret love does not burn within him. For certainly there is something on his mind; and, unnoticed by him, I saw him yesterday, alone in a part of the wood where nobody ever goes.

MÉTAPHRASE: In the remote part of the wood, do you mean to say? a solitary spot, in Latin, *secessus*; Virgil says, *est in secessu locus*—

In the end his disquistions are cut short only when Albert brings in a large bell and rings it loudly at his ear.

The Pursuit of Mastery

Towards the end of the year 1658 Molière brought his company to Court and won royal favour with a repertoire of farces, his own and others'. To those he added, in 1659, *Les précieuses ridicules* (*The Affected Ladies*)—also a farce, but a farce with a mighty difference. Here for the first time the individual style of the author becomes apparent, for *Les précieuses ridicules* is in essence a social comedy. The externals of the plot are not unlike those of many earlier plays—the disguising of a witty servant—but in this case the servant's masquerading has a different dramatic purpose. When Mascarille parades as a marquis it is not in order to cheat an old man and win a lady for his master, but to expose the absurd affectations of the ladies themselves. In the cult of preciosity, fed by the interminable romances of the time, Molière saw an object well worthy of the laughter of social comedy; he sought to entertain, and to reform through entertainment. The Marquis has himself carried directly into the house, and the girls at once are infatuated with his elegant hauteur and languid grace. "My dear," says Cathos, "we should call for chairs"; "Almanzor," replies Madelon to her page, "convey me hither at once the appliances of conversation." To cover her mistake in thus vulgarly alluding to chairs, Cathos turns to the Marquis: "For pity's sake," she begs,

do not be inexorable to that armchair which for the last quarter of an hour has stretched out its arms to you; satisfy the desire it has of embracing you.

The attack on what was then a fashionable diversion of Parisian Society soon had various ladies of the Court protesting violently, and, although Molière assured them that he was but aiming his shafts at absurd provincials, he found that the hornets' nest he had aroused suggested the taking of more cautious steps for at least the immediate future. In *Sganarelle, ou le cocu imaginaire* (*Sganarelle; or, The Cuckold in his own Imagination*, 1660) he accordingly produced an innocuous, and a highly successful, farce in which the citizen Sganarelle thinks his wife unfaithful and yet cannot rouse up courage enough to seek vengeance on her supposed lover. He considers the claims of honour, lets prudence calm his rage, and then, with anger once more rising, comes to his final conclusion. He will address himself to some manly action:

> Yes, my blood is up, I will revenge myself on the scoundrel, I will be no coward! And to begin with, in the heat of my passion, I am going to tell every one everywhere that he is living with my wife.

After a somewhat unfortunate excursion into the field of tragi-comedy (*Don Garcie de Navarre*, 1661) the actor-dramatist once more swung back to social comedy in *L' école des maris* (*The School for Husbands*, 1661), the first truly great comedy from his pen, and one destined for a lengthy career. Although lacking the ease and organic structure of some of his later works, this comedy, based on Terence's *Adelphi* and on Lope de Vega's *Discreta enamorada*, exhibits clearly the qualities that give him his real title to fame—the development of a social comedy in which excesses are ridiculed wittily, good sense is enthroned, and the golden mean is made the prize of man's endeavour. Externally this comedy is, like Ben Jonson's, classically realistic; like the English dramatist, Molière endeavours to present in imaginative terms deeds and language such as men do use; yet there is an essential difference between the two. Jonson bent all his energies to the creation of satire, and the things he satirized were those follies that touched him nearly; for Molière the task was to shed comic laughter on follies he deemed inimical to the social structure. Jonson was ego-centred; Molière's orientation was towards the society to which he belonged.

The School for Husbands is somewhat mechanically planned, but Molière's typical approach is well exemplified in its scenes. The two main characters are set before us at the very beginning—Ariste, who argues that one should bow to the ways of society, and Sganarelle, his brother, who churlishly insists on the expression of his own individuality. "We should always fall in with the majority," says Ariste, "and never cause ourselves to become conspicuous. All excesses are offensive, and every truly wise man ought not to display affectation either in his dress or his language, but willingly follow the changing customs of his time." These two men are revealed in relation to their wards, Isabelle in the charge of Sganarelle and Léonore in the charge of Ariste. Where the socially amenable Ariste allows Léonore her freedom, the puritanically individualistic Sganarelle insists on imposing his will upon Isabelle. The greater part of the play is devoted to showing how this girl, irked by the restrictions imposed upon her, eventually tricks her guardian and marries Valère, while at the end Léonore expresses her willingness to marry Ariste, whose kindness has won her heart. Poor Sganarelle, the misanthropist, is left alone cursing the female sex and the more strongly confirmed in his misanthropy.

Following *The School for Husbands* came the rather slight sketch entitled *Les fâcheux* (*The Bores*), which formed a *comédie-ballet* presented before the

King in 1661. *L'école des femmes* (*The School for Wives*, 1662) soon followed, and in this Molière made a notable advance in his comic art. The serious element is over-pronounced in *The School for Husbands*: brilliant as are many of the scenes, the play is written to a thesis. Far greater freedom and more liveliness in the character delineation animate its successor. The difference between the two comedies may be realized when we contrast the Ariste and Sganarelle of the one with the other's Chrysalde and Arnolphe. Basically they represent the same types, but here the types are made richer and more delicately humanized. Arnolphe is also a surly individualist, but instead of having a philosophy on which his actions are dependent, he is presented as an ambitious, self-confident egotist. Similarly, Chrysalde appears not as a mouthpiece for a particular view of life, but as a good-humoured, cynical man of the world. When the play begins we are shown Arnolphe (who, to shine in society, calls himself M. de la Souche) planning to marry his innocent ward Agnès, a girl as yet wholly ignorant of the world. He explains his belief that if a man is to avoid being made a cuckold he should marry such an ignorant maiden, and keep her ignorant. His assurance is complete: "I am up to all the cunning tricks and ingenious devices which women employ to deceive us," he declares. "As I know that we are always duped by their dexterity, I have taken my precautions against mishaps, and she who is to be my wife has all the ignorant simplicity needed to save my forehead from evil influence." In vain Chrysalde presents before him his worldly wisdom; in vain he argues that no man can count himself safe, and that, if one needs must marry, the best plan is not to worry overmuch about it; the only certain course is not to marry at all. As the play develops we are introduced to this innocent Agnès, whose simple little heart is stirred into love by the gentle courtship offered her by Horace. This young gentleman, however, is rather like the hero of *L'étourdi*, and nearly ruins his own chances by confiding to Arnolphe (whom he does not know to be Agnès' guardian) the whole progress of his love-affair. The first important scene in which Agnès and Arnolphe are shown together is perfect in its simplicity:

> *ARNOLPHE:* It is very pleasant walking.
> *AGNÈS:* Very pleasant.
> *ARNOLPHE:* What a fine day!
> *AGNÈS:* Very fine.
> *ARNOLPHE:* Well, and what news?
> *AGNÈS:* The kitten is dead.
> *ARNOLPHE:* That's a pity: but we are all mortal, and every one must think of himself. Has it rained here during my absence in the country?
> *AGNÈS:* No.
> *ARNOLPHE:* Did you feel dull?
> *AGNÈS:* I never feel dull.
> *ARNOLPHE:* What have you done during these nine or ten days?
> *AGNÈS:* Six nightshirts, I think, and six nightcaps too.

SETTING FOR A PLAY BY CALDERÓN, 1690
From *Lopé de Véga*, by Marcel Carayon (Presses Universitaires de France, Paris, 1929).

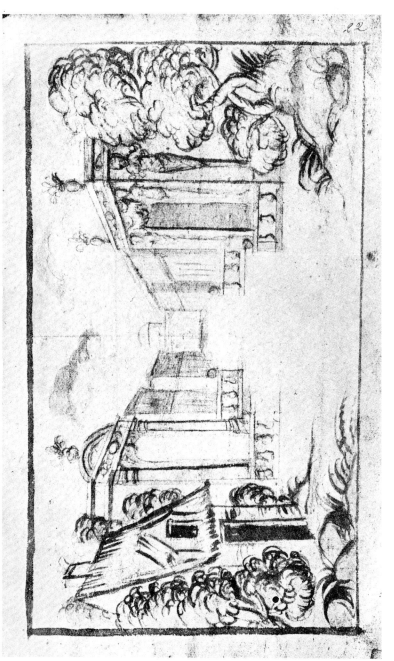

SETTING FOR "PANDOSTE" AT THE HÔTEL DE
BOURGOGNE, ABOUT 1632

Prompted, she tells frankly and openly of her having seen Horace from her balcony, and of her later meeting with him. Arnolphe then announces that he intends to marry her immediately, and reads her a passage from a book entitled *The Maxims of Marriage; or, The Duties of a Wife: with her Daily Exercises*. As her love grows, so Agnès throws off her simple folly; from a desire to have her as his wife because of her innocence, Arnolphe moves to a deeper devotion, but all is in vain; by a sudden turn of the plot Agnès is made free to marry her Horace.

The play immediately made a stir, and there were not wanting moralists and literary critics who attacked its contents and its style, whereupon Molière made dramatic history and added to his stock of comic scenes by penning the first play upon a play—*La critique de l'école des femmes* (*The School for Wives criticized*, 1663). Climène, a *précieuse*, feels faint with disgust after seeing it; Uranie protects it against her strictures; Élise satirically agrees with Climène; a marquis thinks it must be altogether silly because it has proved so popular; the poet Lysidas feigns to praise, but easily allows himself to reveal his belief that such pieces are not true comedies. Into the mouth of Dorante Molière has put his own defence. He argues that the general applause given to the drama is a testimony to its value and to good sense, that the "rules of art" cannot be taken as definitive laws. "I should like to know," he remarks, "whether the greatest rule of all rules is not to please, and whether a piece which has gained that end has not followed the right road."

The controversy continued. Edmé Boursault gave to the Hôtel de Bourgogne his *Le portrait du peintre, ou la contre-critique de l'école des femmes*, whereupon Molière replied with *L'impromptu de Versailles* (*The Impromptu at Versailles*, 1663), in which his actors are gathered together for a rehearsal. Here, again, Molière seems to have been making dramatic history: the play within the play was a well-known device, but this seems to be the first 'rehearsal' piece on record. Ironically he hits out at the style of acting at the Hôtel de Bourgogne. Once more a single individual, Brécourt, is introduced to put forward the claims of common sense. The comic author does not present satirical portraits, he argues: "The business of comedy is to represent in a general way all the defects of men, and particularly those of our own age"—and consequently he ought to remain free from the strictures of those petty individuals who fail to see that in his work is to be found a corrective for society.

The Triumph of the Art of Comedy

Immediately after these plays came a couple of slight *comédies-ballets* —*Le mariage forcé* (*The Forced Marriage*) and *La Princesse d'Élide* (*The Princess of Elis*), both acted in 1664, the one at the Louvre and the other at Versailles. Neither deserves much attention, although the former—which shows Sganarelle anxious to marry, and then, having seen his future wife's flirtatious propensities, at the end aghast at the thought of the wedding—is written with verve and gaiety.

A third time Molière was asked during this year to contribute in the diversion of the Court, but instead of these two flimsy shows his chief offering to the gorgeous spectacle at Versailles, entitled the *Plaisirs de l'île enchantée*, was the first version of his deepest and his bitterest comedy, *Tartuffe, ou l'imposteur (Tartuffe; or, The Impostor)*. We cannot tell precisely, of course, what relationship this bears to the drama we now possess, but the fact that, after its Court performance, it was not again given until 1667, and then was forbidden public representation until 1669, suggests that basically it contained the same material as that with which we are now familiar.

Here was the most complete fusion of comedy and purpose. From the portraits of folly Molière now turns to vice. Tartuffe is a sensual, self-seeking hypocrite who trades on credulity. Fastening upon the dull-witted Orgon, he insinuates himself into his household and threatens to bring it to complete disaster. Only his own lust and his over-confidence, brought to betrayal by the innate honesty of Orgon's wife, result in his unmasking, discomfiture, and punishment. Technically the comedy is a true work of genius. For two entire acts Tartuffe himself does not appear before us, yet a powerful impression of his personality is built up through the references to him on the part of the other characters: thus the looming character of his personality comes upon us with the greater force, while his eventual entry is made the more impressive. In the first scene the bigoted Madame Pernelle, mother of Orgon, gives him praise, while his true nature is hinted at in the words of Damis, her grandson, and the maid, Dorine. The whole family is set before us in inimitably etched lines, so that we are thoroughly acquainted with their personalities before ever the main figure appears—and his appearance is effectively contrived. Dorine, the maid, is on the stage when he enters. Catching sight of her, he immediately turns to his servant:

> *TARTUFFE:* Laurent, lock up my hair-shirt and my scourge, and pray Heaven ever to enlighten you with grace. If anybody comes to see me, say that I am gone to the prisons to distribute my alms. . . . [*Turning to DORINE*] What is it you want?
> *DORINE:* To tell you—
> *TARTUFFE* [*taking a handkerchief out of his pocket*]: Ah! Heaven! before you speak to me, take this handkerchief, pray.
> *DORINE:* What's the matter?
> *TARTUFFE:* Cover this bosom, of which I cannot bear the sight. Such objects hurt the soul, and are conducive to sinful thoughts.

Almost at once we see him making love to Élmire, Orgon's wife; Damis, her son, tells his father, and Tartuffe shows his genius by refusing to deny the specific accusation; instead, he piously declares that he is "a wicked, guilty, miserable sinner," and, when Orgon angrily turns on his son, magnanimously chides his patron:

Ah! let him speak; you blame him wrongfully, and you would do better to believe what he tells you. Why should you be so favourable to me in this instance? Do you know, after all, what I am capable of doing? Do you, brother, trust to the outward man; and do you think me good, because of what you see? No, no, you are deceived by appearances, and I am, alas! no better than they think. Everybody takes me for a good man, no doubt; but the truth is, I am worthless. [*To DAMIS*] Yes, dear child, speak; call me perfidious, infamous, reprobate, thief, and murderer; load me with still more hateful names; I do not gainsay them, I have deserved them all; and on my knees I will suffer the ignominy due to the crimes of my shameful life.

[*Kneels.*]

His unmasking comes only when Orgon is persuaded to listen while he makes further love to Élmire and seeks speciously to argue that she may without sin lie with him because of "the purity of the intention." Even then he is not defeated and almost succeeds in ruining Orgon, who is saved only by direct intervention of the King.

There is an atmosphere here closely akin to that of Jonson's *Volpone*, but, whereas in the English play there is hardly a worthy character among all the *dramatis personæ*, and whereas all these *dramatis personæ* are exaggerated caricatures, Molière's domestic interior, although treated idealistically, is true to life, and good shines among the bad. Madame Pernelle is the typical old bigot, Orgon the besotted fool, Élmire the wife who would rather suffer inconveniences than have trouble in the house, Dorine the keen-eyed little maid, Damis the honest youth who has not tact enough to make his honesty known. In reading *Volpone* we are not concerned with the interests of society; in *Tartuffe* Molière seeks to arouse laughter that he may warn his fellows of an insidious danger.

Tartuffe was a hypocrite: in *Don Juan, ou le festin de pierre* (*Don Juan; or, The Banquet of Stone*, 1665) Molière delineated the atheist for whom no conventional morality has any meaning, the brave soul whose daring leads him to disaster. There is a mood of continual dissatisfaction about his hero; like Faust, although in another way, he seeks for the unattainable:

The true pleasure of love consists in its variety. It is a most captivating delight to reduce by a hundred means the heart of a young beauty; to see day by day the gradual progress one makes; to combat with transport, tears and sighs, the shrinking modesty of a heart unwilling to yield; and to force, inch by inch, all the little obstacles she opposes to our passion; to overcome the scruples upon which she prides herself, and to lead her, step by step, where we would bring her. But once we have succeeded, there is nothing more to wish for; all the attraction of love is over, and we should fall asleep in the tameness of such a passion, unless some new object came to awake our desires and present to us the attractive perspective of a new conquest. . . . I have in this the ambition of conquerors, who go from victory to victory, and cannot bring themselves to put limits to their longings.

Accompanied by the timorous Sganarelle, he is revealed in diverse aspects, in the end—like Tartuffe—donning the garb of the hypocrite in order to effect his purposes, and after this final evil being consumed in hell-fire, while Sganarelle, true to the spirit of comedy, can think only of the money owed him and now lost to him for ever:

> Oh! my wages! my wages! His death is a reparation to all. Heaven offended. laws violated, families dishonoured, girls ruined, wives led astray, husbands driven to despair, everybody is satisfied. I am the only one to suffer. My wages, my wages, my wages!

An apparently more joyous play followed—*L'amour médecin* (*Love is the Best Doctor*), acted in 1665 as part of an elaborate *comédie-ballet*—but the bitter tone apparent in the two dramas immediately preceding cannot quite be concealed by its gaiety. The plot is a simple one. Lucinde, daughter of Sganarelle, pretends illness in order to further her love-affair with Clitandre. Four pompous doctors are called in to attend her, and spend most of their time in boring talk about the social aspects of their profession. Eventually Clitandre dresses as a physician, declares that Lucinde's trouble is mental, and persuades Sganarelle that she must be humoured:

> CLITANDRE: However, as one must flatter the imagination of patients, and as I see in your daughter signs of distress of mind that would be dangerous if prompt remedies were not administered, I have made use of her own fancies and have told her that I was here to ask her of you in marriage. Then her face changed in a moment, her complexion cleared up, and her eyes brightened. If you keep up that delusion in her for a few days, you will see that we shall save her.
>
> SGANARELLE: Indeed, I am most willing.
>
> CLITANDRE: After that we will use other remedies to cure her entirely of these fancies.
>
> SGANARELLE: Quite right!—Well, my daughter, here is a gentleman who wishes to marry you, and I have told him that I am most willing.
>
> LUCINDE: Alas! is it possible?
>
> SGANARELLE: Yes.
>
> LUCINDE: But really?
>
> SGANARELLE: Yes, yes.
>
> LUCINDE [*to CLITANDRE*]: What! are you willing to be my husband?
>
> CLITANDRE: Yes.
>
> LUCINDE: And does my father consent to it?
>
> SGANARELLE: Yes, my child.
>
> LUCINDE: Ah! I am truly happy, if it is really so!
>
> CLITANDRE: Do not doubt it for one moment; my love for you does not date from to-day, and I have long wished to be your husband. I came here on purpose, and if you wish to know the whole truth, this dress is but a mere disguise, and I only acted the doctor that I might better obtain what I desire.
>
> LUCINDE: You give me marks of real affection, and I am as grateful as I can be.
>
> SGANARELLE [*aside*]: Oh! the foolish, foolish, foolish girl!
>
> LUCINDE: You are willing, then, Father, to give me this gentleman for my husband?

SGANARELLE: Yes, yes; come, give me your hand. Give me yours also, sir.

CLITANDRE [*holding back*]: But, sir—

SGANARELLE [*choking with laughter*]: No, no, it is to—[*stifling his laugh*] to soothe her mind. Shake hands, both of you. There, the affair is settled.

CLITANDRE: Accept as a gage of my faith this ring, which I give you. [*To SGANARELLE*] It is a constellated ring, which cures all delusions of the mind.

LUCINDE: Let us write the contract, then, so that nothing be wanting.

CLITANDRE: Alas! I will do so, if you like. [*Aside to SGANARELLE*] I will call up the man who writes my prescriptions, and tell her he is a notary.

SGANARELLE: Very well.

CLITANDRE: Ho! there! send up the notary I brought with me.

LUCINDE: What! you had brought a notary with you?

CLITANDRE: Yes.

LUCINDE: How pleased I am!

SGANARELLE: Oh! the foolish, foolish, foolish girl!

L'amour médecin was followed by what many critics regard as Molière's greatest play, *Le misanthrope* (1666), in which his comic view of life becomes darker and his consideration of man more philosophic. Basically this is a study in the opposition in the human being between his own individuality and his needs as a social animal. The central figure is Alceste, a character akin to the individualist of *L'école des maris*, but more intimately and effectively delineated. The empty politenesses that accompany social life arouse his anger and annoyance; why, he asks, should he praise a wretched sonnet on which his opinion is requested or bow and smile to a man whom he has no intention of seeing again? To his own disgust he finds himself emotionally attracted by the young widow Célimène, a gay, flirtatious coquette, and the greater part of the comedy is occupied with tracing his repulsion to her follies and his paradoxical desire to possess her. Contrasted with him is the good-humoured, complacent Philinte, who, while recognizing the absurdities of the world, is prepared to accept its manners and to comply with its conventions. The two sides of the picture are presented with scrupulous balance. Alceste is undoubtedly a figure that stirs in us both admiration and sympathy; compared with Célimène, he possesses an honesty and integrity wholly worthy. Yet the individualist is an ever-potent menace to his companions; the only logical course for him and for the society to which he belongs is to have him sent out in loneliness to a desert. This, indeed, is the end of Alceste. Célimène's frivolity has been amply demonstrated, but even a realization of her pettinesses cannot kill the love for her he has in his heart: he consents to forgive her, on condition that she will follow him into the solitude where he has vowed to live. "What!" cries Célimène, "renounce the world before I grow old, go and bury myself in the wilderness?" Alceste argues with her:

> But if your love answers to mine, what can be to you all the rest of the world; are not all your desires centred in me?

CÉLIMÈNE: Solitude at twenty years of age frightens me. I do not find in my heart greatness and self-denial enough to yield to such a fate; if the gift of my hand can satisfy your wishes, I am willing; and marriage—

This offer Alceste indignantly rejects, and the play ends with his departure, while Philinte and Éliante prepare for their commonsense wedding, and Célimène retires, no doubt to capture other hearts. These characters are sensible, yet to the very conclusion the balance is preserved: there is a moving quality in the hero's final words:

As to myself, betrayed on all sides and crushed with injustice, I will escape from a gulf where vice triumphs, and look in all the earth for a desert place where one may be free to be a man of honour.

Molière's Last Plays

Laughter, gay and uninhibited, comes again in *Le médecin malgré lui* (*The Doctor in spite of Himself,* 1666), in which a woodcutter, Sganarelle, is mistakenly forced to act as a physician. At the beginning he is cudgelled into his profession, but as he proceeds he finds that he has the audacity sufficient to carry off the trick, and decides that doctoring is better than woodcutting. His patient pretends she is dumb, and Sganarelle is talking with Géronte, her father, who seeks to know the cause of her malady:

SGANARELLE: There is nothing easier; it is caused by her having lost her speech.
GÉRONTE: Yes. But the cause, if you please, for her losing her speech?
SGANARELLE: All our best authors will tell you that it comes from an impediment in the action of her tongue.
GÉRONTE: But still, what is your opinion on this impediment in the action of her tongue?
SGANARELLE: Aristotle, on that subject, says—marvels!
GÉRONTE: I believe you.
SGANARELLE: Ah! he was a great man!
GÉRONTE: Undoubtedly.
SGANARELLE: Altogether a great man. [*Raising his arm above his head*] Greater than I am by all this. To come back to our reasoning, then; I hold that this impediment in the action of her tongue is caused by certain humours, that is to say—peccant humours; for, as the vapours formed by the exhalations of the influences which arise in the region of diseases coming —as it were—to—Do you understand Latin?
GÉRONTE: Not in the least.
SGANARELLE: You don't understand Latin?
GÉRONTE: No.
SGANARELLE [*with enthusiasm*]: *Cabricias, arci thuram, catalamatus, singulariter, nominativo, hæc musa,* the muse, *bonus, bona, bonum. Deus sanctus, est-ne oratio latinas? Etiam.* Yes. *Quare?* Why? *Quia substantivo, et adjectivum, concordat in generi numerum et casus.*
GÉRONTE: Ah, that I had studied Latin!

JACQUELINE [the Nurse]: See what a clever man he is!

LUCAS [her husband]: Sure enough, that's so fine that I can't make out never a bit of it.

SGANARELLE: Now, these vapours of which I have been speaking to you, in passing from the left side where the liver is, to the right side where the heart is, it happens that the lungs, which we call in Latin *armyan*, communicating with the brain, which we call in Greek *nasmus*, by the means of the concave vein, which we call in Hebrew *cubile*, meets on its way the said vapours, which fill the ventricles of the omoplate; and as the said vapours—— Follow closely this reasoning, I beg of you—— And as the said vapours have a certain malignancy—— Listen to this, I beseech you.

GÉRONTE: Yes.

SGANARELLE: Have a certain malignancy which is caused——Be attentive, if you please.

GÉRONTE: I am so.

SGANARELLE: Which is caused by the acrimony of the humours engendered in the concavity of the diaphragm. It so happens that these vapours —*Ossabandus, nequeis, nequer potarinum, quipsa milus*. This is precisely the cause why your daughter is dumb.

When Géronte remarks that he has placed the heart wrongly on the right side Sganarelle can rise gloriously to the occasion with his famous *"Nous avons changé tout cela"*:

Yes, it was, formerly; but we have altered all that, and we now practise medicine in quite a new way.

GÉRONTE: I did not know that, and I beg you will excuse my ignorance.

Many plays were still to follow, although some, such as *Le Sicilien, ou l'amour peintre (The Sicilian; or, Love the Painter,* 1667)—an anticipation of the *opéra-comique*—may be disregarded. *Amphitryon* (1668), except for the vivacious part of Sosie (written for himself), does not add much to the body of his work, and *Georges Dandin, ou le mari confondu (George Dandin; or, The Baffled Husband,* 1668), although replete with verve, is little more than an elaboration of *La jalousie du Barbouillé*, with development of character and the provision of a firmer social background.

In *L'avare (The Miser,* 1668), as in *Amphitryon*, Molière sought his theme among the plays of Plautus, selecting for this purpose the *Aulularia*. Although this play is superior to the other two presented during the same year, it betrays a falling off from the brilliance of *Tartuffe* and *Le Misanthrope*. The miser, Harpagon, is rather farcically conceived, and the plot tends to be confused. One has the double impression that Molière, unlike Ben Jonson, is not at his happiest in dealing with miserliness and that his skill of hand is declining. What is of interest, however, is the manner in which the French dramatist has departed from his original by associating the old man with a large household instead of leaving him an isolated recluse. Within that household, too, there is one person, Maître Jacques, who is a masterpiece of comic portraiture. He is both cook and coachman, and keeps two coats ready for his assumption of either of his two duties. A somewhat stupid but good-willed fellow, he provides much of the laughter of the play.

A *comédie-ballet* entitled *Monsieur de Pourceaugnac* followed in 1669—a merry record of the painful adventures suffered by a provincial lawyer among the professional sharks of Paris. In this piece Molière experimented upon, and considerably improved, the comic-opera style already tried in *L'amour médecin*. The mediocre *Les amants magnifiques* (*The Magnificent Lovers*, 1670) was of the same character, as was also the joyous *Le bourgeois gentilhomme* (*The Bourgeois Gentleman*), produced during the same year. The picture painted of M. Jourdain is superb. A middle-class shopkeeper who has amassed a small fortune, he determines to figure in the world of Society. He enters in dressing-gown and nightcap, having been told that in this wise aristocrats hold their morning levees; amid the dancing- and music-masters whom he has summoned to instruct him he meanders along in simple-minded delight. Soon the professional teachers are at each others' throats, each claiming the superiority of his own subject, until the exponent of philosophy, flying at his companions, remains lord of the stage. "*Nam sine doctrina vita est quasi mortis imago*," declares the philosopher. "You understand this, and you have no doubt a knowledge of Latin?" "Yes," replies M. Jourdain; "but act as if I had none. Explain to me the meaning of it." "The meaning of it is that 'without science life is an image of death.'" "That Latin is quite right," says M. Jourdain. A ludicrous lesson follows, and rises to a culmination in Jourdain's famous discovery that he has been speaking prose all his life without knowing it. Into this world of the fantastically real the Turkish episode at the end fits with perfect harmony: M. Jourdain is made a Mamamouchi by a group of men disguised to hoodwink him, and the play ends with the simple, foolish, and rather pathetic little shopkeeper thoroughly pleased with himself and entirely ignorant of the figure of fun he has become.

In *Les fourberies de Scapin* (*The Tricks of Scapin*, 1671) a return is made to that admixture of *commedia dell' arte* and native farce with which Molière began his work, with Scapin keeping the scenes in constant movement by his skilful impostures. Provincial pretensions are satirized in the rather slight *La Comtesse d'Escarbagnas* (1671), and then, somewhat surprisingly after these efforts, comes the magnificent *Les femmes savantes* (*The Learned Ladies*, 1672). Here the theme is that of education for women. Central in the picture is the pedantic Philaminte, the middle-aged wife of the honest bourgeois Chrysale, who neglects her home for the sake of philosophy. She has two daughters, Armande, a prudish *précieuse*, and the common-sense Henriette. Clitandre is the lover, once the wooer, of Armande, but, disgusted by her affectations, now the avowed adorer of her sister. Philaminte deems him too unlearned to marry one of her daughters, preferring the wit Trissotin. On this basis the comedy proceeds. Armande professes repugnance at the thought that Henriette can even dream of marriage—although secretly and almost unknown to herself she is consumed with jealousy. Poor Chrysale tries from time to time to put in a word, but the masterful Philaminte ever bears him down. One hilarious occasion occurs when the maid Martine is being dismissed. Chrysale tentatively inquires the cause, but is soon forced to berate the girl without knowing why: he eventually discovers that she has been guilty of using a word disapproved of by a famous grammarian. Towards the very conclusion of the drama, when Philaminte seems certain to compel Henriette to marry Trissotin, a *deus ex machina* appears in the person of Chrysale's brother, Ariste, who falsely announces that the family has lost all its money: Trissotin immediately backs out of his pretensions to Henriette, while Clitandre nobly offers the household all he possesses. Anticipating many a later sentimental heroine, Henriette now refuses to wed Clitandre, because she would not burden him with their poverty, when Ariste reveals the fact that his news was merely a device to expose Trissotin. The last words are spoken by Chrysale, anxious at last to assert his authority: turning to the notary, he bids him, "Execute my orders and draw up the contract in accordance with what I said."

The brilliance of this comedy cannot be denied, and yet that last sentimental note is troublesome: it is an indication that a new world is approaching. Molière's own career, however, was now near its end. Suffering from a disease he knew would soon bring his end, he ironically penned his last comedy, *Le malade imaginaire* (*The Imaginary Invalid*, 1673), at the fourth performance of which he collapsed and died. Argan here is a hopeless hypochondriac who surrounds himself with doctors and apothecaries, and it is his person who dominates in the play. Opposed to him is the gay maid Toinette, whose frank enjoyment of life and refusal to think of the morrow provides a vivid contrast to his dark thoughts. A further foil is established in Argan's brother, Béralde, who, mocking the hypochondriac's fancies, counsels a visit to the theatre to see some of Molière's plays. It is in this scene that Béralde quotes the author himself as saying that he will have nothing to do with the doctors:

> He is certain that only strong and robust constitutions can bear their remedies in addition to the illness, and he has only just strength enough to endure his sickness.

Thus closed Molière's career. During its course he had succeeded in creating a comic world which places him among the greatest of comic playwrights. Building from the individual, yet concerned with the presentation of types, he wrote plays in which an inimitable gallery of memorable portraits is placed before us. His fundamental attitude is one of common sense; frankly he accepts the world, and strives to show that excesses of all kinds are fatal to the even tenor of social life. Although his plays include many farces, and even his darkest comedy contains much of hilarity, his greatest power lies in his skill in arousing what has been called 'thoughtful laughter,' where a smile takes the place of the guffaw and in the mind is left a dominant concept. Logical proportion, avoidance of extremes, honest acceptance of the facts of life, the application of reason to social affairs—these were the messages which Molière constantly preached to his fellows even as he contributed richly to their entertainment.

3

THE RESTORATION COMEDY OF MANNERS

SINCE Racine and Molière were so closely associated with the Court of Louis XIV, we might have thought that France would have produced during this time a drama prevailingly aristocratic. It is true that the former's tragedies reflect the modes of High Society and that the orientation of the latter's comedies is towards the manners set by the King and his courtiers; yet both Racine and Molière refuse to be bound by the aristocratic *milieu*. Molière's main strength, indeed, comes from the fact that the interests of the middle class play a part equal to that of the Court's interests; the family that is nearly wrecked by the machinations of Tartuffe is essentially bourgeois, and the numerous Sganarelles are worthy citizens, not noble gallants. The "bon bourgeois," although he may often be placed in a ridiculous setting, is in a sense the true hero of these comedies; if he is exposed to the stings of satire it is for the good of his own soul, not because he seems to a well-born author an object of contempt.

Despite the royal patronage accorded to Molière, therefore, and despite the writing of several of his plays specifically for the delectation of the Court, the strength of this classical French drama rests in its power to take into account all classes in the community. The peasant and the shopkeeper, the coachman and the maidservant, are fully as important as the marquises and the wits, nor is the ridicule devoted to the aristocratic follies a whit less than that devoted to the follies of the others.

For a truly aristocratic theatre in this age we must, peculiarly, go to that country which had dared to set on trial and to execute its sovereign. During the time of the Commonwealth Puritan opposition to the stage had succeeded in closing the theatres, so that for eighteen years the only dramatic performances in England were surreptitious productions liable to be interrupted at any moment by the incursion of Cromwell's soldiery, or else, at the very end of the period, simple shows disguised as musical entertainments. Sir William D'Avenant obtained licence to present 'operas' where he would have failed to get leave for the giving of 'plays.' In 1660, however, the King, Charles II, came back to his own again, and the playhouses were reopened—but under conditions far different from those that prevailed during the days of Elizabeth. The great mass of the citizenry, still dominated by Puritan sentiment, avoided them; the auditorium became filled with courtiers and their attendants.

The Restoration Playhouses

The quality of this audience is the cardinal and determining factor in the development of the Restoration drama. It explains the fact that from 1660 to 1682 only two theatres could keep their doors open in London —and then often at a loss—while from 1682 to 1695 but one stage was active. Innumerable records of these forty years indicate that the courtiers regarded the playhouses as toys of their own; the theatres became almost like clubs attached to Whitehall. Assignations were made there; gallants wandered into the auditorium in search of friends or mistresses; quarrels sprang up while plays were in progress, and duels even were fought upon the stage.

In structure and equipment these stages stood as transitional between the Elizabethan and the modern. The new houses, like those of France, were modelled on the long, narrow, rectangular tennis-court of the time, with the actors placed, not in the midst of the audience, but at one end of the hall; indoor conditions introduced lighting as a theatrical element; memories of the Court masques presented during the days of Charles I, added to the theatrical knowledge acquired by Charles II's little wandering group of courtiers during the time of the Commonwealth, led to the regular presentation of plays with scenic accompaniment. At the same time Elizabethan traditions could not be forgotten. In place of the sharp stage-line characteristic of most Continental theatres, the Restoration playhouse had a curving projection beyond the curtain—technically known as the 'apron,' and obviously the relic of the platform stage of earlier times. Besides this relic another appeared in the presence of two, and sometimes four, doors of entrance set in the proscenium façade. Through these the actors commonly moved on to the stage, and through them they made their exits. Since the apron brought the players nearer to the audience, and since the doors opened on to the apron, we may believe that the greater part of the action took place on the forward area and that the scenery for long remained little more than a background to the actors. It was to be many years before these actors gradually moved back and were content to perform within, instead of against, the settings provided for them.

While there were some particularly spectacular productions during the Restoration period, we must believe also that most of the scenes were simple and that but little endeavour was made to paint new flats for new plays. All the evidence available suggests that the playhouses possessed stock sets of wings and back-shutters, which were used variously in the presentation of their repertoire, and it is noticeable that the writers both of tragedy and of comedy were inclined to fashion their plays in such a manner as to permit of the use of these stock scenes. Unquestionably the introduction of scenery points towards theatrical realism, but the realism of the Restoration stage was by no means particularized. In tragedies the grove, the temple, and the palace hall follow each other in almost monotonous succession, while in comedy appears the corresponding series of bedroom, boudoir, and park.

The audience was self-centred and fashionably noisy, of that we may be sure; and as a consequence histrionic style in serious drama was apt to become bombastic. These young gallants were not qualified to appreciate tragic drama, and a Betterton could capture their attention only by means of flamboyance of utterance. For comedy, on the other hand, they were ready to attend; a scene of wit could rivet their eyes and ears on the stage, for on conversational wit they fed in their daily lives, and a dramatist's skill in sharp repartee, an actor's ease in the delivery of polished lines, immediately aroused their interest.

Here was the aristocratic playhouse *par excellence*—not the temporary Court theatre of the Renaissance with a privileged invited audience, but a public theatre, set in the midst of a relatively small but bustling community, which yet attracted to its performances only those who clustered around the palace either by right of birth or, like Pepys, by reason of their occupations.

The Heroic Drama

Despite the fact that at least one author of eminence and two or three others of fitful genius applied themselves to the writing of serious drama during the latter years of the century, absolutely nothing of sterling excellence in this kind was produced by the Restoration theatre. In France Racine won through to the creation of an adequate form of expression for this age of classical sentiment, but in England conditions were not so propitious. France had no distracting romantic traditions to haunt the imaginations of her playwrights. English playwrights could never forget the glories of Shakespeare's tragedies. The result was that all the efforts made in London to devise a new tragic form were vitiated by confusion of form and uncertainty in orientation.

Typical is Thomas Otway, an author of more than mediocre talent, who made determined attempts to develop a tragic style suited to the conditions of his time. Racine laid a spell upon his spirit, and his early plays, notably *Alcibiades* (1675) and *Don Carlos* (1676), obviously strove (and failed) to capture classical form, yet the Shakespearian influence could not be gainsaid. After a pitiful experiment in trying to turn *Romeo and Juliet* into a Roman *Caius Marius* (1679) he reverted completely to native English models, producing a kind of romantically emotional domestic tragedy in *The Orphan; or, The Unhappy Marriage* (1680) and another romantic tragedy with an Italian setting, *Venice Preserved; or, A Plot Discovered* (1682), which almost achieved true greatness. The age, however, could not cultivate that sternness of spirit out of which the Elizabethan tragedy was wrought, and consequently, noble as is Otway's attempt, the quality of pathos takes from its would-be tragic grandeur. Considered in relation to the development of Restoration drama alone, *Venice Preserved* must be accounted a great play, but when it is set against the background of the theatre as a whole we have regretfully to dismiss it as but a very modest eminence amid surrounding mountain heights.

At the beginning of the Restoration period John Dryden, a worthy successor to the literary giants of the earlier part of the century, sought to evolve a form of 'heroic drama,' penned in couplet verse, harmonious with the classic predilections of his contemporaries. The conflict of love and honour was its staple theme; intellectualism ruled the conduct of its scenes; and inflated bombast was employed in a vain endeavour to arouse that mood of admiration which the tragic drama demands. There are some magnificent things in these plays of Dryden—in *Tyrannic Love; or, The Royal Martyr* (1669), in *The Conquest of Granada by the Spaniards* (1670), in *Aureng-Zebe* (1675)—but their whole atmosphere is false and their conception confused. The Duke of Buckingham had ample justification for his satirical burlesque of the form in his famous *Rehearsal* of 1671.

The failure of this form of drama was tacitly recognized by Dryden himself when he turned, in 1677, to write his blank-verse *All for Love; or, The World well Lost* on the theme of Antony and Cleopatra. The structure here is classical, but the selection of a theme which Shakespeare had enriched indicates an awareness of the impossibility of producing anything of worth in the purely 'heroic' style. Thereafter, for the last quarter of the century, the tragic drama oscillated precariously and uncomfortably among the ideals of classic precision, heroic sentiment, pathetic interest, and Shakespearian grandeur. John Crowne essayed classicism dully in several dramas; Nathaniel Lee mingled mad absurdities with searing flashes of real genius; from John Banks came a series of tragedies in which heroines took the leading rôles—*Virtue Betrayed; or, Anna Bullen* (1682) and *The Island Queens; or, The Death of Mary, Queen of Scotland* (printed 1684) being the best—without, however, in the slightest degree suggesting the subtlety with which Racine had handled similar material.

Surveying this long range of bombastic and pathetic dramas, we must confess that the Restoration genius had but little to offer to the realm of tragedy. The power that had invested the Elizabethan period was gone, yet there did not exist that singleness of aim and precision in form out of which alone strength could emerge from the classic style. Racine's greatness is seen clearly outlined when presented against the array of these works.

Restoration Comedy: John Dryden and Others

If, however, the Restoration audiences could not foster an effective tragic drama they were well qualified to summon forth the comic spirit. The one thing on which their minds were set was social brilliance; fine manners ruled, witty conversation was practised and admired, intrigue formed the daily business of the gallants and their ladies.

To a large extent conditions at the English Court were similar to those at the Court of Versailles, but there was one fundamental difference. Despite the haughty tone of the French nobility, Molière could, as we have seen, bring within his circle the world of the middle class and as a consequence produce a comedy broad in its implications. For the courtiers who thronged Drury Lane, Lincoln's Inn Fields, and Dorset Garden the middle class simply did not exist; these courtiers were interested in their own exclusive affairs, and everything outside was neglected. Thus came into being an entirely new type of play—the comedy of aristocratic manners; and, although it does not have the breadth of appeal which attaches to any dramatic form wider in its range, the accomplishment of the Restoration comic authors is by no means negligible. We may decide that the style of comedy they produced has but limited interest, but in the handling of their material they were undoubtedly accomplished, if characteristically careless, masters.

Already before the theatres closed in 1642 comedy, as has already been suggested, was moving steadily from the humour of Shakespeare and the satire of Jonson to the gay presentation of the witty Cavalier's existence. In the plays of Shirley the atmosphere of the Restoration is clearly adumbrated. When the return of Charles II permitted the actors once more to go about their business the time and the conditions were ripe for the fuller development of the genre sketched in these earlier plays. The courtly society was even more than previously a coherent unity, conscious of its own peculiar principles. By the introduction of scenery a suggestion of immediate reality could be given to the episodes of daily life. The substitution of actresses for boy players permitted a richer development of the sex-duel which formed the basis of so many of these episodes. In the hands of diverse authors the ornate Elizabethan prose periods were giving way to a new, crisp, intellectual prose style admirably equipped to deal with comic dialogue. Above all, there was the model set in France. During the sixties Molière was rapidly making himself the outstanding dramatist of his time, and, although his earliest introduction to the English stage was in a burlesque scene of *The Playhouse to be Let* (probably written by Sir William D'Avenant in 1663, but possibly a burlesque, penned by an unknown author, of his theatrical efforts), there is plentiful evidence in the plays of the time that his works were eagerly and appreciatively read by English dramatists. They found his plots too simple; they rejected much that he had to offer; but for structure and for comic invention they ransacked his writings. Without doubt, despite the difference between his spirit and theirs, he contributed much to the Restoration dramatists of manners.

Even here the theatre is not entirely sure of its aims. There were playwrights such as Thomas Shadwell, who, although presenting scenes in the style of the comedy of manners, fundamentally looked back to the

Jonsonian comedy of humours. In *The Sullen Lovers; or, The Impertinents*
(1668) this author won an instant success; both his skill and his range of
comic invention were displayed in *The Humourists* (1670), *Epsom Wells*
(1672), *The Squire of Alsatia* (1688), and *Bury Fair* (1689). In these the
teeming world of Restoration London is set before us, its wit and its folly,
its uglinesses and its graces; but in writing his plays Shadwell explored
no new territory. His model was Jonson, and to the style of that author's
comedy he added nothing. Other playwrights, like Mrs Aphra Behn,
pursued the comedy of intrigue, especially the Spanish variety beloved of
Charles II. In her *The Rover; or, The Banished Cavaliers* (1677; second part
1680) and *Sir Patient Fancy* (1678), as in John Crowne's surprisingly
sprightly *Sir Courtly Nice; or, It cannot be* (1685), we have little of delicacy in
the dialogue, but much intricacy of episode and bold caricature.

Still other writers, while making passing contributions to the characteristic comedy of manners, displayed a strange eclecticism, indicating
their lack of certainty as to what they wished to achieve. Of these, unfortunately, John Dryden is one. Without doubt the witty lovers of his
early comedies—*The Wild Gallant* (1663), *An Evening's Love; or, The Mock
Astrologer* (1668), *Marriage à-la-mode* (1672)—as well as such pairs as
Celadon and Florimel (*Secret Love; or, The Maiden Queen* 1667,) from his
tragi-comedies, did something towards consolidating the first experimental essays in the new style, but in all of these there is a lack of distinction; the delineation of manners is confused by association with scenes
cast clearly in imitation of Jonson and with episodes inspired by the
Spanish comedy of intrigue.

The Comedy of Manners

For its development the true comedy of manners requires singleness,
and sureness, of aim, and this first was indicated in the work of Sir
George Etherege, a gentleman of fashion, to whom the depiction of the
aristocratic world came easily. His first essay, *The Comical Revenge; or,
Love in a Tub* (1664), in which he mingled comic scenes with heroic,
marked a false start, but in *She Would if She Could* (1668) and *The Man of
Mode; or, Sir Fopling Flutter* (1676) he brilliantly outlined the main features which were to be adopted by all those who applied themselves to
this comic kind. Of these features most significant is the emphasis laid on
the young gallants in their prime quest of amorous adventure. In the
comedy of Shakespeare the lovers generally are not particularly interesting, and, although in Benedict and Beatrice there is a faint suggestion
of what was to come, it is not so much of the lovers themselves we think
when considering his lighter plays as of the atmosphere in which they
appear. Jonson was too intent on his satirical purposes to allow this element free play, and in Molière it is more commonly the wit of a servant
than the liveliness of a gallant that captures our attention. Spanish
comedy, it is true, had made the lover and his mistress central figures,

but always the code of manners in that country prevented the full development of repartee between the man and the woman—between the lover who tried to cover emotion with a veneer of scepticism and the lass who, though coy and affected, would fain be won. During the entire history of the drama this was the first time when conditions of social life and of the theatre were propitious for the development of such scenes as Etherege had to display.

In presenting these lovers to us Etherege paints them in terms of his age. Courtall and Freeman in *She Would if She Could* are portraits of such men as the audience knew—or, rather, we might perhaps say that they were such as the gallants in the audience would have wished to be. This comedy is realistic in that its setting is London and its characters types of that city's men and women, yet it is idealistic in that the dramatist uses his skill to give its life a polish, a grace, and a turn of phrase which but rarely could have been met with in reality. Here is a dream-world of the witty courtier, not fantastic, but based on the familiar and the known.

There is no thought of the past or of the future in this comedy; its men and women live entirely for the present—a present of indolence and pleasure. "Well, Frank," says Courtall at the opening of *She Would if She Could*, "what is to be done to-day?" and Freeman's answer is typical:

> Faith, I think we must e'en follow the old trade: eat well and prepare ourselves with a bottle or two of good Burgundy that our old acquaintance may look lovely in our eyes—for, for aught as I see, there is no hopes of new.

Having thus placed his two heroes, Etherege hastens to introduce us to his heroines—Ariana and Gatty. "My dear Ariana," cries the latter, "how glad am I we are in this town again!" and at once their talk turns to risky adventures. They express envy of the men:

> *GATTY:* How I envy that sex! Well! we cannot plague 'em enough when we have it in our power for those privileges which custom has allowed 'em above us.
> *ARIANA:* The truth is, they can run and ramble here and there and everywhere, and we poor fools rather think the better of 'em.
> *GATTY:* From one playhouse to the other playhouse, and if they like neither the play nor the women, they seldom stay any longer than the combing of their perriwigs, or a whisper or two with a friend, and then they cock their caps and out they strut again.

Very soon the couples have met, the girls masked and the men encountering them in the park:

> *COURTALL:* By your leave, ladies—
> *GATTY:* I perceive you can make bold enough without it.
> *FREEMAN:* Your servant, ladies—
> *ARIANA:* Or any other ladies that will give themselves the trouble to entertain you.
> *FREEMAN:* 'Slife, their tongues are as nimble as their heels.
> *COURTALL:* Can you have so little good nature to dash a couple of bashful

young men out of countenance, who came out of pure love to tender you
their service?
GATTY: 'Twere pity to balk them, sister.
ARIANA: Indeed, methinks they look as if they never had been slipped before.
FREEMAN: Yes, faith, we have had many a fair course in this paddock, have
been very well fleshed and dare boldly fasten.

[*They kiss their hands with a little force.*

The same ease and gaiety attends all their meetings:

COURTALL, FREEMAN: Your servant, ladies.
ARIANA: I perceive it is as impossible, gentlemen, to walk without you as
without our shadows; never were poor women so haunted by the ghosts of
their self-murdered lovers.
GATTY: If it should be our good fortunes to have you in love with us, we will
take care you shall not grow desperate and leave the world in an ill humour.
ARIANA: If you should, certainly your ghosts would be very malicious.
COURTALL: 'Twere pity you should have your curtains drawn in the dead of
the night and your pleasing slumbers interrupted by anything but flesh and
blood, ladies.

This ease and this gaiety reach even finer precision in *The Man of Mode*.
The title character, a delicious caricature of a fop, is cleverly withheld
from us until the play is half-way through; but he is not the mainspring of
the comedy: the true figures of importance are Dorimant and his Harriet. The former is characteristically introduced in the first scene, clad in
dressing-gown and slippers, soliloquizing over a letter he has penned to a
mistress of whom he had grown tired:

What a dull insipid thing is a billet-doux written in cold blood, after the heat of
the business is over! It is a tax upon good nature which I have here been
labouring to pay, and have done it, but with as much regret as ever fanatic paid
the royal aid or church duties.

Harriet is a lady well his match in wit. Both play easily with delicate intellectual fancies, and at heart both feel the force of love, more powerful
than their ready scepticism. By convention Dorimant offers his protestations; by convention she conceals her emotions; but the protestations
now are sincere, and nothing can quite hide the impress that he has made
upon her. She keeps her flippancy to the end, but when Dorimant agrees,
in order to see her, to leave his loved town and endure the miseries of the
country we know that their marriage is assured: the sprightly blade has
been caught and his mistress's armour pierced. Lady Woodvil tells him
he will be welcome at her manor if he cares to visit it:

HARRIET: To a great rambling lone house, that looks as it were not inhabited
the family's so small. There you'll find my mother, an old lame aunt and
myself, sir, perched up on chairs at a distance in a large parlour; sitting
moping like three or four melancholy birds in a spacious volary. Does not
this stagger your resolution?
DORIMANT: Not at all, madam. The first time I saw you, you left me with

the pangs of love upon me, and this day my soul has quite given up her liberty.
HARRIET: This is more dismal than the country!

The painting of this world of fashionable manners requires the most delicate balance, and it is not surprising that few were able to follow Etherege's lead. Individual scenes in the plays of his contemporaries and successors catch his well-poised grace, but of the dramatists belonging to the Court of Charles II only William Wycherley succeeded in capturing his style—and even he exhibited elements alien to this kind of comic expression and dangerously apt to shatter its fragile being. Etherege was born to the manner of the time; Wycherley acquired it. No doubts or fears entered into the former's mind; Wycherley was always liable to view the fashionable world from without rather than from within, and he was, too, always liable to indulge in exaggeration. An accomplished dramatist, with a sure sense of character-drawing, he just failed to move with unthinking ease in the world he chose to depict.

Love in a Wood; or, St James's Park (1671) and *The Gentleman Dancing-master* (1672), his earliest experiments, present gaily the gallants, the fops, and the fools on whom Etherege fixed his attention, but it is not for these plays that he is remembered. In *The Country Wife* (1675) and in *The Plain Dealer* (1676) he produced comedies which at once were recognized as the work of a strong and arresting personality, individual in its outlook. The former of these plays is obviously based on Molière, but there is a vast chasm between the spirits of the English and the French playwrights, just as there is a chasm between the spirits of Etherege and Wycherley. This story of Horner, who, in order to carry on his intrigue among the ladies unhindered by their jealous males, pretends that he has been castrated, has a viciousness lacking in Molière and a sensuality wanting in Etherege. Dorimant and his companions are libertines, yet there is a grace in their lives which gives them distinction: Horner dwells on another plane. Etherege's wit is expended on social raillery; Wycherley's applies itself almost entirely to sexual affairs. There is brilliance here, as in the scene in which the country wife writes her letter to her lover or as in the famous 'china' scene, yet this brilliance is of a kind less airy and more brutal than that which renders the meeting of Freeman and Courtall with Ariana and Gatty a joyous masquerade.

Recognizing these qualities in Wycherley's work, we need feel no surprise in turning from *The Country Wife* to *The Plain Dealer*. Once more Molière is the model, but, whereas in *Le misanthrope* the hero is presented as a man irritated at the follies and insincerities of social life, as one who feels his individuality threatened by the conventions of the world he moves in, Wycherley's hero, Manly, is one obsessed by sexual thoughts. It is not irritation at social conventions that inspires him, but disgust at infidelity. The very plot of the play indicates its difference from *Le misanthrope*. Manly is the misanthrope, whose faith in humanity hangs slenderly on two threads—reliance on his friend, Vernish, and trust in his mistress, Olivia. Returning from a journey abroad, he finds that Olivia has married Vernish, and his fury at the world rises almost to lunacy—would, indeed, have ended in madness had he not discovered that his page is in reality a lady, Fidelia, who has followed him faithfully because of her devotion to him. There is something of an Elizabethan quality in this plot, and the language often reminds us more of Middleton than of either Etherege or Molière. We are being carried in *The Plain Dealer* far from *The Man of Mode*.

The spirit of Etherege, however, had not died; indeed, at the very end of the century it was to reach its fullest expression in the work of William Congreve. Here perfection was attained both in posed acceptance of the social world and in precision of utterance. The very first lines of *The Old Bachelor* (1693) illustrate this fully. Bellmour and Vainlove meet:

> *BELLMOUR:* Vainlove! and abroad so early! Good morrow. I thought a contemplative lover could no more have parted with his bed in a morning than he could have slept in't.
> *VAINLOVE:* Bellmour, good morrow. Why, truth on't is, these early sallies are not usual to me: but business, as you see, sir [*showing letters*]. And business must be followed, or be lost.
> *BELLMOUR:* Business! And so must time, my friend, be close pursued, or lost. Business is the rod of life, perverts our aim, casts off the bias and leaves us wide and short of the intended mark.
> *VAINLOVE:* Pleasure, I guess you mean.
> *BELLMOUR:* Ay, what else has meaning?

The plot much concerns Heartwell, "a surly old bachelor, pretending to slight women," who falls in love with Vainlove's discarded mistress, Silvia, agrees to marry her, and is saved only by a trick at the end. This theme, however, is merely the material fabric of the play: its spirit depends on the adventures of Vainlove and his Araminta; he intoxicated with delight in the chase, but immediately chilled when the object of his attentions shows any fondness, and she, aware of his capricious foibles, dallying gracefully with him. They are in love with each other, this pair, yet the mood of their time keeps them delightfully apart.

In *The Double-dealer* (1693) a similar combination is presented. The action is kept moving through the machinations of Lady Touchwood and Maskwell, and through the follies of Lord Froth, "a solemn coxcomb," his *précieuse* wife, Lady Froth, and the "pert coxcomb," Brisk, but the quality of the comedy depends upon the relations between the young gallant Mellefont and Cynthia, his mistress. In their conversations the wit flows easily and fancies abound:

> *MELLEFONT:* You're thoughtful, Cynthia?
> *CYNTHIA:* I'm thinking, though marriage makes man and wife one flesh, it leaves 'em still two fools; and they become more conspicuous by setting off one another.

MELLEFONT: That's only when two fools meet and their follies are opposed.

CYNTHIA: Nay, I have known two wits meet and by the opposition of their wit render themselves as ridiculous as fools. 'Tis an odd game we're going to play at. What think you of drawing stakes and giving over in time?

MELLEFONT: No, hang't, that's not endeavouring to win, because it's possible we may lose. Since we have shuffled and cut, let's e'en turn up trump now.

CYNTHIA: Then I find it's like cards; if either of us have a good hand it is an accident of fortune.

MELLEFONT: No, marriage is rather like a game at bowls. Fortune indeed makes the match, and the two nearest, and sometimes the two farthest, are together, but the game depends entirely upon judgment.

A certain darkness of spirit lightly clouds *The Double-dealer*; though perhaps a faint shadow yet remains in *Love for Love* (1695), this comedy displays Congreve in the process of fully mastering his instrument. Valentine and Angelica here are the lovers. Because of his extravagance the hero has fallen under the displeasure of his father, Sir Sampson Legend; in a thoughtless moment he agrees to sign a bond, whereby Sir Sampson engages to pay his debts on the understanding that the inheritance will be handed over to his brother Ben, a sailor. Repenting of his action, he later pretends insanity, and is saved, partly through Ben's rough manners, partly through Angelica's presence of mind and wit. This simple plot is complicated by the introduction of many finely etched and amusing characters—Scandal, Valentine's free-spoken friend; the garrulous Tattle; superstitious old Foresight; Mrs Frail, Foresight's amorous sister-in-law; and Miss Prue, a gawky young country girl. There are comic scenes between the irascible Sir Sampson and Foresight, between Ben and Miss Prue, between Mrs Foresight and Mrs Frail. The last-mentioned characters, indeed, provide one of the most exquisite episodes in the play. They are sisters, and the former upbraids the latter for going in a coach to Covent Garden and meeting a friend there. "But can't you converse at home?" she inquires:

> I own it, I think there's no happiness like conversing with an agreeable man. I don't quarrel at that, nor I don't think but your conversation was very innocent; but the place is public, and to be seen with a man in a hackney-coach is scandalous. What if anybody else should have seen you alight, as I did? How can anybody be happy while they're in perpetual fear of being seen and censured? Besides, it would not only reflect upon you, sister, but me.
>
> *MRS FRAIL:* Pooh, here's a clutter! Why should it reflect upon you? I don't doubt but you have thought yourself happy in a hackney-coach before now. If I had gone to Knightsbridge, or to Chelsea, or to Spring Garden, or Barn Elms with a man alone, something might have been said.
>
> *MRS FORESIGHT:* Why, was I ever in any of those places? What do you mean, sister?
>
> *MRS FRAIL:* Was I? What do *you* mean?

MRS FORESIGHT: You have been at a worse place.

MRS FRAIL: I at a worse place, and with a man!

MRS FORESIGHT: I suppose you would not go alone to the World's End!

MRS FRAIL: The World's End? What, do you mean to banter me?

MRS FORESIGHT: Poor innocent! You don't know that there's a place called the World's End? I'll swear you can keep your countenance purely; you'd make an admirable player.

MRS FRAIL: I'll swear you have a great deal of confidence, and in my mind too much for the stage.

MRS FORESIGHT: Very well, that will appear who has most. You never were at the World's End?

MRS FRAIL: No.

MRS FORESIGHT: You deny it positively to my face?

MRS FRAIL: Your face? What's your face?

MRS FORESIGHT: No matter for that, it's as good a face as yours.

MRS FRAIL: Not by a dozen years' wearing. But I do deny it positively to your face then.

MRS FORESIGHT: I'll allow you now to find fault with my face—for I'll swear your impudence has put me out of countenance. But look you here now: where did you lose this gold bodkin? Oh, sister, sister!

MRS FRAIL: My bodkin!

MRS FORESIGHT: Nay, 'tis yours, look at it.

MRS FRAIL: Well, if you go to that, where did you find this bodkin? Oh, sister, sister! Sister every way.

In this comedy as in the others, however, it is the lovers, Valentine and Angelica, whose wooing and whose wit give characteristic tone to the scenes as a whole. The other characters provide merriment, but they form the focus of the dramatist's attention.

Valentine and Angelica are transformed, and enriched in the transformation, into Mirabell and Millamant of *The Way of the World* (1700), Congreve's last and finest comedy. The plot is an intricately confused one, but whatever puzzlements, inconsistencies, and improbabilities occur in the story need trouble us little; Congreve has atoned amply for these in the scenes he has written about the gay Mirabell, in love despite himself, and the affected, coquettish Millamant, jealous of her freedom, yet fain to be won. Well is her entry prepared for. She is so talked of in the first act that we get a glimpse of her from afar, and then in the middle of the second act, as Mirabell puts it, "she comes i'faith full sail, with her fan spread and streamers out, and a shoal of fools for tenders"—or at least with one fool, Witwoud. She is the perfect lady of fashion. Accused of being late for her appointment, she confesses "Ay, that's true,"

O but then I had—Mincing, what had I? Why was I so long?

MINCING: O mem, your La'shap staid to peruse a packet of letters.

MILLAMANT: O ay, letters—I had letters—I am persecuted with letters—I hate letters—no body knows how to write letters, and yet one has 'em, one does not know why—they serve to pin up one's hair.

WITWOUD: Is that the way? Pray, madam, do you pin up your hair with all your letters? I find I must keep copies.

MILLAMANT: Only with those in verse, Mr Witwoud. I never pin up my hair with prose. I think I tried once, Mincing?

MINCING: O mem, I shall never forget it.

MILLAMANT: Ay, poor Mincing tift and tift all the morning.

Rising and falling, the wit flows steadily on until at last love conquers, albeit with effort, the affection of indifference:

MIRABELL: "Like Daphne she, as lovely and as coy." Do you lock yourself up from me to make my search more curious? Or is this pretty artifice contrived to signify that here the chase must end and my pursuit be crowned, for you can fly no further?

MILLAMANT: Vanity! No—I'll fly and be followed to the last moment; though I am upon the very verge of matrimony, I expect you should solicit me as much as if I were wavering at the grate of a monastery, with one foot over the threshold. I'll be solicited to the very last, nay and afterwards.

MIRABELL: What, after the last?

MILLAMANT: O, I should think I was poor and had nothing to bestow if I were reduced to an inglorious ease, and freed from the agreeable fatigues of solicitation.

There follows the delicious proviso scene. "Positively, Mirabell," she says,

I'll lie abed in a morning as long as I please.

MIRABELL: Then I'll get up in a morning as early as I please.

MILLAMANT: Ah! idle creature, get up when you will. And d'ye hear, I won't be called names after I'm married—positively I won't be called names.

MIRABELL: Names!

MILLAMANT: Ay, as wife, spouse, my dear, joy, jewel, love, sweetheart, and the rest of that nauseous cant in which men and their wives are so fulsomely familiar—I shall never bear that. Good Mirabell, don't let us be familiar or fond, nor kiss before folks . . . nor go to Hyde Park together the first Sunday in a new chariot, to provoke eyes and whispers—and then never be seen there together again, as if we were proud of one another the first week and ashamed of one another ever after. Let us never visit together, nor go to a play together, but let us be very strange and well bred. Let us be as strange as if we had been married a great while, and as well bred as if we were not married at all.

It is all very pretty and very fantastic, the last curtsy of aristocratic fashion before the new world is ushered in.

PART VI

THE AGE OF GENTILITY, PHILOSOPHY, AND SENTIMENTALISM

THE AGE OF GENTILITY, PHILOSOPHY, AND SENTIMENTALISM

By the time Congreve was writing a new age was already waiting to take control of the stage. In France and in England alike the serried ranks of the aristocracy were being broken. While the young gallants busied themselves with pleasure, worthy and unworthy scions of middle-class houses occupied themselves with business less witty but more serious, so that the beginning of the eighteenth century found the circle of the élite impoverished and a new circle of *nouveaux riches* ready to pay attention to something more than their counting-houses. When young aristocrats discovered that they could obtain the wherewithal to live only by espousing daughters of the wealthy bourgeoisie the barriers between the classes were shattered, the exclusive families had to admit aldermen and their wives into their drawing-rooms, and the newly arrived guests eagerly, if at first somewhat ludicrously, applied themselves to acquiring the manners of society and to taking an interest in the diversions of the cultured.

This process was, of course, slow in its development. Already in Molière's comedies and in the plays of pre-Commonwealth English dramatists hints are given of what was to come, but only in the eighteenth century does the movement reach a culmination. In France the tax-collectors, made rich through the foolish policies of the Court, established a new class of financiers; in England, less spectacularly, the men of business had built up pretty fortunes from trade and, later, from diverse escapades in the East.

The general result was a new theatrical public, destined to call for dramatic fare different from what had pleased their predecessors. Since, however, this public was not so coherent as that, for example, in Restoration London or so assured in its judgments, the eighteenth-century drama exhibits a strange variety of form. Plays of the most diverse kinds appear on the stage, and at first it seems almost impossible to determine the main currents by which the theatre was carried from the precision of Racine to the romantically melodramatic spectacularism of Pixérécourt. Yet these currents may, with effort, be distinguished and viewed apart, even if they appear at times to mingle their waters confusedly.

One such current may be called *the traditional*, carried forward, although with slackening force, from the seventeenth century. The pseudo-classic tragedy and the comedy of manners continued to persist amid conditions rapidly changing.

The manners, however, were not quite the same. Much as the middle-class members of the audience tried to admire what aristocratic society admired, they could neither appreciate the aristocratic delicacies of style nor quite forget their own moral code. The result of this was that they sought for something more sensational than Racine could give them in tragedy, and that in comedy they were uneasy when polite manners became *risqué*. A man born to the manner may hazard much, for he stands on the firm footing of his birth; a middle-class merchant, admitted on sufferance to this society, has to play safe and is apt to be shocked by freedoms unknown in his own circle. Hence a second main current of the age is that of *the genteel*, insensibly altering the old forms into forms of a new devising.

Beside this is another force. By habit and training the aristocratic society had come to base itself upon precision and convention, and this emphasis on precision and convention it carried over to its literary tastes. Exact comedy and exact tragedy pleased it, and it was quite content to see both presented with a kind of formalism. Not so with those born of the middle class. For them conventions tended to be alien and irksome; they took delight in mixed forms and constantly sought, without conscious purpose, for reality. Realism in itself is obviously hostile to the dramatic tendency to separate plays into diverse genres, for life presents tears alongside laughter and rarely rises for more than a passing moment to either; if tragedy be black and comedy white, then common existence usually manifests itself in a neutral grey. This current of *realism*, even although we may now deem the realism hopelessly artificial, is a potent power in the eighteenth-century theatre.

Allied to that is the current that may be styled *philosophic*. In the past many critics and some playwrights had attempted to demonstrate the moral and even the social value of drama, but they did so only in the broadest and the most general of terms. When we enter the eighteenth century we begin to find, for the first time in modern Europe, a definitely propagandist theatre. Men were beginning in these days to think very seriously about social life; from Addison's gentle essays in *The Spectator* to the revolutionary enthusiasms of Rousseau the age showed itself 'philosophic' in this sense, displaying an almost pathetic belief in the power of reason. Apart from this, and on a more practical plane, the middle-class audience demanded from the theatre the inculcation of those virtues from which—despite attempts to embrace the code of aristocratic society—the bourgeoisie could not escape. The middle-class fortunes had been built up by hard work and application to business; they depended on efforts extending over periods of years; hence the careless freedom of the aristocratic gallants—their concentration on the pleasures of the moment, their destructive duelling and reckless gambling—were to the merchants anathema. What these merchants wanted was a series of plays in which such vices were condemned and the bourgeois virtues lauded. Consequently the drama of the time becomes filled with highly moral 'sentiments,' and, since these sentiments were commonly both facile and superficial, the provision of stock sentiment easily passed into the sentimental colouring which is so typical of those days.

In endeavouring to trace these currents we must observe that in this century the theatre rapidly becomes more international than it had been during the sixteenth and seventeenth centuries. Not only do diverse countries find a drama awakening in their midst, but there is more inter-flow of ideas and forms throughout the whole of Europe. It is true that Shakespeare knew of Italian drama, but the influence was one way only; during the eighteenth century the thought and the creative achievement of England, France, Germany, and other lands move more freely across individual frontiers. Hence the study of the theatre in this time demands, not so much the discussion of national achievements, as the tracing of broad movements within the various countries treated as a whole.

1

TRAGEDY AND OPERA

THE FATE of tragic drama during the eighteenth century was but a sorry one. Despite the fact that playwright after playwright attempted to emulate the triumphs of his predecessors in this kind, the conditions were so unpropitious that but little of worth emerged. Opera, on the other hand, flourished, precisely from the same causes as occasioned tragedy's decline: the audience that could not be moved by austerity or aroused to sincere admiration of tragic grandeur found joy in the less exacting emotions of the operatic, revelled in the splendour of the scenes and the rich music of the orchestra. It was mainly the opera that encouraged the building of new theatres.

The Theatre of the Eighteenth Century

This was the period when the modern type of theatre structure definitely assumed its characteristic form; it was also a period of considerable expansion in stage affairs, not only in the capital cities of the larger countries, but in the provincial centres as well.

In England the patent monopoly established by Charles II in 1662 endured until the nineteenth century overthrew its restrictions, but it is plentifully evident that the growing audiences of the period, swelled by middle-class recruits, were capable of supporting more than Drury Lane and Covent Garden (which supplanted the theatre at Lincoln's Inn Fields). Not only were the patent theatres periodically enlarged within these hundred years, not only did they find more accommodation for spectators by cutting down the 'apron' and putting seats in the space thus saved, but various attempts were made to establish other playhouses in the metropolis. An opera-house in the Haymarket (1705) marked the start of the vogue for musical performances; a smaller theatre in the Haymarket eventually secured a 'summer licence' (1766) under the direction of Samuel Foote: minor theatres, such as Goodman's Fields and Sadler's Wells, succeeded at various times in evading the law and in opening their doors to paying patrons. At the same time the old touring actors of the circuits took on unwonted dignity. All over the country Theatres Royal were being built, and within their walls stock companies presented fare not dissimilar from that which delighted London audiences. By the end of the century hardly a city of importance lacked its theatre, and the stage of the metropolis was constantly being fed by actors who had served their apprenticeship in the provinces.

This was an age of great actors. No doubt David Garrick towered above them all, but the general histrionic quality of the period is indicated by the existence of a brilliant group of players during the first years of the century—including the eccentric Colley Cibber, the sparkling Anne Oldfield, and the tragedian Barton Booth—who handed on the torch to the tempestuous Charles Macklin, the delicate Kitty Clive, and the affected Peg Woffington, until eventually they ceded place to the 'incomparable' Sarah Siddons and her brother John Philip Kemble.

At the same time the French stage likewise gathered to itself a galaxy of splendid performers. Adrienne Lecouvreur won fame for her successful endeavour to supplant earlier rhetorical styles by more realistic interpretation of her rôles; in this she was followed by Mlle Dumesnil (Marie-Françoise Marchand)—although Mlle Clairon (Claire-Josèphe Léris) brought the stage back again to artificial heroics in the grand manner, an effort in which she seems to have been aided by Voltaire's protégé Lekain (Henri-Louis Caïn).

These actors, however, appear to have been less happy in their conditions than their English colleagues. True, they had a national theatre, but their esteem in the eyes of the public was less than Garrick and Mrs Siddons were to enjoy. Yet increase of the French audiences is as clearly marked as increase of the English. Paris had three theatres in 1700; the number was five in 1754, and that had doubled in 1784, when a royal edict gave monopolistic rights to the Comédie Française and the Académie Royale de Musique; in 1791, with freedom restored, fifty-one houses were opened in the metropolis. Meanwhile the provinces showed their own interest in the stage. Almost every large town proceeded to erect theatres of ever greater proportions and richer embellishment. To mention many examples would be tedious; sufficient be it to cite, as illustrative of the general trend, the majestic new playhouse built at Lyons in 1754 and the even more majestic structure of which Bordeaux boasted in 1780. It is indeed a far cry from these monumental edifices to the simple, tennis-court stages of little more than a century previously.

In Spain theatrical affairs were less fortunate. Isabella Farnese, the second queen of Philip V, caused an opera-house to be constructed in 1737, and this, it is true, did have the effect of persuading the managers of the public theatres (still *corrales* in the open air) to think of improving conditions for their audiences; as a result the Theatre of the Cross was established in 1743 and the Prince in 1745. But the spectators at these public theatres were rude and unlettered, and the eighteenth century saw the Spanish drama fall sadly from the heights it had attained in the Golden Age.

Italy too was dominated by opera, and most of the magnificent baroque and classic houses built there were intended for this purpose. Here was constructed the lovely Teatro Filarmonico of Verona (after designs by Francesco Galli-Bibiena), the Teatro San Carlo of Naples (1737, designed by Antonio Medrano), and Milan's famous Scala (1778). For operatic use, too, were intended the rich scenes and the surprising machine effects which Italian architects and designers wrought from their inventive minds. The Galli-Bibiena family of Bologna spread their influence wide, not only throughout their native land, but over the entire European world, and they were companioned by many another artist of rich talent—Filippo Juvarra of Messina, Giovanni Servandoni of Florence, Vincenzo Re of Naples, Giambattista Piranesi of Venice, the various members of the Galliari family of Andorno, whose work, carrying into the nineteenth century, vied with that of the Bibiena. There was, however, in Italy—and especially in Venice—still a dramatic theatre of some general interest, and, although, as in Spanish society, the social vogue was mainly for the opera, just sufficient encouragement was given to the playwrights to keep them creatively productive.

Meanwhile other theatres were awakening in many lands. No doubt patronage was commonly given in most of these countries to the opera, but stages intended for the spoken word arose alongside those intended for recitative and aria. Noble houses designed for the opera were erected through princely enterprise in the Germanic territories—almost every Court of distinction deemed itself uncultured until it had engaged an architect to build it an elaborate operatic stage—but at the side of the companies of singers dramatic troupers were winning their way, surely if comparatively slowly. During the seventeenth century visits of English actors (the *Englische Komödianten*) and of Italian *commedia dell' arte* players prepared the path for native professional troupes. By the twenties of the century following the talented actress Karoline Neuber was establishing her reputation; before the third quarter of the century had been reached the playhouses of Hamburg and of Weimar were welcoming men of such eminence as Lessing and Goethe. In 1800 Berlin had its Royal Theatre, a structure soon to be rebuilt on interestingly new lines under the inspiration of the architect Karl Friedrich Schinkel. Vienna saw the establishment of the famous Burgtheater's tradition in 1752, and this house was soon to be followed by the opening, in 1780, of the Leopold-stadttheater.

About the same time (1782) Stockholm's citizens were introduced to their new National Theatre; Copenhagen's Royal Theatre was opened in 1725; Norway was beginning at the same time to show a faint interest in that form of art from which her greatest writer was to arise. Eastward Russia and other Slavonic lands were wakening to the joys of the stage. Already in 1672, during the reign of Tsar Alexis, amateur performances had been given in the Imperial Palace: further enthusiasm for the drama was witnessed under the inspiration of Tsarina Anna and Tsarina Elizabeth; and finally the great Catherine, herself a dramatic

A PERFORMANCE IN
LE PALAIS-ROYAL,
PARIS
Bibliothèque Nationale

CLASSICAL TRAGEDY
IN FRANCE
By courtesy of the
Metropolitan Museum of
Art, New York. Bache
Collection

author, thoroughly accustomed her nobles to theatrical productions. At first the playhouses were either built within the Court or regarded as appendages to the Court; soon, however, what the nobles enjoyed was handed down to the bourgeoisie. The history of the great Bolshoi Theatre in Moscow goes back to 1776, and, although the building of this house did not come until the nineteenth century, the official sanction for its establishment is symbolic of its age. Petersburg's Bolshoi, or Kamenni, Theatre was opened in 1783.

In 1765 Poland acquired a public theatre. In Prague a playhouse was opened in 1783 for performances of plays and operas, although in that city a long time had to pass before representations in Czech took the place of those in German and Italian.

If thus it was in the East, so was it too in the West. Far off amid the young American colonies, which were to break their ties with England towards the close of this period, stage-playing had begun, and in the rapidly growing cities theatres were being erected. By the middle of the century several of these cities welcomed more or less permanent playhouses: in 1767 New York had its John Street Theatre, and the end of the century saw the opening of the important Park Theatre, destined to be the first of many imposing houses in the commercial and cultural, if not the political, capital of the United States.

This brief conspectus of stage activities from 1700 to 1800 may provide a clue towards an understanding of the drama produced during this age. Everywhere the Courts were sponsoring the opera, and through their sponsorship ever richer scenery and more effective stage machines were being introduced; everywhere the middle classes were beginning to take an interest in the performances of plays. A new audience and new forms were in process of creation.

The Fate of Classical Tragedy

This new audience was not well fitted to take delight in the austere virtues of the tragic drama. It is true that in all countries bewigged and brocaded actors strutted their way across the boards and mouthed speeches replete with impeccable tragic sentiment, but the entire century—at least until the arrival of romantic passion towards its very close—has hardly more than three or four dramas of this kind worthy to be seriously considered. Shakespeare and Racine between them had so far exhausted the possibilities of the dramatic forms they exploited that little remained for their successors to accomplish, while at the same time the social conditions of the period offered but half-hearted encouragement to authors willing to essay this style of composition.

In England at the beginning of the century there was a flutter of excitement over Joseph Addison's *Cato* (1713), but the excitement was political rather than æsthetic. About the same time Nicholas Rowe sought to emulate Racine by penning a series of 'she-tragedies'—*The Fair Penitent*

(1703), *Jane Shore* (1714)—but without achieving more than a rather chill pathos. No finer were the works of his followers: *The Distrest Mother* (1712) of Ambrose Philips is only a dull translation of *Andromaque*; the *Zara* (1736) and *Alzira* (1736) of Aaron Hill are fashioned after Voltaire; James Thomson has a trifle more of vigour, yet his classically conceived *Sophonisba* (1730) and *Edward and Eleonora* (1739) hardly make inspiring reading to-day; even the great Samuel Johnson failed when he tried to awaken the tragic spirit with his *Irene* (1749). Obviously the age, even although it encouraged much critical discussion concerning the nature of tragic drama, did not possess those qualities which might stimulate the creation of further new plays in this style.

The Spanish serious drama was at an even lower ebb. The native style descended from the vigour of Calderón to the depths of absurdity, and the attempt made by Agustín de Montiano y Luyando, with his *Virginia* (printed, in 1750, with a lengthy essay "sobre las tragedias españolas"), to introduce the exacter model of Racine utterly failed to meet the needs of the time; nor did his later Visigothic *Athaulpho* (printed 1753) improve upon his first experiment. Twenty years passed before a tragedy based on the French style, Nicolás Fernández de Moratín's *Hormesinda* (1770), appeared on the boards; its influence was insignificant.

In Germany there were slight stirrings of the dramatic spirit, but the country was divided into small principalities and racked by strife —conditions hardly propitious for the production of any work of value. During the seventeenth century Italian and English players carried their wares to many Courts, and, stimulated partly by their efforts, partly by the work of the Jesuit playwrights, Andreas Gryphius composed a series of largely religious tragedies, thus establishing this form in his native tongue. Thereafter numerous attempts were made in the same direction, all without the slightest grace or consequence. On the popular stages flourished bombastic melodramas—the Haupt- und Staatsaktionen —mere mixtures of gory incident, meaningless mouthings, and such conceits as clownage keeps in pay. Only with the appearance of Johann Christoph Gottsched was any conscious attempt made to encourage higher effort. Realizing the formlessness of the German drama, he concentrated upon the pseudo-classic 'rules' and sought to impose French fashions on the theatre of his time. He translated plays by Racine and others and imitated their style in such works as *Der sterbende Cato* (*The Dying Cato*, 1732). Because of his energy and enthusiastic sense of purpose, and because he succeeded in associating himself with a competent group of actors, among whom Karoline Neuber and Heinrich Koch were the most important, his influence was widespread, and up to the time of Lessing the German intelligentsia aped nothing but the French. Little of value came of his efforts, but no doubt this period of apprenticeship was necessary before maturer achievements could come towards the end of the century.

To Russia, as to other countries, the French influence penetrated, and

Alexander Petrovich Sumarokov for long was the arbiter of dramatic fashion with his classically inspired *Khorev* (1747) and his *Zemir* (1751). It is worthy of note that he was responsible for introducing *Hamlet* (1748), through a French adaptation, to the Russian public. His successor, Iakov B. Kniazhnin, pursued the same path in his *Vadim* (1789), influenced by both Racine and Voltaire.

It is, of course, to France that we should look for developments in the realm of classical tragedy, but the French genius had all but exhausted itself in Racine: although her tragic stage offered a trifle more than that of either England or Germany, the record of serious plays presented during the latter half of the seventeenth and the entire course of the eighteenth century is rather a sorry one. Dramatist after dramatist essayed to assume Racine's mantle, but it would fit none with ease. Except for the work of one author, it produced merely that dull combination of classic chill and of gory incident which formed the staple recipe of the once famous Prosper Jolyot de Crébillon. The single exception is Voltaire (François-Marie Arouet), who won both his contemporary laurels and his later fame more by his incisive sense of purpose than by his theatrical skill: if he made a real contribution to the theatre it was less in form and concept than in extension of subject-matter. His earliest effort, *Œdipe* (1718), was an obvious imitation of Racine's style with suggestions from the Greek, and these influences endured throughout his entire career. He did, however, try both to recall tragedy from its concentration upon love-themes and to widen the range of tragic material beyond the limits of the classical. *Brutus* (1730), *La mort de César* (*Cæsar's Death*, 1735), and *Mérope* (1743) illustrate the first endeavour, while the second is demonstrated by such dramas as *Zaïre* (1732), *Alzire* (1736), *Zulima* (1740), *Le fanatisme, ou Mahomet le prophète* (*Fanaticism; or, Mahomet the Prophet*, 1741), *L'orpheline de la Chine* (*The Orphan of China*, 1755), and the medieval *Tancrède* (1760). Of these *Zaïre* may be taken as typical. Set in Orosmane's seraglio in Jerusalem, it introduces a heroine, Zaïre, who is loved by and loves the sultan. She is in reality a Christian maid, and, unknown to herself, the sister of Nérestan, a youth who has been released from Saracen slavery so that he might return to France in order to raise money sufficient for the rescue of his fellow-captives. Nérestan returns with just sufficient to buy the freedom of Zaïre and a few other prisoners: for himself he proposes that he should remain in durance. Orosmane, however, meets his offer with noble magnanimity, pledging the release of himself and of a hundred Christians, but declaring that the aged Lusignan and Zaïre cannot be of their number. It is at this point that the true tragic conflict begins. Lusignan is discovered to be the father of Nérestan and Zaïre; she is torn between love of Orosmane and desire to follow her Christian heritage; Orosmane is tortured by the fear that Nérestan is her lover. In the end the sultan stabs her, learns the truth, gives orders for the liberation of all the Christian captives, and commits suicide.

All the chief characteristics of Voltaire's tragic style are here. The

Eastern setting gives him opportunity for the introduction of an element of colourful wonder; and perhaps one of his chief contributions to the tragic stage was the introduction of subject-matter apart from the almost exhausted treasury of classical material. Even farther East did he go in *L'orpheline de la Chine*, while in *Alzire*, the sub-title of which is "Les Américains," he voyaged westward to distant Peru at the time of the Spanish Conquest. In *Zaïre* the theme of Christianity and Mohammedanism allows ample chance for the expression of philosophical opinion. There can be no doubt but that there is strength here—yet that strength is not as the strength of Racine. The characters are sentimentally conceived in that their motives spring rather from externally determined principles than from their own inner beings. For revelation of personality in subtle words rhetoric is substituted. It is true that Voltaire had sufficient power to make his plays successful in their own day and capable of retaining their hold in the repertoire of the Comédie Française: he lacked, however, the larger qualities which alone can carry a dramatist's work over the boundaries of his own land. These tragedies certainly did make their appeal to English (and other) contemporaries: they can make little appeal to us to-day.

Typical of his failure is the fact that, while refusing to concentrate entirely on the theme of love in the Racine manner, he yet could not escape from introducing this theme—and, because it did not receive main stress, introducing it unsatisfactorily. In *Mérope*, for example, the principal plot is 'political,' yet Mérope's devotion to her son almost assumes the characteristic of the more familiar forms of love-interest: so too in *Brutus* the austerity of the Roman political scene is softened by Titus' passion for Tullia. Voltaire was, in fact, struggling unsuccessfully against those limitations which Racine had so easily accepted; his sardonic genius was unfitted for the fetters worn so tranquilly by his predecessor.

The truth was, of course, that classical tragedy in France had temporarily run its course. The old 'rules,' certainly, were to continue for years to lay their skinny fingers upon the stage, and even when Shakespeare was first imported across the Channel he was forced by Jean-François Ducis to permit a classic curb upon his romantic fervour: the *Hamlet* that appeared in 1769 and the *Lear* of 1783 were but grinning shadows of their real substance. Nevertheless the domination of the pseudo-classic manner was at its close; it had no longer in it the spirit to inspire new works of quality, and soon it was to be supplanted by other aspirations.

As in England, Germany, Spain, and Russia, the French influence swept into Italy. Her earlier attempts at the development of the classical style had not proved very propitious (for example, the *Medoro* (1630) of Giovanni Delfino), and later there is not much of praise that can be given to such dramas as the *Marco Tullio Cicerone* (1715) of Pier Jacopo Martello, but, with the flowing in of French influence, something more promising made its appearance. In the *Merope* (1713) of Francesco Scipione di

Maffei a tragedy was written in a style which showed that the Italian theatre possessed potentiality of greatness. The time was ripe. France's greatness was behind her; England could not forget Shakespeare; Spain's theatre was debased; Germany's just becoming aware of itself; whereas Italy was now free to experiment freshly and interestingly in the classical form. *Merope*, although not one of the greatest masterpieces of the theatre, has a quality denied to most works of a similar kind produced during the eighteenth century, a quality so marked that it was deemed worthy of imitation by Voltaire himself. There is true character delineation here, and passion is not concealed by cold rhetoric.

After Maffei there came a lull, with the sporadic appearance of tragic essays such as the *Marco Bruto* (1743) and *Druso* (1747) of Antonio Conti or the *Giovanni di Giscala* (1754) of Alfonso Varano, all of them possessing merely minor interest; then appeared the only true master in that age of the classic drama, Count Vittorio Alfieri, who succeeded in infusing new life and force and grace into the old forms. Fundamentally his strength comes from the fire of his own heroic, if undisciplined, emotions and from his drinking deeply at the prime fount of the Greeks. Racine's artificial delicacy, so hard to imitate, is here cast aside in favour of an idealized reality; further strength comes to his work from the way in which he conceives his scenes in terms of the political enthusiasms of his time. There is a drive here, and a fire, lacking in almost all other similar works written during this age.

Alfieri himself has left a clear critical statement of his aims. The tragic, he believed, should concern itself with the most powerful passions, but reveal these in a form of the simplest and most repressed kind. For themes the finest models were to be found among the legends of the Greeks; in exploiting those there was an opportunity for uniting "artistic truth with moral truth, beauty with morality." In his opinion the theatre ought to be a school in which men should learn to be "free, strong, generous, transported by true virtue, impatient of every oppression, dominated by love of their country, truly aware of their individual rights and in all their passions keen, noble and magnanimous." To secure this end he deliberately renounced the use of secondary characters, of tender emotions, of all that savoured of mediocrity.

Among his earliest dramas—there are twenty-eight in all if we include the six comedies written just before his death—is an interesting *Filippo* written on a theme chosen because of the opportunity it gave for the presentation of the liberal-minded Don Carlos in opposition to his father, Philip II of Spain. His masterpieces, however, with the exception of *Saul* (1782) and *Mirra* (1789), are to be found among the groups of plays composed on themes already dealt with by the dramatists of Greece. Of these *Antigone* (1783), contrasting the revolutionary heroine with the tyrannical Creonte, possibly shows his intense political sentiments at their best, but undoubtedly the most powerfully conceived is his *Oreste* (1778). In both, the antique stories are given a new and an interesting development. The first shows Argia, Adrasto's daughter and the widow of Polinice, come to Thebes for the purpose of bearing with her the ashes of her husband. Secretly entering the Theban Court by night, she hopes she may encounter Antigone, and the two women do meet, reveal their identities to each other, and league themselves to undertake the burial specifically banned by Creonte. They are seized by guards; Antigone boldly confesses her action; they are condemned to die, the while Emone, in love with Antigone, pleads for mercy. Discovering his son's infatuation, Creonte changes his plan and offers Antigone the choice of death or marriage to Emone. Stung by pride and determined not to bow to a tyrant's will, she chooses the former. In anger he decrees that she shall be buried alive, but, in carrying out the decree, he finds he has lost his son. Emone enters at the head of an armed band, denies that he has a father, and in misery moves off to his own death, bearing the body of Antigone. In its fundamentals the plot is almost the same as that of Sophocles' drama, but the interpretation of the characters is coloured by modern sentiment; beneath the flow of individual passions runs a powerful political current.

The way in which Alfieri seeks to give reality to the classical legends is well demonstrated in *Oreste*. Even after its treatment by Æschylus, Sophocles, and Euripides, he still is able to find a new approach. Oreste enters after having slain Egisto and also, unwittingly, his mother Clitennestra. Elated, he holds his sword on high, while Pilade trembles at the thought of what will happen when he realizes the truth. "Where is Clitennestra?" he asks, and Pilade evades an answer. Oreste presses him:

ORESTE: Tell me;
  What is't?
PILADE: Stabbed . . .
ORESTE: By whom?
PILADE: Come; let us go.
ELETTRA: Thou hast killed her.
ORESTE: I? A parricide? . . .
PILADE: Thy sword
  Has pierced her breast, as thou, unconscious, blind
  In thy rage, dashed upon Egisto. . . .
ORESTE: Oh, what
  A fear enfolds me! I have killed her? That sword,
  Pilade, give it me. I must . . .
PILADE: It shall not be.
ELETTRA: My brother . . .
PILADE: Wretched Oreste!
ORESTE: Who calls me brother?
  Thou impious woman, perhaps, who hast to life
  And to the murder of my mother saved me?—
  Give me that sword, that sword . . . Oh, Furies?—What
  Have I done? . . . Where am I? . . . Who is by me? . . . Who
  Torments me? . . . Oh, where, where shall I fly? . . . Where

Shall I hide my miserable self? . . . My father!
Dost thou glare at me? Thou askedst blood;
And here is blood . . . for thee alone I spilt it.
ELETTRA: Oreste, Oreste . . . O miserable brother! . . .
    He hears us not; . . . his sense is gone. . . . Ever must we,
    Dear Pilade, stand by his side. . . .
PILADE: Cruel
Inevitable law of fearful destiny!

Alfieri came near towards revitalizing the classical tragic drama, but already by the time he was writing the forces of romanticism were at work—and, indeed, his own passion for liberty was part of the revolutionary movement which animated men's minds towards the end of the century. His influence upon the Italian dramatists who immediately followed him was strong, but little of prime worth emerged from their efforts, and some of these efforts showed clearly that the romantic theme was nearer to the age than the classic. Vincenzo Monti closely imitated Alfieri's style in his *Caio Gracco* (1802) after displaying some faint signs of a romantic spirit in his fundamentally classical *Aristodemo* (1786) and *Galeotto Manfredi* (1788), based on a not entirely unworthy drama of the same name by Carlo de' Dottori (printed in 1670); in the work of Giovanni Pindemonte and of Niccolò Ugo Foscolo, on the other hand, the Alfierian passions were channelled into diverse courses. The former's *Ginevra di Scozia* (*Ginevra of Scotland*, 1795) is thoroughly romantic in concept, while Foscolo is recognized now as one of the stalwarts of the Italian romantic movement. The time was too late to hope for virtue from the pseudo-classic stage.

The Opera, Serious and Comic

Tragic sentiment more easily in that age found its expression in the softened beauties of the opera. This form of drama, born of the Renaissance, rapidly sped from splendour to splendour. Kings and princes vied with one another in building theatres for its production, and during the eighteenth century both courtly and middle-class audiences found it precisely to their taste. Its appreciation required no intellectual effort or exercise of passion; its scenic beauties pleased the eye and its lyrics the ear. Over the whole world it spread, leaving a trail of rich 'opera-houses' in its wake, although for all this period its prime inspiration remained Italian. Giovanni Battista Lulli may have so identified himself with the Paris Court that he became a Frenchman as Lully, but his birth and training belonged to the land whence the opera had originally sprung. Other composers, such as Henry Purcell and G. F. Handel, although introducing original qualities into their compositions, freely fed from this fount.

The story of opera, of course, does not properly belong in a volume of this kind, yet it may hardly be neglected completely. For music Dryden wrote some of his dramas; *The Beggar's Opera* and the later Savoy operas form part of the record of the ordinary theatre; in a poet such as Metastasio the operatic stage found a dramatist of genius; from the opera descended the plebeian melodrama. In order to understand the course of dramatic history from the seventeenth century to the nineteenth century, therefore, it is necessary to glance at least at the development of the musical theatre.

In Apostolo Zeno, Court poet to the Emperor Charles VI at Vienna, the opera acquired a formalizer who sought to refine and polish the work of his predecessors. A learned man, he aimed at giving to the musical drama a dignity and a regularity akin to what was possessed by the classical tragedies, and, although his own talents were not outstanding, he succeeded in his sixty-odd operas in bringing distinction to a form that hitherto had lacked any true sense of proportion. In this task he was aided by his greatest successor, Pietro Metastasio (Pietro Trapassi). Metastasio's writings were universally admired in his own time; Voltaire put him alongside Racine, and most contemporaries would have been prepared to echo the praise of Rousseau: "He is the only poet of the heart, the only genius apt to move us by the charm of his musical and poetical harmony"; even now we can recognize, in the words of Carducci, that he was the finest Italian poet since Tasso and that his lyric talent was not rivalled by any other European poet of his age. To us now his work may seem unduly formal, yet, particularly in those pieces which he wrote during his so-called 'second period'—notably *Adriano* (1731), *Issipile* (1732), and *La clemenza di Tito* (1734)—we find a fine lyrical quality and an economy of means that mark him out as a writer of unquestioned talent.

What, however, is also to be observed is a certain monotony in the character presentation of these works. All are alike in their pattern, and when we note that that pattern always introduces a noble-minded hero, a frail and unfortunate heroine, and a dark villain we realize how fatally easy was the passage from courtly operatic realms to the rudeness of the melodrama. At the same time the fact that his operas could be, and sometimes were, performed as spoken tragedies without the aid of music testifies to the fact that they possessed a quality of which most *libretti* are innocent.

Except for this later development of the melodrama and for the encouragement given to the elaboration of scenic decoration and machinery, the serious opera left comparatively little impress on the drama. Metastasio was a lonely lyric genius, and most of the other *libretti* of the time offer nothing of merit: Paolo Rolli's work makes sad reading after Metastasio's. More and more the composers seized the upper hand. Handel in England, Gluck and Mozart in the German lands, these were the men who dominated in the operatic world. It is also to be remembered that throughout this period the Italian language was universally regarded as the sole tongue fit for chorus and aria, with the result that in no country outside Italy was there any encouragement offered by the serious musical drama to native writers.

The story of comic opera, however, is another affair. The beginnings of this form seem ultimately traceable to Naples, where the exalted court-liness of the grand opera found a rival in a gay, realistic world, of pea-sants instead of princes, of farce instead of formality. When Gennarantonio Federico wrote the words and Giovanni Battista Pergo-lesi the music for *La serva padrona* (*The Maid the Mistress*, 1733) the Neopo-litan *opera buffa* acquired an international reputation. On its own it proceeded to produce works of spirit and of gaiety, culminating in the magnificent *Socrate immaginario* (*Socrates in Imagination*, 1775), in which Giambattista Lorenzi collaborated with the composer Giovanni Pai-siello in presenting a delightfully satirical portrait of the classical en-thusiast Don Tammaro Promontorio; at the same time it spread abroad, and, in the form of the French *opéra-comique*, rapidly was accepted by ordinary theatre audiences (as opposed to the more courtly or more af-fectedly social spectators who flocked to listen to the more ambitious compositions in the tragic style). The *opéra-comique* found a friendly home in Paris, while in England it produced hundreds of musical plays of the lighter kind, from regular comic opera—or 'comedies in music'—to the more interesting ballad operas. Indeed, for a time it seemed as though the ballad opera, in association with related forms, was destined to cre-ate a characteristic kind of dramatic expression apt to meet the needs of the new middle-class English audiences of the time.

When John Gay presented *The Beggar's Opera* in 1728 at the small theatre in Lincoln's Inn Fields he took London by storm, and for the next few years the most popular performances were those of pieces similarly composed or of farcical burlesques, mostly with a political colouring, such as Henry Fielding's *The Author's Farce* (1730), *The Tragedy of Trage-dies* (1731), *Pasquin* (1736), and *The Historical Register* (1737). In these the age was being given what it wanted. These middle-class audiences did not seek for, and perhaps were incapable of appreciating, delicacy of form; they liked to listen to music; they could relish burlesque; and they were actively interested in political personalities even if political prin-ciples were not deeply relished. Gay and Fielding between them went far towards supplying dramatic works well calculated to meet these require-ments. *The Beggar's Opera* owed its success partly to its burlesque atmo-sphere, partly to its gay lyrics, and partly to the fact that, skilfully though it may be constructed, it exhibits none of that precision in pattern which marked the writings of Congreve. Had the ballad opera and the associ-ated political burlesque favoured by Fielding been permitted free range, something of worth might well have arisen from these efforts, but un-fortunately governmental action soon brought its uproarious career to an untimely end. Sir Robert Walpole had been keenly touched in the sallies made by Gay and Fielding, and, determined not to permit further attacks upon his person, he succeeded in obtaining Parliamentary approval for the famous Licensing Act of 1737, by the terms of which the activities of the little theatres (such as had housed the efforts of the offending dramatists) were suppressed, and no plays were permitted to be performed until they had first been approved by the Lord Chamberlain or by his deputy. The ballad opera continued its career, but with marked lack of enthusiasm, while Fielding in disgust turned from the stage to become the first of a great line of English novelists.

2

THE GROWTH OF BOURGEOIS COMEDY

SOME of the interests of the middle-class audiences of the eighteenth century had been met in the work of Gay and Fielding, but these authors did not in any wise reflect what, above all others, was the prevailing characteristic of the time.

With the entry of the bourgeoise into the theatre new demands were being made. The cavaliers and gallants at the Court of Charles II were content to live for the day, to relish carefree laughter, to ignore contemptuously all that did not come within the privileged circle of their aristocratic society. When this circle was broken and daughters of wealthy merchants, marrying scions of the nobility, brought their families into the playhouses, a clearly marked change in audience attitude, and a corresponding change in drama, became apparent. No doubt the bourgeois spectators were willing, in order to keep up with social tone, to simulate enjoyment—if not actually to enjoy—something at least of the manner of Restoration comedy, but, as we move from the seventeenth into the eighteenth century, we observe, first, that the aristocratic atmosphere is being slowly yet definitely restrained, and that the middle classes, less sure of their foothold in society than those born of noble houses, display an anxious concern with respect to all kinds of excesses. A young gallant of Etherege, because he is absolutely certain of his position in society, may permit himself to do anything; a member of a bourgeois family who seeks to keep in society must ever be cautious, lest he be accused of vulgarity and ostracized. Hence the comedy of aristocratic manners gradually evolves, during the eighteenth century, into the genteel comedy.

This, however, represents merely a negative influence exerted by the new audience. Its power was sufficiently great to call forth a positive influence as well. Where the young Restoration gallant was prepared to follow only the pleasure of the moment and to regard money solely as a means of realizing that pleasure, the middle-class spectator, trained in the way of trade, could never escape thinking of the morrow, and certainly might never avoid seeing money as a commodity not carelessly to be dissipated. For him the future came to mean almost as much as the present, and the wisdom of age to be as important as the sprightliness of youth. Still further, this spectator was concerned mainly, not with daring flights of wit, but with material things: he tended to be practical-minded, utilitarian in his philosophy, and realistic in his outlook on the world. Hence he sought for a kind of play utterly diverse from anything that had been produced in the past.

He was prepared to savour a dash of comedy, but not too much; he was willing, indeed, eager, to welcome pathetic situations and to indulge in the luxury of pity, but not to arouse himself to combat with the austerities of tragedy; he demanded a treatment on the stage of what he conceived to be real life; he desired his plays to be replete with moral sentiment; and he relished seeing in them some not too difficult and not too complex social problem. Hence arose, out of these demands, the characteristic sentimental drama of the eighteenth century, and with its establishment the modern problem drama or play of ideas was adumbrated.

The First Steps in England and France

When we survey the plays written during the first years of the eighteenth century in England and in France it is easy to see the gradual and tentative approaches that are being made in those years towards the sentimental drama of the mid-century.

These approaches are, of course, very faint at first. Congreve was followed by Sir John Vanbrugh and by George Farquhar, and at first the two men seem to be nothing but inheritors of the Restoration tradition. Closer scrutiny of their work, however, indicates that both were breathing a new air. Vanbrugh carries us into the country—territory anathema to the town-loving gallants—and his sense of fun is vastly different from Congreve's play of wit; in *The Provoked Wife* (1697) he shows a woman ill-treated by her spouse who yet remains faithful to him, while in *The Provoked Husband* (1728) a reckless and extravagant wife is cured of her follies by her husband's threat of divorce. No less indicative of changing moods are the plays of Farquhar. Both in *The Beaux' Stratagem* (1707) and in *The Recruiting Officer* (1706) the scene is rustic, and there is an evident undercurrent of human feeling below the badinage that marks the arrival of a new style.

In this period, moreover, when Jeremy Collier was startling the theatrical world with his forthright *Short View of the Immorality and Profaneness of the English Stage* (published in 1698), a different class of dramatic author was arising. The successor of the gay Sir George Etherege was the plebeian Colley Cibber, whose *Careless Husband* (1704), in which the libertine Sir Charles Easy is brought to contrition when he discovers that his wife's faithfulness to him is due, not to ignorance of his lapses, but to true love, well displays both the mood of the genteel comedy and the beginnings of sentimental moralizing. At the same time honest Dick Steele (Sir Richard Steele), co-partner with Joseph Addison in the mildly philosophic and essentially middle-class *Spectator*, carried the style a further stage. In *The Funeral; or, Grief à la Mode* (1701), a highly moral play, he concentrates on the elderly Lord Brampton, who pretends to be dead in order to discover the truth in his family circle, thus finds out that his wife has been jealously maligning her stepson to him, and in the end realizes this son's true devotion. *The Lying Lover; or, the Ladies' Friendship* (1703), founded on Corneille's *Le menteur*, didactically attacks the practice of duelling—a delight of aristocrats, but alien to the interests of the bourgeoisie—while *The Tender Husband; or, The Accomplished Fools* (1705) and *The Conscious Lovers* (1722) are full of the most worthy of moralizations and the most pathetic of scenes. Quite clearly we are entering here into a different world, more decorous, more serious, and intent rather on social problems than on character-portrayal or the effervescence of wit.

Similar, although by no means entirely parallel, trends are observable in France. There the comedy of Molière had never exhibited the aristocratic exclusiveness cultivated by the English dramatists of the Restoration, and hence there was no need to react against a tone antagonistic towards the spirit of the new age. Yet even here the middle-class audiences were making new demands. In Molière's plays social conditions are usually neglected, save when they are absolutely necessary for the development of the plots: in those of Jean-François Regnard, his successor and imitator, not only is the range of portraiture widened, but the social *milieu*, especially in its monetary aspects, is considerably more deeply stressed. True, Regnard is a laughing dramatist, not a sentimental, and there are some who, despite his skill in handling intrigue and dialogue, would dismiss his works as mere farce; but the impress of his age is nevertheless upon him. Of his many comedies the earliest were written for the Théâtre Italien, the latest for the Comédie Française. They include the lively *La coquette* (1691), the racy *La foire Saint-Germain* (1695), and the charming *Le bal* (*The Ball*, 1695, renamed in 1696 *Le bourgeois de Falaise*), as well as the better-known *Le joueur* (*The Gamester*, 1696), *Le distrait* (*The Absentminded Lover*, 1697), and *Le légataire universel* (*The Residuary Legatee*, 1708). *Le joueur* tells the story of an inveterate gambler, Valère, who through his excesses loses his Angélique and is left disinherited as the curtain falls. The style and the theme alike recall the plays of Steele. In *Le distrait* the absentminded Léandre complicates a theme of love and jealousy by his truly comic tactlessness. The flavour of Steele's plays also pervades *Le légataire universel*, although the atmosphere is more bitter than in any of the English dramatist's works. We are introduced here to a world of self-seekers. Old Géronte is obviously near his end, and with eager eyes his relatives gaze upon his wealth. In particular his nephew, Éraste, endeavours, by his assiduous attentions, to become his uncle's heir. In love with Isabelle, this Éraste learns to his dismay that the old man proposes to marry the girl, and this proposal is formally approved by her avaricious mother, Madame Argante. By a somewhat strained device, however, Éraste succeeds in persuading this mercenary lady to agree to alter her plans, on the assurance that he will be able to obtain a will from Géronte in his favour; but the young man's hopes are once more dashed when he hears that his uncle intends to leave large sums to a penniless Norman gentleman, his nephew, and to his niece, the wife of an equally penniless baron. This gives excuse for the main scenes of the play, in which Éraste's servant, Crispin, impersonates these relatives; thoroughly successful, he persuades the old man that he ought to leave his money to Éraste. All seems well, when once more the young man's hopes are dashed by news of Géronte's death. Only one solution for the problem remains: Crispin, daringly and a trifle apprehensively, poses before the attorney as Géronte himself and executes a will—and then is dismayed to learn that Géronte has awakened from his death-like trance. Only with difficulty is the old man made convinced that in this trance he has forgotten his immediately preceding actions and is tricked into approving of the false will.

Much of this is, indeed, farce, but beneath the surface we may discern a new current flowing. This current is still more clearly marked in the *Turcaret* (1709) of Alain-René Lesage, wherein money is the sole motive-force, and the French financier (the type of man who had acquired wealth in collecting the king's taxes) is vigorously held up to ridicule. Turcaret, the central figure, is a man astute in his business affairs, but a fool with women. What he earns he lavishly presents to the Baroness, a widow, a coquette, and in reality nothing more than a fashionable courtesan, who, in turn, gives of her money freely to the specious Knight, her lover. As in *Le légataire universel*, there is not a single amiable character in the entirety of this comedy: all are rogues or fools, and the curtain descends on the servant, Frontin, proud of having tricked his master of a formidable sum of money, boasting that Turcaret's reign is now over and his own begins. In spite of the farcical scenes, *Turcaret* is a bitter comedy, and it is interesting to observe how the style of the comedy of intrigue, which, as is clearly shown by such a play as *Crispin rival de son maître* (*Crispin Rival of his Master*, 1707), Lesage learned from the *commedia dell' arte*, could be turned to purposes of moral import.

Money matters also figure largely in the farcical pieces of Florent-Carton Dancourt, whose plays, if individually of lesser value, collectively provide a magnificent caricature of contemporary society. His *Les bourgeoises à la mode* (*The Citizens' Wives in the Fashion*, 1692; first performed as *Les femmes à la mode*), and *Le chevalier à la mode* (*The Man of Mode*, 1687), and *Les bourgeoises de qualité* (*The Middle-class Ladies*; first performed in 1700 as *La fête du village*, and retitled in 1724) may be taken as characteristic. The first shows two middle-class women who render themselves ridiculous by their aping of aristocratic manners, and a couple of husbands made equally foolish by their grasping avarice and arrant credulity. A brilliantly satirical picture of a genteel libertine who courts three women at once appears in the second play. The cynical delineation of social stupidities is carried even farther in the third comedy, where a thin, indeed barely traceable, plot is used by the author for the purpose of presenting four trenchantly drawn portraits of middle-class characters, each of whom seeks to obtain a title. No dramatist of the time has given a more lively, or a more cruelly mordant, display of a society racked by confusion and rapidly sinking into disintegration.

Reflection of changing social modes appears in the plays of Dancourt's companions, Charles-Rivière Dufresny and David-Augustin de Brueys, but, even although the latter's *Le grondeur* (*The Grumbler*, 1691) once received high praise, we can hardly find other than historical interest in their dialogue and action. These writers need not detain us, but at one author we must pause. Dancourt and Dufresny have no living interest now: Marivaux still retains vitality.

If Lesage is bitter, Marivaux (Pierre-Carlet de Chamblain de Marivaux) is genteel. In this author appeared something fresh. Other writers had, without question, accepted Molière as a master: Marivaux sought for a new style in comedy. To describe this new style is somewhat difficult; its very virtue lies in its subtlety; but fundamentally it may be said to depend upon a translation of Racine's tragic method into comic terms and upon a polished variation of the spirit of the Italian *commedia dell' arte*. Already in the seventeenth century, as has been seen, the Italian players won success in Paris, and towards the end of the century a notable development occurred in their repertory when they called in diverse French playwrights to pen scenes intended to be presented in the midst of their improvised action. Many of these compositions were preserved in the famous collection edited by the actor Evaristo Gherardi, and from these it is plain that the French authors—Nolant de Fatouville, Eustache Lenoble, Jean Palaprat, Regnard, and others—eagerly seized on this opportunity of producing realistic pictures of Parisian manners in a fantastic framework. Typical of such pieces are *L'isle des Amazones* (*The Isle of the Amazons*), in which Arlequin and Pierrot are captured, threatened, and then embraced by the lusty Marphise and Bradamante, and *Arlequin invisible* (*Harlequin Invisible*), in which the *commedia dell' arte* hero has gay adventures through the magic device granted him by Asmodée. The whole of French society parades here, from its aristocrats and its wealthy bourgeois citizens to the dregs of the underworld, and the verve with which many of the scenes is written well justifies those who point to the Gherardi collection as containing some of the best comic material between the work of Molière and that of Marivaux.

In 1697 the Italians encountered royal disfavour and their theatre was closed, but they once more appeared at Paris in 1716, and immediately sought to perform plays specially written for them by French authors. By thus as it were naturalizing themselves the 'Italiens' subtly altered the style of the older *commedia dell' arte*: the originally rough serving-maid was transmogrified into the pert and delicate Columbine, the clownish Pedrolino became a sentimentalized Pierrot, and the whole of the action assumed a misty Watteauesque quality. It was here that Marivaux found his spiritual home.

What he did was to take Racine's intimate searching into the human heart, transform it into comic terms, place it against the fanciful background of the *commedia*, use every endeavour to polish and refine his dialogue, and create out of these elements and qualities a new kind of psychological comedy. Racine had dealt with the ardours and passions of fierce love; Marivaux traced the gentle beginnings of affection charmingly, sympathetically, amusingly. The whole process of his art is already revealed in one of his earliest plays, *La surprise de l'amour* (*The Unexpectedness of Love*, 1722), in which we are introduced to a group of five characters—Lélio, the Countess, Arlequin, Colombine, and Jacqueline. Lélio and the Countess have both renounced love, and the whole plot concerns the gradual awakening in them of a new, and largely unwished for, affection.

The pattern is varied in other comedies, but the basic model remains. In *La double inconstance* (*The Double Inconstancy*, 1723), the two main characters think they are in love, but gradually discover their error when true love enters their lives. Arlequin and Silvia are affianced to each other, but the Prince chooses the latter for his bride, and Arlequin discovers that, in truth, it is Flaminia whom he adores. Another, and a still finer, experiment on the same lines is *Le jeu de l'amour et du hasard* (*The Game of Love and Chance*, or *Love in Livery*, 1730), which tells of the device by which Silvia changes places with her maid, Lisette, and Dorante with his servant, Arlequin. As might be expected in a comedy of this kind, Silvia finds herself disgusted by her supposed lover (Arlequin masquerading as Dorante), while at the same time, to her dismay, she is attracted by one whom she believes far beneath her in station. Concurrently Dorante (dressed as Arlequin) discovers, also to his dismay, that he has come to adore the girl whom he thinks a maid. By a tortuous process, in which the emotions are delicately revealed, Silvia and Dorante are enabled to find their true selves. Equally delicate is *Les fausses confidences* (*False Confidences*, 1737), which reveals the way in which an impoverished Dorante wins the heart of a rich widow.

In some of his plays there is an extension of subject-matter beyond such themes, and these bring his work close indeed to the characteristic sentimentalism of his century. *L'isle des esclaves* (*The Isle of Slaves*, 1725) is of a different sort. Here an Athenian general, a lady, Arlequin, and a maid are wrecked on a lonely island, and are forced to change places: Arlequin and the maid become master and mistress, while the general and the lady become slaves. We are entering the world of social ideas here, and in that world we remain throughout the scenes of such dramas as *Le triomphe de Plutus* (*The Triumph of Plutus*, 1728), where the evils of wealth are displayed. Marivaux was no revolutionary, yet in his mingling of the genteel and the social he was unquestionably reflecting an age for which the methods of Molière in comedy were becoming a trifle out of date. In his works, and in the works of his companions, the eighteenth century was feeling its way towards a new form of theatrical expression. On Marivaux' plays much later endeavour was to be based. We shall have several occasions for observing the influence both of his delicately artificial, fantastic style and of his intimate revelations of sentiment.

Gozzi and Goldoni

Meanwhile the *commedia dell' arte* in Italy itself was producing something of related interest. Throughout the seventeenth century the improvising comedians flourished, retaining their traditional vigour, but, as good showmen, ever showing a willingness to introduce such modification in subject-matter, characters, and theatrical tricks as were likely to prove popular among the changing audiences of the time. Increasingly the literary comedy of the baroque age showed clear signs of the impress made by their performances, and these signs appeared both in the writings of authors who applied themselves to the development of dialect comedy and in those of other authors who sought expression in the standard Tuscan speech. Carlo Maria Maggi thus made much of the type-figure of Meneghino in his Milanese pieces, using the theatrical stock person for the purpose of enunciating concepts of a kind far beyond the reach of the popular comedians with their improvised merriment: typical is *Il falso filosofo* (*The False Philosopher*, 1691). Equally patent traces of the *commedia*'s influence are to be seen in the writings of Girolamo Gigli, Jacopo Angelo Nelli, and Giovan Battista Fagiuoli, all of whom eschewed in general the use of dialect forms. The first two of this trio perhaps are of little importance, but Fagiuoli, although no genius, merits some individual attention. Even towards the beginning of his career he could produce a vivid study of contemporary manners in *Ciò che pare non è vero, ovvero il cicisbeo sconsolato* (*Appearance isn't Truth; or, The Disconsolate Gallant*, 1708), and this liveliness continues with him even when his themes grow more serious, as in *La forza della ragione* (*The Power of Reason*, 1712), wherein the rational is made to triumph over the emotional, or *Il marito alla moda* (*The Fashionable Husband*, 1735), with its almost problem theme. His *Gli amanti senza vedersi* (*Love Unseen*, 1734) is an interestingly novel comedy that tells how Lelio, in love with Isabella, seizes her and locks her in his house. Her cries are heard by Federico, who speaks to her in the darkness of the night through a window. As a result of this conversation the couple, without having seen each other, fall in love. Sad puzzlement, however, comes to Federico when he returns in daylight. Lelio has died suddenly, and in the house besides Isabella are his brother, Orazio, and another girl, Lucinda: between the pair of girls poor Federico cannot decide which is the lady of whom he has become enamoured, and only after diverse scenes of 'equivoque' is the tangle straightened out. Another entertaining play by the same author is *L'aver cura delle donne è pazzia* (*Trying to Control Girls is Folly*, 1735), where the story of the young Cintia, determined to have the man on whom her heart is set, proves the truth of the proverbial title.

Even at their best, however, these three comic writers are second-rate and must immediately cede place to two men of unquestioned genius who were their immediate followers—Count Carlo Gozzi and Carlo Goldoni—both deeply imbued with the Italian popular comic tradition, both reared in the midst of the city, Venice, where the *commedia dell' arte* had its deepest roots, yet hopelessly opposed to each other in their ideas as to the use that should be made of this native material.

For Gozzi the *commedia dell' arte* means fantasy and delight. Less delicate than Marivaux, more keenly satirical, and much more apt to fly into a world of wonder and enchantment, he yet is to a certain extent the French dramatist's Italian counterpart. There are no intimate psychological searchings in his plays, but unquestionably the artificiality of the popular comedy appealed to both men in the same way. Each saw in it a pattern into which they might weave their dreams: each eagerly seized on the opportunity it gave them for securing an imaginative contrast between the ideal and the real.

Gozzi's most representative writings are his so-called *fiabe*—fairy-tales with a purpose—grotesque, absurd, full of theatrical wonder, and, at the same time, closely in contact with the real, humorously ironic in concept, interfused with literary satire. Of his first important composition, *L'amore delle tre melarance* (*The Love of the Three Oranges*, 1761), nothing remains save a 'reflective analysis' (*analisi riflessiva*) presenting the outline of the plot, but even this meagre record is sufficient to indicate its quality, and has proved capable of inspiring later theatrical effort of noteworthy quality. The story tells of a melancholic prince, Tartaglia, who, under the curse of Fata Morgana (in league with the traitors Leandro and Clarice), is doomed to die unless he can be made to smile. The faithful Pantalone persuades King Silvio to introduce the laughter-moving Truffaldino to Court in the hope of curing the young invalid, but his utmost efforts fail until Fata Morgana, an old woman, is knocked head over heels by the acrobatic Truffaldino. At this the prince roars with merriment, and the whole Court is rejoiced. His troubles, however, are only beginning. Enraged, Morgana puts a fresh curse upon him: he is doomed to pine for the Three Oranges. These are kept in an enchanted castle many leagues away, and the prince, attended by Truffaldino, sets forth on the perilous journey. Fortunately aided by the magician Celio—Morgana's rival—he obtains the Oranges, gives them to Truffaldino to carry, and is separated from his companion. Although he knows that the Oranges must not be cut open unless a fountain of water is near by, the foolish Truffaldino, consumed with thirst, opens one. A young girl appears from it, piteously pleading for a draught of water. In terror, Truffaldino cuts open the second Orange, intending to give her the juice, and another young girl comes from this, too: both die of thirst. Just as he is about to cut the third Tartaglia enters, angrily takes it from him, opens it and, when a beautiful maiden appears, gets water from a lake, revives her, and learns that she is a princess, the daughter of Concul, King of the Antipodes. The Prince promises to marry her, but, while he goes off to arrange for the wedding, the wicked Smeraldina, a Moorish girl, causes the Princess Ninetta to be turned into a dove and herself takes her place. It seems as though Tartaglia, bound by his promise, must espouse this dark-skinned girl, when Truffaldino succeeds in bringing Ninetta back to her human form, and the play ends happily.

On the surface this is simply a child's fairy-tale, the theme for a sentimental pantomime. It must, however, be remembered that Tartaglia, Truffaldino, Pantalone, and others are characters of the *commedia dell' arte*, performed by actors to whose personal skill was added a rich inheritance from tradition. To them Gozzi makes magnanimous praise-offering. Describing the scene in which Tartaglia finds Truffaldino with the lifeless bodies of the two young girls who have issued from the Oranges, he declares that no words can adequately convey the effect created by the performers. "The witty actors of the *commedia*," he comments, "in scenes like these improvise such graciously pleasing dialogue and action as may not be expressed in written terms and could not be emulated by any dramatic author."

To appreciate *L'amore delle tre melarance*, therefore, we must use every effort of our imagination to reconstruct for ourselves the original conditions of performance. We must also realize that into this framework Gozzi has infused a kind of philosophic content. His chief aim is to entertain, to offer the comic actors a vehicle of wonder for the exercise of their talents, but throughout the action sly satire plays its part. Fata Morgana and the magician Celio are creators of marvels in this fairy-tale: they are also caricatures of those two contemporary playwrights whom Gozzi most detested—Carlo Goldoni and Pietro Chiari. He disliked their sentimental moralizings, he thought they were murdering the theatre of laughter, and, accordingly, in this guise he held them up to ridicule. He held up to ridicule too the dull, bombastic, tragic style of the age, thus making his entire piece, to use his own words, a "fantastic parody."

The same qualities animate all his later *fiabe* (although in these he provided more written dialogue than he had allowed himself in his earliest effort). *Il corvo* (*The Crow*) followed in 1761, and in 1762 came *Il re cervo* (*The King Stag*), *Turandot*, and *La donna serpente* (*The Woman Serpent*). In *La Zobeide* (1763) tragi-comedy ceded to grotesque tragic scenes. This was followed by *I pitocchi fortunati* (*The Fortunate Beggars*, 1764), *Il mostro turchino* (*The Turquoise Wonder*, 1763), and *L'augellin belverde* (*The Pretty Little Green Bird*, 1765), the last described as a "philosophic *fiaba*," and introducing a poverty-stricken couple, Renzo and Barbarina, who breathe the most moral sentiments of the new French philosophy until they become rich, when all their noble professions of faith vanish in pride, ingratitude, and deliberate evil.

In all of these plays some scenes are left for the improvisation of the actors, but most of the action is fully prepared, with dialogue in prose and verse, by the author. Contrast of every kind is eagerly sought —contrast between the fairy-tale atmosphere and reality, between serious scenes and hilarious, between the imaginative and the satiric, between colloquial prose and delicate verse, between the standard Tuscan tongue and the dialects of Venice or Naples—above all, between scenes apparently designed solely for entertainment and scenes clearly based on philosophic reflection.

These qualities are excellently revealed in *Il re cervo*. The plot tells of a King Deramo who has been given two wonder-making marvels by the magician Durandarte. The first of these is a statue which makes signs to its master when he is being told an untruth. Vainly the monarch has been seeking for a bride: every princess and noble lady brought to his chamber has had her duplicity revealed by the statue's movements, and now at last the King has decided to interview anyone, no matter how poorly born, who may care to seek an interview. Among these candidates he includes one who has sought to escape the ordeal—Pantalone's faithful daughter, Angela. She alone passes the test, and, to her joy (for she is secretly devoted to her lord), is chosen to be the bride. This action, however, enrages Tartaglia, who, besides himself loving Angela, had hoped his daughter, Clarice, would have been the queen. Through his machinations the King is transformed, by means of the second marvel, into a deer; he is nearly slain, would, indeed, have perished had the magician Durandarte, in the likeness of a Parrot, not opportunely given him his aid.

All means are taken to enchant the audience. The prologue is spoken by Durandarte's servant, Cigolotti, who hints at the wonders to come; the scenes, constantly changing, present a rich and beautiful variety; Pantalone's homely Venetian dialect breaks in upon Tartaglia's Machiavellian Florentinity; and Angela's devotion is revealed sharply against the duplicities of her companions. Although German romanticists sadly erred in praising Gozzi as a supreme genius (sometimes placing him even above Shakespeare), they were right in recognizing that, in the midst of an increasingly lachrymose age, this author's keen wit and sense of wonder possessed a virtue well worthy of attention and of praise.

Gozzi was an ironic philosopher; Carlo Goldoni tended to be a sentimental one. The former was an aristocrat who might have found himself more happily situated a century before his own time, who contrasted in his mind the courtly ideals of a past age and the hypocritical bourgeois beliefs that animated the intellectuals of the eighteenth century; the latter was born of the bourgeoisie in a bourgeois period. Like Gozzi, he started his dramatic career by writing for the players of the *commedia dell' arte*, but he early came to believe that such buffooneries and fairy-tale wonders as delighted his companion were unworthy of serious attention. His whole inclination was towards the realistic theatre; he came to despise the native popular Italian tradition (even when its impress was laid upon him most strongly) and sought for models in France and elsewhere;

despite his overflowing good humour, his spiritual home was rather in the territory of the sentimental drama than in that inhabited by Pantalone and his companions. The very fact that, after an apprenticeship in Venice and Rome, he moved to France in 1762 and spent many years in writing for the Parisian Théâtre Italien is indicative of the trend of his talents.

Goldoni is an author whose merits are difficult to assess. His pen was ever on the move, and among the one hundred and fifty odd plays of his composition there are many which deserve no attention. Even his best works fail to measure up against the masterpieces written by those —particularly Molière—whom he took as his models. He has an infectious sense of fun which gives vividity to his scenes, but his power of observation is shallow. He senses the force of the new philosophical ideas that are transforming Europe, yet his own moralizations are petty, and his solutions for the problems he introduces often absurd. Fundamentally optimistic, he misses much that gave substance to Molière's work. At the same time hardly any dramatist has shown greater fertility in invention, hardly any has so enriched the stage with scenes of genuine comic spirit, hardly any has given such a variegated and vitally delineated panorama of his age.

His essential aims appear most clearly expressed in a critical work he presented in 1750—*Il teatro comico* (*The Comic Theatre*), in which a troupe of actors, under their leader Orazio, is engaged in rehearsing a Goldoni farce entitled *Il padre rivale del figlio* (*The Father a Rival to his Son*). Here are enumerated the various evils of the stage as the author saw them—the foolish and disturbing claims of individual performers, the interlarding of improvised words by the comic players, the introduction of senseless vulgarity just for the sake of arousing merriment, the lack of moral purpose in contemporary plays. From all of this it is obvious that Goldoni, forced though he was to write for actors of the *commedia dell' arte* tradition, dreamed of a stage in which the dramatist gave words to the performers, in which the comic spirit was employed for noble ends, and in which the purely fantastic was replaced by scenes based on observation of life.

This critical presentation of his attitude towards the stage came, of course, some time after he had applied himself to the theatre, and at an early date he had succeeded both in imposing some of his reforms upon the actors and in sketching out the style he wished to follow. By 1743 he had already written his first comedy with completely expressed dialogue, *La donna di garbo* (*The Worthy Woman*), and succeeding plays reveal his chief interests. In *La putta onorata* (*The Honest Girl*, 1749) the social world of his day forms a vivid background to a story which tells of the devotion of the heroine, Bettina, to the man of her choice, despite the evils that surround her. Although he does not dare to come forth too boldly, the dramatist obviously believes that virtue is to be found rather under the humble dress of the poor than under the brocades of the aristocracy. Such a concept runs through the greater part of his work, reaching culmination in a play like *La famiglia dell' antiquario* (*The Family of the Antiquary*, 1749), in which Goldoni's refashioning of the character of Pantalone is most trenchantly revealed. In earlier days Pantalone had been nothing save a comically conceived caricature of a Venetian merchant, wealthy but stupidly amorous and a fit butt for others' wit. In *La Bancarotta ossia il mercante fallito* (*Bankruptcy; or, The Ruined Merchant*, 1741) Goldoni had treated him in such a way, and even in *La putta onorata* relics of his original character still trailed about him, but already in the sequel to that play, *La buona moglie* (*The Good Wife*, 1749), they are beginning to fall away: through Pantalone's sympathetic efforts harmony is restored in a household nearly wrecked by dissension. From this time on Pantalone becomes in Goldoni's hands a sentimentally drawn character, often proving the means by which the happy conclusion ends a series of confusing and even potentially tragic scenes. In *La famiglia dell' antiquario*, although much of the action concerns the follies of the passionately devoted collector of antiques, the basic theme concerns the fate of Pantalone's daughter, Doralice, married into a rather decadent and impoverished aristocratic household. It is only the virtue, the common sense, and the magnanimity of Pantalone that bring all to rights as the curtain falls. It is only old Pantalone's sympathetic aid that prevents the action of *Il giocatore* (*The Gamester*, 1750) from developing into a distressful drama.

In another comedy produced in the same year, *L'avvocato veneziano* (*The Venetian Lawyer*), the author's serious aims are equally clearly displayed. The hero is the lawyer Alberto, who is engaged to defend Florindo in a suit against Rosaura: with her he falls in love, and is consequently torn between his passion and his duty. Fortunately for him Rosaura loses her case, but is persuaded to find in him a devoted and sincere husband. Although Goldoni cannot resist the introduction of rich and hearty laughter in many of the scenes, the basic theme obviously deals with a subject of moderately serious import involving a moral problem.

If these comedies illustrate certain cardinal characteristics of Goldoni's style, the conflicting elements in his comic conception of life are even more widely exemplified in the total range of the famous set of sixteen plays which, with truly amazing facility, he produced during the one season of 1750–51. Among them are charming pieces, such as *Il bugiardo* (*The Liar*) and *La bottega del caffè* (*The Coffee House*), in which merriment derived from intrigue is mingled with not inexpert delineation of contemporary manners. Witty dialogue gives colour to the scenes of *Il cavaliere di buon gusto* (*The Gentleman of Good Taste*). The character of Ottavio in this play, and that of the aristocratic scandalmonger, Don Marzio, in *La bottega del caffè*, are expanded and diversified in *I pettegolezzi delle donne* (*The Women's Gossip*), where the gay depiction of social life is invested with a slight touch of sentimental purpose. In turn, this sense of purpose becomes more patent in the plot of *L'avventuriere onorato* (*The Honest Adventurer*), and eventually finds itself responsible for the entire colouring of *Pamela nubile* (*Pamela the Maid*), based on Samuel Richardson's famous novel. If Richardson's influence is apparent here, that of Molière is still more potent. After all, Goldoni was a laughing dramatist, and we are not surprised to find among these sixteen comedies both *La finta ammalata* (*The Pretended Invalid*), based on *L'amour médecin*, and *Molière*—the latter an open testimony to Goldoni's sense of indebtedness to his French master.

Perhaps the total spirit investing this extraordinary run of plays, in which Goldoni ran the gamut from seriousness to farcical merriment, is best expressed in *La castalda* (*The Housekeeper*, 1751), with its engaging portrait of Corallina, and in an immediately succeeding comedy, *La locandiera* (*The Mistress of the Inn*, 1753), with its still more engaging portrait of Mirandolina, who astutely benefits from the attentions of the decayed nobleman the Marchese di Forlipopoli and the rich *parvenu* Conte di Albafiorita, gaily plagues the misogynist Cavaliere di Ripafratta, and finally gives her hand to her humble and faithful servitor. Deservedly this has come to be regarded as one of his true masterpieces.

In *La locandiera* another, and a highly significant, quality of Goldoni's art makes its appearance. Although attention is given to the characters, in a sense the comedy has as its chief hero the inn itself, and, noting this, we recall that among the plays mentioned above is one called *La bottega del caffè*, where the locale assumes almost as much theatrical appeal as the persons who frequent it. In a sense, we may say that Goldoni's comedies take the whole of Venice for their subject, and that in his diverse scenes he casts the spotlight now on a building and now on a social group within the larger community, instead of concentrating, as Molière did, on individuals. The very titles of later plays, such as *Il campiello* (*The Public Square*, 1756), *Il festino* (*The Party*, 1754) and *La villeggiatura* (*The Trip to the Country*, 1756), demonstrate how consistently he exploited this device in so far as localities are concerned, and to these should be added others in which the main effect comes from the delineation of particular segments of Venetian society: the household of the would-be gentleman in *Le femmine puntigliose* (*The Punctilious Ladies*, 1750), the boudoir life of *Il cavaliere e la dama* (*The Gentleman and the Lady*, 1749), and of *La dama prudente* (*The Prudent Lady*, 1751), the teeming city life of *Il cavalier Giocondo* (*Giocondo the Gentleman*, originally acted as *I viaggiatori*, *The Tourists*, 1755), the rustic vignettes of *Il feudatorio* (*The Peasant*, 1752), the carnival excitements of *Le morbinose* (*The Merry Ladies*, 1758), or the backstage world at the ballet in *La figlia ubbidiente* (*The Obedient Daughter*, 1752). As typical as any is a scene from *La putta onorata*:

A view of the Grand Canal with gondolas. At one side a wooden booth at the entrance to the theatre. Farther in, the exit-door of the theatre and the little window where tickets for the performances are sold. A BOY *shouts out from time to time: "Get your tickets, sirs, ten soldi each. Here's the cashier, sirs." At the other side a long bench for four people. Here and there lamps such as are usual outside theatres.*

Several masks go by; some go to buy tickets and enter the theatre; some go without tickets and walk off.

NANE, the gondolier, enters with a lantern, conducting masks to the theatre.

A servant, also with a lantern, conducts the MARCHESA BEATRICE, BETTINA, and CATE. MENEGO CAINELLO ushers in the MARCHESE OTTAVIO and four other men, who go into the theatre. During this time the BOY calls out from time to time: "Take your tickets," etc.

From inside a voice is heard: "This is the way out."

A door opens, and MENEGO and NANE come out with their lanterns.

MENEGO: Nane! How are you?

NANE: How are you, Menego?

MENEGO: All's well, then?

NANE: What's the matter?

MENEGO: That bit of quarrel we had.

NANE: It's gone clean out of my head, I assure you.

MENEGO: We're enemies aboard, but ashore we're friends and brothers.

NANE: A bit of a row is sometimes necessary just to keep up one's reputation, even although it doesn't mean anything.

MENEGO: Why do you think I didn't give you right of way? Because of my master? Not at all. Simply because fifty gondoliers were looking on, and of course I had to put up a show.

NANE: You've brought your master to the play?

MENEGO: Yes.

NANE: I'm here with a stranger who arrived this morning. I've served him before, and he treated me well.

As they chatter away the chill night air begins to enter their bones, and while their masters enjoy themselves they think of their own pleasures:

NANE: The wind's rising. I'm cold.

MENEGO: We'll put that to rights with a bottle of wine. [*To the BOY*] Come here, you, ticket boy!

BOY: What do you want?

MENEGO: We're cold here: get us a bottle of wine. Tell the waiter that Cainello has sent you and that he's to give you what he gives to his friends. Understand?

There is vigorous theatrical skill displayed in the presentation of the teeming life outside the doors of a Venetian water-fronted theatre and in the manner by which this general background is used as an animated setting for the particular persons of the play—its servants and its gondoliers, its gallants and its ladies.

Still a further general characteristic of Goldoni's work is revealed in the comedies already referred to. Their very titles indicate how greatly interested he was in the comic presentation of women: *dama* and *donna* are words frequently on his lips. The little follies that accompany the feminine, the gossip in the boudoir, the contrast between outward flattery and inner jealousy—these all caught his observant eye, and some of his most effective scenes are those in which his heroines take a principal part. In *Le smanie per la villeggiatura* (*The Craze for the Country*, 1761), for example, the liveliest and the most delicate episodes are those which show the barbed arrows lurking underneath the outwardly affectionate greetings of Victoria and Giacinta. The consuming, Pandora-like qualities of the feminine heart provide practically all the plot and the interest of *Le donne curiose* (*Female Curiosity*, 1753), wherein a group of women make every endeavour to penetrate into an exclusively male club run by Pantalone and his friends; the title of *Le donne gelose* (*The Jealous Women*, 1752) tells its own story, and the same theme of feminine jealousy appears in *Gli innamorati* (*The Lovers*, 1759); the desire of a lady to have a little court of admirers is the main theme of *La donna bizzara* (*The Capricious Lady*, 1758). In noting the atmosphere of these plays, however, we must contrast it with another atmosphere less satirical. If Goldoni saw feminine follies he did not close his eyes to feminine virtues, and his men are often as petty-minded as his women. Already in the Corallina of *La castalda* and the Mirandolina of *La locandiera* he had drawn sympathetic pictures of capable, attractive, hard-working heroines; and these pictures are paralleled by others, such as that of Giulia in *La donna di maneggio* (*The Housekeeper*, 1760). Besides this, the author's undercurrent of sentimentalism led him to depict the honesty and sincerity of an Eleonora in *Il cavaliere e la dama*, as well as the almost pathetic distresses of a Corallina in *La donna vendicativa* (*The Revengeful Lady*, 1753).

Goldoni's period of richest invention came during the forties and the fifties of the eighteenth century. In 1758 he left Venice and wandered far, first to Rome and later to Paris. Some of his plays written after this date, such as the rather farcical *La donna di governo* (*The Intriguing Woman*, 1758), suggest that his powers were failing, but others amply testify that even after all his early prolific activity he still had strength for considerable comic invention. In *I rusteghi* (*The Boors*, 1760) he presents the excellently drawn figures of the self-opinionated Simon, the stupidly obstinate Lunardo, and the sour old Canciano. *La casa nova* (*The New House*, 1760) pursues the plan of taking a locality and giving it animation: the plot here tells of the troubles of a young husband, Anzoletto, when his thoughtless bride, Cecilia, runs him into debt because she wants her new house to be fashionably elegant, but somehow it is less the married couple than, so to say, the personality of the house itself that comes to true life. Into *La buona madre* (*The Good Mother*, 1761), with its story of the widow Barbara and the way she protects her children, guiding them to socially successful marriage, the inherent sentimentalism of the theme is concealed by sympathetic character-drawing; while in the Venetian-dialect *Le baruffe chiozzotte* (*The Quarrels in Chioggia*, 1762) Goldoni carries to its farthest limits his interesting experiment in the weaving of comedy out of entire social groups—in this instance the inhabitants of a small fishing village.

In France the aging author continued to pour forth his wares. *Il ventaglio* (*The Fan*, 1765) is one of his best-known plays, in which is employed the novel device of making an inanimate object—in this case the fan itself

—form the core of the action. Passing from hand to hand, it connects the characters and gives vividity to the complex plot. In *Le bourru bienfaisant* (*The Kindly Boor*, 1771) he even turned to pen a comedy in French, depicting a crabbed old Géronte, who, however, hides a sentimentally sympathetic heart beneath his rough exterior. Another play in French, *L'avare fastueux* (*The Ostentatious Miser*), followed in 1776, and here sentimentalism triumphs in the fate meted out to the miserly count who is its central figure.

With this play Goldoni's career was at an end. That he had succeeded in making real contribution to the stage is certain, yet outside of Italy he remains—and probably is destined to remain—a name rather than a living presence in the theatre. He possessed true ability and an amazingly fecund invention, but for the deeper qualities that go to make the true masterpiece we seek vainly in his work. In his comedies is to be found charm rather than strength. The charm, however, is not a fleeting thing: springing directly from the vivacious author's own character, it irradiates all his works with the sole exception of those dull, serious dramas, so ill-suited to his genius, that he wrote at the beginning of his career. The sunlight of eighteenth-century Venice shines here for those who will take the trouble to search it out. To neglect his work is to neglect something very delightful, gay, and vivacious.

Both Gozzi and Goldoni were a trifle unfortunate in their circumstances. They both had genius: in both that genius was thwarted. Gozzi found the kind of theatre he wanted in the *commedia dell' arte*—and no doubt recognized, albeit unwillingly, that the style of that comedy had become by his time a thing outworn. For such fairy-tales as he knew so well how to narrate the serious philosophers had but little sympathy. In the *commedia dell' arte* for which he was forced to pen his plays Goldoni sensed only a hindrance to the development of what he wished to give to the world. Had another histrionic style existed in the Venice of his time he might not have had to waste so much valuable energy in effecting the 'reforms' so solemnly expounded in *Il teatro comico*. As it is, instead of achieving what might easily have been a series of pre-eminent masterpieces, each has left little more than a delightful memory of laughter in an age that was becoming so soberly serious.

The Awakening of the North: Holberg

In the year 1720 a company of French actors established themselves at the Copenhagen Court; two years later, in 1722, another Frenchman, René Montaigu, obtained permission to gather a troupe of Danish players and started his season with a Danish version of Molière's *L'avare*. The same season saw the production of five original comedies by Ludvig Holberg, an author who had already acquired a reputation for his burlesque epic *Peder Paars*, and whose residence in France and in England had given him first-hand experience of what the theatres of these two countries were producing.

It is tempting to find praise for this writer, and when one realizes that he was in effect creating not only Danish drama but Danish literature, one is indeed led to treat his works in a kindly spirit. To call him the Northern Molière, however, is to reject all critical values, and it is better to see in him a stalwart soul who, amid many difficulties, succeeded in providing for his native country a series of plays which the kindliest of criticism cannot call great, but which formed a worthy beginning for the Scandinavian stage.

Holberg suffers from many defects. He satirizes broadly, but rarely does he exhibit any clear orientation in his satire. His mind is confused, and amid the changing social conditions of his time he finds it impossible to take a clear stand. Although we feel that in his comedies he desired to arouse his compatriots to improve their somewhat backward cultural state, and although we recognize that in this aim he was aligning himself with Molière, we are bound to confess that he shows himself wholly unsure concerning the nature and quality of the improvements to be sought. The same lack of certainty is exhibited both in the structure and in the characterization of his comedies. There is liveliness in his present-ation of bourgeois Danish types, and he has a number of effective scenes; yet the scenes are often ill-harmonized, and frequently opportunities for the enriching of the characters are sadly neglected.

These defects, along with Holberg's genuine virtues, are well revealed in the two plays by which he is best known outside of Scandinavia—*Jeppe paa Bjerget, eller Den forvandlede Bonde* (*Jeppe of the Hill; or, The Peasant Meta-morphosed*), one of his earliest works, performed in 1722, and *Erasmus Montanus*, a later play, printed in 1731. The former is closely related to the 'induction' of Shakespeare's *The Taming of the Shrew*, in that it shows a poor peasant, Jeppe, taken up by a laughter-loving nobleman and per-suaded that he is indeed a man of rank and wealth whose memories of a poverty-stricken existence are nothing but hallucination. There are social implications here, but when we compare Holberg's treatment of this plot with Calderón's not dissimilar *Life is a Dream* we realize by how much it fails to achieve greatness. Like the hero of the Spanish drama, Jeppe proves tyrannical, boorish, and cruel when he thinks he is a lord; what is lacking completely is Calderón's philosophic reflections and the conclusions he draws from his action. With the one drama we soar into the realms of the imagination; with Holberg's we plod, not unentertain-ingly but a trifle heavily, over much miry ground. In *Erasmus Montanus* an interesting theme is developed. The plot here deals with a peasant who has been sent to the university and returns to his native village full of wis-dom and Latin saws. He can wield the instrument of logic: he knows that the earth is round; he has mastery over books. Unfortunately for him, however, he runs into opposition. The villagers do not take well to his pedantries, while local dignitaries (such as the deacon and the sheriff) are much disturbed lest he take from their importance. Many scenes are amusing in their satirical display of the foolish academicism of the hero, and presumably Holberg's purpose is to indicate that, while there is no merit in ignorance, there is no greater merit in arid learning. On the one hand, Erasmus is right in most of his beliefs, and an infiltration of knowledge could be expected to raise the boorish standards of the village culture; on the other, he himself is made an arrant fool, without enough common sense to avoid being pressed for the army, and is contrasted with his brother, into whose mouth the author puts expressions, evidently sympathetically conceived, of homely wisdom.

Perhaps we shall do best to regard Holberg as we regard a 'documentary.' There is no doubt but that in his plays is presented a lively picture of social conditions in eighteenth-century Denmark. *Hexerei, eller Blind Allarm* (*Witchcraft; or, The False Alarm*; printed 1731) gives an excellent view of the superstitions prevailing in his backward land. Various other plays reveal by incisive touches the growth of a newly enriched bourgeoisie, their ridiculous (and ubiquitous) attempts to copy the manners of high society; in *Den ellefte Junii* (*The Eleventh of June*, 1723) he turns to show the effects of enrichment on a boorish peasantry; in *Mester Gert Westphaler, eller Den meget talende Barbeer* (*Master Gert Westphaler; or, The Very Loquacious Barber*, 1722) and *Den politiske Kandestøber* (*The Pewterer a Politician*, 1722) he ridicules, firstly, the affections of an uneducated man who, having travelled slightly, wishes to dazzle his friends by his conversation, and, secondly, the absurdities of a tradesman suddenly bitten by the desire to shine in the realm of politics. In all of these are presented vivid pictures of the life of Holberg's day, although rather in a series of jerky scenes than in harmonious weaving of plot.

Only in two respects did Holberg make real contributions to dramatic conceptions. Most of his characters are obviously Danish versions of types already dealt with on the stage by Molière and others, but in drawing one figure he achieved real originality. The hero of *Den Stundesløse* (*No Time to Waste*, 1726) is a man who is continually buzzing about, flitting from one job to another, trying to do three things at once, never possessed of a moment of leisure: and in his oddities he is distinctly entertaining. Here, at least, the Danish author was painting straight from life. Something of the same originality enters into the portrait of the heroine in *Den Vægelsindede* (*The Weathercock*, 1722) and into the rehandling of *commedia dell' arte* material in *De Usynlige* (*The Masked Ladies*, 1725), where Harlequin's stupid aping of Leandro's affected love affairs serves to show up fashionable follies. Nor did he have a model for the interesting device employed in *Hexerei*, where several of his own *dramatis personæ* culled from earlier plays are introduced for the purpose of protesting against their having been ridiculed on the stage. The trick almost suggests the style of Pirandello (although, obviously, Holberg makes no subtle use of it), and indicates that this author, awaking the cold and silent North to the joys of the theatre, was not content merely to adapt scenes and characters from French or English masters.

In himself, perhaps, Holberg does not warrant overmuch attention, but he stands forth as a symbolic figure. With the growth of the middle classes the stage is being carried rapidly into lands which had barely felt the impress of the Renaissance, and from those lands was soon to come new strength and fresh inspiration. Holberg, although he applied himself to the Danish drama, had been born in Norway, and not so many generations were to pass before that country produced its giant figure of Ibsen. It is true that the immediately following years offered but little of any value, yet the line from Denmark's first dramatist, through Johan Herman Wessel, sentimental Johannes Ewald, and classically inclined Nordahl Brun, on to the masters of the nineteenth century, is clear. Nor must the influence of Holberg outside his native country be forgotten. It was, for example, his inspiration that produced one of the earliest comedies in far-off Finland—the *Nummisuutarit* (*The Country Shoemaker*, 1864), by Aleksis Kivi.

It was not only in Scandinavia and the North that the awakening was to be found. In Holland were appearing such comedies as the *Weder-zijdsch Huwelijksbedrog* (*Lovers' Deceits, c.* 1712) of Pieter Arenz Langendijk, where Lodewijk, a penniless man of quality, lays suit to a girl, Charlotte, born of poor parents: she is described to him by her maidservant, Klaar, as abounding in riches, while he pretends to be a wealthy Polish count. Underneath the framework of intrigue is obvious an appreciation of social manners and their bearing upon character. In Hungary György Bessenyei produced his rather interesting sentimental satire of sentimentalism in *Philosophus* (*The Philosopher*, 1777). The early theatres of Russia, somewhat later in the century, were seeing the foundations laid for the stage that was to welcome a Chekhov, and their dramatic offerings will later claim our attention. Across the long wastes of the Atlantic, too, a stirring of dramatic desire was leading towards the establishment of a native American drama.

The Last Flickers of Comedy: Sheridan, Goldsmith, Beaumarchais

By the year 1750 bourgeois interests had introduced a new type of comedy into France and England. However, before this new style engulfed the comic stage entirely there was one last flickering of laughter, and maybe it is fitting to contemplate this before turning to examine the growth of the drama of sentiment.

There were, of course, many men during that age who saw the inherent follies of sentimentalism, and some among them tried to stay its course. For such an endeavour three possible means suggested themselves: satirical attacks and parodies, the creation of an entirely new style of comedy, and the revival of one of the older styles submerged by the wave of sentimentalism.

The first of these was tried, but without much effect. In England the cynical Samuel Foote, who became owner of the 'summer theatre' in the

Haymarket, turned out *The Handsome Housemaid; or, Piety in Pattens* (1773), in which he ridiculed the morality of such works as Richardson's· *Pamela*, and others joined him in directing occasional barbs at the lachrymose drama. It is, however, difficult to trace any sure influence of the parodies cast in this mould: men laughed, no doubt, and a few may have heartily sympathized with the effort, and that was all. Sentimentalism pursued its course unchecked.

As we have seen, *The Beggar's Opera* had suggested the possibility of finding a new form for the expression of a comic mood harmonized with the interests of the eighteenth-century audience. This movement was stayed by the Licensing Act of 1737, and the later record of the ballad-opera presents a series of disappointments. The endeavour to evolve a fresh comic style was frustrated.

Something more, however, came from the determined attempt to revive older forms; out of that attempt came half a dozen masterpieces in France and in England, and, even if we are forced to confess that these masterpieces did not establish a tradition, there can be no doubt but that we must welcome and esteem them for their intrinsic accomplishment.

Both Oliver Goldsmith and Richard Brinsley Sheridan were utterly opposed to the mawkishly sentimental, and both looked back with nostalgic regret at the vanished comedy of the past. We must not, however, assume that the gaze of each was directed at the same object. Goldsmith exhibits in his writing something of Shakespeare's mood: humour, not wit, is the instrument he best knows how to wield; and accordingly, in searching for a model to be used in his own dramatic efforts, he fixes his eyes on the romantic comedies of the latter years of the sixteenth century. It is their spirit he wishes to revive. His *Essay on the Theatre; or, A Comparison between Laughing and Sentimental Comedy* (1772) puts his position clearly. He deplores the growth of the sentimental comedy—"a kind of *mulish* production, with all the defects of its opposite parents, and marked with sterility"; he pleads for the return of "humour" and, with it, a franker attitude towards life, a banishing of that fastidiousness which came with genteel comedy and was exaggerated in the sentimental.

His first endeavour to supply a "laughing comedy," *The Good-natured Man* (1768), showed the hand of an apprentice, but its emphasis was unmistakable, and some of the more polite among his audience were inclined timorously to condemn it as "low." This was followed by the brilliant *She Stoops to Conquer; or, The Mistakes of a Night* (1773). Although it is possible to dismiss this play as merely a mild farce, its characterization and its delicacy of dialogue deservedly make it one of the most popular of eighteenth-century comedies. Marlow, "one of the most bashful and reserved young fellows in the world," is drawn adeptly for the rôle he is to play; Hardcastle, the crusty but kind-hearted country gentleman, has vitality and interest; Miss Hardcastle is a heroine of whom even the exquisite Marivaux need not have been ashamed; and Tony Lumpkin is twin-brother to Shakespeare's clowns. Despite the fact that the author obviously finds it hard to maintain credibility in the results of the original mistake (by which Marlow enters Hardcastle's house under the belief that it is an inn), these persons keep our interest alive in the plot. Goldsmith, like Shakespeare, was less intent upon verisimilitude in action than upon the creation of humorous scenes and the evoking of mood.

If Goldsmith discovered his spiritual home in the romantic comedies of the Elizabethan era, Sheridan lived in spirit with the wits who surrounded Charles II. His endeavour was to revive the comedy of manners. At the same time he was an opportunist and himself a theatrical manager, with the consequence that, fundamentally opposed though he was to sentimentalism, he permitted a faint flavour of that style to colour scenes penned mainly for their laughter, and, moreover, soon abandoned the effort to emulate Etherege and Congreve.

His first dramatic work, *The Rivals* (1775), patently revealed what he wanted to do. The hero is Captain Absolute, a witty young gentleman; the heroine is the fair Lydia Languish, whom reading of books from the lending library has made affected and sentimentally absurd. The plot, complicated by the absurd pretensions of the inimitable Mrs Malaprop, the fiery passions of Sir Lucius O'Trigger, and the good-natured blunderings of Bob Acres, eventually leads to Lydia's surrender to reality. We are, no doubt, far off from the cynical libertinism of the Restoration dramatists; if Sheridan calls any to mind it is the late Vanbrugh and Farquhar, in whose works the atmosphere of the comedy of manners was being transformed into shapes which could easily be moulded into the genteel and the sentimental; yet the indebtedness of the author of *The Rivals* to the graceless author of *The Man of Mode* is easily to be traced.

This early essay was followed by *The School for Scandal* (1777), a masterpiece of dramatic construction. Although the basic plot illustrates the way in which Sheridan was prepared to bow to contemporary sentimental tastes, the spirit of wit is admirably sustained throughout. Like many a duller playwright of his age, Sheridan here presents a hero who, although guilty of many follies and even stained with vices, is shown at the end to be a man whose honesty of heart deserves our approbation. This young gentleman, Charles Surface, is contrasted with his hypocritical brother, Joseph. The former loves Maria, the wealthy ward of Sir Peter Teazle; the latter makes suit to the girl in the hope of obtaining her money while at the same time he pursues Lady Teazle, Sir Peter's wife. As the play develops a *deus ex machina* arrives in the person of Sir Oliver Surface, uncle of the two brothers; by his means Charles' nobility and Joseph's duplicity are amply demonstrated, and concurrently Lady Teazle is made to realize the dangers into which she has so nearly fallen.

The School for Scandal is too well known to require lengthy analysis, yet such analysis it fully deserves; rarely has a comic playwright wrought a complicated plot with such exquisite skill.

Both *The Rivals* and its successor were welcomed by the contemporary

theatre, but Sheridan, ever an easy-going character, must have realized
that esteem of them arose in spite of and not because of their relationship
to the mood of the time. As a result, nothing in the same style followed
from his pen. *The Critic; or, A Tragedy Rehearsed* (1779) is a magnificent
satire of many follies in the theatre of his day; only in its attempt to evoke
laughter, however, can it be related to the two earlier comedies. *St
Patrick's Day; or, The Scheming Lieutenant* (1775) is but a flimsy piece; *The
Duenna* (1775), although it includes some lively scenes, does not exhibit
much merit; *A Trip to Scarborough* (1777) is nothing more than a genteel
version of Vanbrugh's *The Relapse*.

The truth is that the age did not really want the comedy of wit or the
comedy of humour; and Sheridan knew it. Some other authors of the
time tried to persuade the audience to like plays in which a strong dash of
sentimentalism accompanied scenes cast in another manner; thus
Arthur Murphy penned *The Way to Keep Him* (1760) and George Colman
the Elder his amusing *Jealous Wife* (1761), while the latter joined David
Garrick, playwright as well as actor, in writing *The Clandestine Marriage*
(1766), one of the best of these mixed comedies. Along with these works
may be mentioned the not unamusing American comedy of sentimentalized manners, *The Contrast* (1787), by Royall Tyler—the first play
from across the Atlantic that really calls for serious attention. Meanwhile others, among whom Samuel Foote was the most successful, kept
turning out short farces in an effort to keep laughter in the theatre. All of
this, however, was of little avail. Men at the close of the eighteenth century were acclaiming George Colman the Younger as Sheridan's successor, and it is depressing to note that this prolific author aimed rather
at the development of qualities later to serve the melodrama than at the
cultivation of wit.

Much the same story is to be told of Beaumarchais (Pierre-Augustin
Caron) in France. Like Goldsmith and Sheridan, he was a lonely figure,
without true successors; like Sheridan—as his *Eugénie* (1767) shows—he
stood in somewhat doubtful relationship to the sentimental drama; like
both, he had a free sense of fun and a genuine dramatic talent.

So far as comedy is concerned, his name will be remembered for two
works, *Le barbier de Seville* (*The Barber of Seville*, 1775) and *Le mariage de
Figaro* (*The Marriage of Figaro*, 1784). The theme of the first is a simple
one. Old Bartolo wishes to marry his ward, Rosine, who for her part
loves a gentleman, Lindoro, who is really the Count Almaviva. To the
help of the young couple comes the Barber of Seville, Figaro, and the plot
is carried forward partly by his intrigues and partly by the various
devices by which Almaviva insinuates himself into Bartolo's house. In
essence the play is thus a comedy of intrigue, with action similar to that
of hundreds of other pieces; it would have remained undistinguished
from them had it not been for two qualities it possessed. Beaumarchais
was an author with a precise and delicate pen: his dialogue—like
Molière's, excessively difficult to translate—gives animation to scenes of

**COMMEDIA DELL' ARTE
CHARACTERS IN J. CALLOT'S
'I BALLI DE SFESSANIA'**

OPEN-AIR PERFORMANCE
IN VENICE
Painting by Gabriele Bella in
the Pinacoteca Querini, Venice.
Photo T. Filippi

action which otherwise might have appeared artificially dull. The second quality concerns the characterization of Figaro. The Barber is no ordinary valet; he is a man of the people; and into his mouth Beaumarchais has placed a number of such common-sense reflections on the ways of the aristocracy as were to give to *The Barber of Seville* an almost revolutionary significance in the changes which so soon were to overturn French society.

Both qualities are marked again in *The Marriage of Figaro*, written obviously in order to capitalize on the success of the former play, and equally obviously invested with greater social bitterness. The Count and his Rosine are now viewed several years after marriage. They are drifting apart. Figaro, the Count's servant, is preparing to marry Suzanne, the soubrette, but Almaviva demands that, in return for favours he has done to Figaro, she should first become his mistress. When foiled in this effort he capriciously tries to marry off the faithful Figaro to the elderly Marceline, while poor Figaro is further plagued because, without his knowledge, the Countess has persuaded Suzanne to agree to an assignation (intending to meet the Count herself and thus endeavour to effect a reconciliation). Peace comes to the troubled household only when the Count is unmasked and when the discovery is made that Marceline is in reality Figaro's mother.

There is much of laughter in this play, but there are darker sounds as well. The plot gives Figaro the opportunity for passing many trenchant remarks on the pride, the worthlessness, and the exactions of the aristocracy. He becomes a figure of honest, sturdy, plebeian heroism, and unquestionably audiences were expected not merely to laugh, but to feel with him as well. Although Beaumarchais may be justifiably regarded as a not undistinguished descendant of Molière, even these two merry dramas bear clear indication of having been composed in a spirit alien to that of the comedy of manners. The last words of *The Barber of Seville* are "Je me presse de rire de tout, de peur d'être obligé d'en pleurer" ("I am anxious to laugh at everything lest I be forced to weep").

The truth, of course, is that Beaumarchais was fully immersed—for all his laughter—in the sentimental stream. His first play, *Eugénie* (1767), with its characteristically English characters, is a seriously composed drama, while *Les deux amis* (*The Two Friends*, 1770) is thoroughly bourgeois in spirit. With two entirely diverse moods thus fighting within him, he provides an excellent means of transition from the old to the new.

3

THE WAVE OF SENTIMENTALISM

WITH HIS *Eugénie* Beaumarchais published an *Essai sur le genre dramatique sérieux*, in which he set forth as clearly as any the basic principles of the sentimental cult. He notes that there are some people who deplore the partiality of the public for the 'serious drama.' To them he answers, first, that the audience must ever be the master of what is provided in the theatre, secondly, that no appeal to ancient models can be allowed, and, thirdly, that it is "permissible to interest a theatre audience and make it shed tears over a situation which, if it occurred in everyday life, would never fail to produce the same effect upon each individual in that audience." The ancient tragedies are barbaric; the persons of the heroic drama rarely appeal to the heart; a prince is a stranger to us, and we can be truly moved only by contemplating the relationship between man and man. "What," he inquires,

> What do I care, I, a peaceful subject in an eighteenth-century monarchy, for the revolutions of Athens and Rome? Of what real interest to me is the death of a Peloponnesian tyrant, or the sacrifice of a young princess at Aulis? There is nothing in that for me; no morality which is applicable to my needs. For what is morality? It is the fruitful result and individual application of certain mental deductions occasioned by an actual occurrence. What is interest? It is the involuntary sensation by which we adapt that occurrence to our own ends; it puts us in the place of him who suffers, throws us into the situation for the time being.

Folly, he thinks, can be ridiculed in laughter, but only too often we are betrayed by comedy into sympathizing with moral vice because of our delight in witty lines and stage tricks. To attack vice men need an emotional drama, a serious drama, moving us "by true and natural means," which may call forth our tears.

The Basis of the Sentimental Drama

These words of Beaumarchais reveal trenchantly that the two essential foundations upon which the serious drama is set are truth to reality and didactic moralization. Both of these, however, are relative terms, and, as a result, much that seemed realistic to the eighteenth century appears now to be highly artificial, while a great deal that the age regarded as profoundly philosophical has become in our eyes shallow and mawkish. In spite of the aims of the playwrights, the serious philosophical lachrymose drama of the eighteenth century has produced little, if anything, that does not seem absurd and laughable. The word 'sentimental,' which we commonly apply to the genre, is an indication of our awareness of the follies and inadequate reflections which crowd into these scenes.

Originally sentimentalism was adumbrated in England, although it was soon to be taken over by Continental playwrights and given firmness of form. Already in the first years of the century Steele's attacks on duelling and his interest in domestic harmony were didactically pointing forward towards a serious treatment of social evils; even before that diverse comedies had been introducing scenes of a deliberately pathetic kind, so that long ere men were aware of the existence of a new form of drama in their midst many of the technical devices and much of the sentimental mood had been clearly adumbrated. In 1740 Samuel Richardson won popularity for his sentimental novel, *Pamela*, to be followed within a few years by *Clarissa* (1747–48), and from that date the theatre fed freely from the fount of narrative fiction.

It must sadly be confessed that there is not a single English play written in this style during the eighteenth century which is worthy of serious criticism. Author after author applied himself to this genre, and all failed dismally. Men like Hugh Kelly and Richard Cumberland won fame for such works as *False Delicacy* (1768) and *The West Indian* (1771); later came Thomas Holcroft with *The Road to Ruin* (1792) and the prolific Mrs Elizabeth Inchbald with her *Such Things are* (1787) and her adaptation from Kotzebue, *Lovers' Vows* (1798).

Although each of these authors brings his own peculiar qualities to the development of character and of scene, a common style appears in all. Each writer strives to be realistic, and each falls far short of his goal: each is interested in preaching, and deliberately designs his action in order to make his moralistic point; each mingles laughable scenes with serious, although quite clearly he will be better pleased if the audience weep at his comedy than roar with merriment. As an example, and a single example will serve, we may take a scene in Mrs Inchbald's *Every One has his Fault* (1793). Lady Eleanor has come to the home of her father, Lord Norland, to beg his clemency on her husband's behalf: in this house lives her little son, who has been adopted in infancy by his grandfather:

> *She is following the Servant; EDWARD walks softly after her, till she gets near the door; he then takes hold of her gown, and gently pulls it; she turns and looks at him.*
> *EDWARD:* Shall I speak for you, Madam?
> *LADY ELEANOR:* Who are you, pray, young Gentleman? Is it you, whom Lord Norland has adopted for his son?
> *EDWARD:* I believe he has, Madam; but he has never told me so yet.
> *LADY ELEANOR:* I am obliged to you for your offer; but my suit is of too much consequence for *you* to undertake.

EDWARD: I know what your suit is, Madam, because I was with my Lord when Hammond brought in your message; and I was so sorry for you, I came out on purpose to see you—and, without speaking to my Lord, I could do you a great kindness—if I durst.

LADY ELEANOR: What kindness?

EDWARD: But I durst not—— No, do not ask me.

LADY ELEANOR: I do not. But you have raised my curiosity; and in a mind so distracted as mine, it is cruel to excite one additional pain.

EDWARD: I am sure I would not add to your grief for the world. But then, pray do not speak of what I am going to say. I heard my Lord's lawyer tell him just now, "that as he said he should not know the person again, who committed the offence about which you came, and as the man who informed against him was gone off, there could be no evidence that he did the action, but from a book, a particular pocket-book of my Lord's, which he forgot to deliver to his servant with the notes and money to return, and which was found upon him at your house: and this, Lord Norland will affirm to be his." Now, if I did not think I was doing wrong, this is the very book. [*Takes a pocket-book from his pocket.*] I took it from my Lord's table; but it would be doing wrong, or I am sure I wish you had it.　　　　[*Looking wistfully at her.*

LADY ELEANOR: It will save my life, my husband's and my children's.

EDWARD [*trembling*]*:* But what is to become of me?

LADY ELEANOR: That Providence, who never punishes the deed, unless the *will* be an accomplice, shall protect you for saving one, who has only erred in a moment of distraction.

EDWARD: I never did anything to offend my Lord in my life;—and I am in such fear of him, I did not think I ever should. Yet, I cannot refuse *you;*—take it. [*Gives her the book.*] But pity me, when my Lord shall know of it.

LADY ELEANOR: Oh! should he discard you for what you have done, it will embitter every moment of my remaining life.

EDWARD: Do not frighten yourself about that. I think he loves me too well to discard me quite.

LADY ELEANOR: Does he indeed?

EDWARD: I think he does; for often, when we are alone, he presses me to his bosom so fondly, you would not suppose. And, when my poor nurse died, she called me to her bedside, and told me (but pray keep it a secret)—she told me I was—his grandchild.

LADY ELEANOR: You are—you are his grandchild—I see—I feel you are; for I feel that I am your mother.　　　　　　[*Embraces him.*

Thus did the sentimental drama seek to display reality.

For the most part it was simply 'serious drama' or 'lachrymose comedy,' but a few attempts of a bolder kind were made during the age to substitute for the older tragedy of royal associations a tragedy of bourgeois proportions. In this sphere George Lillo easily comes first with his mediocre, yet revolutionary and widely influential, *The London Merchant; or, The History of George Barnwell* (1731). Already in Shakespeare's time experiments had been made in the writing of middle-class tragic scenes, but these had been long forgotten, and Lillo's play came as a surprise and a shock to his contemporaries. They were thrilled to find a hero in an ordinary London apprentice and to discover tragic sentiment in a sordid story of his intrigue with a prostitute, of his sinking ever deeper into the abyss, and finally of his murdering an uncle who has ever been his guardian and friend. Typical of the style of this drama is the scene in which the latter walks to his doom: it is night on a lonely lane:

UNCLE: If I was superstitious, I should fear some danger lurked unseen, or death were nigh. A heavy melancholy clouds my spirits; my imagination is filled with ghashly forms of dreary graves and bodies changed by death—when the pale lengthened visage attracts each weeping eye and fills the musing soul at once with grief and horror, pity and aversion. I will indulge the thought. The wise man prepares himself for death by making it familiar to his mind. When strong reflections hold the mirror near and the living in the dead behold their future selves, how does each inordinate passion and desire cease or sicken at the view? The mind scarce moves; the blood, curdling and chilled, creeps slowly through the veins—fixed, still and motionless, like the solemn object of our thoughts. We are almost at present what we must be hereafter, till curiosity awakes the soul and sets it on inquiry. [*GEORGE BARNWELL enters at a distance.*] O death, thou strange mysterious power, seen every day, yet never understood but by the incommunicative dead—what art thou? The extensive mind of men, that with a thought circles the earth's vast globe, sinks to the centre or ascends above the stars, that worlds exotic finds or thinks it finds—thy thick clouds attempt to pass in vain, lost and bewildered in the horrid gloom, defeated she returns more doubtful than before, of nothing certain but of labour lost.

[*During this speech BARNWELL sometimes presents the pistol and draws it back again. At last he drops it, at which his UNCLE starts and draws his sword.*

BARNWELL: Oh, 'tis impossible!

UNCLE: A man so near me, armed and masked!

BARNWELL: Nay, then, there's no retreat.

[*Plucks a poniard from his bosom and stabs him.*

UNCLE: Oh, I am slain! All gracious Heaven regard the prayer of thy dying servant. Bless with thy choicest blessings my dearest nephew; forgive my murderer; and take my fleeting soul to endless mercy.

[*BARNWELL throws off his mask, runs to him, and, kneeling by him, raises and chafes him.*

BARNWELL: Expiring saint! Oh, murdered, martyred Uncle! Lift up your dying eyes and view your nephew in your murderer. Oh, do not look so tenderly upon me! Let indignation lighten from your eyes and blast me ere you die! By Heaven, he weeps in pity of my woes! Tears! Tears for blood! The murdered, in the agonies of death, weeps for his murderer! Oh, speak your pious purpose—pronounce my pardon then and take me with you. He would, but cannot. Oh, why with such fond affection do you press my murdering hand? What, will you kiss me?

[*Kisses him. UNCLE groans and dies.*

Such scenes seemed marvellous to the age, and hardly any play of the time was better known, either in England or abroad, than *The London Merchant*. It shared with Richardson's novel *Pamela* the honour of promoting that veritable 'anglomania' which swept over the Continent towards the middle of the century.

On the Continent sentimentalism grew much as it had done in England, but there it rapidly became more philosophical and conscious of its purposes. In diverse ways these earlier dramatists to whom reference already has been made—Regnard, Lesage, and Marivaux—contributed towards its formation. To their efforts were added those of Philippe-Néricault Destouches, who rather dully strove to clothe moral sentiments in theatrical costumes. His best play is *Le glorieux* (*The Conceited Count*, 1732), in which is clearly marked the opposition between the old aristocracy and the newly rising middle class, although his most influential was the less skilful *Le philosophe marié* (*The Married Philosopher*, 1727), with its strongly moralizing strain. Characteristic of the international style of the new movement in drama, and of the cross-currents that eventually brought it to port, are the facts that Destouches not only wrote this play in England but showed himself inspired by English authors, and that, when adapted by John Kelly as *The Married Philosopher* in 1732, it exercised a powerful force in developing later English sentimentalism.

From Destouches it is an easy step to Nivelle de la Chaussée, who is frequently regarded as the true father of the *comédie larmoyante*, because of such plays as *La fausse antipathie* (*The False Antipathy*, 1733), *Le préjugé à la mode* (*Fashionable Prejudice*, 1735), and *L'homme de fortune* (*The Man of Fortune*, 1751), and even if we decide that the fullest expression of this type of drama was still to come, we must agree that in his writings the orientation was clearly towards that new species of composition which, hovering between the tragic and the comic, seemed most nearly to meet the demands of contemporary audiences.

The sentimental *drame*, however, first received adequate expression in the once famous *Le fils naturel, ou les épreuves de la vertu* (*The Natural Son; or, The Trials of Virtue*) of Denis Diderot. This work, published in 1757, was first acted in 1771. Its author was the central figure in the combination of writers (including Voltaire) who made history through the publication, during the seventies, of the vast, many-volumed *Encyclopédie, ou Dictionnaire raisonné des sciences, des arts et des métiers*, a work destined to have enormous influence on the growth of such 'philosophical' thought as was ultimately to lead to the Revolution. *Le fils naturel* and the accompanying *Le père de famille* (*The Father of the Family*, 1758) were composed much in the spirit of the *Encyclopédie*. They were animated by a didactic aim and sought to teach by moving the emotions of the audience. From Diderot the whole of the French *drame* took its colouring: even the Théâtre Italien was influenced, and a new kind of sentimental comic opera came into being. Play after play concentrated on the enunciation of moral truths, preached the sermon of natural virtues and the crimes of civilization, aroused tearful pity for those cruelly oppressed, and held up the serious middle-class merchant as an object of supreme admiration. Author after author came forward in this style—unhappily for the most part with pieces of little intrinsic excellence even although of contemporary popularity. Michel-Jean Sedaine was among the best with his well-executed *Le philosophe sans le savoir* (*A Philosopher without knowing it*, 1765)—a drama of merchant morality directed against the practice of duelling. *Le déserteur* (*The Deserter*, 1769) by Louis-Sebastien Mercier belongs to the same school of 'bourgeois drama': this play, as well as his *Jennéval* (printed 1769) and *Le juge* (*The Judge*, 1774), had considerable contemporary significance.

Mercier was the author of an important *Essai sur l'art dramatique* (1773), and this fact reminds us of the close association of critical exposition with creative effort in France during these years. Beaumarchais' essay has already been mentioned, and to his work and Mercier's is to be added the notable letter written by Diderot in 1758—*De la poésie dramatique, à Monsieur Grimm*. The reference to Grimm further reminds us that the critical discussion of the new form was rapidly being pursued in Germanic lands as well; soon, indeed, the torch that had passed from England to France was to be transferred to that country.

Diderot's essay is designed as an effort to give philosophical justification for the "serious comedy, whose office it is to depict virtue and the duties of man." With enthusiasm he discovers the rudiments, at least, of the serious type of play in the comedies of Terence, which, he avers, hardly raise laughter, but present "touching scenes based on events, natural in character and harmonized with the customs of the time." Probably the most revealing in all critical documents of this time is the set of arguments set forth by Carl Wilhelm Ramler in the fourth edition (1774) of a translation of a work by l'abbé Charles Batteux (originally published in 1750). Bourgeois drama, Ramler asserts, is in harmony with the middle-class tastes of the audiences and can more easily draw those audiences to sympathy with the characters; it deals with common events and not with far-off Court intrigues; it is easier for actors to portray familiar characters and for dramatists to find such characters fitting dialogue. The stress here is on utilitarian values, not on æsthetic ones; the playwrights of the time constantly confused, as has been said, "the pattern of drama with the pattern of reality itself."

Soon, however, the incipient realism of the sentimental play was to receive a rude check. That check came, not as the result of endeavours to re-establish the laughing comedy, but as the consequence of a force that, absorbing the sentimental into its being, gave to the lachrymose scenes a new direction. Sheridan and Goldsmith failed to alter the course of the drama in England, just as in Italy Goldoni's gaiety was inclined to become confused with moral seriousness, and his followers (for example, Francesco Albergati Capacelli, with his comic gallery of *Il ciarlatore maldicente* (*The Malicious Prattler*, c. 1785), or Simeone Antonio Sografi, with his vividly depicted backstage world in *Le convenienze teatrali* (*Theatrical Manners*, 1794), could not stem the tide of sentimentalism. That sentimentalism spread everywhere. Alongside *Il ciarlatore maldicente* stands the pathetic *Il delatore* (*The Informer*, 1799) of Camillo Federici, where, instead of a social gossip, we are confronted with a kind of noble traitor. The plot of this play, indeed, shows how far authors were prepared to go in devising tearful situations. A poor old woman, Teodora Benamati, is ill, and her two sons, Pietro and Lorenzo, are desperate in their search for money wherewith to aid her. Suddenly an opportunity offers itself. A man has been killed and a reward offered for information regarding his murderer; whereupon Pietro accuses his brother, dashes home with the reward, and as quickly dashes back to the prison, demanding to be substituted for Lorenzo. Only the discovery of the true criminal rescues both of these most noble-minded youths from dire punishment. A similar atmosphere pervades another typical 'comedy' of this time, *La dama di spirito* (*The Lady of Spirit*, 1772), by Francesco Cerlone; here the story is told of a Beatrice who loves Don Luigi, but is separated from him because he has killed her father in a duel. Much distressed, she is saved from the clutches of a wicked duke, Orione, by the fortunate return of her lover, only to find that he has now got engaged to a rich widow. As in Federici's play, happiness comes in the end only through an unexpected discovery—in this case the sudden turning up of the widow's husband, whom all had believed to be dead.

So, in Spain, Gaspar Melchor de Jovellanos produced his characteristically titled *El delincuente honrado* (*The Honest Criminal*; printed 1787, written 1774), a dismal tale of self-sacrifice, remorse, and concepts of humanitarian honour. Less darkly, a similar sentimentalism enwraps the plays of Moratín the Younger (Leandro Fernández de Moratín)—for example, the not uninteresting *El viejo y la niña* (*The Old Man and the Maid*, 1790) and *El sí de las niñas* (*The Feminine 'Yes,'* 1806)—although this author not only conceals much of his sentimentalism under a mask of laughter, but also is capable of turning out amusingly satirical plays such as *La comedia nueva, o el café* (*The New Play; or, The Coffee-house*, 1792). In Germany dramas of a dull and uninspired, if morally worthy, kind —such as Otto von Gemmingen's *Der deutsche Hausvater* (*The German Father of a Family*, 1782)—developed in the hands of Lessing and Schiller into something far beyond the sentimental achievements of other European theatres.

The mention of Schiller's name, however, at once brings us back to realization of the fact that the sentimentally realistic was fated to be swallowed up in a force greater than itself. Many of those very qualities that characterized the serious comedy and the bourgeois tragedy had within them the germs of romanticism, and with the arrival of strong romantic passions during the latter years of the century the sentimental moralizings were rapidly channelled into fresh courses. The historical, even if often ludicrously interpreted, swept back into the playhouse, and domestic interior sets gave way to ancient abbey scenes and scenes placed in the gaunt halls of medieval castles. Without difficulty the sentimental comedy was transformed into the melodrama.

PART VII

THE ROMANTIC THEATRE

THE ROMANTIC THEATRE

THE ROMANTIC movement may be traced far back into the eighteenth century, where it assumes form as an endeavour to break away, now in one direction and now in another, from the classical style which, having temporarily exhausted itself, no longer could offer the inspiration required for the creation of new works of vital artistry.

Classicism fundamentally implies an attempt to delineate the typical and the representative, to show reality through the revealing of such common qualities as are shared by objects of a like nature. The classic artist tends, as far as is possible, to avoid the handling of detail: he is suspicious of the visionary; and he seeks to simplify. At its highest the classic spirit will produce the art of a Sophocles; at its lowest it will yield the formalized 'rules' of the lesser critics.

Obviously, in searching for a method of artistic creation opposed to this classic method, the romantic artist casts aside all the formalized 'rules,' and eschews the attempt to reduce things to simple terms. He is inclined both to rely upon his own individual genius and to find in elaboration of his material an intrinsic virtue. Where the classicist hammers out for himself a straight road, running Romanlike across undulating plain and over steep mountainside, the romanticist finds a joy in deviation, in the tortuous path that curves and bends, that often seems to lose the very sense of direction.

While such a course is characteristic of nearly all romantic art, from the very beginning of romanticism a cleavage within the ranks of the writers makes itself apparent. The opposition to the classic cult of typical form may, and does, assume two distinct shapes: one of these, cultivating the presentation of detail, leads ultimately towards naturalism; the other, making search beyond and behind the world of material reality, eventually loses itself in a realm of the subjective imagination.

At the very beginning of the romantic movement we may thus recognize the realistic poet Crabbe and the visionary Blake as joining in common fight against the classical style, even while at the same time we are fully conscious of the thoroughly divergent trends in their artistry which keep them distinct. And throughout the entire course of this period we can easily see how the spirit animating Crabbe constantly bends ever more and more inward until it reaches the *impasse* of Surrealism.

Although these two strains are of almost equal importance in the development of the nineteenth-century theatre, it is obvious that, in the first flush of revolutionary enthusiasm heralding the breakaway from outworn classic models, the more flamboyant tendencies of the romantic mood found freer expression and almost overwhelmed the realistic. Both made their appearance at the same time in all forms of literature, so that, for example, the epoch-making *Lyrical Ballads* took shape as an amalgam of Wordsworth's poems of common life and of Coleridge's visionary essays; but when we think of the drama of this time it is the latter mood that clearly takes predominance. Reflections of the mood that created *The Rime of the Ancient Mariner* are apparent everywhere: many years were to elapse before the theatre was to welcome the mood that inspired Wordsworth. What confronts us in the playhouse of the nineteenth century is, first, a wild surge of 'gothicism,' with poetic tragedy, melodrama, opera, and fantastic extravaganza carried on its waves, next, a realistic swell gradually gathering force, and, finally, at the end of the period a bitter conflict between the two, during which each current strives to assert its superior force, and frequently the two find their waters mingling in a confused flood.

Socially, the world was at this time passing through a ferment. The French Revolution, combined with the successful establishment of an independent republic in the United States of America, ushered in an era of revolt. Country after country felt the urge towards freedom, and, in evolving a national consciousness, discovered in the theatre a means of arousing sentiments of a patriotic kind. Italian poets thus turned to the drama with fresh enthusiasm, and even in lands where the theatre had had no previous existence revolutionary knights-errant applied their energies to establishing native stages. Hungary provides a good example. Not until 1791 was there a public performance of a play in the national tongue: a few years later, in 1802, a Transylvanian National Theatre was founded, and in 1837 came a Hungarian National Theatre. Conditions elsewhere in Eastern Europe exhibited similar features. The first performance of a Czech play was given in 1785, and a series of successive ventures throughout the century led ultimately to the setting up, in 1862, of a 'Provisional Theatre' for dramas in the native language and, in 1883, to the opening of a National Theatre.

It was not, however, only patriotic sentiment that was being aroused. Social classes that had previously been submerged or had failed to become vocal were now demanding a share in the general life of the community. The old aristocracy and the new wealthy bourgeoisie still maintained their hold in most lands, but the working men were beginning to stir, and even underneath the apparently placid surface of life in Victorian England heavy currents were on the move.

This meant, for the theatre, a new audience and a new liberty. Although the complete freedom given to the French theatres during the first flush of revolutionary enthusiasm was soon curbed, and although the English playhouses were not officially released from the ancient patent monopoly until 1834, the hard control of theatrical affairs was almost everywhere being lightened, and new houses were being built to accommodate a rapidly increasing public. Men who would never have thought of entering a theatre half a century before now demanded their entertainment, and as the industrial cities grew so grew a fresh body of spectators anxious to savour the delights of the stage. From north to south, from east to west, the drama was exercising a novel fascination.

1

FROM TRAGEDY TO MELODRAMA

THROUGHOUT this period almost every poet, major and minor, sought to contribute to a new drama that should be richer than the old, and every one of them gazed with reverent eyes upon the majesty of Shakespeare. Translations of his works multiplied themselves in profusion; on the stage his dramas won wide acclaim; philosophers and critics found in his scenes a wealth of imaginative magic. This being so, we might have thought that the new romantic drama would have attained its greatest achievements in the land of Shakespeare's own tongue and that from the poets of the English romantic revival would have come masterpieces based on his inspiration.

The Failure of the English Poets

It is true that every one of these poets made valiant efforts to achieve greatness in the dramatic form. From the earliest group of writers to the latest all tried their hands at theatrical composition. William Wordsworth produced *The Borderers* (composed 1795–96); Robert Southey and Samuel Taylor Coleridge collaborated in *The Fall of Robespierre* (1794), and the latter later penned his *Remorse* (1813). Lord Byron has numerous dramas, including the once-popular *Manfred* (1817), among his other works; John Keats wrote an *Otho the Great* (1819), and Percy Bysshe Shelley a *Cenci* (1818). Concerning the will towards the theatre exhibited by these men there can be no doubt.

Yet every one of them failed. We may, if we will, discern some virtue in Byron's dramatic efforts, particularly in his *Marino Faliero* (1820) and *Sardanapalus* (1821), and some erratic praise has been given to *The Cenci*, but not the most ardent of romantic critics have dared to find in any of the other dramas matter of abiding interest; even the laudatory comments made by some on Byron's and Shelley's dramas clearly betray a determination to find something to laud, rather than a genuine critical enthusiasm.

This failure to create a vigorous romantic drama cannot be attributed to one cause alone. Byron's plays have much in them that is good, and if we were engaged here in a consideration of the English drama alone we might be prepared to give them greater consideration. What prevents them from assuming higher power is the intensely subjective tendency of Byron's own genius. This was a common feature of the romantic temper, but when seeking for the basic reasons for the weaknesses in the plays of his companions perhaps we ought to give more weight to other considerations.

One such consideration is the cleavage between the poets and the theatre, due partly to defects in the audience, partly to the aloofness of those who would fain have had their plays put upon the boards. Audiences were rough in those years and their tastes vulgar; the poets were inclined towards solitariness; the two trends, reacting upon each other, served to drive the pair apart. The poets came to despise the contemporary stage; the spectators could find no joy in the rather dull poetic dramas which from time to time were set before them. The divorce between literature and the playhouse was well-nigh complete.

Above all, however, was the fact that the English poets were so thoroughly immersed in the Shakespearian style that all their efforts were remote from the spirit of their own age. Imitation of his works was inevitable, yet his style, so perfectly harmonized to the conditions of the Elizabethan age, could not provide the stage utterance needed by an age two centuries distant from Shakespeare's time, while the fact that the author of *Hamlet* had so deeply plumbed the resources of the romantic theatre meant that imitation of his work, in his own tongue, was bound to seem shallowly apish. Audiences and readers familiar with *Lear* and *Macbeth* and *Othello* could not be expected to feel a thrill of wonder and delight in the contemplation of works so closely akin to these in general aim and yet so far removed from them in freshness of imaginative power and execution. The excitement of novelty and the achievement of original form could come only in countries where no looming native colossus cast its heavy shadow on the poets, and where the influence of Shakespeare could enter as a freshening and invigorating breeze from afar.

The Romantic Drama of Germany: Lessing and Goethe

Such a country was Germany. Thus far the diverse Germanic principalities had accomplished nothing particularly noteworthy in the dramatic form, and, although Gottsched had succeeded in imposing a trifle of shapeliness on a hitherto inchoate stage, the shapeliness was of a classic mould ill-fitted to meet the needs of a new generation. The time was ripe here for a great awakening.

That awakening was foreshadowed in the work of Gotthold Ephraim Lessing. In the year 1765 the Hamburg National Theatre was established, destined to become, two years later, the German National Theatre, and with it came a hitherto undreamed-of periodical. Lessing had been appointed *Dramaturg* to the ambitious young playhouse, and, with the sponsorship of its controllers, he started to issue what is the world's first house-organ, the periodical essays issued collectively in

1769 as the *Hamburgische Dramaturgie*.

These essays were not simply occasional reviews of current productions. Throughout Lessing engaged himself in an endeavour, by means of direct criticism, to inspire young writers to turn to the composition of plays and thus to lay the foundations of a national theatrical art. His aim was at once practical and revolutionary: he ever kept the practical stage in view, and at the same time he ever sought to suggest that the pseudo-classic models favoured by Gottsched were not such as his age required. "The one thing we can never forgive in a tragic poet," he writes, "is coldness: if he arouses our interest it does not matter what he does with the petty mechanical rules." What he searches constantly for is form—organic form springing vitally from a genuine harmony between the subject-matter and the poet's untrammelled inspiration; and in his search he preaches the dual truth that the so-called 'rules' were right and proper for the Greek stage, false and improper for ours, and that, whereas the Greeks properly observed certain restrictions precisely because they were organic developments of their theatre form, the French classic authors were forced, while giving lip-service to the restrictions, to seek for means of circumventing them. By such observations and by the general power of his critical thought Lessing was able not merely to accomplish the negative task of destroying the pseudo-classic cult, but also to provide a firm basis for creative artistry of a new and different kind.

He himself endeavoured to put his own theories into execution in a series of carefully wrought plays, but unfortunately we cannot esteem Lessing the dramatist as highly as we may Lessing the critic. The *Hamburgische Dramaturgie* is worthy almost of being placed alongside Aristotle's *Poetics*, but the dramas—*Miss Sarah Sampson* (1755), *Minna von Barnhelm* (1767), *Emilia Galotti* (1772), and *Nathan der Weise* (*Nathan the Wise*, 1779), although all deserving of individual attention, and although vastly superior to anything produced contemporaneously in England, never succeed in capturing that elusive quality from which true greatness springs. All are heavily oppressed by the philosophy of the 'enlightenment' which cast such a spell over the author's mind, and are rather expansions of the sentimental than plays suggestive of a fresh endeavour. *Miss Sarah Sampson*, by the very choice of an English domestic theme and setting, betrays its close association with the bourgeois drama of London, while *Minna von Barnhelm* exploits a sentimental situation such as had already served half a dozen other playwrights of this school. Here the hero, Zellheim, penniless on his discharge from the army, refuses to marry his wealthy love—the heroine who gives her name to the play —and a happy solution is found only when a lost fortune is discovered, and Minna herself, giving out that she has become poor, pretends to refuse him in turn. There is a sense of character in the comedy and a skilful development of the theme, without, however, the creation of anything of first-rate value.

ITALIAN OPERA SETTING BY FRANCESCO GALLI
BIBIENA, ABOUT 1730
Uffizi Gallery, Florence.
By courtesy of the Superintendent of the Florence Galleries

ITALIAN OPERA SETTING BY BERNARDINO GALLIARI,
ABOUT 1780
By courtesy of the Ministero della Pubblica Istruzione, Rome

THE TEATRO FILARMONICO, VERONA
Reconstructed on the original plans of Francesco Galli Bibiena.
From *La Scenografia Italiana,* by Corrado Ricci (Fratelli Treves
Editori, Milan, 1930).

DRURY LANE THEATRE, LONDON, IN THE YEAR 1792

DRURY LANE THEATRE IN 1813
From *Edmund Kean,* by Harold Newcomb Hillebrand (Columbia
University Press, 1933).

BACKSTAGE AT THE DROTTNINGHOLM THEATRE
From *Bilder från Slottsteatern på Drottningholm* (Malmö
Ljustrycksanstalt, 1942).

Emilia Galotti has somewhat greater worth. The story is clearly taken from the age-old Roman tale of Virginia, stabbed by her father in order to save her from a tyrant's lascivious embraces; but the girl is now presented as a member of the bourgeoisie, her would-be seducer is a member of the aristocracy, and a new turn is given to the theme when Emilia is shown by no means unmoved by the lover's advances. Although there are scenes here that speak to us far more powerfully than anything in *The London Merchant*, yet this play too savours of the dramatic style that gave birth to Lillo's tragedy.

A similar judgment must be passed on *Nathan der Weise*, the subject of which had seen a faint anticipation in one of this author's juvenile works, a one-act drama called *Die Juden* (*The Jews*; printed 1754). Its sincerity of aim is unquestionable. Taking Nathan the Jew as his hero, Lessing shows this man, basing his whole life on such a 'natural religion' as was sought after by Diderot and his companions, infinitely superior in morality and in nobleness of mind to those who base their actions upon established creeds. Nathan is a Jew only in name; in himself he embraces all the virtues and none of the vices inherent in the tenets of Judaism, Christianity, and Mohammedanism. By the romantic device of introducing Rebecca, the supposed daughter of a Christian crusader, who falls in love with a Templar—only to discover that both he and she (brother and sister) are in reality the long-lost children of a kinsman of the Sultan Saladin (who had become a Christian just before his death)—Lessing strives to give concrete dramatic expression to his dissatisfaction with all existing creeds and, at the same time, to his belief that in all the creeds reside some elements of divine wisdom. This argument is further pursued when Nathan presents before Saladin his parable of the rings, a parable designed to demonstrate that the only true religion is that which most benefits humanity. The expression of this concept, however, does not equal the vision, or perhaps it would be more true to say that the vision so cumbersomely preponderates that what ought to excite and arouse us remains uninvested with that theatrical fire we look for in the greatest works of dramatic art.

What Goethe said of Schiller might be applied specifically to Lessing and generally to the entire school of dramatic writing that he inaugurated. "Philosophy," said the poet, "injured his poetry, because this led him to consider the idea far higher than all nature; indeed, thus to annihilate nature. He believed that what he was able to conceive must happen, whether it were in conformity with nature or not." Ironically, this criticism applies to its own author as potently as to any. Johann Wolfgang von Goethe was certainly one of the greatest authors of his age; as certainly, he was not one of its greatest playwrights. For one who was so keenly interested in the theatre and so actively engaged in stage affairs his dramas betray a peculiar lack of theatrical sense: his service as director of the Weimar Court Theatre seemed to teach him nothing. Ideas tend to rule in his plays, and intellectual discussions to take the place of action: the true transcendence of the dramatist is lost in the romantic subjectiveness of his art.

With Goethe's works we move into the full flush of romanticism, into the atmosphere of that movement which took its name from the title of a tempestuous drama of Friedrich Maximilian von Klinger called *Sturm und Drang* (*Storm and Stress*, 1776). Goethe's first work for the stage was the equally tempestuous *Goetz von Berlichingen* (1773), with its revolutionary hero battling against the forces of oppression in his day. This tragedy became a kind of Bible for all the young spirits of Europe animated by passion for 'gothicism'; among the earliest of Sir Walter Scott's writings is a translation of its rather turgid dialogue. In its patent imitation of Shakespearian methods of composition, notably the union of tragic and comic scenes, it served to direct attention away from the style of the would-be realistic domestic drama, and in its choice of a medieval theme it led to the vast wave of historical writing that flooded the stage of the time.

Goethe's next drama, *Clavigo* (1774), dealing with the tragic consequences resultant when the hero decides to break his engagement to Maria lest marriage with her should injure his career, has but slight merit, but *Stella* (1775), destined to be taken by English opponents of the 'German theatre' as the very epitome of immorality, calls for attention if only for the boldness of its theme, which shows a hero, Fernando, loving two women almost equally and finally settling down to an unconventional *ménage à trois*. (It is interesting to observe that in a later reworking the conclusion was utterly changed, and, with greater psychological probability, Fernando and the heroine find a solution for their troubles in self-inflicted death.)

The endeavour to preach a message, so clearly marked in *Stella*, becomes even more pronounced in *Iphigenie auf Tauris* (*Iphigenia in Tauris*; begun in 1779, completed 1787), yet perhaps in the end this may be regarded as Goethe's most successful theatre work. With interesting deviations from the original Greek treatment of the theme, he concentrates on the problem confronting Iphigenia. If she saves her brother by a trick—as she may—she will have given over her soul to lying; instead, therefore, she boldly tells the barbarian king who Orestes is, and endeavours, by working on his sympathy, to persuade him to permit the taking away of the statue of Artemis from the temple. Obviously her action is symbolic, but for once Goethe has succeeded in making the symbol concrete and in clothing a living character with the robes of the idea.

Not so much can be said of *Torquato Tasso* (begun in 1780, completed in 1790), which is little more than a psychological study of a morbidly sensitive poet, not dramatized, but merely cast in dialogue form. Tasso, the hero, becomes almost frenzied in his imaginative passions, is tormented by his hatred of the calm statesmanship of Antonio Montecatino, and at the end comes to realize and to admire the very qualities that had driven him to the verge of madness. The last lines, so full of autobiographical implication, by themselves reveal the undramatic nature of the entire work. As Antonio takes his hand Tasso speaks:

> Oh, noble man! thou standest firm and calm,
> While I am like the tempest-driven wave.
> But be not boastful of thy strength. Reflect!
> Nature, whose mighty power hath fixed the rock,
> Gives to the wave its instability.
> She sends her storm, the passive wave is driven,
> And rolls and swells and falls in billowy foam.
> Yet in this very wave the glorious sun
> Mirrors his splendour, and the quiet stars
> Upon its heaving bosom gently rest.
> Dimmed is the splendour, vanished is the calm,
> In danger's hour I know myself no longer,
> Nor am I now ashamed of the confession.
> The helm is broken, and on every side
> The reeling vessel splits. The riven planks,
> Bursting asunder, yawn beneath my feet!
> Thus with my outstretched arms I cling to thee!
> So doth the shipwrecked mariner at last
> Cling to the rock whereon his vessel struck.

Similarly undramatic is *Egmont* (1787), a play, set in the midst of the Inquisition, which deals mainly with the passions of the character who gives it his name. Although a Catholic, Count Egmont deplores the oppressions imposed, in the name of the Church, upon the Netherlands, but fails in his effort to relieve the suffering because his benevolent goodwill is not enough in a world of hard reality. And, finally, there is *Faust* (1808, 1831), a vast amalgamation of lyric and dramatic episode, of psychological probing, and of recondite philosophy. Difficult indeed is the task of discussing such a drama in the present context. Unlike any work in dialogue that had preceded it, the enormous scope of the play renders it unfit for any but a few experimental stage productions, and in this way it cannot be given such rank in the history of the drama as is accorded to the works of Sophocles or Shakespeare. On the other hand —and quite apart from the pre-eminent position the poem holds in the world's literature—there can be no doubt but that its vastness of scope proved a theatrically inspiring force, indirectly if not directly. By it men were taught to see that the dramatic form need not be used only for the presentation of themes narrowly circumscribed in content, and the way was opened for a vast extension of the stage.

Faust opens in Heaven and shows Mephistopheles gaining permission to attempt the destruction of Faust's soul: this permission is granted by God in the belief that, even if Mephistopheles succeeds in his evil intent, Faust will gain in spiritual wisdom through the trial. Then follows the first part of the play—a clear, dramatic story, in which Faust gives his soul to Mephistopheles provided that the latter can grant him a passing minute of perfect joy. The young Margaret is seduced; Faust kills her brother; she loses her mind, destroys her child, and miserably perishes. From this we move to the richly imaginative and exceedingly difficult second part, wherein the image of Helen of Troy is summoned from the dark backward and abysm of time. From her union with Faust is born Euphorion, who ultimately vanishes into thinnest air. Later Faust, growing old, becomes intent on reclaiming some submerged land, and in this task comes to recognize the truth that only through aiding others can real joy be found. In making this confession he acknowledges that Mephistopheles has won, for a moment of perfect satisfaction has come to him: at the same time, paradoxically, Faust too has gained the victory, and his soul passes upward into bliss.

The general philosophical purpose is plain, even if details remain obscure or hard of interpretation. This questing spirit of humanity represented in Faust seeks sensual, worldly pleasure and finds it inadequate; higher it searches in the realms of ideal loveliness (Helen) and of poetry (Euphorion), only to discover the delights of these worlds evanescent; and eventually, on the highest plane, it reaches to ultimate fulfilment of purpose in renunciation of self and thought for others. The mystical concept is a direct development of the concepts out of which were built *Iphigenie auf Tauris*. We are here in the presence of an imaginative vision which, if expressed in a form beyond the scope of the purely theatrical, obviously soars far above the mediocre philosophizings of the contemporary stage.

The Triumph of Schiller

Less gifted with imaginative power, Goethe's friend Johann Christoph Friedrich von Schiller succeeded theatrically where he had failed. There can be no doubt that since the times of Shakespeare, Molière, and Racine no greater dramatist had appeared on the horizon and that his works deserve to be placed, if not on a level with the writings of these men, at least close in their company. There is a comprehensive sweep here that marks the hand of an expert and masterly playwright.

Like Goethe, he commenced his literary career in the midst of an atmosphere of 'Sturm und Drang,' full of dark medieval fancies, the gloom of pessimism, and turbulent revolutionary sentiment. Out of this grew *Die Räuber* (*The Robbers*, 1781), an extraordinary work for a youth of twenty-two, and one that, in spite of some absurdities, has held the stage from its original production at Mannheim until to-day. The robber-hero (conceived in the spirit of a Robin Hood who flees to the forest because of the exactions of tyranny) was popular at the time when the drama was composed, and Schiller acted astutely in choosing as his central figure Karl von Moor. This man, noble in soul, becomes the captain of a band of outlaws, whose sincerity of spirit is contrasted with the evils and chicaneries of the palace hall, symbolized in Karl's ill-souled brother, Franz. The combination of 'gothicism' in the setting, romantic incident in the development of the scenes, and implicit revolutionary sentiment made the drama an immediate success throughout many European lands. Schiller's star, blazing thus brightly on its first arising, was not destined to wait for later discovery.

Immediately following this triumph came *Fiesko* (1783) and *Kabale und Liebe* (*Intrigue and Love*, 1784), both born of the same mood, and produced during the years when the young rebel, having fled from his native Württemberg, was acting as *Dramaturg* at the theatre of Mannheim. Neither adds very greatly to the achievement of *The Robbers*, although both show the poet gaining in his grasp of the stage and in his handling of character. The former is again revolutionary in spirit. Set in Genoa in the year 1547, it concentrates upon the brutal Gianettino Doria, heir to the dominion of his aged uncle, Andreas Doria, and upon the handsome, dashing figure of the hero, Fiesko, Count of Lavagna, one who, in spite of his excellent qualities, is cursed with the sin of pride, and who conceals an element of selfish deceit beneath his noble exterior. In *Intrigue and Love* Schiller turns from the past to try his hand at domestic tragedy cast in the Lessing mould, telling the dismal story of the fair Louisa, a simple civic musician's daughter, who loves and is loved by Major Ferdinand, son of the aristocratic President von Walther. By the intrigue of this proud old nobleman the loves of the young officer and the common maid are destroyed; Louisa pitiably dies, Ferdinand follows her, and the President is left in despair, his household shattered and his character publicly ruined. Although it may be admitted that *Kabale und Liebe* is not one of the world's greatest plays, we must recognize that it was the first domestic drama in Europe to reach something approaching majesty of proportion.

All these plays had been written in prose, but Schiller essentially was a poet, and in his next play, *Don Carlos* (1787), he turned to verse dialogue, producing a work which, despite its inordinate length, indicates a marked advance in dramatic concept. A political theme is here wrought with a tragedy of love. Philip II, the King of Spain, is a brutal tyrant, and against his cruelties, particularly in the Netherlands, his son and heir, Don Carlos, is in sharp revolt. At the same time this prince finds his heart sorely torn, for Philip has married Elizabeth de Valois, to whom Carlos himself had been betrothed and with whom he is still passionately in love. Carlos is the hero of the play, not perfect in his character, but endowed with basic nobility and majesty of soul; at his side stands the devoted Marquis de Posa, his friend and the character through whom Schiller most clearly reveals his purpose. Carlos can think only in terms of passion and violent revolution; the Marquis is a man who sees the world as yet unripe for his ideal, who realizes that "the rage for innovation but serves to increase the heavy weight of chains it cannot break," and who yet succeeds, by the powerfulness and sincerity of his arguments, in arousing the King's conscience when opposition had merely hardened his tyrannical will. As his first flush of success begins to fade and Carlos seems bound for destruction, the Marquis bravely sacrifices

himself, although by that time the force of circumstance has pressed too
far to permit his sacrifice to be other than vain. In a trenchant scene the
King stands before the Grand Inquisitor, abject in front of a power
greater than his own, and gives his son over to the terrible arm of Rome:

GRAND INQUISITOR: I am not minded, King,
  To seek such interviews again.
KING: But one—
  One service more—the last—and then in peace
  Depart. Let all the past be now forgotten—
  Let peace be made between us. We are friends.
GRAND INQUISITOR: When Philip bends with due humility.
KING [after a pause]: My son is meditating treason.
GRAND INQUISITOR: Well!
  And what do you resolve?
KING: On all, or nothing.
GRAND INQUISITOR: What mean you by this all?
KING: He must escape,
  Or die.
GRAND INQUISITOR: Well, Sire! decide.
KING: And can you not
  Establish some new creed to justify
  The bloody murder of one's only son?
GRAND INQUISITOR: To appease eternal justice, God's own Son
  Expired upon the cross.
KING: And can you spread
  This creed throughout all Europe?
GRAND INQUISITOR: Ay, so far
  As the true cross is worshipp'd.
KING: But I sin—
  Sin against nature. Canst thou, by thy power,
  Silence her mighty voice?
GRAND INQUISITOR: The voice of nature
  Avails not over faith.
KING: My right to judge
  I place within your hands. Can I retrace
  The step once taken?
GRAND INQUISITOR: Give him up to me!
KING: My only son!—For whom then have I labour'd?
GRAND INQUISITOR: For the grave rather than for liberty.
KING [rising up]:   We are agreed. Come with me.
GRAND INQUISITOR: Monarch! Whither?
KING: From his own father's hands, to take the victim.

In this drama of *Don Carlos* Schiller demonstrated what he sought in
the exploitation of tragic historical themes. A strong philosophical purpose constantly animated his mind, and in his scenes, without having
recourse to any overt symbolic devices, he strove to present the truth as
he saw it. Aristotle's declaration that the poet presents a more philosophical conception of events than ever the historian can would have won

his complete approbation, and in the several plays he was yet to write on records of the past he consistently endeavoured to weld his material into an imaginative pattern. As a moralist, he believed that herin lay the ultimate justification for the dramatic form.

This sense of philosophical purpose is to be seen nowhere more clearly than in his next play, in which he turned from a Spanish to a German theme. *Wallenstein* is a trilogy consisting of *Das Lager* (*The Camp*, 1798), *Die Piccolomini* (*The Piccolomini*), and *Wallensteins Tod* (*Wallenstein's Death*; both in 1799). Nothing equal to this in scope and performance had appeared since the writing of Shakespeare's history plays, and, despite the fact that Schiller has not proved able to condense his plot sufficiently, we must recognize in these three connected dramas one of the greatest achievements of the stage. There is a sweep here, and a force, which rarely has been paralleled in theatrical composition.

The Camp is to be regarded as a prologue, introducing none of the main characters, but providing instead a magnificent picture of the army commanded by Count Albrecht von Wallenstein, in the name of the Emperor Ferdinand II—a motley collection of men of all nations, held together by the will and genius of their general. *The Piccolomini* shows the growing cleavage between Wallenstein and the Imperial Court. Intrigue is at work, and, now that the army has driven back the Swedes, the palace has begun to look with suspicion and fear upon the instrument of its might. Realizing that a definite break is inevitable, Field-Marshal Illo and Count Terzky by a trick persuade almost all the officers to sign a document pledging their loyalty to Wallenstein alone, hoping thereby that he will be persuaded to take definite action, repudiate the Emperor, and establish an independent state in league with the Swedes. Meanwhile, however, the Imperial Envoy von Questenberg has found an ally in the ambitious Lieutenant-General Octavio Piccolomini, who, pretending to be one of Wallenstein's most devoted followers, is hoping that he himself may become the commander-in-chief. His son, Max, colonel of a regiment of cuirassiers and an upright, noble figure, finds himself torn in spirit. He detests his father's intrigues, yet is tied to him in filial affection: loyalty to the Emperor clashes with his boundless admiration of Wallenstein and with his love of the general's daughter, Thekla. The last part of the trilogy shows Wallenstein driven desperately to throw over his allegiance and deserted by most of his officers through the machinations of Octavio Piccolomini, who, at the very close of the play, achieves his reward in being created a prince.

The entire work is a complex study in pride and ambition. Piccolomini intrigues in order that he may be ennobled, the Irish officer Butler, hitherto faithful to Wallenstein, is persuaded to desert him and to engineer his assassination because of a slight; Wallenstein's own failing is the taint of overweening pride and belief in his ascendant star. One of the most revealing and dramatic scenes is that in which the Countess Terzky plays on the hero's failings and wins him to rebellion:

WALLENSTEIN: If there were yet a choice! if yet some milder
　　Way of escape were possible—I still
　　Will choose it, and avoid the last extreme.
COUNTESS: Desirest thou nothing further? Such a way
　　Lies still before thee. Send this Wrangel off.
　　Forget thou thy old hopes, cast far away
　　All thy past life: determine to commence
　　A new one. Virtue hath her heroes too,
　　As well as fame and fortune. To Vienna
　　Hence—to the Emperor—kneel before the throne;
　　Take a full coffer with thee—say aloud,
　　Thou didst but wish to prove thy fealty;
　　Thy whole intention but to dupe the Swede. . . .
　　　　　　　　On some morrow morning
　　The Duke departs; and now 'tis stir and bustle
　　Within his castles. He will hunt, and build;
　　Superintend his horses' pedigrees,
　　Creates himself a court, gives golden keys,
　　And introduceth strictest ceremony
　　In fine proportions, and nice etiquette;
　　Keeps open table with high cheer: in brief,
　　Commenceth mighty King—in miniature. . . .
WALLENSTEIN [*in extreme agitation*]: Take her away.
　　Let in the young Count Piccolomini.
COUNTESS: Art thou in earnest? I entreat thee! Canst thou
　　Consent to bear thyself to thy own grave,
　　So ignominiously to be dried up?
　　Thy life, that arrogated such a height
　　To end in such a nothing! To be nothing,
　　When one was always nothing, is an evil
　　That asks no stretch of patience, a light evil;
　　But to become a nothing, having been——
WALLENSTEIN [*starts up in violent agitation*]:
　　Show me a way out of this stifling crowd,
　　Ye powers of Aidance! Show me such a way
　　As *I* am capable of going. I
　　Am no tongue-hero, no fine virtue-prattler;
　　I cannot warm by thinking; cannot say
　　To the good luck that turns her back upon me,
　　Magnanimously: "Go; I need thee not."
　　Cease I to work, I am annihilated.
　　Dangers nor sacrifices will I shun,
　　If so I may avoid the last extreme;
　　But ere I sink down into nothingness,
　　Leave off so little, who begun so great,
　　Ere that the world confuses me with those
　　Poor wretches, whom a day creates and crumbles,
　　This age and after ages speak my name
　　With hate and dread. . . .
COUNTESS: What is there here, then,

So against nature? Help me to perceive it!
O let not Superstition's nightly goblins
Subdue thy clear bright spirit! Art thou bid
To murder?—with abhorr'd, accursed poniard
To violate the breasts that nourish'd thee?
That *were* against our nature, that might aptly
Make thy flesh shudder, and thy whole heart sicken.
COUNTESS: Yet not a few, and for a meaner object,
Have ventured even this, ay, and perform'd it.
What is there in thy case so black and monstrous?
Thou art accused of treason—whether with
Or without justice is not now the question—
Thou art lost if thou dost not avail thee quickly
Of the power which thou possessest. Friedland! Duke
Tell me where lives that thing so meek and tame,
That doth not all his living faculties
Put forth in preservation of his life?
What deed so daring, which necessity
And desperation will not sanctify?
WALLENSTEIN: Once was this Ferdinand so gracious to me;
He loved me; he esteem'd me; I was placed
The nearest to his heart. Full many a time
We, like familiar friends, both at one table
Have banqueted together. He and I—
And the young kings themselves held me the basin
Wherewith to wash me—and is't come to this?
COUNTESS: So faithfully preservest thou each small favour
And hast no memory for contumelies?
Must I remind thee, how at Regensburg
This man repaid thy faithful services?
All ranks and all conditions in the empire
Thou hast wronged to make him great—hadst loaded on thee,
On *thee*, the hate, the curse of the whole world.
No friend existed for thee in all Germany,
And why? because thou hadst existed only
For the Emperor. To the Emperor alone
Clung Friedland in that storm which gather'd round him
At Regensburg in the Diet—and he dropp'd thee!
He let thee fall! he let thee fall a victim
To the Bavarian, to that insolent! . . .
WALLENSTEIN: I never saw it in this light before;
'Tis even so. The Emperor perpetrated
Deeds through my arm, deeds most unorderly,
And even this prince's mantle, which I wear,
I owe to what were services to him,
But most high misdemeanours 'gainst the Empire. . . .
Despatch three couriers——

And the die is cast. In the long scene of which the above is but a fragment the Countess has played upon his pride and superstition until he is forced, albeit almost against his will, to take decisive action—the action that his enemies were waiting for and that is to lead to his death.

Than *Wallenstein* Schiller never achieved anything more masterly or more majestic, yet still, despite his rapidly failing health, he had power left to create some plays worthy of regard.

Maria Stuart came in 1800. Imprisoned in England, Mary has a faithful servant in young Mortimer and a weak, innately deceitful one in Leicester. In the key scene of the play, and one by no means without power, the two queens confront each other, and with skill Schiller contrasts them —Elizabeth wary, cautious, apparently frank, Mary apt to let her passions guide her. Almost wearily the latter offers to resign her pretensions to the English throne:

> Then, sister, not for all this island's wealth,
> For all the realms encircled by the deep,
> Would I exchange my present lot for yours.

Such, however, is not sufficient for Elizabeth, and with politic art she flings taunts apt to put into Mary's mouth words destined to doom her:

> And you confess at last that you are conquer'd?
> Are all your schemes run out? No more assassins
> Now on the road? Will no adventurer
> Attempt again, for you, the sad achievement?
> Yes, madam, it is over. You'll seduce
> No mortal more. The world has other cares—
> None is ambitious of the dang'rous honour
> Of being your fourth husband. You destroy
> Your wooers like your husbands.

Despite Mary's cry,

> Sister, sister!
> Grant me forbearance, all ye pow'rs of heav'n!

she is goaded into a wild outburst of fury:

> A bastard soils,
> Profanes the English throne! The gen'rous Britons
> Are cheated by a juggler, whose whole figure
> Is false and painted, heart as well as face!
> If right prevail'd, you now would in the dust
> Before me lie, for I'm your rightful monarch!

Elizabeth retires, and Schiller astutely makes the Scottish queen wholly unconscious of what she has done. All she can think of is her triumph in having abased Elizabeth, and in the glow of the besotted Mortimer's praise she ignores the tremulous fears of her other counsellors and fails to see the axe she has herself poised above her head. In scenes such as these

Schiller reveals his strength, and, though, like all dramatic authors who have dealt with Mary Queen of Scots, he is sentimentally intoxicated with the romantic legend which is hung about her name, these scenes give real distinction to his tragic theme.

Maria Stuart was followed in 1801 with another 'she-tragedy,' *Die Jung-frau von Orleans* (*The Maid of Orleans*), and one, unhappily, still more deeply soaked in romantic tears. Despite the fact that for years it proved popular on the German stage, we cannot esteem it a great play: no valid central idea gives life to the historical record, no power irradiates the character of the sentimentally conceived Joan of Arc. This study of high idealism, sullied by the world and eventually finding self-purification, fails to achieve its object.

As though he himself were aware of the softening of his romantic mood, Schiller turned in his next play, *Die Braut von Messina* (*The Bride of Messina*, 1803), to a would-be classic style—going so far, indeed, as to imitate the Greeks in the use of the chorus. By introducing this element he believed he was declaring "open and honourable warfare against naturalism in art"; by its means, he pleaded, the modern poet might "transform the commonplace actual world into the old poetical one"; through it lyricism might once more return to the stage. In his idea the chorus should and could be "a general conception . . . represented by a palpable body which appeals to the senses with an imposing grandeur." Unfortunately, for all the beauty wrought into this play, we cannot regard it as a real triumph. The old cloying, romantic sentiment vitiates the strength of its tale of fraternal jealousy between Don Manuel and Don Cæsar, both in love with a girl who turns out, tragically, to be their own sister.

His last play was *Wilhelm Tell* (1804). Basically it is a drama apt to make popular appeal, yet in it are clearly to be seen the defects which prevented Schiller from completely rivalling the earlier masters. The desire to inculcate an idea—the determination to resist oppression and to oppose tyrannical power—leads the author into dividing his charac-ters sharply into the good and the bad, the white and black, so that subt-lety is lost and didacticism pervades the treatment of the scenes. Even more serious is the fact that, as the play advances, the hero is left without a genuinely tragic choice. At the beginning Tell is confronted with the necessity of electing death or the trial of his skill by shooting an arrow at an apple on his son's head; bravely he seizes on the former. The test, however, is rendered spuriously melodramatic, since Tell learns that if he does not make the trial both he and his son will perish. Perhaps, how-ever, Schiller inwardly imagined his theme not so much in terms of the romantic trial itself as in terms of the contrast introduced in the last act. Immediately after Tell's famed skill with the bow has vindicated itself he lies in wait for the cruel Governor Gessler and slays him, conscious that he has acted in the interest of his fellows. Later a man clad in monk's robes comes to his house:

MONK: Are you that Tell that slew the governor?
TELL: Yes, I am he. I hide the fact from no man.
MONK: You are that Tell! Ah! it is God's own hand
That hath conducted me beneath your roof.
TELL [examining him closely]: You are no monk. Who are you?
MONK: You have slain
The governor, who did you wrong. I, too,
Have slain a foe, who late denied me justice.
He was no less your enemy than mine.
I've rid the land of him.
TELL [drawing back]: Thou art—oh, horror!
In—children, children—in without a word!
Go, my dear wife! Go! Go! Unhappy man,
Thou shouldst be——
HEDWIG: Heav'ns, who is it?
TELL: Do not ask.
Away! away! the children must not hear it.
Out of the house—away! Thou must not rest
'Neath the same roof with this unhappy man!
HEDWIG: Alas! What is it? Come!
                    [*Exit with the children.*
TELL [to the MONK]: Thou art the Duke
Of Austria—I know it. Thou hast slain
The Emperor, thy uncle, and liege lord.
JOHN: He robbed me of my patrimony.
TELL: How!
Slain him—thy King, thy uncle! And the earth
Still bears thee! And the sun still shines on thee!
JOHN: Tell, hear me, ere you——
TELL: Reeking with blood
Of him that was thy Emperor, and kinsman,
Durst thou set foot within my spotless house?
Show thy fell visage to a virtuous man
And claim the rights of hospitality?

Although he fails to integrate his material successfully, it would seem that Schiller deliberately wrote his entire play for this conclusion; and when we realize this we realize, too, that here, as in all his plays, the idea is predominant. Neither Tell nor Duke John is a real character in the final episode of *Wilhelm Tell*: they are symbols of conflicting interpretations of right and justice. In thus stressing the idea Schiller weakened his own dramatic expression, yet he was at the same time laying the basis for the later development of the nineteenth-century theatre. When we place alongside his dramatization of the philosophical concept those mass scenes in *Wallenstein's Camp* and the scenes of the Swiss mountaineers in his last play—scenes in which the corporate crowd becomes, as it were, a theatrical entity—it is obvious how much the dramatists of the modern era owed to his inspiration. We may smile now at his romantic enthusiasms and recognize their adolescent sentimentalism; but no such smiling can conceal from us their innate, even if not fully developed, strength.

Schiller's Successors

Following Schiller came a long line of German playwrights who tried, generally without much success, to exploit the resources of the romantic drama, and as we contemplate their work we see romanticism gradually becoming ever more and more tempestuous, ever more and more absurd. Morbid themes attract the attention of the playwrights, and the concept of fate, at first held in bounds, is carried to lengths truly ridiculous. Where the extreme of pseudo-classicism ends in chill sobriety the extreme of romanticism ends in dissipated excess: the fate of the minor pseudo-classic writer is to be dull, the fate of the minor romanticist is to be absurd.

Absurdities troop lugubriously on the stage of the German *Schicksalstragödien*, the tragedies of fate, that were so dear to Schiller's successors. Adolf Müllner turns out his *Der neunundzwanzigste Februar* (*February the Twenty-ninth*, 1812), so called because the family of an incestuous forester is slowly cut down one by one, the victims being summoned to their dooms as the extra days of succeeding leap years bring with them their inevitable call of death. In his *Die Schuld* (*The Crime*, 1816) is to be found a very compendium of all the ridiculously gloomy elements beloved of romantic melancholy. A trifle less absurd, but equally sensational, is Zacharias Werner's *Der vierundzwanzigste Februar* (*February the Twenty-fourth*, 1809), in which the hoary tale is told of a poor aged couple who murder a stranger youth only to discover that he was their long-lost son; and in his unfinished *Das Kreuz an der Ostsee* (*The Cross on the Baltic*, 1806), despite the presence of some scenes powerfully imagined, we wallow rather dismally in a world of pagan sentiment and early Christianity. So exaggerated is the *Alarcos* (1801) of Friedrich von Schlegel that it has been called a parody of tragedy; hardly less of a parody is *Die Gründung Prags* (*The Founding of Prague*, 1814), by Clemens Brentano, with its hopeless conglomeration of witchcraft and sensational incident. There are scenes in these works no less amusing than those in the satirical travesties of August von Platen-Hallermünde—*Der romantische Œdipus* (*The Romantic Œdipus*, 1829) and *Der verhängnisvolle Gabel* (*The Fatal Fork*, 1826).

Even those authors gifted with richer qualities sank into the morass, and the fashion spread outward so as to embrace the Austrian as well as the German theatre. A good example of this appears in the work of Franz Grillparzer, some of whose Viennese dramas may hardly be distinguished from the type of play being turned out contemporaneously by the intoxicated poets in the Germanic states. Just before Grillparzer's arising a change had been coming over the Austrian stage. Up to the middle of the eighteenth century it had given welcome, on the one hand, to the great Court operas, largely Italian in inspiration, and, on the other, to crude, if racy, popular farces. In 1752 the great Burgtheater housed a French company, and under its influence the styles of Molière and Racine came to predominate. Then, in the seventies, German actors came to replace the French, and the way was opened for the introduction of the romantic genres cultivated by Schiller. Grillparzer is the first native Austrian dramatist to essay the new forms.

The immediate result was his *Die Ahnfrau* (*The Ancestress*, 1817), wherein a crime committed against a woman of the house of Count Borotin is shown bringing its curse down upon the living Bertha and Jaromir, until the former poisons herself and the latter, after killing his own father, is slain by a fatal kiss bestowed on him by the ghost of the 'ancestress.' Although this drama exhibits a certain skill in the evocation of the eerie, obviously its theme is basically absurd. All Grillparzer's plays are thus wrapped in romantic sentiment. *Sappho* (1819) deals fervently with the love of the Greek poetess for Phaon, a youth who tragically discovers that his supposed passion for the lady was no more than an admiration for her poetic gifts. His awakening true love for the maid Melitta brings the action to a suitably tragic close. Despite the beauty of some of the language, the trilogy of *Das goldene Vlies* (1822) makes rather tedious reading, and as a drama not much can be said of *Des Meeres und der Liebe Wellen* (*The Sea's Waves and Love's*, 1840), in which another classic tale, that of Hero and Leander, is told with romantic fervour. A certain vigour appears in *Die Jüdin von Toledo* (*The Jewess of Toledo*; written 1837, acted 1888); there are excitingly contrived scenes in *König Ottokars Glück und Ende* (*The Fate and Fall of King Ottokar*, 1824); and an inner sensitiveness distinguishes the treatment of *Libussa* (*c.* 1848)—but we cannot esteem the author of these dramas an outstanding artist of the theatre. He is poet rather than dramatist.

More of worth is to be discovered in the writings of the erratic Heinrich von Kleist, who, besides his contributions to comedy, turned out some tragic dramas of a strangely tortured kind, in which the delineation of the passions almost anticipates the studies of similar passions made by modern playwrights. *Die Familie Schroffenstein* (*The Schroffenstein Family*, 1803) treats, rather untheatrically, the subject of the vicious influence exerted by two self-willed old men upon their children. In *Penthesilea* (1808) a morbid, brooding spirit surrounds the Amazon queen, who, consumed by love of her conqueror, finally murders him amid a weltering torrent of emotion. *Das Kätchen von Heilbronn* (1810), which succeeded in attracting some considerable contemporary attention, is equally morbid, depicting, with amorous gloom, a heroine willing to endure every insult and every indignity that her lover cares to put on her. More interesting is *Der Prinz von Homburg* (*The Prince of Homburg*; written 1811), in which a strange story is strangely told. Opening with a peculiar half-symbolical scene of a life-is-a-dream atmosphere, it pursues a love-story alongside a tale of honour and duty. With a perplexing admixture of irony and serious purpose, tension is built up to the striking scene in the third act where the heroic Prince, arrested and condemned to death for a breach of military discipline, suddenly loses courage in the face of death and, like Claudio in *Measure for Measure*, begs abjectly for the right to live. In his terror he is prepared to humble himself before the Elector, but finally, when he himself is bidden to decide, he declares that he ought to die. What gives distinction to this drama is not its almost mystic exaltation of Prussianism, but the way in which Kleist, departing from the straightforward method employed by other romantic historical playwrights, has invested his scenes at once with fantasy, psychological penetration, and humour. With this drama may be associated another, not dissimilar, historical study, *Die Hermannsschlacht* (*The Battle of Arminius;* written 1808, printed 1821). Here Kleist, following the lines set by F. G. Klopstock in his earlier proto-romantic trilogy of *Hermanns Schlacht* (1769), *Hermann und die Fürsten* (*Arminius and the Princes,* 1784), and *Hermanns Tod* (*The Death of Arminius,* 1787), mingles treatment of passion (sometimes skilful, sometimes jejune) with a conscious and dominating political aim.

None of these plays is a masterpiece, yet in each one there appears a frenzied strength that marks them out as the work of a man of genius who himself realized that that genius was flawed by defects.

Vast conceptions apt to shatter the walls of the theatre buzzed in the minds of these men. Typical are the extraordinary productions of Christian Dietrich Grabbe, whose *Napoleon oder die hundert Tage* (*Napoleon; or, The Hundred Days,* 1831) suggests a continent for a stage, and for the actors an entire army. Grabbe's other romantic-historical works —extending from classical themes, such as *Marius und Sulla,* through the fantastic, as in *Don Juan und Faust,* to the realm of German history, as in the 'cycle' of *Die Hohenstaufen,* are all extensive in scope and, although of some literary interest, are not particularly suited for the stage. Among them, however, may be noted the *Hannibal* (1835), distinguished by its interesting attempt to develop a kind of 'one-man' drama and by the vigour of many of its scenes.

There can be no doubt but that within the field of this romantic theatre we can find many elements which were to be seized upon and developed by later writers, but, in general, historical rather than intrinsic interest attaches even to the best of the plays written during these early decades of the nineteenth century. The poetic imagination of their authors was apt to carry them outside the frame of the stage.

The Trend towards Melodrama: Kotzebue

The German romantic movement tended to burn itself out and, as it progressed, to split in two directions. One of these directions is forcibly indicated by that strange theatrical figure August Friedrich Ferdinand von Kotzebue. Generally despised by the literary critic and

often neglected even by the historian of the stage, his was an influence
of profound importance in the growth of early-nineteenth-century
drama. He was the instrument by which Schiller's poetic style was
reduced to popular terms, and with Guilbert de Pixérécourt he shares
the honour of creating the most characteristic playhouse genre of the
time, the melodrama.

Perhaps there is nothing good that can be said of his literary powers;
perhaps his philosophy was insincere; but we cannot escape from the fact
that hardly any other German dramatist was more popular, in his native
country and abroad, than he. Of his many plays no fewer than thirty-six
were translated into English during these romantic years, and of the
thirty-six twenty-two were given stage representation. Among them
were the immensely popular *Pizarro* (1799), adapted by R. B. Sheridan
from *Die Spanier in Peru, oder Rollas Tod* (*The Spaniards in Peru; or The Death
of Rolla*, 1794), and the much discussed *Stranger* (1798), a version of his
Menschenhass und Reue (*Misanthropy and Repentance*; printed 1789). Between
1790 and 1800 there was a positive Kotzebue mania in London, and for
most people 'the German theatre' meant his works. He himself was
much influenced by Voltaire and Rousseau, and to their native France
he returned their ideas, Germanized and made theatrical: his vogue in
London was hardly less intense than his vogue in Paris.

In dramatic composition Kotzebue was the complete eclectic. Nearly
all his plays are deeply coloured by sentimental philosophizing, but he
permitted only so much of this element as he knew his audience would
endure. Of theatrical effect he was a consummate master, and for sensationalism, stage thrill, he was prepared to sacrifice much. He took from
his fellow-romantics their historical, often medieval, themes, and from
the *philosophes* of France their humanitarian interests. His range carried
him everywhere—from the world of the gothic past to the conquest of
Peru, from familiar domestic interiors to scenes theatrically built around
his own experiences in Russia. His was a restless pen.

His characters were composed in terms of romanticized sentimentalism, and it is through these characters, added to his sensational
development of plot, that he becomes one of the founders of the melodrama. The stock figures, the thrilling episodes, the artifically conceived
conclusions of his plays, almost cry out for musical accompaniment, and
it is easy to see how the impress of his style was laid upon that type of play
which formed so much of the world's dramatic fare during the early years
of the nineteenth century.

To attempt any analysis of his works would be futile. At the same time
attention must be drawn at least to a few which proved particularly
popular or received special comment in their time. First comes a group of
dramas, including *Menschenhass und Reue, Armuth und Edelsinn* (*Poverty and
Nobleness of Mind*; printed 1795), *Der Opfertod* (*Family Distress; or, Self-
immolation*, 1798), and *Das Kind der Liebe* (*The Child of Love*; printed 1791),
which excited attention because in them Kotzebue, with a skilled hand,

WATTEAU: "THE ITALIAN
COMEDIANS"
By courtesy of the National
Gallery of Art, Washington

carried the bourgeois stage beyond the position it had reached with Lessing and his companions. In the first he was sufficiently bold to adumbrate that popular late-nineteenth-century heroine, the lady with a past; in the second the tale is told of a man who has rejected the child whose birth caused the death of his dearly loved wife; the third, opening with an effective scene showing a poverty-stricken room in which lives an old blind woman, hitherto used to the constant attention of servants, who is unaware of the change that has come upon the house, deals with a wife, faithful to her husband in his distress and yet deeply in love with another man; the last treats of the fate of a natural child. Such themes for their time were indeed audacious; we can understand how shocking they appeared to some, how daringly novel to others.

In telling these tales Kotzebue makes full use of his theatrical craft and teaches many a trick to the later melodramatists. Here, for example, is the ending of *Poverty and Nobleness of Mind*, as it appeared to English readers in the year 1799. The bereaved father tells of his devotion to the memory of his dead wife:

PLUM: Yes, here she lives—I feel her presence—she is near me—how else could I feel myself so well? On this chair she has sat [*looking on the back of it*]. Here is still a little powder out of her hair, I have carefully preserved it. At this table she has sat and wrote, with this same pen, so many tender epistles to her happy husband! Here are her letters! Every one is a remembrance of her excellent heart! her faithful love! these gloves she knit for me—this waistcoat was a present from her on my birthday—this lock of hair was cut off after her death. Ah! and here is her picture!
[*He tears away the curtain.*
LOUISA [*with uplifted hands at the foot of the picture*]: My mother!
PLUM [*starts trembling back*]: Girl, what are you doing?
LOUISA [*wildly*]: My mother! my mother!
PLUM [*trembling, in unspeakable agitation*]: Speak! who are you?
LOUISA: She was my mother.
PLUM: Louisa!
LOUISA: Your daughter.
[*PLUM wishes to precipitate himself on her, his knees fail, he sinks back in a chair.*
LOUISA [*hastens to him and embraces his knees*]: My father! forgiveness!
PLUM: Are you really my daughter?
LOUISA: Does not your heart say, Yes?
PLUM [*on her neck*]: Yes, you are!
LOUISA: My letters were in vain; I was determined to try if I could not personally succeed in gaining your affection.
PLUM: You have succeeded! . . .
LOUISA: You forgive me?
PLUM: Do you forgive *me*? Oh, how could I so long deny myself this comfort! [*He lifts LOUISA from the ground.*] Beloved child! help me up—my knees tremble—lead me under the picture of your mother, that I there may bless you!

Such sentimental scenes, with just a dash of what to the period was riskily daring, brought Kotzebue much fame, even as similar scenes brought fame to his contemporary, August Wilhelm Iffland, who, less gifted than his contemporary, pursued this path in *Die Jäger* (*The Foresters*; printed 1785) and *Die Mündel* (*The Nephews*; printed 1785). Kotzebue, however, had many other strings to his bow. Another set of his dramas gives expression to the very best of Rousseauesque sentiments and effectively plays with humanitarian feelings. In *La-Peyrouse* (printed 1798) is depicted the fate of a man cast upon a desert island, who, while falling in love with a "young female Savage," Malvina, still retains his devotion for his wife, Adelaide. The conclusion is typical:

> *MALVINA* [*turning affectionately, yet with trembling, to ADELAIDE*]: I have prayed for thee, and for myself—let us be sisters!
> *ADELAIDE:* Sisters! [*She remains some moments lost in thought.*] Sisters! Sweet girl, you have awakened a consoling idea in my bosom! Yes, we will be sisters, and this man shall be our brother! Share him we cannot, nor can either possess him singly. [*With enthusiasm*] We, the sisters, will inhabit one hut, he shall dwell in another. We will educate our children, he shall assist us both —by day we will make but one family, at night we will separate—how say you? will you consent? . . . [*Extending her arms to LA-PEYROUSE*] A sisterly embrace!

Similar in spirit is *Die Negersklaven* (*The Negro Slaves*, 1795), in which the objects of compassion, as has been said, "show a remarkable acquaintance with eighteenth-century philosophy."

Closely akin to such plays, but more romantically sensational, are those written on the conquest of the Americas. Here *Die Spanier in Peru* stands out pre-eminent. From these it is an easy step to dramas of the type of *Johanna von Montfaucon* (printed 1800), and thence to those in which Kotzebue makes use of Russian themes—notably *Graf Benyowsky, oder die Verschwörung auf Kamtschatka* (*Count Benyowsky; or, The Conspiracy of Kamtschatka*; printed 1795). With constant variety he keeps his audiences interested and alert, providing for his successors both suggestions regarding form and hints for later plot development.

The Melodrama in France and England: Pixérécourt and his Successors

During these years when the German theatre was displaying such sudden and unexpected strength Paris had but little of worth to offer to the stage, and the reason is to be sought—apart from the political confusions of the time—largely in the determined retention by the major theatres of the classical ideal. The age was ripe for the cultivation of romanticism, yet Racine, buttressed by all the extensive library of pseudo-classic theory, forbade the development of a new literary style fit for the expression of the changing concepts animating an altered civilization.

At the same time audiences were anxious to see presented on the stage dramas of a kind different from those hallowed by critical approval, and hence arose that peculiar form of play soon to become familiar under the name of the *mélodrame*. Originally the word 'mélodrame' was introduced to France from Italy as a synonym for 'opera,' but by the beginning of the nineteenth century it had acquired its later specialized significance—signifying a popular play, with a sensationally serious plot broken by comic scenes, and accompanied throughout by incidental music. In this kind of production no attempt is made at securing depth of purpose or literary grace; hence the melodramatic characters tend to become a series of stock types, presented in simple terms of white and black, while the author frankly allows action to preponderate over dialogue. In developing and establishing this new genre chief credit must go to the Kotzebue of France, Guilbert de Pixérécourt, who, first coming before the public with his *Sélico, ou les nègres généreux* (*Selico; or, The Magnanimous Slaves*) in 1793, soon formulated all the elements of which his successors were to make free use.

Like Kotzebue, Pixérécourt was an eclectic writer, and, like him, he displayed wide variety in the choice of his themes. Popular novels gave him many a plot: *Les Maures d'Espagne* (*The Spanish Moors*, 1804) and *La muette de la forêt* (*The Dumb Girl of the Forest*, 1828) are from French sources; how far he ranged is shown in *Robinson Crusoë* (1805), *Les chefs écossais* (*The Scottish Chiefs*, 1819), and *Le château de Loch-Leven* (*The Castle of Loch Leven*, 1822). Emulating Kotzebue, he turned out a *Pizarre* (1802) and a *Christophe Colomb* (1815), and even fared eastward (again like his German companion) in *Les mines de Pologne* (*The Mines of Poland*, 1803).

None of these works exhibits any quality worthy of particular examination, yet a judgment must be passed on them similar to that passed on the writings of Kotzebue. Although they have hardly value as literature, their influence on the stage may not be minimized. Pixérécourt's theatrical skill joined with Kotzebue's in forming the brilliant technique of Scribe, and from the spirit of both was born the English melodrama. Although Goethe was no doubt right in resigning from the Weimar Court Theatre when Pixérécourt's *Le chien de Montargis* (*The Dog of Montargis*, 1816) was produced there—believing it beneath his dignity to be associated with a drama in which a dog was a hero—the fact remains that Pixérécourt knew his public and recognized that dogs were precisely to their taste.

It is easy to see how Pixérécourt built his success out of a determined formalization of elements already existent in the Parisian theatres towards the close of the eighteenth century; equally easy is it to trace the movement on the English stage towards the melodramatic form, years before his influence dominantly asserted itself. In 1802 Thomas Holcroft, already possessed of a reputation as an author of sentimental plays, adapted the French author's *Cœlina, ou l'enfant du mystère* (*Cœlina; or, The Child of Mystery*, 1800) as *A Tale of Mystery*, and thereby inaugurated the vogue for the new genre. At the same time the various elements making up this genre are amply displayed in such earlier works as the sensational *Castle Spectre* (1797) of M. G. Lewis or the *Columbus* (1792) and *Zorinski* (1795) of Thomas Morton. The fact is that the theatre, inadequately supplied by the literary authors with dramas of a modern tone, craved for, and in craving created, a popular form fitted to its mood. Pixérécourt and Kotzebue were not so much innovators as creatures of their time, extraordinarily sensitive to the current demands.

In England the melodrama flourished with particular success because of the long-standing monopoly that gave to the two 'winter' theatres (Drury Lane and Covent Garden) and the one 'summer' theatre (the Haymarket) exclusive rights in the spoken drama. Audiences were increasing; many members of these audiences demanded fare beyond that which was provided in the patent houses; and an escape was found by the opening of other places of entertainment—soon to be familiarly classified as the 'minors'—which were enabled to circumvent the law by presenting plays accompanied by music. Thus the melodrama met not only a spiritual need but also a practical need of the time.

In addition it met a theatrical need. Most of the efforts of the romantic poet were vitiated by their being too classical (Alfieri), too Shakespearian (Schiller) or too abstract (Goethe). The new type of modern playhouse called for a correspondingly new technique, and this the poets were little fitted to provide. Before any further advance in dramatic writing could come there was needed a fresh approach to the purely theatrical devices which might be put to the use of the playwrights—and here precisely the Kotzebues and the Pixérécourts were able to give suggestions of a vital kind. It is not too much to say that the line of development towards Ibsen proceeds from the fount of melodrama. What the early authors in this style gave to the stage was taken over by Scribe and later by Sardou; they brought the mechanics of play production almost to a science; and, although the distance from Scribe to Ibsen is indeed a far cry, technically the later author could not have composed his dramas with such ease had his undistinguished predecessor not made the path smooth for him. The melodrama may have nothing to give us of depth of thought or intensity of emotion, but it exerted a potent force in the development of the modern stage.

The Spread of Romantic Tragedy

While the melodrama thus swept over the popular stages of England and France, other countries, some of them for the first time proudly tasting the joys of the theatre, made noble, but in general fruitless, efforts to produce tragic works of majesty and distinction. For the most part these efforts, being pursued by poets out of harmony with the stage of their time, yielded plays which, although possessing literary quality of varying degrees of excellence, are to be regarded rather as texts for the reading than as scripts designed for histrionic interpretation. In view of the fact that our prime interest here is the playhouse, it were needless to linger lengthily over these many tragedies in diverse tongues: all that is necessary is a rapid glance at some of the more characteristic and intrinsically worthy contributions made in the various lands.

In Italy, where the Shakespearian style never took easy root, the mantle of Alfieri, after being handed to Giovanni Pindemonte, whose *Ginevra di Scozia* (1795) shows romantic sentiment imposing itself on classical forms, and whose *Lucio Quinzio Cincinnato* (1804) begins to display awareness of other methods than those established by the followers of Racine, passed into the possession of the great Alessandro Manzoni, whose *I promessi sposi* is one of the finest of the world's historical novels. For the stage Manzoni wrote his early drama *Adelchi* (printed 1822), set in eighth-century Lombardy, with half-real, half-symbolic figures, of whom chief are the King, Desiderio, a man who knows no law save the barbaric rule of the sword, Adelchi, his son, whose nature is transformed by Christianity, and the gently noble heroine Ermengarda. A second theatrical work, *Il conte di Carmagnola* (*The Count of Carmagnola*, 1820), presents a vivid study of a noble general who, enveloped in political intrigue, is condemned by the Venice he has served so well.

These two plays might have been thought capable of reviving Italy's tragic drama, but after Manzoni comes a long, dreary patch of territory stretching onward to the close of the nineteenth century. With his *Polissena* (1810) Giovanni Battista Niccolini had endeavoured without much success to arouse his countrymen to follow the original Greek models rather than those of Racine and Alfieri. This playwright's most significant work is *Arnaldo da Brescia* (1843), wherein is depicted the effort of the hero, aided by Ostasio, Count of Campania, to break the power of the Pope and establish a popular republic on antique lines: Arnaldo's effort is wrecked, partly by the overwhelming power sent against him, partly by his betrayal through the unwilling complicity of Ostasio's wife, Adelaide. In this drama, as in the earlier over-rhetorical *Antonio Foscarini* (1827) and *Giovanni da Procida* (1830), Niccolini's political aims are clearly delineated. Another political author, Silvio Pellico, famed for his fight in the cause of Italian freedom and for the vividly penned record of his life, *Le mie prigioni*, produced in *Eufemio da Messina* (1820), *Ester d'Engaddi* (1832), and *Tommaso Moro* (1833) three similarly conceived works. Patriotic sentiment also pervades the tragedies written by Count Carlo Marenco, all penned in the spirit of romanticism—which this author hailed as "the school of noble feelings": of these, *Buondelmonte e gli Amadei* (*Buondelmonte and the Amadei*, 1827), is especially noteworthy for its not ineffective portrait of an almost saintlike hero. Among the many dozens of similar plays that made their appearance during these years mention may be made of one other—the *Beatrice di Tenda* (printed 1825) of Carlo Tedaldi Fores, who, despite a mixed style compounded of borrowings from authors as far apart as Shakespeare and Alfieri, also succeeds in presenting a portrait of nobility in the figure of his heroine.

Political fire rather than theatrical glows in these dramas. The poets, as elsewhere, are seen to be removed from contact with the popular stage, where audiences who could have found no satisfaction in this rarer philosophic atmosphere eagerly inhaled the cruder air of the romantic opera and the clowneries of farce.

Other countries likewise failed to give any truly noteworthy contributions to the theatre in this style, although it is important to note the fact that it was largely from the romantic movement that diverse lands which so far had lain dormant found inspiration for the awakening of their dramatic genius. Even if little of consequence emerged within these years, the impulse thus provided is obviously of some considerable interest and importance.

Thus, for example, was Scandinavia beginning to stir restlessly in anticipation of an Ibsen to come. In Denmark arose Adam Gottlob Oehlenschläger. Stimulated largely by the influence of Schiller, he produced a defence of barbaric religion in *Haakon Jarl* (*Earl Hakon*, 1807), a tragic treatment of Teutonic myth in *Palnatoke* (1809), and a medieval love-drama in *Axel og Valborg* (*Axel and Valborg*, 1810), crowning these achievements with a not uninteresting work, written in German, *Correggio* (1809). This story of the almost saint-like artist, Antonio Allegri, amid his companions, is infused with much romantic sentiment, in which art is viewed as a kind of counterpart to religion. It is of interest to observe that here may be found the source of those many nineteenth-century plays that base their plots on artists' lives. Through his application to the historical stage Oehlenschläger's influence was widespread and powerful on nearly every one of the later-nineteenth-century Scandinavian playwrights: his dramas, although marked by common romantic weaknesses, had vigour and strength sufficient to make them appeal to minds greater than his own.

Sweden produced Bengt Lidner, whose *Grefvinnan Spastaras Död* (*The Death of Countess Spastara*, 1783) was once highly praised, and he was companioned by Erik Johan Stagnelius, with his poetic *Martyrerna* (*The Martyrs*, 1821–22) and his tragic *Bacchanterna* (*The Bacchanals*, 1822)—both men adding to the inspiring force of Oehlenschläger.

Similarly, an awakening is to be sensed in the far-off Russian realms. Although nearly all the dramatic works produced there before the middle of the century were comedies, we may by no means neglect the long line of efforts made in an endeavour to establish a serious poetic and a tragic stage. The earlier level of development is marked in the activities of Alexander Petrovich Sumarokov, an ardent admirer of the French theatre, deeply influenced by Corneille, Racine, and Voltaire. By the close of the eighteenth century, however, German influence was beginning to modify this Gallic trend, and shortly after came a still further impulse gained through knowledge both of Shakespeare and of Byron. With Vasili Andreevich Zhukovski and Ivan Andreevich Krylov the way was being prepared, and finally a major author appeared in the person of

Alexander Sergeevich Pushkin, more important perhaps as a lyric writer than as a dramatist, yet distinguished also in the latter field by his *Boris Godunov* (composed 1825, printed 1831). Obviously inspired by Shakespeare, Pushkin has here succeeded in presenting a vivid picture of the ambitious pretender who moves to the throne of Ivan the Great by murdering the heir, Dmitri, and is racked, like Macbeth, by the whisperings of his conscience. While not well adapted for performance, the qualities that Pushkin introduced into this drama—notably the treatment of the crowd and the deep moral tone infusing the entire action—render it worthy of highest praise. Unfortunately, beyond this one work Pushkin gave nothing to the drama: compositions such as *Mozart and Salieri* are poetic essays rather in the style of Browning's 'dramatic lyrics' than in that suited for stage interpreetation.

With Pushkin is associated the almost contemporary Mikhail Yurevich Lermontov, also deeply influenced by German and English romanticism. Schiller dominates over his *Ispantsi* (*The Spaniards*, 1830) and Shakespeare over *Maskerad* (*Masquerade*, 1835). Neither is a masterpiece, although the poet's own lyrical passion has given to the latter a quality capable of arousing interest in the theatre. In this bitter story of a man who, loving his wife yet possessed of an almost demoniacal fury, thinks she has been unfaithful to him, poisons her, and, when confronted by the truth, loses his reason, resides a psychological penetration of more than common appeal. Even in our own times *Masquerade* has proved successful on the stage.

Corresponding to the political poets of Italy, Vladislav Alexandrovich Ozerov sought to use the classical tragic form in *Dmitri Donskoi* (1807) for the expression of patriotic sentiment; while, later, Alexei Stepanovich Khomiakov seized upon the romantic style, as in *Ermak* (1827) and *Dmitri samozvanets* (*Dmitri the Pretender*, 1832), for similar purposes. Their efforts were followed by not a few authors of lesser import. These works may be neglected, but if only for Pushkin's *Boris Godunov* the Russian contribution to romantic drama is of considerable significance.

In Poland, too, the romantic spirit found exponents. The stage there had produced nothing of serious worth since Jan Kochanowski's sixteenth-century Senecan and Euripidean *Odprawa posłów greckich* (*The Discharge of the Greek Ambassadors*, 1578)—a play dealing with the Trojan war. Now came the work of Alojzy Feliński, with his *Barbara Radziwiłłówna* (1811), followed, first, by the writings of Józef Korzeniowski, author of *Piękna kobieta* (*A Beautiful Woman*, 1834), and, later, by those of Juliusz Słowacki, a poet who assumes a position only less high than that of Pushkin. Like his Russian contemporary, Słowacki too was largely inspired towards the stage by his discovery of Shakespeare's genius, and his finest dramas all reveal the strong impress of the Elizabethan technique. *Mindowe* (1833) reflects both *Richard III* and *Hamlet; Balladyna* (1839) similarly calls upon *Macbeth* and *Lear; Mazepa* (1840) has echoes of *Othello*. While we cannot rate Słowacki highly as a playwright, his scenes display poetic power, and the later development of the Polish stage owes much to his inspiration.

Precisely the same Shakespearian seal was set on the Hungarian poets. It was after studying the English plays that József Katona produced his *Bánk Bán* (*Viceroy Bank*) in 1819. This not unimpressive tragedy, set in the thirteenth century, tells how Andreas II leaves the governorship of the kingdom in the hands of the Bán or Count Bank, who becomes involved in a frenzied drama of domestic and political passion. The same theme, it may be noted, was treated by Franz Grillparzer in *Ein treuer Diener seines Herrn* (*A True Servant to his Lord*, 1828), and in noting this we may also admit that Katona's handling of the tragic situation contrasts favourably with that of his Austrian contemporary. A couple of years after the appearance of *Bánk Bán* Karoly Kisfaludy produced his *Irene* (1821), another landmark in the development of the Hungarian drama.

Of a significance still greater than all of these was the slow arising of the theatre in America. Up to 1830 the youthful States had produced nothing of fundamental importance, but clearly a giant was in the making. Its first beginnings may be traced back to the start of the eighteenth century (perhaps even beyond that date); definite advance came immediately after 1750; and with the establishment of the Republic there was a great expansive movement, during which theatres rapidly arose in the principal cities and touring companies brought their wares to the farthest frontiers. In the earlier years the actors had been but waifs and strays from London's minor houses; by the middle of the century American-born players were joining companies with some claims to distinction; when the nineteenth century opened many such companies were in existence, and the most prominent stars (Edmund Kean among them) were glad to make tours across the Atlantic.

Naturally the repertory was at first entirely composed of English classics and of more recent London successes; nor did this kind of repertory alter much during the romantic years. As in London, the comedy of Vanbrugh and Farquhar ceded place to the sentimental drama, and that in turn was swallowed up in the great melodramatic wave that came after 1800. Signs, however, were not wanting that this young playhouse desired to try its hand at the production of native works, and, although nothing much came of those desires, the urge was one later to prove fruitful. America's first native tragedy, Thomas Godfrey's *The Prince of Parthia* (1765), was dully neo-classical in the strain of Addison's *Cato*, and equally dull was the first native play on an American theme, *Ponteach; or, The Savages of America* (1766), by Robert Rogers. With William Dunlap arrived the influence of Kotzebue and Pixérécourt, and soon playwrights were nosing around restlessly amid spectacular Indian themes. James Nelson Barker produced his *The Indian Princess; or, La Belle Sauvage* (1808), while John Augustus Stone, capitalizing on this initial effort, won a measure of justifiable success for his *Metamora; or, The Last of the*

Wampanoags (1829). In those same years John Howard Payne, famous as the author of *Home, Sweet Home*, was turning out melodramas, such as *Julia; or, The Wanderer* (1806), and more ambitious 'tragedies,' such as *Brutus; or, The Fall of Tarquin* (1818); while some literary authors of the type of Robert Montgomery Bird, with his *The Gladiator* (1831), were trying to give dignity to the poetic stage. From his efforts stemmed the later and more worthy plays of George Henry Boker, whose *Francesca da Rimini* (1855) is perhaps as vigorous a dramatic work as any produced by the English poets of the age.

Even *Francesca da Rimini*, however, is artificial and lifeless. The American theatre then, and for half a century to come, could do no more than try its hand awkwardly at dramatic composition and give birth to writings of promise rather than of assurance.

Here, as elsewhere, the romantic theatre had little to offer. In the writing of drama control is necessary, and powerful scenes cannot be wrought out of enthusiasm alone. The poets had their minds inflamed and disturbed by political and imaginative visions, which made them incapable of paying due attention to the requirements of the stage; their despised companions, the melodramatists, knew how to pen effective stage pieces, but of higher purpose they had none. Looking at the drama throughout the world from 1800 to 1830, one can see only slender hope for better things; when, however, we take it in conjunction with what was to follow we realize that the seeds were at this time being planted which were destined, fifty years after, to germinate and to flourish.

2

COMEDY AND EXTRAVAGANZA

During this period of romantic gloom and political ferment men still knew how to laugh. The intellectuals at times were inclined to be somewhat ponderous, but the common folk, at least, still retained their good, hearty, healthy sense of fun. As in the realm of the tragic drama, so here a distinction is to be made between the more literary efforts in the field of high comedy and those in less dignified genres intended for popular consumption. To the melodrama corresponds the vaudeville, the extravaganza, and the musical burlesque.

Social Satire in Russia: Griboedov and Gogol

Pride of place, for originality of conception and grace of execution, must go to two Russian comedies—*Gore ot uma* (literally *Woe from Wit*, also known as *Too Clever by Half*; first acted posthumously in 1831), by Alexander Sergeevich Griboedov, and *Revizor* (*The Inspector-General*, 1836), by Nikolai Vasilievich Gogol. In these appears a spirit entirely at variance with anything contemporaneously produced by other European writers—a spirit in which may be discerned the genuine basis of a characteristically Russian comic realism.

Already in the eighteenth century hints had been given of the potentialities of a native satiric comedy. Even Catherine the Great found time from amorous intrigue and the issuing of ukases to pen (in French or Russian) eleven comic scenes, and in them, despite the German origin of their imperial authoress, a peculiarly Russian kind of ironic satire makes its tentative appearance. In *Peredniaia znatnavo boiarina* (*A Great Lord's Antechamber*, 1772) we are presented with a sketch in which a number of optimistic petitioners have their interviews and depart dejected or irate. *O vremia!* (*O Time!*, 1772) castigates provincial affectations and follies in the persons of three pretentious ladies, Khanzhakhina, Vestnikova, and Chudikhina. With genuine comic verve she ridicules absurd superstition in the person of Kalifalkzherston (a caricature of Cagliostro), the chief character of *Obmanshchik* (*The Impostor*, 1786), ridicule that is pursued farther in *Shaman sibirskii* (*The Siberian Sorcerer*, 1786).

That the quality exhibited here—the tendency to look directly at life and to portray its oddities; the desire to display the follies, duplicities, and, especially, the absurdities of men in society; the predilection to prefer a sketch of life to a formalized development of plot—was not confined to Catherine may be realized when we turn to glance at the *Brigadir* (*The Brigadier*, 1766) of Denis Ivanovich Fonvizin. In this entertaining comedy plot counts for far less than depiction of character and atmosphere. There is, certainly, an 'intrigue' by which Ivanushka, the retired Brigadier's son, is betrothed to Sofia, daughter of a Counsellor, while, with his own father for rival, he lays suit to the Counsellor's wife (like him, an ardent reader of French romances); but the real interest of the play, and the source of its comic spirit, rests in its vivid depiction of manners. Fonvizin has another comedy almost equally good, *Nedorosl* (*The Booby*, 1782), where appears a stupid young Mitrofanushka, a gentleman who wants to get married, "to-night if possible" to no matter whom, placed against the appropriate background of his ridiculous family, the Prostakovs. Thoroughly typical of this author's style, too, is his slighter sketch *Vibor guvernera* (*The Choice of a Tutor*, c. 1790), which gaily, if a trifle crudely, caricatures the absurd pretensions of an almost illiterate Count and Countess, who, in seeking to engage a tutor, prefer a French manicurist to a Russian scholar.

Only a few years later came the *Yabeda* (*Chicanery*, 1798) of Vasili Yakovlevich Kapnist, a play that delineates ironically and with a keenly realistic touch the trickeries of provincial magistrates. Another author who took the same path was Mikhail Matinski, whose *Gostinii dvor* (*The Bazaar*, 1791) indulges in similar satire and serves still further to develop the resources of that kind of native comic realism first exploited by Catherine.

Out of this tradition stemmed directly Griboedov's *Gore ot uma*, written in delicate, witty verse, deriving its strength from earlier pictures of life, but giving to these portraits a fineness and a precision such as the Russian drama had not hitherto known. Started in 1821, the comedy did not receive even a partial performance until ten years later, and a rigid censorship prevented its complete stage presentation until the sixties. Nevertheless it was eagerly read, and unquestionably did much to further the progress of the Moscow theatre. In form the play is little more than a series of comic scenes, but the vividness with which these are etched gives genuine distinction to Griboedov's writing. His hero, Chatski, the young man who is annoyed with the follies of society, moves forward with amusing grace to his final discomfiture. True humour is here, and sprightliness, and that peculiar element, so clearly marked in Gogol's work, of laughter concealing tears. Although Chatski obviously expresses many of the ideas of his creator, his intellect and his appreciation of society's faults do not save him; and at the end he remains a lonely figure, bereft of his beloved Sophie. In Famusov, Sophie's father, Griboedov depicts the worldly-wise functionary, against whose subservience Chatski rebels. The latter has just proclaimed his refusal to take a position at Court. "There you are!" cries Famusov,

> you're all so proud nowadays! You ought to inquire how your forefathers behaved: from their example you could profit mightily. Take, for instance, my late uncle Maksim Petrovich. He dined not on silver but on gold. He had a hundred servants in his house. He was positively covered with decorations. He rode in a six-horse carriage. His whole life he spent at Court—and what a Court! The past wasn't like the present. He served Catherine. In those days every one was a somebody. . . . And my uncle! What prince or count could compare with him? Though dignified and austere, he knew when to bow and bend. Once at a levée he tripped and stumbled, nearly breaking his neck. The old man groaned and was rewarded with a smile from Her Imperial Highness —she even laughed. And what did he do? He rose, adjusted his clothes, bowed —and fell again. This time on purpose. His fall was greeted with a roar of laughter, so down he fell a third time. What did everybody think? They thought he was very clever. His fall may have caused him pain, but it caused him to rise. After that, who was most sought after at the whist-table? Maksim Petrovich. Who received the most cordial greetings at the palace? Maksim Petrovich. Who received most attention? Maksim Petrovich. Who led in rank? Who was given a pension? Maksim Petrovich. You modern braggarts are pygmies compared with him.

After this Chatski's famous last speech comes with the force of a blow. "I'm sorry," he says to Famusov,

> every one is trying to explain to me something I cannot understand. . . . I seem to be moving in a dream. [*With passion*] What a blind fool I was! From whom did I hope to get a reward for all my pains? I rushed: I ran: I flew! I trembled, for I thought that happiness was near! [*To SOPHIE*] To whom did I whisper tender words of love? And you! Oh, my God, whom did you choose instead of me? When I think of it, my brains go numb. Why didn't you tell me straight out that you had turned the past into ridicule?—that you had ripped from your memory all the devotion that bound our hearts together? For me, no distance, no amusement, no alteration of place has made me forget, even for a moment, the days of our youth. I lived and breathed and joyed in the past! . . . And you, sir, father of this daughter, you who adore orders and decorations, I shall leave you happily dozing in your folly. I shall not upset you by asking for your daughter's hand. Another more worthy will come along to bend and bow his way to fame—one who may equal the talents of his future father-in-law. Now my illusions are gone and I am calm. The scales have fallen from my eyes: I am awakened from my dream. . . . You have unanimously proclaimed me mad —you, the amorous fools, the spiteful boobies, the sharp-tongued old women, the decrepit old men tittering with senile mirth. And you're right! A man can spend a day with you and not suffer for it; but he who breathes for a time the atmosphere you live in is bound to sink into permanent stupefaction. Away from Moscow! I shall come here no more! I shall speed without rest to seek a corner in the world where my tormented soul can find peace. My carriage! My carriage!

And the final word is spoken by Famusov: "What will Princess Maria Aleksandrovna say?"—the Russian equivalent of the English inquiry about Mrs Grundy.

Out of this atmosphere steps that greatest of all early Russian comedies, *Revizor* (*The Inspector-General*), by Gogol. The hero of this piece is no Chatski. Khlestakov is a young intellectual stranded, for want of money, in a remote provincial town. he is not either an idealist or a thoroughgoing rogue—merely a lively fellow, rather simple, but with an eye on the main chance, and endowed both with a sense of fun and a keenly observant eye. By chance the various officials of the town, expecting the visit of a governmental inspector, come to the conclusion that this young gentleman is that functionary arrived incognito. In the ensuing scenes Gogol, in a riot of laughable episodes, reveals the chicaneries and the peculations of the provincials, who, feeding on bribes themselves, thrust sums of money and other presents upon him, gleefully reflecting that the fact of their acceptance guarantees immunity for themselves. One by one they come before us—the timid Superintendent of Schools, the lazy Judge, the prying Postmaster, the ignorant District Doctor, and, above all, the terrified but forceful Chief of Police. With them other figures are associated—the Chief of Police's intriguing wife and coquettish daughter, the garrulous and stupid country squires, Dobchinski and Bobchinski, even representatives of the peasantry—for in *Revizor* the whole of Russia is depicted. At the end a letter written by Khlestakov and opened by the Postmaster reveals the self-imposed trick to the dismayed crowd, and in the midst of recriminations a servant announces, with due dignity, the arrival of the true inspector.

There is here a peculiar quality, hard to analyse. The satire and the realism alike remove *Revizor* from the range of Shakespeare's comedies, yet Gogol unquestionably shares some of the English writer's humour. A delicate measure is in his laughter; bitter as is the satire, sympathy intrudes. The characters are fools and rogues, but they are our fellow-creatures. When Gogol printed the play he inserted a motto: "The mirror mustn't be blamed if your face is at fault."

The same mood predominates in *Zhenitba* (*Marriage*; printed 1847), in which, farcically—though, by a paradox, realistically—the timorous bachelor Podkoliossin makes arrangements with a professional matchmaker for a bride, persuades a friend to make the proposal, and, after all has been satisfactorily settled, climbs out of a window and escapes—too terrified to go through with the ceremony. With gaiety, and yet with an undercurrent of emotion, the ridiculous situation is presented in such a manner as to throw emphasis not on the episodes themselves, but rather on the characters and, particularly, on the social *milieu* against which these characters are set.

It is interesting to observe that another Slavonic country, Serbia, produced during this time, in the plays of Jovan Sterija Popović, an atmosphere closely akin to the Russian: his *Laza i paralaza* (*The Liar and his Mate*, 1830) typically deals with the affectations of a girl who, after having received an education in the city, returns to her country home despising what she deems to be rustic ignorance and vulgarity; she is suitably shocked into sense when a Baron Holić, who has been flattering her fancies, is unmasked as a mere trickster. As in the Russian plays, the comic spirit derives, not from intrigue, but from the analysis of character relationships and from the presentation of social *milieu*.

The World of Fairy and of Folk

During these years, when Russia was slowly shaping a characteristic form of comic expression, some dramatists elsewhere were developing a dramatic style which, although all too frequently we neglect it in our consideration of the nineteenth-century stage, must be regarded as one of the most potent and fruitful forces of the time.

When we think of romanticism it is its serious 'gothicism' that comes to our mind. We are inclined to forget that the imaginative fantasy which produced the many poetic tragedies was channelled also into comic territory, where it served to irrigate the soil of fantastic extravaganza.

In Germany, within the decades that were giving birth to the tragedies of fate and the melodramas of Kotzebue, two interesting comic forms make their appearance. The one is the half-fantastic, half-realistic ironic treatment of the actual; the other is the exploitation of an impossible fairy-tale world in terms that institute a relationship between the fantastic and the real. For examples we need go no farther than the experiments in comedy made by two authors whose names we usually associate with work of a serious romantic trend.

Heinrich von Kleist's tragic dramas have already been referred to, but in addition to these he wrote *Der zerbrochene Krug* (*The Broken Jug*, 1811). The jug that gives the title to the play is the precious possession of Frau Marthe Rull, and when it is found broken a lawsuit follows. Before the single act is over it is discovered that the judge is the true culprit and that all the confusion has sprung from his libidinous attempt to engage in an amorous intrigue with Frau Rull's daughter. Outwardly we inhabit the real world here, but careful investigation reveals that beneath the actuality rests a kind of metaphysical basis whereby the hilarious plot serves symbolically to demonstrate a deeper theme. Something of the same is true of the farcical *Die Gouvernante* (*The Governess*, 1813) of Theodor Körner and even of *Der Datterich* (*The Braggart*, 1840) by the dialect poet Johann Elias Niebergall.

This comedy may be taken as illustrating one trend. The other appears in the writings of Ludwig Tieck. His *Leben und Tod der heiligen Genoveva* (*The Life and Death of the Holy Genoveva*; printed 1811), although once highly praised, is not very impressive: its tale of a maligned medieval lady who lives six years in a forest cave before she is restored to her husband reeks of the romantic-sentimental. The very similar spirit of *Kaiser Octavianus* (printed 1804), despite the adroitness shown by the author in the rhythmic forms of his dialogue, yields hardly more of value.

There is, however, an entirely different story when we turn from these serious efforts to the series of fantastic, fairy-tale satires that start with *Blaubart (Bluebeard)*, *Der gestiefelte Kater (Puss-in-Boots)*, and *Die verkehrte Welt (The World Upside Down)*—all printed in his *Volksmärchen* of 1797—and proceed farther with *Zerbino, oder die Reise nach dem guten Geschmack (Zerbino; or, The Search for Good Taste)*, *Leben und Tod des kleinen Rotkäppchens (The Life and Death of Little Red Riding Hood)*, both published in 1799, and the later *Fortunat (Fortunatus*, written 1815). In these Tieck does several interesting things. First, he follows Gozzi in investing fairy-tale subject-matter with satirical content. Second, he breaks down the frontiers between the audience and the actors, so that we have here a kind of romantic intellectual adumbration of yesterday's riotous *Hellzapoppin*. And, thirdly, there arises out of these two things a clear expression of that 'irony' so characteristic of Tieck and his circle. In *Blaubart* elements of terror, of symbolic portraiture, and of literary satire are inextricably intermingled. Satire directed against eighteenth-century 'Enlightenment' appears in *Der gestiefelte Kater* along with hilarious scenes in which actors and audience almost come to blows. In *Die verkehrte Welt* spectators actually do storm the stage in order to take sides in the fight between Apollo and the usurper Skaramuz. The plot of *Zerbino* tells how this sentimentally inclined prince sets out on a journey to find good taste and returns home to discover that his house-dog, Stallmeister, has become the Court philosopher: when he calls the dog a dog all are scandalized and he is locked up as a madman. Even more interesting is the treatment of the Little Red Riding Hood story, where the heroine is depicted as the daughter of corrupt parents (her mother is a rationalist and her father a drunkard) and consequently tainted by her environment: she is obstinate, self-satisfied, and overweening, so that when she is gobbled up by the wolf it is as a result not of childish innocence but of innate stupidity. The wolf himself is drawn within this circle: he too is the victim of circumstance, an idealist who has become embittered through disillusionment.

With these plays may be associated another. Among his romantically serious works Christian Dietrich Grabbe has a strange *Scherz, Satire, Ironie und tiefere Bedeutung (Farce, Satire, Irony, and Deeper Purpose*; written 1822), in which appears a wild admixture of characters—the Baron von Haldungen, his niece, Liddy, the poet Rattengift, a writer on natural history, the Devil with his Grandmother, and Grabbe himself. Perhaps this is an extreme example, yet in its very eccentricities it well illustrates the mood out of which these gambollings of the poets, no less than the ruder extravaganzas of the popular hack writers, were born.

In contemplating the development of this fantastic comedy, we recall the intense enthusiasm aroused in Germany by the discovery of Gozzi's *fiabe* as well as by such Spanish plays as Calderón's *Life is a Dream*. Among Schiller's works is a version of *Turandot*; Schlegel produced, in addition to his famous translation of Shakespeare, two volumes of the

Spanisches Theater (1803–9); Grillparzer not only translated Calderón's dream play, but also penned his own, independent *Der Traum ein Leben* (*Dreaming is Life*, 1834), in which an Eastern hero, Rustan, instead of experiencing events which he later believes to have been a dream, dreams in such a way that his real life is influenced by what he has experienced when asleep. This drama, it is true, is hardly a comedy, while the heavy-handed daubing of philosophical concepts in the same author's *Weh' dem der lügt!* (*Woe to the Liar!*, 1840) almost completely removes it from the realm of the laughable, but the spirit that animates these works is not far removed from that which appears in more gaily fantastic essays of the time.

Finally we may turn to the less pretentious and more popular stage pieces of two Viennese authors, Johann Nestroy and his more brilliant earlier contemporary Ferdinand Raimund. In Nestroy appears a combination of elements to be fully, and perhaps sometimes rather tiresomely, exploited during the half-century following his time. His plays are thoroughly irreverent, indulging in much burlesque of the tragic efforts of the time: they frankly exist for the purpose of entertainment and make no apologies for introducing the impossible and the absurd; their style is marked by an accumulation of sometimes amusing, but more commonly over-elaborated, puns. Taking the already existent *Zauberpossen*, or fairy-tale farces, popular on the Viennese stage, Nestroy fashions his eighty-odd comedies either out of folk-tale elements—such as *Eulenspiegel, oder Schabernack über Schabernack* (*Eulenspiegel; or, Trick after Trick*, 1835) or *Der böse Geist Lumpazivagabundus, oder Das liederliche Kleeblatt* (*The Evil Spirit Lumpazivagabundus; or, The Disreputable Trio*, 1833)—or out of non-supernatural material treated in a manner akin to that used for the handling of the miraculous. The latter style led almost to the threshold of the Pirandellesque drama of a century later. For example, in *Der Zerrissene* (*The Broken Man*, 1844) the hero, thought to be dead, lives among his old friends, while in *Zu ebener Erde und im ersten Stock, oder Die Launen des Glücks* (*Basement and First Floor; or, The Whims of Fortune*, 1835) the wealthy man living in a rich upper-floor apartment is forced down to the basement and the poor man vacates the latter to enjoy life upstairs. There is an atmosphere here of the wonderful and the fantastic, even if outwardly the scenes are realistic and all the characters persons of the day.

The *Zauberpossen*, however, found their greatest exponent in the person of Ferdinand Raimund, a man possessed of a dramatic skill far beyond that of Nestroy, and one, too, imbued with a richer vision. In 1823 Raimund produced his first play, *Der Barometermacher auf der Zauberinsel* (*The Barometer-maker on the Magic Island*), the title of which immediately indicates its style. In it a fairy gives three magical treasures to Quecksilber, a Viennese barometer-maker, much in the manner that wizards and supernatural beings bestow their favours in Gozzi's dramas, although the purposes of the gifts imagined by the two playwrights are different. For Raimund the device is employed in order to reveal the worth of good, honest, homespun integrity: despite the facts that Quecksilber has had annoyances in Vienna and that on his magic island all luxuries are provided for him, he is eager, when the time comes, to return to his humble home.

The next year saw th appearance of *Der Diamant des Geisterkönigs* (*The Diamond of the King of Spirits*, 1824). Here the story is told of a young man, the son of a magician, who is promised a statue of diamond if he can find a girl who has never told a lie. After many adventures and many a weary search he discovers this paragon, falls in love with her, and is granted her as wife—a gift that is "the finest diamond" that could be given him.

With increased mastery, Raimund pursues the theme of *Der Barometermacher* further and more effectively in *Der Bauer als Millionär, oder, Das Mädchen aus der Feenwelt* (*The Peasant a Millionaire; or, The Maid from the World of Fairies*, 1826). The entire plot here is concerned with a peasant hero, Fortunatus Wurzel, who is suddenly granted almost unlimited wealth—wealth that brings evil effects both upon his health and upon his character. Misfortune after misfortune comes, until at last his adopted daughter (really a fairy in disguise) flees his house so that she may escape a loveless marriage Wurzel is trying to force upon her. Left alone, the man who at the beginning of the play had been hale and hearty and who now is brokenly aged, repents and goes back to the rude and simple existence that had brought him peace of mind and the sense of security. Although the main emphasis is, as the title indicates, thrown on the peasant hero, the actions relating to him are bound up with fairy-tale material and with material which almost recalls the subjects of ancient moralities. The adopted daughter is a fairychild, and the riches that come to Wurzel are due to the fact that this girl's enemy is none other than Neid (Envy) himself.

This play at once reveals the essential difference between Raimund and Gozzi. In outward form the writings of these two men have much in common. Although the Viennese author does not make use of any stock characters (such as those of the *commedia dell' arte*), he follows a model akin to that of his Italian predecessor, mingling the world of the folk-tale with the world of reality, and seizing every opportunity of employing the contrast for the purpose of commenting upon contemporary life. Beyond this, however, the two differ fundamentally. Gozzi is an aristocrat who looks back nostalgically to the times of chivalry; Raimund is a good, honest bourgeois. The question of money hardly enters into the *fiabe*: as in *Der Bauer als Millionär*, it continually plays a potent part in Raimund's writings. In *Der Alpenkönig und der Menschenfeind* (*The King of the Alps and the Man-hater*, 1828) the central figure, Rappelkopf, has come to detest the society of his fellows, partly because of his unsuccessful matrimonial adventures—he has buried three wives—but mainly because some of his investments have gone wrong. The plot tells how he sets off for a life of solitude, meets the King of the Alps, becomes terrified, and decides to return home to his latest wife (an embodiment of all the virtues). There, however, the King of the Alps follows him in his own likeness—or, rather, in the likeness he had before he set out on his adventures. By means of the double manifestation of his personality at the end of the play the author develops his philosophy in symbolic wise. The false Rappelkopf—that is, the King of the Alps transformed into the Rappelkopf that was—is in utter despair because he sees himself faced with financial disaster, while the true Rappelkopf, now cured of his hatred of mankind and living an existence based on values higher than the material, tries vainly to dissuade him. When the false Rappelkopf dies the latter has been completely cured of his follies.

Obviously the motivation here depends almost wholly on monetary matters, and the same emphasis appears in most of Raimund's work. The very title of *Der Verschwender* (*The Spendthrift*, 1834) indicates how basic to Raimund's creations was the question of money and its effect upon human character. This play is almost a secular, fairy-tale *Everyman*, in which Julius von Flotwell, a reckless spendthrift, is the hero, accompanied by a devoted servant, whose moral qualities may be taken as representing the author's own ideal. Through the interest of his good angel, the fairy Cheristane, a strange beggar appears before him at certain moments in his career, and when, at the age of fifty, he finds himself utterly ruined it is the alms which he has given to this outcast that bring him joy and promise of a new life.

A play produced the following year, *Die unheilbringende Krone* (*The Cursed Crown*, 1829), brought the fairy element into a fresh atmosphere. The chief character here is a general, Phalarius, who, angered at his King, Creon, accepts from Hades a magic crown which will give him unlimited power over man and nature. As he puts this to evil use, the fairy protecting Creon discovers that the crown's fatal power can be counteracted if she obtains three things—a crown belonging to a king without a kingdom, a crown belonging to a hero lacking courage, and a crown belonging to a woman who, while not beautiful, seems so. The way in which these are secured provides most of the action of the play, and in this action, involving the ambitious Phalarius, the easily satisfied Simplicius, and the poetically fanciful Ewald, we recognize that here Raimund's tendency towards the symbolic has reached its extremest expression.

There can be no doubt but that Raimund expresses in vivid and delicate forms certain qualities inherent in the spirit of the age. In his writings is reflected a mixture of elements which appear and reappear in many a comedy of these years—the fantastic Gozzi-like flavour, the world-is-a-dream motif, the sense of life's pathos, and that other mood which delights to contrast the marionette and man—the mood that finds expression, for example, in the *Lustiges Komödienbüchlein* of Count Franz von Pocci, wherein irrepressible Kasperle brings mingled laughter and meditation.

As with the historical poetic plays, so with these comedies of folk and fairy we can find cognate works in almost every country. There is a breath of Nestroy and Raimund in *Kong Salomon og Jörgen Hattemager* (*King Solomon and Jörgen the Hatmaker*, 1826), *Aprilsnarrene* (*The April Fool*, 1826), and *En Sjæl efter Döden* (*A Soul after Death*; printed 1841), by the Danish playwright Johan Ludvig Heiberg. Typical is the last-mentioned comedy, wherein, by means almost Aristophanic, the worthy citizens of Copenhagen are reflected in scenes depicting the best circles of Hell. Akin in spirit is Heiberg's *Elverhöj* (*The Hill of the Elves*, 1828), one of Denmark's most popular romantic dramas. Here a racy fantasy colours a tale of misunderstandings, and lyric sincerity is combined with episodes ironically conceived. The main plot concerns Albert Ebbesen, who, loving Agnete, is bidden by his King (Christian IV) to wed Elizabeth. Fortunately Agnete is a friend of the elves, and their magic sway envelops the hill where the wedding is to take place. Only when Christian himself arrives is their power arrested, but they have already won their victory because, in delaying the marriage, they have given time for the King to discover that, by a change effected years ago in the nursery, Agnete is really Elizabeth and Elizabeth Agnete. The same fanciful quality appears in the Swedish *Lycksalighetens ö* (*The Isle of Happiness*, 1824) by Daniel Amadeus Atterbom—a work clearly influenced by Tieck's fairy-tale style.

In Poland comic peasant material was freely and amusingly exploited by the first truly notable playwright of that country, Count Aleksander Fredro. Some of his writings, such as *Mąż i żona* (*Husband and Wife*, 1822), are clearly based on Western models, but the greater part of his contribution to the stage consists of native farces, such as *Nowy Don Kiszot* (*The New Don Quixote*, 1826) and *Damy i huzary* (*Ladies and Hussars*, 1823), or of more ambitious comedies with a peculiarly individual flavour. Of the last group the finest and most characteristic piece is unquestionably *Pan Jowialski* (*Mr Jowialski*, 1833). This play, which might almost be called "Mr Jolly," is a minor masterpiece, in which an interesting twist is given to a *Taming of the Shrew* plot. The part of Sly is here taken by a novelist who willingly accepts the trick imposed upon him in order to gain insight into the beings of his companions—the members of Pan Jowialski's family circle. Full of fun and thoughtful laughter, *Pan Jowialski* is one of the numerous dramas of the time that deserve translation into English. This comedy is well companioned, too, by *Zemsta* (*The Revenge*, 1835), in which are presented lively portraits of two neighbours, Cześnik Raptusiewicz and the notary Milczek, who, quarrelling over a boundary fence, are involved in complex intrigue which at once springs from and serves to illuminate their characters.

For Italy the development of fantastic comedy presented no problem, since the tradition of the *commedia dell' arte* was still vital there; but it is to be noted that for the moment this strain was confined to the cruder efforts of the dialect theatres. Later the fantastic spirit was to blossom forth in the *teatro del grottesco*, out of which Pirandello sprang; during these early decades of the century Italian comedy of a more literary sort was, rather strangely, in the hands of such men as Alberto Nota, with his sentimental *Atrabiliare* (1812), characteristically set in London, his mechanically plotted *L'ammalato per immaginazione* (*The Invalid in his own Imagination*, 1813), his pathetically conceived *La novella sposa* (*The Newly Married Wife*, 1827), and his sentimental *La fiera* (*The Fair*, 1826). A somewhat similar atmosphere enwraps the plays of Nota's less well-known companion, Francesco Augusto Bon, an author who hardly got beyond the rather feeble satire of current romantic sentiment presented in the person of the *précieuse* Antonia in *La donna e i romanzi* (*The Lady and the Novels*, 1819). Bon's best work is his series of 'Ludro' plays, starting with *Ludro e la sua gran giornata* (*Ludro and his Great Day*, 1833). Still another minor playwright worthy of brief mention is Giovanni Giraud: typical of his writings is *I gelosi fortunati* (*The Happy Jealous Couple*, 1808), where a husband and a wife, each confessing to jealousy, discover that the green-eyed monster is, after all, only an instrument in Cupid's service. Here in Italy was potentiality rather than effective immediate production.

Into France the play of wonder was introduced and won particular success through the association with it of the popular music of Jacques Offenbach: the *féerie* is one of the recognized dramatic genres of the Parisian stage. And with these French plays are closely connected the teeming extravaganzas of the English J. R. Planché, who in turn passes on the tradition to W. S. Gilbert later in the century. In forms both crudely popular, replete with devastating puns and all the roughest kinds of absurdity, and symbolically ironical, the extravaganza spirit thus found expression nearly everywhere, providing at once what is perhaps the most pleasing dramatic compositions of these particular years and the basis for much interesting effort yet to come.

PART VIII

FROM THE MEDIEVAL TO
THE MATERIALISTIC

FROM THE MEDIEVAL TO THE MATERIALISTIC

BY THE year 1830 vast changes both in the social world and in the world of the theatre were in process of accomplishment. It is true that we cannot select a single year or a single decade to mark the frontier between one period and another; it is also true that the work of many significant writers extends over the early decades into the middle of the century; nevertheless there is every justification, particularly in so far as the theatre is concerned, for treating the four decades from 1830 to 1870 as a unit. During these years earlier suggestions for fresh dramatic paths were courageously explored, and during these years still further paths were, in turn, pointed out to the playwrights of the century's final decades.

The full flush of 'gothic' romanticism had passed away by 1830, and a new romanticism was in process of formation. Browning followed Shelley, and Tennyson Keats. Scientific invention, applied in diverse ways, was changing alike the lives of the theatre's spectators and the fabric of the theatre itself, and necessarily the drama, in accordance with new demands, altered its shape, devised for itself a new structure, adopted a fresh orientation.

Fundamentally this period was characterized by rapid industrialization and the coming to power of the bourgeoisie; the trends in those directions evident from the seventeenth century onward now reached culmination. This meant, first, an uneven conflict between the relics of the old aristocracy and the growing power of the middle class; second, concentration upon the city rather than upon the country; and, third, a long, slow movement of political reform. The dying world of Trollope was being engulfed, both physically and spiritually.

In so far as theatre organization was concerned, perhaps the two most potent forces were the substitution of the railway for earlier means of travel and the introduction of gas lighting. The first destroyed the relative independence of provincial theatres, aided the development of touring companies (utterly distinct from the touring actors of the 'circuits'), helped in the extraordinary growth of the principal cities, and brought the theatres of Europe much closer together than ever they had been in the past. Associated with the omnibus, the railway proved a practical means whereby the teeming middle classes could flock into

the playhouses, and, as a result, city after city found its houses of entertainment multiplying themselves. Save where national theatres, such as
the Comédie Française, were enabled by their special regulations and
opportunities to preserve the repertory system, this in turn meant the establishment of the long run and the rapid commercialization of the
theatre. There was money in entertainment, and as a result the playhouses more and more became buildings owned by men whose only interests lay in financial returns, while the companies using these
playhouses were, with increasing frequency, collections of actors engaged for the performance of a particular play, to be disbanded just as
soon as its popularity waned and a new piece had to be substituted for
the old.

To a certain extent the actor-manager system that played such an important rôle in England and in America proved a check to the complete
commercialization of the theatre during these three decades, but the
handwriting was on the wall, and even the triumphs of a Charles Kean
or, later, of a Henry Irving could not conceal the main trends of the age.

Gas lighting was first used theatrically towards the beginning of these
forty years, and soon a profound revolution was effected by its means. So
long as candles and lamps remained the only resources at the command
of actors all attempts at realism were bound to be half-hearted and ineffectual. It is true that from the sixteenth century onward men interested
in the production of plays had sought to devise methods of controlling
stage illumination, and that during the second half of the eighteenth century considerable progress in this direction had been made: when all is
said, however, the fact remains that before the introduction of gas lighting any devices of this kind were bound to be cumbersome and that the
sources of the light—candles and lamps—were bound to remain basically intractable.

The introduction of gas lighting meant, first, that the auditoria of the
theatres could easily be darkened, and, second, that the means of illumination could be completely and readily controlled. Hence the gradual
movement towards the separation of actors and of audience—a movement evident over a period of two hundred years—now became not only
possible but apparently logical, and with this separation the curtain took
on new significance. The curtain became both the symbol of the separation itself and the means by which a new stagecraft could come into
being.

In minor theatres the older staging methods, with the habitual use of
side-wings and back-cloths, persisted well into the modern era, but along
with these methods new principles were coming into operation. In the
main these new principles may be associated together (despite their variety and apparent diversity) as all aiming at the creation of theatrical realism. Throughout these thirty years, and for decades thereafter, the
public took a naïve delight in seeing presented before them stage pictures
which simulated such objects as were familiar to them in their daily lives,

and by an extension of this delight they rejoiced in watching the re-creation, in correct terms, of the life of past ages. Approaches towards both present and historical realism had, of course, been made even in the eighteenth century, but it was only within this time that full oppor-tunities were given for the execution of such effects and that the process was carried to its fullest extent. We need do no more than consider the English theatre and cast a glance, on the one hand, at the historical scenes so carefully devised by Charles Kean and, on the other, at the 'reforms' of Tom Robertson to recognize the truth of this assertion.

A further result is to be observed. Both because of the growth of the oc-casional company, in which actors were assembled for the playing of a particular drama, and because of the increasing importance of the stage picture, a demand was made for the presence in the theatre of a new func-tionary, the 'stage-manager' or producer. In the old days actors perform-ing in repertory were so familiar with one another that there was little need of the services of such a person; a leading player or a prompter could readily act as the convener of rehearsals, and the performance of a play take shape as a kind of collective effort. Now, however, inspired alike by sheer necessity imposed by changed conditions and by desires differ-ent from those in the past, this new figure arose and rapidly came to as-sume an almost god-like stature, co-ordinating all the activities of the stage, determining the type of scenery to be employed, and instructing the actors in the interpretation of their rôles. Within the realm of ordin-ary productions the stage-manager became a necessary part of a theatri-cal enterprise which, however humble, was much more complicated than had been generally known in the past, while within other realms —such as those of the Saxe-Meiningen company or Wagner's Bayreuth —he invested himself with Prospero's mantle and became a wonder-working artisan.

Under these changing conditions several kinds of dramatic effort flour-ished. In the main realism was dominant, although it is necessary to dis-tinguish several movements within this larger field. At the lowest level we may note how the old melodrama, persisting in its hold on the public, gradually moved from the exploitation of the imaginatively romantic to that of the sensationally familiar. Wicked lords of medieval vintage give way to evil squires, and heroines become simple village maidens or, later, honest factory girls. Here realism of effect takes the form mainly of child-like imitations of the actual—snowstorms and the like—or of equally child-like introduction of real objects—live geese or pigs or hansom-cabs. A higher level is marked in the plays written by Scribe's successors, where the formula of the well-made play is applied to episodes and prob-lems of contemporary existence and where the characteristically 'modern' play of ideas is adumbrated. On the third level something much profounder is attempted. In Germany Hebbel aims at the utiliza-tion of the realistic principle for the communication of ideas far beyond the reach either of the melodramatists or of the followers of Scribe, while

Zola tries to carry realism to logical extremes and invents the drama which is, in truth, a slice of life.

Although these realistic activities form the most typical endeavour of the age, we shall err if we concentrate all attention upon them alone. The older forms of romanticism, delighting in the depiction of past epochs, still persisted, if in changed shape, and won success. Indeed, the application of realistic methods of production to the older forms gave to the romantic play a fresh lease of life. And alongside of this we must remember that in this utilitarian age when scientists were busy ousting the elves there remained a strange, persistent, almost nostalgic love of fairyland. Fancy, despised of science, became a familiar stage character during these four decades, and the impossibilities of the extravaganza, summoned forth by her magic wand, were welcomed along with the increasingly grim depiction of the real.

1

THE REALM OF FANCY

PERHAPS it may not be unfitting to consider the extravaganza first, and in doing so we may extend our gaze beyond the stricter limits of these forty years in order to see, if not its culmination, at least its highly characteristic expression in the work of Gilbert. Although the extravaganza is by no means the most representative dramatic trend of the age, so frequently do we permit ourselves to forget the fairy element in our contemplation of austerer realism that there is virtue in thus fixing in our minds what was without doubt a potent theatrical force—one that produced some of the most enduring stage pieces during the age in question and that was destined to influence considerably the course of the drama in the twentieth century.

The Extravaganza and the Fairy Play

The extravaganza did not by any means die out with the first decades of the century, and in many countries—particularly England, the United States, and France—burlesques and similarly conceived pieces continued to attract their enthusiastic audiences. Most of these, it is true, have but little worth. Hack writer after hack writer turned out these works with crudely conceived scenes and with little more than wild collections of puns to maintain the merriment.

In the writings of J. R. Planché, however, we can discern an effort to make of the extravaganza form something of more enduring worth. Planché was no genius, yet his limited measure of success and the fact that he is the lineal ancestor of Gilbert give him a measure of importance. Of particular significance in his work is the conscious exploitation of the fairy play. Although he does not have the power of a Raimund to invest his scenes with a moral purpose, and although his touch is heavier and less expert than that of Gozzi, he has a verve of his own, and his tinkling dialogue, replete with fantastic puns, proved vastly popular in his time. From his first burlesque of 1818, *Amoroso, King of Little Britain*, to his final lyrics in the fairy spectacle of *Babil and Bijou* in 1872 he kept the stage supplied, frequently through material derived from the Countess de Murat's *Cabinet des fées*, with a constant series of extravagant fancies. A common sentiment was expressed in a letter to this author by J.

Hamilton Reynolds in 1850. "What I like about your fairy dramas," he wrote,

> is their truth in delicate humour, and the perfect understanding you shew of the nice art of Burlesque *in flower.* . . . You inform grown-up beings how they may be reflected in fairy mirrors. . . . You put with an elegant manner *our* household words into mouths, and our habits and foolish manners into persons and places I don't know how far off, or how *very* out of sight, and we laugh at, and enjoy ourselves, and our own delectable nonsenses, all because it pleased a French Countess to be a delicate fairy humourist, and you to be a man of a poetical mind who knew how to translate her into the rarest English burlesque. . . . Oh, that you and I, and a few others (*not many*) could charter a vessel for the latter quiet sea-girt retreat. Where is it? *I* do not know. It *must* be somewhere in the Pacific!

For these were the days when the Pacific seemed far away, and atomic bombs were things undreamed of.

With some slight modifications Reynolds' words might even more appropriately have been applied to W. S. Gilbert, who carried on, expanded, and perfected the Planché tradition during the last years of the century. Although a consideration of his work carries us far beyond the period at the moment under survey, the dependence of these plays and operas upon what immediately preceded them and the manner in which they bring to a culmination what had been fully adumbrated before Gilbert's own time justifies an analysis of their characteristics here.

Gilbert started his career by practising in the style of the fairy play, and, in these, outwardly at least, he acts the sedulous ape to his predecessors. He makes a few excusions into farce, it is true, but his representative writings up to the start of the Savoy operas are pieces such as *The Palace of Truth* (1870) and *The Wicked World* (1873). That which distinguishes these essays from the fairy plays of Planché is the personal mood introduced into the treatment of scenes and characters. Reynolds, contemplating the latter's extravaganzas, wished that he and a few boon companions could sail off to an idealistically conceived Pacific; the sense of world-weariness implied in this desire is increased a thousandfold in Gilbert. A concealed sadness gives distinction to his most humorous scenes, and his famous topsy-turviness springs ultimately from a loathing for the things he finds around him. The fever and the fret of mankind weigh heavily on his senses, and, while we must confess that the decorous conventions of Victorianism prevent his achieving such a range and such a freedom as was attained by an Aristophanes, there can be no doubt but that he succeeded in creating a comic realm of his own not entirely unworthy of comparison with that of the Greek master.

To-day, of course, he is known chiefly through the later operas, in which his versifying skill was combined with the kindred musical skill of Sir Arthur Sullivan. The spirit of these operas, however, was no new thing: it was merely a further development of that which had animated his earlier plays. *Iolanthe; or, The Peer and the Peri* (1882) uses the fairy machinery familiar in these works, and the mood of *Broken Hearts* (1875) reappears in *The Yeomen of the Guard; or, The Merryman and his Maid* (1888). It is easy to accept the operas simply as delightful entertainment—and no doubt such is the prime reason for their being—yet we shall be wrong if we close our eyes to their ironic intent. On the surface *H.M.S. Pinafore; or, The Lass that loved a Sailor* (1878) is a carefree extravaganza replete with all the most orthodox patriotic sentiments of Victorian England; on the surface *The Pirates of Penzance; or, The Slave of Duty* (1879) is only a fantasy, in which the wicked buccaneers throw down their weapons in the name of the Queen. Underneath, however, both of these have an ironic tang. It is not so much that Gilbert was writing with his tongue in his cheek as that he could not quite conceal a mood that passed beyond the outward appearances of his scenes. Whereas outwardly his scenes appear to be invested merely with easy laughter and the delicate play of a punning wit, in reality they are informed by a kind of world-weariness. When royalty severely frowned upon *Utopia Limited; or, The Flowers of Progress* (1893) royalty, from its own point of view, was right. In *Utopia Limited* Gilbert had lowered the veil a little too far, and what was seen beyond did not seem so amusing. All the vaunted progress of the century was revealed as a thing of doubtful value, and the whole of life was presented darkly. The royal box may have lost its occupants ostensibly because a Privy Council meeting was turned into a Christy Minstrel show, but Gilbert's barb went deeper than burlesque of such a kind: fundamentally he was guilty of looking with eyes of laughter upon the benefits of science and of mocking that on which Victorian society was founded—the very concept of progress.

The Inheritance of Marivaux: Musset

The concealed melancholy, masked by mocking laughter, in Gilbert's writings assumed a peculiar and a strangely appealing form in the hands of a French author who added to the spirit of fancy a penetrating interest in the human heart. It may seem foolish to associate Gilbert with Alfred de Musset, yet when we think that the latter owes his being to Marivaux, and that Marivaux' genius springs from the *commedia dell' arte*, perhaps the connexion of their names may seem not so extraordinary after all. Although Musset's plays present nothing of the topsy-turvy humour characteristic of the Savoy operas, the fantastic atmosphere is potent in their scenes.

The influence of Marivaux had been hovering in the wings of the Parisian theatres since the beginning of the eighteenth century, prompting the playwrights even while the spirit of Molière held the stage, and it was no wonder that at last a successor came to carry on his style. Not that Musset realized in his earliest efforts what precisely he wanted to do: he began as a serious romantic dramatist, penning works of minor interest, heavily tinged with dark sentimentalism. *La nuit Vénitienne* (*A Venetian Night*, 1830) was deservedly hissed; *André del Sarto* (printed 1833) is boringly verbose, with little credibility in its portrait of the ageing painter; *Lorenzaccio* (printed 1834), although better wrought, is romantically diffuse.

These writings we may ignore, but something different enters with *Les caprices de Marianne* (*Marianne's Whims*; printed 1833) and *Fantasio* (printed 1833). In the former a young man, Célio, falls in love with a married woman, Marianne. She in turn finds her heart moved by his friend, Octave, and through a caprice inadvertently causes Célio's death. The play ends with Octave and Marianne standing by the dead man's tomb: she offers her affections to Octave, but his simple words close the action: "I do not love you, madam: it was Célio who loved you." In *Fantasio* is presented a young hero who, living for pleasure, can yet find no pleasure in anything he does. In a kind of romantic renunciation of the world he dons the dress of a Court fool, and in this rôle succeeds in breaking off a proposed match between his Princess and a boorish Prince.

The plots of these two plays have no other purpose than to provide the author with an opportunity of delving into the human heart and of presenting whimsical contrasts in human value. In a sense the action is real; at the same time, as *Fantasio* demonstrates, the world of the imagination easily superimposes itself upon the world of actuality.

From such pieces it is an easy step to *On ne badine pas avec l'amour* (*No Trifling with Love*; printed 1834), and in taking this step we move into Musset's characteristic realm, that of the *proverbe dramatique* or *comédie-proverbe*. This theatrical genre explains itself in its title. The author here selects a familiar proverb and develops an action illustrative of its significance. Although Musset is its most famous exponent, he was by no means its inventor; indeed, as a number of plays in several tongues cited above must have indicated, it was one of the most popular kinds of drama during the eighteenth century. Even during the period of the Renaissance a tendency to select proverbial titles may be observed among English and Spanish playwrights, and it was a simple task for Louis Carmontelle, a painter whose activities carried him into the sphere of the aristocratic amateur stage, to evolve from earlier suggestions the typical form assumed by the French *comédie-proverbe* in the salons—short, condensed, epigrammatic playlets of comic spirit with serious undertones. His *Proverbes dramatiques*, published in eight volumes between 1768 and 1781, set the pattern for the similar writings of Théodore Leclercq and his companions. Thus was the fashion passed down to Musset.

In his hands the dramatic proverb was refined and made delicately penetrating. *On ne badine pas avec l'amour* introduces as central figure a proud and testy Baron who plans a marriage between his son, Perdican, and his niece, Camille. Like Marianne, this girl has her caprices: she refuses Perdican and yet is stung when he makes a show of indifference, while he, in turn, devotes half-hearted affection to a country girl,

Rosette. Irritated and inwardly loving him, Camille engages in a series of contradictory devices—inducing Perdican to confess his devotion to her, laughing at him when he does so, and attempting to prevent his marriage to Rosette. At the end Perdican surprises her in tears, and through this their mutual love becomes apparent to both: they embrace, only to be confronted by the fact that Rosette, the tragic pawn in their love-duel, has perished of a broken heart and thus presents an inescapable barrier to their union. "She is dead. Adieu, Perdican," are Camille's last, simple words. By means of this plot of turns and counter-turns Musset succeeds in painting a memorable portrait of his heroine and of revealing delicately the strange paradoxes of the human heart, and, as a fine contrast to the serious action, he balances these baffled lovers with an amusing group of humorous figures—Perdican's tutor, Maître Blazius, Camille's governess, Dame Pluche, and the little village priest, Maître Bridaine. Hardly any play of the nineteenth century is subtler than this, or more graciously alert in its analysis of passion.

Le chandelier (*The Decoy*; printed 1835) tells a somewhat similar story of love, with Jacqueline, the amorous wife of the besotted Maître André, as heroine. Her lover is the conceited soldier Clavroche, and in order to distract her husband's suspicions from him she pretends a display of affection for the adolescent clerk Fortunio. This idealistic young poet takes her advances seriously, while she for her part is moved and dazzled attracted by his devotion. Thus once more, with fine precision and nervous tension, Musset presents another picture of love's sadly strange vagaries.

A year later came *Il ne faut jurer de rien* (*You can't be sure of Anything*; printed 1836). Again the plot is simple: no more than the story of a young gallant, Valentin van Bruck, who sets out to seduce a girl, Cécile, and ends by offering her his true devotion. Love here, as in all Musset's plays, is the mainspring of human life, even of the universe. In the final scene of the comedy Cécile and Valentin are seated in a glade by moonlight. "How vast the sky is!" she says; "how happy the world! How calm and kindly is nature!"

> *VALENTIN:* Do you want me to talk to you of science and astronomy? Tell me: in this dust of worlds, is there one star that knows not its path, that has not received its mission when it was first created, that is not willing to die in fulfilment of that mission? Why are these vast heavens not motionless? Tell me, if there ever was a moment in time when everything was created, by virtue of what force have these restless worlds been impelled to move?
> *CÉCILE:* By eternal thought.
> *VALENTIN:* By love eternal. The hand suspending them in space has written but one word in letters of fire. They live because they seek each other: these stars would crumble into dust were one of them to cease to love.

In *Un caprice* (*A Whim*; printed 1837) further development of character appears, not so much in the depiction of the faithful Mathilde and of her erring husband, Chavigny, as in that of Madame de Léry, with her infinitely amusing garrulity and her kindness of heart. Eight years later came *Il faut qu'une porte soit ouverte ou fermée* (*A Door should be either Open or Shut*; printed 1845), where the action consists merely in the fact that a Count pays a social call on a Marquise and ends by offering her a declaration of marriage. And finally there is *Carmosine* (printed 1850), in which Musset's peculiar atmosphere of real unreality reaches its peak. This tale of a maid who loves a King and of a Queen who is so magnanimous as to send her lord to comfort her exists in the world of the ideal, yet paradoxically the sentiments and characters assume a concreteness and an interest of which, in theory, we might well have deemed them incapable.

It is hard, indeed, to give any impression, by a mere outlining of basic plots, of Musset's extraordinary dramatic quality. His triumph lies in the excessive refinement of his style, in the clarity and intimacy of his portraiture, in the strange air of imaginative fantasy with which he invests his scenes, and in his presentation of a kind of modern disillusioned reflection of Marivaux' gracefully artificial and sentimental analyses of the human heart.

The Romantic Poet in Paris

Musset began his career, as has been seen, with a series of romantically conceived tragedies, and his experiments in this style are part of a general movement that swept over Paris literary circles in the thirties. So far France had failed to respond, within the theatre at least, to the romantic enthusiasm of Europe, but a store of explosive material was being gathered during the early years of the century, and a match, lit innocently enough by a company of English actors, set this off in a blaze of flamboyant splendour.

It was in the season of 1827–28 that Paris was visited by the English troupe—a distinguished body of players who presented, among other works, the four great tragedies of Shakespeare. There was an immediate furore. At first glance the excitement thus occasioned seems inexplicable. Shakespeare had been known in France for many years, and although the earlier translations had been sadly defective, draping the robust Elizabethan limbs in the respectably dignified robes of pseudo-classicism or in the more tight-fitting garments of decent bourgeois sentiment, a complete edition of his plays had been issued in 1821 under the combined direction of Guizot, de Barante, and Pichot. Furthermore, the first of these editor-translators, Guizot, had published a capable analysis of the objectives of Shakespeare's art and had made, at least by implication, a defence of his romantic style. Only three years later Stendhal (Marie-Henri Beyle) issued an essay, *Racine et Shakespeare*, in which, albeit with admirable confusion, the cudgel was deliberately lifted in opposition to classicism. The impress made by the English company would appear, therefore, as though beyond the reach of explanation.

The explanation, however, is there. Not only was this the first opportunity granted Parisian audiences to see the plays in their original form,
it was the first opportunity these audiences had had of seeing them, even
in mangled shapes, presented with an appropriate acting technique.
Edmund Kean had served to reintroduce histrionic passion on the
London boards, and as a result the performances came before the public
not simply as 'Shakespeare,' but as something such as no auditor, however well acquainted he might have been with Shakespeare's text, could
possibly have imagined.

In the theatre, watching these productions, was a young French
littérateur, Victor Hugo, and immediately he was inspired to work a
reform, based on what he had seen, in his native theatre. Already in 1824
he had penned his amorphous *Cromwell*, and now in 1827 he issued it to
the public accompanied by a fiery preface which was in effect a trumpet-
call to revolution. Basically his argument is that drama is the greatest
form of artistic expression, that Shakespeare is "its poetic summit," and
that the quality of his genius is to be found in the "grotesque," the characteristic mood of the modern world—"so complex, so diverse in its
forms, so inexhaustible in its creations, and therein directly opposed to
the uniform simplicity of the ancients." From this he deduces that the
drama, instead of being, as some have said, a mirror of life, is "a concentrating mirror, which instead of weakening, concentrates and condenses
the coloured rays, which makes of a mere gleam a light, and of a light a
flame."

From this preface Hugo proceeded to example. It is worthy of note,
however, that his first experiment was an historical drama, *Marion
Delorme* (1831; originally written in 1829 as *Un duel sous Richelieu*), in
which, however, the story of a courtesan, although draped in romantic
robes, has about it an element of the realistic: the pressure of the real and
the actual could deflect even this flamboyant medievalist from his purposes. It was in *Hernani* (1830) that romanticism truly flourished. All
Paris recognized the challenge: the classicists mustered in droves, intent
upon hissing it out of existence and ridiculing its life away; the young,
ardent spirits of Montmartre came to applaud and cheer. It is said that
for a hundred performances the scenes were constantly interrupted by
the conflicting cries of derision and of praise, that frequently the lines
spoken by the actors could not be heard in the confused turmoil. The
cause of the excitement is perhaps just as difficult for us to appreciate,
a century after the event, as the impress made on Paris by the English
players. To us, maybe, the plot of the play seems even a trifle absurd.
Blood-and-thunder here holds the stage. Centrally placed in Donna Sol
de Silva, the ward of Don Ruy Gomez de Silva, who desires to marry her
himself. For her hand, however, there are other suitors, the romantic
outlaw Hernani and Don Carlos, Prince of Spain. Amid confusion, the
story passes from thrilling episode to thrilling episode. Hernani and Don
Carlos pursue their rivalry, and at one point the former would have been

doomed to destruction had not the old de Silva concealed him, while the hero pledges his life to his protector in pawn. Later Don Carlos becomes not only King of Spain, but Holy Roman Emperor as well, displays his imperial greatness by pardoning Hernani, and is thwarted by de Silva's calling on Hernani's pledge. The conclusion is suitably tragic. Seizing a phial of poison, Donna Sol drinks of the liquid:

HERNANI: That philtre leads thee to thy grave.
DONNA SOL: Was not this head to sleep upon thy breast
    To-night? What matters where it sinks to rest?
HERNANI: My father, thy revenge is just—that I
    Forget.   *[He raises the phial to his lips.*
DONNA SOL [throws herself upon him]: Forbear! Forbear!
          'Tis hard to die!
    The poison lives, and round the heart it hangs.
    Like a fell serpent with a thousand fangs.
    Oh, drink it not! Alas! I could not tell
    That earthly pain could match the fires of hell—
    He drinks!
HERNANI [drinks and throws away the phial]: 'Tis done.
DONNA SOL: Come then to meet thy fate—
    Come to these arms. Is not the torture great?
HERNANI: Not so.
DONNA SOL: Behold, our marriage couch is spread!
    Am I not pale for one so lately wed?
    Be calm. I suffer less. Our wings expand
    Towards the blest regions of a happier land—
    Together let us seek that world so fair—
    One kiss—and one alone.
DON RUY: Despair! despair!
HERNANI: Blest be the Heaven which from my birth pursued
    My life with misery, and in blood imbued—
    For it permits me, ere I part, to press
    My lips to thine, and die on thy caress.
DON RUY: They still are happy!
HERNANI: Donna Sol, 'tis night.
    Dost thou still suffer?
DONNA SOL: No.
HERNANI: See'st thou the light?
DONNA SOL: Not yet——
HERNANI: I see it.
DON RUY: Dead!
DONNA SOL: Not so; we rest.
    He sleeps. He's mine—we love, and we are blest.
    This is my marriage couch. What happier spot
    Can the world show? Lord Duke, disturb us not.
                          [Her voice gradually sinks.
    Turn thee towards me—nearer yet—'tis well.
    Thus let us rest.   *[Dies.*
DON RUY: Both dead! Receive me, hell!   *[Kills himself.*

Obviously the main appeal of this drama to its contemporaries lay in its highly coloured setting, in its bold presentation of romantic love, and, above all, in the quality of its bandit hero. Of subtle character portrayal there is none: indeed, the persons in this lurid tragedy so frequently act contrary to their natures that a reader or spectator must often remain in perplexed puzzlement. Yet the individual scenes are sensationally thrilling, and some of the verse, freed from the excessive technical restrictions of the classicists, mightily thunders in the index. Its very clamour was what gave it distinction and inaugurated the full flow of romanticism in France.

In his next play, *Le roi s'amuse* (*The King takes his Pleasure*, 1832)—the basis of the opera *Rigoletto*—the romantic pattern was further filled in by displaying a Court jester, Triboulet, who avenges himself on his lord, Francis the First, for a wrong done to his beloved daughter. Here revolutionary sentiment is added to the general scheme of fierce passion and sensational incident.

Hugo's next efforts were in prose—*Lucrèce Borgia* (1833), *Marie Tudor* (1833), and *Angelo* (1835)—but with the shedding of the verse little remained save melodrama of the crudest sort. We may be prepared to accept inconsistencies amid the flowing speeches of *Hernani*; when we encounter such inconsistencies in plays written without the magic of poetic utterance we can only dismiss the dramas in which they appear as of little worth. The poetry, however, returns in *Ruy Blas* (1838) and once more sweeps us off our feet. Follies and absurdities are here in plenty, but these are forgotten in the surge of the verse and in the exploitation of the 'grotesque' so dearly loved by its author. The same intoxicating vigour appears also in *Les Burgraves* (1843), a drama consisting of a collection of scenes, divided into three episodes, illustrative of life in the time of Barbarossa.

In all these plays Hugo reveals his deep understanding of the stage's requirements. His appreciation of the quality and interests of the contemporary audience is clearly outlined in the preface to *Ruy Blas*:

> Three sorts of spectators compose what we are accustomed to call the playgoing public—first, women; secondly, the intellectuals; and thirdly, the general crowd. That which the last-named group principally seeks in a dramatic work is action; what most attracts women is passion; what the thoughtful seek above all else is the portrayal of human nature. . . . All three groups look for pleasure—the first, visual pleasure, the second, gratification of emotional sentiments, the last, mental enjoyment. Accordingly in my play appear three distinct kinds of material, the one common and inferior, the two others illustrious and superior, but all answering to a demand—melodrama for the crowd, tragedy that analyses passion for the women, and for the thinkers, comedy that depicts human nature.

The recipe is truly Shakespearian, and that Hugo did not reach Shakespeare's level is due, not so much to a failure on his part to comprehend the true aim of the tragic dramatist, as to the fact that his genius was less fortunately adjusted than Shakespeare's to the conditions of his time. Had Hugo lived in the Elizabethan period he might still not have risen to Shakespearian heights, but he certainly would have proved a mighty rival to Marlowe.

Hugo's chief contribution to the stage of his time was an element that we may call vitality. There is nothing petty in his vision. Though he may often sink to bathos, it is because he aims at, and often attains, the grand style. From the time when he produced *Hernani* the careful precision of Racine's plays ceased to be the paramount model of the French stage. Hugo may not himself have been able to set up a new god, but at least he destroyed some idols.

As a companion he had another young writer, destined like himself to become famous as a novelist, Alexandre Dumas, whose *Henri III et sa cour* (*Henry III and his Court*) appeared in 1829. Less ambitious in his revolutionary aims, Dumas is content to use the melodramatic mould of his predecessors and to make no effort to establish a new poetic theatre. The force that inspired him, however, was the same as that which occasioned the preface to *Cromwell*. He has left on record an account of the impression made upon him by the English performances of Shakespeare's tragedies, when he suddenly realized that the Elizabethan dramatist "was the greatest creator after God himself."

And, however melodramatic, *Henri III et sa cour* is a play planned according to the best recipes of the new romanticism. The realistic tendency enters in and causes the author to paint his background not only in general terms but in particular: his courtiers are faithfully depicted in the fashions of their time, and even the games with which they disport themselves on the stage are historically correct. From the melodrama he takes his technical skill and, unlike Hugo, weaves a plot which, however conventional it may appear on analysis, carries the spectator forward with breathless interest. The same qualities made the later *La Tour de Nesle* (*The Tower of Nesle*, 1832) a success such as is paralleled by hardly another play of the time; scarcely less exciting or less skilful in their exploitation of popular romantic elements are *Don Juan de Maraña* (1836), *Kean* (1836), and *Mademoiselle de Belle Isle* (1839).

Just as Hugo veered in one play towards the contemporary realistic, so Dumas interrupted his series of historical dramas to write his *Antony* (1831), a drama set in the surroundings of his time and introducing characters of the middle class. It is particularly interesting because it indicates how easily the powerful romantic passions could be transferred to another *milieu*. This tale of illicit love, with its dark hero, has clear ties with earlier melodrama: it also points forward, and as clearly, towards the sensationally naturalistic drama to come. When the hero, having ravished the heroine, stabs her in order to save her honour, crying "She resisted me and I killed her!" he is at once imitating melodramatic gestures and anticipating the gestures of a later style of play.

Others of the young romantic group essayed the same path. Alfred de Vigny, for example, made fame for himself when his translation of *Othello* (*Le More de Venise*) was performed in 1829, and when, later, his drama, *Chatterton*, was presented in 1835. Despite its apparent following of classic precept, *Chatterton* belongs in spirit to the revolutionary and noisier tragedies of Hugo and Dumas, and its despondent young hero accords exactly, though in sentimentalized manner, with the Byronic figures of his contemporaries. One thing does, however, give this drama very considerable historical significance. As is shown in the prefatory "Dernière nuit de travail," Vigny essayed to establish a new kind of play—the drama of thought ("le drame de la pensée"). Drawing attention to the simplicity of his plot, he asserts that here "the moral action is everything: the action is within a soul delivered over to dark tempests." In this way Vigny therefore becomes the unacknowledged ancestor of the 'impressionistic' theatre of our own century. In his emphasis upon the manner in which an individual can be ruined by society—a theme mordantly dealt with in the one-act 'comedy' *Quitte pour la peur* (*Let Off with a Fright*, 1833)—he likewise anticipates much that was to come.

Although the grandiose emotions so characteristic of Hugo could not be expected to dominate the stage for long, and although even Vigny's subtler presentation of passion found but few followers, the romantic style thus colourfully set upon the stage continued to make its popular appeal for a number of years to come. François Ponsard, it is true, had some success in his endeavour to re-establish the classical forms with his *Lucrèce* (1843), yet even in his writings the romantic note intrudes (as in *Agnès de Méranie*, 1846, and *Charlotte Corday*, 1850). The same is true of several other similarly inclined authors. Although the French romantics of the Hugo school may have burned themselves out by the forties, the impulse that created their works maintained its force for long and could never quite be forgotten.

The Continued Spread of the Romantic

Partly developing from independent sources, partly inspired by the Hugo revolt, this second wave of romanticism swept over the whole of Europe.

While England, for example, had nothing to offer at this time worthy of much praise, something of the same romantic fervour gripped the minds of her poets and even the minds of her lesser hack writers. On the 'literary' level the Poet Laureate, Alfred Lord Tennyson, applied himself, without too great distinction, to his *Queen Mary* (1876), *The Falcon* (1879), *Harold* (1876) and *Becket* (1879), while his fellow-poet Robert Browning turned out his *Strafford* (1837), *The Return of the Druses* (1843), and *A Blot in the 'Scutcheon* (1843). Most of these plays were produced by prominent actor-managers—Macready, Irving, and the Kendals—but none created any particular stir: an audience that knew Shakespeare could hardly be expected to become excited over such works. On a slightly lower plane popular romantic plays were being composed by others. Edward Bulwer-Lytton (Lord Lytton) won an immediate and lasting success with *The Lady of Lyons* (1838) and an almost equally resounding success with *Richelieu; or, The Conspiracy* (1839). Earlier James Sheridan Knowles had valiantly endeavoured to keep the poetic flag flying with his long run of historical dramas, of which one, *William Tell* (1825), deservedly achieved popularity; later Tom Taylor interspersed among his melodramas a few plays of more ambitious intent, while Dion Boucicault, ever adept at sensing the tastes of the audiences of his time, although he began his career with *London Assurance* (1841), soon extended the romantic subject-matter in his series of Irish melodramas—such as *Arrah-na-Pogue* (1864).

There is, perhaps, little here worthy of remembrance on account of intrinsic quality: on the other hand, in later viewing the growth of realism on the stage within these forty years, we must not lose sight of the fact that a great deal of the current stage fare, both then and later, was in the romantic style. Sir Henry Irving's most characteristic play was *The Bells* (1871), as adapted by Leopold Lewis from *Le juif polonais* (a melodrama by 'Erckmann-Chatrian'—the joint pseudonym of Émile Erckmann and Alexandre Chatrian), while the last years of the century saw audiences flocking in their thousands to joy in theatrical representations of *The Prisoner of Zenda* (1896) and *The Sign of the Cross* (1895).

In Spain as in France, although less forcefully, romanticism wrought something of moderate value, worthy of at least passing attention. Throughout the eighteenth century the inheritance of Lope de Vega and of Calderón had been sadly dissipated, and such playwrights as Ramón de la Cruz, author of several hundred stage pieces, popularly exploited the resources of farce and early melodrama. Pseudo-classic models, of the kind set forth in Montiano's *Virginia* or Moratín the elder's *Hormesinda*, produced nothing of consequence, and the earlier sort of romanticism offered nothing better than the mediocre *El duque de Viseo* (*The Duke of Viseo*, 1801), by José Quintana. As a result, when the impress of later romanticism was felt in the peninsula it came as a sudden revelation and as an inspiration.

Influenced by the French school was Francisco Martínez de la Rosa, whose *Abén Humeya, ó la rebelión de los Moriscos* (*Aben Humeya; or, The Rebellion of the Moors*, 1830) not only coincided in date with Hugo's efforts, but was originally written in French and produced in a Parisian theatre. While the dramatic quality of this piece is not particularly outstanding, its historical value is considerable: the author accomplished something of import in applying the new romanticism to a native Spanish theme in scenes wherein is shown the vengeful onslaught against the Castilians led by a Moorish hero. An intrinsically finer work by this author is his later *La conjuración de Venecia* (*The Venetian Conspiracy*), presented in his native country in 1834. These plays created no great stir, but excitement came when Ángel de Saavedra, Duke de Rivas, released his bold *Don Álvaro, o la fuerzo del sino* (*Don Alvaro; or, The Force of Destiny*) in 1835. This drama, concocted according to the fondest prescriptions of the 'grotesque,' immediately captured public attention, and achieved fame outside of Madrid when it was taken by Verdi as the basis of his opera *La forza del destino* (1862). Although less popular than this drama, more poetic power is to be found in Saavedra's later *El desengaño en un sueño* (*The Disabusing in a Dream*; printed 1842), wherein the spirit of Calderón's famous dream-reality play is reborn. Another highly successful opera of Verdi's, *Il trovatore* (1853), was taken from *El trovador* (*The Troubadour*, 1836), by de Rivas' contemporary Antonio García Gutiérrez; this drama, cast in the same style and so near in date to *Don Álvaro*, served to consolidate the new romantic movement in the Spanish theatre.

Season by season the stage of Madrid was fed with the work of young poets, their heads filled with Byronic fancies and all anxious to create a romantic masterpiece. *Ni el tío ni el sobrino* (*Neither Uncle nor Nephew*), by José de Espronceda, appeared in 1834. José Zorrilla y Moral brought out his *Don Juan Tenorio* in 1844—a Don Juan play wherein the hero truly falls in love with one of his intended victims and is saved by her prayers. In 1837 came *Los amantes de Teruel* (*The Lovers of Teruel*), by Juan Eugenio Hartzenbusch, followed in 1838 by his complex and passionate *Doña Mencía, o la boda en la Inquisición* (*Donna Mencia; or, Marriage in the Inquisition*). And eventually arrived a man who, gifted with a genuine theatrical power and well versed in the European literature of the romantic revival, succeeded in consolidating on the efforts of his predecessors. The aim of Manuel Tamayo y Baus was to re-establish a truly national Spanish drama, and through his vigorous contributions he succeeded in bringing to the theatre of Madrid something at least approaching the quality it had possessed in earlier times. Schiller influenced him in his *Juana de Arco* (*Joan of Arc*, 1847) and Alfieri in his *Virginia* (1853); the spirit of both, added to a characteristic strain of his own, appears in *La locura de amor* (*Love's Fool*, 1855). Perhaps his most interesting drama was the un-Calderón-like *Un drama nuevo* (*A New Play*, 1867), in which he showed Shakespeare with his companions rehearsing and presenting a new drama. What is particularly noteworthy here is that Pirandello has been anticipated in his juxtaposition of theatrical sentiment and real passion: the skill with which Tamayo y Baus has dealt with the theme has caused his play long to hold the boards. In the work of this author the door was being opened for the modern flowering of the Spanish theatrical genius.

Meanwhile in neighbouring Portugal, a country singularly undramatic, Visconde João Baptista Almeida-Garrett produced his *O alfageme de Santarem* (*The Armourer of Santarem*, 1842), a drama politically conceived and containing a powerfully drawn portrait of the armourer, Ferrando Vaz, a stout proponent of the people's rights. Although extraordinarily

successful, this author's other well-known drama, *Frei Luiz de Souza*
(1843), with its story of a long-lost husband who returns to a wife now
married to another man, can hardly be esteemed to have any great general interest.

Less fruitful than Spain, Italy, after her contributions to the earlier romantic theatre, has less to offer. Melodrama flourished fitfully, but only
rarely do we encounter there the work of even mediocre talent in this
style. Almost the only author deserving of particular mention is Pietro
Cossa, who exhibits some slight quality of virtue in his historical plays
—notably *Monaldeschi* (1864), *Sordello* (1865), *Nerone* (1871), *Lodovico
Ariosto e gli Estensi* (*Lodovico Ariosto and the Estensi*, 1875), and *I Borgia* (*The
Borgias*, 1878). His companions rarely display any worth, although occasionally interesting qualities are to be found in portions of a few individual plays—as, for example, the broad sweep in some acts of *Elisabetta,
regina d'Inghilterra* (*Elizabeth, Queen of England*, 1853), by Paolo Giacomet-
ti, and the warmth animating certain scenes of *Il fornaretto di Venezia* (*The
Venetian Baker Lad*, 1846), by Francesco Dall'Ongaro.

To Germany the new movement came in the characteristic form of a
campaign styled *Das junge Deutschland*. One of its chief leaders in the
theatre was Karl Gutzkow, and he well expressed the strange mixture of
liberal and national sentiments animating this circle of writers. Here the
excesses of the 'Sturm und Drang' period are rejected; there is a certain
trend towards the naturalistic; and philosophical sentiment once more
dominates. Of all Gutzkow's numerous works most characteristic and
most notable for the sincerity of its utterance is *Uriel Acosta* (1846), a
drama which, in the introduction of a Jewish but free-thinking hero,
demonstrates how *Das junge Deutschland* moved back beyond the earlier
romanticism to the style of Lessing. Besides Gutzkow, one other dramatic author merits attention—Georg Büchner. During recent years his
Dantons Tod (*Danton's Death*, 1835) has been signalled out for praise, and
it may be confessed that in this work by a young disillusioned revolutionary there is unquestioned power. Jerkily composed, it yet suggested
to later dramatists fresh methods of achieving their effects. In place of the
restrained pseudo-classical style based on the example of Racine or the
sweeping romantic style inspired by Shakespeare, Büchner endeavoured, not without success, to adopt a new method. His tale of the
French Revolution—and his portrait of a man who, having helped to
stimulate rebellion, bitterly regrets his action—is presented by means of
a series of staccato scenes almost film-like in composition. In his general
concept of the historical drama, too, Büchner makes interesting deviations from earlier practice. For Schiller the historical play was a means
of presenting moral truths; for Büchner it was a literary medium for the
depiction of the truth of past events. Thus, in writing of the Revolution,
he refused to delineate the leaders of the time as other than they
were—"bloody, energetic, cynical."

The potential power of this young author (he died at the age of twenty-four) is also shown in his unfinished realistic tragedy *Woyzeck* (written 1836), with its flashes of inspired but erratic language and its strange lunatic theme. A pessimist who came to see men as mere playthings of a mechanistic fate, Büchner joins the earlier von Kleist in anticipating much in the drama that was later to be fully developed. Perhaps his actual achievements have been somewhat overpraised by recent critics, but we cannot deny that in these two dramas are, somewhat strangely, combined the seeds of the naturalism and the expressionism to come.

Apart from these two men, Germany did not have much to offer, at this time, in the new romantic style. Writers such as Heinrich Laube, author of *Prinz Friedrich* (1845), a drama which traces the relations between Frederick William I of Prussia and his son much as Kleist had dealt with his Elector and the Prince of Homburg; Emil Brachvogel, whose *Narziss* (*Narcissus*, 1856) once was widely popular; Friedrich Halm (Baron Eligius von Münch-Bellinghausen), author of the equally popular *Der Sohn der Wildnis* (*The Son of the Wilderness*, 1843); and Salomon Hermann Mosenthal, author of *Deborah* (also known as *Leah the Forsaken*, 1850), turned out dozens of capably written acting vehicles or passable romantic reading-plays, but not any of their works possess permanent value.

Meanwhile other countries were taking up the challenge. During these decades Russia felt the first stirrings of liberalism. The Byronic spirit was rampant in Pushkin, and Pushkin's mantle fell on Count Alexei Konstantinovich Tolstoi, whose *Smert Ivana Groznavo* (*The Death of Ivan the Terrible*, 1866), *Tsar Feodor Ivanovich* (1868) and *Tsar Boris* (1870) present a colourful and emotionally arresting panorama of Russian history. The intrinsic quality of this trio of dramas has been well attested by the success that attended their production by the Moscow Art Theatre. No other Russian romantic playwright vies with him at this period; although Ostrovski tried his hand at the style, his efforts are mediocre by comparison; such a writer as Dmitri Vasilevich Averkiev is little more than a sentimental dreamer with a commercial flair; while Apolloni Nikolaevich Maikov, whose rather dull *Dva mira* (*Two Worlds*), a study of paganism and Christianity, appeared in 1873, can be regarded only as a second-rate poet with rather vague philosophical aspirations.

In Poland Count Zygmunt Krasiński composed his powerful *Nie-boska komedja* (*The Undivine Comedy*; written over a series of years during the thirties and forties), which symbolically presents the class-struggle between the relics of the old feudal nobility and the rising proletariat. Not penned specifically for the stage, it has yet achieved theatrical success in modern times, as has the even more poetic *Iridion* (1836). These poetic dramas are of greater significance than those of Józef Szujski, even although the latter author pursued the self-appointed mission of trying to give vitality to the Polish historical drama. More important for the history of the stage are the plays of Cyprjan Kamil Norwid, whose *Wanda* and *Krakus* (both written in the forties) not only give expression to Polish romantic sentiment, but point forward to later romantic practice—particularly in the application of the theory of 'silence' as a force in play construction. Even if his actual accomplishments hardly measure up to his aspirations, Norwid was, in theory, far in advance of his times.

The Serbian stage produced its Laza Kostich, with his *Maxim Crnojević* (1866), based on local legends and influenced by Shakespeare. Schiller's style animates the *Tugomer* (1876) of the Slovene Josip Jurčič, while the spirits of both Schiller and Shakespeare haunt the scenes of the Slovak Jonáš Záborský and P. O. Hviezdoslav: the latter's *Herodes a Herodias* (1909), in particular, is an outstanding poetic achievement. Many of these plays select source material from Slav legends, but occasionally there is a searching farther afield, as in the *Fântâna Blanduziei* (*The Bandusian Spring*, or *Fons Bandusiæ*, 1884), a drama dealing with the life of Horace, by the Rumanian Vasile Aleksandri.

In almost every country national historical dramas and dramas cast in romantically symbolic moulds flourished apace, although perhaps the only play of such kind worthy of special praise is the Hungarian equivalent of the Polish *Undivine Comedy*—*Az ember tragediája* (*The Tragedy of Man*, 1862), written by Imre Madách. Obviously dependent upon Goethe's influence, its theme is based on Lucifer's attempt to destroy man's faith by showing him the growth of corruption and vice in human society. Here the concept of progress, so potent a force in nineteenth-century thought, is being seriously challenged. With this drama may be noted another Hungarian work, by Mihály Vörösmarty —*Csongor es Tünde* (*Csongor and Tünde*; printed 1831), a symbolic work that recalls both the *fiabe* of Gozzi and Raimund's *Zauberpossen*.

Denmark's contribution came through the writings of Frederik Paludan-Müller and Henrik Hertz. The former's lyrical *Amor og Psyche* (*Amor and Psyche*, 1834) and *Kalanus* (1857) have poetic beauty if not theatrical strength; the latter won some contemporary fame for his *Kong Renés Datter* (*King René's Daughter*, 1845), as well as for his *Svend Dyrings hus* (*The House of Svend Dyring*, 1837).

In general this new wave of romanticism between 1830 and 1870 is to be viewed as important not so much for its positive contributions to dramatic literature as for its awakening inspiration. National spirit was everywhere aroused through these efforts, and from the glowing fire of that spirit new theatres arose, enshrining dreams for the future. The impulse, of course, was not so powerful in some countries as in others, and England in particular gained little of worth from the plays either of her Sheridan Knowles or of her Tennyson; in some lands, however, this romantic endeavour meant the very creation of a national literature or else the revivification of that literature with the introduction of new forms and fresh concepts.

Opera in the Romantic Age: Wagner and the 'Gesammtkunstwerk'

During the early years of the nineteenth century the cause of romanticism was mightily served by the operatic stages; and, in taking note of this fact, it is important to remember that this was the period when the opera, even although in certain areas it still depended largely upon courtly patronage, gradually came to appeal ever more and more to the general public, and that these were the years which produced Richard Wagner in Germany and Giuseppe Verdi in Italy, the two composers who fully expressed the divergent romantic strains within their respective countries.

In Germany, and also largely in France, fiends, demons, earth spirits, wraiths, supernatural characters of all kinds tended to haunt the musical theatres. *Undine* and *Faust*, both produced in 1816, set the tone for numerous followers: the former, with music by Ernst Hoffmann, was based on a libretto constructed by Baron Friedrich de La Motte-Fouqué out of his extraordinarily popular romance dealing with the mysterious forces and presences operating upon man's world; the latter, with music by Leopold Spohr, although obviously derived ultimately from Goethe's work, aimed at widening its appeal by associating the Faust theme with several other unrelated legends introducing matter both wondrous and magical. Five years later Carl Maria von Weber produced his widely acclaimed *Der Freischütz*, with a libretto derived from an eerie tale which had originally appeared in a collection of ghost-stories; and shortly afterwards Giacomo Meyerbeer (a composer largely associated with the French stage although he had been born and brought up in Germany) composed the music for a piece destined to be equally renowned—*Robert Le Diable* (1831), based on a text prepared in collaboration by Eugène Scribe and the melodramatic Casimir Delavigne; and almost at the very same time, in 1833, the youthful Richard Wagner was engaged in composing music for a piece quite appropriately entitled *Die Feen* (*The Fairies*).

Die Feen, in itself, is of no importance, yet it stands as a signpost pointing directly forwards to the phantom world of *Der fliegende Holländer* (*The Flying Dutchman*, 1843). And, since the cult of the supernatural was so closely bound up with the cult of the 'Gothic', the road trodden by this musician was a straight one, leading from *Tannhäuser* (1845), *Lohengrin* (1850), *Die Meistersinger von Nürnberg* (*The Mastersingers of Nuremberg* 1867) and *Tristan und Isolde* (1865) downward and upward into the craggy depths and heights of Teutonic mythology as expressed in *Der Ring des Nibelungen*, with its four related parts, *Das Rheingold* (*The Rhinegold*), *Die Walküre* (*The Valkyrie*), *Siegfried* and *Die Götterdämmerung* (*The Twilight of the Gods*). In its entirety this '*Ring*' was first presented in 1876, when a highly distinguished audience gathered together for the official opening of the magnificent Bayreuth Festspielhaus, a building dedicated to the composer and at least to a certain extent planned by him on the basis of designs, never carried into execution, which the talented architect Gottfried Semper had prepared for a new theatre at Munich.

In every way, the inauguration of the Bayreuth opera-house with performances of those four works may be regarded as the final triumphant realization of a dream which Wagner had expounded a quarter of a century previously. In his *Oper und Drama* (*Opera and Drama*), published in 1851, he had, with characteristic self-assurance and vigour, expressed his dislike of and his contempt for all the operas produced before his own time. These operas, he insisted, were by their very nature unsatisfactory and defective artistic creations because the words had been supplied by librettists and the music provided by composers: even if the librettist were a true poet (such as, for example, Pietro Metastasio), and even if the composer were a man of genius, their combined efforts, he insisted, must be lacking in creative perfection. In place of such dual endeavours he pleaded for the establishment of a 'musical drama' for which single richly endowed artists would be responsible for both scripts and scores: only in such a manner could the words and the music be wrought into a powerful unity, the dialogue making its appeal to the minds of the spectators and the music supplementing these words by its appeal to the emotions. Even beyond this his arguments extended. Usually, he observed, the productions of operas resulted from the activities of many individuals, each intent upon his own particular province—the scores and the scripts were placed in the hands of directors, who then handed them over to others concerned with the scenery, the stage action, the performance of the musicians, the vocal and physical interpretations of the singers—the total effort thus being still more regrettably fragmented; and therefore he argued for the establishment of something far more unified and majestic in concept, for the most total of operatic presentations, wherein one godlike creator composed the words, provided the music, and saw to it that this complete work of art should be presented on the stage precisely as he wanted it to be.

No doubt the concept was a grand one, yet nowadays, as we look back on this *Oper und Drama* and on the records of the Bayreuth productions, it is easy to see how theoretical concepts tended to lead Wagner astray. He had, for instance, much to say about a 'mystic chasm' which he wished to establish between his audiences and his performers: this concept was based on, but went far beyond, the ideas of those who sought to suggest that a 'fourth wall' had mysteriously been left out of a scenic room: his 'mystic chasm' was designed to hypnotize the spectators into imagining that, by the exercise of a powerful wizardry, they were transformed into privileged initiates gazing upon the sanctuary of a Teutonic holy of holies —and this sanctuary he sought to put upon the stage in the most 'naturalistic' manner possible. Needless to say, the Bayreuth records indicate that there were many wide gaps between the visionary dream and the actual accomplishment, and, in taking note of these, we are often forced to decide that, while '*The Ring*' in its totality was designed as a temple erected in honour of ancient dark gods, it was also a temple constructed in the name of what was frequently an over-solemn and occasionally a ridiculous romantic spirit.

There may be full appreciation of Wagner's power to devise his not in-effective alliterative dialogue as an accompaniment for his music: but, even so, there must be full recognition of the fact that his great universal '*Gesammtkunstwerk*' is no better than (and many would say, not so fine as) such a near-contemporary triumph as, let us say, Verdi's *Otello*, with its fine music associated with the libretto constructed by Arrigo Boito on the basis of Shakespeare's noble tragedy. And, still further, appreciation of the German composer's power cannot conceal from us the fact that the largely distinct romanticism of Italy possessed a quality of its own which not infrequently carried its masters into an operatic realm more richly endowed than the Teutonic and the French. True, the spectres and the supernatural powers were not unknown to Italian opera-goers, but those fortunate audiences able at that time to attend performances at La Scala, La Fenice and companion playhouses rejoiced in witness-ing the premières of many great achievements within this sphere, the majority of which were of a different kind. Gioacchino Rossini's *Tancre-di*, *Otello*, and *Mosè in Egitto* appeared, respectively, in 1813, 1816, and 1818. The eighteen-thirties saw the appearance of Vincenzo Bellini's *I Capuletti ed i Montecchi* and *Norma*, as well as Gaetano Donizetti's *L'elisir d'amore* and *Lucrezia Borgia*: the forties and the fifties were made glorious by the presentations of the still greater achievements of Giuseppe Verdi—*Ernani* (1844), *Rigoletto* (1851), *Il Trovatore* (1853) and *La Traviata* (1853)—and still to come were this composer's *Aïda* (1871), *Otello* (1887), and *Falstaff* (1893).

These men proved that, notwithstanding all the critical-philosophical diatribes contained in *Oper und Drama*, the kind of opera which had been established at the close of the seventeenth century by Giovanni Bardi's Florentine academy still possessed the power to create things of enduring theatrical worth.

2

THE COMING OF REALISM

The Realistic Melodrama

WHILE Wagner was invoking Nibelungs humbler playwrights were more modestly engaged in preparing the ground for the new realism, destined to be the most characteristic theatrical form of the century.

At the start melodrama had been for the most part sensationally removed from the ordinary world. Deliberately the authors sought to find themes which, because of their strangeness, might capture the attention of the popular audiences thronging the theatres. As we have seen, however, about the year 1830 a change begins to become apparent: the wicked feudal count is transmogrified into the moustache-twisting squire, the forester's virgin daughter wears a new dress as a contemporary village maid, and the hero, instead of being a sympathetic outlaw, is a sailor or a soldier home on leave. In many a melodrama in many a country during the thirties and forties breathes an air of contemporary rusticity, and interest is maintained partly by the surprise of the plot, partly by the all-pervading sentimentalism, and partly by the increasing introduction on to the stage of real objects. Vincent Crummles rules in this domain.

A decade passes, and for the country scene are being substituted scenes in the city. A wealthy financier, as often as not, takes the place of the village squire, the heroine now is a poor working lass, a sempstress or a mill-hand, the hero is a working lad; and in place of pigs and geese brought alive upon the boards real hansom-cabs are wheeled in, and the scenic effects attempt to suggest train-wrecks or fires in factories.

By these steps the melodrama moves forward. It remains romantic in the basic sense of that term, only it passes from the world of the past to the world of the present; it sheds medievalism and becomes material. The process, of course, is a slow one, and the strides forward tentative, often halting. Not until the last years of the century does the train-wreck melodrama—to take a single example—reach its culmination. But, however hesitant and lacking in deliberate purpose is the advance, there can be no doubt of the direction of the general current with which the professional dramatists were content to glide.

Now that the melodramatic form had been established by men such as Kotzebue and Pixérécourt, there was no need for the arising of other authors of independent spirit and invention in this field. For all essential purposes the melodramatic authors of the mid-century may remain anonymous, and to a large extent they may remain stateless. Any attempt to trace the development of melodrama in more than one country during this time would result merely in repetition. In endeavouring to get an idea of the kind of development within this general realm we may, therefore, rest content with the English stage: another would have served equally well.

The movement from such favourites as *The Castle Spectre* (1797 by M. G. Lewis and his successors on to pieces like *Luke the Labourer; or, The Lost Son* (1826; by J. B. Buckstone) may easily be traced from 1800 to 1830. Thereafter, although colourful romance still holds its own, the 'realistic' rapidly gains in strength, and as it proceeds on its course it attracts to its composition authors of slightly more ambitious aims. Dion Boucicault is no literary genius, but he makes some higher pretensions than Buckstone or Edward Fitzball, and in those melodramatic works in which he dealt with Irish and American themes he clearly tried to secure a tone beyond that of his earlier *Vampire* (1852). Such plays as *The Octoroon; or, Life in Louisiana* (1859) and *The Colleen Bawn; or, The Brides of Garryowen* (1860) were successful beyond other more ephemeral productions precisely because they were more carefully and more skilfully constructed. The same judgment is true of Tom Taylor's long-remembered *Still Waters Run Deep* (1855). It is worthy of note that both this and *The Octoroon* deal with problems of sex—a theme taboo in earlier specimens of the kind—and equally worthy of note is the introduction in the former of the world of criminality. Crimes, naturally, had been common in all the melodramas, but it is only when we come to plays like *Still Waters Run Deep* that we find ourselves introduced to the police-court, only in plays like the same author's *Ticket-of-leave Man* (1863) that we find a detective a principal person among the characters. The detective is a city figure, and from this time on the street rather than the hedgerow lane is the typical locale. *Jim the Penman* (1886), by Sir Charles Young, is a logical development from Taylor's play, as is *The Silver King* (1882), by Henry Herman and Henry Arthur Jones.

With Jones, however, we have entered another sphere, for this author, associated with Sir Arthur Pinero, is by common consent regarded as one of the true founders of the modern literary drama. Perhaps the strength of this modern movement in the theatre lies in the fact that we are able to enter its confines not merely through one broad entrance nobly escutcheoned with the arms of literature, but, as it were, through an obscure wicket set unobtrusively in a side-wall. To get at *The Cenci* only the one approach is possible; to come to *The Second Mrs Tanqueray* (1893) a quite legitimate, although not commonly traversed, path is from *The Castle Spectre*.

Scribe and the Well-made Play

Meanwhile a significant development in dramatic technique was being evolved in France. This came partly through the practice of the melodrama and of its associate, the *comédie-vaudeville*, partly through trends in the sphere of comedy.

From the time of the Revolution to the thirties of the nineteenth century French comedy had been unsure of itself. The famous decree of 1791 established complete freedom for the theatres; decrees issued fifteen years later, in 1806 and 1807, not only limited the number of playhouses, but once more set up a censorship; still other decrees, continually changing the regulations, left those concerned with stage affairs never certain by what rules they would next be bound. Such were not conditions favourable for the flourishing of comedy, nor were the general moods of the age apt to encourage the thoughtful laughter of Molière. If, however, little of intrinsic worth was produced, two movements deserve attention.

The first of these may be described as the mechanization of comic-character portrayal. This is marked particularly in the work of Charles Étienne and of Louis-Benoît Picard. As an example may be taken the latter's *Un jeu de la fortune, ou les marionettes* (*Play of Fortune; or, The Marionettes*, 1806), wherein men are depicted as creatures whose actions are determined by the pulling of invisible strings. In a sense this trend may be regarded as the unconscious comic counterpart of the emphasis on fate in the poets' dismal tragedies.

The second movement is that towards realism. Such a play as *Un moment d'imprudence* (*An Imprudent Moment*, 1819), by Alexis-Jacques-Marie Wafflard, shows a new realistic comedy in the making. Life is treated here with interesting vividity, and the adventures of Monsieur and Madame d'Harcourt are dealt with skilfully. These adventures, ultimately determined by economic causes, are given theatrical complexity through the person of Madame de Montdésir, who lives a double life under her own name and under that of Madame d'Ange: to Madame d'Harcourt she is known in the latter guise, while her husband is acquainted with her in the former. Not without some true virtue, and informed with the same materialistically realistic spirit, is *Les comédiens* (*The Comedians*, 1820) of Casimir Delavigne, an author more famous for his rather melodramatic *Les vêpres Siciliennes* (*The Sicilian Vespers*, 1819).

Into this atmosphere stepped Eugène Scribe. A practical man of the theatre, he realized that for the attainment of success a new, foolproof dramatic technique was required, a technique suited for a theatre so vastly different in potentiality and form from those that had housed the plays of Shakespeare or even the tragedies of Racine.

For Scribe that which matters in a play is the plot, and consequently he looks back, not towards Marivaux, whose stories were merely slim excuses for an opportunity to probe the heart and reveal sentiments, but

THE ROYALTY THEATRE, LONDON, IN THE YEAR 1787:
INTERIOR

THE ROYALTY THEATRE, LONDON, IN THE YEAR 1787:
AUDITORIUM

PHELPS AS CORIOLANUS

THE WATER KING IN "THE
SILVER PALACE"

GATTIE AS M. MORBLEU

PITT AS CHARLY WAG

MISS YOUNGE AS ETHELINDA

MISS YOUNGE AS MEROPE

MRS YATES AS JANE SHORE

MRS MELMOTH AS QUEEN ELIZABETH

FOUR EIGHTEENTH-CENTURY TRAGIC HEROINES

towards Beaumarchais, who, although he knew how to delineate character, was fundamentally interested in intrigue and action. Being a practising writer for the theatre, Scribe realized that a popular audience wants, in the first instance, a vividly told dramatic tale; he realized, too, that many of the devices used in the telling of theatrical tales in the past no longer suited the changed stages of his time; and he set for himself the task of devising a formula by which narratives of all kinds —melodramatic, comic, and farcical—could, with a minimum of effort, be rendered appealing when presented on the boards. His success in this task may be gauged from the fact that he was able to set up what amounted to a play-factory, in which stories were found, invented, or paid for and turned, like sausages, into comestibles for which the public was eager to expend its money.

As Alexandre Dumas *fils* saw clearly, Scribe had no "inspiration of idea" and no sincerity save what he devoted to his commercial values. For Musset a play has an artistic being and, however fantastic, an inner reality: for Scribe a play is a play, to be prepared according to a mechanical plan, a thing without organic life. "No one," comments Dumas,

> knew better than M. Scribe—who was without conviction, without simplicity, without any philosophic end in view—how to set into action if not a character or an idea, at least a subject, and above all a situation, and to extract from that subject and that situation their logical theatric effect; none better than he understood how to assimilate the latest ideas and adapt them to the stage, sometimes on a scale and in a spirit absolutely opposed to the combinations of the one from whom he received the idea. . . . He was the most extraordinary improviser we have had in the history of our drama; he was the most expert at manipulating characters that had no life. He was the shadow-Shakespeare.

From this description of Scribe's ability Dumas proceeds to compare him with Musset:

> If, among the four hundred plays he wrote, either by himself or in collaboration, you place *Il ne faut jurer de rien*, or *Un caprice*, or *Il faut qu'une porte soit ouverte ou fermée*—that is to say, a tiny *proverbe* written by the most naïve and inexpert of dramatists—you will see all Scribe's plays dissolve and go up into thin air, like mercury when heated to three hundred and fifty degrees; because Scribe worked for his audience without putting into his labour anything of his soul or heart, while Musset wrote with heart and soul for the heart and soul of humanity. His sincerity gave him, though he was unaware of this, all the resources which were the sole merit of Scribe.

While this is true—that Scribe's many plays go up into thin air when compared with dramas written from the heart—Dumas was too wise to fail to see that the technical skill of the popular dramatist had its own value. The conclusion, he remarks, is that the playwright who knows *man* as Balzac (or Musset) did, "and the *theatre* as Scribe did, will be the greatest of the world's dramatists."

Just as Musset perfected the work of his immediate predecessors, so

Scribe, looking only at theatrical form, perfected the work of others. Fundamentally, his inspiration comes from the writers of melodramas —who, eschewing character studies, were forced to pay particular attention to action—and from those of the vaudeville-farce, a genre which became increasingly popular during the early decades of the nineteenth century. His earliest success, *Une nuit de la Garde Nationale* (*A Night with the National Guard*, 1815), was called a *tableau-vaudeville*, and the vaudeville technique remained with him to the end of his career. This sketch already shows the main elements of his craft. The play begins with a clear presentation of the background, economically but firmly implants in the audience's mind knowledge of the facts on which the subsequent episodes are founded. These facts known by his public, all the author has to do is to start pulling the strings of his puppets: in and out they go, and the resultant intrigue holds the attention, almost makes us forget that they are puppets without life of their own. And the illusion is made the greater by the free use made by the playwright of material taken from the life of the day. Scribe, as Dumas noted, was nothing if not up-to-date.

This does not, of course, imply that Scribe always took his scenes from material familiar to, or closely associated with, the life of the time. Many of his pieces introduce historical matter—however unhistorically treated —and quite a number escape into the world of the fantastic. Towards the very beginning of his career he varied his pattern with a *folie-vaudeville* entitled *L'ours et le pacha* (*The Bear and the Pasha*, 1820), with exciting scenes in the seraglio, designed to titillate the public, and all the mechanism of Oriental wonder.

By this time the talented young author was the rage of Paris; by this time he had become sure of his art and was capable of applying it to subject-matter of any description. The formula of the well-made play—*la pièce bien faite*—was complete. Thenceforward for a period of thirty-odd years he kept the playhouses supplied with a constant series of dramas, nearly all accompanied by music, in which scenes serious, comic, and farcical were wrought into a skilful theatrical pattern. One after another his four hundred plays followed in a constant stream. Here were the sketches from life, such as *La petite sœur* (*The Little Sister*, 1821), *La seconde année* (*The Second Year*, 1830), and *Le chaperon* (*The Hood*, 1832); here were *drames*, such as *Rodolphe, ou frère et sœur* (*Rodolphe; or, Brother and Sister*, 1823) or (turn it about) *Camilla, ou la sœur et le frère* (*Camilla; or, The Sister and the Brother*, 1832); here were sentimental 'tragedies,' such as the once-famous *Adrienne Lecouvreur* (1849), penned in collaboration with Ernest Legouvé, and (with a happy ending) these two authors' *La bataille des dames, ou un duel en amour* (*The Ladies' Battle; or, A Duel of Love*, 1851); here were fantasies, such as *La chatte métamorphosée en femme* (*The Cat metamorphosed into a Woman*, 1827), *Le diable à l'école* (*The Devil at School*, 1842) or *La fée aux roses* (*The Rose Fairy*, 1849); here were Oriental spectacles, such as *Haÿdée, ou le secret* (*Haydee; or, The Secret*, 1847); here were pseudo-historical pieces, such as *La sirène* (*The Syren*, 1844) or *Marco Spada* (1852).

With spirit, gaiety, and a sense of the sensational Scribe makes each one of these exciting and entertaining fare; there is hardly a real character in any, but, as many another author of the time discovered, there is a multiplicity of action and, above all, an almost infallible recipe for the production of similar works. As he showed so clearly in the extraordinarily popular *Une chaîne* (*A Chain*, 1841), Scribe was able to make people believe in his almost wholly synthetic situations, and naturally his companions eagerly examined the secrets of his art. The immediate imitators of Scribe are legion.

What is more important is that his formula for the construction of a *comédie-vaudeville* was found to be applicable also to the writing of more serious dramas. It is not too much to say that, mediocre though his own creations may be, he provided for others precisely what an age of romanticism most needed—a mould into which dramatic thought and passion might be poured. The romantic mind tends to be diffuse and sometimes vague, but diffuseness and vagueness are untheatrical qualities. Scribe accomplished an important task—albeit unwittingly—by emphasizing the importance of action and by showing how necessary for success is careful and deliberate planning of effect.

While the influence of Scribe's works was widespread, extending far beyond the boundaries of France, it is important to remember that even where the impress of his style is patent dramatists of many European lands preserved at least the main elements in their own native traditions and allowed the Scribe formula, when they employed it, merely to make more strongly theatrical qualities stemming from a different source.

Thus, for example, in Spain the Argentinian Ventura de la Vega, in introducing knowledge of the new style to Madrid, incorporated in it features of a purely Castilian sort: his *El hombre de mundo* (*The Man of the World*, 1845) owes its vigour to such a combination of forces. In these efforts he was companioned by Mariano José de Larra, whose *No más mostrador* (*Closing the Shop*, 1831) is confessedly an adaptation, with Spanish elements, of the French 'master.' In Italy, similarly, the spirit of Goldoni and of the *commedia dell' arte* prevented a merely slavish following of Paris models. There is a true breath of Venetian air in *La donna romantica e il medico omeopatico* (*The Romantic Lady and the Homeopathic Doctor*, 1858), by Riccardo Castelvecchio (Giulio Pullè), which deals, rather delightfully, with a young bride, Irene, who is wrapped in dismal sighs contracted from a reading of the best French love-romances.

Poland finds its characteristic spirit expressed in the various writings of Kazimierz Zalewski, with his *Bez posagu* (*Without a Dowry*, 1869), *Małżeństwo Apfel* (*The Apfel Marriage*, 1887), and other dramas of domestic interests. In Czechoslovakia the Scribe style is given an individual twist by Emanuel Bozděch, with his popular *Zkouška státníkova* (*The Politician's Trial*, 1874), and in Austria it is handled by Eduard von Bauernfeld in such plays as *Die Bekenntnisse* (*The Acknowledgments*, 1834) and *Bürgerlich und romantisch* (*Simple and Romantic*, 1835). Hungary too presents a peculiar comedy-drama variant of its own in such plays as the lively *A kérök* (*The Suitors*, 1819) and *Csalódások* (*Illusions*, 1828) by Károly Kisfaludy, while Ede Szigligeti displays Scribe's influence not only in his numerous folk-plays but also in such romantic dramas as *Szökött katona* (*The Deserter*, 1843) and in such historical tragedies as *A trónkereső* (*The Pretender*, 1868). From Sweden comes *Ett resande teatersällskap* (*The Touring Company*, 1842) by August Blanche, thoroughly Scandinavian in character, with a plot confessedly taken from Scarron and planned in a style clearly influenced by Scribe.

In considering such plays every endeavour must be made to assess the two determining forces at work—the force of that powerful French influence which made so many plays in so many lands merely pieces taken 'from the French', and the other force of the dominating national strains which even that influence could not completely banish from the stages of Europe.

'Sardoodledum'

Through a kind of amalgam of Scribe's technique, the suggestions given by the early experiments in mechanistic comedy and the resourcefulness of the melodrama—now directing its attention to materialistic themes—a new form of drama gradually came into being. From Lytton to Robertson in England, and from Augier to Sardou in France, diverse playwrights were engaged in preparing the theatres for what was to come—and, paradoxically, establishing a style against which later writers might react. Although the progress of realism is constant and uninterrupted during these years, yet the realism of one decade has ever seemed absurd to the realists of the next, and accordingly advance has taken the form continually of unacknowledged influence associated with public expressions of contempt. To Robertson Lytton appeared old-fashioned, and to Pinero Robertson was outmoded; nevertheless the line from the first author to the last is absolutely unbroken. Sardoodledum was both an inspiration and a menace for the dramatic authors at the end of the century.

It is, indeed, the prolific and successful Victorien Sardou who, although so much of his work belongs to the final years of the century, provides one of the chief links between the earlier styles and those that were to come. If we take a bird's-eye view of dramatic development in France and England within this period we can easily discern three main currents meandering downward and eventually forming one great stream. One is the melodramatic, represented by Sardou in France and by Boucicault in England. The second is the transformation of comedy-farce: here Eugène Labiche and H. J. Byron may be taken as representative. The third is the tentative introduction of contemporary themes—in particular those of marriage and money—not confined to one author or to one group of authors, but, as it were, welling up from the soil in diverse places almost imperceptibly until suddenly they take shape as a constantly flowing rivulet.

Victorien Sardou was a faithful disciple of Scribe, and his one endeavour was to produce plays likely to prove successful on the stage; he soared to success in 1860 with *Les pattes de mouche* (*A Scrap of Paper*), which long held popular esteem. Accordingly he ranges over vast territory, embracing in his wanderings both the romantic-historical and the realistic. Plot is of more concern to him than either character or idea, and theatricality predominates in his writings. This very theatricality, however, has its values, since he succeeded in enlarging the Scribe formula so as to make it apply to a stage which was becoming increasingly rich in its resources. He knew well how to make use of new scenic effects, and he was even capable of making his own innovations—such as the dramatic use of crowds, the employment of groups of persons not as automaton-supers but as dynamic forces in the action. It was in this and in other ways that Sardou prepared the path for his successors.

His historical pieces, such as *Théodora* (1884), *La Tosca* (1887), *Robespierre* (1899), *Madame Sans-Gêne* (written with Émile Moreau, 1893), and *La sorcière* (*The Witch*, 1903), need not detain us, although some of these are to be remembered because they were written for, and provided highly characteristic rôles for, Sarah Bernhardt. This sphere of playwriting, moreover, provided Sardou with what was one of the most successful and certainly one of the best among his plays, *La patrie* (*The Fatherland*, 1869), in which he piles melodramatic sensation upon realistic scenes and both of these upon the exhibition of tragic, tortured love. Typical is the scene in which Karloo discovers that his revolutionary friends have been betrayed through the ministry of Dolorès. Her husband is going to his death on the scaffold as Karloo and she plan to flee the country together, when suddenly the truth is revealed:

KARLOO: That woman—at the Duke's—this morning! That woman—at the Duke's—last night!

DOLORÈS: Last night?

KARLOO: It is she.

DOLORÈS: No!

KARLOO: It's you. It's you! You have betrayed us! You miserable— Dare you deny that you are the one?

DOLORÈS: Ah, Karloo!

KARLOO: Leave me—don't touch me!

      [*He disengages himself and darts towards the right, where he falls into a chair.*

DOLORÈS: Pity me.

KARLOO: God's vengeance! And I have been looking for her! And here she is. Who else?

DOLORÈS [*who has fallen to the floor*]: Ah, Karloo! Don't curse me! Let the others do that—not you.

KARLOO: Fiend—traitress—coward—coward!

DOLORÈS [*on her knees, making her way towards him*]: You don't know all, my Karloo. He wanted to kill you. When he left me he said: "I am going to kill him!'' I was mad with terror—stark mad—Karloo! I swear I was raving mad! I only tried to save you—I loved you so much! It was for your sake, for you!

KARLOO [*taking her hands in his*]: Your love. Your love has made me a perjurer and a traitor! Your fatal love has brought these poor wretches to the scaffold, and a whole nation to its ruin! Your love is hellish, deadly! I *do* curse you! I execrate, I hate you!

[*He casts her to the floor.*

DOLORÈS: Ah, Karloo, you are killing me!

KARLOO: No, not yet!

DOLORÈS: What are you going to do?

KARLOO [*dragging her to the window*]: Come here, Madam! First, look at your work.

DOLORÈS: Pity me!

[*The windows are red with the reflected light of the faggots. Screams and murmurs of horror are heard.*

KARLOO: Look at it! Look at your faggot-heap—it's burning!

DOLORÈS: Pity me!

KARLOO: Look—count your victims!

DOLORÈS: Karloo—ungrateful—

KARLOO [*raising her and forcing her to look*]: You must accustom yourself to flames—you must have some notion of what hell is like—hell, where your love is dragging us!

DOLORÈS: Mercy!

KARLOO: Listen! They have caught sight of me! Listen now, listen!

THE PRISONERS: Karloo—traitor! Traitor!

KARLOO: Do you hear?

DOLORÈS: My God!

KARLOO: And do you not also hear the dead man crying out: "Remember your oath"??

DOLORÈS [*rising in terror*]: No. No.

KARLOO: "No matter who the guilty one may be, strike, have no mercy!"

DOLORÈS: Karloo, would you strike me?

KARLOO [*drawing his dagger*]: My oath!

DOLORÈS [*wild with terror, as she struggles to free herself*]: With your own hand—no! You wouldn't do that! Pity me—I'm afraid!

KARLOO [*losing his self-control*]: I have sworn!

DOLORÈS: No, no—don't—leave me!

KARLOO: I have sworn, I have sworn! [*He plunges the dagger into her.*

DOLORÈS [*falling to the floor*]: Now go—you have killed me. And I loved you so! I loved you so. [*KARLOO throws his dagger down.*

KARLOO [*nearly out of his mind*]: I have killed you! I! I!

DOLORÈS: At least you can join me, now! Come.

KARLOO [*falling to his knees before her, an inanimate mass, and covering her with kisses, while he sobs*]: I will come with you—I am so miserable! Dolorès, my sweetest love! O God! O God!

DOLORÈS: Come, then.

KARLOO [*standing*]: Wait! I am coming! [*He runs to the window, stands in it, and cries out.*] Executioner [*excitement in the Square*]—you lack one man! Make way for me on your faggot-heap!

DOLORÈS [*rising in order to see him*]: Ah!
KARLOO [*to DOLORÈS, his voice full of loving tenderness*]: You see? I am coming, I am coming! [*He goes swiftly from the room. DOLORÈS dies.*

What popular audience would not be thrilled by such a scene? What lover of truth in the theatre can refrain from a smile or a sneer?

Play after play is cast in the same mould. *Spiritisme* (*Spiritualism*, 1897) exploits current interest in the occult by showing a young wife, Simone, angered at her husband's absorption in spiritualistic research, first taking a lover and later giving herself out as dead. Deserted by the lover, she finds a friend who so works on the husband's mind as to persuade him to summon her spirit back from the shades—whereupon, of course, the real Simone appears. This is the situation of *Much Ado about Nothing* without the poetry. Equally theatrical is *Marcelle* (1896), which, dealing with the story of a woman with a past, characteristically brings her safely out of her troubles to a conclusion vastly happier than any of the realists would have allowed her.

Yet this very theatricality was to be put to good use, both by Sardou himself and by his immediate followers, in the service of the realistic drama. Of such plays his *Daniel Rochat* (1880) may be regarded as typical. Here a free-thinking, 'atheist' hero marries, by a civil ceremony, an Anglo-American girl, Léa, but jibs at following this by a ceremony in church. The entire play is taken up with the struggle between these two, and in the end a somewhat unsatisfactory conclusion is reached. Although not by any means a masterpiece, and although now seen to be replete with many spurious sentiments, this drama illustrates well how the Scribe technique, applied in new ways, was being adapted to the requirements of contemporary themes. In himself Sardou is nothing but a later edition of Kotzebue or of Pixérécourt; as a 'barometer' of Parisian playhouse taste his works have prime historical value; for those who came after him he was a model to be imitated and an idol to be overthrown.

Closely associated with Sardou in his endeavour to feed the stage with successful entertainments is Eugène Labiche. Instead, however, of cultivating the melodramatic, he relies mainly upon comedy farce, applying the now familiar Scribe formula to plays designed mainly for the purpose of arousing laughter. Although he succeeded in presenting a delightful series of amusing pictures of contemporary life, most of his works have little intrinsic value. On the other hand, a few of them—notably *Le voyage de M. Perrichon* (*M. Perrichon's Journey*, 1860) and *La poudre aux yeux* (*Dust in the Eyes*, 1861)—exhibit qualities of a further kind. The former presents a definite thesis, suggesting that men are apt to detest those who do them a good turn, that their affection goes out rather to those whom they themselves have assisted. In *La poudre aux yeux* the plot is based on the idea of being and seeming—the complications arising from the social masks worn by the diverse characters. Perhaps Labiche does not contribute in these works much of great importance for the later development of the play of ideas, yet this incursion of a sense of purpose into the realm of farce is not unworthy of notice. Most of his work, however, is of the delightfully irresponsible kind represented by *Le chapeau de paille d'Italie* (*The Italian Straw Hat*, 1851), in which a worthy young hero is thrown into a maze of unexpected comic trials all because his horse happens to eat a straw hat that has been hung up on a tree.

Along with these two currents we must observe how topics based on contemporary conditions were beginning, even before 1829, to receive dramatic treatment. Two thoroughly minor playwrights, for example, Édouard-Joseph Mazères and Adolphe Empis, collaborated in this very year to produce *La mère et la fille* (*Mother and Daughter*, 1830), a play dealing with marriage in relation to money, while four years later they brought out *Une liaison* (1834), in which appeared a theme later to be more fully exploited—that of the prostitute in the family circle. Even before these dates another minor writer, Casimir Bonjour, wrote his *L'argent, ou les mœurs du siècle* (*Money; or, The Manners of the Age*, 1826), which by its very title indicates its interests.

These are early dramas: Sardou, starting his career in 1854, carries us on into the present century; the work of Labiche appears mainly in the sixties and seventies. Although diverse in date, the three streams may be viewed together if we regard Sardou not so much for himself as for what he symbolized, and if we see Labiche merely as the perfector of a line of comedy-farce the tradition of which he inherited. The realistic melodrama, the realistic farce, and the introduction of the 'thesis' in both laid the foundations of the typical drama of the latter half of the century.

Popular Realism in France

The fusion of these is well revealed in the work of Émile Augier. Starting in the mood of imaginative romanticism, tinged with melodramatic sentiment, pursuing technically the methods of Scribe, he became one of the principal founders of the new style. In 1844 he first came before the public with a verse drama, *La ciguë* (*Hemlock*), an unimportant piece, followed shortly afterwards by a couple of other works in the same medium, *L'aventurière* (*The Adventuress*, 1848) and *Gabrielle* (1849). The interest of these two dramas rests in their subject-matter. *L'aventurière* presents a picture (set in an historical past) of a prostitute, Clorinde, whose entire being is transformed because of her newly awakened love, and draws a sharp contrast between the good sense of the bourgeoisie and romantic follies: in it we are close to *La dame aux camélias*. In the second a definite thesis is introduced. The whole purpose of the play is to prove that it is better for a woman to extract joy and romantic pleasure from living respectably as a wife than to snatch at the illusory delights of being a mistress: here we have entered the sphere of the drama of ideas.

As yet, however, the form by no means harmonized with the content.

The scenes, characters, and ideas belong to the social life of the mid-nineteenth century, but the tinkling verse carries us into the atmosphere of another age. Soon, however, Augier, no doubt inspired by Dumas *fils*, was prepared to find a truer harmony; and as a result of his determination came *Le gendre de M. Poirier* (*The Son-in-law of M. Poirier*), in 1854, written in collaboration with Jules Sandeau, from whose novel *Sacs et parchemins* its plot is derived. There can be no question but this is a minor masterpiece. Its effervescent wit, allied to a serious purpose, gives it a distinction above most of its companions. Fundamentally, the story is based on the clash between two ideals. On the one hand stands the Marquis de Presles, representative of the ancient aristocracy; on the other is the wealthy, middle-class M. Poirier. The latter has caused his daughter, Antoinette, to marry Gaston, a scion of the noble house: Gaston is just on the point of coming to appreciate the virtues of his *parvenu* bride when Poirier starts to retrench, to speak vulgarly of money, to display all his lack of gentility. The conflict between the proud aristocrat, living in the past, idle, domineering, yet gifted with magnanimous qualities, and the hardworking, yet essentially vulgar, bourgeois is delineated with admirable balance and fine restraint. Perhaps the end may appear a trifle sentimental, when Antoinette's native dignity and nobleness of mind succeed in converting Gaston to look upon her with love, but until the very last scenes this play is innocent of the vices which so cluttered up and falsified the dramas of the eighteenth century. Here is a modern spirit: *Le gendre de M. Poirier* can still be read or seen with interest and profit.

Augier's stress on moral ideas is perhaps his greatest contribution to this mid-nineteenth-century realistic movement, and the moral idea becomes even more pronounced in *Le mariage d'Olympe* (*Olympia's Marriage*, 1855), which may be regarded as a kind of answer to *La dame aux camélias*. Augier had been prepared in *L'aventurière* to accept the concept of the reformed prostitute, but he was not prepared to allow her to stain family honour. His Olympe is a woman who, after a life of sin, allows her former life to vanish from memory by the device of taking another name. In her new rôle she marries Henri, nephew of the Marquis de Puygiron, by whom she is welcomed into the aristocratic circle. Her nature, however, is wholly evil: she yearns for the excitements of her early life, and through sheer boredom she starts a scandal concerning the innocent Geneviève. By her own actions she is revealed, and at the end the old Marquis, to protect the honour of his line, shoots her and is shown reloading his pistol, for the purpose of committing suicide, as the curtain falls.

Throughout the course of his later work Augier kept emphasizing his common-sense views on life. He was no revolutionary, and romantic excesses seemed to him a potent danger; his mission, as he regarded it, was to draw lifelike pictures of contemporary society and to plead for the basic virtues. The evils of city life are delineated both in *La jeunesse* (*Youth*,

1858), and *Les lionnes pauvres* (*Dissipation*; written in collaboration with Édouard Foussier, 1858); in *Les effrontés* (*The Impertinents*, 1861) he attacks the enormities of the modern newspaper and the power it puts into the hands of single men; discussion of politics and clericalism made *Le fils de Giboyer* (*Giboyer's Son*, 1862) a *succès de scandale* in its day; divorce is the theme of *Madame Caverlet* (1876). Finer than these is *Les Fourchambault* (1878), in which a study is made of an upper middle-class household, with a vulgar Mme Fourchambault, a libertine son, Léopold, who yet has some good in him, a poor relation, Marie, and a *deus ex machina* in the person of an illegitimate son, Bernard, who sentimentally saves the family from bankruptcy and wins the fair Marie's hand as the curtain falls. In all of these there is a skilful and interesting handling of character as well as a philosophy which, although maybe somewhat shallow, gives to the scenes an individual quality. The plays of Augier proved that the theatre could well serve as a platform for the enunciation of ideas, made interesting because of their incorporation in plots narrated with the technical brilliance which Scribe had taught his followers to cultivate.

Augier's chief companion in this sphere was Alexandre Dumas *fils*, whose career extends from the famous *La dame aux camélias* of 1852 to *Francillon* in 1887. Like Augier, he was serious in his intent; like him, he based his technique on that of Scribe, although to Scribe's influence in this way he added a strength based apparently on careful study of Corneille's style; like him, he set out to explore the reaches of contemporary life. In his writings, however, more clearly than in those of Augier, the characteristic trend of nineteenth-century realism becomes apparent. His persons are treated as creatures of their surroundings, puppets rudely battered as they are jerked to and fro by unseen strings in the blind power of circumstance, and there is a tendency in his writings to assume that the realistic resides only in the darker spheres of life. In their reaction against the prevailing themes of their romantic predecessors, the romantic realists of the age were impelled to abandon the colourful for the sordid.

His characteristic qualities are well revealed in that earliest of his plays, *La dame aux camélias* (played frequently as *Camille*), in which a prostitute, Marguerite Gautier, is made the heroine. Following the Scribe formula, the first act is devoted almost entirely to presenting the general *milieu* in which she moves. This set, the play is then made to march on towards its fatal conclusion. For the first time Marguerite's heart has been touched by love, and she arranges to go off with her Armand to spend the summer in the country. His father arrives, and by his skilful pleading persuades her that, if she truly loves him, it is her duty to give him up. Hereupon she makes the great sacrifice, writing to Armand that she has decided to leave him for another. In drunken anger he insults her publicly, and she, worn out from the passions of these events, falls into a decline. Just as the repentant Armand, having learned the truth, takes her to his arms she dies.

Like a thunderbolt this play descended upon Paris. The whole of the theatre public wept and sighed over the poor Marguerite, and when Augier tried to arouse consideration of other aspects of the problem his *Mariage d'Olympe* had short shrift. This particular kind of realistic drama was firmly established.

It was even more fully established in *Le demi-monde*, of 1855, a play that in its title introduced a new word into the French—indeed, into the international—vocabulary. The 'demi-monde' is the asylum of all those who have left their own social environment, welcoming alike men and women of rank whom fortune has cast down and other men and women who, usually for their own advancement, have climbed up the rungs of the social ladder, but have been unable to enter the closed windows of high life. In this world lives Suzanne, a self-seeking beauty whose one thought is of herself. She entangles in her snares the young hero, Raymond de Nanjac, who is, however, sternly warned of the menace by his gay and cynical friend, Olivier de Jalin, a former lover of Suzanne. A quarrel ensues between the two men, and a duel is fought; but in the end Suzanne's duplicity is revealed, and for the hero all is well.

What attracts our attention here is the manner in which Dumas has concentrated his attention almost entirely on environment. The stress of the play is not so much on the persons as on the social world in which they live: the demi-monde itself, rather than de Nanjac, may be regarded as the central character in the play.

La question d'argent (*A Question of Money*, 1857) followed a couple of years later. Here, instead of developing a *milieu*, Dumas turns to exploit a problem. Fundamentally, this problem is that of the rightness or wrongness of capitalistic finance. The story of the poor-born Giraud, who is prepared to marry Élisa de Roncourt simply for the purpose of obtaining a respectable position in life, does not matter in comparison with the basic question—whether a man has the right to employ duplicity (in this case a pretended absconsion designed to lower the value of company stocks) in order to make an enormous profit from his investments. The theme has been so frequently dealt with since Dumas' time—it has now even invaded the realm of the detective story—that it has ceased to make much impress on our minds, and maybe we must agree that in its structure *La question d'argent* does not exhibit such skill as was revealed in the earlier plays of this author; at the same time, we may readily imagine the impression made on contemporaries by this bold presentation of a problem, adumbrated before, but never so trenchantly expressed.

With *Le fils naturel* (*The Illegitimate Son*, 1858) comes something new: it is now commonly recognized that in this work the modern 'thesis-play' was created. And it was created with conscious deliberation. "'Art for art's sake?'" cries Dumas. "Words devoid of meaning!" And he proceeds to enunciate his belief that it is the mission of the dramatist to preach. The sermon in *Le fils naturel* is illegitimacy, and one of the chief virtues of the drama is that the preacher, instead of merely giving his congregation what it expected to hear, dares to present an idea of his own. Through an exceedingly complex plot Dumas traces the fortunes of the base-born Jacques de Boisceny, who through his own fine qualities succeeds in becoming an outstanding political figure of his time. His father is Charles Sternay, a self-seeking individualist, who has deserted his mistress in order to marry into an aristocratic family. At first Sternay is merely annoyed when his paternity of Jacques is revealed, but as the young man becomes of greater and greater importance in the world of affairs he seeks, in vain, to recognize him as his son. Unquestionably the audience would have expected a sentimental reunion for the final curtain: Dumas, however, has caused his hero to adopt his mother's name and remain unreconciled.

After a number of largely insignificant plays Dumas proceeded to enlarge the scope of his new dramatic invention in *Les idées de Madame Aubray* (*Madame Aubray's Ideas*, 1867), in which appears a kind of study of true Christianity in modern social surroundings. The central character is Madame Aubray, a woman who believes in following the dictates of her own charitable soul rather than the codes of the world in which she lives. Her dearly beloved son. Camille, falls in love with a girl, Jeannine, a presumed 'widow' and in reality an unmarried mother. When Camille asks for his mother's approval Madame Aubray refuses, but after Jeannine, in a moment of noble renunciation, pretends to Camille that she has had many lovers she is so deeply touched that she gives the girl to her son. This is undoubtedly an interesting play, and Dumas has exhibited great skill, not only in revealing the mind of Madame Aubray herself, but, more importantly, in suggesting the influence of her character upon those with whom she comes into contact. Sentimentalism, no doubt, colours the general picture, and the situations are sometimes twisted to accord with the author's purpose, but among the plays of ideas written in the sixties and seventies this stands out for its directness of aim and its sincerity of purpose.

There follows a series of rather conflicting plays on the subject of illicit relations. In the ironical *Une visite de noces* (*A Honeymoon Call*, 1871) a husband is shown attracted towards a former mistress when he thinks she has had many lovers, but immediately repelled when he finds out that she is faithful to his memory: he prefers, rather than resume an illicit attachment to a woman of this kind, to remain with his wife. In *La Princesse Georges* (1871) the irony is of a different sort and bitter. Séverine's husband, a prince, has a liaison with Sylvanie, wife of the Count de Terremonde. Loving her husband, the injured woman informs the count, and then is dismayed to learn that he intends to kill his rival when he comes for his assignation. A shot is heard; Séverine is in despair; then suddenly it is revealed that the slain man is not her husband, but a wretched youth, de Foudette, to whom also Sylvanie had opened her arms and who had, all unwittingly, walked into the trap. The solution is clever—perhaps too clever; for, although in our minds we are prepared to recognize that the author has found an interesting twist for a hackneyed plot—even although we may admit that his purpose is being pursued by indication of the blind fate that operates in this world of the illicit in sex relations—the unexpectedness of the final scene undoubtedly invokes in us an impression of artificiality. Like so many plays of the same kind still to come, there is too much brain-work here.

It is of interest to note—especially when we compare Dumas' career with that of authors immediately following him—that from these purely realistic plays he now turned to a kind of drama which, although maintaining outward realism, became invested with a kind of mystical atmosphere. In his address to the public prefacing *La femme de Claude* (*Claude's Wife*, 1873) he speaks of his latest work as "purely symbolic." "Claude does not murder his wife," he declares; "the dramatist does not murder a woman; together they destroy a Beast." Written after the outbreak of war with Prussia, *La femme de Claude* mingles a spy theme with that of adultery. Césarine is the thoroughly dissipated wife of a great inventor; she becomes involved in the toils of a German agent, Cartagnac, and turns the head of her husband's brilliant assistant, Antonin. In the end, just after she has been foiled in her attempt to steal some military plans, Claude shoots her dead—symbolically with the new rifle invented by Antonin—and the Beast is vanquished.

The symbolic style, no less than that of *La Princesse Georges*, shows at once Dumas' source of weakness and his source of strength. The strength lies in his mastery of what may be called theatrical logic. Although analysis may demonstrate the spurious sentiment apparent in many scenes of *La dame aux camélias*, that irresistible sweep accompanied by economy of means which the author learned from Scribe has made it a popular favourite. Above all other things, Dumas knew how to arrest and to hold the attention of his audiences. At the same time, in this strength lies potential weakness. So long as the dramatist keeps to the level of *La dame aux camélias* all is well; but when he tries to become profound the very artificiality inherent in the 'well-made-play' formula proves his undoing. The scaffolding and the machinery suddenly reveal themselves to us blatantly, and illusion is dispelled.

With Augier, Dumas may be accepted as one of the most influential members of that dramatic group which was intent on establishing the new realism, on introducing social problems into the playhouse, and on using the stage for the purpose of inculcating ideas; but neither was a genius.

Dozens of other writers applied themselves to the new style and wrote abundantly of the problems (mainly marriage and money) of the bourgeoisie. Among them are François Poinsard with his *L'honneur et l'argent* (*Honour and Money*, 1853), Paul Arène with his *Pierrot héritier* (*Pierrot the Heir*, 1865), Théodore Barrière with his *Malheur aux vaincus* (*Woe to the Vanquished*, 1865), Jacques Bornet with his *L'usurier* (*The Usurer*, 1870), Victor Séjour with his *L'argent du diable* (*The Devil's Coin*, 1854). Of such authors few deserve special note. Honoré de Balzac has quality, but even he warrants much more attention for his *Comédie humaine* than for his dramas—*La marâtre* (*The Stepmother*, 1848) and *Mercadet* (1851)—although the latter is an incisively written study of financial chicanery, with some excellent scenes. So, too, individual mention may be made of the interesting *La révolte* (*The Revolt*, 1870) of Count Philippe de Villiers de l'Isle-Adam, a not ineffective anticipation of *A Doll's House*.

There are works of minor interest here, but the real triumphs of the realistic stage were still to come.

Realistic Gropings in England

While the English stage produced no Dumas or Augier, the same movements as dominated in Paris can be traced in London.

In the year 1840 appeared a play called *Money*, by Lord Lytton, and its very title tells its story. Here is the direct equivalent of those French plays which, then and later, explored the problems of wealth and sought to reveal some of the vices of bourgeois society. The scene in which the will of the rich Mr Mordaunt is read indicates its tone. The relatives are gathered, all eager and expectant, with, among them, the poor hero, Evelyn, and his love, Clara. One after another of the richer members of the company are woefully disappointed, and then comes the shock as the lawyer reads on:

> *SHARP:* "And, with the aforesaid legacies and exceptions, I do will and bequeath the whole of my fortune, in India Stock, Bonds, Exchequer bills, Three Per Cent. Consols, and in the Bank of India (constituting him hereby sole residuary legatee and joint executor with the aforesaid Henry Graves, Esq.) to Alfred Evelyn [*pause—a movement on the part of everybody but SHARP*], now or formerly of Trinity College, Cambridge [*universal excitement*], being, I am told, an oddity, like myself—the only one of my relations who never fawned on me; and who, having known privation, may the better employ wealth." And now, sir, I have only to wish you joy, and give you this letter from the deceased. I believe it is important.
>
> [*All rise.*
>
> *EVELYN* [*looking over to CLARA*]: Ah, Clara, if you had but loved me!
> *CLARA* [*turning away*]: And his wealth, even more than poverty, separates us for ever!
> *LADY FRANKLIN:* I wish you joy.
> *OMNES* [*crowding round to congratulate EVELYN*]: I wish you joy.
> *SIR JOHN* [*to GEORGINA*]: Go, child—put a good face on it—he's an immense match! My dear fellow, I wish you joy; you are a great man now —a very great man! I wish you joy.
> *EVELYN* [*aside*]: And *her* voice alone is silent!
> *GLOSSMORE:* If I can be of any use to you—
> *STOUT:* Or I, sir—
> *BLOUNT:* Or I? Shall I put you up at the clubs?
> *SHARP:* You will want a man of business. I transacted all Mr Mordaunt's affairs.

SIR JOHN [*rushing to centre of crowd, and pushing them aside*]: Tush, tush! Mr
Evelyn is at home *here*—always looked on him as a son! Nothing in the world
we would not do for him!
EVELYN: Lend me ten pounds for my old nurse!
OMNES: Certainly! Certainly!
[*Chorus put their hands into their pockets, producing purses, and offering them eagerly.*

No more than this brief extract is required to indicate *Money's* position
in the history of the theatre. Without doubt it stems from the sentimental
tradition: the situation in which Evelyn and Clara find themselves is
similar to that of many an eighteenth-century hero and heroine. At the
same time, its dialogue has not the strained artificiality associated with
the names of Cumberland and Kelly, while its theme definitely aligns it
with the work of the new realists.

In this way the play stands as an excellent example of transitional
drama. Lytton was a writer who, like Scribe himself, was apt in sensing
the trend of public taste. *Money* he wrote because he realized the craving
for the realistic in measured doses: he was also the author of the immensely popular 'gentlemanly melodrama' *The Lady of Lyons* (1838) and
the romantically historical *Richelieu; or, The Conspiracy* (1839), because he
realized that the same public that craved for realism also craved for
romance.

The contributions of Boucicault, Reade, and Taylor have been noted
above, but something new enters into the theatre with the work of Tom
Robertson (T. W. Robertson). It must be confessed that his plays have
little intrinsic importance: he wrote no *Dame aux camélias* or *Gendre de M.
Poirier*. On the other hand, the significance of his writings was, for the
English stage, of very considerable extent, and accordingly their innovations must be surveyed, if not for their own worth, at least for what they
meant to others.

Fundamentally Robertson, who started as a romantic melodramatist,
was the first man in England to conceive of stage realism as a complete
whole. Others before him had penned scenes taken (more or less) from
ordinary life; others too had introduced real objects, or their theatrical
semblances, to the boards. It remained for him to co-ordinate these
efforts. He not only set forth to write plays in which he tried to reflect the
ways of common life; he endeavoured to provide for those plays such settings and such interpretation as fitted their lines. He sought for actors
prepared to abandon the old bold manner appropriate to melodrama
and the romantic play; he insisted that his doors should have real knobs
on them and not simply painted forms.

An excellent, and an essentially truthful, picture of his struggles was
presented by his successor, A. W. Pinero, in *Trelawny of the 'Wells'* (1899),
and nowhere better could one find an indication both of what Robertson
set out to accomplish and what he sought to banish from the playhouse.
If this later comedy is read as a comment on his own works we shall have
a clear mental image of his achievements. After a kind of transitional

play, *David Garrick* (1864), he created in *Society* (1865) a drama that immediately fluttered Victorian audiences, and followed this with a series of similar pieces—*Ours* (1866), *Caste* (1867), and *School* (1869). Of these *Caste* shows his qualities at their best and most characteristic. Whiffs of sentimentalism and romance are to be breathed here certainly. The Honourable George D'Alroy is almost as pure as a hero of melodrama, and Esther Eccles is a true heroine. Beyond this, however, there is a flavour in this comedy-drama of which the melodrama remained innocent. Esther is in danger, but not from any dark-moustached villain: the menace to her life is the snobbery of D'Alroy's aristocratic family. Noting this, we realize that in *Caste* Robertson has moved into an entirely different mental and emotional world. Although he makes use of melodramatic devices, the service to which they are put is far other than that of a few decades before. The very title of his play shows his purpose: above and beyond the characters and the plot there exists a theme, and that theme is 'Caste.' In his own way Robertson was doing for London what Augier and Dumas *fils* were doing for Paris.

One further comment may be made on his significance for the modern stage. Not alone, certainly, yet nevertheless powerfully, he aided in the development of the present-day producer. As the drama increased its scope during the nineteenth century and as the theatres came to enjoy practical resources of which they had no knowledge in the past, the need arose for the appointment of officials responsible for co-ordination of effect. Such need came with the 'historical' productions of Shakespeare's plays by Charles Kean; it presented itself to Dion Boucicault with his new-style melodramas; Gilbert found it essential to exercise control of this kind in the production of his comic operas. Robertson was one of the first in England to demonstrate the need with respect to the realistic stage.

This, of course, is not to say that he achieved anything akin to what was accomplished by the German players who acted under the direction of the Duke of Saxe-Meiningen and whose methods so deeply impressed contemporary theatre workers, but his tentative efforts were in the same direction as theirs. In its tours during the seventies and eighties this company revealed in final form what the stage had been groping towards during the immediately preceding decades. The director became all-important, and every effort was made to secure unity of impression, whether in the presentation of Shakespeare's plays in revival or in the production of the new realistic drama.

The Realism of Hebbel and the Naturalism of Zola

Germany had something else to offer to realism in the theatre.

This was a period when Prussia under the Hohenzollerns was forging an unwieldy collection of dukedoms and principalities into a coherent whole; and with startling rapidity the Reich thus created swelled to giant proportions, stepped beyond its boundaries, and shattered the proud power of France. Perhaps most effort during these decades was devoted to the building of material strength and to the provision of a philosophy, mystical in its quality, likely to serve as a kind of national religion, but the theatre too played its part in the development of nationalism.

Its greatest and most characteristic growth was that of the Wagnerian opera.

At the same time the surge of national enthusiasm could not entirely conceal the concurrent development of social thought, and in Friedrich Hebbel the stage found an author of more than common vision and depth of purpose. A tortured soul inclined by nature and circumstance towards introspection, he succeeded in accomplishing something much more profound than anything achieved either by Augier or by Dumas *fils*. In his earliest drama, *Judith* (1841), the potentialities rather than the actualities of power were displayed: although this rather chaotic, artificially constructed, and bombastically executed tragedy has won some considerable applause from his countrymen, we must deem it nothing save the immature promise of Hebbel's genius. His second important work, however, fully revealed his strength. *Maria Magdalena* (1844), despite its title, was no tragedy based on a Biblical theme. The scene is set in a German joiner's house. This joiner, Anthony, a hard and rigorous although well-meaning man, has a daughter, Clara, and a son, Karl. With grim realism Hebbel traces their fortunes until the girl is forced to cast herself into a well. The end of the play is typical of its general mood. A secretary, in love with Clara, has just come in wounded after fighting a duel with her seducer: Karl has rushed out after a rumour that a woman has killed herself:

KARL [*comes back*]: Clara's dead. Her head's all broken in by the edge of the well, when she— Father, she didn't fall in, she jumped in. A girl saw her.

ANTHONY: Let her think well before she speaks. It is too dark for her to have seen that for certain.

SECRETARY: Do you doubt it? You'd like to, but you can't. Just think of what you said to her. You sent her out on the road to death, and I, I'm to blame that she didn't turn back. When you suspected her misfortune, you thought of the tongues that would hiss at it, but not of the worthlessness of the snakes that own them. You said things to her that drove her to despair. And I, instead of folding her in my arms, when she opened her heart to me in nameless terror, thought of the knave that might mock at me, and—I made myself dependent on a man who was worse than I, and I'm paying for it with my life. And you, too, though you stand there like a rock, you too will say some day: "Daughter, I wish you had not spared me the head-shakes and shoulder-shruggings of the Pharisees: it humiliates me more that you are not here to sit by my deathbed and wipe the sweat of anguish from my brow."

ANTHONY: She has spared me nothing. They saw her.

SECRETARY: She did what she could. You were not worthy that she should succeed.

ANTHONY: Or she, perhaps!   [*Noises without.*
KARL: They're bringing her.   [*Going.*
ANTHONY [*standing immovable till the end, calls him back*]: Into the back room
   with her, where her mother lay.
SECRETARY: I must go to meet her. [*Tries to get up and falls.*] Oh, Karl!
                                    [*KARL helps him out.*
ANTHONY: I don't understand the world any more.   [*Stands thinking.*

All the ingredients of the later naturalistic play are here—the drab, lower
middle-class atmosphere, the sensationalism, the tendency towards
moralization, the conflict of man and society.

In one sense this drama is unique among Hebbel's works, since all his
other plays have historical or legendary themes, but in this mingling of
the contemporary with the mythical he proved himself a companion of
the later Ibsen and Strindberg. He proved their companion, too, in striving to attain a philosophy of the theatre in its relation to social life. In his
critical pronouncements he develops, albeit in a strangely crabbed Germanic style, the concept of a new kind of tragedy—the tragedy, not of the
individual (conflicting with forces outside himself or within his own
being), but of society. Despite all the verbiage with which he invests this
idea, it is obvious that basically it is both pessimistic and authoritarian.
In *Agnes Bernauer* (1852), for example, he shows his fifteenth-century
hero, Albrecht, Prince of Bavaria, resolutely sacrificing his love for the
heroine, the barber's daughter who is nicknamed "the angel of Augs-
burg," in the stern interests of the state which he is destined to rule. For
Hebbel the ultimate Universal is human society, and tragedy is developed when a man or a woman attempts to set his or her individual will
against the basic Idea. Yet the concepts of this individual, paradoxically,
may be those which the Universal, at a later date, will embrace within its
own being. *Agnes Bernauer* thus, in the words of the author,

> simply represents the relation of the individual to society, and accordingly
> illustrates in two characters, one of the highest, the other of the lowest class,
> the fact that the individual, however splendid and great, however noble and
> fair, must under all circumstances yield to society. For in society and its
> necessary formal expression, the state, humanity lives as a whole, while in
> the individual only one single phase of it is unfolded.

Irony lies in the fact that, to quote this author again, "all tragedy lies
in destruction and proves nothing but the emptiness of existence."

The distinctive quality of Hebbel's historical dramas lies in their expression of this philosophy and in their distinctively 'modern' development of motivation. If they were stripped of their decorative costumes
the characters might stand forth as persons of the dramatist's own
time. In *Judith* there is a probing of the heroine's soul; in *Genoveva*
(1843) is an examination of the fate of a woman falsely accused of unfaithfulness; in *Herodes und Mariamne* (*Herod and Mariamne*, 1850) is an

exploration of religious sentiment. Later came *Gyges und sein Ring* (*Gyges and his Ring*, 1855), in which a Greek atmosphere is transformed into German. The story of Kandaules, King of Lydia, who causes Rhodope, his queen, to appear disrobed, with the consequent vengeance taken by the injured woman, is here (somewhat absurdly) invested with would-be philosophical significance. A final proof at once of Hebbel's intimate association with his own time and of his power of anticipating things to come may be found in his trilogy entitled *Die Nibelungen* (1862), professedly designed to draw the "great national epic dramatically nearer to the public"—a romantic monument as florid and pretentious as Wagner's. Including an introductory act, *Der gehörnte Siegfried* (*The Horned Siegfried*), and two complete dramas, *Siegfrieds Tod* (*Siegfried's Death*) and *Kriemhilds Rache* (*Kriemhild's Vengeance*), it forms a vast, lumbering, effusive, two-day production.

What Hebbel lacked was a sense of form. Like Kleist and others, his language tends to be tormented—a chaotic flow illuminated at times by lurid flashes of mighty splendour. Like Wagner, his soul was essentially middle-class. At the same time hardly any other dramatic author of his own time can be accounted his equal. We may detest his philosophy, deplore his cloudy rhetoric, smile at some of his tragic tensions, but we cannot deny his genius.

During these same years another kindred German author was striving to develop a new modern tragic expression. Otto Ludwig shared Hebbel's tendency towards theorizing and his associations with Kleist and the earlier 'Sturm und Drang.' He too feels deeply the fate of the modern artist, denied the free, untrammelled lyricism of the primitive poet and forced to bring intellect into the sphere of the imagination. He too is a soul broken by an inner dichotomy. His interests are almost equally divided between the romantic and the materialistic, and in his critical discussion of the latter he tends to give away the basic secret of much failure in the realistic theatre. "It is no little thing," he pompously remarks, "to keep your eye on eight characters all at the same time." The statement is no doubt true, but the fact, of course, is that the truly great dramatist does not 'keep his eye' on his characters: by a strange imaginative magic he *becomes* those characters: he is the god who has created them and in whom mystically he has his being. In their concentration upon philosophies the realistic playwrights have constantly tended to abrogate their divinity and become spectators of the events they describe—or else they have sought, Byron-wise, to make all their dramatic characters mere replicas of parts of themselves.

Ludwig's concrete contributions to the theatre are *Die Makkabäer* (*The Maccabees*, 1854) and *Der Erbförster* (*The Forester*, 1850), but only the latter has any real significance. This grim tale of crime and passion, in which an old hereditary forester, his mind filled with exaggerated ideas of his own rights, clashes fatally with his choleric master, with its technique confessedly based on the author's own intimate analysis of

Shakespeare's methods, undoubtedly established one more trenchant model for the realistic dramatists to come. Such a work, when taken with Hebbel's *Maria Magdalena*, at once reveals to us what qualities the new realists desired to substitute for the artificialities of the Scribe pattern. No doubt neither achieved more than a partial success, but they both point the way unerringly to Ibsen.

Although the dramatic work of Emile Zola takes us into the seventies of the century, it may be well to consider his naturalistic aims along with these German efforts. In himself Zola is not important as a playwright, but he has tremendous importance on account of the æsthetic philosophy which he tried to establish on the stage. Fundamentally, what he sought was the extreme of objectivity, applied—characteristically enough—only to the gloomiest spheres of human life. In the realm of prose fiction, of course, rests his greatest fame, but of hardly less significance is his contribution to the theatre. *Thérèse Raquin* (1873) inaugurated a style utterly different from anything attempted by Augier, Dumas *fils*, and their companions. The plot is not particularly remarkable—a story of a woman, Thérèse, and her lover, Laurent, who decide to murder her husband, accomplish their crime, and find that they are driven by force of conscience to end their own lives in a suicide pact. It is the way in which this gloomy tale is presented that grants the play its peculiar significance. What Zola wanted was a type of drama which should, without twisting facts in order to prove a thesis, be absolutely true to existence. Where Augier had tried to be realistic Zola endeavoured to be naturalistic. The 'drama of ideas,' the *pièce à thèse*, tacitly assumes that the author devises a plot in such a way as to prove his argument: such an author may present a setting true to the actual in every respect, he may adopt a kind of dialogue faithful to the terms of contemporary speech, but his basic purpose implies that he must so order his material as to accord with his preconceived idea. Zola wanted complete objectivity, the depiction of the real with almost photographic exactitude. He sees his characters as case-studies; he wishes the drama to submit to follow the methods of science by studying men dispassionately. He attacks the old romantic theatre, but at the same time has no desire to revive the classic. "There should no longer be any school," he cries, "no more formulas, no standards of any sort: there is only life itself, an immense field where each may study and create as he likes." The recipe for the well-made play he rejects: "Naturalism is already stammering its first accents on the stage. . . . The drama will either die, or become modern and realistic. . . ." In writing *Thérèse Raquin* he attempts so to present his characters against the background of their environment as to make them "not *play*, but rather *live*, before the audience."

The Realism of Ostrovski and Turgenev

Both Hebbel and Zola, each in his own way, exercised a wide influence on the drama of Western Europe. A third force, working during the same years, was destined for long to remain unknown save in the land of its birth. Hebbel's was German realism, Zola's was French: meanwhile, in Russia, further advances were being made towards the creation of the style that culminated in Chekhov. Moscow had its writers such as Alexei Feofilaktovich Pisemski, author of the Tolstoi-like and powerful *Gorkaia sudbina* (*Bitter Destiny*, 1859)—in which a peasant murders the child born of his wife to a libidinous landowner—who were influenced deeply by current theatrical developments abroad and who sought to construct their dramas according to the recipes popular in Paris or Berlin; but far more important is the gradual evolution of the characteristic methods adumbrated by Gogol and Griboedov. In this field two men, writing during the middle years of the century, are of supreme significance.

The work of Alexander Nikolaevich Ostrovski is not well known outside his own country, yet he is unquestionably one of the most important and interesting dramatists of his epoch: without Ostrovski, Chekhov the dramatist might not have been. His first claim to attention is the fact that he was the first Russian author to apply himself exclusively to a professional stage career. Gogol and Griboedov had entered the theatre lightly, airily; Ostrovcki made of playwriting his entire life's work. In himself he thus symbolized the Russian theatre's coming of age. This, of course, merely gives him historical significance; intrinsic significance is provided by the quality of his writings. Intensely Slav in sentiment, he seized upon and developed the native realistic style cultivated by his predecessors. Instead of concentrating upon plot, he followed them in exploring character; instead of stressing ideas and problems, he set out to depict the life around him, satirically yet with infinite sympathy. Characteristic of all this school of writing is the peculiar orientation of the poet-creator to the objects of his creation. From one point of view we might be tempted to regard Ostrovski's plays as based on the 'slice-of-life' pattern. Their lack of exact structure and the tendency to prefer a series of loosely related scenes to the logical exposition of a theme would seem to give justification for such a point of view. No less than three of his dramas, instead of being called comedies or dramas, are described as "Scenes" or "Sketches" of Moscow or village life —*Prazdnichnii son—do obieda* (*A Holiday Dream—before Dinner*, 1857), *Vospitannitsa* (*The Ward*, 1859) and *Ne vse kotu maslienitsa* (*After the Dinner comes the Reckoning*, 1871). Looking at these, we might indeed be tempted to suppose that Zola's naturalism was here being put into practice. Such a conception, however, would be false: the looseness of structure is apparent merely, and on examination proves itself, like the structure of Chekhov's plays, to be carefully designed. Carefully designed, too, is that quality which so often has puzzled Western critics of this Russian realistic theatre—its seeming uncertainty of mood. Very often we do not know whether to laugh or to cry, whether to praise or to condemn: a character whom we feel to be despicable may suddenly assume admirable virtues; the coarse merchants whom Ostrovski so frequently flays may, in some scenes, be put forward as heroes. The explanation, of course, is that this author, like his companions, is composing his work under the impulse of a peculiar kind of humour: he is satiric, certainly, yet for the things satirized there is in his heart infinite compassion. This is the realm of the so-called *bytovaia komedia*—an almost untranslatable term signifying a play which depicts a way of life—the dramatic expression of the Russian literary movement to which was given the title *Byt*.

With the exception of *Snegurochka* (*The Snow Maiden*, 1873) and his unimportant historical dramas, all Ostrovski's plays are realistic, and, with the exception of *Groza* (*The Thunderstorm*, 1860), *Grekh da beda na kovo ne zhivet* (*Sin and Sorrow are Common to All*, 1863), and *The Ward*, they are comedies in the sense that they end happily, even though their happiness be bitter. Although among the exceptions stands his best-known play, *The Thunderstorm*, his genius was not well adapted to deal with potentially tragic material. *Sin and Sorrow*, which tells the story of Krasnov, a shopkeeper, married to Tatiana Danilovna, who starts an intrigue with a young landowner, has little incisiveness of purpose, and the stabbing of the wife by her husband seems to have no inevitability. Infinitely superior is *The Thunderstorm*, yet even it leaves us unsatisfied. Here a similar plot is used. A young wife, Katia, finds herself neglected by her husband and gives way to a handsome lover. In the end the lover abandons her, and, terrified of the husband's wrath, she commits suicide. Death is avoided in *The Ward*, but the atmosphere is no less dark; the last words are spoken by a maidservant who has been a spectator of all the events—"What's fun for the cat is sorrow for the mouse." The ward is Nadia, and basically the entire action which leads towards her betrothal to a man she detests is designed to reveal the evil unconsciously perpetrated by the rich, domineering, self-righteous old dowager, the lady Ulanbekov.

Bespridannitsa (*The Poor Bride*, 1879) may be taken as transitional between these and the comedies. To a certain extent the plot is tragic in that a girl without a dowry is forced into a loveless marriage, yet the fact that she takes a joy in sacrificing herself, together with the exceedingly vivid manner in which the dramatist deals with the preparations for the wedding, gives the play an atmosphere different from that of *Sin and Sorrow*. Another transitional work is *Bednost ne porok* (*Poverty is no Crime*, 1854), distinguished by the character of Liubim Karpich Tortsov, a sad rogue and a drunkard, albeit lovable, who reveals the pettiness and meanness of his merchant-brother's household and who serves as *deus ex machina* in joining the hands of Liubov and the poor, honest clerk Mitia.

This type of character was a favourite one on the Russian stage, largely because it enabled a contrast to be made with the dull, convention-ridden life of the middle class. Not dissimilar is the Neschastlivtsev of *Les* (*The Forest*, 1871), an actor who, though not as successful on the stage as he had hoped, prefers his way of life to that of his bourgeois relations. The rogue, however, is not always presented in such pleasing form as he assumes in the person of Liubim Tortsov. Among Ostrovski's most successful comedies is his very first, *Svoi liudi—sochtemsia* (1850; with an almost untranslatable title: *It's a Family Affair—We'll settle it Ourselves* is literal, but loses idiomatic significance; perhaps *Birds of a Feather* would best express the theme). In effect, this play is a kind of middle-class Russian *Volpone*. In order to enrich himself a merchant, Bolshov, arranges with a rascally attorney, Rispolozhenski, to fake a bankruptcy: since he has long had loyal service from his clerk, Podkhaliuzin, he decides to pretend to make over certain of his property to him. Podkhaliuzin, however, at once sees and seizes his opportunity, holds on to the assets and finds in Olimpiada, Bolshov's daughter, a kindred spirit. The cold-blooded pair marry, and the wretched Bolshov, all his schemes awry, is hoist with his own petard. Typical of the style are the daughter's long opening soliloquy as she reviews in memory the season's dances, and the final words spoken by Podkhaliuzin. The latter has just indulged in his final trick, bilking the dishonest lawyer, who departs muttering enraged curses and accusing his tormentor of many crimes. Thereupon the hero turns to the audience. "Don't you believe him," Podkhaliuzin says,

> I mean him who was talking, gentlemen—that's all lies. He's just inventing. Perhaps he only dreamt it. The wife and I, gentlemen, intend to open a little shop: do please favour us with your patronage. If you send your little son to us for an apple, you may be sure he shan't be given a rotten one.

Here the villain-rogue triumphs, although in another kindred work, *Na vsiakovo mudretsa dovolno prostoti* (*Enough Silliness in Every Wise Man,* or, *The Diary of a Scoundrel*, 1868), the trickster is outwitted by forces more honest than his own. A comparison of the two plays shows how difficult it is to pin down Ostrovski to any particular moral code: unlike the French dramatists of the ideological school, he is elusive as life itself.

The comedies mentioned above are thoroughly characteristic of Ostrovski's work as a whole, and perhaps are the best of his writings. In the others the picture of Russian life—sometimes realistically displayed, sometimes coloured with the garish tints of caricature—is expanded along similar lines. *Dokhodnoe mesto* (*A Lucrative Job*, 1856) reveals the weakness of the Civil Servants; *Beshenie dengi* (*Rabid Money*, 1870) deals with those financial questions which so worried all authors in this age: in one play after another Ostrovski essayed to reveal some fresh aspect of Moscow society. In all he showed himself a master in portraiture—one who perhaps hardly possessed Chekhov's power of universalizing the particular, yet nevertheless a dramatic artist whose worth has not been sufficiently realized outside his own land.

As a companion he had another author who, despite the fact that his best work was accomplished in the realm of prose fiction, materially contributed to the development of the Russian drama. Where Ostrovski concentrated his attention mostly on representatives of social classes, Ivan Sergeevich Turgenev dealt mainly with the intricacies of the heart. It is true that *Provintsialka* (*A Provincial Lady*, 1851) charmingly makes use of such material as that on which Ostrovski drew for his plots, but the orientation is different. Here Daria Ivanovna, wife of a provincial Civil Servant, is a true creation. We learn that she had been, like Ostrovski's heroine in *The Ward*, a protégée of a rich woman, who had married her off at an early age to the rather stupid, hard-working Stupendev. In her little home she dreams of the joys of life in the great house where she had spent her girlhood, and when she learns that her patroness's son, Count Liubin —now an elderly dandy, but with whom she once had had a flirtation—has arrived in town she eagerly entices him into her net. Turgenev's genius is shown in the masterly comic manner by which he leaves us guessing whether her affections are really aroused or whether all of her sly advances have been made in a spirit of fun. That she wants the Count to obtain a Moscow post for her husband is certain, but how far she is attracted towards the dandy we cannot tell. It is a comedy she is playing, and playing well, as the Count realizes. When he compliments her on her skill her reply is ambiguous: "Count, you know one can only play a comedy well when one feels one's part. . . ."

Not always was Turgenev so gay. In the plays that he wrote during his 'dramatic' years, mostly between 1847 and 1850, the mood varies from laughter to tears. There is a seriousness of purpose in *Razgovor na bolshoi doroge* (*A Conversation on the Highway*), which contrasts an impecunious aristocrat and an honest old servant, while *Mesiats v derevne* (*A Month in the Country*) ends in darkness. This undoubtedly is the greatest of his plays, and at once demonstrates how much Chekhov owed to his predecessors. In dramatic technique and in atmosphere alike the Chekhovian manner is amply apparent. The plot is complex, yet lacking entirely the tight intrigue of Scribe: the characters are revealed, not directly but by implication. In the centre of the picture stands Natalia Petrovna, the twenty-nine-year-old wife of a wealthy landowner, Islaev. She does not really love her husband, nor does her love of Rakitin, her husband's friend, go beyond mild affection and a sense of comfort derived from his constant and unselfish devotion. Trouble enters her life when a young student, Beliaev, is engaged as tutor for her boy Kolia, and when her seventeen-year-old ward, Vera, falls in love with him. Subtly Turgenev shows his heroine inflamed by a passion which her reason tells her is absurd, but which she cannot control.

Had this play been written by a contemporary French playwright it would have been made into a drama of the grand passion or else presented as a social problem; certainly the young man with whom the heroine falls in love would have been made into a hero. In Turgenev's hands the tutor Beliaev is pictured as a most ordinary fellow, himself callow and uninterested in either Natalia or Vera. The result is that opportunity is given for developing psychological studies of the two women: Natalia so loses herself in her frenzied passion that she is even prepared to marry off Vera to an elderly and stupid neighbour; from being an innocent child Vera develops before our eyes into a woman.

In a French play too all the 'intrigue' would have been concentrated and made economic with respect to means: Turgenev not only introduces numerous scenes of no importance for the development of the plot, but brings in lengthy speeches utterly unrelated, except by emotional implication, to the main story. Typical is the opening of the play, with four characters playing at cards, while Rakitin sits reading *The Count of Monte Cristo* to Natalia. The conversation ebbs and flows fitfully, providing atmosphere merely. This is followed by the equally characteristic long narrative of the doctor, Shpigelski, apparently entirely unconnected with the theme of the drama and yet aiding us in the building-up of a total imaginative impression.

A kindred spirit prevails in *Nakhlebnik* (*A Poor Gentleman*). The plot here is of the simplest. A newly married couple, Pavel Nikolaevich Eletski and Olga Petrovna, come to the bride's estate. In the evening the husband and some of his friends, for their amusement, cause a poverty-stricken old man, Kuzovkin, to become drunk. Becoming conscious of their taunts, he suddenly declares that he is in fact Olga's father. It is not, however, the plot that really matters: what Turgenev is interested in are his characters, and particularly he is concerned with the relationships of these characters—the wretched, broken-down Kuzovkin; the steel-like Eletski; the sympathetic Olga; Tropachov, the boorish land-owner; Karpachov, his toady; even the self-effacing and timorous Ivanov, Kuzovkin's friend. The social *milieu* plays its part; but it is what men are and what they may become, it is the contrast between what man dreams of being and what he actually is, that interests Turgenev. When the author devotes so much space to recounting Kuzovkin's dreams of recovering his lost estate he is not wasting time, for herein lies the symbolic core of his play; and typical Russian irony results when the dream is made true, not in the way which Kuzovkin had imagined, but through the fact that his drunken indiscretion forces him to leave the Eletski household—and, incidentally, the daughter whom he loves.

Like Ostrovski, Turgenev played infinite variations on this theme. In *Bezdenezhe* (*Insolvency*) the young Zhazikov plans, in imagination, a new livery for his servant Matvei, even while he is forced to keep in hiding from his creditors. Another aspect of the same contrast between the dream and the reality appears in *Gde tanko, tam i rvetsa* (*It breaks where it's thin*), which shows the ineffective Gorski losing the girl of his heart because he cannot summon up sufficient resolution to win her hand. Often the contrast leads to a half-resignedly sad, half-happy conclusion, as in *Kholostiak* (*The Bachelor*), where a self-seeking young Petrusha becomes the fiancé of Maria, a ward of Moskin's. When, however, an acquaintance complains she is not sufficiently cultured he throws her over, and we are left to understand that she will marry her guardian. The contrast here is between kind-heartedness and self-interest, between passion and sentiment, between dreams of ecstatic devotion and homely affection.

In these plays Ostrovski and Turgenev, building on the foundations set by Gogol and Griboedov, wrought an entirely new kind of comedy. Hebbel's is the realism born of Byronic romanticism: it is bold and blatant. Zola's realism is that which strives to depict a section of life photographically, and, since so many photographs are of the Christmas-card variety, the French naturalist tries to select the darker, cruder scenes of life on which to turn his lens. In the Russian plays we seek in vain either for the boldness of the German or for the external faithfulness of the French; rather do we move within the characters and their environment, exploring spiritual spheres no camera can reach, spheres which boldness of utterance cannot hope to reveal. The result is that even while Ostrovski and Turgenev are realists, their realism induces a kind of poetic mood: the delicate balancing of implications is almost like the poet's balancing of images. We are in the presence of life here, but it is as though, instead of watching the events through a non-existent fourth wall, we were paradoxically at once outside and inside the scenes, watching the characters as they move about and at the same time entering into them. Zola's drama, and Hebbel's too, is the drama of the spectator; Ostrovski's and Turgenev's is the drama of the spectator-participant.

PART IX

REALISM'S TRIUMPH

REALISM'S TRIUMPH

BY THE year 1870 sufficient experiments had been conducted in the realistic style to provide a firm foundation for the work of a culminating master. So far no unquestioned genius in this style had appeared; so far no attempt had been made to select from the diverse forms assumed by the new drama and to establish one single form exactly suited to the requirements of the age. The time for the appearance of such a genius, however, and for such a task of selection was now ripe.

Hebbel had contributed a crude strength; Augier and Dumas *fils* had shown how ideas could effectively be realized; Zola had presented a new naturalistic pattern; while Scribe and Sardou, despised though they might be by the superior spirits in the theatre, had taught men how the common speech of men and the ordinary events of their lives might be given appealing shape in the playhouse.

At the same time two developments were contributing materially towards the culmination of the new style. In France various critics had discussed the qualities to be desired in realistic plays, while in Germany one theorist, Hermann Hettner, a friend of Hebbel's, had produced a slim volume, entitled *Das moderne Drama* (1850), which was destined to prove of considerable importance in furthering the interests of its subject. Fundamentally Hettner's thesis is that Hebbel was pointing the way towards a great dramatic revival, but that he had failed to bring his achievement to the height of his aims; that in the struggles within the social fabric lay the materials for a new form of tragedy; and that in the development of this new form playwrights must strive at once to concentrate on psychological truth and on a deep understanding of social forces. Ibsen himself has left on record a testimony to the impress made upon his mind by this critical essay: it opened up for him fresh avenues of thought and stirred him to new effort.

The social forces on which Hettner laid such stress were, of course, the preponderating power in this age, largely because of the rapid development of scientific activities both pure and applied. The impact of a machine civilization on human beings tended to put man at the mercy of forces beyond his own individual strength, while scientific thought led towards the belief that the human being, so far from having mastery of his fate, is a creature of circumstance, conditioned by his environment, and hence not even possessing a native personality of his own. With the sweeping away of religious and moral concepts came a conviction on the part of many writers that all they could do was to observe life, depicting the miserable sorrows of reality; while other authors saw drama and literature generally, not as the instrument of expressing eternal values (for these were assumed not to be more than figments), but as an instrument designed to ameliorate the conditions of life.

The second development was that of the theatre itself. During these latter years of the century the stage was acquiring equipment by which it could present much more realistic settings than anything achieved in the past. The gas lighting that had been introduced about 1820 remained for many years a crude device, but within the years 1870–1900 the addition of many improvements (such as the new lime-light), together with superior methods of control, rendered it an instrument capable of producing most of the effects desired by the directors. And towards the very end of the period electricity came, gropingly at first, to supplant the earlier source of illumination and to offer still greater flexibility of control. Gradually too the traditional use of wings and backcloths was giving way to the execution of box-sets for interiors and of built-up sets for exterior scenes. With the disappearance of the repertory system in many theatres, obviously greater care could be given to the scenic backgrounds than was usual, or feasible, in days when the bill was changed nightly. When Charles Kean, during the fifties, devoted anxious labour, first, to research into the historically correct dress and surroundings of Shakespeare's plays and, next, to endeavours to reproduce in realistic form the results of his research, he was pointing the way forward with unerring finger.

Even when the repertory system was abandoned, however, the new desires of the directors and of the scenic artists demanded changes in theatrical equipment. It is during these years that machinery enters the stage. In New York that inventive genius Steele MacKaye opened the Madison Square Theatre (1881) and displayed to wondering audiences a double elevator stage by means of which entire sets, with their actors ready placed, could be raised or lowered into position. Shortly before, in 1880, the Opera House at Budapest was equipped with a sectional stage and hydraulic elevators. In Germany similar innovations in stage machinery and lighting were eagerly introduced into numerous theatres, and everywhere the directors were dreaming of still more complex mechanical devices. Thus was the machine age adapting itself to stage requirements: the fresh means were all ready to produce spectacularism or realism, whichever might at the moment be demanded.

One further innovation at this time is worthy of particular note. Realism was obviously desired by the public, and in all countries its sombre joys were exploited. At the same time, in most centres of theatrical activity the enthusiasts forged sadly ahead of the great mass of their contemporaries, so that by the nineties there existed a very considerable gap between what ordinary spectators were prepared to accept and what the more ardent spirits wished to impose upon the stage. The result was the introduction into the theatrical realm of an entirely novel element—the growth of the 'independent' theatre. In 1889, largely owing to the inspiration of Otto Brahm, the Freie Bühne was opened in Berlin, and throughout its career specialized in the presentation of realistic plays too extreme for public representation. Two years earlier a young French devotee of naturalism, André Antoine, succeeded, by the sheer drive from within him, in opening the Théâtre Libre in Paris. This lasted from 1887 to 1894: when it closed much of the enthusiasm that had inspired its efforts was transferred to the Théâtre de l'Œuvre, opened by Alexandre Lugné-Poë in 1893. Again under the inspiration of one man—in this instance J. T. Grein—the Independent Theatre Society was established in London in 1891. While it is true that the effect of these efforts was perhaps felt rather through their offshoots in our own century, we must give them all credit for their experimental aims, for the way in which they spread among their members knowledge of what was being accomplished in countries other than their own, and for their encouragement to new playwrights: Strindberg, Hauptmann, Brieux, and Shaw all stand in debt to the 'independents.'

1

THE TRIUMPH OF REALISM: IBSEN

ABOVE all other dramatic authors of this age towers the rocky figure of Henrik Ibsen, one who suddenly brings the hesitant Norwegian theatre to a position rivalling that of other lands with lengthier stage traditions and far richer heritage of accomplishment.

Not only does Ibsen display a greater combination of assured theatrical strength, of penetrating vision, and of determined purpose than any of his companions, he reveals himself as a kind of massive symbol of all that his age sought for and achieved in dramatic form. Within the course of his works we can see, as though in a concentrating mirror, an image of his age's countenance.

The Historical Plays

When we think of Ibsen now it is usually the author of *Ghosts* who comes to our mind, and we conceive him as a man who wrought a realistic form for himself almost unaided. The first thing we ought to remember is that, as *Dramaturg* and director of the little theatre at Bergen, he had much to do with presenting the plays of Scribe, and that his own primal effort was a romantically conceived *Catilina* (1850). In his apprentice days he was most deeply influenced by the romantic strain of his century, and the first task he set for himself was that of creating a powerful form for historical drama concerned with the traditions of his native Norway. Scribe offered suggestions in so far as technique was concerned; Shakespeare presented visions of greatness; the efforts of the many romantic dramatists from the time of Schiller onward provided immediate inspiration; while the attempts already made by preceding dramatists to put Scandinavian themes on the stage pointed out to him the path he should take.

In 1850 appeared the relatively unimportant *Kjæmpehöjen* (*The Warrior's Barrow*), in which the influence of Oehlenschläger is amply apparent; five years later came the first truly significant piece from his pen, *Fru Inger til Östråt* (*Lady Inger of Östråt*, 1855), where the spirits of Schiller and Scribe vie for pre-eminence. There is strength here, and a sense of character in the depiction of an ambitious woman who succeeds by her machinations only in ruining her son. Individual scenes

display unquestioned skill in the composition, although the play's plan
as a whole indicates that as yet the young Ibsen had not gained mastery.
When the Stranger is suddenly introduced at the close of Act I and Lady
Inger faints we can realize how thrillingly effective the apprentice
dramatist must have imagined this 'curtain' to be; yet it is equally
obvious how ill-adapted the device is to stage requirements. What Ibsen
has forgotten is that an audience must know the circumstances of an
action before it car be moved; he has yet to learn to put himself out of his
study into the auditorium.

Lady Inger of Östråt ushered in a long line of dramas on Scandinavian
themes, each succeeding play demonstrating the author's advance in
theatrical craftsmanship and in grasp of character. *Gildet paa Solhaug* (*The
Feast at Solhaug*, 1856) and *Olaf Liljekrans* (1857) are not of any importance, but *Hærmændene paa Helgeland* (*The Vikings at Helgeland*, 1858) and
Kongsemnerne (*The Pretenders*, 1864), although neither proved an immediate success, fully demonstrated his growing power. Based on the same
sagas as were to animate the soul of Wagner, the former deals mainly
with Sigurd the Strong and his beloved Hiördis, foster-daughter of
Örnulf of the fiords, and the attempt is made, albeit with not a trifle of romantic sentimentalizing, to reproduce in modern form the atmosphere of
the world of ancient myth. In *The Pretenders* the tale is told of two contrasting men—Håkon, sure of himself and with an objective in whose
rightness he has not a shred of doubt, and Skule, his mind filled with
visions, but timorous and hesitant. Although in the latter is a god-given
strength lacking in the former, it is Håkon who becomes King and ruler
of a united Norway. Both plays have vital plots, but clearly *The Pretenders*
is a much greater drama than its predecessor, precisely because in it
Ibsen has concentrated on the inner beings of his characters.

Early Symbolism

In these plays is evident, besides the increasing psychological power,
an increasing sense of purpose: to a certain extent *The Pretenders* may be
regarded as a symbolic tragedy. This symbolic purpose is even more
deeply marked in other works written about this time—diverse in nature
yet all contributing towards the deeper harmonies of Ibsen's composition. In *Kjærlighedens komedie* (*Love's Comedy*, 1862) the symbolic is carried close to the author's own time. An essay on sex relations, it preaches
a gospel alien to that of conventional society: "If you want to marry,"
says Ibsen, "don't be in love; if you love, part." This thesis is presented
by means of a series of couples, each, as it were, in gradation. First comes
the clergyman Straamand and his wife, in both of whom domesticity has
destroyed all vision; next are Styver, the law-clerk, a visionless creature,
and Fröken Skjaere; following them are Lind, a divinity student who
dreams of being a missionary, and his Anna; and finally there are the
poet Falk and Svanhild. Through these pairs Ibsen endeavours to show

that inevitably marriage brings with it a dulling of aspiration and a supine acceptance of conventional codes. For such as Styver and Fröken Skjaere there may be no loss in this, but in marrying Anna, Lind is sacrificing his missionary dream, while for the lyrical Falk marriage would be the death of his poetic power and his revolutionary ardour. Ironically, the truth is shown to this poet by the merchant Guldstad, and, true to her romantic name, Svanhild gives him up at the end of the play: the stage is left peopled by the Straamands and their numerous progeny, while Falk's voice is heard in poetic triumph as he tramps off for a life of adventure with a group of gay, ardent youths.

Although *Love's Comedy* seems to occupy a peculiar place among Ibsen's works, it is a play the understanding of which is necessary for an understanding of the dramatist's entire development and outlook upon the world. Ibsen was by way of being a prophet, and this bitter comedy is an expression of his faith, a challenge cast down to the Philistine, a declaration of his intention to keep unsullied and unimpaired the visions and the dreams that were in him. Clearly it links up with his next three dramas—*Brand* (1866), *Peer Gynt* (1867), and the last of his historical works, *Kejser og Galilæer* (*Emperor and Galilean*, 1873).

After having displayed a caricature of a spineless, worldly-minded, hopelessly conventional clergyman in *Love's Comedy*, in *Brand* Ibsen shows his opposite. The hero of this play, young and vigorous in his faith, goes to a small remote town. Determined not to sacrifice by a tittle the integrity of his vision, he proceeds to follow the dictates of his inner voice even although all are against him—the civic officials of the little community, the whole mass of his parishioners, even men who might have been supposed to sympathize with his point of view. The play is a difficult work to understand, for the likelihood is that in it the young author, now coming to his full powers, wrote more and better than he knew. On the surface *Brand* is a violent outburst on the part of an irate individualist against all the pettiness, triviality, and spiritual squalor of his surroundings. It breathes the spirit of Kierkegaard, whose whole philosophy, opposed to the idealistic absolutism of Hegel, laid stress on individuality and on the painful relation of each individual to his god. Brand looks with horror on his mother, who, having made a marriage of convenience, finds her heart dead and her whole being submerged in the world's common greed. Nobly, he dares to face the dangers that others will not face in an endeavour to aid those in distress, but the very intensity of his passion brings sorrow upon himself. By believing that his duty lies in remaining with his people he virtually destroys his own loved child, who, ailing, could have been saved only by being taken southward to a more clement atmosphere. In the end he stands among the mountains virtually alone with the God whom he has so sternly endeavoured to serve, and, as an avalanche is about to descend upon him, he cries out in misery—his very soul overwhelmed with a weight of doubt as his body will be overwhelmed by the snows—asking bitterly whether "the uncompromising assertion of man's will" cannot bring him salvation. From the empyrean above the answer thunders over the roar of the avalanche: "*Deus caritatis.*"

God is love: this pronouncement at the close of the tragedy in itself suggests that, perhaps without being fully conscious of it, Ibsen saw that his Brand was not a wholly worthy figure. "Brand dies a saint," says Bernard Shaw, "having caused more intense suffering by his saintliness than the most talented sinner could possibly have done with twice his opportunities." Even although Ibsen the prophet did often lack the saving grace of humour and often posed in attitudes ridiculous rather than sublime, one can hardly credit that he was so naïve as to take his hero seriously, all on trust. There can be no doubt that Ibsen detested many elements in the bourgeois society surrounding him, that he found himself frequently thwarted by that society, and that he sought to arouse men towards the freer expression of their own beings, but even if we admit so much we cannot avoid seeing in *Brand* something perhaps just a trifle humorous: this clergyman is as much a caricature as the clergyman of *Love's Comedy*.

In *Peer Gynt* symbolism, serious purpose, a sense of tragedy, and a spirit of fun jostle each other through five long, hell-bubbling acts. There is much here that might well have been omitted; there is much here that reminds us of Goethe's rather clumsy attempts at comedy, as though an elephant, clad in canvas frills, were solemnly trying to emulate on his heavy feet the graceful pirouettes of a ballet-dancer; yet, when all has been said, *Peer Gynt* remains one of the greatest plays produced in the nineteenth century. It is strange that, despite the facts that when this play was written Ibsen was nearing his fortieth year and that he was exhibiting a technical ability of assured competence, here and in *Brand* individual scenes remind us of the work of an adolescent. The very crudity of the central ideas in both these dramas suggests youth rather than maturity, and the 'symbolism,' which elsewhere is subtle and imaginative, frequently sinks to the juvenile quality of the scene of the four merchants in *Peer Gynt*. There a Frenchman, a Swede, a German, and an American stand aghast after having heard Peer explain that he is supporting the Turks against Greece:

MONSIEUR BALLON: I saw myself a conqueror,
    by lovely Grecian maids encircled.
TRUMPETER STRÅLE: Grasped in my Swedish hands, I saw
    the great, heroic spur-strap-buckles!
VON EBERKOPF: I my gigantic Fatherland's
    culture saw spread o'er earth and sea!
MR COTTON: The worst's the loss in solid cash.
    God dam! I scarce can keep from weeping!
    I saw me owner of Olympus.[1]

This is the sort of thing we might have smiled at had we found it in a play

[1] The quotations from *Peer Gynt* are from the translation of W. and C. Archer.

by a youth of twenty: in the composition of a man nearly twice that age the crudity of the satire seems almost unforgivable.

Yet, when all is said, *Peer Gynt* remains a masterpiece of extravagant fancy. With enormous verve Ibsen traces his hero from his early days, when he fills his mother's ears with wild tales of impossible adventure and abducts the bride of a neighbour, to the time when, greyed and failing, he finds his soul being weighed in the scales of judgment. At the beginning he is a graceless rascal for whom we cannot but feel a certain amount of sympathy: his very lies suggest a power of imagination in him, and his escapades, if reprehensible, have a daring quality. This sympathy accompanies him when, having made advances to the troll-king's daughter, he is shown in the hobgoblin Court of that monarch. There then follow a contest with the great Boyg, a figure of crass vulgarity, and a sentimental scene in which a girl, Solveig, innocent and truly loving, comes to share his exile in the mountains. Peer, too, loves her as he has loved no other woman, but, remembering the stains that are on his spirit, he deliberately renounces the idyllic delights of life in companionship with her: she is to him fairest, purest gold, and no alloy can be permitted. In the scene of renunciation the best that is in his character becomes revealed. He remembers that the Boyg had monotonously reiterated the advice to "go roundabout":

> PEER: The Boyg said, "Go roundabout!"—so one must here.—
> There fell my fine palace, with crash and clatter!
> There's a wall around her whom I stood so near,
> of a sudden all's ugly—my joy has grown old.—
> Roundabout, lad! There's no way to be found
> right through all this from where you stand to her.
> Right through? Hm, surely there should be one.
> There's a text on repentance, unless I mistake.
> But what? What is it? I haven't the book,
> I've forgotten it mostly, and here there is none
> that can guide me aright in the pathless wood.—
>   Repentance? And maybe 'twould take whole years,
> ere I fought my way through. 'Twere a meagre life, that.
> To shatter what's radiant, and lovely, and pure,
> and clinch it together in fragments and shards?
> You can do it with a fiddle, but not with a bell.
> Where you'd have the sward green, you must mind not
>   to trample.
>   'Twas nought but a lie though, that witch-snout
>   business!
> Now all that foulness is well out of sight.—
> Ay, out of sight maybe, not out of mind.
> Thoughts will sneak stealthily in at my heel.
> Ingrid! And the three, they that danced on the heights!
> Will they too want to join us? With vixenish spite
> will they claim to be folded, like her, to my breast,
> to be tenderly lifted on outstretched arms?

Roundabout, lad; though my arms were as long
as the root of the fir, or the pine-tree's stem,—
I think even then I should hold her too near,
to set her down pure and untarnished again.—
    I must roundabout here, then, as best I may,
and see that it bring me nor gain nor loss.
One must put such things from one, and try to forget.—

                             [*Goes a few steps towards the hut, but stops again.*

Go in after this? So befouled and disgraced?
Go in with that troll-rabble after me still?
Speak, yet be silent; confess, yet conceal—?

                                    [*Throws away his axe.*

It's a holy-day evening. For me to keep tryst,
such as now I am, would be sacrilege.
SOLVEIG [*in the doorway*]: Are you coming?
PEER [*half aloud*]: Roundabout!
SOLVEIG: What?
PEER: You must wait.
  It is dark, and I've got something heavy to fetch.
SOLVEIG: Wait; I will help you; the burden we'll share.
PEER: No, stay where you are! I must bear it alone.
SOLVEIG: But don't go too far, dear!
PEER: Be patient, my girl;
  be my way long or short—you must wait.
SOLVEIG [*nodding to him as he goes*]: Yes, I'll wait!

The final episode in this section of the drama is the magnificently conceived death-scene of Peer's mother. Miserably he tries to forget that her
poverty has been caused by his extravagance. "Now, mother," he says,

                we'll chat together;
               but only of this and that,
            forget what's awry and crooked,
             and all that is sharp and sore.—
          Why see now, the same old pussy;
          So she is alive then, still?

He tells her a tale, quietly but with conviction, and the old woman, en-
tranced by his eloquence as he sits astride a chair with a string for reins,
imagines herself riding with him far up into the air. The story becomes
more and more vivid, ending with a loud and triumphant laugh. Peer
turns to his mother:

PEER: Ay, didn't I know what would happen?
    Now they dance to another tune!
      [*Uneasily*]
Why, what makes your eyes so glassy?
    Mother! Have you gone out of your wits—?

                              [*Goes to the head of the bed.*

You mustn't lie there and stare so—!

Speak, mother; it's I, your boy!

[*Feels her forehead and hands cautiously; then throws the string on the chair, and says softly.*

Ay, ay!—You can rest yourself, Granë;
    for even now the journey's done.

[*Closes her eyes, and bends over her.*

For all of your days I thank you,
    for beatings and lullabys!—
But see, you must thank me back, now—

[*Presses his cheek against her mouth.*

There; that was the driver's fare.

When next we see him Peer is middle-aged, a prosperous merchant who has made himself rich by trading Negro slaves to Carolina and idols to China and who has dreams of becoming the world's emperor. Deserted by his companions, he turns in abject fear to thoughts of the religion he has ever spurned, but these he soon forgets when luck comes his way again. His life is now, however, a constant decline: he is tricked by a Moorish maiden, caged in a Cairo lunatic asylum, nearly drowned as he sails homeward. The final scenes are mainly concerned with the episode of the Button-moulder, an instrument of divine wisdom, who has come to melt his soul down in a ladle. Desperately Peer argues with him:

PEER: But these, my good man, are most unfair proceedings!
    I'm sure I deserve better treatment than this;—
    I'm not nearly so bad as perhaps you think,—
    I've done a good deal of good in the world;—
    at worst you may call me a sort of a bungler,—
    but certainly not an exceptional sinner.
THE BUTTON-MOULDER: Why, that is precisely the rub, my man;
    you're no sinner at all in the higher sense;
    that's why you're excused all the torture-pangs,
    and land, like others, in the casting-ladle.

To his horror Peer learns that he is neither an heroic sinner nor a virtuous saint and, being neither one thing nor the other, must lose his identity. "Bless me, my dear Peer," remarks the Button-moulder,

there is surely no need
to get so wrought up about trifles like this.
Yourself you never have been at all;—
then what does it matter, your dying right out?

Given a little time, Peer searches desperately to prove that he has had a true self, and fails. He even cannot fathom what this really means, and stands somewhat puzzled when the Button-moulder tells him that "to be oneself is—to slay oneself." Only at the end does he come upon Solveig again: he casts himself in repentance at her feet, and is pardoned. To her he propounds his riddle:

Canst thou tell where Peer Gynt has been since we parted?

SOLVEIG: Been?
PEER: With his destiny's seal on his brow;
 been, as in God's thought he first sprang forth!
 Canst thou tell me? If not, I must get me home,—
 go down to the mist-shrouded regions.
SOLVEIG [*smiling*]: Oh, that riddle is easy.
PEER: Then tell what thou knowest!
 Where was I, as myself, as the whole man, the true man?
 where was I, with God's sigil upon my brow?
SOLVEIG: In my faith, in my hope, and in my love.

It is common to speak of *Brand* as a drama in which Ibsen puts forward a hero who asserts his individuality even at the expense of others, and of *Peer Gynt* as a companion piece in which "the poverty of spirit and half-heartedness that Ibsen rebelled against in his countrymen" were embodied in the character who gives his name to the play. To a certain extent, but to a certain extent only, this is true: what we should realize, however, is that its imaginative vision goes far beyond such a concept. It is, indeed, impossible in logically framed words to define its precise imaginative scope, and just because it does proceed beyond the intellectually logical it assumes its own peculiar quality of greatness.

Ibsen soon was to turn to the exploitation of realism, but before the coming of *Ghosts* he made one last effort in the historic and poetic style. During a visit to Rome his mind became deeply impressed by the presence there of two distinct civilizations—the ancient pagan grandeur and the later medieval grandeur of the Christian Church. Out of this grew a strange work which, while cast in terms beyond those of the stage, may perhaps be regarded—as he himself regarded it—as the most powerful demonstration of his genius. In *Kejser og Galilæer* (*Emperor and Galilean*, 1873) there is a sweep and a vigour that surpasses anything in his other writings. The drama—divided into two parts—is at once an essay in imaginative philosophy and a lengthy study of character, and, in ways similar to those that make *Peer Gynt* so complex, both are presented with peculiar subtlety. At the beginning we are introduced to the main character, Prince Julian, living during the reign of an Emperor who favours Christianity. He is a handsome, brilliant youth, proud of his skill in debate, in love with life and beauty. At the same time the greatness of his spirit causes him to be dissatisfied with such learning as he has acquired, and anxiously, eagerly, he seeks out teacher after teacher, ever striving to reach the innermost core of thought's mysteries. Eventually he encounters the mystic Maximus, who, calling up spirits from the vasty deep, shows him a vision of the 'Third Empire.' Maximus explains:

  There are three empires.
JULIAN: Three?
MAXIMUS: First that empire which was founded on the Tree of Knowledge;
 then that which was founded on the Tree of the Cross—
JULIAN: And the third?

MAXIMUS: The third is the empire of the great mystery; that empire which shall be founded on the Tree of Knowledge and the Tree of the Cross together, because it hates and loves them both, and because it has its living sources under Adam's grove and under Golgotha.

When Julian becomes Emperor he endeavours to establish a reign of tolerance, although, in order to make a break with the immediate past, he himself pours libations to the ancient pagan gods. Gradually, however, he is forced into persecutions real and imagined: since most of the Court officers are Galileans of a time-serving and corrupt sort, he dismisses them, and is accused of attacking the Church; while ardent enthusiasts, eager for martyrdom, act in such a way as to call forth sternest measures. In watching Julian's progress throughout the latter part of the drama we see a man in desperation striving to crush a spirit that is unconquerable and eventually destroying himself in the process. Madness descends on him during a disastrous expedition into Persia; the thought of Christ haunts him wherever he goes and intrudes into whatever he does. Tricked by a Persian spy, he gives orders for the imperial fleet to be burned, and, as the flames mount, bursts out exultantly:

Yes, the fleet is burning! And more than the fleet is burning. In that blazing, swirling pyre the crucified Galilean is burning to ashes; and the earthly Emperor is burning with the Galilean. But from the ashes shall arise—like that marvellous bird—the God of earth and the Emperor of the spirit in one, in one, in one!

Darkness descends deeper and deeper on his spirit: the oracles that Maximus consults on his behalf are silent. In the end he is slain by his boyhood friend Agathon, and dies in the knowledge that the Galilean has triumphed, that the vision of sun-bathed loveliness, of pagan joy, has betrayed him. At the same time we are given the sense that in his failure he has been a tool in the hands of a power greater than either Christ or the old pagan deities:

MAXIMUS: Led astray like Cain. Led astray like Judas.—Your God is a spendthrift God, Galileans! He wears out many souls.

Wast thou not then, this time either, the chosen one—thou victim on the altar of necessity?

What is it worth to live? All is sport and mockery.—To will is to have to will.

Oh, my beloved—all signs deceived me, all auguries spoke with a double tongue, so that I saw in thee the mediator between the two empires.

The third empire shall come! The spirit of man shall re-enter on its heritage—and then shall offerings of atonement be made to thee. . . .

[*He goes out.*

BASIL: It dawns on me like a great and radiant light, that here lies a noble, shattered instrument of God.

We may, if we will, ridicule Ibsen's philosophy here; we may even detest it; but we cannot avoid judging *Emperor and Galilean* a worthy peer of *Faust* and *The Dynasts* in its epically dramatic proportions.

The Coming of Realism

Already, before the composition of this historical and symbolic tragedy, Ibsen had shown signs that he was preparing to experiment in a new
style. In 1869 came the tempestuous presentation of *De unges forbund* (*The
League of Youth*), a highly topical 'comedy' in which the author castigated
local politics and, in particular, the liberal party. Even yet Ibsen was the
disciple of Scribe, and in the rather mechanical structure of this piece,
with its irritating mixture of farce and melodrama, the impress of the
'well-made play' is amply apparent. On the other hand, the realistic dialogue and the portraits of the opportunist Stensgård, of the spirited
Selma, and of the pompous Councillor Bratsberg may easily be related to
other less mechanically composed dramas to be written shortly afterwards. Once more the comedy scenes seem to be elephantine and the
concept diffusely presented, but we may accept the play for what it is
worth—an excellent introduction to Ibsen's most characteristic dramatic work.

Eight years later appeared *Samfundets stötter* (*Pillars of Society*, 1877), in
which again the influence of Scribe and the satirical presentation of
social conventions predominates. Not yet has he succeeded in shedding
all his adolescent fancies. Much better constructed than *The League of
Youth*, *Pillars of Society* essays to expose small-town morality. One of the
pillars is the ultra-respectable, wealthy Consul Bernick, whose wife's
brother, Johan, is spoken of in scandalized tones by local gossips because
he is supposed to have had an affair with an actress and to have stolen
some public money, and whose stepsister, Lona Hessel, is looked upon as
an immoral character. Unfortunately for Bernick, Lona and Johan
return to their native town from America, and it is revealed, mainly
through the persistence of the former, that not Johan but Bernick himself
had been the criminal. At the same time this worthy's selfish plan for self-
aggrandizement through the building of a railway is exposed, and,
touched by conscience, he publicly confesses his errors. The story is told
not without sentimentality, and the curtains—like that at the end of Act I
ending with Lona's "I will let in fresh air, Pastor"—are frequently
designed rather for theatrical effectiveness than for their character
values. The satire, also, exhibits often the heavy-handed quality which is
so patent in Ibsen's earlier plays—as, for example, when Hilmar utters
bold words to the little Olaf as the child is showing him his bow:

> *HILMAR:* Ha—there we have the rising generation nowadays! Goodness
> knows there's plenty of talk about pluck and daring, but it all ends in play;
> no one has any real craving for the discipline that lies in looking danger
> manfully in the face. Don't stand and point at me with your bow, stupid; it
> might go off.

Ibsen obviously was finding it hard to throw off his youth; perhaps, indeed, he never quite grew up.

The following year, in Rome, he was jotting down notes for a new play, a "modern tragedy":

> There are two kinds of spiritual law, two kinds of conscience, one in man and another, altogether different, in woman. . . . The wife in the play ends by having no idea of what is right or wrong: natural feeling on the one hand and belief in authority on the other have altogether bewildered her.
>
> A woman cannot be herself in the society of the present day, which is an exclusively masculine society, with laws framed by men and with a judicial system that judges feminine conduct from a masculine point of view.
>
> She has committed forgery, and she is proud of it; for she did it out of love for her husband, to save his life. But this husband with his commonplace principles of honour is on the side of the law and regards the question with masculine eyes.
>
> Spiritual conflicts. Oppressed and bewildered by the belief in authority, she loses faith in her moral right and ability to bring up her children. . . . Love of life, of home, of husband and children and family. Here and there a womanly shaking-off of her thoughts.
>
> Sudden return of anxiety and terror. She must bear it all alone. The catastrophe approaches, inexorably, inevitably. Despair, conflict and destruction.
>
> Krogstad has acted dishonourably and thereby become well-to-do; now his prosperity does not help him, he cannot recover his honour.

Thus was *Et dukkehjem* (*A Doll's House*, 1879) born, and additional papers from Ibsen's study reveal clearly how it grew. First came a scenario, in which the bare outlines of the plot were presented. Next was a full draft of the play itself, in which mere suggestions in the scenario were brought to life and enriched. From this draft evolved the play as we know it, taut in construction, character-revealing in its subtly framed dialogue. Throughout, the handling of the speech and the planning of the scenes display a masterly hand at work. The story of the play is, of course, too well known to require a précis, but we may pause to consider wherein it soars beyond all previous attempts at the creation of realistic drama. First, there is the skill in the use of words: Ibsen has conquered what, after all, is the basic problem of the realistic playwright—the problem of combining language which shall at once seem natural and be dramatically appropriate. After his long apprenticeship he has at last succeeded in achieving that inner harmony without which the situations must remain bare or artificial. In addition to this, he has learned how to modify the Scribe formula so as to retain the thrillingly effective and at the same time to hide the presence of the machinery. His curtains, looked at objectively, are of the same kind as those employed in the earlier dramas, but the fact that they are built out of character and imaginatively integrated with the basic situation makes us forget the deliberate craftsmanship determining their being. The third element might be described as Ibsen's thought. In France the playwrights could not get beyond themes of marriage and money conceived in conventional terms: to the question of marriage and money Ibsen gives a startlingly new interpretation. The French plays had rung the changes on the social relations between aristocrats and members of the wealthy bourgeoisie, on love opposed to convenience, on the eternal triangle, and on the problems of illegitimacy. Fresh air blew into this salon and café world when Ibsen took a loving husband as his hero and as his heroine a childish creature, adoring her husband and yet, when her eyes are open to his character, determining that she must leave his house. This is the old theme of marriage and money certainly, but presented with such a difference as to make it seem absolutely new. *A Doll's House*, because of this novelty of concept, served as a clarion-call to the younger generation of dramatic realists.

If this play was a clarion-call, *Gengangere* (*Ghosts*, 1881) was a long-drawn-out fanfare. Here Ibsen dared to deal with a topic absolutely taboo, and wrought his modern theme to the pattern of a Greek tragedy. In those ancient plays a fatal curse hung inexorably over a house doomed to the third and fourth generation: in adopting this dramatic situation, for his fatal curse Ibsen substitutes an inherited venereal disease and peoples his drama with ghosts that are no less powerful because they are unseen. To a certain extent *Ghosts* is now an outmoded drama: it is always the fate of the innovator to find that the very qualities that caused such a stir when his works first appeared lose their interest as others exploit the same or similar themes. Indeed, this drama would have proved to be no more than an historical curiosity had Ibsen not cast into it a wealth of character delineation. The portrait of Mrs Alving combines all the solidity demanded of a strong theatrical rôle with subtle implications which make her seem a living character. She is a frigid, conventional woman, whose husband has had intrigues with other women: in order to preserve the respectability of her household she remains with him. Venereal disease contracted by the father is passed on to his son, Oswald, and as the play ends the latter is shown rapidly sinking into insanity. It rests a moot point whether his mother is to give him poison rather than let him suffer in misery. The very fact that Ibsen himself has left us to guess is in its own way indicative of the gulf between him and his French predecessors; whereas they were inclined to tie all their knots tightly and to leave no untidy ends, Ibsen's dramas, like all great works of the theatre, permit at least a little room for our imaginative fancies to play in. Once, when William Archer asked Ibsen whether he intended Mrs Alving to give her son poison or not, the author "smiled and said thoughtfully: 'I don't know. Each one must find that out for himself. I should never dream of deciding so delicate a question. But what is your opinion?' "

The Intrusion of the Symbolic

With *Ghosts*, 'Ibsenism' became an affair of battle. Young enthusiasts in many a land fanatically ranged themselves under the standard thus set up, while the more conservative employed every weapon in an endeavour to destroy what they regarded as a godless and immoral force. In looking back now at records of the strife we are almost reminded of the bitter and unruly theological bickerings at the time of the Reformation.

Meanwhile Ibsen himself showed that his was a nature not content to win acclaim among the ranks of ardent youth by continuing to deal with subjects hitherto denied entry into the playhouse. In his subsequent career, indeed, he succeeded not a little in dismaying and perplexing his followers; some were shaken in their beliefs, and others speculated seriously on the sad falling off of their master's power. Just for a moment, in fact, it seemed as though his own angry spirit and a revival of that adolescent naïveté which is so marked in some of his earlier dramas were to lead him astray. *En folkefiende* (*An Enemy of the People*, 1882) is a good acting-piece, but it is written too irately to be taken seriously. Attempts have been made to suggest that the author himself saw the fun in this story of a Dr Stockman who makes a vast philosophic issue of the contaminated swimming-baths in a small Norwegian town, but the truth is that here the juvenility of Ibsen's mind was once again dominant—a fact that he himself recognized when, in later age, he described his hero as "*ein grotesker Bursche und ein Strudelkopf*" ("an extravagant immature fellow and a hot-head").

Two years later, however, came *Vildanden* (*The Wild Duck*, 1884), and at once we recognize that Ibsen has won through to an entirely new vision, building a structure finer than anything hitherto achieved in the realistic style. There is no petty anger here; instead, a wealth of sympathy, such as had appeared in no other of his plays, enwraps the characters in its folds. Ordinary men and women are frail and pitiable figures as Ibsen now sees them, and in order that they may live they require to have their dreams: for them a word of truth may be fatal. This theme is revealed through concentration on a single domestic interior—the household of the unsuccessful and well-intentioned, although fundamentally selfish, Hjalmar Ekdal. In poverty the members of this household carry on their lives with a certain measure of happiness, their illusions being symbolized in the strange secret of the attic—where a crippled wild duck is kept by the daughter, Hedwig, and her old grandfather: opening the door to that room, they enter into a world of fond dreams and inhabit for a space the mountains and the moors. Into this circle comes the crass young idealist Gregers Werle, who has been so fed by modern theories as to believe that truth must be served at all costs, and that it is impossible for a man to be himself unless he resolutely refuses to allow untruth to clutter his own life or the lives of others. As a result of this 'idealism,' Werle reveals to Hjalmar that his wife, Gina, had been the mistress of Werle's own father, and that Hedwig is not his child; he further persuades Hedwig that it is her duty to make sacrifice of her precious wild duck, with the consequence that the child, all her illusions broken, kills herself with the pistol Werle has practically thrust into her hands.

In this play of infinite compassion Ibsen reaches a dramatic power beyond anything he had hitherto revealed. The characters have a peculiar depth, and the skill with which the plot is unfolded shows a command of material such as could be matched by no other contemporary author. For the secret of his strength we must look to his infinite patience, his painstaking care, and the refusal to be satisfied with anything less than perfection. "I have just completed a play in five acts," he wrote to a friend in 1884, "that is to say, the rough draft of it; now comes the elaboration, the more energetic individualization of the persons and their modes of expression." What that process of elaboration entailed is made amply apparent by a comparison of the happily preserved first writing of the play and the final version. A single example will serve to illustrate this. In the finished play very considerable dramatic significance attaches to weakness of eyesight: Hedwig is threatened with blindness and her father suffers from failing vision. The device has several values: not only does it possess something of a symbolic nature, it also helps simultaneously to reveal the plot and to expose character. Hedwig's relationship to her father is hinted at before the discovery is actually made, and to that relationship is given at least a suggestion of the heritage theme which dominates in *Ghosts*. In addition Hedwig's plight serves to make her the more appealing, while Hjalmar's selfishness is illuminated by his permitting her to injure her eyes further over retouching work that he himself should have carried out. Looked at from these different angles, the stress on this element is realized to be a key to the understanding of the entire drama—from the old Werle's entry in the first scene "passing his hand over his eyes" and being warned that it is very bad for him to stare at the gaily lighted ballroom, to the remarks, so replete with unconscious irony, that Gregers addresses to Hedwig in the last act:

> Oh, if only your eyes had been opened to that which gives life its value—if you possessed the true, joyous, fearless spirit of sacrifice, you would soon see how he would come up to you.

Yet the fact is that not a word is said about weakness of eyesight in the early version: although *The Wild Duck* seems almost to rest on this foundation, the device—symbolic, plot-aiding, and character-revealing—was an afterthought, the result of the process of "elaboration." Nothing, perhaps, better shows Ibsen's imaginative genius at work.

From *The Wild Duck* it is but a step to *Rosmersholm* (1886), in which the outward semblance is realistic, the inner core spiritually symbolic, and in which Ibsen turned to give his attention to the modern emancipated woman. In *A Doll's House* Nora is just becoming free; Rebecca West has no ties to bind her, no soil into which she may cast down roots. A housekeeper in the family of the liberal Johannes Rosmer, a man of breeding and the owner of Rosmersholm, she has set out to become his second wife and inspirer; to achieve her ends she has so worked upon the mind of Beata, his first wife, as to drive her to suicide. It is at this point that the play starts, and through its four acts we are shown the spectacle of this iron-minded female, goading on Rosmer to glorious battle with the entrenched forces of the conservative clergy, gradually broken down by a force greater than she possesses. The spirit of Rosmersholm enters into her being; in the end she and Rosmer go out hand in hand to meet death in the same place and by the same means as carried off the wretched Beata.

There is a peculiar haunting quality about this drama, and Ibsen's delineation of at least one type of the 'new woman' is subtle. As he advanced in his art he was becoming more and more conscious of emotional values, less and less animated by the rather jejune enthusiasms of his earlier years; and perhaps a grim, slightly cynical smile is touching the lips which before had been set in the hard revolutionist's lines.

Most assuredly that grim smile appears in another 'tragic' drama composed four years later and also presenting a portrait of a self-seeking woman—*Hedda Gabler* (1890). In one sense Hedda is the opposite of Rebecca; for she is a woman of birth who thinks she has married beneath her, not one who aims to rise by her marriage; yet fundamentally they are sisters at heart. With consummate artistry (although not without showing to the critical eye evidence of lessons in craftsmanship learned from Scribe) Ibsen reveals this woman to us in the first act, and draws her inevitably to her end in the succeeding scenes. Married to Tesman, she is possessed of a demonic passion for the young genius Eilert Lövborg, and because of the follies into which this brings her she finds herself in the power of the cynical and libidinous Judge Brack, who, when he hears that she has shot herself, sinks back in his chair, crying, "Heaven help us —people don't *do* such things!" With certain reservations, Brack is right, and his words form a motto to the drama, for this is no high tragedy, as some Ibsen enthusiasts would have us believe. Obviously a sentiment such as Brack expresses could never have found a place at the close of the scene when Œdipus tears out his eyes or of the scene when Hamlet sinks to rest; it is entirely appropriate to *Hedda Gabler* precisely because, instead of aiming at the tragic, Ibsen has written what in effect is a high comedy. If we try to interpret all the talk about "vine-leaves in the hair" seriously we immediately find ourselves straining to give solemn interpretation to things at which the comic muse is gazing quizzically; only by realizing that in penning this case-study of a modern neurotic Ibsen is essaying the path taken centuries before by Jonson in his *Volpone* can we really appreciate this masterpiece aright. Hedda is really not frightening: she is mordantly funny.

Before writing *Hedda Gabler* Ibsen had written another study of a woman in *Fruen fra havet* (*The Lady from the Sea*, 1888), in which a not uninteresting story of an idle woman's hallucinations is made just a trifle ridiculous by the pomposity of the symbolism with which the entire action is wrapped. That Ibsen was on the right track in seeking to invest his realistic subject-matter with material of deeper imaginative import is certain; the difficulty is, however, that what so easily may be introduced into a poetic play often becomes rather absurd when it is attached to prosaic dialogue. In *The Tempest*, as in *King Lear*, the symbolism is implicit rather than explicit; we are hardly aware of it consciously, and we realize how powerful it is only after a careful analysis of the scenes. In *The Lady from the Sea*, and in the kindred *Bygmester Solness* (*The Master Builder*, 1892), the symbols stand out aggressively as though they had been intellectually instead of imaginatively conceived, as though they had been nailed on to the text instead of being organically fused with it. The plot of *The Lady from the Sea* tells of a woman, Ellida, who is possessed of a haunting attraction towards the ocean, and this attraction becomes concretized in the debt she imagines she owes towards the Stranger, a man whom she had known in her youth, who has been a seafarer, and who now returns to claim her from her husband, Dr Wangel. In so far as this story is concerned, we have merely a skilful dramatic study of a peculiar neurosis; but, besides that tale, there are two elements in the play of more questionable import. The first is the somewhat naïve solution of Ellida's problem. At the end, after much discussion and bandying to and fro of argument, Wangel suddenly decides to allow his wife freedom of choice, whereupon the lady who feels the sea-waves lapping in her heart equally promptly decides to give up her Stranger:

WANGEL: And therefore—therefore I—I cancel our bargain on the spot. So now you can choose your own path—in full—full freedom.
ELLIDA [*gazes at him awhile as if speechless*]: Is this true—true—what you say? Do you mean it—from your inmost heart?
WANGEL: Yes; from the inmost depths of my suffering heart, I mean it.
ELLIDA: And *can* you do it? Can you carry out your purpose?
WANGEL: Yes, I can. I can—because I love you so deeply.
ELLIDA [*softly and tremblingly*]: So closely—so tenderly have you come to love me!
WANGEL: The years of our union have taught me to.
ELLIDA [*clasps her hands together*]: And I—I have been blind to it!
WANGEL: Your thoughts took other directions. But now—now you are fully freed from me and mine. Now your own true life can return to its—its right groove again. For now you can choose in freedom; and on your own responsibility, Ellida.
ELLIDA [*clasps her head with her hands and gazes fixedly towards WANGEL*]: In freedom—and on my own responsibility? Responsibility too?— That transforms everything!   [*The steamer bell rings again.*
THE STRANGER: Do you hear, Ellida? They are ringing for the last time. Come away?
ELLIDA [*turns towards him, looks fixedly at him, and says with decision in her voice*]: I can never go with you after this.

Intellectually considered, the conclusion is logical: it remains to be wondered, however, whether it has emotional justification. The truth seems to be that Ibsen has allowed himself to become so hopelessly enamoured of his fine symbol that he has subordinated all else to it. By the time we are halfthrough with *The Lady from the Sea* we become rather tired of mermaids and fish-eyes, and Ellida's fancies seem to us excessively boring.

The same dominance of a symbolic concept weighs heavily on *The Master Builder*; indeed, the symbol, here as in the former drama, assumes such a blatant form as to make it seem immature and consequently almost laughable. All the talk in these scenes is of houses built for God or for people to live in, of architects' dreams, of trophies to be placed on high scaffoldings—and the import of this talk is akin to that about brackish waters, seaweed, and drowned sailors on the beach. The plot itself is simple. Halvard Solness is a builder, a man of late middle years, hearty yet feeling the effects of age, and terrified by the thought that youth will come and supersede him. Into his life comes a young girl, her mind gloriously and selfishly set on inspiring him to do great things. Although he knows that his head is not good for heights, he forces himself to climb up to the top of one of his recently constructed buildings, turns sick, and crashes down to his death. Perhaps the story is autobiographical, and, if so, then certain weaknesses in it would be explained. There is strength and there is interest here, yet *The Master Builder*, like others of Ibsen's dramas, appears not a little absurd; it lacks the calm objectivity of true greatness, and its ideas are somewhat shallowly based. At the end of a recent performance a man was heard to remark, "Crude, of course, but a promising play for a young man. The author *is* very young, isn't he?"—and the comment embodies an essential truth. When Ibsen wrote *The Master Builder* he was, technically, a master craftsman; spiritually, he was a middle-aged adolescent.

Lille Eyolf (*Little Eyolf*, 1894) is equally peculiar and equally oppressed by the symbolic. Fundamentally written to show the selfish Allmers and his wife, Rita, finding a new vision after the death of their crippled child, it fails to reach imaginative tensity. We may, if we will, interpret the little child as passive and suffering humanity, Allmers as self-conscious egoism, Rita as unconscious egoism, and the half-sister, Asta, as beneficent love, but the effort hardly enriches our appreciation of the play. What is an inherent weakness in the realistic drama is revealed by a comparison of the original draft for *Little Eyolf* and the finished version. In the former is little more than a straightforward and rather dull domestic tragedy concentrating on a mother's hatred of her sick child; in the latter this theme is complicated by symbolic content. Neither is satisfactory: the one is bare and the other is artificially decorated. Nor can we see any way by which the bare could be made richer or the artificially decorated given vitality. Once more the symbol fails to integrate itself into the organic whole, and the failure is due, not to Ibsen's weakness, but to the intractability of the form in which he is working.

John Gabriel Borkman (1896) displays a greater imaginative power, per-

JOHN OPIE: "BETTY, THE
INFANT ROSCIUS"
*National Portrait Gallery
photograph*

J. ZOFFANY: GARRICK,
AICKEN, AND BRANSBY IN
"LETHE"
*By courtesy of the Museum
and Art Gallery Committee of
the Corporation of Birmingham*

SETTING FOR "NORMA", BY LUIGI BAZZANI

By courtesy of the Ministero della Pubblica Istruzione, Rome

haps because in it the symbolic is, except in a few episodes, laid aside. Instead Ibsen presents a study of a man and of his surroundings. Borkman's vision had been one of wealth and power—not so much in and for itself as for what it could achieve. He had been truly and genuinely inspired by the thought of harnessing the hidden forces of the earth in the service of mankind: he was, in fact, the very image of the great modern industrialist, the Carnegie, whose vast undertakings are dominated by a tangle of inextricably intertwined motives, from selfish love of riches to grandiose dreams of bettering humanity's lot. The man who first markets safety-razors no doubt thinks at one and the same time of gashless chins and the chink of gold. Like many a great industrialist, Borkman has crashed heavily; and after a long incarceration he has returned to his home—to his hard wife, Gunhild, whose one aim is to encourage her son, Erhart, to amass money and so mend the family fortunes, and to her sister, Ella, whom Borkman years ago had loved and left. With powerful intensity, Ibsen shows the broken giant living in his study, waiting vainly day by day for the call which he thinks is sure to come to him from his former colleagues, befriended only by the weak little clerk Foldal, who visits him merely because he finds that Borkman is the one person who will flatter his secret passion to be considered a poet. Perhaps the most poignant scene in the entire play is that wherein Borkman is suddenly stung into revealing the truth and bluntly telling Foldal he has no use for his "poetical nonsense," and wherein Foldal, angered in turn, informs Borkman that he can never hope to come back to the position he once held. The picture is etched firmly and harshly.

One other play was still to come—*Naar vi döde vaagner* (*When We Dead Awaken*, 1899). In this we may see Ibsen's final testament. The hero here is a sculptor, Arnold Rubek, married to a sensuous, empty-headed Maia, younger than he, "with a vivacious expression and lively, mocking eyes, yet with a suggestion of fatigue." Neither is happy. Back into his life comes a woman, Irene, one who had served as model for his greatest piece of statuary and whom Rubek had regarded as no more than an instrument towards the achieving of an artistic result. Hearing him thank her for a "priceless episode," she had left him and had gone about the world as a kind of living corpse; his coldness had slain her:

IRENE: I . . . swore . . . that I would serve you in all things—
RUBEK: As the model for my art—
IRENE: —in frank, utter nakedness—
RUBEK [*with emotion*]: And you did serve me, Irene—so bravely—so gladly and so ungrudgingly.
IRENE: Yes, with all the pulsing blood of my youth, I served you!
RUBEK [*nodding, with a look of gratitude*]: That you have every right to say.
IRENE: I fell down at your feet and served you, Arnold! [*Holding her clenched hand towards him*] But you, you,—you—!
RUBEK [*defensively*]: I never did you any wrong! Never, Irene!
IRENE: Yes, you did! You did wrong to my innermost, inborn nature—

RUBEK [*starting back*]: I—!

IRENE: Yes, you! I exposed myself wholly and unreservedly to your gaze—[*more softly*] And never once did you touch me.

RUBEK: Irene, did you not understand that many a time I was almost beside myself under the spell of all your loveliness?

IRENE [*continuing undisturbed*]: And yet—if you had touched me, I think I should have killed you on the spot. For I had a sharp needle always upon me —hidden in my hair—[*Strokes her forehead meditatively.*] But after all—after all —that you could—

RUBEK [*looks impressively at her*]: I was an artist, Irene.

IRENE [*darkly*]: That is just it. That is just it.

Bitterly she claims that she had given him her "young, living soul"—

And that gift left me empty within—soulless. . . . It was that I died of, Arnold.

In the end, among the mountains, the pair are caught in a storm, but, instead of seeking safety by descending, they agree, like Rosmer and Rebecca, to mount upward towards certain death. The full significance this work held for Ibsen will never be known, but it would seem that thus, at the end of his life, he had come to believe that fullness of emotional existence was all that man should seek in the world, and that devotion to art or industry, if it interfered with that existence, was an evil.

It is hard indeed to estimate Ibsen's spirit aright. As a craftsman his position is secure. Trained in the school of Scribe, he evolved a powerful technique suited to the modern stage; what had been mechanical he made organic. In his casting aside of the older methods of exposition, in his attempt to allow character gradually to evolve as the action proceeds, and in his demonstration of what can be achieved by means of strict economy of form he was followed by many a successor. Besides these things that he taught to others, he was responsible for breaking the ancient five-act division, for suggesting the potential value of the retention of the unity of place, and for pointing out how much a realistic dramatist may convey to actor and reader through carefully worded stage directions. In the field of social and character concepts he wrought a veritable revolution, so that his influence on the intellectual world from 1880 to 1920 can hardly be fully assessed: Shaw's *Quintessence of Ibsenism* is a clear testimony to the impress made by the aging, rugged Norwegian upon the younger spirits of other lands.

His plays have a power beyond that of nearly all other realistic dramas of his time. Partly this is due to the fact that in him a poetic spirit sang lyrical tunes even while he was engaged in handling material of sordid reality: principally it is due to the fact that not one of his principal characters is ordinary or commonplace. It was the professed object of Zola, the confirmed practice of Augier and Dumas *fils*, to depict familiar situations and such persons as in no wise deviated from the regular run of men and women. Ibsen's characters are of an entirely different category. He may depict scenes of middle-class life, but the creatures who inhabit these scenes are not of the middle range of humanity. When we think of them we think of human beings *possessed*. Nora is no ordinary child-wife: she has heard a call that comes from the mountains, not from the market-place. Rebecca West is enthralled, as is Hedda: Solness has heard sirens' songs; Ellida belongs to the sea; and Hedwig is a queen of an enchanted attic. Something from outside, something that suggests the operation of a magic spell, holds these persons in fee. The result is that while outwardly Ibsen's scenes are 'ordinary' and materialistically conceived, inwardly they are extraordinary and at times breathe the atmosphere of Peer Gynt's adventures in the hobgoblin's court.

This gives greatness and enduring interest to his work. At the same time his plays, when placed against the greatest achievements of the theatre, are seen to lack that balance and poise out of which alone the highest dramatic achievements can come. Perhaps for this the historical position in which he found himself was to blame. He was forced to devote his energies to the cultivation of the realistic stage, yet the realistic stage could not offer him the scope desired. As a result, his imaginative development was, to a certain extent, thwarted. Had he grown in the poetic concept his spirit would have expanded: as it was, he lived on into old age a strangely adolescent soul. His writings still have power to appeal to us, yet that appeal is waning. Of the measure of Sophoclean and Shakespearian greatness he has none.

2

STRINDBERG AND THE PLAY OF THE SUBCONSCIOUS

OF PARTICULAR interest to us, when we consider the history of the theatre as a whole, is the fact that Ibsen does not stand alone. Just as Athens produced Æschylus, Sophocles, Euripides, and Aristophanes, as Elizabethan London produced Marlowe, Shakespeare, Jonson, and a score of others, as Spain produced Lope de Vega, Calderón, and their companions, as seventeenth-century France produced Corneille, Racine, and Molière, so the Scandinavian dramatic movement out of which Ibsen sprang brought to birth other talents worthy of being associated with his own.

Björnson and his Companions

The prevailingly characteristic style during the latter half of the century among these Scandinavian playwrights was the realistic, but since the majority of the authors did not succeed in enlarging their vision as Ibsen had done, and since they could not improve upon Ibsen's technique, their works have now become little more than historical curiosities. The Norwegian Knut Hamsun is remembered as a novelist, not as the author of *Livets spil* (*The Game of Life*, 1896); novelist rather than dramatist, too, is Jonas Lie, whose *Lystige koner* (*Merry Wives*, 1894), despite its effectively ironic tone, is by no means a great play; Alexander Kielland is barely to be remembered for his *Tre par* (*Three Couples*, 1886) and *Professoren* (*The Professor*, 1888). Just a trifle better equipped for the stage is Gunnar Heiberg, a dramatist who has at least a considerable local reputation. Starting in the problem-play tradition with *Tante Ulrikke* (*Aunt Ulrikke*, 1884), he soon proceeded to move from the discussion of social problems to treatment of human emotions, reaching his greatest success in two related dramas, *Balkonen* (*The Balcony*, 1894) and *Kjærlighedens tragedie* (*Love's Tragedy*, 1904). In both of these it is the nature of love, not the quality of social evils, that occupies his attention. He still remains aware of political and other similar issues, but his main interest lies in probing the complexities of the individual human soul.

Among these dramatists, however, stands one man of more than common quality, Björnstjerne Björnson, a Norwegian whose life is closely associated with that of Ibsen. Had Ibsen not been, Björnson's reputation assuredly would have stood high; as it is, he has been fated ever to be compared, and always to his disadvantage, with his greater compatriot and contemporary. This has been due, partly to the circumstances that threw them together, partly to the fact that in their dramatic art a peculiar parallelism prevails, and partly because Björnson, while seeing many of the errors in social life that were so patent to Ibsen, inclined to adopt an optimistic and compromising attitude that has little pleased the intellectual or other rebels during the past decades.

His earliest works were composed in the familiar historical mould so popular in his time. From the barbaric Viking material of *Mellem slagene* (*Between the Battles*, 1857), *Halte-Hulda* (*Hulda the Halt,* 1858), *Kong Sverre* (*King Sverre*, 1861), and the long series of episodes in *Sigurd Slembe* (*Sigurd the Bastard*, 1862) he moved to the ever-fascinating topic of *Maria Stuart i Skotland* (*Mary Stuart in Scotland*, 1864). The year following the appearance of the last of this series, however, saw the production of a play in an entirely different style, *De nygifte* (*The Newly Married Couple*, 1865), in which Björnson definitely aligned himself with the realists. Its tone is light and its conclusion happy, but the subject is definitely a 'problem'—that of the young man (in this case a worthy fellow named Axel) who finds his whole being fettered by a child-like wife, Laura, who, in turn, has not sufficiently grown beyond babyhood to escape from the loving chains set about her by her parents. There is a good deal that is artificial about Björnson's comedy, yet one can feel here an easy strength and an agreeable liberalism of outlook eminently admirable.

After nearly a decade of active political work, when Björnson returned to the theatre it was the style set in *The Newly Married Couple* that he pursued. A lone *Sigurd Jorsalfar* (*Sigurd the Crusader*, 1872) testified to his earlier interests; *Redaktören* (*The Editor*, 1874) and *En fallit* (*A Bankruptcy*, 1874) demonstrated clearly that in realism he had found his most effective medium. The former attacked bitterly the weaknesses of journalism; in the business-man Tjaelda of the latter play he reveals the dishonesties which may enter into commercial life, and, through this character's conversion to integrity, trumpets forth the claims of standards based more deeply upon true moral values.

The dull demand for respectability ruling in the society of his time was further pilloried in the interesting *Leonarda* of 1879, in which a woman of sincerest virtue is seen cold-shouldered by society. Leonarda's niece, Aagot, falls in love with Hagbart, nephew of the local bishop, and when this young man shifts his affections to her she deliberately sacrifices herself for the girl's sake. The play contains one particularly interesting character, the old Grandmother, first of a lengthy theatrical progeny of octogenarians, very wise and very tolerant, who are rather amused at youth's belief that they alone have the secrets of freedom, frankness, and independence. Following an unimportant *Det ny system* (*The New System*, 1879) came what is probably Björnson's best-known drama, *En hanske* (*A*

Gauntlet, 1883), where a simple question is asked: has a girl the right to demand from her fiancé the same premarital purity he demands from her? The author has been blamed for leaving his answer unsure, but perhaps such criticism is misplaced: what Björnson was interested in was the voicing of the problem itself, and the fact that he leaves his own answer in doubt makes his play maybe more in tune with the reality than any doctrinaire pronouncement could have made it. The young Alfred Christensen loves Svava Riis, and is repentant on account of an earlier affair of his own, yet not so repentant as to permit him to believe he would have condoned any similar escapade on Svava's part; she is horrified at this realization of the 'double morality,' and her intellect tells her to break the match, yet her affections prevent her from wholly closing the door; her mother is inclined to side with her, yet realizes that the setting up of such severe standards as Svava's would wreck social life entirely.

Over ævne (*Beyond our Strength*, or *Beyond Human Might*, 1883) enters into the realm of religious faith, and presents a tragic picture of the simple Pastor Sang, who believes he has been gifted with the power to work miracles. Extraordinary examples of his healing skill persuade the countryside that he is blessed by God with supernatural talents; only his bedridden wife, although she loves him, sets her will, almost unconsciously, against his, and in the end he dies, broken by the knowledge that his power is not what he has deemed. Perhaps in this drama Björnson has reached his highest and deepest dramatic utterance. Two years later came *Geografi og kjærlighed* (*Geography and Love*, 1885), depicting the utter selfishness of a scholar, Professor Tygesen, who demands that his whole household should be subservient to his needs: although much in the play is feeble, there are several scenes here—notably those in which Tygesen and his rival Turman appear—that are rich in sly, comic values. In 1895 came a second play entitled *Over ævne*, a drama dealing with the problems of capital and labour, introducing four characters from the former play, but fundamentally standing distinct from it. Designed to defy the forces of superstition and to call for a rational planning of human life, Björnson here has entered into the symbolic realm inhabited by the aging Ibsen. The two persons who testify to hope for the future, Credo and Spera, are as much personifications as any allegorical figures in the medieval moralities. A similar style appears in *Laboremus* (1901) and *Naar den ny vin blomstrer* (*When the Vineyards are in Blossom*, 1909). In the former, a powerful play, Björnson castigates in Lydia not merely a woman but a principle—the principle of aggressive individualism which is associated with the Nietzsche cult; the latter drama, infinitely weaker in concept and execution, gives one last fling at the Ibsenian new woman, and shows a middle-aged husband seeking in the love of a young girl for that which his wife is too busily occupied to give him.

In these and other dramas we may, if we will, find much shallowness and perhaps not a trifle of sentimentalism, yet Björnson's works are of value for their healthy sanity, their breezy good-humour, and their constant sympathy even for those characters whom he most condemned. If Ibsen is the Puritan of the nineteenth-century theatre, Björnson is one of its truest humanitarians.

The Early Strindberg

Greater by far than Björnson—and, indeed, a man whose genius, although erratic and strangely tormented by grotesque fancies, may be thought more intense than that of Ibsen itself—was the Swede August Strindberg. His fiery career has been narrated by himself and often retold by others, and from the record it is apparent that his creative career is sharply split in two by the complete breakdown which he suffered in his late forties; in a sense there are two Strindbergs, and, although there are ties binding the man who wrote before the year 1897 with the man whose work appeared after that date, these two may be regarded almost as separate entities.

Among the qualities held in common by the early Strindberg and the late, chief in significance is the intense 'subjectivity' in his art. It was as though he saw the whole of life focused upon himself, as though nothing existed save for the purpose of impinging on his personality. Oppressed by this concept, he continually interpreted events, not in relation to other events, but in relation to things that had happened to him: in his play *After the Fire* the Stranger speaks in the author's name when he declares that

> however life shaped itself, I always became aware of connexions and repetitions. I saw in one situation the result of another earlier one. Or meeting *this* person I was reminded of *that* one whom I had met in the past.

The result is that every one of his plays is a kind of reflection of himself: of the purely objective style in dramatic art he is entirely innocent.

Along with this must be noted a peculiar attitude towards reality which, although appearing in an intensified form only among his later plays, is early adumbrated in diverse scenes. For Strindberg material reality does not possess the same significance it did for Ibsen, and this expresses itself both by a greater selectivity and by a tendency to allow appearances, phenomena, to dominate in his plays. Not only is the spiritual of greater consequence to him than the physical, the physical at times almost seems to cease to exist, to prove itself merely a figment of the mind.

A third characteristic is the fact that, while his genius was a forceful one, hardly any other author of equivalent stature has shown himself so strongly and yet fitfully influenced by others as he has. In philosophy he passes under the spell of Buckle, Kierkegaard, and Swedenborg; in art he is swayed by a variety of writers from Byron to Maeterlinck. The consequence of this is twofold: that often two diametrically opposed styles are apparent at one single period of his career, and that that career exhibits a variety far greater than what is usually to be found in the work of a great dramatic author.

His first compositions intended for theatrical representation were romantic in tone (showing clearly the influence of the Byron-Schiller tradition). For his earliest dramas he made selection of classical subject-matter, but soon, like so many other Scandinavian authors, he turned to the history of his own land, and in *Mäster Olof* (*Master Olof*, 1872) produced his first notable dramatic work. While almost entirely neglected or condemned on its first appearance, this play shows the hand of genius at work, and was destined to win later esteem. The central figure is Olaus (Olof) Petri, the founder of the Swedish Reformation; he is associated with Gustavus Vasa and the Anabaptist Gert, a fanatic printer. The historical plot is concerned with the first struggles that Olof has with the priesthood, his acceptance by Gert as a kindred revolutionary soul, his patronage by the King, and his pursuit of his ideal in compromise manner. Apart from this plot, however, the drama may be looked upon subjectively, and in this manner Strindberg himself probably conceived it. Seen thus, the three persons of Olof, the practical idealist, Gustavus Vasa, the man of affairs who allows no ideal to deflect him from his purpose, and the utterly impractical visionary Gert take shape as projections of parts of Strindberg's own self—for thus early in his career did he recognize in himself a split individuality. The double quality gives to the work, crude though it may be, a distinction among the historical dramas of the time.

A few other similar plays followed, including *Gillets hemlighet* (*The Secret of the Guild*, 1880) and *Herr Bengts hustru* (*Sir Bengt's Lady*, 1882), and then came the satirical fairy-tale *Lycko-Pers resa* (*The Wanderings of Lucky Per*, 1882). This, Strindberg insisted, was intended as a play for children, and, even although it has won much success on the stage among adult audiences, it would seem that his assertion ought to be taken literally. If we judge it as, for example, we judge the similar *Peer Gynt*, then the fairy machinery and the obvious allegory must be condemned as childish; but if it was indeed Strindberg's purpose to make it so, our estimate of the drama's worth inevitably will be of a different kind, and we shall find in its satire of social life a subtle adjustment of means to ends. Particularly effective from this point of view is the scene in the third act wherein we find ourselves in a market-square: in the middle are a Pillory and a Statue of the Mayor. These suddenly become animate and hold a conversation:

PILLORY [*bows to the STATUE*]: Good morning, Statue! Did you sleep well last night?
STATUE [*nods*]: Good morning, Pillory; did you sleep well yourself?
PILLORY: I slept all right, but I dreamt too; can you guess what I dreamt?
STATUE [*testily*]: How should I be able to guess?

PILLORY: Well, I dreamt—can you imagine?—that a reformer had come to the town!

STATUE: A reformer? What! [*Stamps.*] It's deuced cold for the feet standing here, but what does one not do for honour's sake! A reformer? Well, I suppose he will have a statue too?

PILLORY: Statue! Statue indeed! No! He had to stand here at my feet himself like a statue, and I took him by the throat with my two arms! [*The neck-irons rattle.*] You see, he was a real reformer and not one of those charlatans you were when you were alive.

This introduces us effectively to a developing action wherein Strindberg's fantastically conceived satire is displayed with skill and precision.

The Violence of Realism

From the tone of this play it is indeed a far cry to the tortured misery of *Fadren* (*The Father*, 1887), through which Strindberg inaugurated his trenchant series of darkly pessimistic and tortured realistic dramas. The theme of this tragic action is bare, almost gaunt. A Captain, characteristically left without a name, finds his strength and his reason sapped by his wife, Laura. With diabolical cruelty she separates him from his only friend, Dr Östermark, and then proceeds by insinuations deliberately to drive him insane. Beyond and around this bitter tale of two sex-enemies is the atmosphere of feminine power—the monstrous regiment of women—that Strindberg sets as background for the action. The Captain's household is dominated and ruled not only by his wife, but also by those associated with her, and there is a bitter irony in the fact that, at the very conclusion of the play, the strait-jacket is slipped upon him by his old Nurse as she bends over him, whispering motherly words into his ears. Without a doubt this is among the greatest dramas produced by the late-nineteenth-century theatre: its very simplicity of aim gives it a peculiar distinction.

In connexion with this simplicity of aim there should be noted one basic difference between the methods and the concepts of Ibsen and Strindberg. If, for example, we take *Hedda Gabler* for comparison with *The Father* we find that the Ibsen play starts with a meticulously described interior setting, and that as the action unfolds very considerable reference is made to the material surroundings of the characters. *Things* were for Ibsen of tremendous import, and frequently he makes his most telling points by relating his persons to furniture and properties. We can hardly think of this, or of any other of his realistic dramas, separated from the settings. To such a dramatic method *The Father* presents a complete contrast. The room in which the Captain sits—and the very fact that he is called simply the Captain and not given an individual name is in keeping—is described in general terms; almost the only two objects of which dramatic use is made in the whole course of the action are the lamp he hurls after his wife and the strait-jacket by which he is bound at the end.

In effect, *The Father* could quite easily, and perhaps might most effectively, be played on a completely bare stage. With this quality in Strindberg's work may be associated both his reduction of the plot element and his several experiments in writing plays which, unbroken by scene divisions, present one unified action from start to finish, with all stress upon the passions, none upon the intrigue. Strindberg's concentration is wholly on the world of the spirit: his action is of the soul, not of the body.

Precisely similar in character to *The Father* is *Kamraterna* (*Comrades*, 1888), in which a talented artist, Axel, sacrifices his genius for his wife, Berta. During several years of marriage, which she likes to describe as "comradeship," she has forced him to debase his talents by the turning out of commercial work, while she, an artist also, is free to give her time to painting what she likes. So devoted is he to her that when they both prepare pictures for the Salon and when he realizes that his unquestionably will be accepted, hers rejected, he sends his canvas in under her name. When news comes that Berta's picture has been accepted she openly exults, and with unparalleled cruelty arranges that the rejected work should be returned to him, humiliatingly, in the midst of a party. This action finally brings him to a realization of her true nature and of the quality of their relationship: although she pleads with him, he determines that their marriage must be dissolved. He will, he says, take a mistress: "I like to meet a comrade at a café; at home I want a wife," are his final words. Strindberg's genius is nowhere more clearly demonstrated than by the fact that this is one of the few plays in the entire history of the drama that truly conveys the impression of an artist's life. Ibsen's Rubek is by comparison a synthetic composition.

Even more bitter is the tormenting *Fröken Julie* (*Miss Julie*, 1888). The heroine of this terrible "naturalistic tragedy" Strindberg himself describes as a "half-woman, the man-hater"—a tragic type, "offering the spectacle of a desperate fight with nature"; she is a neurotic child of a degenerate aristocracy, proud and yet willing to sink her pride in the frenzied attempt to satisfy her love of sensation. Centuries before, Middleton had depicted just such a character in the heroine of *The Changeling*. Almost hysterically she makes love and gives herself to her valet, Jean, finds herself in his power, and is forced by him to steal money from her own father; in the end Jean callously suggests that her only remedy is to commit suicide, and, as in a trance, she obeys. In telling this gruesome tale Strindberg deliberately sets himself to plan a technique harmonious with his central purpose.

"I have rather broken with tradition," he says,

in not making my characters catechists who sit asking foolish questions in order to elicit a smart reply. I have avoided the mathematically symmetrical construction of French dialogue and let people's brains work irregularly, as they do in actual life, where no topic of conversation is drained to the dregs, but

one brain receives haphazard from the other a cog to engage with. Consequently, my dialogue too wanders about, providing itself in the earlier scenes
with material which is afterwards worked up, admitted, repeated, developed
and built up, like the theme of a musical composition.

The plot is full of possibilities, and since it really concerns only two characters I have confined myself to these, merely introducing one minor character,
the cook, and allowing the father's unfortunate spirit to hover over and behind
the whole. This is because I thought I had noticed that the psychological process is what chiefly interests the newer generation; our inquisitive souls are not
content with seeing a thing happen; they must also know how it happens.
What we want to see is the wires, the machinery; we want to examine the box
with the false bottom, to handle the magic ring and find the joint, to have a look
at the cards and see how they are marked.

In addition he has abolished the act division, an experiment made in the
belief "that our decreasing capacity for illusion was possibly weakened
by intervals in which the spectator has time to reflect and thereby escape
from the suggestive influence of the author-mesmerist."

From these remarks, made by the author himself, it is obvious that the
'naturalism' of *Miss Julie* is something that goes far beyond earlier naturalistic endeavours. There are none of Zola's "supernumerary fools"
here: indeed, Strindberg deliberately rejects "the so-called 'folk-scene'"
as being something likely to destroy the illusion. And as for scenery, he
declares that he has "borrowed from impressionist painting its asym-
metry and its abruptness." Already the stage was moving beyond the
limits of Ibsenian realism.

In *Fordringsägare* (*Creditors*, 1888) the sex-war is still further developed,
and in a form even more abstract. Here, again, only three persons are
introduced: Tekla, a predatory woman writer; Adolph, her husband, an
artist; and Gustav, her former husband, a teacher. The lesson of the play
is that the woman has made her reputation by sucking the strength of
Gustav, and is now similarly sapping Adolph's power. Hardly any
drama of Strindberg's is more compact than this one, and the author's
skill is displayed no less by the incisive etching of his characters than by
the tensity of the emotional atmosphere evoked.

The same year saw the composition of *Paria* (*Pariah*, 1889), a drama in
which for the first time the influence of Poe becomes dominant. Two
middle-aged characters—again typically called simply Mr X (an
archæologist) and Mr Y (an American traveller)—appear, set almost *in
vacuo*. The former, poor yet holding in his hands a priceless treasure he
has unearthed, wonders why he cannot bring himself to take some of the
antique golden ornaments and melt them down for his own use. Something he cannot himself understand, an inner compulsion, holds him
back. His companion turns out to have been guilty of a forgery; and, as
for himself, Mr X reveals that he has been guilty of murder. On hearing
this Mr Y tries to blackmail him, but his strength is petty compared with
that of the archæologist, and it is the man who will not steal who remains

the victor. The play is interesting for its deliberate seeking after an effective and sensational curtain, and for its early treatment of a theme later to press heavily on Strindberg's mind—that of justice.

The sensationalism reappears in the still more Poe-esque *Samum* (*Simoom*, written 1888, printed 1890), where, in the midst of the simoom, an Arabian girl, Biskra, aided by her lover, Yusuf, succeeds by tricks in so working upon the mind of Guimard, a lieutenant of the Zouaves, as to drive him to his death. Another, and even shorter, one-act play of the same time is *Den starkare* (*The Stronger*, 1890), interesting technically because, although it presents two characters, Mrs X and Miss Y, the latter remains silent, and the piece thus takes shape as a kind of monologue. With consummate skill Strindberg succeeds in focusing attention more on the woman who does not speak than on the one who does.

During the following years many other plays succeeded, diverse influences, chief among them that of Nietzsche, ever bringing fresh tones and colours to their composition. *Debet och kredit* (*Debit and Credit*; printed 1893) introduces a kind of bitter laughter in its delineation of Axel, a teacher who, by relying on help from others, has gained a high reputation, but who has no financial means at his command. Pestered by those who think he owes them a return for services rendered, he prepares a set of cynically worded letters, leaving thus the country of his birth and his creditors. Closely akin in spirit are *Första varningen* (*The First Warning*, 1893), in which marital relationships in middle age are treated with a crackling and ironic laughter, and *Leka med elden* (*Playing with Fire*, 1892), where an artist's wife nearly goes off with her husband's best friend. In *Moderskärlek* (*Mother Love*, 1893) he turns to the problem of children and parents, a theme further developed in *Bandet* (*The Link*, or *The Bond*, 1893), which also deals with the question of justice. Here a young Judge is forced to fine a farmer for libel when he knows that the man is perfectly innocent, and then is confronted by the perplexing case of the Baron and the Baroness who seek separation, bitterly accuse each other, and yet are tied together by thought of the child they have brought into the world. In this work the 'abstract' quality of Strindberg's art is more than ever apparent: his mind increasingly is being drawn within itself.

The Later Historical Plays

After he had recovered from his mental breakdown Strindberg's writings assumed diverse forms. Rather peculiarly, one set of dramas is a series of historical studies which catch up, as it were, his earliest efforts. In *Gustav Vasa* (1899), indeed, he actually took over the characters whom, years before, he had shown in *Mäster Olof*, revealing them now in their middle age. *Erik XIV* came the same year, with, as its central figure, Erik, the son of Gustavus. Perhaps the most interesting of all his historical works, its atmosphere is that of "a mad world, my masters." The King lives with his devoted mistress, Karin, but dreams of becoming the husband of Queen Elizabeth of England. His eccentricities, by no means unlovable, drive him into opposition with his hard-headed, ambitious nobles, and the drama ends with a magnificent scene in which Erik's miserable and pathetic Court is shattered by the heavy tread of the Dukes who are to usurp his rule.

In *Folkunga-sagan* (*The Saga of the Folkungs*, 1899) Strindberg turned farther back in the pages of history, and wrote a fascinating study of the weakly tolerant Magnus, setting this King against a background of sex-passions. He is married to Blanche, but she has a 'servant' in Bengt Algotson, while the Queen Mother, Ingeborg, keeps a lover in Knut Porse: against these is set the pathetic child-marriage of the boy Erik and his bride, Beatrix. With extraordinary vigour the author reveals to us this wretched palace, concentrating with particular delight on delineating the vicious Ingeborg and her Porse:

> PORSE [*brutally*]: Can I rely on you?
>
> INGEBORG: You don't love me!
>
> PORSE: Nonsense! Is it for elderly people like us to waste our time on lovers' tiffs? I suppose you expect me, the Duke of Halland, to squat on my knees and pluck the lute while women and boys snatch away the crowns! Be yourself, Ingeborg; be rough, as nature and life has made you; fire for the hovel and axe for the head, mirror of my own soul! Love? Really I never expected that word from you. If we feel drawn to each other, that is not love, but a common hate, hate, hate!
>
> INGEBORG: You frighten me!
>
> PORSE: Are you so easily frightened? I shouldn't have thought so!—Tell me: why won't you marry me? It would make our position safer and dearer!
>
> INGEBORG: I don't see that.
>
> PORSE: Don't you? But consider what may happen. When I have thrown out Erik the crown is mine; I can't offer to share it with you as my mistress, but as my wife I could!
>
> INGEBORG: Time enough to think about that when. . .
>
> PORSE It's too late. . .
>
> INGEBORG: First do your knightly service and clear the way to the throne.
>
> PORSE: For two, or for one?
>
> INGEBORG: That depends on . . .
>
> PORSE: Whether you have to kick me aside then. Show your cards! You want to use me as a broom and then throw me into the fire. It's Aunt Britta's great idea come up again: the sisters are to rule over the brothers; but the brothers are to look after mass, confession, preaching, choir duty, housekeeping, instruction,—in a word—do the brain work, while ignorance and incompetence sit at the helm.
>
> INGEBORG: I hate you!
>
> PORSE: Go on!
>
> INGEBORG: So much that I should like to see your eyes on a fish-hook and your liver chopped up for the cats! I loathe you like garbage and filth; you sicken me like unkempt hair and black finger-nails; I curse the hour your feet brought you my way, and I wish your mother had thrown you on a dung-heap one dark night, to be eaten by the swine!

PORSE: Bravo! Splendid! There speaks my Ingeborg again; the royal mother, the strong, the red-hot. If you knew how beautiful you are now you would never prattle of love. When you talk like this, your words are drums and trumpets, the music of battle in my ear. And now for my knightly guard —even if it means fighting with ghosts and Satan! Hail, Queen!

[*He seizes her and throws himself on her to steal a kiss.*

In this series of dramas, which includes the strong *Gustav Adolf* (*Gustavus Adolphus*, 1900), *Engelbrekt* (1901), *Carl XII* (1901), *Gustav III* (1903), and *Kristina* (*Queen Christina*, 1903)—the last a skilful study of a neurotic and half-deranged woman—Strindberg revealed the power of his dramatic conceptions and the mastery he had acquired of his craft. These later historical dramas are among the most powerful plays of the kind produced in modern times.

The Later Realistic Plays

Another group of plays written at this time recalls, but afar off, the style of his middle period. Typical of these is the strange 'comedy' *Brott och brott* (*There are Crimes and Crimes*), published in 1899 with *Advent* under the general title of *Vid högre rätt* (*In a Higher Court*). Here the theme of justice is caught up with the religious trend, which had already, in 1892, found expression in *Himmelrikets nycklar* (*The Keys of the Kingdom of Heaven*). The scene of *There are Crimes and Crimes* is Paris; but it is a Paris of the mind, not the city of actuality, and the action is one in which the real is subordinated to the imaginative. The main character is Maurice, a playwright who, after years of poverty, is expecting success from a drama about to be produced. He has received devoted love from his mistress, Jeanne, by whom he has a dearly beloved daughter, Marion. On the eve of his victory he meets Henriette, the mistress of his friend Adolphe, and, consumed by a wild passion, goes off with her. The child Marion, however, is a bar to their happiness, and when it dies he accuses Henriette of committing murder, while he himself is looked upon by the law as the probable criminal. The world, which had seemed so full of promise, turns against him, and only at the close is it discovered that Marion had died naturally, with the consequence that he is relieved of the nightmare into which he had sunk. The whole drama, of course, is a kind of impressionistic study of thought, and its ironic conclusion, wherein Maurice agrees to divide his life between prayer and acceptance of the worldly joys now restored to him, is deliberately planned.

Its companion piece, *Advent* (1899), departs entirely from even a semblance of realism, and is replete with Swedenborgian symbolism. The main characters are, on the one hand, a Judge and an Old Lady, essentially evil, accompanied by the Other One, the devil who feels pain in the task assigned to him, and, on the other, by two children, befriended by the Playmate, who is in reality the Christ Child. This entire piece is wrought with a dream-like atmosphere; we are withdrawn entirely from the world of reality; it is a realm of magic we inhabit where objects pass through apparently solid walls: in the court-room scene,

> *The bell rings. The gavel raps once on the table. All the chairs are pulled up to the table at once. The Bible is opened. The candles on the table become lighted.*

Peculiarly effective is the macabre devil-dance episode, in which appear the Prince, Lucifer himself, and the Satanic Master of Ceremonies. The Prince demurs at taking part in the masquerade:

> *MASTER OF CEREMONIES:* Try to do anything but what you must, and you'll experience an inner discord that you cannot explain.
> *PRINCE:* What does it mean?
> *MASTER OF CEREMONIES:* It means that you cannot all of a sudden cease to be what you are: and you are what you have wanted to become.

To this section of his writings belong the several 'chamber plays' that Strindberg wrote specifically for August Falck's Intimate Theatre at Stockholm—a tiny structure that became, to all intents, a Strindberg playhouse. In these dramas the author sought to carry out his original dream of abolishing intermissions, and pursued farther his characteristic treatment of the scenic accompaniment of his actions. The scenery he reduced to quickly interchangeable backgrounds with a few stage properties—just sufficient and no more to provide his characters with a barely indicated *milieu*. Among these chamber plays *Oväder* (*The Thunderstorm*; printed 1907) is notable for its effective picture of old age, presented in a study of the Master, living in an apartment of the house where he had once been happy with his divorced wife, Gerda. To her image he clings, and only gradually does it lose its power as his passions sink to resignation. In the conduct of this piece there is more than a suggestion of a Pirandellesque treatment, with people and their actions viewed from differing standpoints.

Another play of the same kind is *Brända tomten* (*After the Fire*, or *The Burned Lot*; printed 1907). As in *The Thunderstorm* a house of several apartments stood behind the characters, so here the background is composed of the ruins of a burned home, set in a street which, as Anderson the Mason tells the Detective, has the peculiar quality that the people who move from it always must return. "We call it the Bog," he says. "And all of us hate each other, and suspect each other, and blackguard each other, and torment each other." The fire has started gossip, and gossip has widened into accusation: all that is rotten has been exposed to the light; symbolically, a pitiful pile of salvaged goods lies open for all to gaze at. Into this picture steps the Stranger—a portrait of Strindberg himself—philosophically moving amid the wreckage of his world.

Sometimes dark, sometimes with a breaking of light, Strindberg's mind during these years passed in review the fundamental problems of man's life. In *Påsk* (*Easter*, 1901) a religious spirit prevails; the darkness and cold of winter, the dark depression of Elis, burdened with a sense of guilt because of his father's actions, are dissipated as the warmth of the spring sun enters into his life. But the shadows are impenetrable in the terrible *Dödsdansen* (*The Dance of Death*, 1901), which some critics, not without justice, regard as Strindberg's greatest work. Here, in an isolated fort, Edgar, a captain of artillery, and Alice, his wife, have lived for twenty-five years, hating each other with a deadly venom and each wishing for the other's death. Their home becomes peopled with devils, and when Curt, Edgar's friend, comes to stay in it he is caught up in the atmosphere of evil: he falls in love with the wife and becomes her associate in a plot designed to destroy her husband. During a stroke, however, Edgar suddenly gains a new vision of life. He realizes his own errors and pleads for a reconciliation. Thus ends the first part of the drama. The second shows the final triumph of the wife. Remorselessly she drives Edgar to his death—although in the very process of doing so a bitter doubt enters her mind:

> *ALICE:* Do you notice that there is peace in the house now? The wonderful peace of death. Wonderful as the solemn anxiety that surrounds the coming of a child into the world. I hear the silence—and on the floor I see the traces of the easy-chair that carried him away—— And I feel now that my own life is ended, and I am starting on the road to dissolution! . . . While we have been talking here, the image of him as he was in his younger years has come back to me—I have seen him, I see him—now, as when he was only twenty —I must have loved that man!
>
> *CURT:* And hated him!
>
> *ALICE:* And hated!—Peace be with him!

The Development of a New Form: "The Dream Play"

It is the third type of play developed by Strindberg during this time that is most interesting, because most new. Even in *Advent* Strindberg had kept some slight hold on the objective. In *Till Damaskus* (*To Damascus*; Parts 1 and 2, 1898; Part 3, 1904) something different appeared. Here is the true theatre of surrealism, the presentation on the stage of the wholly subjective—the theatrical representation of the dream. This was followed in the same style by *Ett drömspel* (*The Dream Play*, 1902) and *Spöksonaten* (*The Spook Sonata*, 1907).

In writing these Strindberg worked quite deliberately. He had, he declared, "tried to imitate the disconnected but seemingly logical form of the dream":

> Anything may happen; everything is possible and probable. Time and space do not exist. On an insignificant background of reality, imagination designs and embroiders novel patterns: a medley of memories, experiences, free fancies, absurdities and improvisations.
>
> The characters split, double, multiply, vanish, solidify, blur, clarify. But one consciousness reigns above them all—that of the dreamer; and before it there are no secrets, no incongruities, no scruples, no laws. There is neither judgment nor exoneration, but merely narration. And as the dream is mostly

painful, rarely pleasant, a note of melancholy and of pity with living things runs right through the wabbly tale. Sleep, the liberator, plays often a dismal part, but when the pain is at its worst, the awakening comes and reconciles the sufferer with reality, which, however distressing it may be, nevertheless seems happy in comparison with the torments of the dream.

To attempt to describe the kaleidoscopic 'plots' of these works would be futile. *The Dream Play* opens with conversation between a Glazier and his Daughter, looking upon a castle that is growing ever higher and higher "because they have manured it," and that "ought to be blooming soon, as we are already past midsummer." Soon an Officer and his sick Mother are introduced, and before long the stage is peopled with a medley collection of variegated characters—a Singer, a Portress, a Bill-poster. In the midst of these the Prompter enters, followed by a Lawyer and a *corps de ballet*. Poets and miners, personifications of Theology, Philosophy, and Medicine, these are jumbled together with all the inconsequence of a nightmare; yet beyond them all lies the dreamer himself, seeing evil come of the incorporation of the pure intelligence in fleshly form.

In *The Spook Sonata* a similar atmosphere prevails—with an apparition of a Milkmaid, the ghost of a Consul, a Mummy (the Colonel's wife). We are in a world of spectres here, not less terrible and not less real because they are figments of the imagination. The world is one of illusion, guilt, suffering, and death, with only the fitful light of faith to give it feeble illumination. Youth and age alike are bound in a circle of evil, and although the action ends with a strange vision in which "the whole room disappears, and in its place appears 'The Island of the Dead' by Boecklin as background," while "soft music, very quiet and pleasantly sad, is heard" from the distance, the mood is pessimistic, modified only by a kind of Buddhistic resignation towards the miseries of the flesh. The young Student, Arkenholtz, and his sweetheart are as tightly shackled by the terrors around them as the old Hummel and the whitehaired crone who had once been his love.

Closely associated with these dramas is the fairy-tale *Svanevit* (*Swanwhite*; printed 1902), in which the influence of Maeterlinck is, confessedly, dominant. Among the most successful theatrically of all Strindberg's plays, it substitutes the pleasant dream for the nightmare, drawing its portraits of little Swanwhite and her Prince with infinite compassion, though with the same unreality as distinguishes the other plays. With it may be placed another 'folk-play,' *Kronbruden* (*The Bridal Crown*, 1902), of kindred spirit. Here the legend is told of two shepherd lovers, separated by family feuds, but pursuing their life of mutual passion amid a world peopled with characters human and supernatural.

In these dramas, as in the others written during his tempestuous career, Strindberg reveals a power which can barely be matched elsewhere in the nineteenth-century theatre. Even when he is contrasted with Ibsen the impression of this power remains distinct and emphatic. Indeed, it is Ibsen not Strindberg, who suffers in the comparison. No doubt the Norwegian author is the more accomplished playwright, assured in his craftsmanship, while the Swede is erratic and sometimes fumbling; yet the fact remains that after reading or seeing Strindberg's plays Ibsen's seem to us not a trifle dull and dowdy, adolescent, facile, lacking in deep passion. What appeared to us to be granite suddenly assumes the softness of putty. Where Ibsen's scenes are sometimes ordinary, Strindberg's are extraordinary and demonic. His characters possess almost superhuman proportions, and his masculinity triumphs over Ibsen's feminism.

While it is certain that Ibsen writes works better calculated for commercial production, and that most of Strindberg's plays are likely to remain somewhat caviare to the general, these latter plays forge far ahead of the former in vision and concept. Three things in especial Strindberg did. First, in the supreme concentration of the dramas of his middle period, he showed how much even the closely packed realistic plays of Ibsen lacked of essential dramatic economy. Secondly, he came as near as any man towards creating a modern social tragedy. And, thirdly, in his latest works he achieved what might have seemed the impossible—producing theatrical compositions that in effect are wholly subjective. In the long range of his writings his hands touch now the early romantics, now the realists and naturalists, now the expressionists, now the surrealists, and now the existentialists. There is no author whose range is wider or more provocative. In him the entire history of the stage from 1800 to the present day is epitomized.

3

THE INDEPENDENT THEATRE IN GERMANY

THE FORCE that had produced Schiller and Goethe and that later was to foster the works of Hebbel, Ludwig, and Wagner was not yet spent; in Gerhart Hauptmann Germany was to welcome a dramatist only slightly less powerful than the Scandinavian masters.

To a large extent his genius was inspired by the opportunities offered to him by the Freie Bühne, which, created under the enthusiasm of Otto Brahm, first came before the public with a production of Ibsen's *Ghosts* in 1889. Although this venture succeeded in maintaining life for only three seasons, its impetus was perhaps of even greater influence than its own intrinsic efforts. Directly arising out of its example came Bruno Wille's proletarian playhouse, the Freie Volksbühne, of 1890, and the same director's Neue Freie Bühne of 1892; later, in 1895, came the inauguration of the Workmen's Theatre of Vienna, modelled on the People's Independent Theatre Society of Berlin. Through these efforts of the original Freie Bühne the ordinary stages were opened to works written by the new realistic playwrights, and from them sprang, indirectly at least, the manifold activities of Max Reinhardt.

Hauptmann's Predecessors and Companions

Besides the influence exerted upon Hauptmann by this theatrical movement, he owed much to his immediate predecessors in dramatic writing. The works of Hebbel, Ludwig, and their companions have already been noted: slightly later came Ludwig Anzengruber, whose importance lies chiefly in his deliberate attempt to develop a form of dramatic dialogue suited to the new realistic stage which, while based on the forms of speech current in various spheres of ordinary life, should still avoid the monotony consequent upon mere phonographic reproduction of the common tongue.

In structure Anzengruber's dramas are based on the popular and rather melodramatic 'Wiener Volksstück,' from which he borrows sensational effects, looseness of structure, and rapid changes of scene. Thence, too, came his love of music, sometimes introduced merely as background accompaniment, sometimes built into the body of a play. Fundamentally, however, he is interested in developing a realistic form of theatrical expression somewhat along the lines of the experiments made fully a generation earlier by Hebbel and Ludwig. His themes are diverse. In his first drama of this kind, *Der Pfarrer von Kirchfeld* (*The Kirchfeld Priest*, 1870), he chooses a religious subject, showing a young idealistic pastor, Hell, in conflict both with the church authorities and with a local dignitary, Count Finsterberg. Having taken into his service a girl, Anna, he is traduced by evil-minded neighbours and removed from his cure, but, rising out of despair, determines to carry on the good fight. For *Heimg'funden!* (*Home at Last*, 1885) he introduces as the main figure a Dr Hammer who deserts his old mother in order to devote himself to money-making, who is ruined and is on the point of committing suicide when he is persuaded to return to the scenes of his boyhood, there achieving peace of soul. Often Anzengruber strikes a note of sardonic laughter, as in *Der G'wissenswurm* (*The Worm of Conscience*, 1874), with its old farmer, Grillhofer, his poor brother-in-law, Dusterer, and Grillhofer's bright, joyous illegitimate daughter, Liese Horlacher. The scene in which the farmer, persuaded that it is his duty to visit the girl whom he had seduced in his youth, finds in his former flame a termagant mother of a dozen children, has genuine verve and spirit. Clearly, however, this author felt more at ease when his subjects were melodramatically full of exciting incident or when they were dark with disaster. Typical is *Der Meineidbauer* (*The Perjurer*, 1871), in which the main plot is based on the perjury whereby the wicked Ferner robs the heroine, Vroni, of her just inheritance, and which gloomily combines with this dark romantic tale equally dark romantic scenes in the mountains among the haunts of smugglers. Typical in another way is the burlesquely titled *Der Doppelselbstmord* (*The Double Suicide*, 1875), where a pair of rustic lovers, compelled by circumstances, end their lives in a death pact. This is the mood that dominates in Anzengruber's most famous drama, *Das vierte Gebot* (*The Fourth Commandment*, 1877), a play which, because of its bitter attack on the crushing of youthful spirit by the old, was seized upon eagerly by Otto Brahm when he first opened the doors of his Freie Bühne. In this play still another theme much to be exploited by the realistic dramatists of the end of the century—what may be styled the 'generations' theme—made its appearance.

The same year that *Das vierte Gebot* was thus introduced to a Berlin audience the work of two younger writers, *Die Familie Selicke* (*The Selicke Family*, 1890), by Arno Holz and Johannes Schlaf, was produced at the Freie Bühne. Here misery prevails. The family circle is made up of a weak-willed mother whose whole interest is focused on her dying youngest daughter, a father besotten with drink, and a girl who is forced to break her engagement for the sake of her parents. Naturalism of the gloomiest kind is now being introduced to the German stage. In a work of similar tone Schlaf produced later his tortured portrait of a criminal in *Meister Ölze* (*Master Olze*, 1892), thus establishing yet another model for the naturalistic drama.

Others during these years eagerly and viciously pursued similar ideas. Max Halbe, in whom is to be discerned a theatrical power beyond that of most of his companions, delineates a doomed household in *Emporkömmling* (*The Upstart*, 1889), where a son, instead of a daughter, is ruined by a hard, obstinate father—a descendant of Anthony in Hebbel's *Maria Magdalena*. Halbe's most influential plays, however, came only in the nineties—*Der Eisgang* (*The Ice Floe*, 1892), *Jugend* (*Youth*, 1893), and *Mutter Erde* (*Mother Earth*, 1897). Over the German-Polish lovers, Paul and Antoinette, in the first of these heavily burdened dramas hangs the menace of heredity, and in the conflict of son and father clashing social concepts are embodied. *Jugend* tells a terrible story of a girl, Annchen, who, falling in love with a young student, is murdered by her imbecile half-brother, Amandus, who aims his gun at the man and by mistake shoots her dead. In the third play romantic love, carried from youth to middle age, yields nothing but bitterness, and the familiar double suicide closes the action. Equally violent are the dismal themes of *Das tausendjährige Reich* (*The Thousand-year Reich*, 1900) and of *Der Strom* (*The Stream*, 1903). Although Halbe possesses some power, and although his example was of considerable influence during these formative years, there is little likelihood, now that this gloomy naturalism has lost its force, that he will be remembered otherwise than as a writer of temporary appeal. All that can be said is that he is outspoken in his championing of the poor, although generally this championing assumes rather crude form—as in *Die gerechte Welt* (*The Just World*, 1897), where, artificially, the miseries of the simple mechanic Hügel and his sister, Anna, are contrasted with the evil machinations of the capitalistic Grossmann brothers.

Among these revolutionaries, most of them so extreme that their writings could be expected to make appeal only in limited circles, two men in particular were responsible for bringing the naturalistic problem play to the attention of more general audiences. The first of these, Hermann Sudermann, once was hailed as among the greatest of the realistic playwrights of these years, but time has not dealt gently with him, and his reputation now has become rather sadly tarnished. Serious in aim, he is yet seen to have sacrificed honesty of purpose to theatrical effect: the insincerities that were not so obvious to his contemporaries have been blatantly revealed by the light of passing decades.

Die Ehre (*Honour*, 1889), his first play, won him considerable esteem. Presented not in an independent theatre but on a public stage, it must have appeared daring indeed to an ordinary audience: Its object was to delineate, in sensational terms, the vast cleavage in viewpoint between the code of the upper-middle class and that of the proletariat. There is nothing startling here in the discussion of a problem still potent nowadays; there is no vision; there is but mediocre development of character; but unquestionably this young author displayed considerable perspicacity in seizing on the kind of problem for which his audience were eagerly expectant.

If in this play he turned a satiric pen upon a current social code, in his second drama, *Sodoms Ende* (*The Destruction of Sodom*, 1891), he attacked the vices rampant in aristocratic circles. The hero is an artist who is taken up by a rich woman, is seduced by her, and is instrumental in causing misery to more than one of his companions as he sinks lower and lower in the moral scale. A providential, poetic-justice death immediately following a scene of repentance brings to a neat conclusion a play honest in parts and clumsily spurious in others. This work, moderately successful though it was, brought less attention to Sudermann than his once-famous *Die Heimat* (*Home*; usually played as *Magda*, 1893), which might be regarded as *La dame aux camélias* of the nineties. Here a heroine dominates the play—a girl who rebels against the strait-laced morality of her home, works out a life of her own as a concert singer, becomes the mistress of a local dignitary, and bears an illegitimate child; in melodramatic manner her father demands that she marry her seducer and, on her refusal, has an apoplectic stroke and dies.

Illicit love has a fascination for Sudermann. In *Das Glück im Winkel* (*The Vale of Content*, 1896) the heroine, who has married the headmaster of a school, encounters her former lover, who urges her to go off with him. Amid a welter of confused hopes and fears, she confides in her husband, and the curtain falls on a reasonably happy domestic fireside. Less fortunate is Countess Beata in *Es lebe das Leben* (*Long Live Life*, or *The Joy of Living*, 1902): she too has had her lover, but she breaks with him when her husband and he become friends. Most of the plot is taken up with a complicated endeavour to still the voice of slander, and at the end, when the endeavour has proved successful, Beata, rather unnecessarily, puts poison in her glass and dies immediately after proposing a toast to the joy of life.

This last play suggests that when Sudermann treats of upper-class existence he is somewhat out of his element: only when his main characters are of lower-middle class does he reach even slight honesty in portraiture. His picture, in *Die Schmetterlingsschlacht* (*The Battle of the Butterflies*, 1895), of the struggle waged by the courageous widow Fra·¹ Hergentheim to preserve a semblance of respectability for her family is of moderate merit. There is fairly vigorous ironic comedy in *Der Sturmgeselle Sokrates* (*Socrates, Companion of the Storm*, 1903), where the democratic dreams of 1848 are shown amusingly, yet pathetically, pursued by old men, once young and ardent revolutionaries, now washed by time into a backwater. What approaches tragic tension appears in the fated loves of Georg and Marikke in *Johannisfeuer* (*Midsummer Eve's Fire*, 1900), and in the equally dark theme of *Morituri* (1896). This last-mentioned play really consists of three connected one-act pieces, *Teja*, *Fritschen*, and *Das ewig Männliche* (*The Eternal Male*). In each the hero is destined to die. The first deals with a gloomy King of the Goths, trapped near Vesuvius by Byzantine forces; from this barbaric atmosphere we are carried in

Fritschen to the modern world where a young officer is forced into a duel from which, we understand, he will not come alive; in the third play the central figure perishes because of a jest undertaken in all mirthfulness.

By no means a genius of the calibre of Ibsen or Strindberg, Sudermann yet deserves perhaps more praise than critics and historians of the theatre have been prepared to grant him. He may have sought mainly for commercial success, but the stage needs men who, determined to appeal to the general public, are still determined to provide that public with something more than common entertainment.

It is, of course, true that his often sentimental treatment of current problems appears superficial when we compare it with the bold ideas put forward by such men as Otto Erich Hartleben and Georg Hirschfeld. The former approaches the entire subject of moral concepts with a questioning and even anarchic spirit. Indeed, in *Die sittliche Forderung* (*The Moral Demand*, 1896) his heroine, a concert singer like the heroine of *Magda*, laughs at her lover when he urges her to marry him, stating her preference for a life free from the ties of marriage. Like several of his companions, Hartleben exercises his mind mightily over the way in which youth is prevented, through economic necessity, from marrying until an age when healthy passion has become vitiated and dulled. This is the topic that occupies his attention in *Die Erziehung zur Ehe* (*Education for Marriage*, 1893). *Rosenmontag* (*Rose Monday,* or *Love's Carnival*, 1900) attacks the Prussian military code by showing a young officer who feels himself forced to shoot the girl he loves because his colleagues have, in their conversation, spoken slightingly of her virtue. In the same questioning spirit he approaches the entire social life of man in what is his most interesting drama, *Hanna Jagert* (1893), wherein he traces the struggles of a poor girl who moves from the haranguing of a socialistic soapbox to the polite conversation of a baron's hall. Georg Hirschfeld's claim to attention among this group of writers depends partly on his technical skill and dramatic experiments, partly on his power of delineating, in incisive terms, the social *milieu* of his time. His experimental spirit is well illustrated in *Agnes Jordan* (1898), the first drama to attempt the plan —later popularized by twentieth-century playwrights—of presenting a family through the passage of decades. The first act of this work is set in 1865, and the young, optimistic Agnes Jordan introduced to us here is shown as she passes through disillusioned middle life (with scenes in 1873 and 1882) until she reaches the serenity of age in 1896. In the one-act *Zu Hause* (*At Home*, 1893) Hirschfeld displays his extraordinary ability to reveal domestic interiors: this household of Doergens, a good-willed, hard-working tradesman, with its selfish wife, its tragically debilitated daughter, and mean-spirited son, is etched in gloomy but memorable terms. A similar atmosphere is presented in *Die Mütter* (*The Mothers*, 1895), which shows a young artist introducing to his family the mistress whom he has found in a social circle lower than his own; with perhaps slightly unnatural perspicacity she decides that she will merely be a drag upon him, and, without letting him know that she is to bear his child, she pathetically departs.

Among these authors Max Dreyer also deserves mention, both because of the manner in which he explored the possibilities of what may be called the drama of atmospheric realism in *Winterschlaf* (*Hibernation*, 1895), and because of his extending the field of the social-problem play into the sphere of philosophic thought. His *Der Probekandidat* (*The Practice Teacher*, 1899), the first of many works in many tongues dealing with educational problems, takes as hero a young biology teacher, Dr Heitmann, who finds himself forced either to palter with the truth and abandon his Darwinian beliefs or else to lose his position. With this may be associated *Flachsmann als Erzieher* (*Flachsmann the Teacher*, 1900), a witty treatment of scholastic life by Otto Ernst (Otto Ernst Schmidt). For his *Drei* (*Three*, 1892) Dreyer won some fame, and, indeed, this drama—which takes its title from a trio consisting of the nervous *littérateur* Karl Genzmer, his wife, Susanne, and his friend Hans Martiensson—has some value. With skill Dreyer develops his theme—the way in which Susanne is led to fall in love with Hans because of the suspicions expressed by her husband; yet, when the last curtain falls, there is little of abiding interest left in our minds, largely because of the realistic sentimentalism that colours so much of the action.

Although by no means a follower of current Ibsenite ideas, Ludwig Fulda essayed the realistic style in his own way. *Die Kameraden* (*Comrades*, 1894) is an amusing satire, almost Molièresque in its proportions, of the 'new woman.' When Frau Thekla Hildebrand, wife of a rich merchant, leaves his house because it fetters her soul all she gets is a divorce and the chagrin of seeing her husband marry her young friend. Less gay by far are Fulda's earlier writings, *Die Sklavin* (*The Slave-girl*, 1892) and *Das verlorene Paradies* (*The Lost Paradise*, 1890)—plays which, even if not of prime value, served to extend the confines of the social theatre. It is noteworthy that, in addition to penning such works, this author could also produce a romantic *Der Talisman* (*The Talisman*, 1892) and an Arabian Nights tale of the kind represented in *Der Sohn des Kalifen* (*The Caliph's Son*, 1896), where social purpose is clad in richly Eastern robes. In Austria Karl Schoenherr extended the stage's confines still farther by concentrating upon the dramatic world which had already attracted Ludwig Anzengruber and by dealing with its characters and themes still more naturalistically and in a manner more penetrating. In *Der Bildschnitzer* (*The Wood-carver*, 1900) he early displayed his tragically ironic mood with a plot in which a husband consciously seeks death in order to bring happiness to his wife and his dearly loved friend. It was the tragic bitterness of life that appealed to this author—the compelling power of hunger that drives a young boy in *Karrnerleut'* (*Caravan Folk*, 1904) to betray his own father for the pitiful reward of a loaf of bread; the sardonic situation in *Erde* (*Earth*, 1907) where an old peasant causes his coffin to be made while the family quarrel over the disposal of his goods even before he is dead; the infatuation of a woman, in *Der Weibsteufel* (*The She-devil*, 1914), who contrives the deaths both of her weak husband and of her young lover; the fate of three children, in *Die Kindertragödie* (*The Children's Tragedy*, 1919), as they watch their mother engaging in a love-affair. About all of Schoenherr's work lingers a peculiar bitterness and a mood of miserable resignation, made endurable only by his undoubted skill in character-portrayal. With almost adolescent sentiment his companion Felix Dörmann, once one of Vienna's literary lights, treats in *Sein Sohn* (*His Son*, 1896) the story of a maladjusted young sculptor who is obsessed by the thought that his greater sculptor father has by the power of his art deprived him of glory. There is a bottle of poison conveniently handy for the final act.

Hauptmann's eclecticism and Sudermann's flair for the popularizing of the new meet in the work of another Austrian author, Hermann Bahr. Bahr can be amusing in an almost Shavian manner, as in *Josephine* (1898); he can deal comically with social problems, as in *Das Konzert* (*The Concert*, 1909), which presents a portrait of a musician, in love with his wife yet demanding the excitement of other love-affairs; in other plays, such as *Der Meister* (*The Master*, 1903), he can pursue a serious course, in this drama presenting a study of a doctor who, proud of his intellect, seeks to be master of the world surrounding him. Among his dramatic works not least notable is *Das Tschaperl* (*The Fellow*, 1897), in which two contrasting couples are presented: in each case a husband has a wife who wins fame and fortune, one by writing an opera, the other by acting. Jealousy and shattered affection result in the first household; in the other the husband complacently accepts the advantages accruing from the wealth and patronage his wife's beauty brings. It is interesting to note how frequently this theme of the woman artist appears in plays (particularly German and Austrian) of this time: attention may here be called to one other drama of the kind, *Ewige Liebe* (*Eternal Love*, 1897), by Hermann Faber, which deals with the passion of a young professor for a violinist who, although attracted by him, wishes, like the heroines of Sudermann and Hartleben, to be independent and to lead her own life.

All these authors, however, fade in importance when they are put alongside the German Wedekind and the Austrian Schnitzler, and even these two must obviously cede place to the still greater Hauptmann. With Frank Wedekind the realistic drama is seen, as in the writings of Strindberg, to be at the point of shattering its restraining walls. Like Strindberg, he moves from naturalism of the starkest kind to symbolic abstractions; at one moment we are confronted with merciless pictures of the world around us; at the next we are drawn into the haunted realm of the nightmare. Like Strindberg's, too, his dramas are obsessed by thoughts of those sexual relationships which he sees determining men's lives by their terrible power.

Wedekind will certainly never prove a popular playwright: his methods are too blunt and too personal to receive wide acceptance, yet no one can read his plays without feeling that here indeed was a man of genius, even if that genius lacks the balance of form and the assured harmony from which alone true mastery springs. Coming before the world with *Die junge Welt* (*The World of Youth*) in 1890, he showed, in this drama of adolescent dreams in a girls' boarding-school, what was to prove his lifelong obsession. Then, the following year, he startled even the revolutionary enthusiasts with his utterly frank, incredibly brutal, and still strangely beautiful *Frühlings Erwachen* (*Spring's Awakening*), with its mixture of appearance and reality, its naturalism and its symbolism, its lyrical chant of love and its tortured depiction of adolescent imaginings. Suicide, misery, joy, are presented here in a flame of outpouring words. Basically, the story is that of two boys: one, Moritz, commits suicide because of his brooding over sex; the other, Melchior, gets a young girl with child. In a final scene of fantasy Melchior comes to the graveyard, where his friend's ghost bids him take his own life, but from such thoughts he is drawn by a symbolic figure, the Man with the Mask, who leads him back to life. The world of adolescence is changed in *Erdgeist* (*Earth Spirit*, 1895) into the world of later youth, with a tragically symbolic heroine in Lulu, who, evil incarnate, lusts instead of loves; her diabolic power causes her first husband to die by a stroke, her second to commit suicide, while she herself murders her third after she has had an *affaire* with his son. In a sequel, *Die Büchse der Pandora* (*Pandora's Box*; printed 1904), peculiarly written with one act in German, one in French, one in English, this wretched woman is shown moving to a dismal end, even while a spirit greater than hers arises in the person of her Lesbian devotee, the Countess Geschwitz. Equally violent is the action of *Totentanz* (*The Dance of Death*, 1906); of the three connected plays—*Der Kammersänger* (*The Tenor*, 1899), *Musik* (*Music*, 1907), and *Schloss Wetterstein* (*Castle Wetterstein*, 1910); and of *Der Marquis von Keith* (1901). In all of these love, natural and degenerate, and lust are the dominating forces, while the style moves erratically and erotically from the real to the allegoric, with a kind of spluttering lunacy gradually becoming more and more evident. In others of Wedekind's dramas, such as *So ist das Leben* (*Such is Life*, 1902), *Karl Hetmann* (1908), *Simson, oder Scham und Eifersucht* (*Samson; or, Shame and Jealousy*, 1914), and *Herakles* (1917), the lunacy becomes predominant, and we move in a wild, fantastic nightmare of sexual imaginings. Although it is impossible to aver that Wedekind has been grossly underrated, and although much of his would-be tragic vaporizings become simply amusing in their immaturity of expression, it must be confessed that in his dramas resides an inchoate strength and a peculiar intensity of spirit.

Love too dominates in the writings of Arthur Schnitzler, albeit in a vastly different manner. Wedekind was a man who never, in thought, got beyond the sexual torments of a hypersensitive eighteen or twenty; Schnitzler's world is that of disillusioned middle life. He has long passed the adolescence that keeps Wedekind so firmly in its grip; he has acquired the wisdom that recognizes how darkly we are surrounded by illusions, and how much more terrible it is to live without these illusions than to accept them frankly for what they are. In style Wedekind was the type of irritated artist who impatiently shatters existing forms; Schnitzler is of the company of those who frankly accept such existing forms, even although they may realize their inadequacy, and endeavour to put into them fresh content. From one point of view his dramatic structure appears antiquated and artificial, from another its quality is richer than the erratic and discordant venturings which dictated Wedekind's latter plays. Wedekind is the wild-eyed, propagandist rebel; Schnitzler is the sad-eyed, compassionate poet of resignation.

His introduction to the literary world came in the form of a series of one-act plays (perhaps dramatic sketches would be a better description) under the general title of *Anatol* (1893), slightly sentimental, delicately flavoured, the gentle reminiscences of diverse affections. These were followed by a play, *Liebelei* (*Light o' Love*, 1895), by which he is perhaps best known to the outside world. The hero of this drama is a young Fritz Loheimer, whose clandestine association with a married woman, Catherine Binder, is becoming so hazardous that his light-hearted friend introduces him to a girl of lower-middle-class surroundings, Christine, in the hope that a little philandering with her will cure him of his obsession. Fritz lightly toys with Christine, and his shallow love-making is exquisitely contrasted with the deep affection which is awakened in her heart. In the end he is killed in a duel by Binder, Catherine's husband, and gradually the wretched Christine learns the truth. He is dead, he has been killed on account of another woman; he has left her no note; before he went to the duel he had merely casually spoken of Christine among other things. Yet, knowing all this, her loyalty to him still makes life seem meaningless without his presence. Suddenly she turns to his friend Theodore:

> CHRISTINE [*with sudden resolve*]: Theodore, take me to him—I want to see him—once more I want to see him—his face— Theodore, take me to him.
> THEODORE [*with a gesture, hesitatingly*]: No.. . . .
> CHRISTINE: Why 'no'? You can't refuse me that! Surely I can see him once more?
> THEODORE: It is too late.
> CHRISTINE: Too late? To see his corpse . . . is it too late? Yes. . . . Yes. . . .
> [*She does not understand.*
> THEODORE: He was buried this morning.
> CHRISTINE [*with the greatest horror*]: Buried. . . . And I didn't know about it? They shot him . . . and put him in his coffin and carried him out and buried him down in the earth—and I couldn't even see him once more? He's been dead two days—and you didn't come and tell me?
> THEODORE [*moved*]: In these two days I have. . . . You cannot dream all that I . . . Consider that it was my duty to notify his parents—I had to think of many things—and then my own state of mind.
> CHRISTINE: Your . . .
> THEODORE: And then the . . . it was done very quietly. . . . Only the closest

> relatives and friends . . .
> *CHRISTINE:* The closest—? And I—? . . . What am I?

In spite of all, she bids to be taken to his grave, and there she dies. About the entire play, realistic though it is, breathes a peculiar air of melancholy poetry.

Liebelei is thoroughly typical of Schnitzler's art as a whole. Four years before, in *Das Märchen* (*The Fairy-tale*, 1891), he had written a play of social ideas, and a similar style appeared in *Freiwild* (*Fair Game*, 1896) and *Das Vermächtnis* (*The Legacy*, 1898); in these questions were asked such as were being asked by his companions: can a girl who has committed an error in her youth ever be rehabilitated? and, what is honour? But fundamentally such themes were alien to Schnitzler's spirit. Basically alien, too, was the kind of objective case-study of sex which appears in *Reigen* (*Hands Around*; written 1896–97, printed 1900): these were merely pages from the doctor's diary. Much more characteristic were *Der grüne Kakadu* (*The Green Cockatoo*, 1898) and the strangely appealing *Der einsame Weg* (*The Lonely Way*, 1904). In the latter of these two dramas Schnitzler carries his method one stage farther: action almost disappears, and what is set before us is a study, entirely unsentimental yet sadly gracious, of the loneliness of age. Pursuing this actionless theatre, Schnitzler, like his contemporary Maeterlinck, found the one-act form peculiarly suited to his genius, and many of his writings, from this time on, are cast in that shape. In *Der Ruf des Lebens* (*The Call of Life*, 1906) he expresses, even more forcibly than in his earlier dramas, his belief in life, in the open-armed acceptance of experience, and at the same time his belief in the power of devoted self-sacrifice. *Lebendige Stunden* (*Living Hours*, 1901) tells the story of a woman who, realizing that her ill-health is ruining her son's artistic powers, commits suicide: what her death means is trenchantly presented in a contrast provided by the son and by an older man, who had been the mother's lover.

The extraordinary power of Schnitzler's dramatic writing rests in the fact that in it three qualities are merged. He is the scientific observer, objective, unimpassioned; he is the cynic, who sees the follies and the meannessesses of the world; and he is the poet, his heart filled with compassion, a love of beauty, and faith. Thus at one moment he can write his *Reigen*, at another his *Lebendige Stunden*, and at a third sardonically witty studies such as *Zwischenspiel* (*Interlude*, or *Intermezzo*, 1904). His best work is achieved when, subtly uniting these qualities, he depicts the intimacies of the human soul, not in tortured spirit like Strindberg, not blatantly like some of his German companions, but with a strange, resigned, melancholy mood unique in its tone. Such plays as *Komtesse Mizzi* (*Countess Mizzi*, 1909) and *Das weite Land* (*The Vast Domain*, 1910) most perfectly offer him opportunity for the exercise of his peculiar power—a power that draws its strength not from violence and sensationalism, but from quietness and reflection. The same power allows him to create impressive scenes in his *Professor Bernhardi* (1912), where a Jewish doctor refuses to permit a Roman Catholic priest to administer the last sacrament to a dying girl, because she pathetically believes she has been cured and the doctor has not the heart to shatter her illusions. Towards the end of his life, in a manner reminiscent of the pattern set by many another playwright, he tended to let the symbolic and the fantastic take possession of him—witness his *Fink und Fliederbusch* (1917), *Der Gang zum Weiher* (*The Pathway to the Pond*, 1925), and *Im Spiel der Sommerlüfte* (*In the Play of the Summer's Breezes*, 1930)—but these rather tedious works should not allow us to forget the inimitable quality of his writings during youth and middle age.

Gerhart Hauptmann

Titanic as is Wedekind in his frenzied sex obsession, nobly resigned and artistically gracious as is Schnitzler, the writings of both men fall below the broad, if strangely disappointing, accomplishment of Gerhart Hauptmann, the only German dramatist of this period who is worthy of being associated in name with Ibsen and Strindberg.

Hauptmann's contributions to the theatre depend, like Ibsen's, primarily upon the fact that, gifted with keen powers of observation, he succeeded, at one and the same time, in devloping his own individual style and in bringing to culmination the best qualities of his predecessors. His sense of dialect variations was extraordinary; he knew how to construct his scenes so as to give the impression of reality, and at the same time arrest the attention of an audience; he carried a stage farther the Ibsen development of the descriptive and atmospheric stage direction. From Hebbel he inherited the tradition of the bourgeois tragedy; from later naturalistic authors he derived the concept of objective depiction of life, so that he could speak of himself as an Æolian harp whose strings are stirred by every slightest breeze; from others he gained the concept of the social problem drama; and from others still he got the idea of the vaster philosophic theatre, exploring the deeper roots of our being.

His advent was meteoric. In the year 1889 the Freie Bühne staged *Vor Sonnenaufgang* (*Before Sunrise*), and this, his first play, immediately created a stir in intellectual circles. The *Tobacco Road* of its day, it presented an utterly sordid scene of degradation. Two characters only are raised above the bestial level—the young Alfred Loth, who is visiting a Silesian village in pursuit of his economic studies, and Helene Krause, a girl who, though born there, has been educated outside it. Her father is a besotten wretch, who falls so low as to assault his own daughter; Martha, Helene's sister, married to an engineer, is tainted with the taste for drink; her stepmother is carrying on an affair with her nephew, Wilhelm Kahl. Out of this desperate atmosphere Helene hopes to escape with Loth, but he is so shocked by thought of the hereditary vices which must be implanted in her that he departs. The closing of the entire action by means of stage direction is so characteristic of atmosphere and technique that it may be quoted in full. Helene (or Helen) enters the empty room:

She looks about her and calls softly: "Alfred! Alfred!" As she receives no answer, she calls out again more quickly: "Alfred! Alfred!" She has hurried to the door of the conservatory, through which she gazes anxiously. She goes into the conservatory, but reappears shortly. "Alfred!" Her disquiet increases. She peers out of the window. "Alfred!" She opens the window and mounts a chair that stands before it. At this moment there resounds clearly from the yard the shouting of the drunken farmer, her father, who is coming home from the inn. "Hay-hee! Ain' I a han'some feller? Ain' I got a fine-lookin' wife? Ain' I got a couple o' han'some gals? Hay-hee!" HELEN utters a short cry and runs, like a hunted creature, towards the middle door. From there she discovers the letter which LOTH has left lying on the table. She runs to it, tears it open, feverishly takes in the contents, of which she audibly utters separate words. "'Insuperable!' . . . 'Never again.' . . ." She lets the letter fall and sways. "It's over!" She steadies herself, holds her head with both hands, and cries out in brief and piercing despair. "It's over!" She rushes out through the middle door. The farmer's voice without, drawing nearer. "Hay-hee! Ain' the farm mine? Ain' I got a han'some wife? Ain' I a han'some feller?" HELEN, still seeking LOTH half-madly, comes from the conservatory and meets EDWARD, who has come to fetch something from HOFFMANN'S room. She addresses him: "Edward!" He answers: "Yes, Miss Krause." She continues: "I'd like to . . . like to . . . Dr Loth . . ." EDWARD answers: "Dr Loth drove away in Dr Schimmelpfennig's carriage." He disappears into HOFFMANN'S room. "True!" HELEN cries out and holds herself erect with difficulty. In the next moment a desperate energy takes hold of her. She runs to the foreground and seizes the hunting-knife with its belt which is fastened to the stag's antlers above the sofa. She hides the weapon and stays quietly in the dark foreground until EDWARD, coming from HOFFMANN'S room, has disappeared through the middle door. The farmer's voice resounds more clearly from moment to moment. "Hay-hee! Ain' I a han'some feller?" At this sound, as at a signal, HELEN starts and runs, in her turn, into HOFFMANN'S room. The main room is empty, but one continues to hear the farmer's voice; "Ain' I got the finest teeth? Ain' I got a fine farm?" MIELE comes through the middle door and looks searchingly about. She calls: "Miss Helen! Miss Helen!" Meanwhile the farmer's voice: "The money'sh mi-ine!" Without further hesitation MIELE has disappeared into HOFFMANN'S room, the door of which she leaves open. In the next moment she rushes out with every sign of insane horror. Screaming, she spins around twice—thrice—screaming, she flies through the middle door. Her uninterrupted screaming, softening as it recedes, is audible for several seconds. Last there is heard the opening and resonant slamming of the heavy house door, the tread of the farmer stumbling about in the hall, and his coarse, nasal, thick-tongued drunkard's voice echoes through the room: "Hay-hee! Ain' I got a couple o' han'some gals?"

The following year appeared *Das Friedensfest* (*The Feast of Reconciliation*, or *The Reconciliation*, 1890), almost equally sombre in theme and tone, while in 1891 came *Einsame Menschen* (*Lonely Men*, or *Lonely Lives*), in which, with subtle skill, Hauptmann reveals the way in which the ordinary circumstances of life, without the incursion of any evil forces, can suck away joy and creative power. In *Before Dawn* Helene had stood, dismayed, among a group of dipsomaniacs and perverted souls; in *Lonely Lives* Johannes Vockerat is enveloped by the shallowly good. His father and mother, unlike the Krauses, are morally respectable, and they have a real interest in furthering their son's career; his wife, Käthe, is the very embodiment of good nature. What he lacks in his family circle is intellectual companionship: he tries to think for himself, and his thoughts appear merely shocking to these worthy burghers reared in a safe conservative tradition. Into his life comes a young girl, Anna Mahr, attuned to him in spirit, and through association with her he might have risen to something greater; but such intellectual companionship is not understood by his family. Anna has to go, and in despair he commits suicide.

After producing an unimportant *Kollege Crampton* (*Colleague Crampton*, 1892) Hauptmann turned to a new sphere in *Die Weber* (*The Weavers*, 1892), and at once demonstrated that in him lay a quality beyond that possessed by any of his companions. Those earlier plays of his might have been written by one of the others: *The Weavers* was utterly unique both in concept and technique. In general the realistic drama had been tending in the direction of economy in the use of characters; it was no uncommon thing to find, in the early nineties, dramas restricted to three or four main persons; here Hauptmann suddenly set a whole crowd upon the stage, and, in addition, made that crowd the hero of his drama. Even although both Schiller and Büchner had suggested the making of the crowd the central collective figure in a play, new ground unquestionably was being broken here; and new ground too was being broken by the combination of the realistic method and of the historical theme. For the most part, with the exception of Büchner's *Dantons Tod*, the many historical dramas produced during the seventies and eighties had searched far back into the almost legendary past and had treated their characters 'poetically': in *The Weavers* Hauptmann returns to the year 1844, taking his inspiration confessedly from his own father's accounts of the author's grandfather, "who in his young days sat at the loom, a poor weaver like those here depicted," and he deals with these persons as though they were contemporaries. Fundamentally his theme is revolution. The terrible conditions amid which the weavers live are depicted with grim anger; the manner in which the traditional subservience of the mass of the men is changed—partly by the pressure of circumstance, partly by the righteous indignation of Moritz Jaeger, who has returned to his native village after service in the army—into fiery revolt is carefully traced; and the play ends with the crowd sacking the home of the 'capitalist' Dreissiger and meeting the soldiery with volleys of stones.

Nothing quite like *The Weavers* had ever appeared on the stage before, and with it Hauptmann opened up vast possibilities. Hitherto the theatre of the realists had been documentary or concerned with bourgeois problems: Hauptmann first introduced the proletariat on to the boards and suggested a revolutionary theme. Here, however, enters a paradox: a lesser author, thus having accomplished something new, would have proceeded to turn out other *Weavers* by the dozen, and we cannot declare that we should have esteemed Hauptmann more had he pursued such a course. At the same time, when we look at the erratic path of his later career, during which he moved restlessly from style to style, we are almost bound to acknowledge that his violent artistic see-sawing is indicative of a less assured sense of purpose than that we discern in Ibsen or in Strindberg. His next play was "a thieves' comedy," *Der Biberpelz* (*The Beaver Coat,* 1893). With richly ironic comedy, much of the kind that Gay exploited in *The Beggar's Opera*, Hauptmann here takes as his heroine a thoroughly disreputable washerwoman, Mrs Wolff, who, in league with her equally disreputable husband, steals a fur coat and proceeds thoroughly to baffle the addle-pated justice von Wehr-hahn. She stands, as the curtain falls, in meek humility while Wehrhahn lauds her honesty and, shaking her head resignedly, murmurs: "Well, then, I don't know no more what to think. . . ." From this atmosphere Hauptmann next moved into the symbolic and poetic realm of *Hanneles Himmelfahrt* (*The Assumption of Hannele,* or *Hannele,* 1893), a complete departure from his earlier styles. Amid the sordid surroundings of a dirty hospital peopled by the very scum of Berlin's underworld, there mysteriously blossoms forth a strange vision in which the real becomes the ideal, in which concepts of formal Christianity mingle with the spirit of Hans Andersen's fairy-tales. The effect is achieved by introducing into the wretched *milieu* of the outcasts a little girl, Hannele, who, after having been brutally ill-treated and neglected by her besotted stepfather, has been brought there to die. As she lies on her cot she dreams—and the visions that come to her are, quite naturally, a farrago of all she has known and heard. Heaven and Hell are there, the devil and God's angels, the palace of the fairy prince and the glories of paradise. In effect, Hauptmann is employing here the basic methods used in Strindberg's final plays, except that the dream, instead of being presented in itself, becomes a kind of play within a play.

Pursuing his avid search for new forms, Hauptmann next proceeded into the realm of the historical drama, producing in *Florian Geyer* (1894) another play where an attempt is made to treat the life of former generations in a 'realistic' spirit. We are far here from earlier romantic styles; all the flamboyance of the Schiller school has gone, and instead we are regaled with dialogue which the author tries to render at once historically correct and true to life. The treatment of the theme too is different. *Florian Geyer* takes shape as a social drama, with the peasantry of the sixteenth century the hero, and with plentiful display of revolutionary sentiment.

This effort was, to Hauptmann's anger and dismay, ill-received by the public; but he was amply compensated by the acclaim which greeted still another experiment, this time in the style of the symbolic, *Die versunkene Glocke* (*The Sunken Bell,* 1896). The power of this play derives in no little measure from the manner in which it reflects the author's own aspirations and doubts, although in the very process of doing so it indirectly reveals his weaknesses.

THE CHINESE
STAGE: HEROINE
IN A GARDEN

THE JAPANESE NŌ
STAGE: ANCIENT
MASKS

In *The Sunken Bell* this reflection of the author's own uncertainty is presented through the medium of a fairy-tale. Attempts have been made to interpret the drama as illustrating the general problem of the modern artist: rather is it to be regarded as applying solely to Hauptmann's own personality. The action opens with a scene introducing Rautendelein, a sprite of the woods, with some of her elvish companions; one of these, a hob-goblin creature, tells how some men have been dragging a great bell to the church, but have been cheated of their object: the bell has been tipped over a gulf and now is lying at the bottom of a lake. At this enters Heinrich, the maker of the bell, faint and weary; Rautendelein succours him. "Thou art not used to mountain ways," she tells him,

> Thy home
> Lies in the vale below, where mortals dwell.
> And, like a hunter who once fell from the cliff
> While giving chase to some wild mountain fowl
> Thou hast climbed far too high. And yet . . . that man
> Was not quite fashioned as the man thou art.

From this point the symbolic allegory develops. Heinrich is an artist, and he stretches out arms imploringly to this forest maiden, calling her his fantasy. Heinrich is married to Magda, but she cannot share his visions: when he is brought down on a litter from the mountainside she can only rejoice at his being saved, what the loss of the bell means to him she cannot fathom, and when he tells her that his work was faulty, that the bell now lying at the bottom of the lake "was not made for the heights," she is merely puzzled. This was a fine bell, she avers, and fails to understand as he insists that it was merely for the valley, not for the mountain-top. Rautendelein comes to him and saves him from despair, and he goes to the mountains with her, but the ties of the valley are still strong upon him, and in the end he dies, hearing "the Sun-bell's song." The skill by which Hauptmann has invigorated the scenes of this morality play keeps it from being tedious, but as a whole it is sadly representative of his own failure: the varied claims of valley and hill were too strong for his spirit.

After an unimportant *Elga* (1896) and *Das Hirtenlied* (*Pastoral*, 1898) he returned once more to the realistic style in *Fuhrmann Henschel* (*Drayman Henschel*, 1898), a grim, tragic essay in the breaking of a vital soul. Henschel, the central figure, is a sturdy, good-natured, lusty, vigorous man; his wife, dying, makes him promise that when she goes he will not marry another. Soon, however, he is caught in the toils of the ambitious maid-servant Hanne Schäl, and by her tormenting cruelty is driven to suicide. There is a powerful economy here, and a directness of aim that wins our admiration, even although the characteristic German violence makes the entire action darkly sensational.

As though his restless spirit could find no peace anywhere, in his next play Hauptmann veered off again into the realms of the fantastic. *Schluck und Jau* (1899) is "an ironical masque with five interruptions," an elaboration of the ever-popular theme that Shakespeare had exploited in the Christopher Sly scenes of *The Taming of the Shrew*. Jau and Schluck, two peasants, are transformed by a nobleman into a 'prince' and his 'princess.' Out of this story the author extracts much opportunity for philosophizing on the nature of life, with plentiful suggestion taken from Calderón's *Life is a Dream*. When Jau has been returned to his normal state, at first he cannot quite believe that his glory has been taken from him; then slowly the truth penetrates his brains:

> *JAU:*   Ay, ay, tha's right.
>   These ain't nothin' but ol' patched rags!
> *KARL:* Be thou content, my man! Thou hast but dreamed.
>   Yet I, even as thou seest me, and the prince
>   And all his huntsmen and his serving-men—
>   We dream! And to each one the moment comes,
>   Seven times upon each day, in which he says:
>   Thou wakest now and hitherto hast dreamed. . . .
> *JAU:* So I just dreamed that there business! Well, well, well, well! You don't say! Well, I'll be damned! All right then! Things is as they is! How! Tell me this: Ain't I as good as him? He's got a good stomach! I got one, too. Better mebbe 'n his. He's got two eyes. All right. I ain't blind, neither. Has he got four stomacks or six eyes? I sleep all right; I c'n drink my whiskey. I c'n draw my breath as good as him! What? Ain't I right? . . . I tell you, I know, Schluck! I'm a prince an' I'm Jau too. Come, lil' brother. Even if I'm a prince, we'll go over to the inn now an' sit down with plain people an' I'll be reel condescending, reel friendly like!

Back to the darkly realistic came Hauptmann again in *Michael Kramer* (1900), in which, once more, suicide closes the action. The hero is a teacher of painting, who realizes that his own talents have never reached their hoped-for ends, and who dreams of so inspiring his son, Arnold, as to create in him the artist he himself would have wished to be. Unfortunately Arnold's spirit is incapable of scaling the heights. He is a weak, ineffective lad, who makes ridiculous love to a cheaply pert Liese Bäusch, and, mocked by his fellows, tormented at home, ends his miserable life by suicide.

With *Der rote Hahn* (*The Red Cock*, or *The Conflagration*, 1901) we return to the mood of the 'thieves' comedy. Frau Wolff of *The Beaver Coat* is now Frau Fielitz, wife of an elderly shoemaker, and, pursuing her earlier activities, decides to set fire to her house in order to collect the not inconsiderable insurance money. In this case the imbecilic Gustav Rauchhaupt is accused of the crime, and until the end Frau Fielitz cleverly keeps attention from herself—but that end is a grimmer one than the comically ironic lines of *The Beaver Coat*; a bitter sadness envelops the final scene as Rauchhaupt mourns for his boy and the dishonest old woman passes from this life.

The to-and-fro movement of Hauptmann's artistic development

(perhaps 'groping' would be the better word) is shown by the strange mixture of styles in his next three plays—*Der arme Heinrich* (*Poor Heinrich*, or *Henry of Auë*, 1902), *Rose Bernd* (1903), and *Und Pippa tanzt!* (*And Pippa Dances!*, 1906). The first meanders into the world of medieval legend, telling the story of a knight afflicted with leprosy who can be cured only if a virgin is willing to give her blood for him. Ottegebe is prepared to make this sacrifice, and he, after much doubt, at last consents, only to reject the offer when he truly realizes what it means. As a result comes a miracle; he is cured by an act of God, and, restored to his former health, takes Ottegebe as his bride. In this play we are thoroughly immersed in romantic sentiment. Our immersion in the realistic when we turn to *Rose Bernd* is no less complete. Here is nothing but stark misery and sensational violence. Rose Bernd is a young peasant girl who first is the mistress of a neighbouring landowner, Christopher Flamm, and who later is blackmailed by a brutally despicable Arthur Streckmann. Her guilty liaison is made public; she bears a child and smothers it; makes confession of her crime; only in the final words of her fiancé, August Keil, do we rise out of the dark pessimism surrounding all the action. "That girl," he says to the police constable, "what she must have suffered!"—and his simple phrase lets loose a wealth of pity. *And Pippa Dances!* moves again into the symbolic sphere. The first act is realistic enough, with its noisy scene in old Wende's tavern, but very soon we move among shadowy abstractions. Pippa becomes the symbol of beauty sought in diverse ways by diverse men. Old Huhn is the primitive man who wants her simply as a wife; the unnamed Manager of a factory wants her merely as a plaything; for herself, she is attracted by the self-centred artist Michael Hellriegel, while the wise Wann, described as "a mythological character," glimpses something of her mystery. This is a strange drama and perhaps not a very good one: the symbols are at once crude and synthetic, the atmosphere childishly clear in parts, in others mistily obscured.

The truth is that by this time Hauptmann was approaching the end of whatever true artistic power he possessed, and for the most part his erratic questing becomes henceforth blundering and ineffectual. *Die Jungfern vom Bischofsberg* (*The Maidens of Bischofsberg*, 1907) and *Kaiser Karls Geisel* (*Charlemagne's Hostage*, 1908) are of minor interest; *Griselda* (1909) is an uninspired treatment of a theme which, though basically absurd and not a trifle distasteful, has made a deep impress on the romantic imagination. In 1911 came, disconcertingly, *Die Ratten* (*The Rats*), a "Berlin tragi-comedy," with its degraded atmosphere and tone of dejection. Suicide (so familiar a device in Hauptmann's theatre) closes the action, yet many scenes, particularly those in which the irrepressible Harro Hassenreuter appears, are rich in bitter, earthy comedy. Complex in plot, the play suggests that modern style of dramaturgy in which several entirely separate plots run their course with little to unite them save the physical proximity of the characters living in city tenements. Suicide likewise was Hauptmann's solution for the hero of *Gabriel Schillings Flucht*

(*Gabriel Schilling's Flight*, 1912), in which an artist is set between the opposing claims of wife and mistress.

A medley of mainly mediocre work followed: *Festspiel in deutschen Reimen* (*The Festival Play*, 1913), *Der Bogen des Odysseus* (*Ulysses' Bow*, 1914), *Winterballade* (*Winter Ballad*, 1917), *Der weisse Heiland* (*The White Saviour*, 1920), *Dorothea Angermann* (1926), *Die schwarze Maske* (*The Black Mask*, 1929), and so on to *Ulrich von Lichtenstein* in 1939 and *Iphigenie in Delphi* in 1941. Among these perhaps the only dramas of any interest are *Der Bogen des Odysseus*, where the Homeric hero is delineated in modern spirit as a man afraid to return home lest, having been forgotten by his friends there, he may be deprived of his illusions; and *Hamlet in Wittenberg* (1935), which essays to show the young Dane at the university immediately before news comes to him of his father's death. A democratically minded young idealist who has some theatrical and dramatic skill, author of a play on King Cophetua, he is outlined in such a way as to make probable the effect on his nature of the rude shock from outside reality. As friends he has his countryman Horatio, a young Danish student, Wilhelm, and a German aristocrat, Balthasar von Flachus, while among his acquaintances are the ribald vagrants Paulus and Achazius, as well as a riotous swaggerer, Juan Pedro de León. In the first act Hamlet rescues a pretty young gipsy girl, Hamida, with whom he falls in love, but who proves to be one of Hauptmann's characteristic faithless temptress women. The play is interesting rather than appealing.

Hauptmann's career, even up to his latest embracing of the Nazi philosophy, is peculiarly symbolic of the entire German genius. He has inventiveness and the flash of inspiration, but of that deeper desire to reach uttermost perfection in any one style or of consistency in patterning there is in his work no sign. The German drama of the nineteenth century consists largely of a long line of unfinished or shattered monuments, some of them strong, but strong largely by means of their violence. We cannot deny that Hauptmann possesses those qualities that warrant our putting him alongside Ibsen and Strindberg; the structural perfection of the one, however, and the deep intensity of the other fail to find expression in his writings, nor does he provide anything of value to take their place. Among all his plays there is hardly a character whom we can admire; the good characters are weak and pathetic, the strong are brutal. We can have nothing but praise for his energy and his craftsmanship, nothing but regret that that energy and craftsmanship have not been put to service in the creation of something more than the sorry world of his realistic dramas, something firmer than the nebulous realm of his fantasies.

4

THE PLAY OF IDEAS IN FRANCE

FRANCE presents a startling contrast to Germany during these years. The German theatre wins attention because of the contributions made by a number of highly individual playwrights: in Paris there is no single dramatist during these years who deserves to be put alongside even Hauptmann—far less alongside Ibsen or Strindberg—yet the cumulative efforts of a group of late-nineteenth-century writers unquestionably make the French stage of this time assume a position of considerable importance. Although these writers may not have been linked together under a single banner, they did express common ideals, and each in his own way gave something to the development of that play of ideas that had already been adumbrated by Augier and Dumas *fils*.

The Eternal Triangle

When Georges de Porto-Riche published some of his dramas in a collected volume he found for them the general title of *Théâtre d'amour*, and this is symbolic of one extremely characteristic feature of at least a large section of the late-nineteenth-century Parisian stage. As often as not the 'problem' dealt with by the playwright was the problem of wife and mistress: the eternal triangle loomed heavily over the proscenium. It proved both a source of strength and a source of weakness—of weakness because it tended to circumscribe and to fetter, of strength because it led to the development of a number of exceedingly subtle character studies and of skilful analysis of emotional situations.

In this field Porto-Riche is supreme. Essentially a poet, he is obsessed by the omnipresence and predominance of passion. Love is both sunshine and lowering tempest in his dramas. Of these *La chance de Françoise* (*The Luck of Françoise*, 1889)—the story of a wife who, forgiving a husband for his infidelity, saves him from possible death in a duel—was the first to attract wide attention, *Amoureuse* (*A Loving Wife*, 1891) was unquestionably the most effective, and *Le vieil homme* (*The Old Man*, 1911) was the most carefully wrought. In all of his plays appears a woman whose whole being is set upon passion, and who either destroys herself or finds complete satisfaction in the world of the emotions. This passion he often brings into association with other interests, as, for example, he does in *Amoureuse*, where his heroine dominates all the scenes of the drama. Germaine is the wife of a man, Dr Étienne Feriaud, considerably older than herself; wearied of the amorous adventures of his youth, he now hopes for calm and the leisure to work in the warmth of a domestic fireside. This hope, however, is dashed, for Germaine, loving him, makes large demands: he cannot concentrate on his studies; he is forced by her to break his ties with colleagues. The situation becomes so intolerable that he proceeds, quite deliberately, to throw her into the embraces of his friend Pascal—yet at the end, even after she has openly told him of her infidelity, he finds himself so deeply impelled by her physical attractions that he is forced to bid her stay with him. In the unexpected close the ironic spirit of Porto-Riche is perfectly expressed. Fundamentally a dramatist of inner action, he remains uninterested in intrigue for itself, and consequently his plays are cast mainly in the form of discussion pieces: in the ceaseless, subtly delicate play of words rests his dramatic strength.

Emphasis on dialogue and avoidance of violent physical action characterize, too, the plays of Maurice Donnay, a dramatist of wider powers and broader interests. Where Porto-Riche remains baffled by the passions he has observed and portrayed, Donnay presents a wise and halfsmiling tolerance. His *milieu* is much the same, but it is noticeable that while Porto-Riche tends to concentrate his focus on one or two characters, in Donnay's hands a definite segment of life, carefully modelled, is set before us like a set of Dresden figurines. There is ironic humour in his eyes, and a sense of almost Grecian proportion keeps him from entering the realm of hysteria; not without significance is the fact that his first play was a modern version of the *Lysistrata* (1893). The choice of *La patronne* (*The Proprietress*, 1908) as a theme is also typical of his interests; here the life of the *pension* gives him an opportunity of peopling his stage with numerous characters, and likewise offers him the chance of giving concrete expression to his own philosophy of love: love is a pleasant thing, but if the object of one's adoration prove disloyal one should not wreck one's life over the defection or indulge in useless heroics. This is the central theme of the play through which Donnay first came to public attention—*Amants* (*Lovers*, 1895), a study of a youth and a girl, Vetheuil and Claudine Rozay, who, passionately devoted to each other in lyrical ecstasy, yet find themselves prevented by external circumstance from marriage. Many another dramatist would have made of this a tragedy; Donnay, with quiet calm, allows his lovers to separate and each marry another. A series of similarly toned plays followed—*La douloureuse* (*The Aching Heart*, 1897); *L'affranchie* (*The Emancipated Woman*, 1898), wherein a philosopher expresses the belief that women should be kept in the realm of emotion, to which they properly belong, and not introduced into the world of reason; *Georgette Lemeunier* (1898), which presents a variant of the theme otherwise developed by Porto-Riche in *La chance de Françoise*; and *Le torrent* (*The Torrent*, 1899), less successful because the author here has carried his favourite story of unfaithfulness to tragic realms, wherein he moves manifestly out of ease. Then, in 1902, came what is unquestionably his best work, *L'autre danger* (*The Other Danger*). The 'other danger' is revealed in the story of Claire Jadin, who, wearying at last of a husband cowardly, petty, and mean-spirited, finds a new joy in life through the love of Freydières. To her dismay, however, her daughter, Madeleine, meets this man, and rapturously tells her mother of her devotion to him. In order to give Madeleine her happiness Claire renounces the one thing that had made her own existence tolerable. In this play Donnay's attitude to life's problems is made clear: happiness, although the most precious possession, is short-lived, and the wise human being is the one who is ever ready to seize the joy when it comes and to accept with calmness its inevitable loss. While perhaps he is not an outstanding genius, there is a peculiar quality, introducing mingled passion and philosophical resignation, which gives an individual tone to all this dramatist's work.

For *Le mariage de Télémaque* (*The Marriage of Telemachus*, 1910) Donnay worked as collaborator with Jules Lemaître, a man of not dissimilar qualities, evenly balanced, widely observant, gifted with a kind of sadly ironic acceptance of life's vagaries. After a rather uncertain beginning with *Révoltée* (*Insurgent Woman*) in 1889, he produced in *Le député Leveau* (*Deputy Leveau*, 1890) a well-written and characteristic drama, essentially true to life and made theatrically interesting only by the extreme skill with which the characters are delineated and their inner motives revealed. *Mariage blanc* (*White Marriage*, 1891) tells a strained and peculiar story of a consumptive girl, who, about to marry an old roué, is driven to her death on seeing him make love to her half-sister. *L'âge difficile* (*The Difficult Years*, 1895) deals with the problems of middle age, and to this adds satire directed at an attractive 'new woman' whose husband, realizing what advantages she brings him, encourages her in her career as an adventuress. *Le pardon* (*The Pardon*, 1895) essays to give a fresh twist to the triangle. Suzanne, the young wife of Georges, a husband whose work takes him much away from home, finds joyless amusement for her idle hours in a rather pathetic intrigue. Georges behaves in conventional manner, drives her from his house, and sets off to tell his woes to a former friend of his, Thérèse, now herself a married woman. For a time Thérèse vainly tries to soften his anger and to persuade him to pardon his wife, but, as these two are so closely thrown together, the inevitable happens, with the result that the pardon which could not come before now is easily found. Georges realizes that he has sinned as well as Suzanne, and the play ends as they agree to restart their lives on a fresh basis. Irony enters into *La massière* (*The Studio Assistant*, 1905), when a mother who has objected to the marriage of her son with a girl engaged as assistant to her artist husband hastens to approve the match when she finds the latter much attracted by this lady. Lemaître, brilliant as a critic, was gifted with no more dramatic genius than Donnay, but once more we must recognize in his plays suggestions at least of true virtue. His vision is wide and his sense of inner reality by no means despicable.

The Passing of Joyousness

Dozens of other dramas by diverse authors, some of them to be noted below, were devoted to such themes of love, and almost always the sadness of the contemplative mind rather than the lyricism of unreflective youth colours their scenes. Alongside this another current of thought is devoted to consideration either of the changing social world or of the joyless search for pleasure on the part of men and women wearied and forlorn.

In the works of François de Curel, an author of much more distinguished gifts than those possessed by any of the playwrights already mentioned, there breathe constantly a sad nostalgia and a melancholy induced by viewing the decay of ancient culture. His advent upon the stage (that of the Théâtre Libre) was startling: a young dramatist who could present, in the same year (1892), two such powerful and interesting plays as *L'envers d'une sainte* (*The Reverse of a Saint*) and *Les fossiles* (*The Fossils*) obviously was a man of more than common attainments. The first of these narrates a strange story—the story of a woman who, deserted by her lover and driven by her jealous passion to make an attempt on the life of his young wife, enters a convent and lives there for many years. Learning that her former lover has died, she returns once more to the world and seeks to steal away from the hated wife her beloved daughter, only to be thwarted by learning of an affectionate farewell left her by the dead husband. Moved by this, she abandons her vengeance, and the convent embraces her once more. A mere outlining of the plot is unjust to the keen psychological penetration with which the heroine's character is drawn and which gives distinction to the peculiar theme. *L'envers d'une sainte* concentrates its attention wholly upon psychological analysis: in *Les fossiles* the theme of love is allied to contemplation of the decaying aristocracy to which Curel himself belonged. The scene is the country house of the Duc de Chantemelle, who lives there with his duchess and his two children, Robert and Claire. Over the household hangs a heavy shadow, for the heir to the dukedom is dying of consumption. As his end approaches he begs that his mistress, Hélène Vatrin, be permitted to come to him. Claire objects, but his mother tends to welcome the suggestion—the more so as, having formerly suspected a liaison between her husband and this girl, she is relieved to think that her fears were false. When Hélène arrives it is found that she has a child, a boy, and a marriage is planned in order that the tradition of the ancient house be preserved. After several scenes in which the honour of this house emerges more than a trifle tarnished, and the Duke confesses to Robert that in reality Hélène had been his mistress, the dying man discovers a new vision. "Let us forget ourselves for the time being," he says, "and save little Henri: he is the family: think of him!" He himself goes to his death, while Hélène and Claire pledge themselves to devoted care of his son, aiming "to make him first an honest man, and, better, a man capable of dying for the sake of an idea."

The theme of the child, combined with the lengthy dramatic interval used in *L'envers d'une sainte*, reappears in *L'invitée* (*The Guest*, 1893), where a woman abandons her home on learning of her husband's intrigues with other women, only to return after the passing of nearly two decades in order to protect her children, dangerously apt to be ruined by his influ-. ence. That Curel was capable of writing scenes of high comedy is proved in *L'amour brode* (*Love Embroiders*, 1893), in which a widow and her lover play a game of pretence until both get what they want—a marriage. The same mood gives quality to a much later play, *La comédie du génie* (*The Comedy of Genius*, 1918), where a young man becomes a famous dramatist just because one day he sees an actress rehearsing her part at an open window and thinks that her gestures are an invitation to him to enter her apartment. In *La figurante* (*The Ballet Dancer*, 1896) an ironically conceived situation is saved from sentimentalism only by the author's delicate style, and even so there is a sense of strain in the achieving of the effect. If this was somewhat of a failure, *Le repas du lion* (*The Lion's Feast*, 1898) was an unquestioned triumph, perhaps not in the grand style, but at least in a style interesting and not without its own power. Here the atmosphere of *Les fossiles* is further pursued in a form which, abandoning the theme of love, involves the author's entry into the sphere of the social-problem play. The hero, Jean de Miremont, is an aristocrat who, having been inadvertently responsible for killing a drunken workman, is driven by a sense of guilt to devote his life to ameliorating the conditions of the proletariat. By turns Christian socialist and revolutionary, he ends ironically as a great factory-owner, satisfying himself by developing the theory that the workers can best be aided by the expansion of industrialism. This play was followed by *La nouvelle idole* (*The New Idol*, 1899), in which Curel, choosing as his hero a scientist, Dr Donnat, interestingly strives, by showing the struggle within this man's mind between his scientific denial of God and the persistence with which his mind demands belief in a divinity, to suggest the ever-questing spirit of the human race. The plot deals with a doctor who inoculates with cancer a girl whom he (wrongly) has believed dying of tuberculosis, and not the least effective scene of the drama is that in which the victim, learning the truth, accepts her sacrifice for the sake of humanity. Equally interesting is the kindred study of a woman, the heroine of *La fille sauvage* (*The Savage Girl*, 1902), who finds herself between the spirit of animalism and a mystic faith.

In all these plays symbolism is constantly intruding, although it is symbolism of a peculiar kind. When Ibsen or Hauptmann introduce symbols into a drama we can remain in no doubt as to the fact that they are symbols; one of the most perplexing elements in Curel's art is the half-light in which many of his scenes and characters are set, so that we can never be entirely sure when we are on the plane of objective reality and when we move on to a plane of allegory. We see this no less in *La fille sauvage* than in *La danse devant le miroir* (*The Dance before the Mirror*, 1914), *L'ivresse du sage* (*The Wise Man's Rapture*, 1922), *La terre inhumaine* (*No Man's Land*, 1922), and *L'orage mystique* (*The Mystic Storm*, 1927). Of these latter plays perhaps the most interesting is *La danse devant le miroir*, which might almost be regarded as a precursor of psychological dramas to come. Here a man and woman, in love with each other, are yet tortured by doubts, and in the end the former kills himself at the very moment when he sees in the woman's eyes her true devotion to him: he prefers to die on this second of untrammelled joy rather than descend once more into his spiritual hell of uncertainty.

A peculiar inner quality distinguishes Curel's work, and along with that an equally peculiar fastidiousness. He will not stoop to win applause by the introduction of sensational incident, nor will he even pay attention to the commonly accepted conventions of dramatic technique, and consequently his dramas may gather less applause than those of his companions—but there can be no doubt that his influence was strong upon those who in the twentieth century sought to develop the theatre of inner realism.

Closely associated with Curel, yet profoundly removed from him in outlook, is Henri Lavedan. Often the themes chosen by these two dramatists have a passing similarity, but when we search deeper we realize that where Curel's are tortuously composed psychological studies, Lavedan's are competently written surface sketches; a comparison of the two men reveals the distinction between the artist (however minor in worth) and the craftsman. This does not mean that Lavedan's plays are characterless—simply that their characters do not have that brilliant flame that irradiates so many of Curel's scenes which without it would be flat and dull. In *Le Prince d'Aurec* (1892) and *Les deux noblesses* (*The Two Nobilities*, 1894) he surveys the fate of the aristocracy as Curel had done, and perhaps the difference between the two men is shown most clearly by the contrast between their respective methods. Lavedan's plays are well constructed, and the fact that he seems to owe a debt to Augier places him in the tradition that stretches forward from Scribe. The first of the two dramas shows a young aristocrat wasting his patrimony in senseless gambling and finally approaching almost complete ruin, to be saved only through the instrumentality of his mother, who, it is stressed, was born not of an aristocratic family, but of good bourgeois stock. In the second play the fortunes of the d'Aurec family are shown progressing in the hands of a scion of the house who, making a success of business ventures, carries the name of d'Aurec to the plebeian levels of Roche.

In *Viveurs* (*The Rakes*, 1895) Lavedan discovered his true métier. When he tries to be philosophic and to present problems he seems rather out of his element, but when he casts his observant eye upon the jaded, restless troops of Parisian pleasure-hunters and describes their wretched intrigues, their crackling, mirthless laughter, and their inner dejection of spirit, he is thoroughly in his element. The play vastly appealed to contemporaries when they saw on the stage the realistic scenes of a fashionable ladies' tailor's 'studio' and the exact representation of a well-known Parisian restaurant. His attempt in *Catherine* (1898) to contrast aristocratic and middle-class manners is of little worth, but when he carries on from *Viveurs* to pen *Le nouveau jeu* (*The Latest Craze*, 1898), *Le vieux marcheur* (*The Old Reprobate*, 1895), and *Le goût du vice* (*The Taste for Vice*, 1911) he strikes an individual note. The first and the last of these well illustrate his characteristic attitude. In the society he depicts men and women must, in order to be fashionable, profess to be vicious. In *Le nouveau jeu* he shows men and women following society's tone in regarding marriage as a thing to be lightly undertaken and as lightly dropped. Among his characters in *Le goût du vice* are two—a girl, Mirette, who pretends to be as fast as any one of her set, and a man, Lortay, who writes fiction which is on the borderland of the obscene. These two fall in love, and gradually they discover that neither is really vicious, that neither takes pleasure in the evils they talk about so freely. Their taste for vice is merely pretence, imposed upon them by their social surroundings.

The Play of Ideas

In Lavedan's work a moral purpose is obviously present, but that purpose is subordinate to the presentation of sensational scenes. In the writings of the other authors mentioned above the introduction of problems is patent, but in general the problem is subordinate to character. Alongside these men there were others to whom the idea, the social view, was of greater importance than either the development of the intrigue or psychological analysis.

Within this group comes Paul Hervieu, an author of some considerable distinction who permitted his love of the intellectually conceived 'thesis' to rule both the course of his plots and the treatment of his characters. That Hervieu had, in spite of this, the ability to pen dramas of interest and even warmth demonstrates the amount of genuine talent concealed behind his somewhat frigid façade.

His problems are at once varied and restricted. He confines himself almost entirely to the world of 'society,' but within that field he ranges widely. In *Les paroles restent* (*Words Remain*, 1892) it is his object to show that gossip, however innocently retailed, has a power of destruction: words are easily spoken and seem to be slight, evanescent things, yet words can murder on occasion. *Les tenailles* (*The Pincers*, 1895), his next play, and the first of his successes, illustrates well the intellectual patterning of plot that is so typical of his art. This play falls into two parts, perfectly balanced. A wife, tortured by her marriage, seeks divorce, is refused, and takes a lover: such is the theme of the first part. In the second her husband, who for diverse reasons has changed his mind, proposes a legal separation; but now the wife, for the sake of her child (who, ironically, is the son not of the husband, but of the lover), refuses to grant him his wish. The same theme of divorce is dealt with in *La loi de l'homme* (*Man-made Law*, 1897), where a woman is compelled to sacrifice herself for the sake of a daughter. Laure de Raguais discovers that her husband is having an affair with her friend Mme d'Orcieu, and, later, that her daughter, Isabel, and this lady's son have fallen in love. In an attempt to break this proposed marriage she reveals her husband's faithlessness to M. d'Orcieu, but he, to save himself from society's gibes, insists on absolute silence. The woman is beaten by the man-made law.

With *L'énigme* (*The Riddle*, 1901), Hervieu makes a departure almost in the direction of the Pirandellesque concept, but in writing *La course du flambeau* (*The Passing of the Torch*, 1901) he comes back to the same problem, evidently one that affected him deeply, which he had exploited in *Les tenailles* and *La loi de l'homme*. Basically *La course du flambeau* is written to prove that, as generation succeeds generation, the parents always sacrifice themselves in the interests of the young, and that the young, for the most part, accept these sacrifices as their right. The central figure is Savine Revel, a mother with one daughter, Marie-Jeanne, who first puts aside thoughts of a second marriage, next is prepared to steal her own mother's money in order to save this girl and her husband from financial disaster, and finally goes so far as to allow the mother to die simply that Marie-Jeanne may be happy. Naturally the author endeavours to hide the mechanical nature of the theme by every means in his power, but nothing can conceal the fact that the play has been evolved not out of an imaginative concept, but out of a desire to prove a case.

The problem of divorce in a household where there are children occupies his attention in the fairly powerful *Le dédale* (*The Maze*, 1903); the eternal triangle appears in *Le réveil* (*The Awakening*, 1905); the guilty wife once more is introduced into *Connais-toi* (*Know Thyself*, 1909), where a further ironic twist is given to the familiar theme by contrasting a military man's advice regarding the obligations of 'honour,' given to a friend, with his own commonsense complacency when he finds himself confronted by similar circumstances. In all of these there is a contrast set up between social convention on the one hand and natural feeling on the other; in all the basic intellectual problem is the core of the action.

What Hervieu lacks above all is variety of mood. In every scene his style is the same, and as a consequence, despite our feeling that he possesses some strength, we are oppressed by his monotony of conception and utterance. The same judgment might be passed on Henry Becque, were it not that his dramas are illuminated by a peculiar sombre and bitter irony. Where Hervieu possesses a certain calm when confronting his problems, Becque displays irritation, anger, and disgust: throughout his scenes burns a black and turgid fire. It is true that he rarely is successful in penning a drama capable of giving us an harmonious and consistently sustained impression, yet maybe *Les corbeaux* (*The Vultures*, 1882) and *La*

Parisienne (*The Woman of Paris*, 1885) are more powerful plays than any written by Hervieu. Whether Becque was acquainted with Jonson's *Volpone* we cannot tell: the fact is that *Les corbeaux* takes shape as a kind of naturalistic bourgeois replica of that bitter comedy. We are introduced here to the household of a hardworking paterfamilias, Vigneron by name, who, dying suddenly, leaves his wife and three daughters, Judith, Marie, and Blanche, at the mercy of the vultures who eagerly descend to pick at the carcass. Chief of these vultures is Vigneron's rapacious business partner, Teissier. With remorseless truth to the sordid reality, Becque makes scene follow scene in the depiction of the doom settling on this once happy family. The lives of all these helpless women are broken, and in the end Marie, the frankest and most open-eyed of them all, is forced to marry the odious Teissier in order that he may turn on the other vultures, drive them off, and so rescue what little has been left. A similarly gloomy atmosphere pervades *La Parisienne*, which presents, not without genuine comic verve of the mordant sort, a portrait of what Becque regards as a typical Parisian woman, eminently respectable, yet in heart and in action hopelessly depraved.

The last of this group of dramatists is the most extreme. In the work of Eugène Brieux France saw the play of ideas carried to its final conclusion and the stage turned into a platform for the reformer. According to Bernard Shaw, who in 1911 sponsored the publication of three of his plays in translation, "after the death of Ibsen, Brieux confronted Europe as the most important dramatist west of Russia." The claim is a large one, and may hardly be accepted if we look upon the theatre not as a sounding-board for the presentation of ideas, but as a place for the exhibition of artistry. Brieux, it is true, possesses the necessary qualities for putting a story into dramatic terms, but without a doubt his own real interests, and the source of any esteem to be granted to his writings, rests in the boldness with which he put upon the boards vivid representations of broader problems than those which had formed the themes of Hervieu and his companions. The trouble is that these problems, if boldly conceived, are dealt with in a somewhat juvenile spirit: his plays read rather like fiery prize essays written by revolutionary-minded undergraduates upon the enormities of the civilization of their times. With disconcerting fervour, he seizes upon topic after topic, as though his one object was to reveal as many as possible of the errors in life around him. Starting with a rather clumsy series of efforts, he won attention first with *Blanchette* in 1892, produced at the Théâtre Libre, a play designed to demonstrate the difficulties arising from the widespread education of girls. In *Les bienfaiteurs* (*The Philanthropists*, 1896) he proceeds to attack fashionable charity, claiming that the giving of alms without love is worse than futile. In *Les trois filles de M. Dupont* (*The Three Daughters of Mr Dupont*, 1897) it is the loveless marriage imposed by society's conventions that arouses his anger, the theme being revealed through the story of the three daughters—Angèle, who has been forced into a life of prostitution, Caroline, the ugly, soured old maid, and Julie, attractive, driven into a loveless marriage and impelled by circumstance to indulge in sordid intrigues. In *La robe rouge* (*The Red Robe*, 1900) he melodramatically castigates the errors apparent to him in the exercise of justice, by showing a group of provincial judges, all eager for promotion, and the fate of an innocent man who gets caught in the legal machinery. This was followed by *Les remplaçantes* (*The Substitutes*, 1901), where the thesis is directed against mothers who permit their babies to be reared by peasant wet-nurses; and by the best known of his dramas, *Les avariés* (*Damaged Goods*, 1902), where venereal disease is made the subject of a dramatic essay. In it Georges Dupont, just about to be married, discovers that he has syphilis: he undergoes a short treatment by a quack doctor and weds; a child is born, diseased like himself; when the wife at last discovers his fatal secret she is beside herself with angry horror, and only the advice of a *raisonneur* doctor, who suggests that a permanent cure may be effected, prevents the action closing in sensational melodrama.

Brieux' next two plays, *La petite amie* (*The Little Sweetheart*, 1902) and *Maternité* (*Maternity*, 1903), have virtually the same basic subject-matter. In the latter drama two themes run parallel courses, the one depicting the misery of a woman, Lucie Brignac, forced by her husband to have a child every year, and the terrors of Annette, who, about to become an unmarried mother, goes to a quack in order to have an abortion. Annette dies, and the woman-quack is brought to trial, when counsel for the defence causes a sensation by delivering a fiery attack on the girl's lover and on the hypocrisy of society. *Les hannetons* (*The May Bugs*, 1906) demonstrates, with bitter humour, that unmarried love may be more enfettering and enfeebling than a burdensome marriage, the hero, Pierre, being completely enthralled by a woman from whom he could escape —so far as legal ties are concerned—but who maintains her hold fast upon him.

In such wise, with plays coming from his pen in almost annual progression, Brieux ranged over the social vices and the creaking flaws in civilization's machinery. Perhaps he would have achieved more had he himself practised a kind of artistic birth-control: as it is, his dramatic progeny is too numerous and ill-reared. There is a want of classic restraint in his work, a reliance on crude effects, a descent to the use of the melodramatic, a spurious theatricalization of commonplace doctrines. It is to be feared that Bernard Shaw was mistaken.

Brieux' position in the history of drama is symbolic of what the French theatre achieved, in general, during these years. Much of interest is to be found here, yet we can hardly believe that the plays of this period, even the best of them, will continue to give pleasure on the stage. Less than a half-century has passed since once they were applauded, and already they are damned by that most devastating critical judgment—the accusation of being old-fashioned.

5

REALISM IN DIVERSE LANDS: ITALY, SPAIN, ENGLAND, RUSSIA

THE OTHER countries of Europe during the last years of the century all were influenced by the movements which produced Ibsen, Strindberg, Hauptmann, and the French playwrights of the 'problem' variety, but hardly anywhere else was anything of real and characteristic value contributed to the stage.

Italy presents a picture as typical as may be found. Into the midst of romantic melodrama intrudes the spirit of Scribe, and soon plays *a tesi* are being written, with naturalism, in the guise of *verismo*, capturing all the attention of the younger intellectuals and artists.

The movement starts with romantically conceived dramas into which enters a dash of the realistic—such as *Una donna di quarant' anni* (*A Woman of Forty*, 1853) or *Il cavaliere d'industria* (*The Captain of Industry*, 1854), by Vincenzo Martini. In *Il marito e l'amante* (*The Husband and the Lover*, 1855) this author dares (for the first time in the Italian theatre) to deal seriously with the theme of adultery. The conflict between natural sentiment and social convention is the theme of *Il misantropo in società* (*The Misanthrope in Society*, 1858). The development of the new realism may well be traced in the work of his companion, Tommaso Gherardi del Testa. At the start this author's style is fundamentally based on that of Goldoni—as in *Con gli uomini non si scherza* (*Don't Play with Men*, 1846). Then gradually this style becomes altered by contact with the French stage. The *nouveaux riches* form the centre of the picture in *La moda e la famiglia* (*Manners and the Family*, 1857). In *La carità pelosa* (*Selfish Charity*, 1879) a self-seeking philanthropist has his inherent inhumanity unmasked. A kindred mixture of styles is displayed in the writings of Achille Torelli—for example, *I mariti* (*The Husbands*, 1867), a study of social follies. Most of this author's writings deal with the familiar problems of love, sometimes expressed in an appealing manner: *La moglie* (*The Wife*, 1868) presents a vivid picture of a woman's devotion, and *L'ultimo convegno* (*The Last Meeting*, 1898) gives us an understanding portrait of an understanding husband. In the work of Leo di Castelnuovo (Conte Leopoldo Pullè) the moral note is strongly stressed. His *Impara d'arte* (*Getting a Job*, 1872) shows an impoverished nobleman trying to earn a living by learning a craft. Thence the new style develops in the hands of Paolo Ferrari and others during the second stage of its progress. Typical are this author's *Il duello* (*The Duel*, 1868) and his *Cause ed effetti* (*Causes and Effects*, 1871), in both of which appears a mixture of sentimentalism, Scribe-like intrigue, and serious purpose, the amalgam being rendered into a unity by the author's keen interest in character and by the verve he inherits from the Goldoni tradition. With what force that tradition operates on his mind is indicated in the title of one of his best-known plays, *Goldoni e le sue sedici commedie nuove* (*Goldoni and his Sixteen New Plays*, 1851), at once an historical study and an autobiographical document.

After these come the plays of Giuseppe Giacosa. This author began with a series of plays in which he exploited historical and legendary material, principally from the medieval period. Among these perhaps the best are *Il conte Rosso* (1880), *Il fratello d'armi* (*The Brother-in-arms*, 1877), and the delightfully fantastic *Una partita a scacchi* (*A Game of Chess*, 1873). This preoccupation with themes from the past, however, gave way to other interests, and soon he made himself one of the leading exponents of the new realistic drama. His *Tristi amori* (*Sad Loves*, 1888) is a well-wrought play rather in the manner of the French school. The basic situation might be paralleled by reference to half a dozen contemporary Parisian dramas—a wife, who does not obtain all the attention she desires, drifting into a love-affair—although the solution, through which husband and wife agree to live together for the sake of their child, has an individual flavour. *I diritti dell' anima* (*The Rights of the Soul*, 1894) tells of a husband who is full of pride when he finds that his wife's loyalty has succeeded in withstanding the wooing of an ardent lover, but who discovers later that, while her physical loyalty remained unimpaired, in her soul she had responded to the courtier's advances. In *Come le foglie* (*Like Falling Leaves*, or *As the Leaves*, 1900) a lower-middle-class family is presented in the midst of financial decay, while in *Il più forte* (*The Stronger*, 1904) there is a companion picture of a skilful and ruthless business man who, having no scruples, is well qualified to succeed in the money-making world.

Next to Giacosa in importance is Gerolamo Rovetta, whose collected dramas, from *La moglie di Don Giovanni* (*Don Juan's Wife*), of 1877, to *Molière e sua moglie* (*Molière and his Wife*), of 1909, although none of them masterpieces, contain vividly written and well-imagined scenes. Not without human understanding he depicts the little bank clerk Carlo Moretti in *I disonesti* (*The Dishonest*, 1892), and shows him gradually forced into a series of crimes until, no longer able to stand the weight upon his conscience and the fear of discovery, he abandons his beloved family and flees abroad. On account of its unusual theme, *Il poeta* (*The Poet*, 1897) has interest, with its caustic attack on a thoroughly selfish and basically evil youth, Paolo Sardi, who sponges on a worthy humanitarian, Giovanni Vandoni, until his excesses become so foul as to lead to his exposure and dismissal from grace.

With Rovetta is to be associated another author, Roberto Bracco, whose work carries us well into the twentieth century. In *Una donna* (*A Woman*, 1892) he fashions a play which, manifestly influenced by the work of the French school, presents a dismal picture of a woman of easy virtue who falls in love with a poor painter, has a child by him, and eventually, after many trials, commits suicide. Something of the same spirit dominates in *Maschere* (*Masks*, 1893). The influence of Schnitzler becomes evident in *L'infidele* (*The Unfaithful*, 1894). Out of a combination of these two, together with a vivid observation of Neapolitan life, Bracco creates his own characteristic style in *Don Pietro Caruso* (1895). Pietro Caruso is an ordinary little man whose one joy is his daughter, Margherita, and the play concerns itself with showing how this girl, protected by him from reality, becomes the mistress of one of his acquaintances. With an interesting mixture of ironic comedy and seriousness Bracco succeeds in drawing an appealing picture of this couple. The combination of ruthless realism and widespread human sympathy appears also in *Sperduti nel buio* (*Lost in Darkness*, 1901), with its touching picture of a blind man's hopeless passion for a girl who, he thinks, may respond to his affection because he believes her ill-featured, but who in reality is an outstanding beauty. The central figures of these two dramas are of the kind Bracco knows best how to paint, for he is a man of infinite pity for the humble soul—for such a hero as appears, for example, in *Il piccolo santo* (*The Little Saint*, 1909), a man who, having loved and lost, becomes a priest, and years later has the memory of his sorrow return. Bracco is at his best in such 'tragedies of the soul' as are represented in this play or in *I fantasmi* (*The Phantoms*, 1906) and the later *I pazzi* (*The Fools*, 1921). The former shows a widow who has promised her dying husband not to remarry falling in love and finding her vow an impassable barrier between her and a man with whom she might have secured happiness. All this author's characters are simple folk, the sufferers on earth rather than the wilful seekers of power.

Bracco is delicate, reflective, sympathetic in his realism: Giovanni Verga prefers, like the Germans, scenes of brutal violence, of the kind introduced into *Cavalleria rusticana* (*Rustic Chivalry*, 1884—better known in its operatic version), *La Lupa* (*The She-wolf*, 1896), *La caccia alla volpe* (*The Fox-hunt*, 1902), *La caccia al lupo* (*The Wolf-hunt*; printed 1902), and *Dal tuo al mio* (*From Thine to Mine*, 1903). All these are dramas passionate, dark, pessimistic in tone. Less violent, but bitter, are the plays of Marco Praga, a competent craftsman who yet lacks inspiration. Influenced by Ibsen, his drama *Le vergini* (*The Virgins*, 1889) first brought him to notice. The title is ironic, for the 'virgins' of the play are girls who, to serve their purposes, are willing to make any concessions to the men they meet; out of this atmosphere of outward respectability and inner corruption arises a dramatic situation in which one of the women falls genuinely in love, is compelled by a sense of honesty to confess to her fiancé, and remains abandoned by him. Like some, indeed most, of the French playwrights,

Praga is deeply obsessed by the question of sexual relationships, although his manner of dealing with these presents nothing startlingly novel. *La moglie ideale* (*The Ideal Wife*, 1890) sardonically treats its heroine as an 'ideal wife' because she so carefully conceals a liaison from the husband for whom she has affection. A similar secret remains unrevealed for different reasons in *La morale della favola* (*The Moral of the Fable*, 1899), while in *La porta chiusa* (*The Closed Door*, 1913) the results of such adventures are shown when a son escapes from his mother's fond clutches by revealing his knowledge of the fact that he is illegitimate. Both the uncertainty of Praga's philosophic approach and his power of evoking strong scenes is shown well in *La crisi* (*The Crisis*, 1904), with its portraits of the weakly besotted Piero, his strong-minded wife, Nicoletta, and his stern brother, Raimondo.

Something of the same preoccupation with sexual relationships dominates in the rather unsatisfactory realistic dramas penned by Sabatino Lopez, an author whose dramatic career extends from a *Di notte* (*At Night*) in 1890 to a *Luce* (*Light*) in 1937.

Dark pessimism characterizes the plays of Camillo Antona-Traversi, best known for his *Le Rozeno* (*The Rozeno Family*, 1891), but probably reaching greater artistic success in *I parassiti* (*The Parasites*, 1899), a vigorous attack on those members of society who, outwardly respectable, make their fortunes by preying on others worthier than themselves. Camillo's brother Giannino likewise turned his pen, with a lighter satiric touch, against society's villains and fools, achieving his greatest success in *La scuola del marito* (*The School for Husbands*, 1899), a study of a man and woman of the upper class losing their lives in the idle pursuit of pleasure. His work continues well into the modern period.

Such success, however, was at its best but slight. The truth is that *verismo*, or naturalism of the kind exploited abroad, was alien to the spirit of the Italian theatre, which, from earliest days to latest, found its most effective expression in the realm of open and obvious theatricality: the spirit of the *commedia dell' arte* and of the opera suited its temper better than the painful naturalism exploited by these followers of French, German, and Scandinavian masters.

To a certain extent the Spanish stage exhibits similar qualities. Born of romance in the days of Lope da Vega, it never took kindly to the incipient realism of the sentimental movement, and when the influence of later realists came to exert itself the imitation of their methods was either hesitating and unsure or suffered a sea-change. Only one playwright of any distinction appeared in Madrid to cultivate this form of dramatic composition, and even he betrays in his writing dissatisfaction with the style of his adoption; the romantically melodramatic constantly causes his steps to stray from the path of naturalism. This man, José Echegaray y Eizaguirre, once had a wide reputation; nowadays his esteem is moderately low. A romanticist at heart—as is demonstrated not only by his early 'cloak-and-sword' dramas, but by kindred pieces produced throughout his entire career—he endeavoured to capitalize on the new style, as in *El hijo de Don Juan* (*The Son of Don Juan*, 1892), but without achieving more than temporary success. Although in Spain his most famous play is *O locura o santidad* (*Lunatic or Saint*, 1877), in which a generously minded man is hurried to an asylum by his relations, of his works only *El gran Galeoto* (*The Great Galeoto*, or *The World and his Wife*, 1881) has succeeded in winning an international reputation; and even so perhaps its real interest lies less in fineness of craftsmanship and in true vision than in the fact that, historically, it is among the first dramas to suggest, albeit vaguely, the method later to be more fully exploited by Pirandello. Taking a common theme, that of the eternal triangle and the concept of honour, Echegaray gives it a new orientation. The triangle is there, not in reality, but in imagination. The wife, Teodora, is pure-minded: gossip, however, couples her name with that of a protégé, Ernesto, of her husband, Don Julian; at last the husband comes to believe that she has been unfaithful to him, and Teodora is forced, by this pressure of opinion, to take Ernesto as her lover. Outwardly the play shapes itself as a fairly uninspired re-treatment of an old theme, but the operation of public thought, instituting an opposition between what is in reality and what exists no less firmly in imagination, is so far made the core of the plot as to give the action a peculiar flavour of its own.

Echegaray's other plays hardly merit much attention. Desperately he tried to develop new themes in the manner of the French playwrights or of Ibsen. Their problems, however, seem synthetic, the result rather of a desire to make profit out of a new style than of a deeply felt urge to explore fresh territory. Greater sincerity of purpose appears in the peculiar writings of Benito Pérez Galdós—Spain's François de Curel —lacking Echegaray's theatrical sense, although gifted with an appreciation of social values and of character utterly wanting in the other. In his plays the heroine usually takes precedence of the hero, and it is through her eyes that the author presents his view of the world. *Electra* (1900) discusses the problem of the girl who is being impelled towards a convent life for which she is entirely unsuited; *La [Duquesa] de San Quintín* (*The Duchess of San Quintín*, 1894) poses the problem of a young duchess, early left a widow, who has as choice for a second husband a spiritless, conventional nobleman, who has no substance on which to exist save his traditions, and a vigorous, keen-witted, idealistic member of the bourgeoisie; to the horror of her relations, she chooses the latter. Not only domestic and social problems attract his attention: he is prepared also to enter into the then less-explored realm of politics, producing in *La fiera* (*The Beast*, 1896) an interesting dramatic work anticipatory of Spain's civil war, pleading for compromise and common sense in the bitter conflict between the Absolutists and the Liberals. Author of a considerable number of dramas, including *La loca de la casa* (*The Family*

Lunatic, 1893), *Mariucha* (1903), *El abuelo* (*The Grandfather*, 1904)—a Curel-like study of an aging aristocrat who finds peace of spirit in the love of an illegitimate child—and *Alceste* (1914), Galdós certainly is a man of considerable power, although his hesitant handling of dramatic form and his concentration upon purely Spanish questions take from his work the possibility of wide appeal.

Much more sensational, not to say melodramatic, situations appear in the work of Joaquín Dicenta, whose *Juan José* (1895) is a powerful study of a labourer, become a thief through his love of a fickle Rosa and roused at the end to murder both her and her rich admirer. The impress of realism was, however, most clearly to be found during those years in the specifically and intensely patriotic Catalan theatre organized by Frederic Soler, himself author of a number of unimportant pieces. More gifted than he was José Feliu y Codina, author, among several other dramas, of the racily authentic *La Dolores* (1892), the heroine of which is a lovely barmaid pursued by many men, and giving her heart only to one, who is slain by a rival. The outstanding playwright of this movement was Àngel Guimerá, whose works show the familiar pattern in their progress from romantic sentiment, through realism, to symbolic experiments. Among his earlier works *Judith de Welp* (1883) *and Mar y cel* (*Sea and Sky*, 1888) have some value; in the second style he produced *María Rosa* (1890) and *Terra baixa* (*Lowlands*, 1896)—the latter a strong naturalistic study in which a labourer, Mannelich, takes vengeance upon his master, a wealthy farmer named Sebastian, when the latter, after foisting off on him his mistress, Marta, seeks to resume his former intrigue after the girl's marriage; in the third style he wrote *Andrónica* (1905), a play of manifest weaknesses, yet aiming at effects beyond those attempted in his more youthful essays.

Although, naturally, a vast gulf separates these Spanish plays from contemporary English productions, there is a certain historical kinship between the works of Echegaray and the writings of the once famous, now unduly despised Sir Arthur Wing Pinero and Henry Arthur Jones. Like him, both these men were professional dramatic authors intent upon theatrical success; like him, both turned to exploit the new realism; like him both tended to produce plays which, despite their contemporary esteem and influence, have largely failed to maintain their hold on the stage.

Once more we are confronted by the equivocal position occupied by these men. Of their great importance in the development of the English stage there can be no doubt; of their insignificance in the great march of the modern theatre there is equal certainty. Their plays materially aided in the development of the English drama in the twentieth century, yet not one, even the once-lauded *The Second Mrs Tanqueray* (1893), has qualities of permanence.

Pinero and Jones gained much strength from the fact that both allowed their art to grow out of an essentially popular stage tradition. The former's earliest writings were farces, some of them were farces, some of them excellent—*The Magistrate* (1885), *The Squire* (1881) and *Dandy Dick* (1887); the latter began in the melodramatic tradition and won considerable success with his *The Silver King* (1882), distinguished from none of its predecessors save by a greater tightness of structure and incisiveness of dialogue. From these beginnings each proceeded, with characteristic mildness and lack of revolutionary fervour, to exploit the potentialities of the play of ideas. With *The Second Mrs Tanqueray* Pinero startled London society and was acclaimed by the critics as responsible for having produced the greatest drama of his age. Regarding it now from the standpoint of eighty years later, we may agree that, while it possesses unquestioned virtues, its worth appears markedly less than was once imagined. There is not a little of the sentimental in this treatment of a woman with a past who finds that her now grown daughter has fallen in love with her own former lover. Suicide suitably brings the plot to a would-be 'tragic' conclusion, without in the least arousing in us that admiration and that sense of wonder out of which alone the true tragic passion can be evoked. The same judgment must be passed on such an ambitious effort as *Iris* (1901), where the heroine is a woman who, while not natively vicious, has no will-power to keep her on the straight path and gradually deteriorates into a creature of vice. In Pinero's last important drama, *Mid-Channel* (1909), a kindred atmosphere prevails. Here we are presented with a middle-aged couple, Theodore and Zoe Blundell, who after fourteen years of marriage are becoming constantly involved in quarrels and recriminations. They part: Zoe goes off to Italy with a friend of her husband's on a perfectly virtuous and platonic tour, but, learning that Theodore is having an affair of his own, she takes this friend as a lover. On her return home she finds to her dismay that, while she is willing to pardon her husband, he angrily drives her from the house. The result is suicide from a balcony.

Jones was much less interested in the woman who sins, much more in social and religious ideas. These ideas, however, he handled in a manner which showed that, while he had the will to be a thinker, he entirely lacked the ability. *Saints and Sinners* (1884) is both melodramatic and sentimental, and something of those qualities mars the much finer, and relatively significant, *Michael and his Lost Angel* (1896), a drama in which the soul of a Puritanical clergyman is bared for us. Perhaps Jones' importance lies less in what he actually achieved in dramatic form than in his ceaseless and effective championing of a new modern theatre in London. His collected critical studies, animated by a fine enthusiasm, published under the title of *The Renascence of the English Drama* (1895), were of no little importance in directing men's minds towards the potentialities of the realistic stage.

During these years Wilde was penning his witty comedies, and the Independent Theatre Society was discovering the genius of a fiery-headed young Irishman resident in London, George Bernard Shaw; but the former is to be considered rather as a comic writer than as a contributor to the realistic drama, while the latter's greatest achievements belong to the period after 1900. As companions, Jones and Pinero had, during the nineteenth century, only worthy but wholly uninspired writers such as Sydney Grundy, author of the sentimental *A Pair of Spectacles* (1890) and the peculiarly confused *A Fool's Paradise* (1887). It must sadly be confessed that in this kind the English stage had little to offer during the final decades of the century.

In Holland arose one writer of slightly greater promise, Herman Heijermans. Although it is impossible to associate his name with those of Ibsen or Hauptmann, there can be no doubt that he possessed sterling qualities. He has a sure grasp of dramatic technique; he has an observant eye and a reflective mind; and he has true sincerity. On the other hand, all his work has now an old-fashioned flavour: far less than the others was he possessed of the power to incorporate into his realistic scenes elements of an enduring quality. The reason, perhaps, may lie in what was his chief virtue as a man. Where Ibsen, Strindberg, and Hauptmann were self-centred, Heijermans has a broadly humanitarian outlook upon the world; infinite pity is his, and he looks upon the men and women around him with genuine sorrow when he sees them involved in misery and torment. The result is that, even while we appreciate the qualities that animate his nature, we feel in his plays a lack of strength and a want of deeper intensity.

His first success was secured with *Ahasuerus* (1893), and his fame definitely established with *Ghetto* (1899), in which an attempt is made to depict the atmosphere of a typical Dutch Jewish home—the world of youth, inspired by new dreams, rebelling against the Puritan conservatism of the elders. After this exploration of Jewish life Heijermans turned, like the other realists, to deal with a variety of social problems, from those of wide extent, involving whole classes, to those of individuals wrecked by the civilization around them. He thus could present vivid stage studies of individuals—such as that of *De Meid* (*The Maid*, 1905), a penetrating analysis of a girl who, having found a compromising letter belonging to her mistress, derives an evil joy in the power thus given to her: and he could produce his equally effective pictures of social groups, as, for example, in *Op Hoop van Zegen* (*The Good Hope*, 1900), which deals with a fishing community where men's lives are sacrificed to add to the wealth of a callous shipowner. While there is little value in the 'social' message of this drama, Heijermans' skill is evident in the atmospheric quality of the scenes. A similar mood prevails in *Ora et labora* (1903), a miserable picture of small tenant-farmers; in the characteristically named *Schakels* (*Links*, 1904); and in *De opgaande Zon* (*The Rising Sun*, 1908), where his dark-glassed microscope is turned upon the petty shopkeeper.

In all his writings Heijermans betrays the same qualities—a competent knowledge of stagecraft, a sympathetic understanding of character, a genuine sympathy with the underdog, and a complete lack of that spark from which alone can come real and continuing dramatic interest.

To Russia, as has been noted above, the realistic style that was sweeping the Continent during the late nineteenth century had already been introduced by such men as Alexis Feofilaktovich Pisemski, whose *Gorkaia sudbina* (*A Hard Lot*) was as violent and as gloomy as any naturalistic study by Hauptmann. This style, which in effect ran parallel and sometimes clashed with the tradition set by Gogol and Griboedov and carried on by Turgenev and Ostrovski, found a powerful exponent in Count Lev, or Leo, Nikolaevich Tolstoi. Fundamentally, of course, Tolstoi's genius gained deepest expression through the medium of the novel, where the vaster canvas permitted him to reveal his characteristic breadth of vision, and where no narrowly circumscribing conventions detracted from the vigour of his character conceptions. When he approaches the theatre there is amply evident in his scenes an impatience with stage restrictions, so that his plays are often marred by weakness in dramatic structure and by a certain spluttering incoherence. At the same time, the vigour of his own personality and his burning sincerity give to his characters a peculiar intensity and to his scenes a lurid grandeur.

His first approach to the theatre came in 1886, when he wrote a sketch called *Pervii vinokur* (*The First Distiller*), designed as a moral tract whereby to reveal the evils consequent upon drunkenness among the peasantry, and followed this with the tragic naturalistic drama, *Vlast tmi* (*The Power of Darkness*, 1887). In general the atmosphere of this work is akin to that of Hauptmann's *Before Sunrise*—sensational in episode and brutal in conception—to it, however, is given a typically Tolstoian conclusion that removes its Christian fervour from the agnostic pessimism of the German author. The central character is a peasant, Nikita, who has an affair with the wife of the man for whom he works. In order to profit from this situation Nikita's mother, an evil-spirited and avaricious woman, persuades the wife to kill her husband. Thus freed, she marries her young lover, but he now proceeds to seduce her stepdaughter. Once more the mother enters the scene: the child born of this intrigue must die, she declares, and the girl be married off. To her promptings are added those of the wife, who realizes that if Nikita can be persuaded to undertake this crime his soul will be stained by the same guilt as has besmirched her. Eventually Nikita consents, crushes the child under a board, and inters it in a cellar. Almost immediately, however, his conscience begins to work, and, in order to free himself from the weight of his crime, he takes the occasion of the marriage of his mistress to announce publicly what he has done.

In Tolstoi's hands, accordingly, the stark depiction of life's brutalities serves a purpose different from that which it had in the hands of others. The entire drama is shot through with a moral, or religious, concept of a kind which but rarely is apparent even in vaguest form among the works of the realists. The larger social world is depicted in *Plodi prosveshcheniya* (*The Fruits of Enlightenment*, 1891), where Tolstoi takes up—although in vastly diverse terms—a theme dealt with in one of the early comedies of Catherine the Great, that of the toying with the supposedly supernatural. Catherine had laughed satirically at those who followed the lead of Cagliostro; Tolstoi bitterly attacks the parlour spiritualism of his age, and adroitly mingles this topic with the larger one of opposition between peasants and landowners. It is a peasant girl who, pretending to have the powers of a medium, succeeds in helping her fellows to purchase a tract of land from a proprietor who hitherto had refused to sell it to them; it is through the spiritualistic scenes that these peasants are brought to a dim realization of the profitless lives of the aristocracy. Already in 1891 Tolstoi sensed that the class to which he belonged was rudderlessly drifting to disaster.

After this play there was a long dramatic silence. Over twenty years were to elapse before *Zhivoi trup* (*The Living Corpse*, or *Redemption*, 1911; written 1900) and *I svet vo tme tsvetit* (*And Light shines in Darkness*) were published. The hero of the former is a true Tolstoian figure—a man, Fedia, who, discovering his wife's intrigue with one of his companions and himself deeply oppressed by a feeling of his own inner weakness, abandons his home, leaves his coat by the side of a stream, and is consequently thought to have been drowned. Unfortunately one man knows the secret and villainously exposes the deception. Lisa, the wife, and her lover are arrested as accomplices in a supposed attempt to thwart the marriage laws: these laws prohibit divorce, and it is thought that the entire trick was a conspiracy designed to allow a bigamous remarriage. In the end Fedia decides, both to satisfy his own sense of unworthiness and to give happiness to his wife and her lover, that his death is the only solution. In *And Light shines in Darkness* Tolstoi gives a dramatic picture of his own tortured soul. The story of the man who wants to give away his wealth and is thus brought into opposition with his wife, who seeks to inculcate the ideal of pacificism and finds his preaching resultant in disaster, is quite clearly a reflection of the struggles of his own latter days. As might be expected, its action has a luminous intensity, although the nearness of the theme to the author's own personal experiences manifestly detracts—quite apart from the unfinished state in which it was left —from its dramatic value.

During these years when Tolstoi was writing a far greater playwright, Anton Chekhov, was experimenting in still newer forms of realism. Although his earliest dramas belong to the eighties, it may, however, be better to postpone an account of these until an opportunity arises for discussion of the significant productions of the Moscow Art Theatre. Chekhov died at the very beginning of the twentieth century, yet strangely he seems to belong in spirit much more intimately to the later realism than to the realism of the century in which most of his life was passed. In the closely related Slavonic country of Poland Stanisław Przybyzewski contributed to the realistic movement another individualistically conceived treatment. A daimonic spirit somewhat akin to Strindberg, he was a man at once deeply oppressed by sexual preoccupations and one whose soul fared into dim metaphysical realms. Out of the combination of these elements was wrought his series of realistic-symbolic dramas—*Dla szczęścia* (*For Happiness*, 1899), *Złote runo* (*The Golden Fleece*, 1901), *Goście* (*The Guests*, 1901), *Matka* (*The Mother*, 1903), *Śnieg* (*Snow*, 1903), *Odwieczna baśń* (*The Eternal Fable*, 1906), and *Gody życia* (*The Feast of Life*, 1909). In these he expresses forcibly his sense of the sorrows, the confusions, the inconsistencies, of the world. It is himself who appears as the hero of his dramas: he is his own Zdżarski in *For Happiness*, Ruszczyc in *The Golden Fleece*, Kazimierz in *Snow*. To a large extent, therefore, his realism approaches the inward style of Strindberg; the external events of *Snow*, for example, have very much less import than what is symbolized of subjective emotions and of the despairs of dreams. Although an author almost unknown outside of Poland, and although himself a strangely tortured and erratic soul, Przybyszewski possesses a power of no ordinary measure.

The new French realism captured the attention of several other Polish authors during these years, but without enabling them to produce plays powerful enough to appeal beyond their own time and country. Among them Józef Narzymski is worthy of mention because of the extreme enthusiasm with which he embraced the realistic creed and of the way in which he used its style—as, for example, in *Pozytywni* (*The Positivists*, 1872)—for idealistic purposes. Further advanced on the path towards naturalism were the plays of Gabrjela Zapolska, in whom resided a power both of serious purpose and of comic conception; her later *Moralność pani Dulskiej* (*The Morals of Mme Dulska*, 1906) is still remembered. For his *Rozbitki* (*The Wreck*, 1882) Józef Bliziński is also to be remembered in this company.

To the other countries of Eastern Europe also came the new style, although in those areas the familiar realistic problem play was usually diversified by the inclusion of sentimental, legendary or fantastic elements. Hungary thus produced Gergely Csíky, an author who commonly mingled love stories with serious attacks on the standards of middle-class society—as in *A proletárok* (*The Proletarians*, 1880) and *Cifra nyomorúság* (*Misery in Ribbons*, 1881). Keener satirical laughter appeared in the works of the Rumanian Ion Luca Caragiale: his *Conul Leonida față cu reactiunea* (*Mr Leonida and the Reactionaries*, 1880) and *O scrisoare pierdută* (*The Lost Letter*, 1884), although they are nearly centenarians, remain still amusing even when read in translation. In Czechoslovakia Alois Jirásek veered between realistic social episodes and historical themes such as that presented in *Lucerna* (*The Lantern*, 1905), while Ladislav Stroupežnický exploited a kind of Ostrovski-like style in pieces such as *Naši furianti* (*Our Swaggerers*, 1887), in which we see an entire community set in confusion because of a dispute concerning a dowry. Similar satiric shafts, although not so skilled, appeared in plays written for various theatres within what is now Yugoslavia—as, for example, those of Branislav Nušich and Ivan Cankar.

6

NEO-ROMANTICISM IN THE THEATRE

ONE THING must never be lost sight of in surveying the fortunes of the drama during these years. Ibsen and Ibsenism loom up as the great force of the time; the work of the independent theatres, almost wholly devoted to the cultivation of the violently naturalistic stage, seizes primarily upon our attention. Yet, even in the very days when the culmination of this style had barely been reached, there is amply evident a counter-movement designed to combat and, if possible, to destroy the very tenets of naturalism.

This, we must remember, was the age that produced the 'symbolist' movement in poetry, a school adumbrated by the appearance of Mallarmé's *L'après-midi d'un faune* in 1876, and definitely launched as a 'movement' by a manifesto published in *Figaro* during the year 1886. From its inspiration came plays wherein the external reality ceded to the inner. In the original manifesto it was stated that "symbolist poetry seeks to clothe the Idea with a sensory form which, however, would not be its own end." Here logic is completely banished, and Zola's belief that the naturalistic method of composition could ever possess the exactitude of science is utterly denied: words are used not to reproduce life, but to evoke emotions, and objectivity is abandoned in favour of the subjective.

The Neo-Romanticism of Germany

Almost every country during the latter years of the nineteenth century can exhibit dramatic movements of an anti-realist kind, sometimes taking shape as revivals of the earlier romantic styles, sometimes expressive of this later poetic inspiration. Not only so: often these dramatic movements are to be found even among the works of those authors most closely associated with the growth of naturalism. Ibsen thus starts his career with the penning of historical dramas clearly inspired by previous experiments in that form; in *Peer Gynt* he veers off into the world of the fantastic; while the impress of the symbolic sheds a quivering poetic light on his later compositions. His companion Strindberg begins with the historical and fantastic and later returns to both styles. Perhaps most characteristic of this development, however, is Gerhart Hauptmann.

Hauptmann is chief of the realistic school in Germany: he is also the

chief exponent of the neo-romantic movement there. *The Sunken Bell,
Henry of Auë, And Pippa Dances!*, are landmarks in the history of romanticism on the stage, and in these plays he was expressing a need felt by his
contemporaries; he was giving the public that for which, in addition to
the realistic, it sought. The truth of this assertion is demonstrated by
even the most cursory glance at theatrical development from the nineties
of the century onward. When Ludwig Fulda presented his *Talisman* in
1892 its success was so emphatic that no doubt could remain concerning
the will of the playgoers to welcome something poetic and colourful, and,
as a result, the immediately following years show a succession of efforts
to provide these elements in stage form—efforts that gave inspiration to a
number of dramatists who, coming to the theatre after the year 1900,
pursued the same path and sought to reach further goals.

Dominant among Hauptmann's companions is the Austrian poet
Hugo von Hofmannsthal, one who sought through the medium of
romance to provide for the world a great vision of life. In his earliest plays
he wanders lyrically and beautifully in a realm of subjectively conceived
romantic dreams. From *Gestern* (*Yesterday*, 1891) he moves to *Der Tor und
der Tod* (*The Fool and Death*, 1893), eventually collecting together in his
Theater in Versen (1899) and in his *Kleine Dramen* (1906) a series of such
studies, mainly short, one-act pieces—such as *Der Abenteurer und die
Sängerin* (*The Adventurer and the Singing-girl*; written 1899) and *Der Kaiser
und die Hexe* (*The Emperor and the Witch*; written 1895).

At the beginning he is the exponent of the ideal of 'sensations'—the
passive acceptance of experience and of such emotions experience may
bring with it. Gradually this philosophy gives way to an appreciation of
higher and less selfish values, so that *Der Tor und der Tod* is an essay in the
futility of concentration upon those secret passions that were so precious
to the æsthetes of the nineties; while in his latest works he passes into a
sphere where the elements of classical thought are allied to the concepts
of Christian belief. It is certainly of interest that on this final level the poet
found the most fitting medium for the expression of his moods in the
rehandling of ancient themes. For *Elektra* (1903) and *Ödipus und die Sphinx*
(*Œdipus and the Sphinx*, 1905) and *Ariadne auf Naxos* (1912) he turned to
Athens, making the classical figures into tortured neurotics; for *Das geret-
tete Venedig* (*Venice Preserved*, 1905) he found the source in Otway's play;
for *Jedermann* (1911) he sought inspiration in the morality of *Everyman*;
and for *Das grosse Salzburger Welttheater* (*The Great Salzburg Theatre of the
World*, 1922) the Spanish *autos* form a source. Fate looms darkly here;
death is omnipresent; and the dream that is life leaves man strangely
insecure—a creature stumbling his way along paths that lead he knows
not where. The author of the delightfully romantic *Der Rosenkavalier*
(1911) found his true realm in the world of spiritual torment. *Elektra* is a
study of the frenzied psychology of a woman whom hate has made mad;
Ödipus presents a strange treatment of the Greek theme, with Œdipus
hailed as deliverer and the atmosphere of "the blind deed of the gods"

about him.

In all his work Hofmannsthal reveals himself as a poet of high distinction, although a poet whom sheer love of beauty frequently leads astray and whose writings have but little message of hope. Despite his 'philosophy,' he is only a blind prophet whose ears are intoxicated with music, and at the end of his life, as is shown in *Der Schwierige* (*The Fastidious Man*, 1921) and in *Der Turm* (*The Tower*, 1925), with its plot developed out of Calderón's *La vida es sueño*, he felt out of touch with his time, preferring the dream to the after-war reality.

In developing this atmosphere Hofmannsthal is the typical poet of the entire school, finding exquisite expression for the common thoughts and emotions of his companions—such men as the German Karl Gustav Vollmoeller, whose dramatic work, starting in 1903 with *Katharina, Gräfin von Armagnac, und ihre beiden Liebhaber* (*Catherine, Countess of Armagnac, and her Two Lovers*), includes a *Turandot* (1912), based on Gozzi, and the famous *Das Mirakel* (*The Miracle*, 1912), the pantomimic production that gave Max Reinhardt international fame; Eduard Stucken, who exploited the Grail legend in *Gawan*, *Lanval*, and *Lanzelot* (1902–9); and Ernst Hardt, author of *Tantris der Narr* (*Tantris the Fool*, 1908). Besides these avowed disciples of the school were numerous others who, influenced by the wave of enthusiasm that greeted its efforts, essayed individual works in this style. The weathervane that was Sudermann thus produced his *Johannes* and *Die drei Reiherfedern* (*The Three Feathers*) in 1898, while in 1898 Schnitzler caught the mood in *Paracelsus*, and in 1900 followed this with *Der Schleier der Beatrice* (*The Veil of Beatrice*). Later Herbert Eulenberg, after dealing unromantically with an incest theme in *Anna Walewska* (1899), penned his *Kassandra* (1903) in the symbolist style, and neo-classicist Wilhelm von Scholz, whose *Vertauschte Seelen* (*Bartered Souls*) appeared in 1910, was sufficiently influenced to write his mythological *Meroë* (1906), in which father and son are tormented rivals in love. Effectively, although painfully, Richard Voss wrought out of Hans Andersen an engrossing fairy-play in *Die Blonde Kathrein* (*Fair Kathrein*, 1894). Obviously influenced by Hauptmann, he here tells the story of a poor mother's sacrifice to prolong her suffering child's pilgrimage on earth. The older style of romanticism is pursued by Adolf Willbrandt in *Der Königsbote* (*The King's Messenger*, 1894), an historical drama set in eleventh-century Norway.

It cannot be claimed that, except for the plays of Hauptmann and Hofmannsthal, the German theatre produced much of permanent worth in this kind, but assuredly considerable historical interest attaches to these works produced in the very midst of enthusiasm for the realistic. Hardly anywhere more clearly are the trends of the time thus demonstrated in concrete productions. The works of the neo-romantic school when placed alongside the contemporaneous naturalistic dramas help to explain the peculiar eclecticism of the greatest stage director of that time, Max Reinhardt, who seized variously upon the ultra-realistic and the fantastic, the prosaically objective and the subjectively lyrical, who found inspiration alike in the tiny Kleines Theater and in the vast Grosses Schauspielhaus.

Before leaving the German neo-romantic theatre one other thing should be observed. The antagonism towards the naturalistic led some of the younger spirits through incipient romanticism to a new kind of classicism. Typical here is Paul Ernst, who, starting in the realistic camp, soon moved over to the world of romance in *Der Tod* (*Death*, 1900), and thence shifted to a style in art which is definitely based on classical models, tending to rely on intellectual ideas rather than on emotions and to preach the cult of civilization based on order imposed upon the individual. Neither his works nor those of his companions merit the esteem in which they were held in Hitler's Germany, yet the trend marked in them deserves attention, particularly if it is related to the contemporary resuscitation of the classical tragedy in France.

French Fantasy and Flamboyance: Rostand and Maeterlinck

During the years before the appearance of the Symbolist manifesto various playwrights in Paris had been attempting to keep alive the spirit of the poetic theatre. Vicomte Henri de Bornier thus won considerable success with *La fille de Roland* (*Roland's Daughter*, 1875), a vigorous treatment of heroic material, while François Coppée attempted to give new form to the romantic historical drama in such works as *Severo Torelli* (1883), *Les Jacobites* (1885), and *Pour la couronne* (*For the Crown*, 1895). The first, set in fifteenth-century Pisa, tells a melodramatic story of a mother who saves her son from parricide by herself stabbing her former lover; and the other plays introduce similar sensational situations covered with the rich colours of romantic verse. Manifestly stimulated by the writings that had stirred France during the thirties of the century, Coppée brought to the theatre a skilled dramatic craftsmanship, a true sense of effective situation, a bold if not very subtle understanding of character, and a rich poetic eloquence. His *Pour la couronne* is Victor Hugo modernized and tightened in structure. With admirable economy he keeps his eyes fixed on his central situation—that of a son, Constantin, who is faced with the terrible problem of murdering his own father, Michel Brancomir, or of permitting his father to sacrifice his country and his honour. In others of his dramatic compositions, such as the one-act pieces *Le passant* (*The Passer-by*, 1869), *Le luthier de Crémone* (*The Lute-maker of Cremona*, 1876), and *Le trésor* (*The Treasure*, 1879), Coppée shows a grace and delicacy which give to his works their peculiar flavour.

These writings, however, fade in importance when put alongside those of Edmond Rostand, an author of considerably greater strength, and one who has succeeded in gaining both a national and an international reputation. Rostand's success depends upon a number of very definite qualities. He was, first of all, a consummately skilful playwright; indeed, some of his dramas might almost be taken by apprentice writers as models of craftsmanship. To this he added a genuine, if not extraordinary, poetic gift: his words sing, and he combines a skilful handling of words with flamboyant passion. Still further, he succeeds in making the most of two worlds, taking from the older romanticism its vigour and from neo-romanticism its delicacy and novel soul-searching. It was the combination of these diverse elements in his work that gave to him his peculiar position.

His first play, *Les Romanesques* (*The Romancers*, 1894), is a joyous lyrical essay written in a frankly escapist mood—a glove laughingly cast down at the feet of the dismal followers of Zola. This was succeeded by *La princesse lointaine* (*The Far-away Princess*, 1895), in which the medievalism of the neo-romantic movement is exploited. In an almost Pre-Raphaelite manner the tale is retold of the troubadour Rudel whose heart is dominated by a hopeless passion for the distant Mélisande, and who makes his last journey to her Court, there to die in the ecstasy of his bliss. With medieval themes the neo-romanticists frequently combined treatment of themes based on Christ's life, and we need not be surprised to find Rostand next composing *La Samaritaine* (*The Woman of Samaria*, 1897), where the idealistic love of Rudel is translated into divine devotion. The plot is simple: among the Samaritans Christ makes his appearance, and by his gentle words instantly converts the beautiful Photina, who becomes one of his most devoted proponents, one who succeeds in bringing all the natives of Samaria to the worship of the new God.

Perhaps realizing that his true métier did not lie in such realms, Rostand proceeded, immediately after the production of this piece, to startle Parisian society with his swaggering *Cyrano de Bergerac* (1897). In this he abandoned the stained-glass effects of the preceding two plays and developed his theme against a background, carefully and minutely studied, of life in seventeenth-century France. That vivid opening scene set in the theatre, with its teeming humanity and its contrast between the real and the artificial, strikes at once a note entirely fresh. Rudel had no substance, and the Christ of *La Samaritaine* was but a figment of the imagination: in the depiction of the historical Cyrano and his comrades there is solidity and life, so that even when the theme introduces the same story of hopeless passion as already had been dealt with in *La princesse lointaine* we are prepared to listen with a fresh interest and to be moved. It is true that the devotion of Cyrano for Roxane is like that of Rudel for his lady, but the hero is different. Skilfully, Rostand has altered his pattern and found as a barrier to love's fulfilment not an external obstacle, but a characteristic of the hero himself. Rudel's story was a pitiful one of a moth and a flame; that of Cyrano is the story of a man proud, courageous, and witty, doomed by fate to have his spirit encased in a ridiculous frame. About the treatment of the tale too there is an expansive gaiety. Fundamentally the play relates the sad tale of Cyrano, in love with Roxane and driven by that very love to aid the handsome young Christian de Neuvillette towards possessing her, until he dies with his own passion unspoken: it is consequently 'tragic.' Yet our general impression of the action is not one of gloom: rather do we recall such episodes as that in which Cyrano contemptuously teaches the impertinent Valvert a lesson and runs him through with his rapier to the riming music of a ballade.

THE VICOMTE: I shall fling at him now some of my wit! [*Advances towards CYRANO, who is watching him, and takes his place in front of him with a silly air.*]
 You—your nose is—nose is—very large.
CYRANO [*gravely*]: Very!
THE VICOMTE [*smiling*]: Ha!
CYRANO [*imperturbable*]: That is all?
THE VICOMTE: But——
CYRANO: No, young man.
 That is somewhat too brief. You might say—Lord!—
 Many and many a thing, changing your tone.
 As, for example, these:—Aggressively:
 "Sir, had I such a nose I'd cut it off!"
 Friendly: "But it must dip into your cup.
 You should have made a goblet tall to drink from."
 Descriptive: " 'Tis a crag—a peak—a cape!
 I said a cape?—'tis a peninsula."
 Inquisitive: "To what use do you put
 This oblong sheath; is it a writing-case
 Or scissors-box?" Or, in a gracious tone:
 "Are you so fond of birds, that like a father
 You spend your time and thought to offer them
 This roosting-place to rest their little feet?" . . .
THE VICOMTE [*in a temper*]: Buffoon!
CYRANO [*giving a cry like one who feels a sudden pain*]: Oh!
THE VICOMTE [*who was going off, turning about*]: What's he saying now?
CYRANO [*with grimaces of pain*]: I must
 Shake it, because it falls asleep—the fault
 Of leaving it long idle——
THE VICOMTE: What's the matter?
CYRANO: My sword-blade tingles!
THE VICOMTE [*drawing his own sword*]: Very well, come on!
CYRANO: I shall give you a charming little stroke.
THE VICOMTE [*with disdain*]: Poet!—
CYRANO: A poet, yes! and such a one,
 That, while I fence with you, I'll improvise
 A ballade for you.
THE VICOMTE: A ballade?
CYRANO: I suppose
 You do not e'en imagine what that is?
THE VICOMTE: But——
CYRANO [*as if reciting a lesson*]: The ballade, then, is made up of three stanzas,
 Of eight lines——
THE VICOMTE [*shuffling his feet*]: Oh!
CYRANO [*continuing*]: And a refrain of four.

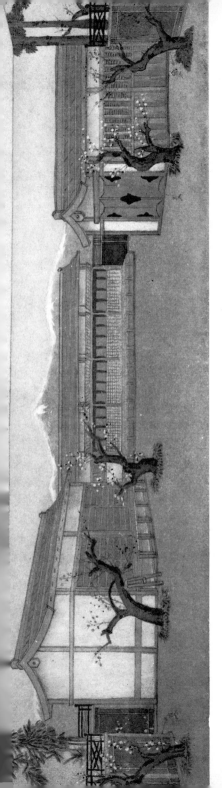

THE JAPANESE KABUKI STAGE: TWO ORIGINAL
DESIGNS FOR SETS

THE JAPANESE KABUKI STAGE: ORIGINAL DRAWING OF
A PERFORMANCE

THE VICOMTE: You——

CYRANO: I'll make one and fight you, both at once.
And at the last verse touch you, sir.

THE VICOMTE: No!

CYRANO: No?
The Ballade of Monsieur de Bergerac's Duel
At the Hôtel de Bourgogne with a Booby.

THE VICOMTE: What is that, if you please?

CYRANO: That is the title.

THE HALL [*excited to the highest pitch*]: In place!—
No noise!—In line!—This is amusing.

[*Tableau. A circle of curious onlookers in the parterre, the MARQUISES and the
OFFICERS mixed in with the TRADESMEN and common people. The PAGES climb
on people's shoulders to see better. All the women stand up in the boxes. To the right DE
GUICHE and his gentlemen. To the left LE BRET, RAGUENEAU, CUIGY, etc.*

CYRANO [*closing his eyes for a moment*]: Wait, let me choose my rhymes—I have
them now:

My hat I toss lightly away;
From my shoulders I slowly let fall
The cloak which conceals my array,
And my swo.˙d from my scabbard I call;
Like Céladon, graceful and tall,
Like Scaramouche, quick hand and brain,—
And I warn you, my friend, once for all,
I shall thrust when I end the refrain.

[*The swords meet.*

You were rash thus to join in the fray;
Like a fowl I shall carve you up small,
Your ribs, 'neath your doublet so gay,
Your breast, where the blue ribbons fall.
Ding dong! ring your bright trappings all;
My point flits like a fly on the pane,
As I clearly announce to the hall
I shall thrust when I end the refrain.

I need one more rhyme for 'array'—
You give ground, you turn white as the wall,—
And so lend me the word 'runaway.'
There! you have let your point fall
As I parry your best lunge of all;
I begin a new line, the end's plain,
Your skewer hold tight, lest it fall.
I shall thrust when I end the refrain.

[*Announces solemnly*]

REFRAIN.

Prince, on the Lord you must call!
I gain ground, I advance once again,
I feint, I lunge [*lunging*]. There! that is all!

[*The VICOMTE staggers. CYRANO salutes.*

For I thrust as I end the refrain.

It proved hard for Rostand to equal this masterpiece of the colourfully romantic. *L'Aiglon* (1900) deals with the 'eaglet,' the son of Napoleon, who, inspired to recapture the empire of his father, has no strength of will or of body to carry out his aims. This play was a manifest failure. Something near to success, however, comes with *Chantecler* (1910) and *La dernière nuit de Don Juan* (*Don Juan's Last Night*; printed 1921). The former, with its richly satirical verse and its general symbolic character, introduces a new element in Rostand's art. His old power of dramatic construction is there, and every scene is carefully planned for its effect: one after another—the coming of the Pheasant, the incursion of the Hunting-dog, the bliss of love, the flight, the despair, and the new-found hope—each aids in contributing to the general impression. The main story is properly simple—the tale of the renowned barnyard cock who believes in his soul that the very sun rises at the command of his proud crowing. Detested by the creatures of night, he is in a dangerous position: if his dream is shattered his sense of the value of life itself will be gone. The Pheasant with whom he goes off wishes to destroy this dream, for she is jealous of Chantecler's devotion to it, but even after she has succeeded in this plot Chantecler regains his confidence in himself, although with a wisdom deepened by experience, and the Pheasant herself, won by his strength of spirit, is content to accept his vision of life. There is nothing very profound in the play's theme or in the hundreds of minute episodes through which the allegory is pursued: nevertheless *Chantecler*, because of its richly lyrical utterance, its vivid sense of character values, and its skilful construction, is one of the most interesting dramas of its period.

Rostand's last play, left unfinished by his death, deals interestingly with the eternally fascinating theme of Don Juan. Opening with a scene in which Don Juan is being taken to Hell by the Statue—and in which the dialogue is, as it were, a continuation of the last lines of Molière's drama—the action presents the hero as granted, like Faust, a respite of ten years ere the Devil calls on him, and finding, again like Faust, that he has gained nothing. At the conclusion he is forced ignominiously into taking a part in the Devil's puppet-show. "I long to suffer!" cries the romantically disposed hero.

> I've never suffered! I've a right to hell!
> I've earned my hell!

To which the Devil makes reply:

> Hell is where I decree;
> I fix its place. Some celebrated men
> Are damned within their statues; thou art damned
> Within thy puppet!

Rostand's gaiety, satire, and irony, combined with his rich appreciation of romantic heroics, give him a secure position in the theatre. He may not have contributed much towards the dramatic interpretation of the neo-romanticism of his time, yet we gladly exonerate him for this, in view of the breezy freshness and vivid colouring that is spread over his three greatest dramas.

For the dramatic interpretation of neo-romanticism the Parisian stage had in the Belgian Maurice Maeterlinck a man who in his youth distinguished himself as a poet of the Symbolist school, and who later deliberately set about the task of translating the quality of this poetry into theatrical terms. Both because he was a pioneer in this realm and because he was possessed of a true, if limited, genius, his influence upon the theatre of the present century has been widespread. We may perhaps have grown out of the mood from which his plays were constructed; his scenes may no longer have the excitement and magic they had for an earlier generation; these things can be readily admitted without our forgetting the debt that the modern stage owes to his work.

In the year 1889 appeared his first drama, characteristically titled *La Princesse Maleine*, and this was followed by a series of similar plays—*L'intruse* (*The Intruder*, 1890), *Les aveugles* (*The Blind*, or *The Sightless*, 1890), *Pelléas et Mélisande* (1892), *Alladine et Palomides* (1894), *L'intérieur* (*The Interior*, 1894), *La morte de Tintagiles* (*The Death of Tintagiles*, 1894), *Aglavaine et Sélysette* (1896). The last of this series was *Sœur Béatrice* (*Sister Beatrice*) in 1901.

All of these, whether exploiting medieval themes or not, are characterized by the same qualities. A thin veil separates us from the characters; a dreaming inactivity replaces the richly moving action of a Rostand; a sense of fatal destiny removes the slightest vestige of human responsibility. Of the medieval-set dramas, *Pelléas et Mélisande* is the finest—a variant of the Paolo and Francesca story placed in a world of dreams. The opening scene strikes the note that is to be heard throughout its entire length. We are placed before a castle gate, and voices are heard within:

MAIDSERVANTS: Open the gate! Open the gate!
PORTER: Who is there? Why do you come and wake me up? Go out by the little gates; there are enough of them.
A MAIDSERVANT: We have come to wash the threshold, the gate and the steps; open, then! open!

Clearly we are in a world beyond reality, and in that world we remain until the doomed lovers are finally laid to rest.

Medieval themes, however, were common among the writings of the romantic poet-dramatists, and Maeterlinck showed far greater originality in his attempt to create a "static theatre" in *L'intruse*, *Les aveugles*, and *L'intérieur*. The first introduces us to death, the intruder in the family circle. There is no plot in the ordinary sense of the word—just a picture of a little group sitting in a small room, while beyond a woman lies in child-

birth. Fitfully the talk drifts, ebbs lightly, and falls silently back, while all
the time we feel death's presence drawing closer:

> *THE GRANDFATHER:* Are the windows open, Ursula?
> *THE DAUGHTER:* The glass door is open, Grandfather.
> *THE GRANDFATHER:* It seems to me the cold is entering the room.
> *THE DAUGHTER:* There is a little wind in the garden, Grandfather, and
> the rose leaves are falling.
> *THE FATHER:* Well, shut the door, Ursula. It is late.
> *THE DAUGHTER:* Yes, Father. I cannot shut the door, Father.
> *THE TWO OTHER DAUGHTERS:* We cannot shut the door.

In *Les aveugles* the situation is equally static—just a group of blind men,
lost in a forest and desperate because their guide, a priest, has died in
their midst. Even less of dramatic action is involved in *L'intérieur*. Here we
stand outside a house and look in through a window at a happy, quiet,
peaceful family scene within. But a girl belonging to this family has been
drowned, and the dialogue of the play comes from one or two neighbours
whose duty it is to break the sad news and who stand hesitating outside.
The real persons of the drama are not these neighbours: they are the
members of the family circle whom we cannot see, whom we never hear
speak: the veil is drawn between us and them.

For the subtlety of these pieces there can be nothing save admiration.
In them Maeterlinck has fully and delicately realized his dream of a new
stage. "There is," he says,

> an everyday tragedy which is more real, deeper and more in keeping with our
> true existence than the tragedy of great adventures. . . . I have come to think
> that an old man, seated in his armchair, simply waiting beside the lamp,
> listening, without knowing it, to all the eternal laws that reign about him, in-
> terpreting, without understanding it, what there is in the silence of the doors
> and windows and in the small voice of the light, undergoing the presence of his
> soul and of his destiny, leaning a little his head, without suspecting that all the
> powers of this world are intervening and watching in his room like attentive
> servants, not knowing that the sun itself sustains the little table on which he
> rests his elbows and that there is not a planet in heaven nor a power of the soul
> which is indifferent to the dropping of an eyelid or the disclosure of a
> thought—I have come to think that this motionless old man was living in re-
> ality a deeper, more human and more general life than the lover who strangles
> his mistress, the captain who wins a victory or the 'husband who avenges his
> honour.'

In his dream of a static theatre Maeterlinck may have been anticipated
by predecessors such as Norwid, but his enunciation of this theatre's
aims no less than his creative interpretation of them still justify us in
styling him an innovator.

From this style Maeterlinck moved, with the production of *Monna
Vanna* in 1902, to another less individual in concept, yet more likely to
win popular esteem. The story here has a ring familiar to those versed in
the romantic drama of the time. The city of Pisa is besieged and starving:

to save it from destruction Monna Vanna agrees to give herself to the general, Prinzivalle, commanding the investing forces, but to her amazement finds in him a chivalrous lover who freely proposes to release her from her promise. When he is about to be arrested as a traitor she brings this hero to her house; her husband suspects the worst; she declares she has not been seduced, but at the threat of torture being applied to Prinzivalle she lies boldly, and we are left to believe that she will rescue him from prison and go off with him. Here is something vastly less interesting than Maeterlinck's earlier work. Unquestionably, despite its theatrical success, this play marks a retrogression in his art: there is some beauty in it, yet there is an irritating quality combined of sexual suggestiveness and vague mysticism.

Joyzelle (1903) introduces more of the mystical, although here too the themes of love and of sexual sacrifice are once more pursued; and both reappear in *Marie Magdaleine* (1910), a somewhat unsatisfactory piece, in which the characters are obvious stereotypes—the Roman soldier Lucius Verus, Marie Magdaleine, the courtesan who becomes devoted to Christ, and the philosopher Annæus Silanus, who quests solely after wisdom.

In *L'oiseau bleu* (*The Blue Bird*, 1908) Maeterlinck discovered fresh and fruitful territory, and the appeal of this play must be fully recognized, even if we may now find much of its allegory childish and most of its philosophy spurious. Perhaps it is best to accept it for what it truly is—a rather sentimental children's fantasy, skilfully planned and expressed with not a little beauty of language. It is easy to sneer at *The Blue Bird*: nevertheless it possesses its own virtues and is a play which, even although its bloom of novelty is now worn off, has an enduring appeal. Not so successful is *Les fiançailles* (*The Betrothal*, 1918), in which the author tried to provide a kind of sequel to his earlier fantasy.

To reach an objective estimate of Maeterlinck's contribution to the theatre is difficult. Posing as a philosopher, he can win little esteem for his thoughts about the mystery of life; beginning his career with a bold new theory of dramatic expression, he abandoned his own position and ended by supplying the public with rather cheap theatrical effects. Yet in the end it is in these early dramas, and the theory out of which they grew, that we find the truest evidence of his genius. No doubt the theatre is too rough and vulgar a place for the exploitation of the purely static drama that he desired to encourage: no doubt the veils he places between his characters and ourselves occasion, if they do not justify, accusations that his art is inherently 'escapist.' On the other hand, those who condemn or dismiss these works will neglect at their peril observation of the wide influence Maeterlinck's style has had on dozens of twentieth-century authors, many of them working in realms apparently far removed from his, and they will fail to assess at its real worth the truly exquisite craftsmanship that these dramas display.

Beyond the writings of the French Rostand and the Belgian Maeterlinck the theatre of Paris has nothing of consequence to offer in the field of romanticism, unless we except *Le chemineau* (*The Tramp*, 1897) of Jean Richepin, that interestingly ironic idyllic picture of a tinker's life, and the dramas, such as *Le cloître* (*The Cloister*, 1900), written in the lyrical strain by Maeterlinck's fellow-countryman Émile Verhaeren. But more was not needed. Rostand and Maeterlinck between them gave to the French romantic play a paramount international import.

PART X

THE DRAMA OF THE ORIENT

THE DRAMA OF THE ORIENT

To INTRODUCE a summary account of the theatres of the East at this particular point in a general history of the stage may seem to be preposterous. We have just surveyed the age of Ibsen and we are approaching the age of Shaw: to divide these epochs by passing in imagination to the countries washed by the waters of the warm Pacific does indeed appear at first glance to be absurd. Chronologically the dramas of China, Japan, and India took their rise during the centuries we style the Middle Ages and the Renaissance; it was at that time that they achieved their richest power of expression; and since that expression commonly was devoted to truths religious, metaphysical, and philosophical, it might well be thought that more appropriately these Oriental plays might have been dealt with in association with the mysteries and miracles of the Catholic Church.

As a justification for the placing of the present section it may be argued that every work of wide general scope—whether it be a universal history of human events or of literature—must select some definite orientation, and clearly what we are most interested in is the development of the Western theatre from its earliest-known days in Greece to its latest manifestations in the playhouses with which we ourselves are currently familiar. If we had turned to treat the Eastern drama along with the medieval mysteries solely because, across a waste of several thousand miles, unknown poets of China, Japan, and India were engaged at the same time in producing religious dramas, we should unquestionably have been falsifying the composition of the picture being painted. The focal point is the theatre of the West, and everything must be dependent upon that fact.

To the Western stage Oriental drama remained almost utterly unknown until the early part of the nineteenth century, and even then its impact on the playwrights was but slight. True, Goethe and others among the German romantics raved over the beauties of Kalidasa's works in the ecstatic terms of praise which they found for all objects of their adoration, but direct influence of these works on contemporary dramatic form is still to seek. All through the century increased knowledge of the Oriental stages was brought to men's attention; from the specialized library of the scholar this knowledge was passed to the theatrical library;

and gradually, towards the end of the century, we begin to discern faint signs of an impact being made by the East upon the West. Linnebach is sufficiently acquainted with certain features of the Japanese stage to borrow from it the device of the revolving platform; the public is being made acquainted with the forms of the plays by a series of translations. India, China, and Japan, with their theatres, are drawing closer to the Occident.

It is, however, only during the present century that this knowledge becomes intimate and begins to influence our drama directly. A Chinese company comes to Paris in 1895, a Japanese to London in 1900; the ancient Sanskrit plays are being looked upon not merely as curiosities or as storehouses of Oriental philosophy: they are adapted to the stage and performed, and even if nearly all these performances make their appeal to limited audiences the fashion has been set for other more popular productions to come. Even in the nineties *The Toy Cart* was something of a success in France: *The Yellow Jacket* (1913), fashioned in Chinese style for the American playhouse by J. H. Benrimo, finds commercial acclaim, and is followed by the frequently acted *The Circle of Chalk* (originally adapted as *Der Kreidekreis*, 1923, by Klabund) and by *Lady Precious Stream* (1934), wherein, with subtle skill, S. I. Hsiung has so adapted the Oriental style to Western needs as to have created a work whose general appeal made it one of the best-known dramas of the thirties.

Along with these developments comes an awakening of interest on the part of the poets in the conventionalities of the Oriental stage. Arthur Waley's renderings of the Japanese Nō dramas are eagerly welcomed, and so, too, are works describing the methods of acting used in the presentation of these and kindred plays. As will be seen, the impress made by the Oriental theatre on the writings of poetic dramatists—particularly in the twenties and the thirties of our century—is by no means negligible.

All of this offers ample justification for the treatment of the stage of the East at this particular position in the general account of the theatre. In a work written by a Chinese theatrical historian concerning dramatic development in his own country Shakespeare and his fellows might occupy a corresponding place, coming along with the record of such native works as first displayed Elizabethan influence. We are dealing here not with actual but with spiritual time.

1

THE SANSKRIT DRAMA

THE THEATRE of India, as has been noted above, first among the Oriental stages impinged itself on the attention of the West. Precisely when the Sanskrit drama arose we do not know, largely because of that almost complete lack of any chronological interest so characteristic of early Indian literature. Traditional myth asserts that the joys of the stage were brought to men by Urvasi, condemned to descend from heaven to earth because, her mind confused by thoughts of her human lover, she had failed to exhibit her accustomed skill before the great god Indra. But when this supposedly supernatural event occurred and who were Urvasi's immediate successors remains utterly unknown. All that can be said even with the faintest measure of assurance is that already towards the beginning of our era a scholar, Bharata, had in front of him a sufficient body of material to be able, Aristotle-like, to compose his exhaustive *Science of Dramaturgy*; that the most famous of all Sanskrit playwrights, Kalidasa, apparently flourished in the fourth and fifth centuries; that before his time there had already been at least one successful playwright, Bhasa (some of whose work may perhaps be included among the dozen early Sanskrit dramatic works discovered some thirty years ago); and that the theatre long remained a distinguished and noble form of artistic expression in Indian Courts.

Concerning the stage used for these productions, much rests unsure, yet a fairly vivid general picture can still be formed both of the methods used and of the social background against which the dramas were enacted. The first thing we have to do in order to place Kalidasa in his setting is to allow our imaginations to carry us back to an ancient Indian palace Court, gorgeous in its appointments, replete with glistening adornments. Within this palace a theatre has been erected, with care and devotion. Prayers have been spoken; the very site has been selected only after meticulous consideration; the ground has been measured out in its minutest proportions; four pillars, symbolic of the four castes, have been erected at each corner to provide the main supports of the building; preceding the ritual when the foundations are laid, the man in charge of the performances has fasted for three full days. The whole atmosphere connected with the establishment of this playhouse is solemn and majestic.

We may imagine erected in this area so carefully chosen a hall about a hundred feet long and about half as wide, divided into two equal parts, the one designed for the King and his courtiers, the other for the performers. Facing the audience is a platform stage, with two compartments at the sides, backed by a curtain which can be drawn when necessary, revealing behind it another stage area ending in a magnificently decorated scenic back-wall.

What is peculiarly characteristic of this theatre, however—and, indeed, of all the theatres of the Orient—is not its physical shape, but rather the conventions on which the entire art of the performance depends. Costumes, make-up, gestures, all are highly stylized, and, since dance and music play a significant part in the production, this stylization is harmonized with the other elements to make one unified whole. Movement of head, eyes, limbs, fingers, all is strictly set. The gestures may or may not approximate to what we should expect in reality: the important thing is that the highly select and cultured audience knows how to interpret the minutest indications given by the actors, translating these into terms of mood or situation. In *Sakuntala* the heroine is called upon to express fear of a bee that is buzzing round her head: this the performer does by moving his head quickly to and fro, while his lips quiver and his hands, with the palms held inward, are pressed unsteadily against his face. In the same drama a character has to pretend to be gathering flowers: here the left hand is extended horizontally in a set position, to symbolize the holding of a basket, while the position of the right is so devised as to suggest the motion of plucking the blossoms and carefully placing them in the basket.

In imagining a performance of a Sanskrit play as it was originally produced we must, therefore, place ourselves within the closely guarded precincts of an ancient and splendid Court and endeavour to think ourselves trained members of an alert audience. The joy of the spectacle will come, not so much from what is new, but rather from the delight in watching highly expert performers reproducing with their bodies the time-honoured gestures appropriate to the scenes in which they appear.

Perhaps Italian audiences in the early seventeenth century derived just such joy from seeing the histrionic exhibitions of a fresh Arlecchino or Pantalone, although in such farcical episodes as were presented by the *commedia dell' arte* companies greater latitude and more individual freedom could be permitted than was possible in the presentation of the seriously conceived romantic plays which formed the dramatic fare of the early Indian Courts. In so far as the emotional content of these plays is concerned, the nearest parallel offered by the Western theatre is perhaps the type of comedy which became so popular in England during the reign of James I, and which may be exemplified by Shakespeare's last writings —*Cymbeline, The Winter's Tale*, and *The Tempest*. Within the Sanskrit theatre there could be no tragedy, since the very concept of the tragic, as interpreted in the West, would have been utterly alien to the philosophic and metaphysical beliefs of this age and clime. The result is that nearly all the plays produced on the Indian stage belong to what we should call romantic tragi-comedy, of a strongly poetic, even lyrical, tone. Serious and distressing scenes are introduced here, but softened in their colouring; comic scenes appear along with them, but with their realism decently veiled.

From the critical writings on the theatre that have been preserved for us it would seem that both structure and characterization were as conventionally controlled as was the actor's gesture. Individuality of conception was achieved by the dramatist through variations in the set pattern rather than through boldness of composition. Of special significance here was the elaboration of what may be styled dramatic moods (*rasas*), each distinct, yet capable of being employed in combination, which the playwright had to try to express. Every play, it was argued, must have its dominant impression—whether of love or of the marvellous or of the heroic—and, even if some scenes might awaken other impressions, the total harmony demanded that these scenes be treated as subordinate to the mood which had been conceived as the major theme. By means of these *rasas* men might classify the plays set before them, and by appreciation of the *rasa* aimed at they could gain delight from contemplation of each production. Again, as with the conventions of histrionic performance, we must assume and make all allowance for a deep and intimate basis of appreciative knowledge on the part of the audience: each drama must have been regarded, not separately, but in association with other dramas of a similar kind and with the vast body of critical precept that presented, in codified form, the principles upon which the whole of the dramatic art was founded.

Kalidasa

The flower of Sanskrit drama appears in the work of Kalidasa, an author whose dates are unknown: some would place him in the fourth century; others aver that he lived in the first century of our era. Of his plays three have been preserved—*Malavikagnimitra* (*Malavika and Agnimitra*), *Vikramorvasiya*, and, the best-known of them all, *Sakuntala*.

Neither of the first two—thought to have been respectively among the earliest and the latest of Kalidasa's compositions—is of any great value. *Malavika and Agnimitra* tells a romantic story of love set against a background of war. The heroine is Malavika, really a princess, but at the moment living unknown as a maid in the service of Queen Dharini, the chief wife of King Agnimitra. Having seen Malavika's portrait, the monarch has fallen madly in love with her, but the Queen's jealousy forbids his meeting her. By a trick of the clown Gautama, however, an interview is effected, although this is in turn interrupted by the angry arrival of one of the young Queens, who sharply upbraids her lord for his defections. Once more Gautama arranges a love-tryst; once more the young Queen, Iravati, intervenes. In the end it is Dharini who gives way and announces that Agnimitra may have his Malavika; while general joy comes to all (save the ousted Iravati) by the discovery that the maid is a princess in disguise.

The main lines of the plot demonstrate clearly how close in spirit is this ancient Sanskrit play to the romantic comedies of the early seventeenth century, even to those produced by Shakespeare towards the close of the century previous. Allowance being made for the social custom of polygamy, the love theme is developed in a manner startlingly akin to these, and there are even some scenes—such as that wherein Agnimit and Gautama hide in a grove in order to see Malavika, while Iravati and her maid similarly conceal themselves—which seem almost identical to episodes of the kind made memorable by Shakespeare in *Love's Labour's Lost* and *Twelfth Night*.

One particular device used in all Kalidasa's dramas strikes an especially 'modern' note. Before the action of *Malavika and Agnimitra* begins the stage-director enters, gives out the title of the piece, and bids the music begin—only to be interrupted by his assistant, who conservatively demands to know whether the writings of the classical masters shall be neglected in favour of the work of a modern author. To him the director replies with epigrammatic verse:

> Not all is good that bears an ancient name,
> Nor need we every modern poem blame:
> Wise men approve the good, or new or old;
> The foolish critic follows where he's told.

This introductory device has the ring of Ben Jonson—and perhaps, too, of still later authors who, stepping outside the frame of their dramatic action, speak to the audience directly. The familiar tone, apparent in the entire handling of the plot material, is here symbolized.

If the chief *rasa* of *Malavika and Agnimitra* is that of love the chief *rasa* of *Vikramorvasiya* (*Urvashi won by Valour*) is that of the marvellous. In it the legend is told of the divine nymph who, famed for her skill in acting before the gods, brings the joys of the drama to human realms, although in treating it Kalidasa has laid less stress on the art, more on the human passion. After rescuing Urvashi and her friend Chitralekha from the power of a demon, King Pururavas finds his heart smitten with love of the celestial maiden. Likewise moved by love of him, Urvashi descends, invisible, to earth and leaves him a message written on a birch-leaf; this is unfortunately found by Queen Aushinari, who indulges in the usual scene of jealousy. From this episode on earth we are now carried back to Paradise, where Urvashi is in disgrace. While acting in a play she is asked, "On whom is your heart set?" and, forgetting her rôle, replies, "On Pururavas." As a result she is condemned to abandon Paradise, being permitted to return only after her lover shall have seen a child born of her human union. The pair are joined in marriage, Queen Aushinari having magnanimously withdrawn her objections, and for a time they live happily. Trouble comes, however, when Urvashi, entering a grove forbidden to women, is changed into a vine, and for long Pururavas is forced in vain to seek her. All the animals he meets he questions, but none of these can help him, and he succeeds in his quest at last only after finding the magical ruby of reunion. Once more united with his love, he is entirely contented, save for one thing, that he has had no son by Urvashi. By a wonderful coincidence, however, a youth is discovered who turns out to be in reality his child: for Urvashi, dreading the decree that will call her back to Paradise, has chosen to abandon her offspring rather than lose her husband. Touched by her devotion, the gods now rescind their order, and she, to her joy, is not only privileged to welcome her child, but also to remain joined till death with her beloved Pururavas.

There is much charm in this dramatic tale, and certain scenes are brilliantly designed, but its theme makes far less appeal to us than that of the better-known *Sakuntala*, which relates another story of a King's love of a beautiful maiden. King Dushyanta, during a hunting expedition, catches a glimpse of Sakuntala, the daughter of a famous sage and foster-child of a hermit. As she is watering the shrubs she is attacked by a bee, and in her attempts to escape it she encounters the monarch:

> *SAKUNTALA:* This impertinent bee will not rest quiet. I must move elsewhere. [*Moving a few steps off, and casting a glance around*] How now! he is following me here. Help! my dear friends, help! deliver me from the attacks of this troublesome insect. . . .
>
> *KING:* An excellent opportunity for me to show myself. Fear not—[*Checks himself when the words are half uttered. Aside*] But stay, if I introduce myself in this manner, they will know me to be the King. Be it so, I will accost them, nevertheless.
>
> *SAKUNTALA* [*moving a step or two further off*]: What! it still persists in following me.
>
> *KING* [*advancing hastily*]: When mighty Puru's offspring sways the earth,
> And o'er the wayward holds his threatening rod,
> Who dares molest the gentle maids that keep
> Their holy vigils here in Kanwa's grove?

Of course, the pair fall in love, and the King decides to encamp near the hermit's cell:

> I have no longer any desire to return to the city. I will therefore rejoin my attendants, and make them encamp somewhere in the vicinity of this sacred grove. In good truth, Sakuntala has taken such possession of my thoughts that I cannot turn myself in any other direction.
>
> > My limbs drawn onward leave my heart behind,
> > Like silken pennon borne against the wind.

The King marries her, but departs for the city, and there a curse is laid upon him: all memory of his wedding vanishes from his mind. By good fortune, however, a ring belonging to Sakuntala and given her by the King is found by a common fisherman in the body of a carp he has caught: on seeing it memory comes surging back to him, and, after a series of romantic adventures (some of them, like those in *Vikramorvasiya*, set in celestial regions), he regains both his bride and the son to whom she has given birth.

In this drama, wherein elements of love and wonder, the comic and the pathetic, are mingled in admirable profusion, wherein time is ideal and the scenes move easily from earth to heaven and back again, is a quality thoroughly typical of the Sanskrit theatre as a whole. The atmosphere is lyrically fantastic, yet reality intrudes and forms a contrast with the more imaginative passages; in general the tone is one of intent seriousness, yet cynical reflections are not unheard from the lips of clowns and jesters.

Since in structure the play bears a close resemblance to the forms assumed by the Western drama (even being composed in the five-act pattern favoured by the Sanskrit critics), and since its spirit is prevailingly romantic, there need be no wonder that when Sir William Jones issued his translation in 1789 it was eagerly seized upon by those young talents who, in love with everything opposed to classical precision, were searching for new objects of admiration. Goethe's praise may be a trifle exaggerated, but it was assuredly sincere and it was characteristic of his age:

> Willst du die Blüte des Frühen, die
>   Früchte des späteren Jahres,
> Willst du, was reizt und entzückt,
>   Willst du, was sättigt und nährt,
> Willst du den Himmel, die Erde mit
>   Einem Namen begreifen,
> Nenn'ich, Sakuntala, dich, und
>   Dann ist alles gesagt.

Other Sanskrit Dramatists

Kalidasa's works do not stand alone, but, with one exception, they remain virtually neglected save by specialists in Sanskrit literature. That exception is *Mrichhakatika*, known as *The Little Clay Cart*, traditionally attributed to King Shudraka—an attribution, however, not supported by modern scholarly opinion. By whomsoever it was written, there is no doubt but that it is a later elaboration of a much earlier work, attributed to Bhasa, called *Daridracharudatta* (*The Poor Charudatta*), which presents an identical main plot without the embellishments of *The Little Clay Cart*. Here, instead of a royal romance, we are introduced to the story of a poor Brahman, Charudatta by name, who falls in love with a courtesan, Vasantasena. This lady comes under the gaze of an evil prince, and the exigencies of the plot force her to bring her jewels for safety to Charudatta's house: the gems are stolen, and the worthy wife of the hero nobly hands over to him her own jewels in order that he may make restitution. From this point on the adventures become complex and involved. The title of the drama comes from an episode when Vasantasena generously fills with diamonds the little toy cart belonging to Charudatta's son; another line of plot development relates how she saves from wrongful punishment a poor peasant, who later turns out to be the true heir to the throne; a third tells how, rejecting the evil prince's advances, she is apparently strangled by him. Charudatta is accused of the crime: he is led off to be executed; in the nick of time witnesses appear in his defence; the true heir seizes the throne; the hero is rewarded by being made a provincial governor; he and his loyal Vasantasena are, at long last, happily united.

This is a composition of a somewhat different cast from that of Kalidasa's plays. The technique is similar and the romantic episodes, although brought nearer to the levels of domesticity, are akin; but the dialogue displays a surprising number of remarks of the kind we should now call 'social comment.' Indeed, an entire section of the work—that in which a judge, although convinced of Charudatta's innocence, is prepared to sentence him to death because he fears the power of the evil prince—is devoted to an exposure of the ways of justice in ancient days: for this is *La robe rouge* of the Orient. Because of these qualities, perhaps, *The Little Clay Cart* won not a little esteem when, heavily adapted, it was first acted in America a few decades ago.

Among the followers of Kalidasa is numbered another royal dramatist, Harsha by name, who has left three plays, two of which are patterned much on this model. In *Ratnavali* (*The Pearl Necklace*) the device is used of a parrot repeating a love message and so revealing to a monarch a girl's devotion to him; in *Priyadarsika* there is a play within the play. *Nagananda* stands distinct, since, unlike the others, it treats of a religious concept. Here a Buddhist saint, Jimutavahana, seeing that his people are being consumed by a devil-monster in the shape of a horrendous vulture, voluntarily sacrifices himself for their sake. In the end he is saved by the fact that this evil creature, converted through his noble action, suddenly has a change of heart and agrees to undo all the depredations of which it had been guilty.

Some centuries later came Bhavabhuti, and with him the classical stage virtually ceased to be. Rather less variegated in their tone than the earlier dramas, his plays are again romantic tragi-comedies—as, for example, the *Malatimadhava* (*Malati and Madhava*), which narrates the crossed loves of a youth and a girl separated by their families. For his style he is praised, but there is less quality in his work likely to appeal to audiences ignorant of Sanskrit. Plays continued to be written in Sanskrit for many years after this date, but all the evidence seems to indicate that after reaching its flower in Kalidasa the drama of India rapidly declined.

Before leaving these plays, however, note must be taken of two works of entirely different kinds. The first is the farcical comedy called *Bhagavadajjukiya* (*The Ascetic transmuted into a Courtesan*), by an otherwise unknown author, Bodhayana. In its intrigue this play sharply recalls the adventures of Puck in *A Midsummer Night's Dream*, for the whole action is based on the mistake of a supernatural messenger of the god Yama. The chief character is a holy hermit who, at the very beginning of the piece, is shown talking to a not-so-holy disciple, Sandilya by name. During this talk the courtesan Vasantasena enters; Sandilya is much attracted by her, when, to his dismay, she suddenly falls dead—for the celestial messenger, bidden to kill a certain woman and mistaking Vasantasena for his victim, has changed himself into a serpent and stung her. Hereupon the hermit, by the force of his art, causes his own soul to enter the body of the woman: when the girl's mother and her lover arrive they are utterly baffled by the sanctimonious discourses that come from the courtesan's lips. Meanwhile the messenger has been severely reprimanded by Yama for having made a mistake: back to earth he is sent to restore Vasantasena's soul, but, finding her body occupied, he inserts it in the body of the hermit, who now begins to talk in the language of courtesans. The theme is amusing, and without doubt the author displays a rich and racy sense of the comic in the handling of his scenes.

The second play mentioned above is the first known example of Buddhist mystery-morality drama—*Prabodhacandrodaya* (*The Rise of Conscience*, eleventh century). Its plot, involving characters all of whom bear names similar to those appearing in medieval English moralities, shows that besides the familiar tragi-comedies the Indian theatre produced dramas of diverse sorts. At the same time, it is the tragi-comedies which, in the end, are of chief significance for us.

As has been observed, most of these dramas, although dealing with social life and episodes far different from our own, do not materially differ in style and structure from Western tragi-comedies and comedies—particularly those of the kind produced by the English Elizabethan and Jacobean playwrights or by Lope de Vega and Calderón in Spain. The result is that, although Kalidasa's works have for long been known and admired, their influence on the West has been but slight. Knowledge of the highly conventional ballet-like methods of performance on their original production has come to us only within comparatively recent years, and, in the absence of such knowledge, the general tendency has been to interpret these Indian plays in terms of the stage known in the Occident. Only within the last few decades has an appreciation of the unrealistic stylization in histrionic method caused them to be related to the kindred style of dramatic artistry created in China and in Japan.

2

THE DRAMA OF CHINA

As IN other lands, the drama in China seems to owe its origin to religious exercises, although the records of the stage there leave many things uncertain and render any attempt at dogmatic assertion dangerous. Apart from the loss of documentary evidence, the relative disesteem in which the theatre has been held in Chinese literary circles has tended to obscure both the story of its development and the account of its growth in later times.

Legend asserts that stage productions began in the Chow dynasty (1122–255 B.C.), and the Emperor Ming Huang of the Tang dynasty was reputedly an eager patron of such shows in the eighth century of our era. The truth is, however, that not until we reach the hundred and thirty-odd dramas preserved from the Yuan dynasty (A.D. 1280–1368) do we have certain evidence on which to base any firm judgments: most of these plays are included in a famous collection titled "The Hundred Yuan Plays," printed about the year 1600. They belong to the highly refined classical tradition.

Popular elements were introduced into the *kun chü*, several centuries later, and further popularization, with the assimilation of certain forms of rustic drama, appears in the modern 'Peking Opera.' In noting these types of play it is important to remember that, while the Yuan dramas provide the basis for much later endeavour, they themselves are now only reading works, in a language which only a few can understand, and that the 'Peking Opera' for the most part is a thing purely of the theatre, rarely put in reading form.

The Chinese Theatre

Perhaps to us the most interesting feature of China's theatrical activity is not the drama itself but the stage.

The actors appear on a platform which, like that of the Elizabethan playhouse, is surrounded by spectators on three sides, the men formerly on the floor and the women in boxes slightly elevated. Above and behind the players occasionally appears a balcony, reserved for the use of heavenly visitants. There is no scenery, although a heavily and richly embroidered curtain forms a background for the action.

Peculiarly characteristic of the performance in this theatre is the appearance on stage of the property-man, who unconcernedly brings on and removes the few pieces of furniture necessary for the progress of the pieces, hands small properties to the actors during the course of their performance, or even attends to their costumes as they proceed with their parts. His presence there indicates at once that for Chinese spectators realism is not only unnecessary but undesired. In the property-man's appearance among the players is, as it were, a visible and constant testimony to the imaginative quality of the entire production.

This imaginative quality controls, too, the use of such furniture as is supplied and governs the histrionic movements. A chair set on its side will serve to represent a rock; a flowered carpet will become a garden; a table will be taken as a mountain. All sorts of symbolic or conventional gestures provide indication of movements not shown in actuality. If an actor has to go through water he displays a little flag painted with fishes: if he is supposed to be riding a horse he takes long strides and flourishes a whip. Instead of imitating reality, the Chinese actor presents a conventional symbol by which the reality may be imagined.

In harmony with this approach, the rôles appearing on the stage are carefully classified, with four main types—the heroic 'baritone,' or 'tenor,' the 'soprano,' the 'bass,' and the clown. To each of these and to others are apportioned certain characteristic tones of voice and gestures. Where the *tan*, or young girl, sways rhythmically in body, the *lao tan*, or old lady, has a conventionalized palsy shake and bending movements. The hero walks in one way, the villain in another, so that, immediately the spectators see a character enter, even before they hear him say a word, they know his rôle in the drama.

The costumes are rich, although not always governed in colour or shape by the requirements of the particular drama being enacted, and the make-up used is so heavy and so stylized as to make some players seem to be using masks. So complex are the indications given to the audience of age, character, and mood by these means that the theatres have before them some two hundred models of facial presentation, each line and each colour having its own special significance.

The Chinese Dramas

Fundamentally the Chinese plays may be likened rather to Western opera than to ordinary tragedies or comedies with spoken dialogue (whether prose or poetic). Music, too loud and clamorous for most ears, accompanies much of the action, and the performers, originally all male, chant their parts in conventional tones and with long monologues. There is some spoken dialogue (sometimes improvised), but the lyrical portions are those on which main attention is set. Like the Sanskrit plays, the Chinese all assume the character of tragi-comedies, although the mixed elements that make up this type of drama appear in forms much coarser than those provided for the highly refined Indian Courts. Pathos is more deeply stressed, clownery is more absurd, sensational incident is more blatant.

Generally short, these tragi-comedies are usually played in series; so that in such a well-known production as *Hsi hsiang chi* (*The Western Chamber*), for example, we have, not one single play, but in reality five plays linked together in general theme. The style prevailing in these pieces may be assessed from such adaptations as S. I. Hsiung's *Lady Precious Stream*, taken from the original *Wang pao ch'mau*, or *The Circle of Chalk*, as devised by Ethel van der Veer from *Hoei lan kia*. The latter tells the ancient, and universal, story which is familiar to us in the Biblical story of the judgment of Solomon. Hai-t'ang is a beautiful girl who, after a miserable youth, becomes the Second Wife of Ma Chun-shing. This gentleman's First Wife, however, has fallen in love with Ch'ao, a Government clerk, and with her lover she poisons her husband. At the same time, in order to obtain Ma's money, she seizes Hai-t'ang's child, claims it as her own, bribes witnesses to appear in her support, and, by giving a present to the corrupt governor So-shun, obtains an order in her favour. Poor Hai-t'ang is arrested and put in chains. Now enters a *deus ex machina* —the supreme judge Pao-ch'ing. Hearing the statements of the two women, he commands a circle of chalk to be inscribed on a bench; the child is placed thereon and the pair of claimants bidden to pull it out of the marked space. Twice Hai-t'ang fails to hold on to the child, and the judge, realizing that this failure is due to her unwillingness to give hurt, decides that her claim is just: Ch'ao is arrested and the wicked governor So-shun deprived of his offices.

In form, all is wrought in conventional manner. Each character on entering announces his or her name, ancestry, upbringing, and present position. Problems are directly outlined in monologue. Villains have no scruples in telling the audience their inmost secrets. Time passes with bewildering rapidity, and localities are established, as need arises, by the words of the characters. These words vary from prose passages to lyrical, the commonest device being the presentation of some informatory lines followed and broken by a chant. Thus, for example, Hai-t'ang appears after her marriage:

> I am named Hai-t'ang. It is five years since I was married to my lord Ma. My Venerable Mother has long ago departed to the Land of the Gods. I do not know the whereabouts of my brother, as since his departure I have received no news of him. The child which I had from my marriage is called Shiu-lang. Since he was three years of age he has stayed by the side of Mrs Ma, who took him to bring up. As to-day is the anniversary of his birth, my lord and Mrs Ma have taken him to all the temples in the city to burn sweet perfumes and to gild the image of Fu. I go now to prepare rice and tea to receive them as soon as they shall have returned. . . . Hai-t'ang, since you have espoused the lord Ma, nothing has interfered with your happiness.

Through the silken curtains
At my window
I contemplate the moon
And its cold shadows.
It shines alike without reproach or passion
Upon my richly embroidered curtains
And upon that street which is the abode of vice.
Could I ever have hoped one day
To abandon that degrading profession,
The companionship of rakes and their mistresses,
With their orgies and licentious songs?
Yet I have for ever said farewell
To that theatre of pleasure.
Let them follow me if they will
With railleries and aspersions.
Never again will I make advances for gain
Nor stretch forth a seducing hand to noblemen.
No more will I make traffic with my beauty
Nor return to the follies of the gay life. . . .
Untroubled by the wickedness of the world outside,
I live the long hours through in tranquil peace.
Even as the wild duck seeks its mate in the grass,
I have found a husband
Whose heart accords happily with mine,
And who each day begs me
To recompense his tenderness.
And so that I may taste with him
The sweetness of slumber
Ere the moon silvers the edges
Of my window curtains.
I send back to her own apartment
That woman so jealous of my serenity.

I await the return of my lord and Mrs Ma. . . . But they do not come. . . . Let us go out for a moment and look for them in the distance.

The romantic tragi-comedy tone is akin to that of the Sanskrit plays, but there are several differences. In style the dialogue is much more conventional and the transitions from one part of the action to another more sharply abrupt. The supernatural is less in evidence, and the atmosphere, instead of being courtly fanciful, descends more commonly to the levels of ordinary life. Rags and poverty make their gaunt appearance on this stage, whereas in the Indian plays they appear only by implication or in forms made gracious by the exercise of the imagination.

Above all, where the dramas of Kalidasa possess a poetic quality which, if it does not justify, at least explains the enthusiasm of Goethe, very rarely in the Chinese stage pieces do we find flashes of penetrating insight and the thrill of the poetic vision. The charm of the theatre of China lies not so much in the dramatic style as in the total effect of the entire production.

It is this total effect that has, indeed, caught the attention of some at least among those interested in the development of a non-realistic theatre in the West. These productions have taught men that it is not necessary, in order to capture the minds of audiences, to depend wholly upon the naturalistic conventions of the fourth-wall stage; they have indicated that it is possible to find in those other conventions of the Oriental theatre different methods for the setting forth of situation, character, and emotional concept.

We should not, of course, assume from the example of *The Circle of Chalk* that the Chinese drama habitually deals with matters of domestic import; indeed, the precise opposite is true. On the stage regularly appear stage representations of the most famous events in the history of the country, sometimes modified by the introduction of legendary material, often keeping with reasonable accuracy to the progress of actual events. The very earliest Chinese play known in the West, *Chao shih ku erh* (*The Orphan of China*), from which Voltaire wrought his *L'orphelin de la Chine*, is of this kind. Although its most impressive scenes have a kind of 'domestic' quality, the main action, recording the brutal persecution of the Chao family by the wicked T'u Anku and the strange manner in which the little orphan is preserved to wreak his vengeance, has an historical flavour. Of such dramas *Hān koong tseu* (*The Sorrows of Hān*) may be taken as typical. The action is opened by some verses spoken by the Khan of the Tartars, Hanchenyu by name, followed by a simple prose statement of his position, the association of his tribes with China, and preceding political events. He has come to demand an alliance with Yuente, the Emperor, one of the Hān dynasty. Immediately thereafter enters the corrupt, self-seeking, and ambitious Minister Mao Yen-shou, who confesses that he has won his present position of importance by deliberately persuading his master to spend all his time, not with his counsellors, but with the women of the palace, and in a following conversation with the Emperor himself we hear him making arrangements for obtaining many pretty girls for the latter's enjoyment. After this prologue the first section, or act, of the play shows the Minister deliberately disfiguring a portrait of a beautiful maiden (who might have been introduced to the palace) because her father has no bribe to give him, and later comes a scene in which the Emperor chances to encounter this lady, Chao-chün by name, who has been brought to the royal household, but kept jealously from the eyes of the Emperor by his avaricious Minister. Order is given for the Minister's execution. In the second act the Khan reveals that the alliance has been refused; Mao Yen-shou enters—having escaped from the palace—and advises him to ask for Chao-chün by name; this message is transmitted to the Emperor, who is swayed by love on the one hand and on the other by fear of the Tartar host now on his borders. The sacrifice is made, but Chao-chün finds she cannot give herself to another and commits suicide. The fourth act shows the Emperor mourning in his palace:

EMPEROR: Since the princess was yielded to the Tartars, we have not held an audience. The lonely silence of night increases our melancholy. We take the picture of that fair one and suspend it here, as some small solace to our griefs. [*To the ATTENDANT*] Keeper of the yellow gate, behold, the incense in yonder vase is burnt out; hasten then to add some more——

Though we cannot see her, we may at least retain this shadow; and, while life remains, betoken our regard.

But oppressed and weary, we would fain take a little repose.

[*Lies down to sleep. The PRINCESS appears before him in a vision.*

PRINCESS: Delivered over as a captive to appease the barbarians, they would have conveyed me to their northern country: but I took an occasion to elude them, and have escaped back. Is not this the Emperor, my sovereign? Sir, behold me again restored.

[*A TARTAR SOLDIER appears in the vision.*

SOLDIER: While I chanced to sleep, the lady, our captive, has made her **escape, and returned home. In eager pursuit of her, I have reached the imperial palace. Is not this she?**

[*Carries her off. The EMPEROR starts from his sleep.*

EMPEROR: We just saw the princess returned—but, alas, how quickly has she vanished!—

In bright day she answered not to our call—but when morning dawned on our troubled sleep, a vision presented her in this spot. [*Hears a wild-fowl's cry.*] Hark, the passing fowl screamed twice or thrice!—Can it know there is one so desolate as I? [*Cries repeated.*] Perhaps worn out and weak, hungry and emaciated, they bewail at once over the broad nets of the south and the tough bows of the north. [*Cries repeated.*] The screams of those water-birds but increase our melancholy.

In bitter sorrow, he mourns, and finds satisfaction only in learning that the evil Minister has been captured. "Strike off the traitor's head," he cries,

and be it presented as an offering to the shade of the princess! Let a fit banquet be got ready for the envoy, preparatory to his return.

[*Recites these verses.*

> At the fall of the leaf, when the
> wild fowl's cry was heard in the
> recesses of the palace,
> Sad dreams returned to our lonely
> pillow; we thought of her
> through the night:
> Her verdant tomb remains—but where
> shall we seek herself?
> The perfidious painter's head shall
> atone for the beauty which he wronged.

One other example may be taken: in the Chinese repertoire no play is more famous than one which goes under a variety of names—*The Ch'ingting Pearl, Demanding the Fish-tax,* or *Fishing and Massacre*—but which is better titled (as it is by its translator, Yao Hsin-nung) *The Right to Kill.* There is at once appeal and an alienating sense of strangeness here. The idea that a poor man, exploited by those granted power beyond his own, has the right to take justice into his own hands is understandable, even if we may not accept the principle involved: what is alien is the Chinese concept that an entire family must be condemned for the excesses of one of its members. Central in this drama is an old fisherman, Hsiao En, with his daughter, Kuei-ying: desperately poor, he is compelled to pay to a local landowner an exorbitant tax on the fish he catches. So hard are his straits that he resists the landowner's minions by force, and as a result is severely punished by the law. In a scene by no means without crude emotional strength we are shown Hsiao En's final decision being made and the timorous, devoted complicity of his daughter:

> KUEI-YING: Father, you have suffered from injustice.
> HSIAO EN: You call this injustice! [*Vehemently*] In addition to this, that thief of a magistrate ordered me to go to Squire Ting's house to-morrow and beg his pardon. Then, I shall have a more complete injustice!
> KUEI-YING [*eagerly*]: Are you going or not?
> HSIAO EN: What are you talking—going or not! I only wish there were a pair of wings under my shoulders. [*Stares straight before him, with an upswelling rage.*] I want to fly! I want to *kill*——!!!

Terrified though she is, Kuei-ying insists on accompanying him. We see them going down to the river to their boat; in midstream her heart almost fails her, then once more she steels herself; they reach the big house and achieve their vengeance.

It is obvious that, while in these episodes resides an unquestioned emotional quality, the dramatic form itself has little to offer to Western playwrights. The Chinese plays possess charm—and, in their methods of production, inspirational quality—but in themselves they present no peculiar qualities likely to stimulate experiment in European tongues. The conventionalism is appealing, but fundamentally the method of outlining the plot is the same as that habitual in the West. For novelty of technical approach men had to wait until the Japanese Nō plays became available in translation.

3

THE JAPANESE DRAMA

IF THE conventionalism of the Chinese stage has made its impress felt during recent years, an even greater impress has been exerted by these Japanese Nō plays, which, still further stylized, possess the literary qualities lacking in the others. Since the appearance in 1921 of Arthur Waley's *The Nō Plays of Japan* the influence on many Western poets of this ancient aristocratic theatre has been widespread.

Kabuki: The Popular Drama

The Japanese playhouse presents to us two distinct types of entertainment. Of these the Kabuki is at once the more popular, the later in origin, and the less significant. Developed towards the beginning of the seventeenth century, to a certain extent it relates itself to the Chinese, although many of its conventions are utterly distinct and its general orientation is different.

For a stage the Kabuki actors use a platform which characteristically was at first surrounded by spectators on three sides. Into the midst of these spectators are thrust two narrow raised *hanamichi*, or 'flower-ways,' regularly used by the players for entrance upon the stage proper. By this means not only is the drama brought within the auditorium, but the acting-areas at the command of the performers are materially increased. As in China, so in Japan the property-man, clad in black, appears alongside the actors, performing much the same duties, although, in view of the greater amount of scenic display presented in Kabuki, employing methods of which the Chinese stage is ignorant.

This scenic display is of a peculiar kind. A great part of the action is, it is true, conducted by means of familiar, conventionalized movements and gestures. The actors indulge in make-up that is fully as complex and stylized as the Chinese. Villains are ruddy, heroes are basically white, but here too every line tells its story of age, social position, temperament, and even of the present situation in which the character may find himself. Many actions are carried out by means of expressive mimicry, without the use of properties. A duel may be fought in a kind of dance movement so that one sword sweeps close to, but never touches, the other; tea may be drunk from cups that are non-existent.

At the same time the Japanese spectators seek for more in the way of scenic decoration than that with which Chinese audiences are content. Behind the actors, in a kind of frame surmounted by a sloping roof, sets of a mixed realistic-conventional sort are presented to feast the eyes. By using a revolving stage and a complicated system of traps changes of locality can easily and quickly be effected, and in general no scene, whether interior or exterior, is permitted to be shown without an attempt to reproduce—mainly through the employment of flat wings—the semblance of reality.

In content and form the plays produced on this stage are, again like the Chinese, operatic, with chanted lyrics and the constant accompaniment of music. Some deal with subjects from common life; most are historical, with frequent use of the popular theme of the forty-seven Ronins. Among the many dramas produced for the Kabuki stage from its origins, and for the very closely related Joruri, or puppet stage, those of one author, Chikamatsu Monzaemon, have achieved something of an international reputation, although those who call him the Japanese Shakespeare perhaps permit their fancies somewhat to run away with them. With him is frequently associated a later prolific author, Takeda Izumo, who with his collaborators ran what amounted to a play-factory. What we do find in these works is melodrama, sensational tragi-comedy, and crude supernatural incident, inventive and vigorous, no doubt, but lacking in any qualities of greatness. Exciting scene is heaped on exciting scene in admirable confusion, and although here and there we come upon situations that make direct appeal, it must be confessed that most of this Kabuki playwriting is vulgar and lacking in true interest. From study of the highly traditional skill of the actors and of the exquisitely planned performances we may gain much of interest and profit, but from the dramas in which these actors appear there is little indeed that can be extracted of worth.

A few typical examples may serve to illustrate their scope. *Chushingura* (1748), written by Takeda Izumo along with a couple of coadjutors, tells in sensational wise the tale of the forty-seven Ronins. Starting with a scene in which a lord commits hara-kiri immediately after giving his final commands to Yuranosuke, the loyal retainer, it proceeds to narrate excitingly the adventures of this band of desperate, masterless men, moving from episode to episode with such bewildering rapidity that only those spectators especially well versed in the ancient legends or in national history could be expected to follow the action as a whole.

Perhaps because of this, many of these dramas seem to exist rather as a series of only slightly related scenes than as artistic wholes. They are written mainly for the purpose of providing opportunities for the actors, and, as the actor depends upon the scene rather than on the whole play for the demonstration of his traditional points, quite naturally emphasis is laid upon the action immediately before us at any one moment instead of upon the relationship between this action and situations following or preceding. Thus it is entirely possible to extract one episode from Takeda Izumo's lengthy *Sugawara denju tenarai kagami* (*Sugawara's Instruction in Calligraphy*), to call it *The Village School*, and treat it as a separate work. Its story is really complete in itself, narrating how Genzo, the faithful retainer of the exiled Sugawara Michizane, in order to protect and conceal the latter's son, disguises himself as a teacher and puts the boy among a group of others in the classroom. By force of circumstance he is compelled to produce the head of his pupil—for his enemies have become aware of the trick. Another retainer, however, with supreme loyalty, has brought his son to Genzo, prepared to allow him to be sacrificed in place of the heir of Sugawara. In a terrible yet intensely dramatic scene this retainer stands with the official while Genzo goes to a room within: a blow is heard and Genzo returns with a box. The retainer opens it, and, though what he sees within is his own son's head, he bravely asserts that this is the young prince. Sugawara's heir has been saved.

To what extent this episodic treatment extended is to be seen in Chikamatsu Monzaemon's classic *Kokusenya kassen* (*The Battles of Kokusenya*, 1710), in which appears a wild story of conflict, murder, treachery, loyalty, and torture. To and fro the events connected with a Chinese Emperor and his Ministers surge on the stage, introducing scenes of a brutal kind apt to turn the stomach of any Western audience, and finally bringing in the great Japanese hero, Watonai, son of the faithful Minister by a woman of Kyushu, a fearful avenging spirit, monstrous in a make-up of fierce black-and-red streaks. To wrest a sense of unity from such a work is a virtual impossibility.

Sometimes the themes embrace the world of the supernatural, as in *Yotsuya kaidan* (*Yotsuya's Ghost*), by Tsuruya Namboku. Here the beautiful neglected wife of Iyemon has her face hideously disfigured through a poison administered by another woman who is in love with her husband. Worn out by her miseries, O-Iwa commits suicide, and Iyemon marries again; but when he raises his new bride's veil, there is O-Iwa's disfigured countenance staring at him. Spectral visitation followed by spectral visitation eventually drives him to his end.

This drama, it is true, has a fairly direct and consecutive plot, but even when we encounter something of such a kind we cannot persuade ourselves that in these popular Japanese dramas is to be found anything likely to inspire fresh dramatic effort in the West. For that we must seek on the exclusively aristocratic Nō stage.

The Nō Plays

Developed during the fourteenth and fifteenth centuries by Kanami Kiyotsugu and his son Seami Motokiyo, the Nō drama was born of the temple, and in latter times became the pastime of the cultured nobility. Some of its elements were later assimilated into the popular Kabuki, but itself it retained all the exact and precise qualities of a specialized form, bound closely by rules rigorous and unbreakable.

The stage used for these Nō productions is of the simplest. About eighteen feet square, it is almost surrounded by the audience; on the right a narrow platform is designed for a singing chorus, at the rear is another platform for an orchestra. The dressing-room is a separate structure on the left, connected with the main stage by a passage, called the *hashigakari*, or bridge, along which the players make their appearances.

Probably because the performances originally took place in a grove, some small trees invariably are set on the *hashigakari*, or bridge, while the 'scenery' consists simply of a wooden panel at the rear, painted on one side with the representation of a pine-tree and on the other with bamboos. Three pine-branches are also attached to the *hashigakari*.

The costumes of the actors are rich and colourful, and the masks worn by the chief characters are marvels of artistry. Some of those made in early times have been preserved, either as heirlooms or as museum objects, and in them is exhibited a care and a skill which demonstrates the devoted, painstaking efforts that went to produce the polished and assured perfection for which the Nō performances are famous. The actors, all men, have been trained in their art from infancy; every smallest gesture is made to yield significance; by the subtlest movement of a fan an emotion is conveyed and an inner story revealed by a stylized movement of the arm. Although there are several officially recognized 'schools' of the Nō, all agree in insisting upon the utmost fidelity to traditional practice, partly handed down from actor-father to actor-son, partly described and codified in written texts. This traditional practice insists, like the Chinese, on the utmost of conventionalism, with the use of properties which merely suggest, and by no means represent, the real objects supposed to be involved in the action.

The effect created by these means is vividly suggested in a letter written by Oswald Sickert to Charles Ricketts in 1916. He is describing the performance of a play in which an angel, descending to earth, loses her flying robe:

> The best single moment I have seen was the dance of thanks to the fisherman who returns to the divine lady the Hagoromo, the robe without which even an angel cannot fly. It seemed to me an example of the excellent rule in art that, if a right thing is perhaps rather dull or monotonous lasting five minutes, you will not cure the defect by cutting the performance to two and a half minutes; rather give it ten minutes. If it's still perhaps rather dull, try twenty minutes or an hour. This presupposes that your limitations are right and that you *are* exploiting them. The thing may seem dull at first because at first it is the limitations the spectator feels; but the more these are exploited the less they are felt to be limitations, and the more they become a medium. The divine lady returned on her steps at great length and fully six times after I had thought I could not bear it another moment. She went on for twenty minutes, perhaps, or an hour or a night; I lost count of time; but I shall not recover from the longing she left when at last she floated backwards and under the fatal uplifted curtain.

Sickert's prose record of the impression made on a Western mind may be related to a poetic reflection by Eunice Tietjens occasioned by a similar performance:

> In a band of perfect silence the Noh dancer is coming.
>
> The air is still, stirred by the small sounds of the musicians, and the bar of afternoon sunlight between the stage and people is warm with overtones of sound.
> Yet the dancer has wrapped silence about him, and time stands back as he moves.
>
> On the narrow raised bridge he is between Here and There, between this world and the next.
>
> Presently, in an æon, when he has reached the stage, he will speak in a strange high treble, at once chant and wail. The words will be unintelligible. Even his own countrymen must know them to understand.
> Then he will be the spirit revenant, ghost of a dead princess, returned at moonrise to lead her lord to the shadow of Buddha.
>
> But now, on the narrow bridge, he is a presence only, a rhythm incarnate, abstraction visible.
> His rich brocaded silks flow stiffly, as stone might flow. The mask of the dead princess might be the moon, so pale, so eerily remote. . . .
>
> The gestures of his coming are complete, each in itself a whole. Perceptibly they shift into one, held into rhythm by his presence.
> Tidally he moves, slow as a planet, ultimate as beauty.
>
> In a band of perfect silence the Noh dancer comes.

Such an art obviously must depend upon not merely long individual training, but upon extensive tradition as well. The Nō stage is one that has passed down with only the barest of modifications from the time of its first development, and even the plays themselves are largely hallowed by antiquity. Of the eight hundred-odd extant scripts (of which about two hundred and fifty are regularly played) nearly half were written before the seventeenth century; compositions in the style of the older masters are still created in modern times, and numerous texts come from the eighteenth century, but Kwanami Kiyotsugu and Seami Motokiyo remain still the dominant literary figures in this composite form of artistry. The only thing, perhaps, that has fundamentally changed is the general appeal of the performance. Originally hieratic, and hence fairly widely popular, so that Seami could declare that "the perfect actor is he who can win certain praise alike in palaces, temples or villages, or even at festivals held in the shrines of the remotest provinces," the Nō productions have become almost exclusively aristocratic, even while retaining their antique forms.

These antique forms control even the plays' order of performance. Although now three pieces are usual in one 'bill,' originally tradition classified the Nō dramas into five categories and insisted that in one performance a play from each category, culled in a recognized order, must be presented, with a *kyōgen*, or humorous piece, separating each successive play from that which immediately precedes it. After a prefatory sketch, in which the sun-goddess is the main character, there first comes a play (*shura-mono*) in which the ghost of a warrior is presented, next one featuring some noble lady (*kazura-mono*), next a supernatural piece, and finally a play dealing with human passions or teaching some specific virtue.

In general, from two to six characters only are allowed to appear on the stage—the hero, or *shite*; his close companion, or *tsure*; the *waki*, or secondary character with his companion; a child (*kokata*); and, when necessary, a supplementary actor, or *ai*. Some of the plays have a structure which, albeit conventional and compressed, deals with their material in what may be called a normal dramatic manner. In these the regular form is for a *waki* to introduce an opening poetic couplet, to announce his identity, and to describe a journey in which he is engaged, and for the hero thereupon to make his appearance and engage in conversation with him, the events proceeding as though they took place in reality. In other dramas, however, appears a method far at variance with this, and so distantly removed from normal dramatic methods as to have made a deep impress on the minds of many modern poets. Here the dramatic action, as it were, unfolds itself in retrospect and, by the introduction of a ghost, joins past and present in one. It is this type of play that has laid deepest spell on the West during recent years.

An example both of the warrior drama and of this dramatic method appears in Seami's *Atsumori*. A priest, Rensei, enters and recites:

> Life is a lying dream, he only wakes
> Who casts the World aside.

In a succeeding speech he reveals that he had been a warrior who has become a priest because of the grief he suffers for the death of Atsumori, who had fallen in battle by his hand. He makes his conventional journey and encounters a chorus of reapers, with one of whom he stands talking. Suddenly this Reaper turns into the ghost of Atsumori. During their conversation the past reshapes itself imaginatively before our eyes; Atsumori's death is re-enacted. Just as Atsumori advances with sword upraised against his foe comes the chant of the chorus:

> "There is my enemy," he cries, and would strike.
> But the other is grown gentle
> And calling on Buddha's name
> Has obtained salvation for his foe;

So that they shall be re-born together
On one lotus-seat.
"No, Rensei is not my enemy.
Pray for me again, oh, pray for me again,"

A peculiar twilight atmosphere, wherein real and ideal become undistinguishable, breathes in the poetic action.

In all this, strange subdued emotional quality resides, as it does, to take another example, in Seami's *Hagoromo*, wherein a Fisherman, Hakuryō by name, picks up the feather robe of an Angel who has come down to earth. Pathetically the Angel pleads:

> Oh pitiful! How shall I cloakless tread
> The wing-ways of the air, how climb
> The sky, my home?
> Oh, give it back, in charity give it back.

At first obdurate, Hakuryō is at last moved by these entreaties. The Angel dances while the chorus records her flight until her form becomes faint,

> Mingled with the mists of heaven;
> Now lost to sight.

This is the drama that Sickert describes.

Hatsuyuki, by Komparu Zembō Motoyasu, tells the story of an Abbot's daughter who has a beloved white bird that she has named "Early Snow." It vanishes from its cage, and in grief its mistress sings a Mass in its memory, whereupon the bird's soul appears in the sky. "Look! Look!" the chorus cries,

> A cloud in the clear mid-sky!
> But it is not a cloud.
> With pure white wings beating the air
> The Snow-bird comes!
> Flying towards our lady
> Lovingly he hovers,
> Dances before her.

THE BIRD'S SOUL: Drawn by the merit of your prayers and songs.
CHORUS: Straightway he was reborn in Paradise.
　By the pond of Eight Virtues he walks abroad:
　With the Phœnix and Fugan his playtime passing.
　He lodges in the sevenfold summit of the trees of Heaven.
　No hurt shall harm him
　For ever and ever.
　Now like the tasselled doves we loose
　From battlements on holy days
　A little while he flutters;
　Flutters a little while and then is gone
　We know not where.

The subject-matter of these plays is various. Seami's *Haku Rakuten*

Contoured stripes as opposite

GORDON CRAIG:
DESIGN FOR
"MACBETH"
From *Theatre Arts
Monthly,*
November 1928.

ADOLPHE APPIA : DESIGN FOR "HAMLET"
From *Theatre Arts Monthly*, January 1925.

might be styled patriotic, since it shows the Chinese poet Haku Rakuten coming to Japan to subdue that country by the exercise of his art and driven back in his ship by the winds raised during a dance executed by the Japanese god of poetry and his companions. Many themes are Buddhistic, as, for example, *Ukai (The Cormorant Fisher)*, by Enami no Sayemon, in which a Priest rebukes a Fisherman for his cruel trade, and in which this Fisherman reveals himself as the ghost of Yama, the lord of hell. "Hell," he says,

> is not far away:
> All that your eyes look out on in the world
> Is the Fiend's home.

It is interesting to observe that, while such Buddhistic concepts form a staple theme of the Nō dramas, quite frequently these very concepts are chosen in the *kyōgen* for parody. Thus *Ukai* is burlesqued in *The Bird-catcher in Hell*, where Yama catches the evil bird-catcher Kiyoyori, who argues so well and gives the demon such a delicious tit-bit that he is sent back to earth to go on with his trade. As in other lands where burlesque has co-existed with serious effort, however, no farcical scenes of this kind take from the deeply imaginative serious appreciation of the deeper and profounder plays.

In this whole sphere of dramatic activity there is so much that is new, together with such a vivid poetic imagination, that we need not wonder at the way in which it has seized upon the spirit of Western artists.

The Conventionalism of the East

It is obvious, too, that the quality of the Nō drama, once appreciated, was of a kind likely to draw men's attentions to other different, though intimately related, theatrical activities of the Orient: to the Sanskrit drama and the Chinese, and, as well, to the entire vast realm of the marionette stage, which, spread over every Asiatic land, achieves its highest form in those half-lifesize Japanese puppets of the so-called Bunraku-za, which are so complex in their manipulation that each has to be controlled by no less than three or four individual attendants. Here, too, is a highly developed, intricate, conventional, and traditional technique, of the perfection of which numerous Western observers have written in glowing terms. "The artists," declares Paul Schiffer,

are so skilful in their manipulation and directing, in the profound godlike attitude they assume toward the creatures in their control, that after a moment they succeed in making us forget their own presence. . . . Delicately and with a sure touch, they pour their very being and whatsoever of thoughts they may have concerning life and human passions and human moods into the puppets which they move. . . . They do not hide, as we do, that they have to make a thousand movements; the puppets are always openly surrounded by these mechanical devices, and because of that they become uncanny. Before our eyes is clearly revealed the means by which the figure nods, rises angrily, throws a sharp glance to the side, or seems to laugh sneeringly. . . . The boundaries between mechanism and inspired existence are, as it were, obliterated.

For these marionettes plays are written not dissimilar from those composed for living actors: many of the dramatists, indeed, applied themselves to works of both kinds, and some of their works—among them the most famous of Chikamatsu Monzaemon's writings, the *Kokusenya kassen* (*The Battles of Kokusenya*)—are performed now on the puppet stage, now on that of the living actors.

The importance of the Oriental puppet theatre lies in the fact that it is, as it were, a concrete symbol of the conventionalism that has everywhere ruled, at least until latest times, on the stages of India, China, and Japan: and it is precisely this conventionalism that has made its appeal during the past few decades in the West. True, conventional forms have not made any very great incursions on to the commercial stages of Europe or America, yet the influence of the Orient has laid its hand upon the Western playhouse and is likely to inspire further stylized productions in the future. As will be seen, such a popular drama as Thornton Wilder's *Our Town* openly reveals the source of its being, while in the field of the poetic drama writers such as W. B. Yeats and Gordon Bottomley have been led, from study of Asiatic technique, to devise new technical devices suited to their own ends. In seeking for an escape from naturalism they have imaginatively started to explore the possibilities of that theatre which forms the utter antithesis of naturalism—and in this exploration they have discovered a method distinct from that of the Shakespearian. During the earlier romantic period the excitement over Kalidasa brought nothing new, for the style of Kalidasa's plays merely corroborated that of Shakespeare, Calderón, and Fletcher; in this latest interest in the theatre of the Orient is not subject-matter that has attracted attention, but basic dramatic form. To realize the impress the conventional stage has made on the modern mind we need only note Lion Feuchtwanger's adaptation of Sanskrit drama, Berthold Brecht's utilization of Chinese plays, and Paul Claudel's experimentation in the style of the Nō stage.

The force exerted by this Oriental theatre is well expressed in some passages of a private letter by Gordon Bottomley. Referring to the "dissociations and symbolisms" of the Nō dramas, "which have given a few poets hope for a renewed poetic drama in which poetry will master the form as well as content," he tells how, about the time of the First World War, these Japanese plays first impinged on his imagination and on the imagination of W. B. Yeats, and how they were made real by the demonstrations of ritual dramatic dance given in London by Ito. After he had been stirred to write his *Four Plays for Dancers* Yeats urged his friends to pursue this style further, with the ultimate result that both Bottomley and Laurence Binyon began, about the year 1927, to experiment in the writing of Japanese-inspired plays for John Masefield's garden theatre:

That stage lent itself to the Nō conceptions. In using it, our lack of a dancer could, we found, be replaced by an element of narrative poetry (thus integrating the poetic content of the stage more completely)—in the person of the Greek messenger.

Thus, in our times, was a deliberate effort made to naturalize an Oriental theatre related to the conventions of that theatre which is the fount of all Occidental drama, the theatre of Æschylus and Sophocles.

PART XI

ENTERING THE TWENTIETH CENTURY

ENTERING THE TWENTIETH CENTURY

THERE can be established, of course, no absolute break in Western dramatic affairs between the nineteenth and the twentieth centuries. The year 1900 by no means marks the end of the old and the beginning of something new; many dramatists, as has already been sufficiently indicated, whose most important works belong to the period before 1900 continued to produce work for the theatre after that date, while not a few, including among them no less a figure than George Bernard Shaw, whose chief contributions were made in the present era, had already approached the stage before the previous century had run its course.

At the same time, full justification does exist for making a pause at the century's end—even if only because Ibsen's last play came in the year 1899. With his departure from the scene new forces, adumbrated perhaps in the earlier years, found freedom of expression, and the theatres of 1920 had before them a variety of styles vastly different from those available to the dramatists of 1900 or of 1890. The first two decades of the new century saw the birth or the maturing of a considerable group of playwrights—Yeats and Synge, Benavente and Sierra, Gorki and Andreev, Lenormand and Bernard—who were destined to enrich the playhouse during the period immediately before or during the First World War, and whose influence was to lead the drama in new directions.

For the most part these first two decades of our century are a time of continual searching and of constant, violent experimentation. New ideas of stagecraft are now beginning to modify the prevailing trends towards the naturalistic and the colourful romantic. In 1895 Adolphe Appia, a Swiss artist and admirer of Wagner, published his *La mise en scène du drame Wagnérien*, and followed this, in 1899, with the more important *Die Musik und die Inscenierung*. Pleading for a theatrical art wherein light and basic form should be combined with the poet's words and the composer's music, he presented in these books a series of designs in which effects were to be secured through the placing on the stage of series of long, low platforms, essentially non-realistic, designed to offer full opportunities for the play of light. The year after the publication of *Die Musik und die Inscenierung* Gordon Craig produced Purcell's *Dido and Æneas* in London, thus launching his long, inspired efforts to startle his contemporaries to an appreciation of theatrical values beyond the realistic. His epoch-making volume *The Art of the Theatre* was issued five years later, the first of a series of studies in which, with fervent enthusiasm, burning words, and soaring imagination, he pleaded for the theatre theatrical.

While neither Appia nor Craig succeeded in making much direct impact on the commercial playhouse within these years, the ideas they expressed were finding reflection in a diversity of quarters. The Moscow Art Theatre, born of the enthusiasm of Stanislavski and Nemirovich-Danchenko, opened its doors in 1897; Jacques Copeau's Théâtre du Vieux Colombier was established in 1913; the famous Granville-Barker seasons at the Court Theatre were inaugurated in 1904; in Germany and Austria Max Reinhardt gave opportunity to dozens of young men eager to present new stage ideas; during the first years of the century Meyerhold was striving to find a fitting medium for his anti-naturalistic visions. Although these various activities assumed many contrasting forms, and although some (such as the work of the Moscow Art Theatre) seemed to be engaged in furthering the cause of the naturalistic, in effect they all combined in enlarging, extending, and pressing beyond the sphere of nineteenth-century realism. The typical independent theatre of the nineties fixed its gaze on the naturalistic presentation of the darker sides of existence; the typical independent theatre at the beginning of the twentieth century was largely engaged in the exploitation of the beautiful and the artistically conventional.

Especially noteworthy during these years is the growth of the repertory theatre, particularly in the English-speaking countries. In effect these playhouses marked a realization on the part of those truly interested in the stage of the peculiar needs of the modern period. Until the second half of the nineteenth century 'provincial' towns had been fairly well served by a widespread, sometimes crude, but always vigorous ring of stock-company theatres and of accompanying touring 'circuits.' Here young men and women planning to devote themselves to the boards might win experience; hereby audiences throughout the country were kept acquainted with the best the metropolitan theatres had to offer. From the recognition that with the disappearance of these older stock-company traditions a great void had been left in the world of the stage, the impulse towards the establishment of the repertory playhouse —generally associated in the first instance with the enthusiastic devotion of amateurs—took its being. The first years of the twentieth century show this impulse in its primal, formative period, while the century's second decade presents it in the full flush of excited achievement. In England the Birmingham Repertory Theatre opened its doors in 1913, just before the outbreak of war, while in America those stages which were to be responsible for the arising of O'Neill came in the very midst of international hostilities.

Mention of O'Neill reminds us that these repertory ventures exerted great influence on playwriting during this time. Again and again we meet with authors whose genius was first fed by the enthusiastic support of some non-commercial theatre. The flowering of Chekhov is associated with the Moscow Art Theatre; Synge comes from Dublin's Abbey; Shaw originally finds an audience among the members of the Independent Stage Society; O'Neill in his youth acts and writes for the Provincetown Players; while both in England and America there begins to emerge, largely sponsored by the little theatres, a long line of local playwrights who seek to exploit the events and characters of the diverse areas in which they live.

The twentieth century, therefore, introduces us to the development of a new theatrical force—the non-commercial stage—which, although shadowed forth during the final years of the nineteenth century, finds fruition only in our own times. In any survey of the contemporary drama the significance of this force must be kept fully in mind.

1

THE RELICS OF THE OLDER REALISM

IN THE commercial playhouses during these years, and even in some advanced playhouses, the earlier styles of realism still attracted wide attention. What had been the cult of the intelligentsia of the nineties gradually became the joy of a larger public, and in some areas where 'Ibsenism' had barely made an impact even on the more progressive the realistic medium was taken up with all the enthusiasm that comes from the delight of discovery. Thus such plays as *A Doll's House* and *Ghosts*, which had been caviare to the general at the time of their composition, came to be accepted without qualms by a later theatre-going public, while the slowly emergent drama of the United States (to take the most characteristic example), which had so far remained only slightly touched by the revolutionary movements in Europe, found its first inspiration at this time from cultivation of the realistic style. In surveying the fortunes of the stage between 1900 and 1920 it is important to remember that all the many experiments in new forms were set, as it were, against the solid background of 'Ibsenism.'

The English Contribution

In England Pinero and Jones, rather sentimentally and without any singular boldness of purpose, had essayed the new form before the opening of the century, and both pursued their dramatic careers in the years immediately following. Their efforts, however, were soon outdistanced by others, and notably by John Galsworthy, who exhibited the rare ability of mastering the divergent techniques of the vast canvas of fiction and of the more economic way of the stage.

Galsworthy's plays are thoroughly typical of what the realistic mood meant to England. There is no violent *Tobacco Road* atmosphere here; there is no self-tortured misery of the kind purveyed by Strindberg; there is no sensationalism of effect: no brutal villain darkens with his shadow the scenes of this author's plays; no doctrinaire preachments colour the development of the action. In Galsworthy we find a perfect mastery of the naturalistic method, a compassionate depiction of humanity, a fine humanitarianism of spirit. Although one of the most famous of his plays effected much-needed reforms in the penal code, his dramas are not designed to argue any case, and it is indeed ironic that, where so many of the Continental plays of ideas passed by without materially influencing the ways of society, *Justice* should be a prime example of a drama which wrought a mighty change in social conditions.

Galsworthy first came to the notice of the playgoing public in 1906 with the production of *The Silver Box*, in which he established a contrast between the comfortable, fashionable household of Mr Barthwick, a thoroughly respectable Member of Parliament, and that of Mrs Jones, the charwoman. Barthwick's son, Jack, is a scapegrace who steals a girl's purse; Mrs Jones' husband, bringing Jack home after a debauch, steals a silver box. In the one case a cheque easily settles the matter; in the other the law is set heavily in motion. In telling this story Galsworthy never permits the introduction of any direct comment, nor does he darken any of his characters in order to point a lesson. Characteristically, he simply sets forward the theme with as exact faithfulness to reality as he can: we are made aware that there is one law for the rich and one for the poor, but that does not imply by any means that Barthwick is a villain or Jones a blameless hero. Similarly, Galsworthy refuses to admit the easy solution of a suicide (so beloved of the German authors) and the absurd attempt to weave a tragic pattern out of untragic material: his play is frankly and professedly a 'drama,' and gains in strength from recognition of the limitations of its kind.

In *Justice* (1910) we may perhaps detect more of a burning emotion, yet even here, where the dramatist's anger is obviously aroused, the method remains the same. In the central figure, William Falder, we are given no 'hero'; instead we have a weak-willed, ineffective little law-clerk who falls pathetically in love with a married woman, forges a cheque in order to obtain money wherewith to go off with her to South America, and is arrested. Condemned to prison, he is put in solitary confinement, and here Galsworthy introduces the wordless scene which so startled contemporaries:

> *FALDER'S* cell, a whitewashed space thirteen feet broad by seven deep, and nine feet high, with a rounded ceiling. The floor is of shiny blackened bricks. The barred window, with a ventilator, is high up in the middle of the end wall. In the middle of the opposite end wall is the narrow door. In a corner are the mattress and bedding rolled up (two blankets, two sheets, and a coverlet). Above them is a quarter-circular wooden shelf, on which is a Bible and several little devotional books, piled in a symmetrical pyramid; there are also a black hairbrush, tooth-brush, and a bit of soap. In another corner is the wooden frame of a bed, standing on end. There is a dark ventilator under the window, and another over the door. *FALDER'S* work (a shirt to which he is putting button-holes) is hung to a nail on the wall over a small wooden table, on which the novel "Lorna Doone" lies open. Low down in the corner by the door is a thick glass screen, about a foot square, covering the gas-jet let into the wall. There is also a wooden stool, and a pair of shoes beneath it. Three bright round tins are set under the window.
>
> In fast-failing daylight, *FALDER*, in his stockings, is seen standing motionless, with his head inclined towards the door, listening. He moves a little closer to the door, his stockinged feet making no noise. He stops at the door. He is trying harder and harder to hear

something, any little thing that is going on outside. He springs suddenly upright—as if at a sound—and remains perfectly motionless. Then, with a heavy sigh, he moves to his work, and stands looking at it, with his head down; he does a stitch or two, having the air of a man so lost in sadness that each stitch is, as it were, a coming to life. Then turning abruptly, he begins pacing the cell, moving his head, like an animal pacing its cage. He stops again at the door, listens, and, placing the palms of his hands against it with his fingers spread out, leans his forehead against the iron. Turning from it, presently, he moves slowly back towards the window, tracing his way with his finger along the top line of the distemper that runs round the wall. He stops under the window, and, picking up the lid of one of the tins, peers into it, as if trying to make a companion of his own face. It has grown very nearly dark. Suddenly the lid falls out of his hand with a clatter—the only sound that has broken the silence—and he stands staring intently at the wall where the stuff of the shirt is hanging rather white in the darkness—he seems to be seeing somebody or something there. There is a sharp tap and click; the cell light behind the glass screen has been turned up. The cell is brightly lighted. FALDER is seen gasping for breath.

A sound from far away, as of distant, dull beating on thick metal, is suddenly audible. FALDER shrinks back, not able to bear the sudden clamour. But the sound grows, as though some great tumbril were rolling towards the cell. And gradually it seems to hypnotize him. He begins creeping inch by inch nearer to the door. The banging sound, travelling from cell to cell, draws closer and closer; FALDER'S hands are seen moving as if his spirit had already joined in this beating, and the sound swells till it seems to have entered the very cell. He suddenly raises his clenched fists. Panting violently, he flings himself at his door, and beats on it.

THE CURTAIN FALLS

This scene, entirely devoid of dialogue, indicates both Galsworthy's own inventive power and the general manner in which the elaborated, 'literary' stage direction, introduced by Ibsen for the purpose of giving realistic background to his characters, was being further developed in the twentieth century. The year before *Justice* appeared Galsworthy had produced his *Strife* (1909), a drama in which again he displays his broad humanitarian sympathies and his wise impartiality. In *Justice* there was no blackening of those responsible for Falder's imprisonment—indeed, there are scenes in that drama obviously planned for the purpose of being utterly fair to such persons as the Governor of the gaol: similarly, in *Strife* the claims of workers and of masters alike are presented with sympathy, the whole drama being designed to show the fatal consequences and the waste resultant from the strife between them. Galsworthy's world knows few villains and few heroes: over all his characters he broods with understanding and pity, baffled by the circumstances that produce misery and disaster without the active operation of human evil.

All his plays have a kindred atmosphere, even as he turns from aspect to aspect of the little universe around him. When he tries to plead too strongly for a particular individual, as he does in *The Pigeon* (1912), *The Fugitive* (1913), and *The Mob* (1914), he seems a trifle out of his element, but when he essays, as in his one-act *The Little Man* (1915) and *Loyalties* (1922), to present his broad, kindly philosophy—the philosophy of the humanitarian gentleman—he exhibits a quality all too frequently lacking in this age of fierce conflicts and melodramatic concepts—applied, not as they properly may be in the theatre, but disastrously in terms of real life.

Along with him stands Harley Granville-Barker, a man of similar broad sympathies and one who vitally influenced the stage by his creative literary efforts, by his new visions of what should be the functions of the theatrical producer, and by his alert critical studies. Starting with an unimportant *The Weather Hen* (written in collaboration with Berte Thomas, 1899), he brought forward during the first decade of the century four particularly interesting plays—*The Marrying of Ann Leete* (1902), *The Voysey Inheritance* (1905), *Waste* (1907), and *The Madras House* (1910)—in all of which he sought to extend the realistic form beyond its Ibsenite bounds. All incline to neglect plot in favour of atmosphere and character: indeed, basically, their stories are of no importance. Ann Leete shocks social conventions because she, well-born, marries her gardener; Mr Voysey, a prosperous solicitor, is found by his son to owe his fortune to the result of successful gambling with his clients' money; a young politician is ruined when his mistress dies in trying to destroy the child he has given her: such are the simple themes Granville-Barker deals with; yet the general impression we have of his plays, because of the subtle detail introduced by the author, is one of complex structure rather than of simplicity.

There can be no doubt but that here realism is carried almost to its extreme verge, yet it is interesting to observe that for such a writer as Granville-Barker realism was not enough. In 1904 he wrote, in collaboration with Laurence Housman, the delicately idealistic *Prunella*; later came *Rococo* (1911) and *The Harlequinade* (in collaboration with D. C. Calthrop, 1913); later still, in *The Secret Life* (1923), the outer is sacrificed completely for the inner vision. Beyond that, Granville-Barker the critic has shown in many essays that his true ideal is, not the realistic prose drama, but the drama of poetic concept. No clearer example could be found of realism's shattering of its own confining walls.

Within these years many other authors, with varying degrees of success, explored the reaches of the realistic social stage, most of them, however, tending to deal rather with provincial life than with studies of a more general kind. The use of dialect, the association of the events with a particular limited area, best harmonized with their purposes and at the same time met the needs of the slowly arising local 'repertory theatres.' From Northern Ireland came St John Ervine with his *Mixed Marriage* (1911), a kind of modern realistic *Romeo and Juliet*, in which the son of a fanatic Orangeman falls in love with a Catholic girl; *Jane Clegg* (1913), a study of a woman who, after trying her best to act as helpmeet to her spineless husband, eventually is forced for the sake of her own self-respect to leave him; and *John Ferguson* (1915), a powerful, unremittingly grim and dark picture of a sternly religious man, whose whole life is ruled by faith in God and the Bible, but who suddenly finds himself, in his old age, overwhelmed by unexpected disasters: at the end, he is miserably shattered, yet still inflexibly constant in his belief.

In England itself the 'repertory' playwrights eagerly essayed the form. St John Hankin produced, among other theatrical writings, *The Cassilis Engagement* (1907), a much-discussed drama of ideas in which a wise mother, objecting to her son's choice of a fiancée, invites the girl for a week-end to her home, guessing that the discrepancy between her ways and theirs will result in the breaking of the match. With her *Chains* (1909) Elizabeth Baker travelled into a London suburb to draw a depressing picture of a poor little clerk whose visions of escape are thwarted by his wife's announcement that she is to bear a child. Famous in his time was Stanley Houghton, whose *The Younger Generation* (1910) is a cynical study of puritanical middle age in conflict with oat-sowing youth, and whose *Hindle Wakes* (1912) fluttered conventional circles by introducing a determined young 'new woman' of the working class who goes off for a week-end with the son of a factory-owner and then refuses to marry him even when both her parents and the parents of the youth are determined that marriage is the only honourable solution for her escapade.

Particularly memorable among these plays are *Hobson's Choice* (1915) by Harold Brighouse, a comedy which still is eminently stageworthy; *Milestones* (1912) by Arnold Bennett and Edward Knoblock, interesting because of its innovating 'generations' theme; *Rutherford and Son* (1912), by Githa Sowerby, with its effective study of the spirit of bleakness that comes from industrialism; *A Bill of Divorcement* (1921) by Clemence Dane (Winifred Ashton), a once-popular and impressive drama on a current social problem; and *The Mollusc* (1907), by H. H. Davies, a well-constructed comedy-drama, both penetrating and delightfully amusing.

The Playwrights of France, Russia, and Spain

There can be no doubt but that the English contributions to the realistic stage during the first two decades of the present century were materially finer in both craftsmanship and concept than those made by their predecessors during the latter years of the century previous—and this even omitting the works of Sir J. M. Barrie and George Bernard Shaw, which, although closely associated with the work of the realistic movement, are obviously of a kind different from that of *Chains* or *Justice*. Yet, when we survey the entire field of the drama at this time it is obvious that the primal force of the older realism was spent. The truth of this assertion is amply apparent when we turn to survey the work of authors in France, Germany, and Scandinavia.

Many of the dramas penned by the French playwrights already examined were, of course, written after 1900. At the same time it is possible, and for critical purposes desirable, to differentiate those authors who had already established their reputations during the last century from others who first came to recognition in our own era. Of the latter group there are many, and only a few of these can here be singled out for mention.

The Franco-Belgian Henry Kistemaeckers may be taken first, not because of the worth of his plays, but because he was the purveyor of popular pieces in which a dash of the drama of ideas was used to flavour well-made works fashioned according to the old nineteenth-century formulas. *La flambée* (*The Blaze*, 1912) might have been written by Sardou, and his other pieces demonstrate clearly that, despite the achievements of Antoine's Théâtre Libre, there was an ample public for the exhibition of scenes in which no more of 'reality' was presented than might serve to give a surface appearance of life. Just a trifle deeper is the work of Henry Bernstein, an author who knows all the tricks of the stage and who skilfully can combine a suggestion of a problem with melodramatic incident. The modern Scribe, he can turn out a sensational *Le voleur* (*The Thief*, 1906) or direct his hand to the exploitation of current psychology, as in *L'élévation* (*The Height*, 1917) or *Mélo* (1929); he is at home in many theatrical realms.

Bernstein's style, though effective, is apt to be sensationally heavy; that of Alfred Savoir is treacherously light, the bright play of a rapier with point sometimes buttoned, sometimes sharply dangerous; while in Alfred Capus appears an ironic resignation concealed by outward jesting. There is more than meets the eye in such brittle plots as serve *Brignol et sa fille* (*Brignol and his Daughter*, 1894)—a tale of how a man near financial ruin is saved when his daughter happens to fall in love with, and marry, his chief creditor's nephew—or *Monsieur Piégois* (1905). The same ironic jesting appears in *L'habit vert* (*The Green Uniform*, 1912), by Gaston-Armand de Caillavet and Robert de Flers, with its mixture of the triangle theme and satire directed against the Academicians. A lighter cynicism colours the writings of Romain Coolus (René Weil). Something of the same admixture of apparent triviality and inner depth gives quality to many of the plays contributed to the French stage by Pierre Wolff and Georges Courteline. Outwardly their plays may resemble such popular farces as were being currently produced by a Tristan Bernard or a Georges Feydeau, but spiritually they are born of a different mood.

In the eternal triangle Félix-Henry Bataille finds his opportunity for the writing of plays outwardly more serious: play after play he turns out with variants on the same theme—extending from *Maman Colibri* in 1904, on through *La femme nue* (*The Naked Woman*, 1908) and *L'Amazone* (*The Amazon*, 1916), to *La chair humaine* (*Human Flesh*, 1922)—a rather tedious collection of pieces monotonously beating the same rhythm on the erotic drum. True, he varies the environment of his plots, as in *Ton sang* (*Thy Blood*, 1897), where the appearance of novelty is given by the fact that the heroine is blind and that the lovers are brothers, but the central theme is nearly always the same. And often the inner action is accompanied by outer violence, as in *La marche nuptiale* (*The Wedding March*, 1905), where an aristocratic girl, marrying her piano-teacher, finds him wanting and dismally commits suicide. Émile Fabre is more obviously the follower of Becque and Brieux. *Le bien d'autrui* (*The Property of Others*, 1897) presents an idealistic young hero who, on discovering that some property left to him was given in a later will to another, and after searching in vain for a means of giving it to the one whom he regards as its rightful owner, proposes to hand it over to the Government. Political ambition dominates in *Les vainqueurs* (*The Conquerors*, 1908), where the central figure is a man who, to further his ends, is content to indulge in blackmail and to accept a sum of money from the lover of his own wife. Seriousness of purpose, with a definitely 'labour' slant, characterizes, too, the plays of Octave Mirbeau, as represented, for example, by *Les affaires sont les affaires* (*Business is Business*, 1903), which shows a wealthy industrialist engaged in seeking means of adding to his wealth even while his domestic life is crashing about him. No less serious, though not so socialistic in his attitude, is Jean Jullien, whose *L'écolière* (*The Girl Student*, 1901) carries the style of Brieux into other realms.

This record of realism on the Paris stage is not exciting, nor is it bettered by the German theatre. The Austrian part of Poland, however, produced Tadeusz Rittner, author of *W małym domku* (*In the Little House*, 1904), the sad tale of a young provincial doctor and his wife, who showed himself gifted with a gentle talent somewhat akin to that of Schnitzler. In Scandinavia the great wave, although losing its earlier power, still had some force. In Norway Nils Kjaer produced a successful satiric *Lykkelige valg* (*The Happy Choice*, 1914) and Oskar Braaten won esteem for his *Ungen* (*The Little Child*, 1915), while about the same time the Swedish Tor Hedberg presented a strong *Johan Ulfstjerna* (1907), telling the tale of a Finnish patriot, and in *Gertrud* (1906) Hjalmar Söderberg wrote a tense drama of the sexes which for the darkness of its spirit almost rivalled the frenzies of Strindberg. Writing in Swedish, the Finnish Mikall Dybeck infused into the Ibsenian formula a peculiarly poetic spirit of his own, but one too national in inspiration to bear transference abroad. Denmark gave the theatre one writer of talent, Gustav Wied, but even his best plays, such as *Dansemús* (*Dancing Mice*, 1905), can be accepted as no more than second-rate and rather precious. Reminiscent of Ibsen and wholly lacking Ibsen's subtlety is the style of *En martyr* (*A Martyr*, 1896), by another Danish author, Sven Lange, while Hjalmar Bergström develops further the Ibsenian concept of the 'new woman,' who can have her fun if she wants to, in *Karen Borneman* (1907). More primitive passion is infused by the Icelandic Gudmundur Kamban into his *Hadda Padda* (1914), a love-story in which attempted murder is followed by suicide, and into his *Vi mordere* (*We Murderers*, 1920). Surveying the Scandinavian stage as a whole during these years, we realize that most of its vitality went into plays of fantastic, historical, or poetic style rather than into dramas of realism.

In Belgium the current vogue of realism produced the plays of Gustave

Vanzype and influenced the writing of Paul Spaak. The romantic meets, and clashes with, the realistic in the dramas of the Latvian Jānis Rainis. Ibsen's influence is clearly marked on the Greek playwright Gregori Xenopoulos, and it crosses the oceans to cast its spell on the Uruguayan Florencio Sánchez and Ernesto Herrera. In none of these, however, do we encounter much, if anything, of permanent and general value.

In Italy Enrico Annibale Butti, who had early essayed the Ibsenite path with *La fine di un ideale* (*The End of an Ideal*, 1898), and who had drawn in *La corsa al piacere* (*The Race for Pleasure*, 1900) a vivid picture of a life devoid of spiritual aims, produced in 1904 his by no means negligible *Fiamme nell' ombra* (*Flames in Darkness*), a study of a pious priest and his sister impatient of convention. As in *Il vortice* (*The Vortex*, 1892) and *L'Utopia* (1894), Butti's philosophy suggests that it is wiser for man to accept than to beat against society's conventions.

The only other Italian 'realistic' author of the time who deserves mention is Dario Niccodemi, and his work can hardly be accepted as anything save the purveying of popular sensationalism with a veneer of *verismo*. An accomplished craftsman, he succeeded by knowing well how to compromise: a cosmopolitan, who could as easily pen a play in French as in Italian, he provided for the public dozens of dramas in which current stage fashions were adroitly dished up in pleasing or thrilling forms. *L'aigrette*, for example, composed in 1912 specifically for production in Paris, and translated by the author for the first Italian performance in the following year, is a somewhat sensational satire in which the 'aigrette' worn habitually by the Countess of Saint-Servan is regarded by her son, Henri, as a symbol of their family honour. Actually the Countess finds it impossible to keep up her estate and indulges in divers tricks to obtain money; in particular she persuades Madame Leblanc, the wife of a banker, to 'lend' her money. This lady has young Henri as her lover, and in the discovery of the Countess's financial intrigues he is so shocked out of his complacency and so involved in a situation of apparently inevitable disaster that only a violent wrenching of the plot enables the author to bring his curtain down on a stage not darkened by suicide or death in duel. Typical of Niccodemi's writing at its best is his achievement in *L'alba, il giorno, e la notte* (*Dawn, Noon, and Night*, 1921), where he keeps three entire acts alive with interest although only two characters, Anna and Mario, are on the stage. At dawn, in a forest, Mario meets a girl and follows her to her house: from their conversation it emerges that he is about to fight a duel with a man with whom he has quarrelled because he had insisted he had seen a ghost in the wood; now it turns out that this 'ghost' was Anna. At noon Mario turns up and expresses his astonishment at finding her, instead of wracked with anxiety on his behalf, engaged in eating lunch; since she has found out that before leaving for the duel he has written a letter to a certain Marion, her replies are tinged with asperity, while he displays jealousy on believing that she is affianced to a certain Paolino. In anger, Mario departs, but, returning at night, he declares his love and is accepted; all the causes of daytime quarrel are found to have been mere figments: Marion never had any existence and Paolino is a brother, not a lover.

Without doubt Niccodemi possesses extreme skill in weaving his scenes delicately together; his dialogue is vividly precise; and he succeeds in presenting lively pictures of the bourgeois world of his time. We cannot, however, place him very high among dramatic authors: he is of the company of the talented, not of the geniuses. A slightly greater interest attaches to one play, *Addio, giovinezza!* (*Adieu, Youth!*, 1911), by Sandro Camasio and Nino Oxilia, but even this capably written and thoughtful study of adolescent intrigue set against a darker background displays little of the quality demanded of greatness. The truth is, of course, that realism of this sort ill-suited the Italian spirit and consequently yielded few fruitful results.

Two countries only have much to offer in this style. In Russia Tolstoi's mantle was cast on the shoulders of Maxim Gorki (Alexei Maxsimovich Peshkov), who, after one or two early experiments, succeeded in fashioning out of the bitterness of his heart the one work by which he will assuredly continue to be known. *Na dne* (*The Lower Depths*, 1902) hardly resembles in technique any of the realistic plays of the earlier years, save, perhaps, Tolstoi's *The Power of Darkness*. It is not described by its author as a drama: rather he prefers to follow the Ostrovski tradition and styles it "Scenes from Russian Life." In these scenes the author descends to "a basement resembling a cavern," where a miserable group of waifs of all ages are wretchedly huddled together. Of plot there is virtually nothing; of plots there are many. The only real 'story' in the work is that which concerns Vassili, who, having an affair with Vaska, the wife of the lodging-house keeper Kostilev (Mishka), is persuaded to leave her and go off with her sister, Natasha: angered, Vaska comes to blows with Natasha, and Vassili, trying to protect the girl, accidentally kills Kostilev. If, however, this is the only apparent plot, Gorki has succeeded in presenting us with an entire series of stories connected with his characters. Imaginatively, from the hints given to us, we follow the degeneration of the broken-down actor until he has reached this pit of horror; we fill in the grim biographies of the out-of-work locksmith Kleshch and his consumptive wife, Anna, of the 'Baron' and the prostitute Nastia, of Kvashnia, the market woman, of Aliosha, the shoemaker. Into this group of cold and hungry derelicts comes an elderly pilgrim, Luka, and it is through him that most of the atmosphere is revealed. His wanderings have given him a philosophy of life. "We're all pilgrims in this world," he says. "I've heard tell that even the globe we're on is just a pilgrim in the heavens." His secret is revealed when he answers the dying Anna:

ANNA: My name is Anna . . . When I look at you . . . you are so much like my own father . . . my own dear father . . . you, too, are so kind and soft . . .
LUKA: The world has kneaded me for a long time, that's why I'm soft.

He knows all the despair of life, yet hope is still in him. "Human beings?" he asks. "They will find. He who seeks will find. He who earnestly desires will find!" Yet in the end Luka's words are at variance with reality; nothing is found here; these wretched creatures have passed through a night of misery, and their misery stretches on into an indefinite future.

In *The Lower Depths* Gorki produced a masterpiece, but, unfortunately, not so much may be said of his later writings for the stage. None is without interest, none without that peculiar bitter strength which was his greatest characteristic, yet not one of his other plays quite captures the magnificent quality that gives to this drama its unique distinction. Against the cosmopolitan intellectuals he directed his *Dachniki* (*Summer Visitors*, 1904), declaring in it that these men, instead of being integrated in Russian life, were merely tourists in their native land. In *Deti solntsia* (*Children of the Sun*, 1905) he turned, rather futilely, to a mixture of an ordinary domestic theme and a larger political problem. Class conflict is the theme of *Vragi* (*Enemies*, 1906), wherein an attempt is made to demonstrate that inevitably an impassable chasm separates capitalists and workers. In *Starik* (*The Old Man*, or *The Judge*, 1915) he wrote a sombre drama showing a man with another (a former fellow-convict) in his power; the latter is driven remorselessly to his death. Plays of these kinds came from his pen between the beginning of the century and the time of the First World War, all interesting and all essentially mediocre.

Then, almost three decades after the composition of *The Lower Depths*, came *Egor Bulichov i drugie* (*Egor Bulichov and Others*, 1932), in which some of his old magic, but by means of a different formula, was recaptured. This play is designed to present a picture of the collapse of the middle class on the approach of the Revolution. Taking as central figure the capitalist Egor Bulichov, Gorki shows the inherent rottenness pervading the Russian society of the time immediately preceding the outbreak of civil violence. For Bulichov we cannot help feeling some admiration: he is a man of character, will, and ability; but his riches are the result of exploitation; the cancer from which he suffers does not prevent him from seeking to add to his wealth; around him are none save fools and leeches. His relatives are self-seeking and credulously stupid; the Church eagerly eyes his fortune. Although the settings are vastly different from that degrading basement in which the lowest depths were reached, the spiritual atmosphere is no less wretched and despairing. Only towards the close of the drama does a note of hope approach. As the dying Egor stands at his window the singing of revolutionaries can be heard from the streets: for him it is an ironic requiem.

Egor Bulichov and Others was planned by its author as the first part of a great trilogy, representing dramatically the early course of the Revolution. That trilogy was rudely broken by Gorki's death: whether it could have been successfully carried out to completion if he had lived we cannot tell, but certainly the second portion, *Dostigaev i drugie* (*Dostigaev and Others*, 1933), displays nothing of the vigour of its predecessor. As a record of historical events it is interesting; drama, however, to be great needs to be more than mere record, and it must be confessed that of true dramatic vigour this last of Gorki's plays has nothing to give to us.

Apart from Gorki's plays, the naturalistic style inspired no notable works on the Russian stage. There was one realistic writer, it is true, Michael Petrovich Artsibashev, whose writings once had a scandalous success, but he has long been forgotten. The hysterical exploitation of frantic eroticism and sensational episode that luridly illuminates *Revnost* (*Jealousy*, 1913) is not of a sort destined to endure: it is easy to see why when these works were new they excited young men's minds; it is equally easy, now, to discern their inherent absurdity.

To turn from Gorki and Artsibashev in Russia to Sierra and Benavente in Spain is to journey from the bitter North to the warmth of the South. Jacinto Benavente y Martínez in fertility almost equalled the records set by Lope de Vega and his followers. (It would be interesting to inquire and to discover, if possible, why the greater Spanish dramatists have been granted so overwhelmingly fecund talents as to make the totality of their works far outdistance the writings of any of their contemporaries in other countries.) From the year 1892, when four short pieces were issued under the general title of *Teatro fantástico*, he has contributed hundreds of diverse dramas to the stage, some of them, it is true, adapted from the plays of other writers, but most of his own invention. Here is Dionysus' plenty—plays short and plays long, plays romantic and plays realistic, farces and fairy-plays, plays sentimental and plays static.

The very variety of Benavente's contributions to the stage indicates that he is no faithful follower of the realistic tradition. Rather might it be said that on the stock of the traditional vigorous Spanish poetic drama he grafts the twig of Ibsen and his followers. His quality, therefore, depends less on his pursuit of the realistic problem play in itself than upon the strength that comes to him from outside that particular sphere; and this fact reminds us that Gorki too owed his power largely to his inheriting, from Ostrovski and Tolstoi, a theatrical form which may have run parallel with but ever remained essentially distinct from the line leading back to the Scandinavian authors and the French problem dramatists.

Even to enumerate the titles of all Benavente's plays would occupy several pages of this volume, and consequently nothing more can be done here than to indicate in general terms the main characteristics of his dramatic work. First is to be noted in him an element of the fantastic, the love for which no doubt led him towards an appreciative interest in the Oriental stage, expressed in such writings as *El dragón de fuego* (*The Fire Dragon*, 1903), inspired by an Indian theme, and *La túnica amarilla* (*The Yellow Jacket*, 1916), adapted from Benrimo's Chinese drama. This fantastic element already was expressed in his first dramatic writings; among the four dramas making up the *Teatro fantástico* is *El encanto de una hora* (*The Magic of an Hour*), which uses the device of animating some statuettes and of playing with their cold passions until one, attempting to kiss the lady of his choice, chips a piece out of her cheek. Throughout Benavente's career the mood that produced this one-act sketch continued to flower, giving us now the *Cuento de amor* (*The Love-story*, 1899), adapted from *Twelfth Night*, now *La princesa sin corazón* (*The Heartless Princess*, 1907), no *El hijo de Polichinela* (*The Son of Pulcinella*, 1927) and *La novia de nieve* (*The Snow Bride*, 1934).

From these it is but a step to the romanticized, artificial, and sentimental comedies of manners represented by *La Princesa Bebé* (*Princess Bebé*, 1904), and the satirically conceived comedies such as *Los malhechores del bien* (*The Evildoers of Good*, 1905). Romantic passion of a stronger kind enters into some of these dramas, but in general his true strength lies rather in the gentler emotions and in the exercise of concealed irony than in the exploitation of burning fervour.

Among such works Benavente included numbers based on the current naturalistic and realistic efforts outside Spain. The life of the peasantry and the farmers, which had attracted the attention of Hauptmann and others, is dealt with in *Señora Ama* (1908) and *La malquerida* (*The Passion Flower*, 1913). In the former a wife who had previously taken pride in the affairs of the heart pursued by her husband changes her ideas when she finds she is to have a child. The latter is one of those rarer plays from his pen in which passion, usually subdued in the Benavente theatre, bursts forth in a torrent of fury. The central figure is a girl, Acacia, who finds herself, hardly realizing the force that possesses her, enamoured of her stepfather, Esteban, a well-to-do farmer. Like a flame, this incestuous frenzy consumes the pair until Raimunda, the mother, deliberately provokes Esteban into killing her, conscious that now Acacia can never give herself to the man who has murdered her parent.

This reads almost like one of the more violent specimens of the naturalistic German theatre. Powerful as it is, other realistic efforts by Benavente are, however, more characteristic and finer in texture. Already in 1896 with *Gente conocida* (*People of Importance*) he had turned his gaze on the aristocratic world of his time; in 1903, with *El hombrecito* (*The Little Man*), he was exploring the life of the bourgeoisie. These realms attracted much of his attention throughout his career, and out of them he wrought what unquestionably are his finest dramas. Peculiarly typical is *Los intereses creados* (*The Bonds of Interest*, 1907). The plot is confessedly derived from the *commedia dell' arte*, testifying to that love of the fantastic that ever coloured Benavente's work; the theme is a social one, testifying to the influence upon him of the realistic theatre. While the atmosphere may be imaginary, the problems are real. Leandro and Crispin arrive, with little money between them, at a strange city. "This is a little play of puppets, impossible in theme, without any reality at all," says Crispin ironically in speaking the prologue. The city is really two cities—"one for people who arrive with money and the other for persons who arrive like us." Crispin pretends to be Leandro's servant, and starts actively to promote that young gentleman's marriage to an heiress. First they put up an outward show by entertaining the Captain and Harlequin; then Crispin starts to foment his intrigue, which, however, is somewhat upset by Leandro's genuinely falling in love with the fair Silvia. The end of the piece shows a happy union, achieved, thinks Crispin, by the material bonds of interest that unite men, by the principles of self-interest, and by the foundations of the market-place:

> CRISPIN: And believe me now, when you are getting on in the world, the ties of love are as nothing to the bonds of interest.
>
> LEANDRO: You are wrong. For without the love of Silvia I should never have been saved.
>
> CRISPIN: And is love a slight interest? I have always given due credit to the ideal, and I count upon it always. With this the farce ends.

Silvia now turns to the audience. "You have seen in the play," she says,

> how these puppets have been moved by plain and obvious strings, like men and women in the farces of our lives—strings which were their interests, their passions, and all the illusions and petty miseries of their state. Some are pulled by the feet to lives of restless and weary wandering; some by the hands, to toil with pain, to struggle with bitterness, to strike with cunning, to slay with violence and rage. But into the hearts of all there descends sometimes from heaven an invisible thread, as if it were woven out of the sunlight and the moonbeams, the invisible thread of love, which makes these men and women, as it does these puppets which seem like men, almost divine, and brings to our foreheads the smile and splendours of the dawn, lends wings to our drooping spirits, and whispers to us still that this farce is not all a farce, that there is something noble, something divine, in our lives which is true and which is eternal, and which shall not close when the farce of life shall close.

Obviously this is not a realistic drama; as obviously it is a drama of ideas, and the ideas are those that colour all Benavente's 'social' works, even although there occasionally creeps into the optimistic philosophy a faint note of scepticism—such, for example, as appears in the sequel to *The Bonds of Interest*—*La ciudad alegre y confiada* (*The Joyous and Confident City*, 1916)—wherein Leandro is shown in a less sympathetic light than he was in the earlier play.

Benavente's studies of the social life of his time are numerous. In *La comida de las fieras* (*The Banquet of Wild Beasts*, 1898) the basic theme of *Timon of Athens* is transferred to modern surroundings. *La gobernadora* (*The Governor's Wife*, 1901) satirizes society's manners, as does *Lo cursi* (*Vulgarity*, 1901). No revolutionary, he reveals his basic attitude in *Campo de armiño* (*Field of Ermine*, 1916), wherein a noble lady takes a boy into her house in the belief that he is the bastard son of her brother, discovers that he has been foisted on her by a group of grasping lower-class characters, in anger dismisses him from her palace, and then finds that love of him compels her to adopt him as her own: the field of ermine in her coat-of-arms is left pure by her yielding to her better emotions. For Benavente love is the mystery of life and the hope of mankind.

The author's dramatic career was a long one—and peculiarly fortunate. After the performance of one of his dramas in Madrid in 1947 the audience rose in a mass, raised the aged playwright on their shoulders, and in triumphant procession bore him from the theatre to his home. Benavente at least was one philosopher who won fame, while living, in his own country.

Next to Benavente in this new flourishing of the Spanish stage stands Gregorio Martínez Sierra, in whose works, with gentle melancholy, much the same atmosphere prevails. He too is influenced by the social drama of the age; he too brings to that realism a peculiar flavour of his own. From his very first play he exhibited the quality that was to dominate in his work throughout the whole of his career—the quality of penetrating sympathy. This quality is carried to full expression in *Canción de cuna* (*Cradle Song*, 1911), a tender, sensitive study of quiet emotion in a Spanish nunnery; a baby girl left in a basket at the gate is reared, under the sisters' care, by their gardener's wife; at the age of eighteen she becomes betrothed to a young man, and in the play we see him visiting the convent to thank the nuns for the care of his future wife. There is no more plot than that, and Sierra's skill is demonstrated clearly by the way in which, with such slender material, he keeps our interest alert and our sympathies keen, yet untouched by the sentimental. A kindred spirit hovers over *El Reino de Dios* (*The Kingdom of God*, 1915), which consists merely of three episodes in a nun's life—as a girl just before taking her vows, as a woman crushing from her heart a human love, and as an elderly woman commanding by her wisdom a crowd of unruly and half-starved orphans. The power of understanding love, in which Sierra believes as fervently as does Benavente, is revealed in *Los pastores* (*The Shepherds*, 1913), where a priest and a doctor, although neither is capable of passing the examinations which authority deems necessary, are shown as true shepherds protecting the souls and bodies of the country people of their rural area.

Even when Sierra turns from the religious field to the secular he bears with him his own characteristic mood. In *Sueño de una noche de Agosto* (*A Dream of an August Eve*, or *The Romantic Young Lady*, 1918), where a girl, grieved because she cannot have adventures like a man, finds such adventure coming her way when the wind carries a straw hat into her room, and when the hat is merely an introduction to the young novelist who has lost it. No matter how flimsy and artificial the plot, Sierra can hold us intent. *El enamorado* (*The Lover*, 1912) tells merely of a self-made factory-owner whose romantic adoration of his queen is such that he follows in her train wherever she goes. One day her carriage is overturned, and he rescues her: she offers to grant him whatever he asks; and his plea is for a railway pass which will allow him always to be close to her. We may smile in superior manner at such fancies, but if we do we smile at something rather fragrant and lovely.

Fragrance and loveliness too, combined with gentle laughter, appear in the writings of the Quintero brothers—Serafín and Joaquín Alvarez —who, like Benavente, have contributed to the theatre several hundred dramas, from short sketches to full-length plays. Best-known of these outside Spain is the delightful *La consulesa* (*The Lady from Alfáqueque*, 1914), with its magnificently drawn picture of an appealing rascal whose manners are so perfect that hardly anyone can take offence at his shameless sponging on others. Closely akin in spirit is *El genio alegre* (*The Merry Heart*, 1906), wherein the austere household of Donna Sacramento is transformed when her orphan niece, Consolación, comes to stay with her, bringing to the house her canaries, her parrots, and her light-hearted *joie de vivre*. The individual flavour of the Quintero stage is likewise fully revealed in *Papá Juan, centenario* (*A Hundred Years Old*, 1909), in which Papa Juan by his wisdom resolves the perplexing difficulties in his large household; chuckling, he pulls the strings so as to engineer a wedding between his beloved great-granddaughter and her gay blade of a cousin. Sometimes their scenes grow darker, as in *Los Galeotes* (*The Two Galeotes*, 1900), which shows ingratitude rampant—even though good triumphs in the end. Even when they introduce evil it is with a gentle smile. In *Malvaloca* (1912), for example, Salvador has seduced the girl Malvaloca. He and his brother, Leonardo, are at the time of the action engaged in remoulding the cracked bell of the convent, and Malvaloca comes to love and to be loved by Leonardo. In the end, as the task is finished and the bell rings out clearly, Salvador is shown ready to depart, while Leonardo protests to Malvaloca that he will seek to recast her life with his love. Somewhat similar to this play is *Amores y amoríos* (*Loves and Intrigues*, 1908). Here the heroine, Isabel, falls in love with a roué, Juan Maria, who, charmed by the atmosphere of an Andalusian spring, makes her a promise of marriage. Back in cold Madrid, he abandons her, but eventually true love conquers over his libertine affections, and in the end the pair are united.

During this time, of course, the major authors were companioned by many other writers such as Manuel Linares Rivas and José López Pinillos, but only a few plays penned by these lesser dramatists have any real interest for us today. Their value rests, not in their individual worth, but in their numbers: collectively they demonstrate how powerfully the Spanish theatre, having shaken itself out of its long hibernation, was recapturing its earlier strength.

2

THE EXTENSION OF THE REALISTIC

IT HAS been noted above that both Gorki and Benavente—each in his own way—introduce into their plays qualities of a kind distinct from those associated with the direct naturalistic tradition and with the tradition of the drama of ideas. Indeed, we might almost aver that the worth of their writings depends basically upon their divergence from, rather than upon their imitation of, the style of theatrical composition established by Ibsen. Their works thus serve as a kind of transition from the typical *Ghosts* and *A Doll's House* to the various experiments made during the years that followed the appearance of these dramas towards the building of still newer dramatic forms.

⊀ The Poetic Realism of Chekhov

Already in the last two decades of the nineteenth century a fresh impulse was being felt in the plays of Anton Pavlovich Chekhov, and, so far as strict chronology is concerned, there would have been every justification for dealing with his work alongside Ibsen's dramas. Although Chekhov started writing for the theatre in 1884, however, and though he himself died before the twentieth century had passed four years of its course, the fact that his fame did not reach fruition until the production, in 1898, of *The Seagull* by the Moscow Art Theatre warrants consideration of his peculiar contributions to the stage, not among nineteenth-century but among twentieth-century dramas. Chekhov was well ahead of his time, and the qualities of his plays find harmony rather with what men were trying to do a dozen years after Ibsen's death than with what they actually accomplished during his lifetime.

For the first years of his dramatic career Chekhov restricted himself to the one-act play form, gaining mastery of situation and of character by means of short sketches of life. His first composition was a sketch, or 'dramatic study,' entitled *Na bolshoi doroge* (*On the High Road*; written in 1884, but for a time denied theatrical representation because of the opposition of the censorship). There is no plot here, just a picture of a number of ill-assorted characters lodged temporarily in a roadside inn. There are touches of laughter, but the atmosphere in general is one of gloom. Quiet, resigned acceptance of life's despairs is the mood of *Lebedinaia pesnia* (*Swan-song*, 1887), in which an ageing comic actor, left alone on the stage of a small theatre, dreams of his past life, of the visions that once were his, and of the reality before him.

This sadness, generally induced by contemplation of life's failures, is an inherent part of Chekhov's being, yet his real strength comes from his mastery of laughter. In one of his earliest sketches, *Medved* (*The Bear*, 1888), an irate young landowner calls on a neighbour lady to demand repayment of a debt: there is a violent quarrel between them, yet before the half-hour's action is over they have become engaged. Here the spirit of Musset is being transformed into Russian terms. *Predlozhenie* (*The Marriage Proposal*, 1889) shows a timorous young suitor calling on the lady of his choice and becoming so involved in an acrimonious debate concerning the ownership of some worthless land as almost to wreck his hopes—and the girl's. For *Svadba* (*The Wedding*, 1890) Chekhov takes as setting a bridal feast, and derives much merriment from the contrasting characters introduced—particularly from those of a retired naval captain who is mightily aggrieved because, snobbishly, he is being introduced to the company as a general and a nobleman, and of a self-effacing clerk who, himself wishing to have been the bridegroom, seeks to pacify his anger by pretending that after all her family is vulgar and ignorant. *Zhubilei* (*The Anniversary*, 1902) is a hilarious study of the celebrations attendant upon the fiftieth anniversary of the founding of a bank —celebrations considerably interrupted by the love-affairs of the bank manager. Laughter too predominates in *Tragik ponevole* (*A Tragedian in spite of Himself*, 1890), where the wretched husband Tolkachov, burdened with commissions imposed upon him by members of his family comfortably established in a country cottage, seeks sympathy from his friend Murashkin. After listening to the tale of woe Murashkin adds a commission of his own, and the sketch ends with poor Tolkachov madly losing his temper, attacking his friend, and crying out hysterically for blood.

An appreciation of these one-act pieces is absolutely essential for an understanding of Chekhov's full-length plays. While it is true that some of the longer works end with suicide, and that all introduce an atmosphere of darkness, it would seem that a true interpretation of their spirit demands a full acceptance of the humorous qualities inherent in their being There is nothing here of the gloomy pessimism characteristic of Hauptmann's *Before Sunrise*, nothing of the frenzied self-centredness of Strindberg's work. A deep understanding of human souls is Chekhov's prime quality, and, together with that, an ability to view life ironically. He is deeply moved as he contemplates his scenes, yet no bitterness, no fervent anger, stirs his being.

In 1887 he first tried his hand at the composition of a long play, and succeeded in turning out what must be regarded, in every respect, as a failure. *Ivanov* nowhere reveals Chekhov's genuine spirit. Unsuited to the expression of his genius is this story of a spineless man who marries a

Jewess, finds his love for her depart, and falls in love with a neighbour's daughter. The wife, he knows, is dying of consumption, and in one terrible scene, when she upbraids him for his intrigue, he flings the knowledge of her close-approaching death in her face. Shortly after this she departs from life: Ivanov, though racked by conscience, plans to go ahead with a second marriage, but when the doctor declares he will publicly expose him he seeks release in suicide.

Except for the fact that Ivanov himself is akin to other characters in the later plays who fail in their adjustment to life, this drama has but little in common with Chekhov's masterpieces. It aims at creating a tragic impression, and for that his powers were eminently unsuited.

His first true triumph came with *Chaika* (*The Seagull*), unsuccessfully produced in 1896, and two years later destined to become the primal glory of the Moscow Art Theatre. *Ivanov* had been constructed more or less along traditional lines, and all stress was laid on one central figure. In *The Seagull* Chekhov abandoned the traditional formulas and set himself to depict a group rather than an individual. To narrate the plot of such a work is almost impossible, so closely intertwined are the characters with one another. Four persons in particular concern us—the successful actress Irina Arkadina, who, despite her reputation, is obsessed by fears of becoming too old for the stage; her son, Konstantin Treplev, gifted with literary powers, yet submerged by the dominant personality of his mother; Trigorin, a fashionable and successful novelist, conscious of the fact that for all his esteem his genius is not of the highest; and Nina, a young idealistic girl who dreams of a great theatrical career. These are the central figures, but even these four cannot be considered in isolation as a group, for their lives are intimately associated with, and illuminated by, other characters—Irina's good-humoured, slightly soured brother, Piotr Nikolaevich Sorin; his steward, Ilia Shamraev; his wife, Polina Andreevna, and daughter, Masha; the doctor, Evgeni Dorn; and the schoolmaster, Semion Medvedenko. All these persons Chekhov has wrought into a harmonious whole, while apparently allowing his action to drift and even to stagnate.

This play too ends with suicide (Treplev's), but it cannot be styled a tragedy. Throughout its length, despite the many soul sorrows that are revealed by the various persons in the action, ironic laughter is rippling: it was, indeed, Chekhov's unique discovery that the spirit of high comedy could be evoked by means of effects which in the hands of another author might have led only to the tragic or the melodramatic. "Why do you always wear black?" asks Medvedenko of Masha at the very beginning of the play, but the reference to her black dress is not, as one might have thought, a symbolic introduction to a tragic theme. Her reply—"I am in mourning for my life. I am unhappy"—at once reveals to us the mood in which we are to accept the following scenes. This is serious, but somehow not tragically serious. Medvedenko is a sorry creature, and so is Masha; when, however, the two start to argue fitfully on which is the more miserable, while each, despite the fact that they are conversing, remains inwardly intent on his or her own thoughts, the mood evoked is an ironically comic one:

> *MEDVEDENKO:* Why? [*Hesitatingly*] I don't understand. . . . You're in good health; perhaps your father isn't very rich, but he's got enough. My life's very much harder than yours. I get twenty-three roubles a month in all, and from that a deduction's made for pension, and yet I don't go about in mourning.
> [*They sit down.*
> *MASHA:* It isn't a question of money. Even a beggar can be happy.
> *MEDVEDENKO:* In theory, yes, but in practice it's like this: I, and my mother and my two sisters and my little brother—with a total income of twenty-three roubles. I suppose we must eat and drink, mustn't we? I suppose we must have some tea and sugar? And tobacco? There's the rub.
> *MASHA* [*glancing at the platform*]: The play will begin soon.
> *MEDVEDENKO:* Yes. Miss Zarechni will act, and the play is by Konstantin Gavrilovich. They're in love with each other, and to-day their souls will unite in the effort to present one and the same artistic image. But my soul and yours do not have any common point of contact. I love you; I'm so miserable I can't stay at home; every day I walk six versts here and six back again, and from you I get only indifference. That, of course, is to be understood. I am without means, I've a big family on my hands. . . . What inducement is there to marry a man who hasn't enough to live on?
> *MASHA:* Nonsense. [*Takes a pinch of snuff.*] Your love touches me, but I can't return it, that's all. [*Offers him her snuff-box.*] Have some?
> *MEDVEDENKO:* I don't want any.

The quality that is in *The Seagull* also renders this play essentially poetic. Here is life apparently depicted with an utterly naturalistic pen, and yet the impression we have in our minds is entirely imaginative. Partly this comes from the way in which unobtrusively Chekhov weaves symbol into reality, so that what in Ibsen remains something tacked on to the action is here so integrated with the outward movement that the two cannot be disentangled. Partly it comes from the sharp juxtaposition of different thoughts uttered by two or more characters as each remains involved in his own meditations: the effect occasionally is akin to the juxtaposition of images in a passage of lyrical poetry: it is as though the imaginative quality of a Hamlet soliloquy were orchestrated for a quartette; it is as though Hamlet and many Hamlets, their tongues incapable of fully expressing their thoughts, were desperately trying to make others listen, without anyone to heed them or to understand.

How difficult was the task that Chekhov had set himself is revealed in his next play, *Diadia Vania* (*Uncle Vania*, 1899). Already in 1889 he had tried his hand at dealing with the theme here presented, in his *Leshii* (*The Wood Demon*). The character of Professor Serebriakov is common to both plays, and Uncle Vanya appears in the former as Uncle George, killing himself at the end of the third act. There is, however, in *The Wood Demon* a jangling of notes, a lack of a central tune, and it is easy to see why Chekhov himself was dissatisfied with it. Even in the rewriting, or rather re-creation, *Uncle Vanya* may be regarded as less powerful than *The Seagull*.

The central figure here is the retired and widowed Professor Serebria-kov, who lives on his small estate with his daughter, Sofia, and his brother-in-law, Ivan Petrovich Voinitski, known as Uncle Vanya. Into this circle the Professor brings a young wife, a woman of twenty-seven, Elena Andreievna. With her Vanya falls in love, and at the same time the man whom Sofia loves, Dr Astrov, is also attracted by her. Serebriakov is a pompous, fussy egoist; Vanya is a man who has sacrificed everything for his dead sister's estate, which he manages; Sofia is a woman, unat-tractive, to whom the joys of life have been denied; Astrov is a strange mixture of the cynic and the idealist, a drunkard who yet has a great vision of afforestation designed to change Russia's climate and better her peoples; Elena is a woman who, after marrying the Professor, discovers that she does not love him and yet is resolved to remain faithful to him. When Vanya learns that Serebriakov intends to sell the estate to which he himself has given his whole life he tries, unsuccessfully, to shoot him, and in the last act we are back, as it were, at the beginning. Vanya and Sofia are left alone; the vision that was Elena has gone; for Vanya there may be release in carrying on the work that no longer gives him satis-faction, for Sofia there is hope only of happiness in a life other than this:

> We shall go on living, Uncle Vanya. We shall live on through a great, great line of days, of long evenings; we shall patiently endure the trials our fate brings us; we shall toil for others, now and when we are old, without rest; and when our time comes we shall die submissively, and there beyond the grave we shall say that we have suffered, that we have wept, that our lives were bitter, and God will take pity upon us, and I and you, uncle, dear uncle, shall see a life that is luminous, beautiful, splendid. . . . In your life you have not known any joy, but wait, Uncle Vanya, wait. . . . We shall have rest.

After this exploration of the human soul Chekhov had acquired suf-ficient power to create his two outstanding final dramas—*Tri sestri* (*The Three Sisters*, 1901) and *Vishnevii sad* (*The Cherry Orchard*, 1904). Here the plots are even less firm and at the same time, paradoxically, more com-plex. All that *The Three Sisters* has to tell is the story of Olga, Masha, and Irina, three sisters living in a small provincial town and ever dreaming of escaping to the joys of Moscow life. In the action of the play we see nothing more than the slow, gradual fracturing of these dreams. What is remarkable in this play is the quality—still more marked in *The Cherry Orchard*—of a strange mood born out of nostalgia for the lovely things of life that are passing and of some dim hope of future happiness. Men and women are at odds here, with one another, with themselves, with their circumstances. Colonel Vershinin, whose own life is a failure, considers the problems of existence: "Well, I don't know," he says:

> It seems to me that everything on this earth must change little by little, that it's actually changing as we look at it. In two hundred years, three hundred, maybe a thousand years—how long doesn't matter—a new, happy life will

arise. We shan't be able to share in that life, of course, but we are living for it now, we're working for it, yes, suffering for it: we are creating it—and in this one effort is the reason for our existence and, if you like, our happiness.

And, as if in comment, comes the stage-direction—"Masha laughs softly." "What is it?" she is asked. "I don't know," she replies. "I've been laughing all day." The close of the play is in keeping with this tone.

Finally comes *The Cherry Orchard*, in which Chekhov finds complete mastery of his medium. The last scene shows the old Firs left alone in a dark and shuttered house, there presumably to die: throughout the course of the action a sad, nostalgic sorrow prevails for the beautiful things that are being sacrificed. "My dear, my tender, beautiful orchard!" sighs Lubov as she leaves. "My life, my youth, my happiness, good-bye! . . . Good-bye!" But before that the student has been speaking to Anya:

> All Russia is our orchard. The land is great and beautiful, there are many wondrous places in it. [*A pause.*] Think, Anya: your grandfather, your great-grandfather and all your ancestors were owners of serfs, holders of living souls —and can you fail to see something human looking at you from every cherry in the orchard, from every leaf, from every stem? Don't you hear voices there? . . . Oh, your orchard is fearsome and frightening; and when in the evening or at night you walk through it, then the old bark on the trees glows dimly and the old cherry-trees seem to be dreaming of all that was a hundred, two hundred years ago, and their visions weigh them down. Well, then, we have remained for at least two hundred years, it means nothing to us, we don't realize our relationship to the past—we can only philosophize, complain of boredom or drink vodka. And yet it's so clear: in order to begin to live in the present we must first pay for the past, make our peace with the past, and that payment can be made only through suffering, through extraordinary, uninterrupted toil. . . . I feel that happiness is coming, Anya, I see it already.

Not that such a speech by Trofimov makes *The Cherry Orchard* into a thesis play. There is nothing intellectual and rational here: all is imaginative and emotional. As the characters are seated outside by the bank of a river, "suddenly a distant sound is heard as from the sky, the sound of a breaking harp string, sadly dying away." "What's that?" asks Lubov, the graciously useless owner of the orchard. "I don't know," replies the wealthy peasant Lopakhin. "A bucket's fallen down a shaft somewhere far off. It's certainly far off." "Or perhaps it's some bird . . . like a heron," hazards the drifting intellectual Gaev. "Or an owl," adds Trofimov satirically. Lubov shudders: "It's unpleasant, somehow," she remarks, and there is a pause. Then the old Firs speaks, he who had been a slave in the days before the emancipation of the serfs: "Before the misfortune the same thing happened. An owl screamed and the samovar simmered without stopping." "Before what misfortune?" Gaev asks, and the old man's answer comes from the depth of memory—"Before the Emancipation."

In this drama, where tears are blended with laughter, hope with despair, Chekhov carries to the farthest limit his peculiar power of suggesting the inner loneliness of his characters. Each one speaks for himself, and there is no one to listen. The talk drifts on, thoughts welling up from within the breasts of these waifs, tossed on the air and vanishing like bubbles. We know these people as we do not know even the strongly delineated types created by Ibsen, for Chekhov's art is a poetic art where implications and associative values fire the creative process in our own minds.

It has taken many years for Chekhov's peculiar artistry to win general acceptance, but that acceptance has now come, and the success which has attended the many productions of his dramas during recent years seems to indicate that he possesses that almost indefinable quality which alone can win universal and enduring life in the theatre. His world is in truth far farther removed from that of London and New York than the provincial-city flavour set as a background to most of Ibsen's plays, and one might well have thought that things so strange could never have been successful outside of Russia. The fact is, however, that, whenever produced, *The Cherry Orchard* and *The Seagull* have demonstrated their power of making a direct appeal in spite of the strangeness of their atmosphere: by some magic, the precise operation of which baffles our intelligence, Chekhov has been able to invest the particular with universal attributes, so that even when his delicately poised dialogue suffers inevitable coarsening in being transformed into another tongue the play of his creative imagination still casts a warm glow over his characters. Although his dramatic work falls quantitatively far below that of Ibsen, of Strindberg or of Hauptmann, perhaps future historians of the theatre, surveying the fortunes of the stage at the turn of the century, may decide that so far as quality is concerned no other author can vie with him: his subtlety is supreme.

The Irish School

Chekhov wrote his plays in prose, yet in speaking of his writings the epithet 'poetic' constantly comes to our lips. His imaginative process succeeds in transforming the real into the ideal, the particular into the universal. A somewhat similar process was at work during those years in another centre from which hitherto little of dramatic value had come.

It is true that Ireland had made many contributions to the English stage. Numerous dramatic authors whose plays were produced in the London theatres from the beginning of the eighteenth century onward were Irishmen who had settled in England: scores of Irishmen won success as actors during these centuries. For the most part, however, neither playwrights nor actors had anything peculiarly their own, with a national flavour, to give to the stage. We may discern, in both, elements of characteristic Irish humour, but it is clothed in an English dress. Only in the time of Dion Boucicault was there any exploiting of Irish themes and dialect, and even then little more than an external veneer was given to melodramatic situations that might have emanated from almost any land or time.

Occasionally original dramas appeared from the pens of Irish authors on the Dublin boards: some have historical interest and a few exhibit intrinsically interesting scenes, but none break away from the basic patterns derived from outside. These earlier Irish comedies are framed on the current moulds of English comedy; Irish melodramas have precisely the same sensational episodes and the same stereotyped figures as may be found associated with *milieux* of an entirely different kind.

When, in 1899, a small band of enthusiasts set up the Irish Literary Theatre something entirely new was in process of being born. Aided by the munificent patronage of Miss Horniman, they were able to establish themselves, barely three years later, in the famous Abbey playhouse, with the poet W. B. Yeats and the versatile Lady Gregory as their leaders. Yeats' entire spirit was, of course, devoted to the purely poetic, but in his protégé, John Millington Synge, appeared a writer, destined to be of great influence both in Ireland and abroad, who made a contribution to the stage by no means dissimilar to that of the Russian Chekhov. In the writings of the two men, far removed from each other in space, strength came through the exploitation of ways of life distinct from those to be found in the larger centres of Western Europe and through the transmutation of the real world around them into something rich in imaginative quality.

It was in 1897 that Yeats, finding Synge wasting his talents in the Bohemian circles of Paris, persuaded him to return to his native country and, in particular, to dwell for a space in the most isolated areas of that land. The life of the Aran islanders entered into his very being: their speech made music in his ears; their simplicity brought to him a deep sense of essential human emotion. As strange to a citizen of London, of Paris, or of Berlin was this primitive existence as the world out of which Chekhov evoked his tragic comedies, and Synge, gifted with something of the Russian dramatist's power, succeeded similarly in so dealing with his material as to make it of appeal and interest to those utterly ignorant of its customs and essentially alien to its spirit. In his own way Synge pursued Chekhov's path—he remained, of course, wholly without knowledge of the Russian's dramatic work—in extending the confines of the realistic, although his steps led him into more diversified territory, where the starkly tragic exists alongside the comic.

His first two theatrical essays, produced in 1903 and 1904 respectively, were a cynically kindly little folk-sketch, *In the Shadow of the Glen*, and the short tragic essay, unrelieved in its tension, *Riders to the Sea*. The former is to be associated with *The Well of the Saints* (1905) and *The Playboy of the Western World* (1907); the latter, although realistically dealing with contemporaries, has affinities in spirit with the unrevised legendary drama, *Deidre of the Sorrows* (1910). In none of these plays, serious or humorous, does Synge deal, even by implication, with the social-political themes so beloved by the stage of the first years of our century. In Holland Ibsen's follower Heijermans can take the tragedies of fisher-folk and make of their story an indictment of the grasping capitalist: Synge's *Riders to the Sea* confines itself entirely to the relations of men with the nature around them. So far as spirit is concerned, for Synge Ibsen and his companions might never have been: although his dramas could not have taken such shape as they did had it not been for the development of a realistic theatrical technique during the latter years of the nineteenth century, the atmosphere he evokes is strangely unlike anything to be found elsewhere, unless perhaps it be in Chekhov's writings —and even there the changing social-economic conditions operative at this time were scenically introduced either directly or indirectly. Synge has no character in any of his plays corresponding to the Lopakhin of *The Cherry Orchard*: no hint of life altering under the impact of industrialism intrudes into his episodes.

Riders to the Sea and *Deirdre of the Sorrows* unite in demonstrating what formed a great measure of Synge's strength. He realized to the full that if the dramatist could produce nothing but pale and pallid words his writings would possess only ephemeral worth, and he early set himself to master a prose style that had within it the richer cadences we associate with the poet while at the same time retaining ties with the common speech of men. In this task he was materially aided by the subject-matter with which he had chosen to deal. In Ireland, among the western peasantry, he could listen to a language which, because it remained close to the soil, because it was enriching itself by borrowings of phrase and rhythm from the neighbouring Erse, provided a basis far stronger and far more flexible than anything that might be heard in England. The result was that he found himself in a peculiarly fortunate position and was enabled to develop a style of dramatic dialogue at once realistic and poetic —uniquely his own, yet gaining strength from the fact that it was not merely the invented form of utterance devised by a single individual.

Without such a dialogue medium as Synge evolved, *Riders to the Sea* would be of little worth: expressed in bare naturalistic tones it could arouse in us no vital response. As it is, the atmosphere evoked here comes close to the true spirit of the tragic. The haunting cadences of the prose speech not only harmonize with the theme, but are inseparable from that theme:

CATHLEEN [*begins to keen*]: It's destroyed we are from this day. It's destroyed, surely.
NORA: Didn't the young priest say the Almighty God wouldn't leave her destitute with no son living?
MAURYA [*in a low voice, but clearly*]: It's little the like of him knows of the sea. . . . Bartley will be lost now, and let you call in Eamon and make me a good coffin out of the white boards, for I won't live after them. I've had a husband, and a husband's father, and six sons in this house—six fine men,

though it was a hard birth I had with every one of them and they coming into the world—and some of them were found and some of them were not found, but they're gone now the lot of them. . . . There were Stephen and Shawn were lost in the great wind, and found after in the Bay of Gregory of the Golden Mouth, and carried up the two of them on one plank, and in by that door.

There is exquisite music here, a music that works upon our senses and charms us into viewing the dark disaster that has fallen on Maurya's little household not with the dark despair which alone the naturalistic playwrights know how to evoke, but with deeper vision.

Riders to the Sea is one of the best-known of all short plays; not so well known is the longer tragedy *Deirdre of the Sorrows*, although Synge's drama of the love of the fair Deirdre, betrothed to King Conchubor, but intoxicated by the passion in her heart for Naisi, is a true masterpiece of the romantic theatre. In itself it combines the best qualities of two worlds: there is about it the twilight spirit of Celtic myth combined with the more flaming emotions of the earlier romantic movement, and at the same time the handling of the characters has a firmness demonstrating Synge's determined grip upon reality: its language is both beautiful and taut.

While Synge thus won success in the sphere of the tragic, perhaps his spirit found most fitting opportunity for expression in the realm of comedy—a peculiar realm of his own invention where cynicism meets and harmonizes with sympathy. *The Shadow of the Glen* takes us to a small cottage in the west where a young wife, Nora, her heart full of visions that carry her far from her home, discovers a certain satisfaction when her husband decides to lie down in his bed and die. To her comes the Tramp, a rascally fellow whom she invests with the robes of her fancy, seeing in him a symbol of all the fun and adventure she has missed in her life. Pleasantly they chat and make plans, when a sudden sneeze from the 'corpse' reveals that the good husband has been merely pretending death. All irate, he drives Nora from his house, and we are left to imagine her trudging down the road with her Tramp, listening to his enchanting blather. A kindred atmosphere envelops *The Well of the Saints*, wherein a couple of aged blind beggars, husband and wife, are given back their sight by means of water which a Saint has brought back with him from a distant holy place. Their eyes thus opened, each gazes with dismay at the lined and ugly countenance of the other: in anger, they come to blows. Once more the blindness returns, and the good saint, pitying them, proposes to repeat the miracle; now, however, the thought of being able to see brings them nothing save fear, and the husband desperately dashes the charmed water to the ground. He prefers to go through the world with his illusory visions rather than have the advantages of sight accompanied by spiritual despair.

The mood of these two short plays is intimately associated with that of *The Playboy of the Western World*, with its delightfully cynical and humorous plot, telling how Christy Mahon, a weak and worthless fellow, becomes a hero among those who have heard that he has had the daring to kill his own father. Pegeen Flaherty decides that her loutish fiancé, Shawn, is but a block in comparison with this mighty man; Shawn is thrown off even although her father tries desperately to speed up her marriage to him:

CHRISTY: And you'll be wedding them this day, is it?

MICHAEL [*drawing himself up*]: Aye. Are you thinking, if I'm drunk itself, I'd leave my daughter living single with a little frisky rascal is the like of you?

PEGEEN [*breaking away from SHAWN*]: Is it the truth the dispensation's come?

MICHAEL [*triumphantly*]: Father Reilly's after reading it in gallous Latin, and "It's come in the nick of time," says he; "so I'll wed them in a hurry, dreading that young gaffer who'd capsize the stars."

PEGEEN [*fiercely*]: He's missed his nick of time, for it's that lad, Christy Mahon, that I'm wedding now.

MICHAEL [*loudly, with horror*]: You'd be making him a son to me, and he wet and crusted with his father's blood?

PEGEEN: Aye. Wouldn't it be a bitter thing for a girl to go marrying the like of Shaneen, and he a middling kind of a scarecrow, with no savagery or fine words in him at all?

MICHAEL [*gasping and sinking on a chair*]: Oh, aren't you a heathen daughter to go shaking the fat of my heart, and I swamped and drownded with the weight of drink? Would you have them turning on me the way that I'd be roaring to the dawn of day with the wind upon my heart? Have you not a word to aid me, Shaneen? Are you not jealous at all?

SHAWN [*in great misery*]: I'd be afeard to be jealous of a man did slay his da.

PEGEEN: Well, it'd be a poor thing to go marrying your like. I'm seeing there's a world of peril for an orphan girl, and isn't it a great blessing I didn't wed you before himself came walking from the west or south?

SHAWN: It's a queer story you'd go picking a dirty tramp up from the highways of the world.

PEGEEN [*playfully*]: And you think you're a likely beau to go straying along with, the shiny Sundays of the opening year, when it's sooner on a bullock's liver you'd put a poor girl thinking than on the lily or the rose?

SHAWN: And have you no mind of my weight of passion and the holy dispensation, and the drift of heifers I am giving, and the golden ring?

PEGEEN: I'm thinking you're too fine for the like of me, Shawn Keogh of Killakeen, and let you go off till you'd find a radiant lady with droves of bullocks on the plains of Meath, and herself bedizened in the diamond jewelleries of Pharaoh's ma. That'd be your match, Shaneen. So God save you now!

Of course, the supposedly dead father turns up; of course, Christy is shamed, and, when he tries to rehabilitate himself by attacking the old man again, the entire village, which had been charmed by the vision of heroism afar off, is horrified. By twists and turns of the humorously comic imagination and by the enriching of his scenes with his treasury of language Synge has created here one of the finest plays that the twentieth century has to offer.

Once more we encounter, in the fortunes of the Irish theatre at this time, the same phenomenon already observed in other lands. The awakening of dramatic impulse is by no means restricted to the work of one man. Although up to these years there had been no school of Dublin playwriting, Synge does not stand alone: a whole group of writers for the stage are his companions. Yeats' writings fall almost wholly within the sphere of the romantically poetic, but close to Synge's humorous spirit is the mood with which Lady Gregory gives colour to many of her short plays. Like him she is closely in touch with the simple folk whom she introduces into her scenes; like him she allows her fancy to give deeper quality to the world of actuality. Again and again she exploits the situation out of which grew *The Playboy of the Western World*—the contrast between the real and what men think is the real. In *Hyacinth Halvey* (1906) a young man struggles in vain against the common belief that he is an image of virtue; in *Spreading the News* (1904) opinion, based on gossip, has a greater power than truth; in *The Jackdaw* (1907) an entire village community is cast into disorder because its men and women come to believe a wholly impossible tale about an easy way of making money. A basically similar contrast provides the pattern for *The Workhouse Ward* (1908), where the kindly efforts of a niece to take her uncle out of the workhouse (an eminently sensible idea) are thwarted by the old man's desire to remain—because in the workhouse there is a crony-enemy of his with whom he has had a lifelong quarrel. Such a concept is carried even farther in *The Image* (1909), which, through a plot telling how a group of villagers lose a couple of whales that have been cast up on the sands because of their interminable debates as to what to do with the oil, deliberately exploits the belief that in the heart of every man there is an ideal, an image, constantly at odds with reality.

We cannot claim Lady Gregory to be a great dramatist, although we must accept her plays as charmingly delightful sketches of life and as indicative in their style of fundamental qualities informing much of the work of her companions. Yeats' early *The Pot of Broth* (1902) was built on the same pattern, narrating how two beggars succeed in convincing a number of peasants that the boiling of a certain stone in the pot will produce a nice thick steaming soup. With more bitter emphasis Edward Martyn selected the contrast between the real and the ideal as the foundation for his tragic *The Heather Field* (1899). Here a landowner, Carden Tyrrell, is dominated by one consuming desire—to make a great waste of heathery moor into fertile fields; into this effort he throws all his money and sinks into debt; even when at the end, a broken man, he dreams that the ideal has been translated into reality he finds the vision shattered. The heather, he thinks, has been conquered, and, lying ill in his house, he lets his mind dwell fondly on what he has accomplished, when, ironically, his little son runs in, flushed and happy, with a bunch of heather he has gathered from the fields. Without a doubt in this drama Martyn is more deeply influenced than Synge or Lady Gregory by the Ibsen style of realistic play, yet the spirit that informs it is typically Irish. The close contact with nature, the flavour of poetic conception, the symbolic connotations are its own. These qualities are even more marked in *Maeve* (1900), where a woman, Maeve O'Heynes, is summoned from the world of actuality into a vision-world, where reigns Queen Maeve, the fairy of the moors and mistress of all things lovely. Maybe the essential difference between Ibsen and such a writer as Martyn is revealed most clearly by a comparison between *The Lady from the Sea* and *An Enchanted Sea* (1902): Ellida is caught merely by a fancy; the kin of Guy Font is of the realm of fairies and the mermen.

Slightly later than Martyn came Lennox Robinson, whose *The Clancy Name* appeared in 1908. A young man, John Clancy, has killed another in a fit of passion: his mother, intent on keeping unstained the family name, tries to prevent him from confessing, but his conscience is so moved that he determines to give himself up, when by chance he is given the opportunity of saving, at the cost of his own life, a child from a runaway horse. He himself dies a hero, and the name of the Clancys is saved. A peculiar cynicism detracts from the value of this drama. Happily, however, Robinson soon evolved a dramatic concept of greater worth. In *The Dreamers* (1915) he essayed, not very successfully, the sphere of the political-historical play, and in *The Patriots* (1912) he had already presented a bitter portrait of an aging revolutionary who, newly released from prison and expecting to be greeted with enthusiasm by his fellow-patriots, is met with indifference and cold neglect. Out of the spirit of these two comes *The Lost Leader* (1918), a clever exercise in dramatic suspense. For years popular belief credited the story that the unfortunate Irish leader Parnell was not dead, but living under an assumed name somewhere in Ireland. In a decayed old innkeeper, Lucius Lenihan, Parnell's features are discovered, and adroitly Robinson keeps us guessing: there are many arguments which seem to prove that he is no other than merely Lucius Lenihan, yet other evidence seems to prove that he is Parnell. Just as final demonstration is about to be made the old man is accidentally killed, and the curtain falls on a question. While this work perhaps has no great depth of character-drawing, its dramatic skill is subtle and assured.

This dramatic skill has enabled Robinson to produce in *The White-headed Boy* (1916) a delightful comedy, almost worthy of comparison with Synge's masterpiece. The central figure here is Denis Geoghan, a light-hearted youth for whom every sacrifice is made by his family. With sparkling humour and pleasantly cynical laughter Robinson traces his adventures until in the end, when all his relatives have been forced to make contributions towards a sum designed to repay John Duffy for the youth's trifling with the affections of his daughter, it is gaily revealed that Denis and she are in reality married: the money goes to the pair as a wedding present, and the merry of heart are suitably rewarded. A companion picture appears in *The Far-off Hills* (1928), still another study of dream and reality.

With these writers may be noted, too, the author of *Maurice Harte* (1912), T. C. Murray. Although, like most Irish dramatists, Murray cannot keep the lilt of poetic utterance completely banished from his stage, the strength of this drama lies in its unflinching display of the thwarted ambitions and useless strivings so common amid the drudgery of ordinary life. The same quality animates *Birthright* (1910) and, richer and more mature, gives to *Autumn Fire* (1924) its peculiar atmosphere of intensity.

Yet another playwright of this school who succeeded in combining diverse qualities in his work is Padraic Colum, a man who, while by no means an important author, has succeeded in *The Fiddler's House* (1907; a revised version of *The Broken Soil*, 1903) in giving his drunken Conn Hourican a certain distinction; in *The Land* (1905) he essays a more realistic study, and by dwelling on the contrast between the call of the city and the ancient appeal of the soil introduces a social note unheard in Synge and his companions; in *Thomas Muskerry* (1910) he descends still farther towards the level of the naturalistic, writing a play which, except for the character of the old piper Myles Gorman, might have been penned by an uninspired Hauptmann. Colum is by way of being a poet, but he differentiates himself from his companions by keeping his whimsy for children's books, by holding his poetic imagination apart from his study of life, and by proving over-serious in his professional patriotism. It is characteristic that he departed from the Abbey Theatre on account of *The Playboy of the Western World* and that the call of another civilization took him to America in 1914. In his work there are already signs of the disintegration of that fertile movement of which Yeats and Synge were the literary leaders.

Barrie and Scots Sentimentalism

From Scotland hailed a prolific and once widely acclaimed dramatist whose true worth is peculiarly difficult to assess. Clearly, present-day disciples of Artaud and Brecht and Genet will throw aside the plays of Sir James M. Barrie in disgust, seeing in them nothing except feeble sentimentalism: yet we cannot dismiss so easily an author whose comedies and dramas manifestly exhibit a masterly skill, who displayed considerable ability in extending the sphere of the realistic theatre, who for many years received highest critical praise, and some of whose plays still can be profitably revived. That he was indeed a sentimentalist may readily be admitted, but at the same time we must agree that this tendency in his attitude to life did not destroy his keen insight into individual human beings—and, after all, it is with human beings that drama is chiefly concerned.

Of his large dramatic output much may be completely neglected; on the other hand, even when this is done, there remain sufficient plays of genuine interest to merit individual attention. *Peter Pan* (1904) may be merely a children's piece, but *The Admirable Crichton* (1902), *Dear Brutus* (1917), and *What Every Woman Knows* (1908) are plays of which no dramatist need have been ashamed. The first adroitly deals with society's conventions. In Lord Loam's household is an ideal butler, Crichton, polite, imperturbable, deferential. With his master and some others of the family this paragon of servants is shipwrecked on a desert island; through his ingenuity and adaptability to circumstances he becomes lord of the altered society imposed on the group by the power of nature. A rescue ship arrives, and the last act carries us back to Lord Loam's domain, with Crichton once more the model domestic. Outwardly the play is simply a charming whimsy; beneath it has all the characteristics of Barrie's philosophy. His mind was essentially childlike, and this story is one such as a child would love and appreciate. He has an observant eye, and he can well pierce beneath the butler's dark uniform to the man below; at the same time what he sees does not set him mounting soapboxes and attacking the aristocracy. He recognizes that Lord Loam's position is founded wholly on convention, yet such convention he is perfectly willing to accept. In all his outlook on the world there is a kind of sadly resigned humour, an almost pathetic willingness to be content, and a smiling tolerance of pretension.

What Every Woman Knows reminds us that Barrie's entire temperament was feminine rather than masculine. It is on his heroine, Maggie Shand, that he lavishes all his affectionate attention here. John Shand is a capable enough man in the rough-and-tumble of political life, but in his immediate relations with others he is a bit of a fool, and it is only through Maggie's astutely discreet guidance that he is prevented from revealing this folly to the world. Through her he rises up the political ladder; through her he escapes ruining himself by involving himself with an aristocratic charmer. Barrie never saw his women as objects of passion: the motherly invariably loomed more significant in his vision than the qualities of the mistress.

In *Dear Brutus* his philosophy of life is most completely revealed. Taking his cue from some famous lines in *Julius Cæsar*, he evolves a poetic-realistic plot in which the central figure is Mr Lob, who is Puck, middle-aged and in modern dress. Mr Lob is host of a weekend party, and all his guests have one thing in common: each is dissatisfied with his lot and deems that, if only he could be granted a second chance, greater things by far might be attained. They are granted their common wish. On midsummer eve they enter an enchanted wood—and find that, released from reality, they remain themselves. It is not in our stars, declares Barrie, but in ourselves that our faults lie. Purdie, who has thought himself unhappily married and who has been indulging in an affair with Mabel, is now married to the latter, with his real wife as the object of his attentions. The butler Matey, who had proclaimed that his dishonesty was merely the result of poverty, is just as dishonest now that he has become a rich capitalist. So it is for all of them, and, as the charm is dissipated, each returns dazed and a trifle chagrined to the world of reality.

The sheer skill with which Barrie has dealt with his material in these three plays demonstrates the quality of his craftsmanship, and his success in putting before us characters so intimately studied proves how penetrating was his vision. These comedies have nothing to say to us about the iniquities of the social world; in such iniquities Barrie was not interested, since he disbelieved in the thesis that man is made by his surroundings. In a civilization highly conscious of economic conditions and dominated by behaviouristic psychology his is a lonely figure, yet no other dramatist of his time was more adroit than he, no other fixed his gaze so intimately upon the vagaries of human nature viewed, not at moments of tempestuous passion, but by the light of the desert island's camp-fire, the gentle glow in the parlour grate, or the moonlight of the enchanted forest.

Barrie has not had many followers, although one other author, Alan Alexander Milne, has essayed the same sentimentally whimsical path. Typical of his work are *Mr Pim Passes By* (1919), *The Truth about Blayds* (1921), and *The Dover Road* (1922). The first deals, in charmingly comic terms, with the flutter in George Marden's family circle when a Mr Pim casually declares that Mrs Marden's former husband (long since presumed dead) is still alive; in the second, a ninety-year-old Oliver Blayds, for years revered by his family as the solitary remaining major poet of Victorian days, announces that all his fame was based on poems stolen from a deceased friend; while in *The Dover Road* appears a Mr Latimer, not unlike Barrie's Mr Lob, who takes a house on the Dover road where he welcomes lovers posting towards France, hoping that by throwing them together for a time they may consider whether indeed they are being wise in abandoning their marriage ties. There is charm here, at times accompanied by strength.

The Teatro Grottesco: The Predecessors of Pirandello

In all these playwrights from Chekhov to Barrie there is one common theme: each in his own way is intent upon the conflict between reality and the dream. The three sisters live in a world dominated by their thoughts of going to Moscow; Madame Ranevski dwells in the realm of the idealized cherry orchard; Christy Mahon becomes a hero of illusion; Mr Lob puckishly pierces the dreams of his guests. In all of these there is emphasis on the distinction between what a man is in reality, what he thinks he is, and what others think of him. From this mood easily arises a fundamental question: what, we ask, is reality?

It was through the dramatic exploitation of this query that Pirandello made his international reputation; nor was it surprising that an Italian dramatist should have been the man to discover the full potentialities of this theme. As has been already observed, the Italian temperament was basically antagonistic towards dramatic realism. In the theatres of Rome and Florence and Milan the stage is characteristically the home of the theatrical: we need not wonder that the opera, with its frank artificiality, found its true home in the peninsula or that the spirit of the *commedia dell' arte* has ever haunted its stage. As a result, the endeavours on the part of Italian playwrights to emulate the styles of Ibsen or of Hauptmann were almost all either half-hearted or expressive of a desire essentially alien to the demands of their audiences.

Throughout, opposition was evident to the realistic trend, opposition that sometimes took the form of a revival of poetic romanticism, sometimes veered off in the direction of more original forms. Already, in 1909, 'Futurism' was born, and by 1915 Filippo Tommaso Marinetti had established his 'synthetic' drama. Besides this, however, was another movement not heralded by any glowing manifesto, that was to prove more harmoniously associated with the Italian spirit.

In various Italian cities, notably Venice, Milan, Florence, Naples, and Bologna, and in the island of Sicily, the long-established native dialect theatres were beginning to display a new lease of life. Venice's lively and delicate civic comedy had been largely dormant since the time of Goldoni: now it started to display a fresh vigour, and in Giacinto Gallina produced a playwright of more than common talent. With his *Una famegia in rovina* (*A Family in Ruin*, 1872), *Barufe in famegia* (*Family Quarrels*, 1872), *La chitara del papà* (*Father's Guitar*, 1875), *Così va il mondo, bimba mia* (*The Way of the World, My Child*, 1880), *Amor in paruca* (*Love in a Wig*, 1880), and *La base de tuto* (*The Root of Everything*, 1894) he exhibited a keen theatrical sense and a unique depth of perception. The plot of *Barufe in famegia* is based on Goldoni's *La famiglia dell' antiquario*, and breathes the very spirit of that eighteenth-century master. With wit and a true understanding of stage requirements Gallina gaily carries us from scene to scene in which gossip and misconception set the fact in conflict with fiction. A quarrel between the young Toni and Orsolina is fanned to a flame by the chatterings of the maidservant Bettina until these characters, Momolo, the father, Emilia, his wife, and Rosa, his mother, are all involved in violent confusion. *La chitara del papà* almost reminds us of Goldoni's *Il ventaglio* because of the device by which the author has bound his plot together by the use of an inanimate object—here a guitar instead of a fan. Similarly derived from a Goldoni comedy, *Amor in paruca* merely tells how Giulia puts tests upon her lover Andrea to see how far he truly loves her. Tiring of this series of adventures and beginning to guess what is afoot, the latter engages in a counter-stratagem when Giulia writes to tell him that through an illness all her hair has come out. He himself puts on a bald-pated wig and calls on her. Before seeing his head, with pretended tears she offers to release him from his promise of marriage: he accepts the offer, and when she flies into a fury, believing that at last she has discovered his perfidy, he sadly declares that he has done so only because he has gone bald. Thereupon she shows him that her story about her own hair was merely a trick and assures him that, despite the loss of his, she loves him sincerely. By removing his wig Andrea ends both the comedy and his series of tests. A different note, however, enters into *Così va il mondo, bimba mia*, where the story is told, sympathetically yet with a certain bitterness, of a child's emotions when she finds her widowed mother about to take a second husband. Even more bitter, and showing awareness of changing social conditions, is the comedy-drama *La base de tutto*. Vidal is a noble-minded father whose morals are based on ancient traditions, but his son, Alviso, has the standards of a new age. The latter seduces a girl, Cecilia, whom he marries off to an unsavoury Carlo Scamoffietoli and is quite content to consider the affair settled by payment of some money. Old Vidal is scandalized, and finds it hard to realize that gold, in this new age, has become "the root of everything." Gallina's genius is perhaps not outstanding, but in these and other plays he has shown ability to give fresh life to the Venetian dialect theatre, and has hinted, at least, at the fundamental cleavage between appearance and reality, between fact and belief.

For the Florentine stage, much the same was being done by Augusto Novelli, among whose many plays one, *L'acqua cheta* (*Still Waters*, 1908), stands out as the finest. Against a background of Florentine life a family picture is presented, with two girls each in love with a young man. One of the lovers is a sincere, honest fellow who, because he is a socialist, finds little favour from the girl's father; the other is a seemingly good match, although in reality all he wants is to get the second daughter into his clutches. The young socialist, of course, proves hero in the end and succeeds both in gaining his own happiness and in rescuing his sister-in-law from the hands of a would-be seducer. In similar wise Aniello Costagliola devoted his attention to the re-creating of a Neapolitan dialect theatre.

Still more important was the development of native Sicilian drama as a direct result of the enthusiasm of Nino Martoglio, who in 1903 realized his dream of setting up a dialect repertory troupe. Here, in place of Venetian gaiety and Florentine seriousness of purpose, theatrical sensationalism found freest scope, although a characteristic kind of comedy too found expression on its stage. Typical of the latter is Martoglio's own *L'aria del continente* (*The Metropolitan Spirit*, 1915), in which a Sicilian Don Cola Dosciu, after having been forced to spend some months in Rome, returns to his native village the complete 'continental' and starts to reform the habits of his neighbours. In this attempt he puts himself thoroughly to shame, and the final scene shows him angrily reverting to the ways of life that he had so lately been treating with scorn.

Already in the last decades of the nineteenth century the Sicilian 'Renaissance' was in the making. Giovanni Verga's *Cavalleria rusticana* had appeared in 1884, and Luigi Capuana, besides making many contributions to native prose fiction and to the stage, had led a crusade for the encouragement of dialect drama, declaring that, while some might argue that broad social movements were the most significant characteristics of the time, more important were the vast psychological and spiritual gulfs existing not only between the peoples of different countries, but also between the inhabitants of regional areas within Italy itself. For the most part Capuana himself keeps to the brutally sensational side of Sicilian existence, where consuming passions are permitted full scope. A wife is murdered by an injured husband in one of his plays; in another the plot tells of the murder of a woman possessed by an evil spirit. It is the flame of strange passion that inspires this author rather than the irony of life.

The influence of these Sicilian dramatists upon Pirandello was direct and strong: at the same time he received inspiration and suggestions from other playwrights who stood outside the dialect theatre movement. One of these is the Neapolitan Salvatore di Giacomo, who exhibits, albeit in lurid flashes, a certain quality of power. Such dramas as *A San Francisco* (*At San Francisco*, 1896), with its ghastly tale of horror and passion, and *Assunta Spina* (1909), with its powerfully drawn portrait of a woman led by her instincts to betray two men, have a vigour of their own and an individual style. Similar individuality of style is obvious in the work of Sem Benelli, an author who, despite the fact that he displays clearly enough the romantic-poetic influence of D'Annunzio, must be definitely taken into account in any consideration of the antecedents of Pirandello. Without doubt the taffetaed *La cena delle beffe* (*The Jest*, 1909) could not have been penned had D'Annunzio not shown the way, yet here and in others of Benelli's dramas are introduced characters who adumbrate the persons who move on the Pirandello stage. The contrast between the vision and reality was suggested in Benelli's early prose-play *La tignola* (*The Bookworm*, 1908), in which a young librarian dreams of abandoning the world of books and living dangerously: the dream realized, the uninspiring desk, where there is at least security, claims its errant wanderer again. In the very title of *La maschera di Bruto* (*The Mask of Brutus*, 1908) the mood of Pirandello's theatre-world is suggested, and something more of that mood appears in *L'amore dei tre re* (*The Love of Three Kings*, 1910).

Throughout these and other dramatic essays produced in Italy during those years hints of the style later to be given the title of 'grottesco' may be discerned—sometimes merely faint wisps, sometimes, as in Niccodemi's *Acidalia* (1919), decisively moving from the ordinary realism popularized by Ibsen into an entirely new world. This 'Teatro del grottesco,' however, was not formally established as a separate form until Luigi Chiarelli came forward in 1916 with *La maschera e il volto* (*The Mask and the Face*), a brilliantly clever extravaganza of human follies. Taking as his central figure a man who professes to live by the ancient code of honour, the author shows him faced with reality (or, rather, for we are now entering the realm of Pirandello, with what he thinks is reality): he believes his wife has been unfaithful to him. The trouble, however, is that this Paolo really loves his Savina, or at least depends on her, and that his loud protestations are merely a robe covering weakness of

nature. Not wanting to kill her, and at the same time afraid of being ridiculed, he packs Savina off, giving out that he has taken her body and cast
it in a lake. Arrested and brought to trial, he is the occasion of a famous
case: he knows, of course, although he hardly admits the knowledge to
his consciousness, that Savina is alive and could at the last resort save
him, but he puts up a brave show as the husband who has dared to protect his honour, and is acquitted amid the plaudits of the crowd. The
town band greets him on his return home; the mayor gives him a civic
welcome; one of his friends, who had hitherto resignedly winked at his
own wife's giddy flirtations, assumes a new sternness and is tearfully
obeyed; ladies send flowers and marriage proposals to Paolo. But new
trouble for the hero now arises. Savina's scarf has been found in the lake,
and it is decided that she must be given a suitable burial service: despite
Paolo's protests, society demands the ritual. As the mourners gather
Savina, completely veiled in black, arrives, determined to be at her own
funeral. Paolo locks her up in his room, thereby arousing not a little
gossip, and, at last realizing that she is necessary for his happiness,
decides that, whatever society says, he must have her as his wife again.

In this grotesquely humorous work the cynical humour of *The Playboy
of the Western World* was carried one stage farther, and Italian dramatists
realized that a new medium was being put at their command. Chiarelli
himself pursued the method of his invention in *La scala di seta* (*The Silken
Ladder*, 1917), introducing still another element in the form of what is
almost allegory. Contrasted with the sincerely honest man is a male
dancer on whom the world showers honours and riches. It is, says Chiarelli, the dancers of life who alone are likely to succeed, and this concept
is demonstrated in action when the dancer, created a Minister of State
and delivering his inaugural address to the populace, mouths out impeccable platitudes while his feet keep moving in rhythmic steps. The structure and tone of this drama reveal one other feature of Chiarelli's work:
with no change in dialogue and merely an alteration of character names,
The Silken Ladder could almost be taken for a *fiaba* by Gozzi. There can be
no doubt but that the 'Teatro del grottesco' is a lineal descendant of the
ancient *commedia dell' arte*. The masks that so often are referred to in these
plays are the masks of Pulcinella and Arlecchino and Pantalone.

In *Chimere* (*Chimeras*, 1920) a darker tone prevails, although the technique is the same. By taking a Claudio who professes, like Paolo, the
sternest rectitude and a Marina who avers she could never be unfaithful
to her husband, and by showing this couple faced with financial disaster,
Chiarelli demonstrates how the ideal is rudely dissipated when confronted by the real. Salvation can come to Claudio and Marina if she consents to give herself to a wealthy banker: she agrees, and her husband is
content. The farcially ironic mood of Chiarelli's first play reappears in *La
morte degli amanti* (*The Lovers' Death*, 1921), in which a romantically
inclined Eleanora arranges a death-pact with her lover, Alfredo, only to
be thwarted of her heroic end by the unfortunate (or fortunate) arrival of

her husband, who turns off the gas in good, practical, bourgeois manner. For the theme of *Fuochi d'artificio* (*Fireworks*, 1923) he turns to a story very close to that used by Benavente in *Los intereses creados*. Gerardo and Scaramanzia have returned to Italy from America absolutely broke: the former, an honest fellow, thinks there is nothing for the future save suicide, but Scaramanzia, posing as Gerardo's secretary, allows every one to think he serves a millionaire, and public opinion creates the lie into the truth.

Even further than Chiarelli went Luigi Antonelli with his *L'uomo che incontrò se stesso* (*The Man who Met Himself*, 1918), *La fiaba dei tre maghi* (*The Fable of the Three Wise Men*, 1919), and *L'isola delle scimmie* (*The Island of the Monkeys*, 1922). The first of these has the advantage of casting a certain illumination on a dramatist whose work has previously been considered. It will be recalled that in dealing with Barrie an attempt was made to indicate the way in which his plays, although now so freely dismissed as merely sentimental, reveal the same features that give distinction to these grotesque plays of Italy: this judgment is concretely illustrated by the fact that the plots of two of his comedies are reflected in that of *L'uomo che incontrò sè stesso*, where Luciano, in despair because he has found that his wife has a lover and chiding himself for not warning her against the wiles of her seducer, laments that he cannot be given a second chance. Fate brings him to a lonely island, and there his wish is fulfilled. He warns his wife, and she behaves just as she had done before. We are close, indeed, here to *Dear Brutus* and *The Admirable Crichton*.

The use of the term 'fiaba' in the title of the second drama once more reminds us of the indebtedness of this whole school to the work of Gozzi, while the third play illustrates well the bitter disillusionment that is a component of nearly all these writings. When monkeys accept the guidance of men and establish what we style civilization they open their lives to all the misery and evil that surrounds humanity—this is Antonelli's thesis.

Much the same quality informs the work of Cesare Vico Ludovici, an author who won some fame for *La donna di nessuno* (*Nobody's Wife*, 1919), and of Carlo Veneziani, whose disillusionment in *La finestra sul mondo* (*The Window opening on the World*, 1918), and *Io prima di te* (*I before You*, 1919) is even deeper than that exhibited by Antonelli. Symbolism tends to become dominant here, as it does in the work of Enrico Cavacchioli. *L'uccello del paradiso* (*The Bird of Paradise*, 1919), by the last-named author, introduces a central character called He who is in part a mere figment of the mind, in part a kind of allegorical abstraction of fate. Similarly, in *La danza del ventre* (*The Belly Dance*, 1920) a typical mixture of morality drama and of the *commedia dell' arte* produces a strange world peopled by Arlecchino, the sexless dancer Nadir, and the symbol of passion, Pupa. Here the 'Teatro del grottesco' is becoming a trifle absurd.

One writer, however, besides Pirandello remains to be considered, and in his work something of true genius is apparent. Piermaria Rosso di

San Secondo, an offshoot of the Sicilian school, brings to the grotesque drama a quality intensely original, vivid, and bizarre. In 1918 he came before the public with his ironic *Marionette, che passione!* (*Marionettes, What Passion!*), in which three characters, wholly unrelated, are thrown together in a telegraph office. All are lonely, suffering souls—a girl who is abandoning a cruel lover, a betrayed husband, and a second man whose heart is torn by some secret inner torment. They arrange to meet at a café: the girl's lover enters and drags her off, the second man takes poison, and the husband is left in his dejection. The mere outlining of the plot must inevitably be inadequate to suggest the strange, haunting, tortured spirit that the author calls forth from his characters, who, puppet-like, are moved jerkily by forces they cannot control.

Throughout all Rosso di San Secondo's score or so of dramas runs a constant disharmony, as though sweet music were being rudely jangled and strings pulled awry. Mystical allegories are woven into plots in which sensationalism is mingled with the symbolic. The season following that in which his first play appeared saw the production of *La bella addormentata* (*The Sleeping Beauty*, 1919), in which the fairy-tale princess becomes a prostitute, but a prostitute who herself is a symbol of beauty desecrated by humanity. With a strange intoxicating mixture of *commedia dell' arte* figures and of poetic fantasy, wherein colours—blue and grey and yellow—assume almost living qualities, the author guides us through a vision fully as inward in its nature as the dream plays of Strindberg. *La roccia e i monumenti* (*The Rock and the Monuments*) came in 1923, and in it a certain alteration in style is apparent. The rock is the marble of Carrara, and there, in the house of the owner of a great quarry, the action takes place. On the surface the characters are ordinary men and women, but as the scenes unfold themselves we realize that the author's purpose is to use his basic setting in order to demonstrate the difference between primitive man, ignorant of any ties beyond those of his own nature, and the marble that has been chiselled by civilization into a new shape. The real and the symbolic, the living things and the inanimate or dead, are united here, as in *Febbre* (*Fever*, 1926), *La Madonnina di Belvento* (*The Little Madonna of Belvento*, 1928), and *L'avventura terrestre* (*The Terrestrial Adventure*, 1924), into a single strange atmosphere where wisdom and folly, deep thought and vulgar rhetoric, sincerity of purpose and frank theatricalism of the cheapest sort, are incongruously jumbled together.

Luigi Pirandello

From this atmosphere arose Luigi Pirandello, already well known as a novelist long before he turned to the stage with his first full-length play, *Se non così* (*If Not So*), in 1915—even long before he had written his first one-act piece, *La Morsa* (*The Vice*, 1898: produced in 1900). From that time on he tended more and more to devote himself to the theatre, and soon became one of the most widely discussed of modern playwrights.

Although it is to be confessed that throughout his dramatic writing he tends to harp on the same string, ever evolving fresh plots founded on the same basic principle, we must at the same time recognize both the sincerity of his aim (for this repetition of theme is not merely the lazy pursuit of a pattern which had already proved itself successful) and the skill through which he continually finds fresh facets of his theme to display to the world.

Essentially Pirandello is a realist whose realism questions the very fact of reality. For Ibsen a character might be complex, but the character was always one despite the complexity: Pirandello splits the atom that is man, and with explosive results. "Each one of us," he says, "believes himself to be one, but that is a false assumption: each of us is so many, so many—as many as are all the potentialities of being that are in us. . . . We ourselves know only one part of ourselves, and in all likelihood the least significant." The concept of the mask and the face is here taken one stage farther.

But the mask has another aspect. There is, as it were, an internal mask seen only by the person who wears it: there is also the external mask, or masks, by which he is known to his companions. This outer mask may be something he himself has created, or, on the other hand, it may be a thing imposed on him by society, which perhaps he would gladly doff, but which the imposition of public opinion insists that he shall wear. Where, asks Pirandello, in this maze are we to find any objective truth or reality? If all is relative—not merely with respect to an individual, but also with respect to different parts, or aspects, of an individual—surely there can be found no certainty anywhere?

From such thoughts he passes to others concerned with the relationship between art and nature. An author, we say, 'creates' a character; in what sense do we use that word? What hope is there for any writer to depict the shifting sands of character? What bearing have these figments of the imagination, the persons who move and speak on the stage, upon the real individuals whom they are supposed to represent? We speak of theatrical 'naturalism,' but if the stage is manifestly false and if in any case we cannot fathom the substance of the natural, the theatre surely can hardly dare to prate of realism.

While it must be confessed that such ideas are reiterated over and over again in Pirandello's long series of dramas, we must, at the same time, recognize that his inventive skill in finding interestingly varied plots through which to give concrete expression to his intellectual concepts gives to the body of his work a variety which we might well have deemed it could not possibly possess. Pirandello's early plays may, on the whole, be neglected, although the already mentioned *La morsa* and the later *Lumie di Sicilia* (*Sicilian Limes*, 1910) were pieces which clearly showed his dramatic skill. His first essay in the style he was to make his own was *Pensaci, Giacomino!* (*Think it over, Giacomino!*), which appeared in 1916. Here no more than the bare outlines of his later philosophy are presented, but clearly the basis is being firmly set. An elderly teacher named Toti exhibits a peculiar whim: finding that his school board is compelled to pay a pension to the widow of a deceased member of its staff, he deliberately marries a young girl, Lillina, who is about to have a child by Giacomino. Toti makes no attempt to take his place as husband: rather does he do all in his power to cement the ties between his wife and her lover. Gossip buzzes, but he remains content: has he not, he asks serenely, acted much more logically and humanely than the wiseacres would admit—has he not succeeded both in deriving pleasure for himself from the satisfaction consequent on doing a good deed and in protecting a girl from being broken on the wheels of the world?

The same year saw the production of *All' uscita* (*At the Gate*), and in 1917 came *Così è se vi pare* (*Right You Are—If You Think You Are*), the latter of which carries us fully into the world of the fantastically rational irrational. So tangled is the plot that a précis is barely possible; yet certain dominant concepts clearly make their appearance. A husband, Signor Ponza, has supposedly lost his first wife in an earthquake and marries again. However, he carefully keeps this second wife apart from the supposed mother-in-law, Signora Frola, of his first wife. This, he explains, is because Signora Frola thinks her daughter is still alive, still Signora Ponza. The mother-in-law, however, has a different story: she says that Signora Ponza is really her daughter, who is forced to pretend to be a second wife in order to humour a whim of her husband's. As for Signora Ponza herself, she is prepared at one moment to tell Signora Frola she is her daughter and at the next to agree with her husband she is his second wife. Wherein lies the truth? We cannot tell, for the arguments used by each one of these persons are so logical, so plausible, that as we listen to them we are compelled to accept each separate interpretation of events, and, in order the further to make his purpose plain, Pirandello introduces a kind of *raisonneur* in Laudisi, a man whose only function in the drama is to underline the author's basic purpose.

Having thus set the stage with this question-mark of a play, Pirandello gave it further movement in his next two works, both produced in 1917, *Il berretto a sonagli* (*Cap and Bells*) and *Il piacere dell' onestà* (*The Pleasure of Honesty*). *Cap and Bells* introduces a fresh motif. Outwardly throughout most of its action it is a typical Sicilian drama, half amusing, half tragic, of jealous passion. In this outward drama the key figure is Beatrice Fiorica, who, owing to the malicious tattle of an old crone, "La Saracena," is consumed with frenzied anger when she believes her husband to be having an affair with the wife of an ugly, almost grotesque-looking, clerk, Ciampa. In order to catch her husband, she gets Ciampa sent off to a neighbouring city and tells the police to raid his house after he has gone. Fiorica is caught there, but now the stratagem recoils on Beatrice's head: if her husband is proved guilty she will have to leave him and her position will not be an enviable one. To add to this thought there is the unexpected attitude of Ciampa—and there we move from the outward story to the inner. Ciampa is ugly and he knows it: the only thing he could do to keep his self-respect was to overlook his wife's peccadilloes and put up a brave front to the world. Although he might suspect, even know, the truth, all was well with him just so long as common opinion thought her faithful. The logical solution, he declares, is for Beatrice to let herself be certified insane: it will mean only a few months in an asylum, there will be no case against her husband, no need of senseless heroics, no tearing off of the mask. In the development of the latter part of the action Pirandello indulges in much talk of 'puppets,' and these references serve at once to indicate the deep impress made on his mind by the *commedia dell' arte*—particularly by its still-living descendant, the marionette show —and to prepare the way for many other plays in which a contrast is effected between the world of life and that of the stage. The real Ciampa has his existence underneath the puppet figure on which his neighbours look.

The Pleasure of Honesty has a different concept to convey. The story tells of life in aristocratic Society. A young girl, Agata Renni, has been seduced by a fashionable married man-about-town, the Marquis Fabio Colli. To hush up a scandal he approaches an impoverished friend, Angelo Baldovino, with the proposal that he should marry Agata—in the hopeful expectation, of course, that under the cover of this wedding he can remain her lover. Baldovino accepts the proposal, but, once married, declares that his wife must conduct herself with rigid propriety. Enraged, Fabio plans a stratagem through which the husband shall appear to be a thief, but this piece of trickery is perceived by the intended victim and the tables are turned. Baldovino, however, assures the lover that, so long as his name is cleared, he is content to depart; and in this assurance a new note is seen to intrude. Up to now Baldovino has been only a puppet husband; but to his inner dismay he finds himself, as a man, truly falling in love with his wife. This dismay is turned into a kind of regretful joy when he later discovers that Agata herself, deeply influenced by his pronouncements of rectitude, has likewise come to regard him as her husband in fact. From one world, the world from which he had endeavoured to shut out all emotion, Baldovino is drawn into the other world of human passion.

In *L'innesto* (*Grafting*), also produced in 1917, Pirandello has hardly succeeded in making his strained psychological analysis either palatable or credible. His next play, however, *Il giuoco delle parti* (*The Rules of the Game*, 1918), presents a grippingly interesting situation—that of a husband, Leone Galla, who so complacently accepts the intrigue of his wife, Silia, with Guido that, enraged, she manœuvres to get her husband killed. Claiming that she has been insulted by a young nobleman, a noted duellist, she declares that Leone must send a challenge in order to protect her honour; in equally complacent manner he does so, naming Guido as his second, but when the time for the combat arrives he refuses to go, knowing that in such cases the second is bound by convention to take the place of the principal. Guido is thus driven into the trap he and Silia have set; he, not the husband, dies.

Ma non è una cosa seria (*He didn't mean it*, or *But it is not a Serious Affair*) came the same year, and was followed by *L'uomo, la bestia e la virtù* (*Man, Beast, and Virtue*, or *Say it with Flowers*, 1919), a play in which Pirandello shows how deeply his dramatic style, for all its novelty, was implanted in native traditions. In effect we are back in the world of *La mandragola*, with all the apparatus of Renaissance intrigue: the difference lies in the bitter twisting of the plot from what would have been a trick designed by a lover to obtain his mistress into a cruelly savage paradox: instead of using a drug to gain his own pleasure, the lover here is forced to employ it for the purpose of throwing his lady into the arms of her husband. This husband, a sea-captain, rarely comes home to his wife, Signora Perrella, and, when he does, he is so afraid of having another child that he seeks immediate opportunity of quarrelling with her and leaving his house. Signora Perrella, however, has been consoling herself with the little schoolteacher Paolino, and unfortunately finds herself pregnant. In order to save appearances, the lover Paolino is thus forced into devising a strategem (including the use of an aphrodisiac) whereby Perrella will be induced to lie with his wife. The whole situation is farcical, but the farce is typically Pirandellian; the laughter is torn by an almost hysterical bitterness.

With *Tutto per bene* (*All for the Best*, 1920) Pirandello returns to the contrast between the image and reality, and in handling this theme he here produces one of his most incisive and moving dramas. Three or four levels of belief confront us. First there is the common belief that the girl who passes as Palma Lori is in reality the daughter of Senator Manfroni: Manfroni has provided the money for her education, and every one accepts this as right and proper. Secondly there is the belief that Martino Lori, her theoretical 'father,' knows of this common opinion and merely pretends to be devoted to Palma, merely simulates the grief he outwardly shows for the memory of his dead wife: he is, accordingly, treated with scant attention by others, and his expressions of love for his daughter are met by her with obvious irritation—for she too thinks that he is aware of what all accept to be true. Thirdly there is Martino's own belief, genuine and deeply felt, that his deceased wife was a saint: his love of Palma is now the only joyous thing in his life. When he first learns of what has been happening his whole world comes crashing down on him: ideas of revenge fill his mind and have to be rejected; and in the end the old position is restored—but with a vast inner distinction. So far as society is concerned, Martino continues his former pretence, but now he does so deliberately, with conscious knowledge; while that which he had lost before, his daughter's love, is now freely given to him, since, in the realization that he had not formerly been merely play-acting, she discovers in her heart admiration and affection for a man deeply wronged and tormented. The surface is the same, but in the depths all is altered.

To deal with all Pirandello's many variations on this concept of the mask and the face would be impossible here, since his output is so large: no more can be done than to take a few characteristic specimens of his later dramas, as examples of the diverse ways in which he explores, now satirically, now with almost tragic intensity, the possibilities of his chosen realm. One line of development is marked by *La Signora Morli una e due* (*Signora Morli Two in One*, 1920; revised in 1926 as *Due in una*), where the author examines the different personalities embraced within a single human being. In the central character of this play he shows us a woman almost equally divided between the gay, thoughtless, frivolous creature who had been the wife of Ferrante Morli and the serious, cautious, respectable housewife she has become in her association with Lello Carpani. Ironically Pirandello makes the former side of her character associate itself with a husband, the latter with a lover, and he is at pains to demonstrate that these two sides are not due merely to change in circumstance, the one following and as it were supplanting the other, but that they co-exist at the same time in her nature.

Immediately after the production of this study in double personality came the famous *Sei personaggi in cerca d'autore* (*Six Characters in Search of an Author*, 1921). The plot of this drama is well known. We are in a theatre as a new play is being rehearsed (the play, indeed, is one of Pirandello's own). Suddenly, illuminated by a light of their own, Six Characters enter. These were creatures of an artist's imagination, some fully developed in personality, others only half developed, and, searching for an author, they are desperately anxious to realize their destiny. The Father, chief of the group, tries stumblingly to explain to the puzzled theatrical director:

> Oh, sir, you are well aware that life is full of infinite absurdities which, since they are true, do not need to seem plausible. . . . I tell you that to try and reverse the process, to aim at verisimilitude, to make these things appear true, is nothing but folly. Yet you will allow me to remark that if this is folly, it is the sole justification for your profession.

In these words Pirandello carries us into the world of appearance and reality, but with a different purpose. These characters have been side-tracked,

> in the sense, you see, that the author who gave us vitality no longer wished or was not able materially to introduce us to the world of art. And this was a real crime, sir; because he who has the good fortune to be born a living character can laugh even at death. He is beyond death! The man, the writer, the instrument of the creation, will die, but his creation never dies. And for this eternal life no extraordinary gifts, no working of wonders, are needed. Who was Sancho Panza? Who was Don Abbondio? Yet they live eternally because—living germs—they had the good fortune to find a fruitful womb, a fantasy that could rear and nourish them—make them live for eternity!

By contrasting the real and the imagined, the genuine passion and its theatrically simulated counterpart, Pirandello directs our gaze upon the inadequacy of the supposed 'realism' that has so long dominated on our stage. In the fantastic outlining of the plot in which the Six Characters are involved he shows the utter impossibility of neatly ascribing 'motives' to their actions and of hoping that their lives can be adequately translated into playhouse terms. The Director is tempted to act their drama and calls to the Property Man for a sofa:

PROPERTY MAN: Yes, sir, there's that green one.
THE STEPDAUGHTER: No, no, not green! It was yellow, ornamented with flowers—very large! Very soft.
PROPERTY MAN: We haven't one like that.
THE DIRECTOR: But it doesn't matter! Bring the one you've got!
THE STEPDAUGHTER: What do you mean—'doesn't matter'?

The Director proceeds to try to cast the characters: he turns to the Leading Lady:

THE DIRECTOR: You, of course, are the Stepdaughter . . .
THE STEPDAUGHTER [laughing]: What? what? I that woman there?
                                              [Bursts out laughing.
THE DIRECTOR [angrily]: What is there to laugh at?
LEADING LADY [indignantly]: Nobody has ever dared to laugh at me! I insist on being treated with respect—or I'll go.
THE STEPDAUGHTER: No, no, excuse me. I'm not laughing at you at all.
THE DIRECTOR [to STEPDAUGHTER]: You ought to feel honoured to be played by—
LEADING LADY [angrily]: 'That woman there . . .'
THE STEPDAUGHTER: But I wasn't speaking of you, believe me! I was speaking of myself. I don't somehow . . . I don't *see* myself in you at all.
THE FATHER: There! That's the point, you see, sir! What we have to express—
THE DIRECTOR: What you have to express! Do you really think you have any power of expression in you? Nothing of the kind!
THE FATHER: What! We don't have something of our own to express?
THE DIRECTOR: Not a bit of it! You can find expression only when the actors give body and form, voice and gesture, to your beings. And these actors, each in his own line, have been able to give expression to much finer material. Yours is so thin that if it does succeed on the stage, the merit, believe me, will rest entirely in my actors.

To and fro the argument goes until at the end a shot rings out and the Boy falls:

THE LEADING LADY [entering in tears]: He's dead! Poor boy! He's dead! Oh, how terrible!
THE LEADING MAN [running in, laughing]: He isn't dead! Pretence! Pretence! Don't you believe it.
SOME ACTORS: Pretence? Reality! Reality! He's dead!
OTHER ACTORS: No! Pretence! Pretence!
THE FATHER [rising, with a cry]: Pretence is it? Reality, reality, sir!

Reality!   [*He rushes desperately behind the curtain.*

THE DIRECTOR [*unable to stand it any longer*]: Pretence! Reality! To hell with
all of it! Lights! Lights! Lights! [*Immediately the whole theatre is illuminated. The
DIRECTOR takes a deep breath as though he had been freed from an incubus, and all
the actors look at each other, puzzled and bewildered.*] Ah! I've never known such a
thing! They've made me lose a whole day's rehearsal!

This might well have been the culmination of Pirandello's work, but
the year following appeared another, and a diverse, study of a variant
aspect of his problem—*Enrico Quarto* (*Henry IV*, 1922). During the celebration of a pageant the hero of this play has fallen from his horse and
has been living for years under the delusion that he is, in fact, the character he had represented in the pageant itself. Surrounded by a bevy of servants, he maintains a royal state appropriate to the position of the
eleventh-century German monarch. After some years, however, his
insanity passes: he realizes who he is, but he realizes too that he so hates
the ordinary world that he prefers to maintain the illusion of his madness
among others. Into this strange Court, wherein 'Henry IV' quite deliberately keeps up his pretence and wherein his attendants comply in the
belief that he is mad, come the Marchioness Matilda Spina, whom
'Henry IV' had loved in the past, her daughter, Frida, and Baron Tito
Belcredi, who had caused the accident responsible for the delusion suffered by the main character. These persons appropriately disguise themselves so as to fit in with the eleventh-century atmosphere, but Matilda
has the uneasy suspicion that he has pierced through their deception. At
the end of the play Henry, after denouncing all of them, snatches a sword
and stabs Belcredi, and the final words suggest that now, sane though he
is, he must continue in his pretence if his life is to be safe. Left on the stage
with his three valets, he gazes round desperately, "with his eyes almost
starting out of his head, terrified by the life of his own masquerade which
has driven him to crime":

HENRY IV: Ah, now . . . yes, now . . . inexorably [*gathers his VALETS around
him as if to protect him*] together . . . here together . . . for ever . . . for ever.

This study of insanity was accompanied the same year by the study of
what might be styled a characterless personality in *Vestire gli ignudi*
(*Naked*, or *Clothing the Naked*, 1922), where Ersilia Drei, a governess whose
drab life has been interrupted by a passing flirtation with a young naval
officer and by an association with her master, takes poison, and, in the
belief that she will die, gives a highly romantic story of her adventures to
a journalist. An elderly novelist, Ludovico Nota, impressed by this
account, takes her from hospital to his rooms. There she pathetically
tries to create a personality for herself, clinging anxiously to the novelist's
interpretation of her actions, but life will not let her be. Nota sees in her
one thing, the young naval officer sees another, and her former master

still a third. Each of these has before him the same set of outward appearances; these appearances each interprets in his own way. The officer tells Nota he is ignoring the facts, and the latter, speaking for the author, makes reply:

> Facts! Facts! My dear sir, facts are what we assume them to be; and then, in their essence, they are no longer facts, but phenomena of life that take on one or another semblance.

Deprived of her attempt to create a being for herself, poor Ersilia takes poison a second time and dies, clearly revealing in her last words the longings she has had. Her fallacious record of her life was made because she had felt herself naked, never had anything beautiful to put on:

> And then . . . and then I wanted at least to have a decent dress for my burial. You see why I lied? For this, I assure you. Never in my whole life have I been able to have a decent dress to make a good appearance in.

Even this is torn from her. "Go and tell it to them," she cries, "that this dead woman—this dead woman here—could not find a dress for herself."

This drama was followed by the effective one-act *L'uomo dal fiore in bocca* (*The Man with a Flower in his Mouth*, 1923) and by another essay in the nature of truth, *Ciascuno a suo modo* (*Each in his own Way*, 1924), in which again the worlds of 'reality' and of the theatre are intermingled. The first act shows a play being enacted on the stage: this finished, we move to the foyer and listen to the members of the audience commenting upon it, and in particular drawing attention to the fact that the fictional story bears a close resemblance to the 'real' story of a woman who sits in the stalls, Delia Moreno. Pirandello himself provides an understanding of what he was attempting to do:

> With this presentation of the foyer and of the spectators attending the first act of the play, what appeared on the stage in the first plane as the representation of a segment of life will now assume shape as an artistic fiction; hence it will accordingly be distanced and pushed back into a second plane. Later, at the close of this first interlude, it will become clear that even the foyer and the spectators will also be, in their turn, pushed back into a plane yet further removed: this will be realized when it is seen that the play presented on the stage is a *comédie à clef*—that is to say, a drama composed by the author on an event supposed to have occurred in real life and currently in the news.

The entirely fictional, the translation on to the stage of 'real' events, and the 'real' itself are thus completely confounded, and, although Pirandello does not specifically refer to this, yet a fourth plane enters in through the fact that the foyer represented on the stage is the image of the foyer used by the audience who have come to see *Ciascuno a suo modo*.

In the plays written after this date the repetition of forms already exploited tends to take from the characters such glow of sympathy as was apparent in the earlier works, while a movement towards the exploitation of symbolic elements brings to their scenes a rather cold, abstract quality. The earlier concepts are pursued in a number of dramas, but only *Questa sera si recita a soggetto* (*To-night We Improvise*, 1930) and *Come tu mi vuoi* (*As You Desire Me*, 1930) warrant particular mention. The former is a further essay on the subject of *Six Characters*, contrasting the actor's pretence of emotion with the emotion itself; the latter reminds us of the theme of *Right You Are*, introducing a woman whom Bruno Pieri thinks is his long-lost wife, Lucia: her memory seems to be returning to her after a fit of amnesia just when another woman is found and claimed by the family to be the true Lucia. A question-mark ends this play, and we are left with the impression so frequently conveyed by Pirandello's dramas that personality is a thing either built up by ourselves or else imposed from without by others.

The symbolic style may be exemplified by such works as *La sagra del Signore della Nave* (*Our Lord of the Ship*, 1925) and *I giganti della montagna* (*The Giants of the Mountain*, 1937). *La sagra del Signore della Nave* presents a single long scene of massed humanity shown in pagan celebration on a saint's-day, with a strong contrast set between the licence of the secular and the solemnity of the ecclesiastical. Written especially for the Teatro Odescalchi, which came under Pirandello's direction in 1925, the play introduces a style distinct from that of his earlier dramas. In *I giganti della montagna* something still farther removed makes its appearance. This, his last play, introduces to us a group of wretched human creatures who live in some hovels under the spell of a Magician, and to them come a number of characters, half real, half illusionary—a Countess who bears with her a play written by a dead poet, a troupe of actors, and a set of figures of a purely allegorical sort, spirits of the mountain who apparently symbolize bestial power. Despite some scenes of haunting if puzzling beauty, the drama shows a disintegration of strength: without being able to capture the imaginative vision that could come only from a poetic treatment of his material, Pirandello here allows his intellectual fantasies to carry him into a world beyond the reach of artistic harmony.

What judgment ultimately will be passed on his work as a whole is hard to guess. One thing, however, is certain: no other author so clearly, and with such skill, has given expression to this contrast between the appearance and the reality which forms a kind of *leitmotiv* in almost the whole of the serious theatre of the between-war period. Pirandello thus assumes a key position in the history of the modern stage. Apart from this, there can be no doubt but that his analysis of the human personality is acute, that he shows a brilliant mastery of his craft, and that he possesses the power to give emotional connotations to concepts which at first seem wholly intellectual. The likelihood is that he is a dramatic artist who will remain long in the memory of the stage.

3

THE THEATRE SYMBOLIC AND THEATRICAL

PIRANDELLO's dramas suggest that symbols might better convey dramatic truth than living characters; they suggest also by implication that the theatre might as well forget its endeavour to reproduce 'reality' and be content with its theatricalism. Neither suggestion was carried to fulfilment in his own work, since he himself was concerned rather with displaying the inadequacy of certain established forms than with the pursuit of other forms likely to lead to concrete, positive achievement. That task was undertaken during these years by two Russian playwrights, Leonid Nikolaevich Andreev and Nikolai Nikolaevich Evreinov.

Neither perhaps can be esteemed a really great writer; but both are of considerable historical interest, and, even although their works are now but rarely presented on the stage, their influence may still be traced in many quarters. In thus linking them together, however, there is no intention to suggest that their styles are the same: indeed, their aims were so entirely at variance that we might well have dealt with them in wholly different sections. The justification for bringing them under one heading here rests on a single consideration, and on a single consideration only —that both endeavours, each in his own way, to release the stage from the incubus of realism.

Andreev's work is best to be understood by thinking of him as standing between Gorki and Maeterlinck. With the former he is bound by his experiments in realistic drama; with the latter he stands because of his several symbolic plays. Introspective, discouraged, fundamentally pessimistic, he is thoroughly characteristic of the period when Russian intellectuals, after the failure of the 1905 revolution, could see no hope in the future and tended to turn in on themselves. Writing a "Letter on the Theatre" in 1913, he clearly revealed his ultimate desires in pleading for a "theatre pan-psyche," imagining—like Maeterlinck—that action, "in the accepted sense of movements and visible achievements on the stage," might well be dispensed with and that the dramatists to come ought to concentrate upon the workings of the soul.

His first four plays—*K zvezdam* (*To the Stars*, 1905), *Savva* (1906), *Zhizn cheloveka* (*The Life of Man*, 1906), and *Tsar-Golod* (*King Hunger*, 1907)—fully illustrate the nature of his questing for form and substance. *To the Stars* is a peculiarly effective drama in which realism and symbolism are combined. The setting is an observatory situated just beyond the Russian frontier; there live Inna Alexandrovna and her husband, an astronomer, Sergei Ternovski. From across the boundary-line shots can be heard, and Ternovski's rapt absorption in his studies, whereby the affairs of men are viewed as infinitesimal when considered *sub specie æternitatis*, is contrasted with the passions of the young Nikolai, an active revolutionary, and his fiancée, Marusia. Although the play has manifold weaknesses, it possesses, by reason both of its theme and of its sharply delineated characters, the true quality of strength. In *Savva* the method employed is more strictly realistic and the endeavour more consciously intellectual: it is, indeed, a kind of propaganda play designed as an attack upon the superstitions encouraged by the Orthodox Church. Realism, however, could not give Andreev what he wanted, and in *The Life of Man* he discovered a style more intimately harmonized with his aims. Even although we have passed beyond the spiritual atmosphere out of which this symbolic fantasy was created, even although we can now discern how trite are some of its philosophical pronouncements, Andreev's achievement must receive at least qualified praise. Man is born in darkness; as he traces his path upon the earth the Being in Grey, a symbol of inexorable fate, stands constantly by his side; and in darkness man dies. The whole spirit of the drama breathes despair and bitterness, and the final scene is a fitting close to the action:

BEING IN GREY: Silence! Man is dead!

[*Silence, absolute quiet. And the same cold, emotionless voice repeats the words from afar off, like an echo:*

Silence! Man is dead!

[*Silence, absolute quiet. Slowly the darkness thickens, but still the mouse-like figures of the attendant OLD WOMEN are visible. Quietly and silently they begin to gather round the corpse—then they begin to sing quietly—the musicians begin to play. The darkness thickens, and the music and the singing grows ever louder, the wild dance becomes more impetuous. Now they are hardly dancing; rather they madly fling themselves around the corpse, stamping their feet, shrieking, uttering wild, continuous sounds of laughter. It is completely dark, save that the face of the dead man grows luminous; then that light too disappears. Black, opaque darkness.*

And in the darkness are heard the movements of the mad dancers, the screams, the laughter, the discordant, desperately loud music of the orchestra. When they reach their highest note all these sounds, all these noises, swiftly pass somewhere afar off and die away. . . . Silence.

Man expires amid the cacophony of jazz and swing.

The same symbolic style dominates in *King Hunger*, where the figure of Hunger appears before the toiling poor, while above their heads the wealthy move in a constant, dancing round of gaiety. Less successful as a whole than *The Life of Man*, this was followed by the extraordinary drama called *Cherniya maski* (*The Black Maskers*, 1908), strangely beautiful and perplexing, where something of the Pirandellian concept is added to the morality atmosphere that Andreev had cultivated in his two preceding compositions. The Black Maskers are the powers whose field of action is the soul of man and whose mysterious nature no one can ever fathom. When they come seeping into the palace the entire stage becomes as it were a concrete image of the human being, although the symbolism is double in that the main plot deals with the fate of Duke Lorenzo, who, oppressed by dark thoughts, has created a kind of evil double of himself. Only when he rises at the end and slays this second self, thus taking action against the besieging forces of despair and dejection, does he come to a vision of what life may be. Lorenzo himself perishes at the end, but in dying he is a soul who, after a frenzied, nightmarish battle with himself, has gained mastery over his fate.

In *Dni nashei zhizni* (*The Days of Our Life*, 1908), *Anfisa* (1909), and *Gaudeamus* (1910) Andreev returns to a more realistic atmosphere, but at the same time continues actively his exploration of the soul. Of these plays the second is without question the most impressive. The dark theme, involving the treatment of incest, is developed with tense and impressive vigour. The central figure, Anfisa, is a widow, the sister of Alexandra, wife of the erratically brilliant but basically weak Feodor Kostomarov. Alarmed at his excesses, Alexandra has brought Anfisa into her home, hoping that her influence will have the effect of restraining him: instead Anfisa herself comes under his influence, and the greater part of the play is devoted to an analysis of the tortured emotions of these three characters—Anfisa, intoxicated by passion and tormented by Kostomarov's cruelty to her, Alexandra, not certain of the truth yet strongly suspecting, and Kostomarov, a creature swayed like a piece of flotsam by his emotions.

The only symbolic element in this drama is the figure of the old nurse, whose presence introduces a faint suggestion of the supernatural and gives a universality to the story it otherwise would have lacked. The supernatural, however, flows in and engulfs the stage in *Anathema* (1909), a rather unsuccessful development of the age-old theme of the Devil descended to earth for the purpose of plaguing an individual human soul. Equally unsuccessful is the satirically comic *Prekrasnie Sabinianki* (*The Sabine Women*, 1912), wherein contemporary politics are clothed in Roman dress. Possibly dissatisfied with these, Andreev tended in most of his later works to content himself with the infusion of a slight element of the symbolic into scenes that outwardly at least were realistic. Such a drama, for example, as *Sobachii vals* (*The Waltz of the Dogs*; written 1914, printed 1922) is thoroughly in the Gorki manner, while *Tot, kto poluchaet poshchechini* (*He Who Gets Slapped*, 1915) introduces symbolic connotations only by implication. If *The Waltz of the Dogs* reminds us of earlier Russian realistic efforts, this last play clearly has affiliations with the Italian 'Teatro del grottesco.' The concept of the mask and the face is inherent in its theme of the lonely intellectual who deliberately covers his personality with the ridiculous make-up of a clown and permits himself to appear before the public as the wretched zany, the man who arouses laughter because he appears as the absurd simpleton, the butt for the jests and the blows of his companions. Even further is the concept carried through the love awakened in the clown's heart by the lovely Consuelo: when he sees her about to be condemned to what he regards as a living death he gives her poison, and is content to think that thus he has saved her spirit.

A good deal of the sentimental enters into this would-be tragedy, and maybe it is this quality in Andreev that is most likely to deny him permanence. He would have liked to have written plays powerful as *Œdipus Rex*, overwhelming as *King Lear*: instead he succeeded only in creating scenes either of a baffling or of a slightly spurious kind. At the same time, he is by no means to be neglected. If he failed he failed because he aimed high and gloriously.

While Andreev was thus struggling to invest the realistic drama with qualities deeper and more penetrating, Evreinov consciously sought to exploit the theatrical. Andreev's mind was oriented towards the tragic; Evreinov's was inclined towards the comic, even if often his comedy was bitter. The former sought for truth in the theatre; the latter believed not only in making the theatre theatrical, but also in exploiting to the full that theatrical quality which he saw everywhere in nature. At the same time he shared with Andreev interest in the complexities of the mind, and succeeded in mingling with his 'theatricalism' not a little of the quality that was expressed in *The Black Maskers*.

For realism Evreinov has utter contempt. In his book *The Theatre in Life* he makes fun of the famous production of *The Three Sisters* at the Moscow Art Theatre. When he saw it, he tells us, he laughed because he realized that this solemnly naturalistic performance was still conventional and theatrical. In order to be thoroughly naturalistic Stanislavski should, he suggests, have rented a small house in the suburbs of Moscow:

> You, a spectator, would come with the other spectators under the pretext of looking for apartments. At the gate leading into the courtyard you would buy an admission ticket. You would be accompanied to the house by a janitor who would give you in a low voice all explanations needed (that is to say, the full text of the playwright's remarks, uttered, if possible, in a 'Chekhovian' tone). In order to see through the keyhole, or through a half-open door, all the scenes of the play (for even in such stage setting one could not very well do without a bit of conventionality), you would have to visit the house quite a few times—in the morning, in the afternoon, and even in the night, when you would behold it in flames (for the fire which must take place in the abode of the three sisters would be, of course, a one hundred per cent. 'real' one).

This concept he treats dramatically in an entertaining two-act comedy *Chetvertaia stena* (*The Fourth Wall*, 1915), where an ultranaturalistic Assistant Producer casts doubt into the mind of a Director who is preparing a production of *Faust*. The operatic form has to be given up; the Russian text has to be abandoned in favour of German; the furniture has to be authentic; the contents of the bottles in Faust's workroom have to be filled with 'real' liquids, including poisons; in the end even a fourth wall has to be built up and Faust seen merely by glimpses at the window of his study. The play ends when the wretched actor who takes Faust's part, unable to stand this any longer, comes out before the audience and, crying "I can't bear it! I can't bear it!" swallows a fatal draught and dies on the attenuated stage.

This piece, besides presenting characteristically Evreinov's contempt for the realistic, well exhibits the qualities of his style. There is a touch of Pirandello here; there is a suggestion of the symbolic quality associated with Andreev's work; and along with this, strangely, there is a flavour of Chekhov. Had Chekhov opposed realism as does Evreinov, this is precisely the kind of play he would have written: its technique and atmosphere recall nothing so markedly as the spirit of the earlier author's one-act comedies.

At the opposite extreme from *The Fourth Wall*, yet closely bound to it in method of composition and in general texture, is another short piece, *V kulisakh dushi* (*In the Wings of the Soul*, or *The Theatre of the Soul*, 1912), a 'monodrama' introduced by a Professor, who carefully explains to us that, instead of there being, as is commonly supposed, a single 'I' for each individual, a human personality is built up of numerous entities—I_1, I_2, I_3, and so on:

> 'I' is not 'I', because 'I' consists of several 'I's.' In practice we may treat 'I' as consisting of three 'I's.'

[*He writes on the blackboard:* "$I = \frac{x}{3}$."

The first is reason, the second is emotion, the third is the eternal. After this introduction we move to a scene within a single human being, with a great heart pulsating in the middle of the stage, and within this scene the various 'I's' play their part in such a manner as to make the man to whom they belong wander distractedly through a maze of a world. Like Pirandello, but in a slightly different way, Evreinov strives to show us, not only that material objects appear to different persons in different ways, but also that even a single person views these objects differently on different occasions. Thus the Woman with whom this man is in love assumes one form when he applies his reason to her, another when his emotional 'I' is dominant. With skilled hand and witty dialogue Evreinov here presents what might be regarded as the seriously comic counterpart of *The Black Maskers*. In the end the Man shoots himself, but the general atmosphere of the piece summons forth laughter rather than tears. At the end the third 'I' "puts on his hat, picks up his portmanteau, yawns," and leaves the empty stage.

Among the shorter plays of this author, *Revizor* (1912) may be noted as a lively skit on diverse productional methods, showing how Gogol's play would be presented by a 'classic' director, by Stanislavski, by Reinhardt, and by Gordon Craig. Akin in spirit is *Kukhnia smecha* (*A Feast of Fun*, 1913), described as an "International Competition in Wit," wherein the same plot is supposed to be dramatized by a German, a Frenchman, and an American. In the symbolist style *Veselaia smert* (*A Merry Death*) ironically plays with characters from the *commedia dell'arte*. More interesting is *Krasivii despot* (*The Beautiful Despot*), which shows an intellectual who, tiring of liberal sentiment, deliberately sets himself back into the year 1808, surrounds himself with servants who are content to be serfs, and goes so far as to be provided even with newspapers of the period in which he is living his dream existence.

In such short plays Evreinov was thoroughly in his element. He failed, however, to translate his buoyant, mordantly satirical spirit into larger terms. Neither his earlier full-length dramas nor his later *Samoe glavnoe* (*The Chief Thing*, 1919), with its symbolic Paraklete who tries to put the author's theories into practice and to bring the drama out of the theatre into life, have much real value, although this last play, developing the idea of happiness being brought to a number of wretched souls through the building of illusions by theatrical means, has both an original concept and some interestingly penned scenes.

The links that bind Andreev and Evreinov to Pirandello and the whole Italian 'Teatro del grottesco' are obvious. In noting them, however, we should not overlook the links that join all of these to that fantastic comedy strain which already has been noted as one of the chief elements in the nineteenth-century theatre, and which stems back ultimately to the *commedia dell'arte*. There is something in common between Gozzi's *fiabe* and Tieck's purposeful fairy-tales; and qualities inherent in these plays are clearly reflected in Evreinov's scenes. Even more clearly are they mirrored in the poetic dramas of Alexander Alexandrovich Blok, where the play of imagination mingles with satirical laughter and ironic fancies. Typical are his *Balaganchik* (*The Puppet Show*, 1906)—which, with its Pierrot and Columbine, its suggestion of the contrast between appearance and reality, and its symbolist tone, obviously is to be related to Evreinov's *A Merry Death*—and *Neznakomka* (*The Stranger*, 1907). Some of the same elements intrude into the 'tragedy' *Roza i krest* (*The Rose and the Cross*, 1913), a rather weak medieval-set drama of a great lady and her hopeless lover. To the same symbolist school belongs Feodor Sologub (Feodor Kuzmich Teternikov), whose *Pobeda smerti* (*The Triumph of Death*, 1907) and other dramas are clearly cast in the same mould as produced the works of Evreinov.

These Russian writers, of course, were reflecting what was a widespread cult in many countries during the earlier years of the twentieth century, a cult which combined several different elements and which expressed itself in a variety of styles. The misty atmosphere conjured up by Maeterlinck was often to be encountered here; death and love were constant themes; and almost everywhere could be seen reflections of the *commedia dell'arte*. There were some authors who constantly remained within the ambience of the stage ruled by Pierrot, Harlequin and Columbine; but, strangely, we can also find here other playwrights who commuted, as it were, between this territory and that of social realism. Already we have seen how Granville-Barker produced his *Voysey Inheritance* and *Madras House*, studies in upper-middle-class business life, while at the same time he found pleasure in concocting, in collaboration with Laurence Housman, a picture of idealized love in a Dutch garden (*Prunella*) and, in collaboration with Calthrop, a kind of dramatic 'history' of the *Harlequinade*. Alfred Sutro, the popular author of *The Walls of Jericho* (1904) and numerous 'realistic' studies of social life, was also translator of several of Maeterlinck's most fanciful plays. Everywhere we look, similar examples can be found. The Swedish Hjalmar Bergman may be taken as a prime representative of this trend. Ibsen strongly influenced him, and his keen comic sense brought him popularity for his *Swedenhielms* (1925) and *Markurells i Wadköping* (*Markurells of Wadköping*, (1929), but he also wrote his so-called 'Marionette Plays' (1917)—a collection of three short dramas, one of them characteristically entitled *Dödens Arlekin* (*Death's Harlequin*) and another, *Herr Sleeman kommer* (*Mr Sleeman is Coming*), showing, in an equally characteristic manner, a young girl, ideally in love with a young forester, who is forced by her relatives to marry an older businessman—the dream and the reality.

The Vogue of the 'isms'

Realism, naturalism, symbolism, theatricalism—these movements have been seen to play a prominent part in the theatre's world during the last years of the nineteenth century and the first years of our own era. Even more pronounced 'isms,' however, were still to come.

Closely connected with Evreinov in Russia was Vladimir Vladimirovich Mayakovski, whose *Misteriya-Buff* (*Mystery-Bouffe*, 1918) won him some fame in the early days of the Revolution, partly because it is an effective piece of propaganda, partly because its fantastic style is handled with consummately skilful showmanship. Mayakovski, however, is admittedly a Futurist, and here we are carried back once more to Italy —not the Italy of Pirandello, but that of Filippo Tommaso Marinetti, who first formulated and defined the movement. Futurism itself gave little to the stage, yet an understanding of its tenets is important if only for the reason that within Futurism is to be found the extreme expression of many of the mood-qualities animating men who are otherwise set widely apart. To a large extent Futurism is a destructive force in that it rejects the 'beauty' of the past and endeavours to overthrow completely that romantic cult of loveliness which, in its eyes, is nothing save futile escapism. At the same time, it attempts to be constructive by clamouring for a new art from which these romantic delicacies have been banished, an art which will reflect the mechanical civilization surrounding us. In place of the rounded line so characteristic of romantic artistry Marinetti boldly demands the straight line of girders and factories; in place of the haunting charms of the poetic he asks for a blatant, staccato form of expression that, if need be, will substitute mere sounds for the richer tones of the human voice.

In so far as the theatre was concerned, these Futuristic tenets obviously tended to lead in three directions: first, towards the substitution of 'mechanical' form in place of the current types of scenery; secondly, towards the subordination of the playwright to the director; and, thirdly, towards an emphasis in acting upon physical movement. All three trends were carried to ultimate fulfilment in Russia.

Trained in the Moscow Art Theatre, Vsevolod Meyerhold gradually moved over to the embracing of non-realistic styles of production. 'Stylization' became with him a watchword, and, in his attempt to break down the convention of the fourth wall, he moved easily from experimentation with Maeterlinckian symbolism to more original and daring adventures. In the actor he found the core of the dramatic performance, and, since a group of actors must clearly be guided by one person, he began to elevate the director into a position higher even than any he had reached before this time. If the actor were indeed the core of the production, he further argued, then clearly the performer should be permitted to exercise to the full all his athletic skill. In the performances he directed theatricalism went rampant.

About the same time came Alexander Tairov, equally opposed to realism, equally intent upon theatricality, and sufficiently influenced by Futuristic doctrines to set his plays on a stage in which platforms, scaffoldings, and ladders at once reflected the 'mechanical' shapes so familiar to us in our daily lives and provided opportunities for actors to run up and down, to demonstrate their agility, to behave like acrobats. Thus Constructivism came into being.

As both Meyerhold and Tairov set the actor and the production above and beyond the play, naturally this movement, although it is associated with the work of Evreinov and Blok, did little to encourage the dramatists; but elsewhere than in Russia the impulse that moved the Constructivists was destined to develop, under the name of Expressionism, a new kind of playwriting which, although in its pure form it was short-lived, has wielded a considerable influence during the past twenty years on writers who otherwise remained far outside the pure Expressionist cult. This, however, is a development which best may be dealt with in a later section. All we need do at the moment is to note the appearance of these diverse theatrical 'isms,' to recognize that in essence they were anti-dramatic, and, at the same time, to see in them a force which, directed into different channels, was to prove of potent influence in later years.

4

THE POETIC STAGE

ALEXANDER BLOK was a poet, but the trends that led to the efforts of Meyerhold and Tairov were in essence so deliberately opposed to romantic aspirations that they may be regarded as a direct attack upon the literary theatre. In stressing the importance of the actor and of the director, in cultivating athleticism and acrobatics among the performers, and in extolling the virtues of improvization, they clearly aimed at taking the theatre out of the hands of the dramatic authors.

This was, in effect, one way of attacking realism. Another way, however, was found in the equally deliberate exaltation of the word instead of the action. When Synge wrote of Ibsen's pallid dialogue and pleaded for the reintroduction to the stage of verbal terms richer and more powerful he expressed what was beginning to trouble many minds, and within a few concise phrases formulated a programme which numerous authors, in diverse ways, were to follow during the twentieth century.

Irish and English Contributions

The Abbey Theatre in Dublin was, we must ever remember, inspired and directed in its first years by the man who is likely to be regarded by future historians of literature as the greatest poet of our time. William Butler Yeats, throughout the whole of the extraordinarily lengthy period of his creative career, was passionately devoted to the stage, and, although his own plays cannot be extolled as works of supreme dramatic mastery, his influence has been widespread and his example powerful.

At the beginning of his theatrical career he sought to establish a new kind of romantic drama which, intensely lyrical, should combine within itself something of the strength of the older romantic stage, something of the qualities associated with the more recent symbolist movement, and something of an individual atmosphere borrowed from the folk-memories of his native Ireland. Thus inspired, he composed *The Countess Cathleen* (printed 1892, acted 1899), wherein a noble heroine offers herself in sacrifice when, during a time of terrible famine, the Demon Merchants are moving about the land mercilessly purchasing souls for the price of bread. Now that fifty years have passed since the publication of this work, its loveliness may seem a trifle precious, its rhythms too exquisitely

THE THÉÂTRE DU VIEUX-COLOMBIER, PARIS
From *Theatre Arts Monthly*, October 1924.

"CARMENCITA": MUSICAL STUDIO OF THE MOSCOW
ART THEATRE
From *Theatre Arts Monthly*, December 1925.

"GORE OT UMA": MEYERHOLD PRODUCTION
From *The Seven Soviet Arts,* by Kurt London (Faber, 1937).

beautiful, its theme too far removed into a world of the romantic imagination. Nevertheless Yeats' effort must be esteemed as one of the most worthy among the many attempts, made over numerous generations, to bring new life to the poetic drama. Unlike most of the poetic dramatists of the nineteenth century, the poet has here abandoned the Shakespearian music and sought to compose a new music of his own.

From the same period come *The Land of Heart's Desire* (1894), in which a mortal woman is shown listening to the call of fairies' horns; *Cathleen Ni Houlihan* (1902), wherein the spirit of Ireland, eternally lovely and incredibly old, is symbolized in the figure of an old crone who becomes transformed into a young girl with the walk of a queen; *The Shadowy Waters* (printed 1900; acted 1904); *The Hour Glass* (1903), in which a Wise Man finds his reason powerless to aid him when confronted with the mystery of life and death; and *The King's Threshold* (1904). In this last play a master-musician, Seanchan, being affronted by his king, Guaire, decides to sit at the royal threshold without food or drink until he dies, thus bringing shame upon the palace. The affront rests in Seanchan's dismissal by the King from the council of state. King Guaire explains:

> Three days ago
> I yielded to the outcry of my courtiers—
> Bishops, Soldiers, and Makers of the Law—
> Who long had thought it against their dignity
> For a mere man of words to sit amongst them
> At the great council of the State and share
> In their authority.

Seanchan's pupils, instead of persuading their master to save his life, support him in his proclamation of the poets' rights, and the little drama closes with a kind of pæan chanted over the dead body of the poet-musician as it is carried away on a litter.

In all probability Yeats soon recognized that he could not proceed much farther along this particular romantic path, and we need not therefore be surprised to find that, as he advanced in his art and in years, other forms came to be adopted for his models. Such a play as *The King's Threshold*, apart from its strongly lyrical note, is cast in a perfectly familiar form. When he pens his *Four Plays for Dancers* (1920) the poet's aims have altered: now he seeks to make use of all the conventionalism that is associated with the theatre of the Orient. The theatrical use of the mask arouses his imagination; the dance-movement of the Japanese No drama he endeavours to harmonize with his words; he even attempts to introduce that retrospective element which is such a characteristic feature of this Eastern stage. The result is the creation of something utterly unlike any previous Western plays. In *At the Hawk's Well* (1916), for example, an Old Man, moving with stylized gestures to the tapping of a drum, makes as if to prepare a fire, the while Musicians describe his actions and chant in chorus:

FIRST MUSICIAN [speaking]:
  He has made a little heap of leaves;
  He lays the dry sticks on the leaves
  And, shivering with cold, he has taken up
  The fire-stick and socket from its hole.
  He whirls it round to get a flame;
  And now the dry sticks take the fire
  And now the fire leaps up and shines
  Upon the hazels and the empty well.
MUSICIANS [singing]:
  "O wind, O salt wind, O sea wind!"
  Cries the heart, "it is time to sleep;
  Why wander and nothing to find?
  Better grow old and sleep."

The entire atmosphere is extra-naturalistic. In searching for escape Yeats has boldly gone for inspiration, back beyond the romantic tradition, to that type of play wherein conventionalism is not merely a useful device, but the very basis of the dramatic movement.

A similar development from work cast in earlier romantic forms to work even more heavily influenced by the Oriental theatre is to be viewed in the writings of Gordon Bottomley. From *The Crier by Night* (printed 1902) onward for fully twenty years this romantic poet, the inheritor of the traditions of the nineteenth century, experimented in an endeavour to develop a style which, while borrowing from the Shakespearian model alertness and vigour, should be more harmoniously bound to the actual utterance of our own times than were the imitative measures of so much of the poetic dialogue penned during the years from Wordsworth to Swinburne. Bottomley's strength here lay in his refusal to wander, as Yeats had done, into a misty world of symbolic shapes. He unquestionably possessed the power to evoke an impression of the shadowy and to make the mysterious seem real, but in his works too there appears an earthy, almost barbaric, strength which gives them a unique quality. It is characteristic of his earlier style that, when he essayed to write two dramas which should, as it were, present the atmosphere out of which the tragic action of a couple of Shakespeare's had been wrought, he selected, in *King Lear's Wife* (1915) and *Gruach* (printed 1921, acted 1923), themes which permitted him to depict an ancient world of bitter struggle and fierce emotion. Like Yeats, however, Bottomley moved from such plays to the deliberate cultivation of a kind of drama based on the structure of the Japanese Nō. Whereas, however, Yeats had dreamed of rather precious productions in drawing-rooms, Bottomley deliberately oriented himself towards the innumerable non-commercial acting-groups which have sprung up so freely during recent years, believing that a revival of the poetic theatre might be effected by interesting these groups in verse plays and so by providing later an appreciative audience for the professional presentation of poetic dialogue on the commercial stage. Nearly all his writings during the twenties and thirties were guided by this purpose, and the structure of the Nō in his hands was wrought to a form adapted for the treatment of Western themes and calculated for less precious productions and for more general audiences than Yeats' drawing-room performances.

As an example of the dramatic method he made his own we may take *Fire at Callart* (1939). The plot is taken from a sixteenth-century legend of a Mairi Cameron who, having angered her family, is not allowed to go down to visit a newly arrived Spanish ship and like her cousins amuse herself in the purchasing of some of the fine silks which the sailors have on display. Locked in her room at home, she hears the gay voices of her relatives on their return, but in the morning there is a dull silence. Terrified, she breaks open her door and finds nothing save bloated corpses: the Black Death has come with the silks. Neighbours arrive with orders to burn the house, but they consent, before doing so, to summon her affianced lover, Diarmid of Lochawe. He arrives, rescues her, and carries her off. In telling this tale Bottomley introduces three men in Spanish costume who, announcing that they "are nameless men in Spain," unfold and fold a curtain patterned with flames. In general terms they outline the plot, fold up their curtain, and move to the side of the stage. After this the story is revealed in a series of episodes, broken and expanded by choral elements. When the family returns, Mairi's little sister, Griatach, comes to bid her good-night. In the darkness

> *The CURTAIN ATTENDANTS speak without moving.*
> *THE CURTAIN-BEARER:* Is that something in the night?
> *THE FIRST FOLDER:* What do you hear?
> *THE CURTAIN-BEARER:* I hear nothing.
> *THE SECOND FOLDER:* Yet you speak as though in fright.
> *THE CURTAIN-BEARER:* There is no sound—but is there no sound?
>   In the air, though not on the ground,
>   Something stirs: is it breath or clothing?
> *THE FIRST FOLDER:* Is it the murmur of very earth
>   After midnight, in the hush?
> *THE CURTAIN-BEARER:* At a time of death or birth
>   There's a tension, there's a massing
>   Of strong silence, moving, passing:
>   Stillness is on us with that rush.
> *THE SECOND FOLDER:* Something happens; I cannot bear it.
>   Agony makes the darkness deeper,
>   Yet is soundless——
> *THE FIRST FOLDER:* For that I fear it.
> *THE SECOND FOLDER:* It goes on: by hour and hour
>   This dread night piles up its power.
> *THE CURTAIN-BEARER:* Slow—slow—slow and slower
>   Alike to sleepless and to sleeper.
> *The darkness yields a little, the CURTAIN ATTENDANTS are visible again.*

And the way is prepared for Mairi's grim discovery in the dawning. By such means Bottomley sought to link past and present, the real and the symbolic, the fact and the poetic comment.

Along with this poet stands Lascelles Abercrombie, who in the course of his poetic career likewise tried, equally deliberately, to establish new rhythmic measures apt to be welcomed by modern ears. His approach is somewhat different from those of Yeats and Bottomley. For the most part he turns, as in *Deborah* (1913), to deal with contemporary subject matter, seeking to evolve a dialogue-form based on the music of common speech. While there can be no doubt but that his experiments have had a considerable (and perhaps not always fully acknowledged) influence, his impress on the theatre has, unfortunately, not been great. More immediate success greeted the efforts of John Drinkwater, who, after writing several impressive early plays, such as *Rebellion* (1914), *The Storm* (1915), and *X=0* (1917), suddenly achieved international fame with his *Abraham Lincoln* (1918). Drinkwater, by no means so powerful a poet as the others mentioned above, possesses the quality that Abercrombie lacks: as a dramatist he has sureness of aim and knows how to concentrate upon the more important elements in his theme. At the same time, despite the extraordinary success of *Abraham Lincoln*, it may be questioned whether his work is likely to stand the test of time. There is virtue here, but it is a virtue of limited appeal.

Still another English poet, John Masefield, applied himself at this time to the stage, but, except for *The Tragedy of Nan* (1908), it cannot be claimed that his dramatic contributions are either of any outstanding importance or are likely to exert any great influence in the future. He too was impressed by the recently discovered Japanese drama, and in *The Faithful* (1915) he wrote a verse play on one of its most famous themes. It is typical, however, that not the structure but the subject-matter of the Nippon stage has here been used: where Yeats and Bottomley endeavoured to find new forms in the conventionalism of the East, Masefield saw there mainly a source for such strong, brutal plots as he had always loved. Typical also is the fact that in *The Tragedy of Nan* he wrote a drama which, despite its unquestioned power, must be regarded as a *tour de force* rather than as a work belonging to any clearly marked tradition or destined to inaugurate a new style. In effect, *The Tragedy of Nan* may be regarded less as a play written for the purpose of revitalizing the theatre by the application to a given theme of the poetically imaginative purpose than as the composition by a man of poetic powers who has been stimulated by the naturalistic style. The dialogue is in prose, and although Masefield invests the speeches of the old Gaffer with a rich, broken music of their own the impression given to us is one of the starkly realistic. His plot Masefield has succeeded in raising above the sordid, so that the roaring of the Severn waters assumes an element of universal, almost supernatural, power; but we cannot believe that other writers would be apt to find in this play any qualities likely to inspire them to further efforts. The truth is that *The Tragedy of Nan*, like its own heroine, is a beautiful but lonely denizen in an alien world.

The Flamboyance of D'Annunzio

All the pent-up romanticism of these decades found flaming expression not in the English theatre (although the *Hassan* (printed 1922, produced 1923) of J. Elroy Flecker came near to giving full scope to the ecstatic luxuries of the late romantic spirit), but in Italy. Gabriele D'Annunzio may not have been so great an author as he thought he was, and we may utterly condemn his philosophy of life, but no one can deny the sharp surge of his enthusiasm and the fervour of his passions. No Pirandellian doubts trouble his soul: for him conscience is an illness from which man should seek to cure himself: a kind of flaring amoral sensuality colours all his scenes. All is fire, all is burning passion, all is vital energy in his theatre.

D'Annunzio first came before the public with *La città morta* (*The Dead City*) in 1898, and at once showed the main trends of his art in the peculiar treatment he gave to an ancient theme. Although he had already written some five other plays, the daring of *La città morta* came as a shock to his contemporaries and immediately set him in the forefront of the young literary rebels of this time. Here the past is carried into the present, the present confounded with the past; here the modern searching of the soul's innermost reaches is allied to the presentation of bold emotionalism; here the prevailing romantic obsession with fate is given a new treatment. In the devising of his plot D'Annunzio undoubtedly displays extreme adroitness. He tells how, living in the country of Mycenæ, a poet, Alessandro, married to a blind wife, is infatuated with a girl, Bianca Maria, who in turn has aroused the incestuous passion of her own brother, Leonardo. On the site of the dead city Leonardo murders his sister, his soul infected by the atmosphere of the ancient curse on Atreus' house. No doubt it is possible to see many absurd situations in the play, yet we must confess that in its tense, brooding atmosphere it creates just that impression of impending doom which it was the author's object to evoke.

The next year (1899) saw the appearance of *La Gioconda*, in which D'Annunzio turns to pen a realistic-symbolic study of love and art. Lucio Settala, the central figure in this drama, is a sculptor, married to Silvia: although she gives him all her devotion, the inspiration he needs is lacking in her motherly being, and he is forced to turn for this life-giving force to his model, Gioconda Danti. The scene that has most deeply impressed itself upon all those familiar with the drama is that wherein Silvia and Gioconda confront each other in Lucio's studio; Gioconda loses her temper and rushes towards his latest marble in a frenzied desire to destroy it. Silvia cries out and attempts to save the work of art, sacrificing herself so much as to let the stone fall upon and crush her beautiful hands. Even this, however, is not enough to bring Lucio back to her: by a force beyond himself, even though his very soul is torn, he finds himself driven to desert her for Gioconda: his art is a force greater than any common human passion.

Such a man as D'Annunzio could not escape writing a *Francesca da Rimini* (1902), and this he did with frank delight in the penning of the more sensuous episodes. More original is *La figlia di Jorio* (*Jorio's Daughter*, 1904), which carries us far into the mountain lands of the primitive and only half-christianized peasantry of the Abruzzi. Mila, the daughter of Jorio, a noted sorcerer, after being protected by a young shepherd, Aligi, goes to live with him in a hilltop fastness. Days of idyllic happiness follow until Lazaro, Aligi's father, comes, attacks the girl, and is killed by his own son. The youth is condemned to a lingering death as punishment for his parricide, when Mila voluntarily takes the guilt on herself and even pleads that she used black magic to conceal her evil from her lover. As a result she is reviled by all as a witch, hauled off to be burned at the stake, and cursed by the very man whose life she had saved by her tragic lies. Perhaps in the end, despite the brutality of many of its scenes, this drama will be recognized by future historians of the drama as D'Annunzio's most powerful play.

There is no need to survey individually his other works: lust, uninhibited exhibition of passion, physical torment, appear as strains in them all, and the constant iteration of the same subjects makes any continuous reading of his work a descent from reluctant admiration to a boredom that cannot even find amusement in those scenes wherein the tumultuous frenzy seems to become almost a travesty of itself. Whatever his limitations, however, D'Annunzio must, if only for the few plays mentioned above, be recognized as a by no means unimportant figure in the European theatre towards the beginning of our century.

The colourful romanticism that he so vigorously made his own was reflected in some of the writings of Sem Benelli, an author whose other affiliations with Pirandello have already been noted. *La cena delle beffe* (*The Jest*, 1909) demonstrates this patently in its story of Gianetto, the butt for the cruel jests of his brothers, Neri and Gabriello, who succeeds in turning the tables in such a manner as to leave him victor, with Gabriello killed through a mistake by Neri, and Neri languishing lunatic in a cell. There is here, in spite of the melodramatic episodes and the obvious spectacularism, a genuine force which gave to the play at least a passing international reputation.

. Rather different in style, although animated by some of the same motifs, are the allegorical dramas written by Ercole Luigi Morselli, notably the mythological *Orione* (1910), where the son of Earth, the symbol of instinctive desire, miserably perishes, and the rather more subtle *Glauco* (1919). In this company, too, may be mentioned Federico Valerio Ratti, whose plays—*Il solco quadrato* (*The Square Furrow*, 1922), *Bruto* (1924), and *Socrate* (1927)—employ historical subject-matter for the purpose of giving symbolic dramatic expression to the tortured soul of man in conflict with society.

There is not much of permanent worth in these Italian experiments, yet they express so vigorously and in such an extreme manner at least one of the main spiritual currents of the age that they deserve attention perhaps beyond their actual accomplishment.

The Poetic-Historical Drama from Scandinavia to Slavonia

The impulse that drove D'Annunzio to his frenzied ecstasies and that led Yeats to a richly new field of poetic endeavour found a voice in almost every country of Europe, without, however, yielding much that was capable of being translated from the land of its birth on to alien soil.

The Norwegian Hans E. Kinck emulated D'Annunzio and Benelli in his *Agilulf den vise* (*Agilulf the Wise*, 1906), *Bryllupet i Genua* (*The Wedding at Genoa*, 1911), *Mot karneval* (*Towards Carnival Time*, 1915), and *Den sidste gjest* (*The Last Guest*, 1910)—in all of which flaring colours and fiery passions find full scope. The choice of Italian subject-matter in most of Kinck's dramatic work was something of an innovation in the Scandinavian theatre, but this shifting from saga material to Italianate love and intrigue was not entirely an individual idiosyncrasy: when we find the Swedish Per Hallström writing a *Bianca Capello* (1900) alongside *Karl den elfte* (*Charles XI*, 1918), Hjalmar Bergman producing a *Parisina* (1915), and the Danish Sophus Michaëlis writing a *Giovanna* (1901), we realize that in the life of the Renaissance men were finding qualities of peculiar and immediate appeal. Throughout these decades the efforts to establish a poetic drama on the Scandinavian stage were vigorous, although in general these efforts, while eminently laudable, failed to rise above mediocrity. We can hardly find much of universal dramatic value in the *Solsagn* (*Sun Legends*, 1904) of the Danish Helge Rode; and, despite Masefield's interest in it, the *Anne Pedersdotter* (1910), by the Norwegian Hans Wiers-Jenssen, a tale of sixteenth-century witchcraft wherein a wife wins a stepson's love by sorcery, cannot be esteemed a masterpiece. The 'poetic' stage in Iceland, also, found enthusiastic exponents at this time, although none have a very great general interest. Following the lead of Indridi Einarsson, whose lyrical *Nýjársnóttin* (*New Year's Eve*) appeared in 1872 and legendary *Dansinn í Hruna* (*The Dance at Hruni*) in 1921, Jóhann Sigurjónsson produced his well-known tragic drama *Bjaerg-Ejvind og hans hustru* (*Ejvind of the Hills*, 1911) and his less familiar dramatic treatment of local folk-tales, *Galdra Loftur* (*Loft's Wish*, 1915). It is in the fantastic, the mythical, and the historic that the Icelandic theatrical genius seems to find its most harmonious setting, and the style thus established by these two men has been carried on by such later authors as Sigurdur Eggerz, with his *Líkkistusmidurinn* (*The Coffin-maker*, 1938), and Davíd Stefánsson, with his *Vopn gudanna* (*The Weapons of the Gods*, 1943).

What is important in these imaginatively inspired historical and folklore dramas is not the individual excellence of any particular plays, but the extraordinarily wide vogue accorded to them. In Czechoslovakia Jaroslav Vrchlický (Emil Bohuš) exercised his lyric talents in several not very inspiring scenes, his most ambitious effort being the romantically conceived trilogy *Hippodamie* (*Hippodamia*, 1889–91); Jaroslav Hilbert varied his excursions into the Ibsenite drama by experiments in the historical style; while Arnošt-Dvořák incorporated modern concepts into a series of dramas mostly based on episodes in Bohemian history. The Slovak Jozef Gregor Tajovský produced *Smrt Ďurka Langsfelda* (*The Death of Durko Langsfeld*, 1923), a drama noteworthy for its realistic treatment of past events. Much of twentieth-century Bulgarian theatrical writing, too, has dealt with the past, generally in poetic terms. In Rumania Lucian Blaga has found his themes mainly in the realm of folk-myth; the symbolic mingles with the historical in the plays of the Croat Ivo Vojnović. Even from distant Armenia there comes to us an interesting play of this kind—*Hin astvadzner* (*Ancient Gods*, 1912), by Levon Sciant. Set in a medieval community inhabiting an island on a lake, it deals with a convent built on the site of an antique temple and subtly reveals the conflict between instinctive pagan passions and superimposed Christian ideals. An interesting companion piece to this Armenian drama is *Advokat Martian* (*The Advocate Martianus*; printed 1913), by the Ukrainian authoress Lesia Ukrainka, where a similar contrast is presented. The action takes place in the third century, and the Christian Martianus, a brilliant advocate, is engaged in defending a number of his coreligionists. To make his pleading the more effective he is bidden by the Church to pretend to be a pagan, and the conflict here is between his desire to confess openly to his faith and the duty imposed on him by those with whom he is associated. At the end, faced with the need of saving a bishop, he not only allows a complete cleavage to separate him from his sons, but even sacrifices a youth who has fled to his house seeking sanctuary. More interesting in this authoress's dramatic poem *Cassandra* (printed 1908), in which the characters of Greek myth are translated into terms of twentieth-century political and social aspiration.

A kindred spirit animates the work of the Lettish playwright Jānis Rainis; his *Zelta zirgs* (*The Golden Horse*, 1910) is a symbolic mythical drama in which national aspirations are clothed in allegoric forms. Similar in treatment is his *Uguns un nakts* (*Fire and Night*, 1900), also based on local legend. Famous in Estonia is the *Libahunt* (*The Werewolf*, 1912) of August Kitzberg—a dramatization of a sensational folk-tale, while Rumania contributes Victor Eftimiu's *Inšira-te, mărgărite* (*A Tale with No Ending*, 1911), an imaginative fantasy woven out of similar material.

Since the drama was born in Greece, it is somewhat hard to believe that, except for eight Cretan plays (themselves based on Italian models) which have been preserved from the early seventeenth century, the modern Greek drama was an entirely new development introduced in the middle of the nineteenth century, and not fully established until our own period. It was entirely proper that the earliest significant play should have been a verse tragedy—*Maria Doxapatri* (1865) by Demetrios Vernardakis. In 1903, Kostes Palamas, the first modern Greek poet to win a wide reputation abroad, produced his very interesting *Trisevgheni*. And, perhaps most important of all, Anghelos Sikelianos began in 1927 to translate the ancient Athenian plays into the familiar current speech, while at the same time, aided by his wife, he attracted both national and international attention to their presentations at Delphi.

In Hungary Jenö Rákosi, Lajos Dóczy, and the better-known Ferenc Herczeg had applied themselves to the exploitation of native folk-legends or local history, and something of the quality they succeeded in bringing into their scenes gives colour to the best of Molnar's work, even although his chosen sphere is that of the common and familiar. National sentiment pervades all these works, as it does Kálmań Harsány's dramatic treatment of the Attila legend, *Ellák* (1923). The poetic-historical and the poetic-fantastic found many other exponents in the eastern countries of Europe, but only one author showed any real power. Stanisław Wyspiański in Poland alone infused into his writings an element of true originality. This originality derived largely from the fact that to native influences he added the strong impress of both the Greek dramatists and of Shakespeare: from these three he wrought a peculiar atmosphere characteristically his own, but unfortunately too deeply encased with national sentiment to permit it to be carried beyond the bounds of his native country. His unquestioned strength still fails to gather sufficient power to transmute the local into the universal.

Although much of Wyspiański's work was accomplished during the last years of the nineteenth century, the special nature of his genius and the appearance of several of his most important writings after the year 1900 gives authority for discussing him here. It was precisely in the first year of the century, indeed, that his finest drama, *Wesele (The Wedding)*, made its appearance. Outwardly this is a simple folk-drama, similar in kind to many peasant pieces turned out in half a score of countries during these romantic years, but Wyspiański has introduced into the folk-canvas individual elements of his own. The subjective and the objective are inextricably intertwined in its action, and the symbolic boldly takes its place along with the realistic depiction of a rustic interior: even the sheaves of corn, the very basis of life for the peasant community, live and move in the appearance of the *chochoł*.

Wesele demonstrates that Wyspiański's genius is peculiarly fitted to weld together elements of the most diverse—indeed, seemingly irreconcilable—kinds, and it is from just such a process of fusion that his better plays derive their interest. In both *Akropolis* (printed 1904) and *Noc listopadowa (A November Night,* 1904), for example, figures taken from classic myth appear in a Polish setting, and the walls of Cracow's Wawel are peopled by ghosts of the past: it is as though the ramparts of Troy were superimposed upon the medieval fortress. In these and in his other plays

Wyspiański shows himself a master of stage effects: a painter himself, he builds many of his scenes with their decorative appearance in view, and at the same time he engages in interesting dramatic experiments, such as the use of crowds in *Legjon* (*Legion*, 1900). This last-mentioned drama, however, serves to indicate why his fame will always remain localized. In creating it the author frankly indicates that he has been dominated by one basic concept—the idea that "Poland is the Christ of Nations"—and at once we realize that such a theme, although it might give him added power as a national writer, is bound so to restrict his appeal as to make his work assume no more than historical interest for others. Wyspiański, indeed, may perhaps be taken as the supreme example of the poet, undoubtedly gifted with genius, who is so rooted in his own land that transplantation is impossible.

5

PURPOSEFUL LAUGHTER: GEORGE BERNARD SHAW

Despite the innumerable experiments in diverse directions made during this time, and despite all the would-be tragic tension, the gloom, the bitterness, and the romantically flamboyant, this age is likely to be recorded in the annals of the theatre as the age of one man—and that man a master of laughter—George Bernard Shaw. Like a mobile and restless colossus, he carelessly straddles over the lesser figures beneath him, and his laughter pricks many a pretentious bubble, whether blown from Ibsen's hard kitchen-soap or from the more perfumed toilet varieties favoured by Maeterlinck and D'Annunzio.

Not, of course, that Shaw stands alone in his world of penetrating laughter. Amid the prevailing darkness of the naturalistic drama and the often absurdly serious efforts of the neo-romanticists some scenes of laughter were permitted to intrude into the theatre of the time, and it is interesting to observe that for the most part these experiments in comedy during the latter years of the century tended to move into the realm of the fantastic—not necessarily the fantastic as exemplified in the invention of an utterly imaginary fairyland world, rather the playing of fancy upon characters and episodes that outwardly have the appearance of the real.

The tone is set, perhaps, in Ibsen's *Love's Comedy*, with its tinkling verse and its fantastification of persons who bear a likeness to those introduced in other dramas more solemn in style. With this play may be associated some of Strindberg's, darker in spirit, it is true, yet clearly exhibiting the operation of the comic mood. Laughter of a bitter sort appears too among the writings of many other authors of the time. There is a play of wit in the work of Arthur Schnitzler; Hermann Bahr's *Das Konzert* is a comedy.

Animated by an original tone is the group of comedies fathered by the German Ludwig Thoma, of which *Moral* (1908) and *Die Lokalbahn* (*The Branch Line*, 1902) may be taken as representative. The former displays the worthy dignitaries of a small town aghast at realizing that all their names are recorded in the account-books belonging to a bawd who has lately been arrested and whom they are consequently now anxious to protect. The same spirit animates *Die Lokalbahn*. The mayor of a little town interviews a high official concerning a proposed extension of a local railway and reports back to his fellow-aldermen how courageously he confronted this dignitary; awed by his courage, they organize a parade in his honour, but, on thinking over the matter, they later decide that he may have harmed the township by his domineering manner; sensing the change in attitude, the mayor promptly modifies his story, and a second parade is organized. Noteworthy, too, is the vigorous little sketch called *Erster Klasse* (*First Class*, 1910), where the scene is a first-class carriage and where the socially important passengers are irritated by the entry of a loud-mouthed peasant—who turns out to be a Member of Parliament. Somewhat akin in spirit is *Der kleine Mann* (*The Little Man*, 1894), where the Austrian playwright Edouard Karlweis (Karl Weiss) satirizes the way in which the wealthy solicit the working-class vote before elections and then promptly forget the 'little man' when the elections are over.

Much more important than Thoma is Karl Sternheim, the nineteenth- and early-twentieth-century master of acidulous mockery, his jests constantly being directed at bourgeois respectability and the unco guid. Nothing quite like the tone of his collected sketches, published as *Portraits of Bourgeois Heroes* (1908–22), is to be met with elsewhere in this period. *Bürger Schippel* tells the amusing tale of an ambitious young workman who adroitly ascends the social ladder, first by gaining admission to the civic orchestra, next by showing his willingness to aid a middle-class widow in her need, and lastly by having the good luck to be victorious in a duel. In *Die Hose* (*The Trousers*) the adventures of a married lady's pants are hilariously recounted; *Der Snob* (*The Snob*) introduces a middle-class hero in Christian Maske, who carries Schippel's social climbing a stage higher by marrying into a noble house and winning respect there by hinting that blue blood, even if illegitimate, flows in his veins, that he has right to a coat-of-arms with the bar sinister; *Die Marquise von Arcis* (adapted as *The Mask of Virtue*) delicately pierces the pretensions of society; in *Die Cassette* (*The Treasure Chest*) a little schoolmaster dreams of inheriting his aunt's riches even while she is writing a will leaving all her possessions to the Church.

In England these were the Gilbert and Sullivan decades, when the mood of the century's earlier fairy comedy and extravaganza was transmuted into the delicate style of the Savoy operas. And, above all, these were the years when Oscar Wilde introduced his own inimitable brand of the comic. Wilde's position is thoroughly characteristic. A poet of the art-for-art's-sake school, he could toy with flamboyant romanticism in *The Duchess of Padua* (1891) and deal with the decadently suggestive in *Salome* (1893); at the same time, he yet finds his fame as a dramatist resting securely on exercises in the realm of the witty and fantastic. *Lady Windermere's Fan* appeared in 1892, *A Woman of No Importance* in the following year, *An Ideal Husband* and *The Importance of Being Earnest* in 1895.

In *Lady Windermere's Fan* Wilde showed clearly what was his aim. This and the immediately following plays outwardly accept the prevailing themes of the current realistic drama. The drama introduces a 'problem'—that of Mrs Erlynne, a woman with a past who is in reality the mother of the proud young Lady Windermere; the woman with a past, together with concealed parentage, reappears in *A Woman of No Importance*; and a somewhat similar person is the main character in *An Ideal Husband*. Obviously, however, Wilde is dealing with these topics with his tongue in his cheek. He makes no serious attempt to follow the new dramaturgy of the revolutionary intellectuals. Asides and soliloquies are used when they can serve his turn, and he permits the machinery to creak. What he is interested in is the play of wit which his scenes of high life permit him to exploit, and it is for the iridescence of epigram and of lightly turned phrase, not for their solemn problems, that these plays are now remembered.

The Importance of Being Earnest sheds all pretence. Here a wholly farcical plot offers gay opportunity for the flinging of jest after jest before the audience. Wilde has now found the perfect medium for the display of his wit, and that wit continually shatters the conventions of the society he depicts. In his art-for-art's-sake æstheticism he had shocked comfortable respectability: his witty farce is simply the obverse of the medal he ironically hung around his contemporaries' necks. Algernon is making love to Cecily:

> *ALGERNON:* I hope, Cecily, I shall not offend you if I state quite frankly and openly that you seem to me to be in every way the visible personification of absolute perfection.
> *CECILY:* I think your frankness does you great credit, Ernest. If you will allow me, I will copy your remarks into my diary.
>   [*Goes over to table and begins writing in diary.*
> *ALGERNON:* Do you really keep a diary? I'd give anything to look at it. May I?
> *CECILY:* Oh, no. [*Puts her hand over it.*] You see, it is simply a very young girl's publication. When it appears in volume form I hope you will order a copy.

These sallies are constant from the very opening of the play:

> *ALGERNON:* Did you hear what I was playing, Lane?
> *LANE:* I didn't think it polite to listen, sir.
> *ALGERNON:* I'm sorry for that, for your sake. I don't play accurately—anyone can play accurately—but I play with wonderful expression. As far as the piano is concerned, sentiment is my forte. I keep science for life.
> *LANE:* Yes, sir.
> *ALGERNON:* And, speaking of the science of Life, have you got the cucumber sandwiches cut for Lady Bracknell?
> *LANE:* Yes, sir.
> *ALGERNON:* Oh! ... by the way, Lane, I see from your book that on Thursday night, when Lord Shoreman and Mr Worthing were dining with me, eight bottles of champagne are entered as having been consumed.
> *LANE:* Yes, sir; eight bottles and a pint.
> *ALGERNON:* Why is it that in a bachelor's establishment the servants invariably drink the champagne? I ask merely for information.
> *LANE:* I attribute it to the superior quality of the wine, sir. I have often

observed that in married households the champagne is rarely of a first-rate brand.

ALGERNON: Good heavens! Is marriage so demoralizing as that?

LANE: I believe it *is* a very pleasant state, sir. I have had very little experience of it myself up to the present. I have only been married once. That was in consequence of a misunderstanding between myself and a young person. . . .

ALGERNON: . . . That will do, Lane, thank you.

LANE: Thank you, sir. [*He goes out.*

ALGERNON: Lane's views on marriage seem somewhat lax. Really, if the lower orders don't set us a good example, what on earth is the use of them? They seem, as a class, to have absolutely no sense of moral responsibility.

Here is the spirit of topsy-turviness, the characteristic of the fairy play, transformed into a new medium; here is the social question treated not with dull seriousness of purpose, but with irreverent gaiety.

The Play of Ideas

So much has been written on almost every conceivable aspect of Shaw's career, and he himself has so copiously annotated his own purposes, that any brief general survey of his work must inevitably prove impossible. At the same time it may be worth while to emphasize here, not the social ideas about which so much has been said, but rather the purely dramatic significance of his plays.

Many of his contemporaries have been taken in by his own emphatic assurances that he has applied himself to the stage only because he finds there the best platform for the preaching of certain moral or social truths and that he is much more of the prophet than the playwright. Undoubtedly there resides a modicum of truth in these assertions. No one needs to be told that Shaw, more than any other playwright of his age, loved to ponder over social problems national and international. In play after play, as in preface after preface, he has presented his analysis of the evils and errors of the time and has indicated his own solutions. From his early study of the circumstances surrounding professional prostitution in *Mrs Warren's Profession* (1898) to the vast survey of human failure in *Back to Methuselah* (1919–20) he has constantly infused into his action ideas of a philosophical and sociological kind, and there can be no doubt but that the stage-platform has given him the opportunity of shattering numerous false idols and of awakening minds to thoughts beyond the shallowly conventional.

At the same time, even while recognizing these facts, we cannot accept the Shavian assurances at their face-value. If, indeed, Shaw's reputation is to stand on his 'prophecy,' its endurance is set on a shaky foundation. The discussion of war in *Arms and the Man* may have seemed incisive and full of basic truth when this play appeared in 1894, but the experiences of two great wars have cut away the very premises on which the author erected his ideas. When we start to analyse the thought in *Back to Methu-selah* all we are left with is the often expressed regret that the ass that is man lies down and dies just when he is beginning to learn some lessons.

In writing his preface to the English translation of some of Brieux' plays Shaw gives the impression that this French writer is his ideal of a dramatist and that he himself is doing in London what Brieux was doing in Paris. Fortunately the truth lies far otherwhere. Brieux is certainly the sociological dramatist, but there is not the most tenuous connexion between his works and those of his adulator. *Damaged Goods* and the rest of the plays of ideas that Brieux turned out are dictated by central 'thoughts': they are admittedly thesis plays: their ideas might just as easily have been formulated in pamphlet prose: the author clearly indicates just precisely where he stands and creates puppet figures, poor, flat pasteboard puppets, for the purpose of driving his lesson home.

True, the same has been said of Shaw, but it has been falsely said; in reality his method is far different. Had he worked as Brieux did, then his fame, even now, would have similarly sunk. The fact that Shaw's plays still hold the stage demonstrates that we must look in them for something more, and this something more obviously has to be a quality distinct from either analysis of social evil or suggestion for its remedy. What we need to do, in fact, is to forget the prefaces and consider the plays.

Exactly how the prefaces are written in time-relation to the dramas they profess to elucidate is not known, and does not matter: the impression they give is that they are, if not afterthoughts, essays penned separately in spirit from the composition of the stage scenes. We might put this in another way by saying that, unlike Brieux, Shaw succeeds, when he is engaged in dramatic composition, in dividing the pamphleteer from the playwright. In the preface he is the pamphleteer, presenting a reasoned argument and pressing home upon us his own particular point of view. Here Shaw the individual and the sociologist is in the ascendant. Never for a moment are we in doubt as to what he thinks and what he wants us to do. The same impression, however, is not with us when we contemplate the plays: in these the pamphleteer, with his clear, incisive reasoning, gives way to another kind of writer.

This other kind of writer is a man who possesses, or is afflicted by, the dramatist's objectivity. When a true dramatist (not a Brieux) lets his mind play over his chosen plot and its characters he enters into a paradoxical state: on the one hand, he is the god-creator, master of these figures of his imagination; on the other, the persons he has evoked out of the unknown begin to assume their own life. The dramatist's task, in effect, is to give as much free play as possible to the various characters and yet guide them all home to a successful conclusion. It is not simply that he keeps some half a dozen different persons in view all the time that he is writing, but rather that, even while remaining the god-creator, he gives himself to each one of the persons as he or she is made to speak. Within a single individual scene, so to say, Shakespeare is at once consistently and continuously absolute lord of the stage and successively Hamlet, Polonius, Ophelia, when these characters are made to utter their lines. Precisely in this paradox rests the peculiar quality of dramatic art.

Frequently the accusation has been brought against Shaw that his characters are not living beings, with the conclusion that because of this his dramatic artistry is of a sort not destined to endure. The truth of the observation may be accepted, without endorsement of the conclusion. We may agree that in the whole range of Shavian drama there are no characters who assume such breathing vitality as we find in the persons of Sophocles or of Shakespeare: but that is because Shaw's approach to his characters is of a different kind. His theatre might well be described as the theatre of ideas, not in the sense that a single thought is imposed, Brieux-wise, on the entire action, but rather in the sense that Shaw possesses the supreme and well-nigh unique power of making the most diverse ideas take on human semblance. His characters are the embodiments of intellectual concepts; his dramas are ceaseless dances of thoughts.

What requires to be stressed is that, precisely as Shakespeare gives himself to his 'living' characters, so Shaw gives himself to his ideas. When Shakespeare throws himself into Claudius he still retains his comprehensive view of *Hamlet* and of Claudius' position in the story of that play: when Shaw throws himself into the embodiment of a particular thought he similarly remains at once true to the thought itself and to the general plan of which the thought forms merely one part. Unconsciously he has described his own power in his *Too True to be Good* (1932). Aubrey is talking to the Patient:

> *AUBREY:* I am a born preacher, not a pleader. The theory of legal procedure is that if you set two liars to expose one another, the truth will emerge. That would not suit me. I greatly dislike being contradicted; and the only place where a man is safe from contradiction is in the pulpit. I detest argument: it is unmannerly, and obscures the preacher's message. Besides, the law is too much concerned with crude facts and too little with spiritual things; and it is in spiritual things that I am interested: they alone call my gift into full play.
>
> *THE PATIENT:* You call preaching things you don't believe spiritual, do you?
>
> *AUBREY:* . . . My gift is divine: it is not limited by my petty personal convictions. It is a gift of lucidity as well as of eloquence. Lucidity is one of the most precious of gifts: the gift of the teacher: the gift of explanation. I can explain anything to anybody; and I love doing it. I feel I must do it if only the doctrine is beautiful and subtle and exquisitely put together. I may feel instinctively that it is the rottenest nonsense. Still, if I can get a moving dramatic effect out of it, and preach a really splendid sermon about it, my gift takes possession of me and obliges me to sail in and do it.

Had Shaw been merely a Brieux all we should have had would have been a series of Shavian sermons; but, Shaw being Shaw, what happens is that, as each idea presents itself, the playwright's gift of lucidity and sensitivity to dramatic effect make him devote all his strength and skill, for the moment, to the one object of producing conviction in the readers or in the audience. The idea steps out of the *corps de ballet* and executes a *pas seul* in mid-stage.

All Shaw's plays reveal this power, but none more clearly than *Androcles and the Lion* (1913), where the concepts of paganism, meek Christianity, and muscular Christianity are each put forward with such vigour, wit, and charm that while we listen to each sermon we are convinced that in it and in it alone must reside eternal truth. From this derives, ultimately, the interest of *Saint Joan* (1923). These are not living characters who inhabit here: they are all incorporations of spiritual things, the embodiments of faiths and beliefs, the human semblances of rationalizations. That extraordinarily powerful tent scene, wherein the Bishop of Beauvais confronts Warwick, gains its stageworthiness, not from such qualities as Shakespeare would have put there, the vivid illumination cast upon human character; not on such qualities as Jonson would have displayed, the juxtaposition of symbols of classes within the body of humanity; not on such qualities as Ibsen would have used, the subtle building-up of character by the light of a Norwegian table-lamp rather than by that of the sunshine flooding in upon an Elizabethan stage; but from the skill through which Shaw makes two ideas assume the medieval garbs of layman and ecclesiastic, take on material form, and confront each other. The Bishop's arguments are so clearly and so trenchantly expressed that it seems they are irrefutable:

> Catholic courts are composed of mortal men, like other courts however sacred their function and inspiration may be. And if the men are Frenchmen, as the modern fashion calls them, I am afraid the bare fact that an English army has been defeated by a French one will not convince them that there is any sorcery in the matter. . . . Sir John Talbot, we all know, is a fierce and formidable soldier, Messire: but I have yet to learn that he is an able general. And although it pleases you to say that he has been defeated by this girl, some of us may be disposed to give a little of the credit to Dunois.

But we have only to listen for a moment to another speaker to hear a sermon equally true and equally sincere. In the final scene of the play the idea that is Joan and the idea that is the Inquisitor are both presented with absolute assurance.

The Comedy of Fun

It is this quality that explains most of the peculiarities of the Shavian drama. Because of this his scenes often rightly become debates, since the spiritual essences with which he deals are more important than their material semblances. Shaw knows usually when to break a scene with the introduction of some flash of colour or rush of physical business, but these are no more than clowneries devised to provide variety of interest.

Because his characters are ideas, too, the atmosphere he invokes is of a kind absolutely distinct from anything the theatre has had in the past. *Saint Joan* ends with the burning of the heroine, but it is not a tragedy: our hearts are, again perfectly rightly, untouched, our withers unwrung. When Joan sits before the Inquisitor's court it is not a girl who is being tried: it is an idea that is being examined. Concepts of tragedy and comedy need never trouble our minds when we enter the doors of this theatre. Even in the most intellectual, the most unemotional, comic drama of the past a faint call of sympathy has come for the characters. We speak of the Restoration comedy of manners as an amoral creation of wit where we are never summoned to praise or blame save in intellectual terms, where we are never induced to feel for any of the dramatist's persons. This is true when the comedy of manners is compared with such plays as the romantic comedies of Shakespeare's middle period, but the truth is, after all, only relative, since in the end we realize that even Congreve's scenes are peopled with living beings. Millamant may be a cold creation compared with Rosalind, yet still there is warmth beneath her brilliant mask of affectation. In Shaw's dramas there is nothing beneath the mask: the mask is the character, of face there is none.

To sport with ideas in this way is fun, and the term 'comedy of fun' seems best to describe Shaw's peculiar contribution to the stage. One play, *Candida* (1895), he wrote in a more conventional style, and it accordingly has perhaps received more praise than most (for we are ever inclined to run in grooves and more readily welcome the known than the unknown): but it may seriously be questioned whether this is, as some have averred, his best play. There are other dramatists who could have written *Candida:* his best plays are utterly unique. In a sense *Candida*, too, is a play wherein the dramatist has fun with the confrontation of ideas, but it is not a pure specimen of the type. Much more individual among the early dramas, and one wherein we can see adumbrated much of Shaw's later style, is *The Devil's Disciple* (1897). This is called a melodrama, and the very designation reminds us that Shaw's lineage stems from that theatre of the nineteenth century which revelled in stage forms innocent of the living character. Melodrama, opera, extravaganza, flourished then, and in none appeared more than pasteboard figures: melodrama's persons were stereotypes, opera's were inflated balloons, extravaganza's were *commedia dell' arte* caricatures. What Shaw did was to take these and make them spiritually interesting. He could treat them with a disrespect which might be permitted towards the creatures of his imagination by no playwright whose object it was to make his inventions seem real. Hence *The Devil's Disciple* can be full of slapstick; *Saint Joan* can start with a frantic cry on the part of Robert de Baudricourt for eggs, and its most serious scenes can be broken by the English chaplain's loyal platitudes; *Back to Methuselah* can move at times into sheer farce of a kind which H. J. Byron and J. R. Planché would have recognized as akin to their own. In *Cæsar and Cleopatra* (1899) Britannus is made to utter sentiments of a purely modern sort, and Shaw's own comment on those who had taken exception to this character's lines demonstrates patently the mood in which these scenes were written:

> I find among those who have read this play in manuscript a strong conviction that an ancient Briton could not possibly have been like a modern one. I see no reason to adopt this curious view. It is true that the Roman and Norman conquests must have for a time disturbed the normal British type produced by the climate. But Britannus, born before these events, represents the unadulterated Briton who fought Cæsar and impressed Roman observers much as we should expect the ancestors of Mr Podsnap to impress the cultivated Italians of their time.
>
> I am told that it is not scientific to treat national character as a product of climate. This only shows the wide difference between common knowledge and the intellectual game called science. We have men of exactly the same stock, and speaking the same language, growing in Great Britain, in Ireland, and in America. The result is three of the most distinctly marked nationalities under the sun. Racial characteristics are quite another matter.... The characteristics of Britannus are local characteristics, not race characteristics. In an ancient Briton they would, I take it, be exaggerated, since modern Britain, disforested, drained, urbanified and consequently cosmopolized, is presumably less characteristically British than Cæsar's Britain.
>
> And again I ask does anyone who, in the light of a competent knowledge of his own age, has studied history from contemporary documents, believe that sixty-seven generations of promiscuous marriage have made any appreciable difference in the human fauna of these isles? Certainly I do not.

Playing with ideas is certainly fun.

From Mrs Warren to Good King Charles

During the earlier part of his career, from *Mrs Warren's Profession*, through *Arms and the Man, Candida, You Never Can Tell* (1898), *The Devil's Disciple, Cæsar and Cleopatra, Man and Superman* (1903), *Major Barbara* (1905), *The Doctor's Dilemma* (1906), and *Androcles and the Lion*, on to *Pygmalion* (1913), Shaw's models were obviously those mentioned above. In each of these appeared an apotheosis of melodrama, opera, and extravaganza. The structure is familiar, although we hardly recognize old friends when they appear before us in fantastic Shavian dress, brilliant of tongue, daring in the expression of idea, and tricked out with the characteristically voluble stage-directions which, instead of serving (as in the melodrama) to describe actions, now describe thoughts. "Surmising that he has no valet," writes Shaw at the beginning of *Man and Superman*,

> and seeing that he has no secretary with a shorthand notebook and a typewriter, one meditates on how little our great burgess domesticity has been disturbed by new fashions and methods, or by the enterprise of the railway and hotel companies which sell you a Saturday to Monday of life at Folkestone as a real gentleman for two guineas, first-class fares both ways included.

By the use of such devices, by the unexpectedness of his thought, and, above all, by the exquisitely modulated prose of which he is such a complete master Shaw gave to the old devices a gloss of novelty and established himself as the most important dramatic author of his time.

In 1912 came a break in his service to the theatre. War was to shatter men's lives within less than a couple of years, and it was not until 1919 that his next full-length play, *Heartbreak House* (1919), made its appearance. Here a new element has been incorporated into his art. The picture of Captain Shotover's ship-like home with its strange collection of drifting inhabitants points unmistakably to the influence on Shaw's mind of the Chekhovian pattern. It is as though, in place of the individualized persons whom the Russian dramatist had loved to gather together in one limited locale, Shaw had taken his method and peopled his house with ideas—the idea of the out-of-date conservative, the idea of the new financier, the idea of the purposeless woman of the world. In the atmospheres of *The Cherry Orchard* and of *Heartbreak House* there is much in common—a mingled nostalgia for something rather lovely that is perishing and a dim hope for the future, a combination of contempt for moral helplessness and of admiration for courage; but whereas we come from Chekhov's play with certain human characters indelibly implanted in our minds, from Shaw's we come with vivid memories of basic philosophies trenchantly expressed.

Back to Methuselah again brings something new: hardly any dramatic work of our time can be compared with it. Here is a vastness of concept akin to that of *The Dynasts*, and at the same time a vivid theatrical power. The philosophy may be of little account, but the experience of seeing, in sequence, the five plays which make up this enormous work is like no other experience to be gained in the theatre.

This was followed by *Saint Joan* (1923), in which the new lessons he had learned were put to fresh use. There is a subtlety here and a breadth of vision beyond anything in his earlier work. Almost the only inharmonious note is the epilogue—not because it introduces a modern strain into an historical theme, but because the trend it displays runs counter to the main trend of the drama as a whole. Its symbolic saint is at odds with the girl possessed of belief in her own righteousness and determined, in the manner of all dangerous fanatics, to press others into her own mould.

In *Saint Joan* Shaw reached the peak of his art. Thereafter discursiveness, an increasing tendency towards the use of symbols, and a failure to bring his themes to any logical conclusion became evident. There were brilliant scenes in *The Apple Cart* (1929), but these scenes are isolated, not firmly bound together in a single unity; *Too True to be Good* (1932) opens magnificently and drifts inconsequentially away; *On the Rocks* (1933) is hopelessly chaotic, as is *The Simpleton of the Unexpected Isles* (1935). Weaker still are *The Millionairess* (1936) and *Geneva* (1938). Only in *In Good King Charles's Golden Days* (1939) does something of the old glitter return.

The truth, of course, is that when a dramatist essays the bold and hazardous path of building his plays out of ideas rather than out of persons he denies himself the possibility of achieving anything between complete success and failure. Shakespeare may not succeed in creating a masterpiece in *Measure for Measure*, but the fact that our sympathies have been excited for an apparently living Isabella, Claudio, and Angelo permits us to overlook the serious structural weaknesses in the drama. Where we have been moved even by a few scenes we are prepared to accept the play in its entirety and are content to view it with interest whenever it is presented before us. In the Shavian type of theatre we cannot do this. None of the characters in these last plays can make appeal to us as human beings: even King Magnus, the most vital of them all, is cast in Shaw's familiar mould. The result is that, without human warmth to arouse an emotional appeal, structural weaknesses become more than commonly apparent, and these are made the more obvious in that, without realizing it consciously, we feel that the figures moving before us are rationalizations, and consequently that any logical failure in the conduct of the action is a betrayal of its very fabric. Logical errors may be condoned—indeed, freely accepted—in Shakespeare because the foundation of his work is emotional; in Shaw they must be condemned.

Despite the decline from the *Saint Joan* of 1923, however, Shaw takes his throne amid modern dramatists without the slightest fear of being challenged by any pretender. He has brought to a glorious consummation that strain of comic fantasy that we have seen threading its way through the vast-spreading territory of nineteenth-century romanticism. For all we know, he may have been utterly ignorant of the very names of Gozzi and of Raimund, yet there can be no doubt but that he is their descendant, the splendid triumph of their lineage.

PART XII

DRAMA BETWEEN TWO WARS

DRAMA BETWEEN TWO WARS

IN THE entire history of the stage nothing seems to be more certain than that theatrical activities within the period from 1900 to the present were sharply divided into three distinct parts. The First and Second World Wars proved to be so devastating in their immediate effects, and their later consequences were so extensive in range, as apparently to give us absolute assurance that the only proper way of considering the course of the drama—an art form always powerfully conditioned by changing social and political forces—during the early twentieth century is to trace a first movement being sharply checked in 1914, to examine the way in which a fresh start was made, with new objectives and different methods, in 1919, to regard this second movement as being brought to an abrupt halt in 1939, and to discern the rise of still another new movement after 1945.

These conclusions appear to be absolutely incontrovertible, yet the thought that any overall survey of the drama, no matter how cursory, shows that theatrical affairs are very rarely as simple as at first glance they may seem to be possibly will urge us to pause for a moment in order to examine the apparently indisputable assumptions with due care and circumspection.

At the start of such an inquiry we immediately encounter a series of historical events which most certainly might be thought to offer ample justification for this treatment of twentieth-century dramatic activities according to a tripartite plan. After the year 1918 numerous maps had to be redrawn; sceptres and crowns came tumbling down; teeming millions of men and women found themselves suddenly thrust into environments wholly novel and strange, and even within those lands where the political systems were not materially altered, the general conditions of life almost everywhere were no longer what they had been only a few years before. The past was truly past; a new present had been born.

Of particular significance for our immediate purposes is the fact that two or three countries which had largely contributed to the world's stage during the preceding decades now had either nothing or at best very little to offer of a like kind. Russia came under a communist control which at first offered encouragement to new theatrical styles animated by the spirit of Futurism, and which later completely changed course by forcing the stage, and indeed all other artistic endeavour, into the straitjacket of 'Socialist Realism.' Neither from the earlier revolutionary efforts nor from the later dully propagandist style came any plays so planned and composed as to enable them to make any real impact on audiences other than Russian. The land of Chekhov was thus effectively alienated from the larger part of the dramatic world. The cherry orchard had indeed been completely hacked down.

In 1922 Mussolini's Blackshirts moved down from the north and seized control of Rome. Certainly several playwrights—including Pirandello within their company—continued actively to write for the stage, but quite clearly the new fascist social structure was not of a kind likely to produce dramas able to appeal largely beyond the limits of the Italian peninsula. A second country was thus almost completely thrust aside.

Just at first, the German playhouse, even in the midst of terrifying economic ruin, exhibited a certain flurry of excitement which attracted attention within at least a few circles in other countries. Violently Expressionistic plays were feverishly turned out by a few young authors; in 1922 Bertolt Brecht started his literary career. Very soon, however, there was an ominous darkening of the scene, and during the early thirties came the triumphant seizing of power by the Nazis, with the result that universal cultural death accompanied the almost unbelievable, yet all too real, demoniacally inspired massacres in the concentration camps. In this way Germany too was erased from the theatrical map. And Spain soon followed. Racked by civil strife, it soon came completely under the control of Franco's Fascist-style dictatorship; its one outstanding modern playwright, Garcia Lorca, was obscurely assassinated; some of his fellow-authors escaped to Latin America, and those who remained found themselves controlled by a stern suppression of free speech. The land of Lope de Vega and Calderón stumbled down the same murky path which had been taken by the land of Schiller, Goethe, and Hauptmann.

To these significant losses must be added a fifth, even although the loss itself was not conditioned by political events. Chiefly because of the inspired literary creations of Ibsen and Strindberg, Scandinavia had proved to be one of the most important centres of dramatic inspiration during the latter part of the nineteenth century and the early years of the twentieth, but now those authors were gone: Ibsen died in 1906, Strindberg in 1912. That they left behind them several by no means unworthy successors is assuredly true, but the basic power inherent in the northern lands was, at least temporarily, gone.

The disappearance of all those sources of inspiration was, of course, partly counterbalanced by the emergence of numerous and varied new forces, many of them consequent upon the political changes which had been the aftermath of war. The breaking-up of the old Austro-Hungarian Empire meant that the entire creaking framework of that vast, sprawling territory rapidly disintegrated, splitting up into its ethnically separate units, and within these now self-governing areas, notwithstanding the very serious physical, material, and other hardships of the post-war years, dozens of young dramatists, deeply breathing in the intoxicating air of liberty, applied themselves with eager and bright-eyed excitement to make contributions to their national stages. The dreams of the past now were suddenly made real and palpable, so that plays celebrating freedom tended to take the place of dramas cautiously hinting at the possibility of insurgence.

There were, of course, many other political developments accompanied, one might say, by dramatic overtones which may be traced in diverse areas from east to west: but in concentrating attention upon all of these we must be careful to recognize that the mere attaining of national independence, or the changing from monarchical to republican forms of government, or the contrary substitution of monarchical control for republican, was not necessarily the only, or even the most powerful influence operative in the theatre during those years. To realize the truth of this statement no far-sought explorations are called for: all that we need do is to reflect that, even when all the dramatic developments within the freshly established independent states are considered as a whole, their combined significance for the theatre of the inter-war period may well appear to be of less general interest than the new movement which suddenly transfigured the theatrical activities of the United States of America and which called into being the genius of Eugene O'Neill.

The thought of O'Neill may well have the effect of making us pause for reconsideration of the seemingly incontrovertible assumptions from which we started out, and in particular for careful scrutiny of the supposition that, so far as the theatre is concerned, the century's first fourteen years are sharply separated from what developed after the world settled down to peace once more in 1919.

Usually we are inclined to think of O'Neill as a dramatist who belongs almost entirely to the twenties and the thirties, one who was, in fact, a typical representative of a post-war world. Probably some at least will feel surprise when they discover, or are reminded, that it was before the outbreak of war—to be precise, in 1913—that this author, then aged twenty-five, was unexpectedly shocked out of his early tempestuous, drunken, riotous, and wandering life into making the determined decision that from then on he would devote himself to the writing of plays. This was no idle resolution, apt to be broken. Lying on his bed in the sanatorium to which he was confined by illness, he made up his mind precisely as to what he ought to do; he must, he thought, not engage simply in undisciplined writing; rather he must proceed as though he were an apprentice learning an art or a craft, and thus he determined to enroll in George Pierce Baker's Harvard '47 Workshop'. His decision to act in this manner may at first seem somewhat surprising, but the surprise is dissipated when we remember that the 'Workshop' stands in effect as a symbol of the sudden dramatic urge which came to the United States during the earliest years of the century. Most certainly, neither the enthusiasm which prompted Professor Baker to establish this centre for the training of playwrights nor the sudden conversion which gave to the young O'Neill a firm sense of purpose resulted from news of the war in Europe.

The further our explorations are extended the more we realize that the pre-war movement in the United States was by no means singular. Pirandello's earliest plays were composed between 1910 and 1915, and Chiarelli, whose important *La maschera e il volto* appeared in 1916, had similarly been attracted to the theatre in 1912: and these Italian examples are paralleled in almost every country. Whether attention is given to what may be called the general current of dramatic activities or to the trickle of avant-garde experiments (a trickle soon to develop into a flood), we are bound to experience a sense of surprise on realizing how widely and how deeply the flow of drama in 1914 dipped into a cavernous underground and then emerged some five years later with unimpeded force.

Quite probably the continuation of established traditions and styles within this particular field of dramatic composition may not occasion any great surprise, but it is certainly rather astonishing to find that precisely the same pattern is presented to us when we turn to regard the avant-garde movements. During the nineteen-twenties, for example, no dramas seemed to be more revolutionary in concept and in execution than those produced by the German Expressionists, and, quite understandably, there is a common tendency to consider these plays as typical products of a disturbed post-war world—a tendency further strengthened by observing that during the first years of the Russian revolutionary movement Mayakovski headed a group of eager young theatre enthusiasts intent upon promoting the same, or at least closely allied, objectives. What, however, must firmly be borne in mind is the basic fact that the German-Russian Expressionism which appeared to be so thoroughly emblematic of communistic aims is barely distinguishable from the *Futurismo* preached by the Italian Filippo Tommaso Marinetti: this Futurism, it must always be recalled, was officially launched as a 'movement' in 1909, was particularly active during the years which preceded the outbreak of war, and later—without any difficulty whatsoever—attached itself to Mussolini's political Fascism.

Nor is this by any means all. Exploring further, we find that the Futurism-Expressionism which thus was hailed as a new development just before and just after the war of 1914–18 had a lineage even lengthier: with perfect justification it may be regarded as having sprung from the 'discovery' of a play which had been written as long ago as 1891, *Frühlings Erwachen* (*Spring's Awakening*) by Frank Wedekind. This drama, performed in 1906, together with August Strindberg's *Spoksonaten* (*The Spook Sonata*), which was published in 1907 and performed the following year, were very definitely ancestors of the aggressively 'modernistic' writings which at first glance had appeared to be so thoroughly characteristic an expression of post-war anger, doubt, disbelief, and revulsion. And the Surrealism which played such a prominent rôle in the later drama (extending even to the present day) which may seem to be firmly dated in 1924 by the appearance of the first *Manifeste* written by André Breton, quite clearly was not invented by that author: the movement obviously goes back to the Dadaism devised and promulgated by the Franco-Rumanian Tristan Tzara fully eight years earlier.

Observing such things, we find ourselves compelled, rather against our will, to reverse almost completely the simple and apparently inescapable pattern from which we started.

The realization that the simpler pattern will not serve our present purposes, however, presents several problems of a kind almost, if not wholly, new.

First it seems obvious that if the progress of the drama during the twentieth century is to be viewed aright it has to be regarded with what Blake called double vision, and this in turn means that, although the following survey is arranged in three sections, 1900–14, 1919–39, and 1945–70, space must be provided for discussing various developments which clearly overleap the gaps in time and give to the whole seventy years a rather peculiar unity of its own.

Secondly, in so far as the present section is concerned, it seems desirable for various reasons to begin the historical account with a kind of emblematic chapter dealing with two kinds of drama utterly opposed to each other—those which came into being during what is here called the 'American Advent,' and those which, just a few years later, were being produced in newly liberated Poland, a country separated from the United States not only by the broad expanse of the Atlantic Ocean but also by the greater part of the continent of Europe from west to east. Those two sets of plays are in many important respects sharply contrasted with each other, and in effect the enormous cleavages which divide them offer an excellent means of appreciating the often violently opposed forces operating within the playhouse realm during those years —and afterwards.

The contrasts are not only numerous but also varied. Although some American dramatists remained content to compose their plays in a familiar realistic style, many of them, from Eugene O'Neill downward, eagerly sought to adopt novel approaches towards their themes and characters, but almost without exception these novel approaches, so far from being inventions of their own, were borrowed from abroad: there is, in fact, such extensive variety here as to warrant the suggestion that these American plays, taken as a whole, offer a kind of panoramic view of nearly all the numerous and diverse theatrical modes developed and cultivated during the inter-war years in dozens of different countries.

What is particularly peculiar is that on the whole these plays have rarely become sources of inspiration for later playwrights, and, still further, have only occasionally been successful in holding the stage. Eugene O'Neill, of course, is widely recognized as a truly great dramatist; his plays are still read (although perhaps less frequently and less enthusiastically now than once they were); there are occasional revivals, but much less frequently than might have been expected; and, most strange fact of all, instances of his direct influence upon later European and other theatrical authors are rare indeed; many dramatists have openly and willingly acknowledged their indebtedness to earlier writers, extending from Chekhov to Synge, but it is surprisingly difficult to find similar acknowledgments of indebtedness to the creator of *Mourning Becomes Electra* and *Emperor Jones*. And in this respect O'Neill stands as an emblematic figure, illustrative of a similar lack of evidence concerning the influence exerted by other American authors.

Thus, unfortunately and rather puzzlingly, the inter-war flourishing of dramatic writing in the United States of America stands in lonely isolation. It is eminently right and proper to start with a reference to this development and to end with a brief survey of O'Neill's works: yet regrettably it must be admitted that, if all the musicals are set apart, the products of the trans-Atlantic stage during this period of its awakening have not proved to be a powerful, widespread international stimulus.

This fact—for as such it must be accepted—is particularly surprising when it is set against another equally assured fact of a paradoxically opposed kind—the numerous 'discoveries' which during recent years have brought to attention many plays, emanating from various countries, which had been almost completely ignored or else misunderstood in their own times and which now are being applauded and imitated both in avant-garde and in popular circles. The catalogue of authors belonging to this company, men of high distinction and men who were oddities, is both lengthy and heterogeneous, including names such as Paul Claudel and Tristan Tzara, Alfred Jarry and Guillaume Apollinaire, Ödön von Horvath and Marieluise Fleisser, Michel Ghelderode and Stanisław Witkiewicz.

It is with the last person in this short list that it may be profitable to pause for a moment. One aspect of the stage during this period is clearly reflected in the range of O'Neill's dramas: the other main aspect, a strange one, is reflected in the violently eccentric plays conceived by Witkiewicz.

1

THE AMERICAN ADVENT AND DRAMATIC REVOLUTION IN POLAND

AN EXAMINATION of what changes came to the American drama during the present century and of the forces which stimulated these changes is of particular interest precisely because during earlier years the playhouses of the United States, although active and widely popular, had so far failed to encourage the development of any theatrical literature of great importance. Students of American stage history will, of course, find many early plays which well deserve to be remembered, but the best will in the world cannot make anyone sincerely argue that even the worthiest of these productions are invested with any broadly universal, as opposed to local national, value. All that can be said is that as the nineteenth century was drawing to its close, and during the first years of the present era, definite signs of a stirring of spirit can be discerned, and, while it must be admitted that no genuinely great achievements are discoverable even within those later years, we can observe how the hitherto largely somnolent American drama was coming near to the time of its awakening.

The Forerunners

Three particular features of what occurred between about 1890 and, say, 1910 are of special significance. First of these was the cultivation of surface realism (the old Crummles variety brought up to date) in such a way as to go far beyond anything to be found elsewhere. It was at this time that David Belasco became the grand master of the theatrically 'authentic', making a fortune from the public's willingness to pay good dollars in order to see in the playhouses replicas of objects and scenes which easily might have been viewed by everyone for nothing outside the auditorium. Realistic scenes of this sort he adroitly combined with melodramatically conceived actions, as in *The Girl I Left Behind Me* (1893), dealing with the Wild West, or as in the notorious *The Heart of Maryland* (1895), set in the time of the Civil War, in which a strong-armed actress nobly swung on the clapper of a great bell in order to silence its tolling and thus to prevent what had been assigned as the signal for her lover's execution. While it is true that Belascoism was rapidly to become outmoded in later years, its influence, both positive and negative, long has continued to be one of the firmest foundation-stones of the American theatre.

During the Belasco period proper it served, of course, to prevent the development of any deeper kind of realism, and its force was augmented by a second. American dramatists of that age were apt pupils in the school of the 'well-made play.' Scores of melodramas and farces and farce-comedies written within the latter years of the nineteenth century and the earliest years of the present exhibit considerable technical ability within the limits of that formula, and because of this it may be agreed that they fully deserved their wide popularity. Their immediate effect, however, obviously was to encourage among the public a love of the sensational and of the sentimentally adroit: when plays are 'slick' and trapped out attractively there is little call for audiences to question their inner truth. During later years, of course, numerous dramatists inspired by higher aims looked back on the past with distaste and expressed their contempt for mechanically fashioned theatrical plots, characters, and scenes, yet the long training in this style continued to remain subtly potent. There were to be many later authors who, while they honestly sneered at the old melodramas and farces, were prepared to borrow from the treasury of theatrically effective situations which had so strongly appealed to earlier audiences.

The emphasis upon outward realism was still further intensified by a third force. Quite clearly, American spectators were mightily interested in watching actions which purported to show the ways of life to be found within the numerous states of the Union or which aimed at reproducing on the stage recent historical events associated with the exciting establishment and growth of their nation. Sufficient evidence of that trend is provided by reference to just four dramas—one each from the four authors whose names come most readily to mind when thought is given to the stage's career within the later years of the nineteenth century. Bronson Howard dealt in *Shenandoah* (1888) with episodes in the Civil War, and, rightly, this play made appeal to thousands upon thousands of spectators in hundreds of performances; James A. Herne, actor and dramatist, won his greatest success in *Shore Acres* (1892), a good 'strong' piece dealing with New England life; *Barbara Frietchie* (1899), dealing with one of America's most renowned folk-heroines, was one of the most popular works produced by the popular Clyde Fitch; Augustus Thomas, among his numerous writings, created an *Alabama* (1891) early in his career, a romantic drama which was not only widely acclaimed for its theatrical quality but was even said to have done much to heal the scars left by the bitter internecine conflict which provided its background. As further evidence of this trend it may be added that Thomas followed his early play with a *Mizzura* (1893) and an *Arizona* (1899), and again, towards the ending of his active career, returned to a Civil War theme in *The Copperhead* (1918). All such pieces worked strongly upon the audiences of the period. The very novelty of seeing stage characters taken

"THE CRADLE SONG": CIVIC REPERTORY THEATRE,
NEW YORK
Setting by G. E. Calthrop. From *Theatre Arts Monthly*, March
1927.

"THE ADDING MACHINE": BOSTON REPERTORY
THEATRE
Setting by Jonel Jorgulesco. From *Theatre Arts Monthly*,
March 1927.

BASIC SETTING BY PETER GOFFIN FOR THE TRAVELLING
REPERTORY THEATRE PRODUCTION OF "IN TIME TO
COME"

from various American regions, of hearing in their talk the tones of the American voice, hoodwinked even the most astute into regarding the sentimental, the farcical, and the melodramatic scenes as realistic, thus further intensifying the long-prevailing trend: but not a single one of these many plays can have any save a nostalgic appeal for the public of to-day.

As the twentieth century moved into its first decade a slow change came to exhibit itself, although it must be confessed that even here the achievements associated with it were notable rather in connection with what was to follow than because of any great virtue inherent in themselves. Edward Sheldon attracted considerable attention with *Salvation Nell* (1908), a sensational study of a woman who refuses to desert her ne'er-do-well sweetheart when drink leads him astray and who eventually succeeds in reclaiming him; the following year, too, saw the appearance of the same author's *The Nigger* (1909), one of the very first among the widening range of dramatic essays designed to stir the public into reflecting upon the complexities of the Negro problem. When, however, we recall that Sheldon was also author of *Romance* (1913) we feel no surprise in observing that his treatment of the plots of both these dramas was, in fact, slabbily thick with sentimentalism. Sentimentalism, accompanied by sensational melodramatic elements, also colours the much more ambitious effort of William Vaughn Moody, *The Great Divide* (1906), a play in which a bold attempt was made to combine two themes —that of the gentle-born New England woman who forsakes the comforts of civilized life in order to remain by the side of the adventuresome man whom she loves, and that of the woman who, violated by a man, comes to feel affection for him growing in her heart. Yet the treatment of this wide-ranging plot now seems artificially stilted, and similarly artificial appear the lighter plays of Rachel Crothers, such as her early study of male-manufactured social conventions, *A Man's World* (1909).

Quite apart from this not uninteresting, yet still not particularly stimulating, dramatic world which was largely confined within the range of Broadway's commercial stages, another and a different world was being brought into being. Far off, at Harvard University, an enthusiastic professor named George Pierce Baker, at the very beginning of the present century, had risked incurring the wrath of his more conservative colleagues by establishing a 'seminar' which was in effect a course in practical playwriting, and, as has been seen, it was into this group that in 1914 the young O'Neill, having determined to become a dramatist, applied for admission, and was accepted. During the same year two forward-looking authors, one a novelist and the other a poet, enthusiastically set to work at establishing a small 'experimental' summer theatre at Provincetown, Massachusetts; one year later the Washington Square Players presented their earliest productions, and, actively continuing their work during the war years, in 1919 boldly created the famous Guild Theatre.

Excitement clearly was in the air during the years immediately before and immediately after the outbreak of the First World War, and this excitement continued to inspire the new school of playwrights who took command of the stage in the twenties and the thirties.

American Eclecticism

Two dominating aspects of this movement are especially noteworthy. Even although there was undoubted strength amply made manifest in the total output of the American playwrights active during the inter-war period, their combined efforts, even when taken together, differ in nature from the productions of all the greater dramatic movements of the past —from, let us say, the Elizabethan English, the seventeenth-century Spanish, the nineteenth-century Scandinavian. Not only did most of the prominent playwrights, including even the towering figure of O'Neill, tend constantly to experiment in the employment of different dramatic styles, only rarely did any one of those authors seek to invent such styles for themselves. O'Neill thus becomes the truly representative and symbolic figure in the midst of what can be described only by the phrase 'creative American eclecticism'.

Some at least among the individual achievements of this group of authors will, of course, be dealt with in the immediately following chapters of the present survey, but there is one aspect of the new theatrical movement in the United States which demands attention here. The '47 Workshop' itself was not copied from something established elsewhere, and, as has already been suggested, it did not stand alone. It is true, of course, that the concept of what may be styled 'special' playhouses was one which first manifested itself in such ventures as the Moscow Art Theatre, the Freie Bühne in Berlin, the Théâtre Libre in Paris, and which continued as an active force in many countries, exemplified variously in the English 'repertory' playhouses, accompanied by almost innumerable semi-amateur, semi-professional acting societies, in the Italian 'carri di Tespi' and the Teatro degli Indipendenti, in the Spanish Teatro del Pueblo and Garcia Lorca's La Barraca, in the Irish Abbey Theatre. The special feature which distinguished Baker's innovating 'Workshop' was its fusing together of the dramatically creative and of the academically critical, and it was this particular quality inherent in its being which, penetrating deeply and widely into almost all countries, has led to the truly surprising extension of theatrical studies in virtually all the world's universities—a development which, in turn, has resulted in far-reaching innovations of various kinds both among professional theatre-men and among informed playgoers.

Baker had fixed his gaze primarily upon young playwrights, but even in its earliest days his 'Workshop' had stimulated some eager young scene-designers, all enthusiastically intent on enriching the quality of stage productions. Already in 1919 arrangements were made for the very first exhibition organized for the purpose of showing to an interested public what was being achieved by artists such as Robert Edmond Jones, Joseph Urban, Lee Simonson, and Norman Bel Geddes—a notable company soon to be enlarged by the inclusion of Donald Oenslager, Jo Mielziner, and others.

New Theatres for Old

Besides being distinguished artists whose many varied, and varying, styles powerfully complemented what the dramatists were seeking to achieve, several of these men applied themselves to the writing of books concerned both with their own individual aims and with attempts to survey what scenic spectacle had contributed in the past to stage productions and to suggest what it might offer to productions in the future. The range of such volumes was wide, extending from Kenneth Macgowan's characteristically titled *The Theatre of Tomorrow*, published in 1923, to Mordecai Gorelik's *New Theatres for Old*, issued in 1940. The interest taken by these theatre-men in the history of the stage and in exploring paths hitherto almost, if not quite, untrodden may, of course, be paralleled elsewhere, but the interest itself seems to have had a peculiarly inspiring power in the United States: if the earliest proscenium-less playhouse was established by Jacques Copeau in the Théâtre du Vieux Colombier in 1913, the theatre-in-the-round (so powerful a concept in later theatrical presentations) appears to have been put to practical use first in the United States, and it was there that the 'off-Broadway' performances, largely if not wholly inspired by university-trained directors and actors, laid the foundations for the teeming range of 'fringe theatres' which are now so characteristic a feature of latter-day stage activities.

The diverse activities of the American scenic artists call to mind those of another artist far removed from them in space and in temperament and in what may be called theatrical position, a man who remained known only to limited audiences within his own country, whose work was appreciated hardly at all until suddenly he became the subject of one of those 'discoveries' which, as will be seen, have been so characteristic a feature of the playhouse world within recent years.

Stanislaw Ignacy Witkiewicz, the son of a Polish painter and a painter himself, was the author of some thirty plays written between 1918 and the early thirties: of these about a third remain unpublished; only a dozen were performed before their creator committed suicide as his country was invaded in 1939; and, notwithstanding the fact that he actively contributed essays to the avant-garde magazine *Skamander* and also published several more extended critical-philosophical-aesthetic studies, he remained almost completely ignored even in his native land, and entirely unknown even by name elsewhere until suddenly, in the late fifties and in the sixties, he became a person of prominence in advanced circles almost everywhere. His writings are tissues of absurdities; and, appropriately, nothing could be more absurd in dramatic history than that this man should have, as it were, no existence during his lifetime and yet unexpectedly become a person of substance when he himself had for many years been a ghost.

Hardly any writer of this time rivalled him in the outpouring of outrageously extravagant scenes influenced by all kinds of cults and philosophical speculations: Freud's world of the subconscious has a strong rôle to play here, but so also have those concepts which were publicized by the Futurists and the Cubists and the rebellious artists in Kraków who preached the doctrine of 'pure form', while the entire conglomeration of thoughts and emotions is invested with despairing and devastating reflections on human life, often expressed in dialogue which in its wild ferment defies any rational interpretation. Everything and everyone around him seems to be mad and menacing: the whole world is bitterly summed up in the title of *Oni (They*, written in 1920, published 1962, performed 1965): dictators are insane and so are ardent communists: this whole wretched twentieth-century culture is crazy and meaningless —and equally so is the entire historical record of mankind: today's cult of science and technology is just as stupid as the boorish brutishness of an early feudal lord depicted in *Janulka, córka Fizdejki (Janulka, the Daughter of Fizdejko*, written in 1923, published 1962): scientists are absurd lunatics in *Metafizyka dwugłowego cielęcia (The Metaphysics of a Two-headed Calf*, written in 1921, performed 1928, published 1962), and naturally priests are just as moonstruck: plays of the far past (say, those by Shakespeare) are ridiculous, and so too are such later works as Ibsen's *Ghosts* and Strindberg's *The Spook Sonata*, both of which are parodied in *Matka (The Mother*, written in 1924, published 1962, performed 1926), and Wyspiański's *Deliverance*, which is mocked at in *Nowe Wyzwolenie (The New Deliverance*, written and published in 1922, performed 1962): there are constant inconsequences, with many scenes of violence, crowding into these plays, as in *Wariat i zakonnica, czyli Nie ma złego, co by na jeszcze gorsze nie wyszło (The Madman and the Nun; or, Nothing's So Bad It Can't Become Worse*, written and published in 1925, performed 1926); there are corpses which are real corpses, mysteriously coming to life again or else rolling about the stage, as in the same play and in *Niepodległość trójkatów (The Independence of the Triangles*, written in 1921, published 1962), and there are corpses which frighteningly turn out to be mere dummies: there are scenes of ominous inaction, and scenes that go round and round in circles, and other scenes, such as those in *Szalona lokomotywa (The Crazy Locomotive*, written in 1923, published 1962, performed 1964), that rush terrifyingly onward in an insane, uncontrollable precipitancy. Omnipresent in all these writings is the spirit which is dominant in what has become Witkiewicz's best-known work, *Kurka wodna (The Water Hen*, written in 1921, performed 1922, published 1962), where two insensitive old men carry on with their ordinary affairs while the whole world around them is crumbling into ruins—a theme which is also central in

Szewcy (*The Shoemakers*, written in 1934, published 1948, performed 1957).

Where, it may well be asked, does this dramatist belong? In the references cited above the dates of composition, publication, and production of the plays have deliberately been set out in full—and when we consider how few of these dramas were presented to the public in or near the years when they were written, when we think of what little attention was paid to those few which were brought forward either in printed form or in stage performance, and when we reflect on the popularity they have acquired for themselves in advanced circles within recent years, it seems evident that they belong neither to the early twenties nor to the fifties and sixties: there is no place wherein they can appropriately be dealt with here except the no-man's-land of this introductory section prefatory to the examination of dramatic development within the course of the past fifty or sixty years.

In briefly considering them here, particularly when they are set in juxtaposition to the plays characteristic of what has been styled the American advent, they provide what is perhaps at first glance a rather startling, and yet on further reflection an illuminating, introduction not only to the theatre of the inter-war years but also, more broadly, to the entire course of stage affairs from the start of the century on to the present. Eugene O'Neill, widely accepted from the twenties onwards as one of the great masters of the drama, has not been dethroned, but, if we want to appreciate aright what has been happening in the playhouse during these latter years we must fully take into account the extraordinary fact that a painter-playwright in far-off Poland who failed in his own lifetime to win attention and acclaim even in his own country has suddenly soared so high in avant-garde reputation as to provide him also with a seat on Olympus —for how long, of course, only time, the master of all things, can tell.

And still a further observation may be made. O'Neill's name is still generally spoken with reverence, yet, despite this, it seems remarkable how seldom his plays have been revived during recent years, and how rarely the younger dramatists of today seem to find inspiration in his works. He stands, as it were, a mighty monument of the past, to be admired but not necessarily followed, whereas Witkiewicz, despite the fact that he was not recognized in his own time, even despite the fact that he has few direct disciples, arouses present excitement. Any anthology of 'avant-garde' drama prepared nowadays almost certainly will include no play by O'Neill, but in it Witkacy (as he called himself) will, without question, be permanently represented.

2

THE DRAMA OF THE INDIVIDUAL

IN THE development of dramatic trends after the cessation of hostilities in 1918 the first broad movement which we must consider is that which inclines towards the focusing of attention upon the individual. This is the subjective theatre and may be associated with at least some of the main qualities characterizing the impressionistic school in the sister art of painting.

The word 'subjective' may, of course, be applied to the theatre in a variety of different ways, and it is important that these should not be confused. A play is subjective when all its scenes and characters, the entirety of its theme, are consistently coloured by the author's own personality: thus, for example, Maeterlinck's *Pelléas et Mélisande* is subjectively conceived in that over the whole of the action is cast one prevailing spirit, persons of the drama appearing, as it were, through a veil, which is the personality—or at least the particular mood—of Maeterlinck himself. *Pelléas et Mélisande* is utterly unlike Strindberg's *The Spook Sonata*, yet the latter, too, can be described as subjective. In using the word for Strindberg, however, we mean that the writer has permitted himself to attempt the dramatic exploitation of his own inner self: he is not merely letting his subject-matter be coloured by a particular sentiment, rather is he putting his soul's adventures on the stage. Nor is this all: in yet a third kind of play the author may select an individual character (not a reflection of himself) and, as it were, present the rest of the play as though it were a projection of that character's mind. A good example occurs in *Beggar on Horseback*, an American comedy written in 1924 by George S. Kaufman and Marc Connelly. Here the central figure is a man, Neil McRae, by nature a musician, but prevented from applying himself to his art because of lack of money. Although in love with Cynthia, he is toying with the idea of marrying the rich Gladys. Up to this point the scenes provide a kind of introduction to what forms the real core of the drama, wherein a nightmare experienced by Neil takes the place of 'real' episodes. Dreaming, he marries a Gladys whose bridal bouquet is made up of banknotes: he is asked to play something for the guests and his hands refuse to turn out anything effective; money is showered upon him, yet when a friend advises him to murder all his wife's family he does so with glee, and at his trial he vigorously defends himself; finally condemned to punishment, he is placed in a prison-like Cady Consolidated Art Factory, where the convicts hammer out music and poetry and painting as though they were breaking stones, picking oakum, sewing mailbags.

Clearly these three species of subjective drama are connected, and equally clearly we must hold them distinct in our minds even while, for the purpose of tracing larger dramatic trends, we are forced to link them together. They are not, of course, entirely new trends belonging specifically to these between-war years; although they reach a culmination in this period, each had been adumbrated during the opening decades of the century. The first, the *Pelléas et Mélisande* type, we have already seen fully developed by the neo-romantic symbolist poets; the second finds characteristic expression in Strindberg; the third finds expression in such works as Ibsen's *Peer Gynt*, Hauptmann's *Die versunkene Glocke*, and Evreinov's 'monodramas.'

There are, however, two further services to which the word 'subjective' can be, and frequently is, put. In Vienna, during the early years of the present century, Sigmund Freud was engaged in revolutionizing previous concepts of human behaviour, in stressing the importance of the subconscious, and in developing the 'science' of psychoanalysis. Naturally his investigations were bound to exert very considerable influence on the creative arts, particularly upon those of narrative fiction and of drama wherein supposedly living persons are presented. Here older ideas of character-portrayal were put aside and an effort was made to probe more deeply below the surface, to make explicit what is generally concealed, to give expression, directly or indirectly, to those elements in the human soul which remain hidden even from their possessor. In dramatic form this endeavour leads, on the one hand, to a kind of theatrical case-history of clinical tendency and, on the other, to studies such as those of the French playwright Jean-Jacques Bernard—and of both the stage between 1920 and 1940 can produce innumerable examples. For many dramatists psychology has been dismissed in favour of psychoanalysis.

Along with this may be taken a trend exemplified in the work at least of a few dramatists who, dissatisfied with the application of reason to all aspects of human existence, seek once more to testify to the predominance of the spirit and introduce religious themes to the stage. During the nineteenth century and the first decades of our own age the theme of religion was almost entirely banished from the theatre, and when it did make its appearance it usually took the form of vast poetic dramas in which the 'gods' were much spoken of and man's life was symbolically set against a great infinitude of empty space. What is interesting during recent years is the development of a dramatic style wherein matters of the spirit are brought into close association with ordinary life, and wherein a quiet utterance, sometimes even moving into the sphere of the comic, is substituted for the grandiose romantic eloquence of earlier writers.

For convenience all these diverse movements may here be assembled under the single heading of impressionism: although varied in character, they manifest certain qualities in common, and it is perhaps more important that we should recognize these bonds between them by thus connecting them all with the attempt to enter inside the human soul, than that we should divide them into separate categories.

The Vogue of Surrealism

The most extreme form may be considered first. In the year 1896 Alfred Jarry wrote his youthful satirical drama *Ubu roi*, destined to be treated by many later writers as a prime essay in the surrealist style; in 1917 Guillaume Apollinaire presented his *Les mamelles de Tirésias* (*The Breasts of Tiresias*) to the public as a "drame surréaliste"; eight years later André Breton published the first of his surrealistic manifestoes. In surrealism we may see both a destructive and a constructive force. The year when *Les mamelles de Tirésias* appeared the nihilistic Dadaist movement was founded in Zurich by Tristan Tzara, Hans Arp, and their companions, and its first manifesto was issued two years later. Between *Dadaïsme* and *surréalisme* there is a close connexion, and when we observe that the former is a perfectly deliberate denial of all values, an anarchistic attempt to mock at everything in life, we recognize that for some of the followers of surrealism the movement meant no more than an excuse for the cynical expression of disbelief in all and everything.

Beyond this, however, the surrealistic enthusiasts, unlike the Dadaists, had a core of positive endeavour in their theories. Having become acquainted with the subconscious, they declared, in effect, that the only true art, and, incidentally, the only true realism, could lie in those regions of the human mind which hitherto had been explored only occasionally in the past (by such artists, for example, as the fifteenth-century Hieronymus Bosch or the eighteenth-century William Blake). In effect, they took the division of the soul outlined by Evreinov, separated man into the rational and the irrational self, and declared that only in the operation of the latter could the source of art be found.

A few of the extremists went so far as to plead that 'art' should consist merely in (*a*) automatic writing or (*b*) the faithful recording of dreams; but the cleverer among the adherents of the movement, realizing that if such a doctrine were adopted, then anybody's dream is as good as anybody else's, and that hence the position of the 'artist' becomes imperilled, allowed themselves to admit an element of the ordering imagination, without, however, abandoning their belief in the fundamental importance, for the creative writer, of the realm of the subconscious.

We all know the kind of paintings produced under the spell of this theory, and, whether we sympathize or not with the æsthetic aims, we cannot deny that some of the artists, such as Salvador Dali, are men highly gifted with technical ability and power of expression. We all know, too, the manifestations of this style of artistic creation in the works of James Joyce and his followers. What is not so well known are the plays executed in an attempt to put on to the boards the subject-matter of the subconscious.

Perhaps we need feel no surprise at this, since fundamentally the theatre would seem to provide a means singularly unfitted for such an endeavour. The dream is always characterized by its shifting forms: one thing fades into another; nothing keeps its shape for long; in sharp juxtaposition appear images of startling clarity and shadowy essences whose lineaments fade perplexingly into their backgrounds. Such things may be able to find expression in the cinema; in general, the theatre is too hard and fixed a medium for their exhibition. As a result, none of the several dramatic essays penned by the avowed adherents of the school has any lasting, intrinsic significance.

Against that, however, we must weigh two considerations: first, that one or two other writers have succeeded in taking the general spirit of the surrealist mood and in producing works of some interest, and, secondly, that elements of the surrealistic style have found their way into many dramas otherwise not in any respect associated with the aims of Apollinaire and Breton.

In the former category stand forward the perplexing plays of that extraordinary French author Jean Cocteau, a man so various that he seems to be, not one, but all mankind's epitome. Starting his career with *Les mariés de la Tour Eiffel* (*The Wedding on the Eiffel Tower*, 1921), he has turned out a *Roméo et Juliette* (1924), *Orphée* (1926), *La voix humaine* (*The Human Voice*, 1930), *Les chevaliers de la Table Ronde* (*The Knights of the Round Table*, 1937), *L'aigle à deux têtes* (*The Eagle has Two Heads*, 1946), and many others in a confusing mixture of styles. In general—and despite the fact that he also veered to the realistic in *Les parents terribles* (*The Terrible Relations*, 1938) and *La machine à écrire* (*The Typewriter*, 1941)—he stands as the spearhead of that phalanx of writers who demand that the theatre should turn from the realistic style and evolve fresh forms of expression. In general, too, he demands that all the thought processes, all the ratiocination associated with the play of ideas, should be abandoned, that the theatre should once more become true to itself and recognize that in pure theatricality resides a virtue with its own inherent value. At the same time he keeps to no set path, and even within the framework of single plays he startles us by the introduction of inconsistencies and disharmonies. At times he can be almost melodramatically realistic, as when in *La voix humaine* he introduces one long monologue spoken by a character into the telephone, ending the flow of words by means of a suicide effected with the flex of the instrument. At other moments, as in *L'aigle à deux têtes*, his mood turns Websterian and romantic. Here he spins a dark fantasy of a peasant-poet who comes to a palace with the intent of murdering his Queen. Seeing her, he falls under her spell and is drawn into a passionate love romance. She and he are wrapped in a passion beyond which there can be nothing of any worth, and the Queen, realizing that on earth their love cannot find consummation, yet that life without him would be empty, goads him into committing the assassination he had come to effect. In another mood he turns to the style of surrealism, and proceeds to take a number of ancient Greek themes for a treatment far removed from that which they had received in Athenian days. *Orphée* has all the inconsequence of a dream, introducing a bizarre mixture of the gay and the terrible, allowing its characters to defy at once the dictates of reason and the laws of gravitation. The same process is followed in *Antigone* (1922), and is carried to most satisfying form in *La machine infernale* (*The Infernal Machine*, 1934). This last play, based on the ever-fascinating myth of Œdipus, presents the gods before us, in the words of its title, as naught save an 'infernal machine,' a vicious power intent on the creating of misery for man. In narrating his story Cocteau completely abandons any attempt to startle his audience by any surprises except those achieved by his own nimble imaginative dialogue and by the contrast between the Greek story and his chosen method of treatment: he causes his chorus not merely to outline the plot, but also to elucidate the course of the spiritual movement of the play. That spiritual movement aims, albeit by means strange and unfamiliar, at the evoking of a tragic mood by showing a human character who, while not himself of great stature, achieves unwonted dignity by passing through the fire of torment. In this effort Cocteau has displayed consummate skill in craftsmanship, power over words, and innate wisdom in his choice of material. The surrealist (and other anti-realistic) styles can easily lose themselves in an incomprehensible medley of subjectively conceived imaginings: in selecting stories well-known and hallowed by previous handling the author at once permits himself the opportunity of achieving effects from the contrast between the old and the new, and secures a firm basis in dramatic unity and in fundamental clarity of purpose. At the same time in Cocteau's work we always feel that something is lacking. Without doubt he has the power to create scenes which, even when not fully intelligible, are instinct with emotional quality, but it must be admitted that throughout his work we are uneasily conscious of a certain insincerity: we suspect that the surrealistic technique is employed, not because of a deeply felt belief in its virtue, but because he imagines that, handled with his adroit skill, its very novelty is bound to attract attention.

Another dramatist, the Franco-Belgian Fernand Crommelynck, has likewise found the surrealistic methods of some service. From that school he learned how to mix scenes of violently contrasting qualities, to set crudest farce alongside potentially tragic material, to make a dream sequence follow or precede a scene of almost naturalistic kind. Outside of France he is best known for the overflowing vitality and gusty humour of *Le cocu magnifique* (*The Magnificent Cuckold*, 1920), but others of his plays perhaps may be considered in the future as even richer in quality and more vivid in execution. An irrepressibly eccentric author, he has an extended career from the beginning of the century on to the thirties—from *Le sculpteur de masques* (*The Maker of Masks*, 1908) and *Le marchand de regrets* (*The Merchant of Regrets*, 1913), through *Les amants puérils* (*The Childish Lovers*, 1921), *Carine* (1930), and *Tripes d'or* (*Golden Tripe*, 1930), to *Une femme qu'a le cœur trop petit* (*The Woman whose Heart is Too Small*, 1934) and *Chaud et froid* (*Hot and Cold*, 1934). In all of these the same qualities are apparent—the rich outpouring of words, the skilful theatrical situations, the intermingling of the rational and the irrational. In *Une femme qu'a le cœur trop petit*, a strange play that takes as its heroine a woman, Balbine, whose emotional life is suppressed by her concentration on the petty things of domestic existence, we move from scenes of the outward to scenes of the inward, while in others we can hardly tell which particular region we inhabit at any precise moment. In this connexion it is interesting to compare the methods of *Beggar on Horseback* and *Tripes d'or*. Both present fundamentally the same theme—that of a young man in love with a girl, yet prepared to forsake her for money. Whereas Kaufman and Connelly, however, never leave us in doubt concerning the nature of their scenes and eventually reach a nice sentimental conclusion, Crommelynck brings the inner and the outer together and produces a bitter irony all his own. One of the most effective scenes in this play shows the hero, Hormidas, in his room. We know that he adores Azelle, but adroitly Crommelynck has kept her off the stage: we know her, we feel, but only through what others have said of her. Now we learn that she is coming to see her Hormidas, and her knock sounds on the door. In silence he pretends not to hear, and for a brief space we are kept in suspense, then we listen to her steps retreating. The scene is real and yet it is symbolic; it is outward and yet it concerns rather the adventures of the soul than those of the body.

In many different ways the surrealist cult was propounded and practised by numerous devotees. In *Victor, ou les enfants au pouvoir* (*Victor; or The Children in Power*, 1928) another French author, Roger Vitrac, satirized society's follies and evils by creating an impossible world in which a child nine years old speaks and acts like a man. The connection with *Ubu Roi* is obvious, and no surprise need be felt when it is found that Vitrac was co-founder of the Théâtre Alfred-Jarry in 1927, and that he was an active disciple of the Dadaist movement—which, of course, spread the doctrine of 'automatic writing'. His associate in this venture was Antonin Artaud, actor rather than dramatist, theorist rather than creator, who spent much of his time in developing his own 'philosophy'—a revolt against reason and a plea for a return to animalistic 'instinct'—and his cult of the 'theatre of cruelty.' A clear line of development, therefore, may easily be traced from the play which had been just a schoolboy's joke to a theatrical concept which is treated solemnly in at least some present-day theatrical circles. Nor is that by any means the end of the trail, since it is important to observe that this whole movement has connections with the excesses of the romantic spirit. It seems almost incredible that the atmosphere of early nineteenth-century 'Gothicism' should still be cultivated after the passage of more than a century and a half: yet this is a definite fact to be reckoned with. Crommelynck's fellow-Belgian, Michel de Ghelderode, fed his imagination with a somewhat dangerous mixture of romantic and surrealistic dishes, intermingling everything from tales such as might have pleased 'Monk' Lewis on to Jarry's and Vitrac's eccentric concepts. In his own time de Ghelderode was largely ignored, except in Belgium, but from 1950 onward many of his plays have cast their spell on a number of younger writers. Undoubtedly he exhibited a measure of daimonic power in his fifty-odd dramatic works, but it must be borne in mind that his inspiration derives from the past, and that it is often associated with a kind of feverish frenzy.

The Entry of Psychoanalysis into the Theatre

More common was the introduction to the stage of psychoanalytic method, and here Henri-René Lenormand may be taken as a prime representative of a loosely affiliated school of writers. Lenormand comes before us as the brutal naturalistic dramatist turned inward. In his scenes are sensational crudities that remind us of the early Hauptmann's imaginings—with this difference, that the focus is always less on the events themselves than upon the subconscious workings of his characters' beings. One of his better-known dramas, *Le mangeur de rêves* (*The Eater of Dreams*, 1922), indeed, goes so far as to psychoanalyse a psychoanalyst, the central figure being a professional exponent of this 'science' who himself is so unbalanced as deliberately to drag from his patients' souls secrets which should never have been brought to light: he thus demonstrates to a young girl that a display of jealousy in her childhood (which she had entirely forgotten) was responsible for her mother's death. In *Les ratés* (*The Failures*, 1920) two wretched people, an author and his actress wife, both of them wholly unsuccessful, are relentlessly brought from step to step down the ladder until the man murders the woman and commits suicide. The inner life of a Don Juan is revealed in *L'homme et ses fantômes* (*Man and his Phantoms*, 1924), with the psychoanalytic explanation that the hero has passed restlessly from one mistress to another because all his life he has been unconsciously seeking his mother; a perverted soul is dissected in *À l'ombre du mal* (*In the Shadow of Evil*, 1924); while in *La dent rouge* (*The Red Tooth*, 1922) the story is told of a sophisticated girl's marrying an unlettered mountaineer, finding herself surrounded by the fantastic demons of the popular imagination as she sits virtually alone in her snow-bound hut, and finally being accused of witchcraft. *Le simoun* (1920) narrates, in the arid setting of the Arabian desert, the story of a father's incestuous love of his daughter; *Le lâche* (*The Coward*, 1926) cruelly analyses the soul terrors and weaknesses of a man who, during the war, has sought escape in Switzerland. There is not, perhaps, very much of real worth in Lenormand's work, and occasionally we may suspect there is a good deal of nonsense, but his position in the history of the drama is an important one and his influence has not been by any means meagre.

Not unlike in spirit is Paul Raynal, author of *Le maître de son cœur* (*The Master of his Heart*, 1920), *Le tombeau sous l'Arc de Triomphe* (*The Tomb beneath the Arc de Triomphe*, or *The Unknown Warrior*, 1924), *Au soleil de l'instinct* (*In the Sunshine of Instinct*, 1932), and *La Francerie* (1933). The first of these deals trenchantly with the affection of two friends broken by the machinations of a woman; the second, a more powerful drama, shows a soldier on leave from the front and carries its tense scenes forward with merely three persons—the soldier himself, the girl to whom he is betrothed, and his father. Unlike Lenormand, Raynal is rather the romanticist of psychoanalysis than its naturalist. Lenormand's words are bare; Raynal's pour forth in a wild torrent; his figures, although also laid on the dissecting table, have their nakedness wrapped up in the rich folds of his lyrical utterance.

There are others, however, who take a quieter course, and here the once esteemed but now somewhat neglected Jean-Jacques Bernard may be regarded as typical. Some few years ago critics were raving about his works: later re-reading suggests that, despite the unquestioned skill of his dramas, their themes are a trifle thin and their characters too delicate to be real. Take, for example, *L'âme en peine* (*The Soul in Pain*, or *The Unquiet Spirit*, 1926), where an attempt is made to show a woman, Marceline, married to a man she loves, yet strangely tortured in mind, restless, losing energy she knows not why: the explanation is that she has a twin-soul, a man she never meets, but whom we see drifting near to her on several occasions; and we are given to understand that her separation from him torments her subconscious spirit. There is some subtlety here, yet, when we have done with the play, we realize that it is no more than a new treatment of Maeterlinck's neo-romantic *Blue Bird* fantasy of boy and girl souls being divided by the exigencies of their incorporation in human bodies. All Bernard's dramas are of a similar kind: like Maeterlinck, he argues for a 'static' drama; like Norwid, he believes in the drama of silences. *L'invitation au voyage* (*The Invitation to a Voyage*, 1924) shows a young wife morbidly dreaming of a young engineer who has gone off to the Argentine; she is shocked into a realization of fact when she meets him again on one of his visits home. In *Le feu qui reprend mal* (*The Sulky Fire*, 1921) a soldier returns from the front and is racked by jealousy because his wife has had an American billeted in the house; in *Martine* (1922) a country girl, married later, finds her heart throbbing for a youth whom she had met casually years before; in *Le printemps des autres* (*The Springtime of Others*, 1924) a mother finds herself moved, beyond her will, to love her daughter's husband, until, in the end, she forces herself to separate from her child (as the two women part there is "a very long silent gaze between them, the understanding gaze of woman to woman"); *Denise Marette*

(1925) narrates the story of an artist's daughter who puts forth her work as his and is visited by a perplexing ghost who appears now as an angry stranger, now as the father whom she had idolized. It is all very pretty, all very sentimental, and all very thin.

Closely associated with Bernard is Charles Vildrac (Charles Messager), author of *Le Paquebot Tenacity* (*S.S. Tenacity*, 1919), *Madame Béliard* (1925), *Le pèlerin* (*The Pilgrim*, 1926), *La brouille* (*The Estrangement*, 1930), and *L'air du temps* (*The Atmosphere of the Times*, 1938). Intimate in portraiture, gentle in emotion, sad of mood, he has turned out some appealing plays, although not such as are likely to endure. *Le pèlerin* is a kind of tender *Three Sisters* in which the impact of the outside world impinges on a narrow provincial home: listening to her uncle's stories of life in Paris, an awakening dream and a wonder comes to birth in the heart of the little Denise. In *Le Paquebot Tenacity* two ex-soldiers, waiting for the ship that will carry them to Canada, are shown in love with a pretty waitress at a café: the more idealistic of the pair loses her, his bolder friend carries her off. Such simple situations appeal to Vildrac, and he makes them appealing to others by means of a skill in the revealing of secret sentiments and in the evoking of mood.

The psychology of love is the general theme also of nearly all the rather disappointing works of Paul Géraldy. In *Les noces d'argent* (*The Silver Wedding*, or *The Nest*, 1917) he returns to the problem which had so exercised the thought of some nineteenth-century authors and treats of the neglect of the middle-aged and the old by their children. *Aimer* (*To Love*, 1921) interestingly deals with the eternal triangle by concentrating the whole of the attention not on the woman and the lover, but upon the husband and wife. This concentration on a couple of persons appears again in *Robert et Marianne* (1925), where the contrast between sexual desire and love is handled with some real penetration. So he proceeds with similar themes in the bitter *Christine* (1932) and in the less gloomy *Do-mi-sol-do* (1934) and *Duo* (1938), without achieving more than the fashioning of sincere, yet uninvigorating, dramas of meagre worth.

Among all these authors one more stands out—Jean Sarment. There are others, such as Jean-Victor Pellerin, with his interesting study of a will-less character who cannot take his part in life in *Têtes de rechange* (*Spare Heads*, 1926), or Simon Gantillon, with his once much-discussed *Maya* (1924), in which a Marseilles prostitute becomes to diverse men what they desire her to be—but the one man who seems to have the qualities necessary for enduring worth is the creator of *Le pêcheur d'ombres* (*Fishing for Shadows*, 1921), an amazing study of insanity, in which a poet, whose memory has gone, can find peace for his spirit only by remaining, deliberately, within his world of shadows. The play recalls the psychological studies of Pirandello, but still more it savours of the spirit that produces the *proverbes dramatiques* of Musset. Pirandello's music may be 'cerebral' and sometimes hard to follow, but his notes are clear: Sarment plays continuously on muted strings. All his plays have similar qualities.

In his first piece, *La couronne de carton* (*The Pasteboard Crown*, 1920), the Pirandellesque quality is shown in the story of a woman who does not appreciate a man when he is himself; he can arouse her love only when he pretends to be what she thinks he ought to be; and, so far as he is concerned, the confusion of appearance and reality brings to his heart wisdom, perhaps, but also, and more powerfully, a great weariness of spirit. The connexion between Pirandello and Barrie has already been noted; Sarment too becomes Barrieesque in *Le mariage d'Hamlet* (*Hamlet's Marriage*, 1922), where Ophelia, her father, and the hero are given a second chance; Hamlet endeavours to accept his trials less passionately, but soon tires of his static rôle. The contrast between the ideal and reality gives the sadly resigned theme of *Je suis trop grand pour moi* (*I am Too Noble for Myself*, 1924), and variations on such contrasts furnish the mainsprings of *Les plus beaux yeux du monde* (*The Most Beautiful Eyes in the World*, 1925), *Madelon* (1925), *Léopold le Bien-Aimé* (*Leopold the Beloved*, 1927), *As-tu du cœur?* (*Have you No Feelings?*, 1926), *Le plancher des vaches* (*Terra Firma*, 1931), *Le voyage à Biarritz* (*The Trip to Biarritz*, 1936), *Mamouret* (1941), and many others. In all of these are men and women haunted by visions whose airy wraiths are dissipated by reality, shattered by the breaking of their ideals, yet finding the best part of themselves in the sorry remnants of what they had dreamed. There may be no great strength here, but there is undoubtedly magic of a kind.

The English dramatist who perhaps approaches more closely than any other to these French playwrights is Charles Morgan, and that perhaps is why his reputation both as dramatist and novelist was always greater in Paris than it was in London. *The Flashing Stream* (1938), *The River Line* (1952), and *The Burning Glass* (1954)—all are intent upon the exploration of human character set against dominant social, political, and philosophical problems of our age. Pregnant thought and subtle analysis of emotions give distinction to all of these.

The Play of Faith, Space, and Time

For some authors the search inward implies a hard, sometimes cruel, scientific dissection of the soul; for others it implies an exploration of that irrational quality of mankind to which we give the name of faith. This may take the form either of excursions into the field of the religious drama or else of experiments in the writing of plays which, outwardly realistic, focus attention on the spirit.

The former endeavour obviously carries us close to the mood of earlier romanticism, although the demands of the modern world call for scenes less flamboyant and decidedly less rhetorical. Thoroughly characteristic of this sphere of dramatic writing is Paul Claudel, whose *L'otage* (*The Hostage*, 1910) presents a heroine set in much the same situation as some heroines of Maeterlinck, faced with the dilemma of carrying out her duty or of forgetting duty in abandonment to love. Essentially Claudel was a poet who found himself most at home with figments of his own imagination. Early in his career he penned a strange drama, *La ville* (*The City*, 1893), which indicated the general trend of his art. In the midst of the abstractions with which he peoples this play we move darkling; any attempt to find rational explanations of the scenes presented results in a breaking of the charm; only through a frank devotion to the emotional can we hope to sense the author's purpose. Hardly less abstract are the figures introduced into his study of profane and spiritual love, *Partage de midi* (*The Midday Break*; printed 1906). It is true that in his later dramas the characters assume more of human semblance, but always in Claudel's work we sense the hovering of invisible presences, and, at the same time, we feel that within any single one of his works there is incorporated a wealth of imaginative experience which only vaguely is expressed in the plot before us. Maybe his early plays were too fragile to permit them to flourish freely within the walls of the theatre. Most appealing of all his works is unquestionably *L'annonce faite à Marie* (*The Tidings brought to Mary*, 1912), in which the author's simple faith makes memorable a play of quiet emotion. Through her unquestioning assurance in the all-loving God the leprous Violaine effects a miracle and brings back to life the dead child of her sister Mara. Claudel's later *Le soulier de satin* (*The Satin Slipper*; printed 1930, acted 1943) presents to the public a perplexing double action which, however, becomes irradiated by the peculiarly imaginative style and by the almost mystical philosophic light in which its scenes are presented. Religious faith and quiet reflection rule throughout nearly all his thirty-odd dramas.

For Henri Ghéon (Henri Vangeon) the medieval period, with its orthodox faith, proves happy hunting-ground: *Le mystère de l'invention de la Croix* (*The Mystery of the Finding of the Cross*, 1932), *Violante* (1933), and *L'histoire du jeune Bernard de Menthon* (1925) may be taken as typical of his work in general, although it should be noted that he was also gifted with a keen sense of the comic. For a Biblical drama, *Noé* (*Noah*, 1931), André Obey won considerable attention when it was toured through various countries during the thirties by the Compagnie des Quinze, an offshoot of Jacques Copeau's venture at the Vieux Colombier. Obey's other writings, however, carry us out of the religious field: *Le viol de Lucrèce* (*The Rape of Lucrèce*, 1931) is a stylized modernistic treatment of the story that Shakespeare immortalized; *Maria* (1946) is a kind of mixture of Thornton Wilder and Pirandello, the action taking place on a bare stage while a play is being rehearsed, and introducing the familiar contrast between the world of reality and the theatre's fictional realm; all of these exhibit his interest in dramatic experimentation. Clearly associated with Claudel and other playwrights of this group is another French author, Boussac de Saint Marc, with his peculiar *Le loup de Gubbio* (*The Wolf of Gubbio*, 1917), in which a wild outcast is cared for by a girl strong in her unquestioning faith, and *Moloch* (1928), a drama that seeks to delineate the all-devouring maw of the artistic impulse.

With these dramas may be associated *L'autre Messie* (*The Other Messiah*, 1923) of the Belgian Henri Soumagne, an author responsible also for a less successful, although still interesting, drama of the Resurrection, *Madame Marie* (1928).

In Germany the *Totentanz* (*Dance of Death*, 1921) of Leo Weismantel springs from the same impulse that led French experimenters to make use of medieval material. A similar trend appears in the work of the Austrian Max Mell, the titles of whose *Das Wiener Kripperl von 1919* (*The Viennese Manger of 1919*, 1921), *Das Schutzengelspiel* (*The Play of the Guardian Angel*, 1923) and *Das Nachfolge-Christi-Spiel* (*The Play of the Imitation of Christ*, 1927) sufficiently indicate their inspiration. The way in which this exploration of the supernatural meets with the widespread dramatic interest in the folk is made apparent in the writings of another Austrian author, Richard Billinger, in whose works the ideas of Christianity are mingled with the pagan memories jealously guarded by the peasants of the Tyrol. *Das Perchtenspiel* (*The Perchten Play*, 1928) thus bases its plot on the operation of the powers possessed by the 'Perchten' who haunt the mountainside; *Rauhnacht* (1931) celebrates that December eve when these and other supernatural creatures roam the land; and these preoccupations have continued to dominate in his mind even up to his *Bauernpassion* (*The Peasants' Passion Play*) which in 1960 provided a kind of comprehensive epitome of all his favourite themes.

The range of this religious drama is to be realized when we set these imitations of the medieval theatre and these explorations of folk myth alongside such Catholic essays as have been prolifically produced by the Spanish José María Pemán y Pemartín from *El divino impaciente* (*The Anxious Saint*, 1933) to *Callados como muertos* (*Silent as the Dead*, 1952)—which in turn lead us to a series of plays wherein the metaphysical is theatrically exploited in terms not specifically associated either with Christian dogma or pagan legend.

In England Sutton Vane created something of a stir with *Outward Bound* (1923), a skilful, and theatrically a most impressively effective, presentation of the world after death as a ship carrying souls from the country of the living to heaven's custom-house. Since then, both in England and in America, many experiments have been made in this sphere, and perhaps one of the most notable things about the modern stage has been the freedom with which it has seriously exploited the supernatural. Except for some melodramatic experiments made during the early nineteenth century, it might almost be said that the European and American drama remained entirely ghostless from just after the time of Shakespeare until our own period; we think nothing now of accepting a blithe spirit from the other world in a Noel Coward comedy or of welcoming the presence of the devil in a James Bridie fantasy. Thoroughly characteristic is *Father Malachy's Miracle* (1937) by the Canadian author Brian Doherty. With charming power, this author persuades us that little Father Malachy is truly gifted with the miracle-maker's gifts. Declaring that a night club of which he disapproves will be removed from the city of Edinburgh to the lonely Bass Rock, he finds, to his dismay, that his prophecy has been taken by the heavenly powers at face-value. For himself only trouble can come from this manifestation of supernatural power: the Church will certainly want to know all about it, and charlatans will plague him. In despair he racks his brains for a solution and finds it in uttering a second declaration to the effect that the night club will be removed back to Edinburgh again: it is, and the curtain descends on a Father Malachy mightily relieved in spirit.

The mood animating *Father Malachy's Miracle* is somewhat akin to that from which the plays of the Irish dramatist Paul Vincent Carroll draw their distinction, although in this author we sense the presence of a strange dichotomy. On the one hand, we feel that the impulse which has driven him to turn to the theatre is the desire to preach a message of liberal thought; on the other, his most memorable scenes are those wherein his message is forgotten and the light hovering of supernatural wings trembles above his human characters. This dichotomy is to be seen nowhere more clearly than in the play, *Shadow and Substance* (1934), which, after the relatively unsuccessful *Things that are Cæsar's* (1932), brought him to fame. In one sense *Shadow and Substance* may be regarded as a realistic problem drama in which the author contrasts the narrow, reactionary clericalism of Canon Skerritt and the broad-minded, forward-looking idealism of the liberal teacher O'Flingsley. What gives to the play its peculiar intensity, however, and raises it far beyond the reach of the ordinary play of ideas is the imaginative quality that surrounds the character of Brigid, an unlettered country girl on whom the hand of the eternal spirit has descended. Like Joan of Arc, Brigid sees visions beyond the limits of the phenomenal world, and in listening to her words we are rapt into the realm of faith.

Most unfortunately Carroll has not succeeded in rising again to the quality of this drama. *The White Steed* (1938) is disappointing, partly because it does not have the richness of texture that makes *Shadow and Substance* memorable, partly because its 'problem' theme is virtually the same as that of the earlier play, and partly because the sense of the miraculous is summoned forth with far less subtlety. Even weaker seems the confused and confusing *The Wise have not Spoken* (1944), a play in which incoherency beautifully reigns.

Closely associated with such plays are those in which exploration is made of space-time concepts or of subject-matter in which, without the direct or indirect interposition of divine powers, the normal sequence of events in real life is interrupted. A typical example may be found in the play *On Borrowed Time* (1938), wherein the American Paul Osborn tells a strange story of a man who succeeds in temporarily staying the power of death. The author, however, who has most consistently applied himself to this field is the English John Boynton Priestley. His earliest theatrical essays, such as *Dangerous Corner* (1932) and *Laburnum Grove* (1933), give no more than a hint of what he was to make his later speciality. These works indicated that he possessed (rather surprisingly, in view of the large canvas of his novels) the true dramatist's gift: *Laburnum Grove* is a skilfully constructed work in which the contrast between crime and quiet suburbia is excellently handled, and *Dangerous Corner*, with a greater anticipation of his later style, is inherently of the theatre. So, too, is his later *The Linden Tree* (1947), a study of ordinary life amid modern doubts and the clashing of values.

Priestley's 'speciality,' if so it may be called, appeared first full shaped in four dramas released in 1937 and 1938—*Time and the Conways, I Have Been Here Before, I'm a Stranger Here*, and *Music at Night*: in diverse ways the same 'time continuum' concept provides the mainspring for *They Came to a City* (1943), *Desert Highway* (1944), and *An Inspector Calls* (1946), although in another work, *Ever since Paradise* (1947), he has moved into a different kind of experimentation, bringing characters in and out of a play-within-the-play being enacted in their midst. Without doubt all of these possess individual and appealing qualities. In *Music at Night* the playing of a violin concerto releases a group of characters from their outer selves and permits the author to make stage presentation of the subconscious. The plot of *Time and the Conways* allows him to build his scenic picture of life independent of the commonly accepted sequence of minutes, days, and hours. In *Desert Highway* past and present meet on one plane; the action of the first part, involving the adventures of a tank crew stuck in the illimitable waste of sands, is related to action belonging to the eighth century before Christ. Fully into the realm of the imaginative he moves in *They Came to a City*, which shows a crowd of diversely assorted characters, each representative of a class within the community, coming to a great majestic walled town. They find that here civilization has reached perfection. Work is play here; there are no wars; bitterness of spirit is a thing unknown. As Priestley develops the action he seeks to show how the diverse persons from our imperfect social world react to the wonders of this world of wonders. For some it is bliss; for some it is hell. Still another experiment is tried in *An Inspector Calls*. Here a family circle is presented before us. From outside the walls of their home comes a piece of news, the death of a girl, which at first sight seems to have no more to do with them than a mere item of interest in a newspaper. When an Inspector calls, however, he gradually relates each member of this comfortable group to the girl's fate; inner secrets are dragged to light, concealed hopes and fears are laid bare on the dissecting table. Naturally there is consternation, but this is dismissed when it seems that the supposed Inspector was, in fact, a mere impersonator. Then suddenly the telephone rings: it is a call from the police station to say that an officer is on his way to interrogate the group concerning a girl's suicide.

Whether these experimental dramas will continue to 'live' in the theatre is at present uncertain: all that can be said is that the play recently selected by the National Theatre for production on the occasion of the author's birthday is *Eden End*, described by Priestley himself as "rather Chekhovian" and one for which he himself still has "a great affection". Presented originally in 1934, *Eden End* certainly has symbolic overtones, but it has no connection whatsoever with the 'time continuum' plays which were its companions in the thirties and forties.

A consideration of these dramas reminds us that similar topics were being dealt with during these years, and even earlier, on several European stages. In the year following the Armistice (1919) Henri Lenormand in France produced *Le temps est un songe* (*Time is a Dream*). This drama clearly anticipates Priestley's exploitation of the time-continuum concept when it shows the suicidal death of the hero revealed, some time before its actual occurrence, to the girl with whom he is in love. The English author's *An Inspector Calls* reminds us too that there are several present-day dramatists who, interested in personality, employ the device of inserting into a chosen *milieu* some person, such as Priestley's Inspector, who possesses a catalytic force almost supernatural in its capabilities. Very close to *An Inspector Calls*, for example, are several plays by the Italian Ugo Betti. Betti's form is, like Priestley's, outwardly realistic, yet his characters and plots are constantly invested with symbolic significance. Representative of his style are *Frana allo scalo Nord* (*Landslide at the North Slope*, 1935), *Notte in casa del ricco* (*Night in the Rich Man's House*, 1942), and *Ispezione* (*Inspection*, or *The Inspector Calls*, 1947). The first introduces an accident during civic excavations; even as each person involved endeavours to disclaim responsibility, the circle widens until the entirety of the city is involved, and until the secret souls of the individuals directly concerned are bared. Into the realistic setting something of the supramundane enters: the victims of the accident appear to rise again, and the advocate is transmogrified into the judge; for human errors only pity remains. As the play ends, Parsc, a counsellor, speaks in a thundering voice, giving judgment:

PARSC: Taking into consideration that they suffer, yet wish to suffer; they suffer when they own their land and when they work for others; when they are reputed good and when they are reputed evil, when they oppress and when they are oppressed, when they cheat and when they are cheated; they suffer, yet they wish to suffer because they breathe, because they are men, because they wish to live, weep, hope and advance their interests. . . .

GOETZ: For these reasons . . . [*All remain motionless, with heads bowed.*

PARSC [*stretches forth his hand, takes the documents, raises them*]: For these reasons. In the name of God; in the name of the law; we declare that these men . . .

GOETZ [*provokingly*]: Proceed, Parsc. Pronounce the sentence!

PARSC: We declare that these men have pronounced—that every day they pronounce—through their lives, through their labour, the just sentence; they themselves will find their own certitude. And maybe from the hands of justice they may have something else, something higher—pity. Pity.

ALL [*in a low tone*]: Pity . . . Pity . . .

About the whole of his action Betti throws this veil of uncertainty, doubt, condemnation, and compassion.

Notte in casa del ricco shows Betti developing the idea that all our present is bound up in the past. Tito expresses its philosophy. "Yes," he says,

> For example, I want to go there. [*Points in one direction.*] But I cannot. Because of an action that I committed long ago, here I am now; almost without realizing it, without having the freedom to go where I want to go, I find myself *there*.
> [*Points in another direction.*

Ispezione draws this author nearest to Priestley. Into a household come two inspectors; they rake up things hidden, and depart. "We are going," declares one of them at the end of the drama.

> THE INSPECTOR: We are going. We have nothing more to do here.
> ANDREA: You're going?
> THE INSPECTOR: Yes.
> ANDREA: You're leaving us in this way?
> THE INSPECTOR: What do you mean?
> ANDREA [*suddenly, with anger*]: And the dispositions? The directives? At least we can learn why you came here? You'll surely tell us something!
> THE INSPECTOR [*suddenly, with sombre vehemence*]: You yourself don't know what you want, and you have the impertinence to think you know what others want? Very convenient! These are your affairs: and you must puzzle them out alone: reach to an understanding of them all alone. Every one by himself alone. [*With a thunderous tone*] By himself alone! You can be assured that no one will help you!
> [*Goes to the door and disappears with his companion.*

If we have been led to a consideration of Betti's work through consideration of Priestley's plays, Betti in turn leads us to Jules Romains (Louis Farigoule). Like his Italian fellow-dramatist, Romains stylizes reality, and, like him, he sees the individual human being at once as a lonely entity and as a mere part of a larger whole. His philosophy is that of 'Unanimism'—the invisible society that exists among men united by a physical or a spiritual link. A family circle is an example of unanimism; so is a nation, a church, the community of a city—even the passengers in a bus, if something happens to make them conscious of their common interests, can become such a unit. In his plays Romains constantly provides, generally in mocking tones, examples of such unanimity. In *L'armée dans la ville* (*The Army in the Town*, 1911), a play dealing with the question of resistance to imposed authority, the occupying forces form one unit, the townspeople another. Characteristically, *Cromedeyre-le-vieil* (1920) is given a title from the name of the village in which the fantastic action takes place, and the better-known *Knock, ou le triomphe de médecine* (*Knock; or, The Triumph of Medicine*, or *Dr Knock*, 1923) gains all its comic power from exploitation of this concept. The little village of Saint-Maurice here is at once recognizable and a figment of the imagination:

Romains' hero, Dr Knock, who comes to take the place of the old-fashioned Dr Parpalaid, and who succeeds in persuading all the people in this community that they are ill, is both man and symbol. Human beings are thus given unanimity in that every healthy man becomes a potential patient.

The same spirit animates the two plays dealing with *Monsieur Le Trouhadec* (1923 and 1925); in the former we are presented with the 'unanimisme' of the Casino at Monte Carlo; in the latter the hero of the play ironically is shown founding and leading "The Honest Men's Party." Irony colours the whole of *Musse, ou l'école de l'hypocrisie* (*Musse; or, The School of Hypocrisy*, 1930), wherein the little man, Musse, in discovering that a great philanthropist is a completely selfish libertine, comes to the conclusion that the only way of living a quiet life is to be a hypocrite himself; more bitter is *Le dictateur* (*The Dictator*, 1926), which shows an erstwhile revolutionary accepting a king's commission to form a strong (and therefore dictatorial) government. These, unfortunately, are less powerful than the brilliant *Knock*; even the film-like satire *Donogoo-Tonka* (1930), telling how a number of crack-pots try to establish a town in America, although interesting, lacks the graceful verve of that comedy, while *Boën* (1931), displaying the effects of sudden wealth upon a relatively honest middle-class man, wants both vigour and clarity of orientation. In *L'an mil* (*The Year One Thousand*, 1947), one of his most powerful plays, he pursues his aims by taking us far back into the past and by relating that past to the present.

Plays of the Soul

Romains probably takes us rather far from the impressionism from which we started, but in the work of an American playwright, Philip Barry, we clearly find ourselves in close association with the most characteristically 'impressionistic' writers, and from a consideration of his writings we realize the ties that bind together those who are led into the dim regions of the psyche and those who are drawn within the equally dim regions of the symbolic. About Barry there is an aura that reminds us of his Scottish namesake Barrie; that aura, however, also reveals shades reminiscent of Maeterlinck, Pirandello, Bernard, and Sarment. Barry secures an individual note by taking symbolic forms and clothing them with delicate laughter. Often he is spoken of in terms that suggest that his chief interest lies in the development of a modern comedy of manners; in reality his spirit is close to those writers of the 'impressionistic' tradition with whom we have just been dealing. *Hotel Universe* (1930) is a strictly psychoanalytic and 'time-space' play which shows a group of tortured souls gathered together in a house inhabited by a (supposedly) great scientist whose views on the nature of man and of the universe have made him seem mad to his relatives. However, by his influence all the tormented characters, by having their thoughts turned to persons whom they had loved and forgotten, are brought back to mental health. There is no depth in this drama, and (despite the esteem in which it has been held) there is a vast amount of absurdity in its dialogue. No one can deny, perhaps, the simple-minded sincerity that gave it birth, but in the theatre neither simple-mindedness nor sincerity alone is likely to achieve anything of worth. The title of *Hotel Universe* itself well displays Barry's attraction towards the almost childishly 'symbolic,' and this tendency is further exemplified in the Globe Theatre wherein the persons of *Here Come the Clowns* (1938) indulge in their metaphysical meanderings. Some good theatricalism is present in its scenes, but we shall err sadly if we assume that its story of a scene-shifter seeking God and much impressed by the tricks of a charlatan who seems to be an embodiment of the Devil has any profundity of thought or intensity of emotion. On analysis the entire content of the drama is found to be mushy; there is no firm substance fit for dissection. Even a clearer example of the juvenile symbols so dear to Barry appears in *Liberty Jones* (1941), in which Uncle Sam and Liberty rather tediously give expression to the very best, and the most obvious, of sentiments.

Along with these plays Barry has penned many others, and in some at least he happily forgets the pseudo-mystical and engages in purely comic exercise. *The Animal Kingdom* (1932), with its triangle and its paradoxical treatment of the mistress who takes on the qualities of a wife, might have been written by one of Paris's lesser playwrights; *Paris Bound* (1927) unites a Catholic concept to a theme apt for comic treatment in emphasizing that a little defection on the part of a husband need not, and should not, ruin a marriage; *Holiday* (1928) is a rather thin study of love and life cast in sentimental terms, but made gracious by its delicate dialogue; in *Philadelphia Story* (1939), more successfully, he pens a comedy which perhaps may be regarded as the peak of his achievement as an artist.

In general, we may say that Barry is an author some of whose scenes are enjoyable, whose skill in writing we may admire, but whose spirit is apt uneasily to stray into realms he is utterly unqualified to understand or appreciate. Akin to him in some respects, yet outwardly far apart, is William Saroyan, whose continual reiteration of facile philosophic sentiments and apparently novel methods of play construction once persuaded many critics that in him great genius was to be found. It is observable, however, that after the excitement of *My Heart's in the Highlands* (1939) his enthusiastic supporters have tended to become ever less and less vociferous. This, his first play, characteristically mingles together an outwardly realistic scene with elements of the symbolic and with a method of episodical display of material which has the appearance of being new: colloquial dialogue, suggesting naturalistic effect, is set close against flights in a poetic vein. But on reflection we can find but little in these sentimental pictures of poverty-stricken young poets and of broken-down actors who play on trumpets with such Orphean charm that all the neighbourhood comes rapt to listen. This drama was followed by the more ambitious *The Time of Your Life* (1939), where again the scene, a wretched San Francisco saloon, gives the semblance of reality. Following the line of Chekhov, Saroyan here dispenses with plot and causes his characters to philosophize mightily and mistily about life, its wonders and its despairs, its sorrows and its joys. In the centre of the motley group of characters drifts a person named Joe, eternally drunk and eternally buying toys: we learn that this is so since he remembers that as a child he once stopped crying because a toy was given to him. In addition the spectators are provided with a diversity of other strange oddities, for Saroyan also brings in a number of broken-down 'bums,' a prostitute, and a midget barely three feet in height. In *The Beautiful People* (1941) once more a philosopher and a poet are introduced (this time father and son), with a plot which tells of a family living on pension cheques due to the defunct owner of the house in which they dwell. During the next season (1942) a Saroyan Theatre, presenting *Across the Board on To-morrow Morning* and *Talking to You*, was opened in New York, and closed rapidly. His later play, *Jim Dandy* (1947), has as its setting

> all or part of a transparent egg shell which is broken and open along one side. Inside the shell are miserable and majestic ruins. These ruins represent immemorial and immediate reality, as thrown together by time, nature, art, religion, labour, science, invention, plan, accident, violence of war, and wear and tear of weather.

This is all very mysterious, but at least it may be said that these plays have more substance than the shadow that was Gertrude Stein's *Four Saints in Three Acts* (1934)—a musical play that uses four acts to present fifteen saints uttering sentiments wholly incomprehensible.

In diverse ways and in several lands these styles have been cultivated. The plays of Miguel de Unamuno, known as one of the foremost of Spanish philosophers, delve far within the recesses of the soul. Of external action in *Fedra* (1918)—a modern-dress and modern-spirit reworking of the perennially interesting Greek myth—there is virtually nothing, and the very title of *Sombras de sueño* (*Dream Shadows*, 1930) indicates its quality: this is a kind of mystical essay in Pirandello's favourite theme of double personality.

In Italy itself Pirandello's mantle has been given a fresh satirical twist in the writings of Massimo Bontempelli, whose *Nostra Dea* (*Our Dea*, 1925) is an outwardly farcical, inwardly bitter, revelation of a woman who, naked, is nothing, but who assumes diverse personalities in accordance with the dresses she chooses to wear. A kindred mood animates *Il calzolaio di Messina* (*The Shoemaker of Messina*, 1925), by Alessandro di Stefani: here the central figure is a man who, obsessed with the concept of justice and angered because he sees so many criminals escape the law, himself assumes the rôle of judge and executioner. In one instance, however, he finds he has made a mistake, killing an innocent victim, and as a result, his ideal broken, he takes his own life. The same author's *Pazzi sulla montagna* (*Madmen on the Mountains*, 1926) seeks to demonstrate that only the fools among men are wise. Another Pirandellesque author is Guglielmo Zorzi: his *La vita degli altri* (*The Life of Others*, 1926) is a study of a woman who wears like a cloak the personality of her husband, and *La vena d'oro* (*The Vein of Gold*, 1919) contrasts a young mother as she really is with what her son deems her to be. In *Il fiore sotto gli occhi* (*Circles under the Eyes*, 1921), by Fausto Maria Martini, a strange story is told of a poor school-teacher and his wife who, terrified of the monotony of their lives, start deliberately to live the fiction that they are passionate lovers; similarly, in *L'altra Nanetta* (*The Other Nanette*, 1923) the contrast is presented of a woman as she is and as she pretends herself to be. These themes are obviously Pirandellian in character, although Martini succeeds in giving them his own individual flavour by the subtlety of his character delineation and by his technique of understatement.

The Pirandellian style is obvious also in Denmark's *Circus juris* (1935), by Svend Borberg, an interesting drama dealing with the several 'individualities' within a single individual. Among other contributions in this kind may be noted those of two Polish authoresses, Marja Pawłikowska-Jasnorzewska and Zofja Nałkowska, both of whom, profiting from the earlier example of Przybyszewski, followed a line parallel with that taken by Lenormand, Bernard, and others. The former's *Niebiescy zalotnicy* (*Heavenly Lovers*, 1933) and the latter's *Dzień jego powrotu* (*The Day of His Return*, 1931) are by no means unworthy examples of psychological 'impressionism.'

3

THE EXPRESSIONISTIC MOVEMENT

IMPRESSIONISM is characteristically French: expressionism is characteristically Germanic. Impressionism is a term that applies to a mood, or to an æsthetic endeavour merely: there is no particular dramatic form or technique (if we except the theories concerning 'static drama' and the 'drama of silences') associated with its aims. Expressionism, on the other hand, implies both a definite manner of approach towards theatrical material and a fresh means of treating this material.

Such distinctions between the two movements would suggest that expressionism might be explained and defined in simpler and clearer terms than is possible where we are concerned with the diverse schools of dramatic inwardness, yet, strangely, the precise opposite is true. Developed in Berlin between 1910 and 1920, the expressionistic style has embraced within itself the most varied talents, and, by concentrating on one or another of these talents, the several critics who have applied themselves to analysing the general qualities of the style as a whole find themselves seriously at odds both with regard to their diagnosis of the movement's origins and with regard to its particular manifestations.

For the most part the divergences in opinion are due to two causes: first, a confusion between the means and the aims; and, second, a failure to see that the expressionist movement, fundamentally anti-realistic in its objectives, gathered to itself a considerable number of adherents whose ideals were far other than those of the men who stood at the core of the school. Thus, for example, it is easy to see that some of the *methods* used by Strindberg and Wedekind anticipate the methods which the expressionists eagerly adopted as their own, but any attempt to prove that the aims of these two earlier authors were 'expressionistic' is false and confusing. In searching for a true definition of what these German revolutionaries sought when they established Expressionismus as an artistic objective we must, therefore, endeavour at once to separate in our minds the technical devices they employed and the ideals for which these devices were but the means, and to track down the core of the true expressionistic spirit amid the confusion of contradictory aims apparent in the works of those who attached themselves directly or indirectly to the school.

The Aims of the Expressionists

In general the expressionist dramatists seized upon and developed further the kind of dramatic technique in which diverse experiments had already been made by Hauptmann, Wedekind, and Strindberg. Short scenes took the place of longer acts; dialogue was made abrupt and given a staccato effect; symbolic (almost morality-type) forms were substituted for 'real' characters; realistic scenery was abandoned, and in its place the use of light was freely substituted; frequently choral, or mass, effects were preferred to the employment of single figures, or else single figures were elevated into positions where they became representative of forces larger than themselves.

These means, being new, exercised a peculiar fascination on many minds during the twenties, and often we find them employed for purposes far removed from those which explicitly were announced as the aims of expressionism. In particular they were seized upon eagerly and exploited by some writers who, excited by the new psychoanalytic researches, sought to develop a 'subjective' theatre. What we have to recognize—if the picture is to be kept clear—is that, so far from aiming at the subjective, the true expressionists are in conscious revolt against the whole impressionistic theatre of inwardness. Instead of searching into the reaches of the individual soul, they seek to put upon the stage representations of man in the mass: if they are influenced by psychoanalysis it is the crowd emotions they desire to display. Indeed, we might almost say that, while the impressionists are the last descendants of the romantic poets, the expressionists belong to a modern classicism.

Fundamentally, what these men sought to do was to escape from the detailed exploration of the psyche and from the rounded, indirect methods implied in the entirety of neo-romantic endeavour, and to substitute therefor the typical representation of humanity along with a sharp, economic, straight-line effect. In method the expressionists are closely associated with the school of cubism, which, born at Paris in 1908, endeavoured to get beneath the curves of reality to express basic flat planes, and with Italian futurism, which, established by F. T. Marinetti in 1909, similarly aimed at the exploitation of the straight line and the 'synthetic.' In 1915 the first of futurism's theatre manifestoes stressed these qualities: it was specifically called a "Manifesto del teatro futuristo sintetico." Out of the futurist movement developed two cardinal concepts: the idea or sense of space based on appreciation of flat planes, and the idea or sense of function, wherein all romantic ornament was stripped away until only the absolutely essential (the typical) remained. The connexion between these various movements has been well summarized by Anton G. Bragaglia in *La maschera mobile* (1926). Trenchantly he stresses there the relationship between the German revolutionaries and those men—Marinetti, Boccioni, Carrà, Soffici, Depero—who headed the Italian futurist school. In both, he notes, is apparent an antagonism to 'verismo' (realism or naturalism); in both an attempt at the synthetic is the dominant aim. "By the word synthetic," he adds, "is not meant the gallery scene of one colour to which this word is often applied, but those scenes which, by an admixture of design and colour, provide a disciplined and stylized representation of reality, recorded, not re-copied —what Boccioni called the ideal abstraction of typical forms." With minor changes that sentence might have been applied to the aims of classical art two hundred years before.

The development of the new style is intimately bound up with a realization of the mechanistic nature of our civilization. For the neoromanticist there is always the desire to escape from the machine —escape into a world inhabited by Pelléas and Mélisande, escape into the realm of vague emotional symbols, escape into the misty reaches of the human soul. In effect, the mechanistic is here deliberately avoided and, if possible, forgotten. The true expressionist takes a different line. Whether he shares Marinetti's enthusiasm for the machine or whether he stands aghast at the way in which the machine is gradually imposing itself on the living organism, he accepts its existence and endeavours to deal boldly with the problems it raises. The expressionist often is a tortured, sometimes a desperate, soul, but he does not wish to abnegate the world he lives in, and thus, so far from exploiting the dream realm in Strindbergian style (as some critics of expressionism have averred), he takes a firm stand in a position diametrically opposed to that of the subjective impressionist.

German Expressionismus

In the theatre the expressionistic style is clearly exemplified in the work of Georg Kaiser, and particularly in his *Gas* (two parts, 1918 and 1920), a drama which provides a kind of vast morality showing the effect of industrialism on society. The very title of the play indicates its purpose and demonstrates that the author's object, instead of being directed towards the exhibition of individual characters, is to portray the larger elements of collective man. After a kind of prelude in *Die Koralle* (*The Coral*, 1917), in which a former labourer is shown building up a vast factory, the two sections of *Gas* trace the fate of the industry in the hands of this man's son and grandson: both try to help the workers, both are thwarted, until in the end only annihilation of the human race seems left as a solution for a problem thus symbolically presented in a concrete instance.

Kaiser is not a great dramatist, but he is one characteristic of his time, and although he makes free use of effects which would have been styled melodramatic had they appeared in plays of earlier vintage, there does exist in him a kind of tormented daimonic force. Starting with a relatively unimportant satiric *Die jüdische Witwe* (*The Jewish Widow*) in 1911, he produced a not ineffective *Die Bürger von Calais* (*The Citizens of Calais*) three years later, and then, in 1916, startled his contemporaries by the boldness of his *Von Morgens bis Mitternachts* (*From Morn to Midnight*). In this last work he takes as central figure a petty bank-clerk, but in true expressionistic manner makes this character a symbol of a large class rather than an individual. Stealing some of his employers' money, the clerk is shown, in violently anti-realistic scenes, passing through a series of adventures in which his dreams of a fine and exciting life gradually crumble or are rudely shattered. All the persons he meets are symbols or type-representations of human groups: to condemn the author for failing to draw interesting individual characters here is absurd, since his central aim is to avoid that method of dramatic composition and to achieve, by other means, a larger concept than could otherwise be attained. We may legitimately condemn the object: we have no right to seek in such a work something which the playwright specifically sought to exclude.

Beyond these plays Kaiser has little to offer to us. His *Der Brand im Opernhaus* (*The Fire in the Opera House*, 1918) is unimportant; no vigour appears in *Kolportage* (*Hawking*, 1924) or *Zweimal Oliver* (*Twice Oliver*, 1926); a faint sign only of the quality animating *Von Morgens bis Mitternachts* appears in *Gats* (1925). Among his various posthumous works acted in recent years, perhaps only *Das Floss der Medusa* (*The Medusa's Lifeboat*, 1945) calls for attention, and that rather on account of its form than because of its excellence in style. This play is almost unique in that it is written for a company of thirteen children—their adventures in shipwreck being used to suggest the evils in the world surrounding us. Interesting though *Das Floss der Medusa* is, however, it is by no means a masterpiece. The truth is, of course, that Kaiser was one of those dramatists who, having said one thing, have nothing more to say.

Closely associated with his writing is the work of Ernst Toller, whose first play, *Die Wandlung* (*The Transformation*), a study of the growth of revolutionary sentiment in an artist's being, appeared in 1919. This made no particular stir, but excited enthusiasm greeted *Masse-Mensch* (*Man and the Masses*) two years later. Here, again, the typical takes the place of the particular. "These pictures of 'reality' are not realism," writes Toller, "are not local colour; the protagonists are not individual characters." Sonia, the chief person in the drama, is a representative of all idealistic revolutionaries, a woman who leads the crowd of slave-workers to throw off their chains, who tries in vain to curb them when they institute a social rebellion, and who in the end is executed for a movement she had done her best to check. The language used is violently staccato; all shadings are abandoned; the characters appear violently illuminated against a Cimmerian background; exhortation and exclamation are substituted for ordinary conversation; scenes of fantasy are intermingled with scenes of stylized 'reality.' Over the entire action breathes an atmosphere of hysteria. Characteristic is the end of the third 'picture,' in which the heroine speaks to The Nameless One, who is the spirit of the mob, and the beginning of the fourth 'picture,' a dream fantasy:

> *THE NAMELESS ONE:* Keep silent, comrade!
>   The cause demands it.
>   What does one person matter?
>   His feelings? or his conscience?
>   Only the Mass must count!
>   Just think of it: a single bloody battle
>   And then, eternal peace.
>   No empty peace, a mask of mockery,
>   Hiding the face of war,
>   War of the strong against the weak,
>   War of exploiters, war of greed.
>   Think of it: the end of misery!
>   Think of it: crime a half-remembered fable!
>   It is the dawn of freedom for all people! . . .
>   You think I reckon lightly?
>   It is no longer a matter of choice.
>   War's a necessity for us.
>   Your advice means discord.
>   For the sake of the cause,
>   Keep silent.
> *THE WOMAN:* You . . . are . . . Mass.
>   You . . . are . . . right.
> *THE NAMELESS ONE:* Beat in the pillars of the bridge, O comrades!
>   Drive over every one who stands in our way,
>   Mass is action!
> *CROWD IN THE HALL* [*as they storm out*]: Action!   [*The stage darkens.*

FOURTH PICTURE
(*Dream-picture*)

A court with a high wall is suggested. On the ground in the middle of the court, a lantern which gives a miserable light. WORKER GUARDS suddenly emerge from the corners of the court.

> *FIRST GUARD* [*sings*]: My mother
>   Bore me
>   In the mud of a trench.
>   Lalala, la,
>   H'm, H'm.
> *SECOND GUARD:* My father
>   Lost me
>   In a brawl with a wench.
> *ALL THE GUARDS:* Lalala, la,
>   H'm, H'm.

After some more singing The Nameless One confronts a Prisoner:

> *THE NAMELESS ONE:* Condemned
>   By the tribunal?
> *A GUARD:* He brought death

Upon himself.
He shot at us.
THE PRISONER: Death?
THE NAMELESS ONE: It frightens you?
Listen:
Guard! Answer me.
Who taught us
Capital punishment?
Who gave us weapons?
Who said "Hero" and "noble deed"?
Who glorified violence?
THE GUARDS: Schools.
Barracks.
War.
Always.

In such wise is the basic theme revealed in jerky progress of dialogue and scene, the angularity of the whole assuming features that are precisely parallel to those aimed at in contemporary cubist and futurist painting.

The year following the appearance of *Masse-Mensch* came *Die Maschinenstürmer* (*The Machine-wreckers*, 1922), wherein Toller turns to write of the Luddite riots of 1812–15 in terms outwardly more realistic, but basically wrought out of the same artistic desire. In *Der deutsche Hinkemann* (*The German Hinkemann*, 1923) the story is bitterly told of an ex-soldier (again a type-figure, not an individual) who returns home sexually incapable and finds his wife accepting the caresses of another man. Toller's anti-realistic tendencies well up once more in the strange, and not very successful, *Die Rache des verhöhnten Liebhabers, oder Frauenlist und Männerlist: ein galantes Puppenspiel* (*The Revenge of the Rejected Lover; or, Male and Female Craftiness: A Puppet-show of Gallantry*, 1925), as well as in *Hoppla, wir leben* (*Hurrah! We Live!*, 1927), a disillusioned picture of post-war existence.

This last play, which shows a revolutionary returning from a spell in an asylum only to find his comrades turned sadly respectable, is interesting because of the introduction into it of a device which came to be rather freely employed in the expressionistic theatre—whereby dramatic scenes were accompanied by the sporadic display of cinematographic films. The object of this device is amply patent, and, although it must be confessed that hitherto no satisfactory fusion of the two forms has been achieved, we can easily see how tempting must have seemed the use of the film among those authors who aimed at the creation of this vast theatre of humanity.

These early German expressionists were clearly animated by several quite distinct concepts, both political and stylistic —disillusionment, a general opposition to the standards and beliefs of bourgeois society, a trend (sometimes tentative, sometimes bold) towards Marxism, a clash between artistic aims and a desire to use drama for propagandist purposes, and an interest in a new kind of staging which should be 'total' in its use of almost every conceivable theatrical device, no matter how bizarre. Among those who later became most influential within this sphere were two men who for a time worked in close collaboration—Erwin Piscator and the redoubtable Bertolt Brecht—and it is interesting to observe how both of them combined creative endeavour with critical, theoretical disquisitions on the stage.

In considering Brecht's writings it is important to remember, not only that his true power was not recognized until after 1945 but also that it seems most doubtful whether his earlier plays, if they had comprised the whole of his dramatic compositions, would even now be regarded with such high esteem if it had not been for the works which he produced during the later forties, for his active association with the Berliner Ensemble after 1949, and (perhaps particularly important) for his flow of critical studies. Nowadays every smallest aspect of his career and every word he has penned are being examined minutely; but, if we wish to be honest with ourselves, we must confess that the only truly effective drama written by him and produced before 1939 is *Die Dreigroschenoper* (*The Threepenny Opera*, 1928)—and even this piece is, as everyone knows, an adaptation of Gay's original *Beggar's Opera. Aufstieg und Fall der Stadt Mahagonny* (*Rise and Fall of the City of Mahagonny*, 1929) seems more interesting as a piece of political propaganda than as a play; even the best of his other pre-war plays, *Trommeln in der Nacht* (*Drums in the Night*, 1922), while no doubt it deserved the Kleist Prize awarded to it in 1922, appears to be rather dated; although some of his other works have received great praise in recent times, there is becoming apparent a trend of thought which would select *Mutter Courage und ihre Kinder* (*Mother Courage and Her Children*, acted Zürich 1941, published 1949) as the first drama fully to show the strength of his genius.

Reinhard Sorge's *Der Bettler* (*The Beggar*), an hysterical portrait of a poet to whom men will not listen, appeared in 1912, followed by diverse other similar dramas, ending with *König David* (*King David*) in 1916. Violent effects and equally violent emotions were infused into *Vatermord* (*Parricide*, 1922), by the Austrian Arnolt Bronnen, a man who continued to vex the theatre with pretentious sensationalism in such plays as *Rheinische Rebellen* (*Rebels in the Rhineland*, 1925) and *Reparationen* (*Reparations*, 1926). *Mörder, Hoffnung der Frauen* (*Murderer, Hope of Women*, 1907) and *Orpheus und Eurydike* (1918), by Oskar Kokoschka, indicate how closely associated is the expressionist movement with the effort to explore what might be called the hidden wells of humanity. Something of the same quality, although with a more assured lyrical tone, appears in *Himmel und Hölle* (*Heaven and Hell*, 1919), by Paul Kornfeld, and in *Liebe* (*Love*, 1916), by Anton Wildgans. Wildgans perhaps deserves a trifle more attention than some of his fellows because of the imaginative atmosphere he can at times evoke: he has, too, an innate sympathy with individual human beings of a kind often lacking amid the vaster concepts of the expressionists. *Armut* (*Poverty*, 1914), for example, despite its sentimentalism and rhetorical excesses, does succeed in making us believe in its wretched hero, Spuller. In *Die Seeschlacht* (*The Sea-battle*, 1918) Reinhard Göring cleverly causes reality to subserve expressionistic aims by making his sailor characters appear in monstrous-seeming 'mechanistic' gas-masks. In many of these dramas, which remind us of nothing so much as the absurd early efforts of the 'Sturm und Drang' period, the expressionistic devices were used most commonly for non-expressionistic ends; here psychoanalysis was rampant and complexes had the time of their lives.

The motley crew exploiting the new style was numerous. The most talented of its members later sloughed off the blatant wrappings of the expressionist style, but few who had been caught up in its delirious ecstasy succeeded in returning to sanity. One or two, such as the Austrian Franz Csokor, author of *Die rote Strasse* (*The Red Road*, 1918) and the German sculptor-playwright Ernst Barlach, were tormented by religious questings and doubts—the latter's first drama, indeed, *Der tote Tag* (*The Dead Day*, written in 1910, produced in 1919) introduces the spectators to an enormous darkened space in which a son, tormented by symbolic spirits, seeks despairingly for his deceased father, and in the end discovers that in reality he had been engaged in a search for God. Not surprisingly, the mood and style of that early play soon led to the sprawling *Die echten Sedemunds* (*The Genuine Sedemunds*, 1921) which also starts with a young man, but which places him, as it were, in an inverse position: it is his mother, not his father, who is dead. Here, instead of the dimly lit space, we are confronted by a church and a churchyard, placed close to a public house and a circus-ground. In the circus the hero encounters a former friend, Grude, who has just been released from an asylum and who is incidentally responsible for causing the youth voluntarily to enter a madhouse himself. The grotesque and the obscure are here mixed up with vague religiosity, and also with a mood (not unknown to psychologists) which induces some folk to think that everyone they meet is insane.

Usually, however, politics, not religious questings, form the core of these expressionistic scenes: and it need hardly be said that, while the majority of young rebels pursued the course taken by Friedrich Wolf, whose communistic *Matrosen von Cattaro* (*The Sailors of Cattaro*), once was greeted with applause by the enthusiasts, the mood of rebellion could easily lead others, such as Hanns Johst, to embrace and to laud the Nazi philosophy.

To determine which of these plays have real value is an almost impossible task. We feel something of quality in the dramas of the poet Fritz von Unruh, notably *Ein Geschlecht* (*One Race*, 1918), yet reperusal of this piece, set in a churchyard where a mother is burying the son she regrets having brought into the world, is apt to induce smiles rather than sympathy because of its exaggerated style. Follies in abundance, alongside

some impressive scenes, are to be found in the works of Walter Hasenclever. *Der Sohn* (*The Son*, 1914) virtually upholds a youth's right to destroy his father, simply because he believes that the free expression of his
individuality is being curbed: in *Die Menschen* (*Humanity*, 1918) the
macabre note appears in the introduction of a corpse as a central character: in *Jenseits* (*Beyond*, 1920) the ghost of a dead husband takes centre
stage. On the other hand, despite the follies, there is a vigour in
Hasenclever's writing denied to many of his companions—and we must
duly take note of the fact that later he cast off the absurdities of the expressionistic style and turned to comedy. What troubles us here is that,
although his stylistic gifts are manifest, we can never be sure of his sincerity of purpose while he is weltering in the dark joys of the psychoanalytic, or, at the next moment, moving gloomily among the spectres of
the later romantic imagination, or else exploiting the extremes of the expressionistic method, or, in the end, laughing cynically. Our doubts, or
at least questionings, in attempting to determine his worth may, perhaps, be intensified when we compare his plays with a later expressionistic drama, *Wunder um Verdun* (*Miracle at Verdun*, 1930) by Hans
Chlumberg, which deservedly gained an international reputation because of its sincerity, directness of purpose and trenchant style.

A consideration of all these plays demonstrates two things: first, that
the expressionistic technique, appealing because of its novelty, could be
applied for a diversity of ends, and, second, that the expressionistic objective, while no doubt helping to extend the narrowing confines of the
drama, was apt in its purer form to lead towards just such absurdities as
characterized the excesses of the early romantic poets. In some of the
devices used by the expressionists still resides an element of potential
strength, but that strength will probably be found rather in an indirect
acceptance of the expressionist objective than in its bolder and unchas-
tened exploitation.

The Spread of Expressionism

In France the expressionistic movement found little support, but in
Eastern Europe it served to stimulate the genius of Karel Čapek, whose
R.U.R. (1921), written in a modified form of the technique of expressionism, well reveals the central objectives of that movement in its
imaginative picture of a world mechanized. *R.U.R.* is Rossum's Universal Robots, an industrial organization that mass-produces mechanical
figures capable of acting as slaves of men. Gradually something begins to
stir in the chill beings of these automata: they rise in rebellion against
man: apparently the world is doomed to an existence completely controlled by the mechanical when, at the very end, the playwright shows
the first glimmerings of love stirring the mechanized hearts of two of
these monsters and, with the arising of love, the growth of alien sentiments of self-sacrifice and loyalty. Out of the mechanistic, life is being

reborn. Although expressionistic in origin and choice of theme, *R.U.R.* possibly owes its success largely to the fact that here Čapek has succeeded in moulding well-established melodramatic practice to the needs of his own generation and school.

That Čapek too was gifted with a vision which sets him apart from most of the rather callow Germanic philosopher-dramatists from Kaiser onwards is shown clearly in *Věc Makropulos* (*The Macropulos Secret*, 1922). Such a work as *Ze života hmyzu* (*The Insect Comedy*, or *The Life of the Insects*, 1920) may seem on reflection somewhat obvious in its symbolism and shallow in its thought, but the man who could argue that the lengthening of life would be a curse, and not, as Shaw thought, a blessing, was certainly gifted with an independent mind. In collaboration with his brother Josef he penned a possibly over-ambitious philosophical drama entitled *Adam stvořitel* (*Adam the Creator*, 1927), wherein Adam, having blown the world to dust in a fit of horror at its errors, is bidden, ironically, by God to refashion it anew. Despite his efforts and enthusiasm, the new earth is found to be precisely similar to the old. This is by no means a great work, and the truth seems to be that Čapek's genius exhausted itself in *R.U.R.*, with only just sufficient left to give some colouring to a couple of other plays. By himself Josef Čapek penned his *Země mnoha jmen* (*Land of Many Names*, 1923), but this satirical essay presenting the discovery of a new continent and showing what it means to various persons (romance, economic freedom, opportunity for financial exploitation) barely reaches above the ordinary.

Amid plays of other styles, in which the lyrical sharply confronts the naturalistic, a Polish dramatist, Karol Rostworowski, has presented one drama of the expressionistic kind, *Miłosierdzie* (*Charity*, 1920), wherein the problem of the poor in modern society is dealt with in symbolic style. In Sweden Pär Lagerkvist, a disciple of Strindberg, has turned out his expressionistically inclined *Sista människan* (*The Last Man*, 1917), and *Himlens hemlighet* (*The Secret of Heaven*; printed 1919; 1921); but this style he has tended to modify in his effective later writings—particularly *Bödeln* (*The Hangman*, 1934) and *Låt människan leva* (*Let Man Live*, 1949).

In the English-speaking theatre several of these Continental plays have been given notable productions, and the expressionistic style has been attempted by a considerable number of dramatists—although it is observable that in England itself only one author, C. K. Munro (Charles Kirkpatrick MacMullan), and then only in a single work, succeeded in producing an expressionistic play of any worth. *The Rumour* appeared in 1922 and attracted some attention, partly because it introduced the new technique to London, and partly because its author had discovered an interestingly novel idea—the tracing, through a series of short scenes, of a rumour, idle and relatively innocent, which eventually leads two countries into war. When he tried to capitalize on his first success, however, Munro found that his *Progress* (1924) sadly failed to recapture the first enthusiasm out of which *The Rumour* was born.

More emphatically, expressionism made appeal among the young theatrical (and social) revolutionaries of America. From the time when John Howard Lawson presented his *Processional* (1925) sporadic utilization of the German methods have appeared on the American stage, the more particularly on those boards dedicated to the inculcation of radical ideas. *Processional* is an unquestionably effective drama, in which, ironically set against a background of jazz, Lawson deals with a bitter and bloody strife between a group of miners and the police-supported owners. Central in the picture are the symbolic figures of Sadie Cohen and her seducer, Dynamite Jim, with the child to be born of them, the future leader of the workers. Although the social philosophy is crude and several scenes somewhat absurd, *Processional* has a sincere, burning power in it that holds our attention. Less effective, yet still noteworthy, is the *Machinal* (1928) of Sophie Treadwell, a thoroughly characteristic work, in which the heroine, called simply The Young Woman, vainly seeks for romance in a world of machines and commerce.

With much greater result, the expressionistic form seized on the ever-questing imagination of Elmer Rice, one of that powerful group of young playwrights who so ably provided a rich background for Eugene O'Neill in and around the years of the First World War. From the very beginning of his career Rice exhibited an eagerness for any new devices likely to make his themes more effective, and from the beginning, too, he showed a strong, constant sympathy with the oppressed. In his first play, *On Trial* (1914), he indicated without doubt what were his aims when he dealt boldly with a social problem and gave novelty to his treatment of it by introducing a trick—the 'flash-back'—borrowed from the cinema. It was no wonder, therefore, that when knowledge of the expressionistic style came to America he should seize upon it with avidity. In *The Adding Machine* (1923) we are given a vigorous and effective theatrical study akin in spirit to the writings of Toller and Kaiser. The hero is an elderly clerk, Mr Zero, who, when dismissed from his post because mechanical adding machines can do his work more accurately and more economically, goes mad and murders his employer. For this crime he is executed, and his spirit wanders through eternity until, reaching heaven, he is set to work on a monstrous adding machine. This was undoubtedly Rice's most powerful essay in this particular kind of dramatic technique, but the expressionistic method, although not in such extreme terms, has ever laid its spell upon him. Something of the method he had learned in *The Adding Machine* is utilized in his *Judgment Day* (1934), based on the Reichstag Fire trial; signs of its operation are evident in *A New Life* (1943), an allegory of a child surrounded by good (the friends of its mother, honest, hardworking folk) and evil (its father's relatives, idle, rich, and reactionary), as well as in *Dream Girl* (1945), wherein the expressionistic technique is used, as so often it had been used before, for the purpose of exploiting psychoanalytical scenes. All of these dramas have quality, although all are rendered less interesting because of Rice's tendency to see everything in terms of white and black: his anger at social evils inclines him both to lose objectivity of approach and to obscure a sense of colour values.

The expressionistic aims and methods are to be found in many quarters. They have influenced considerably the writings of several poets, in particular Archibald MacLeish and W. H. Auden; they are plainly evident in such a work as *Johnny Johnson* (1936), Paul Green's plea for pacifism; and they have played their part in forming the styles of other authors, such as Thornton Wilder, whom we should not normally think of as belonging to this school. Thornton Wilder, indeed, may well provide for us an example of the spirit out of which expressionism grew: although he himself is not swayed towards embracing the more bizarre among the technical devices cultivated by the followers of Kaiser, his whole creative work is animated by a desire to escape from the trammels of particularized realism, and a consideration of the ways in which he has sought to effect this escape helps to explain the aberrations of the extreme revolutionaries. Gifted with a fine sense of style and a wisely humanitarian outlook upon life, his theatrical writings show that consistently he has endeavoured to find means whereby the modern stage can be released from the narrowness of the ordinary domestic scene and at the same time can be revitalized by the introduction of appropriate conventionalism. For that reason various manifestations of dramatic form have particularly appealed to him—the Elizabethan, the Oriental, and the expressionistic. On the other hand, he does not wish to set any one of these in imitative fashion on the modern boards: rather does he try to employ their principles in an individual manner. *Our Town* (1938) is not, as some critics were inclined to think, a play written in a manner designed merely to excite by reason of its novelty. When Wilder takes a story of characters belonging to a small New England town and sets it forth without the slightest vestige of scenery he is not playing any tricks; nor is he playing tricks when he causes these characters to be introduced by a stage-manager, who, standing at the very edge of the proscenium, addresses the audience directly. These things are introduced because what Wilder wishes to do is to present not merely a particular story of Grover's Corners, New Hampshire, but a typical picture of New England life, because he desires his public, not to sit back and objectively observe the action, but to be drawn over the footlights among the actors. In effect, Wilder is aiming at imaginative participation. Still further, although he is animated by no doctrinaire social theories, he seeks to deal both with the general social life of man and with the deepest, most universal things in man's existence—love and birth and death.

We may be far off here from the staccato rhythms of *Masse-Mensch*, of *Gas*, of *The Adding Machine*, but there is still something in common between the spirit of these plays and Wilder's work; and the connexion becomes clearer still in that strange, exciting, yet by no means wholly satisfying later play, *The Skin of Our Teeth* (1942), which, by its story of

Mr and Mrs Antrobus and Sabina, the maid, seeks to put the entire history of mankind into a single dramatic framework. Without a doubt *The Skin of Our Teeth* could not have been written had Toller and Kaiser not shown the way.

Sean O'Casey

Much of Wilder's writing is cast in a strictly realistic form; besides *The Adding Machine*, Rice pens the ultra-naturalistic *Street Scene*; expressionism and realism meet also in the work of that great Irish successor of Synge, Sean O'Casey.

When *The Shadow of a Gunman* appeared at the Abbey Theatre in 1923 there was general recognition that a new star had come into the theatrical firmament. Here was the advent of a young author whose rich sense of language, keen insight into character, and broad, firm handling of dramatic material immediately set him forth as a worthy successor to the first playwrights of the Irish renaissance. And, in succeeding to this tradition, he indicated, with bold, strong fervour, that he was not prepared merely to follow: if to the tradition he owed his being, he was determined to add to it and enlarge its confines. Yeats had brought the poetic drama to Ireland: Synge had explored the realms of the peasantry: O'Casey set himself the task of interpreting the lower-class life of the city. A born fighter, he had identified himself both with the Irish labour struggle and with the national uprising, yet, despite his direct involvement in these tumultuous movements, he retained a vigorous independence of mind and was prepared to startle his fellow-associates by his unflinching condemnation of some among their most deeply cherished fancies. A man with a definitely tragic attitude towards existence, he has shown himself capable of producing scenes of gorgeous laughter, deep-rooted in a profound knowledge of human life.

The Shadow of a Gunman reveals clearly the chief qualities of his early style. Irony appears in this tale of a loud-mouthed, self-esteeming revolutionary whose romantic pose takes in his associates and, with more serious consequence, leads to the death of a brave young girl. Even finer in quality were the two plays soon to follow, *Juno and the Paycock* (1924) and *The Plough and the Stars* (1926). In these the comic scenes are more harmoniously woven into the tragic texture, the characters are more sharply etched, the episodes more skilfully wrought. Once more, the former introduces a romantic boaster, the 'Paycock' himself, Captain Jack Boyle, fit companion for the lovable yet utterly useless Joxer Daly. Round these persons the family circle is drawn—a fatal circle, poverty-stricken, with death and the breaking of dreams leaving it shattered at the end, yet strangely ennobled by the figure of Juno, the Paycock's wife, a figure into whom O'Casey has cast all his pity and his love. As a background to the action of this drama is set the Irish revolutionary movement: this is brought to the front of the stage in *The Plough and the Stars*, where, almost without a plot, the author has created a series of vivid scenes of darkness irradiated by bitter laughter. There appears, however, to be a change in spirit from *The Shadow of a Gunman*. While still O'Casey is sympathetic towards those who had the courage to fight for the ideal of national independence, we realize that he is becoming more intent upon the general evils in our civilization, deeper and more vicious than those evils against which Jack Clitheroe takes active battle and over which Fluther Good wastes many besotted words. His vision has grown wider and deeper; it is no longer merely Irish.

With this inner development it is not surprising to find him turning from the realistic style to the expressionistic in *The Silver Tassie* (1928). No play better than this illustrates the spiritual essence of the latter form or demonstrates more clearly the impulse that has led so many moderns to seek in it a medium for the display of their dramatic truths. O'Casey's object in *The Silver Tassie* is to show a man of powerful physique broken by the war and turned from a being proud of his healthy body into a cripple. The first act places him: hilariously acclaimed by his friends for having won the 'silver tassie,' the football trophy cup, he has just played his last game before setting off with the army. Another dramatist with aims less wide than O'Casey's would have proceeded throughout in a realistic manner, but for O'Casey the problem of the individual man is dwarfed by the problem of men. After this first act he wants to show the horror of war. Were he to do this in the style of *Journey's End* our attentions would still be riveted on the single hero, and the breadth of effect desired would be lost. Hence abruptly O'Casey changes his method: from the realism of the opening scenes he moves to an expressionistic, symbolic treatment of the trenches. This done, and the background set, he is free to turn back to the particular, knowing that, if we have imaginatively given ourselves to his vision and have been willing to accept the sharp juxtaposition of dramatic methods, the story of his hero will have been enlarged because of what we have heard and seen of the hell through which he has passed.

Having thus experimented with a single scene in the expressionistic manner, O'Casey has found that only this form can give him the opportunity he seeks of presenting his vision of life. *Within the Gates* (1934) is written entirely in the anti-realistic manner. We are within the gates of Hyde Park, but the characters, instead of being individualized, are type creations—a Poet Dreamer, a Young Whore, a Bishop and his Sister. As the scenes develop we learn that the Whore is the illegitimate daughter of the Bishop: sick and near to death, she finds consolation and a spirit of hope not in the dogmas of the Church, but in the arms of the Poet. While this play may be by no means entirely successful, it possesses a wealth of imaginative power and a richness of utterance such as few modern plays have to offer us.

From this time on the expressionistic has been O'Casey's chosen form of dramatic composition, his torrential outpouring of words finding fitting channel in those freer and uninhibited realms which Toller and Kaiser had substituted for the tight and economical Ibsenian structure. In 1940 he wrote for the Unity Theatre *The Star turns Red*, and followed that with *Purple Dust* (1940) and *Red Roses for Me* (1942)—the last a magnificent colourful fantasy, with a poetic dialogue that soars and sears, with a fine distillation of that tragic sense, that irony, and that comedy he is so skilful in intermingling into an impressive whole. There is a central figure here in Ayamonn, but again the vision goes beyond the individual. What is memorable in the play is the mass effect of the whole, the miseries and the splendours of the unemployed and the flower-girls, the quiet searching of the uttermost reaches in the ironic graveyard scene, the philosophical atmosphere which enwraps the entirety of the action. O'Casey has no need to prate about an epic theatre: by his genius, whatever its failures, he has succeeded in creating a theatrical impression of the epic sweep which goes far beyond anything achieved by any of his contemporaries.

The movement called expressionism would have fully justified its existence even if O'Casey's plays alone were the products of its germinating impulse.

4

REALISM, SOCIAL AND OTHERWISE

WHILE the expressionistic movement thus rebelliously set out to shatter the realistic form of drama the various influences, already discussed in brief outline, tending towards a retention of the late-nineteenth-century pattern were being augmented by developments such as the nineteenth century could not have dreamed of. The result has been the paradoxical coexistence of the most bizarre forms the theatre has ever known and of the continued popularity of one of its most narrowly restricted genres.

Socialist Realism in Russia

When the Revolution first laid its impress on the stages of Moscow and Leningrad enthusiastic producers indulged in a riot of eccentric styles which, stemming ultimately from the more radical works of the immediate pre-war years, embraced all the 'isms' and added some more to their number. These were the heydays of Meyerhold and Tairov.

Soon, however, violent changes arrived. Partly impressed by the need of utilizing the theatre as a kind of lecture platform and of making plays serve the needs of mass education, the authorities proceeded to curb the excesses and to demand the realistic. This statement, of course, must not be taken to imply that there has been a complete reversion to the old proscenium-frame, peep-show type of stage. The exact opposite is the case. All kinds of methods of production are employed. It is true that Meyerhold's 'biomechanical' stylization has fallen by the wayside and that Tairov's 'synthetic' theatre is no longer looked upon with favour, but we have only to consider the various experiments made by Nikolai Okhlopkov at the Realistic Theatre or by Alexei Popov at the Central Theatre of the Red Army in Moscow to recognize that, in so far as productional methods are concerned, there is no tying of actors or directors to a set pattern; and it is in the U.S.S.R. that experimental forms of theatre construction find their freest scope.

Method, however, is one thing and basic aim another; there may exist a vast difference in the impress of an idea upon the literary art of the drama and upon the interpretative art of the stage. In imposing Socialist Realism on the arts in Russia the central authorities, beyond curbing extreme naturalism on the one hand and extreme stylization on the other, may have left room for a considerable amount of diversity in the manner of presenting plays, but on the playwrights themselves they set a firm decree. According to the manifesto issued in 1932 by the All-Union Congress of Soviet Writers, this Socialist Realism,

> being the fundamental method of Soviet writing, whether creative or critical, demands from the author a truthful, historically concrete representation of actuality in its revolutionary development. Above all, the truthfulness and historical concreteness of the artist's representation of actuality must be united with the problem of the spiritual fashioning and educating of the workers in the concept of socialism.

This means, when applied to dramatic art, that all plays must be both informative and propagandist. They have to be propagandist because their object is to educate the workers: at the same time they ought not to distort their subject-matter (whether that be contemporary material or historical), but endeavour to be true to all aspects of life in a given period, interpreting these, of course, in communist terms. In effect, what this implies is that the old Russian theatrical ideal of *byt* has been extended and applied to the newer Marxist ideals.

We are not, however, so much concerned with theory as with results, and the results indicate that the application of the dogma of socialist realism has the effect of compelling the authors to produce dramas which seek to combine a whiff of the schoolroom with a steady breeze of Marxist propaganda, and that in style these authors are forced to follow realistic methods of character-displayal and development of dialogue.

From the statistics that are available no country shows a greater wave of theatrical activity than the U.S.S.R. Native-language stages have multiplied themselves constantly during the past decades, and even in Great Russia itself the expansion has been extraordinary. By 1936 it was calculated that, apart from several hundred workers' playhouses, there existed more than six hundred and fifty theatres spread over the whole of the country, with an audience throughout the year of fifty million persons. In these theatres scores of new plays are presented annually, and, as has often been justifiably pointed out, the young dramatist in Russia is offered material opportunities that might well make him an object of envy to his Western colleagues. The fact remains, however, that during the past half-century few Soviet dramas have risen above mediocrity, and none, apparently, have been produced of a kind likely to achieve an international reputation. Symbolic is the fact that a State competition of 1934 yielded 1200 plays, of which not one was deemed worthy of an award.

Among the authors certain major distinctions can be made. First come those who, having had their training before the Revolution, adapted themselves, sometimes enthusiastically and sometimes with effort, to the new conditions. Of this group Alexei Nikolaevich Tolstoi and Anatoli Vasilevich Lunacharski have contributed little of any consequence, but some quality resides in the writings of two of their companions. Early in the last war a German bomb was responsible for the death of Alexander Nikolaevich Afinogenov, undoubtedly one of the most gifted of modern Russian dramatists, but at the same time one who, in 1938, fell under the dire suspicion of the Government. With ardent revolutionary enthusiasm, this writer started his career by the penning of dramas which were designed either to show the development of the social struggle in various countries or to give simple admonishments to his audiences. Most of these early works, although wrought with some skill, are negligible. Nothing much of value can be expected of a theme indicated by a title such as *Keep Your Eyes Open* (1927), a play wherein the story is told of a young communist student who carelessly allows his party card to be used by an acquaintance, and who is aghast to find that it has subserved counter-revolutionary purposes. In 1930, however, came a much more important drama, *Shtrakh* (*Fear*), in which appears an interesting and sympathetic study of an old-time scientist, Professor Borodin, who finds himself so surrounded by Marxist inhibitions that he deems the whole of Russian life to be dominated by fear. The interest of the play consists in the fact that, although the ending demonstrates that the hero is wrong, the analysis of his mood is executed with deep sympathy and alert understanding. Some of Afinogenov's work reminds us of antiquated formulas for play construction, and other dramas, like *Saliut, Ispaniya!* (*Hail, Spain!*, 1936), are, as their titles indicate, largely hysterical *pièces d'occasion*. With *Dalekoe* (*Distant Point*, 1935) we fortunately move back to the mood of *Fear*. In a manner that indicates how deeply he has been influenced by Chekhov, Afinogenov here presents a quiet picture rich in emotional power. The locale is a small Siberian village far removed from wider civilization: its inhabitants quarrel and are at odds with one another. Hither arrives, in the course of a journey from the East, a Soviet general, and through his greatness of soul and sympathetic understanding the confused community life is directed towards a universal united endeavour. Whether in Afinogenov's return to communist grace he would have been likely, had he lived, to enrich his art further, we cannot tell: his comic *Mashenka* (1940) is negligible, and *Nakanune* (*On the Eve*, 1942), while interesting, does not measure up to *Fear*.

Konstantin Andreivich Trenev, a younger contemporary of Afinogenov, is worthy of mention because of his *Liubov Iarovaia* (1925, original version; rewritten 1936). In essence this is a good old melodrama, with a heroine perplexed as to whether she shall save her husband—whom she still loves, but who has joined the Whites—or, by denouncing him, save her comrades. No doubt the thrills and the scenes of suspense are exciting, but, beyond the introduction of some boldly drawn character types, we can hardly esteem the play an important work of dramatic art.

About the same time Michael Afanasevich Bulgakov produced in *Dni Turbinikh* (*The Days of the Turbins*, 1926) another essay in Chekhovian style, one distinguished by its skilful, sympathetic study of an old-time family confronted by the Revolution. For one man the Revolution means the complete negation of all he has known and loved; for another it means simply confusion of spirit, where ancient loyalties batter against human sympathy; for a third it implies a fresh challenge. The final lines in effect tell its story. "Gentlemen," says Nikolka, "do you know, this evening is a great prologue to an historical play"—to which Studzinsky replies, "For some a prologue—for me an epilogue." This is at once among the most powerful and the least typical of Soviet theatrical productions.

Companions of Bulgakov are Alexei Mikhailovich Faiko, author of *Chelovek s portfelem* (*The Man with a Portfolio*, 1928), Vsevolod Viacheslavovich Ivanov, whose most important play is *Bronepoezd No. 14–69* (*The Armoured Train*, 1927), and Valentin Petrovich Kataev, distinguished for his comedy *Kvadratura kruga* (*Squaring the Circle*, 1928). None of these plays is truly valuable, but all are interesting. *The Man with a Portfolio* is a kind of melodramatic *Fear*, and does succeed in presenting, albeit with many sensational incidents, the progress of an intellectual during the first years of the Revolution. Born in an aristocratic circle, Professor Gratanov starts by secretly doing all he can to sabotage the communist government. As he advances in honour and position, however, his sentiments change, and he becomes sincerely anxious to work for the common good. Friends from his past now bring him new dangers, and in desperation he resorts to murder, endeavouring thus to obliterate what he thinks will ruin him, and in the end is forced into confessing his crimes. Crude though portions of this play are, Faiko comes very close to arousing a genuine tragic mood; but very close is not final achievement, and the scenes remain in the melodramatic, not in the tragic, realm. Even more melodramatic is *The Armoured Train*, which does little more than narrate, excitingly, the adventures of a trainload of revolutionary soldiers in conflict with the Whites. *Squaring the Circle* deserves its place in the list because it is one of Russia's few modern comedies: here the fortunes of two ill-assorted couples who are compelled to inhabit a single room is told with gaiety, but at the same time in terms which savour rather of antiquated farce than of recent experiments. It is with some surprise that we find in this proletarian *milieu* precisely the same theme as that which appears in Noel Coward's *Private Lives*.

Beyond a few sensational propaganda pieces apt to arouse political emotions in the audience this first group of authors has not much to contribute to the stage. For the most part their minds were too confused, or else they strove too hard towards a semblance of conforming with the new conditions to permit them to develop a free and unhampered form of expression.

But if they have failed, an even greater failure must be recorded for their successors. Their many patriotic-historical studies are dull, and their dramas of contemporary life wholly propagandist. There is a strange coldness about the majority of these works, as though all the shadings that humanity can give to a work of art were banished in favour of metallic and mechanical darkness and light. Some acclaim has been given to Nikolai Fedorovich Pogodin, but his *Tempo* (1930) rather crudely draws in Boldyrev a portrait of the spotless communist hero; *Aristokrati* (*Aristocrats*, 1935) inclines to creak; and although there is some humour and understanding of humanity in *Chelovek s ruzhem* (*The Man with a Gun*, 1937), we seek in vain here for anything apt to arouse our deeper praise: this also is a drama made to order wherein characters behave, not as they do in real life, but as they ought to do according to Marxist theory. *Inga* (1929), by Anatol Glebov, finds its main interest in discussing the position of woman in the new socialist society. *Konstantin Terekhin* (translated as *Red Dust*, 1927), by Vladimir Mikhailovich Kirshon, gives a tantalizing glimpse of possibilities as each scene moves on its predetermined propagandist way. *Khleb* (*Bread*, 1930) has some effective short scenes, but as a whole is nothing more than a tract preaching the necessity of following the party line.

With regret, it must be admitted by all that from 1920 to the outbreak of war the land which had called into being the genius of Chekhov produced no new dramatic masterpieces. While we can understand the enthusiastic reception given to such a stirring work as *Russkie liudi* (*The Russian People*, 1942) by Konstantin Simonov, we can hardly attribute this reception to its artistic qualities. What's to come is, of course, still unsure; but certainly the first thirty years of the Revolution, despite active cultivation of the theatre, succeeded in bringing to birth little more than a series of informative and doctrinaire plays strangely old-fashioned in their realistic and melodramatic styles. Up to 1941 the tale of the Soviet stage was that of six hundred theatres in search of an author.

The Realistic Drama in America

Realism is deeply implanted in the theatre of the United States, and during the thirties of the present century the natural pre-disposition towards the realistic was very markedly augmented by the arising of a group of young enthusiasts eager, like their Russian colleagues, to use the stage for social purposes.

Despite the fact that the various Continental 'isms' were joyously seized upon and exploited by the leaders of what may be called the American Renaissance, realism and naturalism remained to dominate most of their work. We may think of O'Neill chiefly as the author of stylized and symbolic dramas, yet it was by writing a series of one-act studies of life that he first made his name. If the name of Elmer Rice associates itself with *The Adding Machine*, equally fittingly is it associated with *Street Scene* (1929) and *Counsellor-at-Law* (1931). The former play, as its title clearly indicates, is an essay in locale. It is the street that acts as hero, and the several characters—Frank Moran and his wife, the happy-natured Italian musician, the Swedish janitor, the old folks and the children—serve only to enrich the painting of the setting.

Here is an exceedingly effective experiment in a naturalistic form familiar to us from other examples produced during the years 1890–1910. In the second play Rice reverses his technique, throwing all stress on one central figure—the successful attorney whose past error leads to his professional and social disgrace. How closely Rice copies life may be realized from such a passage as the following—the chatter of Bessie Green, switchboard girl for Simon and Tedesco, lawyers, as she answers calls, talks on another line to an admirer, and occasionally throws a reprimand at the office-boy:

> Say, listen, how many people's work do you think I'm goin' to do around here? . . . Simon and Tedesco—Oh, it's you, is it?—Why, I thought you was dead and buried—No, I don't look so good in black—Yeah, sure I missed you: like Booth missed Lincoln—Well, what do you think I've been doing: sittin' home embroiderin' doilies? Gee, I'm glad I'm wearin' long sleeves, so's I can laugh in 'em—All right, now I'll tell one. [*A buzz.*] Wait a minute—Simon and Tedesco—Mr Tedesco hasn't come in yet—Any minute—What is the name, please?—How do you spell that?—Napoli Importing Company?—All rightee, I'll tell him—Hello—Yeah, I had another call—No, I can't to-night—I can't, I'm tellin' you—I got another date—Ask me no questions and you'll hear no lies—How do you know I want to break it?—Say, you must have your hats made in a barrel factory.

Hardly any American dramatist has his ear more closely attuned to the rhythms of metropolitan speech than Rice.

Another, but a less vigorous, playwright of the same generation, George Kelly, has (among other lesser works which extend as far as the rather futile *The Fatal Weakness* of 1947) contributed one effective drama in this style, *Craig's Wife* (1925), a study of a domineering wife who keeps her husband securely under her thumb until by chance she acts in such a way as to show him precisely in what bonds of slavery he dwells. Similar in tone are the works of Susan Glaspell, who, early on the scene with her *Trifles* (1917), won success as late as 1930 with her play on a poetess, *Alison's House*. Sherwood Anderson first appeared about the same time as Susan Glaspell's début, and, without ever achieving greatness, succeeded in giving to the stage a number of at least capably written dramas, mostly reportorial in kind. Local realism displaying the American West appears in the plays of Lynn Riggs, whose best play, *Green Grow the Lilacs* (1931), with its sentimental flavour, gives a measure of his importance; similarly local in atmosphere is the once bepraised *Hell-bent fer Heaven* (1923), a naturalistic study of a religious enthusiast among the mountaineers, by Hatcher Hughes.

Sternly realistic in tone and treatment is Sidney Howard's *The Silver Cord* (1926), a vigorous essay in the terrors of mother-love, showing a Mrs Phelps who breaks the engagement of one of her sons and nearly shatters the married happiness of his brother. Although gifted with no very great power as a dramatist, Howard has succeeded in leaving behind him a number of fairly memorable plays, works hardly likely to find a permanent place in the repertory, yet possessed of such serious-ness of purpose and such integrity as to mark them out from the run of their companions. Intimate pictures of California life are painted in *They Knew What They Wanted* (1924), a play marked by kindly understanding; *The Late Christopher Bean* (1932), adapted, like Emlyn Williams' similarly named play, from René Fauchois' *Prenez garde à la peinture*, ironically deals with the fate of an artist who has become famous in death; *Alien Corn* (1933) narrates the romance of a mid-Western piano-teacher; in *Dodsworth* (1934) the impossible almost reaches achievement and the widespread canvas of Sinclair Lewis' novel is compressed, with moderate success, into the more restricted framework of the stage. Superior to these is *Yellow Jack* (1934), where again a broad area is covered, Howard's endeavour being to put into dramatic terms the long, painful, and at times seemingly hopeless struggle of man against the disease-carrying mosquito. It is a high testimony to Howard's skill that he has been able to wrest so much of warm human interest from a theme essen-tially historical and scientific.

Yellow Jack reminds us of *Men in White* (1933), by a younger contem-porary of Howard's, Sidney Kingsley. Kingsley's most successful play was *Dead End* (1935), a work in which, with a strange reversion to almost Belascoish methods of handling material, he endeavoured, starkly and yet sentimentally, to prove that criminals are made, not born. Despite the acclaim that greeted this drama, however, it is perhaps in *Men in White* that he has exhibited most dramatic power, and, apart from the in-terest inherent in his treatment of his subject, there is here the added in-terest that rests in his choice of theme. When we look at the plays of the latter part of the nineteenth century and of the first decades of our own era we must be struck by the extraordinary appeal made to the drama-tists by what may be called the artist hero. Ibsen, Strindberg, Haupt-mann, together with dozens of their companions, have put painters, writers, and sculptors upon the stage, frequently—indeed, generally —endeavouring to present a contrast between the claims of a consuming passion for artistic creation and the claims of ordinary life. The trailing relics of this tradition are clearly to be viewed in the artist of *The Late Christopher Bean* and the musician of *Alien Corn*. *Yellow Jack* and *Men in White* carry us into another world wherein the scientist, whether he be hardworking general practitioner, aspiring young medical genius, or great inventor, becomes the hero. No doubt Kingsley allows more than a dash of that sentimentalism which ever seems to be the companion of the realistic to enter into his theme of a doctor who has to choose be-tween the claims of romance and the demands of his career, but at least in his choice of that theme he shows himself attuned to the spirit of the thirties.

Something finer in texture and more philosophic in outlook appears in the writings of Robert Emmet Sherwood, who inaugurated his thea-trical career with *The Road to Rome* in 1927. From this comedy-drama on to his latest work we have the impression that here walks a thoughtful playwright puzzled by the contours of the land he is traversing, anxious to discover his orientation yet lost without a compass, and inclining to steer his steps now towards one landmark, now towards another. In *The Road to Rome* Shaw's influence is obvious, and the action takes shape as a modernistic treatment of a section of classical history, inspired not merely by the detestation of war, but also by the sentimental assumptions that wars are caused by stupid individual heroics and that the bubble of these heroics can be easily pricked by common sense. Rome, threatened by the might of Hannibal, is protected from ruin by the realistic wit of Amytis, wife of Fabius, not by Fabius' armies. The gay spirit of thoughtful wit also animates *Reunion in Vienna* (1931), a delightful fantasy which presents a gathering of Habsburgs, now scattered over the earth and sadly decayed in grandeur, in the home of their former colourful existence. Adroitly Sherwood, in this latter comedy, contrasts both the relics of aristocratic pride with existing poverty and the relics of the code of honour with bourgeois morality, wrapping the entire action in a vesture as witty as it is colourful.

This author's purpose, however, is too serious to permit him to find full satisfaction in the comic realm, even although the laughter be shot through with grave reflection. Already in *Waterloo Bridge* (1930), with its story of a young soldier and a prostitute, he had essayed something darker, and five years later he reached mastery of expression when he turned to write *The Petrified Forest* (1935). With a peculiarly appealing style, he here depicts, in Alan Squier, an unsuccessful, highly cultured poet wandering wearily over the Arizona desert, symbolizing the sense of spiritual disillusionment out of which the entire drama grows. Every one of the characters, indeed, is symbolic; yet every one is real. Duke Mantee, the gangster, stands for the new spirit of adventure, adventure that has been forced to become evil; Gabby, the girl with whom Squier falls in love, represents the hope that lies, rather precariously, in the future. Despairing though the spirit of this play is, it has a warmth and a breadth wanting in many other realistic works of the age. At least Sherwood does not concentrate his attention on eternal triangles, neurotics, or criminals created by society. *Idiot's Delight* (1936) carries on and perfects the style of *The Petrified Forest*. Again the characters are both real and symbols—the German scientist, the French munitions manufacturer, the American 'hoofer,' the English honeymoon couple—and again the emotional tension rises steadily until it ends in the staccato of explosions. Only this time the explosions are not the petty gunfire between gangsters and police, but the dull echoing of bombs amid the mountains. There can be no doubt that this is one of the most effective realistic dramas the twentieth-century theatre has to offer us.

Much less satisfactory, *Abe Lincoln in Illinois* (1938) turns to explore the early life of a recent yet already mythical American president. Then in 1940 Sherwood produced, in a white heat of passion, *There shall be No*

Night, a grimly tense testimonial to the Finns in their struggle to preserve their independence. Perhaps it is typical of the author's wandering path that, soon after the appearance of this work, he found himself as passionately aroused by the German menace, so that, while he was himself devoting his time to the war effort, he allowed the subject-matter of *There shall be No Night* to be translated into terms of invaded Greece. There is probably something of a spiritually autobiographical character in Sherwood's later play, *The Rugged Path* (1945), which shows a liberal newspaperman, Vinion, who, after roaming far through the world, returns to edit his home-town newspaper, becomes involved in a struggle with conservative, 'isolationist' elements, and only by enlisting in the navy succeeds in recapturing his faith in humanity.

The Theatre of the 'Socially Conscious'

With the coming of the depression diverse social strains, amply evident in the earlier American drama, came to the surface. Class-consciousness developed rapidly, and most of the younger theatre enthusiasts were prepared to mingle admiring imitation of Stanislavski with ardent inculcation of socialism. The Group Theatre was thus formulated out of a Theatre Guild Studio; more radical in aim, the Theatre Union bravely struggled on for some years; a New Theatre League came into being; at the extreme left agitated the Theatre of Action and the Labor Stage (the theatre unit of the International Ladies Garment Workers Union). Not only did these organizations present their own repertory (and in one instance develop their own playwright), but the spirit they so eagerly expressed spread over to influence the current fare in the commercial theatres.

Naturally the dramatic results of this movement were various and of varying quality. At the Theatre Union the dramas inclined to be solemnly sincere, melodramatic, sensational, and sentimental. Here appeared *Peace on Earth* (1933), by Albert Maltz and George Sklar, who had already collaborated in a tense and in its way effective indictment of the iniquities of American justice in *Merry-go-Round* (1932). Although the theme of *Peace on Earth* has virtue—it is an attack on munitions-makers and their influence—the handling of the plot is reminiscent of nineteenth-century melodrama. A similar criticism may be passed on *Stevedore* (1934), written by Sklar in conjunction with Paul Peters, and on *Black Pit* (1935), by Maltz. Characteristic of the qualities introduced into these plays is the Theatre Union's final production—*Marching Song* (1937), by John Howard Lawson, author of the expressionistic *Processional* of 1925. Taking as centre of his picture a wretched family, compelled to live in a disused factory building because they have been turned out of their home by the 'capitalists' (who disapprove of the father's radical agitation), Lawson develops his story along familiar lines. The other workers go on strike; the father is given the alternative of having his job back and betraying his fellows or of living with his family at starvation's edge; gunmen engaged by the factory owners resort to murder; the strike spreads, and amid cries of jubilation the capitalists are brought to their knees in abject surrender.

Something rather richer in texture appears in *Let Freedom Ring* (1935), by Albert Bein, chiefly because the setting—a mill located in the Kentucky mountains—permits of the introduction of a more variegated dramatic personnel than can appear in a city-set labour drama. Still richer is *The Cradle will Rock* (1937), by Marc Blitzstein, a play to which flavour is given through the employment of the operatic technique for the expressing of socialistic propaganda. Richer yet is the long one-act drama by Irwin Shaw called *Bury the Dead* (1936), with its gripping (and almost expressionistically developed) theme of the soldiers rising from their trenches and being frantically told by all the living—from their generals to their relatives—that they must remain in the land of the lifeless. Irwin Shaw unquestionably has an original talent denied to most of his fellow-enthusiasts, as is shown by one of his following plays, *The Gentle People* (1939), the tender fantasy of which contrasts vividly with the white-hot bitterness of his first work. The gentle people are two cronies, a Jew and a Greek, desperately poor yet gathering money gradually wherewith to purchase a boat large enough to allow them to fulfil their dream of sailing off far into a warm South. A gangster appears and demands tribute from them, whereupon this innocent and mild-mannered and timorous pair lure him into their little fishing-skiff, row him out to sea, and drown him: the curtain falls upon them as, returned home, they sit, quiet and satisfied, dreaming their dreams.

While the Federal Theatre Project (1935–39) stimulated the labour theatre, in itself it did not do much to encourage dramatic talent. Under its auspices appeared interesting productions—such as the Negro *Macbeth* and *The Swing Mikado*—but of new plays there was a dearth. For the Project Sinclair Lewis and John C. Moffitt wrote the anti-fascist *It Can't Happen Here* (1936): this, however, is a rather lonely effort, and most of the playwrights' energies went into the preparation of 'Living Newspaper' material of Soviet style (such as *One Third of a Nation*, 1938).

For writers of power we must look beyond this venture, and particularly to the talent sponsored by the Group Theatre. This unit brought forward a dramatist with a peculiar quality of his own in Robert Ardrey, author of a fairly feeble 'labour' play *Casey Jones* (1938) and of a truly interesting *Thunder Rock* (1939). The latter, which strangely failed to win any acclaim in America, but was a great success in London, displays extraordinary power and deep-searching vision in its picture of the lonely lighthouse and the shades of the past meeting the forms of the living. Whether American or British audiences were right, unfortunately this author has not succeeded in fulfilling the promise which seemed to many spectators so brightly shining in his early writing.

Beyond all others of this group, however, towers Clifford Odets. When his *Waiting for Lefty* appeared in 1935 it was easy to see that the labour stage had gained a literary artist whose abilities carried him beyond the cliché and the hysterical appeal towards 'action.' No doubt the emotional effect of this one-act drama depends more on the author's skill in arousing political emotion than upon his æsthetic effects, but, even so, the arousing of the political emotion is achieved by means far subtler than had been used in the Theatre Union's melodramas. With skill, Odets has raised before us a vivid picture of the absent Lefty, so that when news comes of his murder by agents of the capitalistic owners we feel almost as though we had heard of the death of a friend. Odets' second play, *Awake and Sing* (1935), demonstrated equally clearly that here was an author not content to rely on the facile sentiments of the ordinary propagandist drama. No doubt the flame at the heart of these bitter scenes is the flame of anger; at the same time, the picture of the Berger family circle, impoverished and destined by circumstance to have all its dreams broken, gains its power from the author's grasp of character and his almost Chekhovian sense of human relationships. One by one, we see these characters going their ways—the old grandfather, to his death; the son Ralph, to a shattering of his romance; his sister, Hennie, to a loveless intrigue. The atmosphere is thoroughly realistic, yet Odets has the power to make his words sing; here is a force akin to that of the young O'Casey.

In *Paradise Lost* (1935) something of the magic vanishes, but sufficient remains to make this too a notable drama: what is missing here is the power so markedly present in the earlier plays whereby the individual action was given general overtones. There is a descent to the melodramatic in *Paradise Lost*, and we feel that the cards have been carefully stacked: in the story of Ben Gordon and his ending under police gunfire we are given something that strains our belief and renders us unable to accept either the characters or the plot as representative in the larger sense. *Golden Boy* (1937) is also melodramatic, particularly towards the conclusion of the piece, yet in this play we sense a return to the quality that gave distinction to *Awake and Sing*. Joe Bonaparte is drawn in terms that bring him to life on the stage, a character at once admirable and weak, a study unmarred by the black-and-white portraiture so often found in the theatre of social realism. This man, a violinist, with the soul of a musician, gives up his art to become a prize-fighter. Money is in the ring, and money he craves, both because he can give of it to the woman he loves and because deep within himself resides a passion for the worldly power that riches can procure. Throughout the play Joe's mental agonies are skilfully revealed in taut, nervous dialogue that, when need arises, has the strength to borrow the qualities of music and to sing. In the end the strain on him is so great that he feels the desire to fly from the world of his own creating, and to crash. He has killed a man in a contest; he has abandoned his violin; his hands, trained to fight, have no longer the skill to play; and in the wild motor-drive which brings death to Lorna and himself he seeks his release. Odets' power of rising to the demands of an emotional climax is revealed nowhere more vividly than in his hero's despairing and exalted pæan in praise of speed:

> *JOE:* But I *did* it! That's the thing—I *did* it! What will my father say when he hears I murdered a man? Lorna, I see what I did. I murdered myself, too! I've been running around in circles. Now I'm smashed! That's the truth. Yes, I was a real sparrow, and I wanted to be a fake eagle! But now I'm hung up by my finger-tips—I'm no good—my feet are off the earth!
>
> *LORNA* [*in a sudden burst, going to JOE*]: Joe, I love you! We love each other. Need each other!
>
> *JOE:* Lorna darling, I see what's happened!
>
> *LORNA:* You wanted to conquer the world—
>
> *JOE:* Yes—
>
> *LORNA:* But it's not the kings and dictators who do it—it's that kid in the park—
>
> *JOE:* Yes, that boy who might have said, "I have myself; I am what I want to be!"
>
> *LORNA:* And now, to-night, here, this minute—finding yourself again—that's what makes you a champ. Don't you see that?
>
> *JOE:* Yes, Lorna—yes!
>
> *LORNA:* It isn't too late to tell the world good-evening again!
>
> *JOE:* With what? These fists?
>
> *LORNA:* Give up the fighting business!
>
> *JOE:* To-night!
>
> *LORNA:* Yes, and go back to your music—
>
> *JOE:* But my hands are ruined. I'll never play again! What's left, Lorna? Half a man, nothing, useless . . .
>
> *LORNA:* No, *we're* left! Two together! We have each other! Somewhere there must be happy boys and girls who can teach us the way of life! We'll find some city where poverty's no shame—where music is no crime!—where there's no war in the streets—where a man is glad to be himself, to live and make his woman herself!
>
> *JOE:* No more fighting, but where do we go?
>
> *LORNA:* To-night? Joe, we ride in your car. We speed through the night, across the park, over the Triboro Bridge—
>
> *JOE* [*taking LORNA'S arms in his trembling hands*]: Ride! That's it, we ride —clear my head. We'll drive through the night. When you mow down the night with headlights nobody gets you! You're on top of the world then —nobody laughs! That's it—speed! We're off the earth—unconnected! We don't have to think! That's what speed's for, an easy way to live! Lorna darling, we'll burn up the night!

Although this scene betrays the weakness common to many young American dramatic authors of the thirties—an inordinate tendency to feel sorry for themselves in the midst of plenty—yet Odets' power is sufficient to carry us past and above the rather lachrymose sentimentalizing. These few lines of dialogue alone are sufficient to testify to his power over theatrical words.

In *Rocket to the Moon* (1938) Odets turned to write a play more puzzling than any he had previously composed. The plot drifts along with the inconsequentiality of a Chekhovian drama, although we feel that it lacks that essential quality which makes Chekhov's plays great. In the works of the Russian dramatist an inner symphonic harmony gives purpose to the least (and perhaps, at first sight, meaningless) episode; in *Rocket to the Moon* we are troubled by a sense of confusion—and for this the cause is to be sought in what Harold Clurman has to tell us of its inception. *Rocket to the Moon*, he comments,

> contained some of Odets' most mature writing and two of his finest characters. The play as written, however, was thematically quite different from what had been implied in Odets' original sketch of it. . . .
>
> As originally planned, the play was about a meek little dentist ravaged through the love of a silly girl. Regardless of its object, love was to give this man a depth of experience and thus a stature beyond his normal scope. The dentist then was the central character, and the play was his play. In the actual writing of the play the theme was transformed to that of the difficult quest for love in the modern world. The person who embodied this quest was the little girl, uneducated, childish, rattle-brained, and true. She had become the centre of the play, a person who despite her 'ordinariness' was what the author called a moral idealist, whose pathos arises from an inability to find realization through connexion with any of the representative middleclass men she meets in the course of her quest.

As a result, Clurman points out, the original scheme was to present a man with a choice of women—a nagging wife and a trivial child mistress. But

> when the girl at the end of the play matured sufficiently to express the essence of her experience—and the playwright's thought—a good part of the audience was bewildered by her transformation and the unexpected turn the play had taken.

This example, perhaps, has the quality of illustrating Odets' main dramatic weakness. He has power over character and his words are rich, but he has not that larger constructive sense which alone can produce unity of impression and of concept.

Unfortunately, he succeeded in producing no other dramatic works of any real strength. *Night Music* (1940) presents some delicately comic scenes, but it lacks the core of an imaginative idea. Much darker in tone is *Clash by Night* (1941), but the darkness, instead of being tragically effective, is put before us with dreary solemnity. Apart from all of these stands *The Flowering Peach* (1954), a play which sets in front of us the familiar Biblical story of the Flood as it might have been told in the intimacy of a humble Jewish house—an experiment which is not very satisfactory. Perhaps, for all his gifts, Odets was a writer not intimately attuned to the stage.

In one particular realm the socially conscious theatre of the United States has found a native theme whose seriousness and dramatic potentialities have been diversely exploited. The Negro problem is one unique to that country, and it is not surprising that almost every one of her playwrights, each in his own way, has tried to deal theatrically with its perplexing issues. Far back in the nineteenth century the ever-inventive Boucicault won success by his melodramatic treatment of *The Octoroon* (1859), and since then scores of dramas have set the opposition of whites and blacks upon the stage. Even those authors who show themselves intent on larger questions feel impelled to turn to this subject: O'Neill pens his *Emperor Jones* and *All God's Chillun Got Wings*, while Anderson gives us his *Wingless Victory*.

The variety of approach here is, naturally, great. Some authors burn with a sense of immediate and urgent purpose. Thus John Wexley, who had, very melodramatically, attacked capital punishment in *The Last Mile* (1930) and ill-treatment of workers in *Steel* (1931), was inspired by a notorious trial of Negroes to write his would-be flaming, but in actuality merely spluttering, *They Shall Not Die* (1934). At the opposite extreme comes the attempt simply to present a theatrical record of Negro psychology. Of this kind of play the delightful *Green Pastures* (1930) of Marc Connelly easily ranks highest—a skilful and sympathetic presentation of a Negro minister's idea of heaven and the history of the world. With a deep understanding of the primitive mind, in which the abstractly symbolic disconcertingly jostles against the common things of the day, Connelly has produced a play that assuredly will remain among the treasures of the world's lesser drama. There is a peculiar direct simplicity of appeal here that captures our attention. "I kin out-trick you an' de Lawd too!" cries Pharaoh, and Moses replies:

> *MOSES* [*angrily*]: Now you done it, ol' King Pharaoh. You been mean to de Lawd's people, and de Lawd's been easy on you caize you didn't know no better. You been givin' me a lot of say-so and no do-so, and I didn' min' dat. But now you've got to braggin' dat you's better dan de Lawd, and dat's too many.
>
> *PHARAOH:* You talk like a preacher, an' I never did like to hear preachers talk.
>
> *MOSES:* You ain't goin' to like it any better, when I strikes down de oldes' boy in every one of yo' people's houses.
>
> *PHARAOH:* Now you've given up trickin' and is jest lyin'. [*He rises.*] Listen, I'm Pharaoh. I do de strikin' down yere. I strike down my enemies, and dere's no one in all Egypt kin kill who he wants to, 'ceptin' me.
>
> *MOSES:* I'm sorry, Pharaoh. Will you let de Hebrews go?
>
> *PHARAOH:* You heard my word. [*AARON is lifting his rod again at a signal from MOSES.*] Now, no more tricks or I'll—
>
> *MOSES:* Oh, Lawd, you'll have to do it, I guess. Aaron, lift de rod.
>
> [*There is a thunderclap, darkness, and screams. The lights go up. Several of the younger men on the stage have fallen to the ground or are being held in the arms of the horrified elders.*]
>
> *PHARAOH:* What have you done yere? Where's my boy?
>
> [*Through the door come four men bearing a young man's body.*]

FIRST OF THE FOUR MEN: King Pharaoh.

[*PHARAOH drops into his chair, stunned, as the dead boy is brought to the throne.*

PHARAOH [*grief-stricken*]: Oh, my son, my fine son.

[*The courtiers look at him with mute appeal.*

MOSES: I'm sorry, Pharaoh, but you cain't fight de Lawd. Will you let his people go?

PHARAOH: Let them go.

[*The lights go out. The CHOIR begins, "Mary Don't You Weep," and continues until it is broken by the strains of "I'm Noways Weary and I'm Noways Tired."*

Between the extremes of *They Shall Not Die* and *Green Pastures* rest most of the works of Paul Green, a Southerner who has made the depiction of the Negro and of the 'poor white' his life's task. When his *In Abraham's Bosom* appeared in 1926 it was immediately realized that its author was a man of no common ability. Taking as his hero a half-caste who determines that the only hope for the Negroes lies in their fuller education, Green shows his Abraham McCranie struggling both against the indifference of his black cousins and against the evil animosity of his white, until, driven desperate by the callousness and evil around him, he is led to murder his own half-brother, a man from whom he had sought aid and who had betrayed his trust by stealing from him his few last possessions. This drama was followed several years later by *The House of Connelly* (1931), in which the crumbling of the old Southern aristocracy is displayed in the gradual disintegration of one single great estate. Through the marriage of Will Connelly, weak-willed and decadent, and Patsy Tate, a girl belonging to the 'poor white trash' whom the Connellys despise, but who possesses vigour and initiative, Green seems to suggest that only through an infusion of new blood into the dry veins of the aristocrats can there be any hope of saving a dying segment of the nation. In a sense Green is thus merely transferring to an American *milieu* what had been hinted by Goldoni nearly two hundred years before, and what had formed the major theme, in the late nineteenth century, of plays by Augier and Lavedan. In subsequently written dramas, many of them one-acts, Green has sought to explore further diverse aspects of life in the South, but without achieving unquestioned success. There is in Green a burning sincerity unfortunately not accompanied by that technical mastery and abounding strength which are required by the most exacting of all literary arts.

With Paul Green may be associated Du Bose Heyward, famous for his *Porgy* (1927), dramatized from his own novel and later made into operatic form (1935), with music by George Gershwin. The importance of this work rests in its departure from themes of miscegenation, of sharecroppers and the like, depicting instead Negro life as it is carried on in Charleston. There is no colour problem here, simply a well-wrought drama with the crippled Porgy as its hero, surrounded by the self-seeking Bess, the flashy Sportin' Life, the murderous Crown, and a variety of other characters making up a vividly drawn picture of a kind that hitherto the American stage had not known. Another drama on similar lines, *Mamba's Daughters*, a collaborative work of Dorothy and Du Bose Heyward, appeared in 1939.

Through these and other plays the Negro definitely entered the New York theatre. *Cabin in the Sky* (1940), by Lynn Root and John La Touche, showed an imaginative sense and suggested fresh proportions; although melodramatic, *Native Son* (1941), by Richard Wright, possessed a vigour of peculiar intensity; Hall Johnson's *Run, Little Chillun* (1933) had an intimate quality that demonstrated how far the drama of colour had moved from the artificialities of *The Octoroon*. All-Negro casts were now by no means rare, and in 1946 theatrical history was made when a Negro actor, Canada Lee, reversed a tradition of generations and, after essaying the rôle of Caliban in *The Tempest*, played a part in *The Duchess of Malfi* in white-face. Thus did coloured actors gradually win a distinguished position on the serious stage, and thus did Negro authors start to have their plays produced. A new area of dramatic writing was in process of being established.

Current American Realism

With the Negro, as has been indicated, is connected the poor white, and for a time the rage of New York was a rather sordid piece called *Tobacco Road* (1933), adapted by John Kirkland from a novel by Erskine Caldwell. The authors may have been inspired by the desire to present a sociological document: audiences almost certainly flocked to see the play out of itching curiosity. This is the *Before Sunrise* of the thirties.

The writer who has most specialized in gaunt, stark pictures of depressed areas and depressing types is John Steinbeck, a novelist who won some theatrical fame when his *Of Mice and Men* was turned into a play in 1937 and when his *The Grapes of Wrath* was made into a film in 1940. Steinbeck has all the true characteristics of the naturalist—his love of the gloomy *milieu*, his implied sense of social purpose, and his inescapable sentimentalism. *Of Mice and Men* is typical, with its deceptively objective yet sentimentally weak portrait of the gentle-hearted, half-witted giant who kills unwittingly the things he loves. The same sentimentalism runs amok in the popular but trivial *The Moon is Down* (1942), which demonstrates in its strained action a worthy idea, no doubt, but one which startlingly fails to do justice to the real events it celebrates: larger problems cannot, it would appear, come satisfactorily within the framework of the realistic drama. This attempt in the American theatre to reproduce the tough naturalism of the Hauptmann period does not seem to offer much hope of worthy results. Even the novelist Ernest Hemingway's *The Fifth Column* (published 1938; acted 1940), although it does succeed in painting a powerful portrait of Philip Rawlings and in making us understand his actions, is vitiated by the same weaknesses as mar Steinbeck's work.

Within the realm of what may be called commercial realism no author has recently shown more skill or won more fame than Lillian Hellman, who first came before the public with *The Children's Hour* in 1934 and followed this with *Days to Come* (1936), *The Little Foxes* (1939), *Watch on the Rhine* (1941), and *The Searching Wind* (1944). In these she stands about midway between the social playwrights and those realistic writers who are intent upon depiction of character. Her not very powerful *Days to Come* deals with labour problems, but obviously this is not the sphere in which she is most at home, and her best, most characteristic scenes appear in such works as *The Children's Hour* and *The Little Foxes*. It is the vicious soul that attracts her most: her understanding of human evil is acute, and she knows how to make it theatrically effective. Indeed, we might almost say that she has won her success by devising a formula for an up-to-date melodrama where the villain, instead of being a black-moustached squire or factory owner, is revealed unexpectedly as a child possessed of inherent wickedness and where the dialogue is impeccably true to the tones of current speech. The theme of *The Children's Hour* might perhaps be described as the effect of an original lie working on a gossip-ridden community, but the real dramatic interest of the play lies in its vicious little Mary Tilford, whose original hint that her school-teachers, Karen Wright and Martha Dobie, have Lesbian relations succeeds not only in arousing this community's anger against a couple of largely innocent women, but also in infecting their souls with ugly thoughts. This is by no means so great or so original a drama as was once thought; we cannot, however, deny its impressive technical ability. *The Little Foxes* varies the pattern slightly. Here the evil force is a woman, Regina Giddens, who practically murders her husband and robs her brothers in order to gain control of a factory. For *Watch on the Rhine* the villain becomes a more familiar figure—a Rumanian count who is in reality a Fascist agent and who is killed by the worthy hero, a mild-mannered German refugee. Perhaps because she was dealing here with somewhat alien matter, Lillian Hellman's hand seems not so steady and her scenes not so effective, nor has she succeeded in rehabilitating herself in *The Searching Wind*. Perhaps in *The Children's Hour* and *The Little Foxes* she has exhausted her treasury of wickedness: this, indeed, is suggested when we find her, in a later play, *Another Part of the Forest* (1947), returning to the latter's domestic *milieu*.

A companion authoress, but one less gifted with original vision, is Rose Franken, whose *Another Language* won some attention in 1932. Later her *Claudia* (1941) attracted audiences not so much because of its dramatic power as because its subject—the difficulty experienced by a girl in casting off her mother's influence and becoming a responsible wife —seemed to many to be new. In *Soldier's Wife* (1944) the problem of the readjustment of the army man to civilian life is discussed, while *Outrageous Fortune* (1944) runs through a gamut of problems from homosexuality to anti-Semitism.

Besides these authors numerous others contributed to the New York stage plays, objective or intense, in the realistic kind. Most of them assuredly were forgotten within a few decades, yet in several reside qualities which we might well have wished to be incorporated in less mortal shapes. There is, for example, an element of strength in *The Criminal Code* (1929), a study by Martin Flavin of honour among thieves; sympathetic portraiture appears in *The Barker* (1927), by Kenyon Nicholson; an affecting story of the impress of divorce on a child's mind is told by Leopold Atlas in *Wednesday's Child* (1934)—we might extend the list by enumerating scores of titles, all worthy yet all certainly lacking the quality of permanence. Once more we are confronted by the fact that, in general, the realistic drama but seldom rises (and then usually by means of extra-realistic elements) to a plane above that of the immediately popular.

The Continuance of the Realistic in England

In England the realistic strain was pursued throughout these years with far less vigour and far less fervency than in the United States. Young American dramatists in the twenties found all the excitement of handling a form new to them, and in the thirties there was the socially conscious theatre to urge them forward: by comparison their English companions in this field seem just a trifle bored and consequently unable to wrest virtue from a long-tried style.

Among these writers John Van Druten takes prominence, if only because of the consistency in his application to the stage. His formula is composed of an apparently realistic setting, characters apparently true to life, the suggestion of a problem, and a strong dash of genteel sentimentalism; through the handling of this material with an undeniably skilled hand, he has won success for many of his pieces. *Young Woodley* (1928), his first, captured attention because of its interesting theme of an elder schoolboy's infatuation for the young wife of his master and because of its excellence of construction. Since then he has produced numerous similarly conceived dramas—*Diversion* (1928), *After All* (1929), *There's Always Juliet* (1931), *The Distaff Side* (1933), *Old Acquaintance* (1939), *The Voice of the Turtle* (1943)—wherein we constantly feel that the author, while gifted with a strength out of the ordinary, always fails to bring to the stage more than a series of relatively trivial plays, each likely to be a current success and each likely to be forgotten once its run is over.

At one moment it looked as though, with the appearance of *Journey's End* (1928), by R. C. Sherriff, a brilliant new dramatist had entered the theatre's doors: his later works, however, have failed to capture the amazing success of this his first play. Unfortunately, J. R. Ackerley deserted the theatre after his extraordinarily successful *The Prisoners of War* (1925), a study of conditions in a military camp which exhibits real tension and sense of character values. Still another war play that remains the solitary notable achievement of its author (H. B. Trevelyan) is *The*

Dark Angel (1928), in which a blinded soldier returns to find his sweetheart devoted to a second man.

The 'repertory' tradition during these years was carried on by Allan N. Monkhouse, with ability but without high distinction. *The Conquering Hero* (1924) is a good play of its kind—a kind that is not good; and *First Blood* (1924) seems a very tame study of strike conditions when we compare it with its American cousins. The early death of Ronald Mackenzie may have cut off (as some think) a true dramatic promise, yet objective analysis of *Musical Chairs* (1931) suggests that it is not nearly so fine a play as many critics once thought it, while *The Maitlands* (1934) hardly suggests developing talent. Slightly more difficult is it to estimate the value of the numerous contributions to the theatre made by Emlyn Williams. Starting with a couple of sensational pieces, expertly planned, *A Murder has been Arranged* (1930) and *Night Must Fall* (1935), he showed even in his first works a firm grasp of character values and an adroitness in the devising of stage situations. *The Corn is Green* (1938), with its interesting treatment of a village teacher and her prize pupil, seemed to set him on a higher level, although we can hardly maintain that his subsequent dramas, all of them marked by a sentimental flavour, have served to keep him there. The study of the drunken actor in *The Light of Heart* (1940) does not penetrate very deeply; *The Morning Star* (1941) is obviously *a pièce d'occasion; The Wind of Heaven* (1945) offers somewhat more, with its strange metaphysical atmosphere, although perhaps it has been over-praised; *Spring 1600* (latest version, 1945) merely presents a pleasing dream of Elizabethan London; and *Trespass* (1947) is a somewhat artificial theatrical essay in ghosts and mediums.

There is entertainment in this realm; what is lacking is broader vision. C. L. Anthony (Dodie Smith) can turn out a graceful *Autumn Crocus* (1931) and an equally graceful *Dear Octopus* (1938); Mordaunt Shairp can engage in psychological studies in *The Offence* (1925) or, more brilliantly, in *The Green Bay Tree* (1932); Keith Winter can pen a would-be tragic study of the grand passion in *The Shining Hour* (1934); others there are who might similarly be recorded—and when the catalogue is done we must acknowledge that, despite the excellencies apparent in diverse individual dramas, we are left in the end with nothing of enduring force. The field is barren and can produce no satisfying crops.

Further Relics of the Realistic

The same story must be told of the progress of the realistic play in Ireland. O'Casey and Carroll, by infusing into the form elements of another character, have achieved some considerable distinction, but because of these other elements they have called for discussion in earlier sections of this survey. Among the Irish authors who have pursued the strictly realistic path hardly any can be esteemed to have produced work likely to remain. Best of them is George Shiels, a man who gained some success with *The New Gossoon* (1930), *The Rugged Path* (1940), *The Summit* (1941), and *Tenants-at-Will* (1942). The first of these is a comedy, defending youthful gaiety against age's solemnity; the last grimly deals with a period of famine. Between these two extremes come the companion plays, *The Rugged Path* and *The Summit*, concerned with the way in which a lonely Irish community is tyrannized over by the members of a ne'er-do-well and criminal family—a study that is highly reminiscent of the many American between-war dramas that deal with life in the Kentucky mountains. In *Marrowbone Lane* (1946) Robert Collis deals with Dublin's slums; the potato famine of 1847 is the theme of Gerard Healey's *The Dark Stranger* (1947).

Greater value attaches to a few plays in which the approach is more fanciful. Anthony Wharton (Alister McAllister) produces in *The O'Cuddy* (1943) a pleasingly satiric picture of a stupid man who is argued into believing that he is the heir to a long line of Irish kings, and Brinsley Mac-Namara presents a series of hilarious dramatic escapades from *The Rebellion in Balleycullen* (1919) to *The Three Thimbles* (1942). A kindred mood prevails in the plays of Denis Johnston, who first acquired fame with *The Moon in the Yellow River* in 1931. This is an interesting drama, concerned mainly with the struggle of an idealistic Irish revolutionary to prevent the erection of a power plant near Dublin; he has fought for the freedom of his country, but he wants her freedom to be more than political; Ireland, he dreams, should be the one place on God's earth which remains green and unpolluted by industrialism's evils. Unfortunately Johnston's later plays have hardly approached the brilliance of this early work. *A Bride for the Unicorn* (1933) is confused in its mingling of common reality and of symbolism; neither *Blind Man's Buff* (1936) nor *The Golden Cuckoo* (1938) possesses the peculiar appeal of the visionary who follows the moon's gleams in the muddy waters. The Irish genius finds its spirit expressed perhaps more freely in the imaginative than in the realistic style, and maybe its mood is better caught in Micheál MacLiammóir's *Ill Met by Moonlight* (1946), with its modern atmosphere charmed into strangeness because the house in which the characters dwell has been built upon a fairy ring.

Just before the outbreak of war a revival of dramatic power seemed imminent in Scandinavia, but not sufficient of worth came from that area before 1939 to warrant any sure guess as to what might have been achieved had Norway and Denmark not been rudely occupied by Teutonic forces. Apart from Helge Krog, whose work is referred to elsewhere, the most important writer here is the Norwegian Nordahl Grieg. In all, his writings suggest that, had his short life not unfortunately been ended in the War, he might have proved the greatest dramatist of his generation. Starting his career obviously influenced by Ibsen and Pirandello, he first produced *En ung manns kjærlighet* (*A Young Man's Love*, 1927) and *Barrabas* (1927). Then, some five years later, he essayed a new style in *Atlanterhavet* (*The Atlantic Ocean*, 1932), where a striking contrast is drawn between the fate of those engaged in a dangerous transatlantic flight and the preoccupations of a newspaper editor interested only in the publicity values of their exploit. *Vår ære og vår makt* (*Our Honour and Our Might*, 1935) similarly introduces vivid contrasts—in this case between a German submarine crew and their hapless victims. In his last play, *Nederlaget* (*The Defeat*, 1937), he turned to deal with an historical theme of the time of the Paris Commune, but obviously his interest in this powerful drama lay not in illustrating the past, but in giving himself an opportunity for commenting indirectly on current life. Very close in spirit and atmosphere are the plays of the Danish Kaj Munk, an author who also perished during the War. His career started with a drama on Herod the Great, *En idealist* (*An Idealist*, 1928), was carried on in *Ordet* (*The Word*, 1932) and the patriotic *Egelykke* (1940), and closed with a vigorous drama, *Niels Ebbesen* (1942), which deals with a Danish hero who kills a brutal German officer. Among these dramas interesting, too, is the work of Kjeld Abell, whose rather immature *Melodien, der blev væk* (*The Melody which was Lost*, 1935) found an abler successor in *Anna Sophie Hedvig* (1938), a strange drama in which the chief character, a rather timorous rural schoolteacher, is shown murdering an evil-minded woman who is about to be made director of her school, and who, in that position, would be likely to ruin the lives of the children placed in her care. The murder is clearly symbolic, and the symbolism becomes manifest when at the end we find the heroine, along with a soldier, waiting for a firing-squad in Spain. There is virtue also in his *Silkeborg* (1946), a play wherein middle-aged bourgeois prudence under the occupation is contrasted with youthful defiance. Less likely to pass beyond the bounds of their own country are the numerous plays, including *Den heliga familjen* (*The Holy Family*, 1932) and *Modern och stjärnen* (*The Mother and the Star*, 1940), in which the Swedish Rudolf Värnlund has found expression for social-realistic studies: these can hardly be esteemed richer in content, deeper in psychological penetration, or more exciting in form than the hundreds of other similar plays with which the twentieth century has provided us.

Although the realistic style was cultivated in numerous other countries, both by authors who sought for no more than immediate popular success and by others who aimed at creating things deeper and (hopefully) more enduring, there are only three or four who call for individual attention. In Austria Karl Kraus deserves to be remembered partly because of the way in which he created a peculiar composite style of his own —a style fundamentally realistic, yet strangely intermingled with symbolic, expressionistic and other elements—and partly because of his similar mingling of actions, characters and attitudes which might at first appear to be hopelessly opposed to each other. When it is observed that in 1923 he produced his *Wolkenkuckucksheim*, a *Cloud-Cuckoo-Land* inspired by *The Birds*, we might almost be prepared to describe his dramatic approach as being, in general, essentially Aristophanic, ironically attacking all the intellectual and other follies of his time. At one moment he is launching out against the journalists, at the next he is showing, in *Traum-theater* (*Dream Theatre*, 1924), the follies of the psychoanalysts: some of his pieces are firmly realistic and essentially stageworthy, yet his enormous *Die letzten Tage der Menschheit* (*Mankind's Last Days*, published 1922), a 'tragedy in five acts with a dramatic prologue and epilogue', twists its seemingly interminable, expressionistic, length along beyond even the bounds of *Back to Methuselah*. In France, Gabriel Marcel attracts notice because, both as formal philosopher and as playwright, he is the exponent of an elusive creed, his "existentialisme chrétien", which has much to say about souls wandering about the world in exile. Among his dramas, *Un homme de Dieu* (*A Man of God*, written in 1925 but not produced until 1949), a study of a minister and his wife tortured by doubts and fears concerning their own actions, *Le coeur des autres* (*The Heart of Others*, 1921), a kindred study of an artist's inner being, *Le dard* (*The Sting*, 1938), concentrating its attention upon the souls of a revolutionary and a man who is 'uncommitted', and *Le chemin de Crête* (*Ariadne*, 1953), may be cited as examples of the diverse, yet strangely related, themes with which characteristically he was concerned. Another French playwright stands in a somewhat similar position: Denys Amiel assuredly is gifted with an individual style and with considerable creative power, yet he has failed to give to his writings an enduring force. Perhaps this is due mainly to the fact that he is inclined to harp on only one string, to concern himself with more or less dark studies of strange marital problems and, above all, to cling uninspiringly to the cult of the 'theatre of silence.' *La souriante Madame Beudet* (*The Smiling Mme Beudet*, 1921, written in collaboration with André Obey) and *M. et Mme Un Tel* (*Mr and Mrs So-and-so*, 1925) deal obscurely with hatred and animosity between married couples, while *Le mouton noir* (*The Black Sheep*, 1946) deals with the love of a husband for his stepdaughter.

Plays of such kinds, unless composed with consummate skill, are apt to fall by the wayside.

5

THE COMIC SPIRIT AND SOCIAL UNREST

ALTHOUGH most of the more ambitious authors who devoted their attention to the between-war stage tended to be bitter, over-serious, or hysterical in their denunciations of society's errors, there still were among them some prepared to take a gayer path, and others anxious to laugh even while engaged in their task of castigation.

Laughter Merely

It was primarily for the English stage that Bernard Shaw penned his roguishly witty scenes and for English readers that he wrote his serious prefaces; and it might well have been thought that his influence upon the younger writers of his time would have been widespread. Surprisingly, however, the socially conscious comedy on the whole flourished less freely in London than it did in many other areas—and perhaps this was due to what the present century's comic stage had inherited from the past.

The latter years of the Victorian era had succeeded in producing an interesting kind of comedy-farce, almost completely lacking in social implications, swift-moving in action, with boldly and effectively drawn theatrical characters and, mercifully, without the almost constant stress upon extra-marital adventures which was a preoccupation of Parisian farce. W.S. Gilbert's delightful *Engaged* (1877), Charles Hawtrey's somewhat less distinguished *The Private Secretary* (1883), A. W. Pinero's adroit *The Magistrate* (1895) and *Dandy Dick* (1887) and Brandon Thomas' apparently everlasting *Charley's Aunt* (1892) passed on their styles not only to other later farces, such as *When Knights Were Bold* (1907) by 'Charles Marlowe' (Harriet Jay), but also to many comedies produced during the Edwardian era and later. A. P. Herbert permits but little of any serious concept to intrude into *La Vie Parisienne* (1929), *Tantivy Towers* (1931) and *Derby Day* (1932). When C. K. Munro, St John Ervine and John Drinkwater turn to comedy, they write, respectively, *At Mrs Beam's* (1921), *The First Mrs Fraser* (1929) and *Bird in Hand* (1927)—comedies which are all free of any revolutionary social messages. Among the most successful comedies presented within this period were the bucolic *The Farmer's Wife* (1916) and *Yellow Sands* (1926) by Eden Phillpotts. Even in comedies with more serious plots, such as Frederick Lonsdale's intriguing *The Last of Mrs Cheyney* (1925) and his treatment of trial marriages in *On Approval* (1926), the stress is definitely upon characters and certainly not upon social theories. The same is true of Terence Rattigan's brilliant comic scenes in *French Without Tears* (1936): and, of course, it was within this milieu that the comedies of Noel Coward were brought into being.

Noel Coward may be taken, indeed, as a symbol of twentieth-century English comedy. Although at the beginning of his career he produced a spuriously serious psychological study of a mother and a son, *The Vortex* (1924), and a tense domestic drama, *The Rat Trap* (1924), and although in later years he has sporadically turned to such patriotic efforts as *Cavalcade* (1931), his strength rests in the easy persiflage of his comic style. *The Young Idea* (1922) exhibits this style at its earliest stage; *Hay Fever* (1925) and *Private Lives* (1930) gloriously display it in mature form; its further graces appear in numerous plays up to and beyond *Blithe Spirit* (1941). In these he makes his prime contribution to the comic stage: no doubt many of his scenes exhibit wit, but his characteristic skill lies in his investing with laughter dialogue which, rejecting the epigrams which Wilde made so popular, presents a series of remarks made memorable and amusing either through their inconsequentiality or their counterpointing. Here, for example, are Amanda and Elyot, in *Private Lives* (1930), seated at the dinner-table, she wearing pyjamas, he in "a comfortable dressing-gown":

AMANDA: I'm glad we let Louise go. I am afraid she is going to have a cold.

ELYOT: Going to have a cold; she's been grunting and snorting all the evening like a whole herd of bison.

AMANDA [*thoughtfully*]: Bison never sounds right to me somehow. I have a feeling it ought to be bisons, a flock of bisons.

ELYOT: You might say a covey of bisons, or even a school of bisons.

AMANDA: Yes, lovely. The Royal London School of Bisons. Do you think Louise is happy at home?

ELYOT: No, profoundly miserable.

AMANDA: Family beastly to her?

ELYOT [*with conviction*]: Absolutely vile. Knock her about dreadfully, I expect, make her eat the most disgusting food, and pull her fringe.

AMANDA [*laughing*]: Oh, poor Louise.

ELYOT: Well, you know what the French are.

AMANDA: Oh, yes, indeed. I know what the Hungarians are, too.

ELYOT: What are they?

AMANDA: Very wistful. It's all those Pretzles, I shouldn't wonder.

ELYOT: And the Poostza; I always felt the Poostza was far too big, Danube or no Danube.

AMANDA: Have you ever crossed the Sahara on a camel?

ELYOT: Frequently. When I was a boy we used to do it all the time. My grandmother had a lovely seat on a camel.

AMANDA: There's no doubt about it, foreign travel's the thing.

ELYOT: Would you like some brandy?

AMANDA: Just a little.

So it goes on, with light dalliance. For those who are more animated by a desire to present their political views than to promote the interests of the drama, there is nothing here of any interest, and it is completely futile for the friends of Coward to plead, unconvincingly, that beneath the light brittleness of the dialogue can be found a measure of social criticism. Coward must be taken as he is—a true master in that realm of comedy which exists purely to give us delight.

In Paris a kind of Noel Coward appears in the person of Sacha Guitry, facile creator both of a series of biographical plays (which merit attention later) and of a number of lightly witty comedies—extending from *Nono* (1905), *La prise de Berg-op-Zoom* (*The Taking of Berg-op-Zoom*, 1912) on to *Le nouveau testament* (*Where There's a Will*, or *The New Testament*, 1934) and *Quand jouons-nous la comédie?* (*When do we begin to Play?*, 1935). All these works are of a piece, cleverly turned, skilfully constructed, wholly unbelievable, and for the most part lacking entirely any foundation of thought. As typical as any is *Le veilleur de nuit* (*The Night Watchman*, 1911), in which the author delicately plays on the conventions connected with the eternal triangle and shows a professor who, on discovering that his mistress is being unfaithful to him, acts most magnanimously.

Sacha Guitry's style is crisp and incisive; with him may be considered the skilful and facile but rather puzzling Jacques Deval, creator of *Une faible femme* (*A Weak Woman*, 1920), a study reminiscent of the style of Jean-Jacques Bernard, of *Mademoiselle* (1932), a brilliant portrait of a private teacher, and of *Tovaritch* (1933), an effervescent fantasy which shows the gay Grand Duchess Tatiana and Prince Mikhail Alexandrovitch merrily applying themselves to their domestic duties in the house of the bourgeois M. Dupont.

Invested with a gentler spirit are the light extravaganzas of Léopold Marchand, a writer welcome in the world of modern cynicism, but the cynical reappears in the equally extravagant scenes devised by René Fauchois, such as *Le singe qui parle* (*The Monkey who Talks*, 1924) and *Prenez garde à la peinture* (translated as *The Late Christopher Bean*, 1932), and in the less ambitious but eminently popular farce-comedies of Louis Verneuil.

The Comedy of Manners

With Deval we move close to the spirit of the comedy of manners and to that kind of high comedy where occasionally the very ripple of laughter dies away, where a chastened mood brings serious reflection. In Coward's works even we feel ourselves close to the kind of comedy for which the Restoration dramatists won fame, although when we watch his scenes there is the impression that Congreve's heady port, which can bring moments of reflection as well as of merriment, has been replaced by a carelessly tossed-off cocktail or a glass of champagne.

Nearer to the atmosphere of English Restoration comedy—to Wycherley if not to Congreve—stands Somerset Maugham. Some of his earlier plays, including the popular *East of Suez*, which came in 1922, will almost certainly be forgotten; but with equal certainty he will be remembered for *Our Betters* (1917), *The Circle* (1921), and *The Constant Wife* (1926). Despite the air of easy sophistication that enwraps the action of these plays, their author has succeeded in giving at once a sharp edge to their wit and a penetrating depth to their situations. The basic plot of *Our Betters*, in which an American girl, Elizabeth, turns back to her honest American sweetheart, Fleming Harvey, after she has been shocked by the escapades of her cosmopolitanized sister, Lady George Grayson, is trite: the dialogue, however, possesses a peculiar brilliance and gives to a stock situation a quality of bitterly amusing interest. The same interest attaches to *The Circle*, with its magnificently planned parallelism in structure, and to *The Constant Wife*, with its novel interpretation of that theme so beloved of modern playwrights, the double standard in marriage. Maugham is on safer ground here than when he tries to deal with serious scenes: such a play as *For Services Rendered* (1932) seems sadly exaggerated and melodramatic, indicating that for the successful treatment of potentially 'tragic' material its author's talent is nowise fitted.

Close to Maugham stands Frederick Lonsdale, whose *The Last of Mrs Cheyney* (1925) deservedly is remembered as a skilful exercise in comic antitheses and in slightly acidulous irony. Here, too, may be mentioned J. B. Fagan, skilful applier, in *And So to Bed* (1926), of modern society's facile witticisms to the age of Charles II.

In Italy something of the style of Maugham, modified by memories of Pirandello and insensibly influenced by native comic tradition, appears reflected in the works of several authors. Obviously Pirandellian in concept is the *Il cuore in due* (*The Double Heart*, 1926) of Cesare Giulio Viola, which deals entertainingly with the story of two men, brothers, who collaborate in the writing of novels: together they present a whole and interesting human personality, but separately each is only half of a man. How potent even yet is the long-enduring dialect-theatre tradition is to be seen in the work of Gino Rocca, whose several plays include comedies written both in standard Italian and, more characteristically, in his native Venetian speech, wherein he amply pays tribute to the still-abiding and vital influence of Goldoni. The comedy-drama style is preferred by Giuseppe Lanza, who might perhaps most properly be called the Italian Somerset Maugham. *Esilio* (*Exile*, 1929), with its tale of the sarcastic Conte Enrico Sanfiorenzo, his wife, Marta, and the young writer, Luciano Vergati, might easily be related to the high-comedy forms cultivated by that English writer; something of the same quality pervades *Ritorni* (*Returns*, 1929). Perhaps Lanza's most interesting play is *La buona sementa* (*The Good Seed*, 1934), wherein a wisely observant magistrate, Sademo, penetrates to the secret of the shooting of a man, Ranza, who has been found seriously wounded in the house of his friend Viario. Sademo knows that the person directly responsible is Viario's wife, Irene, yet he succeeds in convincing the husband that ultimately his was the fault. At the end of the drama Viario, under Sademo's influence, is ready to start a new life with Irene, but she rejects his offer, declaring that she must sacrifice the rest of her life to caring for Ranza.

Elsewhere, in Norway, Helge Krog has tried to develop a style of love comedy of his own, a kind of sophisticated modern version of Marivaux. He is much concerned with the ages of his lovers, and takes pains to indicate not merely the diverse shapes that love assumes at different periods in a man's or woman's life, but also the call of one generation to another. This is revealed trenchantly in *Konkylien* (*The Whispering Shell*, 1929), where the heroine is shown at the age of seventeen attracted by the nineteen-year-old Axel; at twenty she is the mistress of Inge, thirty-five years old; at twenty-two she has become the mistress of twenty-six-year-old Gustav; at twenty-three she finds her Axel again (now aged twenty-five): and presumably she will proceed as before. Something of the same pattern is used for *Trekland* (*Triad*, 1933), where Agnete, aged thirty-four and married to the forty-three-year-old Georg, becomes the mistress first of Emile, in his thirties, and later of a young architect. Krog's philosophy, such as it is, is expressed in a scene which shows Georg, Emile, Peter, and Agnete seated at a café table:

EMILE [*drinking deeply*]: The wandering of souls. . . . Do you remember what you said once about the wandering of souls, Agnete? From woman to woman. From man to man. Hop-skip-and-jump. The fable of the three billy-goats. You know that little fable? Well, once upon a time three billy-goats, one ordinary-sized, one big, and one *tremendous*, were crossing a bridge one after the other; the first explained to the hungry giant that met him there, that there was a bigger one coming behind, and so went free. The second did the same. Same result. But when the *third* one came along—why, it simply put down its head, and flattened him out! Your health, Mr Malling!   [*Drinks. PETER does not touch his glass.*

GEORG: Migration of souls. Do you travel in souls, Agnete?

EMILE: Yes, and it's like walking on treacle! The soul sticks; it clings fast. And therefore a man meets many men in every woman, and a woman meets many women in every man. . . . Your health again, Mr Malling!

PETER: And yours! [*Takes just barely a sip from his glass.*] By the way, do you know the story of the boy and the worm?

EMILE [*uninterested*]: The boy and the . . .? No.

PETER: The boy finds a worm and feels sorry for it because it looks so lonely. So he cuts it in two in order that it may have company. Is that clear?

EMILE [*laughing*]: As clear as daylight!

PETER [*slowly and deliberately*]: But there are people who are so deadly afraid of being alone that they cut themselves in two in order to have company.

In Krog's work there appears an able handling of dramatic material and an interesting diversity in treatment—qualities that enable him to deal with situations hovering between the comic and the psychologically serious.

The essays in the comic spirit during the twenties and the thirties have been various, much of them tinged with the tone of cynicism, it is true, yet, perhaps because of that, making definite contributions to the style of the comedy of manners. In Germany, Bruno Frank is perhaps too seriously aroused to permit him to catch the right quality in his *Perlenkomödie* (*Pearl Comedy*, 1928), or *Sturm im Wasserglas* (*Storm in a Teacup*, 1930), but Austria and the eastern lands of Europe still preserved sufficient balance to capture the elusive comic mood. Nostalgically, Stefan Kamare (Cokorac von Kamare) turns back to a gayer Vienna of the past in *Der junge Baron Neuhaus* (*Young Baron Neuhaus*, 1933); a more bitter laughter invests *Die Gartenlaube* (*The Summerhouse*, 1929), by Hermann Ungar. Incisive satire, sometimes moving, as in *Čaroděj z Menlo* (*The Magician of Menlo*, 1934), to angry attack is directed at modern technology by the Czech Edmond Konrád, but neither he nor his companion-playwright, Ivan Stodola, has succeeded in appealing to audiences outside their own land. Slightly more fortunate is the Hungarian Melchior Lengyel, whose early sensational drama *Tájfun* (*Typhoon*) was widely popular between 1910 and 1912; *Antónia* in 1925 brought his name once more before playgoers in several countries; and if the popular film of *Ninotchka* (1939) was not based on one of Lengyel's plays, at least it came from a short story of his composition.

To find a richer manifestation of the spirit of thoughtful comedy, however, we must turn to the American Samuel N. Behrman, a man who, despite the unevenness of his accomplishment, manifestly possesses true dramatic strength. Behrman's great achievement is to have established an American comedy of manners, but, characteristically, that comedy, even when it deals with those upper-class persons amid whom flourish the social conventions out of which this kind of drama grows, is built upon a seriously conceived foundation—so serious, indeed, that sometimes the rocky basis on which his houses are set is permitted to jut through the ballroom floor. He starts his career with *The Second Man* (1927), a comedy-drama showing a successful novelist who, facing a dilemma in his life, elects to take the safe path rather than to essay one which, while perhaps more heroic, might lead him to disaster. Already a social interest is apparent in Behrman's work, and this becomes further marked in *Meteor* (1929), in which the story is told of a man, Raphael Lord, who rises to self-made wealth, fails, is deserted by his friends, and, undaunted, starts on his own to retrieve his fortunes. In *Brief Moment* (1931) we have a study of a wealthy young man who weds a night-club singer precisely because she does not have the manners of his set, and to his dismay finds her, after marriage, imitating badly all the social tricks from which he had hoped to escape. The political world intrudes, in the person of Leander Nolan, into *Biography* (1932), a rather overpraised comedy concentrating upon the character of a woman painter, Marion Froude. If, however, this comedy ranks not quite so high among Behrman's works as some critics were inclined to believe on its first appearance, it does mark a very definite development in the author's work, since it brings into play the quality which was destined to give distinction to all his later works—the weaving into the action of a great deal of philosophical and social discussion. The truth is that Behrman is a man who, gifted with the truly comic view, is puzzled by life and desperately seeks an answer to his puzzlement. Like all those gifted (or cursed) by the comic mood, he sees that man has made a stupid mess of his existence, and yet, at the same time, he realizes that recognition of man's follies is not enough, since besides folly there is evil, and evil must be combated.

We can follow this progress of thought in Behrman through *Rain from Heaven* (1934)—a play which is really an essay in political discussion —and *End of Summer* (1936)—wherein the opportunistic doctor is contrasted with the honest, socialistic, poverty-stricken young novelist—on to *Wine of Choice* (1938) and the characteristically titled *No Time for Comedy* (1939), wherein the author almost pathetically displays his own realization of the dilemma in which he is placed: his talent is a talent for comedy, yet there are things in the world so dark and menacing that he would fain take sword in hand to fight them. Behrman's provisional answer, in *The Talley Method* (1941), was not successful: the attempt made here to identify discipline and Fascism failed precisely because Fascism and discipline, contrary to his philosophy, lie poles apart. In *Jacobowsky and the Colonel* (1944), he suggests that he is on the way towards finding a satisfactory compromise, whereby the content of his work may be harmonized with the style of which he is a master. True, we may with justice complain that the subject-matter of his play (based on a piece by Franz Werfel) is no matter for laughter: but, if we can succeed in separating the worlds of reality and of the theatre, we may well agree that *Jacobowsky and the Colonel* is one of the most adroit and delightful comedies of modern times. Unfortunately his last play, *But For Whom Charlie* (1964), proved disappointing on the stage because its general structure lacked strength, balance and an ability to convince: but even here the author's innate brilliance shone brightly through in his dramatic portrait of the eternal postgraduate scholar who, without being able or willing to accomplish anything, pursues an easy existence supported by a succession of 'Foundation' grants.

Social Comedy

Behrman's interest in social conditions is thoroughly symbolic of the American stage. His fellow-authors can, on occasion, turn out farcical comedies which aim at no more than the arousing of thoughtless laughter. Thus J. C. Holm and George Abbott, in *Three Men on a Horse* (1935), present their delightfully impossible and mirth-moving story of a timid little non-betting clerk who discovers in himself the power of correctly guessing the winners on the racecourse. This is a successor to the record-breaking *Abie's Irish Rose* (1922) of Anne Nichols and a partner to the hilarious presentation of Hollywood's absurdities in *Boy Meets Girl* (1935) by Bella and Samuel Spewack. Here the typical American crackle of fantastic laughter is to be seen at its most typical. The story-writers are in conference with a film producer:

> *BENSON* [*crosses back to desk; sighs; indicates script*]: You were saying that this is one of the greatest picture scrips ever written.
>
> *C.F.* [*with a superior smile*]: Now, just a minute—
>
> *LAW* [*quickly*]: And do you know why? Because it's the same story Larry Toms has been doing for years.
>
> *BENSON:* We *know* it's good.
>
> *LAW:* Griffith used it. Lubitsch used it. And Eisenstein's coming around to it.
>
> *BENSON:* Boy meets girl. Boy loses girl. Boy gets girl.
>
> *LAW:* The great American fairy-tale. Sends the audience back to the relief rolls in a happy frame of mind.
>
> *BENSON:* And why not?
>
> *LAW:* The greatest escape formula ever worked out in the history of civilization. . . .
>
> *C.F.:* Of course, if you put it that way . . . but, boys, it's hackneyed.
>
> *LAW:* You mean classic.
>
> *C.F.* [*triumphantly*]: *Hamlet* is a classic—but it isn't hackneyed!
>
> *LAW: Hamlet* isn't hackneyed? Why, I'd be ashamed to use that poison gag. He lifted that right out of the Italians. [*PEGGY enters and crosses to her chair and sits.*] Ask Peggy.
>
> > *PEGGY puts the bowl now half filled with water down on the desk.*
>
> *BENSON:* Yes, let's ask Peggy . . . if she wants to see Larry Toms in a different story. She's your audience.
>
> *PEGGY:* Don't ask me anything, Mr Benson. I've got the damnedest toothache. [*She takes C.F.'s hand and looks up at him suddenly.*] Relax!
>
> > [*She begins filing.*
>
> *BENSON* [*wheedling*]: But, Peggy, you go to pictures, don't you?
>
> *PEGGY:* No.
>
> *BENSON:* But you've seen Larry's pictures and enjoyed them?
>
> *PEGGY:* No.
>
> *BENSON:* . . . As millions of others have . . .
>
> *LAW:* Why, one man sent him a rope all the way from Manila—with instructions.
>
> *C.F.:* Boys, this isn't getting us anywhere.

In many of these comedy-farces, however, even in *Boy Meets Girl*, an underlying social purpose is apparent. What on the surface seems nothing but gaiety reveals on examination a kind of crude philosophy—at times, perhaps, a concealed bitterness. A single example will illustrate this clearly. In 1936 Moss Hart and George S. Kaufman collaborated in producing *You Can't Take It with You.* Outwardly this is a piece penned according to early recipes and well flavoured with just such indigenous exaggeration as had animated the plays of American popular comedians, like Edward Harrigan, more than half a century previously. *You Can't Take It with You* is, however, not a simple farce. No doubt it exists primarily for the purpose of arousing laughter; no doubt the aim of its creators was to win immediate popular success. Nevertheless the action of this crazy comedy has a purpose, and that purpose is definitely drawn to our attention in the title. There is almost as much 'philosophy' here as in any of the solemnly serious melodramas produced by the Theatre Union.

Nor is *You Can't Take It with You* an aberration on the part of Kaufman and Hart. This pair of writers, either in collaboration with each other or separately in collaboration with others, have made the New York stage gay with many another merry piece in which the sense of fun is associated with social or political satire. *Once in a Lifetime* (1930) turns the spotlight on Hollywood just at the time when that city of silent lots was fluttered by the sudden irruption of sound. How basically serious are the two authors appears in the fact that within a few years of the writing of this joyous onslaught on the films they joined in composing *Merrily We Roll Along* (1934), a play in which a story with a goodly message is told backward. As the curtain rises we find ourselves at a party given by a successful playwright, who, despite his success, is seen by his friends to have sacrificed integrity for the sake of money. Having thus set the scene, Kaufman and Hart carry us back seven years to 1927, and so by a series of reverse chronological steps we end in 1916 and listen to the future playwright as he stands delivering the valedictory address in the chapel of his college, and ending with the words—"This above all, to thine own self be true."

The spirit in which this drama is written must be borne in mind when we turn to those musical burlesques *Of Thee I Sing* (1931; by Kaufman and Morrie Ryskind) and *I'd Rather be Right* (1937), which were among the most original contributions of the New York stage during the thirties. Taking a suggestion from Gilbert and Sullivan and applying the style of burlesque musical comedy to contemporary politics, the authors here present a parody of the life of their time. In *Of Thee I Sing*—the title being taken from the well-known patriotic anthem—John P. Wintergreen is hustled into the Presidency through his slogan, "Love is sweeping the Country." His excesses, however, are discovered, and he is on the point of being impeached when it is learned that Mrs Wintergreen is about to have a baby; on the basis of the slogan that "Posterity is just around the corner," Congress permits them to remain in the White House. In *I'd Rather be Right* Phil Barker meets Roosevelt in Central Park and puts to him his dilemma: he cannot marry Mary Jones unless he gets an increase in salary; he cannot get that increase in salary until his employer's business gets better; the business cannot get better unless the country's budget is balanced. Roosevelt is touched and convinced: he goes off determined to balance his budget so that Phil and Mary may wed.

In the collaboration of Kaufman and Hart we have the modern American counterpart of the seventeenth-century collaboration of Beaumont and Fletcher, and the facts that they are both so thoroughly identified with the ordinary commercial playhouse, that they are so obviously in harmony with each other, and that beneath their outward merriment courses such a clear current of serious purpose make their works of considerable historical importance. To the writings mentioned above should be added two (quite diversely styled) 'dinner' comedies—the satirically serious *Dinner at Eight* (1932), by Kaufman and Edna Ferber, and the wickedly hilarious *The Man Who Came to Dinner* (1939), by the familiar partners.

Something of the same current flows through dozens of other American comedies and farces, variously displaying itself, for example, in *Having Wonderful Time* (1937), by Arthur Kober, a comedy-drama of life in Camp Care-Free, or in *The Pursuit of Happiness* (1933), by Lawrence Langner and Arminia Marshall, which, though set in Revolutionary times, has obvious contemporary implications. As characteristic as any is the long series of comedies contributed by Rachel Crothers, from *The Three of Us* (1906) to *Susan and God* (1937).

Another style of American realistic comedy displays its interest in the social scene in a diverse manner. From the time when Ben Hecht and Charles MacArthur won resounding success for their noisy, quick-tempo *The Front Page* (1928) to the appearance of *The Women* (1936), by Clare Boothe, the American theatre has developed one peculiar kind of drama of its own—a kind wherein sensational scenes are scrambled up with scenes of raucous laughter, wherein the actions and the characters are given a spurious air of naturalistic authenticity, and wherein vituperative rudeness of phrase is substituted for wit. Although we may readily conceive that journalists testify to the exactitude with which *The Front Page* reproduces American newspaper life and that Clare Boothe has faithfully recorded the conversation of the ladies' retiring-room in *The Women*, both of these thoroughly typical plays are to be seen, on examination, as conceived in terms of modern melodrama. How true this is becomes apparent when we see Clare Boothe, after the incivilities of *Kiss the Boys Good-bye* (1938), turning to write her anti-Nazi thriller, *Margin for Error* (1939).

These plays, while they may contain matter fit for satire, are not created in the true satiric mood. For that bitter ingredient we must turn to France. There, for example, Marcel Pagnol is coldly enflamed to use laughter for purposes wholly satiric. His first success, written in collaboration with Paul Nivoix, was a bitter attack on war profiteers, *Les marchands de gloire* (*The Merchants of Glory*, 1925), in which an ambitious father is shown in dismay when his soldier son, supposed dead, returns; for the sake of his own career, largely based on the esteem given to the 'dead' hero, he persuades the youth to remain unknown and to live under another name. *Jazz* (1926), ironically vivacious, sufficiently indicates its theme by its very title. In *Topaze* (1928) the charlatanism of the world of modern finance is revealed; disillusionment colours the depiction of the ironically conceived action in the later *Marius* (1929), *Fanny* (1931), and *César* (1936) where Pagnol uses his art to depict a section of Marseilles life.

Satirical purpose of an equally bitter sort inspires Édouard Bourdet, a purpose so bitter that his comedies often have the flavour of tragedy. He started his career with a cheerless love tale, *L'heure de berger* (*The Gloaming*, 1922), and four years later won international fame, or notoriety, for *La prisonnière* (*The Prisoner*, 1926), a study of homosexuality in which a heroine is shown powerless to escape from the chains of her unnatural passion. Since then he has devoted himself mainly to the darkly comic exposure of society's errors: true, his last piece, *Hyménée* (1944), deals almost entirely with a love theme, but this is in marked contrast to his more typical writings—*Le sexe faible* (*The Gentler Sex*, 1929), *Les temps difficiles* (*The Difficult Years*, 1934), and *Fric-frac* (1936). We cannot claim this author as a great artist: on the other hand, his keen eye—particularly for things on the darker side of life—and his unquestionably skilled hand merit our giving him at least a measure of attention.

Grotesque Comedy

At a pole diametrically opposed to such comedies as endeavour to hold the mirror rudely before society's unmade-up face there are others, equally characteristic of these our times, which thrive in the realms of the fantastic and eagerly seek for the grotesque.

In France a kind of link between the two kinds appears in the brilliant comic essays of Alfred Savoir, witty, mordant, with concealed barbs underneath their cloak of hilarious laughter. Most characteristic and interesting among his works is the series of allegorical farces which he penned towards the close of his career—notably *La huitième femme de Barbe-Bleue* (*Bluebeard's Eighth Wife*, 1921) and *Le dompteur, ou l'anglais tel qu'on mange* (*The Lion-tamer; or, English as it is Eaten*, 1925), wherein an English lord goes round with a circus, always hoping that he will see the lions eat their trainer; it is he himself who in the end is eaten. The trainer is, of course, the symbol of Fascist tyranny; the English lord is the image of philosophic liberalism.

The circus atmosphere, treated more sentimentally and with no political connotations, appears also in the first play, *Voulez-vous jouer avec moâ?* (*Will You Play with Me?*, 1923), in which Marcel Achard came to public attention. This study of three clowns and a poet possesses a peculiar limpidity and sensitiveness in character presentation and adumbrates the style which reached fruition in *Jean de la Lune* (1929), a study of touching faith, with Jean de la Lune absolutely devoted to his Marceline, even although she tricks him continually, and eventually arousing her admiration. The same qualities—of delicate poetic fantasy and a delineation of sentiment that ever hovers on the border of the sentimental without crossing that treacherous boundary—are carried on in *La belle marinière* (*The Pretty Barge Girl*, 1929), with its memorable heroine, and in *Domino* (1931), a fanciful picture of the world of roués. *Le corsaire* (*The Pirate*, 1938) introduces something different: partly this play is a satiric comedy directed at Hollywood; partly it is an imaginative, almost Barrie-esque fantasy of a pirate's love for a girl he has captured and of the repetition of that love when the pirate's story is being made into a film. Achard loves to play with time in his comedies, and in this manner his later play, *Auprès de ma blonde* (*Beside My Blonde*, 1945), is thoroughly characteristic—a comedy of marriage which starts in the old age of the present and moves back to the youth of sweetheart days.

Satirical extravaganza of a more bitter sort appears in the work of Bernard Zimmer, notably in *Bava l'Africain* (1926), in which a little clerk with dreams succeeds in persuading the world that he is a great explorer; the fairy-tale takes theatrical form in the fantasies of Alexandre Arnoux, of whose writing *Petite Lumière et l'ourse* (1924) and *Huon de Bordeaux* (1922) are perhaps most characteristic; in the plays of Jean Giono, such as *Lanceurs de graines* (*The Sowers*, 1932) and *Le bout de la route* (*Journey's End*, 1941), a poetic mood enwraps all the action—the former presenting a contrast between true love of nature and the desire to exploit nature, and the latter treating with strange and appealing delicacy a simple story of the heart.

Among the writers who have most powerfully contributed to this style of drama is the Scots James Bridie (O. H. Mavor), an author who, although by no means all his works are comedies, clearly demands attention here, since even his most gruesome scenes are inspired rather by the comic than by the tragic muse. Although he has not succeeded in producing any single play to mark him out for secure fame, the totality of his writings are such as to make him the one modern British dramatist who merits a place close to that of Shaw. He has, like Shaw, a deep foundation of philosophical (rather than social) purport, which gives both a firmness and an interest to his dramas, and he shares in Shaw's sense of fun. What prevents his plays from having attained a greater position than they at present occupy is a tendency, apparent in almost all, to bring a promising action to an inconclusive end: we almost have the impression that his mind is so alert, his spirit so inventive, that before one theme has been completed another has sprung into being in the author's vivid imagination, and that, as a result, he would fain be off from the old, before the old is done with, to the new.

Starting, obscurely, with farcical fantasy, light laughter and 'problem' comedy, he came before the large general public in 1931 with a grim drama, *The Anatomist*, telling of Edinburgh body-snatchers engaged in their dark task at a time when the law prevented medical workers from obtaining the bodies they required for their training and experiments. From this he moved to *Tobias and the Angel* (1931), followed by *Jonah and the Whale* (1932), and it was immediately apparent that in these plays he had found the proper medium for his genius. The Biblical stories and atmosphere permitted him to introduce an element of the philosophic; the fantastic quality of both the tales accorded with his own love of the extravagant; while the contrast between the ancient world inhabited by his characters and the modern implications of their adventures offered full scope for the exercise of his own peculiar style in comedy.

In *A Sleeping Clergyman* (1933) Bridie returns, in a way, to the mood of *The Anatomist*, essaying the difficult task of demonstrating the close connexion of genius and criminality in the human soul. This he does by opening the action with a brilliantly sordid scene in which a poverty-stricken medical student, gifted with a vision beyond that of his age, but at the same time utterly without any ordinary sense of moral values, is shown dying of tuberculosis. He leaves behind him an illegitimate daughter, who inherits only the criminal side of his nature, but she is succeeded in her turn by twins, a man and a woman, in whom the vision is renewed and who succeed in saving the world from the menace of a new plague. Except for the final scenes set in the future—and scenes placed in the future hardly ever can be made convincing in the theatre—this play deserves to be regarded as one of the boldest, most satisfying, and most powerfully conceived dramas of that time.

When we consider the scenes of *Tobias and the Angel* along with those of *A Sleeping Clergyman* we obtain a measure of Bridie's wide dramatic range. In the former he can let his fancy play lightly with the episodes of the journey undertaken by the timorous young Tobias and his guide, Raphael in disguise. The latter has encouraged the boy to use his own initiative in killing a great monster of a mud-fish and has further incited him into outfacing a Kurdish bandit. Tobias boasts of what he has done to the fish. "And," he adds,

> what I did to that atrocious, fire-breathing river demon I shall do to you, you hairy-toed polecat, you son of a burnt father, for I am only beginning the carnage I feel I must make before sunset.
> *THE BANDIT:* Who are you, my lord?
> *TOBIAS:* I am Suleiman-ibn-Daoud, and this is one of my Afreets.

The bandit slinks off, and, left alone, Tobias turns exultantly to Raphael:

> *TOBIAS:* I certainly seemed to be able to speak up to that bandit once I got started. I told him off properly, I think. The words seemed to come, somehow. I heard them at the jetty, but I hoped I had forgotten them. And I did very well with the fish too, didn't I?
> *RAPHAEL:* Yes. But there was no need to lie to the bandit.
> *TOBIAS:* I didn't lie to him.
> *RAPHAEL:* You did. Your story of the fish I forgive you. Everybody exaggerates about fish. But you said you were Solomon. That is very far from being true.
> *TOBIAS:* I didn't know what I was saying. I was excited. I wish I weren't such a coward. . . . I was right in one thing I said to the bandit.
> *RAPHAEL:* What was that?
> *TOBIAS:* I said you were an old Afreet. So you are.
> *RAPHAEL:* There are no such things as Afreets. Come along.

This scene has but to be compared with the terrible and powerful opening episode of *A Sleeping Clergyman* for a realization of the ample stops in

Bridie's organ. The tubercular genius Cameron is lying near death in his wretched Glasgow lodgings, and with conscious irony he makes a promise to marry a girl, Harriet, whom he has got with child. Harriet goes, and Cameron is left alone:

> Most touching. Most affecting. What memories to weep over, my dear, twenty years ahead. Your miserable, begrutten face! And now I'm going to die. I've bilked you, you bitch.

His landlady comes in and threatens to send him away:

> You'll go out of here to-morrow, so you will. How I'll ever let this room again, I'm sure I don't know. A perfect pigsty. I'm sure I don't know what sort of home you come out of. And that young lady, too, that I was in the house of the day she was born. I little knew, I've kept myself decent and my premises decent till the black burning day you came, Mister Cameron. Never mind. Out you go to-morrow's morning. And you'll pay for the carpet, and the clock you broke, and the holes in the mantelshelf you burned with your pipe, and the antimacassar you tore. You'll pay. And you needna pretend to be asleep. You know as well as I do . . . as I do . . . Jesus, Mary, and Joseph. He's dead.

From the thirties onward Bridie contributed many plays of diverse kinds to the stage. Among them may particularly be mentioned *The King of Nowhere* (1938), a comedy in which a study of insanity is combined with an analysis of the Fascist mentality, and *Mr Bolfry* (1943), a delightful essay in the fantastic, wherein the devil is charmed up from the nether regions in the likeness of a Protestant minister. Laughter and philosophic purpose meet in both of these, and in their combination amply testify to the originality of talent and to the technical skill of their author.

Allowing for the vast differences in intellectual climate, the mood out of which these plays are built may be related to that inspiring Ferenc Molnár, the dramatist who stands most clearly as the theatrical representative of his native Hungary. He too has his serious pieces; he too succeeds best when laughter and fantasy meet. One of his first works was *Az Ördög* (*The Devil*, 1907), in which the satanic agent appears garbed as a man of the world, while the play on which the author's fame principally rests, *Liliom* (1909), exists in the main for the sake of the scene in heaven when the hero, an unsuccessful waif who has committed suicide, is arraigned before a higher court. Pathos rules here, and some others of Molnár's dramas are tragically or philosophically conceived—witness the symbolic *A vörös malom* (*The Red Mill*, 1923), the characters of which are God, Lucifer, and a perfect human being, and *Az üvegcipö* (*The Glass Slipper*, 1924), in which fantasy of a sentimental sort enriches an outwardly realistic action. Usually, however, at its finest Molnár's talent, like Bridie's, finds itself oscillating between philosophic seriousness and incisive wit. In *A testör* (*The Guardsman*, 1910) laughter triumphs in the plot devised by a jealous husband to test his wife, the curtain ironically falling at the end on a man thoroughly baffled by woman's wit. *A hattyú* (*The Swan*, 1914) pursues a skilful way between ironic comedy and sentiment, telling the story of a princess who, falling in love with her tutor, decides to remain a swan majestically floating on her own watery element rather than step in awkward manner on to common ground:

> *DOMINICA:* I fancy he has had enough. But I shall kiss . . . your daughter.
> *ALEXANDRA:* Dear Aunt . . . if you deem me worthy . . .
> *DOMINICA:* Entirely, my dear daughter, with only this suggestion: that you remember now and again that your sainted father used to call you his swan. Think often of what it means to be a swan . . . gliding proudly . . . majestically . . . where the moon gleams on the mirror of the water . . . gliding always in that purple radiance . . . and never coming ashore. For when a swan walks, my daughter . . . when she waddles up the bank . . . then she painfully resembles another bird.
> *ALEXANDRA* [*softly ironical at her own expense*]: A goose?
> *DOMINICA:* Almost, my girl. Natural history teaches that the swan is nothing but an aristocratic duck. That is why she must stay on the mirror of the water. She is a bird, but she may never fly. She knows a song, but she may never sing until she is about to die. Yes, dear, glide on the water . . . head high . . . stately silence . . . and the song—never! [*There is a pause.*
> *CÆSAR* [*entering at right*]: Breakfast is served.

Úri-divat (*Fashions for Men*, 1914) is an ironic comedy of a hero, Peter, who acts with magnanimity when his wife runs away. His reputation for saintliness, however, brings its own rewards, and his business is shown prospering mightily from the esteem he has won for himself. The general mood which had led the author on the one hand to the gay cynicism of *The Guardsman* and on the other to the fantasy of *Liliom* finds final expression in *Játék a kastélyban* (*The Play's the Thing*, or *The Play in the Castle*, 1926). In this last piece we are, indeed, almost completing the circle and returning to Pirandello. Albert Adam, the young fiancé of the actress Ilona Szabo, by chance overhears her making love to another man, whereupon one of his friends, a dramatist, hastily concocts a one-act play in the dialogue of which the overheard words are included. The result is that when he listens to the rehearsal of this piece Albert is happily convinced that the love-scene was fictional, not real, and thus for him the imaginary becomes the actual.

The spirit of the grotesque is to be widely traced during these between-war years. From Germany Carl Zuckmayer brings, besides his fantastic *Der Schelm von Bergen* (*The Rascal from Bergen*, 1934) and his rustic comedy, *Der fröhliche Weinberg* (*The Joyous Vineyard*, 1925), an excellent satire, *Der Hauptmann von Koepenick* (*The Captain of Koepenick*, 1931), which aptly takes off the pretensions of the old German Junker class. Zuckmayer was among those few German playwrights who succeeded in returning to the stage after the end of the War, but his post-war dramas, not surprisingly, are grimly serious, not grotesquely comic. In Spain, alongside comic dramatists such as Pedro Muñoz Seca and Enrique Suárez de Dezo, who follow more realistic methods, the fantastic appears in diverse quarters. Among writers in this style Carlos Arniches and Ramón del Valle-Inclán deserve particular mention, the former because of the verve with which he presents his extraordinary situations and eccentric characters, and the latter for his 'comedias bárbaras' and for the other poetically conceived dramas that spring from their spirit. In the work of Ramón del Valle-Inclán appears in an extreme form that love of the fantastic, that fascination for the man or woman whose personality deviates from the commonplace, and that tendency towards the introduction of a lyrical quality into the treatment of the action which may be found expressed in diverse ways on the Spanish stage. Whether we look at the almost wholly 'literary' *Cara de plata* (*Face of Silver*, 1923) or at the fantastic *Farsa y licencia de la reina castiza* (*The Farce of the True Spanish Queen*, 1920) these qualities are amply apparent.

With this variety of kindred works before us, from countries as far removed from each other as Scotland and Spain, we cannot escape the conclusion that in the comic grotesque (as opposed to Victor Hugo's tragic grotesque) there lies a quality apt to appeal to, and well calculated to express, the spirit of our age.

6

THE VOGUE OF THE HISTORICAL PLAY

LOGICALLY it is incorrect to set a discussion of the historical drama in juxtaposition to discussions of such dramatic styles as impressionism and expressionism or of such forms as comedy. Historical subject-matter may be, and has been, used for a diversity of purposes: the poets have found therein opportunities for the revealing of their imaginative concepts; some authors have employed historical themes for the exercise of psychoanalysis; there are historical comedies, tragedies, and problem plays.

At the same time the vogue of the historical drama during the between-war years is so marked that it positively demands independent examination: exhibiting itself in all lands, it forms one of the chief trends in the twentieth-century theatre and testifies to the fervent seeking on the part of our contemporaries for comfort or for help in the past. This trend is potent no matter what political systems or social conventions the countries concerned may have. With the historical play in France, Britain, America, we are familiar: equally widespread has been the invocation of former times in Soviet lands. The long series of Russian dramas dealing with the revolutionary years were already 'historical plays' when they appeared in the late twenties and early thirties: Trenev takes an eighteenth-century theme for *Pugachevshchina* (*The Pugachov Rebellion*, 1925), Alexander Evdokimovich Korneichuk, whose *Gibel eskadri* (*The Sinking of the Squadron*, 1934) had dealt with the scuttling of the Black Sea fleet in 1918, goes a century earlier for the plot of his *Bogdan Khmelnitski* (1939), and numerous other authors similarly explore episodes of bygone times.

The prevalence of this almost universal interest, therefore, justifies our considering the historical drama by itself, although, in doing so, we must remember that in the examination of impressionism, expressionism, comedy, and the like we have already covered part of the field. Several of Bridie's plays and of Sherwood's, for example, seek their plots in recorded history, and even such a composition as *And so to Bed* is an historical comedy.

The Historical Play in France

The fortunes of this type of drama in France are typical, clearly revealing that which is most significant in the modern development of the form—its sudden departure from a generally misty and often 'escapist' handling of colourful material, and the evident endeavour of the authors to bring their selected actions into association with the events of to-day. A new note is struck here, a note different from that which Schiller and his followers made resonant.

Take, for example, the *Elizabeth, la femme sans homme* (*Elizabeth, the Woman without a Husband*, 1935), by André Josset, wherein, as it were, the psychoanalyst's piercing eye is turned on the Queen's escapades with her Essex. By leaving out the novel trappings and cutting down on the familiar doublet and hose, Josset succeeds in isolating his characters and giving them human proportions. The theme of Elizabeth and Essex has been put upon the stage many times, but rarely with such vigour. Although the same author's *Les Borgia, étrange famille* (*The Borgias, a Strange Family*, 1938) hardly captures the intensity of his *Elizabeth*, there is no doubt but that, even if for this one play alone, Josset is a dramatist worthy of our attention.

Something of a quality different in kind yet akin in virtue appears in the *Napoléon unique* (*The One and Only Napoleon*, 1936), by Paul Raynal, an author already noted in another connexion. Here too the supernumeraries are all dismissed, and attention is focused on the Emperor and his Joséphine. Action disappears; two souls are drawn out of the past, and are revealed to us with dazzling and even disconcerting clarity.

Into this realm the Belgian Herman Closson brings a spirit of daring, of adventure, of joyous quest, and at the same time of satire. His *Godefroid de Bouillon* (1933) and *Les quatre fils Aymon* (*The Four Sons of Aymon*, 1941) stand out among other works of the kind for their colour, their vivacity, and their wit. Another play by this author is a picture of Elizabethan life —*Shakespeare ou la comédie de l'aventure* (*Shakespeare; or, The Comedy of Adventure*, 1938).

In this particular style no writer has achieved more during recent years than François Porché. His earlier pieces are unimportant, but when we come to *Un roi, deux dames et un valet* (*A King, Two Ladies, and a Valet*), in 1934, we recognize that we are in the presence of a play to be remembered. The King (Louis XIV) is kept off stage during the entire action, and the focus is upon Madame de Maintenon, Madame de Montespan, and the valet Bontemps. Under the most delicate Court polish, emotions struggle to be given birth; indeed, the tension of the drama comes from the manner in which Porché has secured a kind of ironic counterpoint between the artificial manners of Louis' entourage and the passions concealed under flowered brocades and impeccable courtesies. The same treatment gives distinction to his *La vierge au grand cœur* (*The Great-hearted Maid*, 1925), wherein his choice of a theme already well familiar to the stage—that of Jeanne d'Arc—is justified by the imaginative penetration into the inner emotions of the heroine. Another notable piece is his *Le lever du soleil* (*Sunrise*, 1946), written in collaboration with Mme Simone.

From dozens of hands the Parisian stage has been supplied with works of this kind. The plays of Romain Rolland, almost all historical in subject-matter and, for preference, dealing with the period of the French Revolution, extend from a *Danton* of 1901 to *Le jeu de l'amour et de la mort* (*The Play of Love and Death*) in 1925. The general trend of this author to make his subject-matter serve symbolic purposes is shown clearly when we compare his historical pieces with the strange farrago of imaginative-type characters who inhabit his satirical extravaganza *Liluli* (1919). Sacha Guitry interrupts his series of comedies to produce *Deburau* (1918), *Pasteur* (1919), *Béranger* (1920), and *Mozart* (1925), just as Édouard Bourdet varies his satirical career by dealing, in *Margot* (1935), with the reign of Henri III, as Jean Sarment casts in among his other plays a *Madame Quinze* (1935), and as Jules Supervielle presents us with his *Bolivar* (1936). With these authors may be mentioned Paul Demasy, on account of his series of Biblical and classically inspired dramas—of which *Dalilah* (1926) and *La tragédie d'Alexandre* (*The Tragedy of Alexander*, revised version 1931) are the most important.

One principal interest for these dramatists in themes taken from the past lies, of course, in the manner through which comment on the present day may be made through the choice of subject-matter from past ages, and for some there is the added incentive which comes from realization that only through the handling of a 'distanced' story can there be even a hope of approaching the quality of tragedy. It is obvious, therefore, that the same motives which lead some authors to select actual historical events will induce others to turn to ancient legend. Realizing this, we may well feel justified in associating with the authors mentioned above the name of that playwright who has so distinguished himself for his treatment of the legendary, and who, in the end, will perhaps be recognized as the greatest French dramatic writer of the thirties—Jean Giraudoux.

Giraudoux' plays have taken diverse forms. In 1928 he first appeared before the public with a strange allegorical drama called *Siegfried*, in which he tells the story of a wounded French soldier who, rescued by a German woman and on his recovery utterly forgetful of his former life, so identifies himself with his new country that he becomes a prominent leader in a reviving Reich. Such a theme, however, obviously does not offer to this author the scope best calculated to bring forth his talents: that scope is seen immediately we turn from his first play to his second, *Amphitryon 38* (1929). Since then he has contributed to the stage numerous dramas, among which may be mentioned *Judith* (1931), *Intermezzo* (1933), *La Guerre de Troie n'aura pas lieu* (*The Trojan War will not Take Place*, 1935), *Électre* (1937), *L'impromptu de Paris* (1937), *Cantique des cantiques* (*Song of Songs*, 1938), *Sodome et Gomorrhe* (1943), and *La folle de Chaillot* (*The Madwoman of Chaillot*, 1945). Varied as these are, from the artificial

comedy of *Amphitryon 38* to the essay in theatrical imagination that
appears in *L'impromptu de Paris*, from the bitter reflection of *La Guerre de
Troie n'aura pas lieu* to the tragic sentiment of *Électre*, there runs through
all a single though complex strain, composed of a precise and penetrating intellectualism and a richly poetic emotion. The range of his
work can perhaps best be appreciated by taking in conjunction those two
plays of his that are based on classic legend—*Amphitryon 38* and *Électre*.

In the former Giraudoux takes the myth which has so often seized
upon the imagination of playwrights in the past; this version of his he believes must be the thirty-eighth treatment of the theme—hence the title
of his piece—and to it he brings both a graciously piercing wit and a fine
sense of character values. Anyone who saw the brilliant original performance of this play, in which the acting, direction, and décor were all
harmonious with the dramatist's purpose, will agree that *Amphitryon 38*
has been but ill-served by its production in English. The adaptation was
one of S. N. Behrman's less inspired efforts, and on the stage the heavy-
handed treatment of the action, for which presumably Alfred Lunt and
Lynn Fontanne must share the blame, somewhat dissipated the peculiar
grace investing the French scenes. Something very delicate and exquisite
in its proportions was here brought to earth and vulgarized.

From the comic action of this play we move to the tragic of *Électre*,
which, besides the time-honoured characters of the ancient story, introduces a number of persons of Giraudoux' own invention. The mood of
the play is well suggested at the very start when a Stranger (Oreste)
enters escorted by three little girls, the young Eumenides, and meets the
Gardener of the palace:

FIRST LITTLE GIRL: How handsome the gardener's looking!
SECOND LITTLE GIRL: Why not? He's to be married to-day.
THIRD LITTLE GIRL: There it is, sir, your palace of Agamemnon!
THE STRANGER: A curious façade! . . . Isn't it out of balance?
FIRST LITTLE GIRL: No. The right wing isn't there. You think you see it,
   but it's just a mirage. It's like the gardener who comes here to speak to you.
   He doesn't come. He can't say a word.
SECOND LITTLE GIRL: He'll just bray or mew.
THE GARDENER: The façade is in balance, sir. Don't pay any attention to
   these little liars. What cheats the eye is the fact that the right wing is built of
   stones from Gaul that sweat during certain periods of the year. The villagers
   say then that the palace is weeping. The left wing is made of Argive marble
   which—no one knows why—sometimes shines of a sudden, even at night.
   When that happens they say that the palace is laughing. What's happening
   now is that the palace is laughing and crying at the same time.

As they talk the little girls demand leave to act a piece of their own:

FIRST LITTLE GIRL: Are we to act or not?
THE STRANGER: Let them act their piece, gardener:
FIRST LITTLE GIRL: We shall act Clytemnestra, mother of Electra. Are
   you ready for Clytemnestra?

SECOND LITTLE GIRL: We're ready.

FIRST LITTLE GIRL: Queen Clytemnestra has a bad complexion. *She puts rouge on her face.*

SECOND LITTLE GIRL: She has a bad complexion because she sleeps badly.

THIRD LITTLE GIRL: She sleeps badly because she's afraid.

FIRST LITTLE GIRL: Of what is Queen Clytemnestra afraid?

SECOND LITTLE GIRL: Of everything.

FIRST LITTLE GIRL: What is everything?

SECOND LITTLE GIRL: The silence. The silences.

THIRD LITTLE GIRL: The noise. The noises.

FIRST LITTLE GIRL: The idea that midnight is coming. That the spider on his web is about to move from the part of the day which brings happiness to that which brings misfortune.

SECOND LITTLE GIRL: Everything is red because it is blood.

FIRST LITTLE GIRL: Queen Clytemnestra has a bad complexion. *She puts blood on her face.*

THE GARDENER: What stupid stories!

SECOND LITTLE GIRL: It's very nice, isn't it?

FIRST LITTLE GIRL: The way we catch up the end with the beginning, it couldn't be more poetic, could it?

The play develops as a tense study of a woman's hate for a woman, told in a series of passionate scenes, of which, in particular, the conversation of Oreste and Électre in the first act and the confrontation of Égisthe by Électre in the second reach a height of true tragic utterance. As the plot develops the Eumenides grow from children to womanhood, while the theme of the action is symbolically revealed in the speeches of the Beggar, a kind of one-man chorus. In choosing the legend of Electra Giraudoux dared boldly, and his daring has been justified.

Werfel and Others

Emotions and artistic needs not dissimilar seem to have driven the Austrian Franz Werfel to the writing of historical plays. Better known, perhaps, as a novelist, he has still devoted considerable time to the theatre, where he has veered from experiments in poetic drama to attempts in the direction of revitalizing bygone ages.

Towards the beginning of his career he was caught up in the expressionistic movement, and under this influence produced a fairy romance entitled *Die Mittagsgöttin* (*The Goddess of Noon*, 1919) and a nobly ambitious but rather boring work entitled *Der Spiegelmensch* (*The Man in the Mirror*, 1920), which confusedly sought to reveal the duality of human nature, one part extending love towards fellow-creatures, another part selfish and enclosed within itself. The dual personality, treated almost clinically, is the theme likewise of *Schweiger* (1922), in which we find a Franz Schweiger who is really a child-murderer, Franz Forster, cured from his madness by hypnosis: his wife discovers the truth, leaves him, and returns after he has heroically rescued a group of children—too late, however, for she finds he has committed suicide. Neither of these is particularly important, but *Bocksgesang* (*Goat Song*, 1921) introduces us to something different. In this peculiarly effective tale of a monster who springs from the loins of a normal man and who, although slain, leaves his seed to carry on his terrible race, Werfel presents an effective picture of the beast that lurks under the semblance of human civilization. The symbolism is clear and simple, perhaps even over-obvious, but it is not the quality of the symbols that gives this play distinction: what raises it above the mediocre mass of its companions is its genuine, intense theatricality and its power to rise, at least in certain scenes, towards the rarely scaled heights of the tragic.

Hardly the same may be said of *Juarez und Maximilian* (1924) and *Paulus unter den Juden* (*Paul among the Jews*, 1926), while the spectacularism of *The Eternal Road* (1935)—for which, of course, Max Reinhardt must be held mainly responsible—can readily be forgotten. The first of these is a sincere attempt to portray the combined idealism and ineffectiveness of the unhappy Maximilian, caught in the web of his own blind liberalism, of European politics, and of incipient Mexican nationalism: what is lacking is the quality of strength that fired the scenes of *Goat Song*. Werfel forgot that a play on this subject which does not introduce Juarez is equivalent to *Hamlet* without the prince, and that tragedy demands admiration as well as sympathy. Philosophic concepts take, likewise, from the strength of *Paulus unter den Juden*, a study of the differing attitudes towards the new Christian religion exemplified by Paul on the one hand and by Peter on the other.

Far less successful are the plays of Werfel's compatriot and fellow-novelist, Emil Ludwig (Emil Cohn): although sincerely wrought, and although presenting some interesting scenes, his *Bismarck* (1922–24) and *Versailles* (1931) make but dull reading to-day. Nor can a higher judgment be made of the *Kalkutta, 4 Mai* (*Calcutta, May 4th* or *Warren Hastings*, 1916), of still another German author, Lion Feuchtwanger. A trifle more of interest attaches to the Austrian historical studies of Hans Sassmann, Ferdinand Bruckner (Theodore Tagger), Friedrich Schreyvogl, and Erwin Kolbenheyer. Of these Bruckner is probably the most important, with his *Elisabeth von England* (1930) and his two Napoleonic dramas —*Napoleon der Erste* (1936) and *Heroische Komödie* (*Heroic Comedy*, written 1942, acted 1946).

So widespread has been the cultivation of such historical material in numerous countries that, apart from those who have explored this realm in England and America, no attempt can be made here to do other than mention briefly a few dramatists who may be regarded as representative of the movement as a whole. In Spain the historical playwrights are headed by the two brothers Manuel and Antonio Machado, whose first drama, *Desdichas de la fortuna ó Julianillo Valcárcel* (*The Blows of Fortune; or, Julianillo Valcarcel*, 1926), set in the times of Philip IV, immediately demonstrated their unquestioned gifts—a rich sense of verbal values, a keen penetration into character, and a power to make their situations bold and interesting. For Poland we may turn to Adolf Nowaczyński, whose *Car Samozwaniec* (*The Pretender*, 1908) treats of a theme which has inspired many Slav authors, and whose *Wiosna ludów w cichym zakątku* (*The People's Springtime in a Quiet Corner of the World*, 1929) has the merit of originality in that it treats of an abortive revolution, not in terms of tragic gloom, but with infective gaiety. In Czechoslovakia the same trend leads to the writings of Stanislav Lom (Stanislav Mojžiš), such as the histori-cal-legendary *Děvín* (1919) and *Žižka* (1925).

Italy presents us with several dramatists of this order. Giovanni Cavic-chioli turns for inspiration to the half-barbaric times of early Rome in his *Romolo* (1923) and *Lucrezia* (1925). Less gifted with literary talent than Cavicchioli, but a far more accomplished craftsman, Giovacchino For-zano became at one time the most commercially popular of modern Ita-lian playwrights, and in his latter years he achieved notoriety, if not fame, by collaborating with none other than Benito Mussolini. Among his many works the most outstanding is the set of four dramas dealing with the progress of the French Revolution—*Il conte di Bréchard* (1924), *I fiordalisi d'oro* (*The Golden Fleur-de-lis*, 1924), *Danton* (1929), and, with Mussolini, *Campo di Maggio* (*The Hundred Days*, 1930). None of these pos-sesses any permanent value, but all are written with assured theatrical skill.

The Historical Play in England

As in France and other European lands, so in England the predilection for historical themes has proved a marked feature of theatrical activity from 1920 to 1940, and it is clear that the impulse has not yet died out. Here, however, a peculiar paradox is to be observed. In Drinkwater's *Abraham Lincoln* and Shaw's *Saint Joan* the English stage gave the world two dramas obviously inspired by the desire to use historical material for the purpose of illustrating a philosophy; in the events of the American Civil War and in the conflict between France and England during the fif-teenth century these two authors saw characters and issues such as would meet their larger needs. The paradox enters in when we note that, despite the two great examples, English playwrights as a whole have not sought, when treating historical subjects, to make the past a commen-tary on the present. What characterizes their plays is, in general, their frank endeavour simply to revivify the past or to use the historical method for the purpose of finding escape from the trammels of realism.

The Barretts of Wimpole Street (1930), by Rudolph Besier, and the *Vic-toria Regina* (1934) of Laurence Housman are thoroughly representative of this trend. The first is an excellently planned work which seeks to do no more than create an appealing drama out of the Browning-Barrett romance; the second seeks only to present, in a series of episodes, the career of the great Queen from her accession to the throne until her last days. In precisely similar manner Gordon Daviot (Elizabeth Mackintosh) covers the ground already trodden by Shakespeare in *Richard II*, presenting a colourful and sympathetic portrait of that unfortunate monarch in *Richard of Bordeaux* (1932); her later drama, *The Little Dry Thorn* (1947), goes far further back in history to deal with the Biblical story of Abraham and Sarah. The life of Charles Lamb is dramatized by Joan Temple in *Charles and Mary* (1930) and that of Henry VII in *The Patched Cloak* (1947); Reginald Berkeley brings Florence Nightingale to theatrical life in *The Lady with a Lamp* (1929); in *The Brontës* (1933) Alfred Sangster turns to present portraits of a famous literary family; Norman Ginsbury, after dealing with the Duchess of Marlborough in *Viceroy Sarah* (1934), moves a century forward in time to depict the Prince Regent in *The First Gentleman* (1945).

In not one of these plays is there any 'social criticism'; in not one is an effort made to make the recorded events commentaries on our own existance. The authors are all intent, first, on producing effective dramas, second, on revealing character, and, thirdly, on faithfully evoking the spirit of the times with which they deal. In addition, most of them clearly manifest a joy in finding themselves amid surroundings where style in conversation and grace in living are more apparent than they are amid that life which we presently lead.

This last quality becomes even more evident when we move from the realm of the authentic historical to that of the imaginative—for English between-war playwrights, not satisfied with what history could in fact give them, frequently proceeded to create episodes for themselves, fancifully set in some past age, or else sported with characters such as had already been given imaginative being. In this way St John Ervine took the persons of *The Merchant of Venice* and carried them a stage farther on their life's journey in *The Lady of Belmont* (1923). Thoroughly characteristic of these trends are the works of Ashley Dukes, who, besides penning a *Tyl Ulenspiegel* (1927), gave to the theatre one of the most graciously written and fancifully conceived period comedies in *The Man with a Load of Mischief* (1924).

In his search for style and in his discovery that the opportunity for exercising style is to be found in settings from the past, Dukes is companioned by an author, Clifford Bax, who more consistently than any other has sought departure from the contemporary scene. His work extends from free fantasies of the kind represented in *Midsummer Madness* (1923), through historical dramas like *The Rose without a Thorn* (1932), a memorable play on the subject of Henry VIII, on to such experimental essays as *Socrates* (1930), wherein an attempt is made to grant theatrical quality to the Socratic dialogue. As this last-mentioned drama suggests, Bax is less interested in action than in style. It is on his dialogue he concentrates, and few writers of his time had a finer sense of the jewelled phrase than he. The trouble is that, as was made manifest in his *The Golden Eagle* (1946), yet another drama on Mary Queen of Scots, he was inclined to lose dramatic effectiveness for the sake of rich words.

Maxwell Anderson and the Historical Play in America

No less than in other countries the popularity of the historical drama is to be seen in the American theatre. Despite the strong impress of the realistic style on the New York stage, playwright after playwright has turned to the past. It is, however, to be noted that, whereas in general the English writers tended to avoid using material from the past as commentary on the present, American authors have tended to pursue a path diametrically opposed to this and to seek for themes which might aid them in expressing social judgments on the twentieth century.

All through these decades this nostalgic interest in bygone years has given colour to a stage that otherwise might have been severely drab. Sometimes this takes fantastic shape of the kind exemplified in the *Berkeley Square* (1926) of John Balderston, wherein a man of to-day is sent magically back into the eighteenth century; sometimes it finds expression in such musicals as the radiant *Oklahoma!* (1943); occasionally, as in Dorothy Gardner's *Eastward in Eden* (1947)—a study of Emily Dickinson—it merely seeks to record; most frequently it assumes the form of reasonably faithful recordings of past events with stress laid on those features of the selected episodes which appear to offer contemporary parallels. E. P. Conkle thus writes his *Prologue to Glory* (1938), which deals with the adolescence of Abraham Lincoln; in *The Patriots* (1943) Sidney Kingsley selects the times of Jefferson and Hamilton for his theme; *Harriet* (1944), by Florence Ryerson and Colin Clements, treats of Harriet Beecher Stowe. These three examples may be taken as typical of numerous others produced during the two decades from 1920 to 1940.

In this sphere one particular author calls for special examination. As a whole, the plays of Maxwell Anderson may be considered disappointing, but they are disappointing in a grand way. No dramatic author of our age has higher or clearer concepts of what he wants the theatre to be; no other author has made more determined efforts to replace the figure of tragedy in the niche that for so long has been left empty. "I have found my religion in the theatre," he has said recently, "where I least expected to find it, and where few will credit that it exists. But it is there, and any man among you who tries to write plays will find himself serving it, if only because he can succeed in no other way. He will discover, if he works through his apprenticeship, that the theatre is the central artistic symbol of the struggle of good and evil within men." Anderson has the true vision. He recognizes that our present-day playhouse has sacrificed broader interests to the presentation of merely passing entertainment, and he is convinced that unless the quality that evoked an *Œdipus Rex* or a *Hamlet* can be restored to it the theatre will die of inanition or sink to becoming a thing of no consequence in our lives. Even those writers who have most at heart the desire to introduce things vital and appealing have, as he sees it, failed to do more than bring to the stage the elements of journalism.

Throughout his career as a dramatist Anderson has sought, in diverse ways, to realize this vision. His very first play, *White Desert* (1923), was an essay in the tragic. When this failed he set himself to pen a number of dramas in a more realistic style—*What Price Glory* (with Laurence Stallings, 1924), a bitter unveiling of the 'heroic' soldier, *Saturday's Children* (1927), a bourgeois comedy, and *Gods of the Lightning* (with Harold Hickerson, 1928), in which his anger over the Sacco-Vanzetti case makes some of his scenes almost incoherent.

During this time, however, an inward dissatisfaction with realistic prose dialogue makes itself apparent, so that we feel no surprise in finding Anderson turn, in 1930, to history and verse in *Elizabeth the Queen*, followed in 1933 by a companion piece, *Mary of Scotland*. Between these comes an Indian play, *Night over Taos* (1932), also in the poetic style, and a sudden incursion into the mood of political satire, *Both Your Houses* (1933). In *Valley Forge* (1934) he again seeks historical subject-matter, this time in the life of George Washington, and the following year he startles theatre-goers and critics by presenting a gangster drama in verse (*Winterset*, 1935). *Wingless Victory* (1936), a poetic study of the colour problem placed in the nineteenth century, proves thoroughly unsuccessful, but again something new is attempted in the verse comedy *High Tor* (1936). In *The Masque of Kings* (1937) he seeks his theme in Vienna and the unsolved question of how Prince Rudolph came to die; *Knickerbocker Holiday* (1938) is a gay, yet indirectly biting, musical fantasy of old New York; for the story of *Key Largo* (1939) he goes to the Spanish Civil War; *Journey to Jerusalem* (1940) carries us back to Biblical Palestine; *Candle in the Wind* (1941) deals with an imagined episode in the Second World War, and this war also provides the setting for *The Eve of St Mark* (1942) and *Storm Operation* (1944); the difficulties experienced by the young in finding readjustment to civilian life is the topic of *Truckline Café* (1946); in *Joan of Lorraine* (1946) an experiment is made in a kind of Pirandellian style, with a play in rehearsal while the actors discuss the way in which the characters shall be treated.

There is an almost disconcerting variety here, and the variety itself is symbolic of Anderson's failure to discover a medium that shall thoroughly satisfy his needs. He is a prophet vainly dreaming of the temple appropriate to his vision and visiting now one and now another among many houses of worship. What we have here is not a shifting of aim such as marred the creative work of Hauptmann, but rather the restless search for a means wherewith a single dominant purpose may find realization.

In general, perhaps we can admit that the main reason why the purpose has not found concrete embodiment in dramatic form rests rather in our present age than in Anderson himself. No doubt there are among his plays many pieces of lesser import. No doubt his Elizabethan dramas are vitiated by Shakespearian echoes. No doubt his last works in particular fail to rise to the majesty of the occasion they celebrate—so that we are compelled to admit that the story of the American actress, in *Candle in the Wind*, who saves her French officer lover and remains herself in the hands of the Gestapo, seems artificially conceived, and that the theme of *The Eve of St Mark*, with its central figure of Quizz West, appears rather sentimental in concept. No doubt, too, the philosophic speeches in several of the dramas must strike us as lacking in firmness and, so far as the expression is concerned, framed in words which produce a static effect rather than the dynamic impression which greater authors know how to evoke by means of moving imagery and the use of restless words.

All these things can readily be admitted, yet the fact remains that the man who created the Esdras scenes in *Winterset* has in him a vision and a strength denied to most of his companions:

> *ESDRAS:* Yes, if you hold with the world that only
> those who die suddenly should be revenged.
> But those whose hearts are cancered, drop by drop
> in small ways, little by little, till they've borne
> all they can bear, and die—these deaths will go
> unpunished now as always. When we're young
> we have faith in what is seen, but when we're old
> we know that what is seen is traced in air
> and built on water. There's no guilt under heaven,
> just as there's no heaven, till men believe it—
> no earth, till men have seen it, and have a word
> to say this is the earth.
> *GARTH:* Well, I say there's an earth,
> and I say I'm guilty on it, guilty as hell.
> *ESDRAS:* Yet till it's known you bear no guilt at all—
> unless you wish. The days go by like film,
> like a long written scroll, a figured veil
> unrolling out of darkness into fire
> and utterly consumed. And on this veil,
> running in sounds and symbols of men's minds
> reflected back, life flickers and is shadow
> going toward flame. Only what men can see
> exists in that shadow. Why must you rise and cry out:
> That was I, there in the ravelled tapestry,
> there, in that pistol flash, when the man was killed.
> I was there, and was one, and am blood-stained!
> Let the wind
> and fire take that hour to ashes out of time
> and out of mind! This thing that men call justice,
> this blind snake that strikes men down in the dark,
> mindless with fury, keep your hand back from it,
> pass by in silence—let it be forgotten, forgotten!—
> Oh, my son, my son—have pity!

Maybe there is in these speeches a sign why Anderson has been prevented from achieving more. "There's no heaven," says Esdras, "till men believe it"—and men in our days have ceased to believe. We might almost say that there can be no tragedy without belief, for tragic drama is essentially metaphysical and religious. Thus, in the want of a common faith in our midst, the playwright who aims at tragic expression is given no basis on which to stand. One phrase that, slightly varied, finds continual echo in Anderson's plays is that of Mio's in *Winterset*: "The bright ironical gods!" he cries. "Dark gods," "cruel gods," they appear elsewhere, and the very fact that divinity is thus spoken of in the plural tells its tale. The phrase is empty of meaning because there is no belief behind it, and as a result when Anderson confronts life's miseries he can only sink into despair. When Lear addresses the heavenly powers in the storm scene we know that his arms are stretched upward towards a real presence; when Mio addresses the bright ironical gods he is turning towards a great empty void of interstellar space. The conditions of the world in which we live well-nigh deny the playwright to reach, as Anderson would fain have reached, the exhilarating terror and the agonized serenity of the true tragic concept.

Biblical Themes and Themes from Ancient Greece

Among Maxwell Anderson's plays there are two which call for attention, not so much, perhaps, because they are rated among his best as for their being illustrative of a force which became particularly noticeable from the mid-thirties onward: the first of these is *Journey to Jerusalem,* presented in 1940, the central theme of which is the visit of Jesus to the temple where He is told by Ishmael that He is the Messiah, destined to suffer for mankind and eventually to die a terrible death; the second is *Barefoot in Athens* (1951), with Socrates as its chief character—a Socrates who deliberately rejects an opportunity of living as a guest in the palace of Sparta's tyrannical ruler and who prefers to drink his hemlock in a democratic Athens. Not only do these two plays reflect the truly remarkable exploration of ritual and myth which has been so eagerly pursued within recent decades by both believers and unbelievers, they also remind us that the two lands which above all others have provided Western man with his greatest store of ancient fact and of primeval legend are themselves suggesting that their own creative powers do not lie wholly in the past.

Already, of course, in the references to individual authors mention has been made of not a few modern dramas dealing with Biblical material, both from the New Testament and from the Old—dramas stretching from Claudel's symbolic retreatment of *The Tidings Brought to Mary* (1912) to Giraudoux' parable of *Sodom and Gomorrah* (1943)—and to these might be added many others, among them the powerfully poetic and visionary trilogy composed by the Austrian Richard Beer-Hofmann, *Jaákobs Traum* (*Jacob's Dream*, 1919), *Der junge David* (*The Young David*, 1933), and at least the beginning of the third part, *Das Vorspiel auf dem*

Theater zu König David (*The Prelude to the Theatre of King David*, 1936). In considering these and other kindred writings, it may be noted that, although modern Hebrew dramatists themselves are largely concerned with subjects related to current social problems, there are some signs that the Biblical store of legend and of fact may be further explored in divers ways, and that new theatrical themes may be discovered in early Jewish history. The modern Hebrew drama was, in fact, firmly established by the Habimah company in 1936 when it presented Nathan Bystrytsky's *Be 'Layil Zeh* (*On That Night*), a play dealing with the Zealots who fought against Roman power. Obviously the chief source of information here was the well-known history written by Flavius Josephus: this man is himself made to appear in person in the same playwright's *Yerushalayim ve' Romi* (*Jerusalem and Rome*, 1941); and similar use of related historical events is made by Nissim Aloni in his *Akhsar Mi'kol Ha'Melekh* (*The Most Cruel of All was the King*, 1953). The Biblical account of Job is taken by Aaron Megged as a kind of symbolic background for his treatment of the Nazi extermination camps in *Ha' Onah Ha' Boeret* (*The Season of Burning*, 1967).

So too in Greece: and here there is particular interest in observing that, while numerous dramatic authors have concentrated their attention upon contemporary local, social problems in more or less realistic manner and while others have lately been engaging in experiments within the realm of the absurd, several of the most serious and talented dramatists have been more attracted towards the imaginative and poetic treatment of historical events and persons, sometimes taken from the days of ancient Athens but also—and interestingly—from the Byzantine period. Typical are the works of Anghelos Terzakis, extending from his *O avtokrator Mikhail* (*Emperor Michael*, 1938), *O stavros kai to spathi* (*The Cross and the Sword*, 1939) and *Theophano* (1956) on to *O progonos* (*The Ancestor*, 1970), a study of guilt and justice which interestingly demonstrates how, even in a play not directly based upon mythical or historical material, what may be described as myth-inspired concepts predominate. In 1956 Nikos Kazantzakis published a novel entitled *Bios kai politeia tou Alexi Zormpa* which brought him universal fame when it was filmed as *Zorba the Greek*. This, of course, has no concern for us in the present context, but very considerable interest does attach to the fact that during 1955 and 1956 he also published three volumes of collected plays—the first containing four "tragedies with ancient themes": *Prometheus, Kouros, Odysseus* and *Melissa*; the second including four "tragedies with Byzantine themes": *Christos, Ioulianos o Parabates, Nikephoros Phokas* and *Konstantinos o Palaiologos*; and the third having four "tragedies with mixed themes": *Kapodistrias, Christophoros Kolombos, Sodoma kai Gomorra*, and *Boudas*. Most of these are unknown outside of Greece, but *Sodoma kai Gomorra* (*Sodom and Gomorrah*, dealing with the same subject as had attracted the attention of Giraudoux in 1943) was performed in the U.S.A. as *Burn Me to Ashes* in 1956. And with these dramas may be associated the *Alcibiades* (1959) of Giorgios Theotokas, the picture of a general possessed by the same dream which later seized upon the imagination of Alexander the Great, a subject dealt with as though it were a myth but also as if its easily discernible 'sub-text' were designed to have present-day applications.

The appearance of these and many other similar plays should be set against a background which recently was summarized by Anghelos Terzakis. "The spate of theatrical activity going on in Athens today", he has said,

> has reached such a pitch that it is posing special problems of its own. Besides the State companies, there are so many privately-run theatres that Athens has now outstripped Paris and New York, not merely in proportion to the size of its population, but in the total number of theatres in operation.

And although in many of these the latest novelties are being reflected, there is always behind them, above them, and around, the ancient dramas, most of them historical and all of them richly poetic, which yearly cast their spell upon teeming audiences at Epidauros, Philippi, Thasos, Dodona and Thessaloniki.

7

THE REVIVAL OF POETIC DRAMA

IN ATTEMPTING to create a tragic drama out of contemporary subject-matter Maxwell Anderson dared more courageously than any play-wright of the past. From Æschylus onward the playwrights have found that distance in time or place is well-nigh essential for the full and satisfying exposition of tragedy's spirit, and perhaps even Anderson himself was conscious of the unlikelihood of his achieving perfection of utterance in a theme selected from the underworld of his own day.

Yet the attempt forms a symbol and a challenge. Through writing *Winterset* Anderson shocked many of his companions into a recognition that the theatre of our time, if it is to win greatness, must once again be prepared to welcome the poetic imaginative processes couched in appropriate language; and there is no other modern playwright who has done more towards trying to bring this poetic concept within the framework of the common commercial playhouse.

Poetic Experiment in America

Although Anderson himself is rather heavily influenced by Shakespeare he realizes that if this attempt is to succeed some other form than the Shakespearian must be found. Even in *Winterset*, with its modern gangster story, echoes of *Hamlet* are plainly visible in the creation of Mio; one of the chief scenes in the drama is modelled upon the storm scene in *King Lear*; while the Mio-Miriamne story bears close connexions with *Romeo and Juliet*. Despite this, Anderson has sought, in his four-beat line with all the licences which he permits himself, to develop an instrument better harmonized with the speech of to-day than the blank-verse line of the Elizabethans—and in the fashioning of this instrument he shows himself in accord with what must be regarded as among the most hopeful portants of our stage.

It is only within the past few years that poet-playwrights have come to understand that before there can be any revival of poetic drama in our midst a medium of expression must be found which shall bear the same relationship to our current speech as the sixteenth-century blank verse bore to the current speech of Shakespeare's companions. All the efforts to re-establish the poetic drama in the nineteenth century failed precisely because the Elizabethan rhythms were regarded as a model towards which later writers should work, and, as a consequence, what once had been vital because organically bound to living reality became artificial, dull, or, at its best, falsely rhetorical.

Anderson's experimentation in technical form of expression is, therefore, of prime importance; and our sense of the importance of his effort is increased when we observe how his work is companioned by that of many others. In *Panic* (1935) Archibald MacLeish consciously set himself the task of listening to current American talk and of fashioning a verse formula harmonized with it. The result, perhaps, was not entirely successful; what was significant was the recognition of the need and the deliberate attempt to meet it. Since then, apart from the production of several memorable radio plays, of which *The Fall of the City* (1937) was the most impressive, he won popular success with his *J.B.* in 1958.

Earlier than this Edna St Vincent Millay had sought, in the style of an earlier generation, to start a new poetic drama in her *Aria da Capo* (1921), a rather artificial but still graceful one-act piece in which Pierrot and Columbine, lightly dallying, are set in juxtaposition with the tragic actors Thyrsis and Corydon. This first effort, however, was not followed by any notable successors. *The Lamp and the Bell* and *Two Slatterns and a King* (both 1921) are negligible as plays, and only *The King's Henchman* (1927), a libretto written for the music of Deems Taylor, warrants even modified praise—and that rather for her originality in selecting Saxon England for her subject than for the excellence of her treatment of the plot. Edna Millay is decidedly rather poet than playwright.

Despite all the numerous experiments, however, and despite the fact that Maxwell Anderson did succeed in winning popular success with his several poetic dramas deliberately penned for the commercial stage, it must be agreed that the American drama is still heavily dominated by the realistic pattern. A revulsion may come, but until that happens we can record only brave attempts such as *Winterset*, largely isolated from the world in which they make their appearance.

T. S. Eliot and the Revival of the Poetic Play in England

We must note, however, that the writer who has been most markedly responsible both for the development of a new poetic orientation in England and for encouraging a rebirth of verse drama there—T. S. Eliot —was born an American. Already in 1928 he had published an important *Essay on Poetic Drama*; seven years later, in 1935, he produced a play, *Murder in the Cathedral*, which at once was hailed as a work better fitted than any other twentieth-century composition to mark the foundation of a modern poetic theatre. Although penned for, and originally produced at, Canterbury Cathedral, it proved its stage-worthiness when transferred from these ecclesiastical surroundings to the public playhouse, and since its appearance it has clearly exercised a widespread influence.

What distinguishes *Murder in the Cathedral* from all preceding verse plays is its method of approach. So far as the subject is concerned, it is just another historical drama, telling of the assassination, at Canterbury's high altar, of Thomas à Becket, the archbishop who had dared to oppose King Henry II. This ancient tale, however, Eliot has raised to the level of the philosophic. Thomas is a man fated for martyrdom, yet conscious that under the cloak of the martyr many evils may lie hid. Four tempters come to him. Three of these he easily thrusts aside, but the fourth, almost a replica of himself, he finds difficult to reject, for this figure dangles before his eyes an intangible bait—the hope of heavenly glory after death. At last Thomas reaches his decision:

> Now is my way clear, now is the meaning plain:
> Temptation shall not come in this kind again.
> The last temptation is the greatest treason:
> To do the right deed for the wrong reason.

So he goes to his death, while the Knights who have slain him attempt, in almost burlesque manner, to justify their action, and from the chorus of the women of Canterbury comes a great piercing cry of lamentation and self-abasement. In this chorus Eliot has sought to symbolize the cheap, common world, intent on its own safety, unable to reach to the vision of its Thomases:

> Forgive us, O Lord, we acknowledge ourselves as type of the common man,
> Of the men and women who shut the door and sit by the fire;
> Who fear the blessing of God, the loneliness of the night of God, the surrender required, the deprivation inflicted;
> Who fear the injustice of men less than the justice of God;
> Who fear the hand at the window, the fire in the thatch, the fist in the tavern, the push into the canal,
> Less than we fear the love of God.

By reintroducing the use of the chorus Eliot has taught his companions what virtues this dramatic device can bring with it. A whole human background is provided by these old women of Canterbury for the figure of Thomas; the commonplace unanimity of the mass is, through them, set against the extraordinary stature of the hero; by means of the chorus the poet gains a means of presenting indirect commentary on his action; and, above all, the lyrical opportunities thus offered give excellent means both of enriching the speech of the play and of arousing imaginative receptivity on the part of the audience. When, for example, just before the murder, Eliot desires to awaken in us a sense of invading, invisible evil it is the chorus that supplies him with his instrument:

> We have not been happy, my Lord, we have not been too happy.
> We are not ignorant women, we know what we must expect and not expect.
> We know of oppression and torture,

We know of extortion and violence,
Destitution, disease,
The old without fire in winter,
The child without milk in summer,
Our labour taken away from us,
Our sins made heavier upon us.
We have seen the young man mutilated,
The torn girl trembling by the mill-stream.
And meanwhile we have gone on living,
Living and partly living,
Picking together the pieces,
Gathering faggots at nightfall,
Building a partial shelter,
For sleeping, and eating and drinking and laughter.

God gave us always some reason, some hope; but now a new terror has soiled
us, which none can avert, none can avoid, flowing under our feet and over
the sky;
Under doors and down chimneys, flowing in at the ear and the mouth and the
eye.
God is leaving us, God is leaving us, more pang, more pain than birth or death.
Sweet and cloying through the dark air
Falls the stifling scent of despair;
The forms take shape in the dark air:
Puss-purr of leopard, footfall of padding bear,
Palm-pat of nodding ape, square hyæna waiting
For laughter, laughter, laughter. The Lords of Hell are here.
They curl round you, lie at your feet, swing and wing through the dark air.
O Thomas Archbishop, save us, save us, save yourself that we may be saved;
Destroy yourself and we are destroyed.

There is to be found no nobler language in the theatre of our times.

Murder in the Cathedral was followed, in 1939, by *The Family Reunion* and, in 1949, by *The Cocktail Party*. Both of these made powerful impact, but *The Confidential Clerk* (1953) and *The Elder Statesman* (1958) seemed to indicate that Eliot's later endeavour to build a 'poetic' theatre out of commonplace dialogue was not likely to produce the effect desired. After all, the history of the stage shows that, in those ages when the imaginative verse drama flourished, it sought for themes and characters removed from the ordinary world of its time. True, the theme of *The Family Reunion* is based on the antique legend of Orestes, and the juxtaposing of the modern on the ancient produces a peculiar imaginative tension; but the endeavour itself is so much more difficult and hazardous than any task set to himself by a Sophocles or by a Shakespeare that one questions whether this is the path which the poetic drama will take in the days immediately to come.

Somewhat in the same mood that inspired Eliot to write *Murder in the Cathedral*, Dorothy L. Sayers penned her *The Zeal of Thy House* (1937) and *The Devil to Pay* (1939). More significant are the plays of W. H.

"RAZBEG": OKHLOPKOV'S REALISTIC THEATRE, MOSCOW
From *The Seven Soviet Arts*, by Kurt London (Faber, 1937).

"BLITHE SPIRIT": THE PICCADILLY THEATRE, LONDON, 1941

Raymond Mander and Joe Mitchenson Collection

Auden, who first reversed Eliot's career by moving from England to America and then back again. In 1935 he collaborated with Christopher Isherwood in producing *The Dog beneath the Skin; or, Where is Francis?* in which still another approach is made to the revivification of verse drama. Here fantastic satire takes the place of tragic tension. The chorus in melodious verse introduces us to a kind of idyllic Auburn, village of our dreams, and then harshly shatters the dreams by hinting that here too

> Corruption spreads its peculiar and emphatic odours
> And Life lurks, evil, out of its epoch.

In telling his story of the man who disguises himself as a dog Auden endeavours to make dramatic use of diverse measures and, in particular, to employ for his own purposes both popular jingles and forms of verse already associated with special situations. The first act, with its stanzaic forms, suggests the opening of a medieval morality play; a moment later we are listening to octosyllabic couplets; these change to dimeters; prose and a kind of blank verse follow. Witty, impudent, embittered, the play breathes the spirit of the intellectual who has just looked upon the world and found it wanting. *The Ascent of F.6* (1936), once more written in collaboration with Isherwood, has more of a story to narrate—that of an expedition sent out by the British Government to scale a mountain, marked F.6 on the maps and never yet conquered. Since the natives of the region regard it as sacred, and since Britain's rival, Ostnia, is proposing to mount to its summit, the expedition headed by Michael Ransom thus has a political significance—and the two authors seize every opportunity of indulging in vicious, embittered satire at political chicanery and intrigue. Unfortunately they also introduce a strain of the psychoanalytical, which serves to confuse a drama that otherwise might have had considerable directness of appeal.

A third play by the same authors, *On the Frontier* (1938), hardly improves upon these earlier efforts. The story of how war between a Fascist and a democratic nation is prevented by the will of the people has in it more sentimental wishful-thinking than sense. Where Auden fails is in his subject-matter. Not one of these plays presents a strongly imagined theme, and each one is cluttered up with inconsequentialities. This fact is peculiar in that the two poets, deeply concerned about the fate of the world, would wish to make direct appeal to their contemporaries, and we may well deem it ironically paradoxical that the writers most anxious to have their words heard and most intent on utilizing every possible device, including popular songs, to capture public attention should remain farther removed from the public stage than Eliot, with his medieval theme wrought into a drama for presentation in a cathedral.

Several other English poets have applied themselves similarly to the stage during recent years. Louis MacNeice, besides having made numerous contributions to the poetic radio play, and besides having prepared one of the finest existing translations of Æschylus' *Agamemnon*, produced one interesting drama of this kind, *Out of the Picture* (1937), a study of a young artist and the girl by whom he is killed. The year following the appearance of this work Stephen Spender published his *The Trial of a Judge*, a bitter and at times even hysterically violent denunciation of Nazi ideology and practice.

Although *Murder in the Cathedral* in one sense seemed to arrive unexpectedly in 1935, it was, of course, the almost inevitable consequence of much dramatic endeavour from the beginning of the century onward. The efforts of Yeats, Bottomley, Drinkwater, Abercrombie, and others, even although most of them remained strictly caviare to the general, had provided a relatively firm platform for Eliot's play, and the success of J. E. Flecker's *Hassan* in 1923 showed that, when poetic dialogue was accompanied by firm dramatic action, there was a fairly large number of playgoers who craved for something more than the common familiar domestic sets, the drab costumes, and the often barren speech associated with the realistic dramas of the time. *Hassan*, indeed, testified to something more than that: since it possessed sufficient strength to warrant later revival in the playhouse and presentation on the television screen, it indicated that this craving on the part of at least a section of the public has remained fairly constant throughout the whole of this present age.

Nor must we, in considering this development of the verse play, forget how materially the poets were assisted by numbers of other dramatists who, although eschewing the employment of formal 'poetic' dialogue, sought to prepare general audiences for the appreciation of the imaginative in concept by dealing with fanciful themes expressed in various kinds of heightened prose. Masefield's work in this style has already been dealt with, and with him may be associated Lord Dunsany (Edward Plunkett, Baron Dunsany)—perhaps not a truly great dramatist, yet one who certainly deserves to be given an honourable place among those twentieth-century playwrights who consistently sought to make the theatre a place for imaginative experiences. Early in his career, in *The Glittering Gate* (1909), he had carried his audiences to the very portals of whatever heaven may be; and in essence the spirit animating this one-act piece was akin to that which invested his lengthier and more effective dramatic work, appropriately called by the title of *If* (1921), wherein the hero, a little London clerk, is shown in the midst of a series of romantically extravagant adventures (extending from chieftaincy of a Middle Eastern tribe to abject poverty) which might have been his if only he had not missed his regular 8.10 train on one particular morning years ago.

Poetic Experiments from West to East

Almost every country experienced not dissimilar visions. Paris, too, had its group of enthusiasts who dreamed of the possible revival of a poetic stage, and several dramatists sought in diverse ways to transform the dream into reality. All through his lengthy career, Paul Claudel had spent much of his time in seeking to establish a firm foundation for a poetic style apt both to appeal to modern audiences and to prove capable of expressing modern concepts: clearly, he realized, the lyrically romantic style which had appealed in the past was now outmoded, and what he searched for was a pattern likely to startle and delight by its novelty and, as it were, to ring true amid changed social conditions. Even more persistently Jules Superveille applied himself to a similar objective, yet it is not difficult to see why he also failed to achieve his inner aims. Like Claudel, he realized that in the Paris of the thirties there was no room for the rich romantic verbal ebullience or the poetic fancies of yesteryear. Although some of his dialogue assumes patterned forms, a great deal of it is in ordinary prose: and in so far as his themes are concerned we hardly need go further than a consideration of his *La belle au bois* (*The Sleeping Beauty*, 1931). The title of this piece shows that we are in the realm of fairy-tales, and in fact the author has run three such stories into one single plot. In doing so he has transformed them all. The core of the play is the story of the beautiful maiden, sunk in slumber, who is awakened by a young, handsome prince. Here, however, we find that years and years and years ago, when the world was young and beautiful, this sleeping beauty had been in love with Bluebeard, but, having discovered—and having been revolted by—his barbarity, she had voluntarily consented to drift into this state of slumber and forgetfulness. When she is awakened she discovers that the man whose kiss had brought her back to realization of the world surrounding her is a present-day intellectual fool and a crashing bore—certainly no Prince Charming; and, to her dismay, she also finds that memories of Bluebeard still remain with her. Thus she is entirely content to drift into sleep once more. The symbolic import of the play is patently clear—maybe too patently evident.

There is interest in observing that Superveille, although half-French, had not only been a long-time resident of Uruguay but in particular was a keen student of the Spanish stage—a stage which clearly offered to poets a welcome more inviting. Already in the first years of the twentieth century Eduardo Marquina, in Madrid, had been vigorously engaged in seeking to revive the glories of the Golden Age, and it was not long before he was encircled by a little group of disciples eager-eyed in their attempts to support him. At the start their themes tended to be romantic, but gradually, almost insensibly, they began to devise ways by which their plots, even if set in earlier epochs, might be related to contemporary affairs. Marquina's own development, indeed, illustrates this development excellently. Throughout the whole of his career, the dominating impress of Lope de Vega is manifest in his writings, and occasionally we find, as in *Las flores de Aragón* (*The Flowers of Aragon*, 1914), that he has actually borrowed plot-material and characters from that author. Nevertheless, as we survey his dramatic output in its entirety, we cannot fail to discern the very considerable difference both in concept and in style between his earlier dramas—say, *El pastor* (*The Shepherd*, 1902), *Las hijas del*

Cid (*The Daughters of the Cid*, 1908), *En Flandes se ha puesto el sol* (*The Sun has set in Flanders*, 1909) and *El gran capitán* (*The Great Captain*, 1916)—and such a later play as the more richly imaginative, and 'modern', *Fuente escondida* (*The Hidden Spring*, 1931).

With Marquina may be associated Jacinto Grau Delgado, less lyrical in style, but similarly inspired. Of particular interest among his dramas is *El señor de Pigmalión* (*Mr Pygmalion*, 1923), both because of its skilful planning and because, even while its dialogue displays an indebtedness to Lope de Vega, its theme connects it with dramatic essays by Shaw in England and by Čapek in Czechoslovakia. Here an inventor, Mr Pygmalion of the title, so successfully constructs several large mechanical figures that he falls passionately in love with one of them and is finally shot by another. The inspiration from the past of the Spanish theatre thus could prove potent even when the new themes were fantastically modern, just as it could when the plots were made to deal with historical and legendary actions other than those familiar in the time of Lope de Vega and Calderón—as, for example, in the *Ollontay* (1938) which the Argentinian Riccardo Rojas based on an ancient Inca tale.

When we consider this tradition we need feel no surprise in finding that Spain stood alongside England, Ireland, and the United States in bringing this poetic endeavour to full fruition: Federico García Lorca stands alongside Eliot, Auden, Anderson, and Yeats. Nevertheless, it is essential fully to recognize that this Spanish author occupies a very peculiar historical position and that his dramas for the most part are so intimately connected with the singular social life of his native country as to render them difficult of full appreciation by playgoers outside the Hispanic area. Not only are his dramatic writings split into two distinct sections but what may be called the reception of his plays is divided into two separate parts: one García Lorca was known up to 1939, and, although the dramatist was murdered in 1939, another García Lorca came to public notice after 1945. During the earlier period his reputation as a poet-dramatist was high in Spanish theatrical circles, and outside of his own country at least two of his plays, *La zapatera prodigiosa* (*The Shoemaker's Prodigious Wife*, originally produced in 1930 and published in a revised version in 1938) and *Bodas de sangre* (*Blood Wedding*, 1933), were being talked about by a few knowledgable persons, chiefly within university circles. Beyond these two pieces, one an extravagant farce and the other a tragedy, little was known about him save by one or two Hispanologists. At the time of his death hardly anyone was acquainted with his *Yerma* (acted 1934, published 1937), and virtually no one was aware that he had left behind him another tragic drama, *La casa de Bernarda Alba* (*The House of Bernarda Alba*, written 1936, published and acted 1945).

In effect, therefore, he came before the world almost as though he had been two separate individuals. The first of these was a man who might have seemed, and indeed did seem, to be the Spanish equivalent of the

Irish Synge. *The Shoemaker's Prodigious Wife* is an uproarious piece, introducing an elderly cobbler who, having married late in life, finds that he has got a shrew as his wife—a woman who berates him because he does not come up to her romantic ideals and who becomes a scandal in the village because of her constant revilings and her general conduct. At last the poor husband leaves home, but he finds himself forced secretly to return in disguise. After having talked to his wife, he suddenly cannot refrain from revealing himself, crying out, ecstatically, "I can't bear it any longer! Wife of my heart!" In her surprise she remains for a moment speechless. Jeering voices of neighbours can be heard outside. Then, starting to attack him, she cries out in a mixture of tears and laughter:

> Vagabond! Oh, how happy I am you've come back! What a life I'm going to lead you!

In reply, as he settles down comfortably at his familiar cobbler's bench, all he can say is "House of my happiness!" Unquestionably there is much here that is akin to the spirit of *In the Shadow of the Glen*.

Alongside the comedy-farce stands the grim *Blood Wedding*, a play in which folk passions are presented in an admixture of the realistic and the imaginative—and, now that all García Lorca's works are known, we can easily see how this work came into existence. Partly it was a development out of his penning of fanciful 'symbolic' pieces such as the rather feeble and jejune *El maleficio de la mariposa* (*The Butterfly's Charm*, 1920), a drama in which most of the characters are given poetically 'type' names (such as The Mother, The Fiancée, The Groom, The Bride) and which associates these persons with allegorical figures such as Death and Moon. But also partly—in fact, as the poet's brother has informed us, mainly—it came into being after a reading of *Riders to the Sea*. Thus did García Lorca prepare himself for the composition of the realistic-imaginative *Yerma* and *The House of Bernarda Alba* which theatrically belong to the post-war period.

8

EUGENE O'NEILL

IF WE put aside Bernard Shaw as an author who, while producing some of his finest work during the twenties and thirties of this century, established himself on the stage before the outbreak of the First World War, we must all recognize that the dramatist who during this period most clearly displayed the qualities of true genius belonged to the American theatre. Eugene O'Neill is not only a symbol of the dramatic movement that flourished so rapidly and with such resultant fruitfulness during the century's third and fourth decades; he also stands, a powerful and vibrant figure, over and above all his playwriting colleagues throughout the world.

He has genuine dramatic stature, yet the colossus does not by any means plant itself firmly upon the soil, nor is it lacking in cracks and fissures. Richly endowed with genius, O'Neill presents himself as a man who, whatever his strength, is wanting in that one final element of power and balance out of which greatness is born. He has strength of passion; he is not content to serve the stage merely with trivial themes of domestic interest; he ponders deeply upon man in relation to the universe in which he lives; more nearly than any author writing in English he approaches the great entrance-hall to tragedy's temple.

Two things only are lacking. First, we sense in O'Neill's career a strangely uneasy relationship between the man and the theatre of his time. When we confront such dramatists as Sophocles, Shakespeare, Molière, Racine, we feel that there is a perfect adjustment between their desires and the stage for which they write. At times they may endeavour to seize from the theatre effects almost beyond its reach, but in general they restrain themselves, with apparent content and harmony, within limits set by the very nature of the theatrical art of their ages. Not so does O'Neill impress us. All too often he suggests that he is impatient of the restrictions and that he is attempting to shatter them or to wrest from within them something the theatre is incapable of yielding. Frantically, almost hysterically, he turns from style to style, from device to device. Realism, expressionism, impressionism—all these paths are tried; he experiments with the use of masks and of the chorus; he takes the old theatrical convention of the aside and seeks to force from it new dramatic effect. Not content with the play of normal length, he pens a work which takes many hours to set upon the stage, and then proceeds farther towards the design of penning nine dramas as a kind of long-drawn-out theatrical cycle reminiscent of medieval amplitude.

This constant and restless movement in his career, this phrenetic seizing upon new devices, maybe ultimately depends upon his unconscious recognition of the essential lack in him of what is the essential instrument of the great playwright. With the deepest regret we must confess that O'Neill is not a finished literary artist. No words of rich import and beauty wing themselves from his pages; we remember his scenes but not the language in which they are couched; again and again as we reach an emotional climax in one or another of his dramas a wave of disappointment comes flooding in upon us. Where we had confidently expected to find lines instinct with loveliness and majesty all we have heard are sharp cries, broken phrases, the clichés rather than the originalities of expressive language. How far and how deep this defect in O'Neill's writing extends may be realized fully if we open any one of his printed plays at an episode of intense emotion: like a schoolgirl sending an epistle to her friend and conscious that she has not the power to wield her words so as to wring from them true record of sentiment or emotion, O'Neill falls back on the useless device of spattering his speeches with exclamation-marks. As a sort of shorthand stage direction for the actor the use of such exclamation-marks may be justified; but that use is not justified when it is a symbol of all that an author would have liked to say and cannot.

The whole trouble is that O'Neill had been at once fortunate and unfortunate in his training and in his career. A playwright can ask no better destiny than to be born the son of an actor, and from James O'Neill his son must have learned much. We observe, however, that the future author of *Mourning Becomes Electra* soon absented himself from the theatre's realm and spent several years in adventure afloat and ashore. No doubt these years yielded him much experience which later he put to use, but the fact remains that during the formative years when he ought to have been training himself as a writer he displayed hardly a single glimmer of having any sense of purpose in his life—a life which he once tried, with characteristic lack of success, to end by suicide. The entire record of his first twenty-five years is a sordid one, apparently that of an unredeemable wastrel, habitually sodden by drink, consorting with rough companions, sleeping in shady hotels which were perhaps hardly more than doss-houses, occasionally wandering away to take some temporary job or else to sail off before the mast, then drifting back again to resume a miserable, purposeless existence in New York or some other city. Characteristically, the writings of Nietzsche seem to have impressed him most powerfully during those years, but even this influence appears to have been a vague one unaccompanied by any clear firm response from within himself. Certainly, later on, he claimed that these early adventures were of considerable value to him when eventually he did settle down to write his plays, but this is an afterthought concerning which we may be prepared to have our doubts.

As we have seen, his decision to become a dramatist was not made until 1913, and by that time much damage had been done.

From "Thirst" to "All God's Chillun Got Wings"

In 1914 there appeared at Boston a volume which is now excessively scarce, *Thirst and Other One-Act Plays*. *Thirst* itself was given, rather obscurely, by the Provincetown Players at their Wharf Theatre in 1916, and at last the errant playwright's career had been started. All the short pieces in this Boston collection belong to one style, and that style also appears as the dominant force in several other apprentice works of these years. *Bound East for Cardiff* is related in subject-matter and characters to *In the Zone* (1917), *The Long Voyage Home* (1917), and *The Moon of the Caribbees* (1918); and as a result these have occasionally been grouped together and given a general title, *S.S. Glencairn*. In addition, several other one-act dramas of kindred mood saw early production by the amateurs with whom O'Neill was associated—these were *'Ile* (1917), *The Rope* (1918), and *Where the Cross is Made* (1918).

The general judgment which can be passed on these works is that they are strong, sometimes melodramatic, authentic studies of human passion, unflinching in their delineation of rougher, though not necessarily darker, scenes of human life. Of the four *S.S. Glencairn* playlets the first concentrates on a sailor, Yank, who, dying on board his ship, dreams of the peaceful farm he would have wished to have; the second shows a dim-witted but sympathetic Swede, dreaming of visiting his mother after long absence, shanghaied for a vessel bound across the Atlantic; the third reveals a group of sailors in the war zone desperately afraid of sabotage and suspicious of a black box owned by one of their number—till they find it contains nothing more explosively inflammatory than love-letters; in *The Moon of the Caribbees* nothing happens save the coming on board a ship of a group of native women who are entertained by all the sailors except one—Smithy, who sits by himself reading a love-letter. *'Ile* is a trifle more complex—the study of a whaling captain whose wife, nervously ill, begs him to return to port: after long pleading he agrees, but suddenly another whale is sighted and he turns his ship back again; the curtain falls on his wife gone utterly insane. More conscious irony appears in *The Rope*, where children avid of gold search for a miser's treasure, and where, at the end, one lad, not knowing the value of money, sends the coins skipping out over the calm sea-water immediately beyond the barn in which the treasure has been located. The same theme occurs in *Where the Cross is Made*, a play later expanded into *Gold* (1921).

What we have here is either melodramatically conceived irony, as in the last dramas mentioned, or else gripping studies of situations—the fear of the black box, the riotous orgy of sailors and native women, a sailor's dying aboard ship far from home. The language is sincere and realistic, the characters well known to the author. Over all the episodes hovers a highly charged atmosphere, tense and sometimes ominous: throughout these episodes we feel the presence of an author intent on saying more to his audiences than the pretty nothings of social comedy or the trivialities of the domestic problem drama. Even at the very beginning of his career O'Neill is intent on the eternal verities: the sea is as much his hero as man, and the gold of *The Rope* and *Where the Cross is Made* assumes symbolic quality.

In 1920 his first full-length play was produced—*Beyond the Horizon*—a work clearly born out of his experimental essays. In effect this drama takes shape as an extended study of one character, Robert, who, reversing Yank's dreams in *Bound East for Cardiff*, would fain have been a sailor, set against the foil that is his brother, Andrew. The pair are farmers: Robert is about to realize his dream of voyaging when he falls in love with Ruth, marries her, and prepares to settle down on the farm. Andrew goes in his place aboard ship, but when he returns, instead of having let the sea liberate his soul, it is found that his interest has been in amassing a hoard of money in the Argentine. Robert, thwarted, and his visions shattered, dies gladly, and finds in death the joy denied him in life of sailing 'beyond the horizon.' The symbolic use of the sea and of gold, representing good and evil; the nature of the characterization; the overlying mood of irony—all these recall the spirit of the experimental one-acts.

Then came the exciting *The Emperor Jones* (1920), in which a new style was tried: expressionism takes the place of realism in a drama which is, in effect, one long dramatic soliloquy revealing the terror that enters a Negro's soul as, driven into the jungle, he flies in terror from the beating of the drums. Already, however, in this play O'Neill was beginning to let his weaknesses take hold of him. In an interview he stated that, having read of the Congo drums, he immediately asked himself: How would this sort of thing work on an audience in a theatre? The question is revealing, since it indicates the beginning of his search for theatrical means outside the use of words for the arousing of imaginative impression; and when we observe how carefully he has sought to build up his effect by other non-literary means—scenery, lighting, and so on—we realize that, effective as is *The Emperor Jones*, its author was stepping out on a dangerous path.

Like Hauptmann, however, O'Neill was not prepared to move from one kind of endeavour to another in artistic progress. Although he had turned here to the expressionistic style, he was by no means done with realism. A month after the appearance of *The Emperor Jones*, *Diff'rent* was given by the Provincetown Players; six months later came *Gold*; and six months after that appeared *Anna Christie* (1921). The first of these is an unsatisfactory piece of work, a rather crudely artificial study of sex-suppression that becomes either brutal or absurd. Briefly the story tells of a woman, Emma, who, believing that her sweetheart, Caleb Williams, is "diff'rent" from other men, breaks off her engagement when she hears that he has been entangled with another woman. The second part of the play shows her a woman of fifty who, because of her suppressed desires, allows herself to be taken in by a self-seeking young soldier just returned from France. For good measure O'Neill throws in a double suicide at the close. If *Diff'rent* is unsatisfactory *Gold* may be called disappointing. The theme is interesting, but the machinery creaks, and the dialogue fails to illuminate this tale of a sea-captain who, again despite the pleadings of a wife, is proposing to set sail in search of buried treasure and is bilked by his companions and even by his own son. The problem here—as so often in O'Neill—is that there is a great yawning gulf between conception and achievement. Stevenson's *Treasure Island* is a thoroughly satisfying masterpiece because it does exactly what it sets out to do: it is a romantic story of adventure told with the consummate skill of a man who knows that the first duty of a writer is to learn how to write, that no artist is any good unless, by diligent application, he makes himself an able craftsman. O'Neill obviously wishes to invest his story of a desert island, a treasure-chest, and a ship of ill-assorted gold-seekers with a symbolic and tragic significance, and because he has failed to make himself a craftsman and because he merely blunders his way through the scenes, the discrepancy between aim and execution becomes often ludicrous.

Anna Christie is more harmonious in its parts, since it is nothing beyond what it sets out to be, because it avoids the sensational, and because from such a realistic theme as it presents we ask in words no more than the actual speech of common life. The play is deservedly popular, yet we may well inquire whether this is the kind of drama we expect from a man of O'Neill's unquestioned genius. There are other playwrights who might have written this rather mediocre sentimental tale of a golden prostitute. At the beginning we are shown the heroine as a cheap, vulgar streetwalker; then we learn that she has had to adopt this profession because of circumstances; and later we discover that, in spite of all the filth through which she has passed, her soul is pure within her. This is simply the eighteenth-century sentimental libertine-hero who sins not from innate evil, but because he has had bad associates. No doubt O'Neill intended more than the play presents, but it is the play, after all, upon which alone we can base our judgments; and the judgment that must be passed on *Anna Christie* is that, although effective as a stage piece, it is no great contribution to the theatre's treasury.

Amid some other writings of lesser import—*The Straw* (1921), with its scene in a sanatorium, *The First Man* (1922), the study of married torment, *Welded* (1924), and the rather weak *The Ancient Mariner* (1924)—O'Neill turned back from the realistic to the expressionistic style in *The Hairy Ape* (1922) and, at least in parts, in *All God's Chillun Got Wings* (1924). The former is a long character portrait somewhat in the style of *The Emperor Jones*, showing Yank, a person so dark on his chest that he is nicknamed "The Hairy Ape," trying to find out where he belongs. Again the symbol intrudes. Writing about this drama in 1924,

O'Neill asserted that the play was intended as "a symbol of man, who has lost his old harmony with nature, the harmony he used to have as an animal and has not yet acquired in a spiritual way." In a series of scenes, some of which are 'realistic' and some cast in a form akin to that of other 'expressionistic' dramas, we see Yank moving from stokehole to Fifth Avenue and from there to a branch office of the I.W.W., until eventually he gets to the Zoo, tries to shake hands with a gorilla, and is crushed to death. There is strength of conception here, yet, when all is said, *The Hairy Ape* is not a play we would care to see often. At its first impact it impresses us by its novelty and by the obvious sincerity of the author, but once we have heard the lines there is no point in our hearing them a second time. In the scene on the upper deck of the ship we get dialogue like this:

> *AUNT:* But don't you have to have the captain's—or some one's—permission to visit the stokehole?
> *MILDRED* [*with a triumphant smile*]: I have it—both his and the chief engineer's. Oh, they didn't want to at first, in spite of my social-service credentials. They didn't seem a bit anxious that I should investigate how the other half lives and works on a ship. So I had to tell them that my father, the president of Nazareth Steel, chairman of the board of directors of this line, had told me it would be all right.

Down below there is a babel of noise:

> *VOICES:* He ain't ate nothin'.
> Py golly, a fallar gat to gat grub in him.
> Divil a lie.
> Yank feeda da fire, no feeda da face.
> Ha-ha.
> He ain't even washed hisself.

And so on. At the end Yank's long soliloquy before the apes' cage is nothing but a series of staccato phrases and sentences freely bespattered with exclamation-marks:

> What de hell! T'hell wit it! A little action, dat's our meat! Dat belongs! Knock 'em down and keep bustin' 'em till dey croaks yuh wit a gat—wit steel! Sure!

We certainly gain nothing from listening to such dialogue twice.

All God's Chillun Got Wings has the virtue that, while dealing with a question, miscegenation, that stirs human passions to white heat in America, O'Neill has with almost Olympian wisdom concentrated his attention, not on the social problem, but upon his chief characters. Had it not been that such a story as he has selected here cannot hope to escape from being interpreted in social and political terms, it might almost have been said that in this play he came as near to complete fusing of concept and execution as he did in the entire course of his work. There is a peculiar intensity and a directness of purpose in its scenes that carry us triumphantly onward from the opening episodes, wherein we see black and white children playing thoughtlessly together, on to the painful last moments when Ella, half recovered from the fit of insanity during which she has tried to murder her Negro husband Jim, sits with him on his knees before her:

> JIM: Forgive me, God, for blaspheming You! Let this fire of burning suffering purify me of selfishness and make me worthy of the child you send me for the woman you take away!
> ELLA: Don't cry, Jim! You mustn't cry! I've got only a little time left and I want to play. Don't be old Uncle Jim now. Be my little boy, Jim. Pretend you're Painty Face and I'm Jim Crow. Come and play!
> JIM: Honey, Honey, I'll play right up to the gates of Heaven with you!

These lines, however, in themselves indicate what the drama is not. It has been described as a tragedy, but in tragedy, in addition to pain, we want to experience an emotion of admiration, of wonder. Jim is a kindly-souled Negro who at the same time is a failure; Ella is an ordinary girl who, broken in the world, has found temporary refuge in Jim's love. Neither character has the least glimpse of greatness, and, as a consequence, while we may hail *All God's Chillun Got Wings* as an affecting play, we cannot in any wise relate it to those dramatic works of the past to which we give the name of tragedy.

From "Desire Under the Elms" to "The Iceman Cometh"

The excitement occasioned by *All God's Chillun Got Wings* was repeated when *Desire under the Elms* appeared in 1924. Here O'Neill turns to the stark New England countryside and presents to us the Puritanical old farmer Ephraim Cabot, married to the much younger Abbie. Between Abbie and Cabot's thirty-two-year-old son Eben there is strife, for he feels that she has stolen what should have been his birthright: but this strife Abbie turns aside by deliberately enticing him to become her lover, proceeding thereafter to get her husband to sign a deed granting the farm to the child which Ephraim believes to be his. Enraged, Eben tells his father what has happened, while she, now consumed by a genuine passion for her lover, murders her own babe to prove her devotion to him. In the end Eben and Abbie, arrested for the crime of child-murder, go together to gaol, intent only on one another.

There can be no doubt but that *Desire under the Elms* possesses an almost daimonic strength, and O'Neill has been completely successful in presenting his contrast between the hard religious atmosphere, so thoroughly in keeping with the rocky soil, and the volcanic passion aroused in this pair of semi-incestuous lovers. At the same time we do not have here anything that surpasses some of the earlier works in the naturalistic style, while, once more, it must be emphasized that to call this drama a tragedy is completely to deny the only true meaning of that term. *Desire under the Elms* is a powerful play of sex-repression and of sex-satisfaction;

of the metaphysical qualities out of which tragedy arises it has none.

A peculiar, romantically conceived piece, *The Fountain* (1925), followed, illustrative of O'Neill's own restless quest. In effect it is a fairy-tale, of almost Maeterlinckian sentimentality, narrating how Juan Ponce de Leon dedicates his life to a search for the Fountain of Youth, and ends, not by discovering it, but by coming to realize that love is the secret of youth. Again the exclamation-marks bespatter the scene of climax:

> Juan Ponce de Leon is past! He is resolved into the thousand moods of beauty that make up happiness—colour of that sunset, of to-morrow's dawn, breath of the great Trade Wind—sunlight on the grass, an insect's song, the rustle of leaves, an ant's ambitions. I shall know eternal becoming—eternal youth!

Then came *The Great God Brown* (1926), in which O'Neill tries another device—the use of masks—for the purpose of presenting what he obviously intended to be a great philosophic drama, but which can only confuse and perplex. His hero is Dion Anthony, a man within whose self, as the author explains, is combined the quality of Dionysus—"the creative pagan acceptance of life"—and of St Anthony—"the masochistic, life-denying spirit of Christianity." For heroine he has a Margaret, Faust's Marguerite, "the eternal girl-woman with a virtuous simplicity of instinct, properly oblivious to everything but the means to her end of maintaining the race." Brown "is the visionless demi-god of our new materialistic myth—a Success—building his life of exterior things, inwardly empty and resourceless, an uncreative creature of superficial preordained social grooves, a by-product forced aside into slack waters by the deep main current of life-desire." With these and other characters, each possessing masks and donning first one and then another, we get a drama, animated no doubt by the highest motives, that seeks to do in the theatre what the theatre by the very nature of its being cannot attain.

Much the same impression is provided by *Lazarus Laughed* (1927). Here also O'Neill has a basic philosophy to present. Lazarus, having died and returned to earth, has a message to give to men: death is not to be feared, and in God's house there is only laughter. Unfortunately, this idea is constantly driven at us in each scene of the play, while the dramatist, not possessing literary means to arouse our emotions, so constantly falls back on hysterical outbursts of staccato phrases as to make the entire play a wearisome series of echoes of itself. When it first appeared its novelty must have been appealing, but now that the novelty has worn off, *Lazarus Laughed* can be accounted nothing save another grand failure. Even while rejoicing that a playwright of our time has such vision as is exhibited in this play, we are forced to acknowledge O'Neill's inability to incorporate the vision in theatrical form likely to make enduring appeal.

The attack on the materialistic is carried a stage farther in *Marco Millions* (1928), where the famous Italian venturer to the East is shown, with mordant satire, passing on his way through the ancient world of the

Orient blind of eye and heart, intent only on his own commercial advancement. To point his message O'Neill causes an epilogue to carry the spiritual action into the present. As the spectators rise they find to their surprise that one of their number is, in fact, Marco Polo. Dressed in Venetian garments, he "conceals a yawn in his palm, stretches his legs as if they had become cramped by too long an evening," and moves towards the exit door, looking a trifle puzzled. Then, as he nears the street and he finds himself in his familiar materialistic surroundings, his countenance clears. A luxurious limousine arrives: "he gets in briskly, the door is slammed, the car edges away into the traffic, and Marco Polo, with a satisfied sigh at the sheer comfort of it all, resumes his life."

Once more a novel theatrical device is introduced into *Strange Interlude* (1928), a drama made extraordinarily long by its somewhat tedious and fundamentally undramatic elaboration of the quite worthy convention of the 'aside' into a pretentious artistic instrument. The story of this play is, in the main, concerned with the heroine, Nina Leeds, who, having lost in the war the one man who might have satisfied her whole nature, drifts from male to male. Finally we find her with her three lovers—her husband, Sam, Dr Darrel, by whom she has had a son, and Charles Norsden, a novelist who tends to look on her as though she were his mother. It is all very psychoanalytical and very subtle and very long.

With *Dynamo* (1929) we are back again in the mood of *The Great God Brown*, with an increase in the use of symbolism. The son of a Christian rejects his father's religion and goes out into the world to seek a god: this he finds in Electricity. He is, however, in love with the daughter of an Atheist, and, having been cheated by her, he kills her and finally electrocutes himself in the great Dynamo which is the idol of his faith. A tragic dramatist is always unfortunate when one of his chosen themes reminds us of a similar theme comically treated, and O'Neill's Electricity has an uncomfortable resemblance to the hilariously conceived Clouds which Aristophanes makes an earlier truth-quester adopt as his god.

Dynamo is one of O'Neill's mistakes: in *Mourning Becomes Electra* (1931), however, he comes as close to realization of his tragic purposes as in any of his works. Here he escapes from the rather jejune allegory of the machine; here his modern characters are ennobled by their association with that story which, above all others, has seized on the imagination of successive dramatists from the majestic times of Æschylus to the not-so-majestic of Sartre. Composed in trilogy form, the play takes shape as one long drama with three separate parts, *The Homecoming*, *The Hunted*, and *The Haunted*, narrating a story set just after the close of the American Civil War. Head of the Mannon household in New England is General Mannon, married to a woman, Christine, who is a stranger to the district: there is a son, Orin, passionately devoted to his mother, and a daughter, Lavinia, as passionately devoted to her father. During the General's absence at the war Christine has had a love affair with a certain Adam Brant, one of O'Neill's men of the sea, who turns out to be the illegitimate son of Lavinia's grandfather and thus half-brother to the General. Terrified of her husband's homecoming, Christine poisons him and departs to live with Brant. Her crime might have lain unsuspected had it not been for Lavinia's hate. The girl discovers the dark secret and, with much difficulty, convinces Orin of the truth; he shoots Brant almost before the very eyes of Christine, who, her life broken, takes her own life. In order to escape from these memories, brother and sister go away on a long voyage, but during this time Orin finds all the devotion that was once given to his mother turned upon Lavinia, and when he learns that she proposes to marry he is horrified. In the end he commits suicide, while she, her heart torn, shuts herself up in the ill-fated Mannon house and settles down there to self-tormented solitude.

The scheme of the drama is excellent, and O'Neill has been successful in making us believe in the terrible story. Subtly, yet boldly, the characters are revealed before us; although no concrete representation of the Eumenides is put before us, the author almost makes them seem to live upon the stage. At the same time we do not encounter here that great vision which we look for in tragedy. O'Neill has presented a memorable picture of a sex-repressed family finding its passions released in strange, dark, ugly ways, but the mood in which the action opens is carried through to the very end without relief or the enlarging of outlook. This is rather a magnificently presented case-study than a powerful tragic drama. Almost the last words are those of Lavinia addressed half to herself, half to her faithful servant Seth:

> Don't be afraid. I'm not going the way Mother and Orin went. That's escaping punishment. And there's no one left to punish me. I'm the last Mannon. I've got to punish myself! Living alone here with the dead is a worse act of justice than death or prison! I'll never go out or see anyone! I'll have the shutters nailed close so no sunlight can ever get in. I'll live alone with the dead, and keep their secrets, and let them hound me, until the curse is paid out and the last Mannon is let die! [*With a strange, cruel, smile of gloating over the years of self-torture*] I know they will see to it I live for a long time! It takes the Mannons to punish themselves for being born!

In this speech is a symbol of O'Neill's final inadequacy in language. As in his earlier plays, the multitude of exclamation-marks is a confession of weakness—nor do these appear only in passages that are almost soliloquy. Here, for example, is the scene, towards the end of *The Hunted*, wherein Orin tells his mother of Brant's death:

> *CHRISTINE* [*stupidly*]: You didn't go—to Blackridge?
> *ORIN:* We took the train there but we decided to stay right on and go to Boston instead.
> *CHRISTINE* [*terrified*]: To—Boston—?
> *ORIN:* And in Boston we waited until the evening train got in. We met that train.
> *CHRISTINE:* Ah!
> *ORIN:* We had an idea you would take advantage of our being in Blackridge

to be on it—and you were! And we followed you when you called on your lover in his cabin!

CHRISTINE [*with a pitiful effort at indignation*]: Orin! How dare you talk—! [*Then brokenly*] Orin! Don't look at me like that! Tell me—

ORIN: Your lover! Don't lie! You've lied enough, Mother! I was on deck, listening! What would you have done if you had discovered me? Would you have gotten your lover to murder me, Mother? I heard you warning him against me! But your warning was no use!

CHRISTINE [*chokingly*]: What—? Tell me—!

ORIN: I killed him!

CHRISTINE [*with a cry of terror*]: Oh—oh! I knew! [*Then clutching at ORIN*] No —Orin! You—you're just telling me that—to punish me, aren't you? You said you loved me—you'd protect me—protect your mother—you couldn't murder—?

This is not such language as we look for from a truly great dramatist.

Throughout the entire course of his career we can see O'Neill constantly struggling to find what might be effective means of expressing his concept of life. Sometimes the means which he adopted must be considered inadequate, unsatisfactory, even restrictive: but the struggles themselves were clearly those of a giant, and, even when some particular drama seems to be a failure we recognize that our disappointment comes from our realization that we are in the presence of true greatness and that, in his personal grandeur, this strange, tortured, almost Titanic author is representative of the American theatre as a whole during the twenties and the early thirties. These decades were described some time ago by an active stage director as the "Fervent Years" and by an equally active critic as the "Golden Age". Even before the outbreak of war the gold was being replaced by baser metals and the fervency was tending either to become muted or to express itself somewhat frenetically; but fortunately O'Neill himself continued majestically to march along the road which he had chosen for himself. In *Ah, Wilderness!* (1933) he elected to search back in his memories to see himself as a youth, twenty-five years earlier, endeavouring to find his true self in the midst of a disturbing world and being sympathetically counselled by an understanding father. The mood called forth in this autobiographical play persists in *Days without End* (1934), but it seems clear that the mood itself was so personal that even he could not find fit means for expressing it clearly on the stage. In seeking to express his image of the 'tragedy' of John Loving, a man who has forgotten his early visions and who is, as it were, shocked back to his God, the rather forced theatrical device which he employs seems strangely cumbersome, artificially conceived and ineffective.

Fortunately, however, these were not his last works. Immediately following the appearance of *Days without End* O'Neill let it be known that he was engaged in composing a great cycle of dramas depicting a section of American life. Just as the war reached its end, the first contribution to this vast project—the project conceived in the mind of a dramatic giant —came to notice with the performance and publication of *The Iceman Cometh* (1946), a play which had been composed some seven years earlier: but since the great sequel to that drama (although written in 1941) remained virtually unknown until its publication in 1955 and its production in 1956, this final triumph, *Long Day's Journey into Night*, must be dealt with in a later section of the present survey. What, however, may be said here with assurance is that O'Neill, even when these final works are put aside, exhibited a vitality and strength which—despite the fact that the vitality sometimes expressed itself in over-violent terms and the strength occasionally crushed that delicacy which the theatre at its best demands—cannot be matched anywhere else during those years.

PART XIII

CHANGES AND CHANCES

CHANGES AND CHANCES

W HEN we think of the drama's course during the three decades since the end of the Second World War the first words likely to come into our minds are 'confusion,' 'doubt,' 'variety,' 'complexity.'

This feeling of uncertainty which thus comes to us as we scan the disturbed, and often disturbing, stage activities to be encountered almost everywhere is, of course, closely connected with—and indeed, largely a reflection of—the social and political changes and disturbances which have been experienced by so many countries since 1945, some of them the result of revolutionary actions, some of them the consequence of technological innovations, and some of them involving both of these forces. Since hardly any two countries have developed in quite the same way during the course of these post-war decades, obviously the plays produced in the various regions demand examination against the divergent backgrounds provided by the societies amid which they have come into being. Nevertheless, although such procedure is absolutely essential when we are engaged in an effort to assess the dominant qualities, so diverse in kind, which are manifested in the dramatic writings produced within the scope of individual countries, it is also essential to consider, at least in a summary manner, certain stage developments and certain attitudes towards the stage which, so far from being restricted to particular territories, are in essence peculiarly international in their range and in their influence.

The Theatre's Rivals: 1. The Cinema

Just as soon as we begin to think of what has happened during these latter years—mentally contrasting the present period with what had gone before—we must surely realize that the theatre's position in the midst of its social environment has markedly altered from that which it had held throughout many centuries, and in particular we must observe that the word 'dramatist' nowadays bears a significance far less precise than it had when, in the form of 'dramatourgos,' it was invented in ancient Athens or than it was, in not too distant days, when an Ibsen, a Strindberg, a Shaw, and a Chekhov were active.

Between Æschylus and Chekhov, of course, there are to be found many ages when playhouses were completely unknown, and when playwriting ceased to be: still further, during those periods when theatres were active, and producing dramatic works of considerable significance, there almost always were other attractions apt to draw away audiences, including the rich and the poor, the stupid and the intelligent, from the enjoyment of watching great actors interpreting great comedies and tragedies. In ancient Rome, Plautus and Terence frequently found that they could not effectively compete against the thrills and excitements provided by rope-dancers and gladiators; and even in Shakespeare's time the same playhouse building might be used on one afternoon for the performance of a poetic tragedy or comedy and on the next for an exhibition of the horrors of bear-baiting. And today, no particular surprise is expressed when some skilful footballer is accorded greater attention than a prominent actor, and when more persons are likely to know the scoring records of the various competing clubs than to be familiar with even the titles of the most outstanding modern plays.

All of this is incontrovertible, yet it is absolutely essential to observe that never until now has the theatre had any rival closely akin to itself, and that throughout all the centuries when stage-performances flourished only one single meaning attached itself to the term 'dramatist.' Everyone knew that a dramatist was an author who wrote plays, and that plays were pieces composed in such a way as to make them suitable for interpretation by actors speaking their lines on a stage before an assembled audience. The texts might, of course, also be perused in solitude by individual readers, and even from the very start there is evidence which proves that the Greek dramatic poets often had in mind individual readers as well as the massed audiences who gathered in their thousands for the festival performances on the slope of the Acropolis: but, while the double appeal was present from the beginning, obviously plays during those early days, and in later times, basically belonged to the theatre —and the theatre, despite the fact that it was occasionally used for purposes other than the presentation of tragedies and comedies, never had any competitors whose appeal was similar to that of dramatic productions.

During the nineteenth century the competitors tended to increase, with circuses, music-halls, and variety houses drawing away many members of the public who otherwise might have attended the performances of plays, but, although the shows presented by those competitors occasionally came close to the theatres' fare, in general their offerings bore little resemblance to the dramas, no matter how trivial or eccentric in form, offered to theatre audiences.

Then suddenly, just about the year 1900, appeared something entirely new—and also something which, to the surprise of many, rapidly expanded from a humble start into a vast, sprawling industry. At the beginning, what was called the kinematograph had little to offer save short, cartoon-like films and brief knock-about sketches, but it was not long before the more ambitious studios found themselves actively engaged in turning out film versions of popular stage plays as well as specially prepared 'epic' spectacles, while concurrently the possibilities presented by the new medium for providing spectators with records of current events were eagerly exploited by specialists in 'news' items. An ever-increasing public welcome was given to these efforts, so that within a very short time the makeshift premises which had served for the display of the earliest 'moving pictures' were soon supplanted by sumptuously appointed 'palaces.'

As year succeeded year the films themselves improved in quality and, somewhat surprisingly, became altered in form through the means of two following inventions. During the first part of the century they had been silent, but towards the close of the nineteen-twenties, to everyone's amazement, they marvellously became vocal. The earlier primitive titles were dispensed with; no longer was there any need to have a pianist or an organist occupied in the strumming out of suitable tunes as accompaniments for the episodes projected onto the screens: the actors now had the opportunity of adding words to their mimic actions, and, when occasion called for it, the sound of music, specially composed for each particular film, could delight the listening onlookers.

Nor was this all. Before a further dozen years had elapsed, the black-and-white 'talking pictures,' which had already captured so many thousands of spectators, became riotously rich in colour, and the latest attraction made cinema audiences still larger than they had been previously.

Needless to say, this popular new form of entertainment brought changes to the world of the stage, but on the whole these changes were not fundamental, so that the theatre succeeded in holding its own against the rival attraction. Certainly many persons who would normally have gone on expeditions to the playhouses found that visits to the local picture palaces were less costly, besides offering monstrously impressive close-ups of virile heroes and delectable heroines performed by actors and actresses whose lives and doings (particularly in Hollywood) were ever more and more providing copy for popular magazines—yet the theatres, even although they thus lost part of their clientèle, continued to survive. The picture palaces may have been glitteringly impressive and their seats pleasantly comfortable, but the 'living theatre,' as it now came to be called, still retained its thousands of patrons, who discovered that the warm social atmosphere provided by its audiences, and the resultant pleasure of becoming part of the show, had delights to offer which outweighed the allurements of its competitor.

In so far as the drama is concerned, the influence of this first, tripartite, rival to the stage has been largely peripheral. During the nineteen-twenties, just before the arrival of the 'talking pictures,' various youthful members of the intellectual avant-garde found themselves captured by a critical philosophy which praised the virtues of the 'language of movement,' which looked back at the early successes of the *commedia dell'arte*, which focused much of its attention upon the skill of Charlie Chaplin, and which occasionally tended to contrast the supposedly greater effectiveness of cinematic action with the spoken words on which the theatre normally depended: but naturally this particular philosophy lost its force just as soon as the pictures ceased to be silent. Later on, particularly during the nineteen-thirties when the talking films were proving so popular, a few dramatists experimented in novel structural forms which clearly were inspired by cinematic methods—toying with flashbacks, episodic narratives, and the like: but, apart from releasing the playwrights from a too strict dependence upon the technique of the wellmade play, these experiments have little more than a passing interest. Certainly, several dramatists found themselves tempted to accept invitations from Hollywood to spend time there as 'writers', only to find that, when they arrived at their destinations and were provided with offices, desks, and typewriters, they often were given no work to do: the experience provided some amusing material for one or two farces, and virtually that was all. When everything has been said, it would appear that the two kinds of entertainment—theatre and film—in spite of their apparent likenesses to each other, proceeded in general to settle down to a reasonably amicable and often mutually profitable association with each other. This first rival did not, in fact, introduce any serious problems for the playwrights.

The Theatre's Rivals: 2. Radio

The kinematograph, however, was by no means the only rival to the stage which was brought forward during the first half of the present century. Just about the time when a few inventive technicians were actively engaged in experiments designed to add sound tracks to the pictorial films, a second novelty, after a hesitant start, suddenly became universally popular. The crystal-and-cat's-whisker contraption, often with a brass fender used as an aerial, was converted into the radio, and within a very short time it came to be realized that this 'wireless' was something which could be linked with ever-increasing and ever-stronger bonds to the activities of actors and dramatists. When precisely and in what country the first broadcast play was sent into and over the air probably can never be determined with any assurance, but at least one thing is certain—the earliest dramatic piece formally commisioned by the original British Broadcasting Company was written by the Welsh playwright Richard Hughes: his tense mine-disaster piece, called *Danger*, was given to the listening public on January 15, 1924: this led, the following year, to Reginald Berkeley's lengthier and more ambitious *The White Château*, and thence, in a constantly expanding stream, to Dylan Thomas' *Under Milk Wood* in 1954 and to the multitudes of radio plays written, performed and published within recent years. In other countries the same story is repeated. Dürrenmatt, for example, began with a radio play called *Der Doppelgänger* in 1946, and even after he had become universally famous as a stage author he could still write his *Der Richter und sein Henker* for broadcasting, without having a theatrical performance in view: although Beckett won wide esteem for *En attendant Godot* in the early fifties, he turned to the radio when he wrote *All that fall* in 1957, and *Embers* in 1958: Frisch's *Biedermann und die Brandstifter* was originally composed as a radio play in 1953, as was his *Andorra* in 1959.

The facts are plain and incontrovertible. Lucrative opportunities are offered to young writers by the broadcasting authorities, and even authors who have won success and fame in the theatre can still be attracted by the radio's appeal. Tom Stoppard speaks for many of his companions when he tells of his delight in contemplating the fact that any one of his broadcast plays will have an "enormous audience," so that a single recording is heard by more individuals than could be accommodated within a medium-sized playhouse during the course of a fairly long run; and, even more significantly, he is spokesman for numerous authors when he lauds the freedom, the lack of restraint, offered by this new medium. 'The lovely thing about radio," he declares, "is that it's liberating. . . . There are no limitations at all."

"There are no limitations at all." It sounds an idyllic and an ideal environment in which to work, but not much reflection is required to convince us that for any young playwright whose ultimate aim is to apply himself to the theatre freedom unrestricted is not, in fact, necessarily the best apprenticeship which he could have. And even more serious doubts may arise when we consider the implications of the radio's "enormous audience." An author engaged in preparing a radio script and an author occupied in fashioning a text intended for stage presentation are alike in that their medium of artistic expression is verbal and that they must, or should, have in their minds thought of the audience to which their words will be addressed. Nevertheless, a great gulf yawns between them, and their audiences are wholly unlike each other. As he pens his lines, the theatre dramatist must surely have in his imagination, not simply the thought of several hundred individuals assembled within an auditorium, but the thought of a collective entity, a coherent group, composed of men and women who will normally, save for intermissions, watch and listen to the actors from the start to the conclusion of the evening's performance. For the writer of a radio play the imaginative vision of thousands upon thousands of listeners no doubt is awe-inspiring, but he cannot —indeed, he must not—consider them in terms of an assembled audience. These listeners will turn on the radios in their scattered homes, often devoting only half-attention to what is being spoken as they busy themselves with house affairs, frequently having their attention interrupted by the ringing of door-bells and the trilling summons of the telephone.

In effect, therefore, there is justification for suggesting that the time has not yet come for an attempt to determine precisely what effects the 'theatre-of-the-air' will ultimately have upon the theatres-on-the-ground and upon their drama. It is certain that radio plays do have ample virtues of their own, but at the same time no profit can arise from confusing the one form of playwriting with the other: rather it may be a salutary exercise to explore the differences between them, recognizing that the new form has introduced a doubly distracting force which operates both on authors and on those to whom their words are addressed, fully realizing, too, that with the establishment of this novel invention, the word 'drama' no longer means just one thing. The arrival of the 'radio play', in fact, has made it necessary for the term 'play' to be qualified for distinction's sake when it applies to 'stage plays'. No clearer sign could be found to show that, at last, after the passage of many centuries, the art-form established by Æschylus was confronted by a truly potent rival.

The Theatre's Rivals: 3. Television

Nor did this rival remain solitary for any length of time. Broadcasting had been a novelty introduced during the first 'post-war' years, and by a coincidence the second 'post-war' age saw the introduction of another novelty which in certain respects approached even closer to the theatre, and which sometimes tended to edge the older 'wireless' into a subordinate position. While it is, of course, entirely possible that technology will in the future come along with some other invention—perhaps of a kind as yet completely unimagined—television seems, at the present moment, to offer a final summation of all that has been happening since the first years of our century witnessed the development of the cinema from an amusing toy into an industry of vast range and untold wealth.

The television picture appears on a screen: hence television is akin to the moving pictures. The ubiquitous 'box,' on the other hand, is a homely object, to be watched and listened to from a convenient armchair or sofa: hence it is similar to that other box, the wireless set. Obviously it combines within itself elements characteristic of the theatre, the cinema, and the radio, and it is not surprising that already two kinds of TV dramatists have firmly established themselves. On the one hand, there are writers who apply themselves wholly or mainly to television—men such as N. J. Crisp, the appearance of whose name before the presentation of a TV play guarantees that the action will be skilfully managed, with sensitivity, balance, and, above all, adroit adjustment to the opportunities and restrictions inherent in this particular kind of dramatic composition: and on the other hand there are authors such as David Mercer, who, in a recent interview printed under the title of 'Birth of a Playwriting Man,' incisively indicates the attraction which television can have even for those who still wish to maintain direct, and perhaps chief, contact with the stage. In spite of the well-nigh incredible rubbish which those in charge of the programmes sometimes feel compelled to present to the teeming millions of box-watchers incapable of appreciating anything except the boorish, the crass, and the garish, the best writings of these two groups already give full warrant for employment of the term 'television art,' and there may even be some justification for the belief expressed by some of its more enthusiastic proponents that gradually it will shake off all its remaining associations with the playhouse and develop what has been called a "distinctive grammar of its own."

This, however, is a theme which cannot be discussed in the present context: consideration of the possible future of the 'TV drama' lies outside our scope. Virtually the only aspect of that theme which can have pertinence here is the influence exerted by the newly invented form upon the activities of dramatists writing for the stage and upon the audiences which give these dramatists support. 'Radio drama' has already secured a firm foundation for itself, and there are numerous signs pointing to the likelihood that this 'TV drama' will build for itself a foundation even firmer. David Mercer's remarks, clearly expressing the spell exerted upon him by this medium, must constantly be kept in mind, and to those remarks have to be added Kenneth Tynan's unqualified assertion that if he were a young man today he would "undoubtedly prefer to work for TV" rather than to write for the stage.

Theatrical Theorizing and the Movement Forward

With the arising of these three rivals must be associated another characteristic feature of the age.

In the general survey of dramatic development from 1900 on to 1939, attention has already been drawn to the fact that this period of nearly forty years provided a particularly happy hunting-ground for theatrical theorists. Almost everywhere dramatists took delight in seizing upon novel—or at least supposedly novel—ideas, and at the same time scores of fervently enthusiastic acting groups were formed for the purpose of pursuing the various -isms which at that time were scampering around in the art world. The attention of some was set upon naturalism; for others impressionism was the object desired; there were those who would consider nothing save expressionism; and there were those for whom only surrealism mattered. Almost infinite variety was to be encountered here, and eager clashings of opinion were frequent. Nevertheless, despite all the conflicting and confused diversity of opinions, one dominant central aim was common to all those numerous theorists who devoted so much time and effort towards promoting the interests of the 'art of the theatre.' No matter how much they might differ in their particular objectives and methods, practically all of them definitely and firmly focused their attention upon the work of the playwright; and thus the prime aim of those intent upon supporting and encouraging the interests of the stage was to do all in their power to cultivate the composition of 'good drama.'

This fact requires to be very firmly emphasized because today, when we cast our minds back to the earlier years of the century, our first thought might well tend to be that this was the period which produced the revolutionary concepts of Gordon Craig, of Vsevelod Meyerhold, of Antonin Artaud, and of Erwin Piscator—all the prophets currently being worshipped by so many intense devotees, and all of them tending to be more interested in 'theatre' than in 'drama.' If we are to gain a clear and valid concept of what was happening in the playhouse from the start of the century up to the close of the nineteen-thirties, it is essential to bear in mind that those four innovators have found active followers only within very recent years. Certainly the name of Gordon Craig was widely known before 1939, and there was almost universal recognition of his genius as a graphic artist, but even among his very few faithful disciples hardly a single one was prepared to accept as holy writ his basic judgment—that the art of the theatre, like all other arts, must give supreme power to a single 'artist,' and that the only person who could possibly fill that role was a director invested with unrestricted authority, one who might, if he so desired, make his actors into mere puppets. A very few members of the avant-garde occasionally murmured Meyerhold's name, but usually without appreciating what his theory of 'Biomechanics' really implied, and usually without any direct knowledge of his directorial activities. Artaud's Parisian Théâtre de la Cruauté opened and shut in almost record time, with considerable financial loss. Little attention outside Germany was paid to Piscator's theory and practice, and even Brecht's writings, except for *Die Dreigroschenoper*, remained largely unknown.

It is true that during the nineteen-thirties there was a little flutter of excitement among playgoers in New York when they were presented with the productions of the left-wing Theatre Union and of the Group Theatre, but, despite the fervour animating those concerned with these organizations and the genuinely warm welcome given by many members of the public to the plays of Clifford Odets, grave doubts prevailed concerning these and other attempts to substitute propagandist messages for what was commonly regarded as the proper objective of the stage. Even although it was generally recognized that the best and longest-enduring plays, whether tragic in theme or comic, were usually invested with serious concepts, there was almost universal agreement that such an appeal for direct action as appeared in John Wexley's *They Shall Not Die* (1934) was inherently dangerous. And virtually the same attitude was adopted in London by nearly all playgoers not actively concerned with Labour political views when they looked at the efforts made by the St Pancras Unity Theatre Club to promote an 'agitational' playhouse.

Such, then, was the prevailing attitude to the stage in most of the non-communist and non-fascist countries before the outbreak of war. The coming of peace, naturally, found a world vastly altered materially and spiritually, but within those territories which maintained democratic systems of governmental control this traditional concept of theatrical art remained unaltered, and indeed usually unchallenged, for at least a few years. As before, the word 'theatre' commonly called into being thought of 'playwright', 'players', and 'audience' in that order, with 'director' occupying an indeterminate position which varied according to the different kinds of production which happened to be in question.

The Concept of the Popular Theatre

While this general attitude towards the playhouse remained largely unchanged, however, it is important to pay due attention to the active expansion between 1945 and 1950 of a particular concept—that of the 'popular' or 'universal' theatre—which had been voiced in the pre-war years by various persons interested in the stage, but which rarely had been carried into practice. This requires at least a few explanatory comments.

The Unity Theatre Club was representative not only of the scattered theorists who wished to use the stage for political purposes but also of those who revelled in little theatres. There were, however, other theorists, equally interested in encouraging the social significance of the stage, who concentrated their attention upon the basic fact that, while other arts made their appeals to individual viewers or listeners, the theatrical performances were addressed to assembled audiences. From that observation, they proceeded to argue that the finest achievements of this art could be summoned forth only when audiences were broadly representative of their communities as a whole: was not the glory of Athenian drama evoked when practically the whole community attended the performances, and was it not clear that the Globe theatre in Shakespeare's time gathered within its rounded frame representatives of all classes within Elizabethan London? It was only natural that, during the years immediately after 1945 when anxious attempts were being made to rebuild the shattered fabric of civilized life, these thoughts should lead towards careful consideration of the role which the theatre ought to play within the social structure, and, in particular, towards attempts to make playhouse audiences more 'popular' and 'universal' than they had recently been. This trend may be exemplified by reference to two quite distinct movements, one in Britain and the other in France.

It is well known that London never had been graced by a national theatre and that successive governments had turned a deaf ear to the various pleas which from time to time were formulated by idealists who argued that a playhouse of this kind ought certainly to be erected and that, furthermore, public-supported theatres in centres other than the capital were needed quite as much as public-supported museums and libraries; and it seems quite probable that the governmental ear would have remained stone-deaf if it had not been for two war-time developments. In 1939 practically everyone had assumed that, if the theatre did succeed in maintaining its existence, the public would wish for nothing save the most trivial of frothy shows, and great was the surprise when the immediately following years were distinguished by a truly extraordinary series of impressive revivals of great plays which attracted large audiences both in the metropolis and on tour. Shakespeare's appeal was widespread, with important productions of *King Lear, The Tempest, Macbeth, Othello, Hamlet,* and *Richard III*; Donald Wolfit's repertory company found eagerly receptive audiences wherever it went; Sybil Thorndike took her performances of *Macbeth* and *Medea* with impressive success even into the far-off reaches of Welsh mining villages. The second fact is that in December 1939 a small group of interested individuals, fearing lest the arts might be completely blacked out, succeeded in securing modest grants from the Pilgrim Trust and the Ministry of Education for the purpose of establishing a Council for the Encouragement of the Arts (familiarly known as CEMA). At the start this Council's activities were very modest in scope, but it was able to inspire and encourage a number of small touring companies, such as Martin Browne's Pilgrim Players, which tirelessly took simple productions of interesting plays to widely dispersed war-time factories. Then with startling suddenness the bombings of 1941 demonstrated the true value to the community of these modest touring groups—with the result that in 1945 CEMA was transformed, under the new title of The Arts Council, into a permanent, officially sponsored organization. Steadily it has gone ahead, bringing a National Theatre at last into being and providing many provincial centres with their very own state-aided playhouses. It seems likely, indeed certain, that almost any person in 1933 who might have read in the newspapers that the annual grant to some organization called the Arts Council was to amount to seventeen million pounds would have closed his eyes in utter disbelief, but in 1973 this announcement was accepted with complete equanimity.

Thus bold attempts were being made in Britain to render the stage as popular as possible. 'Popular' is indeed the operative word here, and in order to appreciate its full force it is necessary to cross the Channel. Paris, of course, had for many long years enjoyed the possession of just such a national theatre as London had lacked; but the same kind of anxious consideration of the theatre's role in the community as had resulted in the establishment of the Arts Council in Britain drew attention to two facts—first, that the habitual theatre-goers in Paris were for the most part middle-class and upper-class, and, secondly, that French playhouse activities were mainly concentrated in Paris. Considerable discussion, therefore, was devoted to schemes for stimulating stage activities in outlying centres and for widening the social range of the spectators in the capital. Prominent in these discussions was Jean Vilar, a director inspired and inspiring, and in 1951, when means had been found for the establishment of a characteristically named Théâtre National Populaire, it was obvious to everyone that no person was better qualified to guide it on its course than he was. At the TNP he found full opportunity of bringing his dreams to reality: this organization had twin centres, one in Avignon and the other in Paris, where the vast Palais de Chaillot, with its enormous auditorium capable of seating 2,700 playgoers, was sufficiently large and sufficiently well endowed to permit the management to set their admission prices so low that crowds of humbler members of the working class as well as impoverished students were attracted into its interior. Those who had thus been enticed to become regular members of the audience immediately found themselves enveloped in what can be described only as a lively community where they were invited not only to attend the performances but also to join the actors in eager debates concerning the functions of the stage and the qualities exhibited in the plays. The simplicity with which most of the selected dramas were presented at the TNP strangely strengthened the warm feeling of intimacy which Vilar succeeded in conjuring up within this vast structure. As a director, he had ever been intent upon encouraging his actors in two essential ways—by refusing to permit their artistry to be swallowed up in a welter of stage effects (whether old-fashioned scenic spectacle or modern stage machinery), and by urging them to avoid all modish tricks and to rely chiefly upon controlled movement and clear, effective delivery of their lines. Always he had been eager to increase the appeal of the theatre for all kinds of playgoers, and most of the dramas which he selected for performance at the TNP were masterpieces from the past: Corneille, Molière, Shakespeare, Victor Hugo, Chekhov, Racine, de Musset, Sophocles, and Aristophanes appropriately headed the mighty roster of his chosen authors. Everyone entering the vast structure had the feeling that something truly important was happening, something in which each individual had a share. No one who had the good fortune of visiting this playhouse when it was under Vilar's direction can ever forget the great waves of animated excitement which invigoratingly brought the immense concourse into a spiritual unity such as hardly could be paralleled elsewhere in the world. The Palais de Chaillot was indeed the prime symbol and achievement of the ideal—the 'popular' or 'universal' theatre—which was such a basically inspiring force during the late forties and early fifties of the century.

The Concept of the Total Theatre

Nevertheless, even although this was the most characteristic feature of the period, signs were by no means lacking that other forces were also at work, forces which were opening up the way for many complexities to follow. If Jean Vilar stands forward as the living emblem of those theatrical endeavours which aimed at the cultivation of the popular playhouse, with stress boldly placed upon great dramatic works interpreted subtly, yet straightforwardly, by the actors, with a general rejection of all directorial temptations to display novelty at all costs, and with an accompanying avoidance of mechanical stage tricks, another great French actor-producer, Jean-Louis Barrault, may be taken as the outstanding symbol of the other spirit at work during this time. Just at first, if some of his pronouncements and productions are considered in isolation, it might well be thought that he and Vilar were controlled and inspired by identical objectives. At various times Barrault, in outlining his aims, emphasized the basic importance of the dramatist's work; he too stressed his belief in the essential quality of the theatrical art as something evolved from an emotional union of players and public; on various occasions he also uttered words of warning concerning the activities of those who were inclined to overload the stage and make too much use of stage machines; and, in describing the combined effect of the 'escape and illusion' produced by playhouse performances, he associated himself with others in stressing the combined artistic and social values of these experiences.

Yet, in spite of these pronouncements, Barrault stands apart from Vilar, frequently presenting himself as a living image of a peculiar theatrical philosophy which was destined gradually to take the place of the earlier concept of the universal stage. This philosophic trend, which was to play such an important part during the later fifties and the sixties, rightly deserves to be described as peculiar because it sought to be, and confidently assumed that it was, startlingly modern, while quite clearly it was largely dependent upon avant-garde theories which had been formulated during the earlier part of the century. One of Barrault's acknowledged holy scriptures was Gordon Craig's *On the Art of the Theatre*, originally published in 1911. His first production was a mime-play concocted by himself, *Autour d'une mère*. In its own time, this piece won ecstatic praise from Antonin Artaud, exponent of the 'theatre of cruelty' and author of the philosophic *Le théâtre et son double* (1938)—which was another of Barrault's scriptural texts. Despite his adverse critical pronouncements regarding stage spectacles, his presentations of *Le soulier de satin* in 1943 and *Christophe Colombe* in 1953 proved to be epoch-making displays of what, in the new avant-garde circles, was being called "total theatre."

Without any doubt whatsoever, Barrault was one of the greatest men of the theatre active during the years immediately after the end of the war, but if his philosophy and practice are carefully examined it becomes clearly evident that, unlike the equally distinguished Vilar, he was definitely tending to move from the comparatively simple ambience of the TNP towards something much more complex—and at the same time much more confusing. A motto applicable to his entire creative career is perhaps to be found in the title which he gave to an article written and printed in 1950—*Mes doutes et ma foi*.

Doubts and Questions

The doubts and the faith which he experienced were shared by many others.

EUGÈNE
IONESCO,
"LA CANTATRICE
CHAUVE"
Agence Bernand

JEAN
GRAUDOUX,
"LA FOLLE DE
CHAILLOT"
*French Cultural
Services*

STANISŁAW
WITKIEWICZ,
"WARIAT I
ZAKONNICA",
"THE MADMAN
AND THE NUN"
*Państwowy teatr
śląski*

If we move outside the enchanted atmosphere of the TNP we must become conscious of what, during the late forties and early fifties, must seem to be a truly potent and characteristic theatrical development—a development which may be described as an ever-increasing series of questions. After the darkness and terrors of the war years, it was natural that spectators in nearly all countries should avidly seize every opportunity of enjoying the brilliance, the sense of escape, the illusion of the stage. There were teeming audiences everywhere, yet, beyond the joy they took in the brilliance, the escape, and the illusion, they found that they could not give themselves completely to this theatrical realm. They knew that the world was still in an unsettled state; they sensed that all was not well either internationally or within the range of their own separate communities; they were, perhaps, unconsciously aware that, whereas in the immediate past many outstandingly great playwrights had been at work, the new dramas which were now being presented lacked the strength for which they were instinctively craving; and they observed that, despite such ventures as the TNP, the audiences in most of the playhouses, instead of being made more widely representative, were tending, season by season, to become ever more and more middle-class.

A certain state of unease began to make itself evident. In the United States, the thoughts of many men of the theatre started to go back to rosy memories of what Harold Clurman had called the 'Fervent Years' when the Group Theatre, socially committed, had been active in New York: and in many countries not dissimilar thoughts were being expanded, particularly in intellectual circles, by an increasing awareness of the theories and accomplishments of two émigré German activists—Erwin Piscator and Bertolt Brecht. The former had been for several years actively engaged in directing the Dramatic Workshop of the New School for Social Research and thus had an opportunity of indoctrinating his students with the ideas expressed in his 'philosophical' volume, *Das politische Theater*—an uncompromising disquisition seeking to prove that the only kind of playhouse worthy of esteem in modern times is one concerned with inculcating political truths, a playhouse of propaganda. Brecht had fewer opportunities of gathering disciples, but he also was resident for a time in the United States: it was there and in Norway that he wrote several of his most important plays, including *Mother Courage* and *The Life of Galileo*, and there he elaborated his critical approach to the theatre. Even although a full decade was to pass by before he became widely known, during those years his name, some of his writings, and some of his ideas concerning the stage were beginning to be discussed in at least a few interested circles.

The result of the uncertainties, the sense of unease, and the spread of relatively new ideas was that in many areas of stage activity questions began to be asked—and among them was one basic query which, although not infrequently expressed in complex and esoteric forms, was essentially direct and simple: "What is the theatre *for*?" At first this was heard only in small avant-garde circles or among youthful students, but soon it was to branch out widely, so that serious-minded delegates at international conferences could engage enthusiastically in examining its import, while at the same time it infiltrated into less formal discussions among members of the public. "Is the theatre an effective force in our time?" asked one inquirer; another posed the question, "Is it educational?" another "Is it something which can aid men towards an understanding of their environment?" another "Is it an instrument to serve democracy?" another "Is it a truly revealing mirror of our times?" And gradually these questions began to alter in several circles, taking positive form as imperative demands, inquiring "Is it calling attention to the defects in our society?"

Thus slowly the theatre's environment began to change. 'Meaningful entertainment' no longer was regarded as its greatest mission, and soon there came into being a new spirit with positive statements taking the place of queries.

The New Wave of Dramatists

There are always manifest pitfalls in dealing with any form of artistic activity in terms of 'movements,' and perhaps the hazards involved in considering the course of dramatic writing in such a manner are more dangerous than are the corresponding dangers associated with a similar approach to other literary forms. Even so, it is virtually impossible to avoid the conclusion that about the year 1955 the theatre experienced a sudden general change—a change which is evidenced by scores of interesting examples, with arresting plays emanating not only from countries which had previously been in the theatre's vanguard but also from countries which in the past had had either little or nothing of value to contribute to the stage.

In 1952 Beckett's *En attendant Godot* was published; the following year it was produced in Paris, and, in the English version prepared by its Irish author, it was presented to London audiences in 1955. Without any doubt whatsoever, *Le Ping-Pong* (1955), a fiercely satirical attack upon the increasing mechanization of life, marked a new development in the work of Arthur Adamov—a Russian settled in Paris. One of his companions was Eugène Ionesco, also a French citizen but a native of Rumania; already in 1948 he had written *La cantatrice chauve*, but when it was performed in 1950 little attention had been paid to it; audiences at that time were not yet conditioned into accepting what it had to offer: very different indeed were the effects of *Amédée, ou comment s'en débarrasser*, (1953) with its monstrously expanding dead body, and *Rhinocéros* (1959). *Biedermann und die Brandstifter* was written by the Swiss Max Frisch in 1953 as a radio play, and four years later was converted into a stage drama. At approximately the same time another Swiss author, Friedrich

Dürrenmatt, was actively engaged in establishing his reputation. During these years, too, the Berliner Ensemble, founded in 1949, gradually brought Brecht to general attention; this encouraged many playhouses elsewhere to present the plays which he had written during his period of exile; and naturally his theory of 'alienation' was eagerly discussed. Artaud had died obscurely in 1948, but soon his ephemeral 'Theatre of Cruelty,' which had appeared and vanished in 1935, became an object of interest; the letters which had passed between him and the well-known Barrault, published in 1952, were widely read; and, as is the way of the public, general attention to his life was attracted when it became known that he had spent most of his final years in various asylums for the insane. Although it cannot be said that any close connections are to be found between these Continental activities and the work of John Osborne, it must be observed that the arrival of the 'new wave' in England is commonly associated with the production of *Look Back in Anger* in 1956. And above all, serving as a sign that these and associated developments were truly international in scope, there is the rather surprising fact that in the same year, 1956, the Twentieth Congress of the Soviet Communist Party suddenly, unexpectedly, and completely overthrew the Stalinist ukase which had accorded favour only to socialist realism—thus not only bringing a change to the Russian theatre but also, much more widely, releasing a new theatrical force in Poland and other East European countries.

Even these few facts must convince us that from the early nineteen-fifties onward for several years a broadly extended new force was at work in the theatre generally; and of particular significance is the fact that this new force was stimulated and directed in several distinctly different ways. With the appearance of Frisch and Dürrenmatt a country which previously had contributed very little to the drama suddenly assumed a dominating position, with the result that the dramatic writings of these two authors require to be examined not only in terms of the language, German, in which they are composed, but also separately as inspired by the intellectual and emotional qualities of their native land: the question of the Swissness of the Swiss has, as it were, been added to the many other questions confronting the explorer of mid-twentieth-century drama. Even beyond this we must go, since a new phenomenon which can be described only in general terms as 'the concept of Africa' now suddenly emerged to lay its spell upon numerous avant-garde theatrical enthusiasts. When this spell is examined it becomes clear that it includes within itself three quite distinct elements. There are, first of all, the writings of American Negro authors to be taken into consideration. Plays emanating from this source are continually increasing as year passes year, and, when we find the dramatic universe presented in the works, for example, of LeRoi Jones described as owing its distinctive quality to the fact that this well-known playwright has seized upon "all the materials discarded by White America, by inverting its rituals and making a linguistic assault on its verbal orthodoxies," we must admit that here is something which we can disregard only at our peril. Secondly, within this sphere, there are the dramas (also as yet relatively few in number, but constantly growing) written by natives of various African nations. Such works, of course, are of diverse kinds, but perhaps those composed by Wole Soyinka, a native of Western Nigeria and a member of the Yoruba community, may be taken as a not uncharacteristic example. Educated in England and familiar with its stage, he has, as it were, sought to fuse some of its characteristic qualities and styles with his own native tribal beliefs and methods of expression—producing something completely without precedent. And, thirdly, there are all the African ceremonials, sometimes pungently scented with the odour of magic, which of late have been fascinating numerous theatrical individuals and groups, who occasionally have proceeded to adapt them in wondrous strange ways. Already, of course, even before the outbreak of war there were some theorists who had started delving back into the realm of tribal rituals, but most of these men, such as Artaud, had tended to wander (at least in fancy) among remote American Indian tribes rather than among African communities, and their explorations must be regarded as being in themselves primitive when they are compared with the latest investigations and experiments.

The appeal of this ancient, yet theatrically new-found land, together with its effect upon at least some Western stage endeavours, are made manifest in numerous recent statements and experiments, of which two examples may be sufficient here. There is, for example, the expedition in 1972 of Peter Brook and his players across Africa in search of pastures new. "We want," he has said,

> to be as far away as possible from any theatre where a million thoughts and traditions have already been established. What we are seeking is a genuinely empty space, but one in which a culture already exists, nourished by the world of the imagination. Virgin territory is useless. There's a lot to be said against virgins. But we need somewhere free from preconceptions. It's in this area that the genuine theatrical experience exists.

The second example which may be referred to here is a comment made by Richard Schechner, former editor of *The Tulane Drama Review* and latterly director of the acting company known as "The Performance Group." This comment appears in an article entitled "Actuals: Primitive Rituals and Performance Theory," devoted mainly to a description and examination of ceremonials traditionally conducted by a New Guinea tribe. Carefully he describes the *hevehe* masks, commenting upon their significance, and the description induces him suddenly to turn to what in his opinion is a modern Western counterpart. "Joan MacIntosh," he writes, "playing Dionysus in *Dionysus in 69*, had to start her performance each night by emerging naked amid an audience of 250 and saying, 'Good evening, my name is Joan MacIntosh, and I am a god.' Only by finding, releasing, and showing her deepest impulses of fear, hilarity, fraud and humiliation could she begin to cope with the actuality of her preposterous situation." "Her claim to divinity," he opines, "is thinkable only in the terms" of an episode which he had previously described as occurring during the course of one of the New Guinea ritual performances.

'Fringe' Performances and Happenings

'The Performance Group' is, of course, one of the numerous small acting associations which during the past twenty years sprang into existence, first in New York and then later in almost all the large cities of the world: and this reference to *Dionysus in 69* offers an apt cue for considering the significance of a theatrical development which, manifesting itself in scores of different ways, has completely altered the general pattern of playhouse activities.

It has already been stressed that one of the most characteristic trends during the early part of the century was the establishment of numerous 'Little Theatres,' 'Art Theatres,' 'Free Theatres,' and the like, companioned by a truly startling proliferation of play-producing societies, some professional, some amateur; and it is at first both easy and tempting to suppose that a close connexion exists between those earlier activities and the teeming world of 'Fringe,' 'Off-Broadway,' 'Off-Off-Broadway,' 'Laboratory,' 'Workshop,' and 'Underground' ventures which have multiplied so mightily during recent years. In view of that temptation (which, like most temptations, directs attention away from the truth) it must firmly be emphasized that a very serious mistake will be made if these two groups are not held strictly separate and distinct from each other.

For convenience, the associations established during recent years may be divided into two groups. The first of these are characterized in general by aims which are essentially extra-theatrical. Thus, for example, those concerned with 'educational theatre' have in mind only the thought of using stage performances for the purpose of teaching—either by presenting performances contrived in such a manner as to bring certain facts effectively before audiences of children or by encouraging the children to act out simple, but purposeful, scenes: those concerned with 'therapeutic theatre' similarly look upon the stage as a possible means of curing or remedying psychopathic and other disorders. While all such aims are certainly worthy, it seems evident that those who are wholly intent upon activities of this kind can have little specific interest in either playhouse or drama. Somewhat more difficult to deal with are those who are concerned with the 'political theatre', 'documentary theatre,' or 'agitprop theatre', since, while some activists of this kind simply use the stage as a convenient pulpit or lecture platform, others do try to combine their propaganda with new styles of playwriting and with interestingly imaginative production styles. Bertolt Brecht and the Berliner Ensemble immediately come to mind as representative of what the propagandist theatre can achieve at its best—and of course dozens of plays and presentations becloud our minds as we consider the ordinary course of the no doubt well-meaning, but generally rather dull, tendentious theatre which seeks to persuade audiences to adopt particular political attitudes towards this, that, and the other.

When these associations inspired by extra-theatrical ideals have been put aside, the other diverse acting groups may at first appear to be a very motley crew parading in so many directions as to suggest that they must be considered separately, each one of them regarded as a separate entity distinct from all its companions. Further examination of their stated objectives and of their productions, however, serves to convince us that many of them, if not all, share basic concepts and tendencies in common. The 'Happenings' contrived by several Off-Broadway associations, the shows presented before tiny, deliberately restricted audiences by Jerzy Grotowski's 'Laboratory Theatre' at Wrocław, those devised by the Odin Teatret of Holstebro, the various stormy efforts of the 'Living Theatre,' the 'Open Theatre,' and dozens of other kindred groups—all these unite in exhibiting certain common features.

First of all, it may be observed that many of these novel ventures are inspired by two thoughts which, when they are examined in conjunction, may well seem to be in conflict with each other. The first thought is that whereas such arts as painting and sculpture have become 'modern' during recent years by deliberately shaking off all their 'traditional' features, the theatre has not followed them in their bold careers, so that a desperate effort must now be made to force it into line: the second thought is that, in a world where the playhouse has such prominent rivals as the cinema, radio, and television, an effort ought now to be made to give it a form distinctively its own. Thus, for instance, Tadeusz Kantor, creator of the Polish acting group called 'Cricot-2,' has declared that he deliberately took "the experience of painting as a basis" for his stage experiments—not because he himself is a painter, but because

> painting is the only art which has been able to negate itself, the only one which after the war was submitted to a process of permanent revolutionisation. Geometrical abstracts, *l'art informel*, new realism, happenings, conceptual art, ephemeral art—these are only some of the stages of the development of painting, through such trends negating its traditional function.

Such remarks, of course, will immediately be recognized as typical of the claptrap jargon so prevalent in the artistic circles where the word 'tradition' signifies all that is considered despicable, evil, and worthy of immediate destruction. This artistic nihilism cultivated by Kantor seems very close in essence to the differently expressed ideas promulgated by his fellow-countryman Grotowski—a director who recently was lauded because he had "taken upon himself the task of discovering the theatre anew—a theatre reduced to its own possibilities, a theatre that differs from cinema, television and other communication media." In this way the two thoughts come together and are made one.

"A theatre reduced to its own possibilities" implies, for these men and for many others, a theatre in which directors and actors are in complete command—and in so far as the latter are concerned, physical ability counts for much more than vocal power. "It is not the word," declares Grotowski, "which is at the forefront here," but "the body subjected to merciless training in which hands learn how to laugh, legs to weep, and muscles of the face to form themselves into a mask." "This body," he informs us, "is at the same time trained for independent thinking, and from these fragments of the bodily confession the whole sequences of scenes are formed to which afterwards the text is added, introducing a certain order to the whole." His vision of the theatre is akin to that of Allan Kaprow (who may perhaps be regarded as the American inventor of 'Happenings'), who saw the ideal stage performance as one in which the actors' bodily movements were all-important and in which speech was banished in favour of animalistic grunts and snorts and cackles.

So widespread has been the display of 'Happenings' during the past ten or twelve years that in 1970 there was actually put on show at Cologne and Stuttgart an exhibition of diverse objects connected with over five hundred presentations of this sort stimulated by some forty or fifty different 'artists.' *Happening und Fluxus* was the rather pompous title of the show, and according to the basic logic of these performances the various manifestoes which sought to explain their nature—usually expressed in dimly mystical terms—indicated that the dramatists were all being thrust back into the lowly position which properly belonged to them, and that a new approach was being made towards the actor-audience relationship.

This, of course, is not the place for an examination and discussion of the various devices employed. In so far as the spectators are concerned, it is sufficient to recall what is already well-known, that here all attempts are made to get away from the familiar pattern of the ordinary play-house: Grotowski sternly limits his audience to eighty persons, in the 'Liquid Theatre' spectators are blindfolded and led along as they are stroked, kissed, caressed, by the 'actors,' and during the final throes of the 'Living Theatre' it is reported that those who had come to see the show were actually invited to come on stage and embrace the performers. Presumably all these efforts are in the interest of 'ritual', a term dear to many of the fringe companies, and one which seems usually to combine three or four divergent elements—an attempt to return to a world of primeval myth, a vague (and often apparently spurious) religiosity, a strong emphasis upon the sexual, and frequently an attempt to mingle the primordial and the modern, the scriptural and the scatological.

In certain productions the verbal element (sometimes reduced mainly to animalistic grunts and similar noises) is evolved by a kind of improvising process—although it must be noted that some of these groups try carefully to distinguish their own particular kinds of improvisation from the improvisation of the past: in other productions, an already existent drama is taken and twisted into new shapes. Thus, for instance, a masterpiece such as Sophocles' *Oedipus* can be selected, put in a pot, flavoured with fragments taken from Seneca's drama on the same theme, and boiled into a monstrous brew while little bits of contemporary spices are stirred into the mixture—as when, in a scene wherein announcement is made of Oedipus' impending marriage with Jocasta, a newsboy runs over the stage crying "Extra! Extra! Oedipus to marry the Queen Mother! Read all about it!" Another kind of procedure is illustrated by Kantor when, in a recent interview, he described what occurred in the preparations for his presentation of *The Madman and the Nun*. At the beginning there certainly was a text in the shape of a surrealist play, *Wariat i zakonnica* (1923), in which Stanisław Witkiewicz had anticipated by thirty or forty years many dark thoughts concerning twentieth-century civilization by setting his action in an institution which combines the worst features of both a prison and a lunatic asylum and by making his villains take the emblematic parts of Science and Religion. "The text of the drama," says Kantor, "was discussed,"

> the actors commented on it and dropped it, went back to it, recited the words, but never identified themselves with the text.

This process, he explains, was designed to result in "the nihilisation of events," involving their "invalidisation," wherein the words were (quite properly, in his view) "put into a state of insignificance"—so that he was able, in the end, to create a "zero theatre" in which the creative force was "accident."

The trend towards the rejection of the dramatist, particularly when accompanied by much esoteric verbiage concerning ritual, has thus spread widely during the sixties, embracing both the large and the small. At one extreme we find a critic, John Peter, lugubriously recording his impressions of a student drama festival at Durham. Heading his survey with the title *PLAYS WITHOUT PEOPLE*, he closes his account with what he calls his "moment of truth" when he was afflicted by a home-brewed play presumably intended to be an allegory about God and Mankind:

> Three groaning blindfolded men in loin-cloths groped for each other; a fourth, with a savage, idiotic grin and a limp, stalked round them and dealt them fearful blows with his massive crutch. The blows were real enough; red welts rose on the men's bodies and one of them was bleeding from the forehead. It was when he crawled towards me, his loin-cloth alarmingly disarrayed, and started sucking and licking my neighbour's left boot, that I began to compose a desperate letter.

This letter he addressed to Grotowski—advising him that "things are getting rather out of hand." Even while admitting that all this was being done with deep commitment and savage precision, Peter declared that it was

> self-defeating as theatre, banal as moral comment and dangerous as therapy. Who gets what out of it? You wrote about the actor making a total gift of himself to the audience; but what if the audience doesn't want the gift?

From Durham to Persepolis is a far cry, yet the one may serve to call to mind the other. In 1971 Peter Brook concocted at his International Centre of Theatre Research in Paris a 'production' which he grandly presented amid the majestic ruins of the Persian capital. Although some critics who are inclined towards keeping in with the latest experiments had kind things to say about this extraordinary show (which, in the midst of ancient monuments illuminated by flaring torchlight, must certainly have had its share of the effective), and although a day-by-day detailed 'account of the experiment' narrated by A. C. H. Smith has appeared in book-form, a factual report prepared by Ossia Trilling seems best calculated to convey to readers a balanced impression both of the interesting and (shall it be said?) the not so interesting aspects of the venture. In so far as drama is concerned, the most significant feature of the entire show is that Ted Hughes, associated with others, actually devised a completely new language with elements taken from many sources, from classical Greek (although confessedly no one is absolutely sure how that speech was pronounced in ancient times) on to Spanish, and with considerable reliance on elements derived from a long-lost Avesta utterance: despite the fact that, apparently, knowledge of this utterance is to be discovered only on some cowhides unearthed in Persia about two thousand years ago, a student of the tongue, Mahin Tadjadod, felt sufficiently certain that she had so completely mastered its secrets that the company was drilled by her in the pronunciation of its strange 'physiological' sounds. Thus was the manufactured language of Orghast brought into being—a language, it has been said, "that reveals the body as a map of human experience."

When this exercise is related to the various experiments in 'visceral language' it seems evident that, whereas some other left-wing theatrical enthusiasts have sought to expunge from the stage any forms of expression save the 'visceral' and occasional animal-like noises, here a deliberate effort is being made to create, as Peter Brook himself has asserted, a completely new "language of sounds." In effect, as one observer noted, the invention of this 'Orghast' was the result of reflections concerning the breakdown in communication among men in modern times—an attempt which might be described as a mystical rehabilitation of language through the devising of a speech which, because artificially constructed, could have no direct 'meaning.' Orghast was the language, and *Orghast* was also the spectacle, which (it has been reported) was described officially as stemming from certain basic myths—the gift of fire, the massacre of the innocents, the imprisonment of the son by the father, the search for liberation through revenge, the tyrant's destruction of his children: and the search for liberation through knowledge—as reflected in the hymns of Zoroaster, the stories of Prometheus and Hercules, Calderón's *Life's a Dream*, Persian legends and other parallel sources.

Orghast does not stand alone. In 1972 there was the Persian Shiraz Festival, described in brilliantly derisory phrases by Irving Wardle. The two dominant figures here, we are told, were Karlheinz Stockhausen and the American director Robert Wilson, "two intuitive specialists in fragmentation with aspirations to universal communication." The latter's dramatic concoction was "a 168-hour happening running night and day for the whole length of the festival." The experience of watching even part of it was, we are reliably informed, one of "stupefying vacuity"—

On the first night Mr Wilson (a Lincoln-like figure) appeared in a flour-impregnated suit together with an immobile black girl, with her back to the audience, two women in long skirts, and a little girl in a Disney-land sweat shirt. Off-stage, a voice inaudible beyond the first rows read from *Moby Dick* and the Book of Jonah. Now and then the figures made imperceptible movements; walking somnambulistically round the platform with a knife; speaking detached words into a telephone. Presumably they were intended as an average American family. Dialogue consisted of detached grunts and falsetto squawks; except towards 2 a.m. when Mr Wilson staggered schizophrenically towards the front-stage scaffolding and pointed outwards with an accusingly dislocated gesture: "Why are you-oo lee-ee-vv-inn-g?"

Subsequent encounters only repeated the initial experience. A question-and-answer session turned out to be another extension of the play, with Mr Wilson attired in a woolly red beard and responding to direct questions with sibylline remarks about children dying of old age; supported by a veiled lady assistant who backed him up with pop quotations from Yeats and Hopkins, and folded written questions into aeroplanes. The Cretan jail experience was also built into the play. A guard lugged Mr Wilson behind a Jail House flat; whereupon two girls inched over towards it and asked "Can we see our friend?" "LSD? No!" he barks. "Oh", they moan, "Whatever shall we do?", and inch back to the starting point.

The Play's the Thing?

These 'productions' devised by Peter Brook and Robert Wilson came respectively in 1971 and 1972, and now, in 1973, there are many voices uttering words of grim import. "We are groping in the dark," declares a Frenchman. "All of yesterday's certitudes have crumbled—that of the 'popular theatre' and that of the grouplet auto-revolution." "The theatre is in a period of recension," asserts an English critic, while a very prominent English director senses that "the theatre now is reflecting—which is why there are so many questions abroad." Vast spectacular shows in Persia, no doubt, have very little interest for ordinary playgoers, yet, having listened to Irving Wardle's description of Robert Wilson's *Shiraz* prodigy, we may find it of interest to compare that account with Harold Hobson's record of a recent visit to the TNP in Paris. Jean Vilar, alas, has now gone, and his magnificent theatre has been placed in the control of four directors, of whom Patrice Chéreau is one, and, in Hobson's words, Chéreau is a man prepared, "with Cartesian logic," to carry

> to extreme lengths a theory of which we have in England seen the timid beginnings, but as yet only the beginnings. This is the theory that machinery and accessories are more important than human beings.

Characteristically, the play presented to the public at the Palais de Chaillot was a concocted one—a *Massacre à Paris* devised by Jean Vauthier out of Marlowe's queer drama. This piece, writes Hobson,

> is about the massacre of St Bartholomew's Eve in which metaphorically the protagonists waded through blood. M. Chéreau makes his players wade through water, real water, 8,000 gallons of it. The players do more than wade; they sit down in the water, they lie in it, and when one of the characters, like the Queen of Navarre, dies, she is compelled to do an underwater swim before she can climb into the air offstage. This production is likely to leave a greater legacy of rheumatism, fever, dropsy, chilblains, and common colds than any other in the history of the theatre.

Here, it is the TNP and its once so invigorating ideal of a universal stage which are being massacred: no longer is emphasis placed on the presentation of great plays simply and directly presented to vast popular audiences. And it is particularly important that we should observe that this murder of Vilar's basic concept is strangely paralleled by numerous other kindred events. If the spirit of the TNP has passed away, so too has the spirit of the Berliner Ensemble—that organization which proved such a stimulating force during the latter nineteen-fifties and the nineteen-sixties; and with the disintegration of the Ensemble, suddenly, and in many different quarters, an increasing dissatisfaction is being voiced concerning Bertolt Brecht himself—and, as everyone knows, no other man, throughout the course of some twenty years, had been more widely acclaimed as a creative artist and as a theatrical theorist. Just a short time ago, Jerzy Grotowski was said to have left his 'Laboratory' and to have later returned to it a changed man: if we are to take at face value a statement which he made in 1970, it would appear as though he no longer has the same interest in the theatre as inspired him during earlier years. Even the 'Living Theatre,' after a scandal in France when the company trooped out into the streets, calling upon their followers to break down the gaols and release the prisoners, is reported to have ended its somewhat erratic career. And in 1973 the members of the 'Open Theatre' have announced that they intend to break up their confederation.

The fringe theatres had always been inclined, on the whole, to disparage the work of the dramatists, but, since they *were* fringe efforts, appealing only to small groups of spectators, it was relatively easy to disregard the theoretical pronouncements made by divers thoughtless and servile lackeys of the Grotowski cult, who prided themselves in having rejected "the intervention of an author" and who extolled the communicative virtues of "visceral language." A feeling of chill may, however, seize upon us when lately we find similar sentiments repeated by such a distinguished director as Peter Brook—and still more, when we encounter the not so dissimilar but more dangerously subtle arguments presented by Peter Hall—a director equally distinguished, and one who has hitherto maintained his belief in the supremacy of the play. His latest philosophical position seems to be that words, the words of the playwright, are both good and bad things in the theatre: no doubt they have value, but their greatest significance rests in their power to "define silence": thus "verbal poetry is the least poetic thing about a truly poetic theatre—the least."

That there is some truth in these assertions is certain, yet the greatest of caution must be exercised before we accept their terms without question. At first glance, Peter Hall's comment that

> four hundred years of mounting concern with the text, with the playwright and his literary values, have made a lot of people very suspicious

may appear to be fair comment—until we call to mind that it is based on a false premise. The true, the great, playwright is not concerned with "literary values": his dramas derive their worth from the fact that he is intent upon the theatrical quality of his words. And anyone who considers the history of the stage during past centuries must be forced to agree that in the playhouses numerous texts—and particularly the texts of Shakespeare's tragedies and comedies—have been mangled and mauled by actors and directors, many of them, like Caesar's murderers, most honourable men, yet dominated, like many honourable men, by overweening belief in their own superior skills and rectitude. Not only so: there is also the fact that the supposed mounting concern with the playwright is distinctly *not* a recent development. At the theatre's very start in ancient Greece, this concern was much greater than it ever has been in recent times—and for a clear and incontrovertible sign of this we need go no further than a law passed by Lycurgus in the fourth century B.C. Æschylus, Sophocles, and Euripides were by that time deceased, and various actors, when playing the old parts, began to take the liberty of introducing such adjustments in the dramatists' lines as might make the texts more aptly harmonize with their own individual histrionic styles: the new law declared that official copies of the original tragedies should be deposited in the archives of the state, and that any actors who deviated from these texts should be subject to fines. This, surely, must be recognized as an expression of "mounting concern with the text" which surpasses anything known within the last four hundred years: never has Shakespeare's language received such tender legal protection.

What demands particular consideration here is, however, something much more important, something that is quite distinct from questions and problems arising from reflections concerning the relationship between plays and players. The rejection of the dramatist which has been so common a feature of recent avant-garde theatrical activities generally tends to be the result, not simply of a desire to free the performers from restraint, but, much more significantly, from a deeply felt 'philosophical' concept. In effect, it is the end-result of a gloomy contemplation of the fate of our contemporary society during a period when human beings are being swallowed up, and corrupted, and polluted by the consequences of what some people still call 'technological advance.' The experimenters who reject words do so because they deem words to be, not merely void of meaning, but, still more dangerously, misleading. Consequently, in rejecting the 'literary' play they are in fact suggesting that the theatre should make its own physical protest against the defects they discern, or think they discern, in man's present-day society. This is part of the counsel of despair inherent in such ventures as Kantor's 'Zero Theatre.'

If such theatrical experimenters are right, if this is to be accepted as the only possible procedure for those interested in making the stage prove a potent force within its social framework, then certainly no more can be said—the dramatist's task is done. Before such a judgment is accepted, however, it must be remembered that plays are still being written, that many theatre-goers still enjoy attending what may be styled 'traditional' performances wherein the play's the thing, that many other former playgoers are tending to limit their visits to the theatre, or even to abandon such visits completely, precisely because they refuse to accept the conclusions reached by the experimenters, and that there still remain many persons who, while believing that the stage has a salutary social mission to perform, not only insist that pursuit of this mission does not necessitate a break with the traditional structure of playhouse activities, but go still further by insisting that such a break must inevitably prove to be self-defeating.

Since several anti-dramatic statements have been cited above to illustrate the philosophic cult, expressed in so many different ways, which has latterly become fashionable in many quarters, perhaps the best and most effective way of ending this rapid sketch of conflicting thoughts on the theatre is to make reference to a remarkably perceptive essay, printed in 1972, by Robert Brustein, an actor, director, and critic, author of *The Theatre of Revolt, Seasons of Discontent, The Third Theatre,* and *Revolution as Theatre*—most assuredly a man who could never be accused of being insensitive to the aims of modern rebellious and experimental acting groups. As the sixties have moved on to the seventies, he has here expressed his awareness that something is going wrong with the modern stage, and he has decided that this something wrong is not unconnected with the complete freedom which the playhouse has now gained for itself: outwardly, nothing now is forbidden, but inwardly the theatre has become "rather hollow", "has lost the power to reach us"—

And so, at the very moment when true freedom has at last become possible, after years of timidity, censorship and inhibition, there may be nobody around capable of enjoying it.

Interestingly, Brustein's note of gloom has harmonized with a number of end-of-the-year surveys written in December 1973 by some of his fellow-critics in several countries. In these assessments there have not been absent numerous hints that the more penetrating spectators of the theatrical scene are inclining to be more than a little bored with all the previously fashionable talk about 'visceral language' and the like, and that some of them are becoming disturbed by the many attempts made in the nineteen-sixties to shatter the traditional concept of what the playhouse has to offer. There are suggestions in these surveys that at least some of the authors would be prepared to agree with a boldly phrased statement made by Brustein in a recent discussion. Asked about his views concerning 'creative' and 'interpretative' contributors to theatrical productions, he unhesitatingly declared his belief that the only person in the complex realm of theatrical art who might have the right to regard himself as creative is the dramatist: actors, directors, designers, he firmly asserted, are "collaborative" and "interpretative": and his statement ended with the firm pronouncement that "the playwright remains the most important figure in any theatre situation."

Here, without the shadow of a doubt, the wheel has unexpectedly come round full circle, and, despite the numerous attempts to destroy the traditional concept, we are back again with Æschylus in Athens.

At least, we are back with him in spirit. Obviously, in order to determine whether we can regard ourselves as back with him in practice, it is necessary to turn from consideration of the teeming theories to an examination of at least some of the plays which have been written, and which are now being written, in this puzzling theatrical age of ours.

PART XIV

THE TRANSFORMATION SCENE: 1945–73

INTRODUCTION

THE PROLIFERATION of theories, the acknowledged or unacknowledged desire to alter completely the traditional nature of the theatrical experience, and the impacts made by the three powerful forces of cinema, radio, and television—these have largely been responsible for creating the confusions, the doubts, the deviations, and the complexities nearly everywhere apparent in the development of the drama during the middle years of the present century. Nevertheless, when attention is directed away from contemplation of the theatre in general to an examination of the activities of individual playwrights it must immediately be realized that the chances and changes which the stage has experienced from the forties to the seventies were largely dependent upon the operation of that force which has determined the theatre's activities from their very start —the force of the social-political environment within which the playhouse has its being.

There is no one who needs to be told that, if the world was mightily altered after 1919, it was still more mightily changed after 1945. So far as the drama is concerned, however, a considerable difference is to be observed between those two periods of change. During the inter-war years there were so many novel experiments made in the various countries that stepping from playhouses in one land into the playhouses of another often seemed at that time like travelling from one universe into a universe entirely different. Yet within those twenty years it still remained possible—although often rather surprisingly—for interested individuals to secure for themselves valid, personally acquired panoramic views of what was being evolved within the theatres of all those scattered and politically contrasted territories. The changes were most certainly numerous, and the complex chances often perplexing, yet what was being presented on those stages could be mastered and appreciated.

Astonishingly, however, the obtaining of similar panoramic views within the period from 1939 to the early seventies is by no means so easy —astonishingly, because at first glance it must assuredly seem that conditions for surveying the theatre as a whole are far more auspicious today than they were during the earlier part of the century. Travel from country to country has been made swifter, easier, and more common, so that physically theatre-going in foreign countries has become a fairly simple exercise; 'international seasons' in some of the world's larger capitals more frequently provide opportunities whereby companies from abroad can perform before audiences other than those of their native lands; informative reference works abound, from many-volumed encyclopaedias to paperback dictionaries, providing easy access to information which previously had often been difficult to secure; the multiplication of drama departments in colleges and universities has stimulated the preparation and publication of hundreds upon hundreds of plays in translation and of scores of critical-historical studies; and theatrical journals, many of them seeking to be not only up-to-date but also up-to-the minute, have multiplied almost beyond belief. If we believe that the effect of television performances is the same as, or at least close to, that which comes from stage presentations, then to the many new sources of information concerning what foreign theatres are engaged in presenting there must be added the various 'World Theatre' programmes which are brought to thousands upon thousands of homes for individual viewing.

On the surface, therefore, everything now appears favourable for any person anxious to discover and to comprehend what is happening in playhouses here, there, and everywhere.

There is, on the other hand, a very serious—although often not fully appreciated—problem which must not be ignored. Without doubt what may be called the aids to the acquiring of knowledge have increased a thousandfold, and equally without doubt the playhouse realm has in many respects become considerably more international in its range than it has ever been in the past, yet the difficulties confronting individuals who seek to survey this area as a whole have immensely increased both in substance and in spirit. The expansion in geographical range which has been noted above—the truly tremendous social and political changes resultant from what happened during the Second World War—the numerous idiosyncratic differences which subtly separate what superficially may well appear to be similar, even identical, forms of dramatic expression—the proliferation of so many theatrical theories, several of them closely connected with conditions peculiar to individual territories—the impact made by these theories upon dramatists who otherwise remain far removed from each other—the numerous efforts made to translate these theories into practical stage terms—the almost frenetic indulgence in experiments ever more and more bizarre—the varying impacts made in different countries by the theatre's rivals, and the divergent ways in which the activities of those rivals have been accommodated within the many disparate social systems—the strangely contrasting attitudes taken towards the introduction of political material into dramatic writings—the conflicting answers given to the basic question concerning the proper place of the theatre in social life—and, above all, the equally conflicting attitudes taken towards the rôle of the dramatist within the theatre's hierarchy—all these and dozens of other similar reflections combine in forcing upon us the conviction that nowadays the contemporary drama can properly be surveyed only by those who, apart from an intimate knowledge of the theatrical activities within the various areas, have an equally intimate acquaintanceship with the particular patterns of social life amid which these activities have their being.

Such a conclusion, of course, means that the inner spirit informing the plays produced within any one country or area usually cannot satisfactorily be observed, explained, and assessed by any save fellow-countrymen of the dramatists concerned, or at least by fellow-residents in their midst. The practical consequence involved in accepting that conclusion has been that only one valid course seemed to offer an opportunity of providing an intimate picture of the drama's intricately varying patterns during the past thirty years—the presentation of a number of specially prepared surveys devoted to some at least among the more important theatrical territories of the present age. The adoption of such a plan, naturally, has meant that the procedure employed in the earlier sections of the present volume has had to be abandoned: thus, for example, the emphasis upon general trends—such as impressionism and expressionism, realism and naturalism—necessarily had to be abandoned when the focus was shifted to the overall activities within the boundaries of these selected key areas. This also explains why it was deemed essential, or at least desirable, to preface this series of independently written essays by a general introduction concerned, not with individual plays from particular lands, but with widely ranging theories and trends.

The following series of surveys might, of course, have been arranged in many different ways, and no doubt a few brief comments are desirable concerning the order selected here for their presentation. For two reasons it seemed appropriate to begin with the United States of America, since this permits us at one and the same time to see how that giant of the past, Eugene O'Neill, the playwright with whom the pre-war survey ended, could still take a further great stride into the post-war age with his *Long Day's Journey into Night*, and to observe how the early Off-Broadway groups were beginning to engage in various experimental productions destined to find many imitators in other countries. This article on the American drama seemed to demand that it should be followed by the essay on English dramatists and on the English-language plays composed by some Irish authors. The French-language stage appeared to have its proper place immediately after that contribution, partly because it includes the work of another Irishman, Samuel Beckett, and partly because of the widely spread influence of several of its dramatists. Obviously the German-language drama had to come next, since the extensive range of its playwrights in the FDR (the Federal Republic of Germany), the GDR (the German Democratic Republic), Austria, and, not least important, Switzerland, had spread its various styles widely over the whole world. A broader range of languages is included within the article which deals with the Scandinavian countries, and equal variety appears in the essay concerned with the USSR and the communist lands in Eastern Europe. These are followed by shorter surveys devoted to the 'Hispanic' sphere and to Italy, while the series is completed by brief accounts of the new movements within Australia and Africa.

Almost automatically, these essays have ranged themselves in order, emphasizing not only the manner in which novel dramatic patterns have come into being but also the way in which, now as in the past, theatrical inspiration has tended to move from land to land. Thus, for example, Switzerland, a tripartite territory which formerly had virtually had little of significance to offer, suddenly during the fifties and sixties produced a series of peculiarly interesting plays—although here it must not be forgotten that this wealth came from only one of the cantons: amid all the excitement among the German-speaking communities, the French and Italian remained almost wholly silent. A kindred observation, too, must be made concerning the vast communist territories. Theoretically, all of these countries should have been presenting plays and productions of like kind, yet clearly the facts by no means corresponded with the theories: little of interest is to be found in Moscow and Leningrad, but many eager eyes have of late been turned to Warsaw, Cracow and Wrocław.

Thirty years have passed by since the end of the War. For the theatre three full decades is a fairly lengthy period of time, and, as has already been indicated, there are now numerous signs of dissatisfaction in many quarters, and one has the feeling that in the near future some new styles will arrive to take the place of those which have recently tended to be dominant. If these styles are indeed established, of course, there is no means of determining from what quarters they will come. Prognostication is impossible, but at least two concluding comments may be hazarded with a measure of assurance. The first is that the theatrical advent of what originally were colonies in South America, Australia and Africa cannot fail to exercise a new force; and the second is that, if the course of dramatic writing in any way follows the pattern dominant during past centuries, it seems most probable that any new movement which arrives to take the place of the still currently fashionable 'absurd' will arise, not in those countries which have of late been contributing most, if not all, the predominating models for today's playwrights, but unexpectedly in some land which has contributed comparatively little to the stage during the past three decades. What we cannot possibly guess is whether this land will be one, such as Italy, which has had a long dramatic history but which has recently been overshadowed, or whether it will be some area far removed from the present centres of theatrical activity.

This, however, seems to be a speculation which in fact is immaterial. What basically is important is the fact that, no matter how powerful are its present rivals, and no matter what serious problems confront the stages of today, the theatre clearly not only maintains its power but within several important areas has assumed fresh strength and vision.

POST-WAR DRAMA IN THE U.S.A.

ARTHUR WILMURT

The Plays of Disillusionment

THE AMERICAN theatre had scarcely begun to adjust itself to peace-time expectations after the Second World War when the predictable plays of disillusionment began to appear. Arnaud D'Usseau and James Gow had *Deep Are The Roots* on stage before the end of September, 1945; *Home of the Brave*, by Arthur Laurents, followed in December. The earlier play depicted the humiliation of a medalled Negro veteran by the white citizens of his home town; the later struck down a sensitive Jewish soldier with a crippling trauma when he was almost called a Jewish bastard by a dying friend. These were hotly and skilfully written plays, but not until Arthur Miller's *All My Sons* appeared in 1947, showing how an industrialist's zeal for profit resulted in the death of twenty-three American pilots, including his own son, was the cynical theme developed with enough complexity and insight to suggest the arrival of a new important dramatist.

Meanwhile it was becoming evident that, with one exception, the playwrights who had dominated the pre-war scene would not recover their eminence. Only Eugene O'Neill's fire blazed again. His *Long Day's Journey into Night*, produced in 1956, has an emotional force he had never equalled. Autobiographical plays often derive their poignancy or their piquancy from the fact that the author is writing about himself. *Long Day's Journey* lives its own life. As full of pity as it is of terror, this dissection of himself, his brother, his father, and his mother, tortured by their interlocked loves and hates and their awareness of themselves, is totally devoid of self-pity. O'Neill's long-standing debt to Strindberg, so often noted, may be said to have been paid here: the love/hate drama of the Tyrones is unfolded with more compassion and objectivity than can be found in any of Strindberg's variations on the theme.

New figures were emerging to dominate the scene as the forties moved to a close. The technique of *All My Sons* had been glaringly Ibsenesque, causing sceptics to wonder if Miller could keep up with a more expansive theatrical age. *Death of a Salesman* (1949) stilled all doubts. The dramaturgy here moves fluidly in and out of reality, memory and fantasy, making the audience aware to exactly the same degree as the protagonist which area is being occupied at any moment. Willy Loman, travelling salesman over sixty years old, no longer competent or needed, haunted by distracting fantasies that mingle what might have been with what was, struggles frantically to maintain his image of himself as the successful head of the family. One of his sons, knowing how false the image is, explodes in an outburst of contempt and despair: "Pop! You're a dime a dozen and so am I!" and then collapses in surrender to pity and love. Whereupon Willy offers one last sacrifice to his rickety values—his life for an insurance payment that will show his sons his worth. Few dispute the psychologists who have analysed the complex relationships Miller perceived among the play's characters. Whether this drama can be termed 'genuine tragedy' is still being debated.

Miller's own belief that the common man can achieve tragic stature was reasserted in *The Crucible* (1953). Its protagonist, John Proctor, is the obverse of Willy Loman: young, strong, perceptive and independent. But he too is thrust into a struggle to maintain his image of himself, and he chooses death rather than the publication of a false confession that would "rob him of his name." His battleground is the witch hunt that racked Salem, Massachusetts, in 1692, and the play's theme of justice crushed by fear caused it to be taken as a commentary on recent events in Washington, D.C., while its driving energy and its strong contrast between self-sacrificing virtue and craven evil caused it to be put down as melodrama. To these observations Miller replied that the analogy was coincidental and that the decision to deal with positive contrasts simply manifested his concept of what constitutes drama.

The Crucible develops Miller's most intricate action, *A View from the Bridge* (1955) his most straightforward. Metaphorically, the "bridge" links the docks of Brooklyn with the ancient Mediterranean world where perverse familial relationships, resolved by violence, produced what late ages have identified as 'tragedy': there is, in fact, a twisted evocation of *Hippolytus* in the play. Eddie Carbone, a longshoreman, passionately desires his niece; she has a Dionysian suitor; Eddie's inadmissable jealousy drives him to a reckless, degrading course of action involving slander, treachery, and finally his violent death. Miller may try a bit too hard to convey his feeling that the play is the stuff of Greek tragedy, but Eddie Carbone stands beside Willy Loman and John Proctor as exhibiting Miller's concept of the tragic hero. Each puts every available resource into a struggle to maintain his chosen image of himself—Miller contends that this is the prime criterion.

After 1955, Miller's concern for the tradition of tragedy seemed to subside, but the struggle for the image remained basic. It was active in an unconventional 'Western' film, *The Misfits* (1961), and it appeared in

After the Fall (1964) as a struggle generally taken to be a paraphrase of Miller's own. In the area just beyond frank autobiography Miller is no match for O'Neill: Quentin, unlike Edmund, the author-figure in *Long Day's Journey*, talks mostly about himself, taking the audience into his confidence as if it were his psychoanalyst. One sequence in Quentin's confidences leaves a strong impression: his courting and wedding a wayward, hopelessly neurotic popular singer. Here is a memorable character, and here the play comes nearest to achieving the independence from autobiographical reference that distinguishes O'Neill's masterpiece. But *After the Fall* seems mainly to be a struggle to construct and display an image interesting primarily because one assumes it to be the author's own.

In his next play, although he returned to the realistic convention, Miller succumbed to a desire to speak his mind rather than write a dramatic action: *Incident at Vichy* (1964) is a discussion of the plight of the Jews. In *The Price* (1968) he revived his earliest form and situation—a tightly unified structure of cumulative revelations concerning the betrayal of two sons by their father.

Tennessee Williams also continually returned to the theme of his earliest plays, the conflict of sacred and profane love. This was handled with great delicacy in *The Glass Menagerie* (1944), then orchestrated fortissimo in *A Streetcar Named Desire* (1947). In the earlier play, Laura was so fragile that profane love never had a chance. In the later, Blanche DuBois was driven insane by an internal struggle between adoration of the sacred and a too available gratification of the profane, aggravated by the spectacle of a pair who seem to have found in earthly love a passage to heaven. In *Summer and Smoke* (1948) Williams distilled the conflict to its essence. On one side is Alma, a spinsterish parson's daughter, on the other is John, M.D. and rake. At a timely moment in the play's structure her suppressed desire for his body and his unconscious adoration of her soul brush past each other. The outcome is already all too clear: John is betrothed to a nice lively girl and Alma embarks on her first try at harlotry.

In a robustious comedy, *The Rose Tattoo* (1950), the recurring conflict was at last resolved in a happy ending, when a lusty Sicilian-American's loyalty to her dead husband collapsed before the amorous onslaughts of a man with an identical tattoo. Even more robustious was *Camino Real* (1953), Williams' freest, boldest, play. In a pseudo-Latin-American plaza are trapped the world's greatest romantic adventurers: Don Quixote, Byron, Casanova, Marguerite Gautier, walled in by the most oppressive elements of today's life. Among them comes Kilroy, a legendary figure of the Second World War, known only by a message left behind: "Kilroy was here." *Camino Real* has the earmarks of a complex allegory, but Williams described it as a fairy tale, and it may be best to take it for its fairy-tale theme—that what is sacred is adventure, and that "Kilroy was here" means that adventure is always further along the camino whose name, Williams insisted, should be pronounced as in English, 'real.'

Williams continued to populate his sensual-spiritual conflict with a succession of colourful characters. These, and the playwright's vivid, precise, musical language, sustained him while his obsession with the kinship of beauty and violence mounted to a culmination in *Suddenly Last Summer* (1958). Here the issue was the desirability of a frontal lobotomy to prevent a young woman from repeating a story involving homosexuality, child-debauching and cannibalism. More disturbing than the content of the play is an inference it prompts—that the homosexual aesthete who debauched the children and was eaten by them is Williams' personification of spirituality destroyed by an insensitive world.

In this play Williams experimented with a dubious form of dramaturgy, enormously extended monologues. The young woman's narrative and the lengthy reminiscences of the dead man's mother are absorbing *tours de force*, but audiences did not continue to respond enthusiastically to his repetition of the device.

As Miller's style grew more meditative and Williams' more operatic, a new fortissimo crashed out: Edward Albee's *Who's Afraid of Virginia Woolf?* (1962). Albee had already attracted attention with four acrid short plays, the last of which were reminiscent of American forays into expressionism in the nineteen-twenties. *Virginia Woolf*, on the other hand, recalls the naturalistic Strindberg. It is, on the surface, a night-long, sado-masochistic wrangle between a college professor and his wife. Lurking below is the theme of truth-or-illusion: George and Martha have pretended for twenty-one years that they have a son; it is part of their game to keep this pretence a secret. As the Walpurgisnacht thunders on, George and Martha humiliate a pair of guests, Martha humiliates George by seducing the male guest, and is herself humiliated by his failure, while finally George takes his revenge for the insult never consummated by publicly destroying the private illusion. Presumably this clears the air, but the dawn that is rising as the curtain falls holds an ambiguous promise for George and Martha. The effect of the play was gorgon-like. It turned to stone the hearts of the middle class, who flocked to it and gleefully identified the characters with their neighbours. Thoughtful members of the audience, looking for a more substantial metaphor, came up with a variety of them: the homosexual life (it was rumoured that all the characters should be played by men), the ferocity of children's play (the first act was indeed entitled 'Fun and Games'), the confrontation of the past and future (George teaches history, his guest is a geneticist), and the history of the United States, ending with the destruction of the American Dream. No more sardonic play has been fixed in the canon of American drama.

Advancing more swiftly than Miller and Williams, Albee next presented his most complex and mysterious play. In *Tiny Alice* (1964) the surface level itself is fantastic: in a vast house which contains a model of itself which in turn contains a model, etc., a woman whose untold wealth alone is enough to make her unreal, conspires with her lawyer and her butler, both former lovers, to corrupt a middle-aged lay-brother named Julian. Having done all they can about this, they kill him. Murkier fantasies underlie the story. Alice buys the lay-brother from the Catholic Church for two billion dollars. Julian suffers from a basic confusion about sex and his rôle in it. The occurrences in the house also occur in the model, and it may be that the actors'-size house is itself a miniature (which Alice is tiny?). Here perhaps is the theme of sacred and profane love gone mad; the fantasy seems to be, ultimately, the private indulgence of the author.

In 1966 Albee edged back toward the recognizable world with *A Delicate Balance*, an absorbing play whose theme is uncomfortably recognizable—that the balance between generosity and self-protection is not merely delicate, it is insupportable. In 1967 came his most cynical drama to date: *Everything in the Garden* (derived from Giles Cooper's play of the same name). Here four housewives maintain their families' ex-urban status by a sideline of prostitution; at the end their four husbands murder a man who threatens to expose the remunerative arrangement. Greed could hardly be dramatized more trenchantly; one only wishes that Albee, whose view is wry and ironic, were also capable of the comic gusto of Ben Jonson.

One might also wish that the black cynicism of *Virginia Woolf* and *Everything in the Garden* were delicately balanced with the "indulgent cynicism" with which, Somerset Maugham said, the follies and vices of the leisured class were treated in the comedy of manners. Comedy of manners fared badly after 1945, perhaps because there was in post-war America no genuinely attractive leisured class, and no indulgence for irresponsibility. Popular comedy's foremost creator in the period was Neil Simon, whose comic figures, in an overwhelming procession of successes beginning in 1961 and continuing into the seventies, were of the wage-earning set. Their folly was a desire to cope with the values of the middle class, and the status of most of them as comedians depended largely on Simon's genius for jokes.

Other names lit up the sky momentarily. William Inge, with *Come Back Little Sheba* (1950); Robert Anderson, with *Tea and Sympathy* (1953); Paddy Chayevsky, with *The Middle of the Night* (1956), were all acclaimed, with some justification. But these instant successes seem to have demonstrated a general phenomenon: a playwright had to be at his best to get his first production. Having won his accolade, he could then profit by a new interest taken in his earlier works, or try to repeat himself, or belabour the remains of his dramatic imagination, or step into the parlours of the film and television producers. Like a baker's dozen of their compeers, the promising trio subsided into a bland world from which only a Chekhov could wring riches—a world in which everyday people shuffled through their everyday lives, sometimes funny, sometimes pathetic, sometimes rueful, occasionally witty, but always soothingly small. Men as they ought to be were not welcome.

Murray Schisgal's *Luv* (1964) should have put the genre in its place. The triangle in this farcically lugubrious triangle-play comprised Ellen, who could demonstrate her husband's conjugal inadequacy with a pull-down chart; Harry, whose life had been twisted by an early confrontation with a small incontinent dog; and Milt, who could claim equal status thanks to childhood breakfasts of used coffee-grounds with no sugar. But Schisgal's hilarious interlude had no effect; impervious to satire, the insipid flood purled on.

Late in the period fresh life boiled up—life in the Negro world. Generations of white playwrights, in such plays as *The Octoroon, In Abraham's Bosom, All God's Chillun Got Wings*, and *Deep are the Roots*, had indulged in a kind of helpless sympathy for the Negroes' exclusion from the white world. Even the first popularly successful play by a Negro, Lorraine Hansberry's *A Raisin in the Sun* (1959), was about a proud Negro family stubbornly moving into a white neighbourhood. But another Negro, Louis Peterson, had, in *Take a Giant Step* (1953), taken what was actually a very tentative step in another direction: into the theme of self-sufficiency for Negroes, as individuals and as a race. Fifteen years later there appeared in quick succession three noteworthy plays about the lives of Negroes by men who knew: *In the Wine Time* (1968), by Ed Bullins; *No Place to Be Somebody* (1969), by Charles Gordone; and *Ceremonies in Dark Old Men* (1969), by Lonne Elder III.

Not surprisingly these plays are in the naturalistic style. As with Hauptmann and Gorki, the aim is to depict, with as much objectivity as the writer can muster, a way of life made unacceptable by injustice and deprivation. Only *Dark Old Men* develops a genuine plot. *No Place*, although irritatingly interrupted by a narrator, is a harsh version of Saroyan's *The Time of Your Life*. *In the Wine Time* is *Street Scene* improved by Bullins' perception that the scene is not truthfully depicted by a collection of stagey events and vignettes of "colorful characters."

Three other plays by Bullins, all introduced in 1968, revealed the range of his dramaturgy. In *Goin' A Buffalo* there are reminders of *The Lower Depths*, although the characters, social outcasts in a Los Angeles flat, are by no means as completely realized as those in Gorki's classic, and the structure is not so expertly casual. *The Electronic Nigger* is not necessarily a Negro play at all; it is a wisely derisive sketch of life in a Creative Writing classroom. *A Son, Come Home* skilfully and gracefully manipulates time as it brings a young Negro back from an unsuccessful venture into the world to find his mother, who means home, irretrievably lost to him. The sum of strength, controlled anger, judiciousness, and tenderness in these plays puts Bullins among the foremost American playwrights of the sixties and seventies.

Ossie Davis and Douglas Turner Ward enlivened their objectivity with the best non-musical satire of the period. Davis' *Purlie Victorious* (1961) is a stereotype Negro preacher revealed as flagrantly disingenuous, confronting a stereotype Southern colonel so graniticly idiotic that when the tables are turned and the mortgage on Purlie's church is paid off he "drops dead standing up." Ward's *Happy Ending* (1966) presents two Negro servants bemoaning the domestic break-up of their kindly Master and Mistress. What grieves them, we learn, is the loss of graft, thievery, and reckless charity that has kept them on the edge of luxury in their off hours. So we view with indulgent cynicism their rejoicing when Master and Mistress find reconciliation. *Day of Absence* (1966) jokes wildly about the plight of a Southern town on a day when all the Negroes vanish. What with the white men having to do without shoeshines and their women having to tend their own children, it is a fearsome day indeed.

Ironically the more emphatic expressions of outrage are less memorable. James Baldwin's *Blues for Mister Charlie* (1964) is essentially a conventional melodrama of oppression, freshened by one surprising accomplishment—a convincing, perceptive characterization of a white oppressor. LeRoi Jones, a poet and a social activist, wrote several short, raging plays, most notably *Dutchman* (1964), in which a young Negro who is quietly trying to cross the reef that separates the races is teased, tormented, and finally murdered by an aggressively 'advanced' white woman, infuriated by his refusal to assert his blackness. Unfortunately, at the climax Jones has given the boy a two-page speech in the style everyone wishes he could muster at the appropriate moment.

Most of these plays found their stages in the lively area called "Off-Broadway." The epithet is both geographical and figurative. A range of small theatres made out of all sorts of spaces, from warehouses to defunct public libraries, sprang up in areas removed from New York's "theatre district," where producing and theatre-going could afford to be rebellious. Into these theatres flocked artists and audiences who wanted to get off the standard Broadway fare.

What was presented was enormously varied. A quaint musical fantasy derived from Edmond Rostand's *Les Romanesques* had given about four thousand performances by the autumn of 1972. Revivals of plays that had gone down to defeat on Broadway, such as *Summer and Smoke* and *The Iceman Cometh*, revealed values previously unappreciated. Plays that Broadway dared not touch ran proudly, among them many that were at once ugly, satiric, painfully just, and artistically made. Plays flourished on the exploitation of the freedom of language, theme, and spectacle that had been granted by a series of legal judgements concerning pornography.

Gradually Off-Broadway lost its noble dedication and took to pursuing the will-o'-the-wisp, On-Broadway. It became necessary to invent Off-Off-Broadway. Here playwrights became the willing servants of improvisors. Plays were not written, they were rewritten from spontaneous repartee. Plays were replaced by erratic mimes. Plays became games of chance, or inner-directed posturings, or bloated agit-prop. Audiences, because their hosts considered it good for them, were urged, or forced, to endure deafening cacophonies, insults, besmirchment, projection into simulated orgies. The movement was epitomized by the activities of Judith Malina and Julian Beck, a team whose deliberate artlessness was originally stimulating. Working at first with the scripts of playwrights, they systematically moved away from conventional drama. By 1970 their performances included the harassing of audiences with verbal attacks, the presentation of haphazard living statues, the elaborate simulation of onsets of plagues, and a dismally brainless kind of political-social-economic propaganda. The troupe disintegrated as the decade closed.

The 'Musical'

Shortly before the period under discussion, the musical show *Oklahoma!* had made an extraordinary impression. Thanks to a comparatively interesting libretto, a sunny score, lyrics whose content was delightful rather than witty or sentimental, and choreography related to contemporary dance, *Oklahoma!* persuaded people that it had revolutionized musical comedy. Actually this "revolution" is a periodic occurrence in America, always marked by an adjustment of words, music, and spectacle that gives the impression of a newly invented integration. But, revolutionary or not, *Oklahoma!* fixed in the world's mind the conviction that America's forte was the musical show. (Although generally called 'musical comedy,' and sometimes, grandly, 'the musical play', these pieces, from *The Black Crook*, the hit of 1866, to *Applause*, the hit of 1970, make the most of the element Aristotle called the least: spectacle.) The passion for the musical show continued to pervade the theatrical scene. Librettos were culled from every source. Some bold authors toyed with psychological dramatics, advanced music, unconventional rhythms, and sophisticated verbiage. The great successes ran for five years and upward. Occasionally genuine originality emerged: *Hair* (1967) made a boisterous spectacle of raffishness; *Godspell* (1971) made a genial spectacle of the Gospel According to Saint Matthew. Dominance in the field apparently remained secure; eventual abandonment of the *Oklahoma!* formula seemed possible.

Recent Trends

The last quarter of the century found the American theatre drifting without a coherent form or aim. The established playwrights and their emulators seemed to aim only at maintaining their position in the establishment. The small theatres chose an equivalent security, to be found in revivals, collections of little sketches, and anthologies gleaned from the libraries of literature and music. Sometimes they brought out an unestablished, even unconventional, playwright, but after one appearance these figures usually moved on or vanished. In the vast area to the west and north and south of the city of New York some dozen 'regional theatres' maintained a sturdy, if modest, professionalism against constant financial and cultural odds. For them too security lay in the Classics; only rarely did they, or the far more numerous academic theatres, propel a new dramatist into the floodlight of national attention.

Considerable energy was being expended on a movement to pull down the entire theatrical structure. A number of lively persons had subscribed to the proposition that the theatre of the Western world had forged ahead so far in the wrong direction that it had to be returned to its aboriginal beginnings. Primitive rites come upon in New Guinea fired enthusiasm; *The Bacchae* was awarded pre-eminence among the world's dramas; acts of public copulation and animal sacrifice were contemplated. The atavists conceded that it would be difficult to persuade urban audiences to rise to the ecstasies of maenads and bushmen but they hoped that education would bring them round.

For the moment, at least, the hope seemed a forlorn one. The small segment of the nation's population that attended the theatre continued to prefer classic revivals for culture, scenes from daily life for comfort, and musical shows for uplift. The health of the American theatre remained as it had always been: precarious.

POST-WAR DRAMA IN ENGLAND AND IRELAND

GARETH LLOYD EVANS

From 1939 to 1946 the London stage pursued a surprisingly active and often distinguished career, although, of course, with not a few interruptions and amid many hazards. Several of the dramatists who had been most prominent during the thirties continued to bring forward divers new plays, among them several works which seemed to exhibit increased rather than diminishing power on the part of their authors. And, since many of these writers pursued their activities into the post-war period, collectively they provided a bridge carrying the drama from the time before Hitler had unleashed his hordes upon Poland on to the period of adjustment following the end of hostilities.

Noel Coward's *Blithe Spirit* (1941) gave to his witty style and adroit grace a fresh dimension, and, even although his later *Present Laughter* (1942), *Nude with Violin* (1956), and *Waiting in the Wings* (1960) may be thought not to have borne this style and grace to still other achievements, the importance of the fact that he had thus triumphantly stepped across that bridge cannot be minimized. Coward's ghostly Elvira—a most fascinating wraith—reminds us that thousands of Londoners groped their way through the darkened streets in order to revel in the amusingly thoughtful wizardry of James Bridie's *Mr Bolfry* (1943), but, with memories of that play in our minds, we must deeply regret that, despite what seemed to be a clear yet tantalizing new-found strength in *Daphne Laureola* (1949), Bridie's crossing of the bridge was hardly so steady-footed as Coward's. Emlyn Williams' *The Corn is Green* (1938) had appeared just before the outbreak of war, and 1945 saw the production of his effective *Wind of Heaven*—so effective, indeed, that, with the interests of the drama in mind, we may regret that this most accomplished actor-author later abandoned the writing of plays for his brilliant solo-performances. In 1936 Terence Rattigan had won his first great success (and he has had several such) with the sparkling farce of *French without Tears*, but in the wartime *Flare Path* (1942) he exhibited a hitherto unsuspected power of dealing with tense, serious situations, and later he won still further approbation from the public for his well-etched and well-wrought *The Winslow Boy* (1946) and for his excellent melodrama of a failed schoolmaster, *The Browning Version* (1948): a few years later *The Deep Blue Sea* (1952) provided a still more effective demonstration of his skill in the composition of tautly structured dramas designed to satisfy that deep underswell of public expectation—the ebb and flow between a willing disbelief and a desired belief—which seems to remain a constant in the theatre despite all innovating experiments. The last, but most decidedly not the least, of these dramatists, J. B. Priestley, also owed his earlier high reputation partly to a similar skill in craftsmanship, but this skill he combined with the philosophic 'seriousness' of his themes and with hints of still greater depths beneath the surface of his plots and characters. The possession of these qualities fully entitles him to claim that in his writings there is at least something of a Chekhovian approach to human existence. His remarkable *Johnson over Jordan* (1939) and *They Came to a City* (1943), followed by *The Linden Tree* (1947) and *An Inspector Calls* (1946), showed how steadily firm were his steps forward, through war, into the post-war period.

Two other authors may be added to this list—the first (paradoxically) because of the disappointing paucity of his writings and the second because of his extensive dramatic output. There was a time when Peter Ustinov, with his *House of Regrets* (1942), *The Banbury Nose* (1944), and the lively political allegory, *The Love of Four Colonels* (1951), seemed set fair to be one of the country's most eminent purveyors of stage illusion, but, despite the fact that he himself remains as delightfully witty and irrepressible as ever, none of his few later plays succeeded in achieving the sparkling inconsequentiality of those earlier compositions. By this time he might have been an *éminence grise*, instead of which he has joyfully insisted upon remaining an *enfant terrible*. Utterly different has been the steady career of William Douglas-Home, a dramatist who, after winning public esteem within the course of a single year, 1947, for two completely contrasting works, *Now Barabbas*, a prison drama, and *The Chiltern Hundreds*, a political satire, has kept successive audiences delighted by his elegant, well-constructed but, in the final analysis, essentially trivial contributions to post-war theatre.

The Poetic Drama

During the years when those authors were active, the London playhouse public witnessed a rise and fall of poetic drama which is less easy to assess, and explain. In the thirties it had appeared likely that there was to be a substantial flourishing of this kind of play: T. S. Eliot (then at the height of his fame) presented *Murder in the Cathedral* in 1935 and *The Family Reunion* in 1939, and his influence encouraged a number of enthusiastic young authors and actors. Theory and speculation were turned into reality when a Poets' Theatre was established immediately after the end of the war. A small but keenly interested public welcomed plays such as Ronald Duncan's *This Way to the Tomb!* (1945) and Anne

Ridler's *The Shadow Factory* (1945). Eliot's *The Confidential Clerk* (1953) and *The Elder Statesman* (1958) appeared in the West End, and, most important of all, the writings of Christopher Fry, ushered in with *A Phoenix Too Frequent* (1946) and *The Lady's Not for Burning* (1948), glowed in the sky like a divine promise. Then, with startling suddenness, the iridescence vanished. Duncan's *Don Juan* (1957) and *The Death of Satan* (1957) aroused no particular interest, nor did Anne Ridler's *Henry Bly* (1950). Those who had dedicated themselves to encouraging the poetic stage tried their best to arouse interest in Eliot's later plays, but even they were compelled to admit, even if only secretly to themselves, that these dramas appeared to be strangely and sadly tired. The conjunction of Fry's *Ring Round the Moon* and *Venus Observed* alone seemed to suggest that all had not been lost, but his *The Dark is Light Enough* (1954) failed to arouse enthusiasm, *Curtmantle* (1962) gave the impression of being forced, and, sadly, the first performance of *A Yard of Sun* (1970) offered no hope that either a personal or a general revival is in sight.

Perhaps the truth must be faced that unfortunately we live in a prosaic age where the accepted norm of nearly all verbal communication is clipped, harsh and jargonated. The resources of poetry have almost completely vanished from the stage, and even when we listen to cadence, rhythm, and evocative phrasing in a few plays—of which Peter Terson's *The Mighty Reservoy* (1967), Robert Bolt's *A Man for All Seasons* (1960), and Tom Stoppard's *Rosencrantz and Guildenstern Are Dead* (1966) are good examples—we may be forced, with at least a slight sense of shock, to recognize that the pleasure which we derive from the dialogue comes from what is nowadays an old-fashioned virtue, style.

Rebels Without a Cause

During the early fifties there was much talk, sometimes denunciatory but on the whole hopeful, of John Whiting. That he excited dissension seemed in itself to imply his worth: eminences such as Peter Brook, Tyrone Guthrie, Peggy Ashcroft and John Gielgud spoke of him as a potential saviour of the theatre: yet now we must feel that the hoping was merely an urgent desire for wish-fulfilment. It is, of course, not difficult to understand why *Saint's Day* (1951) was greeted both with optimistic enthusiasm and with disappointment. Its theme, declared by Whiting himself to concern self-destruction, is embedded in a number of tensely stated generalizations about the meaning of life. These certainly appealed to intellectuals, among whom the war had left serious doubts about the validity of the old faiths. Here, it seemed, was a man facing up to the truth of things: "I tell you, do not fear, for there is no light, and the way is from darkness to darkness to darkness": here was a man who was eloquent, capable of creating remarkable dramatic tensions governed almost entirely by his deployment of terse phrases interspersed with longer rhythmical passages and by pregnant silences. Nevertheless,

A FRENCH PRODUCTION OF
"LA CASA DE BERNARDA ALBA",
BY FEDERICO GARCÍA LORCA
Agence Bernand

A CZECH PRODUCTION OF "MUTTER
COURAGE" BY BERTOLT BRECHT
Photo Dr Jaromir Svoboda

these virtues could not be properly appreciated by many because of the author's puzzling and often cerebral symbolism; nor did the symbols in *A Penny for a Song* (1951) and *Marching Song* (1954) seem any less obscure. More success was granted to *The Devils* (1961), although this was largely due to its production by the Royal Shakespeare Company. Vast claims for its profundity were made, but it can now be regarded as no more than a competent *coup de théâtre*, even although, in saying this, it is fair to add that it was one of the first of our permissive plays, exposing a topic which could hardly have been previously put upon the stage—the 'possession' of a group of nuns by dark forces, treated in modern terms as neurosis and sexual libertinism. It must be remembered that Whiting died at the early age of forty-five, but even so, despite his ability to create some compelling scenes, his dramatic power cannot, in retrospect, be deemed as great as once it was claimed. He was not, in any significant sense, a revolutionary; and about all his plays there is a withholding quality, as if the essential transference from the deeps of the imagination into embodied fiction, the true essence of drama, is only partial.

Whiting's name was at one time often mentioned in association with that of Robert Bolt, although nowadays it is difficult to understand why the latter considered himself to be, or was considered by others as being, in the van of a new movement. Inexorably, time has shown that his dramas have more affinities with the conventions of the West End play than with anything more outré. *Flowering Cherry* (1957) is a clearly written, romantically conceived study in self-delusion, not unlike Arthur Miller's *Death of a Salesman*: it is in no way a blistering comment on society's iniquities, nor is it innovative in treatment. His later plays are memorable for their 'realism,' their ability to depict events both of high moment and of domestic intimacy in flexible verbal terms encompassing a supple dignity and a sharp idiomatic pungency. His best drama, *A Man for All Seasons* (1960), a psychological study of a great man, Sir Thomas More, whose private strength is not matched with political ability, has some slight but obvious affinities to Drinkwater's historical dramas. It is impaired by its Common Man, an 'alienated figure' seemingly derived from Brecht. This figure is an embarrassing bore and well illustrates the general inability of British playwrights to grasp Brechtian theory and practice, however much they may profess the profundity of his influence. *The Tiger and the Horse* (1960) is splendidly well made, as is his latest drama, *Vivat! Vivat Regina!* (1970), but both—the one in a modern setting and the other in an Elizabethan—reveal the author as a revolutionary who never was, as a very worthy creator of those elegant scenes which he was so curiously given to reject in his earlier days.

Kitchen Sink and So On

A few dates in the history of the stage seem to mark new directions: the building of The Theatre in 1576, Garrick's formal debut in 1741, the first performance of John Osborne's *Look Back in Anger* by the English Stage Company on May 8, 1956. Yet the more we consider these (and other similar) historical events the more difficult it becomes to disentangle cause and effect. Osborne's play is not great; it is not even particularly original; innumerable critics have regarded, and indeed still regard, it as of immense importance in modern theatre history: yet was it really a cause, or was it simply a first symptom, of the events which were to follow? The policy of the English Stage Company was to encourage young dramatists who found the prevailing West End theatre atmosphere depressing; and certainly *Look Back in Anger* became symbolic of a reflex attitude of youth to its environment. The anti-hero, Jimmy Porter, unattractive, undistinguished, reflects the disaffection of young people in the fifties, when the country was left feeling more defeated than victorious, about to be bereft of the material possessions for which in part it had fought: there were, of course, the benefits of the Welfare State, but these might be seen as a curtain-raiser for the sixties and the seventies when a materialistic philosophy and the assertion of permissiveness are largely a surrogate for the great psychological and spiritual effects of declension from Empire, from power and from religious certainty. With national status reduced and vague, the individual unconsciously turns to an assertion of self and attacks what seems to be a guilty establishment. Jimmy Porter, with no 'causes' to fight for, is angry—yet the play is remarkable in not being specific, in spite of its title, about the source of the anger: Jimmy flails with verbal vigour and intellectual incontinence at everything from the Government to his wife and his mother-in-law. The rawness of the language and the irreverence caught a prevailing mood of the times—but there is another aspect of the play which may suggest that the ill-aimed, if venomous, shafts of anger were conceived by Osborne as a part rather than the whole of his hero. If so, it may be that the play came to be representative partly by accident, since there is evidence that a character of greater psychological subtlety was struggling to emerge—a Jimmy Porter who, feeling not merely angry but also deprived, turns upon his 'privileged' wife. He feels he has suffered, and this is expressed in a speech of extraordinary self-indulgence when, describing his father's death, he suggests that he, the observer, suffered more than the victim. We discover that he really needs protection: the bombastic and belligerent attitude which he assumes is that of a frightened child.

In order to establish such a contradictory character, the other persons had to be relegated to the dramatic status of shadows, and thus this play is virtually a dramatic monologue with interruptions. *The Entertainer* (1957), although to an extent also overweighted in this respect, is also in two quite distinct ways superior. On one level it is the story of a broken-down, third-rate comedian and of his relationship with his physically and spiritually defeated wife, his cheerfully nondescript son, his militantly left-wing daughter, and his father—the only repository of pride and will in the family. On another, non-realistic, level a number of music-hall scenes make comments on Archie Rice's world, and ours. Archie is less angry, more truly mordant, than Jimmy, and, because of the double aspect of the drama, he is more credible. There is a deeper dimension here, and in none of his later writings has Osborne matched its widely ranging dialogue deployed in styles ranging from biting naturalistic prose to tinkling doggerel.

The World of Paul Slickey (1959) may be dismissed as an ill-directed barrage of social criticism, *A Patriot for Me* (1965) as a tediously romantic account of a real-life spy, and *The Hotel in Amsterdam* (1968) as offering little more than an opportunity for Paul Scofield to display his technical prowess: but now and again throughout this period Osborne continued to suggest that he might break out beyond his earlier weaknesses and virtues. *Inadmissible Evidence* (1964) is a remarkable study in both self-destruction and self-analysis, and *Luther* (1961), in its demotic way, is as effective a piece of history in dramatic form as can be found in this century. In watching both of these, spectators must often feel that they are in the presence of a prolonged autobiography, and in feeling thus they may cast their minds back to the time when the names of 'Jimmy Porter' and 'Osborne' were almost interchangeable. This autobiographical implication gives these plays their urgent immediacy, their sense of truth, yet one has a strong sense that two opposed creative forces are at work—the one, anger and fear concerning society, and the other, self-condemnation, intellectually and emotionally masochistic. In craftsmanship, too, a similar dualism seems to be operative: inside a writer whose urgent desire to communicate often gives to his language a kind of tousled quality there seems to co-exist another possessed by an almost puritanically severe determination to find poise and severity of expression. Perhaps Osborne, still in his early forties, may yet reconcile the two forces which every great playwright has had to make into a single unity—inner compulsion and the rigours of achieved art.

Osborne's early success undoubtedly encouraged the English Stage Company and other young dramatists. Among the latter John Arden is one of the most important—and no less an enigma. This author's work is very uneven in quality, partly because of his restless inventiveness in style and form, and partly because, like so many of his generation, left-wing in persuasion, he is inclined to fall into the trap of believing that the most significant art is that which has a palpable political or sociological design upon its audience. Robert Brustein's comment on the fuss relating to *The Island of the Mighty* (written jointly by Arden and his wife, Margaretta D'Arcy, 1972) that "good theatres begin to decline when they choose plays for political rather than artistic reasons" might profitably have been heeded both by playwrights and directors in the sixties and the seventies, a period when too often the demands of political ideology were put before the compulsions of artistic creation. The best in Arden revolves around his attempts to forge a genuinely flexible modern dramatic language through the intermingling of prose, songs, free verse, and other devices, associated with his effort to break through traditional realistic forms of presentation. He seems deeply committed to exposing what he believes are the evils of society, and where Osborne generalizes he particularizes. Yet there is in his exploitation of this theme a very interesting and characteristic feature. *Live Like Pigs* (1958) is concerned with the welfare state, *Serjeant Musgrave's Dance* (1959) with a wartime situation, *The Happy Haven* (1961) with the problems of old age, but his characters are, in a sense, dissociated from those topics. There is, instead, an unnerving objectivity in his approach: it is as though he is warmly condemnatory of certain evils but in the end has accepted the fact that no-one, or everyone, is to blame. We in the audience see a succession of characters who are never judged by their creator; nor is their point of view ever approved or disapproved by him. They just 'are,' and often, therefore, their behaviour seems bizarre or motiveless. Arden, in truth, is nearer to Pinter than many of his critics have recognized—not only in his attitude towards character, but also in his ability credibly to inject the unexpected, the sensational, the violent into an apparently ordinary situation. *Serjeant Musgrave's Dance*, his most successful play and his best, exemplifies his customary approach. In 1880 the serjeant and his men arrive in a town on the pretext that they are recruiting; initial suspicion is overcome; suddenly Musgrave reveals that his purpose is to take his own reprisals upon those in authority; other soldiers arrive, Musgrave is disarmed and the re-establishment of order is celebrated. Within this apparently straightforward narrative the issues of pacificism and war are presented in a convoluted, and sometimes baffling, manner: arguments for and against are given equal force, and the dialogue tends at times to be elliptic—so that, because of his unusual approach to characterization and his stylistic waywardness, Arden's audience is left in a kind of excited puzzlement. It is true that such a supple play as *Armstrong's Last Goodnight* (1964) deals directly and in a mood of controlled emotional ferocity with a primitive borderer come face to face with civilization, but against this might be cited *The Workhouse Donkey* (1963) where, apart from the customary puzzlement, we find it hard to decide whether this is comedy, or satire, or maybe even tragedy.

Few of the other young dramatists of the fifties have progressed far. Nigel Dennis won some praise for his extravagant *Cards of Identity* (1956) and *The Making of Moo* (1957), but subsequently faded. Ann Jellicoe's *The Sport of My Mad Mother* (1956) and *The Knack* (1961) hardly seem of much importance now—but she must be noted as one of the most successful exponents of an early form of absurdism. To apply this label to N. F. Simpson is misleading, and might perplex even more those who find his plays troublesomely baffling. *A Resounding Tinkle* (1957) and the superbly comic *One Way Pendulum* (1959)—the latter presenting a scene in which an attempt is made to teach five hundred weighing machines to sing the Hallelujah chorus—are less truly absurdist than absurd, closer to Lewis Carroll than to Pinter. Simpson's logic is the logic of fantasy, with no Q.E.D.s at the end: his world is entirely of the imagination, and however grotesquely extravagant his plots may be, they somehow present a certain calm, a still point, where pure language takes control of everything. Simpson's work, regrettably meagre, was and still remains a welcome antidote to the countless plays committed to social comment which dominated those years.

Shelagh Delaney became as well known as Osborne for her raw and tender study of the relationship between a homosexual and a young pregnant girl in *A Taste of Honey* (1958), but its graphic theatrical effect owed much to the ministrations of the dynamic if occasionally reckless director of Theatre Workshop. *The Lion in Love* (1960), less tautly expressed although having a few speeches of hard lyrical poignancy, lacked the sense of authenticity; it showed that while Delaney had the ability to depict life in her native Salford with emotional sincerity, her talent was, in fact, a minor one. Henry Livings also was associated with Theatre Workshop, and this association, even if it was as actor rather than as playwright, has clearly been of influence upon him. *Stop It, Whoever You Are* (1961), *Big Soft Nellie* (1961), *Nil Carborundum* (1962), *Eh?* (1964) and *This Jockey Drives Late Nights* (1971) are all angrily, sometimes self-consciously, realistic in both location and character-presentation: the recurrent theme is "that of people who have no choice but to go with the fierce steel wheel of their work and the life it makes them lead." Livings' strength rests in his ability to control his comic moods with bitter irony: his weakness is verbal prolixity. Theatre Workshop also clearly influenced Bernard Kops, even although he was never closely involved in its activities. His East End Jewish background dominates such dramas as *The Hamlet of Stepney Green* (1958), described as a sad comedy with songs, *Change for the Angel* (1960) and *The Dream of Peter Man* (1961), providing both their weakness (a ground-swell of sentimentality, sometimes becoming sententious with homespun philosophy) and their compelling force (flexibility of communication, ranging from flat, coarse idiom to rhythmical evocativeness). Thematically, they tell of man's hates and loves, with no attempt at profundity: had they been a little more intellectually severe, they might have escaped the suggestion that they are inclined, emotionally, to protest too much.

It is necessary, also, to remember that Arnold Wesker is Jewish if we are fully to understand the motivations in his plays. His family has a history of deprivation, like his race; his immediate background has inclined him to left-wing political views; his Jewish temperament gives him a warmth of feeling, a sincerity of belief, a respect for education, civilized pursuits, a strong sense of verbal rhythm, and a characteristic sentimentality which frequently makes him incapable of distinguishing between what is dramatically valuable and what is emotionally trivial. The famous 'Trilogy' (*Chicken Soup with Barley*, 1958; *Roots*, 1959; *I'm Talking about Jerusalem*, 1960) contains both the best and the worst of his writing. In this quasi-epic history of two families we can observe his double-focus on existence: he depicts and regrets the economic exploitation of the working class, particularly in the thirties, and in a bright-eyed way he revels in its guts, its defiance, its determination. He is optimistic about the possibility of building a better world, but characteristically he does not confine himself to the proposition that this will be achieved just by concerted action: much emphasis is placed on individual responsibility: for him politics and mass action can go only so far.

This complex way of looking at the world has advantages and disadvantages. *Chicken Soup with Barley*, for instance, seems to be fighting battles already won: when it was produced, working-class power—the great political and social revolution of the sixties—was well on its way to establishment, while Wesker appeared to be saying that the struggle naught availeth unless supreme effort and sacrifice were brought into action: and, in addition to this, his backward view into the thirties curiously depersonalized his writing, making it seem like a rather out-of-date political manifesto. On the other hand, his wide scope enables him to create a great range of diverse characters and—especially if two later plays (*The Kitchen*, 1959, and *Chips with Everything*, 1962) are seen, thematically, as part of his 'epic'—also a wide range of locale. All of these seem authentic not only because Wesker was drawing on his own experience but also because, except when he is proselytizing, his ear for speech and his eye for place are finely attuned. What may well rescue his plays from an oblivion to which his excessive polemics and occasionally undisciplined emotions might doom him is the passionate sincerity of his desire to move the deprived towards a true self-realization by acquiring a sense of dignity, a mental alertness, and, above all, a verbal articulateness —the qualities stressed by Beattie in *Roots*, during the course of a remarkable speech which in itself is worth all the traditional left-wing polemics—and dramatically is much more durable.

Wesker's more recent dramas—perhaps because of his over-optimistic tenacious but abortive attempt to bring the arts to a wider working-class audience—have been far less naturalistic in every way, and less explicitly concerned with the class struggle. *The Four Seasons* (1965), attempting a heightened form of speech, merely revealed that more than a genuine feel for rhythm and sound is needed to create dramatic poetry: *Their Very Own and Golden City* (1966) proved embarrassing in its reflection of the author's own attempts to create his Centre 42: *The Friends* (1970) was filled with verbal and psychological longueurs. It is one of the theatrical tragedies of this century that Wesker, a man of truly great talent, has apparently seen (but as yet has seemed incapable of accepting) the ruthless lesson that in drama sincerity is not enough.

Pinter and Absurdism

Unquestionably the most prominent playwright of the post-war period in England is Harold Pinter, commonly regarded as this country's Absurdist, an opinion justified by the author's own acknowledgment of the debt he owes to Ionesco. His plays almost always involve small groups living in enclosed areas beyond whose bounds the characters never let their thoughts drift, or, if they are forced to do this, they find themselves regarding the outside world as a source of unknown tribulations and terrors. It is rare that anything pleasant lies beyond Pinter's doorways: whatever intrudes from outside seems almost always sinister, malevolent, or disturbingly indefinable. Goldberg and McCann in *The Birthday Party* (1958), Nick in *The Caretaker* (1960), Ruth in *The Homecoming* (1965), the Matchseller in *A Slight Ache* (1961) are all threats because what lies, absurdly, outside the immediate conscious experience is, because it is unknown, unamenable to conventional definition, and must be regarded as potentially dangerous.

Essentially, he is a poetic dramatist. The realistic elements in his plays always—whether implicitly or explicitly—denote symbolic levels of meaning: his characters can always be reflected upon in connotative terms: even objects, such as the Buddha in *The Caretaker*, are found to have associations beyond their mere appearance. If it be protested—and many have so protested—that these dimensions in Pinter's plays are elusive, puzzling, perhaps merely figments of the commentators' fancies, a valid answer may lie in a careful consideration of the essential features of nearly all great plays, from Shakespeare's poetically imaginative scenes to Chekhov's realistic ones. All of them unfold in terms of metaphor and simile, and all of them do so in different ways: Shakespeare uses verse: Chekhov freely indulges in conflicts between one character's thoughts and the thoughts of the person to whom he is speaking: the metre, so to say, of a Pinter play is formed of the architectonics between language and silence. A Pinter pause is not a theatrical gap between words but a resonance of speech: his repetitions do not appear for the sake of emphasis, they are both part of a rhythm and an indication of character. It is essential, too, to realize how closely both words and pauses are bound up with action.

Pinter certainly is a controversially innovating dramatist, yet, although he has cut through many of the accepted conventions of playwriting, it is surprising how traditionally he maintains strict discipline in the creation of his plays. He has blurred the old distinctions between comedy, farce, tragedy, and he has restored a poetic flavour to the drama without seeming to have done so. Blessedly, too, at a time when the director has become all-powerful, god-like, he is an actors' dramatist: in the presentation of his dramas the performers' playing of the score counts for more than the conducting.

During the past few years no significant new trend either in theme or in form has made its appearance. What might be called 'the Pinter mode' is frequently to be encountered, although a few authors, searching for a fresh kind of dramatic language, have, like Tom Stoppard in his *Rosencrantz and Guildenstern Are Dead*, turned to the exploitation of what basically may be defined as 'wit.' Ideas are presented here in a quasi-philosophical manner, accompanied by a humanizing, and often extremely amusing, manipulation of irony, satire, the framing of conundrums, and the making of jokes. The overall effect is of a twentieth-century 'Restoration' manner in which language is, as it were, placed at one remove from character, is almost made into a *dramatis persona*.

Osborne and Wesker, too, remain powerful influences, although their acerbic generalizations about deprivation have largely been replaced by attempts to explore working-class thought and sentiment more deeply. Here it is as if the dramatists, taking Wesker at his word, have decided that he was right in his declarations that a discovery of self is a large part of the answer to social underprivilege. Within this area, several authors have made particularly notable contributions—Willis Hall, in *The Long and the Short and the Tall* (1959), *Last Day in Dreamland* (1969) and *Celebration* (1961); Alun Owen, in a number of television plays and also in his earlier *Progress to the Park* (1959), and Peter Terson, in *I'm in Charge of These Ruins* (1966) and *All Honour Mr Todd* (1966). In this connection, reference may be made to one minor, although significant, offshoot of the working-class revolution—the raising of Football, in both social and symbolic status. The footballer's growth in material affluence has been accompanied by his translation into a kind of myth, so that he has become the equivalent, both tragic and triumphant, of the traditional hero. Terson's *Zigger Zagger* (1967) is a notable example of this small but important sub-cultural phenomenon.

A list of plays written since the mid-sixties would certainly include a large number which gained critical acclaim and popular approbation, yet this cannot be taken to indicate their true worth, since a marked characteristic of these years has been a progressive facileness of critical appraisal: swiftly disseminated approval or disapproval, hectic inflation, and creation of reputation, have made the period critically suspect. To a large extent the lowering of standards has been nurtured by the worst features of mass-media (particularly television, voracious appetite for what is immediate and its unique ability to proliferate the views of alleged pundits which too often subsume what is valuable).

The dramatists who seem to have contributed more than the merely modish are remarkably few. The so-called 'theatre of cruelty' has attracted a number of young authors—perhaps largely through the influence of Peter Brook, who became an ardent admirer of Artaud's philosophizings, particularly those which proclaimed the theatrical spectacle as a means of releasing man from his inner tensions and of forcing him to see himself morally and psychologically 'naked.' Thus, for example, in Joe Orton's *Entertaining Mr Sloane* (1964) a new lodger admitted to a suburban house murders the father of the cosy landlady and of her homosexual brother: the audience might expect that he will terrorize them, but instead they proceed to blackmail him. In David Rudkin's

Afore Night Come (1962) we are introduced to what seems to be a rural Midlands documentary, with dialect smacking as much of invention as of authentic representation of the real: by the end we find ourselves immersed in a grotesque fantasy involving ritual murder committed in an atmosphere of horror. Although this 'theatre of cruelty' remains erratically esteemed in a few circles, mostly pseudo-intellectual, it seems to have only passing (and very slight) significance.

Edward Bond's first play, *The Pope's Wedding* (1962), aroused hardly any attention, but he acquired notoriety for an over-publicized and largely misunderstood incident in his second work, *Saved* (1965)—a scene which shows a baby stoned to death. Violence is characteristic of his writings, but in his hands it is always an integral part of the theme, not gratuitously sensational; and, after the frequently cold objectivity of Absurdism, his committedness, if shocking, is entirely acceptable and even curiously comforting. The incident in *Saved* is a moving indictment, expressed from a moral, not a political, standpoint, of what society does to itself through individual capitulation to expediencies of all kinds: much of its verbal pattern is hardly language—rather it has an almost animalistic terseness and viciousness of sound which stirs the heart like a distant howl, or a bark, or a whimper of pain. *Narrow Road to the Deep North* (1968), set in Japan after the coming of Westerners, may perhaps be thought to be his best play to date, and undoubtedly it is the most successful attempt by a British dramatist to follow the Brechtian style; but unfortunately his recent *Lear* (1971) can be deemed no more than a great disappointment—regrettably so, since few other playwrights seem to be so totally wedded to their craft and art, few are so involved in the effort to master theatrical technique, few are so compassionate in the creation of their themes.

About Tom Stoppard's place in dramatic history there must as yet be doubt, since to date his bravura has dominated over all his other qualities. What can be said is that *Rosencrantz and Guildenstern Are Dead*, *The Real Inspector Hound* (1968), and *Jumpers* (1971) leave us feeling refreshed by contact with true ingenuity of form, exhilarated by language, and (to a lesser extent) excited by intellectual subtlety even while we are left wondering whether the author will be able to stay the course. The first play is certainly subtle in its implied argument concerning the nature of illusion and reality, but the second shows how easily he can be carried away from what might have been a penetrating study by his own virtuosity and sense of fun. John Mortimer has given evidence in *The Wrong Side of the Park* (1960) and *A Voyage round My Father* (1970) that he may well prove a worthy successor to Rattigan. Peter Shaffer's *Five Finger Exercise* (1958), *Black Comedy* (1965), and *The Royal Hunt of the Sun* (1964) are also basically traditional, but they are given distinction by their engaging crispness and variety of style. In *Little Malcolm and his Struggle against the Eunuchs* (1964) David Halliwell produced an outstanding example of the kind of quasi-absurdist play seen at its best in Ann Jellicoe's writings, but for the time being he seems to have run out of steam. It is difficult to see any coherence of style and approach in the three plays which gave David Mercer his prominence, *Ride a Cock Horse* (1965), *The Governor's Lady* (1965), and *Belcher's Luck* (1966). In these the one thing in common seems to be an obsession with disintegration, whether slow or quick: one shows the protagonist descending into infantilism, the Governor of the second piece turns into a gorilla, and, so far as the theme of the third can be clearly ascertained, the chief concerns are those of fertility and impotence.

Impotence. In several respects Mercer is symbolic of the present situation, for this country's theatre exhibits more than a few signs of decay. Subsidies cannot always disguise the fact that audience figures are not satisfactory, nor is the general excellence in acting standards matched by robust standards in the writing of plays. Too many of these seem to reach the stage in a partial state of completion. The over-powerful influence of directors often results in wayward presentation and interpretation. In numerous quarters the cult of new fads seems to be regarded more highly than the maintenance of traditional values. The theatre in general is in fact reflecting its society perfectly. While, however, we may regret much of what is being reflected, perhaps there is some hope in the mere fact that this mirroring is still permitted, and that what society sees in its looking-glass *may* cause it carefully to consider where and how it stands.

Irish Epilogue

No account of the fortunes of drama in Ireland during the past quarter of a century can ignore two most potent influences. The first is the terrible and continuing internecine strife, and the second is the brief, violent emergence of Brendan Behan. If a remark that the one is in a way a reflection of the other appears to be too glib, it may be pointed out how both generated a peculiarly Irish form of self-destruction, both exhibited the eloquence attendant upon that destruction, and both created an astonishing and frightening mixture of the comic and the tragic, of the absurd and the pitiful, of the eminently reasonable and the moronic, which seems an inherent characteristic of the Irish people.

Much of Irish drama written during the post-war period, quite apart from Behan's plays, has of course inevitably been concerned in one way or another with some aspect of the country's own frightening tragicomedy: nor have the effects of religious dissension, political crisis, censorship, emigration in any way dampened its consistently active dramatic spirit. Although the Abbey Theatre has not maintained its dominant position as the chief nourisher of Irish dramatists, it has—not without a sense of the miraculous—survived physical destruction as well as fierce and unceasing internal dissention. Only two dramatists of real distinction have lately been nurtured there, Seamus Byrne and Walter Macken. The former's *Design for a Headstone* (1950), with its controversial treatment of prison life, is in some respects a forerunner of Behan's *The Quare Fellow*, and the latter's *Home is the Hero* (1952) is a powerful, realistic study of Irish contemporary life. To a considerable extent the seminal role of Dublin's most famous playhouse was taken over by a virile company founded in 1951, The Group Theatre. Here the well-known actor Joseph Tomelty discovered his remarkable dramatic talent. His *The End House* (1944) is an unsentimental and tense study of life in the slums, and *Is the Priest at Home?* (1954) proved that he was able to handle characteristically Irish themes and situations without becoming lost in a welter of polemics: there is no other play of the period which treats so calmly and with such detachment the potentially explosive theme of the Priest's position as both a religious and a political element in Irish life. And, as well as Tomelty, there is Brian Friel, one of the few contemporary Irish playwrights enjoying an international reputation. His *Philadelphia, Here I Come!* (1966) and *Lovers* (1968) demonstrate that he has looked well beyond the prevailing, conventional Irish influence—the combined force of Synge and O'Casey—in order to absorb expressionist influences from other countries. Inventiveness in plot and language is the keynote of his writings—and here too there is a refreshing absence of polemics. Still another influential theatre organization, the Lyric Theatre, has encouraged two of the most distinguished writers of poetic drama of the post-war period—Austin Clarke, whose *The Moment Next to Nothing* (1953) conjures up memories of Yeats' excursions into Irish legend, and Donagh MacDonagh, whose delightful 'melodrama in ballade,' *Happy as Larry*, won a high reputation after its production in 1941, and whose later writings, *Step-in-the-Hollow* (1957) and *Lady Spider* (1953), give further testimony to his inventiveness and subtlety.

Above these authors, of course, towers Brendan Behan—member of the I.R.A., imprisoned at the age of sixteen, deported, imprisoned again at the age of twenty-four, very much of a roaring boy, who became, despite himself, a dramatist acceptable to London's West End and New York's Broadway because of his sheer theatrical splendour and his depth of human compassion. His first play of consequence, *The Quare Fellow* (1956), is obviously based on his own experience of prison life, with the effect of an execution its central theme. The Quare Fellow is the condemned man, whom we never see although his spirit pervades the whole atmosphere. Naturalistic in its minute presentation of the growing horror of those inside as contrasted with the indifference of the outside world, it yet rises into symbolism with its irony, pathos, and grim comedy—for the 'hanged man' is society's eternal victim. *The Hostage* (1958) deals with a theme not dissimilar, its central figure being a cockney soldier captured by militant republicans, and its tensions arising from a clash between an I.R.A. which is depicted as mindless and reactionary, and the new youth representing compassion and understanding. In both of these dramas Behan employs idiomatic dialogue, songs, jokes, parody, farce, satire, in such a way as to create a rhythm of mood and style entirely original, preserving the naturalistic even while creating a haunting timelessness. Although he was no great plot-maker, he still is in the classic line of Yeats, Synge, O'Casey, and Ireland has suffered yet another tragedy in his self-consuming, untimely death.

And finally, in speculating on what Ireland has recently contributed to the drama, reference cannot be omitted here to one who was greater still, who, born near Dublin, was most certainly Irish, yet who might be styled an English dramatist, and who even could be classified as French. No play has achieved greater fame or exerted more influence during recent years than *Waiting for Godot*, and it must be remembered that this drama was originally performed in 1953 as the author had written it, *En attendant Godot*. It is a fact, at once strange and inevitable, that the Irish playwright whose writings have had such universal appeal has had, during the entire course of his life, hardly any associations with the playhouse of his native land.

POST-WAR DRAMA IN FRANCE AND BELGIUM

PIERRE PAUL AUGER

In 1928 and 1929 Louis Jouvet, at that time in charge of the Comédie des Champs-Élysées, presented two magnificently directed and brilliantly acted dramas, *Siegfried* and *Amphitryon 38*, the first stage writings of Jean Giraudoux. These productions achieved almost immediate success, and from that time onward to the appearance of *Ondine* at the very threshold of war in 1939 this dramatist steadily increased his reputation until in the opinion of most critics and playgoers he stood forward as the chief playwright of those years, the author who most clearly and most firmly expressed the theatrical ideals of his age. He believed in, and firmly insisted upon, the paramount importance of language: over words he himself had complete command, so that, as need might arise, his wit could be delicately incisive, his rhetoric powerfully impressive, his poetic style penetratingly imaginative. Nevertheless, he was an author who always thought first of the actors who were to take control of his lines on the stage and of the audiences to whom those lines were addressed and who, he hoped, would be collaborators in the total dramatic experience. He displayed his power by stepping forward boldly on his own path without permitting himself to be distracted by any modish experiments; and this power was further revealed by the constant variety apparent in his themes and scenes. Instinctively he knew that writing for the stage, if it is to be successful, requires firmness and diversity. And he believed that the appeal of the play should always be to the emotions and imaginations of his auditors.

Throughout the whole of his work a definite consistency in approach is clearly evident, so that even when in his last plays—those which particularly concern us here—there is a tendency for his view of life to become ever more troubled, his wisdom and his sense of balance remained unimpaired. Even here laughter can enrich the theatrical quality of subjects basically dark and serious. *Sodome et Gomorrhe* closes with the roaring of flames and the crashing down of walls as the Biblical cities are being destroyed, but when the irate voices of Jean and Lia, angrily berating each other, are heard rising above the sounds of destruction, audiences hardly know whether to laugh or weep—and perhaps, if they are moved as

Giraudoux wished them to be, they indulge in both. It is true that *Pour Lucrèce* (1953, translated as *Duel of Angels*), presents a situation so polluted that nothing is left for the heroine, save suicide, but it is significant that by far the most powerful of these final dramas, *La folle de Chaillot* (*The Madwoman of Chaillot*), offers a kind of summation of all Giraudoux' dramatic qualities—the seriousness, the laughter, the sympathy and the contempt, the imaginative scenes and the penetratingly realistic. In 1945 the spectators, on looking at their programmes, saw that the fictional time and place of action in that play was 'Paris: One day next spring'— and all succeeding audiences have known that this 'next spring' is as apt a time for themselves as it was for those who attended the première. A Prospector has just declared his belief that there is oil to be found under the Chaillot district of Paris, and frenziedly a group of money-grabbers is engaged in an effort to gain access to the source of this liquid gold. It seems as though nothing can stop them, for they have influence, and they are prepared to bribe. Unfortunately for these 'developers', however, there are two humble forces opposing their plans. The first consists of just a single young man, Pierre, the Prospector's hireling, who summons up enough courage to disobey an order to set a charge of dynamite below-ground. The second includes a motley crew of apparently disreputable characters—a demented Countess, ridiculously dressed in late-nineteenth-century attire, three other madwomen, a dish-washer named Irma, an old-clothes-man, and a man who works in the sewers. After a brilliantly amusing and penetrating lunatic mock trial of the 'pimps' who are trying to take control of the world, the Countess neatly foils their schemes. She owns a shabby café, disseminates a rumour that the supposed oil is directly underneath, tricks them into going down into the sewers, slams down a heavy stone slab upon them, and gleefully leaves them to perish. At once the stage becomes joyously illuminated; happy music sounds; a mysterious voice acclaims the Madwoman, giving her thanks on behalf of humanity. Nor is her task yet completed: the youthful Pierre has been so miserable in working for the Prospector that he determines to kill himself, but she has seen that he has been attracted to Irma and that this poor girl is in love with him; so she talks the lad out of his dismal thoughts and persuades the pair to kiss and get married. As the curtain begins to make its final descent, it might seem that the author has been indulging here in a sentimentally conceived dream, and also that his drama owes its being to social-political concepts: but Giraudoux was no sentimentalist, and he was never directly doctrinaire. Even if there is a happy ending, even if he shares in the Madwoman's chuckling delight as she drowns those rats down in the sewers, even if his money-grabbing villains are rich and titled while their opponents are a wretched group of slum-dwellers, he leaves the audience with the thought that in this world only the mad are happy, and that for them too life is often dismally unpleasant: the Madwoman herself tells us that, although from time to time she gets the chance of having a good laugh, every morning she has to take her hair out of a bedside drawer and her teeth out of a glass.

Jean Anouilh: 'Pièces Noires' and 'Pièces Roses'

Thus Giraudoux carried the drama of the thirties into the forties, and by a coincidence he was immediately followed by another dramatic master, Jean Anouilh, who not only carried the drama of the forties on to the seventies but who shared many of his predecessor's qualities. He too was eminently 'theatrical', an author who also constantly composed his scenes with thought of the stage in mind, who instinctively knew when to change step from slow to fast and from fast to slow, and who was adroitly adept in mingling the real and the fantastic. Although he had started writing plays in the early thirties, it was not until about 1937 and 1938 that he succeeded in establishing himself with *Le voyageur sans bagage* (*Traveller without Luggage*), *La sauvage* (*The Restless Heart*), and *Le bal des voleurs* (*Thieves' Carnival*). Even in these plays, however, he had not succeeded in finding the full means of expressing his true power, so that his genius was not completely revealed until, during the war years and in those immediately following, he proceeded to compose the lengthy series of plays which included *Léocadia* (*Time Remembered*, 1940), *Le rendez-vous de Senlis* (*The Rendezvous at Senlis*, or *Dinner with the Family*, 1941), *Eurydice* (*Legend of Lovers*, or *Point of Departure*, 1942), *Antigone* (1944), *Roméo et Jeannette* (1946), *L'invitation au château* (*Ring Round the Moon*, 1947), *Ardèle* (1948), *La valse des toréadors* (*The Waltz of the Toreadors*, 1952), and *L'alouette* (*The Lark*, 1953).

Throughout, although his plays exhibited almost kaleidoscopic variations in style and in mood, his basic playwriting technique and his outlook upon life remained both constant and sure: like Giraudoux, he was sufficiently master of himself to maintain his own forms and modes of expression and to prevent him from becoming a follower of newly invented trends. Anouilh's ever-lively theatricality also restrained him from the danger of merely repeating himself, yet there is one pervading and characteristic concept, which is expressed in many different ways throughout his writings—a peculiar kind of sadness consequent on an awareness by his heroes and heroines that, although they themselves wish and strive for the good, the pure and the clean, there is something in the very nature of the world around them which is apt to thwart their best efforts. Love is the theme which most attracts him, yet rarely are his lovers happy: again and again they are confronted by barriers which they find it impossible to surmount. Sometimes, it is true, these barriers are set up by the surroundings into which his characters are born, yet, again like Giraudoux, Anouilh generally refrains from suggesting that it is social conditions alone which are always responsible for the world's unhappiness. Certainly he discerns the evils in modern civilization; certainly he shows the emptiness and the hypocrisy of what is called 'society'; but most definitely his attitude to the life around him is not that of the propagandist political reformer.

Everyone knows that Anouilh loves to classify his plays in his own particular manner: he has his '*pièces roses*' when his mood is inclined towards fantasy and towards at least a measure of happiness, his '*pièces noires*' at those times when his mood is dark, his '*pièces brillantes*' when eyes are all a-glitter, his '*pièces costumées*' when he feels like putting on fancy-dress, and his '*pièces grinçantes*' when teeth grind together as the contrast between dream and reality becomes peculiarly bitter and hard to endure. There are forty of these dramatic pieces, sufficient in their number, their variety, and their style to make Anouilh the grand-master of the French stage during the later years just as Giraudoux had been master of the earlier.

In a sense the *roses*, the *noires*, the *brillantes*, the *costumées*, and even the *grinçantes* were all anticipated within the scope of the play which brought him his first truly great success, *Le bal des voleurs*—a play which he himself called a '*pièce rose*'. The setting is a charming villa, surrounded by a delightful garden, belonging to an elderly Lady Hurf. Here there is a carnival ball; lovers kiss; lights sparkle; music accompanies the action; a young Juliette gains the Gustave to whom her heart has been given. Yet behind and beyond all the charm and the delight there is sadness. Lady Hurf, who largely controls the play's events, is old and bored, and her self-appointed rôle as fairy godmother is taken up simply because she wants something to do: Gustave has come on stage finely attired as a Spanish aristocrat, but this is merely a disguise: in truth he is only a thief who has intruded into the party because he has his eyes set on Lady Hurf's jewellery. No doubt the play ends in merriment, yet at least some of the laughter is forced, and Lady Hurf is about to be left again to her weary thoughts. The '*pièce*' is '*rose*' only because of two whims of circumstance—the elderly woman's boredom and the extraordinary claim by her even older companion, Lord Edgard, that Gustave is his long-lost son—a claim which may be excused only because the said lord is almost in his dotage. Perhaps, when we consider its plot and characters very closely, *Le bal des voleurs* is not so far apart from *La sauvage*, the heroine of which is a pure, idealistic Thérèse to whom fate has not been so kind as it was for Juliette. This Thérèse has been born into a disreputable family of fourth-class itinerant cheap musicians: her father is dissolute, her mother has a lover. When she falls deeply and sincerely in love with a rich, handsome, successful young composer who asks her to marry him she is forced to look into her own heart and find the strength to leave him: for her, she decides, no such happiness is possible.

We are indeed close here to *Eurydice*—one of Anouilh's most powerful plays, in which his sense of disillusionment and pity and understanding go even further. This Eurydice may have the name of a mythical Greek heroine, but in fact she is only a poor touring actress, dragged down into slime because of her wretched surroundings although still preserving a dream of purity in her imagination: Orfée here is no divine harpist but an impoverished musician who wanders from saloon to saloon. These two meet on a station platform: they fall in love: they walk together to an hotel: in the morning she goes out, and within a short time news comes that she has been killed by falling under a bus. Orfée is bowed down with grief. Then comes Anouilh's most effective twisting of the classical legend. Death, in the form of Henri, a commercial traveller, tries to help him, brings Eurydice back to him, but warns that he must not look at her until the morning. Orfée, however, is so anxious to find out the truth of her love for him that he starts to question her: she tells him about the life she had hitherto led, about her sudden pure passion for him, about her committing suicide in her misery: and Orfée, desperate in his anxiety to discover whether she is in fact telling the truth, is forced to look into her eyes—and she vanishes. Orfée cannot forget her: although he is loath to die, he turns to Henri for help, and Death, pityingly, tells him how he might find her again. In their quiet conversation Anouilh brings onto the stage a strangely affecting atmosphere of tenderness, of deep understanding and of tranquillity. "My dear!" murmurs Eurydice when she sees him, "How long you have been!"

In an equally effective manner his theatrical power is demonstrated in *Antigone*. The events and the characters are fundamentally the same as those in Sophocles' tragedy, but the emotions aroused are vastly different. This play was, of course, written and presented during the war, and quite clearly it reflects the problems which confronted many persons in the France of its time, but most certainly it is a drama which possesses far more than a merely temporary and topical significance. In effect, what Anouilh does is to give a different shape to the conflict which forms the core of Sophocles' work, and this he does by developing still further the contrast, already expressed in *Eurydice*, between the appeal of death, with all its finality, and the appeal of life, which frequently might mean a sordid and uninspired passing on from day to day until an end accompanied by just such boredom as was experienced by Lady Hurf. This Antigone, therefore, does not act simply because of love for her dead brother or because of religious convictions; she rejects life because of her belief that death alone could hold inviolate the purity of her new-found vision.

Two other '*pièces noires*' followed, and then Anouilh issued his light *L'invitation au château*, introducing to us a pair of identical twins—a simple-minded, romantically inclined Frederic and a mischievously cynical Horace, two characters designed to be performed by the same actor. The former is engaged to an heiress, Diana; in a Puck-like spirit, the latter engages a poor actress, Isabelle, to attend a ball and to do all she can to turn poor Frederic's head. Complications follow when Isabelle falls in love with Horace, and these complications are not dismissed until a wise old aunt (like Lady Hurf, playing the part of a fairy godmother), realizing that the girl is in love only with Horace's outside, directs Diana's attention to Frederic, and is even clever enough to play the part of matchmaker for Diana and Horace. Death, however, still held his court in Anouilh's imagination, and just one year after the appearance of this gay invitation to a ball came the bitter and tormenting *Ardèle*, a piece indeed *grinçante* in which a dark theme is made darker still by its association with some grotesquely comic interludes. The woman who gives her name to this terrible play never comes on stage: all we are told about her comes from the lips of her thoroughly upperclass (and thoroughly disreputable) relations, who declare that she is a contorted hunchback, forty-four years of age, of whom they are ashamed and whom they keep out of sight in an upstairs room. They are now confronted with what seems to them the uttermost horror: this deformed woman and a similarly deformed tutor have fallen in love, and of course they agree that such a union must be prevented at all costs. The play ends with the tutor slipping into Ardèle's room and joining her in a double suicide. Since we see neither the tutor nor Ardèle, we are left with the feeling that perhaps what these terrible relatives detest is, in fact, the purity of their love—a purity which to them seems deformed. Certainly in a play which followed only two years later, *La répétition* (*The Rehearsal*, 1950), an idle group of upper-class characters, when confronted by true love, try their best to shatter it—chiefly because it shames them.

Although Anouilh was to write several light plays from this time onward, in general his mood continued to tend towards the dark. Two bitterly quarrelling characters from *Ardèle* are introduced into *La valse des toréadors*; in *La grotte* (*The Cavern*, 1961) the audience is led downstairs from the drawing-room into an ominous kitchen: a dinner-party in *Pauvre Bitos* (*Poor Bitos*, 1956), with the guests dressed up as characters from the period of the French Revolution, brings together a repellent present and an equally repellent past; death, naturally, hovers over the Joan of Arc in *L'alouette* and the central character in *Becket, ou l'honneur de Dieu* (*Becket, or The Honour of God*, 1959). Sadness, often associated with regret, is all-pervasive: the ironic title of one of his latest plays, *Tu étais si gentil quand tu étais petit* (*You Were so Sweet when You Were Little*, 1972), might well be taken as a symbolic motto expressive of his general vision of life.

Unquestionably, the judgments passed upon his work as a whole will in the future be diverse—as, indeed, Anouilh himself predicted in his *Cher Antoine* (*Dear Antoine*, 1969): many of his plays may well be allowed to fall by the wayside, but it seems improbable that those who look upon the more arresting works within his rich dramatic world can fail to see in him one of the truly outstanding dramatists of the present century.

By his side stand many other noteworthy authors. Nearest to him in spirit is Armand Salacrou, a writer who first attracted attention by his surrealistically inclined *Patchouli* (1930), who won popular success with *Atlas-Hôtel* (1931), and who finally found his true sphere in *L'inconnue d'Arras* (*The Unknown Girl of Arras*, 1935). In this last-mentioned play an ordinary middle-class man has just committed suicide, but in the fractional moment as the shot rings out episodes from his life come flooding in upon his memory while time is mysteriously arrested—and, strangely, among all these recollections, strongest of all is that of a girl he had once seen, merely in passing, when he was visiting Arras. Unfortunately however, nearly all his later plays just miss that elusive quality which gives distinction to those of Giraudoux and Anouilh. *La terre est ronde* (*The Earth is Round*, 1938), set in the Florence of 1492 when Savonarola's mobs were ruling the city, suggests in its title that what happened yesterday has come again in Hitler's Germany, and that something similar is almost sure to return tomorrow: but somehow it does not fulfil its promise. *Les nuits de la colère* (*The Nights of Wrath*) was unquestionably a powerfully appealing play in 1946, with its grim debate concerning collaboration and resistance, involving men dead and men living: yet it too seems wanting in enduring strength. Something of Anouilh's sadness appears in *Histoire de rire* (*When the Music Stops*, or *No Laughing Matter*, 1939), but little of his incisiveness and theatrical skill. It seems as though Salacrou can give of his best only when he invents, or adopts, some unexpected dramatic device, as he did, for example, in *L'inconnue d'Arras* and in his later *Sens interdit, ou les âges de la vie* (*No Entry*, or *Life's Ages*, 1953), where the characters start old and grey, proceed backwards to youth, and end in nothingness.

Both Anouilh and Salacrou suffer because they feel that life does not measure up to their dreams of what it might be, but neither defines this sense of dissatisfaction in precise terms, and both of them seek escape, when they can, in an admixture of laughter, irony, and tears. By their side, however, stand several other playwrights who express their bitterness in terms more sharply defined and more starkly uttered. Henry de Montherlant thus emerges as a figure who might be regarded as an aristocratically Gallic counterpart of the democratically American Hemingway—a vigorous athlete, a proud bullfighter, a man possessed of a strong and stern personality, yet one who at times is apt to exhibit unsuspected facets of his nature. Although he had toyed with the stage many years earlier, his first play was, in effect, *La reine morte* (*Queen after Death*, 1942), a work which at once established him as a dramatist of importance. The central character here is King Ferrante of Portugal, a strong-willed man subject at times to sudden doubts. He has set his heart upon a royal marriage between his son Pedro and the Infanta of Navarre, discovers that the prince is secretly married to Inés de Castro, and in a fit of passion orders him to be imprisoned. Although this action leaves him exhausted, afflicted by a great weariness of spirit, rage swells up in him once more when he further learns that Inés is with child. At once he commands her death, but the effort costs him his own life: he dies just as her corpse is borne into the palace. The play ends with Pedro, now King, collapsed in despair over the body of his 'Queen after death.'

Nearly all this author's dramas are, like this one, dark studies of human character, and most of them, similarly set in times past, intro-

duce religious themes. *Port Royal* (1954) obviously is concerned with the
fierce conflict between the Jesuits and the Jansenists: faith, doubt,
obedience, rebellious thought all confusedly afflict its spiritually tortured characters. *Malatesta* (1948) deals with a bitter disappointment,
different from but no less painful than, that suffered by Ferrante. The
hard, cruel, indomitable tyrant of Rimini dreams always of future fame
and engages a chronicler to be constantly at his side recording his actions
and his thoughts. Gradually, however, the rock-like ruler, tormented by
fears, grows weak, and the last scene shows the poor scribe poisoning his
master. As the venom takes possession of his body, Malatesta experiences a vision not unreminiscent of the nightmare which tortured
Richard III, while at the same time he sees the chronicler slowly, deliberately, tearing up the Malatesta record, destroying the pages one by one
in flames. Still more effective, but at the same time more perplexing, is *Le
Maître de Santiago* (1947), a largely static work which concentrates on the
ageing Don Álvaro Dabo, devoted knight of the Order of Santiago, who
clings so tenaciously to his rigid religious beliefs that, under his influence, his daughter, as if in a trance, has a vision which causes her to see
her father's face on the figure of Christ before which she kneels in prayer.
In the end she abandons her hopes of a happy marriage in order to accompany the devout Master into a dark cloistered life of unending
prayer.

The atmosphere of this drama is not unlike that pervading two plays
by François Mauriac—*Asmodée* (*Asmodeus*, 1937) and *Les mal aimés* (*The
Ill-beloved*, 1945), the first showing a woman strangely dominated by the
stern religious fanaticism of her son's tutor, and the second showing a
girl who, like de Montherlant's heroine, abandons her own visions of
happiness for the sake of her father—although here this father, instead of
being a devoted knight of a religious order, is a drunkard. The disappointments thus revealed are not dissimilar from those exhibited by
Anouilh as he watches suffering individuals failing to escape from the
sometimes invisible, yet invincible, forces surrounding them. The more
these five playwrights are examined together, the more they appear,
despite the truly vast differences between them, to belong to the same
world: collectively they are modern representatives of the classical
French tradition which stretches back to the seventeenth century.

The Theatre's Discovery of Paul Claudel

And with those five must be associated still another author who, even
more than they, served in a double manner to link the past with the present. Paul Claudel, born in 1868, had written the first version of his earliest play, *Tête d'or*, in 1889; in 1912 he had achieved considerable
success, not only in France but also abroad, with his *L'annonce faite à
Marie* (*The Tidings Brought to Mary*); and by 1939 his published dramatic
works included some twenty-five titles. Yet, although these texts were

available in printed form, and although the author's reputation as a poet stood high, only a limited number of these dramas had been seen by pre-war French audiences: some of his plays remained wholly unproduced, some had been presented only by small acting groups, and some—such as *Le pain dur*, published 1918, acted at Oldenburg in 1926, and *Le repos du septième jour*, published 1901, acted at Warsaw in 1928—had been staged only in other countries and in translated texts. Thus, despite his literary eminence, there was a general opinion that his dramas were, on the whole, too 'special' for theatrical performance: both his highly indi-vidualistic verse forms and his frequent refusal to accept the limitations commonly accepted by stage writers seemed to indicate that he would remain a closet dramatist. And, since in 1939 he himself was seventy-one years of age, it appeared improbable that this judgment was likely to be changed. Then something extraordinary happened. In 1929 Claudel had published, in two volumes, a very lengthy poetic play, *Le soulier de satin* (*The Satin Slipper*), described as an '*action espagnol en quatre journées*', the thematic range of which was confessedly world-wide, even if it was mainly concerned with the sixteenth and seventeenth centuries. Almost all who had perused its text tacitly assumed that this most certainly was a work which could have a place only in the study. There was, however, one prominent director, Jean-Louis Barrault, who believed that it might prove the basis for a great theatrical spectacle, and in 1943 he succeeded in producing its extensive scenes in what was an exercise in 'total theatre.' Its poetic lines were carefully and painstakingly delivered by the actors according to a text (actually printed in a special edition) which indicated the values—in rhythm, emphasis and pitch—which were to be given to the author's words.

For war-time playgoers *Le soulier de satin* proved to be a wonder and a revelation, and during the later forties and the fifties it was followed by performances of others among Claudel's plays, notably *Le livre de Chris-tophe Colomb* (*The Book of Christopher Columbus*, published 1933, produced 1953) and *L'histoire de Tobie et de Sara* (*The Story of Tobias and Sarah*, written 1938, published 1942, produced 1947). In considering these perform-ances, however, it is essential to bear in mind Claudel's peculiar position within the range of modern French literature. Not without justification, he has been likened—in his historical position, if not in his positive achievements—to Homer, Virgil, and Dante, three poets who were akin in delivering final farewells to certain great ages. If this proposition is accepted, each of Claudel's more significant dramas may thus be regarded as a curtain falling upon a period of civilization which has reached its end, and thus we must see him, even although he emerged as one of the outstanding theatrical figures during post-war years, even although he himself lived on until 1955, as a distinguished author stand-ing apart from the new epoch which was engaged in acclaiming his achievements. This clearly means that, while we can fully appreciate what deep impact these stage productions made upon thousands of playgoers, there must also be full appreciation of the fact that his works marked the culmination of a tradition, not something new, and that he himself was, after all, more poet than dramatist. He was, indeed, an author destined to tower up alone, without close companions and without immediate disciples, in lonely grandeur.

Surrealism and Existentialism

Claudel's unique position during those years is made manifest when he is set alongside another distinguished author, Jean Cocteau, just twenty years his junior, most of whose plays had also been composed during the pre-war period, but whose relationship with the post-war stage is markedly different. Both were poets, but Cocteau often tended to equate the 'poetic' with action rather than with words: it is thus significant that whereas Claudel's first full-length play was a lyrical *Tête d'or* (*Golden Head*), written in the year when Cocteau was born, the latter's entry into the theatre, in 1912, was as a deviser of ballet actions. Both were Catholics, but *Tête d'or* was based on the theme of vanity of vanities, all is vanity, while Cocteau made his earliest significant bow to the public as a dramatist with an extravagantly avant-garde *Les mariés de la Tour Eiffel* (*The Wedding on the Eiffel Tower*), jauntily constructed in surealistic style.

Jaunty though Cocteau may seem to be, he nevertheless revealed himself, even in his pre-war works, as a deeply troubled playwright, one whose basic attitude to life was not unlike that expressed by Giraudoux. If Lia and Jean are constantly quarrelling in *Sodome et Gomorrhe*, *Orfée* displays its legendary lovers at bickering odds with each other; if Giraudoux' characters are often shown confronted by forces operating upon them beyond their control, *La machine infernale* depicted man at the mercy of cruel gods. Even Cocteau's later *L'aigle à deux têtes*, with its final scene in which two hapless lovers bring death upon themselves, might have been devised by Giraudoux, and his final, strange *Bacchus* (1951) presents several features recalling his companion dramatist's style. The setting in that drama is sixteenth-century Germany, the central character a peasant, Hans, who, after having been tormented by some sadistic aristocrats, had lost his wits, had later recovered, but had decided to maintain a pretence of being unbalanced. During the week of a 'Bacchus' festival, this man is chosen to be a carnival lord, absolute in power for his brief spell of majesty, and he proceeds to use his authority in an effort to promote love and kindness, to banish hate and fear. As he proceeds to put this ideal into practice, the entire community rises up against him: even the Church, in the person of a Cardinal, decides that such hopelessly extravagant vision, if carried into practice, would result in more evil than good. At the week's end, the mob howls for his death at the stake, an execution from which he is saved by a bullet fired by one of his few admirers, and only by exercising devious methods is the Cardinal able to have poor Hans' body laid to rest in sanctified ground. Manifestly there is a deep sadness, a profound disillusionment, here.

The surrealism which had attracted Cocteau was, in the main, expressive of the mood characteristic of the pre-war years: the philosophically existentialist attitude exposed in the plays of Jean-Paul Sartre and Albert Camus, despite the fact that it owed much to the earlier experiments, was something distinct, and, just as the comparison between Claudel and Cocteau is of assistance in any attempt to enter into an appreciation of their respective achievements, so it is profitable to compare Cocteau with these two younger contemporaries of his. Born in 1889, Cocteau was fifty-two when France was occupied by the Germans, and his reputation was high in many lands: in 1941 Sartre was only thirty-six, a teacher of philosophy who had as yet no connections with the playhouse: in the same year Camus was barely twenty-eight, and although his first drama, *Caligula*, had been written in 1938, this piece was not published until 1944 and not acted until 1945. In considering the long range of the theatre's affairs, the passing of decades is often of but slight significance, but here the movement from year to year brought mighty changes, sharply separating the old from the new. This separation was rendered still firmer by the fact that whereas Cocteau had pirouetted to the stage door from artists' ateliers and musicians' salons, the youthful Sartre had been brought up under the control of a Calvinist grandfather and began his career as an author with the publication of a philosophical study of 'being and nothingness' and of *Nausée* (*Nausea*) an autobiographical-philosophical novel, while Camus, after an even harder upbringing and an academic training in philosophy, similarly started his literary career with a deeply thoughtful novel, *L'étranger* (*The Stranger*, 1942). Despite Sartre's willingness and Camus' refusal to accept the label of 'existentialist,' the two writers were fundamentally at one: both of them were men of the Resistance; both of them, concentrating upon the basic fact of death and upon the presence in man of reason and of forces far beyond reason's control, tended to express a view of life which was grimly dark; both, although they devoted much time to the writing of their plays, providing them often with actions violent and arresting, regarded these dramas rather as philosophic exercises than as contributions to the theatre's treasury; both made notable contributions to the stage of the dark forties, yet it is without surprise that we observe two things—that, in spite of the almost melodramatic episodes introduced into their writings, their stage actions often seem to be rather awkwardly arranged, and that their reputations tended to decline as the years went by.

Concerning the immediate effect of Sartre's *Les mouches* (*The Flies*) there is, of course, not the slightest doubt. This metaphysical and political document, this patent allegory of men confronted by totalitarian forces, was, as it were, impertinently presented to the French public in 1943 under the very noses of the German authorities. Orestes, returning to his native Argos, finds its people abjectly passive under a plague of monstrous flies controlled by Zeus: although at first he had intended to remain an unattached observer, Orestes suddenly decides to act, kills Ægisthus and Clytemnestra, and finds that this deed gives him the power to defy Zeus: his action, freely and independently undertaken, gives him a peculiar power, making him independent both of other men and of the gods. Sartre, of course, was an atheist: the gods for him had no existence, and their Heaven was a myth: and in his next play, *Huis clos* (*No Exit*, 1944) he set out to demonstrate that Hell was, in fact, nothing but "other people." In this one-act piece, three characters, a man and two women, recently dead, find themselves in a handsomely appointed Second Empire drawing-room, confronted by the terrifying certainty that for all eternity they are doomed to continue together in desolation and nerve-strung agony. These two dramas were composed with effective skill, but in his later writings, for various reasons, Sartre's handling of his dramatic material tended to become less skilful. Theatricality— sometimes theatricality of a sensational kind—is present in each play, yet the clarity of vision which gave distinction to *Les mouches* and *Huis clos* is apt to become blurred. *Morts sans sépulture* (*The Victors*, or *Men without Shadows*, 1946), with its picture of Resistance fighters murdered by men of Vichy, is accompanied by *La putain respectueuse* (*The Law-abiding Whore*, 1946), set in a southern part of the USA; *Les mains sales* (*Dirty Hands*, 1948) rather confusedly presents a young hero's existentialist choice, even although decision means death, in a communist land where the Party line has been changed; *Le Diable et le Bon Dieu* (*The Devil and the Good Lord*, 1951), set in sixteenth-century Germany, has a rather cumbersomely allegorical parable of a plot which rambles on in an attempt to prove that there is no God, that "the Church is a whore, selling her favours to the rich," and that attempts by men to achieve total goodness are futile; a double suicide, carried out in a misery of self-abasement, brings an end to the interesting, but equally cumbersome, plot of *Les séquestrés d'Altona* (*The Condemned of Altona*, 1959).

Not surprisingly, therefore, whereas the name of Sartre was one to conjure with in the years immediately following the end of the war, his theatrical popularity markedly declined as the fifties moved into the sixties: and much the same may be said concerning his one-time associate, Albert Camus. *Le malentendu* (*Cross Purposes*, or *The Misunderstanding*, 1944) proves, in retrospect, to be a not very inspiring re-treatment of the folk-tale which had attracted the attention of George Lillo in 1736, with focus set upon ideas rather than upon characters; *Caligula* (1945) presents, rather extravagantly, the picture of a man who, on realizing that death is inescapable, engages in a frenetic career of complete nihilism— this, according to the author, being a "tragedy of the intellect"; *L'état de siège* (*State of Siege*, 1948) must be judged ineffective in its effort to be an example of 'total theatre' and inadequate in its lumbering allegory, directly introduced by the stage persons of Plague and Death, which relates the menace of pestilence with that of dictatorial tyranny. That Camus exerted and still exerts considerable influence is certain—but perhaps more through such of his non-dramatic writings as *Le mythe de Sisyphus* (1942) and *La peste* (1947) than through his plays; equally certain is the fact that Sartre's impress has been just as strong—but, again, probably more through his philosophic study, *L'être et le néant* (1943), accepted by scholars as having hardly less significance than Heidegger's *Sein und Zeit* (1927), than through his contributions to the theatre. In so far as the stage is concerned, the significance of both men rests largely in the fact that, independently and unwittingly, they encouraged their successors to explore and exploit what has now become familiarly known as absurdism.

The Arrival of the Absurd: Ionesco and Adamov

During the years when Sartre and Camus were active, various young avant-garde playwrights and directors, rather surprisingly, turned back for inspiration to the past—the main road which they chose for their regressive journeys being that which was boldly signposted with the title of Jarry's *Ubu Roi*, that extraordinary piece which had been produced in the dim, distant past of the year 1896. The discovery of Jarry did not by any means stand alone. Travelling along this road, the excited young writers rushed pell-mell towards his friend Guillaume Apollinaire, whose *Les mamelles de Tirésias* in 1917 had been the earliest theatrical demonstration of the surrealist style, and who later led a gibbering and disoriented rabble towards the dead-end of Dadaism. André Breton's 'manifestoes' relating both to the surrealistic and dadaist 'philosophies' were eagerly perused, and even the utterly ridiculous 'science' of 'pataphysics' invented by Jarry led to the creation, in 1949, of the nonsensical Collège de Pataphysique, a Collège to which many authors, some of them men of eminence, devoted much of their time. Still mightier treasure-trove came from the study of Antonin Artaud, an author-director who had started as a surrealist but who soon proceeded to evolve his own 'theatre of cruelty.' It was at this time, too, that another discovery was made: the French-language plays by the Belgian Michel de Ghelderode came to the notice of the Parisian progressives. Some of this author's works had, of course, been well known in earlier years, but others, such as the '*tragédie-bouffe*' called *Fastes d'enfer* (*Chronicles of Hell*, published in 1929, produced in Paris 1949) did not come before the public until after the war, so that in general there had not previously been full realization of what grotesquely grim and gruesome scenes, melodramatically romantic in the familiar 'Gothic' tradition, were to be found among his numerous works. Ghelderode's style, with its admixture of all kinds of apparently discordant elements both in form and in content, characteristically Flemish in its inspiration, added further suggestions for the young French playwrights intent upon establishing a new kind of drama. His free use of

almost every kind of theatrical device, from poetic speech to unexpected
and often cacophonous sounds, from medieval formalism to circus clowneries, from devotion to savage irreverence, from the bliss of Heaven as
seen by some early Renaissance painter to the tormented Hell of Hieronymus Bosch—all these elements added more conceits for the new
authors.

By far the most immediately influential of these new writers is, obviously, Eugène Ionesco, whose 'anti-play,' *La cantatrice chauve* (*The Bald
Soprano*, 1950), soon spread its absurdity over many European countries:
nothing could resist the appeal of this piece which, according to its
author, had initially come into his head by chance—which, so far from
having been designed as a comedy, had originally seemed to him an excellent example of "the tragedy of language," and to which for some considerable time he could not attach any appropriate title. In *La leçon* (*The
Lesson*, 1951), *Jacques* (written 1950) and *Les chaises* (*The Chairs*, 1952) he
travelled farther along this new-found path, mixing together collections
of common phrases culled from various sources for the purpose of creating an impression of life's meaninglessness, and of the positive dangers
inherent in the use of words. Thus in *The Lesson* a girl-student comes to a
professor's house for an hour of coaching: first, in a fairly quiet manner,
he discusses several geographical matters, starts to become excited when
he turns to mathematics, and finally, in proceeding to linguistic matters,
completely loses control of himself and stabs his pupil. A maidservant
now enters to scold him because this is his fortieth victim for the day: she
reminds him that she already had given him a serious warning that
"mathematics almost always proceeds to philology, and philology proceeds to crime." In *Les chaises* the stage is provided with seats for an audience who are to listen to a great pronouncement by an Orator—but the
seats remain unoccupied and the Orator turns out to be a deaf-mute.

Thus Ionesco found his true sphere in a nightmare world in which the
frightening absurdities of language are combined with the terrors associated with material objects and with other people. *Amédée, ou comment s'en
débarrasser* (*Amédée, or, How to Get Rid of It*, 1954) introduces a monstrous
corpse which from moment to moment grows frighteningly larger and
larger. Simple, familiar things assume horrific dimensions: eggs become
menacing in *L'avenir est dans les œufs* (*The Future is in Eggs*, 1953); masses of
furniture, unaided, bear down upon an entire city in *Le nouveau locataire*
(*The New Tenant*, 1955). Then comes *Tueur sans gages* (*The Killer*, 1958),
introducing in the person of Bérenger a symbol of the ordinary man in
the midst of an ominous world; and this leads on to *Rhinocéros* (1959)
where the same character, Bérenger, sees the whole of humanity being
turned into rhinoceroses. He is terrified; although a friend assures him
that this is nothing save a slight epidemic of rhinoceritis, he suspects instinctively that there is something evil here, swears he'll never join the
others, and then, suddenly feeling his utter loneliness, is cast into despair
because he is now different from all the rest: only at the very end of the

play does he succeed in summoning up courage to defy this insidious monstrosity. Other similar plays followed, culminating in the strange *Macbett* (1972), which has been described as Shakespeare cross-fertilized with *Ubu Roi*.

In such a way the theatre of the absurd was fully established, and it received a formal blessing in 1970 when Ionesco was made a member of the Académie Française. Meanwhile, it was receiving further extension in the early plays of Arthur Adamov, notably in *Ping-pong* (1955), which reveals the meaninglessness of ordinary life as it traces the careers of two young men while they move on to old age, its conclusion being a frightening ping-pong game in which the pair become ever more and more excited—until one of the pair collapses in death. Ritualism, eroticism, still more violence, were added to the absurd by Jean Genet in *Le balcon* (*The Balcony*, 1956), in *Les nègres* (*The Blacks*, 1959), and finally in *Les paravents* (*The Screens*, 1961), a pretentious drama, introducing nearly a hundred characters, which concentrates upon the person of Saïd, a wretched Arab who deliberately seeks to secure an identity for himself by rejecting everything and everyone. Here the connection between existentialism and the later absurd becomes amply apparent; and it is not surprising that, while the Académie Française blessed Ionesco and Cocteau, Genet was blessed by Sartre in his biographical *Saint Genet, comédien et martyr*. If Genet, as is suggested by this canonization, feels that human beings have fallen from grace, Jacques Audiberti in his sextormented dramas tends to view the absurdity of man's condition as an inevitable consequence of his having separated himself from the natural grace of the animal kingdom; and if Ionesco derived his reputation largely from his monstrously expanding corpses, his rhinoceroses, and the like, Boris Vian presents in *Les bâtisseurs d'empire* (*The Empire Builders*, 1959) a kind of diminishing mirror-picture in which an apparently ordinary family, tormented by a strange, inexplicable noise, grows smaller and smaller, forcing themselves into ever more restricted quarters, until in the end the father dies, all alone, in an attic. The excitements and the oddities which so easily and endlessly could be multiplied in the theatre of the absurd, together with the opportunities offered by this dramatic style for the association of the ridiculous with the cruel and the erotically perverse, and the scope which it gives for out-of-the-way stage presentations, have naturally drawn many youthful avant-garde writers within its embracing sphere. And if we wish to select a piece which is, as it were, emblematic of all these elements and conditions, we need hardly go beyond *Le cimetière des voitures* (*The Car Cemetery*) as it was produced at Dijon in 1966 by the Argentinian director Victor Garcia. All the fashionable features were here—the pollution of the modern age symbolized by the setting, the filthy desolation of a space (established almost in the midst of the audience) with a mass of heaped-up, battered, broken, rusting automobiles, the miserable people who dwell in its midst, the absurd fact that in several respects they are given service as though they were in an hotel, the terrifying and almost casual violence, the grotesque ritualistic element wherein a modern Christ-figure suffers flagellation and then is crucified on a police motor-cycle. Essentially, all of this was derived from a playlet written by Fernando Arrabal in 1958, but, since the text was too brief for a full entertainment, the Dijon performance was confessedly "a spectacle by Victor Garcia" concocted out of four pieces, *Le cimetière des voitures* itself, and three other brief playlets by the same author, *Oraison* (*Orison*), *Les deux bourreaux* (*The Two Executioners*), and *La communion solenelle* (*The Solemn Communion*).

Waiting for Nothing?

Within this sphere there is one writer and one play which imperatively demand particular attention, even although the creator and his creation occupy a triply anomalous position.

First of all, *En attendant Godot* (*Waiting for Godot*, 1952), although originally written in French, is the work of an Irish author. In one sense, therefore, it does not belong here in this brief account of post-war French drama: yet most certainly it came into being within the world of the Parisian avant-garde: it is, indeed, difficult to think of any other environment which could so effectively have brought it into existence. This play, as everyone knows, has probably had more, and greater, and wider, influence in dozens of countries than any other 'absurdist' dramas except for some of the writings of Ionesco, but here another anomaly becomes apparent: it is, apparently, the only full-length dramatic work brought into being by its author. In itself it is a peculiarly subtle achievement, a largely static play which succeeded in producing a strangely hypnotic effect, a work which has a seemingly simple theme and yet which includes scores of tantalizingly perplexing speeches and actions. No one need wonder why its appeal was so great: no-one need regard its constant repetitions of ideas and situations as other than a necessary device to evoke the all-pervading atmosphere of continual waiting in vain for something which does not, or at least may not, exist. But here enters in a third anomaly—one which has a very direct and important relevance to consideration of the theatre of the mid-twentieth century.

The repetitions *within* this drama may certainly be essential for suggesting the atmosphere which Beckett desired to envelop its entire action: but when we look at his work as a whole we cannot avoid observing that his other dramatic writings tend constantly to repeat the one basic thought that life is not worth living, and that in general they incline towards becoming ever shorter and shorter. It is true that *Happy Days* (*Oh, les beaux jours*, 1961) includes two scenes, but *Fin de partie* (*Endgame*, 1957) is a trailingly long one-act with a central Hamm, in a wheel-chair, attended by his servant-slave Clov, a pair which mirrors the blind Pozzo and Lucky: this play is almost completely motionless, a quality emphasized by the presence on-stage of another couple, husband and wife, immobile in two large ashcans. Words disappear completely in *Acte sans paroles* (1957), followed in 1960 by *Acte sans paroles II*. *Krapp's Last Tape* (*La dernière bande*, 1958) has just one character who, listening to a tape-recording of his own made many years before, erratically provides comments on its contents. The already-mentioned *Happy Days* repeats the ashcan device by showing a woman buried in the ground, first up to her waist, and then later up to her neck. The brief *Va-et-vient* (*Come and Go*, 1966), deliberately described as a 'dramaticule,' is almost wholly silent, although, as the title indicates, there are occasional entries and exits. There is an uninterrupted impression here of things becoming ever smaller and smaller—and this impression is certainly not dissipated by the appearance of *Not I* (1972), in which all that the spectators see is a mouth, with its tongue, in Beckett's own words, "flickering away like mad."

Presumably the absurd can go no further. *Not I* has been described as "a miniature *Œdipus Rex*," but, if so, magnificent grandeur has indeed been reduced to a ridiculous microcosm.

Samuel Beckett is, of course, a distinguished author, and to him the term 'genius' is commonly applied. Our concern here, however, is specifically directed towards the drama, and that being so, it would indeed be startlingly ironic—a final anomaly—if the admittedly gifted author of *En attendant Godot* were to be found largely responsible for something which of late has been worrying many persons intimately associated with the French playhouse. This something is a fear lest the drama—that drama which has been made glorious by Molière, Corneille, Racine, Marivaux, Claudel, Giraudoux, Anouilh and their many companions, the drama which until now has played a significant rôle in the development of French civilization—is at last being brought to an end.

GERMAN-LANGUAGE POST-WAR DRAMA
(FDR, GDR, AUSTRIA, SWITZERLAND)

HILDE HAIDER-PREGLER

DURING the past few decades the development of German-language drama has been largely determined by political forces. The Nazis had broken the continuity of the theatre in Germany by their witch-hunt against 'degenerate art,' driven out many of the leading theatrical figures, directed dramatic writing into channels favoured by the party, and thus isolated Germany (and later, Austria) from the outside world. It is therefore not surprising that the two authors who helped this German-language stage to regain an international reputation in the fifties, Max Frisch and Friedrich Dürrenmatt, belonged to Switzerland. During the earliest post-war years in West Germany and Austria the cultural climate was dominated by an almost hectic desire to catch up with plays elsewhere, and also, of course, with those produced by the émigrés. At the same time a whole generation of aspiring young playwrights began to seek for personal means of expression in the most widely differing, and often disorientated, styles, and finally during the sixties, when the wave of the absurd had died away, found what seemed to many of them a satisfactory dramatic form in the documentary theatre and the new realism. Naturally, during these same years, the drama presented in the German Democratic Republic developed in an entirely different manner, with party directives determining both form and content for all stage efforts.

Dramatic Models

One powerful personality, however, played a dominating role in the post-war theatre both in the East and in the West—Bertolt Brecht, a man who fused playwriting, dramatic theory, and the technique of play-direction into a single entity. No-one could escape from a confrontation with Brecht—whether he was admired, or directly imitated, as the greatest theatrical master of the age, or whether he was boycotted because of his political views (in 1948 he decided to leave for East Berlin and to accept the Party line of the German Democratic

Republic). The form of his "epic theatre", involving "alienation" in dramatic structure, stagecraft, and acting, has, as is well known, become so widely familiar as to take its place in almost all discussions concerning the theory of drama and performance.

For Brecht these attitudes towards the theatre resulted from his ideological concepts in general: when he embraced Marxism in the twenties he became convinced that both man and society could be intellectually analysed, and that therefore both could be portrayed and altered. The theatre, while still preserving its function as a provider of entertainment, should, he thought, aim at providing an intellectual insight such as was essential for the alteration to a positive attitude. For him a general, overall, view could be secured only by moving back from the subject to a correct distance—by the substitution of 'alienation' in place of illusion.

From 1933 onward Brecht wrote in exile a series of plays dealing with the problem of Fascism—*Die Rundköpfe und die Spitzköpfe* (*The Roundedheads and the Pointed-heads*, 1934); *Furcht und Elend des Dritten Reiches* (*Fear and Misery of the Third Reich*, 1938), a cavalcade of twenty-four scenes showing how this regime of terror gained its power through intimidation of individuals; *Die Gewehre der Frau Carrar* (*Señora Carrar's Rifles*, 1937), a play about the Spanish Civil War; *Der aufhaltsame Aufstieg des Arturo Ui* (*The Resistible Rise of Arturo Ui*, written 1941, published 1957), a parody of Hitler's career set in gangster-ridden Chicago; *Schweyk im zweiten Weltkrieg* (*Schweyk in the Second World War*, written 1941–43, published 1957), the story of an artful fellow who acts on the theory that only the survivor can be right. It was during his refugee period, too, that he wrote his last great works: *Das Leben des Galilei* (*The Life of Galileo*, performed at Zurich, 1943); the magnificent chronicle play concerning the Thirty Years' War, *Mutter Courage und ihre Kinder* (*Mother Courage and Her Children*, performed at Zurich, 1941), a drama in which he exposes war in all its cruelty, with in the centre the formidable figure of the canteen-woman, Anna Fierling, nicknamed "Mother Courage." There is a poetic atmosphere in *Der gute Mensch von Sezuan* (*The Good Woman of Setzuan*, written 1938–40, performed at Zurich, 1943), in which a former prostitute, Shen Te, comes to grief because of her good qualities and the difficult situations in which she is placed; there are excellent parts in *Herr Puntila und sein Knecht Matti* (*Mr Puntila and His Man, Matti*, written 1940–41, performed at Zurich, 1948), designated by Brecht himself as a *Volksstück; Der kaukasische Kreidekreis* (*The Caucasian Chalk Circle*, written 1944–45, published 1949) introduces a fresh treatment of the judgment of Solomon, wherein the maid Grusche, at great personal sacrifice, brings up the child of the hard-hearted governor's wife, and in the end is recognized as the 'real' mother.

The discussion concerning Brecht is still far from finished, but unquestionably he can be regarded, with justice, as one of the 'classic authors' of the twentieth century.

By 1960 the ground was prepared for the rediscovery of a long-underrated writer, the Austro-Hungarian Ödön von Horvath, whose so-called 'folk-plays' did not originally receive the attention they deserved, because the public and the critics failed to see, beneath the apparently realistic, dialectically coloured colloquial language and the idyllic surface pattern of bourgeois and proletarian existence, the indifference, the heartlessness, the constant bestiality of a social life wrapped up in sentimentality. "All my plays are tragedies," declared Horvath, "There are only two things I attack—stupidities and lies—and only two things I champion—common-sense and honesty." His *Geschichten aus dem Wiener Wald* (*Tales from the Vienna Woods*, 1931) uses elements of the traditional cosy sentimentality of the Viennese operettas for the purpose of emphasizing the underlying reality, evil, chilling, and cruel. *Kasimir und Karoline* (1932) sets a story of inner misery against the merriments of the Munich Oktoberfest, and *Italienische Nacht* (*Italian Night*, 1931), which was accepted in its own time as a light-hearted romp, can now be seen to be a bitter and ominous forewarning of the Nazism to come. With von Horvath may appropriately be associated Marieluise Fleisser, who, after the rather stormy receptions of her *Fegefeuer in Ingolstadt* (*Purgatory in Ingolstadt*, 1926) and *Pioniere in Ingolstadt* (*Pioneers in Ingolstadt*, 1928), both of which swept away the small-town idyll, has only recently come to be fully appreciated. In fact, von Horvath and she may be regarded as the inspirers of what, for want of a better term, must be called the 'new realism': both are now cult figures for a whole generation of young dramatists. Another author whose plays have only now come on to the stage is Elias Canetti, whose *Hochzeit* (*Wedding*, 1931–32, first performed 1965) presents a marriage party in a Viennese suburb which is expanded into an apocalyptic vision, a dance of death, a lascivious witches' sabbath, an image of humanity driven on by sexual passion and the lust for possessions. The *Komödie der Eitelkeit* (*The Comedy of Vanity*, written 1933–34, first performed 1965) shows, in a series of scenes, the mass-hysteria generated in a society where the citizens are rendered incapable of knowing themselves because a totalitarian regime has banned all mirrors, pictures, and photographs. Confrontation with death and general despair provide the basic themes in *Befristeten* (*Men with a Time Limit*, written 1952) showing a civilization in which men and women have their death-dates allotted from birth; they answer, not to their names, but to their life-spans.

The 'Lost' Generation and the Traditionalists

Of the 'lost' generation—those youths who returned from the war bewildered and hopeless and who found, when they reached home, nothing save misery and ruins—only one succeeded in giving to a personal testament the power of appealing to others. *Draussen vor der Tür* (*Outside on the Doorstep*, or *The Man Outside*), originally written as a radio play, was produced at Hamburg in 1947 the day after its author, Wolfgang Borchert, died at the early age of twenty-six, and thus almost literally it stands as a

A POLISH PRODUCTION OF "OLD TIMES",
BY HAROLD PINTER
Photo Edward Hartwig

"RENGA MOI", DEVISED AND DIRECTED BY ROBERT SERUMAGA

monument to the unknown soldier of the Second World War. In it Beckmann returns home after three years as a prisoner in Siberia, to find his wife with another man, his child (whom he had never seen) killed by bombs, and his parents (who had been unimportant fellow-travellers) driven to suicide. There is no work for him, and no one can rid him of the searing pangs of conscience caused by the fact that, blindly carrying out his orders, he had led eleven of his comrades to death. In successive scenes, some realistic and some expressionistic, visions inspired by fear are set alongside the rubble-strewn dreary daily existence: here God Himself appears as a helpless dotard, and Death, the Undertaker, is monstrously fattened by the victims with whom he has to deal.

Borchert's confessional play was also a farewell. Much more difficult was the task imposed upon other young dramatists who had to prove themselves over a longer period, and until the establishment of the theatre of the absurd at the close of the fifties uncertainty prevailed. Leopold Ahlsen, who soon elected to devote himself to television, produced a pathetic study, in *Philemon und Baukis* (1955), of an old couple who had succoured not only some partisans but also a German soldier, who are condemned to death, and who go to meet their ends drunk and hand-in-hand. More effective is *Die Illegalen* (*The Law-breakers*, 1947) by Günther Weisenborn, the first play to deal with the German Resistance movement, and there is some considerable force in the Brecht-like *Ballade vom Eulenspiegel, vom Federle und von der dicken Pompanne* (*The Ballad of Eulenspiegel, Federle, and Fat Pompanne*, 1949). Karl Wittlinger cleverly mingled elements of the theatre of the absurd with popular cabaret-style material, as in *Kennen Sie die Milchstrasse?* (*Do You Know the Milky Way?*, 1956). The absurd style is still stoutly championed by Wolfgang Hildesheimer, a style to which he has given a new dimension in an 'historical' *Mary Stuart* (1970). The well-known novelist Günther Grass has so far not succeeded in gaining any large following for his black comedies, although *Die Plebejer proben den Aufstand* (*The Plebeians Rehearse the Uprising*, 1966) has won some attention outside of Germany because of its imaginary presentation of Brecht.

These and other younger dramatists have experimented in divers styles, but at the moment it seems an almost impossible task to determine which of their plays are likely to be remembered. Among all the anxious searchers for new forms and themes, the experienced theatrical practitioners who returned from exile had little difficulty in impressing their decisive stamps upon the German post-war stage. Carl Zuckmayer aroused heated discussions with his *Des Teufels General* (*The Devil's General*, 1946), a well-wrought theatre piece in which various questions such as active resistance to the Nazis and the problem of the army code versus the political are effectively presented: no post-war play was more frequently performed, but in 1963 it was withdrawn by the author lest it should be wrongly reassessed as "the excusing of a certain type of fellow-traveller." Far less satisfactory is *Der Gesang im Feuerofen* (*The Song in the Fiery Furnace*, 1950) where the action involving the massacre of a group of French Resistance fighters is unfortunately intermingled with symbolic scenes dealing with such figures as Father Wind, Mother Frost, and Brother Fog—a style utterly alien to this dramatist's talents. There is solid theatrical craftsmanship in *Barbara Blomberg*, 1949), a comedy about the ageing mother of Don John of Austria, but all his later plays, from *Das kalte Licht* (*The Cold Light*, 1955) onward, are of lesser value. The position of the Austrian-Swiss Fritz Hochwälder appears at the moment to be much the same. He became famous almost overnight through his drama concerning the early seventeenth-century Jesuit state in Paraguay, *Das heilige Experiment* (*The Holy Experiment*, or *The Strong Are Lonely*, 1943), written and produced in Switzerland. Without doubt this author is possessed of a vital theatrical instinct and his characters are well-drawn, but only too often he descends to introducing sensational effects which tend to mar his work. These virtues and defects are clearly evident in *Der öffentliche Ankläger* (*The Public Prosecutor*, 1947), an historical play mainly concerning the methods used by the courts during the French Revolution to obtain confessions "in the name of the people"; in *Donadieu* (1953), another historical drama set in Huguenot times which focuses on a central character who, by rigorous self-mastery, abandons personal revenge on a man who had injured him; and in *Die Herberge* (*The Inn*, 1956). Later he was unsuccessful in following up the stage success of these plays either in his modern mystery drama, *Donnerstag* (*Thursday*, 1959), or in his comedy, *Der Himbeerpflücker* (*The Raspberry-Picker*, 1965).

Dürrenmatt and Frisch: The Tragedians' Renunciation of Tragedy

It is, then, clear that the international acclaim given to German-language drama during the post-war years was largely due to the works of the two Swiss authors, Friedrich Dürrenmatt and Max Frisch.

The former, a vicar's son born in the Canton of Berne, has never made things easy for himself, his audiences, or his critics. He studied a variety of subjects—German literature, philosophy, science, theology—without taking a degree; he tried his hand as a painter, displaying distinct talent; he became a theatre critic and, later, a freelance author turning out short stories, detective novels, radio plays, and, above all, stage dramas. It is evident that everything concerned with the theatrical profession fascinates him: he theorizes about the stage, about plays, about the theatrically creative process, while at the same time he inveighs against theorists. A cardinal element in his critical approach to the playhouse is his conviction that in our time comedy is the only valid form, since comedy is in its element when an ordered world disintegrates, whereas tragedy demands an ordered environment. His own comedies combine keen intellectual dissection of society enlivened with the witty lines of a born playwright, while, cynically and often cruelly, he opens the curtains to reveal a sick world all around. Even while he revels in laughter, however, he always reveals himself in his writings as a strict moralist. Those who are responsible for the sickness are men—not, as for Brecht, social conditions.

His first play to be produced, *Es steht geschrieben* (*It is Written*, 1947), caused an uproar: to many its portrayal of the Anabaptists at the time of the Thirty Years' War seemed blasphemous: but probably the trouble really lay in the fact that he had treated his theme in a tragic manner foreign to his genius: years later, in 1967, he presented the same subject in a specifically 'comic' manner under the title of *Die Wiedertäufer* (*The Anabaptists*). This comic style he first found in *Romulus der Grosse* (*Romulus the Great*, 1948), a play in which he invented his own individual style both in dialogue and in characterization. Then came the real breakthrough in *Die Ehe des Herrn Mississippi* (*The Marriage of Mr Mississippi*, 1952), an hilariously garish morality, the penny-dreadful amusingly presented as an art form, with numerous 'asides' interrupting the action, which itself is presented in an intentionally naive serious manner. Various radio plays were written before the appearance of *Der Besuch der alten Dame* (*The Visit*) in 1956, a drama which has already become one of the classics of the post-war German stage. Claire Zachanassian, born many years ago in Güllen as Kläri Wäscher, here makes an impressive return to her poverty-stricken, run-down home-town. Her objective is to take her revenge on Alfred Ill, now a respected shopkeeper, who had made love to the seventeen-year-old Kläri, denied responsibility when she found herself with child and even bribed witnesses to declare on oath that they had slept with her. Leaving Güllen, she was forced to enter a brothel, but in various ways she had succeeded in amassing an enormous fortune; and now she offers the town a thousand million for Ill's death: so certain is she of the citizens' acceptance that she has thoughtfully brought with her a coffin for the corpse. At first the townsfolk are horrified, but Claire can wait—just as once, after a long search, she had tracked down the two false witnesses at her trial: castrated and blinded, they have for long years formed part of her grotesque retinue. Of course, the inhabitants of Güllen succumb to the lure of money, and the last scene shows her leaving in triumph with the dead lover of her youth, intending to build him a mausoleum in Capri. Dürrenmatt's own comment on this 'tragic comedy' is thoroughly characteristic:

> *The Visit* is the story of something which happened somewhere in Central Europe, written by someone who does not dissociate himself from these people and who is not sure if he would have acted differently himself.

Die Physiker (*The Physicists*, 1962), equally successful on the stage, shows his comic style in a more serious vein. In a private asylum three patients feign insanity—one is a world-famous physicist who pretends to be mad so that he will not be forced to reveal the secret of a potentially world-destroying discovery, while the other two are secret agents posing as Einstein and Newton. These three men finally give up pretending to one another and they decide to remain in the asylum with their fictitious lunacies. But it is too late: the chief psychiatrist, a Dr Mathilde von Zahnd, turns out to be the only truly mad person in the play; long since she had got hold of the formula and handed it over to a world-dominating trust.

By this time Dürrenmatt may perhaps have reached the conclusion that his own particular dramatic style was becoming old-fashioned when compared with the documentary plays being produced by Weiss, Kipphardt, and Hochhuth; and possibly he was mirroring his own position in *Der Meteor* (*The Meteor*, 1966) which is enriched by a clever basic idea —the interpretation of the 'immortality' of a great literary figure in an absolutely literal manner. Here a brilliant playwright, who has been awarded the Nobel Prize, cannot die despite all the doctors' death certificates. That the writing of this drama was not unconnected with a personal, social, and aesthetic crisis experienced by the author himself seems to receive further confirmation when we note that during the next four years he produced, apart from the new version of *The Anabaptists*, only four adaptations from other authors' works, followed by a strange *Porträt eines Planeten* (*Portrait of a Planet*, 1970), dealing with the destruction of the earth by a "cosmic accident" in a mixture of historical revue with cabaret gags, political innuendoes, and metaphysical 'end-games.'

Max Frisch, until 1954 a practising architect, stands in the forefront of German post-war literature both as an epic and as a dramatic author. His plays, all of them parables, clearly show the influence of Brecht, although quite obviously the two writers approach their subject-matter from two different points of view. Brecht describes by placing on the stage what he regards as a picture of reality—the portrayal of an historical or social event, based on his socio-economic analysis of the facts. Frisch, on the other hand, is a linguistic sceptic, one who believes that language is incapable of reproducing reality. In his critical comments published after the writing of his play *Biografie* he definitely rejected the *Dramaturgie der Kausalität*, the 'dramaturgy of causality,' which he had previously followed, since it could lead to nothing save an 'imitation of life' on the stage. The theatre, he insisted, ought to reflect, not imitate: "There is nothing more superfluous than reality," he said, "we have quite enough reality." However, as *Biografie* demonstrates, his recommended 'theatre of possibilities' is not without its own problems.

Frisch's development as a dramatist seems to have been largely determined by experimental probings; plays concerned with the search for identity have alternated with others politically inspired; and, like Dürrenmatt, he has presented several of his works in more than single versions, all his variant texts having obviously been written in an effort to clarify his objectives. It is thus significant that his first two dramatic essays were *Santa Cruz* (1944), a romance concentrating upon a woman's dreams as she finds herself attracted at one moment by exciting, although possibly hazardous, adventure and at another by stable order, and *Nun singen sie wieder: Versuch eines Requiems* (*Now They Sing Again: An*

Attempt at a Requiem, 1945), in which he stood firmly forward as the first and as the most clear-minded playwright to come to terms with the past. These two contrasting works were followed immediately by *Die chinesische Mauer* (*The Chinese Wall*, 1946), which although labelled by the author as a farce is a warning of the atomic threat looming over mankind —and at the same time a sardonic statement of belief that nothing can be done about it, since "There is no Noah's Ark against radioactivity." Less successful is *Als der Krieg zu Ende war* (*When the War Was Over*, 1948), and none of the three versions of *Graf Öderland* (1949, 1956 and 1961) is truly satisfactory: the former play is a study of a German woman, her war-criminal husband, and a Russian officer, while the latter takes shape as a perplexing fantasy of a distinguished judge who suddenly becomes director of a terrorist gang animated by anarchist dreams of complete personal freedom. World-wide success, however, was attained by *Biedermann und die Brandstifter* (*Biedermann and the Fire-raisers*, or *The Fire Raisers*, 1958), a "morality without a moral" with a direct political objective—the unmasking of the typical narrow-minded bourgeois public as the henchmen of violence and terror; always there is the inherent menace of the highly respectable, tolerant fellow-travellers who see the approaching disaster but ignore it, and sometimes even assist it on its course. The central character, Gottlieb Biedermann, is a diligent reader of the newspapers, and he is thus fully aware of the increasing number of outrages perpetrated by the fire-raisers, yet when they come to his house he lets them in, allows them to store their petrol in a loft, makes friends with them, even hands matches to them. The consistent intensification of the grotesque situation is a masterpiece of dramatic construction as Biedermann behaves more and more genially towards his visitors the more openly they explain their intentions and methods to him: joking, they inform him, is the third-best kind of camouflage, the second-best is sentimentality, but the best of all, and the most certain to prevail, is "the plain and unadorned truth." "Funnily enough," he is told, "nobody believes it".

Andorra (1961) was at first celebrated in Germany as the most valid and important contribution to coming to terms with the past, but latterly it is being judged more cautiously—as it was, in fact, regarded at its first presentation elsewhere, in New York, for example. Andorra is an imaginary country inhabited by a worthy, self-righteous people who firmly believe in their own tolerance, while in the nearby state of the 'Blacks' cruel persecution of the Jews is rampant: the plot is complex, but basically it is designed to illustrate the force of public opinion, the horrors of racial prejudice and mankind's way of twisting even the best-intentioned actions into evil forms. After this play, Frisch developed his "dramaturgy of chance" as presented in *Biografie* (*Biography*, 1968), showing, by means of a 'stage-rehearsal' method, a man trying to go back to selected points in his past so that he might shape his life in a new way—and continually failing in his efforts.

The 'Documentary Theatre' and Peter Weiss

At the beginning of the sixties there became evident an increasing dissatisfaction with the traditional theatre, however experimental and modernistic it might pretend to be in its absurd and surrealistic forms. In the midst of heated discussions following the collapse of the Nazi period, many people at first took refuge in entirely non-political, subjective, and uncommitted attitudes, but gradually there was an approach towards a belief that political intents do not by any means imply adherence to some one-party doctrine but rather are essential if the individual is to take a responsible place within society. One possibility of rescuing the stage was seen in the 'documentary theatre', wherein invention is cast aside in favour of 'authenticity' which sometimes includes agitation in its aims. Rolf Hochhuth, a completely unknown writer, became world-famous overnight when Erwin Piscator first produced *Der Stellvertreter* (*The Deputy*, 1963), wherein the failure of the Pope and of the Catholic Church to prevent the persecution of the Jews is attacked: the play is far too lengthy and burdened with explanatory notes, but the controversial nature of the theme made it a subject of wide discussion. In *Soldaten* (*The Soldiers*, 1967) he again displayed his eagerness to poke at wasps' nests, but with less success; his *Guerillas* (1970) showed up the naiveté of his thinking as well as his tendency towards verbosity and his associated inclination to assume that his particular interpretation of 'facts' is correct. The true documentary method was pursued more consistently by Heinar Kipphardt with his *In der Sache J. Robert Oppenheimer* (*In the Matter of J. Robert Oppenheimer*, 1964). In a 'politrevue,' *Toller* (1968), Tankred Dorst's best piece, the action is deliberately stated to be merely "a particle of reality," while Dieter Forte claims that he is presenting his highly individual historical documentary, *Martin Luther und Thomas Münzer, oder, Die Einführung der Buchhaltung* (*Martin Luther and Thomas Münzer, or, an Introduction to Bookkeeping*, 1970), as a theme for discussion.

The approaches made to this type of drama are various; but among them all that of Peter Weiss is unquestionably the most important, and at the same time the most interesting. For long years this author, an émigré in England, Czechoslovakia, Switzerland, and Sweden, had wandered homeless, and his first, unsuccessful, Kafkaesque plays give the impression of having been written in an attempt at self-discovery. Only as he was nearing his fiftieth year did he win wide attention for his '*Marat-Sade*' drama (1964), with its somewhat pretentiously long-drawn-out title:

> *Die Verfolgung und Ermordung Jean Paul Marats dargestellt durch die Schauspielgruppe des Hospizes zu Charenton unter Anleitung des Herrn de Sade—*
> *The Prosecution and Assassination of Jean Paul Marat performed by the Play-acting Group at the Charenton Asylum under the Direction of the Marquis de Sade.*

This work obviously reflects—and indeed might almost be taken as a demonstration of—three attitudes towards society and the stage. The now well-known plot, set in a lunatic asylum, shows the Marquis de Sade supervising a performance by patients of the murder of Marat: Marat's position is that of the active ideologist, the revolutionary convinced of the necessity of revolution, de Sade is the intellectual, the individualist who takes a subjective view even of revolution. This group reflects the transitional situation in which Weiss found himself at the time when he conceived the play—a man standing between the independence of a 'third standpoint' not committed to any particular ideology and a Marxism which would like to assist politically through playwriting in changing society, but without abandoning a formal claim to art.

The '*Marat/Sade*' could not have appeared at a more favourable time: it was associated with the interest awakened by Hochhuth in historical events and personalities: it was presented as total theatre, in which intellectual interest was combined with emotional shock in the Grand Guignol manner: and it appealed to the apostles of the recently discovered Artaud. During the following year, in his *Die Ermittlung (The Investigation*, 1965), an 'oratorio in eleven cantos', Weiss made a most significant contribution to 'coming to terms with the past'. Based directly on the Auschwitz Trial, the machinery involved in the process of annihilation—the arrival of the prisoners, the organization of the camp, the torturings, the killings, the gas-chambers, and the crematoria—is comprehensively brought forward for judgment. The accused appear under their own names, although the witnesses remain anonymous, since, as Weiss says, "Personal experiences and confrontations must yield to anonymity." The whole work has a peculiarly effective power: here an historical event is analysed in all its horror and not crushed down into the dimensions of a private conflict by concentration upon the fate of a selected individual.

Some political-agitational-didactic pieces followed—*Gesang vom Lusitanischen Popanz (Song of the Lusitanian Bogey*, 1967), *Trotzki im Exil (Trotski in Exile*, 1969) and the *Viet Nam Diskurs (Vietnam Discourse*, 1968)—the last with its characteristic and revealing long-drawn-out title:

Diskurs: über die Vorgeschichte und den Verlauf des langanhaltenden Befreiungskrieges in Viet Nam als Beispiel für die Notwendigkeit des bewaffneten Kampfes der Unterdrückten gegen ihre Unterdrücker sowie über die Versuche der Vereinigten Staaten von Amerika, die Grundlagen der Revolution zu vernichten.

Discourse concerning the Origin and Course of the Prolonged War of Liberation in Vietnam as an Example of the Need of the Oppressed to Take up Arms against their Oppressors, as well as of the Attempt by the United States of America to Destroy the Basis of the Revolution.

And these were succeeded by his *Hölderlin* (1971), a drama which made the didactic documentary theatre of agitation out of date, and yet one which is 'political' in its own way. Hölderlin, the revolutionary poet, is driven into the exile of his tower and is deemed by everyone to be insane: he who had been demanding Utopia has to come to terms with those who, by their actions, have adapted themselves to their surroundings—men, for example, such as Hegel, Fichte, Schelling, Schiller, and Goethe. *Hölderlin* is not a comfortable play—indeed, for many it may be more uncomfortable than the more superficial didactic works. But then Weiss never was a 'comfortable' author—either for himself or for his audiences.

'Angry Young Men' and the 'New Realism'

In addition to the brash politicizing of the stage by the documentary theatre—a movement which could hardly prove to be a final solution for the increasingly evident crisis in dramatic affairs—other alternatives to the esoteric goings-on in the absurd and poetic spheres were crystallized in the sixties. Young authors produced much critical and aggressive social criticism, using some elements of conventional psychological dramatic theory alongside other elements taken from the epic theatre, applying themselves to the renaissance of the 'unpleasant' *Volksstück* after the rediscovery of von Horvath and the later discovery of Marieluise Fleisser, and unmasking from various points of view objectionable patterns of speech and behaviour. Their seriousness of purpose by no means excluded the use of comic methods—which, so far from trivializing, often intensified their exposures of society's evils.

Martin Walser is among the more conventional writers, an analyst of the middle-class citizenry of the Federal Republic. He deals with the opportunistic adaptation of former Nazis to life in this prosperous, affluent society, the confrontation of the younger generation with the guilt of their parents, and the all-prevailing omnipotence of money. His greatest success so far, *Die Zimmerschlacht* (*The Battle of the Room*, 1967), shows the 'solid middle-class marriage' in its death-throes, and *Kinderspiel* (*Child's Play*, 1971) gives to the device of 'playing a part' some radical variations in the author's search for a new dramatic form as he deals with the rising post-war generation. Hans Günter Michelsen has attracted some attention, especially with his one-act *Helm* (1965), in which a former slave of the Wehrmacht takes Old-Testament-style vengeance on his former superior. With deliberate employment of clichés, Jochen Ziem, in *Nachrichten aus der Provinz* (*Provincial News*, 1967), presented a depressing set of thought and behaviour patterns in the economic wonderland, and, in *Einladung* (*Invitation*, 1967), gave an equally depressing view of the petit bourgeois existence as a family get-together of East and West Germans is set on stage.

The young Martin Sperr takes as his target the social conventions of village and small-town life, showing how behind the simple-minded 'cosiness' of 'respectable' citizens there lurk barbaric and cruel mass instincts, which erupt when the characters are confronted by social outsiders. Sperr is an author who can create strong parts, and his means of expression is a pointed, apparently realistic (but actually artificial) language suggestive of South German idiom. He had a sensational début with his *Jagdszenen aus Niederbayern* (*Hunting Scenes from Lower Bavaria*, 1966), a work which later he turned into a trilogy by adding *Landshuter Erzählungen* (*Tales from Landshut*, 1967) and *Münchener Freiheit* (*The Freedom of Munich*, 1971), thus progressing from a village via a small town to "the world-famous Munich city."

Sperr seems to be the most legitimate successor to von Horvath, but the very prolific Franz Xaver Kroetz also claims kinship to that author. His concern is chiefly directed towards the underprivileged in a society which still distributes its favours according to the standards of the educated middle class. Unlike Sperr, he presents characters who have not much to say. "Language does not work for my persons," he declares; and, in general, he wishes to break away from the theatrical convention of "volubility." Thus his stage figures tend to be creatures whose expression is largely restricted to their bodily functions: they eat, they digest, they copulate, and they have abortions, but their words are few. In *Wildwechsel* (*Deer Pass*, 1971) a young girl incites her boy friend to murder her father—who is an obstacle to her happiness; *Heimarbeit* (*Home Crafts*, 1971) deals with the monotony of marriage, with deception, with attempted abortion, and with child murder; abortion is successful in *Michis Blut* (*Michi's Blood*, 1971); *Lieber Fritz* (*Dear Fritz*, 1971) deals with the vain attempt of a sex criminal to lead a normal life; *Stallerhof*, with its sequel *Geisterbahn* (*Ghost Train*, 1971), shows that the respectability of Bavarian peasants is only a veneer covering horrifying hardheartedness and lack of understanding. Plays of this kind are characteristic of his repertoire.

For a time Kroetz worked at the 'anti-theatre' in Munich run by Rainer Werner Fassbinder, a many-sided, talented writer from the 'underground,' whose works defy categorization: maybe his most characteristic theme is that of brutalizing actions displaying themselves as a reaction to social pressures and mechanization. Whether Heinrich Henkel will be able to follow up the decisive success of his *Eisenwichser* (*The Iron Polishers*, 1970) only time will tell: in that play he concentrated on two characters, one old and one an apprentice, in order to show how the monotony of industrial work brings men to complete apathy.

Various members of the young generation in Austria are eagerly suggesting fresh impulses for the contemporary theatre. Wolfgang Bauer's dialect plays are based on his own experiences. *Magic Afternoon* (1968) presents a picture of a clique of beat-generation youngsters with its boredom, drinking, smoking, a little sex and drugs, while the deliberately trashy thriller called *Change* (1969) presents glimpses of the Viennese 'culture-world' with little attempt at disguise. Peter Turrini, from Carinthia, is actively engaged in giving to the familiar dialect play a new, surrealist form. In particular, he delights in presenting a contrast between everyday language in completely realistic settings and highly improbable plot developments with symbolic overtones, the clash between those two producing the desired shock effects. Also from Carinthia comes Peter Handke, an author who created a stir in 1966 with his *Publikumsbeschimpfung* (*Abusing the Audience*) in which four actors in ordinary dress speak to the spectators directly in a sort of word game which attacks and provokes those who are seated in the auditorium, which exposes clichés and which denies any kind of stage 'reality.' The problems presented by language are shown even more impressively in *Kaspar* (1968), where a dumb man is taught to speak—and thus immediately becomes a victim of rule-ridden conformity. Even if these and later writings by Handke, all concerned with the theatre's possibilities (*Quodlibet*, 1969) and *Der Ritt über den Bodensee* (*The Ride across Lake Constance*, 1970), for example, may be criticized for their artificiality, they still form a substantial contribution to the debate concerning the modern theatre.

The two stage essays of Thomas Bernhard stand like eccentric blocks in the field of contemporary German drama—*Ein Fest für Boris* (*A Party for Boris*, 1970) and *Der Ignorant und der Wahnsinnige* (*The Ignoramus and the Madman*, 1972). In these the author presents 'end-games' of man as a social being in his relations to the world around him: language produces sounds, but it has no communicative power to create mutual understanding: everyone is left to himself; all that man can do is to imagine reality according to his own preconceptions: life is a continual confrontation with death. "Death is my theme", this author declares, "because life is my theme, incomprehensible, unmistakable".

Developments in the German Democratic Republic

The development of post-war drama in East Germany is directly bound up with the political structure of the 'Workers' and Farmers' State': here the Socialist Unity Party determines the guidelines for its artists. The dramatist's position is important because he can play an active part in building a socialist society and because the function of the theatre is to educate the 'new man'. Dramatic themes usually are derived from everyday occurrences, and 'socialist realism' determines the style. It is, of course, obvious that plays produced under these conditions can hardly have any real appeal for those who live under different political conditions.

During the first few years after the war the theatre was concerned primarily in settling accounts with the past: the question of the guilt of the German people, the glorification of Marxist resistance fighters, the condemnation of the war, the fates of returning soldiers, and the urgent need of rebuilding society were dealt with by such émigrés as Friedrich Wolf, Hedda Zinner, and, of course, Bertolt Brecht, who obviously left all the rest behind. A committed communist for many years, Wolf has called the drama "a weapon against those who are backward-looking" and "a tool for building a new world." His plays encouraged the spectators to identify themselves with the characters on the stage and thus developed a new, socially relevant catharsis, entirely different from Brecht's intellectual attitude. As for Brecht himself, his own dramatic activities were more or less completed when he moved to East Berlin in 1948, but, as everyone knows, the following years were of prime importance because of the '*Modell-Inszenierungen*' presented by the Berliner Ensemble —productions highly significant for both theatrical practice and aesthetic debate.

Hedda Zinner's plays concentrate mainly on the Nazi past, either through the presentation of fictitious plots, as in *General Landt* (1947), or through such historical reconstructions as *Der Teufelskreis* (*The Devil's Circle*, 1953), dealing with the Reichstag Fire trial of 1933, and *Ravensbrücker Ballade* (*Ballad of Ravensbrück*, 1961).

Gradually the old guard gave way to a new. Hermann Werner Kubsch in *Ende und Anfang* (*End and Beginning*, 1949) combined the problems of returning soldiers with a call for socialist reconstruction: its plot shows Georg discovering that his wife Ellen has taken a lover during his absence —but nobly both seek comfort in work for the State and this, it is hinted, may perhaps save their marriage. Harald Hauser attracted attention with his *Am Ende der Nacht* (*At the End of the Night*, 1955), in which a well-educated engineer finds difficulty in adapting himself to the new classless society, but is brought to a right way of thought through the selfless aid given to him by a Russian colleague. With his *Im himmlischen Garten* (*In the Heavenly Garden*, 1958) he gives an artificially conceived picture of Tibet as it is reconstructed on a socialist basis with the aid of China, and in *Weisses Blut* (*White Blood*, 1960) he turns to attack the USA and the German Federal Republic as imperialistic forces whose actions might cause an atomic war. Divers young dramatists have produced a mass of village plays: Erwin Strittmatter constructed his *Katzgraben* (1953) under the direction of Brecht, intending to show how a backwoods community transformed itself into a socialist collective; Alfred Matusche produced his similar dramas, *Die Dorfstrasse* (*The Village Street*, 1955), *Nacktes Gras* (*Naked Grass*, 1958) and *Lied meines Weges* (*Song on My Way*, 1969); and Fred Reichwald companioned them with his *Das Haberfeldtreiben* (*The Field of Oats Affair*, 1957), dealing with the first period of land reform, and *Das Wagnis der Maria Diehl* (*The Daring Stroke of Maria Diehl*, 1959), showing us the public and private problems of the chairwoman of a village collective; in a similar way, Helmut Sakowski deals with *Die Entscheidung der Lene Mattke* (*The Decision of Lene Mattke*, 1959) when a capable farmer's wife takes precedence of her drunken (but violently protesting) husband.

During the late fifties 'didactic teaching theatre' was encouraged, presenting revues and plays with familiar themes treated in the same predictable manner. Helmut Baierl in *Die Feststellung* (*The Discovery*, 1957) shows a peasant couple who had fled to the West penitently returning to the East, and in a *Volksstück*-like comedy, *Frau Flinz* (1961), he presents a hard-working, stubborn woman who is gradually wooed from an attitude of 'I've got no time for politics' to acceptance of the new order. Among numerous other pieces of a like kind, attention may be drawn to one which is constructed in an interesting manner—Herbert Keller's *Begegnung 1957* (*Encounter 1957*, 1958). The plot deals with a communist in the West and an anti-communist in the East, each wanting to leave his own part of Germany for the other; and the two characters, at the instigation of the director, are encouraged to engage in what appears to be free improvising, acting out important events in their respective lives.

In 1963 the Sixth Party Conference of the SED decided that the restructuring of society had been achieved, that accordingly the earlier theme of conflict in a class society could be abandoned and that attention should now be given to the position of the 'new socialist man' in his own environment. The plays of Heiner Müller, Volker Braun, Claus Hammel, Horst Salomon and Peter Hacks well illustrate the effects of the new directive. The last-mentioned, in particular, has attracted some attention outside of the Democratic Republic, largely because, although he is a committed communist, he often refuses to be tied down to the exposition of party doctrine: he has had several conflicts with the authorities, and some of his plays actually had their first productions in the West. Hacks is a master in the art of the historical picture-strip spectacle, a kind of performance which he handles with restraint and elegance of form and in which the didacticism is made entertaining. His first drama, *Eröffnung des indischen Zeitalters* (*The Start of the Indian Age*, 1955) deals with Columbus; *Das Volksbuch von Herzog Ernst* (*The Chapbook of Duke Ernst*, written 1953, first produced 1967) is concerned, according to the author, with "basic features of the Gothic—military Gothic, class Gothic, sexual Gothic, judicial Gothic"; *Margarete von Aix* (*Margaret of Aix*, 1969), introducing the performance of a play at the court of the last King of Provence, deals with the relationship between art and politics; *Die Schlacht bei Lobositz* (*The Battle of Lobositz*, 1957) is a comedy which might be described as showing an anti-hero in the Seven Years' War; and *Der Müller von Sans-Souci* (*The Miller of Sans-Souci*, 1958) dissects a popular legend in Marxist terms. Among this author's several adaptations, his version of *Amphitryon* (1968) deserves special attention because of the adroit manner in which he has turned the ancient comedy into a parable concerning the political man of action (Amphitryon himself) and the intellectual (Sosias).

Recently a considerable stir has attended Ulrich Plenzdorf's study of the problems of youth in his *Neuen Leiden des jungen W.* (*New Sorrows of the Young W.*, 1972). In its title there is, of course, an ironic bow towards Goethe and incidentally towards the artistic values of the whole humanistic tradition. The play deals with a revolutionary youth animated by pacifist-anarchist ideals who seeks for death as a final solution. Is it suicide? Is it an accident? Who can tell? One thing, however, is certain—that here is the portrayal of a generation unsure of itself, whose ideals have been shattered—a theme of conflict which has an interest for everyone all over the world. In so far as subject-matter is concerned, the drama of the German Democratic Republic seems to have emerged from its isolation.

POST-WAR DRAMA IN SCANDINAVIA (DENMARK, SWEDEN, NORWAY, FINLAND, AND ICELAND)

JENS KISTRUP

Denmark

Between 1918 and 1939 the theatre flourished in the Scandinavian countries, and particularly in Denmark. The age was generally felt to be 'dramatic'—politically, psychologically, and poetically—and it was natural that this mood should be reflected in the theatre itself. On all sides, among all sections of the various communities, there was interest in encouraging an active playhouse—a playhouse inspired by the great external and internal conflicts of the time, intent upon influencing social developments, upon warning the public of the dangers inherent in the rise of dictatorships, upon striving to make man more happy and more free.

For the most part, the drama that followed in the years after the Second World War had ended must be regarded as a continuation of what had gone before rather than as something new, even although the greatest Danish dramatist, Kaj Munk, had been murdered during the German occupation. Certainly many of his plays were frequently performed and remained popular during the later period, but in effect his particular 're-theatralization of the theatre' died with him. There still were, however, numerous personal links between the old and the new. The tetralogy of modern life which had been inaugurated by Carl Erik Soya in 1940 was completed in 1949 with a bitterly farcical fourth part, and he also presented another play dealing with the German occupation of his country, *Efter* (*Afterwards*, 1947), a stingingly sardonic picture of the collaborators who, after the passing of a few years, were loud in their praise of the resistance movement. In 1942 Knud Sønderby's 'generations' play, *En kvinde er overflødig* (*A Woman is Superfluous*), proved to be one of the chief dramatic events during the war years, but unfortunately he has not followed this play with any other similar work. More productive was Leck Fischer, a playwright who has excelled particularly in presenting on the stage arresting pictures of the dreamers in the social world, the losers in life, those who struggle against everyday existence and who sometimes escape from it: the best, and perhaps the most characteristic of his works as a whole, is *Frisøndag* (*Free Sunday*, or *Sunday, Day of Rest*, 1954), a drama thematically and technically influenced by Arthur Miller's *Death of a Salesman*.

Among all these authors, however, the one whose influence was a dominating force up to about 1960 was Kjeld Abell, and at the same time the one who, in a spirit of deep personal commitment, most effectively expressed the problems of this time. In his *Anna Sophie Hedvig*, presented in 1939, he had made an unreservedly passionate attack on dictatorship, tyranny, political and social injustice; and his first play after the war was *Silkeborg* (1946), a picture of Danish society seen from the point of view of a resistance fighter. Instead of merely expressing joy at the victory which had been won, and instead of suggesting that the defeat of Hitler opened up the way to a splendid future, he demonstrated in this drama a profound concern about man's future. As year by year went by, the concern gradually turned to despair and desperation. In *Dage på en Sky* (*Days on a Cloud*, 1947) he expressed his conviction that the whole of mankind will be destroyed unless the scientists deliberately decide to recognize their duty to the world by rendering their own inventions powerless to damage or destroy the world. Three years later came *Vetsera blomstrer ikke for enhver* (*Vetsera Does Not Come Out For Everyone*, 1950), in which his fears and anxieties were even more trenchantly expressed, and that play was followed by *Den blå Pekingeser* (*The Blue Pekingese*, 1954), his greatest, most profoundly inspired, and most penetrating stage fantasy, a subtle and powerful dream-play in which the limits of space are abolished: here the past, the present, and the future have become one, here the dead, the living, and the unborn appear side by side. Although he had still several important plays to contribute to the stage, including among them one the title of which—*Skriget* (*The Scream*, 1961)—might well be taken as symbolic of his bitterness, *The Blue Pekingese* stands out as the work which marked the climax in this powerful writer's last phase.

In line with Kjeld Abell, but composing his plays in a much more naturalistic-traditional manner, is H. C. Branner whose writings, among which *Søskende* (1952) and *Thermopylæ* (1958) are particularly noteworthy, are also contributions to the anxious debate concerning the 'crisis of humanity,' that theme which most clearly reflected the post-war searchings of conscience and the almost desperate quest for a new way of thinking and a new way of living. "The time of miracles has gone: now we have to make miracles ourselves," *Søskende*'s key line, applies firmly to this period—or, as the same thought is expressed in *Thermopylæ*, "We must look at the world with new eyes—or else be destroyed."

During the late fifties and the early sixties three forces from outside had an invigorating effect on the Danish stage and also, to a certain extent, on the Danish drama: these three impulses were the Brechtian theatre, the French drama of the absurd, and the contemporary English drama, and in combination they served to push the playwrights over the dead centre which for a time had seemed to hold them stationary. With the operation of these influences, too, came the rapid development of radio and TV drama, both of which provided a kind of State-subsidized experimental stage for new apprentice playwrights. During those years it is easy to see the deepening of thought concerning political and social problems, the increasing eagerness to use the stage in a new way, and the experimentation, particularly among the smaller theatres, in the handling of new dramatic forms.

It is thus significant that the most talented young dramatist of the fifties, Finn Methling, has developed his highly individual style most freely in his writings for the radio: his finest stage drama, too, is not unlike in form—a monologue called *Rejsen til de grønne skygger* (*Journey to the Green Shadows*, 1952), the story of a woman's life from birth to death. And with Methling may be associated the poet Erik Knudsen, with his satirical-absurd, topical, and political mini-comedies and revues, of which *Frihed—det bedste guld* (*Liberty—the Best Gold*, 1961) is a particularly interesting example.

The chief weakness of the Danish drama during the forties and the fifties was its general blindness to the revolution which was taking place in Danish society. A new mass welfare and consumption social structure was in fact turning all the patterns and objectives of life upside down, and yet only a few playwrights seemed fully to appreciate what was happening, and most of them still sought to maintain the old standards as if nothing had happened. The major dramatists—Kaj Munk, Kjeld Abell, and H. C. Branner—had been more interested in the 'large' than in the 'small' world, and this trend in their writings produced in the works of their successors and imitators a fatal distance from the life that was all around them. This is the chief reason why the elimination of the gap came mainly, at the start, not within the official 'theatres' but through radio sketches and amateur experiments, not by means of formally constructed 'plays' but by means of revues and satirical musicals.

Thus such authors as Klaus Rifbjerg and Jesper Jensen gave fresh spirit to the revue in *Gris på gaflen* (*Pork on the Fork*, 1962), *Hvá skal vi lave?* (*What's to Do?* 1963) and *Diskret ophold* (*Discreet Residence*, 1964); and the final establishment of the new trend came when Ernst Bruun Olsen, after having written several successful radio plays, had his definitive breakthrough with the satirical musical *Teenagerlove* (1962), the story of the pop-singer Billy Jack, with a wide-ranging criticism of contemporary society. In his later stage writings Olsen has made this critical trend still clearer and stronger: his *Bal i den Borgerlige* (*Ball in the Civic Club*, 1966), for example, seeks to show how the current Social Democracy works against the interests of the working class, while in *Hvor gik Nora hen, da hun gik ud?* (*Where Did Nora Go, When She Went Out?*, 1968), he takes Ibsen's Nora and makes her realize what her own personal protest meant socially and politically.

Among all these new dramatists, Leif Panduro has reached the largest audience—but characteristically this audience has not assembled in playhouses, but has been made up of the hundreds of thousands listening to his grotesque radio sketches or watching his more restrained TV pieces. In these writings he continually questions the world around him, and he also reflects the sense of desperation behind the apparent harmony, the sense of insecurity behind apparent security, the sense of conflict behind the affluent social world of the sixties and seventies. Although an account of TV drama lies outside the scope of the present survey of the Danish theatre, it is important to observe that Panduro's writings for the television screen, from *En af dagene* (*One of These Days*) in 1963 on to *Hjemme hos William* (*At Home with William*) and *Rundt om Selma* (*Round About Selma*) in 1971, may well be regarded as the most significant and representative dramatic works produced recently in Denmark.

For Klaus Rifbjerg playwriting has been one form of expression among numerous others: apart from his contributions to the stage, he is also well known as a lyric poet, a journalist, and a film-writer. His real debut as a dramatist came with *Udviklinger* (*Evolutions*, 1965) a play reminiscent of Pirandello's theatre, taking shape almost as though it were a dialogue within the author's brain, introducing constant changes in attitude. Among his later works most striking have been his black study called *Voks* (*Wax*, 1968) and the quiet recalling of memories of the occupation, *År* (*Years*, 1970).

The fact that the new writers have applied themselves indiscriminatingly to playhouse stage, TV, and radio inevitably means that any attempt to view the new Danish drama as a whole must result in a picture which is rather confused, and which introduces conflicting elements. Leif Petersen's very considerable skill in the penning of dialogue and in the planning of effective dramatic situations has thus developed in all these different kinds of composition, even although it may be admitted that the playhouse has given him the greatest opportunities for the exercise of his talents. His *Alting og et posthus* (*Everything and a Post Office*, 1969) is a most effective piece of theatre, as is *Nu går den på Dagmar* (*Now It is Played on the Dagmar*, 1970), while his *Rene ord for pengene* (*Plain Speaking*, 1972) proved to be a most suitable and highly original festival play presented on the two hundred and fiftieth 'birthday' of the first Danish permanent stage, that for which Ludvig Holberg wrote most of his comedies. In a similar manner, Jess Ørnsbo, author of an interesting absurdist stage play, *Dværgen, der blev væk* (*The Dwarf Who Disappeared*, 1962, performed 1966), Svend Åge Madsen and Inger Christensen, author of *Intriganterne* (*The Intriguers*, 1972), have all spent much time in experimenting in the field of radio drama.

If any generalization is to be made, this might well assume the form of a statement that in Denmark the most prominent feature of dramatic activities during the sixties has been the development of stage, TV theatre, and radio theatre as one coherent whole, a development which has radically changed the playwright's position and enormously expanded his field of activity. After the 'great' years during the thirties the position of the Danish drama did not by any means stand high, but since 1960 it has been experiencing a fresh movement forward.

Sweden

The same generalization may be made, too, concerning post-war drama in Sweden, although here this observation ought to be associated with the noting of another, and a very important, trend. In Sweden the theatre has been flourishing more strongly and more luxuriantly than in any other Scandinavian country, and there has been an opportunity, lacking in Denmark, of creating a close collaborative association between dramatists, actors, and directors, an association which extends from the activities of the little theatres to the collective group experiments organized at other centres, notably the municipal theatres at Stockholm and Göteborg. In this connection it may also be noted that not a few actors—notably Erland Josephson, since 1966 head of the Swedish National Theatre, Allan Edwall and Kent Andersson—have applied themselves energetically to the writing of plays.

During the forties and fifties Swedish drama did not succeed in producing much of enduring interest. The majority of plays were composed by writers for whom theatrical works were sidelines, authors such as Vilhelm Moberg, Björn Erik Hoijer, and Sara Lidman. Several men, such as Ingmar Bergman, have similarly turned from their activities within the fields of film and radio to contribute plays to the stage, and one or two lyric poets—Werner Aspenström and Sandro Key-Åberg, for instance—have experimented in the writing of dialogue. The former's *Poeten och kejsaren* (*The Poet and the Emperor*, 1956) has interest because of its attempt to present a picture of the poet's role in the world, and his *Det eviga* (*The Eternal*, 1959) takes its place among other essays in the absurd by showing a group of monkeys trying, by means of tape recordings and of films, to recall from the past a world that has vanished in ruins. The most important of these authors is, perhaps, another lyric poet, Lars Forssell, most of whose plays are poetically humorous melodramas dealing with characters and situations in the near or distant Swedish past, although his fertile imagination and active pen have also expressed themselves in plays of varied kinds, extending from his first dramatic work, *Kröningen* (*Coronation*, 1956), a new treatment of the ancient theme of Alcestis, on to one of his latest plays, *Show* (1971), dealing with the career of the American variety star, Lenny Bruce.

Essentially, however, the renewal of the Swedish drama has come about not so much through the efforts of a few great authors as through what can be categorized only as a social renewal. The initial breakthrough was *Hemmet* (*The Home*, 1967), a collaborative production of the writer Bengt Bratt and the actor Kent Andersson which, in a light manner reminiscent of the revue style, describes life in an old people's home for the purpose of demonstrating the lack of solidarity and communal spirit in society as a whole. The same two collaborators followed up their success in this play by writing *Tillståndet* (*The Condition*, 1971), a kind of companion piece set in a home for the mentally sick.

During the year when *Hemmet* appeared Kent Andersson produced his first play, *Flotten* (*The Raft*, 1967), a work which adumbrated his later prevailing interest in political and social themes. The following year saw the presentation of *Sandlådan* (*The Sand-box*, 1968), where he concerned himself with the life of children in a modern society dominated by adults. From these he has proceeded until in *Agnes* (1972) he has experimentally created a new kind of social drama, less direct in its presentation of a theme and more poetical in its style. It may be noted here that the play with which Bratt made his debut, *Sorgen och ingenting* (*The Sorrow and Nothing*, 1963), was also concerned with young people, and there is further interest in observing that some of his best original dramas have been written for radio and TV—particularly important being his *Exercis* (*Drill*, 1968) which is both a plea for pacifism and an effective picture of the authoritarian spirit in modern democratic society.

The collaboration between Bratt and Andersson is paralleled by a similar co-operation, based on the ideas animating the group theatre, between two actors, Hans Bendrik and Jan Bergquist, both belonging to Stockholm's municipal playhouse. These two men have written and arranged several revue-style topical plays with strong polit-ical-propagandist trends: *Ivar Kreugers svindlande affärer* (*The Outrageous Transactions of Ivar Kreuger*, 1969) concerns the capitalist world, *Mr President* (1971) deals with the assassination of John F. Kennedy. Such dramatic presentations of political themes have also been prepared by other young dramatists, such as Lars Ardelius, Lars Björkman, Agneta Pleijel, and Ronny Ambjörnsson: the two authors last mentioned, for instance, were responsible for *Orden råder i Berlin* (*Order Reigns in Berlin*, 1969) in which the German Social Democrats during the years following the First World War are severely criticized. This new social wave in Scandinavian (and particularly in Swedish) drama has indeed become so powerful that it has, at least temporarily, almost closed the road for any other kinds of writings for the stage, and in this connection it is significant that most of the plays written by such a dramatist as Lars Gustafsson have had to be presented outside Sweden.

Many of Sweden's dramatic successes have been staged in the other Scandinavian countries, but movement in the opposite direction has been rather modest. Partly this may be explained by the fact that countries such as Norway, Finland, and Iceland have had very few new dramatists capable of creating dramas likely to appeal outside their own theatres—and this general assertion includes even authors like Johan Borgen, Jens Bjørneboe, and Klaus Hagerup in Norway, Johan Bargum in Finland, and in Iceland the Nobel prize-winner Halldór Laxness: but partly the explanation is to be found in the fact that, although the Scandinavian countries have much in common, there is at the same time much that estranges them from each other both politically and culturally.

POST-WAR DRAMA IN EASTERN EUROPE
(BULGARIA, CZECHOSLOVAKIA, HUNGARY, POLAND, THE SOVIET UNION)

MAŁGORZATA SEMIL-JAKUBOWICZ

'Socialist Realism'

The fundamental fact about post-war drama in Bulgaria, Czechoslovakia, Hungary, Poland, and the Soviet Union—five countries which, for want of a more precise term, may be referred to collectively as 'Eastern Europe'—is its intimate ties with the recent social history of these lands. The aftermath of the war, involving political upheavals which culminated in the establishment of a new social system, naturally provided powerful, fresh stimuli for the writing of plays concerned directly with the resultant problems, both general and particular. Much has been done to promote the development of theatre for its own sake, and this preoccupation with social affairs, which in any event may have been expected, has been further encouraged by the authorities, who have seen in the theatre (and indeed in all the arts) a valuable instrument for the illustrating, explaining, and promoting of the new social policies.

Already, of course, in the Soviet Union 'socialist realism' had been proclaimed by the Writers' Congress of 1934 as the only true progressive literary genre, and this style continued to reign supreme for several years—one exception being the highly original *Drakon* (*The Dragon*, written in 1943, produced in 1961) by Yevgeni Shvartz, in which the terrors of the totalitarian Nazi machine are treated, not realistically, but as a poetic tale for adults, tinged with an ironical, occasionally even cynical, humour. In the other four Eastern European countries, when playwrights and those associated with theatrical affairs began to pick up the pieces and to build a new life, the new plays tended to be markedly diverse in style and widely varying in range. An excellent example of this may be found in a trilogy written by the Slovak Peter Karvaš, actually begun before the fighting had ended and not completed until 1948: the first part, called *The Meteor*, is a symbolic presentation of our world as an isolated little sphere in space threatened by the fall of a blazing star; the second play, *The Fortress*, takes shape as an historical fresco, depicting the struggle of the Slovaks for national and social freedom; while *A Return to Life*, the concluding drama, is a psychological study showing the difficulties experienced by individuals who had spent years in Nazi concentration camps in their efforts to readjust themselves to normal life.

Gradually, however, socialist realism gained a firm foothold in the other Eastern European countries, a process hinted at in *Dwa teatry* (*The Two Theatres*, 1946) by a distinguished Polish writer, Jerzy Szaniawski. Defined in a vague formula which insisted that plays should be "socialist in content and national in form," this style was, in fact, the application of the archaic, middle-class *pièce bien faite* and *pièce à these* to modern conditions, with, let us say, real tractors being substituted for the plush settees of the nineteenth century. According to the formula, playwrights were expected to deal with current social situations in a spirit of optimism, to present positive and negative aspects of these situations in a sharply contrasted manner, to aim at influencing the spectators' views and at encouraging them to take an active part in the firmer and better establishment of socialistic endeavour. In addition, the formula also encouraged the writing of plays concerned with the heroic struggles of the various peoples for liberation and with the consolidation of the world's progressive forces—and it may be noted that the choice of such themes led to the creation of several dramas of lasting value. In Poland, Leon Kruczkowski offered in his *Niemcy* (*The Germans*, 1949) a penetrating examination of the social, psychological and moral forces in wartime Germany and the powerlessness of middle-class liberalism when confronted by Nazism. Gyula Illyés, Hungary's outstanding poet, has similarly produced two dramas of much more than passing interest—*Ozorai példa* (*The Example of Ozora*, written in 1945, acted 1952) and *Fáklyaláng* (*Torchlight*, written in 1947, acted in 1952): both of these deal with the rising of 1848 and offer a profound analysis of the Hungarian national existence. The same subject has also attracted another distinguished playwright, Lásló Nemeth, to compose his *Az Árulo* (*The Traitor*, written in 1954, acted in 1967). And there were also other authors who found that the choice of historical themes gave them an opportunity to by-pass the otherwise persistent demand for unquestioning, affirmative involvement in current affairs.

A turning-point, however, came with the 20th Congress of the Soviet Communist Party in 1956. Here the tight corset of narrowly interpreted realism was unlaced, and at the same time the East European theatre was introduced, first to Brecht, and later to other 'Western' authors, with a resultant turbulent change and an effort to explore new dramatic dimensions. Each country revived its own earlier avant-garde traditions and embarked on a determined effort to shape its own individual theatrical style; the scope of realism was enlarged; political problems were tackled more boldly; over all these lands a wave of 'stock-taking' rolled. Various dramatists probed such themes as the transformation of revolutionary fervour and vigilance into fanaticism and distrust, of revolutionary discipline into fear-ridden conformism. Gyula Illyés bitterly attacked the personality cult in *A kegyenc* (*The Favourite*, published 1963, acted 1965), where the present was reflected in a fifth-century Roman past, when a courtier is shown sacrificing everything—family, dignity, morality—for the favours of a sadistic Emperor, until finally he realizes that "not even God can be served by man's debasement," kills the tyrant, and commits suicide. The views of the Bulgarian 'hard-line' and liberal groups are contrasted and explored by Georgi Dzhagarov in *Prokuroret* (*The Prosecutor*, 1966), while in the Soviet Union itself distortions in social life are examined in such plays as *Druzya i godi* (*Friends and Years*, 1961) by Leonid Zorin, *Naznacheniye* (*The Nomination*, 1963) by Alexander Volodin, *Pered uzhinom* (*Before Supper*, 1962) by Victor Rozov, and *Cherniye ptitsi* (*The Black Birds*, 1956) by Nikolai Pogodin. Pogodin, in his later years, also reflects another development in East European dramatic writing—a return to psychological and/or poetic realism. Whereas in most of his earlier plays (such as those comprising the Lenin trilogy) he had dealt with issues of historical importance to the nation, in the fifties he turned to comedies about contemporary youth—*Malenkaya studentka* (*The Little Girl Student*, 1959) and *Sonet Petrarki* (*A Sonnet by Petrarch*, 1957). About the same time, Leonid Leonov, another eminent Soviet dramatist of the older generation, also infused poetic and symbolist elements into straight realism, presenting bitter pictures of highly complex human experience. His *Zolotaia karieta* (*Golden Chariot*, written in 1947, acted in 1956) thus scrutinizes the moral and psychological dilemma faced by a woman who is forced to choose between a soldier who has lost his sight in the war (a favourite Leonov hero—a man sorely tried but refusing to give in) and a younger man who owes his high social position entirely to his father's position.

With the domestic drama may also be associated the Rumanian Paul Everac, author of *Simple coincidente* (*Simple Coincidences*, 1964), and Alexandru Mirodan, who wrote several lyrically sentimental tragicomedies such as *Seful sectorului suflete* (*Chief of the Soul Department*, 1963). The Bulgarian Dimitr Dimov was particularly successful in his intimate portraits of women, such as *Zheni z minalo* (*Women with a Past*, 1959) and *Potchivka v Arco-Iris* (*A Short Rest at Arco-Iris*, 1963). Psychological drama was popular in Hungary, and Imre Sarkadi used it to give expression to his generation's *Weltschmerz*: his *Oszlopos Simeon* (*Simeon Stylites*, written in 1960, acted in 1967) and *Az elveszett paradicson* (*Paradise Lost*, 1961) both deal with disillusioned intellectuals: in the former, nihilistic rebellion against the supposedly absurd 'normal' world ends in defeat; the latter's hero, after suffering from an acute crisis of values, is saved from utter ruin by a budding love. In such ways an extended, enriched range of theme brought something new to the drama about the year 1956, and with it came a bolder use of form. The older-established pattern was now replaced by complex action, episodic structure, epic narration, flashbacks, simultaneous scenes, and similar novel theatrical devices.

In Bulgaria this new trend was introduced a few years later and has endured under the general title of the 'poetic wave.' More importantly, the Soviet Union found a harbinger of things to come in Alexey Arbuzov. His *Irkutskaia istoriya* (*The Irkutsk Story*, 1959), which has been called the "Soviet *Our Town*," sets a tenderly told love story against the background of a great production plant in Northern Siberia, making free use of flashbacks, choral and epic monologues—devices which had previously been little used on the Soviet stage. With his lyrical approach, his good-natured humour, and his psychological insight, as in *Moy biednii Marat* (*My Poor Marat*, 1965) and *Skazki starovo Arbata* (*The Stories of Old Arbat*, 1970), Arbuzov is clearly a descendant of Chekhov and Afinogenov, while at the same time he may be described as the founding father of a long line of younger dramatists—Leonid Zorin, Victor Rozov, Alexander Volodin, and, Edvard Radzinski, Mikhail Roshchin and Alexander Vampilov. Alongside their favourite psychological studies, particularly concerned with young people's hopes and fears, some of these new playwrights have produced several notable historical dramas, mainly in the matter-of-fact style, with particular emphasis being placed on an attempt to look upon the October Revolution of 1917 with an abandonment of what might be called the romantic legends which had come to be associated with it, although of course with full approval of what it had achieved. Mikhail Shatrov's *6 Iula* (*July 6th*, 1964) and *Bolsheviki* (*The Bolsheviks*, 1966) thus dispassionately reconstruct the actual events from a study of contemporary documents, concentrating on the intellectual and emotional experiences of the revolutionaries and their resultant political decisions. The last-mentioned drama was presented in 1967 as the third part of a trilogy, which started with Zorin's *Dekabristi* (*The Decembrists*) and included Alexander Svobodin's *Narodovoltsy* (*Members of the Narodnaya Vola Party*). One of the most interesting works in this trend has been *Odnazhdy v dvadtsatom* (*Once in Nineteen Twenty*, 1967) by Naum Korzhavin: here the characters, all prisoners in one cell, represent various attitudes and social philosophies of the time—the tragicomic 'episodes' of the play providing a philosophical and sociological analysis of the epoch and demonstrating the relationships among the various historical forces then at work.

And, in thinking of Soviet drama, it is important to remember the very considerable contributions made by dramatists from various republics outside of Russia proper—such as Alexander Korneichuk of the Ukraine, who has always remained true to socialist realism; Juozas Baltushis of Lithuania, whose plays, such as *Gieda gaideliai* (*The Cocks are Crowing*, 1947), likewise tend to be sharply naturalistic; Andrey Makayonak of Byelorussia; and the interesting Estonian Juhan Smuul, the author of *Lea* (1964) and *Polkovniku lesk* (*The Colonel's Widow*, 1968), a comedy bordering on the grotesque.

The Grotesque and Absurd Drama

This reference to the plays of Smuul reminds us that the East European dramatists in general eagerly seized the opportunity of transcending the confines of realism, although, as might have been expected, the wave of grotesque and absurd plays showed considerable variations from one country to another.

The earliest intimations that this new style was on the way came from Poland, where a trend towards the grotesque had for long manifested itself, with antecedents going back to the Romantic period. During the inter-war period it had shown itself in the works of such avant-garde authors as Bruno Jasieński and Stanisław Ignacy Witkiewicz (Witkacy)—the latter being one of the most puzzling and fascinating dramatists of this century who, long before Ionesco's *The Bald Soprano*, wrote several absurd tragi-farces which broke loose the stultifying bonds of middle-class drama. And Witold Gombrowicz, even although he left Poland in 1939, also exerted an influence on the playwrights of his native land through such works as *Iwona, Księżniczka Burgunda* (*Ivona, Princess of Burgundy*, 1938), and *Ślub* (*The Marriage*, written about 1946, published 1953). Grotesque tendencies, too, briefly made an appearance in such early plays as *Papuga* (*The Parrot*, written before the war, acted in 1946) by Kazimierz Korcelli and *Święto Winkelrieda* (*Winkelried's Feast*, written in 1944, acted 1956) by Jerzy Andrzejewski and Jerzy Zagórski. Only in the late fifties, however, did the grotesque and absurd drama come to stay in Poland. A rapidly increasing number of student theatres and cabarets with their parodies, nonsensical humour, and irreverent treatment of history aided the establishment of this style, while in Jerzy Broszkiewicz appeared a playwright whose *Jonasz i Błazen* (*Jonah and the Clown*, 1958), *Głupiec i inni* (*The Fool and Others*, 1959) and *Dziejowa rola Pigwy* (*Quince's Historic Role*, 1960) combined irony, a perverse humour, and a grotesque presentation of reality for the purpose of making a statement on subjects then obsessively haunting Polish spectators—problems of power, of human relationships, and of current social and psychological change.

Then appeared Sławomir Mrożek and Tadeusz Różewicz, two outstanding dramatists. The former is, above all, a satirist gifted with a rare depth and analytical insight. In general, all his twenty-odd plays (many of them short) are governed by the iron laws of a crazy logic which reduces every normal situation to total absurdity and, in addition, presses every absurd initial situation to its perfectly logical conclusion. His first drama, for example, *Policja* (*The Police*, 1958), is set in a totalitarian state where the police have stamped out all political crime: consequently, in order to keep in business, they are forced themselves to organize such crime—with the officers finally arresting one another and being locked up in jail. *Tango*, which may be regarded as his most profound work, appeared in 1964. Here Mrożek shows the world as a system of social forces, which at the present moment is suffering from a crisis of values, in the midst of which man is powerless in the face of his alienated products—and, in particular, of the 'myths' he himself has created to justify his actions. The play's hero, young Arthur, disgusted with his family's disorderly life, sets out to reintroduce old 'form.' This old form, however, he discovers is no longer relevant to the times: he looks for another idea, or 'myth,' and finds it in power and the threat of death. Arthur thus seeks for the tragic in a world where everyday life is a mere farce: so he feels that someone must ceremonially die in order to give his idea the breath of life. At this point the 'myth' itself sets to work in reshaping reality. Arthur himself lacks real power, and before he can bring about someone's death he is overpowered by Edek, who represents brute, unthinking force, and who proceeds to establish his own totalitarian order.

In nearly all his plays Mrożek uses a similar interplay between reality and 'myth' in order to show up all kinds of beliefs, including the old Polish literary and national traditions which place a constraining force upon contemporary life: the device is especially noteworthy in *Indyk* (*The Turkey*, 1960) and *Zabawa* (*The Party*, 1962).

The other major figure in post-war Polish drama is Tadeusz Różewicz, a distinguished poet, whose ten plays have more than once been described as forming one great work. His method is that of 'open dramaturgy' where a stream of life is set moving across the stage, a collage of naturalistically observed situations, dramatic episodes, lyrical scenes, and 'ready-made' texts, such as passages quoted from speeches and newspaper reports, yet at the same time a collage which, governed by intuitive poetic logic, forms an organic whole. In effect, Różewicz seeks to show the world dissected into its component pieces, which then are reassembled into a whole which may explain our own lives. Both in *Akt przerywany* (*The Interrupted Act*, 1964) and *Grupa Laokoona* (*The Laocoon Group*, 1961) he ridicules and totally rejects older forms of art and the theatre, which he considers banal, empty, and meaningless; and throughout his writings he shows himself dominated by revulsion and compassion in his contemplation of the human condition. The hideousness of old age, and the absolute dictates of nature by which men and women go on eating, drinking, sleeping, and procreating again and again are obsessive themes in his dramas. Although rarely referred to directly, war is also one of the common underlying motifs in his work: indeed, he made his debut in 1960 with *Kartoteka* (*The Card Index*), which was an apt summing-up of the feelings and anxieties of a generation of Poles who grew up in wartime and who were left empty-handed and empty-hearted, with a sense of utter bankruptcy. In *Świadkowie, albo nasza mała stabilizacja,* (*The Witnesses, or, Things Are Almost Back to Normal*, 1962) three unconnected dialogues show people so strongly attached to their newly won affluence that all sense of humanity has been obliterated. *Stara kobieta wysiaduje* (*The Old Woman Broods*, 1968) totally condemns the world, showing it as a huge, apocalyptic rubbish-heap. Some individuals try to restore order and to make it a livable place, but without success: their aims are praiseworthy, yet in these circumstances merely grotesque and absurd. A similar conflict between man's ambitions and the transient nature of his existence forms the central theme in his latest, strongly autobiographical, work, *Na czworakach* (*On All Fours*, 1972), in which the hero, Laurenty, a doddering, nearly senile, author, represents the contrast between the heights of man's psychological and creative potentials and his physical weakness.

Różewicz may be regarded as one of the most consistent and original of post-war playwrights, whether in Poland or in Eastern Europe as a whole. He has, however, been accompanied by numerous other talented dramatists, such as Stanisław Grochowiak, Bohdan Drozdowski, Ireneusz Iredyński, Jarosław Abramov, and Janusz Krasiński. Their chief preoccupation is the situation in Poland—a theme strongly marked in Abramov's and Drozdowski's writings—although statements of wider validity are also attempted, as in *Chłopcy* (*The Lads*, 1964) by Grochowiak and in Iredyński's *Jasełka moderne* (*A Nativity Play à la mode*, 1962). The former is set in an Old Folks' Home, which serves as a symbol of society, while the latter examines man's debasement and sublimation by showing the inmates of a wartime concentration camp who are ordered by the commandant to perform a nativity play. Among the latest arrivals on the Polish stage are Ernest Bryll, Helmut Kajzar, Jarosław Marek Rymkiewicz, and Jerzy S. Sito, several of whom have made their mark with dramas in the native grotesque tradition with particular emphasis upon national and romantic themes: Ernest Bryll, a well-known poet, is of particular importance. His plays, such as *Rzecz listopadowa* (*The November Theme*, 1968), *Kurdesz* (1969), *Kto ty jesteś?* (*Who Are You?*, 1970) and *Co się komu śni* (*Who Dreams of What?*, 1972) are penned in verse, ranging from political discourse expressed in metaphorical language, and topical satirical sketches. They paraphrase and mock romantic drama, challenge its ideas, ridicule contemporary manners, and hold up a surrealistic mirror to today's Poland.

The grotesque drama made its appearance in Czechoslovakia somewhat later than in Poland, and its ties are with theatre, not with literature. From the time of the First World War onward various satirical cabarets and small stages became a breeding-ground for the likes of Jaroslav Hašek, remembered for his nonsensical humour and his 'Party of Small Progress within the Revolution,' and among them we should recall particularly Yindřich Honzl's 'Unfettered Theatre' (Ozvobozené Divadlo) which, during the twenties and thirties, developed a specific kind of performance which dealt with political affairs in a characteristically zany manner and which rejected all officially recognized styles. In the late fifties this special kind of humour was revived when many nightclubs and cabarets sprang up in Prague, followed by several small playhouses such as 'The Theatre on the Balustrade' (Divadlo na Zabradli).

Among the authors associated with this particular playhouse was Václav Havel, a sharp satirist whose style has frequently been compared with that of Mrożek. His first full-length play, *Zahradní slavnost* (*The Garden Party*, 1963) typically introduces one of his chief preoccupations, the relationship between man and his society. The central character has become so fully adjusted to the demands of the system as to be wholly stripped of all individual qualities: because he thus conforms to the system's dictates and its irrational logic, he rises fast through the ranks, incidentally helping to consolidate the framework within which he is set: in this way the individual is seen as the product of the system—and vice versa. *Vyrozuměni* (*The Memorandum*, 1965) makes system and bureaucracy identical. A department is ordered to employ Ptypede, an artificially constructed language which, it is alleged, will streamline the work and increase efficiency. In practice, however, it is soon found that this man-made language plays havoc, completely altering the power structure and human relations within the department, giving some clerks tyrannical power over others. Mrożek's influence makes itself clearly evident in this piece: as in *The Good Soldier Schweik*, the idiocy of bureaucratic decisions is amply revealed when they are accepted at face value and conscientiously put into operation. In a later drama, *Ztížená možnost soustředění* (*Puzuk, or The Increased Difficulty of Concentration*, 1968) the emphasis is shifted from society to the individual's inner life. In a frantic search for an existence richer than his everyday experience, the hero takes one mistress after another, only to find that each affair is a carbon copy of his dull marriage.

Ladislav Smoček's one-act *Bludiště* (*The Maze*, 1966) touches upon a somewhat similar theme, man's attitude to the workings of a vaguely defined system, here represented by a maze, an absurd institution from which there is no exit. Another one-act play by the same author, *Podivné odpoledne dr. Z. Burkeho* (*Dr Zvonek Burke's Extraordinary Afternoon*, 1966) has an air of Dürrenmatt about it: Dr Burke, an old-fashioned eccentric and philanthropist, finding himself in an extraordinary situation, murders several real and imaginary enemies in order to protect his way of life. An atmosphere of insecurity, of persistent menace, accompanied by a realization of the futility of trying to come to terms with one's environment, also permeates Alena Vostrá's Kafkaesque *Na ostří nože* (*Things Come to a Head*, 1968), a play which exhibits a definitely darker atmosphere than that presented in her earlier *Na koho to slovo padne* (*Whose Turn Next?*, 1966) in which a group of young people are shown engaged in a constant game of clowning, amusing themselves with wild plays upon words, dreaming up nonsensical situations which they themselves accept as real—all this in an effort to breathe some life and sense into the world surrounding them.

Alena Vostrá is one of several authors, such as Pavel Landovsky and Josef Topol, who, instead of creating plays in a spirit of pure absurdity, have sought to inject grotesque elements into basically realistic plays in order to stress the correspondingly grotesque aspects of reality. All the members of this group spring from and work with the fringe theatres which arose in the fifties, and all are much concerned with the problems of the young. Topol, for example, deals with the clash between youth and age in *Jejich den* (*Their Day*, 1959) and concentrates exclusively upon the rising generation in his later *Konec masopustu* (*The End of the Carnival*, 1963) and *Kočka na kolejích* (*Cat on the Rails*, 1965). Among still other writers who departed from the purely realistic style in the sixties may be noted the Slovak dramatist Peter Karvaš. His *Parochňa* (*The Big Wig*, 1964) dealt symbolically with the question of arbitrary power, while *Experiment 'Damokles'* (*The Damocles Experiment*, 1967) presented a grotesque theme reminiscent of Dürrenmatt's *Ein Engel kommt nach Babylon*, introducing a parable concerning human behaviour in face of a menace.

This avant-garde style took a longer time to find a place for itself in Hungary, and for this there were three obvious reasons: in that country there had been no strong earlier tradition, the theatre had had an over-long exclusive emphasis upon narrowly understood socialist realism, and there was in the background the powerful influence of the national-historical drama, represented by such writers as Illyés, Németh, and Gyula Háy.

The first tentative departures from realism during the early sixties passed by unnoticed. In 1960–61 Háy wrote *A ló* (*The Horse*), a comedy showing signs of Dürrenmatt's and Ionesco's influence, which, dealing with Caligula's elevation of his horse to the rank of Consul, offered a sharp critique of totalitarian régimes: but comparatively little attention was paid to it. A couple of years later Miklós Mészöly composed *Ablakmosó* (*The Window-cleaner*), clearly inspired by Ionesco and Beckett; but this had only a very short run in the provinces, while his second play *Bunker* (*The Bunker*) never even saw the footlights.

Not earlier than 1967 came the decisive break-through with the production in Budapest of *Tóték* (*The Tot Family*) by István Örkeny. This drama is set in the time of the Second World War—an era used by many Hungarian playwrights as a period with a clearly defined political context and a familiar set of circumstances against which to set their dramas of the absurd. The plot shows a village family which, in order to protect a son at the front, has to endure the outrageous whims of a visiting officer—but in the end the head of the household, weak and terrified although he is, rebels against this tyranny and the officer is killed.

Violence and response to violence, the individual's inner freedom, the merits and demerits of compromise and active struggle, of opportunism and non-involvement—all these are recurring themes in Hungarian drama, beginning with the historical plays by Németh and Illyés and ending with those by Örkény. In *Komákasszony, hol a stukker?* (*Musical Chairs*, 1968) by Gábor Görgey, five representatives of various segments of society are shown locked up in a shelter, playing a game of musical chairs in which the winner is always the current possessor of the only gun. *Hordók* (*The Barrels*, 1968) by István Eörsi contrasts the non-involved position of an intellectual with those who engage in an active fight against evil.

Another dominant theme in Hungarian drama is the criticism of petty bourgeois concepts and popular ambitions. Károly Szakonyi, in his *Adáshiba* (*A Fault in Transmission*, 1970) presents a family so engrossed in watching television that it has completely lost the ability to pay attention to anything else: not even the coming of Christ with his miracles can draw their eyes away from the insidious box. In *Ki lesz a bálanyia* (*Fall Guy for Tonight*, 1969), by István Csurka, an endless game of poker reveals to four middle-aged semi-successful professional men the total meaninglessness of their lives: one of them, indeed, discovers that the only thing he can do in order to escape the trap is to commit suicide. Another play of special interest is Örkény's latest work, *Macsakajáték* (*Cat's Play*, 1971) which depicts, with great subtlety and psychological insight, two elderly women representing different attitudes to life—of resignation and of a refusal to give in to age: particularly affective is the presentation of one of these characters as she seeks for love and is treated with indifference by all those surrounding her. These last-mentioned plays seem to suggest a new and promising course for Hungarian drama, a fusing of the grotesque with the realistic comedy of manners. In fact, despite the considerable numbers of 'absurd' plays produced in its theatres, these dramas, when examined as a whole, seem to be less innovative than the corresponding works produced by Polish and Czechoslovak authors, and also to be less penetrating: the desire to entertain has nearly always restrained the desire, exhibited elsewhere, to break through accepted patterns.

In Rumania the generation gap is so pronounced that an author's age proves a good clue to the kind of drama he is likely to write. The new wave of young dramatists appeared in the late sixties, and these now are firmly established alongside the members of the older generation, represented by such men as Aurel Baranga, Alexandru Mirodan, and Horia Lovinescu. The first sign that this new band of writers was coming appeared in Ecaterina Oproïu's *Nu sint turnul Eiffel* (*I Am Not the Eiffel Tower*, 1965) where the action deals with the problems of contemporary Rumanian youth—and the writers among this contemporary youth followed her in a desire to do away with old forms. They have yet to establish a recognizably fresh identity: they make their plays ever more and more bizarre and unrealistic; they create grand metaphors and theatrical parables; their styles and forms are manifold—philosophical dramas, poetic dramas, lyrical comedies, absurd plays, and historical plays (the last-mentioned usually bearing symbolic significance, as in *Viteazul* (*The Valiant One*, 1969) by Paul Anghel); and it is worthy of note that a fair number of their writings take shape as short, one-act pieces.

By far the most interesting among these diverse writings are the works of the poet Marin Sorescu: typical is his monodrama *Iona* (*Jonah*, 1969), a parable concerning the meaninglessness of human life. Another poet, Josif Naghiu, is the author of *Intunericul sau gluga pe ochi* (*Darkness*, 1971), an absurd drama dealing with the various kinds of human limitations—lack of knowledge, of imagination, of intellectual freedom, and the like.

Radu Dumitru goes in another direction. His first play, *Portocala verde* (*The Green Orange*, 1969), strongly reminiscent of Ionesco's *The Bald Soprano*, introduces four characters who have lost all human traits except a defective memory and a limited vocabulary, and who spend their time in an apparently meaningless discourse, ever turning round and round the connotations of words. Still another writer worthy of attention is Teodor Mazilu, whose *Tandreţe si abjecţie* (*The Tender and the Abject*, 1969) also explores the comic qualities of ordinary speech, of everyday sayings, of newspaper slogans and, likewise, of 'educated' semi-philosophical utterances—all of them demonstrating both human stupidity and the banality of everyday life.

On the whole, this grotesque drama has so far failed to establish itself in one particular European country—Bulgaria. The modern drama of that land consists mainly of the psychological drama of manners, represented in the works of Nikola Khaitov, Georgi Karaslavov, Dragomir Asenov and Dimitr Dimov, although it is true that in the sixties a new 'poetic wave' did appear in the writings of Ivan Radoev, Ivan Paichev, Valeri Petrov, Georgi Dzhagarov and others. It is also true that this 'poetic wave' has made some attempts (fairly timid) to enrich dramatic form by the introduction of such elements as episodic structure, free use of time and space, expressive imagery, metaphorical language, and the like. Some of these plays, such as *Posestenie v minaloto* (*A Trip to the Past*, 1965) by Bozhidar Bozhilov, try to rise above immediate social problems by dealing with more universal moral and philosophical issues within the framework of the lyrical drama.

Perhaps the most interesting author here is Yordan Radichkov, who combines satirical observation of reality with poetic sensitivity. His *Sumatokha* (*The Row*, 1967) thus shapes itself as a satire on the Bulgarian peasantry, their obsessions and weaknesses, composed of folk humour, the nonsense-talk of village simpletons, and grotesque popular fantasies.

The 'row' of the title stands for all world-wide and local anxieties and upheavals, which throw up menacing shadows and on which every man must willy-nilly take a stand. The theme of this particular play thus might be seen as symbolic of all those social topics and issues which have served as the main frame of reference for the bulk of contemporary East European drama. The social situations may change, but the plays change with them. As has been noted, after the period of Socialist Realism, the pendulum has in general swung over sharply to the other side, towards the grotesque and the absurd, and, although predictions are always hazardous, it looks as though at the present moment, and maybe for the immediate future, most dramatists are intent upon steering a course between these two extremes.

POST-WAR HISPANIC AND BRAZILIAN DRAMA

RODOLFO CARDONA

The Spanish Drama

Spain, in one sense at least, stands apart from most other European countries: it was ravaged by bitter military conflict, but its post-war period began, in 1939, at the very time when the rest of Europe was beginning to suffer from the first onslaughts of a devastating conflict destined to endure for more than five years, engulfing ever more and more territories in its destructive course. This basic fact, in so far as the drama is concerned, has two inescapable consequences. First, in order to compare the Spanish 'post-war' with the immediately preceding 'pre-war,' it is necessary to move back in time by almost an entire decade from what was the 'pre-war' elsewhere, and, secondly, it must be recognized that theatrical conditions after the conclusion of the Spanish Civil War markedly differed from those prevailing elsewhere.

Already in the early thirties several Spanish playwrights had been indulging in interestingly novel experiments. Among these playwrights one, Federico García Lorca, was at that time becoming recognized internationally as an author of prime distinction: his reputation was high even at the time when the Second World War broke out, and this reputation was raised still higher when in 1945 *La Casa de Bernarda Alba* was published. What, however, remains still not widely realized is the fact that during the years immediately preceding his death in 1936 this author's experimental boldness was extending far beyond the range of his better-known works. *Así que pasen cinco años* (*And Thus Five Years Pass By*), although written in 1930, was not published until 1937 and remained largely unknown until after 1945. This drama, described by Lorca himself as a "mystery about time", shows the five years speeding in their course within the mind of a young man during the brief hours immediately preceding his death. While it is true that some 'surrealist' and other dramatists elsewhere had previously taken many steps into this realm of the theatrical subconscious, García Lorca's 'mystery' has a power peculiarly its own. And by its side stands another play, *El público* (*The Public*), written about 1933, so eccentric in its form and so daring in its style that even its author thought· that "no company would dare to produce it" and that "no audience would be capable of sitting through it without becoming indignant." This strange piece has never been published in its entirety, but an account given by R. M. Nadal of the existing manuscript clearly indicates that it includes elements of what later became known as 'theatre of the absurd,' 'epic theatre' and 'theatre of cruelty': indeed, it stands so far ahead of its time that we can see in it even that exploitation of interaction between public and actors which the 'Living Theatre' has so assiduously pursued, together with the accompanying exploitation of another avant-garde innovation, stage nudity.

Nor was García Lorca entirely alone in his experimental endeavours. In 1931 Rafael Alberti composed *El hombre deshabitado* (*The Hollow Man*) as a kind of 'unsacramental' '*auto sacramental*' wherein God is placed in the dock and judged directly responsible for the failure of mankind. Similar novel features are to be found also both among his 'committed' political dramas and among his poetic plays, several of them written in exile: his best-known and possibly his best work, *Noche de guerra en el Museo del Prado* (*A Night of War in the Prado Museum*), set in the time when the Civil War erupted in 1936, was in fact not composed and printed until twenty years had passed by and the author was an exile. Another émigré playwright, Alejandro Casona, who in 1937 organized a company which toured throughout Latin America and who lived in Buenos Aires from 1939 to 1963, tended in his dramas to deal with themes fantastic and marvellous: when his critics attacked this style as being a 'theatre of evasion' he defended himself by declaring that, living and working in Argentina, he was compelled to write on topics not too close to the conditions prevailing in Spain. By contrast, however, exile in Mexico did not deter Max Aub from devoting himself to a 'committed' theatre, which took shape in three distinct periods. From 1923 to 1935 he was influenced largely by avant-garde aesthetics, his best play of that time being *Espejo de avaricias* (*Mirror for Misers*: written in two variant versions, 1927 and 1935): the second period, extending from 1936 to 1939, the years of the Civil War, inspired him to deal with the contemporary events directly and concretely in what he himself called his 'theatre of circumstance': the last and most important period began in 1943 and produced his great works, *San Juan* (*Saint John*, 1943), *Morir por cerrar los ojos* (*Die to Close Your Eyes*, 1944) and *El rapto de Europa* (*The Rape of Europa*, 1946), as well as an interesting series of one-act plays.

These Spanish playwrights in exile were all actively in touch with what was being done in the theatre elsewhere, and the chief among them were consciously endeavouring to bring their plays into the mainstream of European and American theatrical developments. Unfortunately, however, the richness and excitement so clearly evident in the best Spanish drama produced before, during, and after the Civil War (the last by the authors living in exile) are nowhere evident during the first ten years of theatre life in post-war Spain—a depressing picture of the consequences of an ironclad dictatorship, heavily censoring what was put on the stage. The censorship, in fact, has operated with particular severity upon playwrights, since the Government has shown special sensitivity concerning the media which make a direct impact on the public or are too readily accessible. Thus the censorship of books (especially expensive volumes addressed to a cultured minority) has been far less stringent than the censorship of magazines, newspapers, television, film, and theatre.

Between 1939 and 1949 there was practically nothing of any value presented on the Spanish stage. Some of the new plays tended to be artificially constructed pieces in which Benavente's formula of harmless social criticism prevailed: others carried on the earlier comic tradition but without the brilliance exhibited, for example, in the earlier adroit writings of Carlos Arniches. Thematic monotony and the dulness of an unadventuresome realistic pattern prevailed. The solitary exception, perhaps, may be found in *Tres sombreros de copa* (*Three Top Hats*) and even that well-known play by Miguel Mihura Santos, although performed for the first time in 1952, had been written twenty years earlier.

The 'new' Spanish drama tentatively made its appearance in 1949 with *Historia de una escalera* (*Story of a Staircase*) by Antonio Buero Vallejo. Here he demonstrated that he was not prepared to evade the surrounding reality or to permit his public to find satisfaction in an easy escapism: his scene is set in a poor district of Madrid: we see the fond dreams of youth being inexorably shattered: and then, within a time-span of thirty years we are shown how the dreams of a younger generation are similarly destroyed by harsh reality. Strangely, however, Buero Vallejo succeeds in investing his basically bleak and pessimistic picture with a quality which justifies us in regarding his total dramatic output as a kind of theatre of redemption and, therefore, of hope. *The Story of a Staircase* is realistic, but most characteristic of his theatrical method is his series of historical plays wherein adroitly he relates the past, and even the future, with the present. Thus in *Las meninas* (*The Ladies-in-Waiting*, 1960) he deals with the artist Velázquez in such a way as to make the audience aware that his treatment of seventeenth-century problems is conditioned by his keen awareness of the problems of today. *El concierto de San Ovidio* (*The Concert on Saint Ovid's Day*, 1962) carries us back to Paris in the latter part of the eighteenth century and directs its attention to a miserable group of blind men in the Hospice des Quince-veintes and, as we listen to the hero, Valentin Hauy, declaring that he is determined to teach them

> to read, and to place in their hands books printed by themselves: thus will they be able to write signs and to interpret their own writing,

it is clear that the dramatist has the not-so-veiled intent of alluding to his fellow-Spaniards. And in *El tragaluz* (*The Skylight*, 1967) he introduces a kind of transformed, or reversed, historical perspective by making two symbolic characters, named just He and She, living in some vague period of the future, view and dissect the problems confronting a present-day Spanish family suffering from the consequences of the Civil War.

Alongside Buero Vallejo stands the sometimes rather perplexing and puzzling figure of Alfonso Sastre, a man thoroughly dedicated to an attempt at renovation of the Spanish stage and yet one whose position is by no means so high as might have been expected. He has worked hard: apart from his lengthy list of dramatic writings, he has been active in practical theatre affairs, responsible for founding several play-producing groups—'Arte Nuevo' in 1945, 'Teatro de Agitación Social' in 1950, and 'Grupo de Teatro Realista' in 1956; each of these ventures has been accompanied by theoretical 'manifestoes,' and with these may be associated his two critical volumes, *Drama y sociedad* (*Drama and Society*, 1956) and *Anatomía del realismo* (*Anatomy of Realism*, 1965). In general, however, it may be thought that both his theoretical exercises and his creative dramatic work suffer from a certain amount of confusion. At one moment we find him declaring that 'social' objectives are far more important than 'artistic' achievements: a moment later, he is emphasizing that "only an art of the highest aesthetic quality is capable of transforming the world" and that "a poorly-wrought work of art" is essentially useless. Nor is this confusion in thought unrelated to a weakness evident in many of his plays wherein he displays an inability to translate his 'ideas' into effectively dramatic terms. Among his score of plays, perhaps the most truly effective is *La Cornada* (*The Death Thrust*, 1960), an excellent piece, well planned and full of dramatic suspense, concerned with the relationship between a bullfighter, his impresario, and his wife. Even here, however, Sastre cannot leave well alone: his achievement is lessened, not enriched, when he pretentiously presents this theme as a reinterpretation of the Chronos-Saturn myth.

Buero Vallejo and Sastre have been largely responsible for encouraging a number of younger authors to apply their talents to the theatre of protest, although the realistic style cultivated by these masters tends occasionally to be mingled with expressionistic elements, many of which, when examined carefully, appear to have been inspired by fresh examination of the fantastic elements in the plays of Valle Inclán. Some of the younger authors belonging to this group have run foul of the censor —as, indeed, Sastre himself did on several occasions: but on the whole they have tended to deal with problems and social injustices of which the Government is well aware and which it would like to solve (or at least which it pretends to want to solve): and thus, however deeply felt and vigorously stated their dramatic 'protest' may be, their plays are passed for performance. An excellent example of this is Lauro Olmo's first work for the stage, *La camisa* (*The Shirt*, 1961), which forcefully and trenchantly deals with the miserable conditions prevailing among members of the working-class, driving them in desperation to thoughts of emigration.

This particular theatre of protest, however, is associated with another group of young authors who are generally known as the 'underground playwrights' because most of their writings have been systematically banned both for theatrical presentation and for publication, and also because their revolutionary dramatic devices are neither understood nor appreciated by directors brought up in a purely neo-realistic tradition. It is of interest to observe that, although this group is made up of numerous individuals, each working alone and independently—so that they cannot be regarded collectively as forming anything like a 'school' of playwrights, their dramas are strangely alike in expressing a new sensibility and in employing technical devices surprisingly akin to each other. Whereas the 'neo-realistic' group have tended to criticize social injustices generated by the political situation, to develop positive characters with whom the spectators may easily identify, and to develop themes within what may be called a rational framework (even although solutions may not always be offered), these 'new wave' authors tend to present negative characters with whom no one can identify, to select irrational themes developed with still further irrationalities designed to produce a reaction from, not an identification with, the audience. Both make use of allegory, but the first group tends towards the use of historical allegories, whereas the second group delights in abstract allegories not dissimilar from those employed by Calderón and his companions in the seventeenth century—the chief differences being that they are less conceptual and thus are easily appreciated even by an uninitiated audience, with symbols easily recognizable.

The Drama in Spanish America

Obviously, the general conditions prevailing in Spanish America differ completely from those operative in Spain itself: and here the year 1945 marked the start of a new era in which the dramatists brought their thematic objectives and their styles into harmony with those of the postwar European and American theatre.

In its earliest beginnings, Spanish-American drama had either been wholly subservient to Spanish models, or else, after the various wars of independence, had sought to develop a distinctive presentation of national features separating their own customs and ways of life from those of their former rulers or of more recent European immigrants. Thus emerged a popular theatre of manners, making particular appeal to the middle and lower classes, searching for and offering a sense of national identity. It is certainly true that, as the years passed by, this theatre of manners occasionally became deeper and richer by dealing with national problems and even by tending to become a theatre of commitment, striving to influence spectators politically. Nevertheless, it is only during more recent decades that the Spanish-American drama has acquired real significance by developing its own expressive language and techniques even while it has channelled its efforts into the two great streams which have dominated the world stage during the past twenty or thirty years—the Camus-Sartre-Beckett-Genet stream with its existentialist-ontological examination of character and situation, and that other stream which confronts the individual with his social environment, as in the works of Brecht, Dürrenmatt, Frisch, and in the later writings of Valle Inclán.

At the very start, particular mention should be made of two important theatrical groups which were established in the two great cities of Spanish-speaking America, Mexico City and Buenos Aires, both establishing centres which clearly pointed the way towards the future—the 'Ulysses Theatre' founded in 1929 in Mexico City by two poets, Xavier Villaurrutia and Salvador Novo, and the 'People's Theatre,' established in Buenos Aires in 1930 by Leónidas Barletta. Later other cities such as Montevideo and Santiago de Chile saw the development of stages similarly motivated, and during the post-war period, largely but not exclusively through the influence of universities, dramatic activities expanded widely even in the smallest of the Spanish-American republics.

The forms, styles, and aims of the new dramas are numerous and diversified. Demetrio Aguilera Malta, an Ecuadorian, has, for example, wrought out of the realistic theatre of manners which had been so popular during the earlier part of this century a kind of 'magic-realistic' drama which is as it were the theatrical reflection of Henri Rousseau's paintings or of novels conceived by Asturias, García Marques, and Carpentier. Perhaps the best examples of his playwriting style are *El Tigre* (*The Tiger*, 1956) and *Infierno negro* (*Black Hell*, 1967). Several other authors, presenting realistic situations with overt political overtones, put into service almost every available technical device known to the modern stage: typical examples of such works are *La muerte no entrará en Palacio* (*Death Shall Not Dare to Enter the Mansion*, 1957) and *Los soles truncos* (*The Fanlights*, 1959) by the Puerto Rican René Marqués, *Lo que dejó la tempestad* (*What the Tempest Left Behind*, 1961) by the Venezuelan César Rengifo, *Y nos dijeron que éramos immortales* (*And They Told Us We Were Immortal*, 1963) by the Argentinian Osvaldo Dragún, and *Yo también hablo de la rosa* (*I Too Speak of the Rose*, 1966) by the Mexican Emilio Carballido.

Still other dramatists prefer to employ a more fantastic method, exhibiting strong overtones of the European 'theatre of the absurd,' for the purpose of exposing social and political injustices, and occasionally the same style is employed for the presentation of concepts of still wider application, as for example in the writings of the Argentinian Griselda Gambaro: her masterpiece is *El campo* (*The Camp*, 1967), which exhibits the slow encroachment of totalitarian practices within a social unit, ruthlessly revealing human tendencies towards aggression and submission. Other successful achievements in the same style are *Los invasores* (*The Invaders*, 1962), by the Chilean Egon Wolff, a blood-curdling nightmare of the "inevitable" attack on the wealthy by the dispossessed, *El día que saltaron los leones* (*The Day they let the Lions Loose*, 1963) by Emilio Carballido, a fanciful picture of social revolution, and *La biblioteca* (*The Library*, 1959) by the Uruguayan Carlos Maggi, in which the bureaucratization of Spanish-American society is carried to its logically absurd conclusion.

Maybe the most original, and therefore the most interesting, trends exhibited in a few of the best Spanish-American dramas is a return to ritual. Carballido's *La hebra de oro* (*The Golden Thread*, 1956) thus explores the depths of perceivable reality by combining dance, music, pantomime, strange visual effects, in a sort of total theatre addressed to the senses rather than simply to the mind; in *La orgía del mulato* (*The Mulatto's Orgy*, 1966), the Mexican Luisa Hernández employs the same combination of diverse devices in a ritualistic manner to provide a vision of protest, a plea for freedom; and, in a different manner, the Cuban José Triana, in his brutally impressive *La noche de los asesinos* (*The Night of the Assassins*, or *The Criminals*, 1964), employs the ritualistic element in a different way by showing two sisters and a brother evoking a spirit of incantation as they prepare to murder their parents. Such presentations of ritualistic elements clearly are to be associated with Artaud's plea for the creation of a theatre "whose only value rests in its excruciating, occult association with reality and dangers: indeed, it may be asserted with confidence that in some of the most effective South American dramas composed in this style we are confronted by the most effective examples to be found anywhere of this French author's 'Theatre of Cruelty.'

In their search for viably expressive dramatic devices, these Spanish-American dramatists have (perhaps not so surprisingly) consciously gone back to the Spanish seventeenth-century tradition of the '*auto sacramental*', and even to still earlier types of religious plays, adapting their style to purposes quite other than the religious aims of their original models. The Colombian Enrique Buenaventura, for example, seized upon the traditional *mojiganga* and used it to present an allegory with socialist implications in his *Á la diestra de Dios Padre* (*At the Right Hand of God the Father*, 1960). Both the Guatemalan Carlos Solórzano and Emilio Carballido have actually described some of their own dramatic writings as *autos sacramentales*. The former's *Las manos de Dios* (*The Hands of God*, 1956) is an imaginative attempt to show the Devil as a Promethean figure whose mission—which he tries in vain to fulfil—is to save mankind from superstition, ignorance, and injustice: the latter's *La zona intermedia* (*The Intermediate Zone*, 1948) deals whimsically and apparently lightly with the idea of the Last Judgment, but, beneath the lightness, displays his very serious concern concerning man's responsibility in the world—the final justification for his existence. In more anguished terms, the same plot is dealt with by the Panamanian José de Jesús Martínez in a drama which he expressly entitles *Judicio Final* (*Final Judgment*, 1962).

The Brazilian Drama

The Brazilian theatre demands separate consideration, even although several of its problems and characteristics parallel aspects of the Spanish-American stage which have already been outlined above.

The present development of this Brazilian drama starts in 1943 with the production at Rio de Janeiro of *Vestido de Noiva* (*The Wedding Gown*) by Nélson Rodrigues. In this production a group called 'Os Comediantes' ('The Players'), led by the Polish director Zbigniew Ziembiński, introduced Rio's spectators for the first time to expressionistic lighting methods and to new rhythmic movements aimed at underlining and emphasizing the play's theme.

After this presentation 'Os Comediantes' took charge of the aesthetic reform of the city's stage. One of their first and most important innovations was to diminish the importance of the leading actors and instead to place the control of the entire company in the hands of a director. The conjunction of Nélson Rodrigues (who broke with current dramatic conventions) and of Ziembiński (who demonstrated the effectiveness of the best American and European production standards) succeeded in stimulating an entirely new dramatic movement which from Rio spread to other centres. Highly 'professional' amateur acting groups soon sprang into existence, and one of the best among these associations, the 'Teatro dos Amateurs' of Pernambuco, made it a rule to engage foreign directors for their productions. During the fifties, São Paulo gradually began to take the lead, with the 'Teatro Experimental' (founded by Alfredo Mesquita) and the 'Grupo Universitario do Theatro' (founded by Decio de Almeida Prado) proving the most influential acting companies: while, about the same time, the Italian industrialist Franco Zampari generously provided the funds which permitted the building in that city of the 'Teatro Brasileiro da Comedia' which presented to the Paulista audiences excellent productions, both of classical and of modern plays, imported from Europe and the United States.

Naturally, this enthusiastic theatrical activity soon encouraged the development of a new drama. Jorge Andrade, starting with *A Moratoria* (*The Moratorium*, 1955), produced a series of plays dealing with the social and psychological decline of the region's wealthy plantation owners, thus carrying on the new spirit in the Brazilian theatre which had been introduced a decade earlier by Nélson Rodrigues. Silveira Sampaio, abandoning his medical profession to become a self-made actor-director-playwright, composed a distinguished *Trilogia do Héroi Grotesco* (*Trilogy of the Grotesque Hero*, 1948–49) in which he treated, in a bold and frank manner, several subjects which hitherto had been considered taboo for the theatre—incest, prostitution, and marital infidelities. Among the younger members of this group, Ariano Suassuna de Paraiba won success with his *Auto da Compadecida* (*Play of the Compassionate Woman*, 1957), in which he skilfully combined elements of Brazilian folklore with '*candomblé*' (the religious practices of the Brazilian black and mulatto population which combine Catholic rites with magical and ritualistic forms originally introduced from Africa). A similar conflation of Brazilian folklore and '*candomblé*' also appears in the Brazilian play which so far has achieved greatest recognition abroad, *O Pagador de Promessas* (*Payment as Promised*, 1960). And Suassuna de Paraiba is accompanied by an active, and on the whole successful, group of young dramatists, such as Augusto Boal, Oduvaldo Viana Jr., Millor Fernandes, Antonio Callado and, perhaps the most outstanding among them, Gianfrancesco de Guarnieri, author of *Eles não usam black-tie* (*They Don't Wear Evening Dress*, 1958) and *Gimba* (1957), plays which are both thoughtful and theatrically effective.

As a global conclusion for this section one might stress the fact that during the post-war period, and particularly during the last fifteen years or so, Latin American theatre has come into its own. Quite recently it was not uncommon to read in manuals of Latin American literature that drama was an inferior genre in comparison to lyric poetry and the novel. Today we can point to a very rich and novel dramatic production in all of the countries, even in the smallest, which is beginning to compete successfully with the contemporary novel, whose 'boom' has been so much publicized.

As for Spain, a slight relaxation in the censorship during the last five years has allowed wider experimentation in the production as well as in the publication of plays. Still, however, a fine Catalonian playwright such as Manuel de Pedrolo (*Cruma, Homes y No, Tècnica de cambra*, to name a few titles) remains better known abroad than within his own country. Apart from *The Foundation* (*La fundación*), the latest play by Antonio Buero Vallejo, the most important theatrical productions have been revivals of plays by Valle-Inclán (*Luces de Bohemia, Divinas palabras*) and García Lorca (*Yerma*). The impact of these productions, one hopes, will help to pave the way for the presentation of works by the most talented among the playwrights of the 'new wave.'

POST-WAR DRAMA IN ITALY

Amid the rather confused and not infrequently perplexing extension of dramatic and theatrical styles from 1945 onward one thing seems to be absolutely and irrefutably clear—that during these thirty-odd years, and particularly within the decade of the nineteen-sixties, the minds of 'advanced' playwrights almost everywhere from the U.S.A. and its near neighbours on to the majority of European countries have been particularly affected by a relatively limited number of themes, patterns and fashions, and that beyond all other attractions the appeal of the absurd has proved especially potent.

Thoroughly characteristic of what has been happening lately are the records of two plays. The first is that of Ionesco's 'anti-play,' *The Bald Soprano*, which, originally produced in 1950 and published in 1954, swept over almost all frontiers and stimulated the writing of not dis-similar pieces here, there, and everywhere: the second concerns the fortunes of *En attendant Godot*—originally composed by an Irishman resident in Paris, published in 1952, acted at a small French playhouse in 1953, performed at the Arts Theatre in London two years later, translated and acted in almost all languages, and finally, in 1966, being provided with a sequel by the Montenegrin Miodrag Bulatović, *Godo je dosao* (*Godot Has Arrived*), which shows the hitherto unseen title-character coming at last to those who have been waiting for so long, and being rejected by them because he appears in an unexpected guise.

There is not the slightest doubt but that this cult of the absurd has thus spread almost everywhere. Nevertheless, it is important to observe that, while the impact of the cult was almost if not quite universal, the plays composed under its influence in the various countries differed markedly from each other, assuming diverse forms which clearly were either unconsciously patterned upon, or else positively determined by, the prevailing dramatic styles in which the moods and feelings of the several communities had previously found theatrical expression. This observation must be associated with another, that the absurd, in its more extreme manifestations, has been given a reception much more enthusiastic in some areas than in others, and that in particular the United States and England have on the whole been far less affected by its spell than many lands within the continent of Europe. It is true that this term is difficult to define precisely and exactly, but it may be agreed that, during the years when dozens of European playwrights have been tumbling over each other in frantic endeavours to devise ever greater and greater absurdities, the mainstreams of the American and English stages have, by comparison, pursued a fairly steady course, and that in general the more significant authors who have in any respect been influenced by this style have employed its methods and objectives in characteristically independent manner. Thus, for example, although Harold Pinter has freely acknowledged his indebtedness to Ionesco, his plays, so far from being imitative, obviously have their own highly individual idiosyncratic forms and objectives. Certainly in both countries there are a few writers, such as Edward Albee, who exhibit in some of their works elements akin to those which distinguish dramas produced in the original homes of the absurd; certainly, too, 'absurdism' has been freely exploited by various groups of the 'off-Broadway' kind: but, even when all these are put together, it seems amply clear that American and English plays of this sort do not loom so large as those brought into being within the range of many European dramatists.

The 'Teatro del Grottesco'

When we consider these European countries as a whole, however, one peculiar anomaly becomes apparent. Quite frequently the term 'absurd' occurs alongside the term 'grotesque', so that the two words appear to have one and the same significance, yet the land which was the original home of the 'teatro del grottesco' and which still produces at least some plays influenced by that tradition has largely pursued a dramatic course characteristically its own.

Here several pertinent facts must be held steadily in mind. The first, and the most important, of these is that the word 'grotesque' can have two quite distinct meanings, one of which applies properly to the Pirandellesque productions of the Italian stage and the other applies with equal propriety to the absurd-grotesque plays which have come from French, German and allied theatres. Put simply, the latter reflects the significance of the term as it was used by Hazlitt for what in his time was commonly called the Gothic, by Ruskin to describe the conjunction in art of startlingly opposed elements or symbols, and, more recently, by Wolfgang Kayser to describe artistic efforts designed for the purpose of invoking and subduing demonic forces in the world. In perfect accord with these and similar interpretations, the terms 'grotesque' and 'grotesque-absurd' may properly be employed to describe the atmosphere evoked by Michel de Ghelderode, Jean Genet, and the disciples of Antonin Artaud's 'theatre of cruelty.' Those playwrights, however, are clearly very far removed from Luigi Chiarelli, who seems to have been the first to speak of the '*teatro del grottesco*', and from his still greater companion, Luigi Pirandello. The Italian '*grottesco*' may not be invested with the savage power and terror which has been so freely manifested on the stages of Paris, Zurich, and Berlin: what it does characteristically exhibit is a peculiarly pointed grace, a delicacy, a penetrating intimacy.

With this consideration must be associated a second. Quite frequently, discussions of the modern 'absurd' have related it, directly or indirectly, to the *commedia dell'arte* tradition—but when we consider this matter with care it must appear obvious that this tradition can be connected with the writings of Ionesco and Dürrenmatt, Adamov and Genet, only by a process of artificially forced argument, while on the contrary the Italian Chiarelli and Pirandello are without the shadow of a doubt modern descendants of those theatre-men who, in Renaissance times, developed the characteristic kind of masked comedy which spread widely outward from its original Tuscan-Venetian homeland. And, finally, this thought leads to the realization that, save for one or two unimportant exceptions (and, of course, for certain avant-garde 'fringe' activities), the post-war Italian playwrights have shown comparatively little interest in the 'absurdism' of Central Europe. It is by no means without significance that when the popular Ezio d'Errico was persuaded to enter the world of Beckett and Adamov by writing his *Il tempo di cavallette* (*The Time of the Locusts*, 1958) and *La foresta* (*The Forest*, 1959), these pieces had their premières, in German translations, at Darmstadt and Kassel respectively. During the past three decades the masters of the Italian stage have been Pirandello and Betti, not the disciples of Jarry and Artaud.

The Searchings of Ugo Betti

Without doubt, Ugo Betti, who, in spite of the dismal social-political world created by Mussolini and his Fascisti, had succeeded in making a name for himself even before the outbreak of war, was the greatest of all recent Italian dramatists. During the forties and onward to his death in 1953, he produced a series of sensitively profound theatrical works in which, instead of repeating the absurdists' constant and often tedious generalizations, he concentrated upon individual characters and upon themes which frequently dealt with crime, redemption or punishment. Thoroughly typical is his *Corruzione al Palazzo di Giustizia* (*Corruption in the Palace of Justice*, 1949), a study of three judges—the relatively young and very ambitious Cust, the equally ambitious but ailing Croz, and the distinguished Vanan, elderly and indeed near to retirement. There is serious suspicion of judicial corruption in the court, and an inspector arrives to conduct an inquiry, during the course of which he discovers that indeed there have been malpractices, that each judge blames one of his colleagues, and that each one of them has things to conceal. Had this been all, the drama would not have risen above the level of a commonplace detective piece, but into this situation Betti places a girl—Elena, the daughter of Vanan. In herself she is not of major importance, but through her presence the dramatic plot is moved up onto another plane. She is devoted to her father, and in his integrity she has absolute belief —so that when Cust accuses Vanan with what on the surface appears to be incontrovertible evidence of guilt she is so utterly broken in spirit that in desperation she seeks escape for herself in suicide. Vanan resigns his post, and Croz, suffering from an incurable disease, dies without having an opportunity of revealing what are in truth completely valid and devastating proofs which he has found to demonstrate Cust's transgressions. Thus Cust appears to have reached his goal, but what Croz had foreseen soon follows: the criminal, with the thought of Elena's miserable suicide in his mind, is racked by conscience and voluntarily confesses his crimes.

This drama, therefore, is not (as any audience might at first have reasonably expected it to be) an exposure of corruption in the highest places: it is not in any respect a critical study of social affairs, either in general or in particular: all its strength—and of theatrical strength it has much—is inward, not outward: it is concerned with men's souls, not merely with their actions. Obviously, therefore, the whole play is a development and conflation of two kinds of dramatic studies which had occupied Betti's attention during earlier years, and which have already been referred to elsewhere: on the one hand, it exhibits certain features of *Ispezione*, which had been written in 1941, although it was not published or produced until 1947, and even some which are reminiscent of *Frana allo scalo nord* (1936), and, on the other, there is in it something of the inner world which is to be found in *Una bella domenica di settembre* (*A Beautiful Sunday in September*, 1937): and both these elements are bound together by the introduction of a third, and fresh, element, that of religious thought.

Betti's new-found dramatic sphere was expressed, somewhat melodramatically, in *Lotta fino all'alba* (*Strife unto Dawn*, 1949) and in the passion-fraught *Delitto all'isola delle capre* (*Goat Island*, 1950), both of them 'strong' plays, but both far surpassed by the peculiarly interesting *La regina e gli insorti* (*The Queen and the Rebels*, 1951), a complex work which has as its setting an imaginary country in which a group of insurgents have bloodily seized power. Anxious to arrest the Queen, they keep watch at a border village; the action starts with the examination of a coachload of travellers, and, in so far as 'plot' is concerned, this examination proceeds throughout the four acts until, at the very end, "a burst of gun-fire" indicates that the Queen has been identified and executed. That, however, is merely the outward, what might be called the physical, part of the drama. The inward part, and that which unquestionably led Betti to construct this play, concerns just one single character, a common prostitute named Argia, one who has struggled through difficult times, knowing what it feels like to

lie huddled on the hard floor of an all-night bar, learning the pleading smile of poverty. . . listening to the cheap jokes of the barman, with an anxious smile on her face; soothing and flattering the bad-tempered taxi-driver.

She is among those who have been stayed for questioning, and beside her cowers the Queen, disguised as a peasant-woman, terrified, abject and cowardly. Out of pity, Argia, almost against her own will, tries to help her, until suddenly, when the Queen swallows poison and lies dead on the ground, she rises and addresses the chief interrogator, Commissar Amos: "Not every eye shall look on the ground," she says:

> There shall still be someone to stand before you. Yes, *I* am the Queen!

And at the end, partly to save the real Queen's son but chiefly because she has summoned up a majestic dignity of which this real Queen had no command, she calmly walks out to her death in a spirit of proud serenity: as she reaches the door, she pauses for a moment to look out upon the landscape. "How lovely and serene it is over the mountains," she murmurs,

> and the star Diana is still there in the sky. Unquestionably, this is a seat for kings, and in it we must try to live regally.

Presumably, when Betti called his drama *The Queen and the Rebels*, in his imagination the true Queen was indeed the poor prostitute.

Beyond even this realm he ventured in his final plays. Courtroom dramas had been popular among a number of twentieth-century realistic dramatists, and it might have been assumed that in selecting a murder trial as the theme of *Il giocatore* (*The Gambler*, 1951) Betti had been attracted principally by thought of the opportunities which such an action offered for tense theatrical situations. This courtroom, however, is one with a vast difference: the author is concerned wholly with metaphysical concepts of guilt and judgment—actual guilt and guilty thought, judgments legal and Judgment divine. The element of the mysterious, the unearthly, and the symbolic is here boldly set by the author before the eyes and ears of the audience. This same element, although presented in a less direct manner, reappears in the final mountain-scene of *Acque turbate* (*Troubled Waters*, written in 1951, published 1955) as well as in another mountain-scene, made mysterious with its visions, which is introduced into *L'aiuola bruciata* (*The Burnt Flower-Bed*, 1953, a play which is structured in much the same way as *The Queen and the Rebels*. When the spectators find that the action here is specifically set by Betti in "the present" and in a secluded spot on the border between two enemy countries, they may feel themselves fully justified in believing that the play which they are about to see is politically motivated, and this belief will certainly be increased when they further find that much of the dialogue is devoted to discussion of a meeting which is planned for emissaries of the opposed lands. Soon, however, they must come to realize that it was not these political matters which were of primary interest to Betti: it was the struggle within which seized upon his mind and his imagination. The burnt flower-bed is a symbol; onto this spot, some time ago, a young lad aged fifteen had fallen to his death from a lofty window; and the spiritual presence of this boy is subtly kept before us until it is revealed that, in fact, his death was self-inflicted, a suicide committed because of his realization that the social-political world in which he lived was arid and waste—"just one great barren devastated flower-bed." This discovery does not end in despair: instead, characteristically, Betti makes the boy's death into something which stimulates faith and the striving for something better.

Religious and Psychological Questionings

Betti's *Ispezione* had appeared in 1947: Diego Fabbri's *Inquisizione* (*Inquisition*, 1950) was performed three years later. There is no similarity in their plots, nor in style is there any sign that the earlier drama had any influence on the latter: yet these two titles indicate that Betti and Fabbri inhabit the same spiritual world. Both are concerned with individual men and women confronted by a mysterious universe; both are searchers after truth; both realize that truth is difficult to determine and to grasp; both refuse to restrict their choice of themes to an examination of purely social forces. *Ispezione*, as has been seen, ended with a strange, perplexing question-mark: *Inquisizione* concerns itself with just four characters—a young priest who is losing his faith and who has almost decided to abandon the Church, a young troubled husband and wife, and a very old priest who devoutly believes in miracles even although nothing of this sort has ever come his way; at the close of the play this old man talks quietly to the other three, and infuses into his words such simple, effective sincerity that he brings peace to their disturbed souls. When they have gone we see him on his knees, thanking God for this miracle which has just been vouchsafed to him. Fabbri's works are many, and perhaps the most impressive of all is his *Processo a Gesù* (*The Trial of Jesus*, but translated as *Between Two Thieves*, 1955), a strange drama possessed of a peculiarly incantatory power. Every night, it is supposed, a 'Processo a Gesù' is performed by a wandering group of German-Jewish actors. In part, the text of this performance is definitely fixed and unalterable: the rôle of the Judge is always given to Elias, whose son Daniel had been murdered by the Nazis, and always Pilate is deemed guilty: yet, strangely, his fellow-actors cast lots for the other parts in the play. When judgment has been passed, however, the performance is by no means at an end, since members of the audience (of course, actors pretending to be spectators) rise to express their views on what has been presented before them, on related metaphysical questions, and on the nature of Christianity itself: there is even a sudden violent intrusion as one of these speakers feels himself compelled, in deep disturbance of spirit, to confess that he had been partly responsible for Daniel's death. Hardly any one among the scores of dramas composed in the play-within-the-play tradition can quite compare, or vie, with this work of Fabbri's in subtlety and effectiveness. Religious questionings of various kinds appear frequently on the Italian stage, sometimes indirectly as in Betti's writings, sometimes perplexingly as in Fabbri's *Processo a Gesù*, sometimes accompanied by historical panoply as in Ignazio Silone's *L'avventura d'un povero cristiano* (*The Life of a Humble Christian*, 1968)—a play which deals with a medieval Pope. Nor can this religious questioning be disassociated from the numerous attempts to penetrate into the innermost, secret recesses of the human personality. As in other countries, thought of what the atomic bomb may do to mankind has attracted the attention of more than one Italian dramatist, but at least two plays on that theme have qualities of a distinctive kind: Riccardo Bacchelli's *L'alba dell' ultima sera* (*The Dawn of the Last Evening*, 1949) concentrates mainly upon one single person, a scientist whose thoughts and emotions are subtly analysed as he comes to the decision that he would rather suffer death than reveal the secret of a new stupefying and potentially devastating discovery which he has made, while Carlo Terron, dealing with the same basic problem in his *Avevo più stima dell'idrogeno* (*I Used to Have a Higher Opinion of Hydrogen*, 1955), surprisingly bathes his scenes in laughter until at the conclusion the scientists join the rest of humanity in universal destruction. Individual and universal guilt is probed by Enrico Bassano in *Uno cantava per tutti* (*One Sang for All*, 1948), and his *Come un ladro di notte* (*Like a Thief in the Night*, 1953), amid talk of an impending obliteration of mankind, focuses attention upon the strange, enigmatic figure of a lonely hermit—who may perhaps be just one other commonplace human being, or a second John the Baptist, or, maybe, Christ Himself in a second coming. Compassionate incisiveness gives distinction to Valentino Bompiani's quest for truth and righteousness in *Albertina* (published 1945, performed in Paris 1948 and in Bologna 1949), while in his impressive *Anche i grassi hanno l'onore* (*Honour, the Braggart's Last Refuge*, 1950) he shares with Betti the belief that avenging conscience is the true punishment for guilt. Rightly, Bompiani has described his plays generally as being a 'theatre of remorse.' Although several of Vitaliano Brancati's dramatic works are politically motivated, it may well be thought that his true power is most fully demonstrated when he too seeks to explore similar psychological problems. It is the inner thought of guilt which drives his seemingly upright and high-thinking heroine to suicide in *La governante* (*The Governess*, published 1952, performed 1965). Even more profoundly, even more intimately down into the obscure depths of the human soul, Silvio Giovaninetti descends exploringly in his powerful and terrifying psychoanalytic study appropriately called *L'abisso* (*The Abyss*, 1948) and in his agonizingly subtle investigation of the theme of incest in *Sangue verde* (*Green Blood*, 1953), a drama which also ends in self-inflicted death. Despite the laughter-arousing outpouring of words in Natalia Ginzburg's prize-winning play, *L'inserzione* (*The Newspaper Advertisement*, 1968), the true interest and value of this study of an over-talkative abandoned wife rest in its penetrating insight into the human mind and soul.

All of these, and others—even Dino Buzzati's strange *Un caso clinico* (*A Clinical Case*, 1953)—are imbued with the same spirit, are characterized by the same immediately recognizable approach. This last-mentioned drama, indeed, might profitably be taken as a prime example for the purpose of demonstrating the subtle distinction which separates the Franco-German 'absurd' from the Italian '*grottesco*'. In its many episodes it shows a rich businessman, who has been suffering from nervous strain, being sent to hospital after examination by a medical consultant. On arriving there he finds that this building is arranged and operated in a strange manner: it has seven floors, each of which has a particular significance of its own: the lowest is reserved for patients most seriously ill, indeed for those virtually beyond hope of recovery, and the others rise up in gradation from 'dangerously unwell' to merely 'under observation'. Naturally, the businessman is relieved to find that he has been assigned a bed on the top floor, but in the various scenes which follow we watch him being shifted down to a bed on the sixth floor, then to one on the fifth, to one on the fourth, to one on the third, to one on the second and, finally, to one on the lowest, where he dies.

It cannot be denied that both in this play and in his novels Buzzati was influenced by the writings of several French, German, and Austrian authors, and in particular by Franz Kafka's works; yet fundamentally *Un caso clinico* must be seen as being much more in debt to Pirandello than to those non-Italian novelists and playwrights, and as exhibiting the spirit of the '*grottesco*' rather than that of the 'absurd.'

Buzzati's drama, indeed, may well be taken as a marker indicating just how far the Italian theatre as a whole cares to go in the direction of the latter style; and precisely because there is such a limit beyond which few playwrights or none are prepared to pass no doubt explains why the modern Italian theatrical authors are less well-known and canonized in avant-garde circles elsewhere than are numbers of their French and German fellows.

Comedy and Drama, Italian Style

This thought carries us directly to consideration of the activities of Eduardo De Filippo, undoubtedly one of this century's most brilliant actor-directors, and also one of the most penetrating modern writers of what may properly be described as serious comic dramas, yet knowledge of his work outside his own country is remarkably meagre; and, moreover, such reputation as he has gained is largely based on the screen-play called *Marriage, Italian Style* which was concocted out of his subtly amusing and delicately subtle *Filumena Marturano* (1946). Filumena, previously a prostitute, has been living for some twenty-odd years 'respectably' as the mistress-housekeeper of Don Domenico Soriano. He is now aged fifty-two and she is forty-eight. Lying in her bed supposedly ill unto death, she easily tricks him into granting her a last wish—that he should marry her. This effected, she quickly recovers her health and shocks him by revealing that she has three grown-up sons whom she has secretly reared with such monies as she has been able to save from her housekeeping allowances: moreover, she points out, since he is now her husband, he has legally become their father. Naturally, he storms and fumes, declares he will have the marriage annulled, hesitates a moment when she adds that one of the youths is, indeed, his own son, and then stalks out of the house. Ten months later he returns, contrite: neither can he do without his Filumena nor can he refrain from wanting to meet this unknown son of his. A second marriage is celebrated, but still she tantalizes him, refusing to reveal the identity of his own son and declaring that he must accept all the three as his children: they are all good-looking and well-mannered fellows, they all call him papa, and so the comedy ends amid smiles and tears, as Don Domenico is persuaded to strum his guitar while all the others join in song.

Absurd? No. Pirandellian grotesque? Yes. And it is particularly important to observe that behind and beyond Pirandello stands a stage figure from the past—Pulcinella, prime symbol of the Neapolitan commedia dell'arte. Openly De Filippo has acknowledged his indebtedness to the creator of *Six Characters in Search of an Author*, and the connection between the one and the other is clear to sight. Essentially Pirandello is realistic, not fanciful and preposterous, even when unnamed persons such as the Father, the Stepdaughter, the Director are dealt with: yet at the same time he is also essentially theatrical; *Six Characters* begins with a supposed stage rehearsal, and it ends with what might seem to be a crudely 'strong', extravagantly melodramatic speech which the Stage Director greets delightedly with his "Splendid! Splendid! Curtain down!". In similar manner all of De Filippo's writings are basically realistic and yet also magnificently theatrical. And, above all, there is a further similarity to be observed in considering the total dramatic output of these two authors. Pirandello's life was one afflicted by disasters, misfortunes, torments, and reflections of these are clearly to be seen in his plays, yet when he called most of them '*commedie*' it is obvious that he did not interpret that term in its usual Italian indeterminate sense of simply 'plays': in employing that term he had in his mind the original Greek significance of the word, the significance which it still bears in English usage, as a stage performance which, however serious its theme may be, is bathed in laughter. So, too, in the works of De Filippo there are dark themes —murder, suicide, hallucinations, ugly episodes taken from the seedier ranges of ordinary life: yet all of these are treated in such a manner as to make them not only arrestingly theatrical but also truly comic.

There is an exquisite balance here. De Filippo neither wallows in the dark waters of complete despair, as for example does Witkiewicz, nor does he toy with absurdities just for their own sake, as sometimes Ionesco seems to do. Maybe the word 'mellowness' most aptly expresses the characteristic mood reflected in all his best plays, and possibly their style is most clearly emblematized in his *Sabato, domenica e lunedì* (1959) where Saturday brings threat of stormy weather which envelops the characters ominously on Sunday morning but which begins to quieten down in the evening, and where Monday brings with it glimpses of sunshine which seem all the brighter and all the more welcome because of what had intervened.

Without any doubt whatsoever Pirandello had constantly looked back to the tradition of the commedia dell'arte, with its prevailing admixture of the dark and the light and of scenes and persons which are, at one and the same time, both real and unreal; and even more deeply De Filippo has penetrated into the secrets of that peculiarly Italian theatrical world. It is thoroughly appropriate that one of his latest plays, *Il figlio di Pulcinella* (*Pulcinella's Son*, 1962), should admittedly have been composed with the specific aim of demonstrating that the ancient masked character is as alive today as he was in the seventeenth century.

Equally appropriate is the title of another half-serious, half-comic play, *La grande magia*, *The Grand Magic*, which, produced in 1949, offers a fitting description of all his three-score dramas—dramas which, although they derive their particular, peculiar quality from an ancient tradition, are distinctly modern; which, although they often deal with grave themes, never abandon laughter completely; and which, even although they are not so widely known in advanced theatrical circles as are some other modern plays, serve to indicate that there is more of genuine worth outside of certain currently lauded styles than frequently is allowed for. His comedy-dramas are, in essence, completely different from the plays conceived by Genet and Adamov, Dürrenmatt and Frisch, Camus and Beckett. These authors habitually elect to deal symbolically with the horrors of Hell-upon-Earth: invariably De Filippo prefers to concern himself with an Earth which, however murky it may be, is irradiated at times by a spotlight directed from Heaven through an opening in the theatrical clouds.

Just at the present moment, when our civilization might appear to be tottering towards its ruin, the darker view may seem to be the one more properly fitted to adopt towards what now confronts us. But, as Thornton Wilder has demonstrated, mankind has on several occasions been threatened with utter ruin and yet has strangely succeeded in surviving, even if only by the skin of its teeth; and probably humanity will somehow succeed in surmounting its present trials, troubles and tribulations. In securing this survival the theatre may still have a potent rôle to play—a rôle which is neither that of a pantomimic Demon of Despair nor that of a saturnalian Master of the Revels, but which, as De Filippo suggests, is rather that of a masked Pulcinella, a person who is, of course, the boon companion of irrepressible Arlecchino.

POST-WAR DRAMA IN AUSTRALIA

KATHARINE BRISBANE

The colony of Australia was first established when a shipment of convicts, soldiers and a few administrative officials were landed at Port Jackson, New South Wales, in 1788. During its formative years there entered into the Australian theatre a prevailing working-class taste, an important Irish Catholic influence, and an admiration for the outlaw, together with a suspicion of law-enforcement. These traditions, which flourished in the nineteenth-century theatre of spectacular melodrama, farce and burlesque, remain potent to this day.

With the Great War, during which so many men went overseas, and were faced for the first time with the 'real' civilization, Ibsen and Shaw invaded the stage. While the cinema emptied the popular theatre, a white-collar drama, largely amateur, developed and gained influence. It found its first professional expression with the rise of radio drama in the thirties.

In 1941 listeners first heard the blank-verse play *The Fire on the Snow*, Douglas Stewart's evocative word-picture of Scott's fatal Antarctic expedition which has become a radio classic. The following year *Ned Kelly*, though intended for the stage, made its debut on radio, as did *The Golden Lover* (1944) in which a Maori legend was given dramatic form, and *Shipwreck* (1947), dealing with the sinking of the *Batavia* off Western Australia in 1629. Stewart's strength was lyrical rather than dramatic, but his success brought prestige to dramatic writing at a time when the indigenous theatre was gathering confidence for a new advance.

In 1953 the Australian Elizabethan Theatre Trust was created to establish a national theatre, opera and ballet—though it was not until the Australian Council for the Arts (now the Australia Council) superseded the Trust in 1968 that continued assistance was offered to young playwrights.

It was this Trust, however, which sponsored the première of Ray Lawler's *Summer of the Seventeenth Doll* (1956), a drama of middle-age in which two cane-cutters and their women face the passing of a romantic dream. This play for the first time brought awareness to Europe and the

United States of the fact that a new drama was slowly being brought into being within the Australian continent, and it remains Australia's favourite play. Four years later came *The One Day of the Year*, by Alan Seymour, a moving study of a failed man's need to restore his dignity with memories—one which within Australia shares pre-eminence with Lawler's play, but is less well known abroad.

In this encouraging atmosphere Patrick White's earliest play *The Ham Funeral*, written in 1947, was given its first performance in 1961. White succeeded in what Douglas Stewart and other poets before him had attempted—in breaking through the conventions of naturalism to make visual on stage the landscape of the mind. In this, though he abruptly terminated his stage career in 1964, White was an influential precursor of the new school of playwrights who, during the sixties, finally broke away from foreign techniques in order to deal theatrically with the rhythms and shapes of their Australian environment. The recurrent theme of White's plays is the awakening of the innocent to the relentless cycle of life.

The Ham Funeral is set in a seedy London boarding house where a romantic young poet is torn between the spirit and the flesh; this environment is transferred to Sydney in *The Season at Sarsaparilla* (1963), in which the author gives force to the suburban round of birth, death and taxes; and in *A Cheery Soul* (1963) a powerful character study of an interfering old spinster which in the second half imaginatively elevates her to the status of martyr to a generation of discarded lives. The fourth drama, *Night on Bald Mountain* (1964), moves Ibsen-like towards a form of expressionism as the figure of Miss Quodling, a goatherd, broods upon the domestic drama being enacted within an academic household. Patrick White's poetic challenge was pursued by some of his companions. *Burke's Company* (1968), by Bill Reed, treats the fatal story of the explorers Burke and Wills with a haunting shadowy quality. Dorothy Hewett, who turned to the theatre in 1965, is preoccupied with the emotional desert at the heart of much Australian life, and with the power possessed by the artist to realize existence in his—or, more particularly, her—own way. *The Chapel Perilous* (1971), an epically inclined comedy-drama concerning a rebellious poet, introduces a heroine who pursues spiritual and moral freedom with a Lawrence-like passion, one who almost always makes the wrong decisions and who moves inevitably towards conservatism as the years pass by. The play itself is given strength by the inclusion in it of a number of lyric poems and songs—a dramatic style which this authoress had further developed in her later works, some of which freely mingle material from many sources—literature, vaudeville, Hollywood movies and contemporary pop material.

During the sixties these formal developments were accompanied by the appearance of another kind of theatre cultivated by a number of young writers, mostly working-class in upbringing but with university education, and also mostly of Irish Catholic descent. In Melbourne a number of undergraduates thus formed the La Mama company and later, in 1970, the Australian Performing Group. Among their leaders were the playwrights Jack Hibberd, John Romeril, Barry Oakley and David Williamson. As director and prolific author, Hibberd produced the early experiments in form and ritual which gave a characteristic style to the group. Most of his writing is iconoclastic and accusatory, expressed in language which delights in exotic revelations of the power of the vernacular. Sexual repression and insecurity are his chief targets, ranging from male bar-room rituals to censorship laws and the exploitation of women by society. Especially important is his *A Stretch of the Imagination* (1971), which takes shape as a comic and poetic monologue by an old hermit who expresses the traditional paradox of the classically educated white man coming to terms with the barren world around him as he moves cheerfully towards a lonely, inevitable death.

Among these new authors of the seventies David Williamson has had the widest popular success. His plays are, in style, naturalistic comedies, written with a keen eye and ear for the absurdities of domestic life, and with a disarming acknowledgment of his own confusions: among them all he is the one who is most comfortably familiar to his Australian audiences, and who at the same time has exhibited the power to have his writings made familiar in London and elsewhere. *The Removalists* (1971) and *Don's Party* (1971) have had the widest popular success, exhibiting his peculiar power, as Harold Hobson expressed it, of taking 'an old form' and breathing 'into it new life and emotion'. In *The Department* (1974), about a college staff meeting, his style moves from engaged reportage to a more contemplative study of the triviality of most human confrontations.

John Romeril remains the most socially committed of contemporary Australian playwrights, and his work examines the social pressures which have gone into the making of the Australian working-man. The treatment is sometimes political, sometimes domestic: in *Chicago, Chicago* (1969) Australia's sense of inadequacy looms large through a lampoon of American politics; and in *I Don't Know Who to Feel Sorry For* (1969) he plays domestic games on the theme of poverty. In *The Floating World* (1974) his outlook expands again as he studies Australia's xenophobic fear of Asia, both in war and in trade relations, through Les, a former prisoner of war, now a tourist to Japan.

Like Williamson, Barry Oakley, who is one of Australia's most popular novelists, is much concerned with the absurdity of domestic and literary life. His earlier plays were composed in the satirical improvising manner made fashionable by the Australian Performing Group, but manifestly his best drama is his later *Bedfellows* (1975), a formally structured sex-comedy with side-swipes at literary pretensions.

Meanwhile Sydney followed Melbourne's lead by encouraging another group of young authors—all of whom tend to be more extrovert, more relaxed and sentimental and definitely less propagandist. A seminal work was *The Legend of King O'Malley* (1970) by Michael Boddy and Bob Ellis, which with its vaudeville style reaffirmed the taste for a popular theatre. Today the most skilful writer remains Alexander Buzo, an author possessed of a rich verbal style which seizes upon the Australian vernacular with the same glee as that exhibited by Hibberd, Williamson and Romeril, but which at the same time has the power to transform the vulgar into the exotic. The occasional secret surfacing of the poetic from inside the convention-ridden minds of his characters gives his writings a double-edged cruelty and sympathy. Moving from his one-act dialogue between a storeman and a Pakistani student in *Norm and Ahmed* (1967) on through *Rooted* (1969) and *The Front-room Boys* (1969) to *Coralie Lansdowne says 'No'* (1974), he has clearly displayed his power to move from simpler things to a more complex and sensitive comedy of manners.

In Sydney also the young enthusiasts succeeded in opening their own Nimrod Street Theatre, which, starting with much improvised theatricality, later turned to present more finished scripts.

Here appeared Peter Kenna's *A Hard God* (1973), a mature work about an Irish Catholic family by a contemporary of Ray Lawler, written in a style which mingles the familiar Irish flair for anecdote and comic illogic ability with a flavour truly poetic. Realistic in language, it is experimental in form, moving in two emotional time planes between the slow life of a middle-aged family rich in memories of the past and a brief, swift affair between guilt-ridden teen-aged youths.

The Nimrod Street Theatre has also provided a stage for Jim McNeil, a playwright standing apart from the others, uninfluenced by any of the current fashions. Actually, his career began when, as the member of a debating society in Parramatta Gaol he discovered his power over words—a power manifested, for example in *How does your garden grow* (1974), which, written in a style spare and contemplative, offers a sympathetically gentle account of the measures taken by prisoners to preserve their private dignity. In this drama there is distinctive quality and depth.

Thus did the decade from 1965 to 1975 completely change the style and form of the Australian indigenous theatre. From a rarity the local play has become a majority choice, and sometimes it has succeeded in travelling from its own side of the world to the other: and clearly its career is by no means ended. A characteristic Australian style is being evolved: it was originally the writers who gave new life to the stage, and now they are moving forward, strengthened from their experience towards a greater, and deeper, simplicity of expression.

POST-WAR DRAMA IN AFRICA

LEWIS NKOSI

THE VAST continent of Africa obviously presents a wide range of diverse cultures, and in considering, even briefly, its dramatic activities, it is essential to bear steadily in mind the fact that within these enormous territories is to be found an extensive variety of contrasting styles. Here things ancient and indigenous co-exist with other things not only modern but also, more significantly, born out of entirely different social environments, religious beliefs and fundamentally variant objectives.

Prime examples abound. At the ancient Yoruba town of Oshogbo, in Nigeria, for instance, there are to be seen annual performances of a ritualistic drama, *The Imprisonment of Obatala*, wherein the God of Creation, on his way to visit Sango, the Thunder God, is so tricked by a mischievous fellow-deity named Eshu that Sango, failing to recognize him, causes him to be cast into prison—with the result that for a time no child can be born, no seeds can germinate: only when consultation of the Oracle reveals the truth and Obatala is released does the world escape the terrors of famine, drought and disaster. So, too, the annual 'Igogo' festival at Owo, in Western Nigeria, takes shape as a vegetation rite with as its chief character a forest creature named Orosen. During the early part of the present century the Dahomey cult dramas attracted considerable ethnological attention, and various other similar and related performances are still to be seen in the seven-day epic performance *Ozidi*, given by the Ijaw people on the Niger, in the *Egungun* and *Oro* of the Yoruba, in the *mmo* mask performances of the Ibos, and in the dance-operas wherein South African Zulus depict salient events in their history.

At the opposite extreme, recent years have seen these traditional festival shows suddenly, and often incongruously, companioned at various centres by performances far different in kind—the presentation of plays composed according to Western European conventions and dealing with the affairs of the bourgeois élite in a number of newly established African states. Thus, for example, the writings of Sarif Easmon of Sierra Leone and J. C. de Graft of Ghana are closely akin in style to hundreds of realistic Western plays, and, like them, are designed to present social messages. In the former's *Dear Parent and Ogre* (1960), the plot deals mainly with a brilliant lawyer-politician who is the successful aspirant to the office of Prime Minister but who at the same time is a lamentable failure as a father. Not dissimilar in style and in aim is his *The New Patriots* (1966), a play which concentrates on the twin chief maladies of contemporary Africa—tribalism and administrative corruption. In much the same manner de Graft's *Sons and Daughters* (1964), mixing together themes of generation conflict and social comment, seeks to focus attention on the not very attractive qualities manifested among the Ghanaian middle-class communities.

No matter how well-intentioned they may be, the obvious trouble with plays such as these is that the attacks on African philistinism are carried out only in the presentation of the themes and the characters, without any attempts being made to devise fresh theatrical conventions different from those which are themselves the product of these social evils. When this has been said, and when we look around for playwrights gifted with deeper vision, two names immediately come to mind—those of Wole Soyinka and John Pepper Clark, both products of the University College of Ibadan, in Nigeria. In 1959 the former first attracted wide attention by the production at the Ibadan Arts Theatre of *The Swamp Dwellers*, a study of village life under the stresses of social change, and of an excellent comedy, *The Lion and the Jewel*, which shows an ageing chief and reactionary lecher winning (against the expectations of the audience) a local belle from his rival, a progressive but ineffectual school-teacher who becomes the chief butt of the author's humour. *The Trials of Brother Jero* (1960) shows Soyinka pursuing and enriching his comic satire in a style which eventually was to reach its finest expression in *Kongi's Harvest* (1966), a bitter attack on power corruption in a West African state. It was still further enriched in *A Dance of the Forests* (1960), a play, written for the Nigerian independence celebration, in which he turned a jaundiced eye on the "gathering of the tribes" and mocked the august assembly as an occasion for noisy bickering among the returned spirits of potentates, royal prostitutes and power-hungry artists who have been recalled from the other world to share in the proceedings. As in his almost mystical *The Road* (1965), the writing in this *Dance of the Forests* is dense, enigmatic, gnomic, with symbols and motifs drawn chiefly from Yoruba lore. The same darkness of spirit pervades *The Strong Breed* (1964), a revenge tragedy. In this and some of his other dramas he has sometimes been justly criticized for being too cryptic in his use of symbols, yet no matter how obscure the language and the themes, he has never abandoned his determination to maintain his dramatic hold upon his audiences. "My prime duty as a playwright," he has said, "is to provide good theatre" so as to make sure "that the playgoers do not leave the theatre bored." His latest drama, *Madmen and Specialists* (presented in the U.S.A. in 1970), demonstrates in a practical manner how significantly he has been moving away from the exhibition of verbal pyrotechnics towards a richer dramatic style.

His fellow Nigerian, John Pepper Clark, an Ijaw from the delta region, shows himself more deeply steeped in strictly African imagery. His *Song of a Goat* (1961) takes shape as a verse tragedy mainly concerned with a man's sexual impotence, itself associated with a darkly symbolic theme. Three years later, in *The Raft* (1964), he moved almost entirely from the private world to the public, presenting four lumbermen adrift on the Niger—characters who offer a commentary on the situation within his country just before the outbreak of the 1967 civil war (the lumbermen, of course, representing the four regions of the republic). Perhaps these two dramas may be regarded as having been trial essays in preparation for his *Ozidi* (1966), an epic work which has not only strengthened his reputation but has also clearly demonstrated his power to break new ground. This recasting of an annual festival drama has had a revitalizing effect on his earlier rather precious 'Elizabethan-type' language: here drums and masks are freely used; here there is a deliberate attempt to free himself from European tutelage.

Two women playwrights, both from Ghana, have during recent years made deep impact upon the stage in English-speaking West Africa. Efua Theodora Sutherland, whose work has been closely associated with the activities of the Ghanaian Writers' Workshop, has been responsible for more than half a dozen dramas, including an effective *You Swore an Oath*, *Odasani* (a Ghanaian version of *Everyman*), *Foriwa*, a communal drama (1964), and a children's play, *Ananse and the Dwarf Brigade*, based on the African equivalent of Western fairy-tales. Most powerful and the best known of all her writings, however, is *Edufa* (1964), which shows a wife, through the workings of the supernatural, dying a "substitute death" in the place of her husband. The second woman playwright is Christina Ama Ata Aidoo, whose *Dilemma of a Ghost* (1965) deals with the conflict between a Ghanaian husband and his American-born wife, set against the background of traditional African culture. Both of these last-mentioned plays are concerned with exploring the differences and the meeting-point between African and European value-systems; both present interestingly unusual subject-matter; and both display complete mastery of their individual styles.

Although its quality is somewhat patchy, and the level of its achievement is not as high as that in Nigeria, French-speaking West Africa has also a well-established theatrical tradition which originally, during the thirties, received its impetus from the setting-up in Senegal of the Daniel Sorano National Theatre at the William Ponty School. At that time the school's pupils were encouraged to collect traditional local folk-lore and legends, and these were later used as the basis for plays, composed in French, but fundamentally concerned with African culture. Since those early days, apart from the works of the much-venerated President Senghor, at least three Senegalese dramas have won praise—*Les derniers jours de Lat Dior* (1965), by Amadou Asse Dia, *L'exil d'Albouri* (1967), by

Cheik N'Dao, and *El Hadj Omar* (1968), by Gerard Chehet. All three deal, in one way or another, with episodes in African history.

Dramas dealing with historical characters, usually ancient heroes, are, in general, popular among the new playwrights. President Senghor's *Shaka*, concerned with the famous Zulu king, was presented at the Ife Festival in 1966; dramas such as *La rencontre secrète de l'Almany Samory et de Tieba* by Mamadou Cuttara of Mali, *Tanimoune* by André Zalifou of the Niger Republic and, in South Africa, the historical dramas concerning Zulu monarchs written by the late poet and playwright H. I. E. Dhlomo, all form parts of a widely sweeping trend. Indeed, it might be said that the popularity of the historical play is rivalled only by dramas dealing with cultural conflicts—works such as *L'Oracle* by Oaul Mayenga of the Congo Republic and *L'appel du fétiche* by Moctar Fofana of Mali—both of which deal with the fascination exerted by witchcraft and the supernatural upon heroes and heroines who seek to live "modern" lives.

Next to such themes comes that which is concerned with the impact of European colonialism in divers areas, a prime example of which is Bernard Dadié's *Monsieur Thôgô-Gnini* (1967), where an attempt is made to present a clear and dramatic picture of the so-called "civilizing mission" in French West Africa.

Until recently, East Africa has tended to lag behind West Africa in theatrical activities, but even there the past few years have been marked by what may almost be described as intense activity. In Ethiopia, Tsegaye Gabre-Medhin, director of the Haile Selassie Theatre, has already written many plays in Amharic, and one, *The Oda Oak Oracle* (1965), in English. In Kenya, Rebecca Njau has won acclaim for a poetic tragedy, *The Scar* (1963), and in Uganda, despite the fact that the political climate has tended to inhibit pursuit of the arts, Robert Serumaga's theatre company has displayed such ingenuity, inventiveness and skill that it has already made wide European tours, giving performances in France, Holland, Belgium and Yugoslavia: its reputation, indeed, has had even wider dissemination through other expeditions which have carried the company to various parts of the Asian continent and to the Caribbean. Serumaga's best-known creation, *Renga Moi*, skilfully and impressively exploits various traditional African theatrical elements—dance movements, much use of drums and other percussive instruments and great variety of mimed action. It was produced in London in 1975.

The return to traditional African theatrical forms is by no means confined to the performances of this one company but is to be found in many widely extended territories. What may be called "traditional folk opera" has been actively pursued in Nigeria, with plays by Kola Ogunmola, Hubert Ogunde, Duro Ladipo and Obutunde Ijimere particularly noteworthy; and in South Africa a similar movement pursued by the Zulu Theatre Company has led to the presentation in London (in 1972) of *Mabatha*, the "Zulu Macbeth".

Naturally, South Africa's racial policies have tended to thwart the development of indigenous drama: funds which might have given welcome aid to such ventures frequently go to the support of White companies whose standards imitate those of London's fashionable West End. Despite this, however, several courageous Whites have sought to break away from the provincial insularity of this style of theatrical presentation—and here Athol Fugard, who has consistently sought to derive inspiration by working in close collaboration with both Black and White actors, stands forward as a prime symbol. In *The Blood Knot* (1961) and in his collection of Port Elizabeth plays, *Boesman and Lena* (1970), *Sizwe Banzi is Dead* and *The Island*, he has dramatically presented, in an effective manner, the recondite mysteries of *apartheid*, sometimes with desperate rage, sometimes with sardonic humour.

Among Black South Africans jazz opera has lately proved a popular area of activity. *King Kong*, with a libretto by the novelist Harry Bloom and music by the late Todd Matshikiza, aroused great excitement when it was first produced in 1959—but unfortunately, as local and overseas impresarios jostled with one another in their attempts to capture the production in Europe, it was gradually watered down in attempts to turn it into an exotic imitation of a typical Broadway musical.

Regrettably, most South African dramatists now live in exile. Thus Lewis Nkosi's *The Rhythm of Violence* (1965) was written in the U.S.A., and has since been presented in West and East Africa as well as in Great Britain: another South African exile, Arthur Maimane, is author of *The Prosecution*, presented in London together with Nkosi's *Malcolm* in 1973.

Although no one can possibly predict what will happen in the future, a consideration of these diverse activities suggests that during the years immediately to come the African theatre will almost certainly move away not only from the naturalistic forms of the three-act realistic drama of the European stage but also from the various attempts now being made in various countries to establish new theatrical patterns, and will strive to create a theatre capable of exploiting traditional modes of expression for contemporary purposes.

INDEX

Dates of birth and death are inserted after the names of dramatists

Budapest, theatre in, 438
Buenaventura, Enrique, 878
Buero Vallejo, Antonio (*b.* 1916), 874, 880
Bugbears, The, 141
Bugiardo, Il, 318
Bulatović, Miodrag (*b.* 1930), 881
Bulgakov, Michael A. (1891–1940), 691–2
Bulgaria, 863, 864, 871
Bullins, Ed (*b.* 1935), 802
Bunker, The, 869
Bunraku-za, Japanese puppet drama, 553–4
Buona madre, La, 321
Buona moglie, La, 318
Buona sementa, La, 714
Buonaparte, Niccolò, 156
Buondelmonte e gli Amadei, 365
Burbage, James, 203
Bürger Schippel, 628
Bürger von Calais, Die, 677
Bürgerlich und romantisch, 411
Burgraves, Les, 395
Burgtheater, in Vienna, 358
Burke's Company, 892
Burlador de Sevilla, El, 187
Burlesque plays, 305
Burn Me to Ashes, 739
Burned Lot, The, 471
Burning Glass, The, 663
Burnt Flower-Bed, The, 885–6
Bury Fair, 280
Bury The Dead, 698
Business is Business, 568
Bussy D'Ambois, 228
But For Whom Charlie, 717
But it is not a Serious Affair, 602
Butterfly's Charm, The, 749
Butti, Annibale (1868–1912), 569
Buzo, Alexander (*b.* 1944), 893
Buzzati, Dino (*b.* 1906), 888
Byelorussia, 864
Bygmester Solness, 455, 456
Byrne, Seamus (*b.* 1904), 818
Byron, George, Lord (1788–1824), 342, 463
Byron, H. J. (1834–84), 412, 634, 818–9
Bystrytsky, Nathan (*b.* 1896), 739
Byzantium, drama in, 99

Cabinet des fées, 387
Cabin in the Sky, 704
Caccia al lupo, La, 505
Caccia alla volpe, La, 505
Caccini, Giulio, 145–6
Cæsar and Cleopatra, 53, 634–5
Cæsar's Death, 246
Caillavet, Gaston-Armand de (1869–1915), 567
Caio Gracco, 303

Caius Marius, 277
Calandria, La, 139–40, 154
Calcutta, May 4th, 732
Calderón (Pedro Calderón de la Barca, 1600–81), 40, 173–89, 211, 220, 298, 323, 375, 399, 460, 518, 748, 786, 876
Caldwell, Erskine, 704
Caligula, 831, 832
Caliph's Son, The, 480
Calisto y Melibea, La comedia de, 186
Call of Life, The, 484
Callado, Antonio, 880
Callados como muertos, 665
Calprenède, Gautier de Costes de la (1614–63), 246
Calthrop, D. C. (1878–1940), 565, 614
Calzolaio di Messina, Il, 672
Camasio, Sandro (1884–1913), 570
Cambises, 200
Camilla, 410
Camille, 418–19
Camino Real, 799–800
Camisa, La, 875
Cammelli, Antonio (fourteenth century), 143
Camp, The (Gambaro), 877
Camp, The (Schiller), 351
Campaspe, 206, 207
Campiello, Il, 319
Campo, El, 877
Campo de armiño, 574
Campo di Maggio, 733
Camus, Albert (1913–60), 831–3
Canace, 144
Canada, 665
Canción de cuna, 575
Candida, 634, 635
Candle in the Wind, 736, 737
'candomblé', native Brazilian rites, 879, 880
Canetti, Elias (*b.* 1905), 840
Cankar, Ivan (1876–1918), 514
Cantatrice chauve, La, 778, 834
Cantique des cantiques, 729
Cap and Bells, 600
Capacelli, Francesco Albergati (1728–1804) 335
Čapek, Josef (1887–1945), 683
Čapek, Karel (1890–1938), 682–3, 748
Capitano, stock type in Italian *commedia dell'arte*, 151
Capitano, Il, 140
Capraria, La, 141
Caprice, Un, 391–2
Caprices de Marianne, Les, 390
Capricious Lady, The (Goldoni), 321
Capricious Lady, The (Lope de Vega), 172
Captain, The, 140
Captain of Industry, The, 503
Captain of Koepenick, The, 725
Captives, The, 86